LAW AND SOCIETY IN ENGLAND

1750–1950

AUSTRALIA AND NEW ZEALAND
The Law Book Company Ltd.
Sydney : Melbourne : Perth

CANADA AND U.S.A.
The Carswell Company Ltd.
Agincourt, Ontario

INDIA
N.M. Tripathi Private Ltd.
Bombay
and
Eastern Law House Private Ltd.
Calcutta and Delhi
M.P.P. House
Bangalore

ISRAEL
Steimatzky's Agency Ltd.
Jerusalem : Tel Aviv : Haifa

PAKISTAN
Pakistan Law House,
Karachi

LAW AND SOCIETY IN ENGLAND 1750–1950

By

W. R. CORNISH,

LL.B., B.C.L., F.B.A.

Professor of English Law,
London School of Economics and Political Science

And

The Late **G. de N. CLARK,**

B.A., LL.B.

Lecturer in Law,
University College,
University of London

LONDON
SWEET & MAXWELL
1989

Published in 1989 by
Sweet & Maxwell Ltd. of
South Quay Plaza,
183 Marsh Wall, London
Computerset by Promenade Graphics Limited, Cheltenham
Printed in Great Britain by BPCC Hazell Books Ltd,
Member of BPCC Ltd, Aylesbury, Bucks, England.

British Library Cataloguing in Publication Data
Cornish, W.
  Law and society in England 1750–1950.
  1. England. Law. Social aspects, history
  I. Title   II. de N. Clark
  340'.115'09242

  ISBN 0–421–31140–1
  ISBN 0–421–31150–9

PREFACE

This book seeks to break new ground. It sets the history of substantive law and legal practice in the two centuries since industrialisation beside the surrounding politics and, even more, beside the economic and social conditions which gave the law its essential significance.

How far the book attains this ambitious objective is not something on which critics are likely to agree. If it succeeds even in pointing the way for the next generation of scholars it will have done much of its work. It is written primarily with the law student in mind, though its discussion of legal materials may hold something for students of other disciplines. It will be evident that it has derived much from the work of economic, administrative, social and political historians, for whom legal events, activities and attitudes are one strand in a richer fabric.

The book was conceived over twenty years ago, at a time when study of the recent history of English law was still neglected. Geoffrey Clark and I felt keenly that the omission of this history from the stuff of legal education weakened its very texture and needed fundamental repair. The result of trying to remedy old neglects is a long book. Even so, it is only a work of survey and ordering. It provides rather more than most law students want or need to digest in any short term. It has always been our hope, nevertheless, that it will prove a useful tool for special courses devoted to the study of its period; and that more generally, students with an instinct for historical appreciation will want to have it by them as their studies progress in various directions. It should be stressed in this connection that, while the text seeks to point up the links between legal and related elements, it makes no attempt to supply a systematic account of political events or of economic and social change. It assumes that the reader has a working knowledge of such material.

In 1972, Geoffrey Clark died after painful illness, aged only 49. Both his faculty at University College, London and the larger world were deprived tragically of a considerable scholar. Without his knowledge and enthusiasm, it was hard to keep work going on the book. Although he had finished drafts of Chapters 2, 4, 5 and 7, there remained much more to be done. At the time of his death, the fruits of post-war historical work were only beginning to be harvested. The knowledge and shape of many subjects dealt with in the book were being transformed. Accordingly it has proved a much larger task to arrive at a completed text than either of us appreciated in those early years. The detailed writing no longer contains much of Geoffrey's drafts and it would certainly be wrong to assign posthumous responsibility to him for what is finally appearing. But it has seemed broadly satisfactory to adhere to the breakdown of subject-matter and to more detailed sub-divisions within chapters which we settled upon long ago.

In a book that has been slow a-coming, it would be foolhardy to name those who have helped as it has gestated. The list would be long and would probably neglect some who fully deserve inclusion. All those who have given assistance, great and small, must rest content with this general expression of heartful thanks. I do, however, wish to acknowledge the patient encouragement afforded to me since Geoffrey Clark's death by his literary executors, Anne Gilman, Patricia Millner and Professor Paul O'Higgins. For their fortitude, the reward is a book at last in hand. The publishers also deserve special thanks for their patience and helpfulness in processing a difficult manuscript.

There is one other acknowledgment that is not to be suppressed. The book was generated in the Law Department of the London School of Economics, where Geoffrey Clark was a law student and where I have spent most of my teaching life. The Department's motive force has long been that the study of law be grounded in a broader study of society. This book is one expression of that belief. It owes much to the fact that the intellectual life of the School is devoted to the social sciences in a widely conceived and integrated sense. Particularly since I am about to remove myself to Cambridge University, I must record that it was in the special environment of the L.S.E. that the whole project began and remained possible.

London, May 1989   W. R. Cornish

BIBLIOGRAPHICAL NOTE

This book could lead to a wide range of further reading in primary and secondary sources. I am proposing to provide some detailed guidance, particularly on primary sources for modern English legal history, in a separate Handbook. This is currently in preparation. Even in the realm of secondary sources there is a considerable volume of material on the many subjects covered in this book. A short list of important further reading is given at the end of each chapter. Where a book or article is on this list, it appears in the footnotes only by author's name and year of publication. In addition, two authors are cited throughout the book in abbreviated form:

Blackstone, *Commentaries*: Sir W. Blackstone, Commentaries on the Laws of England, 4 vols. (1765–1769)

Holdsworth: Sir W. S. Holdsworth, A History of English Law, 16 vols. and Index (1903–1952)

Since this is a book intended to make connections between legal and other history, no simple lines of demarcation can establish what can properly be included in the Further Reading lists and the footnotes. Readers who need to cast widely may be helped by general histories of the period. A list of these is attached separately at the end of Chapter One.

At the end of the book, a Biographical List gives brief details of many persons who play a role in this history. A list of further references is to be found there.

W.R.C.

CONTENTS

Chapter Five
THE FAMILY

Chapter Six
POVERTY AND EDUCATION

Chapter Seven
ACCIDENTS

Chapter Eight
CRIME

Chapter One

INSTITUTIONS AND IDEAS

PART 1: INDUSTRIALISATION 1750–1875

I. SOCIETY AND LAW

This book explores the history of legal institutions and doctrines within the economy and society which generated them. It seeks to account for the political pressures which affected their shape over time and for their own influence on the range of debate about public policy. In order to emphasise the thrust of the treatment, the ensuing chapters draw together congeries of subject-matter which are rather broader than the traditional classifications of legal history books. This first chapter, however, lays a foundation for all that follows. It ranges over a considerable ground-plan and its coverage has accordingly to be rather summary.

The Chapter divides the time-span of the book into two Parts, making its break at 1875, when Britain still stood unchallenged in her economic dominance. It was the year when, as a reflection of that reality, the English legal system was finally given a more coherent structure, to be operated, more than ever before, by the lawyers. In the middle of each Part, accordingly, stands a description of the court systems and the legal professions. But in each case, this is preceded by some discussion of the relation of law and the legal system to society in general, and to the economy and the organisation of politics.

It is succeeded by an account of the growth of bureaucracy at central and local levels. For here lay the real power activating the social programmes that became a necessary response to conditions of urban, industrial life. Finally each part turns to that most enticing of historical subjects, the interrelation between intellectual debate and the course of social and political events. Since ideologies have the capacity to appear both to shape basic perceptions of social existence and to operate as rationalisations of a world driven by far more elemental forces, assessing their influence may seem intriguing, but ultimately baffling. Yet in a history of law conceived as a branch of social history, the task is a necessity.

The changes that thrust Great Britain forward from her mid-Georgian to her mid-Victorian condition were the most considerable in her history. Taken in the round they conjure metaphors of transformation or revolution. The population more than trebled—from something over six millions in 1750 to nearly 18 millions in the census of 1851 and 22.7 millions 20 years later. The country moved from being a young blood contending among the nations of Europe for colonies and wealth to become the all-father of industry and com-

merce. The impact of these changes—demographic and economic—
has many social measures, to which we shall in due course come. But
we shall start with perceptions of society rather than its structure.

It has become almost an axiom of social history that eighteenth
century society saw itself in terms of ranks or stations in which the
links were ordered vertically; the nineteenth century however moved
to a perception in which the main links were horizontal, with deep
clefts of antagonism lying between.[1] These graphic images are an
attempt to define backwards. By the middle third of the nineteenth
century a society that was increasingly industrial and urban
expressed its elemental divisions as those of class. Typical members
of the upper, middle and working classes corresponded to the
notional actors of classical economics—the landowner who took rent,
the capitalist who competed for profits, the labourer who drew
wages. These divisions implied social barriers of education and work
experience, of accent and culture, which were inherently difficult to
bridge. The nineteenth-century world of market-place competition
was not however the successor, as it was to be in many parts of continental Europe, to one bi-furcated by a massive division of lord from
peasant. On the contrary the society that was passing had contained
many levels, between which a degree of movement was common.
The successful tenant farmer might become a small squire and the
ambitious apprentice might advance to journeyman and eventually
to master and alderman.

The eighteenth century world, dominated by a ruling class whose
wealth lay primarily in agricultural land, was nonetheless one in
which the myriad gradations of social rank were keenly observed. In
the higher reaches equals treated each other according to an elaborate code of refined manners and formal honour, in which rank insults
were settled by duel and proprietary grievances by a Chancery suit.
Those above expected, but did not always receive, from those below
a loyal subservience. The counterpart of this deference was a
measure of paternal responsibility, rough or oppressive though it
might become. The propertied divided amongst themselves, according to rank, responsibility for maintaining the poor and disciplining
the vagrant, pursuing the criminal to justice and maintaining the
roads, bridges and river-banks of the locality. In every advancement
a man or woman looked to the patronage of "friends."[2] The system of
government bred a plethora of offices which could be used to satisfy
such demands. Some of these places were complete sinecures, others
carried more or less arduous duties. Some could be made to generate
quite remarkable incomes. Nowhere was the network of place more
evident than in the manifold clerkships, masterships and steward-
ships of the courts and legal offices. Justice after all was a major
activity of government, central and local.

The ensuing chapters of this book start with the legal strands

---

[1] On this theme, see esp. Briggs (1959), 8–20; Perkin (1969) Chap. 2; P. Laslett, *The
World We Have Lost* (3rd ed.; 1983); Porter (1982) Chap. 2.
[2] "Friendship" could span large social distances: "Lord Sydney was my friend,"
claimed Mary Burgess, one of the first convicts transported to Australia, "and I
understood I was not to be sent abroad": M. Ignatieff, *A Just Measure of Pain* (1978),
p. 92.

entwined in this layered society and then follow their changing position as the whole fabric is re-woven. The tensile strength which laws and constitutional assumptions already imparted to it would contribute to the nation's ability to become the first to industrialise. We may usefully isolate two aspects of this power at the outset. First is the virtual absence of laws whose overt purpose was to segregate special elites or to restrain upward social movement. There were no separate estates of nobility, clergy and bourgeoisie, each subject to its own legal regime; although the common law allowed scope enough for the vagaries of local custom, it was nevertheless opposed to legal pluralism on such a scale. At the top of the pyramid the aristocratic elite had not sought purity of caste by defining the group within which its members might marry.[3] At the bottom, feudal serfdom had disappeared over time, the depopulation of the fourteenth century contributing much to the process. There remained only the bound condition of the Scottish miners (until 1796)[4] and the enslaved Africans in the towns (until their grudging emancipation conferred by Lord Mansfield in 1772).[5] Physical movement in search of better prospects was to some extent curtailed by the laws of settlement; but their effect was undoubtedly less drastic than Adam Smith supposed in his attack.[6] The major limitations in the law were of political rights—to franchise and to office.

Secondly, preference for individual private property over notions of obligation to family or larger community had been growing over a long period. In law this was marked particularly by rules allowing alienation of land upon death as well as during life, a process that had been much advanced in 1540 when freehold land became open to testamentary disposition. Even in the twelfth and thirteenth centuries, England may not have been a peasant society (if indeed it ever had been) in the sense that lands would be held by all the members of a family, and the head of each generation would have the limited powers of a custodian. So Macfarlane had posited, relying partly on the state of the common law itself and partly on the frequency and variety of transactions in land from that period onwards.[7] Whatever the ultimate merits of so challenging a thesis, by the seventeenth century private property had become deeply entrenched as the fundament of most political thought. Whether society was perceived as the result of a social contract or the accretion of historical experience, it had become an ordering which preserved individual property before all else through the law and the organs of the state.[8]

The emergence of a middle class with interests opposed to the old landed order is rooted in economic circumstance. The vast upsurge of productivity swelled the middling ranks to a size and proportion that compelled a political reckoning. Here were people who were learning

[3] Significantly, not all the children of peers were ennobled; and the Crown preserved its prerogative to create new peers, see below p. 9, n. 28.
[4] See, e.g., R Page Arnot, A History of the Scottish Miners (1955) Chap. 1. The bondage was lifted by statutes of 1774 and 1799.
[5] Somersett's case (1772) 20 St. Tr. 1.
[6] See below, pp. 419–421.
[7] A. Macfarlane, The Origins of English Individualism (1978).
[8] See esp. C. B. MacPherson, The Political Theory of Possessive Individualism (1962).

that capital must be made to work, and that to such an end labour
must be set to an arduous, unvarying regime. With time they were to
see their interest as lying in the freedom to compete in markets rather
than in protection from foreign and colonial trade. The food needed
for a bounding population gave these new perceptions a sharp focus.
The wars with France at the turn of the eighteenth century made the
supply of corn from continental markets difficult, pushed up home
prices and induced a major wave of inflation. Agricultural owners
and producers at home shared in a novel prosperity which rescued
many from long-borne debt. The process lasted long enough for a
new order of expectation to grow, only to be rudely unsettled with
the ending of hostilities. The Corn Law of 1815 involved no new
principle in its imposition of a duty on imported corn until the price
rose above a set level. But in raising that level from 66s. to 80s. it
erected a barrier which had a real impact on the lowered prices of
peace-time. Forty years before, when Adam Smith wrote, it had been
the agricultural progressives who had been seeking free trade in corn
and the new manufacturers who wanted more protection. From 1815
the positions were reversed: the protection of corn became a guarantee of agricultural incomes and this would mean a reduction of
manufacturing profits through the higher wages needed to sustain
the labour force.

At this point the watershed divided.[9] The proportion of the labour
force in agriculture, which half a century before had been predominant and was still about one-third at the turn of the century, soon fell
to below a quarter.[10] The proportion working in industry, trade and
transport, already over 40 per cent in 1801 was to climb steadily until
a century later the proportion would be two-thirds. Town after town
was beginning its dramatic surge in size, drawing its people partly
from the surrounding countryside but more from families already
there. The pattern of economic life in the countryside was changing
to a capitalistic form as the proportion of hired labourers to employing farmers increased.[11] In the towns an equivalent process was over-
taking the old "guild" arrangements of the craft trades, replacing
them increasingly with wage labour. The flexible concept of the
labour contract would allow this process to take place without
serious impediment.[12] The strain upon legal resources would be felt
more in other novelties of urban existence: in the provision of housing; protection against unemployment, sickness, old age, accident;
reduction of the horrifying conditions that squalid proximity would
induce; suppression of the "dangerous classes" who lived off urban
predation.

In town life the various levels that came to regard themselves as
"middle-class"—the burgeoning professionals, tradespeople and
shopkeepers—began to feel their common interests in combating the
highly restrictive franchise and in airing other grievances against the
landed class. They were also coming to see that those with higher

[9] On this, see esp. Perkin (1969) Chap. 6.
[10] Thereafter its decline would be more gradual, until at the end of the century it was
under 10 per cent.
[11] An estimate of some 4:7 around 1700 had become 4:11 a century later.
[12] Below, p. 286ff.

manual skills, though not easily distinguished in earnings or prospects of advancement from the lower middle classes, were acquiring a distinct consciousness of their economic and political potential. The balance of power was already very different from a quarter-century before when the first shock waves from France stirred radical embers in constitutional clubs and dissenting meetings.

II. Economic Growth and Law

The astonishing process by which production, as well as population, came in late eighteenth century to grow in multiples rather than fractions is the stuff of economic histories. It can be measured in terms of production: the 5 million lbs. of cotton being processed in 1771 had by 1818 become 164 million lbs; the 70,000 tons of iron produced in 1790 had become 400,000 tons by 1820; the 10 million tons of coal in 1800 had become perhaps 2 million tons by 1830 and grew rapidly thereafter with rail transport. It is imprinted in the changes in production methods: in the domestic workshop, the value of equipment per worker was some £2–£3; in the factory it soon became £40–£50 per worker. It is registered in the growth of exports, which between 1800 and 1815 grew some 30 per cent., even though thereafter the same rate was not again achieved until mid-century. The export figures indeed underscore the vital role of the domestic market in creating demand for the new industrial products. This in turn comes back to that layered structure of society which so readily fostered the spirit of emulation. Desire for comforts and luxuries in cheaper versions stimulated invention and investment and the results in turn bred desire.

These developments underlay the shifting social allegiances after 1815. The battle against the Corn laws was not an isolated campaign; it was repeated in much the same terms against a range of barriers to foreign and colonial trade and industry. This run of opinion so strongly in favour of free competition in international trade was to lead Dicey and his followers to label the First Reform Act years an "age of laissez-faire."

To that characterisation of the period itself we shall return.[13] First it is necessary to see the process in earlier perspective, for the role of law in the regulation of trade already had a lengthy history. Tudor government had drawn upon a mosaic of medieval regulation, much of it local, to devise an embracing policy of central direction over trade, industry and the economy more generally. In a nationalistic spirit, the business of mercantile and colonial adventures to the new continents was given direction and aid, the amassing of precious metal and other wealth at home was shored up against removal abroad, new industries were fostered by invention patents and other monopolies, frequent attempts were made to steady domestic production, employment, food prices and provision for the poor.[14] Aware that deep misery could produce a dangerous restiveness in

---

[13] Below, p. 69ff.
[14] Holdsworth IV, pp. 314–407, surveys this body of law.

the populace, the Privy Council had grown more and more active in its interferences, using royal proclamations and statutes to prescribe rules, and a whole range of connections—with gilds, boroughs, justices of the peace, special commissioners and courts—to provide an administration for collecting information and enforcing directives. Under Elizabeth, this mercantilist direction was taken to its furthest point. By the time of the Restoration, the crucial administrative movers in the machine had disappeared. What remained was a mass of statute, sometimes to be refashioned by further legislation, or rehoned by proclamation. But the effectiveness of it all, so far as domestic affairs were concerned, was left largely to interest groups. Without a central intelligence that concerned itself with wage regulation and price fixing, the operation of markets grew apace, the law confining itself effectively to the recognition and protection of property and the enforcement of contract in the terms set by the parties. Traders and masters could try their own policing of older constraints; but their insistence upon their monopolies of sale in their towns, and upon seven-year apprenticeships for new entrants to their crafts, was steadily undermined.[15] Local restrictions of these kinds were losing acceptability, but it was only beginning to dawn that monopolies in trade, if they were to have the force of law, must depend upon more esoteric knowledge than that needed for the manufacture of things: such privileges would be reserved for the services offered by the modern skilled professions. And their monopolies would have to be upon a countrywide rather than a local level.

III. POLITICS AND LAW

In the internal struggles of the seventeenth century, rival claims to ultimate legal authority had placed the idea of law at the heart of political debate. The Settlement of 1689, by which the two Houses of Parliament offered William of Orange and his Stuart consort the Crown on terms acknowledging the supremacy of the King-in-Parliament, was in time to establish itself as a final outcome. It was a victory for the organised strength of landed wealth over royal absolutism, for regular law over the vagaries of prerogative, for Whig over Tory (in the original thrust of those soubriquets). It was not easy to foresee that the aggressions and jealousies of the powerful would in the succeeding century be turned outwards, to the tensions among the nations of Europe on battlefields of the old world and the new. The political theory and constitutional organisation of the internal state continued to be matters of high debate among gentlemen. The conditions on which their rule and their law ought no longer to command obedience, were root issues which only gradually lost their immediacy. With time the critical events of 1688 could acquire the air of resolution rather than revolution: there had been no break, Parliament had merely filled the gap occasioned by James II's flight.

The Hanoverian succession, finally assured by the failure of the second Stuart rebellion in 1745, put paid to ideas of royal absolutism.

---

[15] See below, pp. 292–293.

Montesquieu's vision of a state in which power was divided and balanced by law gained its immediacy from the new shapes emerging in the British constitution.[16] A great literature of political thought, from Locke, through Hume, Smith and Millar, to Burke and Paine—examined its implications from a variety of perspectives. But it was Blackstone who gave it that peculiar legitimacy which stems from describing its legal sub-frame. Since his *Commentaries on the Law of England* (1765–69) took constitutional principle as the first level in the whole edifice of the common law the impression was the more imposing.[17] Blackstone did not ignore philosophical debate, but borrowed eclectically.[18] He espoused from Grotius, Pufendorf and Burlaquami a natural law established through divine revelation and human reason, and used it to illumine the perfection of the common law.[19] He derived from John Locke a contractual theory of the formation of society and a labour theory justifying the recognition of private property.[20] His contractualist view was notional rather than real; if he could not, with Hume or Burke, discount all such imaginings as fanciful, he at least accorded an important place to historical justification—some of it drawn from Roman analogy, more from an English inheritance stretching back to a golden Saxon age.

Yet, for Blackstone that deep attachment to the ideal of individual liberty, which already touched so many practical issues of government, was the real bedrock upon which law at this level was founded. Robustly, if rather derivatively, he pronounced the right of personal security, the right of personal liberty and the right of private property to be *absolute*. It was his manner to follow dogmatic assertion by almost offhand qualification: there were indeed exceptions where the great liberties "required by the laws of society to be sacrificed to public convenience." Nonetheless, individual freedom remained the presumptive condition against which all else was to be measured, beginning with the elements of the constitution[21]: that separation of legislative, executive and judicial powers so striking to a Frenchman such as Montesquieu[22]; the sovereign Parliament which took the advantages, but avoided the disadvantages of monarchy, aristocracy and democracy by combining all three elements in King, Lords and Commons; the system of courts through which all persons had access to the law's protection; the rights of each subject to petition the King or either House of Parliament and to protect himself by bearing arms (suitable to his condition and degree).

The positive ability of each House to initiate bills and the negative

---

[16] *L'Esprit des Lois* (trans. by Nugent, 1752).

[17] A selection (with a useful introduction concentrating on fundamental principles) is by G.H. Jones, *The Sovereignty of the Law* (1973).

[18] See P. Lucas (1963) 7 A.J.L.H. 142.

[19] He nowhere averted to the possibility of statute failing to be law because it contravened natural law. There was an innate positivism about his refusal to follow Locke into speculation about any ultimate power to remove the legislature: "No human laws will . . . suppose a case, which must at once destroy all law and compel men to build afresh upon a new foundation . . . " (*Commentaries*, I Chap. 5).

[20] *Commentaries*, I Chap.4.

[21] See further, below, p. 10.

[22] It was the British constitution which exemplified much of *L'Esprit des Lois*.

power of each to veto them, in accordance with well-elaborated procedure, was held to invest the King-in-Parliament with "sovereign
and uncontrollable authority . . . To do every thing that is not naturally impossible."[23] And from this stemmed the limitations, both legal
and political, upon the powers of the other two branches of government. The monarch, still in reality the source of all executive power,
could act under his prerogative only to the extent that it had not been
overtaken or curtailed by statute. He might retain a wide discretion
to conduct relations with foreign states; but his army was allowed
him by Parliamentary vote each year, and his power to tax his subjects, whether to pay for wars or for any other purpose, had to be
assigned by legislation introduced first in the Commons.[24] As new
departments came to be added to the central bureacracy—such as
those of the Secretary of State for War and the Postmaster-General—
it was Parliament which empowered them. The monarch no longer
had the power to suspend statutes generally or to dispense with their
application to particular cases. Even his role in the legislature was in
practice becoming formal, since the power to disapprove a bill sent
forward by both Houses was no longer used.[25]

At the outset of the seventeenth century struggles, Chief Justice
Coke had pronounced the independent authority of the common
law; with time this might have developed into an ultimate standard
against which the judges could measure the validity of statute. But
while in the succeeding century, the vestige of this desire might
occasionally surface, the courts mounted no direct challenge to the
legal supremacy of Parliament. Whatever the notion of the rule or
reign of law might now imply, however much the common law
might be paraded as an emanation of natural law declared by the
judges on the basis of immemorial custom, whatever the defects to
be found (by Blackstone's account) in most statute law, the judges'
powers were confined to interpreting its meaning in order to apply
it. The freedom thus left to them was not inconsiderable, particularly
since the Act of Settlement 1701 guaranteed their enjoyment of office
against dismissal by the monarch and so rendered the grotesque
manipulations of Charles II and James II a regrettable interruption in
a much longer tradition of judicial independence.[26]

The theory of parliamentary sovereignty was pragmatic dogma
lying beyond proof. One factor which supported its appearance of
inevitability was the host of rules, some enshrined in statute, some
contained in Crown Charters or through other exercises of the royal
prerogative, some fixed by long usage and perhaps supported by
decisions of the courts, which defined each constituent part of the
legislature. The monarchy was an inheritance determined, since the

---

[23] *Commentaries*, I Chap. 5.

[24] *Ibid.* Chap. 8.

[25] Anne had rejected the Scots Militia Bill in 1707, since when the veto had not been
used, though it would occasionally be used against colonial bills in the ensuing century.

[26] The Act (12 & 13 Will. III c. 2, s.37) applied to the judges of the common law courts,
their independence being completed when George III forswore his right to appoint
afresh on ascending the throne (a position at once affirmed by Parliament: 1 Geo. III,
c. 23).

Act of Settlement 1701, by the legislature's will rather than by divine ordination.[27] The House of Lords was composed of all English peers temporal, together with the two archbishops and 24 bishops representing the established Church and the 16 representative peers of Scotland.[28] Most complex of all, the Commons consisted of the 92 county members and the 421 representatives of the chartered boroughs; to which union had added 36 county and nine burgh members for Scotland in 1707.[29] In the English counties the franchise was uniform and relatively straightforward, belonging to the 40s. freeholders. In the boroughs, it varied with the charter, which was often obscure in initial terms or had become so through the subsequent manipulations of monarchs eager to control their Parliaments. Much therefore had come to depend on local custom. Only a few had an occupier franchise, rather more a householder qualification (measured mostly by liability to poor rate) and some a freehold or burgage tenure basis. Many were controlled by the freemen and more by the borough corporation, a self-perpetuating clique; some, where the town had decayed away (like Old Sarum), were the fief of a few plot owners, making the "rotten" borough an entirely saleable property.[30]

Parliaments, moreover, had been extended from three to seven years maximum at George I's accession,[31] so that the business of election, for all that a serious contest might arise,[32] was intermittent. At once one encounters the gap between constitutional description and political reality. The representation of landed property, so admired by Burke as the wisest way of "holding all physical and moral natures each in their appointed place," was secured through various types of influence. The Lords were themselves leading figures among the landowners, great, substantial and moderate. But it was their very considerable control over Commons seats which made them the fulcrum of the "balanced constitution." Yet the Crown as a great landholder had its share of interest in the Commons; and if the Hanoverians could no longer employ the royal prerogative to rewrite borough franchises, they and their intimates still used the power of purchase and reward to increase the strength of the Court "party." The legacy of Stuart ambition meant that such manifestations of influence were watched with particular jealousy: the country "party," with a centre of gravity among the county members of the Commons, was the grouping from which the King and his advisers might most consistently expect opposition.[33]

---

[27] Blackstone, *Commentaries*, I Chap. 6.

[28] *Ibid.*, 155–157. Heirs with courtesy titles were not members. Union with Ireland in 1800 added 28 representatives. The royal prerogative to create new peers was preserved without impediment in 1721 by a Commons eager for honours. See generally, Maitland (1908), pp. 347–351.

[29] Union with Ireland would add 64 county and 36 borough members, giving a total house of 553.

[30] See generally, Maitland (1908), pp. 351–357.

[31] 1 Geo I. 2 c. 38.

[32] Contests were not common but could become very expensive.

[33] On the controversy over principle vs. politics in reign of George III, see now the (embattled) views of J. C. D. Clark, *English Society 1688–1832* (1985) Chaps. 6–8 and *Revolution and Rebellion* (1986) Chap. 6.

In Blackstone's legal perceptions, the monarch was the figure in which all executive power coalesced. The one constitutional means by which he was provided with advice was through his Privy Council.[34] But that body was much too large and independent of mind for it to be a manageable *modus operandi*. Government was becoming a matter of continuous administration on numerous fronts—the collection of revenue, the organisation of the forces, the supervision of the overseas trade and colonies, the maintenance of civil peace. However much the domestic economy might be freed from state regulation, central government was the subject of constant accretion. When royal authority depended so much on influence bought through the rewards of office, the growth was limited only by the size of the Crown's revenue. The various departments of State were presided over by the holder of an ancient office, notably the Lords Commissioners of the Treasury,[35] or one of the Secretaries of State (originally a Tudor office)[36] or an office-bearer established by more recent statute. These executive chiefs gained their positions as the confidants of the monarch and tended to form an inner circle of advisers. Queen Anne had held regular "Cabinets" and the idea persisted, dividing at some stages into inner and outer ranks, but still contributing to a process in which the monarch would play a decisive personal role. The chief among these ministers, forerunner of the modern prime minister, remained so long as he kept the royal confidence, though it was already part of that favour that he should also enjoy the support of the Commons on most issues. His relationship with his king was a personal one and his dismissal did not precipitate as of course the resignation of the rest of the cabinet. It needed the revision of the franchise in 1832, combined with the transfer of departmental financing from the king's civil list to the consolidated fund,[37] for the convention of ministerial responsibility to the Commons to begin its growth.

The telling image of the eighteenth-century constitution is of balance rather than of separation. Between the three constituent parts of central government there continued to be a host of linkages: the king's ministers were normally members of one or other House, the House of Lords kept its function as the ultimate resort within the system of courts, the Lord Chancellor, a royal nominee with a Cabinet seat, functioned as both judge and legislator. In the small world of national politics, the cross-functions could head off frontal collisions, while still doing something to ensure that no one person—not even the monarch—thrust out beyond the bounds of critical constraint. In the worlds of more direct consequence to the great bulk of the populace, the government of shire, borough and parish, no such

---

[34] *Commentaries*, I Chap. 5.

[35] From this office in commission, the First Lord would, in the nineteenth century, come normally to be the Prime Minister and the Chancellor of the Exchequer the finance minister.

[36] For most of the eighteenth century there were two—by the 1780s a Home Secretary and a Foreign Secretary. In 1801, a third became Secretary for War and the Colonies, the office not being divided until 1854.

[37] This transfer, begun in earnest in 1816, was carried much further between 1830 and 1837.

systematic distinctions could be observed. Powerful local families and individuals found less formal ways of accommodating their rivalries and treated their charge over most local activities—as Lords Lieutenant, justices of the peace, commissioners, trustees and the like—as natural adjuncts of their social supremacy. The justices organised prosecutions, sat as judges and maintained gaols; they prescribed rules for dispensing the poor rate, supervised the overseers of the poor in the parishes and heard appeals from disappointed applicants; borough corporations determined rights to trade by issuing bye-laws and granting individual freedoms.[38] Interweaving of functions exemplified how difficult it would have been in practice to distinguish between the legislative, executive and judicial elements of local government.

Those aspects of government which imposed obligations on individuals (and most came to this in the end) required the authority of law. Without it any interference with person or property would in principle be a legal wrong. The jurisdiction and other powers of the justices was very largely to be found in statute, that of manorial tribunals was mostly a matter of custom, corporations might look to the express terms or the implications of their charters. The courts of common law, as we shall see,[39] were becoming increasingly eager to try questions of jurisdiction or authority to act, taking an interferer's view of those special processes which Lord Mansfield would group together as the "prerogative writs"—notably habeas corpus, prohibition, mandamus and certiorari. Typically King's Bench under Mansfield would subject the bye-law-making power of a borough corporation (conferred in very general terms) so that it was used only to regulate and not to restrain trade[40]: the decisions had a dramatic effect in breaking up the local monopolies of trade gilds.[41] But not all "governmental" decisions were yet subject to such external discipline. Borough corporations were still regarded by Lord Eldon as free to take self-interested decisions about expenditure of their own monies.[42] But this was a last bastion of privilege reflecting the curious function of boroughs in the constitution of the Commons. Against it courts of equity would soon begin to turn soon afterwards. Monies held upon charitable trusts had long been useable only for the purposes prescribed.[43] Particular, and then more general, funds of boroughs came to be treated in similar case.[44] The change was virtually complete by 1835, when new municipal corporations replaced

---

[38] See below, pp. 30ff., 551ff., 561ff.
[39] Below, pp. 31–33, 35.
[40] e.g., Harrison v. Godman (1756) 1 Burr. 12.
[41] See, for an example, R. S. Neale, Bath 1680–1850 (1981) pp. 63–69.
[42] Mayor of Colchester v. Lowten (1813) 1 V. & B. 226 (corporation entitled to pay bill of costs of Town Clerk's agent in fighting an election to the office—this was sufficiently "connected with Corporate Purposes").
[43] When in the early nineteenth century, reformists sought once more to insist upon this principle, borough corporations were found to be among the most neglectful of charity trustees: see below.
[44] Funds raised by rate or duty for the execution of public works by virtue of statute were held on trust: Att.-Gen. v. Brown (1818) 1 Swans. 265; Att.-Gen. v. Mayor of Dublin (1827) 1 Bligh N.S.P.C. 312, (1834) 3 Cl. & F. 289. Likewise lands and revenue held for public purposes by virtue of charter or custom: Att.-Gen. v. Gort (1816) 6 Dow.

the boroughs, their powers and duties carefully delimited by statute.[45] These were some of the last steps in the process of establishing
and refining a Rule of Law highly sensitive to individual liberty and
private property, and insistent upon the accountability of all action
in the name of government.

The theme was already one of central significance to eighteenth
century political life. It became, in the early years of George III's
reign, the focus for a growing dissatisfaction with the results of 1689.
John Wilkes and his associates astutely twisted the tails of ministers,
first by securing the rulings of Common Pleas that general search
warrants, allowing fishing expeditions for evidence of crime, were
against the liberty of the subject guaranteed by common law.[46] Then,
the freeholders of Middlesex thrice elected Wilkes a county member,
and each time the Crown, by alleging seditious libel against him, had
the Commons refuse him membership, on the third occasion substituting Colonel Luttrell—its own man and second in the race. Thus
was demonstrated both the extent of royal influence in the lower
chamber and the fundamentally undemocratic way in which it might
be used.[47] The stage was set for a persistent radicalism mainly preoccupied with means rather than ends, with access to power rather
than the substance of social change.[48] Its main achievements would
come only in 1832, after the long history of wars with the American
colonists and with France and the observation (much of it fearful) of
experiments in constitution-making in both those countries.

So long as the wars lasted, ministries which took to calling themselves "Tory" could rule virtually uninterrupted. They could attack
any threatening signs of dissidence with the might of the law, their
train of prosecutions against authors, printers and radical activists[49]

136; *Att.-Gen.* v. *Heelis* (1829) 2 Sim. & St. 67. Old boroughs could not pay over any of
their income to support local churches: *Att.-Gen.* v. *Aspinall* (1837) 2 My. & Cr. 613;
Att.-Gen. v. *Wilson* (1840) 1 Cr. & Ph. 1.

[45] In particular the borough fund was to be used only for given purposes and any surplus was to be applied for the public benefit of the inhabitants and the improvement of the borough: 5 & 6 Will. IV, c. 76, s. 92.

[46] The cases disapproved warrants to search for and arrest the authors, printers and
publishers of the *North Briton* No. 45 (*Wilkes* v. *Wood* (1763) 2 Wils. K.B. 203, 204;
Leach v. *Money* (1765) 19 St. Tr. 1001—KB cautiously upholding CP); then dis-
approved warrants to arrest the plaintiff and seize his papers on suspicion (*Entick* v.
Carrington (1765) 2 Wils. K.B. 275; *Wilkes* v. *Lord Halifax* (1769) 2 Wils. K.B. at 1406).
The Englishman's home was re-affirmed his castle: "with respect to the argument of
State necessity . . . the common law does not understand that kind of reasoning,"
said Lord Camden (2 Wils. K.B. at 1073).

[47] The argument came to rest chiefly on the scope of Commons privilege: having
expelled Wilkes (which had first occurred five years before), could the House declare
him an incapable candidate so that votes given him were wasted? It assumed power
to do so, but powerful voices at the time (led by Burke and Grenville) strove to
maintain the decision in *Ashby* v. *White* ((1704) 2 Ld. Raym. 938) that the *existence* of
a privilege was a matter either of statute or common law, not of resolution by the
House concerned. Eventually, the Commons expunged its record of the Middlesex
elections: see Holdsworth, X, pp. 539–44.

[48] See H. T. Dickinson, *Liberty and Property* (1977) Chaps. 6, 7.

[49] While Tom Paine was successfully prosecuted *in absentia* for seditious libel in the
The Rights of Man, Part II (1792), prosecutions against Horne Tooke and others were
dismal failures; the colourful advocacy of Erskine did much to shame even special
juries into acquitting: see L. P. Dykstra, *For the Defence* (1949); E. P. Thompson, *The
Making of the English Working Class* (1963) Chap. 5.

being supported by new legislation on the definition of treason, seditious meetings, illegal oath-taking and mutiny, a prohibitive stamp duty on the popular press and even a temporary suspension of habeas corpus. But the intensification of such measures in the troubled years after 1815, culminating in the Six Acts and the extravagant attack on the Peterloo crowd listening to the democratic rousings of Orator Hunt, gave focus to a new unease.[50] Industrialisation and urban growth had come far enough for a real conflict of interest to be felt with the agricultural protectionism of the governing class. The heirs of Charles James Fox, now the out-of-office "Whigs," could discover their reformist leanings and allow Lord John Russell to emerge as the respectable champion of moderate change in the Commons franchise.[51] The systematisation of that franchise was indeed the issue best calculated to induce perceptions of large horizontal affinities within society; and so the language of class began to penetrate the hustings.

Only a fringe contemplated physical violence as the means towards reform, the bulk of radicals accepting that Parliament itself, unrepresentative as it was, could be induced to make its lower house appreciably more so: a democracy of manhood suffrage according to the real radicals, a revised representation of the propertied (following a plenitude of different proposals) according to the less extreme.[52] In the event, the spectre of civil unrest loomed large enough to goad even a highly reluctant House of Lords into acquiescence in the Reform Bill (in its third revision) promoted by Grey's Whig government. In 1830 the new revolution in France, replacing the autocratic Charles X with Louis Philippe, seemed to be sparking the "Swing" outbreaks of violence and threats in the agricultural south and west of England. The mass demonstrations and alarming disturbances which followed the Lords' rejection of the Reform Bill of 1831 contributed to the divisions among the Tory opposition. Grey was ultimately able to persuade William IV to pledge the creation of new peerages enough to carry the Bill. Before so terrible a threat the Lords capitulated.[53]

Disenfranchisement of rotten and pocket boroughs, even when balanced against increased representation for burgeoning cities, reduced the number of borough members from 465 to 399, while county seats rose from 188 to 253. In England and Wales, the vote went in the counties to the 40s. freeholders (for the most part), the £10 copyholders and long leaseholders and £50 tenants on shorter terms and at will[54]; in the boroughs to the £10 occupiers who also

---

[50] See below, p. 595ff.

[51] In 1821 he secured the disenfranchisement of the rotten Cornish borough of Grampound: 2 Geo. IV, c. 47.

[52] Brougham, for all the alarm that he caused his leaders on the subject, did not dare to go so far on the abolition of rotten boroughs.

[53] 2 & 3 W. IV, c. 45. For this complex story, see esp. P. A. Brown, *The French Revolution in English History* (1923); J. R. M. Butler, *The Passing of the Great Reform Bill* (1914); M. Brock, *The Great Reform Act* (1973); J. Cannon, *Parliamentary Reform 1640–1832* (2nd ed., 1980); J. C. D. Clark, *English Society 1688–1832* (1985), Chap. 6.

[54] Shorter leaseholds were those from 20–60 years; in the case of the tenancies less than these, the measurement was £50 rent rather than annual value.

satisfied residence and ratepaying qualifications.[55] The electorate grew by a half (to 652,000)[56] but the results were in many respects short of the expectations of those who had battled most persistently for reform. At a few points there appeared to be decisive change. The constitutional relationship of central executive to legislature at last emerged in essentially modern form, even if there was much still to come in the full political sense. The Crown lost its direct influence over Commons seats and the personal direction of the monarch over the course of executive government received its final ousting: in 1834 Peel could not sustain office against repeated Commons defeats, for all the King's support. Collective responsibility of Prime Minister and Cabinet and the individual responsibility of Ministers for the activities of their departments were to establish their conventional character under repeated resort. Constitutional historians and theorists recognised the peculiar force of these and other practices in the very structure of the State.[57] Not until their treatment by Dicey as constitutional conventions would they find any adequate status in terms of law.[58]

The relation of legislature and executive came under novel strains because—and this was the real mark of 1832—both began to enter upon new realms of activity. Parliament ceased to be an institution largely preoccupied with the initiatives of individuals, and local and private groups. As had already begun to appear in the twenties, cabinets would expect to foster regular programmes of general legislation for the governance of the whole Kingdom and its clutch of colonies. Law was becoming a positive instrument of social engineering and this would often take the form of introducing new institutions of central and local government or would confer new executive powers on existing authorities. As Dicey remarked, the franchise reform of 1832 stands as a clear example of how law can affect and lead "public opinion" as distinct from responding to it.[59] The very idea that legislation might remake the world is perhaps the profoundest element in that influence.

The mutual antagonisms of upper, middle and working classes, so heightened by the events of 1830–1832, soon appeared to be little altered by the outcome. Middle-class representation in the Commons had increased only modestly: there were a number of radicals—particularly on the Whig fringe—but still some 500 members were for the landed interest, a figure which would slip by only a fifth in the period to 1865.[60] Prime ministers and cabinets came very largely from

---

[55] The latter conditions were designed to stop the multiplication of votes; so was the exclusion of some freeholders. They did not succeed.

[56] Out of a population for the Kingdom of £13.9 millions (1831 census).

[57] Thus E. A. Freeman (*Growth of the English Constitution from the Earliest Times* (1872) Chap. 3) wrote of "certain" traditional maxims, which limit the exercise of all political powers . . . for the most part unwritten and conventional . . . (which) embody the matured experience of successive generations of statesmen in the conduct of public affairs and are known as precepts of the constitution." See O. Hood Phillips (1966) 29 M.L.R. 137.

[58] A. V. Dicey, *Introduction to the Study of the Law of the Constitution* (1885) Chap. 14.

[59] Dicey (1914), pp. 42–43.

[60] Until well after 1867 a considerable proportion of seats would not be contested: T. Lloyd (1965) 8 Hist. J. 260.

the landed class, whether government was Whig and Tory. The working-class activitists who had debated and organised in favour of reform took their bitter disappointment and frustration into the groupings which, because of their fragmentation, make up the complex phenomenon of Chartism.[61] The People's Charter of 1838, a temporary common denominator, expressed a continuing belief in change through the machinery of law. It set forth once again the demand for universal manhood suffrage, together with five other claims that had been widely debated for a decade and more; two of these—annual parliaments and the secret ballot—had been placed out of prospect by Grey before the first Whig Bill had been presented.[62]

Middle-class concerns, however, were brought to bear on substantive issues by the campaign for repeal of the Corn Laws. The protection of domestic agriculture was the result of a long series of enactments, and Wellington had accepted in 1827 that legislation should be used to temper their impact. Now their very existence was threatened by class arguments that sensed well enough the need to win working-class allegiance for the future: the protection of agriculture meant high food prices that ate into wages (the more so, if the nostrum of a "wages fund" was accepted). Against such high rhetoric, whipped up by Cobden, Bright and their fellows in the Anti-Corn Law League, the protectionist case that the whole campaign was a conspiracy to lower wages made little ground. Peel was persuaded and went out of office with the Tory party severed on the issue. The advocates of the "entreprenurial ideal" (to use Perkin's phrase) achieved their victory with ease under the ensuing Whig government.[63] The middle classes found that they had an influence even for causes that ran counter to the agricultural interest. In a world troubled by the rumblings of Chartist violence and demands for a ten-hour day, to say nothing of the numbing misery in Ireland, they could accept the settlement of 1832 as a sufficient representation. The regular testing of ministerial responsibility in the 1850s gave a satisfying patina to the theory of Parliamentary sovereignty. The fluidity of politics—enhanced by the split between Peelites and Protectionists and by a loose notion of party loyalty which allowed considerable play for individual conscience and interest—bolstered the primacy of the lower house in the new constitutional order. In the fifties Bright and his friends could test opinion by promoting further reform bills, Lord John Russell could waiver in his adherence to "finality," but Palmerston and other grand figures could brush the question easily aside.[64]

[61] The first outcome was the short-lived Grand National Consolidated Trades Union and its sorry tail-piece, the prosecution of the "Tolpuddle Martyrs" of Dorset in 1834: see below, pp. 309–312.

[62] Of the others: the property qualification for MPs would be abolished in 1858, payment of members would have to wait until 1911. For equalisation of electoral districts and the secret ballot, see below p. 82ff.

[63] 9 & 10 Vict., c. 22; For details of the campaign and aftermath, D. G. Barnes, *A History of the English Corn Laws from 1660–1846*; N. McCord, *The Anti-Corn Law League 1838–1846* (1958).

[64] In a period when much earnest consideration was given to the "industrious classes," there was toying with "fancy franchises"—entitlements to vote based on

It was not to be dismissed even for a generation. By the death of
Palmerston in 1865, influential opinion had shifted, mysteriously but
somehow decisively, in favour of a second prescription of reform, in
a dosage that would make full adult suffrage ultimately irresistible.
There were already democratic precedents to bolster the argument:
in the United States (where freedom had brought civil war), in the
colonies, in the municipal corporations and the poor law unions of
the new local government, more liberal franchises were known. But
the real stirrings that brought Russell and Gladstone, and then Derby
and Disraeli, to advocate positive proposals were the product of
numerous forces. By the time the details had been thought through
and the political advantages of particular formulae had been reckoned, the final bill was passed by an anxious Parliament, leaping
with Derby into a democratic dark only because the present had been
too harshly spot-lit as unrepresentative.[65] So it is the initial impetus
which is the crucial issue.

The Second Reform Act in the end gave the vote to all male householders in the towns, as well as lowering the rating limit for
occupiers in the counties to £12, thus increasing the electorate from
just over one million to almost two millions.[66] It was primarily a
reckoning with the upper ranks of the working class, the skilled
workers who by earnings and an eagerness for education had
marked themselves out as an "aristocracy of labour." This back-
bone of the workforce had begun to acquire an organised strength,
through its trade unions, and to an extent through political
societies, which drew a novel, grudging respect. The comfortable
classes were beginning to feel the wisdom of finding the workers a
place before too late in a capitalist world, with a measure of political entitlement, access to regular schooling for their children and
some better understanding about collective bargaining in the
workplace. To this attitude the orderliness and high moral tone of
the great suffrage meetings contributed significantly. The two main
outbreaks of violence, both in Hyde Park, came relatively late and
were not supported by the crowds' leaders. If anything the events
helped to foster the general view that "the power of mere
numbers" was better contained by concession at once than put
down by confrontation later.

The debates on the Bill raised the position of women as a serious
issue for the first time, pricking a little the assumption that they were

educational achievement and other solid indicators of responsible citizenship. Even
Palmerston flirted with the possibility, notably in a bill that he felt obliged briefly to
support in 1859. In the early stages of the 1866 agitations, the "fancy franchises"
were prominent; but Disraeli dropped them when he agreed to a wide occupier
basis.

[65] The image was found by Disraeli for his leader, though he himself saw well-enough
the chances in the deal he had secured. For the view that fear was a predominant
motive, see R. Harrison, *Before the Socialists* (1965) Chap. 3; and an attempt at countering, M. Cowling, *1867; Disraeli, Gladstone and Revolution* (1967). Also, F. B. Smith,
The Making of the Second Reform Act (1966); G. Himmelfarb (1966) 6 J. Brit. St. 97.

[66] 30 & 31 Vict. c. 102. There was a redistribution of 25 county and 15 town seats. Five
large cities acquired a third seat, but only under a limitation of each elector's votes
to two, which was added by the House of Lords (s.9).

inferior and dependant beings.[67] The democratic radicals and Chartists had, not surprisingly, been able to devote little energy to the female suffrage.[68] But the conventions which condemned middle-class ladies by social propriety, limited education and professional embargo to a life of child-bearing and domestic supervision was beginning to produce a profound reaction, particularly amongst the able and under-occupied.[69] J. S. Mill's dignified plea in the Commons for the admission of women to the suffrage on the same property conditions as men met the standard conservative reaction: that they would only abuse it, through ignorance and an innate emotionalism.[70] But the defeat (196 to 73) was by no means humiliating and the campaign secured their admission to the municipal franchise two years later—a victory indeed.[71] There would soon be consequential gains for women in other fields: married women's property, wife battering and the treatment of prostitutes.[72]

IV. The Legal System

(a) General

Before Parliament became a regular source of legal change on a national scale, the chief burden of propounding law lay with the courts. They teased it out of customary expectations, their own previous decisions and established procedures, adding twists and refinements of their own as they felt the need. For the country as a whole this constant process had given rise to the twin systems of common law and equity and to that *tertium quid*, the rules of civilian origin applied in the ecclesiastical and admiralty courts. In local communities there were numerous other jurisdictions, some clearly within the common law frame, others applying discrete forms of local custom or other, more amorphous principle. In the period up to 1875 a certain measure of rationalisation was brought to this array of jurisdictions. In tracing its outline, two underlying determinants of its shape emerge. One is the desire to impose unity in place of diversity, so that the law could be presented as equal, raising for all the same fear but no favour.[73] The other, running in a different direction, is the

---

[67] See generally, N. St. John-Stevas in R. Graveson and F. R. Crane, *A Century of Family Law* (1957) Chap. 11; E. Campbell (1961) 1 Adelaide L.R. 190.

[68] Despite the appearance of Mary Wollstonecraft's *Vindication of the Rights of Women* in 1792, Bentham prevaricated on the subject and James Mill opposed.

[69] The journals of the sixties marked such women out as "the Girl of the Period," learning the need of liberty at the feet of J.S. Mill and replacing her family creed with the positivist humanism of Auguste Comte.

[70] P.D. 1867 CLXXXVII 817–29. Mill's *The Subjection of Women*, written in 1861, was only published in 1869.

[71] Municipal Franchise Act 1869, ss.1, 9; closely followed by the Education Act 1870, s.29, which gave women the right to be elected to school boards. But the common law disability of married women was held still to exclude them: *R. v. Harrald* (1872) L.R. 7 Q.B. 361.

[72] See below, pp. 398ff., 391–392. For the later history of political and professional rights, see below, pp. 82–83.

[73] A perspective explored *in extenso* by Arthurs (1985).

inclination to conserve the basic features of the English system—in particular that judges would continue to be drawn from the practising bar rather than from a separate cadre; and that the "high priests" among them would remain a very small band, whose decisions alone would be the regular source of common law and statutory interpretation.[74]

(b) Central and Local Elements

(i) Jurisdictions

Tables I–III (pp. 19–21) give a first impression of the range of court systems around 1800 and the extent to which they were to change during the nineteenth century. Civil and criminal jurisdictions are presented separately, for, despite a few awkwardnesses of fit, this had become the basic distinction in the minds of lawyers. The constitutional struggles of the seventeenth century had put paid to any structural division between private rights defined by common law and a "public law" by which government might employ a dispensing power to override those rights.

The presence of the common law judges at the centre of both the civil and the criminal jurisdictions is a first feature of the whole. Their ubiquity had long been a crucial part of English government. The web of central control which Norman and Plantagenet kings had spread across the country had depended substantially on these judicial elements, particularly the twice-yearly circuits of pairs of royal judges to the county assizes. The eighteenth-century monarchs and princes on the European continent might face grave difficulties in extending their law and authority throughout their realms.[75] By contrast, the Hanoverian Kings found that the fibres of the judicial system encompassed not only England but also Wales. The accommodation with Scotland, while leaving the Scots judicature intact, had placed it under the ultimate sovereignty of Parliament and there, at least after 1750, the rule of the chiefs did give place to the King's law.[76] It was Ireland that was the case apart. But the Irish problem was scarcely one of competition between judicial systems; it was the much graver difficulty of securing English authority, including its legal institutions, against ever-brewing insubordination.[77] The case of Ireland gives immediate proportion to arguments about "pluralism" in the judicature of England and Wales.

Each of the three common law courts consisted of a chief justice and three puisne judges;[78] and the Court of Chancery was composed

---

[74] See Simpson in Allsop (ed.) (1970).

[75] See, e.g. H. E. Strakosch, *State Absolutism and the Struggle for the Rule of Law* (1967) 7–14.

[76] Subject, that is, not only to enactments of Westminster but also to a final right of appeal to the House of Lords (as was Ireland). The delaying effect of Scots appeals made them comparatively popular by the eighteenth century: see Stevens (1978) pp. 7–10, 15–16.

[77] See e.g. R. B. McDowell, *Ireland in the Age of Imperialism and Revolution 1760–1801* (1979), esp. Chap. 16; S. Clark and J. S. Donnelly (eds.) *Irish Peasants* (1983), esp. Chaps. 1, 4.

[78] Known in the Court of Exchequer by the titles of Chief Baron and Baron.

simply of the Lord Chancellor and, beneath him, the Master of the Rolls, until in 1813 a Vice-Chancellor was added. Here was the most distinctive characteristic of the entire common law system, particularly to those accustomed to the large ranks of career judges in the civilian systems of Europe. The beginnings of this crucial divergence of structure lay in the thirteenth century when the civilians had turned to a system of inquisition by judge as the form of trial, while English common law had begun to build up the system of jury trial.[79] The difference indeed gave the English system the appearance of marvel, a conjuring trick made possible only by the constant resort to lay participation, not only in the form of juries, but also through the benches of justices of the peace in the counties and boroughs. These two institutions must accordingly be brought into account at an early stage. They bound central justice organically to each region, allowing the propertied ranks of the locality a considerable autonomy but subjecting them to strategic elements of control. In consequence, the main judicial system itself was neither "unified" nor "plural."

(ii) Juries and Justices

The jury, the earlier of these institutions, was to be England's longest surviving instance of government by rotation. By the eighteenth century it had assumed various forms: the trial jury, which is our prime concern; the grand jury of 12 or sometimes many more members, which presented serious crimes for trial; the coroner's jury which considered cases of suspicious death; and various juries of presentment which investigated neglects and nuisances before local courts. The trial jury (of 12) had undergone a process of transformation: the medieval jury, which had decided cases of its own collective knowledge, had given place to a body which decided (still unanimously) upon evidence given before it in court. Yet the jury allowed the law to remain close to local sentiment. Common jurors, who tried the general run of cases, might include small shopkeepers and agricultural labours,[80] men well below the "esquires, merchants and bankers" of a special jury.[81] The possibility that either side, in misdemeanour trials as well as civil proceedings, might require a special jury suggests one way in which there was scope for social manipulation in the system.[82] Equally, since juries always tried cases under the direction of a judge or bench of justices, there was room for influence upon their deliberations and even in some instances the power to refuse to accept their verdict.[83] But the greater wonder was

[79] For a structural and political explanation of the divergence, see J. P. Dawson, A History of Lay Judges (1960), esp. pp. 129–136.

[80] The standing of assize jurors was generally higher than at Quarter Sessions: E. Halévy, England in 1815 (9th ed.), pp. 112–115. Until 1825, the qualification to be a common juror was obscure being left largely to petty constables and under-sheriffs. By 6 G. IV c. 60, s.1, common jurors had to occupy premises of £20 annual value (£30 in London and Middlesex).

[81] The judges did not allow special juries in the most serious criminal cases—treason and felony.

[82] Hence the widespread allegations of jury-fixing in the sedition trials of the 1790s; see, e.g., J. Bentham, Elements of the Art of Packing as applied to Special Juries (1821); above, p. 12.

[83] For the development of such controls, see below, p. 201.

that the jury continued to be a necessary element in all trials at common law. In 1670, the Court of King's Bench had held that juries were no longer liable to attainder for refusing to convict a person accused of crime.[84] This sovereign power of acquittal, together with habeas corpus, soon became elemental to the liberty of the free-born Englishman, envied by Montesquieu and proudly proclaimed by Blackstone and many others, apologists and radicals alike.[85] Governments had to take their comfort from the popular character of the tribunal and the greater acceptability of any verdict that they could procure from it.

The office of justice of the peace, firmly established by the fourteenth century, had become in post-feudal England a prime institution of the governing class. Compared even with juries, the justices were a body remarkable for their degree of independence. Correspondingly, in social origin they were confined more closely to the apex,[86] particularly in the countryside where squirearchy and clergy predominated—a mixture of decent Allworthys and rumbustuous Westerns.[87] In the towns, they might be degraded to the level of the "trading justices" of London, implicated, for instance, in dealings over stolen goods; and as the new manfacturing districts developed, the mill- and mine-owners were drawn onto benches, to continue there the hostilities over discipline and conditions that infected many work-places.[88]

The first concern of the justices was with the command structure of social control, over outbursts of rioting as well as and day-to-day crime. They were the representatives of civil power when armed force was called in, the supervisors of police, the main prosecuting authorities, and often enough the judges. At their quarter sessions (held in each county and borough four times a year) they would sit with a jury to try serious offences which did not carry a mandatory death sentence. In their own localities they would sit, mainly in pairs, to dispense summary justice (at what became known as petty sessions) under an ever-growing catalogue of minor regulatory legislation.[89] Beyond this, as we have already noted, they provided their districts with most of the local government necessary.

The nineteenth century was to make the deployment of both juries and justices more selective. The jury system was gradually confined to the trial of the most serious criminal offences, together with those in the medium range where the accused (or sometimes the prosecution) was not content with summary trial before magistrates.[90] Special juries lost their importance, but common juries continued to be selected by a householder property qualification. This was rela-

---

[84] *Bushell's Case* (1670) 6 St. Tr. 999, Vaughan 135—one of the most singular dissociations of the common law from royal influence.

[85] Green (1985) Chap. 6.

[86] In 1733 (5 Geo. II c. 11) had imposed the property qualification of an annual income of £100 (it would remain until 1906). The appointment lay with the Lord Chancellor—for the counties, on the recommendation of the Lord Lieutenant; for the boroughs, on the corporation (until 1835).

[87] On composition, see esp. E. Moir, *The Justices of the Peace* (1969) Chaps. 4–7.

[88] D. Philips, (1976) 3 Midland Hist. 161; and below, *e.g.*, pp. 297–298.

[89] See below, p. 546ff.

[90] See below, p. 618.

tively radical when set in 1825 by Peel's reforming legislation but had taken on anti-democratic air long before its abolition in 1971.[91] In civil matters a gradual preference emerged for the Chancery mode of trial—by judge alone, with appeal to further judges; but this development lay mainly in the period after 1875.

The justices were to shed many of their general functions in local government. This began in the boroughs, with the introduction of elected municipal councils in 1835.[92] The governance of the shires was to remain headed by quarter sessions until the creation of elected county councils in 1888. In criminal justice, the appearance of modern police forces between 1829 and 1856 provided new prosecutors and left the justices in a supervisory role.[93] Their responsibility for local gaols was ceded to the national system in 1877.[94] Increasingly they became a judicial body and so contributed much in relieving the work-load upon the central judges. In London and a few other cities, the lay justices were replaced or supplemented by stipendiary magistrates, who came to be drawn from the bar.[95] But, for all the antagonism that from time to time the lay justices aroused, the system was too deeply entrenched for the movement towards professional substitutes to be other than marginal. The lay magistracy has proved the least transferable of English institutions of government, but at home it has shown great resilience, being used not only in minor administrative-cum-judicial tasks, such as issuing warrants of arrest and liquor licensing, but also to conduct the bulk of criminal business and to exercise important jurisdictions over family matters and landlord-tenant relations.[96] Throughout this evolution the justices have remained barometers of local power. The system of selection has continued to be hidden and undemocratic but has responded in its own gradual way to the rise of new political forces. The very nature of the institution, requiring substantial, intermittent service without salary, has ensured that benches, whatever their composition in terms of party, are strong in loyalty among themselves and towards the police and others who run local services.

(iii) Judges

In a structured world, where condescension mirrored dependence, the royal judges needed a considerable social position. They were, after all, to carry central authority to the shires and in particular to the county benches with great landowners on their commissions. Among Victorian amateurs of Self-Help, judges were the shining exemplars of social ascent, men who by their determined brilliance could rise from humble to noble rank, through the bar to the bench. Such admiration must, however, be read to scale: true, Abbot, Lord Tenterden, was the son of a Canterbury barber, Copley, Lord Lynd-

---

[91] See W. R. Cornish, The Jury (1968), pp. 26–27.
[92] At the same time the borough benches were reformed—in the Webb's view the principal function of the Municipal Corporations Act 1835: S. & B. Webb, The Manor and The Borough, (1908), p. 727.
[93] See S. & B. Webb, The Parish and the County, (1906), pp. 578–580.
[94] Below, p. 585.
[95] See R. M. Jackson (1946) 9 M.L.R. 1.
[96] Below, pp. 391–393; 135–136, 184–187.

hurst, the son of an American painter, and above all the Scott brothers (Lords Stowell and Eldon) the sons of a Newcastle coal merchant. But in the period 1760–1832, they were a small minority, the great bulk of the judges coming equally from landed and professional families. It would have been remarkable had it been otherwise. Those who acquired highest office were expected to purchase an estate commensurate with their station[97]; and they had all to show the social accomplishment befitting their place in the order of precedence. Perhaps of more interest is that, in the ensuing 75 years, the judiciary became increasingly of middle-class stock, the proportion from professional (particularly legal) backgrounds increasing to 60 per cent, and those from the landed class giving place in considerable measure to those from the entrepreneurial class.[98] The polite professions of the eighteenth century—the church and the armed and civil services—remained for much longer the preserves of the old upper ranks.

Since the appointment of judges was to remain a matter for government, the upper benches were largely inhabited by men who had participated in political life. Those who filled the "political" judgeships—the Lord Chancellorship and the Chief Justiceships— had frequently served as Law Officers of the Crown.[99] Many puisnes were previously M.P.s or candidates (though this may well have been mainly with a view to the bench). Throughout the nineteenth century, they were more likely to be preferred when their own party was in power.[1] Even after 1875, the sprinkling of mediocre Tories among Lord Halsbury's judicial appointments aroused criticism in and beyond the legal professions.[2] It is only in modern times that such party connections have ceased to play a significant part in most appointments to the bench. Yet at all stages, political affiliation must

[97] F. M. L. Thompson, *English Landed Society in the Nineteenth Century* (1963), pp. 51–58. D. Duman, *The Judicial Bench in England 1727–1875* (1982), pp. 126–134, for details of judges' wealth; and for their earnings on the bench, pp. 117–126. In 1750, the puisne judges earned a salary of £1,000 and fees from suitors; gradually the former was increased and in 1825 set at £5,500 (£5,000 in 1832); at the same time, after a Benthamite onslaught, the fee element was removed. The Chief Justices, and even more, the Lord Chancellor, earned more from both sources but in addition held the appointment to many offices. This patronage largely disappeared in 1825. In 1832, the Lord Chancellor received £10,000 (and £4,000 as speaker of House of Lords), the Chief Justices £8,000).

[98] D. Duman, (1973) 17 Am. J. Legal Hist. 353; and above, n. 97, Chaps. 3, 4.

[99] J. L. Edwards, *The Law Officers of the Crown* (1964) Chap. 5; Duman (above, n. 97), pp. 87–88. Lord Mansfield (for substantial periods) and Lord Ellenborough (briefly) were both members of Cabinet while Chief Justice of King's Bench; thereafter, as the Cabinet acquired its modern significance, only the Lord Chancellor was a member. The tradition (never a strict convention) that the Chief Justiceship of the King's Bench (later the Lord Chief Justiceship) would be offered to the Attorney-General of the day survived into the twentieth century. But the manipulation by which the office was kept for Sir Gordon Hewart Att.-Gen. (1921–1922) damaged the very notion of judicial independence: A.T. Lawrence J. took the office *pro tem.* after signing in advance his letter of resignation.

[1] Of 139 judges appointed in the period 1832–1906, 80 had been MPs and another 11 candidates: H. J. Laski, *Studies in Law and Politics* (1932), pp. 168–169. Of these 61 held seats at the time of appointment.

[2] They were by no means all bad. Heuston (1964) Chap. 5 reckons 7 out of 30 appointments to the High Court to have been "dubious."

be ranked a secondary factor, below the homogenising influences of social class and professional experience. These elements of common background were shared by the new ranks of judges as barristers were appointed to the County Courts (after 1846) and to the courts of colony and empire. They formed a body of men whose mutual loyalty and respect were crucial to an expanding common law.

With so much by way of background to those with the power of decision, let us turn to the courts themselves, seeking to identify in their jurisdictions and procedures the factors which become vital to the substance of later chapters.

(c) Civil Courts

(i) Courts of Common Law

The royal courts occupy the centre of Table 1 (p. 19). The three courts of common law—King's Bench, Common Pleas and Exchequer—had evolved as distinct institutions during the Middle Ages. So long as the judges and lesser officers lived by their fees, competition between the three, as well as with jurisdictions outside, was a vital motive in their development. Acceptance of the central courts as a state service, funded out of general revenue as well as litigants' fees, grew in the eighteenth century alongside notions of judicial independence. It produced a new frame of reference, one that was a necessary precursor to the unification of the legal system. Even so, the process of dismantling the offices of profit within the courts proved particularly laborious and costly.[3]

The royal courts had developed over a long period towards a balance between competition and cooperation. Common law actions had to be instituted in King's Bench, Common Pleas or Exchequer and the initial, documentary stages of the litigation were a matter for that court alone, including the argument of preliminary points of law on demurrer.[4] This took place during a law term before the court sitting as a bench of judges in Westminster Hall. However, the action was rarely tried there but was dealt with on an Assize circuit under the *Nisi Prius* system.[5] The judge might be any one of the 12, not necessarily from the court of the proceedings; and the jury would be summoned to the assize court from the county. If the result of the trial went on review,[6] the case would pass back to its own court; but after that there was the possibility of an appeal by writ of error to a body drawn from the other judges.[7] Maintaining the equilibrium of this bifurcated system was inherently difficult and depended upon two factors: the generation and recording of substantive rules and the development of formal procedures. The royal judges had begun the process of formulating a discrete common law of civil obligation—rules that applied between one individual and another as

---

[3] For a full account of these offices, distinguishing those which had become complete sinecures, see Holdsworth I, pp. 246–252 (common law), pp. 435–442 (chancery); and numerous official investigations in the nineteenth century.

[4] See below, p. 25.

[5] *Nisi prius*: unless the case had already been heard at Westminster.

[6] For the techniques, see below, p. 26.

[7] Below, p. 25.

well as between Crown and subject—even before their courts emerged as bodies distinct from the Royal Council. In a world where legal rights were barely distinguishable from customs of the locality, there had been a novel self-consciousness about constructing rules that were common to the country, principles which would determine what were wrongful invasions of land and injuries to it, wrongful misappropriations of chattels and damage to them, wrongful interference with expectation, whether in the fulfilment of agreements or the maintenance of good reputation.

A hard crust of rule had crystallised gradually upon a bedrock of procedural constraint. The number of writs and bills available to commence a common law action was always limited and it was for the judges to determine what factual circumstances would justify an action under any one of them. This provided the other half of the restrictive process; the need to find a form of action gave that element of uniformity and certainty which is a necessary condition of a rule. The process made it natural for the common law to carry forward its settled rules into changed times where they might withstand pressures for alteration. Yet there was also room within for adaptations, as the resort to incontrovertible allegations and to fictions of various kinds makes plain. The idea of judicial precedent coalesced around the acceptable forms of action and the written pleadings that were introduced to support the plaint and defence to it. The sufficiency of the formally pleaded case was the issue that could be raised before the full court on demurrer and the defendant who chose to raise it had to forego his trial with a jury on the merits.[8] Before the age of print, the precedents on sufficient pleadings were collected in the tutoring manuals that we now know as Year Books, and from the sixteenth century in collections of private law reports.[9]

As jury trial gradually became the standard method of the common law courts, pleadings took the appearance of a corollary to it. The pleadings recorded the allegation and defence and came, as jurors became less and less likely to know anything personally of the merits, to be supported by evidence at the trial. The pleadings would fine down the area of contention between the adversaries and would (at least ideally) give notice of the disputed facts, which it would be for one or other to make out if he could.[10] The use of a tribunal to judge fact which could be brought together only with difficulty, and which would not necessarily be literate, held its own imperatives: the trial had to take place at one time, and to be as brief and as much in oral form as possible. As evidence came to be admitted and the skills of lawyers expanded from the drafting of pleadings to the examination of witnesses and the argument of cases to juries, there developed new refinements. Not only were the parties incompetent

---

[8] The history of the common law, as it developed through the writ and pleading system, is now treated with great authority and subtlety by Baker (1979) and Milsom (1981); for details of the techniques, see also R. Sutton, *Personal Actions at Common Law* (1929).

[9] On the history of private law reporting, see J. W. Wallace, *The Reporters* (1882); W. S. T. Daniel, *The History and Origin of the Law Reports* (1883); Holdsworth XII, 101–162; J. P. Dawson, *The Oracles of the Law* (1968) Chap. 1.

[10] See, however, below, p. 41.

as witnesses, so were others interested in the outcome of the suit.[11] Rules, such as that against hearsay, would disallow evidence that a jury could not be trusted to weigh. Judges would not only direct the jury on the applicable law but would rule that certain issues were for them to decide as matters of law. Not surprisingly these included all questions upon the construction of documents: but there came to be numerous others, as judges felt a growing need to curb the sympathetic enthusiams of juries.[12]

That the corps of judges was so tiny reinforced the adversarial nature of litigation in the common law courts. The main initiatives in furthering an action or defence were not directed by the court but left to the parties; and so for a litigant to act without professional assistance was hazardous. Here was a natural environment for technical objections and procedural stratagems: these choking, fee-sucking devices were the bane of eighteenth-century litigation.[13] Lord Mansfield, while Chief Justice of King's Bench, did seek to free the main branches of process; but under his successors, the parasitic growths crept back.[14] Since costs had long been on an indemnity basis, the loser paying a substantial portion of the winner's costs, a common law action was not worth risking for relatively small sums or injuries and was in any event beyond the means of much of the population.[15]

There was another way in which litigation was tending to grow more complex. The traditional process, working towards a jury's verdict, did not encourage the development of an appellate structure. To the written record of a suit, formed from writ and pleadings, objections in point of law lay initially by demurrer[16] and this stage came to be open to higher review: the writ of error allowed argument of the same type to be put to a further body of the judges[17] and from them error could be taken to the House of Lords.[18] The trial itself had no formal record which could be open to the same challenge. Yet, as witnesses became a regular phenomenon, some corrective device seemed necessary to ensure that the growing body of procedural and

---

[11] Jeremy Bentham's ridicule of the rules excluding all interested persons as witnesses was the first pinnacle of his critique of evidence law: *Collected Works* (1843) VI, pp. 487–89, 506–17.

[12] See below, pp. 201, 496ff.

[13] We lack detailed evidence of the business of the common law courts in this period; but there are impressions enough of the problems to be had from the reported cases and elsewhere.

[14] For details, see C. H. S. Fifoot, *Lord Mansfield* (1936) Chaps. 3, 8.

[15] For working-men plaintiffs, see below, p. 496.

[16] With time it became possible to raise objections to the pleadings after the trial by means of a motion in arrest of judgment or for judgment *non obstante veredicto*, both before the full bench. Too often, it seems, these became devices for delay after losing at trial: see generally, Sutton (above, n. 8), pp. 129–132.

[17] In the case of Kings Bench and Exchequer, this body (the Court of Exchequer Chamber) consisted of the judges of the other two common law courts; in the case of Common Pleas error lay to the Kings Bench. In 1830, the three courts were put on the same footing, appeal lying to an Exchequer Chamber consisting of the judges of the other two courts: 11 Geo. 4 & 1 Will. IV, c. 70, s.8.

[18] English appeals to the Lords were rare until the nineteenth century. To answer difficult questions, the Lords might seek the advice of all the judges. See generally, Stevens (1978) Chap. 1; A. S. Turberville, *The House of Lords in the Eighteenth Century* (1927) and (1936) 52 L.Q.R. 189; L. Blom Cooper and G. Drewry, *Final Appeal* (1972) Chap. 2.

evidential rules were duly applied and that the judge's summing up on the evidence was good in law. From the late seventeenth century, a succession of techniques were tried, some operable only with the cooperation of the trial judge—notably the taking of a special verdict[19] and the statement by him of a special case for the opinion of the full bench.[20] One, however, the motion for a new trial, depended only upon counsel raising an objection at the relevant point in the trial. These were important developments in the evolution of the common law towards a less formal process with a regular right of appeal on legal and procedural issues arising out of the trial. But in their eighteenth century forms, they shared the general inability to resist factitious gamesmanship. While Blackstone could find the motion for a new trial a considerable improvement upon any alternative, within a century Mr. Justice Maule was condemning it as "incomparably the worst" mode ever invented of administering justice.[21]

(ii) Chancery: the Administration of Equity

The Court of Chancery, which administered the distinct set of principles known as equity, was by the eighteenth century no longer a thrusting competitor of the common law.[22] The Lord Chancellor had first acquired jurisdiction as the royal officer who reviewed petitions to the monarch, the ultimate fount of justice. His interventions had long been principally in the interests of the propertied private suitor and his court had escaped the annihilation that had swept away such instruments of state policy as Star Chamber and High Commission. In the Tudor and Stuart period, the Chancellor's responsiveness had not only swelled his caseload (and concomitant fees) but had provided a major technique in stepping beyond bounds set by common law doctrine. From this process emerged such crucial ideas as the settlement of land and other trusts of property, the conception of mortgage as a security interest and the assig-

---

[19] This required the jury to answer a set of specific questions about the facts so that the full bench might rule on their actionability in law. It displaced the device of a demurrer to evidence: see *e.g., Lickbarrow* v. *Mason* (1787) 4 Bro. P.C. 57; *Gibson* v. *Hunter* (1793) 6 Bro. P.C. 235.

[20] This followed upon the taking of a general verdict. One variant allowed the judge to take a verdict subject to argument upon a point reserved by him for the full bench; if this succeeded, a contrary verdict would in effect be substituted. This device limited counsel to arguing the specific point reserved.

[21] *Commentaries*, III Chap. 24, W. F. Finlason, *An Exposition of Our Judicial System* (1877), p. 359. The only record of the objection would be in the judge's note: the formal bill of exceptions (which became common in Scots procedure) was not allowed to blossom in England. The trial judge might not be a member of the full bench. Counsel supporting the verdict was obliged to argue its correctness first, before knowing necessarily the real objection being raised. The procedure was perhaps allowed to remain so unhelpful because it could be followed even when the judge would not cooperate. Probably the point-reserved procedure (referred to in the previous note) was the improvement that the judges did permit.

[22] For this growth, see Holdsworth, I Chap. 5; Milsom (1981) Chap. 4; Baker (1979) Chap. 6. The Court of Exchequer, as the court peculiarly concerned with the Crown's property and revenue, had acquired a similar jurisdiction in equity; this was passed to Chancery in 1841, 5 Vict., c. 5, s.I; see W. H. Bryson, *The Equity Side of the Exchequer* (1975).

nability of debts.[23] In addition, Chancery had its own prerogatives in the matter of remedies. It did not in general award monetary amounts; damages or debts due were for a jury's verdict at common law. Instead Chancery directed its orders to the person of the defendant, and backed them by imprisonment for contempt: from this came the remedies of specific performance, rescission, rectification or cancellation of documents, and above all of injunction. Injunctions were in general prohibitory but could be mandatory. They were to give equity a significant place in the control of public authorities as well as private litigants.[24]

In the eighteenth century equity was fast becoming a body of settled doctrine which formed an addendum to the substantive rules and remedies of common law. True, equity had the power to override common law where a difference arose. But this was no longer a matter of virulent contest as it had been under James I. The central courts did not need to jockey for constitutional position; within the new vision of statehood the common law courts had acquired an independent judiciary. Their interest, as well as that of the politically dependant Lord Chancellor, was to build interconnections between law and equity. It had become merely curious that equity could be applied in one only of the group of central courts.[25] The oddity, however, was structural. It would require a whole series of interstitial reforms before the administration of both could be brought under the single roof provided by the Judicature Acts 1873–75.[26]

Part of the structural difference lay in procedure. Chancery had not dealt with the severe limitations upon its judicial manpower by resorting to jury trial. Suits were in consequence likely to come before the Chancellor or Master of the Rolls at various stages, there being no trial in the common law sense to give focus to the whole.[27] The court, moreover, delegated ministerial tasks such as the taking of accounts and the holding of trust funds to lesser officials, notably the Masters in Chancery.[28] The processing of Chancery litigation was even more dependent than that at common law upon the written record; the originating bill and subsequent pleadings held labyrinthine mysteries which would give reforming lawyers in the nineteenth century much cause for jocular impatience.[29]

Yet Chancery also drew upon the tradition of lay assistance. If litigation did require evidence from witnesses, it was not heard in court but was commissioned. Formal questions (interrogatories) were pre-

---

[23] Matters to which we return, *e.g.* below, pp. 127–128, 228.

[24] See, *e.g.* below, pp. 95ff., 154ff.

[25] According to Blackstone (*Commentaries*, III 441), "there cannot be a greater solecism than that in two sovereign independent courts, there should exist in a single instance two different rules of property, clashing with and contradicting each other."

[26] Below, pp. 43–45, 92–93.

[27] In 1813, a Vice-Chancellor was added, and in 1841, two more. From them, as from the Master of the Rolls matters could be reheard before the Chancellor.

[28] There were also the Examiners, the Registrars and the notorious Six Clerks: and see below, pp. 40–41.

[29] As in the essays by Lord Bowen, *Selected Essays in Anglo-American Legal History* (1909), I p. 516; and A. Birrell in W. B. Odgers (ed.), *A Century of Law Reform* (1901) Chap. 6.

pared by a party and notified in advance; the examiner or commissioner (outside London a local justice or person of similar standing) would then record answers to them under oath. In addition,
the idea of referring disputes to an arbitrator for settlement was a
widespread phenomenon, offering an alternative to formal court
proceedings.[30] Chancery became accustomed itself to appointing
arbitrators to reach decisions on such sensitive matters as the application of charitable funds and the apportionment of lands in an
enclosure.[31]

(iii) The Civilian Jurisdictions: Ecclesiastical and Admiralty

The ecclesiastical courts, together with the Court of Admiralty,
ranked as "civilian"—that is, they applied rules and followed procedures that grew originally in the canon and mercantile laws of continental Europe.[32] In London at least, they were served by their own
corps of professionals, the advocates and proctors of Doctors' Commons,[33] the judges for the various London courts being largely
drawn from among the advocates.[34]

The number of ecclesiastical courts was large, for each archdeacon
had his own court, and there were additional franchises (the pecu-
liars), giving some 330 throughout England; above these came the
courts of the bishops, then the Provincial courts of the Archbishops
of Canterbury and York and finally the High Court of Delegates, acting in the name of the monarch.[35] The medieval system of church
courts had been reshaped only marginally by Henry VIII and had
continued to exercise a wide jurisdiction over the spiritual and
material life of the community at large, not merely over the clergy.
Some aspects of this were in essence punitive.[36] But the ecclesiastical
courts also dealt with matters of church property, notably the vexing
issue of tithes, and with matrimonial disputes and the probate of
wills,[37] so far as the estate consisted of personal property rather than
freehold land. In the seventeenth century, the courts intervened
actively in many disputes important to the equanimity and orderliness of local communities.[38] A century later this constant interference
was losing its vitality. Nonetheless the probate business, most of it
not immediately contentious, was a legal process that continued to

---

[30] See further below, pp. 36–38.

[31] It was not the only court to make use of arbitrators.

[32] For the evolution of the civilian jurisdictions, see Holdsworth, I, pp. 544–568.
(admiralty), pp. 598–632 (eccesiastical).

[33] For their qualification, see below, p. 49.

[34] While there had normally been at least one permanent judge, all the advocates
might sit as surrogate judges and courts were frequently so constituted until mid-
nineteenth century; Wiswall (1970), pp. 78–80, 82; G. D. Squibb, *Doctors' Commons*
(1977).

[35] But this simplified description disguises a web of intricacies.

[36] Below, p. 546.

[37] And grants to administer the estates of those dying intestate. See generally, A. H.
Manchester (1968) 6 Sydney L.R. 25.

[38] Below p. 544ff.

provide the ecclesiastical courts with a regular function. It gave a steady flow of work to local attorneys, who looked anxiously upon any proposal for reform for fear that the work might be removed to a distance.[39] There was also a jurisdiction in matrimonial disputes, but it was only of limited importance in the absence of judicial divorce in the modern sense.[40]

The Court of Admiralty administered laws of sea use which had come to form part of the general law merchant of Europe. Though its commercial jurisdiction had been roughly appropriated by the seventeenth century common lawyers,[41] it survived with power to try cases on seamen's wages, collisions and other torts at sea, salvage, droits (perquisites) of the Lord High Admiral in wrecks, and in war-time prize. With the growth of British merchant shipping in the nineteenth century the court of Admiralty was once more to acquire a swelling case-load.[42]

(iv) Local and Special Courts

On the left-hand side of Table I stand a plethora of institutions that defy real classification, let alone exhaustive description.[43] At one pole are those which were in a sense regional substitutes for the central courts: the Great Sessions of Wales, a court of pleas established by Henry VIII as a bond in the complete union of Wales and England[44]; and the Courts of Pleas and Chancery in the Palatinates of Durham and Lancaster.[45] Among the jurisdictions for some special purpose are courts which recur in different parts of the country, such as the courts of the various forests[46] (here also the assize judges presided at the highest level); and the commissioners of sewers who oversaw the drainage of land and its protection from the sea. Other courts belonged to particular localities. London had its own hierarchy of sheriffs' courts, mayor's court, royal judge on commission and finally House of Lords. In Devon and Cornwall the

---

[39] As became evident before the Ecclesiastical Court Commission, see its Report, pp. 1831–1832 (199) XXIV; for the continuing opposition to reform and the eventual absorption in 1857, see below, pp. 385–386; A. H. Manchester (1966) 10 A.J.L.H. 51.

[40] See below, pp. 374–375.

[41] See Holdsworth, I pp. 568–573.

[42] See generally, Holdsworth, I pp. 544–568, Wiswall (1970) Chaps. 1, 2.

[43] A good starting point is Blackstone, *Commentaries* III Chaps. 4, 6; and see Manchester (1980), pp. 118–124, 151–159; Arthurs (1985) Chap. 2.

[44] As a court of record, it was subject to the supervision of King's Bench by writ of error; and since the common law courts came to acquire co-terminous jurisdiction in most instances it declined into a species of local court. Brougham and the first generation of reformers were particularly scathing about it and it was abolished in 1830: see Holdsworth, I pp. 122–132; Arthurs, (1985) p. 18.

[45] In these courts there had long been a tendency to follow common law and equity, which with time had increased by appointing the central judges to the court of pleas: Holdsworth, I pp. 109–117. The third county palatine to survive was Chester, with its own Chief Justice who also sat in the Great Sessions of Wales. Its courts came under the same obliquy and were abolished at the same time (see n. 44).

[46] Their jurisdiction in the early eighteenth century provides much of the evidence for E. P. Thompson's *Whigs and Hunters* (1974).

Stannary courts dealt not only with claims to mining rights but with disputes more generally in their communities.[47] In Oxford and Cambridge the Chancellors held courts for civil suits involving members of colleges and other privileged persons.

At local level there were a multiplicity of courts, some lively, a great many moribund. The ancient communal courts of county and hundred had largely ceased to function, save in a few places.[48] But the courts of the manors,[49] inherent once in feudal lordship, had survived longer. One part of their jurisdiction was over the copyhold land in the manor, the court standing guardian of such customary rules as those determining inheritance and the lord's right of heriot, and equally acting as register of transactions in the land.[50] Alongside this a general court of the manor for civil suits might or might not be functioning. A borough was generally granted one or more courts under its charter and where the town itself continued to flourish, so in all likelihood did its tribunals.[51] At the time of market or fair, there might still be a summary court of piepowder dispensing rapid justice to traders and customers.[52] Here also the notions of a general law merchant were likely to have a place.[53] If the town was a port, it would have a court of admiralty to deal with a range of shipping and wharving disputes.[54]

But the older institutions in the boroughs were often wanting. From around 1750 new courts began to be instituted by local Act. Commonly known as courts of requests or of conscience, they spread as local initiative dictated, hearing claims for small amounts, mostly debts, before a tribunal drawn from local merchants and other borough worthies, sitting without a jury.[55] The courts were frequently directed by their statutes to try cases according to "equity

---

[47] R. R. Pennington *Stannary Law* (1973) Chap. 1. These courts were reformed in 1836 and absorbed into the county court system in 1896. For traces of other mining courts, see Arthurs (1985), p. 22.

[48] Hence they are not included in Table I.

[49] Originally comprising the court baron (a court of claims) and the court leet (essentially a local criminal jurisdiction) the two had often with time become confounded. See generally, S & B Webb *The Manor and the Borough* (1908) Chaps. 1, 2.

[50] See below, p. 132ff.

[51] The Tolzey Court of Bristol, the Liverpool Court of Passage, the Norwich Guildhall Court and the Salford Hundred Court were proud and much-used institutions which continued past the nineteenth century reforms until 1971. A great miscellany of local courts (listed in *Halsbury's Laws of England* (3rd ed.), IX paras. 1169–1335) were formally abolished at that juncture.

[52] S. & B. Webb, *The Manor and the Borough* (1908), pp. 453, 499, 661, give examples of such courts functioning in the 17th and 18th centuries; *cf.* Holdsworth, I p. 540.

[53] The medieval merchant courts of the Staple had given place by the 16th century to a preference for arbitration among leading traders and financiers such as insurers. This kept the ideas of the law merchant alive and they were absorbed over time into the common law: see below, pp. 198–199; and J. H. Baker [1979] C.L.J. 295.

[54] Webb (above, n. 32), pp. 359–360, gives a number of examples.

[55] Modelled probably on the City of London's Court of Conscience, which was created as early as 1517 by the Common Council: Webb (above, n. 32), p. 661. See generally Winder (1936); A. L. Cross (1932) 30 Mich. L. Rev. 369; Arthurs (1985), pp. 25–49. A well-known account of the Birmingham Court by a leading commissioner is William Hutton, *Courts of Requests* (1787); *cf.* J. Parkes, *The Fate of the Court of Requests and the Public Office of Birmingham* (1828).

and good conscience" (rather than by common law)[56]; and even more importantly a "no certiorari" clause made review by the King's Bench possible only in rare cases.[57] In this way there built up over the period to 1845 some 400 of these courts, all limited in their geographical jurisdiction, some limited to claims of £2, others of £5, a few of the latest to £10 or even £20. Nonetheless, those in popular areas were receiving 20,000 or more plaints each year by 1830 and adjudicating many of them.[58] They became the civil equivalent to the summary jurisdiction of the justices on the criminal and administrative side, meeting the widespread demand for debt recovery that was a concomitant of a society reliant on credit.

The comparison with the justices is important, for the commissioners in the courts of requests were largely the same, or very similar, men to the borough benches, and interference by King's Bench was likewise precluded in some of the new minor jurisdictions being conferred on the justices.[59] But while the justices were to blossom in the nineteenth century into an even more significant lay tribunal, the courts of requests were to be displaced by lawyers' courts—the modern county courts, whose judges were drawn from the ranks of the bar. As we shall see, this was a parting of the ways crucial to the Victorian reforms of judicature.[60] Even before those reforms, the common law courts had sought to exert some ultimate control over the mass of local courts. So long as the prime motivation for this lay in competition for jurisdiction, the judges had been willing enough to remove cases wholesale for trial in their own courts. Writs existed, for example, by which a party could have a case in an ancient county or manorial court removed to Westminster; Blackstone blamed the decay of these courts on this very possibility.[61] But as the judges became concerned with their authority, rather than the amount of business before them, forms of intervention were fostered, in which judgements given below were scrutinised for errors of law or procedure.

Within their own immediate sphere, we have seen how the common law courts expanded their supervision from review of the case as pleaded to review of it as proved; and how one major difficulty was to provide an adequate summary of events at the trial upon

[56] Arthurs (1985), pp. 29–34, claims that this indicates an approach to decision at odds with the common law. It is difficult now to assess how far the directive to follow equity and good conscience (which Winder (1936) says was omitted in later statutes) produced different results.Certainly the courts examined parties on oath, and ordered debts to be paid by instalments, which were departures from common law. In the common law courts the verdicts of local juries determined the outcome, which was another way of admitting local understandings and prejudices (see below, p. 36).

[57] See below, p. 35.

[58] A detailed picture can be found in the Court of Requests Return, P.P. 1839 (338) XLII. See the App. to the Small Debts Courts Act 1846 for the courts abolished. One objection to the courts of requests was that they encouraged the too liberal granting of credit: see also below, pp. 229–230.

[59] The general property qualification for commissioners was land of £5 per annum or personal property of £500; 26 Geo. III, c. 38 (cf. above, p. 20, n. 86). Their number was often large. For a different comparison of the two, see Arthurs (1985), pp. 32–34.

[60] See below, p. 38ff.

[61] *Commentaries*, III 33–37.

which to conduct a review that was not a re-trial.[62] The same dilemma arose in developing procedures for the review of inferior jurisdictions. Once the lower court's judgement had been executed, a collateral action could be brought at common law alleging that the execution constituted a wrongful invasion of personal or property rights. This could serve to raise an objection that the lower court lacked any jurisdiction in the matter; but since the officers of the lower court were thereby exposed to personal liability, the tactic was reserved for blatant excesses. If the lower court was a court of record (as were, for instance, the market courts of piepowder) the writ of error lay to King's Bench to raise errors of law that appeared on the face of the written record: and from other courts much the same result had been achieved by use of the prerogative writ of certiorari.[63] Here too the search was often said to be for lack of jurisdiction; this was a counter-strategy against "no certiorari" clauses in Acts of Parliament. There was a manifestly greater readiness to use certiorari rather than a collateral action as a medium of interference, whether put in terms of jurisdiction,[64] action or error on the face of the record. The King's Bench in Lord Mansfield's time further expanded its scope by receiving affidavits from witnesses to the lower proceedings.[65] In non-criminal cases particularly,[66] this became a significant way of acquiring an account of what had happened, since the "record" below was usually elliptical, omitting any reference to the proof. Overall, the court was "inundated" with applications for certiorari.[67]

This increased significantly the chance of imposing a standard interpretation upon a great host of statutory rules and in principle the cause of legal unity advanced notably. But, as elsewhere, too much came to depend upon the niceties of form. Opportunities proliferated for exhausting an adversary by stratagems of delay and cost, certiorari being notoriously expensive.[68] The procedure applied even more to criminal than to civil process and its debilitating effects in the hands of the astute and unscrupulous will be discussed again in that context.[69] The fear of central review spread to such an extent that

---

[62] See above, pp. 25–26.

[63] The process of extending certiorari beyond the realm of courts of record had a long history and had become especially important as the justices acquired new powers. It was effectively completed by Holt C.J. in *Groenvelt* v. *Burwell* (1700) 1 Ld. Raym. 213: S.A. de Smith, *Judicial Review of Administrative Action* (4th ed., 1980), pp. 587–590.; A. Rubinstein, *Jurisdiction and Illegality* (1965), p. 70. For the early history, (1923) 32 Yale L.J. 523 E.G. Henderson, *Foundations of English Administrative Law* (1963).

[64] One device used in furtherance of certiorari distinguished "want of jurisdiction" sufficient to found a collateral action and "excess of jurisdiction" for which there could be certiorari: Rubinstein (above, n. 63, pp. 66–67).

[65] *R.* v. *Wakefield* (1757) 2 Ld. Ken. 164; *R.* v. *Hitcham* (*Inhabitants*) (1760) 2 Burr. 910, 1035 (1735) Hard. 169. *cf. R.* v. *Oulton* (*Inhabitants*) Cas. t. Hard. 169.

[66] For the position in criminal cases, see below p. 35.

[67] Or so it is said (de Smith (above, n. 63), p. 590); but the state of the records forbids any quantitative investigation as yet: Arthurs (1985), pp. 44–46.

[68] In particular, 5 Geo. II c. 19, s.2, required the defendant and two sureties to enter recognisances each for £50, from which costs would be extracted if he failed; whereas if he succeeded he was not entitled to costs, J. Chitty, *The Practice of the Law* (1834), II p. 225–226.)

[69] Below, p. 35.

Parliament was constantly besought to introduce protection in this or that instance by means of the "no certiorari" clause.[70] Here was a prominent motive behind the creation of local courts of requests for the collection of small debts. The amounts at stake demanded a rapid, cheap, and above all final, process in which lawyers' ceremony could not obstruct commercial necessity. The insistence of the rising class of traders upon new local tribunals of their own, rather than an adapted version of some ancient court,[71] registers the strength of feeling against the litigation system under the common law's surveillance.

(d) The Criminal Courts

By the eighteenth century, the processes of the criminal law were conducted very largely in the name of the central state, though there was much about them that maintained a local character. Certainly it was on the monarch's behalf that offenders were prosecuted. The courts mainly concerned are indicated in Table III (p. 21). The most serious offences—those carrying the penalty of death—would almost always be tried before a royal judge sitting with a jury at assizes. Under the "Bloody Code," these would include not only murderers and rapists but the robbers, burglars, forgers, serious thieves and others who committed one of the great splay of capital offences against property. The non-capital crimes that were classified either as felony or misdemeanour would mostly be dealt with by the justices of the peace sitting with a jury at their Quarter Sessions. Minor offences could be disposed of summarily by the justices in their home districts, sitting in pairs or sometimes singly.[72]

The ecclesiastical courts still kept their separate power to police the morals of their flock, where the wrong lay outside the compass of the common law. In the seventeenth century, the archdeacon's court would hear a regular string of cases involving minor defamations, drunkenness, swearing, brawling, adultery, failure to attend church and other spiritual lapses. Really serious offences might warrant excommunication, but more frequently the punishment was an expiatory confession or a payment in lieu.[73] But as the eighteenth century drew on, it was this part of jurisdiction that fell most evidently into decline, the inadequacies of the sanctions being accorded the blame. The legislature could have altered them if it chose; a deeper *malaise* seems to have been at work, a loss of respect for the authority of the established church which had to do with the gentrification of its

---

[70] A very restricted view of lack of jurisdiction, when challenged by collateral action, was taken by Commons Plea in *Brittain* v. *Kinnaird* (1819) 1 Brod. & B. 432 (the "Bumboat" case) and followed in other decisions. All concerned attempts to make justices pay damages for exceeding jurisdiction, a hazard from which they were eventually protected by statute in 1848 (11 & 12 Vict., c. 44). These cases were not allowed to make much impact on the availability of certiorari.

[71] Blackstone (*Commentaries*, III pp. 81–83) lamented the loss of jury trial and pointed to the revival of the ancient county court of Middlesex by statute (23 Geo. II, c. 33) as the proper model; but in vain.

[72] Below, pp. 546–548.

[73] See J. A. Sharpe in J. Bossy (ed.) *Disputes and Settlements* (1983) Chap. 7.

clergy. In many cases, the parson ceased to be an intermediary between the village and its governors, becoming instead a "squarson" with a substantial tenanted farm. The enforcement of order passed to the landed class, the clergy finding their way onto the bench of justices as administrators of the secular morality of the state.

A very considerable transformation of the criminal process was set in train in the 1820s. In place of exemplary execution and transportation abroad, imprisonment at home became the chief instrument for punishing serious crime. Professional police began to replace the amateur arrangements that had sufficed for so long.[74] An essential concomitant of these steps was to confine the justices more distinctly, if not entirely, to an adjudicatory role.[75] As we shall see,[76] the magistrates' courts, as well as holding preliminary inquiries into charges of indictable crime that were destined for trial at assizes or quarter sessions, came to try an increasing proportion of all criminal charges. Lesser indictable offences could be dealt with by them summarily, in most instances, at the option of the accused. The list of such offences would grow longer as the work of higher courts grew unduly burdensome.[77] Here too a technique for avoiding the ritual of jury trial was quietly developed. Though it was not in the end carried so far, a broadly similar process was at work to that in the civil courts. Adjustments were introduced which fined down the gravest cases to a number which could be supervised by a small central judiciary.[78]

One element in this was a determination not to allow indiscriminate opportunities for upsetting convictions. Criminal procedure had long contained a variety of guarantees that were essential to any real notion of a rule of law. Habeas corpus, which was available in any common law court and Chancery, restrained both unauthorised detention and undue failure to put on trial.[79] In addition, the accusation—indictment being the usual form, for serious crime[80]—had to specify all the essential allegations which made up the offence; and as evidence came to be introduced, a number of restrictive rules developed, such as those keeping previous convictions and involuntary confessions from the jury. Law of this kind burgeoned in the eighteenth century, as those accused of crime came a little more regularly to have the advantage of legal representation. Indictments grew to be subject to the kind of scrupulous criticism that infected the pro-

---

[74] Below, p. 587ff.

[75] They would continue such administrative tasks as issuing warrants and granting alehouse licences.

[76] Below, p. 618.

[77] The process began in 1854 (17 & 18 Vict., c. 125, s.3): see R. M. Jackson, (1937) 1 M.L.R. 132.

[78] Assisted in increasingly generous measure by barristers sitting part-time as recorders and deputy chairmen of Quarter Sessions.

[79] Blackstone, *Commentaries*, III, pp. 131–133; R. J. Sharpe, *The Law of Habeas Corpus* (1976).

[80] A grand jury had, as a preliminary measure, to find that an indictment was "true." This protection was denied when the crown proceeded by way of information: this was only open in cases of misdemeanour, but was used, for instance, in seditious libel prosecutions.: see below, pp. 545–546.

cess of pleading in civil actions.[81] The casuistries of the law on the subject suggest that they were being used as an escape route from the exigencies of the Bloody Code, a way out largely confined to those who could employ counsel to argue the objection.

Even so, objections to these defects in the process had in the main to be taken at the trial itself. Opportunities for removal of cases out of assizes and local jurisdictions were few, the main exception being that statutes creating summary offences often allowed the case to be entirely reheard at Quarter Sessions. The chance of review after conviction was likewise constricted. Objections to an indictment had to be taken to the King's Bench by way of writ of error, and so were confined to objections evident in the document itself. Points of law or of evidence arising at the trial could only be aired there and then, unless the judge could be persuaded to reserve a point (after a special verdict) for the opinion of his brothers. This process was eventually expanded (so as also to cover Quarter Sessions) with the establishment in 1848 of a Court of Crown Cases Reserved; but even after this there was no *right* of appeal.[82] The judges held over only a handful of cases each year for further argument.

At the summary level, the chance of raising similar points increased significantly from the mid-eighteenth century. Certiorari from King's Bench would lie to the justices and that court began to require (if necessary by mandamus) the lower court to state all facts (and the evidence for finding them) necessary to give jurisdiction.[83] As in civil cases, Parliament sought to provide against this new interference by enacting "no certiorari" clauses; but here too the court refused to read these as referring to issues of "jurisdiction"; and it took such an extensive view of what went to jurisdiction as to allow almost any error of law to be raised by certiorari.[84] Parliament only arrived at a true means of inhibition when it began to prescribe short forms for the recording of convictions.[85] The record once more became faceless and certiorari lost its impact. By 1857, the government felt obliged to provide a way of raising points of law from magistrates, but without the laboured formalities of certiorari: it did so by giving both defence and prosecution the right to have a case stated for the opinion of Queen's Bench or other common law court.[86]

---

[81] J.F. Stephen, *History of the Criminal Law in England* (1883), I pp. 273–294, who takes to task the Victorian reforms of the subject.

[82] 11 & 12 Vict., c. 78; and see below, pp. 609, 619ff.

[83] Rubinstein, (above, n.63), pp. 71–73. The decisions could be most scrupulous: *e.g. R. v. Daman* ("a gentleman") (1819) 2 B & Ald. 387—conviction for taking fish quashed for failure to state that the owner of the fish had prosecuted.

[84] Chitty (*Practice of the Law* (1834), II p. 224) gave the propensity of justices to convict for game offences without just cause as the reason. As with civil causes, the court would on occasion supplement its view of the lower proceedings by receiving affidavits: *ibid.* 223–224.

[85] For early experiments, see the Malicious Damage Acts, 7 & 8 Geo. IV, c. 29, s.71; 9 Geo. IV, c. 31, s.27. The provision was made general by Jervis' Act, 11 & 12 Vict., c. 13, s. 17.

[86] Summary Jurisdiction Act 1857, ss.2–7. Sir George Grey, the Home Secretary, said that "otherwise they could not give the magistrates a large increase in jurisdiction": P.D. 1857 CXLVI 1020.

(e) Dispute Settlement Beyond the Courts

Courts are institutions developed by state authority to decide disputes on the complaint of one party and empowered by that authority to enforce their orders. But in any social organisation, respected figures are likely to emerge to whom disputants may together refer their differences; resolution will then come from the outsider's own judgment or from his proposal of solutions which the contenders are persuaded to accept. Certainly the idea of turning to outsiders to arbitrate or mediate disputes was deep-rooted in English life. In the seventeenth century personal quarrels, after erupting into the ecclesiastical courts, often went to arbitration by a local gentleman.[87] Arguments over the terms of labour, whether they concerned entitlements already earned or the conditions of future service, were settled in this way in the eighteenth-century and a series of Acts would seek subsequently to bolster the process.[88] Most commonly, disputes among merchants and also between them and their customers went to arbitration.[89]

Putting out issues for settlement occurred in so many circumstances that it was very difficult for the central courts to fix upon a clear line of policy towards the phenomenon as a whole. Arbitration could be preferable to court process for a host of reasons: because for instance, it was speedier, or cheaper, or more private; or because it would provide a more informed judgment upon the issues, or would be based upon more acceptable norms; or because it would more easily enable the disputants within a community to go on living and dealing with each other. If the reason why a court could not offer the same advantages was inherent in its structure, it might welcome the spread of arbitration. In the sixteenth century, Chancery, the Star Chamber and the Council had all referred disputes to arbitrators as a means of expanding slender resources. But the common law courts of the early modern period, in their hunger for jurisdiction, seem to have adopted a more antagonistic view. As they did in this period with the lesser courts, they might insist that a dispute be removed into their court. In the case of arbitration this was achieved by allowing one party who had submitted to arbitration nonetheless to bring a common law suit at any time before the arbitrator made his award.[90]

But here too the common law judges began to move from expropriation to strategic supervision. So far as concerned commercial disputes, the eighteenth-century judges, led by Lord Mansfield, made a determined effort to absorb into the common law itself principles of the law merchant governing the circumstances of trade. By a master-

[87] Sharpe (above, n. 73).

[88] See below, p. 295ff.

[89] As merchants ceased to travel, their need of local courts (staple, piepowder) tended to diminish. Once they directed operations from a home base, they turned naturally to dispute settlement by arbitration, see Holdsworth, XIV pp. 187–198; Lord Parker of Waddington, *The History and Development of Commercial Arbitration* (1959); P. L. Sayre (1928) 37 Yale L.J. 595; Sir L. Macassey (1938) 24 A.B.A.J. 518; Arthurs (1985), pp. 52–54; and for the old common law, S. Kyd, *Law of Awards* (1791).

[90] *Vynior's Case* (1610) 8 Co. Rep. 796 81b came to be treated as the basic authority for this rule. For other severities in the early law, see Holdsworth, XIV pp. 191–195.

stroke, Lord Mansfield used the jury, the common law's own machine for bringing communal understanding to the determination of disputes, for this process of development: but his jury comprised special jurors from the City of London, many of them sitting regularly to determine crucial cases on the import of financial, insurance and trading customs.[91] By this approximation many of the obvious differences between common law rules and commercial arbitration disappeared. Even so, arbitration lost nothing in popularity, since there were other reasons enough for preferring it; and the common lawyers were in no position to take over all the work, even if they had wanted to.[92] Instead an atmosphere of accommodation was fostered by the creation of machinery for enforcing the submission to arbitration and the arbitrator's award through court process,[93] and later for allowing the arbitrator to state a case for the court's guidance on a matter of law.[94] After the Judicature Acts this was to become open to demand by one party.[95] The judges' attitude by 1800 is probably best understood in the way that it was described a century later by a leading commercial judge, Scrutton L.J.:

"In countless cases parties agree to submit their disputes to arbitrators whose decision shall be final and conclusive. But the Courts, if one of these parties brings an action, never treat this agreement as conclusively preventing the Courts from hearing the dispute. They consider the merits of the case, including the fact of the agreement of the parties, and either stay the action or allow it to proceed according to the view they form of the best method of procedure; and they have always in my experience declined to fetter their discretion by laying down any fixed rules on which they will exercise it."[96]

Only thus is it possible to understand two centuries of case-law in

---

[91] See below, pp. 198–199; F. M. Burdick in *Select Essays in Anglo-American Legal History* (1909), III 34; L. S. Sutherland (1934) 17 T.R.H.S. (4th ser.) 149; F.D. Mackinnon (1936) 52 L.Q.R. 30.

[92] See Arthurs (1985), pp. 62–77. Compare the position in a number of US jurisdictions, where, according to Horwitz, nineteenth-century courts made a determined effort to suffocate arbitral proceedings: *The Transformation of American Law 1780–1860* (1977) Chap. 5.

[93] Arbitration Act 1698 (9 Will. III, c. 15). One view is that in consequence the common lawyers, hugging bear-like, insisted that arbitrators follow their rules: see Parker (above, n. 89) at p. 13. But this is to underplay the willingness of the common law to adapt and the equivocation about interference that continued despite occasional sweeping pronouncements. The procedural reforms of 1833 (3 & 4 Will IV, c. 42, ss.39–41) required the court's leave before revoking a submission to arbitration under the 1698 Act, and gave further assistance.

[94] Common Law Procedure Act 1854, s.8.

[95] By the Arbitration Act 1889, s.19; Lord Bramwell's original bill, however, had provided only for a power to state a case: see E. J. Cohn, (1941) 4 U. Toronto L.J. 1 at 19. The change to compulsion aroused no real comment and was probably treated as one more step in the process of replacing the tribunal's discretion with a party's right to review of the law by a higher tribunal. Within the structure of the courts proper this had been a long development recently completed with the Judicature Acts.

[96] *Czarnikow* v. *Roth Schmidt* [1922] 1 K.B. 478 at 487–88.

which the courts chose to interfere only intermittently with the arbitration process. They held moreover that the parties might agree that no action could be brought on a contract until the amount due had been settled by arbitration.[97] Sanctity of contract permitted so much, though "public policy" would not allow a total ouster of jurisdiction.[98] This left an ultimate power to direct and control, enough to preserve the rule of the common law. The judges could still insist on procedural fair play; and more fundamentally they could try to insist upon their own standards of "public policy" should any obvious conflict of objectives emerge. Arbitration was, after all, a common condition on which the economically powerful did business, and through which they might seek to sustain their monopolistic control of a market.[99]

(f) Reform of the Courts

In the half century after 1830, the overgrown thicket of civil courts was formed, by hard pruning and some replanting, into an ordered plantation. Much of its characteristic shape would nonetheless remain. The largest change came not in the regrouping of superior courts (which occurred finally with the Judicature Acts 1873–75) but in the creation of a complete system of county courts. The Small Debts Act 1846 created some 500 county courts for the whole of England and Wales, arranged into 59 circuits, each with its judge, a barrister of at least seven years' standing.[1] They were lawyers' courts, in which the judge sat with a five-man jury only if a party requested it, and they mainly replaced the courts of requests staffed by lay commissioners or part-time professional judges.[2] The right of representation was confined to members of the bar and attorneys.[3]

A trend that local trading interests had been fostering for a century was decisively reversed. Coming at the very moment of the free-trade victory, the county courts were the lawyers' particular spoil in

---

[97] *Scott* v. *Avery* (1856) 5 H.L.Cas. 81; so held by the House of Lords after considerable division among the judges. The decision was the more striking in that the only legal action permitted by the agreement to arbitrate was to enforce the award; accordingly the arbitrator in effect had power to settle all issues in disputes between the parties in the course of reaching his award. Large organisations might thereby, if they were not careful, lose the support of the legal process: building societies found themselves unable to recover the debts of their members (*Municipal B.S.* v. *Kent* (1884) 9 App. Cas. 260)) and needed the Building Societies Act 1884 to rescue them.

[98] The limit began to be expressed in this way from about the middle of the eighteenth century; see *e.g., Kill* v. *Hollister* (1746) 1 Wils. K.B. 129; *Thompson* v. *Charnock* (1799) 8 T.R. 139; *cf. Wellington* v. *Mackintosh* (1743) 2 Atk. 570, *per* Lord Hardwicke L.C.

[99] As to this concern, see below, p. 270ff.

[1] 9 & 10 Vict., c. 95. The courts were so named in order to create a sense of lineage (which was largely wishful-thinking); *cf.* H. Smith (1969) 13 A.J.L.H. 126). Because the judgeships were part-time, the judges were at first paid by litigants' fees, though in 1850 salaries (£1,200–1,500) were substituted.

[2] Some of the part-time judges were taken over into the county courts—according to Judge Snagge as an act of kindness: *The Evolution of the County Court* (1904).

[3] 9 & 10 Vict., c. 95, s.91.

the overall thrust of middle-class confidence.[4] The movement gained some of its impetus from the swelling ranks of both legal professions.[5] The campaign was begun in earnest by Henry Brougham who made an eloquent speech in support of his reforming bill of 1830[6] and continued his attack on ascending the Woolsack in the same year. He dwelt upon the inadequacies of the courts of requests and other local civil courts, scattered in small pockets, their jurisdictions limited in different ways and their authority to compel appearance and enforce judgment often insecure. Brougham's proposals ran into the personal opposition which he so often generated, in this case from the erstwhile Lord Chancellor, Lyndhurst, who had his own ideas on judicial reform. But Lyndhurst also gave voice to feelings widely shared: that a phalanx of courts under lawyers' control would create a large new patronage for the Lord Chancellor, would endanger the idea of a central bar and would rob the existing tribunals of their simplicity and their sensitivity to local expectations (including a natural inclination to see traders' debts enforced—though this was scarcely emphasised). Certainly such anxieties were aired in legal journals and by witnesses before the Common Law Commissioners, to whom the dispute was referred. But that reform-minded body of lawyers came down firmly in Brougham's direction, not hesitating to disparage the courts of request for lacking the restraining hand of the common law and its procedure.[7] They were even said sometimes to be wanting in impartiality, though precious little was offered by way of substantiation.[8]

Even so, the change had to await two experiences. One was the introduction of the various commissions and inspectorates—over poor law, factories and tithe, for instance—which suggested new chances for a scrupulous and dedicated public service. This did a good deal to dissipate fears that new posts multiplied nothing but patronage and place. The other was the preoccupation, which became intense after 1838, with sanctions for recovering debts and in particular with the role that should in future be allowed to imprisonment for debt. The striking of a new accord on the matter was, as we shall see, a protracted business in which the new county courts were to form an important element, their lawyer judges appearing to stand apart from any creditor interest.[9] By the 1840s both political parties favoured a version of Brougham's bill, Lyndhurst taking it up for the Tories and Cottenham pushing it through for the Whigs.

Within ten years, during which there were some important modi-

---

[4] There was some disgruntlement—attorneys were not allowed to become judges, and the fees for appearance were set low enough to start immediate campaigns for their increase—which brought changes in 1850; but this seems secondary. *Cf.* Abel Smith and Stevens (1967) 34–37.

[5] See below, pp. 48, 51. On the reform campaigns, see Cross (above, n. 55), Arthurs (1985), 34–49.

[6] *Speeches* II, 489.

[7] Fifth Report, P.P. 1833 (247) XXII.

[8] *cf.* Winder (1936) at p. 378 with Arthurs (1985) at pp. 41–42 on the "Hackney Map" case. Occasionally a court of requests became the focus of a popular hostility, but the cases seem to have been very intermittent.

[9] Below, pp. 229–230: another precursor was the increasingly frequent appointment of barristers as part-time judges of courts of requests.

fications of detail, it became clear that the county courts were a success.[10] For traders they handled a very large number of small claims
for debt, their maximum jurisdiction being raised from £20 to £50 as
soon as 1850.[11] Most significant of all, they taught that the convoluted
rituals of the superior courts were capable of amendment even
within an adversarial process under the control of lawyers. Their
judges tried the great bulk of cases by themselves without juries
being called for. The courts took over from the courts of requests the
initiatory process by simple plaint, without adherence to forms of
action or scrupulous pleading. Likewise they continued those courts'
practice of allowing parties to appear as witnesses. A method was
devised of appealing on a point of law (to two judges of a superior
court sitting out of term) which was not allowed to disintegrate into
expensive caprice.[12] The courts showed that they could handle a
variety of jurisdictions and indeed during the rest of the century
were the regular recipients of work under new statutes.[13]

Beside such Victorian plainness, the superior courts appeared a
minaretted extravagance, embodying everything capricious and self-
serving in Georgian public life. Jeremy Bentham had taught younger
radicals to rank "Judge & Co." at the head of the demonship.[14] Beginning with the Select Committee procured by Michaelangelo Taylor
into the workings of the Chancery court in 1811, they were a regular
target of invective, in Parliament and outside[15] Successive editions of
John Wade's *Extraordinary Black Book* listed in relentless detail the
earnings and perquisites of office-holders in the courts, and the
opportunities for expensive delay which each party could turn
against the other and lawyers could turn to themselves.[16] By 1824
even Lord Eldon was obliged to preside over a Commission into
Chancery. "The general plan" appeared to the Commissioners to be
"as well calculated as any system that could be devised"; but 188
recommendations for minor improvements did emerge.[17] Occasionally, a determined man might seek to straighten some part of the edifice—as when Lord Mansfield had cut away at procedural
complexities and delays in King's Bench,[18] or when Brougham

---

[10] This was the verdict of a County Courts Commission chaired by Lord Romilly M.R.:
P.P. 1854–55 [1914] XVIII.
[11] In March–December 1847, the courts handled 429,215 plaints, claiming an average of
three guineas and recovering about a half the total claimed (many claims being
effectively uncontested). Between 1859 and 1891, the number of plaints would grow
28 per cent. while the population increased 44 per cent.: see Sir J. Macdonnell (1894)
57 R. Stat. Soc J. 452 at pp. 500–504. Acts of 1856 and 1867 allowed the court jurisdiction over larger claims by agreement and penalised in costs superior court proceedings which could have been brought in a county court: Smith (above, n. 1) at p. 131;
and see his article more generally on the non-use before 1880 of the county courts as
a forum for accident claims.
[12] 13 & 14 Vict. c. 61, s.14.
[13] Snagge (above, n. 2).
[14] For instance, in "Truth v. Ashhurst", *Works* (1843) V 231–37.
[15] See P.P. 1810–1811 (244) III; 1812 (273) II.
[16] *e.g.* the edition of 1829, Chap. 8. See generally, E.R. Sutherland (1926) 39 Harvard
L.R. 725.
[17] P.P. 1826 (56) XV.
[18] C.H.S. Fifoot, *Lord Mansfield* (1936) Chap. 3; Holdsworth, XII 588–605.

worked his way unremittingly (if perfunctorily) through the backlogs
of Chancery. But the direct passages which they unblocked had a
habit of resealing themselves. Five years after Brougham's departure
from the Woolsack there were 850 suits awaiting trial in Chancery
and a practitioner could write: "No man, as things now stand, can
enter into a Chancery suit with any reasonable hope of being alive at
its termination if he has a determined adversary."[19]

The major efforts to subject the superior courts to even a first
measure of utilitarian efficiency divide into three stages. The first,
which occurred in the years around and after 1832, had greater
impact on common law than on chancery. This was the period when
Brougham's onslaught[20] led to the investigations of both the Common Law Commissioners[21] and the Land Law Commissioners.[22]
Dominated by lawyers of moderately reformist bent, the thrust of
their recommendations was towards making the old formal system
more efficient upon its own premises. The forms of action were
purged of outmoded relics, such as the ancient real actions for the
recovery of land, and some procedures were markedly simplified.[23]
Above all, under the influence of Sergeant Stephen[24] and Baron
Parke, the system of pleadings was subjected to a new drive for
scientific accuracy. The Hilary Rules of 1834 curtailed the ability of
the defendant to defeat the true purpose of pleading by hiding
behind the General Issue—that blanket denial ("Not guilty") of all
the plaintiff's allegations, which gave nothing in advance away.
Instead, specific excuses (in the form of confession and avoidance)
had to be specially pleaded.[25]

These shifts unquestionably sprang some of the man-traps of common-law litigation. But being impelled by formal accuracy, they harboured their own power of ambush. Some of the judges, notably
Parke B., could insist upon correctness in pleading even against the
perceived merits of the case.[26] Opinion was soon to swing against
this novel scientism. The Common Law Commissioners of 1851 felt
obliged to speak of "technical and captious objections . . . not only
useless but mischievous."[27]

The succeeding stage—the 1850s—saw a new round of investi-

---

[19] G. Spence, *Equitable Jurisdiction of the Court of Chancery* (1839) Preface.
[20] Notably his marathon speech in the Commons in 1828: *Speeches* (1838), II 319;
Holdsworth, XIII 296–308.
[21] Their first three Reports concerned the common law courts: P.P. 1829 (46) XI, 1830
(123) XI, 1831 (92) X; for their other work, see below, p. 229 and above, p. 39.
[22] See below, pp. 173–174.
[23] For ensuing legislation, see in particular 2 & 3 Will. IV, c. 39, on uniformity of process.
[24] For Stephen as an advocate of scientific pleading, see his *On Pleading* (1824).
[25] W. S. Holdsworth (1923) 1 C.L.J. 261.
[26] "His keenest delight was to non-suit a plaintiff in an undefended action for some
inaccuracy of expression": C.H.S. Fifoot, *English Law and Its Background* (1932),
pp. 154–155; and for examples of Parke at play, see the same author's *Lord Mansfield*
(1936), pp. 236–241.
[27] P.P. 1851 [1389] XXII, 33. They nonetheless acknowledged the very real advance
secured by the 1834 Rules. Procedural points may arise in abundance even after the
adoption of a "liberal" regime such as that of 1883: see Lord Parker, (above, n. 89),
p. 20.

gation and recommendation.[28] It was at this point, in the wake of the county court reforms, that perhaps the most substantial changes were initiated. First, there was a very real shift in favour of a more flexible procedure, in which formalities were reduced and formal errors lost much of their consequence. At common law, the choice of a form of action ceased to govern the whole exercise from the outset. The form did not have to be indicated in the writ but only in the plaintiff's first pleading; all relevant forms could be used in a single action and incorrect choices saved by amendment.[29] The forms ceased to be structural and under the Judicature Acts their entire abandonment could follow.[30] A few, such as Parke B., looked upon the change as incorrigible laxity. But on the whole the common lawyers were content with other buttresses, such as the expanded bases for appeal and the growing control by judges over juries. More generally, insufficiencies of pleading became curable by amendment. No longer could a "relevant" variance between facts pleaded and facts proved of necessity defeat a claim or defence at trial.[31] Even the parties at last became competent to give evidence.[32]

Secondly, the movement to coalesce the various courts advanced. Not only were the ecclesiastical jurisdictions transformed,[33] but a cultural exchange began between common law and equity. In Chancery the oral examination and cross-examination of witnesses was admitted in 1852 (though until the Judicature Acts it continued to take place before separate examiners).[34] It became possible for Chancery to decide questions of common law for itself—a shift which much advanced the prospect of speedy relief.[35] Each jurisdiction was empowered to award the remedies that previously had been the preserve of the other: chancery to give damages, common law to grant injunctions, specific performance and other types of equitable relief.[36] Moreover, the increasing pressure of work in Chancery led to one major change in structure there. In 1851, a Court of Appeal in

---

[28] Common Law Commission: 1st Report (forms of action, pleadings) P.P. 1851 [1389] XXII; 2nd Report (parties as witnesses, discover, trial by jury, remedies) 1852–53 [1626] XL; 3rd Report (common law and chancery) 1860 [2614] XXXI. Chancery Commission: 1st Report (procedure) P.P. 1852 [1437, 1454] XXI; 2nd Report (probate reform) 1854 [1731] XXIV; 3rd Report (evidence) 1856 [2064] XXII. Both commissions were composed of leading judges and barristers. They were preceded by a number of Select Committees much concerned with costs and delays.

[29] Common Law Procedure Act 1852, 15 & 16 Vict. c. 76, s.3.; see C. M. Hepburn in *Essays in Anglo-American Legal History* (1909) II 643.

[30] Judicature Act 1873, s.3. The Commissioners of 1851 boldly recommended abandonment forthwith: Report (above, n. 28) at pp. 34–35.

[31] 14 & 15 Vict. c. 99, s.13. "Material" variances of no injurious consequence had already gone: 3 & 4 Will. IV, c. 42, s.23.

[32] 14 & 15 Vict. c. 99, s.2; "interested persons" had been admitted, to a small degree, by 3 & 4 Will. IV, c. 42, s.26, but mainly by Lord Denman's Act, 6 & 7 Vict., c. 85.

[33] In 1857, the probate jurisdiction was at last transferred to a new probate court, which had district registries for the use of provincial solicitors; and a new Divorce Court was created to handle judicial divorce; for the latter, see below, p. 374ff.

[34] 15 & 16 Vict., c. 86, ss.28, 29 (part of a very substantial reform of Chancery procedure).

[35] See below, p. 155.

[36] Lord Cairns' Act 1858—a jurisdiction so evidently useful that, even though it may have been repealed in 1884, was considered by the House of Lords to have survived as a matter of practice: *Leeds Industrial Cooperative v. Slack* [1924] A.C. 851.

Chancery, composed of the Lord Chancellor and two Lord Justices, was interposed between first instance and the House of Lords.[37]

The stones raised by the changes of the 1850s were overturned by the third stage, the administrative reforms of the Judicature Acts 1873–75.[38] These alterations were the most striking of all, at least if attention is confined to appearances. The three courts of common law, and the courts of chancery, admiralty, probate and divorce were all made part of a Supreme Court of Judicature. The new Supreme Court was divided into a Court of Appeal and, below it, a High Court of Justice composed of Divisions reflecting the old jurisdictions (see Table II). All parts of this new structure were empowered to apply the rules of common law, equity and the civilian courts.[39] But the amalgamation was one of jurisdiction, not of doctrine. Each body of law was to be preserved as a setting for its particular rules. The few instances of direct clash were dealt with either by specific statutory provision or by the general rule that equity was to prevail over common law.[40] The changes that came were accordingly not so much a matter of power as of influence, and chief among them was to be the effect of the more numerous common law judges upon the distinct traditions of equity.[41]

The superior courts—now the exclusive domain of the bar and the bench drawn from it—were kept distinct from the inferior civil courts and the general run of criminal courts, despite proposals for more complete integration.[42] The separation was not a complete one, since oversight from the centre continued to be an important function. Within each High Court division, three of its judges would sit as a Divisional Court constituting an appeal court from the county courts and magistrates' courts.[43] The Queen's Bench Divisional Court, moreover, exercised the main jurisdiction to issue the prerogative writs against inferior tribunals and public officers of all kinds. The old scheme of assizes, by which royal judges conducted both civil and criminal trials in the provinces, was retained. The one important alteration was that the courts were to function in London and at assizes at the same time. An old pattern of life at the common law bar was broken up amid dismayed regret.[44]

---

[37] 14 & 15 Vict., c. 83.

[38] Preceded by an imposing Royal Commission on the Judicature: 1st Report: P.P. 1868–1869 [4130] XXV (need for supreme court); 2nd Report: 1872 [C. 631] XX (county courts). For the first attempts at implementation, see Abel-Smith and Stevens (1967) 48–51.

[39] Judicature Act 1873, s.24.

[40] Ibid., s.25.

[41] See below, p. 220ff.

[42] See Judicature Commission, 2nd Report (above, n. 38), p. 13; Lord Hatherley L.C.'s Appellate Jurisdiction Bill of 1870 proposed an integration of criminal with civil appeals; but nothing came of it: Abel-Smith and Stevens (1967), p. 49.

[43] Originally the Divisional Courts were to be courts of reference by individual judges of the division, after the practice of the common law courts: Baker (1979), pp. 122–23. Lord Hatherley's attempt in 1870 to implement the plan included an integration of criminal with civil work to the extent of giving the Court of Appeal jurisdiction over both. A regular court of appeal for criminal cases would have to wait for a considerable time more: see below, p. 619ff.

[44] See below, pp. 93–94.

The new structure was a response to demand for the services of superior courts, above all from the great interests, industrial, commercial and financial, which had built up Britain's economic triumph. In making the case for reform, the Judicature Commissioners were able to dwell upon the inconsistencies and inconveniences of commercial litigation which arose from the separations of jurisdiction: the difficulties that came, for instance, from treating company directors as agents at common law and as trustees in equity; or from the different rules of liability for collisions at sea applied by common law and admiralty.[45] Yet it was a measured response, in which the needs of business were balanced against the interests of lawyers. To an extent both groups shared the same concerns. There was increasing dissatisfaction over the waywardness of juries in handling commercial questions—invention patents, for instance, or bills of exchange. The way out was no longer to develop the use of special juries in the manner of Lord Mansfield but to increase the court's discretion to order trial of a common law issue by judge alone. The Judicature Commissioners heard much evidence in favour of the introduction of commercial courts with businessmen among the judges, after the model, for instance, of the French *conseils de prud'hommes*. For the previous twenty years this prospect had been steadily canvassed and had attracted the interest of chambers of commerce and trade councils.[46] But the Commission voiced the antagonism of leading lawyers to any such idea. Nothing was to be done until new embarrassments induced the creation of a Commercial list for the Queen's Bench Division in 1895.[47]

To a significant degree, therefore, the Judicature Acts turned the judges away from outside influence.[48] Some sat mainly in London, an increasing proportion of cases were heard without a jury, the appellate judges no longer doubled as trial judges but worked in the rare atmosphere of their own courts. Indeed this separation of appeals completed a development which had been slow to evolve because it ran counter to the notion of final disposal by a jury. As we have seen, even when methods of raising issues of law were extended from the pleadings to the actual trial, the judges did a good deal to preserve their discretion over the referral of issues. A losing party's *right* to question the outcome of the trial was the subject of difficulties which were only resolved in the latter stages of reform.

Indeed, if Gladstone's government had had their way, this new apartness would have been even more complete, for the initial Judicature Act abolished the appellate jurisdiction of the House of Lords. Only an upsurge of romantic conservatism, not from the Lords themselves but from Tory lawyers on the Commons back-benches, saw to its preservation.[49]

In the upper house the judicial business was by now distinct from

---

[45] 1st Report (above, n. 38), at p. 7ff.
[46] A. R. Mersic, *Parliament of Commerce* (1960); Arthurs (1985), pp. 56–61.
[47] See below, p. 93; and note the Arbitration Act 1889, above p. 37.
[48] On this theme, see A. W. B. Simpson in P. Allsop (ed.) *Then and Now* (1974), p. 51; on the achievements in detail, *cf.* I. H. Jacob *ibid.*, p. 159.
[49] R. B. Stevens (1964) 80 L.Q.R. 343.

the political, in the sense that lay peers did not vote.[50] Even as its appellate business had built up during the nineteenth century, it had somehow been handled by a small coterie of lawyers, current and former Lord Chancellors and a few ennobled judges.[51] In 1876 they were at last supplemented by other very senior judges, who were made life peers (Lords of Appeal in Ordinary).[52] So this third tier became the rarely accessible apex of the superior court pyramid—a structure which at once confirmed the bar's exclusive rights of practice and its role in supplying the judges of consequence. In their adapted environment, the judicial Lords (who were also the main members of the Judicial Committee of the Privy Council for the Empire) could manage with a peculiar finesse the tensions between the professional and the political that are the lot of ultimate courts everywhere. They could continue to announce themselves pure declarers of common law, mere fixers of the dictionary meanings of statutory words.[53] But they were not, on the domestic side, constantly having to interpret a single constitutional document; and on the colonial side there was a distance of superiority as well as geography. Their interventions in matters of first political water would remain sporadic enough for claims to a perfect objectivity to get by. It could be for insiders alone to appreciate that from time to time the course of the law would incontrovertibly be set by the current judges and by them alone.

(g) The Legal Professions

In manufacture and commerce the bastions of monopoly, such as the guilds, had been disintegrating since the seventeenth century and were to disappear almost entirely with the freeing of international trade in the period to 1850. Yet it was in this period that the first examples of the modern professional monopoly in services began to blossom. Their growth was led by the two legal professions, the bar and the attorneys (or solicitors, as they later, more decor-

---

[50] The convention became plain in the 1840s but took 50 years to be settled beyond question. Lay members were still regular in the Judicial Committee of the Privy Council in the 1860s: Stevens (1979), pp. 29–34.

[51] In the 1820s, when business first accelerated, lay peers were drafted in to make a quorum on an extraordinary rota: Stevens (1978), pp. 19–23. After that there were just enough "law lords" to cope—though there were crises in the mid–50s and late 60s. The Judicial Committee of the Privy Council had taken over its appellate business from the civilian courts and the colonies in 1833 at Brougham's instigation. He had larger visions of a single court of final appeal with himself as President, which had some effect on the failure of his campaign: D.B. Swinfen (1974) 90 L.Q.R. 396.

[52] An attempt to make the great Baron Parke a life peer had been defeated in 1857 because such an undermining of established tradition was said to be beyond the royal prerogative. Parke (by then childless) became Lord Wensleydale in the ordinary way: Stevens (1978), pp. 39–44; F.M.L. Thompson, English Landed Society in the Nineteenth Century (1963), pp. 51 55.

[53] The keystone in the doctrine of stare decisis—the rule that the House of Lords bound even itself—was fixed in position: London Street Tramways v. London County Council [1894] A.C. 489: adopting the view taken earlier in Beamish v. Beamish (1861) 9 H.L.C. 274: Stevens (1978) Chap. 3.

ously, became).[54] By no means all who aspire to the status of the "professional" today have acquired the imprimatur of an exclusive right of practice and it is a condition under industrial capitalism that has nothing natural about it: the case has always to be fought for initially and guarded thereafter. The argument depends upon an expertise which can be acquired only through training in the specialised art and which ought therefore to be practised upon the public only by those shown to have acquired the skill. The admitted practitioners can often claim to be the only proper judges of the attainments of new entrants and of the failings of their peers. An essential independence of judgment can then be maintained in these and other ways even when the state becomes the major provider of the services (as it has, for instance, of medical services in Britain).

Expertise of this kind has mostly depended on scientific, technical or managerial advances in the wake of industrialisation. Sociologists who have analysed the professionalisation process as a whole have accordingly treated the modern forms as a nineteenth-century phenomenon differing radically from independent occupations which in the preceding centuries had become acceptable pursuits for cadets of the aristocracy and gentry, such as commissions in the armed services and the better livings in the established church.[55] The value of general typologies, however, has its limits, and nowhere is this more apparent than in the history of the two legal professions.[56] Each grew over a longer span than the industrial period itself; each developed idiosyncrasies that stem partly from the work undertaken and partly from being such early examples. The bar, as the senior branch, had acquired its monopoly over the right to represent clients as advocates in the courts of common law and equity by the late middle ages. With this had come self-governance by the Inns of Court and a developed system of formal training.[57] In 1729 the attorneys gained a monopoly over the institution of litigation on behalf of clients, and the preparation of its documentation. Their monopoly over conveyancing, shared with the senior branch, was given in 1804. The younger Pitt, seeking to increase the stamp duty upon attorneys' practising certifi-

---

[54] Attorneys had originally been attached to the common law courts, solicitors to Chancery, but eighteenth century practice was to admit them to both (see esp. 23 Geo. II, c. 26, s.15). However, something of the distinction in respectability would continue for much longer.

[55] Work on the British professions with a strong historical bent includes A. M. Carr-Saunders and P. A. Wilson, *The Professions* (1933); W. J. Reader, *Professional Men* (1966); M. S. Larson, *The Rise of Professionalism* (1977); T. J. Johnson, *Professions and Power* (1972); R. Dingwall and P. Lewis, *Sociology of the Professions* (1982).

[56] The earlier literature, in the tradition of Weber, regards the professions as modern-day equivalents of the older, non-entrepreneurial occupations (see esp. Carr-Saunders and Wilson (above, n. 55)). But it is naive to assume that what is broadly true of salaried, bureaucratic services is a dominant characteristic of the "private" professions.

[57] For the early history of the legal professions, see Baker (1979) Chap. 10; Holdsworth, II pp. 311–19, 484—512, 556–66; XII 4–101; W. R. Prest, *The Inns of Court . . . 1590–1640* (1972); W. R. Prest (ed.), *Lawyers in Early Modern Europe and America* (1981) Chaps. 1–5; W. R. Prest in Rubin and Sugarman (1984) 300–20; G. Holmes, *Augustan England* (1982) Chap. 5, M. Miles (1981) 23 Bus. Hist. 127; on more recent developments, there is much statistical information in Abel (1988).

cates and articles of clerkship conceded this as a quid pro quo.[58] Its value then lay primarily in the surrounding business that conveyancing attracted, but conveyancing itself would come in time to provide the ballast stabilising the entire solicitors' profession. The practice of an attorney was scarcely proper for an eighteenth-century gentleman. But not only was there an upper echelon of solicitors who provided discreet and highly valuable services in organising the settlements and legal business of aristocracy and gentry[59]; flourishing beneath them were successful and respected men, providers of legal and financial services to the growing middle classes, agricultural and commercial.[60] The doubtful reputation came from the lower end of the trade, the "pettifoggers" who fomented Dickensian litigation in order to live off the proceeds. It was indeed against the worst of them that the monopoly of 1729 was granted.

If attorneys already varied considerably in their positions and interests, so to a lesser extent did the bar. Although a much smaller, closer-knit body, it had long since ceased to be merely an adjunct of the landed class. A substantial proportion of its clientele came from a lower social order; so also did a good number in its own ranks.[61] The esoteric skills demanded in its practice called for those whose cleverness and determination would secure great practices before leading to judicial and occasionally to high political office.[62] At the same time there was room for those of more modest ambition, including members of the gentry who acted during local assizes but otherwise devoted themselves to the life of the family seat.[63]

Unlike the many professions that were to emulate the law, monopoly status for the bar and the attorneys was not preceded by the formation of a national association to lobby for it. On the contrary, central organisation, with control over training and admission, gradually assumed the character of necessity after the elite position had already been secured.

(i) The Bar

In the later eighteenth century the practising bar was very small, though its size cannot be measured with accuracy. Many who were called to the bar never practised, or did so only occasionally, a fact

---

[58] The stamp on annual practice certificates was first imposed in 1785 (£5 in London, £3 in the provinces—doubled in 1804). The stamp on articles began in 1794 (£100 in London, £50 in the provinces—increased by 10 per cent. in 1804; never a tax objected to by those concerned with barriers to entry). In addition, a conveyance had since 1785 attracted a stamp if drawn by an attorney, a burden which helped the argument that unqualified conveyancers should be excluded. See Robson (1959) Chap. 2; Kirk (1977), pp. 130–131.

[59] These led in the formation of the Society of Gentlemen Practisers: below, p. 51.

[60] For examples see Birks (1960) Chaps. 8, 9, 11; Robson (1959) Chap. 9; M. Miles in Rubin and Sugarman (1984) 470; G. Holmes (above, n. 57). P. Aylett (1987) 5 L. & Hist. R.I.

[61] See Prest (1981, above, n. 57), Chap. 3; Duman (1983), pp. 9–29, giving a detailed picture of the geographical, social and educational background of barristers, mainly in the early and late nineteenth century.

[62] See, *e.g.* many of the biographical entries in the List, p. ix.

[63] For an example, R. Cocks (1978) 8 Kingston L.R. 37.

that indicates something of its special status.[64] By 1835 Duman estimates that the number lay between 450 and 1010; by 1885 between
660 and 1450. He also shows that the number of initial admissions to
the Inns fluctuated considerably, a peak of over 300 per annum in
1835 falling rapidly thereafter to a number perhaps half that in 1858,
before climbing again to a steadier mid-point.[65] These are not the
statistics of major growth or even of steady progress.[66] The 1840s
were years of serious overcrowding in the bottom ranks and a time
too of much hostile criticism from outside, some of it rooted in simple envy. Yet there remained about the bar a special aura that combined glamour with dignity. The criminal and (later) the divorce
courts provided newspapers with dramatic fare and leading counsel
acquired familiar names.

Despite its small numbers, the bar could afford some diversity in
its organisations. Its peculiar combination of camaraderie and com-
petitiveness made its groupings social first and professional
second.[67] In London, the four Inns of Court (Inner and Middle Temple, Lincoln's and Gray's Inn) acted as dining clubs, often boisterous,
sometimes solemn. Each was presided over by a self-perpetuating
Bench which was responsible for admissions and calls to the bar and
which administered formal discipline.[68] The Inns were active during
the four short terms of the common law year. But as much of the bar
went off with the judges on assize, a similar life centred around the
Messes of the different circuits. These were comradely bodies without formal powers.[69] Nonetheless they played a vital role in building
and maintaining those practices that preserved and spread business
within the circuit: barristers from outside it could appear only if the
client paid a "special" fee and offered a brief also to a circuit member; King's Counsel were generally expected to appear with a junior;
and the junior was to receive two-thirds or three-fifths of his leader's
fee.[70] The Messes would retain their distinctive vitality until the
Judicature Acts. It was then that the new overlap between London

---

[64] For more than a century before this a successful career at the bar had been a glitter-
ing prize: Holmes (above, n. 57), p. 125ff.

[65] Duman (1983), pp. 6–9. See also Abel (1988), Table 1.1, 1.10–12.

[66] At the same period, the number of solicitors with practising certificates remained
virtually stationary (see Kirk (1976), p. 42), despite the considerable rise in population. One part of the explanation must lie in the reforms of court process. The bar,
by contrast, was providing the means of entry to county court judgeships, legal positions in the colonies, and positions in the new central and local bureaucracies.

[67] For the origins of these arrangements, see A. W. B. Simpson [1970] C.L.J. 241.

[68] The judges had become members of the separate Sergeants' Inn (which survived
until the Judicature Acts). The 12 common law judges acted as visitors to the Inns,
which was held to exempt them from supervision by mandamus: R. v. Gray's Inn
(Benchers) (1780) 1 Dougl. 353; and see R. v. Lincoln's Inn (1825) 4 B. & C. 855. The
Benchers insisted on their right to refuse admission as they chose until 1837, when,
in the face of considerable criticism, they ceded a right of appeal to the judges:
Abel-Smith and Stevens (1967) pp. 63–64.

[69] For their role, see esp. R. Cocks (1976) 6 Kingston L.R. 36; and Cocks (1983), pp.
147–153.

[70] The view of Abel-Smith and Stevens (1967), p. 220ff. that these restrictive practices
were formalised and tightened in the wake of the Judicature Acts is probably inac-
curate: see R. Cocks (1976) 92 L.Q.R. 512; (1978) 94 L.Q.R. 505; cf. Sir A. Johnston
(1977) 93 L.Q.R. 190. For numbers of silks, Abel (1988), Table 1.24.

and assize sittings was to bifurcate the bar's world and new organisations would become necessary for its cohesion.

The eighteenth-century bar required no formal training of its entrants, but merely a period of five years between admission and call to practice during which dining rites in the Inns were to be observed. The earlier function of the Inns as educational bodies had disintegrated, leaving a gap which was not filled by the ancient universities. On the continent the universities assumed such a primacy in legal education and in the associated process of providing a rational coherence for law that it has seemed an elemental part of emergent capitalism.[71] In England, however, only the small band of civilians drew upon this tradition, receiving their degrees in civil law from Oxford or Cambridge before entering practice at Doctors' Commons. Entrants to the common law bar were left to fit themselves for practice, doing their own reading and becoming pupils to barristers, special pleaders or conveyancers as they chose. The establishment of English law chairs at Oxford (1758) and then Cambridge (1800) had no effect on professional qualification. Apart from Blackstone's distinguished tenure of the Vinerian Chair in the former, the posts became sinecures for practitioners.[72]

In 1762, the Inns accepted some need to improve the quality of entrants by allowing Oxford and Cambridge graduates to be called after only three years.[73] But it was not until the mid-nineteenth century that even a few leaders of the profession were to take a serious interest in systematic learning as a pre-requisite for practice: both Bethell (afterwards Lord Westbury L.C.) and Palmer (afterwards Lord Selborne L.C.) were prominent advocates of reform. A Select Committee of the Commons in 1846 recommended the properly scientific teaching of law in the ancient universities and examination for both admission and call to the bar.[74] A Royal Commission in 1854 espoused Westbury's case for a "Legal University" formed in London out of the Inns of Court (and financed from the considerable funds which they took from students).[75] Selborne later ran a sustained campaign to establish a "General School of Law" which would provide a common training for entry to both legal professions; he presented bills on the subject to Parliament between 1871 and 1876.[76]

To such pressures the bar was obliged in some measure to respond, for these were years when lawyers attracted prominent hostility in the press and elsewhere. In 1852, the Inns joined in a Council of Legal Education, which established five readerships in basic subjects; in order to be called, a student had now to attend the lectures or

---

[71] M. Rheinstein (ed.) *Max Weber on Law and Society* (1954) Chap. 7.
[72] See H. Lawson, *The Oxford Law School 1850–1965* (1968); P. Lucas (1962) 77 E. Hist. R. 456.
[73] Later extended to graduates of Trinity College, Dublin and (in the case of the Middle Temple) of the new universities of Durham and London (1840s). On a different tack, the Inner Temple insisted on a preliminary test in the classical languages (1829–1854).
[74] P.P. 1846 (686) X; for the malaise of the period, Cocks (1983) Chap. 2.
[75] P.P. 1854–55 [1998] XVIII; Cocks (1983), pp. 93–102.
[76] See Cocks (1983), pp. 172–180; Abel-Smith and Stevens (1967), p. 76.

pass an examination.[77] In 1872, the examination before call was at last made compulsory, though the standard was scarcely demanding. No formal qualification was imposed on initial entry as a student; and the larger plans for a General School foundered upon a lack of any sustained concern and antagonism to the idea of joint training for the two branches.[78] Oxford and Cambridge in their turn, together with newer institutions such as the University of London colleges,[79] began at last to build up their teaching of law, but in an historical, theoretical and universalist mode, which contrived both to allay academic suspicions and to refrain from intruding upon the technical mysteries of practice.[80] The first generation of law teachers in the universities contained scholars of considerable distinction: Maine, Bryce, Pollock, Holland, Anson, and above all Dicey and Maitland. But the coming leaders of the bar were rarely their pupils and the practising profession could afford to take only spasmodic notice of their writings. It had not had to espouse education as a pre-condition of its professional status and it continued to believe that the advocate's craft was to be learned in life at the bar rather than in letters.

Advocacy had long ceased to be a pursuit of gentlemanly leisure. The barrister's skills were needed at the hard edges of existence and success was measured in brief fees. Perhaps in consequence, this tough, competitive reality was encased in a peculiarly refined etiquette. In modern times this is marked by forms of dress and address which remain rooted in the eighteenth century.[81] Even at that period, it was accepted that barristers did not form partnerships; neither (by and large) did they take clients directly but only through the instruction of an attorney.[82] Their fees were in nature honoraria[83]: they did not sue for them, but neither did they owe duties to attorney or client to conduct a case with due care or indeed at all. When facing the client, they could remember their duty equally to assist the court; when facing the court they could hold out their responsibility to represent whoever first sought their advocacy. The whole amounted to a deeply individual code of professional honour whose keeping lay not

---

[77] Cocks (1983), pp. 97–100 gives details of what was taught.

[78] In 1877, Lord Cairns and Holker A.-G. promoted a bill to set up an educational council for the Inns alone; but this was not proceeded with.

[79] In true utilitarian endeavour, University College, London, established chairs in English law and jurisprudence (first held by Amos and Austin) in 1826; its orthodox rival, King's College, also introduced some teaching of law from an early stage: J. H. Baker (1977) 30 C.L.P. 1; Abel-Smith and Stevens (1967), pp. 165–168.

[80] International and Roman law, jurisprudence and the history of the constitution and the land law predominated. For the rôle of textbooks, cf. A.W.B. Simpson (1981) 48 U. Chicago L.R. 632; D. Sugarman in W.L. Twining (ed.), Legal Theory and the Common Law (1986) Chap. 3.

[81] For his own time, Blackstone likened the relation of suitor and counsel to that of cliens to the ancient Roman orator: Commentaries, I Chap. 14.

[82] But the bar long avoided having to admit this as a strict rule of etiquette, fearing the power that this could confer to wreck individual careers: Brougham was once so threatened. It became a matter of particular tension in the 1840s when numbers at the bar rose steeply. The Act of 1846 creating the County Courts expressly precluded barristers from direct access; but in 1852, Brougham procured a reversal of the rule and a provision that attorneys might not instruct other attorneys as advocates there: Abel-Smith and Stevens (1967), p. 57; and see, W.W. Pue (1987) 5 L. & Hist. R. 135.

[83] Their clerks could set fees by negotiation with attorneys. The only control exercised by the courts lay in their power to tax the costs payable by one side (normally the loser) to the other.

so much in formal powers of the benchers of the Inns as in the informal approval or disapproval that came constantly from judges and fellow counsel, and, in their deferential but decisive way, from instructing attorneys. It is in the intensity of these beliefs, and in the admirations and the loyalties, and the fierce judgments and hostilities engendered by them, that the historian will find the clue to the unique forms of the institution. In turn, its closeness to the state, coupled with the determination to stand disinterestedly apart, suggests why these gentlemanly trappings should remain so urgent a part of the profession's self-conceit.

(ii) Attorneys

If, in the eighteenth century, the social condition of individual attorneys could vary considerably, their ranking as a group was undoubtedly moderate. They bore the stamp of the tradesman, an apprenticeship of five years in articles of clerkship being treated as the condition of the court-work monopoly granted in 1729.[84] More damagingly, the image of the pettifogger, clinging leech-like to his client, persisted in literature as in life. The nineteenth-century rise of this second tier of legal practitioners to the status of solicitors was accordingly a considerable movement, which approximated more closely than did the bar to the rise of the modern professions in general. Actual numbers are not known for most of the eighteenth century but by 1800 there were about 1,800 practising attorneys in London and perhaps 3,500 outside.[85] By 1841 the total (measured by numbers of practising certificates) had risen to just over 10,000, a figure which was to remain roughly consonant for another thirty years before rising to a peak of around 17,000 in 1911.[86] The mainspring of the movement was the emergence of capitalist organisation, for attorneys played a vital role in the process of coalescing and managing large agricultural estates and then in the organisation and financing of industry, commerce and communications. In directing the energy released, a professional organisation which claimed to speak for the whole body, rather than for some narrow enclave, played some considerable part; it was not however so central a role as Larson claims to be typical.[87] The first major step towards monopoly in 1729 came before the emergence of any body of this kind: the Society of Gentlemen Practisers was formed only in 1739, when the 1729 Act was renewed.[88] The Society was active in trying to rid court practice of unqualified pettifoggers.[89] It was strong enough to challenge the important local monopoly over document writing enjoyed by the Scriveners Guild in the City of London[90] and it negotiated

---

[84] See Kirk (1976), pp. 72–73. An attorney would be expected to use the tradesman's entrance when calling at a barrister's residence.

[85] Robson (1959), App. 4.

[86] A figure not to be exceeded until after 1945: see Kirk (1976), p. 108.

[87] See above, n. 57.

[88] Birks (1960), pp. 144–51; Kirk (1976), p. 23.

[89] In 1748 the Society procured legislation preventing the backdating of admissions: 22 Geo. II, c. 46, o.12.

[90] Litigation on the question lasted from 1749–1760: see *Harrison* v. *Smith* (1760), Holdsworth, XII 71; the conflict is a good instance of the replacement of local by national monopoly.

with Pitt over the conveyancing monopoly in 1804.[91] Yet the Society
was from the outset an elite group of leading London attorney,
whose unrepresentativeness stood out as numbers expanded. Eventually it was absorbed into an Incorporated Law Society, which was
founded in 1823 and received a royal charter in 1831—a broader institution which was to become the modern Law Society.[92] It was to
establish for the rest of the nineteenth century an influential position
as the body to which governments turned on questions of legal and
professional moment and it became closely involved in the veritable
stream of legislation which came to affect solicitors' practice.

Yet it would not be until the twentieth century that the Society
could claim as members more than half of those with practising certificates.[93] The profession divided not only, as did the bar, between
the well-established and the new entrants but also between the
metropolis and the provinces.[94] Given a court structure with so
strong a centralising tendency, the rift was of long standing and bred
a succession of country solicitor associations, the best-known being
the Metropolitan and Provincial Law Association which flourished
in the tense middle years of the nineteenth century.[95]

The establishment of the Incorporated Law Society had one early
consequence: in a new effort to protect the monopolies and to discomfort the unqualified, the cause of formal education was taken up
positively. The judges had long admitted attorneys to practice, but
the step was a final formality after articles.[96] In 1836 masters of court
and ILS examiners were empowered to test the legal knowledge of
candidates. Levels were not high, but the Society began to provide
lectures in the main fields (common law, equity, bankruptcy, conveyancing and criminal law). In 1860, it was able to add a preliminary
examination in general knowledge; growing respectability was
underpinned by this impediment to entry from the lower classes,
which operated particularly against the managing clerks of attorneys
themselves.[97]

The monopoly over court work, if it carried no educational pre-
condition when it was created, did not come entirely without supervision. The judges held the power to strike an attorney from the roll
for misconduct, either in the processing of litigation or in handling a
client's money or other affairs.[98] Given the lack of training in
accountancy, the absence of any duty to file accounts, and the
increasing involvement in conveyancing and other property dealings, financial defalcations were to increase with industrialisation.
Disciplinary proceedings before the court were an embarrassment to
the whole profession, admirably calculated to fan old prejudices. The
Law Society would have liked a larger say in the process, hoping

[91] See above, pp. 46–47.
[92] Birks (1960), pp. 155–57; Kirk (1976), pp. 29–30.
[93] Kirk (1976), p. 42.
[94] See Birks (1969), pp. 151–155.
[95] Birks (1960), pp. 212–213. Its organ was the *Law Times* (from 1857 the *Solicitor's Journal*).
[96] Birks (1960), pp. 171–172, taking the enrolment of William Hickey as illustration.
[97] The Solicitors Act 1860, s.8, however, gave the judges power to grant exemptions
    which they exercised freely; the ILS took a further 20 years to get what it wanted in
    practice.
[98] Kirk (1976), p. 72ff.

thereby to deflect the public gaze; but until the last quarter of the century it still lacked the measure of trust and influence that such a demand would need by way of support.[99]

By the period of the Judicature Acts, the solicitors had acquired a social acceptability, which the rules on education and accountability served to buttress. But props are not foundations. The new status came from the services which solicitors offered to increasingly prosperous classes of property owners, whose own successes added constantly to their needs. So considerable had these become that the solicitors were more preoccupied with preserving their acknowledged territories than in expanding their frontiers. They could allow others with organisational and managerial skills to occupy adjacent preserves: accountants, land agents and surveyors, estate agents and auctioneers, patent agents, bankers, insurers, friendly and building society managers. The solicitors did little to impede the arrival of these more junior professions and less to merge with them or absorb them. Their main hostility was directed towards encroachment on their court work and conveyancing monopolies.

V. Executive Government and Law

In the First Reform Act years, Parliament created a succession of national corps, where previously there had at most been local initiative, to regulate and administer economic and social life at crucial points. The massive new problems of population growth, urban existence and industrial production demanded no less. One eventual consequence was the emergence of a modern civil service of the British type: salaried, selected by merit, permanent, anonymous. As "the monarchy rose above party, so the civil service settled below party. Constitutional bureaucracy was the counterpart of constitutional monarchy."[1] The very different experience of central administration that preceded it contributed something to its shape. The old notion of office as a piece of freehold property fostered ideas of permanence and kept down a tendency towards a "spoils" system, under which the senior administrators would share the sympathies of the politicians currently enjoying executive power and would go out of office with them.[1a] The personal relationship of the Hanoverian kings to their chief advisers contributed to the same end, since it inhibited the definition of ministries by clear party allegiance.[2] With the emergence after 1832 of collective responsibility of the executive to the Commons, a nominate political figure would have direction

---

[99] See below, p. 107.

[1] Parris (1969) 49, and see generally, Chap. 1; E. Cohen *The Growth of the British Civil Service* (1941); on "neutrality", G. Kitson Clark (1959) 2 Hist. J. 19.

[1a] Parris (1969) 26–33; and on the Northcote–Trevelyan reforms, J. Hart in G. Sutherland, *Studies in the Growth of Nineteenth Century Government* (1972) Chap. 3; MacDonagh (1977) Chap. 11.

[2] But the tendency had deeper roots: the Stuart habit of revising the commission of justices after Parliamentary elections survived under George I but then died away: see L. J. K. Glassey, *Politics and the Appointment of Justices of the Peace, 1675–1720* (1979).

over and responsibility for a bureaucracy, which in turn would for the time pursue his policies.[3] On the whole, with the substitution of salaries for the perquisites of office and the replacement of friendship by merit in matters of recruitment and advancement, these bureaucracies would, provide a reasonably efficient and dedicated service. But there was little enough reason to suppose in advance that anything beneficial to the public weal could emerge from the sudden growth of new offices, just when such energy was being devoted to proscribing the old.

There were those wider trends—notably the de-regulation of foreign trade—which contributed to suspicion of all manifestations of government and gave an appearance of paradox to the new agencies. Indeed they were established at all because governments in particular, and Parliament and informed opinion more generally, had to admit some measure of restraint and mutual accommodation amid such rapid social change. There were myriad issues of what and how, which gave opportunity to express mistrust of the novel developments. One characteristic is plain: most of the intervention by the central state was to regulate the activities of private enterprise; factories, mines and workshops, railways and shipping, land rights and finance in the agricultural sector—all were to be affected, as we shall have much occasion to note in subsequent chapters. Few schemes were run centrally in the public name, the exceptions being the postal service, and to an extent the poor law and the prisons. Public health legislation, which had to tackle an accumulation of dangers, began as regulation of the outworks of the free market; but a more interventionist, managerial form would emerge, as local government, to an extent under central supervision and financial assistance, entered the business of water supply, sewage disposal, burial of the dead and eventually slum clearance, housing provision and an outcrop of municipal services. It was *this* shift from "individualism" to "collectivism" that was to prove the great change of gear.[4] Yet the gradualness with which it occurred is one of the clearest measures of that deep and abiding faith in the virtues of private initiative to direct an economy growing with unique speed and good fortune.

There is another measure of that same attitude. MacDonagh and other writers have given a particular impulse to administrative history by emphasising the internal energies of the new bureaucracies.[5] According to MacDonagh's "model" of government growth, the administrative unit (typically led by inspectors) was created only after a scandalous state of affairs had been revealed and Parliament had made an ineffective attempt to abolish it by general legal prohibitions or the conferment of powers on local authorities. Once the bureaucracy was installed, it would assess the factors that would make for at least common-sense remedies. Soon enough it would

---

[3] Parris (1969), pp. 93–105, Chap. 5.

[4] H. Perkin. *The Structured Crowd* (1981) Chap. 4.

[5] Macdonagh (1958) and applied by him in *A Pattern of Government Growth: The Passenger Acts and their Enforcement* (1961); interestingly developed by I. Paulus, *In Search of Pure Food* (1974). The controversy over the relationship of this thesis to the influence of ideas is discussed below, p. 63ff.

find its legal powers in need of strengthening and it might well press for central direction that would bring with it ministerial responsibility for the operation. Eventually it would work itself into a position where it had the power to establish a full administration, attacking the continuing problems by publicity, persuasion and, where necessary, prosecution (or other adjudicative process); assembling statistics; initiating and following up technical advances; conducting experiments that might lead to new general policies. By this stage a new breed of administrator would have emerged, equipped with a professional expertise directed to the range of tasks.

This driving energy, a distinctive counterpart to the aggressive thrust behind industrialisation, was the more marked for the opposition that it had to meet—an opposition which, whether from simple self-interest or from higher-minded ideals, could invoke the dangers of governmental interference and the debilitations of legislation as matters of high principle. It explains why there was so much pre-occupation with legal powers at the stage in MacDonagh's time-sequence after the first introduction of the central bureaucracy.

The opposition could take a considerable variety of forms, the significance of each varying from case to case. At this point we may list the forms as strategies, which may help to bring out the significance of particular developments as they arise in later chapters. There was in the first place the business of Parliament itself, since new governmental bodies unquestionably needed legal authority for their range of activities—for all decision-making, executive and judicial, as well as the acquisition and dispensing of moneys.[6] The powerful groupings like the railway interest, whose chances constantly depended on the course of legislation, could achieve a great deal by the "friendship" of members of each house. They could be called upon to argue against or "amend away" proposals for increasing bureaucratic powers.[7] Occasionally they could be used for positive attack, for instance, by procuring counter-enactments.[8] Resistance to new legislation might be looked for in other quarters—where for instance the interests of professional groups (such as the lawyers) would be affected, their own spokesmen could be enleagued. Equally, since government servants were a far from uniform breed, there might be help from a man in senior post who shared a mistrust for accretions of bureaucratic power.[9]

Secondly, as an answer to difficulties in procuring new legislation, the bureaucracy might seek delegated authority to make orders or rules. As early as 1833, Parliament was prepared to concede such authority to the new factories inspectorate and a year later to the poor law commissioners. Gradually standard types of delegated legislation would develop: if made by central authority, it would be subject to tabling before Parliament or very occasionally to approval

---

[6] For the position of earlier local authorities, see above, p. 21, as for ministries and "the Crown", see below, p. 58.
[7] e.g. below, pp. 175ff., 302ff., 515ff.
[8] e.g. below, pp. 229, 517–518.
[9] e.g. below, p. 162.

by affirmative resolution; if made by local authority, it might well need the approval of a minister.[10]

The pressure for delegated powers came from experience with many types of regulation. If businesses were to fall under constraints they would be anxious to know the standards they had to meet and would proclaim it a particular burden to be left to the discretion of an inspector. The enforcing officers themselves would be in favour of clear standards when these could be prescribed, for they would then be empowered to act in a uniform manner and to draw moral support from doing so.[11] Yet powers of delegation were often resisted and inspectorates left to struggle on, perhaps proclaiming their policies through circulars, notices and the like.[12] These would lack legal authority and might at any stage be challenged as an overreach, or an advance fettering, of discretion.

Thirdly, there was the question of political authority, which was an intimate part of emerging notions of ministerial responsibility to Parliament. The conception of a ministry—that each main department of central government would be headed by a member of Cabinet who would answer for it in one or other House—had become well-enough settled. But one eighteenth-century practice, designed to curb excesses of individual authority, had been to place this political overlordship in the hands of a board rather than an individual. The idea of a board, however, acquired an extension, principally after 1832, when it was conceived as a way of conferring semi-autonomous authority for a particular function; this achieved a certain distancing from the immediately political. "Boards" were indeed to have a long and varied history.[13] But the immediate experience demonstrated that any activity that was constantly controversial must be made the direct responsibility of a minister with real authority. The Poor Law Commissioners, appointed as an independent "board" to give central direction to the revised policies of 1834, were to suffer for their independent structure and were re-constituted with Parliamentary representation in 1847 (as the Poor Law Board).[14] The Railway Department in the Board of Trade (1840) was to become a "Board" (still departmental—1844) and a Commission (independent—1846) before being re-absorbed *de facto* (1849), then *de jure* (1851) into the Board of Trade.[15] Between the 1850s and 1906 those boards which constitutionally remained distinct from ministeries were in all important cases placed under some form of ministerial

[10] The diffusion of delegated legislation remained problematic for much of the nineteenth century: see J. E. Pemberton, *British Official Publications* (1971) Chap. 10. Just as they had supervised the bye-law making of the old, so the courts required the new corporations not to make bye-laws that were "manifestly unreasonable": *Kruse v. Johnson* [1898] 2 Q.B. 91.

[11] See MacDonagh (1958) 2 Vict. St. 29; and in R. Robson (ed.) *Ideas and Institutions of Victorian Britain* (1967) Chap. 3.

[12] It is only in the 1850s that the new central bodies began to acquire significant powers to make orders and the like: Parris (1969), pp. 188–196.

[13] Willson (1955) 33 Pub. Admin. 43 gives lists of the ministries and boards existing in 1832 (12 and 9 respectively) and for ensuing years (by 1855, 15 and 21); and see Parris (1969), pp. 80–93.

[14] Below, p. 429ff.

[15] H. Parris, *Government and the Railways in Nineteenth-century Britain* (1965).

supervision.[16] The orthodoxy of responsibility to Parliament was settled, despite the doubts of a few theorists.[17] The "board" idea would re-emerge only as government became more widely interventionist and managerial.

Fourthly, and significantly in a world directed to regulation, there was the question of adjudicative power. If they could have been treated by the assumptions surrounding the justices of the peace, the new inspectors could have been given the authority not merely to find that individuals were transgressing legal standards but to adjudge them in the wrong and impose fines or other punishment upon them. The first factory inspectors were indeed each put in the position of a magistrate for the purpose of enforcing the Factories Act 1833. Hostility to factory inspectors led the Home Secretary to direct them not to use their judicial powers, and after a decade these powers were removed from the statute book.[18] Instead, as in so many other instances, the new inspectors were confined to the role of prosecutors and the tribunals before which they had to take their complaints, if they could not negotiate an informal solution, were the justices in petty sessions.[19] It becomes part of the essentially "judicial" conception of the justices' functions that time and again they should be called upon to administer the minor criminal jurisdictions of administrative regulation. "Interfering" administration was thus made subject to "law" as seen by a less than impartial outside body. On the bench of justices, the attitudes of many of those most directly being regulated might find strong representation. In the boroughs the landlords of insanitary housing and the purveyors of adulterated food, in industrial areas the mill-owners and workshop proprietors, could muster a substantial presence, either personally or through their families and friends. The reports of the early factory and mine inspectors make clear how nakedly partisan the justices could be in resisting attempts at enforcing new legislation, even when its terms were clear enough.[20]

Fifthly, there was the issue of supervision by the central courts over the new bureaucracies. Here, so far as central government was concerned, the approach had to depend on whether the body was a ministry and therefore entitled to the exceptional privileges that still in law enswathed "the Crown"; or whether, as a creature of statute, it had been given an independent existence as a "Board." In the former case, the rule that the Crown could do no wrong precluded suits against it entirely in the case of torts[21] and created special difficulties

---

[16] Willson (above, n. 13) gives details.

[17] Bentham (in his Constitutional Code) had planned for an executive with a right to speak but not vote in the legislature. J. S. Mill wanted general use of the advisory boards that were becoming a prominent feature of Indian government. Bagehot and Todd maintained the virtues of British practice: B. B. Schaffer (1957) 3 Aust. J. Pol. Hist. 60; F. Rosen, *Jeremy Bentham and Representative Democracy* (1983), p. 136.

[18] See below, pp. 304–305.

[19] See Arthurs (1985), pp. 103–115.

[20] See below, pp. 306–308, 517–518.

[21] The only hope was therefore an *ex gratia* payment. The position was not to change until the Crown Proceedings Act 1947: see L.L. Jaffe, *Judicial Control of Administrative Action* (1965), pp. 198–212.

in the case of repossession of land and breach of contract.[22] Mandamus would not lie against the Crown to compel the performance of any duty. This was some shackle upon any complete idea of a rule of law; but nonetheless Crown servants were individually liable for legal wrongs which they committed.[23] The Poor Law Commissioners, by contrast, were liable to the same general extent as local authorities. The limited range of functions of most central authorities made this difference less striking than might at first appear. Yet any body which was not the Crown had potentially to face a wider array of challenges. The Attorney-General once went so far as to advise that the Poor Law Commission was only able to act if all its members were present to take decisions; otherwise it would be in breach of the rules of natural justice and open to review by certiorari.[24] Because of the preference for giving adjudicative decisions over to the ordinary courts, there were few central bodies which regularly and obviously exercised judicial power. Where they did, as in the case of the tithe and enclosure commissioners it was usual to provide expressly for a right of appeal,[25] just as was happening with the general courts themselves.

Lastly, there was the role of law in the relations between central and local authorities. Those who believed, or professed to believe, that the novel interference from the centre broke a fundamental understanding of the constitution found the romantic theorisings of Toulmin Smith on the theme of local autonomy much to their taste.[26] A tension over central–local relations built up, which became a powerful current in its own right.[27] Corporations and parishes were ready enough to resist impositions upon them if they could find the legal means of doing so.[28] In any case the most that Parliament would do in many circumstances was to empower the local authorities to take action; time and again (particularly since a mere power conferred no implied authority to interfere with private rights)[29] the consequence was simple inaction or the keenest parsimony, which neither central government nor potential beneficiaries could impugn.

The matter was more complex however than issues of duty versus discretion. An elaborate notion of accountability by law was beginning to affect both the collection of revenue through taxes and rates, and its disbursement. At the centre the Treasury's methods, which

---

[22] The proceeding was by petition of right and needed the fiat of the Attorney-General. It was somewhat improved by the Petition of Right Act 1860. The procedure for a declaration only became general in the present century.

[23] The Crown remained protected from vicarious liability until 1947, whereas other governmental bodies became subject to it in 1866 (see below, pp. 492–493). In the case of mandamus not even a Crown servant could be compelled to perform a duty owed solely to the Crown. (R. v. Commissioners of the Income Tax (1888) 21 Q.B.D. 313, 319.

[24] Arthurs (1985), p. 141.

[25] Or even Parliamentary supervision (see below, p. 140).

[26] See below, p. 162.

[27] For the thesis that it is a major determinant in the growth of bureaucracies after 1832, see W. C. Lubenow, The Politics of Government Growth (1971).

[28] e.g. certiorari lay to quash an order of the Poor Law Commissioners requiring the establishment of a Board of Guardians, when the existence of such a Board already precluded their power: R. v. Poor Law Commissioners for England and Wales, re St. Pancras Parish, (1837) 6 Ad. & E. 1.

[29] See below, p. 163.

had retained an extraordinarily cumbersome, pre-banking character, were in 1833 placed under the careful administration of a Comptroller-General, who presented regular accounts to Public Accounts Commissioners.[30] Moneys collected for the consolidated funds were held by the Bank of England and disbursed upon the Comptroller-General's authority, he being responsible for seeing that it was employed only for purposes sanctioned by Parliament. These were developed by Gladstone's financial reforms into the modern institutions of Comptroller and Auditor-General and Public Accounts Committee of the Commons.[31] Eighteenth-century practice, which had allowed paymasters and money-holders to put funds to personal use until paid out, was replaced by severe scruple at all stages.

To bring the myriad local authorities under financial scrutiny was not an easy undertaking. It was, for example, essential to the policy embodied in the Poor Law Amendment Act 1834 that a new degree of financial control should be given to the Poor Law Commissioners (then Board) over the guardians of the poor law unions: the crucial elements of audited accounts and personal liability to surcharge for amounts expended on non-permitted purposes (such as toys for workhouse children) were part of the original scheme.[32] These were then strengthened: the justices lost a right of alleviation in 1844, the Board itself, as an alternative to the courts, became a tribunal of appeal in 1847; and in 1868 it acquired the power to appoint the district auditors, who in 1879 became civil servants under the Local Government Board.[33] By then they had acquired the audit of local education and sanitary authorities and were given similar powers over the new county councils and district councils, when county government was finally subjected to democratic ideas.[34] Only the municipal corporations, perhaps because their basic reform came as early as 1835, stayed partly beyond the reach of central audit. The new corporations had been subjected to statutory limits upon their purposes, but they retained the right to elect their own auditors.[35] The stick of central audit did reach them to the extent that they bit the carrot of central–local relations: the grant-in-aid. First applied to promote simple popular education in the 1830s,[36] it became a regular factor in other programmes of positive action from the 1850s onwards. It was introduced then for local police forces and brought with it not only financial inspection by central audit but substantive inspection for "efficiency."[37]

The first period of growth towards modern government was thus one of considerable antagonism, marked by constant resort to legal discipline. It was an experience to give particular urgency to Dicey's affirmation of the rule of general, "ordinary" law in contradistinction

[30] 4 & 5 Will. IV, c. 15.
[31] Exchequer and Audit Departments Act 1866.
[32] 4 & 5 Will. IV, c. 76, s.15; See S. and B. Webb, *History of the Poor Law* (1929), II pp. 210–214.
[33] See, 7 & 8 Vict. c. 101, s.37; 11 & 12 Vict. c. 91, s.4; 30 & 31 Vict. c. 91, s.4; 31 & 32 Vict. c. 122, s.24; 42 & 43 Vict. c. 6.
[34] See County Councils Act 1888, s.71(3); District Councils Act 1894, s.58.
[35] The position survived until 1972.
[36] Below, pp. 439–440.
[37] Below, pp. 594–595.

to a *droit administratif*; special courts and judges might all too easily
allow government a discretion to intervene in private rights and
affairs in the interests of state.[38] Yet by the time that Dicey wrote
there would be signs that the aggressive legalism of mid-century was
becoming tempered. A process of learning had been continuing on
all sides. Administration was becoming accepted as an inevitable
necessity; central departments and local authorities were acquiring
powers wide enough for the legal to be replaced at the forefront of
argument by the political and economic. It was a shift in perception
that, as we shall see, would find an appreciation among the judges.[39]
The administrators themselves learned much about the art of regulation. They were obliged by the hostility they faced on many issues to
adopt conciliatory tactics against the powerful. They relied very substantially on persuasion which appealed to a sense of social responsibility, and which might on occasion be allied with a realisation of
long-term economic advantage, or at least the hope that the cost of
regulation would bear harshly on competitors. It became clear that
systems which interposed this stage of negotiation would achieve a
measure of acceptance denied to older processes comprising only the
blunt instrument of adjudication by courts.[40]

VI. THE INFLUENCE OF IDEAS

(a) Ideologies

In any society where political processes are influenced by a considerable number of people, there emerge congeries of beliefs and
attitudes for which the term "ideology" is made to do service. It is a
useful concept since what has to be described is a condition that is
much less precise than a philosophy or any other systematically elaborated set of beliefs. An ideological position attracts for its
emotional as much as its rational appeal and draws upon the great
variety of psychological and social factors which condition individuals. The term carries the added overtone that much justification
offered for policy and decision dresses up a narrow self-interest in
the finery of large, unselfish principle. Any form of social history
seeks to elucidate the ideological because of its inevitable force in
shaping social life. Part of the difficulty in doing so is that ideas and
attitudes of apparently different depths appear in overlay, producing
complex and changing positions in individuals and in groups. For
our purposes what is important is to identify those ideologies which
were mainsprings for political action and so were likely to affect the
deployment of legal machinery. A helpful first step is to set out three
recurrent dichotomies which frequently underlie ideological positions thus understood, and which contribute to their formation at

[38] *Introduction to the Study of the Law of the Constitution* (1885), Chap. 12; for the significance of his discussion of the subject through succeeding editions, see F. H. Lawson
[1959] 7 Polit. St. 109, 207.
[39] Below, p. 95ff.
[40] See below, p. 164ff.

least among the politically influential. These are the distinctions between individualism and collectivism, between idealism and utilitarianism, and between a belief in the perfectability of man and in his innate viciousness.

(i) Individualism/Collectivism

We start with a substantial ambiguity. These terms may be used to describe the approach to an analytical problem. The individualist aims to isolate the particular characteristics which distinguish the individual inhabitant of a larger world; it is typically the method of the biologist.[41] The collectivist, by contrast, aims to show the interrelationship of function between integers in a complex whole; here lie many of the preoccupations of chemistry and physics. But in the study of societies, where description so easily slides into prescription, the terms have come to be used not merely to identify different ways of analysing man in society but to express the first premise of a political philosophy. Thus individualism has often been associated with liberalism, with pleas for a social organisation which leaves the individual free to realise his own abilities and desires so far as is compatible with the same wish in others. Collectivism has become allied with socialised or communistic organisation in which the interests of the individual become subjugate to the higher good of the state or the local community. It is where the terms are used in their methodological sense that they take the appearance of a precondition to ideology. It by no means follows that an individualist in this sense is necessarily an advocate of minimal government. Thomas Hobbes, first individualist among English philosophers, was a deep pessimist who argued that society was a necessary protection against violent destruction and that it must involve unquestioning subjugation to a sovereign ruler.

(ii) Idealism/Utilitarianism

The idealist takes as his premise that persons and things have an essential quality or ideal which it is the object of human inquiry to discover and promote. In Christian societies, idealistic philosophies held a long dominance, finding expression in the various social theories based upon the idea of a natural law. In the eighteenth century, deductions about the essential needs of man would acquire individualistic connotations in theories of organisation based upon a social contract; and they would be allied to libertarian ideals in the demands for the natural rights of man. But idealist positions could lead equally to views of an ordered society in which each man had his place and function within the collectivity.

The utilitarian, repelled by the innate metaphysic of the search for an ideal, started from the pyschological observation of the human tendency to maximise happiness and pleasure and to minimise unhappiness and pain. Social action was explained and moral injunctions were prescribed by reference to this one motive force. In

---

[41] In this sense, for instance, Jeremy Bentham was clearly individualist: Hume (1981), pp. 58–62.

the age of the Enlightenment, with its rationalistic concern for the betterment of the human condition, utilitarian analysis gained wide ground among European thinkers. Utilitarian premises were applied equally to an analysis of the economic functioning of society and to the organisation and activities of government in every aspect of its business. The overriding objective of government was, in Bentham's phrase, to procure the greatest happiness for the greatest number.

(iii) The Perfectability/Non-perfectability of Man

The conception of original sin—alluringly symbolised in Adam's plucking of the apple for Eve—has attracted the pessimists among theologians and philosophers of the Christian tradition, distinguishing them from optimists who in varying degrees have believed that man is capable of a utopian existence in which his inherent abilities are fully realised. A dismal view of man's spiritual fate posited an after-life in the flames of torment. Indeed the protestant ethic—the desperate struggle of the Calvinist to redeem himself through unrelenting work—was taken by Weber and Tawney to be a mainspring of capitalist endeavour[42]: an ideology in itself. If that description must now be treated as an exaggeration, a belief in man's essential nastiness remains nonetheless a crucial starting point for many in the overall formation of ideologies, just as for others it was the belief that essentially all is for the best. Where rational calculation has largely replaced obeisance, the same dichotomy continues. Halévy's well-known contrast between Adam Smith's belief in the beneficence of pursuing of individual self-interest (the "invisible hand" of God still remaining the ultimate guide) and Bentham's increasing fear of the abuse of power and the need to find ways of guarding the guards, represents an important tension with many echoes in the period of industrialisation.[43]

From such elements, the eighteenth-century ruling class generated grand theories of their society and state that were highly self-confident, containing much for their own freedom of action, little of the fear of God. These were couched either in idealist or utilitarian terms. The idealist tradition of Locke was carried forward by, for instance, Blackstone, for whom the very constitution was merely a part of the Rights of Persons. The state arose from a social contract between the "original founders" and existed solely for the protection of each individual's life, liberty and property. And of these three the greatest was property, since nothing "so generally strikes the imagination, and engages the affections of mankind."[44] Limited recognition of property is held to have existed from the earliest ages "by the law of nature and reason" and to have broadened its character out of the need to increase sustinence for a growing population. Property in land is a natural adjunct of occupation for production; property in its produce a recognition of the labour needed to secure

---

[42] M. Weber *The Protestant Ethic and The Spirit of Capitalism* (1900, trans. 1930); R. H. Tawney, *Religion and the Rise of Capitalism* (1926).

[43] E. Halévy, *The Growth of Philosophic Radicalism* (1901–1904, trans. 1928).

[44] *Commentaries*, II Chap. 1.

it.[45] Here begins the association of labour with property, and its economic counterpart, value, that will eventually found the whole Marxian critique of capitalist exploitation.

In the end there is much of the utilitarian about these calculations of what "natural justice" demanded or the social contract implied. A tradition of thought which saw society solely in terms of its historical experience had as its spokesmen, Hume and his followers (including Smith and Millar) in Scotland, and then Burke. As the Rousseau-inspired rhetoric of natural rights was turned against the French court and its aristocracy, the conservative implications of this opposite approach inspired Burke's greatest eloquence.[46] All that people could look to for protection against internal strife and tyranny was their own institutions and traditions; change which did not evolve gradually from that experience would throw a society back to its primitive, bounden condition. Britain had evolved by hard-won struggle a government in which those with greatest stake in the property of the nation were represented, and under that system a freedom of mercantile transaction was creating an ineluctable capacity for growth. Thus the conservative tradition, which was to have such a prominent place in the coming course of English history, received its classic formulation, at a time when the few had much to conserve and when the idea of conceding any substantial power to the multitude was scarcely on the horizon of political debate.

(b) An Age of Laissez-faire

With his nose for provocative generalisation, Dicey characterised the years between the first and second Reform Acts as an Age of Laissez-faire, preceded by an Age of Tory Paternalism and succeeded increasingly by an Age of Collectivism; against this last it was his whole object to warn.[47] The "public opinion" that dominated his middle period he saw as both utilitarian and individualistic, deriving from one man, Bentham, and proselytised by his disciples, the Benthamites. Historians have fought quite as hard over *Law and Public Opinion* as have lawyers and political scientists over *The Law of the Constitution*. The objectors fall into two types: those for whom the entire conception is unhelpful—"an encouragement to error"[48]; and those for whom the ultimate characterisation remains in essence accurate, though its association with Bentham and his "disciples" is treated as in various ways misleading.

Not surprisingly, critics of the first school have been led by administrative historians, whose focus of interest has been on that remark-

---

[45] Without property there would be "innumerable tumults"; and the same fear is used by Blackstone to justify the most contentious of all aspects of property, the right of inheritance by the family. Blackstone's rationalisations were eclectic enough in technique to excite some modern scholars to high scorn: see esp. D. Boorstin, *The Mysterious Science of the Law* (1941); D. Kennedy (1979) 28 Buffalo L.R. 205; cf. H.L.A. Hart (1956) Butt. S. African L.R. 169; J.M. Finnis (1967) 12 Nat. Law Forum 163; M. Lobban (1987) 30 Hist. J. 311; J.W. Cairns (1984) 4 Ox. JLeg. St. 318.

[46] *Reflections on the French Revolution* (1790).

[47] Dicey (1914).

[48] G. S. R. Kitson Clark, *An Expanding Society* (1967) 162.

able shift from the selfish, amateur, public-cum-private, conduct of affairs to the bureaucratic organisation of government. The criticism has not been merely that this change began in earnest in the wake of 1832 but that it was so extensive a phenomenon; hence it is seriously distortive to claim that the essential trend of opinion at just this time was against governmental interference. There had, after all, been a movement over a long period of time to remove legal and official constraints on freedom of individual action, which in a sense had already culminated half a century before in Adam Smith's *The Wealth of Nations*; in the interim Parliament had heard a great deal of the virtues of "Laissez-faire" and had not hesitated to act in consequence. It was part of Macdonagh's purpose, in developing his model of government growth,[49] to suggest that the middle third of the nineteenth century was not a period peculiarly committed to an unbending liberalism, but rather that, in facing its own social problems, it found by experience that new forms of disinterested intervention were needed. What is more this experience was diffuse and gradualist, a much broader phenomenon than the plannings of a few determined Benthamites intent on procuring effective government.[50] It is an approach with an appeal to all who see the nineteenth century in pragmatic, conservative terms.

Part of the limitation inherent in viewing the matter from an administrative perspective is that so much early administration was preoccupied with the regulation of social problems—end products of the whole economic system. That they arose as they did was the result of views about the functioning of the economy in terms of private enterprise and market forces—the essentials of laissez-faire policies which, in the great debates about the corn laws and other forms of protection against foreign competition, received triumphant endorsement in the 1840s after powerful opposition. Whatever its ultimate merits, criticism of this kind puts in focus what is worth debating. The issue is one of ultimate judgment, which can be attempted only by drawing together evidence which is touched upon in every chapter of this book. We ourselves are of the view that "Laissez-faire" encapsulated an ideological attitude that for large numbers of people, and particularly those with real political influence, was a root position.[51] But it is a matter to which in the end every student of the period will bring his own nuances.

At this level of criticism it is important to remain fair to Dicey, since he is easily parodied.[52] He himself disclaimed any suggestion that mid-century government actually withdrew to the cranky, mini-

---

[49] See above, pp. 54–55.

[50] A line pushed to extremes in belittling Bentham's personal influence by D. Roberts (1959) 2 Vict. St. 193. He and Macdonagh are convincingly answered on this theme by H. Parris (1960) 3 Hist. J. 17, and J. Hart (1965) 31 P. & P. 39; compare more generally, Roberts' *Victorian Origins of the Welfare State* (1960) and S. E. Finer's *Life and Times of Sir Edwin Chadwick* (1952). On the nature of Bentham's own proposals for regular revisions of his all-embracing codes of law, see L. J. Hume (1967) 10 Hist. J. 361.

[51] Following Hobsbawm (1968) Chap. 12; A. J. Taylor (1972); R. L. Crouch (1967) 35 Manchester School 199.

[52] Atiyah (1979), pp. 232–235 comes close to this in associating him with literary critics of the concept, notably Dickens in *Hard Times* (1854).

malist position of Herbert Spencer's *Social Statics*.[53] He saw other ideologies at work, to a limited degree achieving legislative and other change, but restricted enough in their flow to be pictured as "counter-currents" and "cross-currents." His history, like J. S. Mill's economic policy, was presumptive in character: a natural inclination prevailed against intervention by government, which at all stages, from first principles to the details of practice, could be reversed only by highly persuasive argument about the need for action.

The second line of criticism, which concerns the place of Bentham and his followers, is much more persuasive. At the outset, there is the considerable difficulty of how Bentham's ideas were diffused. He produced no *Koran* or *Kapital*, nor was he even a Blackstone or an Adam Smith. Occasional pieces of his massive oeuvre reached a reasonably wide public directly. But more became better known abroad through publication there, and much more, including his long final labours towards a Constitutional Code, was left unfinished.[54] Any major influence thus occurred through a complex process of absorption and interpretation by others, to which Finer has attached the "Benthamic" labels of *Irradiation* (acceptance by a circle of intimates), *Suscitation* (propagation by means of reviews, carefully orchestrated investigations by parliamentary committees, royal commissions and the like, and circulation of their findings to the influential), and *Permeation* (working within bureaucracies established to promote utilitarian policies).[55] The circle into which James Mill drew Bentham in the second decade of the nineteenth century included such notable figures among the political economists as Ricardo, Grote, McCullough, Senior and Tooke; the radical lawyers, Romilly, Brougham, Bickersteth, Parkes and Austin; as well as political figures such as Hume, Place and Roebuck. Through them there were links to the younger leaders of the Whigs, such as Althorp and Lord John Russell. Hume and Place demonstrated the suscitation of Select Committees in the 1820s[56] and the technique was taken up in the 1830s and 40s, notably by Edwin Chadwick, but also by others in the circle. Chadwick would also become a highly public permeator, in the central administration of first the poor law and then public health; there were many others, including Kay (Kay-Shuttleworth) and Southwood Smith who worked with him on health aspects of poor relief,[57] and Poulett Thompson who became President of the Board of Trade (under Melbourne) in 1834.

Men such as these knew much of the techniques for fostering ideas and pressing practical plans; in a changing world they would have an undeniable impact. But still the "philosophical radicals," as J. S. Mill christened them, remained an allegiance primarily intellectual and only incidentally political. They did not seriously consider forming a

---

[53] See Dicey (1914), pp. 17–18.
[54] Some of it appearing in his posthumous *Collected Works* (1843, ed. Bowring) IX; see now L. J. Hume (above, n. 11); F. Rosen, (above, n. 17).
[55] S. E. Finer, in G. Sutherland, *Studies in Nineteenth Century Government Growth* (1972) Chap. 1.
[56] Below, p. 298.
[57] Below, pp. 159–160.

separate party and their associations with the radical fringe of the Whigs was loose and shifting. They were a debating club without any common line upon the dictates of policy. Between them they pursued a number of striking ideas; but they were only one set of contributors to a larger whole.[58]

Then there are questions raised by the labels "utilitarian" and "individualist." Bentham was undoubtedly a source from which argument by utilitarian calculation was culled. We remember him today for the engaging persistence of his balancing of pleasures against pains by "felicific calculus," with the object of supplying codified laws for the "greatest happiness of the greatest number." But the idea of utilitarian prescription was as old as parenthood and for many it would be more comfortably learned from such popular sources as Archdeacon Paley's *Moral and Political Philosophy* (1785). Paley had a natural attraction for those who regarded the insistent calculation of necessary reform by reference to carefully garnered statistics as unduly subversive.

Most problematic of all, is the question whether Bentham is to be regarded as an "individualist." Certainly he was known as the author of a *Defence of Usury* (1787), in which, at a time when he was learning the precepts of political economy, he capped Adam Smith by arguing for repeal of the Usury Laws. But his wrestling with economic concepts, as a sequence of unpublished writings now shows us,[59] led him away from Smith's world where, in general, the enlightened effects of individual self-interest required markets to be left free and competitive. Bentham came to contemplate state intervention in order to maintain investment and employment, compulsory saving and state participation in life assurance and friendly societies, the storing of food supplies and regulation of the maximum price of staple foods. The circle of his old age must have known something of all this. He himself had by then become less concerned with the perfection of a market economy and more preoccupied with a structure of government in which a functioning democracy could curb the self-interested instincts of those with power.[60]

By this period, political economy had reconsidered Smith's benign view of a society growing naturally in response to an increasing division of labour. Malthus' warnings of the tendency of population increase to outstrip food production, with the inevitable result that the mass of people must remain condemned to a bare subsistence, seemed all too apparent in contemporary events.[61] His was an explanation of the high economic rent that the landed classes had enjoyed during the war period and a justification of their subsequent inter-

---

[58] W. A. Thomas in P. Hollis (ed.) *Pressure from Without* (1974) Chap. 3.

[59] W. Stark (ed.) *Jeremy Bentham's Economic Writings* (1952–54).

[60] See T. W. Hutchinson (1956) 66 Econ. J. 288, reviewing the *Writings* in the Stark edition (see previous note). J. B. Brebner's identification of Bentham as "the archetype of British collectivism" ((1948) 8 J.Ec.H. 59, 61) set the whole modern debate in motion.

[61] *Essay on the Principle of Population* (1798); see below p. 426; upon the assumption that each couple would produce twice as many children, Malthus pronounced that population grew geometrically while food supply could at best grow arithmetically.

ventions to protect the price of corn. His popularity with them was heightened by his support for conspicuous consumption among the few and his view that the poor law was an artificial interference which, by stimulating the birthrate and lowering the death rate, could only exacerbate the root problem.

Malthus' view of the Corn Laws was attacked by Ricardo in his systematic analysis of economic functioning.[62] Here was the root attack on agricultural rent as a depletion of the capital otherwise available for industrial investment. From it came a true realisation of the conflicting interests of land-owning and manufacturing classes. At the same time, for all his emphasis on labour as the measure of value, Ricardo affirmed that the labouring class must take its earnings from a free and fluctuating market unsupported by poor law allowances or legal limitations upon hours or conditions. This provided the one efficient way of dividing the "Wages Fund," that share of national income which was available to the needs of labour.[63]

In the hands of economists such as Senior and McCullough these arguments would be transmuted even more directly into prescriptions of policy. These they sometimes chose to express in terms of unremitting laissez-faire, as did the economic politicians of the "Manchester school," and the newspapers and populists who followed them.[64] On other occasions they were more circumspect, particularly as they grew older and less doctrinaire. They could feel that utilitarian calculations of the behaviour of economic man did not always dictate that government should "Be quiet!", that sometimes the effective way of tackling new social problems was well-directed, adequately supervised intervention.[65] Even then their plans were drawn so as to leave as much scope as practicable for the free market. The case for the protection of factory children against intolerable hours was made out; but for Chadwick and his associates on the Factories Commission any solution must interfere as little as possible with the freedom of adult operatives to work as long as they had agreed.[66] The presumption remained.

One reason why the utilitarians cannot be regarded as more than a contributory, and sometimes muted, force in building the non-interventionist ideology is that to claim more for them ignores the massive influence of the spiritual, moralistic movement that is labelled Evangelicalism. The fat and easy comfort of an assured place in God's

[62] *Principles of Political Economy and Taxation* (1817).
[63] It would remain a standard tool of analysis until disproved by J. S. Mill, *Principles of Political Economy* (1848), pp. 337–354.
[64] On these, see W. D. Grampp, *The Manchester School of Economics* (1960); H. Scott Gordon (1955) 63 J. Polit.Econ. 461; Harriet Martineau's *Illustrations of Political Economy* in the 1830s gave her "undisputed pre-eminence" as vulgariser of classical economic theory: Taylor (1972), p. 27.
[65] L. C. B. Robbins, *The Theory of Economic Policy in English Political Economy* (1952) puts high the revisionist case that the classical economists tempered their views on non-intervention; cf. S. G. Checkland (1953) 20 Economica (N.S.). 61. See further J. Viner (1927) 35 J. Pol. Ec. 198; (1949) 39 Am. Ec. R. 360; (1960) 3 J.L. & Ec. 45. And for the varying attitudes revealed among politicians by their speeches, W. O. Aydelotte (1968) 11 Vict. St. 225; G. Watson, *The English Ideology* (1973).
[66] See below, pp. 303–304.

estate, which characterised so much of the established church's perception in the eighteenth century, had been disturbed by a new,
anxious desire for salvation from original sin.[67] Rooted partly in the
Calvinist traditions of the Old Dissenters, it had been heightened by
the sober, committed orderliness of the Methodist sects which
sprang from Wesley's beginning, and it found its way into the
Church of England through the campaigning of the Clapham Sect
and a wider missionary zeal. Here in various guises was a vital religion which demanded an act of profound submission and re-orien-
tation in order to be saved: the subject must undergo within himself
a conversion to the Lord and must thereafter work constantly and
unselfishly for the good of others rather than himself. It was a profound source of inspiration for the whole spirit of self-help, that a
moral force within was the only guide to righteousness.[68] The eagerness to mould others sometimes, as in the new regimes imposed
upon prisons, took on the appearance of force-feeding[69]; but even
there, as more benignly in the churches' arrangements for popular
education,[70] there was a ready recognition that an individual could
in the end only find himself.[71]

As a utilitarian calculator, a man such as Chadwick could be drawn
by experience of the intractable problems facing the state to an ever-
louder call for intervention and regulation. An evangelical of the
mould of Ashley, Lord Shaftesbury, could equally ally his inspiration
with the older beliefs of his aristocratic background: from the emergent state he was not afraid to demand a paternalistic responsibility.
But as the fate of so much that they attempted will show, such people
met a great wall of hostility—from grand denunciations of principle
to penny-pinching refusals to provide financial support[72]—which in
the end supports the view that they were only a counter-current. It is
because the streams of economic rationality and religious feeling
both ran so strongly in the opposite direction, that in Dicey's broad
sense laissez-faire seems after all to be the tide of the day even if he
gave a very imperfect account of its motive force. In Hobsbawm's
words, "by the middle of the nineteenth century government policy
in Britain came as near *Laissez-faire* as has ever been practicable in a
modern state."[73]

---

[67] See I. Bradley, *The Call to Seriousness* (1976).

[68] 1859, the year when Darwin's *Origin of Species* and *Essays and Reviews* planted profound seeds of doubt, was also hailed as a year of Revival, spreading onwards from
New York. A Bishop of Durham wrote; "hundreds of people of that time were
awakened, awed, more conscious of eternal realities. And a goodly number of these
shewed in all their after life that they were indeed new creatures born again to a living hope and to a steadforth walk. A great social uplifting, wholesome and permanent, followed the Revival. In particular, a vigorous movement for temperance and
thrift arose spontaneously among the work-people . . . " H. C. G. Moule, *Memories
of a Vicarage* (1913) p. 50.

[69] See below p. 578ff.

[70] Below, p. 438ff.

[71] The evangelical spirit was strongly alive in popularisers of economic *laissez-faire*,
such as Harriet Martineau and Samuel Smiles.

[72] On this aspect, see esp. Taylor (1972), pp. 58–62.

[73] *Industry and Empire* (1968), p. 197.

(c) Ideology and the Judges

The small band of men who occupied the senior judicial positions held an unusual power of decision: they had regularly to apply general rules to particular circumstances that were ambiguous enough to provide scope for real argument. They did so under public scrutiny: their decisions were often open to appeal; and their judgments, at least if they were reported, acquired authority as precedents. Since they were led inevitably behind the terms of explicit rules of statute or case-law to larger points of reference, these underlying assumptions have a particular importance, both in the history of the law and as a *catalogue raisonée* of accepted attitudes among those who governed.

It is possible to think in terms of an ideology of the judges for two rather different reasons. First, the "law-fixing" function of judicial decisions gives its own coherence to the cumulation of opinion and attitude. With their severe limitation of numbers, the superior judges adopted that special respect for earlier precedent encompassed in the doctrine of *stare decisis*, under which even single decisions of a higher court or the court itself would in essence be regarded as binding for future cases "on all fours." This eminently conservative principle did a great deal to cement common judicial attitudes which accordingly grew step-wise rather than by ellipse.

To some extent paths might still diverge. The structural divisions before 1876 allowed equity to pursue a paternal protectiveness somewhat at variance with the severer individualism of the common law.[74] To a degree also the judges differed in their political leanings and in more fundamental attitudes. A few stood out for the strength and openness of their personal beliefs: Brougham, the advocate of radical reform, St Leonards, the heir to Eldon's fear-laden conservatism, Bramwell, the unbending liberal for whom property and contract defined the world. But still the structure as a whole, with its increasingly collegiate character, made for a uniformity much more persistent than the idiosyncrasies and differences. The truly oracular figures were men like Parke and Blackburn who brought to the pronouncement of law a weighty abstraction that commanded a deep respect and appeared to remove the rationalisation of judicial decisions from any sphere of simple political preference.

This factor adds complexity to the process of plotting judicial ideology. Yet it fulfilled a significant function. The English tradition left the judge free to discourse in judgment as he thought fit; yet there was a strong preference, which does not vary much over time, for reasoning which finds pre-existent law and fits the particular facts within it.[75] This allowed the judicial function, under the conditions

---

[74] See below, p. 202ff.

[75] A vogue in American scholarship has aligned styles of judgment with different historical periods, a "grand style" of plain speaking about policy being associated (so it is claimed) with the proto-industrial period before the Civil War, a "formal style" of reference to precedent and statute (though it is scarcely the formalism of eighteenth century common law or of European judicial practice) taking over as capitalist enterprise becomes dominant: see, for a recent version M. Horwitz, *The Transformation of American Law* (1977) Chap. 8. The same approach, adopting a different periodisation, is applied to judgments of the House of Lords by R. B. Stevens (1978). We,

of the post-1832 constitution, to be represented in terms of a simple positivism: law, the sovereign's command, was interpreted by grammatical rules and dictionaries if it took statutory form and "declared" if it was part of the common law.[76] When the judges did venture beyond such confines it was often to find what was "reasonable," what made "common sense"—crypto-utilitarian judgments, one might say, impregnated with a deep respect for established practice. As the nineteenth century progressed, overt pronouncements of "public policy" would be reserved very largely for major political confrontations, notably those involving organised labour.[77] Mystificatory concepts—vires, consideration, duties of care— would grow in importance and the old attachment to correctness of form and procedure would assume novel, "reformed" guises.

The judges made a fundamental contribution to the gradual accretion of libertarian beliefs and practices. In part this was a contribution to the constitutional struggles which curbed the Crown's power to deprive of personal liberty and to invade the domestic hearth. Even more fundamentally, it involved elevation of private property into an instrument capable of manifold uses and divisions at the option of the owner and an equal readiness to allow contract and associated institutions (including important equitable concepts such as the trust) to be employed in an ever-widening variety of applications as economic circumstance demanded. In the period after 1832, these developments were carried a very considerable distance with the evolution of modern doctrine of contract which gave equal emphasis to freedom in contracting and to the sanctity of bargains once struck, but only so far as the parties were concerned.[78] Yet it is part of the essential conservatism of the judges' contribution that this was only a particular stage in a course which had long since been set.

It has been claimed that the post-Revolution judiciary in the United States became a major instrument in the middle-class capitalist challenge to the interests of an established governing class: to this end the judges reoriented common law principles by lifting legal inhibitions upon the full economic potential of land and other assets.[79] As far as concerns English judges such a movement is more easily discernible two centuries before, during the rise of the landed aristocracy and gentry, with its demand for complex ways of holding and manipulating property. Chancery then emerged as the court par-

---

however, prefer the view, well-demonstrated by R. B. Ferguson, that the dominant style of English judgments cannot be said to vary significantly over time: (1980) 7 Brit. J. Law & Soc. 141. There has been one established tradition which allows for a fair measure of individual idiosyncrasy. Compare the much more plausible thesis of Atiyah (1979) that there was a strong pressure on judges in the mid-nineteenth century to enunciate clear, general rules even at the expense of harsh applications to fringe cases: see, esp. pp. 388–397.

[76] John Austin, in The Province of Jurisprudence Determined (1832) provided a careful and elaborate statement of this position. As Cocks (1983) Chap. 1 shows, the practising profession felt some initial attraction towards Austin's ideas; but his poor presentation and the abstraction of the ideas meant that they found no regular place in legal education. When Dicey gave them more practical expression in The Law of the Constitution (1885), they were a great success.

[77] See below, p. 312ff.

[78] Below, p. 200ff.

[79] M. Horwitz, The Transformation of American Law, 1780–1860 (1977)

ticularly sympathetic to the needs of this growing elite and provided machinery which would foster the accumulation and retention of land and its ability to put capital to those uses which prepared the country for its take-off into industrialisation. From the eighteenth century the demand for judicial creativity lessened. Parliament provided the major machine for further adjustments of rights: while its control was in the hands of a small and relatively homogenous group, the private bill procedure catered adequately for many of their initiatives. After 1832, general legislation rapidly became the major instrument of legal change. By then the judges as a group had for long been used to a close association with the landed interest, providing them with an important service as barristers and expecting to move into their number, insofar as they were not in any case from a landed background. It was not for them to undertake, explicitly or by gradual slide, any substantial undermining of all that private property had come to mean to the owners of estates: the entitlement for instance to most generous compensation where the development of a transport artery compelled acquisition, or the right to object to damage to the environment from the effluvia of towns.[80]

For the most part, the judges stood apart even from the pressure groups formed to procure reforming legislation. Lawyers, particularly barristers, might play prominent roles in the Society for the Amendment of the Law and then the National Association for the Promotion of Social Sciences, in both of which Brougham was much involved. But once they attained the bench, their desire to stand apart worked with the considerable calls upon their time to keep them at a distance. Only in matters of direct relevance to the practice of the courts and the functioning of the legal system were they regularly involved in the political process. There the strong determination to retain and strengthen the system in which they had been bred took hold as a powerful ideology in its own right. Nonetheless, in this relatively passive sense, most Victorian judges had an undoubted sympathy with the broad spirit of laissez-faire—with a view of the world in which the state and its law kept the civil peace, secured property for its owners and upheld bargains.

(d) Stirrings of Socialism

An ideology of labour, a belief that the working class had a mutual interest at odds with those of landowners and capitalists, a determination to lift the yoke of wage slavery, had its first significant manifestations in the 1790s and from that point spread alongside the industrialisation which was its necessary condition.[81] Measuring this rise in consciousness of class has been a preoccupation of critical historians since the Webbs' generation. In our own the case for its cohesiveness and effectiveness has been fervently made by E. P. Thompson.[82] Criticism of his picture as overdrawn was only to be

---

[80] See below, pp. 153, 157.
[81] For general surveys, Beer (1919); Cole (1953–1960).
[82] *The Making of the English Working Class* (1963, revised 1968).

expected, though it has received some interesting support from intensive local studies.[83] It is in the end an extremely difficult field of investigation, since the written record is a very patchy indicator of a culture that lacked much organisation for its educational, political and social activities.

Enough certainly was done for the precepts of political and economic argument to be re-worked in ways that challenged the orthodoxies of the powerful and propertied. There was a usefulness in utilitarian calculation, particularly in the democratic conclusions that Bentham and some of his followers drew from it. Its basic method encouraged detailed factual investigation of the condition of society for purposes of statistical and other comparison. The calculations of Dr. Charles Hall and Patrick Colquhoun began to show the true shape of the emerging capitalist society and the proportions of national income which each drew.[84] But it was the idealistic case for man's natural rights, tested by the French revolution and set in British context by Tom Paine's *Rights of Man* which was the more telling. His case against the unscrupulous appropriation by the king and the great estate-owners through their control of the political system was read and re-read in the constitutional clubs of the 1790s and for generations thereafter. In developing an attack on the Ricardian assumption of the capitalist's right to take the profit of the production that he has organised,[85] Thomas Hodgskin was drawn into an attack on legislation and the utilitarian theory which denied that rights existed apart from and anterior to positive law.[86] His whole object was to show that the only natural right of property was in the maker of the thing and that any positive law which gave ownership to another was artificial, distortive, and, above all, oppressive.

In Paine's own period the first ideas were beginning to be formulated of a future ideal state. He himself advocated the use of taxation as a weapon of redistribution to those in social jeopardy,[87] an idea that would have to wait a century for implementation. Other more extreme precepts were canvassed. There might be no apparatus of the state: in Godwin's vision, the height at once of atomism and optimism, the abandonment of protection for private property would leave each with a frugal sufficiency, making him independent of others.[88] Thomas Spence advocated the revival of local communities by the parishes re-annexing their lands for letting out to tenants; their rents would be a sufficient tax to provide the needs of government.[89] What was absent was the idea of national control of land as the ultimate resource of society.

---

[83] *e.g.* J. Foster, *Class Struggles and the Industrial Revolution* (1974); R. A. Sykes (1980) 23 Hist. J. 167; *cf.* D. S. Gadian (1978) 21 Hist. J. 161.

[84] C. Hall, *Effects of Civilisation* (1805); P. Colquhoun, *Treatise of the Wealth, Power and Resources of the British Empire* (1814).

[85] For this, see his *Labour defended against the Claims of Capital* (1825).

[86] *The Natural and Artificial Rights of Property Contrasted* (1832), a riposte to Brougham's espousal of utilitarian law reform in the Commons.

[87] In *The Rights of Man*, Part II and *Agrarian Justice* (1795).

[88] *Political Justice* (1793).

[89] See esp., *Constitution of the Spencean Commonwealth* (1798); *The Restorer of Society to its Natural State* (1800). For the resurgence of the "single-tax" idea, see below, pp. 169–170.

As far as concerned the means of implementation, advocacy of change by violent overthrow was of necessity muted by the government's readiness to prosecute treason and sedition. And until 1832, the campaign for Parliamentary reform by legislation held a real prospect of success on a substantial scale. In any case there was a third possibility: that example would lead to emulation without the need for arms or statutes. The ideas of Robert Owen, which made such a distinctive contribution to socialist ideology in Britain, underscored this prospect.[90] Owen's answer to the oppression of competitive capitalism was a communism born of cooperation. He did not look to the state but to far-seeing paternal individuals (such as himself) who would establish productive factory-villages with a view to providing the workers with a decent environment for living as well as working and a share in the profits of their production. Their evident superiority would be enough.

Owenite communities for cooperative production were set up but in England they failed to establish any permanent foothold. It was to be in the simpler activity of cooperative distribution, and in mutual insurance and financial services, that a very substantial movement would grow. Its practical achievements would foster a working-class ideal that retained much of Owen's essence: an optimistic belief that mutual action would of itself bring the working people a greater share in the national prosperity. It was to be a significant factor not only in developing the trade union movement but in convincing those above that below them were emerging "industrious classes" with whom it was on balance profitable to treat over political and legal rights.

Much less peaceable were many of the voices associated with the Chartist movement. Amid all the rhodomontade and carefully qualified incitements to physical force, two ultimate plans could be discerned. One, essentially radical and individualist, sought to foster the spread of independent peasant farming through the establishment of small freeholds; it thus ran in tandem with the freehold movements of the Manchester school, though without the same overt intention of multiplying votes in the process. This was associated mainly with Feargus O'Connor, who regrettably proved to lack the managerial skills to make his Chartist Land Company a viable institution.[91] The vision of returning to a simple rural existence was, however, to have an unending appeal to the factory-tied labourers of the towns.[92]

The other, explicitly socialist, was chiefly the brain-child of Bronterre O'Brien. It was a plan for the progressive acquisition by central government of the land—in other words, land nationalisation. In order to be acceptable it would take place upon death, the heir being paid some compensation for his deprivation. The land would then be let out at competitive tender to tenants; but the farming would have to conform to a plan which would assess national needs for foodstuffs and other natural produce. O'Brienite groups would survive the final end of Chartism itself. His ideas would re-emerge as one

---

[90] *Observations on the Effect of the Manufacturing System* (1815); *A New View of Society* (1816); *Report to the County of Lanark* (1820).

[91] J. MacAskill in A. Briggs (ed.) *Chartist Studies* (1959) Chap. 10; A. Hadfield, *The Chartist Land Company* (1970).

[92] See below, p. 169ff.

strain in the land reform movement that became increasingly insistent after 1867.[93]

It took the land as a case apart—the resource of uniquely limited capacity. O'Brienite ideas did not extend to the socialisation of all the means of production and distribution with which Marx was to become preoccupied in the 1860s. There was a movement for nationalisation of the railways, but it was chiefly a middle-class vehicle by which commercial users of rail transport sought to attack the freight rates of the companies. While this was carried, in Gladstone's Act of 1844 (even after a battering at the hands of the railway interest), as far as to give an option of state purchase after 21 years, it was on such generous terms as to preclude the prospect ever being taken up. Freights came to be regulated instead and calls for nationalisation took an ancillary place in periodic confrontations on the subject. So the case would remain until the organisation of railwaymen gained strength enough to shift the whole balance.[94] But that would not be until the new century.

PART 2: PASSING GREATNESS 1875–1950

I. SOCIETY AND LAW

Inevitably the government of the country became more complex, indeed more perplexing, as democracy made strategic advances. At the same time the population continued its upward statistical course[95]; while sheer fertility was beginning to fade, the chances of staying alive at last began noticeably to improve, particularly for young children.[96] A growing proportion of the whole population was to be found in the confines of the cities and towns.[97] The 37 "great towns" of 1871 had become 75 by 1901 and 113 by 1931.

As a refraction of the constitutional advances, social perceptions—particularly those of class—were beginning to shift from their mid-century forms. The old antagonisms between landed governors and trading middle classes, so intense in the 1830s and 40s, were coming to mean less. In the wake of spreading prosperity, the two groups were becoming blurred—by an intermingling of wealth and occupation, an intermarrying, a sharing of education and so of speech and culture. In particular the immense privilege of land-owning was to be tempered through economic change and political necessity so as

---

[93] See Barry (1965) Chap. 1.

[94] *Ibid*, Chap. 3.

[95] The population of England and Wales would jump from 22.8 million to 26 million in the decade, 1871–81 (an increase of 14 per cent.). Thereafter it would reach 32.6 million in 1901, 37.9 million in 1921 and 41.7 million in 1941: see generally D. C. Marsh, *The Changing Social Structure of England and Wales 1871–1961* (rev. ed. 1965).

[96] This became pronounced only in the Edwardian years. Overall the population would remain young, with an average age in the twenties. The even distribution of the sexes would be disturbed by the death tolls of world war, but not to the extent commonly supposed. For family limitation through a high age of marriage, and the growth of contraception, see below, p. 357ff.

[97] *i.e.* towns of 50,000 population or more: see Marsh (above, n. 95), pp. 66–76.

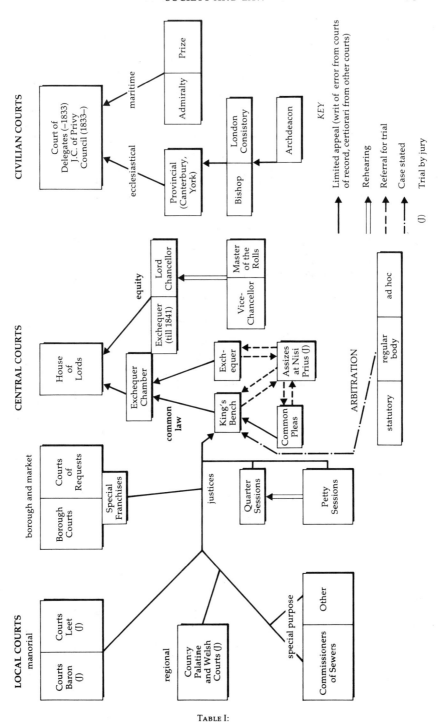

KEY

Limited appeal (writ of error from courts
of record, certiorari from other courts)

Rehearing

Referral for trial

Case stated

(J)   Trial by jury

TABLE I:

MAIN COURTS AND OTHER BODIES DEALING WITH NON-CRIMINAL DISPUTES

before the reforms of 1851–75

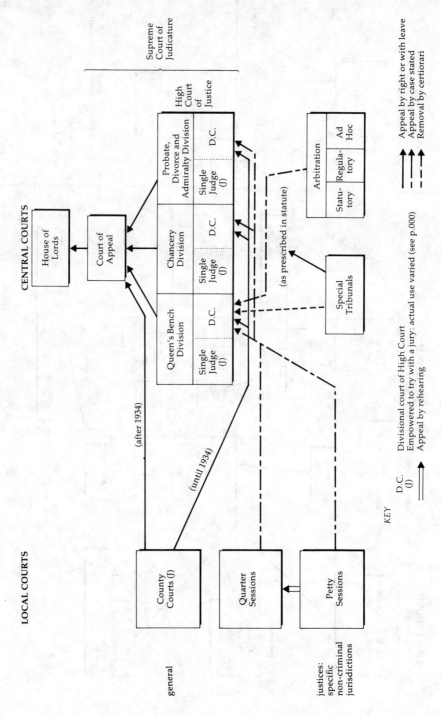

TABLE II:

COURTS AND TRIBUNALS DEALING WITH NON-CRIMINAL DISPUTES AFTER 1880

TABLE III:

MAIN CRIMINAL COURTS IN THE 19TH CENTURY*

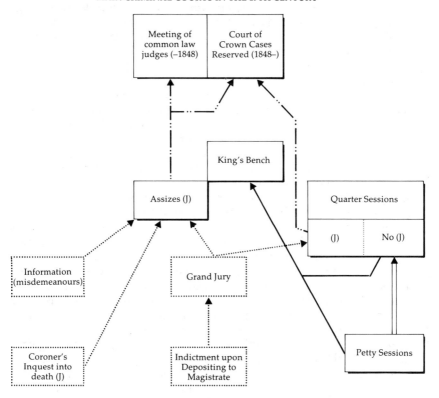

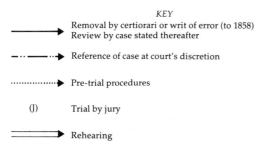

KEY

Removal by certiorari or writ of error (to 1858)
Review by case stated thereafter

Reference of case at court's discretion

Pre-trial procedures

(J) Trial by jury

Rehearing

* Not included: the rare cases of impeachment by Parliament, trial of peers by House of Lords and trial at bar of King's Bench, quasi-criminal jurisdiction of ecclesiastical courts over moral and minor wrongs, presentment by the ancient sheriff's tourn, courts leet and forest courts.

to effect, in at least some measure, a re-distribution of national wealth.[98] After the Edwardian period, many of the great estates would be split up, passing in farm-sized lots to previous tenants or to newcomers. The patronising snobbery of the high Victorian age would be a long time dying, for the habit of class distinction had been engrained deep. Despite it a coalescence was forming which made property owners of all kinds more often think of themselves as united than divided.

With the expansion of the Parliamentary franchise, the mob was becoming part of the people. The wage-earning working class was at last beginning to receive from the increases in productive capacity some improvement in living standards.[99] But most of them remained bound to a life of frugal subsistence or worse. In a whole variety of matters—religion, political allegiance, regional affiliation, occupation, earnings—there remained as many social distinctions among the working class as among those who thought themselves middle- or upper-class. Yet the root stratification was coming to be that between the class with property and that without.

The economic underpinnings and political consequences of this realignment would bring legal reorientations in many forms, which permeate the latter parts of each of the succeeding chapters. Laws which explicitly discriminated by class or rank had rarely proved necessary in the past; where they had emerged they marked a point of severe social tension—as with the Master and Servant Acts—and they could not survive in a post-1867 world.[1] "Class law" could also arise by implication: in rules like the "fellow servant" defence to accident claims against employers which effectively operated against the working class alone.[2] Laws which specifically disadvantaged the least well-off seemed to belie the very equality inherent in a "rule of law"[3]; and if that notion could not be maintained, respect for the whole edifice of proprietary, contractual and associated rights and duties built up by common law and statute might be in jeopardy.

More than ever before, law came to be used as an instrument of positive discrimination. As the organisation uniquely powerful in a society of proliferating groups, the state would use legislation and bureaucracy to benefit those—largely from the working class—who were unable to support or help themselves against the vicissitudes of old age, sickness, unemployment and bad housing. The costs would have to be met out of one or other form of taxation, unless it could be provided in advance from the contributions of those who were to benefit. Again, it was accepted, though not without protest, that taxation might be graduated to fall more heavily on those with greater wealth. Inevitably the feeling of common cause among the upper and middle classes grew in the face of such determination to place collective responsibility upon individual property.

---

[98] See below, p. 169ff.
[99] See below, p. 323ff.
[1] See below, p. 320.
[2] See below, p. 520ff.
[3] Only the most extreme defenders of property would object to the Housing of the Working Classes Acts: see below, p. 182ff.

II. Economy and Law

The crucial counterpart of the changes in social relationships was the decline of the country's economic predominance. Britain would not again experience quite the bullishness of the early 1870s. In agriculture, the vast profitability of corn production would be hit by competition, mainly from the North American prairies; domestic meat production would have to face foreign imports made possible by ship refrigeration. The "great depression" of the later 70s and 80s, patchy though it was, would produce a new economic stability only in the Edwardian years; and in the process the aura surrounding land and its great owners would dim.[4]

In industrial production and export trading, the supremacy of mid-century would increasingly be challenged, by a Germany unified under Prussian leadership and, in its vast home market particularly, by the United States. Those countries, and lesser powers like France, began to move from a freeing of the barriers around their own markets back towards higher protection. This raised for the British the future of Cobdenite free trade. A "fair trade" lobby began to demand retaliatory discrimination in British markets, or even a systematic policy of preference between the still expanding units of the British Empire. These challenges only held attention during the worst moments of trade depression; they gained no real momentum until taken up by Joseph Chamberlain in 1903 under the banner of "tariff reform."[5] Thereafter the idea would have an allure for Conservative leaders, seeking an answer to unemployment and other social problems in some form of securer economic prosperity rather than state relief. The electorate, however, adhered to old faiths: protection still meant dear food. Balfour in 1910 and Bonar Law in 1922 saw the danger in time, Baldwin fell victim in 1923. Only the catharsis of the international economic collapse in 1929–32 would make protection seem inevitable. It was instituted under Neville Chamberlain's guidance in 1932, so as to include an Imperial Preference which meant little else than that British farmers would have to share their home market with Dominion producers.[6] A state which in living memory had intervened in the economy only in war-time (and would soon do so again on a more complete scale), had assumed a decisive role as a peacetime planner. Many producers acquired a new dependence upon regulation, and thus upon the goodwill of politicians and bureaucrats.

Alongside the spread of international competition came a growth in the scale of domestic industry. The mid-Victorian formula of the joint stock company with limited liability, formed as of right by a simple process of registration, proved to be readily suited to industrial concerns as they outgrew the ownership and management of a single family or partnership.[7] The corporation became the typical form of business organisation, not merely as a means of raising stock

---

[4] See S.B. Saul, *The Myth of the Great Depression* (1969).
[5] See B.H. Brown, *The Tariff Reform Movement in Great Britain, 1881–1895* (1943).
[6] The major dominions already had protectionist inhibitions on British imports where their domestic producers needed them.
[7] See below, p. 266ff.

market finance and limiting the liabilities of share-owners, but as a basis for employing career managers and of defining chains of command and responsibilities. The law imposed no constraints on the financial structure that might be chosen. Nor, save for an experiment with workmen's compensation for accidents, did it oblige employers to look to the welfare of their labour force; instead the State set up its own schemes, and, in the case of national insurance against sickness and unemployment, required both employer and employee to contribute to the cost.[8]

The extreme openness of the law of incorporation allowed endless adaptation within a frame of legal efficacy. The same flexibility would permit the absorption of smaller businesses into larger corporate units, a process which became significant in the 1920s under the catch-word, rationalisation. It would lead after 1926 to larger groupings in successful, newer industries, such as cars (Austin, Morris), tobacco (Imperial Tobacco), rubber (Dunlop) and food (Unilever, Cadbury-Fry) and to national units that were related to international cartels, for instance in nickel (International Nickel) and chemicals (Imperial Chemical Industries). In the staple industries, "rationalisation" in the wake of the 1929 crisis, meant a call for statutory backing. Marketing boards were established for coal, shipbuilding and agriculture in 1931. It was a move above all in the interests of the owners and underpinned a "monopolistic competition" in their joint interests.[9] In the threatening economic conditions it became acceptable for the state to use its law-creating powers in support, just as ten years previously it had assisted rationalisations of the transport and power industries—railways, electricity, gas—which would deflect the brief post-war interest in nationalisation.

The legal framework of capitalist enterprise contained within it a certain freedom even to operate beyond the discipline of the legal system—to work by way of gentlemen's agreement, to establish internal systems of control and to use private arbitration, on occasion in order to apply rules contrary to the general law. On the whole this proved politically acceptable in a country which still applied the market discipline of free trade and which accordingly saw most attempts at cartelisation and other forms of mutual protection as a defensive response mainly to foreign competition. It did not therefore require regulation in its turn.[10]

To commerce and finance such freedom carried implications for the rights of labour to organise collectively and to use the power of strike and boycott which were a concomitant of such association. In the aftermath of 1867, when the main unions were still confined to the skilled and semi-skilled trades, a new moderation entered labour relations. Older hostility against them, given force by repressive, abnegating law, was replaced by organizational rules for unions (subject—at the unions' behest—to a substantial measure of freedom from supervision and enforcement by the courts) and a considerable

[8] See below, pp. 449ff, 454ff.
[9] For the rationalisation movement, see L. Hannah, *The Rise of the Corporate Economy*, (1976) Chap. 3, and below, pp. 272–273.
[10] See below, p. 268ff.

freedom to withdraw labour and to support this with picketing activities.[11]

When, twenty years later, mass unionism embracing the unskilled began to take shape, there was a frightened reaction against this generosity, in which the judges played a prominent part. But its direct result would be a new set of concessions to a politically organised labour movement, which the Liberal government of 1906 felt obliged to make. It would become plain in the years immediately preceding the outbreak of European war that the unions were acquiring a new scale of industrial power and might constitute a permanent threat to a capitalist economy. The prospect that the political wing of this movement might become a truly independent Labour Party did at least rouse hope of an accommodation within the forms of Parliamentary government, rather than through some extreme form of industrial democracy.

The pre-war talk of combined union action—the triple alliance of railway, dock and coal workers to effect, if necessary, a general paralysis of the economy—seemed to acquire new impetus in the charged atmosphere of the war's end. It led the coalition government to convert war-time powers for repressing opposition, disaffection and interference with pressing needs into a peace-time equivalent.[12] The Emergency Powers Act 1920 allowed the government to proclaim a state of emergency and issue orders for preserving safety and securing supplies.[13] Designed primarily to deal with major industrial conflict, the Act would in the main come to demonstrate the histrionic and minatory potential of ultimate legal powers. It was, however, to be given full rein in the General Strike of 1926 when it was used not only (as on other occasions) to put the armed forces to running essential services but also to commandeer land and vehicles, to issue special licences to drive, to suppress meetings and to create special offences of spreading dissension.

In the failure of the General Strike, legal process and the idea of legality played an interesting, but essentially secondary, role.[14] The major unions were not able to sustain their position and unity in 1926 because of weaknesses in the British industrial structure which had been manifest since the sudden collapse of the post-war boom in 1920. If Britain weathered that first crisis without the financial chaos that overwhelmed Germany, she was left with endemic unemployment that would prove hard to lift. And when the great collapse of 1929 came it would hit the country with particular virulence.[15] The twenties provided an anxious experience which turned many towards a far greater involvement of the state in planning and adjust-

---

[11] See below, p. 314ff.
[12] The regulations under the Defence of the Realm Act 1914, wide-ranging in their curbs upon civil liberties, had been used particularly to put down strikes and other labour trouble on Clydeside and elsewhere. See G.R. Rubin, *War, Law and Labour* (1987).
[13] After one month, the state of emergency required Parliamentary approval. *Inter alia*, special courts of summary jurisdiction would be set up; for the administrative structure that operated the Act under Conservative and Labour governments, see R. H. Desmarais (1971) 6 J. Contemp. Hist. 112; (1973) 8 *ibid.* 165.
[14] See below, pp. 349–350.
[15] See below, p. 459ff.

ment of the economy than had previously been contemplated save by those on the extremes of political debate. Law would be used not merely in support of private property and market transactions; it would make the state an owner and exploiter of crucial resources, a regulator of major industries and financial institutions and guardian of the essential pre-conditions of a decent life.

III. POLITICS AND LAW

(a) Parliamentary Democracy

The semi-democracy of 1867 was sustained by no compelling logic. In 1884 Gladstone saw to an extension of the householder franchise to the rural population, as well as urban.[16] In this he was urged by his own instinct for "the people," by the Chamberlainites and by the Irish MPs (elected, since the secret ballot of 1872, without direct pressure from landlords' agents). The third Reform Act extended the franchise from about one in three adult males to two in three. The qualifications, however, became more complex than ever before, turning in particular on a residence requirement of one year for householders and others.[17]

Gladstone made the case for treating householdership as a rough correlative of the maturity and responsibility required in an elector. The continued exclusion of women who were householders from the franchise, even when as ratepayers they would enjoy a number of local franchises, was not so easy to sustain.[18] That it continued was one measure of the emotional depth to the male notion of women as denizens of a different sphere, bearers of children, helpmeets, graceful ornaments who would be blemished by sharing in men's tasks and aspirations.[19] A small band of suffragists would keep up the case for the female parliamentary franchise. Exasperation would eventually allow the Pankhursts and their "suffragette" followers to mount their highly agitating campaign of civil disobedience.[20] Politicians felt obliged to resist such direct challenges to the authority of government, as much as they had ignored the more seemly protestations of the suffragists. But they were ready enough to use the

---

[16] Representation of the People Act 1884. Lodgers whose lettings were for £10 annual value or more were included. Owners of businesses and graduates continued to have more than one vote. At the same period the electoral process became more respectable: Corrupt and Illegal Practices Act 1883. See generally, C. O'Leary, *The Elimination of Corrupt Practices in British Elections 1868–1911* (1962); L.M. Helmore, *Corrupt and Illegal Practices* (1967).

[17] Registration Act 1885. The lodger provision proved so difficult that it was only returned in marginal constituencies: N. Blewett (1965) 32 P. & P. 27; and *The Peers, the Parties and the People* (1972) Pt. I.

[18] See above, pp. 16–17.

[19] See B. Harrison, *Separate Spheres* (1978); leading figures across the political spectrum held fervently to this position (Barker (1978), pp. 111–122); for the judges, see A. Sachs in P. Carlen (ed.), *The Sociology of Law* (1976) p. 104.

[20] In a considerable literature, see (for grand style) G. Dangerfield, *The Strange Death of Liberal England* (1936), pp. 121–177, 293–311; and R. Fulford, *Votes for Women* (1957); C. Rover *Women's Suffrage and Party Politics in Britain, 1866–1914* (1967); A. Rosen, *Rise Up, Women!* (1974); D. Morgan, *Suffragists and Liberals* (1976).

sudden drafting of women into the war-time economy as a reason for conceding the vote in the last year of the war.[21] By then also the peculiar virtues of householdership (which would have continued to exclude most women, just as it excluded most men who lodged or still lived with relatives) no longer set a dependable barrier. A democracy of all adult residents and occupants, each with a single vote, was established[22]—though women had to wait another ten years for real parity.[23]

The admission of rural householders to the Commons franchise in 1884 demanded a major restructuring of constituencies, for the increase in numbers of voters (from 3 to 5 millions overall) would have suddenly swollen the representative responsibilities of county members out of all recognition. Notions of proportional representation were canvassed; but representation from localities was much too ingrained an idea.[24] Instead, in the re-division of 1885, single member constituencies were introduced and the number of seats overall increased from 416 to 643.

The Liberal and Conservative parties, which had grown out of earlier roots after 1867, believed that they could manage a further intensification of democracy—indeed that they could remain the poles of the Parliamentary magnet even after such a reform. Most leaders of the trade union movement in the 1880's saw Parliament in broadly this form as the continuing centre of politics. When Keir Hardie launched an Independent Labour Party in 1893, few felt it had much prospect.[25] Even the turning of ultimate legal weaponry—the civil remedies of injunction and damages—on trade unions which organised strikes, seemed in the short term to provoke a reaction in favour of the Liberals.[26]

In their massive electoral victory of 1906, there were also elected 29 Labour Representation Committee candidates and 24 miners and "Lib-Labs." But there would be little future for an independent labour movement, if the unions could not support Labour MPs financially—and in the *Osborne* judgment of 1909, the House of Lords ruled that they could not do so. The reaction to this second legal attack was, however, the direct payment of MPs, which became law in the unsettling year of 1911; and then legislation allowing unions to

[21] Representation of the People Act 1918. The Act also removed the disqualification upon those in receipt of outdoor poor relief.

[22] Electors could qualify in more than one constituency but could not vote more than once, with an exception for the last plural franchise, the university constituencies (which survived until 1948): Representation of the People Act 1918.

[23] In 1918, the vote was restricted to women aged at least 30; the "flapper vote" was admitted in 1928 and produced the awful reality of a preponderance of female electors. The Sex Disqualification (Removal) Act 1919 admitted women onto juries, as MPs and to all universities, offices and professions (with surviving limitations, particularly upon married women in the Civil Service). It was held however not to have affected the exclusion of peeresses in their own right from the House of Lords: *Viscountess Rhondda's Claim* [1922] 2 A.C. 339.

[24] There would however remain advocates of proportional representation and the idea attracted a following lasting to the final dose of Parliamentary reform—in 1918: see M. Pugh, *Electoral Reform in War and Peace 1906–18* (1978) Chap. 11.

[25] For the evolution see esp. H. Pelling, *The Origins of the Labour Party 1880–1900* (1965); *Popular Politics and Society in Late Victorian Britain* (1968).

[26] See below, p. 328ff.

establish separate political funds which members would contribute to unless they specifically contracted out of doing so.[27]

Democratisation of the Commons brought with it a new discipline for its parties. Both Liberals and Conservatives began to build national machinery which would ensure that there were suitable candidates in position to contest elections.[28] The leaders of both government and opposition would expect their elected members to follow their lead in the voting lobbies and imposed their will (as on hounds) by their whips.[29] As part of its appeal to voters, each party would pledge itself more or less specifically to a programme, and with a dependable parliamentary party, the victors would then begin to turn their platform into operative legislation.

They would come under kaleidescopic "pressures from without." From 1832 onwards, the business of lobbying was a prominent part of all the restless organising for economic advantage and social improvement: factory conditions, corn law repeal, temperance, compulsory education and a host of other causes. But now, more than before, there were pressures from within. For government had moved on from being a passive, sanctioning tool. Central bureaucracy acquired its modern, professional accoutrement when in 1870 recruitment to the higher grades of the civil service was finally made competitive.[30] Departments had come to be in charge of all the major activities of central government and they now contained permanent experts to advise ministers on policy, to press for increases in their own authority, to fight for their financial needs and to monitor their own administration and that in local authorities and even private enterprises. The question of who really governed was acquiring a new, more complex meaning.

While either party could expect to have its way in the House of Commons so long as it commanded a working majority, it was very much part of the late Victorian realignments that only the Conservatives could count upon support in the House of Lords. The rough parity of Whigs and Tories among the peers up to 1867 quickly gave way to a permanent predominance of Conservatives, as financial and commercial interests, the old landed Whigs and finally the Unionists deserted the Liberal ship. Under Salisbury's scrupulous command, the Lords tempered their inclination to govern even when in opposition, accepting the third Reform Bill and its attendant redistribution of seats, and even putting through the democratisation of their

---

[27] See below, p. 341ff.

[28] See esp. R. Blake, *The Conservative Party from Peel to Churchill* (1970) Chaps. 4, 5; J. Vincent, *The Formation of the Liberal Party* (1966); D. A. Hamer, *Liberal Politics in the Age of Gladstone and Rosebery* (1972) Chaps. 1–3.

[29] At the same period, other forms of discipline had to be built into Commons procedure, particularly in face of philibustering by Parnell's Irish cohort. The Speaker's guillotine upon debates, instituted in 1882, was one crucial step towards government control of the Parliamentary time-table. See A. L. Lowell, *The Government of England* (1917) Chap. 35; E. Hughes in R. Pares and A. J. P. Taylor (eds.) *Essays presented to Sir Lewis Namier* (1956), p. 289.

[30] The Treasury's Order-in-Council was the culmination of reforms under the Civil Service Commission which followed upon the high, exaggerated criticism contained in the Northcote-Trevelyan Report of 1853.

own heartlands, the counties.[31] But once the Liberal government of 1906 began to feel that their party's future lay in social reform and wealth redistribution, the Lords made a succession of direct challenges.[32] Lloyd George drew them into the dangerous game of rejecting the finance bill which embodied the People's Budget of 1909. They proved to lack the command of old positions which might have preserved their traditional powers; only their prestige allowed them to survive as an almost supernumerary brigade in the constitutional ranks.[33]

(b) Local government

In 1884, English local government was a hotch-potch. At its upper level, the justices whose sessions governed the counties were still appointed by mysterious nomination; yet the boroughs had acquired elective representation with a franchise based on a double test of rate-paying and residence. At the lower level—primarily the 15,000 parishes—various forms prevailed: the old meeting of parishioners in open vestry, the closed self-perpetuating vestries secured by private Act or customary practice, the elected vestries of Hobhouse's Act 1831. In any case, some of the most important local functions had passed to special bodies; the boards of guardians administered the poor law and had in many cases acquired public health and highway functions; school boards and school attendance committees were the instruments of compulsory education; a variety of special institutions, such as turnpike trusts, were still in existence from an earlier age.

In 1888, the Conservatives chose to create elected councils for counties and county boroughs, in large measure depriving Quarter Sessions—"the rural House of Lords"—of their administrative functions. Salisbury, once an Abdullamite resister of the second Reform Bill, had learned the virtues of strategic concession, and he saw the advantage in cementing his new association with Joseph Chamberlain by such an apparently radical measure.[34] In the event, the new county authorities, which were elected upon the same franchise of rate-liability and residence that had been given to the reformed boroughs in 1835,[35] had much the landed complexion of sessions: old partners for modified dances.[36]

The Liberals, who were the real progenitors of the move, followed it up by the creation (in 1894) of parish councils, and urban and rural

---

[31] See below, next heading.
[32] In particular, the Education Bill 1906 and the Licensing Bill 1908 were at the centre of inter-party controversy; and see below, p. 89ff.
[33] See below, p. 90.
[34] Local Government Act 1888. See generally, B. Keith-Lucas, *The English Local Government Franchise* (1952) Chap. 4.
[35] Outside the boroughs, the electorate comprised those who had the £10 occupiers' franchise for Parliament: County Electors Act 1888.
[36] This despite the absence of any property qualification for councillors, or of ex officio positions for magistrates, or any plural voting for "property." There were sixty-one county boroughs, more than originally proposed. To the London County Council, the Conservatives would add 28 Metropolitan Borough Councils in 1899.

district councils[37]—lower-level, elected bodies to take over the main
secular functions of the parish vestries and similar bodies, which
covered public health, lighting, highways, public baths and libraries,
and burial grounds. Through them, the guardians of the poor would
in future be nominated.[38] All county and Parliamentary electors had
a single vote.[39] Then in 1918, the wives of occupiers were added[40]:
this, the franchise for all local authorities, retained until 1945 a connection between property and political entitlement that had been
abandoned at the national level.

Arguments for efficiency and professional management justified
passing the more important functions of local government to the new
county and county borough councils. It was a process fraught with
political tensions—for education, for instance, in the Edwardian
years; for poor relief in the uneasy conditions of the twenties.[41] There
would be strain on the one hand between central and county authority, and on the other between county and district levels. The legal
bases of these power relationships were accordingly of first importance; so were those between elective bodies, such as the county and
district councils, and specialised committees and boards, often containing nominated experts, which would be concerned in the
detailed administration of new schemes of social protection.

(c) The Cost of Government

As the cost of government rose, the question of who should pay for
it became a front marker of politics. Pressing needs could be
financed, as they had long been, by loans.[42] But loans had to be ser-
viced and ultimately to be repaid. Since central government provided
little by way of profit-making services, and local government had
begun to do so only where the notion of municipal enterprise was
catching on, the bulk of expenditure had to be met, immediately or in
the long run, from taxes or rates. Central government had traditionally raised most of its revenues by indirect taxation upon commodities produced (excise), imported (customs) or sold (sales tax) rather
than by taxation proportional to the income or wealth of individuals.
Customs and excise duties, regressive in that they fell as a higher
proportion of income on the less well-off, were relatively easy to collect. They could be assessed without investigation into personal
affairs that was implicit in any tax on personal income or capital.
Income tax had not proved wholly escapable. Under the younger Pitt

---

[37] Local Government Act 1894.
[38] This ended the property qualification for guardians and the ex officio position of
justices.
[39] Women had continued, as in the past, to be qualified for the local franchises where
they satisfied other requirements. The Court of Appeal, however, held them
excluded from election to the county councils (*Beresford-Hope* v. *Lady Sandhurst*
(1889) 23 Q.B.D. 79) and this continued until the Qualification of Women Act 1907.
[40] Representation of the People Act 1918: the wives newly admitted had to be over 30
until 1928. The requirement of occupation was still for six months (reduced in 1926
to three months), a complicating factor which in practice kept many from voting.
[41] See below, pp. 474ff, 461–462.
[42] Both central and local governments had done much to give a function to the London
and other stock exchanges: see below, p. 247.

it had largely taken over as a war-time tax from the earlier land tax, both taxes being upon annual accruals, declared or estimated.[43] Peel had revived the income tax in 1842, following the legal patterns set in 1799 and 1802,[44] and thereafter it never entirely disappeared, though Gladstone in particular was committed to its repeal and took this prospect as a pretext for refusing to make its incidence more just. In the run-up to the general election of 1874, when both parties were advocating abolition of the income tax, it was bringing in £5.7 million, while customs and excise were accounting for two-thirds of a total expenditure of £77 millions.[45]

The only point at which capital itself was taxed was on death, when, for a long period, a jumble of duties had been extracted— inheritance duty on realty, probate duty on personalty and legacy duty from collateral and unrelated successors. The Conservatives had begun the process of reform in 1888, but it was the Liberals, with the declared intent of increasing revenue,[46] who substituted a single estate duty payable on all wealth at death. The notion that taxation should be proportional—advocated by J. S. Mill for its equity and practised by Peel and Gladstone for its political appeal—was replaced by one of social responsibility. The estate duty was graduated; 1 per cent. was payable on estates under £500, but then the rate climbed, being 5 per cent. between £25,000 and £50,000 and 8 per cent. above £1 million.[47] Here was a machine that future Chancellors could use to extract increasing returns from those who had done best.[48] Equally clearly, the latter would now devote considerable endeavours, with the aid of highly-skilled lawyers and accountants, towards averting the pressure upon them. In this they would be successful enough to make estate duty, in large measure, a voluntary tax.

The principal means of local taxation was the rate, which had come over time to be a levy on the estimated value of land to its occupier. Rates were also relatively easy to impose (since, as with the land tax and the income tax upon land occupiers, they were based on a notional assessment of receipts less maintenance costs) and to collect. Rating was only gradually becoming standardised. Previously there were the wildest variations in estimated valuations for rates and in the extent to which the poorest plots and cottages bore any liability at all. In the towns, the practice grew up of "compounding" the rent and rates of domestic lettings into a single payment to the landlord, who was then responsible for the actual rates to the local authorities, but at a discount for his agency. Rates accordingly had an incidence that affected farmer, businessman, professional and owner-occupier much more graphically than his income tax.

No simple test could determine what should be paid for locally and

---

[43] Pitt's income tax of 1799 had to be repealed in 1816 under fire marshalled by the young Brougham. See Sabine (1966), pp. 26–46.
[44] Addington's Act of 1803 had introduced the five Schedules (A–E) of returns for particular sources of income, which would have a long influence on the form of the tax.
[45] In contrast, by 1914 direct taxes were accounting for 60 per cent. of a much increased revenue.
[46] Particularly to meet naval expenditure.
[47] Finance Act 1894, Pt. I.
[48] Goschen called it "scaffolding for plunder"; but as Conservative Chancellor of the Exchequer he had made the 1888 moves.

what nationally. Between the evident cases (rubbish removal and street lighting, as distinct from foreign affairs and defence) stood divided ground whose shape changed over time.[49] As rates continued to rise, agricultural occupiers (and owners) claimed that they were bearing a special burden; while radicals insisted that most of the increases were being recovered from urban property, where rising rateable values accompanied the main growth in municipal expenditure.[50] The issue became central to the party divide, the inclination towards active change lying with the Tories. Disraeli's wisdom in treating town and country alike was ceasing to be conventional; the party swung towards favouring its agricultural supporters by rating relief coupled with grants-in-aid from central to local government.

Mid-Victorian Parliaments had occasionally accepted the concept of a central contribution for a specific aspect of a local service, most notably when the counties were obliged to establish professional police[51]; but these were special cases.[52] In 1888, as part of their new deal at the county level, the Conservatives sought a new, more general settlement of financial relations between central and local government: The Chancellor of the Exchequer, the ex-Gladstonian, Goschen, replaced the particular contributions to local expenditure by an assignment of nominated portions of national revenue. Initially, these were certain licence fees (arms, dogs, game, male servants, various forms of retailing etc.) which had a local feel about them, together with part of the probate duty, (the death duty on personalty), which was intended to represent a contribution of personal wealth to local services. In 1890, Goschen added beer and spirit "surtaxes" ("whisky money"), and hoped that he had achieved a lasting compromise.[53] But home government stood on the threshold of massive expansion. By 1912, the expenditure on local services of poor relief, mental health, police and prosecutions, main roads, sanitary officers and education would grow three times (from £18 m. to nearly £55 m.). To this central government would contribute a proportion which in 1890 was 40 per cent. and which would continue at just under that figure. Central government would be unable to resist reverting to financial arrangements that gave it more control. An ever-watchful Treasury could scarcely accept the automatic payment over of sums collected in its name. Some services—notably the reorganized education system of 1902—demanded separate treatment. For the politicians, grants for particular services enabled them to encourage acceptable spending, and, in a world where populist majorities were no longer merely theoretical, to discourage what they disapproved of.

---

[49] Thus the maintenance of highways would seem more naturally a national concern when long-distance use predominated; this it did in the coaching era and again towards the end of the nineteenth century, but not in the "railway age."

[50] This long and intricate debate is unravelled by Offer (1981) Chaps. 10–14.

[51] See below, p. 595.

[52] The other instances were the contributions to costs of prosecution (1835) and of poor law medical officers (1846).

[53] Edward Cannan called the result as "atrocious jumble": *The History of Local Rates in England* . . . (2nd ed., 1927) p. 145, and see generally Chap. 6.

Rating relief of agricultural occupiers, likewise, was not an entire novelty in the late nineteenth century, since agricultural land had occasionally been exempted in part from particular rates.[54] The Conservatives finally introduced it as a general rule in 1896[55]; farmers were relieved of one-half of their liability to rates,[56] the shortfall being made up from general taxation through grant-in-aid (but only to the extent of the loss in 1895–96). This was followed by a broadly similar reduction in the rate on the clergy's tithe rent-charges, a departure from Disraelian orthodoxy for a second favourite.[57]

Here was a significant element in the Liberals' Parliamentary victory of 1906 and one which pulled them along their collectivising, interventionist track. By way of countering the Tory favouritisms, they began to examine once more not only out-and-out land reform (such as nationalisation and smallholdings) but also taxing the special increments to land values that stemmed from social prosperity.[58] This meant a tax on capital value separate from that arising on death, implying a valuation of the land itself (as distinct from its annual value for rates) and in all probability an official compilation of land ownership.

These would provide the most provoking elements in Lloyd George's "People's Budget" of 1909.[59] During his spell as Chancellor of the Exchequer, Asquith had already introduced a measure of differentiation into the income tax, adopting as his point of departure, the distinction between earned and unearned income.[60] Lloyd George proceeded not only with an increase in the levels of this income tax[61] but would add to the burdens of the wealthy a supertax of 6d in the £ over £5,000 upon the amount that the income exceeded £3,000.[62] He proposed doubling stamp duty, increasing the rates of estate duty and the taxes on tobacco, spirits and liquor licences, and introducing taxes on cars and petrol. By themselves all these would likely have been accepted as the prerogative of government. But the proposals for 2d in the £ on the capital value of vacant land, the same rate on mining royalties, a 10 per cent. reversion duty on benefits to the lessor at the termination of a lease, and above all a 20 per cent.

---

[54] *e.g.* under the Watching and Lighting Act 1833, a rebate of one-third was given; and under the public health legislation, a rebate of a half in urban districts.

[55] Agricultural Rates Act 1896.

[56] Subsequently the rebate became 75 per cent. in 1923 and the rating was abolished entirely in 1929.

[57] Tithe Rent-charge (Rates) Act 1899; the loss was in this case passed back to other ratepayers: Cannan (above, n. 53), p. 156.

[58] See Offer (1981) Chap. 19; a leading role was played by the Scottish law officers, Shaw and Ure; they promoted such a tax for Scotland in a 1907 Bill which the Lords threw out.

[59] In which generally see H. V. Emy, *Liberals, Radicals and Social Politics* (1974) Chaps. 5–7.

[60] Following the recommendation of Sir Charles Dilke's Select Committee on Income Tax, P.P. 1906 (365) IX, the new tax imposed a standard rate of 1s. in the £, with a reduction to 9d in the £ for earned income under £2,000 (the Select Committee had proposed £3,000 as the limit). There had been abatements before, *e.g.* on land and houses in Harcourt's Budget of 1894, but their level was less distinctive.

[61] He raised the standard rate to 1s. 2d. and added an intermediate rate of 1s. on earned income from £2,000 to £3,000.

[62] A super-tax had been proposed by the Dilke Committee (above, n. 60).

duty on the incremental value to land which had accrued at transfer (by sale, gift or on death), were too much. Attached to them would be an inquisitorial valuation of the land which would (somehow) attribute separate values to site and buildings. The Lords staged a revolt which could be put down only by an election reconfirming Asquith's government in office (January, 1910).[63] The Lords, moreover, were obliged to accept unequivocal statutory limitation of their powers. But here too the Parliament Act 1911, with its removal of the Lords' veto on money bills and its constriction of their power over other bills to a delay of two sessions, could be obtained only by a second election (December, 1910—again sufficiently in Asquith's favour) and by making known George V's undertaking to create as many Liberal peers as would be needed to ensure the bill's passage.[64]

With this victory, the flight from landed property would begin in earnest. The yield of the land taxes would in fact prove to be disappointing. But the increment value tax, particularly once the courts held it to apply to the profits of speculative builders,[65] had a depressing effect on housebuilding and a shortage began to threaten.[66] The municipalities continued to press for more help and Lloyd George was moved in 1914 to adopt the Tory tactic of increased grant-in-aid. This was one of numerous reasons for needing once more to raise the major taxes and duties, so that his 1914 Finance Act pushed the top rate of income-cum-super tax to 13 per cent. on £9,000 and more. Wartime taxation would soon make even this seem modest.[67]

For all the apparent danger to land, the hazards in organising the new taxes on it—and in particular the complex new valuations for increment value tax—proved extraordinarily difficult. In 1914, Scrutton J. held that the value of grass and other uncut crops (a constantly fluctuating figure) had to be included in the "gross value" of farms, but deducted from the "full site value"—an administrative nightmare.[68] Lloyd George had been waiting for completion of the valuations before imposing that long-held objective of single-taxers and other reformers, a tax on the capital value of the site as such. In 1914, he sought to appease the municipalities partly by converting this into a rate on site values; but his plan was submerged first under an argument about how far it could be included in a money bill and then by pressure from industrial and other antagonists in his own party. Here was a sign that the whole Land Campaign was faltering.[69]

---

[63] The Finance (1909–1910) Act was finally passed in April, the Lords accepting the verdict of the electorate.

[64] For the politics in full colour, see G. Dangerfield, *The Strange Death of Liberal England* (1935) Chap. 3. The Parliament Act 1911 also reduced the maximum life of a parliament from seven years to five.

[65] *Lumsden* v. *I.R.C.* [1914] A.C. 877 (a 2–2 decision of law lords with Liberal connections; the issue well illustrated the intractable problems of detail that the whole endeavour invoked).

[66] Lloyd George kept up heat on the land question by instigating a Liberal Land Enquiry, which produced detailed reports in 1913 (rural problems) and 1914 (urban).

[67] In 1918, the top rate for supertax payers became 10s. 6d. in the £ (52.5 per cent.).

[68] *I.R.C.* v. *Smyth* [1914] 3 K.B. 406.

[69] See generally Offer (1981) Chap. 22.

After the war, it would receive a rapid *coup de grace* from Austen Chamberlain.[70] The Land Campaign thus achieved much more by what it threatened than by what it extracted. Lloyd George continued to devise ways of giving it new life, so that the Liberal Party in the late 20's had weapons in its armoury more radical than most of the Labour party's[71]; yet the lack of impact of these ideas became one measure of how far Liberal politics had lost way. Land was passing from the estate-owning class to those who exploited it. Meanwhile all income recipients—earners and non-earners—were having to meet taxation demands which even the Labour leaders had not publicly contemplated before the war. There was some reduction to fit peace-time; but the basic rate of income tax—a central barometer of all the pressures in public finance—would stay at 4s. 6d. in the £ (22.5 per cent.) or more, save for four of Churchill's budgets as Chancellor (1925–29). It would then climb gradually to cope with the difficulties of depression and recovery, until in 1938 Sir John Simon would carry it to 5s. 6d.

At the outset of the period, an influential royal commission recognised that the principle of graduation had become an accepted starting point and made a number of recommendations for rationalising the allowances and reliefs that helped those with small incomes and for rendering the supertax (or surtax as it would become) progressive in stages.[72] These proposals were taken up in subsequent Finance Acts. There was also a certain amount of political preferment—the Labour party, led on finance by Snowden, seeking to load additional taxation directly on the rich, the Conservatives showing some liking for indirect taxes on commodities, which would bear "equally" across the board. In two decades of predominantly Conservative government, Britain would become known as a country of high taxation.[73]

The problems posed by evasion and avoidance of tax became correspondingly more acute. Evasion had been a difficulty associated in particular with the income tax, though to some extent the requirement of proper accounting had been side-stepped by notional assessments—for instance on the annual rental value of land. In other cases, it could be overcome only by bureaucratic prying.[74] Avoidance—reducing one's tax liability by means within the law—posed problems of legal boundary rather than of concealed fact. In 1874, in a shift truly Diceyian in significance (for all that it went unremarked), the Commissioners of the Income Tax, General and Special, had become subject to appellate review by the common law courts. A

---

[70] In his 1920 Budget.
[71] *Land and the Nation* (1925) proposed the substitution of tenants under county committees for owners of agricultural land and so was the subject of high controversy. *Towns and the Land*, its urban counterpart, had nothing so spectacular to say. See T. Wilson, *The Downfall of the Liberal Party* (1966) Chap. 17.
[72] Royal Commission on Income Tax, P.P. 1920 [Cmd. 615] XVIII.
[73] See generally, Sabine (1966) Chaps. 10, 11; U.K. Hicks *The Finance of British Government 1920–1936* (1938).
[74] The fear of this for long kept the collection of taxes primarily in the hands of local worthies, who were appointed Commissioners for the purpose. Even the Board of Inland Revenue, which replaced earlier arrangements at the centre in 1853, did not get power to appoint all Commissioners until 1931: see Sabine (1966), pp. 15, 29, 187.

regular stream of tax decisions flowed from this source, judges and counsel assuming with equanimity that the interpretative task was one exactly suited to their skills.[75] Arguments were devised by resort to a mixture of dictionary reference to the meaning of statutory words, grand "principles" of the common law (sometimes banal, sometimes historically dubious) and appeals to "common sense." The judges fashioned their views out of like material. They showed little inclination to resort to developed notions of economic theory, sensing perhaps that such theory was unlikely to provide any sophisticated answer to the line-drawing exercises in which they were mostly engaged. Nor did the judges show consistent favour towards either tax-gatherer or tax-payer. At a time when the Millian ethic of equality grounded most taxation, and income tax rates were minimal, any decision to protect one category of payer could be treated as passing the burden to others.

In the period between the wars, these attitudes changed. There was a new emphasis on strict interpretation against the Revenue; and beneath it a hostility against taxation as confiscation.[76] The Duke of Westminster, instead of paying his employees in full, granted them seven-year covenants, which had the effect of transferring the covenanted amounts from his own income to theirs without his incurring any liability to tax. This was, in the House of Lords' view, a permissible device.[77] Other avoidance schemes proliferated, many of them using the machinery of the private company or the discretionary trust. The annual finance acts began to accumulate, from 1922 onwards, the counter-measures which were an inevitable part of this "undignified game of chess." When the Revenue promoted its own strategies through legislation, there was rarely any protest in Parliament[78]; the matter was essentially whether the Chancellor of the day was prepared to include the Commissioners' proposals in his Finance Bill. Meanwhile the judges had reached one of their strict adhesions to the letter which signal a deep-felt repugnance.

IV. Judges and Courts

In the period up to the Judicature Acts the restructuring of the judicial system had been marked by a cautious determination to conserve.[79] The "unity" of the whole was heightened; the primacy of lawyers was confirmed, particularly over the question of businessmen judges; the superior and inferior levels stayed apart so that a strong central bar might maintain an exclusive preserve, and the highest judges might command with a splendour remote.[80]

---

[75] For details, R. Cocks in Rubin and Sugarman (1984), p. 445.

[76] R.B. Stevens (*Law and Politics* (1978), pp. 204–209) traces these shifts in House of Lords' judgments from the Lloyd George years.

[77] I.R.C. v. *Duke of Westminster* [1936] A.C. 1. For seven-year covenants, see below, p. 471.

[78] Sabine (1966), pp. 181–184, 190–191.

[79] See above, p. 40ff.

[80] In 1876, the Supreme Court of Judicature opened with a complement of judges (and Blackburn and Gordon joined the House of Lords as Lords of Appeal in Ordinary—life peers at last). In 1920 there would be 23 judges and 7 Law Lords; in 1940—31 and 7.

The Judicature Acts were to prove a terminus rather than a staging-post. In an age of democratic politics, as the relations of state and people became more intense and complex, the courts did adapt themselves in a measure to mass demands for adjudication. The county courts would hear much of workmen's compensation and rent restriction.[81] Magistrates would deal with security of tenants against eviction and maintenance of deserted wives.[82] After the disruptions of the first world war, the demand for divorce would mean that its deliberate restriction to London had to give way and a limited number of assizes began to be used.[83] The need for expedition in commercial litigation, impelled by the increasing resort of disputants to arbitration, saw the establishment in 1895 of a "Commercial Court" within the Queen's Bench Division, with judges of special experience, an accellerated procedure and fixed dates for trial.[84] But all this was change of a secondary kind. The only real alteration of structure came with the creation in 1907 of a Court of Criminal Appeal, giving those convicted of serious criminal offences by assizes or quarter sessions the right for the first time to appeal against either conviction or sentence.[85] Parliament, with its sizeable representation of JPs in both houses, had long refused to take the step; but the misconviction of Adolph Beck for a series of frauds upon women provoked a sense of outrage which could be dispelled by no lesser shift.[86] Leading lawyers had, on the whole, given the idea little support. But the creation of the new court did complete the supervisory net of the senior judiciary over civil and criminal jurisdiction in its "ordinary" sense. One consequence was that county quarter sessions began to seek legally qualified chairmen who would have the skill to avert criticism from above.[87]

Most other dissatisfactions with the courts proved capable of resistance—by the judges, by practitioners or by government. London remained the centre of the legal universe, the provinces making do with the assize system and the inferior jurisdictions. The assize arrangements had been somewhat expanded with the Judicature Acts, giving the busiest centres a sitting three or even four times a year. But the distribution proved not to coincide with demand from litigants and the amount of travelling provoked the judges. By the end of the century, cases awaiting trial were banking up in London and the delays were grudgingly met by the appointment of two more

[81] See below, pp. 533ff., 184ff.
[82] See below, pp. 135–136, 391ff.
[83] See below, p. 396.
[84] This was the final upshot of the long campaign for special tribunals to hear commercial cases (for which, see above, pp. 36–38, 44). It was also sparked off by the ineptitude of J.C. ("Long") Lawrance J. in trying the case of Rose v. Bank of Australasia [1894] A.C. 687; see also T. E. Scrutton (1921) Camb.L.J. 6; P. D. Mackinnon above, p. 37, n. 91; Lord Parker, above, p. 36, n. 89.
[85] The cause had a long, fruitless history; see below, p. 609.
[86] See below, p. 619ff.
[87] By 1936 a Royal Commission on the Despatch of Business at Common Law would recommend that most chairmen be legally qualified (P.P. 1936 [Cmd. 5065] VIII paras. 208, 212, echoed by the Committee on Quarter Sessions P.P. 1936 [Cmd. 5252] VIII. This was given effect from 1938 as chairmen retired, over the objection of Attlee, Cripps and others, who wanted the existing amateurs removed at once: Abel-Smith and Stevens (1967), pp. 107–108.

judges, assigned to the King's Bench Division, and by minor adjustments in assize arrangements.[88]

There was regular discussion of increasing the monetary limits upon county court jurisdiction. In 1903, indeed, the indomitable Sir Albert Rollit, MP, President of the Law Society and representative alike of the chambers of commerce and the municipal corporations, pushed through an increase in the maximum claim from £50 to £100.[89] But he had to outface the opposition of the Lord Chancellor, Halsbury, and all further movement in this direction was blocked until 1938, when a compromise increase to £200 was introduced, a defendant sued for more than £100 retaining the right to remove the case into the High Court.[90] On the criminal side, by contrast, the process of shifting the trial of medium-range offences into the summary jurisdiction of magistrates and away from the burdensome ritual of jury trial proceeded more readily, the two largest moves coming in 1879 and 1925.[91]

The temporary abrogation of civil juries during the first World War had a subsequent effect: in the inter-war period the use of trial juries became markedly more selective.[92] In the ordinary courts the business of judging was passing, on the one hand to professional lawyers and on the other, to the justices of the peace. The magistracy was stripped of its most evidently squirearchical marks with the abolition of the property qualification in 1906 and the admission of women in 1918.[93] It also acquired a measure of specialisation with the creation in 1933 of a juvenile court panel within each bench.[94] But the appointment of justices continued to be by the Lord Chancellor, very largely on the recommendation of the Lords Lieutenant of the counties: and they in turn came to be advised by small committees with a secret membership—an adaptation recommended by a Royal Commission and quietly taken up by Loreburn as Liberal Lord Chancellor.[95] In the period to 1945 the magistracy changed only peripherally in social composition, partly because of the selection arrangements, but partly because the appointment needed a regular and voluntary commitment of time during the working week. Magistrates' courts could be relied upon to underpin the interests of the state, supporting the police in their day-to-day work and denouncing the disrupters in times of tension, such as the General Strike.

Novel demands for adjudication arose amid the outworks of a

---

[88] For details, Abel-Smith and Stevens (1967), pp. 93–98; and for the inter-war period, *ibid.*, pp. 100–107.

[89] This was the limit for debt and other common types of action: County Courts Act 1903, s.3.

[90] Abel-Smith and Stevens (1967), pp. 92–93, 109.

[91] See R.M. Jackson (1937) 1 M.L.R. 132.

[92] After 1883, when it became the rule that common law actions would be tried by jury only if one side requested it, about 50 per cent. of actions were tried by judge alone. In 1918 the court was in most actions given its own discretion to refuse a jury. Although the previous position was reverted to in 1925, the 1918 provision was again substituted in 1933: see Jackson (above, n. 91).

[93] One year before, women were admitted to juries; but there they still had to meet the householder property qualification.

[94] See below, pp. 628–629.

[95] See generally, Moir (1969), pp. 182–188.

modestly collectivising state. At those points where the price mechanisms of free bargaining were no longer to determine who should
have what, a new complexion coloured allocation. Power of office—
that dread eighteenth century shade—threatened to darken fresh corners. Only detailed regulation could hope to confine the opportunities for corrupt preference and malign deprivation that were the
sombre side of broad discretion. And regulation would cast its own
shadows of penumbral uncertainty as its classifications were pro-
jected upon the myriad circumstances of ordinary life.

The superior courts had early signalled how unequal they were to
the task of non-market allocation by their failure to deal with railway
rate-fixing in a manner acceptable either to the companies or their
customers.[96] When they were drawn into the workmen's compensation scheme of 1897 they brought an elaborate procedure and a
heightening of tensions which was widely disliked.[97] They were
accordingly given no equivalent rule in the new institutions of social
security. Old age pensions, sickness insurance, unemployment
insurance, would all breed special tribunals for determining challenges by claimants to unfavourable decisions by administrators.[98]

Before this, the growing range of powers by which politicians and
bureaucrats could directly affect the rights and freedoms of individuals had been subject to some degree of control by the ordinary
courts. The early forms of regulation—of factories, mines, ships and
so on—had required a criminal prosecution, normally before magistrates, as the sanction for failure to comply with the demands of an
inspector. So equally with the exceptional compulsions of primary
education and smallpox vaccination.[99] Later, as positive intervention
was added to regulation, and political choice become a necessary part
of governmental action, the question of how far any decision could
be reviewed became more complex and difficult; but the procedures
mostly remained the same. Now, over entitlements that appeared
relatively precise (and accordingly "justiciable"), the task of reviewing was passing either to those politically responsible (such as ministers) or to bodies which were much like courts but which would have
an expertise in their own subject, knowing through familiarity the
problems that administrators were having to solve with limited
resources.

The judges had perforce to accept these new bureaucratic procedures. Their sense of propriety was in some measure appeased by
two factors: in some cases, they were still placed in the position of
ultimate arbiters upon the scope of legal powers by typically Victorian provisions allowing an appeal from the tribunal to the High
Court (or the statement of a case on a point of law)[1]; and where these
mechanisms did not operate, the courts might still have resort to the
old prerogative writs, so much in use a century earlier, as a tool of
central supervision and by no means supplanted by all the interven-

---

[96] See below, p. 269.
[97] See below, pp. 533 535.
[98] See below, pp. 455–457.
[99] See below, p. 445ff.
[1] See, *e.g.*, below, p. 456.

ing regularisation of appeals and references.[2] Certainly two well-known judgments of the House of Lords—*Board of Education* v. *Rice*[3] and *Local Government Board* v. *Arlidge*[4]—took an essentially accommodating line: interventionist government must needs have regular decision-making powers, some of them leading to the disturbance even of property rights, without regular supervision by the independent judiciary. Such adjudication had only to keep within the terms of the empowering statute and, where it was "judicial" or "quasi-judicial" in character,[5] to comply with the basic standards of natural justice—no man to be judge in his own cause, every person affected to have the right to be heard, though not necessarily on the strict lines of common law procedure. Thus the *Arlidge* case upheld the ministerial practice of deciding to order the closure of premises for overcrowding after taking submissions from the occupier and receiving the report of a local inspector, but without showing that report to the occupier.[6]

These were influential precedents but they could not guarantee a uniform line from a judiciary sensitive to Dicey's peculiarly English version of the "Rule of Law." A local authority bent of heterodox social policies, as the London Borough of Poplar had been for a quarter-century, could still draw the House of Lords into interpreting a statute in a way that enmeshed the actual text in a web of larger preconceptions: according to *Roberts* v. *Hopwood*[7] the Council's statutory authority to pay its workers had to be exercised "reasonably," which meant keeping to market rates, and observing such differentials between male and female employees as the market dictated. Councillors who acted otherwise exposed themselves to the penalties of ultra vires action: disallowance and personal surcharge (to which legislation then added disqualification from office).

There were also judges ready to suspect that bureaucrats were manipulating the rules of parliamentary sovereignty in order to shelter from judicial scrutiny. There were, for instance, statutes in which delegated legislation, after being put through a prescribed procedure of laying before Parliament, was deemed to form part of the very Act. Eventually the House of Lords would rule that such a formula could not preclude the courts from considering whether the delegated legislation was ultra vires.[8] Then there were provisions, dubbed "Henry VIII clauses," which gave ministers the power by regulation

---

[2] See generally above, p. 32ff.
[3] [1911] A.C. 179. For the political background to this complex case, see below, pp. 475–476.
[4] [1915] A.C. 120. The members of the House had all been Liberal politicians: Stevens (1978), pp. 197–198 (under the rubric, "The Tragedy of Public Law").
[5] "Quasi-judicial" decision-making was to be distinguished from merely ministerial: it involved some measure of choice, as a matter of policy, among feasible alternatives, and so was not merely the application of law to given facts; but still it called for an assessment upon a proper collection of information: for a significant instance, see *R.* v. *Electricity Commissioners* [1924] 1 K.B. 171.
[6] The ruling would, however, be criticised by the generally supportive Donoughmore-Scott Committee (below, n. 11).
[7] [1925] A.C. 578.
[8] *R* v. *Minister of Health ex p. Yaffe* [1931] A.C. 494, reversing the tendency first shown by the House of Lords in *Institute of Patent Agents* v. *Lockwood* [1894] A.C. 347.

to vary the terms of an Act, a procedure sometimes used to settle the relation of a complex new statute to other Acts. Both practices were denounced by Lord Hewart C.J. in *The New Despotism* (1929) as autocratic devices which made the *droit administratif* of France appear a paradigm of responsibility under law.[9] He likewise had dark things to say of non-appealable tribunals in ministries, whose unpublished judgments formed no kind of precedent and were not always supported by statements of reasons.[10]

This curmudgeonly outburst was answered urbanely by the Donoughmore-Scott Committee on Ministers' Powers, which took much the line found earlier in the *Rice* and *Arlidge* judgments: all was essentially as it had to be; bureaucrats were not in the habit of betraying the trust given them; the only case was for marginal improvements—in standardising the steps for making delegated legislation, improving publication arrangements for the more important types, ensuring—by Standing Committees of each House—that Lord Hewart's pet bugbears made no unnecessary appearances in statutes, and securing ultimate powers to refer questions of law from administrative tribunals to the ordinary courts where the function was strictly "judicial."[11]

As we shall see, in the inter-war years the new forms of state provision, above all for the relief of unemployment, fell under extreme pressure and would accordingly be enmeshed in a tangle of alterations—by statute and delegated authority—and of disputes, which were handled in thousands by special tribunals. The county courts and magistrates' courts had managed to absorb some important new business, at points where private relationship had been subordinated to legislative guarantees. But it is hard to see how they could have been adapted to provide any regular supervision or adjudication within the massive growth of administration. The logistic difficulties help to explain why the protests of leading lawyers were so infrequent and marginal.[12] But in addition there was plain hostility towards giving either type of lower court—professional judge or bench of justices—a role in direct social provision by the state. It came not only from bureaucrats and politicians but also from the labour movement. Some disputes could be conducted before special instances; the rest had almost always to be raised by political, rather than legal action. In this way the British reached a balance between

[9] pp. 45–46. Chap. 10 listed 22 instances of "as if enacted in the Act" and "modifying the Act" clauses. The problems posed by delegated legislation in modern government were undoubtedly serious; they were reviewed in more temperate terms by, *e.g.*, C.T. Carr, *Delegated Legislation* (1921) and C.K. Allen, *Bureaucracy Triumphant* (1931).

[10] "It is a queer sort of justice that will not bear the light of publicity": see pp. 46–49. Hewart also castigated the Ministry of Justice plan (see below, p. 101) and a proposal to consult the courts for an opinion before litigation on the meaning of a statute: see Chap. 7.

[11] Committee on Ministers' Powers P.P. 1931–1932 [Cmd. 4060] XII.

[12] The general attitude of the courts towards the validity of administration made it easy for them to accept what was done in wartime under massive emergency powers: this extended even to remarkable infractions of personal liberty: see esp. *R.* v. *Halliday, ex p. Zadig* [1917] A.C. 260; *Liversidge* v. *Anderson* [1942] A.C. 206 (with its well-known dissent by Lord Atkin); on the latter case, see A.W.B. Simpson, *Rhetoric, Reality and Regulation 18B* (1987).

the sovereignty of parliament, ministerial responsibility to parliament and the Rule of Law that would last until the 1960s.[13] Then, as two centuries before, the judges would attempt to stand as arbiters of fair and acceptable administration.

V. The Legal Professions

According to Perkin, the years before the first world war saw a decampment of those sharing a middle-class "entrepreneurial ideal" to the Conservative Party, leaving the Liberals to radical leadership embodying the "professional ideal." As he shows, the proportion of professional men on the Liberal benches in the Commons increased and, in particular, lawyers became prominent among the leaders: Asquith, Lloyd George, Loreburn, Haldane.[14] But lawyers went into Parliament for a variety of reasons: some were pure politicians; some used a Commons seat as a step towards the judicial bench[15]; some were looking for a second career in a ministerial post.[16] It would be a mistake to infer from evidence about the background of MPs that the general run of either barristers or solicitors did not keep broadly in step with the entrepreneurial middle-class. The "professional ideal" which Perkin sought to typify was, after all, that of the expert whose secure position enabled him to espouse a relatively disinterested concern for the public good. By contrast the legal professions had remained "free," separated by the fee-paying of their clients from the state in whose activities they played so distinct a part. To many of them undoubtedly it was an older, more competitive liberalism which spoke ideological truth.

The peculiar importance of retaining the liberal character of the two professions stamps much of what is significant in their recent history.[17] There was indeed a strong hostility to the institution of state legal services in any province already colonised by private practice. For instance, as the modern administration of the criminal law grew, there arose a persistent campaign for a state-run prosecution service as an adjunct and a regulator of the professional police forces. Yet a long succession of bills to Parliament secured no more than a modest concession, the office of Director of Public Prosecutions.[18] On the civil side, the solicitors attacked vehemently the Land Registry's proposals for its own conveyancing service and, more generally, ran

---

[13] It was a compromise bred of experience and attitude and owed little, as Ernest Barker regretted, to any systematic theory of the state: (1914) 1 Polit. Q. 2; see also W.J.L. Ambrose (1910) 26 L.Q.R. 53.

[14] H. Perkin, *The Origins of Modern English Society* (1969), pp. 437–454; and in J. Butt and I. F. Clark (eds.) *The Victorians and Social Protest* (1973), p. 206.

[15] 80 out of 133 judges appointed between 1832 and 1906 were MPs at the time (another 11 had been candidates); moreover 63 of them had been appointed when their party was in office: H. Laski, *Studies in Law and Politics* (1932) Chap. 7. On Halsbury's judicial appointments, see R. F. V. Heuston, *Lives of the Lord Chancellors 1885–1940* (1964) Chap. 5. Note also Duman (1983), pp. 106, 108–109.

[16] Duman (1983), pp. 184–191.

[17] The World War would reduce the number of practitioners savagely, but this seems to have produced no shift in the central attitude.

[18] Below, p. 608.

a long campaign to prevent the spread of registered conveyancing.[19] To these and other illustrations we shall come in later chapters. Here we may note the impress of the same tendency upon six other matters: legal services in government, political responsibility for legal administration, legal services for the poor, legal education, accountability to the public and relations between two professions themselves.

(a) Government Legal Services

As government became more complex, it could not do without internal legal services, from advice on foreign affairs and high domestic policy to the collection of taxes and the conduct of its own conveyancing.[20] There had indeed long been a small group of legal advisers, over and above the Lord Chancellor and Law Officers appointed by each government, the chief among them being the Treasury Solicitor.[21] In the 1870s a legal service under him was to grow somewhat.[22] Even so, the contrast with continental bureaucracies, chiefly composed of men who had studied law in a university, could not have been more striking. Following the advice of a Committee chaired by Lord Jessel, M.R., the Treasury Solicitor developed a roving service of legal advisers available to all departments.[23] Many of its members were not permanent civil servants, but came for a limited period out of private practice. This slender provision was able to survive until 1919, when a permanent staff became the regular arrangement. But, in the main, it was still possible to continue a small specialised service.[24] This derived from its centralisation a measure of detachment rather like that claimed by the Law Officers in relation to the Cabinet; but at the same time it stood at a distance from the core of decision-making. Even its members who were drawn from the bar did not "practise,"[25] and cases in the superior courts, together with much opinion work, was given over to counsel in private practice, who were retained generally or specially by the Treasury or another department. The central government legal service was small and self-effacing—loyal to traditions and etiquette of the private professions in which its members trained.

In local government much larger numbers came to be involved but traditions scarcely differed. Solicitors had long acted as clerks of the peace to borough justices and county quarter sessions and as clerks

---

[19] Below p. 176ff.

[20] See generally, G. Drewry (1981) 59 Pub. Admin. 15; also J. L. Edwards, *The Law Officers of the Crown* (1964) Chap. 8.

[21] The office can be traced back to 1655; the term "solicitor" here and elsewhere in government is not related to the junior branch of the private profession.

[22] The special business of drafting legislation was only gradually turned into a professional task, the office of Parliamentary Counsel being established in 1867: Sir C. Ilbert, *The Mechanics of Law Making* (1914) Chap. 4.

[23] The new staff were not within the administrative grade and twenty years later, leading civil servants were still scoffing at the possibility: Drewry (above, n. 20), pp. 23–24.

[24] Centralisation would not be entirely maintained, the Post Office and the Inland Revenue in particular needing their own solicitor.

[25] Those who were qualified as solicitors did not have to keep up their practising certificates.

to local justices.[26] With the growth of local bureaucracies, town and county clerks were frequently solicitors. In large cities and major counties, these offices became highly responsible posts dealing with major issues of policy and administration. In lesser places, the link with the free professions was maintained by having a clerk on a part-time basis. A similar kind of linking occurred with the registrarships of the County Courts of 1846.[27] It was part of a web, still largely unstudied, which allowed private practitioners to move in mid-career to offices in government and the courts.

(b) Court Administration: A Ministry of Justice?

The courts were in their own right a major government service, depending for their professional judiciary almost entirely on the experienced stratum of the bar. The relationship was one of nice balance, for the number of superior courts in operation affected the size and earnings of the bar and in turn its ability to provide judges of suitable quality. Within government, the main responsibility for them lay with that protean figure, the Lord Chancellor, and the small office (composed mainly of barristers) that he had acquired a decade after Judicature Acts.[28] To him fell the duty of appointing the judges, court officers and justices of the peace. But it was not an exclusive responsibility: the Treasury dealt with the administrative side of the courts; and the Home Secretary, as well as having close associations with criminal justice by his charge over prisons and police, appointed the metropolitan and stipendiary magistrates and the recorders and legally qualified chairmen of quarter sessions.[29]

This historical mixture was said to combine the virtues of associ-ation (since the Lord Chancellor was always a leading member of the bar) and diffusion (since some of the appointments lay with a minis-ter who would likely not be a lawyer). Certainly proposals to create Ministry of Justice, covering courts, appointments, law reform and the legal professions, attracted little following. There had been occa-sional suggestions of this kind in the nineteenth century,[30] but the argument was most prominently made by Lord Haldane during the

---

[26] The Justices' Clerks Society was formed in 1839, well before the Magistrates' Associ-ation: R. M. Jackson, *The Machinery of Government in England* (7th ed., 1977) pp. 315–317.

[27] For them, see P. W. J. Bartrip in Rubin and Sugarman (1984), p. 349.

[28] Muir Mackenzie was the first Permanent Secretary (1885–1914) and was succeeded by Claud Schuster (1914–44): see G. Drewry (1983) 61 Pub. Admin. 396, 399–401.

[29] This would in the event continue until 1949, despite the recommendation of the Macdonnell Royal Commission on the Civil Service (6th Report, P.P. 1914–1916 [Cd. 7832] XII Chap. 4 para. 4) that all appointments should pass to the Lord Chancellor.

[30] These had varied starting points:
  (i) Lord Langdale M.R. had seen it as a means of distributing the burdens of the Lord Chancellorship: see, *e.g.*, P.D. 1836 XIV 44.
  (ii) The inadequacies of Lord Cranworth's Statute Law Commissioners in the 1850s had suggested a full-time body to deal with consolidation and law reform: see, *e.g.*, P.D. 1857 XLVI 790, 793.
  (iii) During the Judicature Acts reorganisation, the Legal Departments Commission had actually proposed the establishment of a single Ministry: Second Report, P.P. 1874 [C.1107] XXIV, pp. 104–105.

See further, New Fabian Research Bureau, *A Ministry of Justice* (1933), pp. 4–5.

first World War. The version advocated by him, as chairman of the Ministry of Reconstruction Committee on the Machinery of Government, would have given all judicial appointments to the Lord Chancellor but other judicial and legal concerns to a Home Office renamed Ministry of Justice.[31] This was for a time taken up by the Law Society; but it was opposed by the Conservative Lord Chancellor, Birkenhead, from a brief written by Sir Claud Schuster, the adroit Permanent Secretary of the Lord Chancellor's Office: the Lord Chancellor, it was claimed, was an essential buffer for workable relations between executive and judiciary.[32] Hewart, then Attorney-General, was to absorb from this episode the implacable belief that Schuster was after a Ministry of Justice for himself—to Hewart this was bureaucratic manipulation that threatened truly inviolable territory. Accordingly in 1934 he denounced a mild plan to appoint a Vice-President in the Court of Appeal as the thin end of this very wedge.[33] The sensibility may have been absurd; the general feeling behind it was certainly shared by leaders of the bar. After the war, radical lawyers would press the cause of a Ministry of Justice which had attracted them since around the time of Hewart's outburst.[34] But the Lord Chancellor, Jowitt, reacted with almost equal vehemence. Nothing was to come of it even under a majority Labour government.

The real novelty of Haldane's plan was that officials of the proposed Ministry would watch over law reform and would study the development of each subject at home and abroad. The growth of central government in the previous century had meant that, in the particular fields that it supervised, there was frequent legislative change from within.[35] But no tradition of regularly overseeing the general law had developed and the stimulus which had earlier come from without, particularly through such lawyerly organisations as the Society for Promoting Amendment of the Law and the National Association for the Promotion of Social Science,[36] had dwindled. The Victorian commissions and committees which had responded to these thrusts with large plans for reforming statute law and codifying criminal law and procedure[37] had themselves led to little change. In the years after the Judicature Acts, the main achievements were the four statutes which codified particular aspects of commercial law and this was at the behest of the mercantile rather than the legal com-

---

[31] Report, P.P. 1918 [Cd. 9230] XII, Chap. 10. See generally, G. Drewry (above, n. 28); also Lord Schuster (1949) 10 Camb. L.J. 175.

[32] Lord Birkenhead, *Points of View* (1922), I p. 92.

[33] P.D. (Lords) 1934 XCV 224–237. The first bearer of the title would have been Slesser L.J., who had been Solicitor-General in the first Labour Government.

[34] See R.S.T. Chorley (1933) 4 Polit. Q. 544; Chorley was also the author of the Fabian pamphlet (above, n. 30).

[35] See, *e.g.*, the growth of law on factories (below, p. 302ff.), poor law (below, p. 429ff.), housing (below, p. 179ff.).

[36] See above, p. 71.

[37] See below, p. 598ff. Most was achieved in the relatively modest, but significant, field of consolidating successive statutes, a subject on which Lord Cranworth began a great project in 1853: see Sir C. Carr, *A Victorian Law Reformer's Correspondence* (1955) pp. 8–9; A.H. Manchester (1973) 2 Anglo-Am. L.R. 395. Neither this nor later arrangements were as productive as might have been, had there been a minister with overall responsibility. See Lord Jowitt, *Statute Law Revision and Consolidation* (1951).

munity.[38] Through the Edwardian years a long wrangle, intimately connected with the solicitors' interests in conveyancing, was taking place over the reform of land law.[39]

While it received little overt comment, there can be no doubt that an increase of bureaucratic interest in the run of law reform might have a displacing effect on the influence of practising lawyers. The failure of the Ministry of Justice plan meant that any systematic strategy could be left on one side throughout the twenties. Each subject in contention could be handled ad hoc, with resort to official committees to deal with particular pressures.[40] Eventually in 1934, Sankey established, under Lord Chancellor's Office auspices, a Law Revision Committee with standing functions. But on it, beside the Permanent Secretary to that Office, were four judges, five barristers, two solicitors and two professors of law. Initiatives might now come from officials but it was plain that recommendations were to be left predominantly to representatives of the legal professions; they would work with a deliberation dictated by their various preoccupations elsewhere.[41] So it would remain for another three decades.[42]

(c) Legal Services for the Poor

The nineteenth century legal system, with its absorption in individual rights, was largely the province of those who could afford legal advice and assistance. The coming world of social claims could not operate upon such a basis, and the courts were to play only a secondary part in it. Yet their exclusion from "mass law" was by no means entire and this gave a special urgency to questions of legal assistance for the poor. In an adversarial system, professional help was a veritable pre-condition for penetrating an otherwise incomprehensible maze. The most obvious cases where help was essential were accident claims (particularly under the workmen's compensation scheme of 1897) and divorce (much in demand after the upsets of war).[43] But there were other matters that went on a large scale to the courts: housing, crime, agricultural tenancies, rating appeals, debt enforcement.[44]

As a whole they raised two spectres for the legal professions: one

---

[38] See below, pp. 206, 258.

[39] See below, pp. 178–179.

[40] As happened for instance over divorce and other civil jurisdiction, legal education and the treatment of children; see pp. 107, 396–398, 628–629.

[41] Three more academic lawyers were added in 1937 in the hope of speeding progress. The Committee reviewed a number of aspects of what became the Law Reform (Miscellaneous Provisions) Act 1934 and the Law Reform (Married Women and Joint Tortfeasors) Act 1935. (See P.P. 1933–34 [Cmd. 4540, 4546, 4637] XI, 1934–1935 [Cmd. 4770] X) and then reported on limitation of actions, the Statute of Frauds, consideration, frustration and contributory negligence (see P.P. 1936–37 [Cmd. 5449] XIII; 1938–39 [Cmd. 6009, 6032] XII).

[42] The pre-war committee would be revamped in 1952 as a Law Reform Committee, with in addition a Private International Law Committee (1952) and a Criminal Law Revision Committee (1959). Not till 1965, with the establishment of the English and Scottish Law Commissions would law reform come of age. See generally, J. Farrar, Law Reform and the Law Commission (1974) Chap. 1.

[43] See below, pp. 533ff., 396ff.

[44] See below, pp. 184ff., 618–619, 136, 229–230.

was of litigation upon a profit-sharing, "contingent fee" basis—a practice which, despite the temptations to grab cases and win at any cost, was becoming an established feature of litigation in the United States. The other was of a subsidised, state-run service of advice and representation for the poor. Contingent fee practice surfaced, as it was bound to do, within a system which offered the impecunious plaintiff practically no other recourse, and it had its appeal for those at the bottom end of the professions. But to the leaders it was anathema. For the solicitors it raised the old smear of "pettifogging"; for the bar it disturbed the balance between duties to court and client which was considered the nub of the adversarial process.[45] But equally, the prospect of state legal services was disturbing. They could be attacked for their capacity to proliferate unwarranted claims and unjustifiable defences. But their root offence was that they might deprive private practitioners of business.

The royal courts had long provided some means for an utterly poor person to bring a civil action (but not to defend one). By the *in forma pauperis* procedure, if a plaintiff had no assets of more than £5, the Lord Chancellor would assign counsel and attorney to conduct his case for nothing. But fear of vexatious suits had always infected these arrangements: by 1774 the pauper had first to secure counsel's certificate of the merits of the claim, which doubtless called for strong tugs upon the ties of "friendship."[46] Even when the rules were finally reformed in 1883, raising the capital limit to £25 and admitting defendants as well, these preliminaries were made so daunting that the procedure was still used only rarely.[47] On the criminal side, the court again might provide some primitive assistance, nominating a defender from counsel robed in court to any pauper who could raise £1 3s. 6d for a "dock brief." This at least provided an advocate, if not an attorney to seek out evidence.

By these means the courts dispensed a mite of charity through the cooperation of the professions. In the last decades of the century, as the respectable came to their first real perception of urban poverty, "Poor Man's Lawyer" organisations began to offer free advice and sometimes more substantial assistance in working-class neighbourhoods.[48] The mesh of motives behind these initiatives was complex. Much of the most helpful work stemmed from a genuine revulsion against the outworks of industrial progress. There were many lawyers who felt that, as professional men with a protected status, they— or at least their brethren—could do no less. Moreover, since charity was the keynote, the donors could control what was done and so could sift the meritorious from the stirrers of trouble and the artful dodgers. Equally, if there was control—as there was in the advice

---

[45] The common law had long treated maintaining proceedings for another, and—even worse—doing so upon a champertous arrangement to share the proceeds, as a criminal and civil wrong: P. H. Winfield, *The History of Conspiracy and the Abuse of Legal Procedure* (1927) Chap. 6.

[46] Egerton (1946) Chap. 7, who notes that that counsel and attorneys thereafter began to claim fees from the proceeds of successful actions (and costs) brought by paupers.

[47] *Ibid.* pp. 8–9.

[48] They began with the university settlement movement in the East End of London; for an account of 50 years development: *ibid.*, Chap. 5.

organizations—it could ensure that there was no diversion of work that would otherwise be paid for. But the schemes for aid in litigation were run ultimately by the courts, rather than the professions, and accordingly posed some threat to private practice.

Certainly this last consideration dominated Law Society attitudes after 1914 when a revised Poor Persons Procedure[49] coincided with the war-time upsurge in the demand for divorce. The new arrangements placed legal aid for High Court litigation in the hands of a court department but depended on the cooperation of barristers and solicitors prepared to work for nothing.[50] As we shall see,[51] their response fell far short of need; but the Law Society did little enough to encourage change until it was allowed to assume responsibility for the scheme.[52] Once handed over, it set up panels throughout the country which quickly reduced the backlogs. It then insisted, for the rest of the inter-war period, that this scheme should be purely voluntary and should not slide into any form of cut-rate or contingent fee work.[53] By the late 1930s this led the Society into serious conflict with Welsh solicitors, for whom the effects of economic depression were long-lasting. But it maintained its position until the next war brought an even larger wave of demands for divorce.[54] Some form of payment became essential if this work was to be coped with, and during the war itself special departments had to be set up.[55] The Society's longer-term strategy, however, shifted: civil legal aid would become a state-subsidised service for county courts as well as the High Court and above, organised under its aegis and conducted by solicitors in private practice. The inter-war experience put the Society in a strong position to demand what became the crucial features of the modern system, set up in 1949.[56] Both barristers and solicitors were to be paid at something below normal professional rates from government funds. While taking on a new type of state service, the profession was able to preserve the marks of its freedom to a unique degree.

[49] The Poor Person's Rules 1914 were brought into effect only after considerable modification in the light of objections from both professions: Egerton (1946) pp. 10–13; Abel-Smith and Stevens (1967) pp. 140–142.

[50] The new Poor Persons' Department operated by referring applications to barrister and solicitor volunteers for reports, on the basis of which the court decided whether to issue an aid certificate. Applicants had to be worth less than £50, or £100 in special circumstances.

[51] Below, p. 395ff.

[52] For the bargaining of the Society before the Poor Persons' Rules Committee (the second of two under Lawrence J.), see Abel-Smith and Stevens (1967) pp. 147–148 and below, p. 396.

[53] This conviction was (inevitably) shared by the Treasury: P.C. Alcock (1976) 3 Br. J.Leg. St. 151, 165. It carried over into the Final Report of the Finlay Committee on Legal Aid for the Poor, P.P. 1928 [Cmd. 3016] XI, which rejected any state scheme of aid or advice outside the High Court: Kirk (1976), p. 162.

[54] For this, see Egerton (1946), pp. 15–17; Abel-Smith and Stevens (1967), pp. 158–164.

[55] These were established by the Law Society, first for service personnel and subsequently for civilians: Egerton (1946), pp. 18–19.

[56] Legal Aid and Advice Act 1949, based on the recommendations of the Rushcliffe Committee, P.P. 1944–1945 [Cmd. 6641] V. Various European countries and U.S. cities already had more thorough-going provision, as E.J. Cohn's article ((1943) 59 L.Q.R. 250, 359) made clear. For the pressure groups, see Abel-Smith and Stevens (1967), pp. 318–319.

Significantly, the history of aid for criminal defendants took a different course towards its modern form. The Law Society did not find the same need to insist upon control, or upon charity; but then the pool of paying clients was unquestionably restricted. From 1903, the dock brief largely gave way to a system that was in principle more adequate: the magistrates or the trial court could grant representation by both counsel and a solicitor to a poor prisoner being tried on indictment. What is more, the defence became entitled not only to reasonable expenses but to a modest fee, paid for out of local rates.[57] In 1930 the same approach was extended to summary charges when they were unusually grave or otherwise exceptional.[58] The original step in 1903 derived at least part of its support from those who, five years earlier, had secured the criminal defendant's right to give evidence with the purpose of obliging him to submit to cross-examination or risk the consequences. In similar spirit, poor persons' defence was available only to those who would reveal their defence in advance, thus allowing a preliminary judgment upon it and an important advantage to the prosecution. Only a very small proportion of criminal defendants ever sought help on such terms.[59] But the seed was planted for an aid system from public funds and was to grow on the civil side after 1949 and the criminal after 1960. While this became common ground, the separation of the two in terms of administration would persist, the courts continuing in charge of the criminal side, the Law Society of the civil.

(d) Professional Education and Entry

Because law remained a craft mystery practised by the two private professions, new entrants, whatever their social background, had not, in the past, thought to study the subject in advance in any systematic way.[60] If they went to university it was to acquaint themselves with a literary or mathematical guise of gentlemanly learning.[61] Only gradually would those who entered the professions take one of the law degrees which the universities were establishing.[62] For the most part they would acquire their legal knowledge through practical training in articles (solicitors) or pupillage (barris-

---

[57] Poor Prisoners' Defence Act 1903. For details of the scheme, Egerton (1945), pp. 20–22.

[58] Poor Prisoners' Defence Act 1930, based upon the First Report of the Finlay Committee on Legal Aid for the Poor, P.P. [1926] Cmd. 2638 XIII. The Committee rejected the creation of a Public Defender as too expensive and difficult. For the background, see Abel-Smith and Stevens (1967), pp. 153–156.

[59] See Abel-Smith and Stevens (1967), pp. 152–153.

[60] See above, pp. 49–50, 52.

[61] In the nineteenth century, over half the bar would be graduates, the proportion of attorneys and solicitors much smaller: R. Abel (1986) 49 M.L.R. 3, 4; and Abel (1988) Tables 2.2, 2.3

[62] The provincial universities—starting with Manchester, Birmingham, Bristol, Exeter—would introduce law teaching, mainly for Law Society examinations and only in the new century.

ters),[63] and through undertaking the professional examinations. The solicitors, it will be recalled, had introduced examinations with some eagerness, the bar with measured disdain. These attitudes would carry forward. In 1877, the Law Society succeeded in gaining control of the solicitors' qualifying examinations.[64] This led to a raising of pass levels and some increase in the Society's lecturing, by extending it from London to a number of provincial centres.[65] In 1903 it established a School of Law in London[66]; and in 1922, upon the initiative of its head, Professor Edward Jenks, attendance at lectures was made a pre-requisite to entering the examinations.[67] This in turn led to Law Society activity not only in maintaining provincial lectures of its own but in fostering law teaching in local universities.[68] The teaching was towards its own examinations and made considerable use of part-time instruction by members of the profession. It was a development which left the Law Society largely in control but brought a decorous association with higher learning.

The bar, on the other hand, was frequently pressed, within and without, to adopt an educational plan of greater purpose.[69] In particular, the notion of a legal university in London refused to die away: first an "Albert University" was proposed with King's and University Colleges (1884); then University College sought a charter for a separate university (the "Gresham" charter) and wanted collaboration with the Inns and the Law Society (1891); the Herschell Commissioners, appointed to reorganize the University of London, sought to attract in the Inns by offering them a very considerable measure of autonomy to run a law school (1899). Nothing transpired, for in each case there proved to be intransigent hostility in some quarter of the Inns. It was built upon the combined beliefs that external schools could not profess to teach what was needed, that the true skills of the advocate could be learned only by practice, that any collaboration might lead to a combination of education with solicitors, which in turn might threaten the separate existence of the bar; and that outside education might in the end provoke a scramble of entrants such as had occurred fifty years before. The bar continued to prefer its rather feeble examination system, for which scant teaching would suffice, knowing that launching a career in any case depended upon finding a place in chambers and attracting work through the clerk and solicitors. A Committee under Lord Atkin in 1934 quickly

---

[63] Even pupillage was not strictly required until 1959. While the earlier nineteenth century practice may have been for a long pupillage (two years), it seems that the habit dwindled: Abel (1986, above, n. 61).

[64] Abel-Smith and Stevens (1967), pp. 169–170; Abel (1988), Table 2.10.

[65] Birmingham, Liverpool, Manchester and Newcastle were the first such centres: *ibid.*, pp. 170, 178.

[66] For preceding attempts to secure that some of the sums resulting from selling off the old Inns of Chancery should be devoted to professional education, see Abel-Smith and Stevens (1967), pp. 174–175.

[67] Solicitors Act 1922, s.2, exempting (after a determined campaign) managing clerks admitted under the 10-year rule established in 1860 (above, p. 52, n. 97), those with approved degrees and those geographically remote.

[68] In London, however, the private school, Gibson & Weldon, attracted more candidates than the Law Society's School. The two were not merged until 1962.

[69] See generally, Abel-Smith and Stevens (1967), pp. 168–180.

concluded that legal education needed no basic improvement, and certainly no real enhancement of the provision in the universities.[70]

(e) Accountability to the Public

The Law Society had one further objective in the cause of autonomy, and this for a particular reason. Monopoly brought with it some public accountability for charges to clients and the professional body could never hope to bring the systems of taxing fees[71] within its own control. But it did seek a role in disciplining solicitors who had defalcated or otherwise been guilty of professional misconduct. The bar, after all, dealt with such matters itself through the benchers of the Inns[72]; yet solicitors came before the judges. No publicity could better stoke the fires of derision and mistrust. The change was not easily secured from Parliament: in 1888, the Law Society was permitted a committee to conduct preliminary investigations of alleged misconduct before any airing in open court; but not until 1919 did a Disciplinary Committee of Law Society Council members take over the whole matter, subject to a right of appeal to the High Court.[73]

It was a true investiture of respectability achieved despite a regular trickle of disenrolments. At the turn of the century, indeed, there had been a number of prominent scandals[74] and the Society was obliged to seek power to refuse an annual practising certificate to solicitors who were undischarged bankrupts.[75] In 1907 an internal committee favoured a stringent series of measures in the keeping of accounts, including a separate clients' account for moneys held on trust and (by a majority) the annual auditing of books. It was not however until after the Solicitors Act 1933, when the Society finally acquired power to prescribe rules of good conduct, that the first of these proposals was implemented; and the second came only in 1945.[76] It was always difficult to persuade the membership that business practices which ought to have been regarded as common precaution should be imposed by rule, even one that was internally agreed.[77]

---

[70] Committee on Legal Education, P.P. 1934 [Cmd. 4663] XI. The Committee was established by Sankey L.C. upon the urgings of Professor Harold Laski that England needed an equivalent of the Harvard Law School. The Committee did urge the creation of an Institute of Advanced Legal Studies; in 1948, the University of London undertook this.

[71] For which, see above, p. 50, n. 83.

[72] Formal disciplining through disbarring or other penalties was very rare, the spokesmen of the bar making much of the informal pressures that arose from Inn and bar mess life, together with the constant overseeing by judges in court: Duman (1983) pp. 34–37.

[73] See generally Kirk (1976) Chap. 4; Abel-Smith and Stevens (1967), pp. 188–190; Abel (1986 above, n. 61).

[74] Including one ex-president of the Law Society; see Kirk (1976), pp. 97–99.

[75] Solicitors Act 1906. It also promoted the Larceny Act 1901, making fraudulent conversion of funds held by an agent an offence.

[76] Birks (1960), pp. 273–275, Kirk (1976), pp. 105–106. In 1943 a compulsory compensation fund was established by the Law Society: Abel-Smith and Stevens (1967), p. 192.

[77] Kirk (1976), pp. 100–105; Birks (1960), pp. 272–275.

(f) Relations between the Two Professions

As free professions, both barristers and solicitors offered their services to the public at large. Accordingly, they played down the extent to which some among them might do all or most of their work for particular clients.[78] But the structures within which they maintained this freedom were at once different and interdependent: accordingly they were always a potential source of friction. The bar pursued its individualism to the extent of precluding partnerships.[79] At the same time its work depended largely on introduction from solicitors. The exposure to risk which stemmed from this combination made the bar most reluctant to acknowledge, as a strict rule of etiquette, that solicitors were their only source of clients.[80]

To keep the matter equivocal at least provided ammunition if the solicitors should attack other points along the existing line of understandings. Of these the most vital was the bar's exclusive right of audience in most superior courts: its preserve included not only the royal courts of justice but assizes and those quarter sessions where the bar had asserted itself by regular attendance. With this the solicitors were never entirely happy and watched for chances of circumvention. The moves to increase the monetary limits to county court jurisdiction and to pass divorce work down to these courts were obvious instances.[81] On a lesser scale, the solicitors fought for and eventually obtained certain rights to appear at quarter sessions on licensing appeals and then rating assessment appeals.[82]

With grudges about the distribution of work between the professions went an irritation over the barriers placed by the benchers of the Inns in the way of a solicitor switching to the bar. A certain looseness in the relationship had survived into the eighteenth century, when the Bar had seen to it that attorneys were wholly excluded from the Inns of Court.[83] This had been followed by a tightening of the requirement that, before applying for admission as a student of an Inn, an attorney must cease to practise and have his name removed from the roll. In the name of preventing any partisanship for former clients (or favoritism from them), the effective waiting period had,

[78] The bar insisted that only those who engaged in free practice could enjoy its rights of audience. But it did not restrain such practices as the payment of retainers by clients to secure the services of counsel over time. Solicitors in the service of a business or government had only to take out a certificate in order to preserve their right of practice.

[79] Victorian barristers mostly worked alone with their own clerks; gradually chambers sharing a clerk developed, though sets were typically only of four or five in the 1930s: Cocks (1983), p. 9; Duman (1983), p. 83.

[80] In mid-nineteenth century, while this was the general practice for superior court work, it did not wholly prevail in the criminal and bankruptcy courts. Even when the Bar Committee acknowledged it as the rule for contentious work in 1888, subsequent statements would not be so unequivocal: see Kirk (1976), pp. 172–174; Abel-Smith and Stevens (1967), p. 222.

[81] See above, p. 94, below, p. 394.

[82] See Abel-Smith and Stevens (1967), pp. 236–238; Kirk (1976), pp. 155–162.

[83] See Kirk (1976), pp. 22–23. The attorneys and solicitors were thus left to make use of the Inns of Chancery; these however were always too small and local to serve as a professional institution; hence their winding up in the late nineteenth century (see above, n. 66).

after 1834, become a prohibitive five years. In the 1870s the Law Society kept up pressure on the subject, itself improving the ability of barristers to become solicitors and then demanding reciprocal advantages. Under threat of legislation, the Inns eventually altered the position so that a solicitor of five years' standing could sit the bar's final examination after one year's wait.[84] The difference was reduced, but continued to rub, along with a number of other aggravations: the various practices by which the bar sought to spread (and to increase) its work; the peculiar condescension which left counsel free from obligation to appear on a brief and under no liability for negligence; above all, the exclusive entitlement to all the senior and many intermediate judicial offices, at home and in the colonies— leading to suspicions that, whenever new posts were created, the bar employed its parliamentary strength to annex them for itself.

As the junior branch, the solicitors undoubtedly had the more immediate need of a professional body to defend its interests and in the 1870s the Law Society was able to confirm its primacy by absorbing its most substantial rival, the Metropolitan and Provincial Law Association.[85] By the eighties there were sectors of the bar which were becoming distrustful of their leaders' organisations. The Inns were becoming more remote, since, with the disbanding of Sergeants' Inn at the time of the Judicature Acts, the judges were returning to the Inn benches. When accordingly the Rules Committee of the Supreme Court chose to tackle the rising costs of litigation by clipping away at the procedural luxuriance which was such a stay to the junior bar, it suddenly realised how ill-represented it was. It insisted on forming a Bar Committee, which would be consulted before similar changes were made in future. Pressure followed on the benchers to convert the Committee into a Bar Council which could represent the whole bar and which would have the financial support of the Inns. In 1895 this arrangement was finally conceded in grudging terms chiefly notable for the undertakings not to trespass upon the traditional pastures of the Inns' authority: admissions, formal discipline, education. The Council survived in this ancillary form since it proved a useful channel by which to decide questions needing a single voice—for instance, upon matters of bar etiquette—and through which to negotiate such issues as it suited the Inns to have it settle.[86]

The bar could afford so conservative a response because in the end it faced little more than niggling at the margins. The grand issue of fusion with the solicitors, though it had occurred in some of the colonies and in the United States, refused stubbornly to take hold in the home of the common law. It could not go entirely undiscussed. There were moments of special uncertainty in the bar's history when its less assured members began to feel the attractions of partnership and

---

[84] See Kirk (1976), pp. 179–181; Abel-Smith and Stevens (1967), pp. 226–227; Abel (1988), Table 1.9. The period became six months in 1928.

[85] See above, p. 52.

[86] See generally, Abel-Smith and Stevens (1967), pp. 211–220: Duman (1983), pp. 68–71; these developments made it harder to distinguish the organs of the bar from trade unions than it had been for Dicey, writing in the *Fortnightly Review* in 1867: Cocks (1983), pp. 127–130.

direct access to clients. Outsiders, who naturally tended to doubt a professional division which doubled the manpower engaged in higher litigation, were likely to stir the pot at such times: and so did *The Times* in a substantial article in 1884. Calls for fusion were also likely to find a response amongst the upper echelons of solicitors, always well-represented on the Law Society. Yet the bar did not have to reckon on serious difficulty from the lower branch. For when the Law Society did test the issue among its members there proved to be a consistent majority against fusion. The smaller firms and one-man offices saw their guarantee of independence from their larger brethren in their ability to obtain expert advice and aid from counsel.[87]

The ideal of liberty had its workings at every level of professional arrangement. It could scarcely fail to colour judgment upon larger issues, social and political. Samuel Smiles had taken the lawyer as the epitome of Modern Man Self-helped by "plodding industry."[88] The attitudes and assumptions behind such achievements were likely only to intensify in a world moving towards political democracy, collective labour and social support of the poorest by the wealthy.

VI. IDEOLOGIES AND DEMOCRACY

We return finally to the larger world of ideas and the place within it of thinking about law and legal institutions. The democracy heralded in 1867 would produce not only the realignments of a propertied class facing a wage-earning class but a broader ideological shift towards collectivist organisation. To conservers of the older liberal tradition, like Dicey, the new prospects of state regulation and direction were an incoherent but many-sided threat posed by legislative interference, bureaucratic inspection, "gas-and-water" municipal socialism, the increasingly defiant organisation of labour and the emergence of an Independent Labour Party. Collectivism, said Dicey, was "rather a sentiment than a doctrine," a current of opinion that could not be "connected with the name of any one definite school."[89] It was, of course, Dicey's mission to parade the influence of "Benthamite individualism" upon thinking and events in the preceding period and it is always easier to impose unitary causal explanations upon the course of the past than upon the confusing ebb and flow of the present. But for his distaste, he might have allowed more for the deep earnestness with which many in his own time not only furthered campaigns of social reform, but sought a justification for their programmes in philosophic or economic theory.

Their anxious studies were the product of revelations about the underside of industrial society. These came of age in detailed surveys of working-class households by Booth and Rowntree. They were supplemented by the personal experience of "East-ending" at Canon Barnett's Toynbee Hall and the university settlements and the sight

---

[87] Abel-Smith and Stevens (1967), pp. 227–230, 235–236.
[88] See *Self-Help* (1859) Chap. 7. Certainly not *Woman*, whom both the Inns and the Law Society kept from admission before 1918: see *The Times*, December 3, 1905 (refusal to admit Bertha Cave to Gray's Inn); *Bebb* v. *Law Society* [1914] 1 Ch. 286.
[89] Dicey (1914), pp. 64–65, 67.

of meetings and demonstrations by the unemployed. They were part of a wealthier, more experienced and more sceptical world, one less frightened of immediate violence but more aware of gulfs that might in the end mean deeper subversion. No longer was there so easy an acceptance of that rather blinkered calculation of human affairs which put its faith in functioning of free markets. J. S. Mill, in restating classical political economy upon a presumption of non-interference by government, had found a growing range of justifications for overturning the presumption, and his influence for a modified liberalism was very considerable.

Of the many manifestations of classical economics, Malthus's answer to the threat of rising population—that the fittest must be left to survive—had subsequently found wider intellectual repercussions. From it had stemmed the proofs of biological evolution provided by Charles Darwin and T. H. Huxley; and from them in turn came interpretations of the development of societies in evolutionary terms. To neo-Malthusians, such as Herbert Spencer, further progress demanded an even greater withdrawal of the state.[90] But many others would argue the converse: that the state must use its authority to advance the coming of a condition in which wealth and life chances were more evenly distributed among the population as a whole. Indeed to those drawn to the potentially sinister science of eugenics, that authority might be harnessed to biological improvement of the national stock, at least to the extent of preventing the feeble-minded, habitually criminal and mentally disturbed from reproducing themselves, and of excluding incursions of aliens.[91]

Ideas of historical progression, broadly affinitive in character, informed the positivist philosophy of Auguste Comte. He saw morality moving from a theological beginning, through a metaphysical staging-post to a scientific end-point, in which tenets would be tested by "positive," rational enquiry, and which could encompass even a religion of common humanity. In the 1860s and 70s his ideas would enjoy a considerable English following, led by academic figures such as Richard Congreve and Frederic Harrison.[92]

Comte was heir to the rationality of the French enlightenment, Karl Marx to the shrouded metaphysics of Hegel. In Marx, historical evolution became a dialectic struggle between social classes formed from

[90] See, in particular, *Social Statics* (1851), *Synthetic Philosophy* (10 vols. 1862–96), *The Man versus the State* (1884); for which see J. F. Burrow, *Evolution and Society* (1968) Chap. 6. His position was given political focus in the 1880s by the Liberty and Property Defence League (for which, see E. Bristow (1975) 18 Hist. J. 761) and for a leading luminary, C. Fairfield, *A Memoir of Lord Bramwell* (1898)). Even more extreme liberals approached an anarchism which nonetheless remained distinct from that of figures on the far left such as William Morris: see Barker (1978) pp. 50–60, 71–79.

[91] See, *e.g.*, C. D. Darlington, *Genetics and Man* (1966) Chaps. 13, 14; G. R. Searle, *Eugenics and Politics in Britain 1900–1914* (1976). In different ways, the concern for the condition of the national stock touched the Webbs, G. B. Shaw and H. G. Wells. Its legal repercussions can be seen in the conversion of incest into a common law crime and the measure for putting away habitual criminals in 1908, and the restriction of alien immigration in 1905; see below, pp. 611–613.

[92] Harriet Martineau, the economic publicist, was the first to provide an English paraphrase of Comte's ideas; and J. S. Mill lent a generally sympathetic weight to their spread (*Auguste Comte and Positivism* (1865)). See generally, M. S. Vogeler, *Frederic Harrison* (1984).

the very modes of economic organisation. Using essentially the tools of the English political economists, he re-analysed elements in industrial capitalism to show an expropriation by the bourgeois owners of the surplus value of labour; but the process of competition must in time squeeze the amount thus made available for the formation of new capital; inevitably a crisis must occur—indeed in the most developed economies it was imminent—from which the working class would emerge to claim their real share of value and so be released from wage slavery to personal fulfilment. In the wake of this revolution, the state and law, instruments of bourgeois domination, would wither.

As Marx was translated from the German, he was studied in intellectual circles as one source of inspiration for the fight against the grossly unequal capitalist condition.[93] But he was read together with, for instance, the Gotha Programme of the German Social Democrats and with O'Brien, Henry George and other nationalisers or capital taxers of land.[94] Marxist ideas acquired a following in the Social Democratic Foundation, founded and dominated by H. M. Hyndman, and in some of the splinter movements from it.[95] But any real presence would have to await the creation of the British Communist Party in the wake of the Russian Revolution.[96] The socialism of the Fabian Society, as it came under the leadership of Sidney Webb, was a pragmatic programme of amelioration by the increasing intervention of the state, which was at no great remove from the thinking of radical liberals.[97]

By and large those who took an intelligent interest in social issues were in search of ways of adapting and conditioning the known world of private property and free contract; they were at least suspicious of any dramatic breach with that present. Moderate radicals of a theoretical cast of mind might accordingly be drawn to the teaching of the Oxford philosopher, T. H. Green and his Balliol circle. As with Marx, Green was led away from what appeared a calculating opportunism in utilitarian thought to seek more fundamental values in German idealist philosophy. His concern remained essentially with the conditions for the fulfilment of individual moral choice. In arguing that a society must act to secure the basic conditions that would make such choice meaningful for each member within it he was seeking to preserve the essence of individualism in a "positive liberty."[98] Many who were not attracted by the philosophic underpinning, welcomed the justification of state intervention, whatever its effect upon a strict freedom of contract, to secure public health by

[93] See, *e.g.*, S. Pierson, *Marxism and the Origins of British Socialism* (1973); K. Willis (1977) 20 Hist. J. 417.
[94] See above, pp. 73–74 and below, pp. 169–170; N. and J. Mackenzie, *The First Fabians* (1977) Chap. 4; A. M. MacBriar, *Fabian Socialism and English Politics 1884–1918* (1958).
[95] See C. Tsuzuki, *H.M. Hyndman and British Socialism* (1961); H. Collins in A. Briggs and J. Saville (eds.) *Essays in Labour History 1886–1923* (1971), p. 47; Barry (1965) pp. 136–144.
[96] For which, see J. Klugmann, *History of Communist Party of Great Britain* (1980).
[97] Mackenzie (above, n. 94) Chap. 7.
[98] *Liberal Legislation and Freedom of Contract* (1880); *Principles of Political Obligation* (1886); M. Richter *The Politics of Conscience* (1964); D. Nicholls (1962) 56 Am. Pol. Sc. R. 97.

slum clearance and house-building, to promote moral well-being by supporting temperance and above all to provide compulsory education so that all children might escape "that kind of ignorance which practically excludes them from a free career in life."[99]

Green was to influence some of the coming Liberal leaders—among them Milner, Asquith and Haldane—but he remained a somewhat withdrawn academic figure.[1] In the next generation the revision of liberalism, shorn of idealist preamble, was argued forcefully, in the press as well as more scholarly books, by the sociologist, Leonard Hobhouse and the economist, J. A. Hobson.[2] Hobhouse saw a process of growth from a world of myriad individual relationships through the development of associations such as trade unions and trading cooperatives, all of them voluntary collaborations, to association at national level expressed in legislation: legal regulation of activity by the state was thus a higher condition of what had gone before, higher because it replaced the debilitating inequities of the competitive order. If this was socialism it was a liberal form, distinct from a Marxian socialism devoted to state ownership of the means of production and distribution and to exploitation through central planning. Equally it was distinct from the "official socialism" (promoted by the Webbs and other Fabians) in which the dedicated expert became the essential creator and manipulator of social progress. It was, in other words, an attempt to articulate a distinct liberal position among political theories all of which accepted a very substantial role for collective organization in modern industrial society.[3] In any state which was to surrender or qualify the self-generative mechanisms of the market, the expert administrator was destined to assume a position of leadership. A figure of Platonic ancestry, he had appeared as the founder of Owenite communities and the priest in the Comteian religion of humanity. He was undoubtedly an important figure in the thinking of many Edwardians who worked on plans for educational and social reform.

His appearance was as likely in the thinking of the right as of the left: immense in his denunciation of liberal capitalism, Thomas Carlyle had been equally massive in admiration of leaders of Hegelian stature, such as Cromwell and Frederick the Great.[4] Legal scholars, who remained faithful to the philosophic roots of Benthamism, nevertheless drew from them markedly anti-populist conclusions. Maine despaired of democracy as a cloak for petty corruption and party manipulation; it led, if not to repressive autocracy, then to intervention in ways which stultified the original, progressive ideas of the creative few.[5] This was an argument for entrusting govern-

---

[99] Green (1880, above, n. 98).
[1] B. Semmel, *The Rise of Free Trade Imperialism* (1970); H. G. C. Matthew, *The Liberal Imperialists* (1973).
[2] For their relationship and generally, see P. F. Clarke, *Liberals and Social Democrats* (1978); M. Freeden, *The New Liberalism* (1978); S. Collini, *Liberalism and Sociology* (1978); P. Weiler, *The New Liberalism* (1982).
[3] See, esp. *Liberalism* (1911); *Social Evolution and Political Theory* (1922); and in Various, *Property: its Duties and Rights* (1913) Chap. 13.
[4] See B. E. Lippincott, *Victorian Critics of Democracy: Carlyle, Ruskin, Arnold, Maine, Stephen, Lecky* (1938).
[5] See esp. *Popular Government* (1885); J. W. Burrow (above, n. 90) Chap. 5; G. Feaver, *From Status to Contract* (1969), pp. 227–242; R. Cocks, *Sir Henry Maine* (1988).

ment to an enlightened oligarchy. FitzJames Stephen, equally from a utilitarian foundation, glorified the enlightenment of a great imperial power such as Britain and saw in its influence alone the hope of improving the condition of the native peoples over whom sovereignty was so largely asserted.[6] Dicey deplored the collectivist consequences of expanding the electorate; and he became an obsessed campaigner against Irish Home Rule, in his eyes a semi-independence which would muddy the responsibilities of sovereign power.[7]

There remained, however, a polar distance between such castes of mind, which conceived the wise to know both the limits and necessities of government, and that of the Fabians (or at least the more consistent of them), intent on using the power of government for social betterment. The Webbs, for instance, saw the need for democratic participation, but wanted it carefully conditioned: expert central planning under the general authority of Parliament was appropriate for national needs; local decision-making should be by units of area large enough to provide all the necessary services, spread the burden of rates and avoid petty dog-fights and self-aggrandisement. It was not enough to adopt Hobhouse's optimism over the democratic expression of the general will; there must be careful calculation—expressed in legislation—of the relation between centre and localities, and between elected representatives and salaried bureaucrats.[8]

There was however a novel and quite separate dimension to arguments about the future of democracy. Collectivities distinct from political institutions and their franchises had arisen to advance mutual interests in myriad ways: institutes and committees of agricultural, industrial and financial interests, chambers of commerce, cartels, professional bodies, trade unions, friendly societies, building societies, religious, charitable, cultural and learned bodies—all these and more lobbied constantly for or against legislation and the activities of executive government, and negotiated with opposed interests and with consumers (so far as they had any coherent voice). A world of cohesions seemed to be arriving in which the individual's real hopes for personal security and satisfaction lay in his membership of the mutual interest groups to which he most naturally affiliated.

From various points of the political spectrum there was accordingly interest in pluralist theories that would accurately and helpfully express this new complexity. In Britain they would not, however, receive the extensive treatment that was to be found among French writers such as the jurist, Duguit, the sociologist, Durkheim, or the political theorist, Sorel. Juristic interest flourished particularly in F. W. Maitland's subtle historical investigations of mutual association and his interest in legal recognition for collectivities as they arose.[9]

[6] For Stephen, see J. A. Coliaco, *James Fitzjames Stephen and the Crisis of Victorian Thought* (1983); E. Stokes, *The English Utilitarians and India* (1959) Chap. 4.3; and for the connection between idealism and imperialism, his lecture, *The Political Ideas of English Imperialism* (1960). The prime critic in the period was J. A. Hobson, *Imperialism* (1902); see Clarke, above, n. 2, Chap. 3.

[7] See R. A. Cosgrove, *The Rule of Law* (1981) Chaps. 6, 7, 10.

[8] Their most extensive proposals (with strong pluralist leanings) were in *A Constitution for the Socialist Commonwealth of Great Britain* (1920).

[9] See below, p. 332, and Maitland's Introduction to O. Von Gierke, *Political Theories of the Middle Ages* (1900) and *Collected Papers* (1911), III pp. 210–404.

For a time Harold Laski was engaged against the idealist buttressing of the state as an over-competent sovereign; he sought a balance that would decentralize power in the interests of both groups and individuals.[10] At the level of political activism, union leaders after 1910 were turned by Tom Mann and Ben Tillett towards notions of syndicalist organisation in which workers were chiefly represented through their unions in political as well as economic matters, and the institutions of democracy became proportionately less significant.[11] In place of political lobbying there would be collective bargaining, in place of legislation the adhesion contract.

On the continent of Europe, the thrust of such thinking would have immense consequences in the inter-war period. States which abjured the centrist socialism of the Russian example were turned by Fascist leaders towards forms of mass organisation which replaced democratic politics with the solidarities of workplace and militaristic groups. In Britain, the experience of representative government proved sufficient for its institutions to survive as vital organs of the state.[12] The shop stewards movement, which during the first War marked an advance for the syndicalist cause, lost way as the unions sensed the chance of a Labour party victory at the polls.[13]

The minority Labour governments of 1924 and 1929 were achievements scarcely conceivable before the War. At the same time, the electoral course of the period showed that the working class was by no means a solid rank behind the workers' party and was unlikely to become so in the foreseeable future. The Labour Party's leaders and theorists stood a considerable distance from root-and-branch rejection of capitalist, market organisation. Under Ramsay MacDonald, the Party's manifestos proclaimed a new society in which the chances of benefit would be more evenly distributed, an achievement to be sought by experimentation and through democratically elected institutions.[14] The party looked for intellectual guidance to such men as the English Weberian, R. H. Tawney, who drew inspiration both from the Christian socialism of F. D. Maurice and Canon Scott Holland and from the anti-materialism of Ruskin and J. A. Hobson. He taught the need for moral re-direction away from selfish acquisition and socially irresponsible use of wealth. This re-direction must come from an internal co-operation, democratically expressed. There could be no quick solution through the medium of central state socialism; Tawney saw greater hope in the pluralist notion of professional and guild associations as guardians of enlightened stan-

---

[10] *Studies in the Problems of Sovereignty* (1917).
[11] See B. Holton, *British Syndicalism 1900–1914* (1976). Also significant in the pre-1914 years, were the distributist ideas of Hilaire Belloc and G. K. Chesterton, the associated hostility to government interference of Stephen Reynolds and the ideas of G. D. H. Cole and other Guild Socialists. See Barker (1978) pp. 63–65, 84–91, 98–104.
[12] For Mosley's British Fascist Party in the 1930s see R. Benewick, *The Fascist Movement in Britain* (1972).
[13] On this period, see M. Cowling, *The Impact of Labour 1920–24* (1971).
[14] For MacDonald's thought, see R. Barker in A.J.A. Morris (ed.) *Edwardian Radicalism 1900–1914* (1974). And see the Labour Party documents, *Labour and the Social Order* (1918—mainly by Sidney Webb), *Labour and the Nation* (1928—mainly MacDonald); Barry (1965), pp. 203–205, 280–284.

dards and conduct.[15] In counter-balance, Harold Laski had moved on from his examination of pluralist political theory to assert that, while groups had an important role to play, they could not be left as ultimate repositories of power. The democratic state must be the consumers' arbiter of the claims of producer organisations.[16]

Already during the second Labour government, there were signs that, in the competition among political theories, those favouring elite direction over democratic choice were in the ascendant. Herbert Morrison, as Minister of Transport, created for the metropolis a London Passenger Transport Board.[17] It was to be a significant precursor of post-1945 events—the nationalisation of industries under boards and councils, the introduction of extensive social security arrangements under a new ministry, the creation of a national health service in which the serving experts—doctors, dentists, pharmacists—would gain a significant place in decision-making.[18]

Political organisation was for many an adjunct to more fundamental plans—social policies which would secure to all a "national minimum of support," economic policies by which government would adjust and direct the course of events and private enterprise would be subjected to a very different wave motion from the crests and troughs of free market capitalism. In these fields, the moulders of opinion who came to consolidate leading positions in the 1930s were the social planner, William Beveridge, and the economist, Maynard Keynes. During the second war, as the Labour party under Attlee not only joined in coalition government but planned for electoral victory once peace was restored, it drew heavily on the proposals of these two men, for all their old associations with Liberal legislation and policy. Beveridge's celebrated report of 1942 laid the foundations for a universalist system of basic social security[19]; Keynes not only promised the public, but was beginning to persuade the Treasury, that government intervention in the economy could secure full employment as the basic guarantee of a quite novel prosperity for the mass of people.[20]

A weary but victorious Britain was ready in 1945 to trust the party which more evidently planned to use the powers of the state to intervene on a quite new scale in stimulating growth and protecting those in need. Despite the memories of inter-war depression, it was commonly assumed that Britain would emerge as one of the richest, most productive, most advanced nations, supported in her position by a large empire, which would resolve into a commonwealth of associated nations. Equally it was supposed that the private enterprise centre of the economy would remain intact. Accordingly the old need for a legal system which protected private property and gave cer-

---

[15] See esp. *The Acquisitive Society* (1921); *Equality* (1931).

[16] *A Grammar of Politics* (1925); *Parliamentary Government in England* (1938); B. Zylstra, *From Pluralism to Collectivism* (1968).

[17] The model was the Conservatives' Central Electricity Board of 1926; see Barry (1965), pp. 290–294.

[18] See below, p. 468ff.

[19] See below, pp. 464–466.

[20] See R. Skidelsky in W. Mommsen (ed.) *The Emergence of the Welfare State in Britain and Germany* (1981) Chap. 9; P. F. Clarke, *The Keynesian Revolution in the Making* (1988).

tainty to transactions and transfers that concerned property would continue unabated. But there would be points at which the old enthusiasms for leaving individuals to operate these legal safeguards to their personal advantage would have to give place to overriding regulation in aid of the weak, the oppressed, the ignorant. Legislation—the great formal instrument of intervention—would mould, constrain, encourage as never before. It would give bureaucracies wide, but by no means unlimited or unsupervised, powers of intervention and discretionary judgment.

In each of the succeeding chapters we pursue the process of legal change to this peculiar point of historical flux, observing how it responded to, and to some extent constrained, social shifts and economic developments. For optimists and radicals this recovery from war was a moment of immense opportunity, a chance to harness the resources of the state towards a true collectivity. For pessimists and conservatives, the task of rebuilding was intrinsically hard, and made even more difficult by the new determination to constrain the capitalist economy by ideas of social responsibility. Ground positions were being laid for great conflicts of modern Britain.

FURTHER READING

Government, Politics and Law

Cannan, E., *The History of Local Rates in England* (2nd ed., 1912).

Emy, H.V., *Liberals, Radicals and Social Policy* (1974).

Finer, S.E., *The Life and Times of Sir Edwin Chadwick* (1952).

Hart, J., "Nineteenth Century Social Reform: A Tory Interpretation" (1965) 31 P. & P. 39.

Hume, L., *Bentham and Bureaucracy* (1979).

Lubenow, W.C., *The Politics of Government Growth* (1971).

McDonagh, O., *Early Victorian Government* (1977).

McDonagh, O., "The Nineteenth-Century Revolution in Government: A Reappraisal" (1958) 1 Hist.J. 52.

Parris, H., *Constitutional Bureaucracy* (1969).

Parris, H., "The Nineteenth Century Revolution in Government: A Reappraisal" (1960) 3 Hist. J. 17.

Roberts, D., *Victorian Origins of the British Welfare State* (1960).

Sabine, B.E.V., *A History of the Income Tax* (1966).

Thomas, M.W., "The Origins of Administrative Centralization" [1950] C.L.P. 214.

Webb, S. & B., *English Local Government: I The Parish and the County* (1906); II–III *The Manor and the Borough* (1908).

Legal system, judiciary and legal professions

Abel, R., *The Legal Profession in England and Wales* (1988).

Abel-Smith, B. and Stevens, R.B., *Lawyers and the Courts* (1967).

Allsop, P. (ed.), *Then and Now* (1970): Simpson, A. W. B., "The Survival of the Common Law System" (Chap 3); Jacob, I.H., "Civil Procedure since 1800" (Chap. 8).

Arthurs, H.W., *"Without the Law": Administrative Justice and Legal Pluralism in Nineteenth-Century England* (1985).

Baker, J.H., *An Introduction to English Legal History* (2nd ed., 1979).
Birks, M., *Gentlemen of the Law* (1960).
Blackstone, Sir W., *Commentaries on the Laws of England* (1765–69).
Cocks, R., *The Foundations of the Modern Bar* (1983).
Dawson, J.P., *A History of Lay Judges* (1960).
de Smith, S.A., *Judicial Review of Administrative Action* (5th ed., by J. M. Evans, 1980), App. I.
Dicey, A.V., *Law and Public Opinion in England in the Nineteenth Century* (2nd ed., 1914).
Duman, D., *The Judicial Bench in England 1727–1875* (1982).
Duman, D., *The English and Colonial Bars in the Nineteenth Century* (1983).
Duncan, G.I.O., *The High Court of Delegates* (1971).
Edwards, J.L.J., *The Law Officers of the Crown* (1964).
Egerton, R., *Legal Aid* (1946).
Fifoot, C.H.S., *Judge and Jurist in the Reign of Victoria* (1959).
Green, T.A., *Verdict according to Conscience* (1985).
Holmes, G., *The Augustan Age* (1982) Chap. 5.
Holdsworth, Sir W., *A History of English Law* (1903–72) esp. vols. I, XV.
Howell, P.A., *The Judicial Committee of the Privy Council 1833–1876* (1979).
Ilbert, Sir C., *Legislative Methods and Forms* (1901).
Jackson, R.M., *The Machinery of Justice in England* (7th ed., 1977).
Kirk. H., *Portrait of a Profession* (1976).
Larson, M.S., *The Rise of Professionalism* (1974).
Laski, H.J. "The Technique of Judicial Appointment" in *Studies in Law and Politics* (1932) Chap. 7.
Manchester, A.H., *Modern Legal History of England and Wales* (1980) Chs.
Moir, E., *The Justices of the Peace* (1969).
Offer, A., *Property and Politics* (1981).
Radcliffe, G.R.Y. and Cross, G., *The English Legal System* (5th ed., 1971).
Reader, W.J., *Professional Men* (1966).
Robson, R., *The Attorney in Eighteenth Century England* (1959).
Rubin, G.R., and Sugerman, D. (eds.), *Law, Economy and Society 1750–1914* (1984).
Stevens, R.B., *Law and Politics* (1970).
Winder, W.H.D., "The Courts of Requests" (1936) 52 L.Q.R. 369.
Wiswall, F.L., *The Development of Admiralty Jurisdiction and Practice since 1800* (1970).

Ideas and Law

Atiyah, P.S., *The Rise and Fall of Freedom of Contract* (1979).
Barker, R., *Political Ideas in Modern Britain* (1978).
Barry, E. E., *Nationalisation in British Politics* (1965).
Beer, M., *History of British Socialism* (1919).
Bradley, I., *The Call to Seriousness* (1976).
Clark, J.C.D., *English Society, 1688–1832* (1985).
Cole, G.D.H., *History of Socialist Thought* (1953–1960) I–V.

Dickinson, H.J., *Liberty and Property* (1977).
Greenleaf, W.H., *The British Political Tradition* (1983).
Halévy, E., *The Growth of Philosophic Radicalism* (1928).
Houghton, W.E., *The Victorian Frame of Mind, 1830–1870* (1957).
Kitson Clark, G., *The Making of Victorian England* (1962).
McGregor, O.R., *Social History and Law Reform* (1981).
Perkin, H., *The Origins of Modern English Society* (1969).
Roll, E., *History of Economic Thought*, (2nd ed., 1953).
Roberts, D., *Paternalism in Early Victorian England* (1979).
Taylor, A.J., *Laissez-faire and State Intervention in Nineteenth-century Britain* (1972).
Thompson, E.P., *The Making of the English Working-Class* (1963; rev. ed. 1968).

General

There is a great range of books of general, political, economic and social history which might profitably be consulted for information and views on matters touched upon in this and subsequent chapters.

A reader in need of guidance might well start with one of the series:

Oxford History of England: for 1760–1815, J. S. Watson (1960), 1815–70, Sir L. Woodward (2nd ed., 1962); 1870–1914, Sir R. Ensor (1936); 1914–45, A. J. P. Taylor (1965).
Pelican History of England: for the 18th century, J. H. Plumb (1950); 19th century, D. Thompson (1950); 20th century, D. Thompson (2nd ed. 1981).
Pelican Social History of England: for the 18th century, R. Porter (1982); 1914–45, J. Stevenson (1984).
History of England (Longman): for the 18th century, D. Marshall (1965); 1780–1870, A. Briggs (1959); 1868–1914, D. Read; 1914–64, W. N. Medlicott (1967).
New History of England (Edward Arnold): for 1714–60, W. A. Speck (1977); 1760–1815, I. R. Christie (1982); 1815–65, N. Gash (1979); 1865–1914, E. J. Feuchtwanger (1985); 1914–45, M. Beloff (1984).
History of England (Blandford): for 1689–1793, R. W. Harris (1963); 1793–1868, J. W. Derry (1963); 1868–1965, T. L. Jarman (1963).
Foundations of Modern Britain: for 1660–1783, G. Holmes; 1783–1870, E. J. Evans (1983); 1870–1975, K. Robbins (1983).
History of England (Norton Library): for 1714–1815, J. B. Owen (1974); 1815–85, D. Beales (1969); 1885–1955, H. Pelling (1960).
History of England (Paladin): for 1865–1915, R. Shannon (1974); 1915–64, Lord Blake (1985).
Social History of England (Hutchinson): for 1700–80, R. W. Malcolmson (1981); 1780–1858 (rural), P. Horn (1980) and 1776–1851 (urban), J. Walvin (1984).
History of England (Fontana): for 1700–1820, M. Berg (1984); 1815–1914, M. Bentley (1984).

Also of particular value are:
Best, G., *Mid-Victorian Britain 1851–1875* (1971).
Burn, W.L., *The Age of Equipoise* (1964).

Checkland, S.G., *The Rise of Industrial Society in England 1815–1885* (1971).

Halévy, E., *History of the English People in the Nineteenth Century* (2nd ed. 1949–52) I–VI.

Harrison, J.F.C., *The Common People* (1984) Parts III, IV.

Hobsbawm, E., *Industry and Empire* (1968).

Young, G.M., *Victorian England: Portrait of an Age* (2nd ed., 1953).

Chapter Two

LAND

Rights in land were as crucial to the layered structure of the eighteenth century as the obligations of feudal tenure had been to the early Middle Ages. The two worlds were separated by a process of evolution which had been as long as it had been precocious and which had played a distinctive part in preparing England for industrialisation. But because the development was for the most part gradual there remained vital connections with what had gone before which the law acted to enforce and maintain. Even today the land law can be properly depicted only by drawing in the long lines of its history.

At least until the end of the nineteenth century land was a key to political power as much as to wealth as such. Yet the two aspects were closely intertwined. The feudal order had meant that, in return for the physical and political protection of the lord, the vassal had typically to provide military services or a portion of his agricultural produce. With the advent of ordered society under pervasive central government, these units of labour had acquired a quantifiable value. Money could buy off the obligations not only of freemen but of villeins. In this process land came to be a marketable commodity and, already in the fourteenth and fifteenth centuries, the buying and selling of interests constituted an active market in some parts of the country. The process was never to reverse. Depopulation in the wake of the Black Death was to be followed by the soaring demand for wool and the first marked phase of enclosure. In the sixteenth century the Church lost many of its estates. The Crown granted away large tracts of land and the class of gentrified land-owners grew and consolidated.

The marks of the transition upon the law were legion. The most fundamental included the following:

(i) The types of land-holding came with time not only to include the freehold tenure first granted to the freemen, but also the copyhold tenure of those emancipated in a manor and the miscellaneous leasehold tenures. As the feudal obligations attaching to the various sub-divisions of freehold were lifted, this tenure drew as close as theory would permit to complete ownership of land. Freehold was still held of the Crown, but the State, deprived of feudal dues, maintained itself instead by taxation. This would include a land tax, which, in the war years of the eighteenth century, was to reach very substantial levels.

(ii) Rights in land tended to the individual rather than the familial: by the thirteenth century the common law had allowed alienation of freehold to any stranger or to any member of the next generation of the family during the holder's lifetime

121

without the consent of his heir. It took longer for freedom to transmit by will upon death to establish itself, being securely acknowledged only by the Wills Act 1540. While the children may have had no more protection than this, the wife of a freeholder had, from the thirteenth century, an inalienable right of dower during her life in one-third of her husband's freehold; but eventually this was transmuted into the jointure arrangements of marriage settlements.

(iii) A strong tendency to pass freehold by right of primogeniture was manifest.[1] That the eldest surviving son should be sole heir was the first of the common law's rules of inheritance. Until it became possible to dispose of land by will this would be the automatic consequence of leaving land unalienated at death; thereafter it became the first rule of descent only if there was an intestacy. The same principle did not establish itself so potently for the lesser tenures of copyhold and leasehold. Descent of the former would depend on the custom of the manor; the latter was treated as personal rather than real property by the common law and so would pass with the chattels on an intestacy in a partible succession.

(iv) There had over a long period been experiments with legal conceptions that would allow a separation of managerial responsibilities over land from shares in its beneficial value. From this, in the early modern period, the equitable concept of the trust has established itself and had been given a vital function in the strict settlement of land, a device which allowed an elaborate balancing of familial against individual interests. At much the same time the mortgage was converted by equity into a flexible instrument for deploying land as security for a loan.

By the eighteenth century, there was little hint anywhere of the *Gemeinschaft* model of early communities developed by Tönnies, marked by the relative lack of separation by rank and the subjugation of the individual's interests to those of the whole group. A rugged self-interest, typical rather of the competitive *Gesellschaft*, had been dominant enough to produce the considerable variety of communities in existence. To this the range and adaptability of legal interests had certainly contributed. Agricultural historians are now using evidence gathered from estate surveys, enclosure awards and land tax returns to distinguish typical formations of land-ownership and to plot their frequency. One measure of distinction is between the characteristics of hamlets in the pastoral areas and of villages and townships in the champion (arable) districts; a cross-measure is that between open communities, where smallholdings and large population densities predominated, and closed communities, compact and small, where substantial holdings in one or two hands provided a strong manorial tradition, whether or not there was a resident lord.

---

[1] There were parts of the country where other traditions survived: *e.g.*, divided inheritance by all the sons (Kentish gavelkind); ultimogeniture (the Borough English of a few towns and manors): see Holdsworth, III pp. 256–275.

Open communities predominated in pastoral territory, while there would be a mixture in champion. For the whole of England, save the far north, Holderness estimates that by 1750 some 20 per cent. of villages were closed, the proportion rising to 40 per cent. in some places.[2]

Such distinctions are useful in the comparative analysis of many basic social characteristics: economic development, poverty, population growth, housing, religion, social control. It can be seen how the open often provided labour for the closed and that the differentiated structure of the closed might foster the introduction of subsidiary industry, such as domestic weaving. Likewise the relative freedom from labour in pastoral agriculture left opportunity for outside employments of the proto-industrial kind.

Our concern is with the legal understandings and transactions which underpinned this elaborate patchwork and we begin, in this Part, with their place in a rural world only beginning to be touched by demands for greater productivity. The new pressures had legal implications which we examine in Part II. In Part III, attention shifts to urban conditions, where there was immense investment in building that would house the teeming life of city and town. Here we will find that analysis can be more coherently related to type of legal tenure than in rural areas. It has been estimated that by the late nineteenth century something under 10 per cent., of the town population lived in housing that was their own, the rest being in rented accommodation, from the detached villa to the shared room. More than half of this renting was from owners of the freehold, the rest by way of sub-tenancy from a builder or other entrepreneur who was himself the tenant of a ground landlord. Some housing development was by large landowners, who either sold off freeholds or remained as landlords. But there is no strong evidence that their dominance was such as to allow them much market power; rents responded to supply against demand in markets essentially competitive, where small capitalists were likely to be active. The result was a supply of housing and an urban environment that became a major source of tension in the evolving democracy. While radical and socialist campaigns on the Land Question would fall well short of many objectives, they would create the conditions for major changes in ownership, for public controls over old freedoms of the private market, and for the emergence of a public housing sector built up by local authorities. These shifts are the subject of Part IV.

PART 1: AGRICULTURAL EXPLOITATION 1750–1850

I. Strict Settlement of Landed Estates

The organisation of great wealth—its administration as well as its distribution—calls for considerable legal sophistication. In the latter seventeenth and eighteenth centuries conveyancers and judges

---

[2] B. A. Holderness (1972) 20 Ag. Hist. R. 128; D. R. Mills, *Lord and Peasant in Nineteenth Century Britain* (1980).

engineered for the aristocracy and gentry the strict settlement of their landed estates, just as in the nineteenth century lawyers and legislature were to devise for the owners of capital the joint stock company registered with limited liability. In their complexity, adaptability and range of usefulness, these two institutions stand apart. There are indeed points of comparison between them which serve to underscore the special significance of each; to these we shall come.

The strict settlement used as its primary building blocks the three estates which the common law recognised in freehold land, the estate for life, the estate in fee tail and that surrogate for full ownership, the estate in fee simple. All three estates had medieval origins and any understanding of their evolution is a skilled business, which it would be foolhardy to summarise. On no subject is it easier to misperceive the earlier by the light of the later.[3] Centuries of experimentation had settled the ways in which the different estates could be posited one after another. A dialectic process had been at work, often described as a tussle between those with dynastic ambitions, who sought to tie up their estates within their family for succeeding generations, and those who feared the consequences of allowing this to happen without check. Dynasty-mongering is after all of elemental political significance.

In considering first the "classical" strict settlement we are looking at the synthesis which emerged from earlier argument and which was acknowledged as such: an accepted set of bounds within which the courts of common law and equity worked.[4] Both these systems made distinctive contributions to the whole and these can be taken as a starting point.

(a) The Common Law

The basic premise of strict settlement was male primogeniture. In a typical case the head of a family would decide to bring his lands into settlement as part of the arrangements for his eldest son's marriage.[5] His object was to divide up his fee simple estate in the land in ways that would limit the interest of himself, then the eldest son and finally the first grandson of the marriage. He could not go further down the generations because general principles against perpetual limitations (the rules against perpetuities) prevented him. The settlement gave him a life estate, and then conferred estates in remainder on the son for life and the grandson in fee tail male. Against predictable hazards, such as the son failing to produce any grandson who would live to maturity, there would be alternative provisions creating similar interests in the son's second and subsequent sons (and in each case their heirs), then the father's second and subsequent

---

[3] For current learning, Milsom (1981) Chaps. 8, 9; Baker (1979) Pt. II; Simpson (1986) Chaps. 8, 9.

[4] For a detailed description of the contents, see English and Saville (1983), pp. 17–30.

[5] Marriage settlements of this type were one reason for the settlement of land; but settlements also occurred regularly on death by will: see English and Saville (1983), pp. 32–40.

sons, and providing, if need be, for descent through the female line or a collateral branch of the family. The ultimate part of the father's original estate would be left as a remainder in fee simple to himself and "his own right heirs."[6]

Those who had life estates under such a dispensation enjoyed the land and its profits during the continuance of the life but that was all: in principle this was the only interest of which they could dispose.[7] Before the eighteenth century, however, it was by no means clear how far this really held. A prime concern for the devisers of the strict settlement had been to find a means that would deprive the life tenant of an ability effectively to dispose of the whole fee simple. It was equity which produced the solution and we shall come to it in a moment.

Those who held an estate in fee tail had an interest which notionally would endure as long as the original estate-holder had descendant heirs (as distinct from collateral heirs); if the entail was male, then only male descendants would count. This however was only one half of the conception. An estate tail could in some circumstances be "barred" by its current holder—converted by him into a full fee simple so as to make it a freely disposable asset. What the fee tail had come to achieve was a temporary constraint upon the ability to treat it as such an asset. A tenant in tail could not bar the entail until his majority. Moreover, if there was a preceding life tenant still in possession, the barring would be fully effective only if the life tenant joined in the disentailing deed.[8] This was the factor relied upon to secure the continuance of the settlement, while allowing it to be modified to meet the circumstances of the next generation. Upon his majority or marriage, the grandson would be induced to join first in a disentailing and then in a re-settlement, the main feature of which would be that, instead of a fee tail, he would have a life interest, and his own first son, (*i.e.* a great grandson) would become remainderman in fee tail male.[9] The prime inducements offered to the grandson were normally an immediate income until his life interest should fall into possession, provision for his wife, or preference for his daughters over his younger brothers and their sons. The constraint on free alienation was accordingly reimposed for another genera-

---

[6] Henry VIII's Statute of Uses 1536 and Statute of Wills 1540 had disruptive effects on the developing law which took a century and a half to resolve. For their contribution to the emergence of the strict settlement, see Milsom (1981), pp. 218–239; Baker (1979), pp. 237–244.

[7] Permanent values in the land—notably minerals and timber—presented a difficulty, since their commercial exploitation had a "once-for-all" quality. The life tenant who realised them was entitled only to the income from their value unless declared to be "without impeachment for waste": see *Waldo* v. *Waldo* (1841) 12 Sim. 107; Holdsworth, VII 275–281.

[8] The technique that proved most efficient was to suffer a "common recovery," a fictitious action of considerable complexity (see Simpson (1986), pp. 129–138) which was much simplified in the first procedural reforms at common law: Real Property Commissioners, First Report, P.P. 1829 (263) IV, pp. 20–38; 3 & 4 Will. IV, c. 74.

[9] The tenant in tail could act without the life tenant by "levying a fine" which would create a "base fee," barring only those subsequently entitled under the entail and not reversioners or remaindermen: the fact that it was odd did not prevent it from occurring from time to time. George Eliot used it accurately in *Felix Holt.*

tion, after which once more the family circumstances would be reviewed.[10]

(b) Trustees and the Role of Equity

The concept of trust, by which the Court of Chancery required the owner of property at law to hold it for beneficiaries in equity, reached something approaching its modern form at much the time that the strict settlement came to maturity. Some settlors indeed used the machinery of a trust as the central organising frame of their landed settlement. The form was particularly useful when the immediate beneficiary was an infant, or mentally unstable, or distrusted as a spendthrift. But a trust of this type would make the trustee party to managerial decisions to an extent that most heads of family would resent for themselves and would not seek to impose upon their heirs. Moreover it was not easy to find trustees to assume active duties, for they were mostly sought from the landed class and so would have to be found among "friends."[11]

In the classical strict settlement trustees were accordingly given a strategic, but secondary emplacement, "something like the constitutional safeguards of a complex political system."[12] Two of these purposes stand out. First, there was the need to prevent the incumbent life tenant from disposing of the entire estate (or, indeed, from losing it through forfeiture to the Crown—in the seventeenth century an evident political hazard). In common law doctrine, this could occur so long as the fee tail given to the first grandson was a contingent remainder—i.e before his birth gave him an identity that would make his remainder *vested*. The cunning invention of Bridgeman, Palmer and their fellow conveyancers was to give trustees an interest during the life of the life tenant, "to preserve contingent remainders." The device would work only if their own interest, which came after that of the life tenant, could be classed as a vested remainder; and since it only took effect upon attempted alienation by the life tenant (or deprivation from him), this was by no means clear. But Bridgeman had been in a position, as Lord Keeper, to hold it effective; and eventually in 1740 the House of Lords found reason to approve it—by then it was standard practice in the property arrangements of the ruling class.[13]

The second use of the trust was to secure limited shares in the estate, or some part of it, by way of jointure for the widow of the life tenant; and by way of portion for the younger brothers and the sisters of the life tenant. The jointure was normally an annual income

---

[10] Not all the literature distinguishes initial settlement, commonly on marriage, from resettlement, when the heir's majority might provide the reason. But sometimes the settlement at 21 was temporary until marriage: Trumbach (1978), p. 73. The occasion could provoke hard bargaining.

[11] Hence Lord Hardwicke's aversion to an attempt by a trustee to extract a fee: *Ayliffe* v. *Murray* (1740) 2 Atk. 58.

[12] Pollock (1883), p. 112.

[13] *Dormer* v. *Parkhurst* (1740) 6 Bro. P.C. 351; and see *Garth* v. *Cotton* (1750) 1 Ves. Sen. 546; learned conveyancers would continue to doubt its principle, if not its expedience: *e.g.* H. W. Challis, *Law of Real Property* (3rd ed., 1866), pp. 144–146.

and was given in place of the widow's dower—her old common law right during widowhood to a one-third interest in the land.[14] Portions typically were lump sums payable to younger sons in order to buy them a place or commission or to launch them on some other career; and to a daughter as a dowry on marriage.[15] The sums were often raised by mortgage on the estate (for which power would be given) thus spreading the burden over time or, where the estate was over-committed, adding to a well-nigh irremovable burden.

Distinctive as they were, trusts were not equity's only contribution to the mechanics of strict settlement. The common law courts had recognised the concept of the power—a mandate or authority that might be used to deal with many kinds of future contingency. But the Court of Chancery had added modifications and extensions to the common law concept and had thus increased the range of possibilities open to a settlor.[16] The main discipline that Chancery insisted upon was that a power must be exercisable only within the period allowed under the rule against perpetuities. This was one indication that many types of power—particularly powers to appoint persons to take interests, and powers to revoke the interests of some in order that others should take—were themselves treated as a type of property interest. Powers could equally pertain to the realisation of interests: often enough the life tenant's power to mortgage was restricted to raising the portions of his younger brothers and his sisters. Or they could concern managerial strategy, such as the power to grant long leases—perhaps with a view to mining or urban development. One thing, however, was plain: the considerable choice of arrangement which the rules opened up to the settlor could not be liberally adopted by him if he wished to keep his settlement *strict*. If he left others with the ability to choose for themselves, he necessarily conferred an ability to jeopardise the future of the family's estate. Complaint, when eventually it surfaced, could only be against the undue caution with which settlors were said to use a device that could be operated in many ways.

In a manner similar to its intervention over powers, equity also transmuted the mortgage of land. This was a development by no means confined to settled estates, for the mortgage became a general tool in the capitalist development of land. In that context, we shall look at it again.[17] The emergence of its modern form belongs here because of its place in the structures of large landholding. Land could be used as security for money lent by machinery that operated purely under rules of common law. Indeed these had long been employed. The borrower's legal estate in the land could be conveyed to the lender, subject to a covenant to re-convey the estate when the loan was repaid on the due date, but that otherwise it was to be forfeit. This risk-pledge did not give rise to the objection of usury where there was no direct charge of interest; nonetheless, if the forfeit

---

[14] See below, p 174
[15] The dowry might well be brought into a marriage settlement, together with property of the husband; for the family interests in these, see below, pp. 368–369.
[16] See generally, Holdsworth, VII pp. 149–193.
[17] See below, p. 237.

occurred, the profit might be great.[18] By the early seventeenth century, just as a measure of interest was beginning to be permitted on loans, equity insisted that the borrower be given time to repay beyond that set by the mortgage; and in the hands of Lord Nottingham and Lord Hardwicke this right grew into a proprietary interest—the mortgagor's equity of redemption. It could itself be settled in fee tail and would pass on death as real estate to the heirs.[19] From the mid-seventeenth century onwards, other practices confirmed the device as a security: the mortgagee did not go into possession before default in repayment; nor were the rents and profits used directly to pay interest or to repay capital.[20]

The device was thus adapted to become an instrument for long-term lending. It appealed to lenders for its low risk and its flexible duration, the mortgagee's interest being regularly assignable. It attracted borrowers by the correspondingly moderate rates of interest on offer. The convoluted forms of the law raised imponderables of theory: was, for instance, the mortgagor left in possession as a tenant at will, or on sufferance, or was he not a tenant at all? Until the reforms of 1925 the expensive formality of a re-conveyance was needed to close the transaction.[21] The odd circumstances that equity qualified common law rules led to the sometimes arbitrary concepts of consolidation and tacking.[22] But chiefly remarkable is the determination with which Chancellors shaped unwieldy concepts into a regular commercial institution. Mortgages came to stand alongside the government funds and land itself as the typical resorts of the eighteenth-century investor.

(c) The Uses of Strict Settlement

All in all, even the creator of a settlement who was most intent upon dynastic conservation soon came against the barriers placed by the law in the way of his ambitions. Entails were not, as in Scotland, unbarrable[23]; and contingent remainders were effectively confined to the first generation as yet unborn at the date of the settlement.[24] The compromises thus defined had been laborious to secure; they were moreover on terms relatively favourable to settlors. Here then is some explanation of why no significant attempts seem to have been

---

[18] See R. H. Tawney (ed.), Wilson's Discourse upon Usury (1925), pp. 31–42.

[19] R. W. Turner, The Equity of Redemption (1931) Chaps. 3, 4. In consequence, a mortgagor in possession retained the franchise: ibid., pp. 183–185.

[20] The "Welsh mortgage," by contrast, had the opposite features.

[21] Equity came to treat informal practices such as the deposit of title deeds with the lender as creating a purely equitable mortgage.

[22] For these and other details of the developing law, see Holdsworth, VI pp. 663–665.

[23] Scots settlements were brought into line with the English in 1848, 11 & 12 Vict., c. 36: see generally, C. F. Kolbert and N. A. M. Mackay, History of Scots and English Land Law (1977).

[24] Other future interests had to turn from contingent into vested interests within the perpetuity period. This period was fixed in principle by Lord Nottingham in the Duke of Norfolk's Case (1680–1683) 3 Cas. in Cha. 1; 2 Swanst. 454, and finally determined as a life in being and twenty-one years thereafter: Cadell v. Palmer (1833) 1 Cl. & Fin. 372. Lord Nottingham's opinion was more generous towards perpetuation than that of the common law judges: G. L. Hoskins (1977) 126 U.Penn.L.R. 19; and see D. E. C. Yale (1954) 73 Selden Soc. lxxiii–xci.

made in the eighteenth century to lengthen the span for which settlements could be rendered unalterable. But in any case, re-settlement
was not just a matter of legal necessity; it was positively, indeed
vitally, useful.

First, re-settlement fostered the whole pattern of familial expectation in the aristocracy and gentry. In particular, the fixing of portions for younger sons as interests ranking ahead of that of the eldest
helped to make primogeniture acceptable to the group most likely to
proclaim its inequity. Reconciling the younger sons was feasible only
in an economy that could offer other sources of income for which the
portion purchased an entitlement.[25] The army and the church, and to
some degree the navy and the bar, provided opportunities in professions; the branches of civil government bred a swarm of positions
(with more or less substantial duties attached to them).[26] Likewise a
dowry set a value upon a daughter in a market eager for rewarding
alliances.[27] The eighteenth century preferred to fix its amount in
advance, rather than leave the matter to negotiation.[28] Its concomitant was the jointure by which the estate would provide for the
endowed bride if she were widowed; the regular rate of jointure was
an annuity of one-tenth her dowry.

Secondly, re-settlement played a role in determining the level of
debt which the estate would carry forward as a drain upon its
income. Though it was not so labelled, settlement was in reality a
regime for limiting capacity and therefore liability. Without it, the
current head of family would have been able to mortgage or sell any
part of the land to raise funds for whatever purpose, and in addition
his ordinary creditors could have had half the land sold in execution
of debts pursued to judgment.[29] As a life tenant his ability to use the
land as mortgage security would arise only by power expressly conferred, which might well be confined to the raising of portions. For
his personal debts—not secured upon the land—the creditor had
redress only against his income from the estate for the time being (in
respect of which he might have to suffer the indignity of a receiver-
ship) and property which he owned outright.[30] The moment of disentailing could well provide incumbent father and inheriting son
with their one chance (before the new settlement) to sell off or mortgage so as to eliminate or reduce the personal indebtedness of either
or both, or the debts binding the estate.

Thirdly, there were the professional interests of the conveyancers
whose intricate machine, with its mesh of precautionary and subsidiary clauses, proved to need re-assembly once a generation. An

[25] See Thompson (1963), pp. 70–73.
[26] Even in estates where otherwise little use was made of settlement, it was employed
to secure portions: E. Spring (1964), pp. 218–220 (Lambton), 220–222 (Fitzwilliam).
The portion itself rarely had to be laid out in land: Clay (1967).
[27] A substantial jointure could be a lure for that most desirable of quantities, an heiress. Patrick Colquhoun reckoned that the "20,000 gentlemen and ladies living on
incomes" contributed £14m. a year in purchasing power to the economy: see
F. M. L. Thompson (1969), pp. 58–59.
[28] Trumbach (1978), p. 70.
[29] See below, p. 229.
[30] See, e.g., the bankruptcy of the Duke of Newcastle in 1870: English and Saville
(1983), p. 90.

enclave of Chancery solicitors, who knew the inner workings of the great families, managed this crucial aspect of their affairs in consultation with the specialist counsel and conveyancers at the bar. Equally those respectable attorneys who were becoming the property organisers of the lesser gentry and tradespeople were finding settlement business to be an appreciable part of that vital asset, their practice in conveyancing.[31] Some part of the work, especially for the largest estates, might be in drafting a private Bill and cossetting it through Parliament; or a dispute in the family might become so intractable as to provoke a Chancery action. But for the most part, the delicacies of settlement transactions could be kept private, understood in full, perhaps, only by the discreet men who organised them.

(d) The Rise of the Great Estates

What then was the contribution of the strict settlement to the rise of the great estates of the eighteenth and nineteenth centuries? Habakkuk placed settlement, together with the flexible-term mortgage, at the centre of causation.[32] He detected a tendency among the gentry in the earlier seventeenth century, before perfection of the two devices, to leave their landed property divided among their children rather than primarily to the eldest son. In his depiction, trusts to preserve contingent remainders made primogeniture dynastically safe, keeping the estate in the family yet providing an acceptable measure of support for its main members in each generation. The result was an accumulation of land large and secure enough to be uniquely capable of new growth—by calculated marriage, by the use of surplus income in the purchase of new land or the consolidation of old (with or without an enclosure), by alone being in a position to buy land at high prices, by introducing new crops, improved beasts and production methods to increase yield.

This simple causal picture has been received with some scepticism. Investigations of general factors, both economic and demographic, as well as of particular estates, suggest that the law's role was not so much to provide catalytic means as to underpin the social perceptions and desires that called forth the means in the first place. Land retained a price and a certain shortage value because of the prestige of land ownership, even through a long period before 1750 when agricultural prices were far from buoyant.[33] And when eventually they rose, land itself did not accelerate dramatically in value and there were always factors bringing it onto the market. The period

---

[31] There were in addition attorneys who took a more practical hand in the day-to-day management of estates (see, e.g., D. Spring (1963) Chap. 3); they might well become involved in settlement drafting for the less grand, as well as drawing leases and similar matters. Mr. Tulkinghorn, acknowledged by all in the Dedlocks' drawing room, is Dickens' portrait in Bleak House.

[32] Habakkuk (1940), (1949); and in J.S. Bromley and E. Kossman (eds.), Britain and the Netherlands (1960), p. 155; (1965) 20 Annales 649. All his writing is suggestive rather than dogmatic in character and the author has accepted much of the cases made by his critics, while providing further evidence of settlement practices, in (1978) 29 Tr.R.H.S. (5th) 187; 30 ibid. 199; 31 ibid. 195.

[33] On these issues, see esp. F. M. L. Thompson (1964), (1967); Clay (1974); Beckett (1977), (1984); P. G. Lane, (1972) 3 Ec. & Soc. R. 413.

in which the proportion of small landowners declined and the larger estates increased—the first three-quarters of the eighteenth century—came before the most noticeable increases in value and profitability. In the forty years after 1775 there was if anything an increase once more of small owners, many of them absentee investors, who sold out again in the uncertainties of the period after 1815.

There was also a significant demographic factor which curtailed the restraining potential of settlement in the earlier eighteenth century. For the peerage and upper gentry at least this was an age of considerable dynastic uncertainty. Marriages might produce no children or children relatively late; fathers might die before eldest sons married.[34] These were events which could make the settlement terminable without strings.[35] What stands out in the history of a number of estates is not that settlement operated to pass title down a line of first-borns; rather, that when the estate passed to a tenant who could bar the entail without having to submit to terms, he would do so for himself but create a new settlement at his death.[36] The freedom that had been his by chance he would not allow to his successors; the code of his caste dictated otherwise.

Birth and survival rates had improved by the end of the century and this must have increased the likelihood of regular re-settlement. Even so there were many ways of varying the balance between preservation and exploitation in the arrangements then determined. Moreover, it was not uncommon, particularly in the largest estates, to put only a part of the whole into settlement, leaving the current head of family a free hand with the rest.[37] There could be a re-writing of settlement terms in interim periods by resort to private Act of Parliament, if the current beneficiaries could agree upon a scheme. In a typical eighteenth-century year there would be 20–30 estates bills promoted; they would be referred by the House of Lords to two judges for a report on the general propriety of what was proposed. Any family in its senses used this procedure, costly though it was, in preference to a suit in Chancery, whose ruinous toils stood as an awful warning to those who could not compound their differences.[38] Our traditional picture of settlement derives from highly conservative conveyancers of the stamp of Sugden (Lord St. Leonards) and from liberal critics of the landed system towards the end of the nineteenth century who saw it as the great barrier to free trade in land.[39] When Pollock compared the severity of settlement to "the customs of an oriental despotism," with the settlors themselves as "powerless as the great kings of old to alter their decrees," the exaggeration of the

---

[34] The passing of an estate to an indirect relation might well lead to its sale, because the new incumbent was not prepared to service the existing level of debt or because of some other inconvenience to him. For the strategems adopted to keep estates in the family, see esp. L. and J.C.F. Stone, *An Open Elite?* (1984) Chap. 4; but *cf.* Bonfield (below, n. 41).

[35] Clay (1968); Bonfield (1983), p. 102; English and Saville (1983), pp. 114–115.

[36] For the histories of particular settlements, see esp. English and Saville (1983) Chap. 2; Trumbach (1978).

[37] For examples, see E. Spring (1964).

[38] See English and Saville (1983), pp. 48–51.

[39] In addition to his technical books, his *Handy Book of Property Law* went through numerous editions.

image is apparent.[40] Even in 1880 the device was a flexible tool that the landed could adapt at least once a generation to meet their family case.[41] Such "strictness" as by then there was should certainly not be read back into the age when as a class they were assembling together the whole basis of their prestige and wealth.

There is more to say on the subject of settlement, and the later controversies which afflicted it. But "land reform" was to encompass much else in the ownership and management of agricultural estates; it had to do notably with landlord-tenant relations and with lawyers' interests in the business of conveyancing. These must be introduced next, as must something of the legal machinery for developing urban property.

II. LEASEHOLD AND COPYHOLD

The essential counterpart of the large and medium estates, whether the land was settled or unsettled, was the system of farming through tenants. While there were many variations, larger farms (over 100 acres, perhaps 300, occasionally 1,000) were becoming more common, the farmer of the unit being the provider and organiser of the necessary labour and the supplier of at least working capital, such as stock or seed.[42] The basis on which he held this land, if it was not itself freehold, was as leasehold or copyhold. These tenures together had provided a legal foundation for England's precocious break from feudal regimes of unfree labour service. Copyhold was initially the more characteristic of that process. As the economic and social crises of the fourteenth and fifteenth centuries had led the serf to seek emancipation, the land he worked came to be held of his lord on customary terms that could be enforced in the manorial court: the court rolls provided the "copy" that, as the proprietary character of the right became more pronounced, constituted title. The incidents of copyhold thus varied from manor to manor, though the central courts were to intervene in support of the copyholder, insisting upon the permanence of his interest and subjecting local variations to tests of "reasonableness" at common law. Their interference, particularly in the sixteenth century, was of high significance: it reflected a determination above all else to secure stability at a crucial level of the agricultural hierarchy.[43]

As a distinct concept, the idea of letting seems first to have evolved for the working of the home farm of the manor and the lease for a money rent had an early association with land as security for a loan. In the later middle ages, leases of various kinds developed and by the Tudor period were frequent enough for the common law courts to be expounding an elaborate set of rules for the press of cases before them.[44] By the eighteenth century, leasehold had become the forward-looking arrangement adaptable to the needs of market agricul-

---

[40] Pollock (1883), p. 113.

[41] For the long significance of this, see esp. L. Bonfield (1986) 39 Ec. H.R. (2d) 341.

[42] By 1851, one-third of cultivated acreage was in farms of more than 300 acres, with a quarter in farms of 50–100 acres: Chambers and Mingay (1966), p. 93.

[43] See Holdsworth, VII pp. 296–312.

[44] See Holdsworth, VII pp. 238–296.

ture. It was a flexible concept admitting of innumerable variations which could meet changes in farming practice and adjustments in rent payable to the land-owner. Copyhold, by contrast, was weighted in favour of traditional practices, giving in some of its manifestations an ownership close to freehold and in others a value-sharing relationship close to some types of lease, which was nonetheless erratic and difficult to adjust.

Since, through their different histories, leasehold and copyhold both came to admit of many varieties, any comparison between them as types can only be approximate: it is best begun with the two most crucial characteristics of land-holding, the duration of the estate and the return expected for it by the grantor, be it a payment in kind, a money rent or a more spasmodic payment (generally called a fine).

A typical characteristic of leasehold was that both duration and rent were set by the terms of the letting itself, supplemented by general rule to some extent when terms were left unspecific. The lowliest tenancies—for instance the cottage plots of labourers—might be held at will or on sufferance, or at most from week to week; they were accordingly terminable at once or on a week's notice. Farms were often let from year to year, which meant that notice to quit must coincide with the ending of any year of the letting.[45] The more substantial leases would be for a specified term—seven years or even twenty-one for agriculture, longer if the purpose was mining or house-building.[46] Rents for the shorter, indeterminate terms were periodic—weekly, monthly, quarterly, annual. Non-money rents, consisting for instance of a portion of the crop, were still known and so gave a measure of profit-sharing—with the risk, however, that large harvests would bring low prices. Leases for a term of years might be based upon a fine rather than a regular rent. Overall the movement during the eighteenth century was towards "rack-renting"—the charging of a regular rent at whatever rate the market would bear and, so far as the law was concerned, adjustable only if the lease itself provided an express arrangement.[47] The most that Chancery did was to allow time to pay overdue rent despite the landlord's suit for forfeiture; it did not alter rents with changes in market prices.

Copyhold, by contrast, was often tied to older ideas. At least in its traditional form, it was a property right of indefinite duration, being capable of alienation during the holder's life and on his death, save to the extent that the manor's custom dictated otherwise. Commonly, if it remained his until his death, his widow enjoyed free-bench in a half or a third of it so long as she did not remarry. Copyhold could end only upon escheat to the lord (for instance when the copyholder died intestate and without heirs) or upon agreement between lord and copyholder to convert the interest into freehold or to substitute a lease. Rights of the copyholder often stretched across the manor, giv-

---

[45] Note however, the fifteenth and sixteenth century difficulties over tenancies not for fixed terms: Simpson (1986) pp. 252–256.
[46] Notably in the West Country, the lease for a life, or (as was common) three lives, survived on into the eighteenth century.
[47] On the church's shift as a landlord from uncaring to grasping, C. Clay (1980) 87 P. & P. 128.

ing pasturage, turving and other profits from commons and other land. Upon the entry of a new copyholder, the lord often had the right to take a heriot (the most valuable beast or chattel) and to require a fine. If the fine had been specified long before, it could be nominal in value, and the state of the holding would be close to freehold. If the fine was "arbitrary," the common law insisted that the lord only demand a reasonable amount, which was normally set at two years' value of the land as improved.[48] This brought the interest closer to a long-term lease subject to fine.

According to the Real Property Commissioners, "a considerable proportion of the land" was in copyhold, though much of this was in small lots, often enough defined without precision.[49] As reform-minded lawyers, the Commissioners found copyhold anachronistic: it inhibited economic growth by its rules on arbitrary fines (which amounted to a tax on improvements made by the copyholder) and by the frequent custom that lord and copyholder had to agree upon the cutting of timber and the exploitation of minerals; it provoked aggression (from lords) and fraud (from holders) in the matter of heriots; it was ill-run by manorial stewards who were labelled "ignorant and negligent"[50]; and it was the most prominent example of law fashioned out of local custom, some of it preserved only in oral tradition, much of it uncertain and so provocative of litigation. The Commissioners would have liked to eradicate copyhold by compulsion, after the manner about to be applied to tithes.[51] But they drew back, seeing in the process of valuing the lord's interests complexities that would often be too costly to unravel. Instead they only recommended inprovements in the machinery for voluntary enfranchisement. Parliamentary opinion was with them: legislation followed in 1841 and a decade later this was made to encompass enfranchisement at the request of either party.[52] Under the 1925 legislation the remaining vestiges of copyhold could be disposed of by compulsory machinery.[53]

The writers on agricultural improvement of the late eighteenth century considered that leasing practice had a vital bearing upon increased production. Arthur Young recommended leases for terms of 21 years, renewable at the tenant's option, as a means of securing investments by the tenant in buildings and fencing, manuring and other measures that were boosting the agricultural revolution.[54] The leaders of the new agriculture used their leases to prescribe regimes for their tenants: on the Coke estates in Norfolk, for instance, a four-year, and then a six-year, cycle for arable was required, as well as sufficient manuring and grass-sowing.[55]

Term leases grew more common during the eighteenth century,

---

[48] This did not, however, apply to a building grant.
[49] Third Report, P.P. 1831–1832 (484) XXIII, pp. 14–20.
[50] For instance, they would allow subdivision of lots, but not their merger, because fees on enrolment of conveyances went by the piece.
[51] See below, p. 143.
[52] 4 & 5 Vict., c. 35 (with amendments, 6 & 7 Vict., c. 23, 7 & 8 Vict., c. 55); 15 & 16 Vict., c. 51.
[53] Law of Property Act 1925, Sched. 12.
[54] *Political Arithmetic* (1774) 15, a view adopted by many agricultural improvers.
[55] R. A. C. Parker, *Coke of Norfolk* (1975), pp. 55–57, 100–105, 138–152.

when moderate prices placed tenants in a relatively favourable position. But the great opportunities of profit presented by the scarce war years around 1800 induced a reversal of pattern. This was to continue into the unsettled years of peace and it received a further stimulus from the admission of the £50 leaseholder to the Parliamentary franchise in 1832. The periodic lease (say) from year to year provided the landlord with a recurrent chance to set a bad tenant loose and, until the secret electoral ballot of 1872, this could include a test of the tenant's political loyalty. In bad times, when the tenant could not meet his rent, the landlord's discretion increased: he could waive part or all that was owing, or take payment in kind for what it was worth. The tenant's lack of security was a sharp discipline, social and economic, tempered mainly by the market for satisfactory tenants and the need to keep the whole tenanting system acceptable.

Alongside the notice to quit, the landlord had at his disposal the old self-help remedy of distress[56] with which to recover outstanding rent—a remedy which had grown both in significance and efficacy with the prevalence of rack-renting.[57] The landlord was entitled to seize any personal property, which would include tools, stock and produce, that he could find on the leased premises.[58] If the tenant did not retrieve them by payment, the landlord could sell them in satisfaction of the rent due.[59] No ordinary creditor enjoyed so wide-ranging and summary a right, but it would not be until the latter nineteenth century that the movement for land reform would begin to trim away at excesses.[60] Landlords would fight hard to retain this form of preference among creditors.[61] There were of course tenants whose visible assets were slender enough to make distress a shadowy advantage, a matter which was to become pressing as domestic lettings in the cities grew. In 1838, the year in which summary arrest of debtors was abolished,[62] landlords were quick to secure themselves a new advantage. The magistrates were given jurisdiction to order the eviction of defaulting tenants who had not complied with a notice to quit, where the tenancy was for less than £20 per annum.[63] The army of private bailiffs who already executed distress found a

[56] For its origins, see, e.g., Pollock (1883), pp. 139–140; and for its nineteenth century deployment, Englander (1983) Chap. 2.
[57] A succession of statutes (beginning with that mentioned in n. 59) had removed hazards in the landlord's path.
[58] The property did not have to be the tenant's but might, for instance, belong to a sub-tenant, lodger or customer of the tenant; no notion of contractual privity prevailed here.
[59] The power of sale had been accorded only in 1689 (2 Will. & Mar. c. 5), a typical example of landed self-interest. A feeble attempt to eliminate the predations of bailiffs (1817, 57 Geo. III, c. 95) had no impact: see Englander (1983), pp. 24–25.
[60] In 1871, lodgers received some protection against having their goods seized (Lodgers' Goods Protection Act); and in 1883 the Agricultural Holdings Act substantially reduced the scope of distress for agricultural leaseholds. It also instituted a requirement that bailiffs be approved by a county court judge. This was made general in 1888: Englander (1983), pp. 26–27.
[61] See below, p. 242.
[62] See below, p. 229.
[63] 1 & 2 Vict., c. 74. For the passing of the Act and its consequences, see Englander (1983), pp. 12–21; Daunton (1983), pp. 148–154; and below, p. 180ff. There were "anti-flitting" provisions, allowing the police to stop and search furniture carts, in the Metropolitan Police Act 1839 (3 & 4 Vict., c. 47, s.67).

new outlet for their talents. The justices of the peace kept this jurisdiction even after the county court system of 1846 became the standard machinery for small debt collection; in the matter of overdue
rents, the justices could be trusted to know their duty.

The contractual element in leasehold was no novelty of the industrial period. There was however some tendency to heighten this
aspect of the relationship by refusing to add implied terms to
expressed obligations. Typically this was led by the Court of Exchequer. In the 1840s it held that there was no implied covenant that,
irrespective of the landlord's fault, buildings should be habitable or
that the land should be usable for the tenant's purpose—for instance
as pasture.[64] The one exception was that a *furnished* letting bore the
implication that it would be habitable—not infested by bugs or
structurally unsafe.[65] Somewhat earlier Lord Ellenborough had
refused to imply a term in an agricultural lease that the tenant might
remove his fixtures at the end of the lease, although it was well-
settled that the opposite applied to a trade tenant: the baker might
take out his ovens, the dyer his vats.[66] The main thrust of such
decisions was in favour of landlords but it did not travel entirely one
way. In the absence of an express covenant, tenants were not held
liable for non-repair. The courts refused to resort to earlier notions of
"permissive waste" to fill the gap, though some obscurity continued
to haunt the question throughout the nineteenth century.[67]

III. Land as an Agricultural Resource

In the enveloping wave of engrossments, which coalesced agricultural holdings into large farms worked by tenant farmers and their
labourers, there lay two specific types of change: the enclosure of
common fields, common grazing and waste and the commutation of
the church tithes. The scale on which they occurred in the early
industrial period was much greater than that of the compulsory
acquisitions needed for canals, roads and railways.[68] The Parliamentary enclosures which typify the period after 1760 affected perhaps a
fifth of all land in England and stretched in a great belt from the mid-
south to the north-east. Tithe commutation or its exoneration in the
course of enclosure occurred in the great bulk of parishes. The tithe
issue generated prolonged acrimony, playing a noteworthy part in
revising the relations between established church and state. Enclosure, by contrast, in its eighteenth century, Parliamentary form, provided a relatively "efficient" vehicle for even more fundamental
change. From it there was much to be learned about the process of

---

[64] *Sutton* v. *Temple* (1843) 12 M. & W. 52 (manure heap poisoned without landlord's
knowledge); *Hart* v. *Windsor* (1843) 12 M. & W. 68 (bug-infested house); in effect
reversing earlier cases: *Edwards* v. *Etherington* (1825) Ry. & M. 268; *Collins* v. *Barrow*
(1831) 1 M. & Rob. 112.

[65] *Smith* v. *Marrable* (1843) 11 M. & W. 6 (short let of house at Brighton to titled family).
See further, below, p. 511.

[66] *Elves* v. *Mair* (1802) 3 East. 38; and see below p. 171. For the emergence of a countervailing "Lincolnshire custom," see R. J. Olney, *Lincolnshire Politics* (1973), pp. 41–43.

[67] *Herne* v. *Benbow* (1813) 4 Taunt. 764; *cf.* Jones v. *Hill* (1817) 7 Taunt. 392.

[68] For this, see below, p. 151ff.

government and we shall consider it first. There will in addition be a third factor to discuss—investment in land drainage, which thanks to technical improvements, was showing signs of profitability in the 1840s. The owner of estates would be granted both financial assistance towards drainage and, where necessary, a lifting of constraints in their settlements. The results would not bring the marked yields of enclosure, but the process played its part in qualifying older notions of the family's relationship to the land.

(a) Enclosure

After nearly a century's historical work, enclosure has emerged as anything but a uniform process.[69] The distinction between enclosing the great communal fields of medieval cultivation and enclosing the commons and wastes over which villagers held joint rights of pasturage, timber, fuel and the like, is only one starting point. The process of dividing off private fields by hedge or ditch might well begin piecemeal, as might a complementary movement consolidating private closes into larger farms. The more general re-arrangement of holdings in the interests of profitable efficiency might well come only at an advanced stage in the whole process.[70] It might indeed be undertaken largely to confirm title rather than to initiate change[71]; or it might be set in train but never carried through to the actual re-division. Enclosure was certainly not the single cause of engrossed farms or of surplus labour that was driven away to the factories.[72] But it remains a distinct contributory factor in the transformation of the countryside and its people and one that was sufficiently disturbing to proliferate only under the impetus of a rapidly increasing demand for food.[73] It would reach its peak as the agricultural sector saw both increased profits for landlords and tenants and serious poverty among paupered labourers. It demanded systematic management if its disruptive potential was to be contained.

Some measure of enclosure had been in process since at least the fourteenth century. The profitability of wool-farming was an early incentive. Indeed the Tudors and Stuarts, in their most ambitious piece of agricultural planning, had restrained the conversion of arable to pasture out of a fear for the food supply.[74] Early enclosure involved much commandeering on the part of the powerful—rough injustice and gross pressuring that could provoke violent reaction. Later, the process began to acquire a more seemly aspect of negoti-

---

[69] For useful reviews of the literature, see Chambers and Mingay (1966) Chap. 4; Yelling (1977).

[70] Sometimes enclosure had the initial effect of increasing the number of separate holdings. For an instance of subsequent reductions, see W. A. Hoskins, *The Midland Peasant* (1965) Chap. 10.

[71] Gonner (1912), p. 60.

[72] See J. D. Chambers (1953) 5 Ec. H.R. (2d) 319.

[73] A move to large tenanted farms at rack-rents could mean an increase in rents of 50–200 per cent: Tate (1967) Chap. 15. Yelling (1977), pp. 110–111, challenges the earlier view of Johnson that most of the land so treatable had been enclosed by 1780.

[74] Such enclosure had produced significant displacements of population with consequent dangers to civil peace. Eighteenth century enclosure was not in the main from arable to pasture and so did not produce social disturbance of this order.

ation; influence was more subtlely applied and the resulting agreement might well be enshrined in a decree entered upon the record of the court of Chancery.[75] The Parliamentary process, for which occasional precedents begin in the seventeenth century, forms a contrast to both simple annexation and to Chancery enrolment, importing a new degree of formality, partly legislative and partly bureaucratic.[76] To no other purpose did the aristocracy and gentry use their legislature more regularly for the adjustment of private rights. By mid-eighteenth century it had become the predominant technique for enclosure.

The Parliamentary stage began with a petition, naming the petitioners and describing the land.[77] Unless this was rejected, a friendly member would then present the bill, which, after second reading in the Commons, would be examined by a committee and reported on; then the Lords would deal with it (perfunctorily) before it became law. By Commons Standing Orders in 1774 not even the petition was to be presented before a notice of it had been posted in the parish church for three Sundays in August or September. Surprise was probably one of the advantages of the private Act in its earliest years. But Parliament could scarcely overlook the dangers of becoming implicated in secret advantages. Instead its process was turned towards eliciting whatever opposition there was and confining it to the issue of principle, before the business of actual division got under way. Parliament's most delicate role was to judge whether opposition could safely be ignored. This it was mostly prepared to do if the objectors amounted to no more than a fifth or a quarter of the landowners by value (not number). Significantly no precise proportion was ever laid down, nor how the valuation was to be arrived at (whether by acreage, or annual value, or land tax assessment, or poor rate liability). The legislature moreover insisted on keeping the public inquiry stage to itself, and rejected all efforts, even when the need to increase food supplies became acute in the French wars, to give it over to others.[78] The most it would allow was a "general clauses" Act, (1801) setting out some forty provisions that could in future be incorporated by reference. An early instance of an important technique, the Act was frequently adopted, in whole or in part, and did a certain amount to reduce detail, length and thus expense. It helped in the process of evolving normal expectations.

Standard clauses were needed since, typically, the Act was more about procedures to be followed than about entitlements. For the administrative stage, commissioners would be named who were to investigate claims and to prescribe in detail the terms of a fair redistribution of the lands to be enclosed. While after 1774, the propor-

---

[75] For the era of Chancery enclosure, see Holderness (1976), pp. 59–60.

[76] For the chronology of Parliamentary enclosure, see Turner (1980), Chaps. 6–14.

[77] For detailed description of the Parliamentary process, Hammond (1927) Chap. 2; Tate (1967) Chap. 12.

[78] This despite pressure from the semi-private Board of Agriculture, (which was involved in four previous bills) and the existence of such legislation for Scotland (since 1695). There were other reasons: the inevitable interest of the private bill promoters; and the church's interest in insisting on its tithe case by case.

tions to be given to the lord of the manor and tithe-owner had to be specified in the Act, it was for lesser proprietors to submit their claims to the commissioners by a given date. The commissioners' discretion was wide indeed, for there were rarely precise norms about measuring existing interests or assessing the terrain for distribution in order to take account of variations in productivity and workability.[79] Moreover it was a prime object of many Acts to preclude review of their decisions by *certiorari* or other process which could have deflected the whole scheme into the courts. An appeal to quarter sessions was often the sole right allowed, although according to Lord Thurlow, sessions did not have the time necessary to consider such cases.[80] Another technique was to require disputes to be referred to arbitrators, when much would depend upon who was appointed to act.

The Parliamentary enclosure commissions—some 5000 in all—make up a significant experience in the breeding of experts.[81] In the early eighteenth century, influence and friendship could play an evident part—the commission might well consist of a dozen men, giving honorific service after the manner of a grand jury. But there soon emerged, as more or less regular commissioners, men drawn from the class of land managers—attorneys, stewards and other agents. In part they conceived the work as an office of profit for which charges were either prescribed in the Act or left to their own discretion.[82] A few of them appear to have become rich men as a result, their fees contributing to enclosure costs which in some cases became enormous.[83] At the same time they were representatives of interests. It became common practice to appoint three commissioners, one of whom was to represent the lord of the manor, one the owner of the tithe and one the remaining proprietors. The "regular" commissioners would act repeatedly for one or other of these interests and doubtless built their reputation upon their representative skill. But from the process was generated a larger expertise. Each new commission was no longer without precedents or accepted standards. An element of objectivity could be brought to the resolution of what were after all property questions of the highest sensibility.

Eventually, in 1836 and 1845, Parliament could be persuaded to go further. The 1836 Act allowed a two-thirds majority of land-owners (still by value) to appoint commissioners without resort to Parliament and a seven-eights majority to proceed without even a commission, the award being enrolled at quarter sessions with the clerk of the peace.[84] In 1845 came a permanent bureaucracy, in the form of a three-man Enclosure Commission, working with assistants and

---

[79] During the course of their survey and deliberations, the Commissioners often had power to direct the course of husbandry: this became a part of their expertise.

[80] Hammond (1927), p. 35.

[81] Their minutes are an historical source which is only beginning to be tapped: M. E. Turner (1973) 21 Ag. Hist.R. 35.

[82] The Commons Standing Orders of 1774 sought for the first time to limit the most outrageous claims.

[83] For a regular commissioner who left a fortune of £600,000 at his death, see Tate (1967), p. 112.

[84] 6 & 7 Will. IV, c. 115, s.2, 40.

drawn from the professional experts who by now knew the business well.[85]

As a body with power to distribute new interests by the measure of old entitlements, the Enclosure Commission had a function peculiarly on the border between the judicial and the administrative. Exceptionally, the duty of supervising it was retained by the legislature, since each year's proposals became operative only upon the enactment of a statute covering them all.[86] Under this dispensation, the new Commission—which must rank as one of the earliest administrative tribunals—saw to the enclosure of a further 600,000 acres over a quarter-century. It never rejected a scheme entirely and kept the process out of the public eye.[87] Only when the enclosure of commons became an urban issue—rousing those who fought for open spaces against the encroachments of house-builders—did the matter return to Parliament and further checks were instituted.[88]

It is for its place in the transformation of agriculture that enclosure remains central to the history of social institutions. In the first generation of historians to study the subject in detail, the Hammonds depicted its impact on village communities as devastating and later historians have agreed that this was often the result at the bottom end of the scale.[89] The Hammonds went further, assembling instances which suggested that this outcome was the product of callous manipulation: the promoters of a bill would rely on "friendship" to push it through against any opposition and then upon a nice legalism to deprive all but substantial property owners of their expectations. The resulting havoc might provoke rioting, arson and other protest for years afterwards. In addition, if costs of enclosure remained high, they could be expected to undermine many who got so far as to substantiate their claim to an allotment, forcing them to sell up sooner or later under their mortgage burden. There was in this account some exaggeration. Subsequent work suggests that violent reaction, such as the Hammonds found at Otmoor in Oxfordshire, was exceptional rather than typical.[90] Likewise, a largely landed Parliament had little doubt of the need for enclosure in general. Population growth, and then fear of war-induced famine, propelled the process, acting at once as goad and seduction. But there is not much evidence that Parliament let particular members push through their own schemes by organising a job.[91] In addition, recent

---

[85] 8 & 9 Vict., c. 118. It was preceded by a Select Committee, chaired by Lord Worsley (P.P. 1844 (583) V), before which the radical case for better community provisions—roads, drains, village greens—had been well-canvassed.

[86] Enclosures of open fields were only made subject to this in the substantial amendments of 1852: 15 & 16 Vict., c. 79 (an Act, typically, which the Commissioners themselves had much to do with).

[87] Despite doing very little to provide public amenities or allotments for the poor: see Tate, (1967), p. 138.

[88] For this campaign and the ensuing legislation (Metropolitan Commons Act 1866; Commons Act 1876), see Tate (1967) Chap. 13.

[89] Hammond (1927) Chaps. 2, 3; Chambers and Mingay (1967), pp. 96–104; Tate (1967), pp. 88–90, 174–175.

[90] Hammond (1927), pp. 63–72; see also J.M. Neeson (1984) 105 P. & P. 114.

[91] The Hammonds' instance—King's Sedgmoor—was one where the cause was lost: (1927), pp. 40–46.

work on the records left by sets of commissioners suggests how scrupulously they went into claims, surveying and allotment.[92] At this level their attention to legal rectitude clearly provided a hedge against unscrupulous cupidity. There has been considerable doubt over the costs of enclosure, though modern studies seem to be substantiating the Hammonds' first hunch that they were often considerable.[93] Meeting them in some places undoubtedly led to substantial selling up of smaller holdings, though there is evidence that this may have been mainly by absentee-investors.[94]

(b) Tithe

The tithe interest often held a strong bargaining position during enclosure because the tithe was in any case the source of disruptive contention. The tax in kind had originally lain due from parishioners to their incumbent for the church fabric and the poor as well as for himself. But it turned with time into an individual right of property, any communal obligation being transmuted into the tithe-owner's liability to pay tax, including the poor rate.[95] In about a third of all parishes the "great tithes," (on corn, hay and wood) had passed to a lay impropriator,[96] perhaps the local squire or a large landowner, who would pay the incumbent an annual stipend or allow him a portion of the tithe or let him a farm. The tithe might be sought in kind by its owner, or he might collect it through an agent or even grant a lease over it. The business of assessing what was due on which products and of collecting the actual portion was a regular source of argument despite the recording of parish practice in "glebe terriers." Litigation proliferated and elaborate law accumulated upon the subject.[97]

These difficulties had over time produced a tendency to transmute tithe in kind into a fixed money payment, which, if it had become legally binding by custom, was known as a modus. It might apply, for instance, to a parish or to a particular product, notably if it were something such as milk which had otherwise to be constantly reckoned. Such payments in lieu were likely to spread in periods of stable prices and to be challenged in times of inflation. If it came to proof, the common law rules had to be satisfied: that there was no reason why it should not have existed since 1189 and that the memory of living man did not run to the contrary. In consequence tithe had a varied impact both on the landowners, farmers and cottagers who had to produce it and on the clergy, who might be more or less directly dependent on it. It helped to mark out the considerable gap between the well-connected incumbent of one or more rectories and the poor country parson or curate who, despite his degree from Oxford or

---

[92] Gonner (1912), pp. 75–83; W. E. Tate (1944) 44 E.H.R. 238; (1948) 19 Ag. Hist. R. 137.

[93] J. M. Martin (1964) 9 U.Birm. H.J. 144; M. E. Turner (1973) 21 Ag. H.R. 35; cf. W. E. Tate (1952) 5 Ec. H.R. (2d) 258.

[94] J M Martin (1979) 32 Ec. H.R. (2d) 328.

[95] See Evans (1976) Chap. 5.

[96] Mainly upon the dissolution of the monasteries.

[97] For legal texts and collections of cases, see Evans (1976), pp. 175–177.

Cambridge, had to supplement a meagre tithe or stipend by farming or schoolmastering.

With the upswing of agricultural prices in the late eighteenth century and the accompanying drive towards capital improvement in farming, tithe ceased to be a source of sporadic bickering and became a focus of wide discontent. The rising prices stimulated clergy and lay impropriators alike. The governing establishment of the church became an active instigator of change, prompting incumbents to insist upon their full entitlement, especially upon taking up office. In particular, alleged moduses were challenged by demands once more to exact the tithe in kind. With this came a new grievance, since tithe was an entitlement to a tenth of the gross produce, without any allowance for what it cost to enhance production. Tithe-payers and agricultural improvers alike were quick to point the lesson: that tithe acted as a disincentive to capital investment and experimentation, particularly with new crops such as potatoes and turnips. "Tythes," wrote Arthur Young, "are so powerful an obstacle to all spirited husbandry that it can never arise under the extreme burden of their being taken in kind."[98]

In such a hostile climate, litigation now spread in earnest. Issues over proportions due and collection were still tried in the ecclesiastical courts,[99] but question of title, including the question whether a modus had replaced entitlement in kind, had been taken over by the central courts. The existence of the custom might be put to juries (common or special) whose tithe-payer sympathies made them anathema to tithe-owners. But even if the verdict of a common law jury was sought, the process would most likely be begun in an equitable jurisdiction (the Court of Chancery or—even more likely—the Court of Exchequer) in search of injunctive relief.[1]

The consequences could be extraordinary. A dispute at Kendal lasted for nineteen years, cost some £20,000 and had to be ended by private Act. It was not uncommon for a tithe action to cost £3,000–£4,000 and to last 10 years. A wide range of people learned bitterly the costs and hazards of major litigation—in particular that those who won were often those with economic power and social position.[2] A substantial rector might well force smaller farmers into an expensive compromise; but an ordinary incumbent who dared to take on a great landlord might find himself exhausted by interminable stratagems of procedure devised by the best counsel and solicitors.[3] The whole experience must rank (like nuisance actions and

---

[98] *Annals of Agriculture* (1784) I, 73; and see Adam Smith, *Wealth of Nations* (1976 ed.), II pp. 836–40.

[99] In 1696 (by 7 & 8 Will. III, c. 6), the justices in petty sessions were given a default jurisdiction (with distress as a sanction) for tithe due, to the value of £2 (increased to £10 in 1813—53 Geo. III, c. 127, s.4). The church courts also heard other tithe disputes through the eighteenth century: Evans (1976), pp. 44–45.

[1] See Evans (1976) Ch. 3.

[2] See E. J. Evans (1974) 74 Trans. Westmoreland and Cumb. Ant. Soc. 159.

[3] In the case of Quakers, the objection to paying tithe was conscientious and, in the late seventeenth and early eighteenth centuries, they had been the subject of quite substantial persecution. Subsequently, it seems that for the most part ways were found by which the tithe owner could extract his due while allowing the Quaker

workmen's compensation later on) as one of the truly striking lessons in the exacerbative potential of litigation.

The church itself came to see that insistence on tithe in its original form could not survive into an age of high farming and a money economy. As long as Parliamentary reform could be forestalled, it did not need to act; but in the disestablishment storms of the 1830s, tithe in kind was soon offered as a hostage to fortune.[4] In 1836, the Whigs pushed through an Act creating compulsory machinery for the commutation of tithes into annual rentcharges upon land, calculated on the average over the previous seven years (taking some account of collection costs) and adjustable for subsequent shifts in agricultural prices in accordance with a set formula.[5]

Three central commissioners and a staff of assistants (following the model of the poor law commission) were to work across the country settling the amounts due under this novel form of church rate. They were first to seek arrangements by agreement (the sole procedure that the church and Tories would have admitted) and this they managed in nearly 60 per cent., of parishes. In the other cases disputed rights had to be adjudicated and the decisions settled many questions of modus and exemption through enclosure which had waited for years to be resolved in the courts. A right of appeal lay to courts of equity; it seems however not to have been greatly employed.[6] It was clear that commutation had brought to an end the church's hope of raising its tithe revenues by the dramatic multiples that it had looked for and sometimes achieved in the preceding half-century. The Commissioners and their assistants, many of whom were experienced as administrators of enclosure, brought an expertise that was trusted by the main protagonists. Moreover they opened a prospect of permanent solution rather than a temporary truce. The great bulk of their work was completed by the early 1850s. It rescued the Church from a wave of rural antagonism which might otherwise have swamped the tithe entitlement completely.[7] It was a signal victory for bureaucratic directness over judicial super-erogation. Introduced at a time when the principal combatants were

---

some way of symbolising that he did not participate voluntarily—for instance, by "forcible" removal of produce; the process was part of a larger accommodation of old dissent. See Evans (1976), pp. 58–62.

[4] In 1832 itself, Lord Tenterden's Act (2 & 3 Will. IV, c. 100) imposed a limitation period of 30 years on challenges to moduses. But it first allowed a year within which to begin proceedings on older issues. This had the effect of turning many into "active" disputes, some of them still outstanding over a decade later: Evans (1976), pp. 122, 143. For other curbs upon litigation, see 4 & 5 Will. IV, c. 83, 5 & 6 Will. IV, c. 74; and see generally G. F. A. Best, *Temporal Pillars* (1964), pp. 465–79; W. R. Ward, *Religion and Society in England 1790–1850* (1973), pp. 111–24.

[5] Tithes Commutation Act 1836, 6 & 7 Will. IV, c. 71. For a detailed account, see Evans, pp. 129–31.

[6] A number of disputes about their powers also found their way to Queen's Bench by prerogative writ: see 7 Will. IV & 1 Vict., c. 69, s.3 and *e.g.*, re *Ystradunlais Commutation* (1844) 8 Q.B. 32; re *Dent Commutation* (1845) 8 Q.B. 43; re *Appledore Commutation* (1845) 8 Q.B. 139.

[7] As it was, the rentcharge was to survive despite the dragging effects of agricultural depression, until 1936, when its exoneration was settled over a period of 60 years; the massive inflation that has since intervened produced a crippling result for tithe owners: Evans (1976) Chap. 8.

wearying of conflict, the Commission was allowed to perform an adjudicative function as a very distinct administrative tribunal. Its success certainly led to the creation of the Enclosure Commission with its similar functions.[8] Both were prime examples of what specialist administrators alone might achieve.

(c) Loans for Improvement

In the 35 years from the repeal of the Corn Laws in 1846 some £13.5 million for capital improvements was borrowed by landowners (in addition to the considerable expenditure which they found from current income). This was not only deployed in drainage, though technical advances made this a prime concern[9]—farm buildings, cottages, roads, even rail links across farmland would eventually be within the special schemes.[10] The Treasury itself provided £4 million[11] in the early stages as a sop to the protectionists and a desirable end in itself to land improvers like Peel and Prince Albert.[12] But soon private funds supplied through land development companies became a more popular source. The private Acts by which they were established permitted them to offer more favourable terms.[13] A modest measure of discrimination allowed the state to withdraw from active participation to the safer realm of regulation.

Because the loans were being made to aristocratic and gentrified proprietors, the land could be charged with the debt only if the terms of settlements could be made sufficiently broad. The Enclosure Commissioners acquired the function not only of sanctioning the expenditure of the Treasury money but of approving all loans which needed special authority for a mortgage. It was one more displacement of Chancery, which had been given similar functions under two sterile Acts of 1840 and 1845.[14] The Commissioners' duty was to see to the standard of work and the likelihood that the loan would improve income to the extent that it would pay for itself within "a specified number of years so that it would not rest a permanent burden upon succeeding generations." Their decision-making, for all the adjudicative elements within it, was not subject to any right of appeal. In the event they rarely ruled outright against an improvement, their inspectors acting as consultants and asserting authority

---

[8] Into which, in 1851, the Tithe Commissioners were absorbed.

[9] Chambers and Mingay (1966), pp. 175–177.

[10] See the terms of the Improvement of Land Act 1864, 27 & 28 Vict., c. 114.

[11] The first Public Money Drainage Act in 1846 (9 & 10 Vict., c. 101) gave £2m for Britain (most of which went to Scotland) and £1m for Ireland. The second, of 1850, gave £2m, much of it earmarked for England and Wales. Loans could be made to fee simple owners as well as to life tenants.

[12] See D. Spring (1963), pp. 149–150; Chap. 5 is a detailed account of the politics and administration of the Acts.

[13] The best known were the West of England and South Wales Drainage Co. (1848), the General Drainage and Development Co. (1849) and the Land Improvement Co. (1853); others followed, leading to general legislation in 1864. See D. Spring (1963), pp. 152–159 for their various powers, which depended to some extent upon the Private Money Drainage Act 1848 (11 & 12 Vict., c. 119).

[14] These acts—the first becoming known as Pusey's Act after its progenitor, a Conservative landowner—at least helped Parliament to accept the notion of interfering with the terms of settlements.

largely by prescribing their requirements in advance.[15] Once more their intervention attracted approval; they were considered an effective "public trustee" acting on behalf of those who would inherit the land in the course of settlement.

No equivalent method of by-passing settlements was devised in the mid-century years for approving the grant of long leases or the selling up of land. The black years of Ireland's famine produced a precedent there for intervention,[16] and in 1856 Lord Cranworth piloted through a bill giving English tenants for life the right to apply to Chancery for power to sell for re-investment in other land and the power to lease for farming, building and mining for various maximum terms.[17] He proposed that the court would act in accordance with the precepts by which Parliament approved private estate Acts—a typical change of procedure for its period. Despite some modifications and extensions[18] the Act was little used, for the process remained cumbrous and expensive. It was the response of reform-minded lawyers to Cobdenite attacks on the settlement system; at root defensive, it was an apparent concession that gave nothing much away. Only when a much longer and more persistent campaign for land reform had run its course, would the tenant for life acquire powers of management and sale without official supervision.[19] In the interim, the Commissioners were able to do a good deal to lift constraints on the life tenant's ability to undertake development for himself.

PART 2: URBAN CONDITIONS AND LAND VALUES

The industrial towns began their rapid sprawl by filling fields and absorbing villages, many of which were themselves the work-centres of a proto-industrial world. An accumulation of factories and workshops, businesses and shops would be interspersed with housing. The desire to live apart from the workplace began to spread through the middle classes and with the development of transport arteries they tended to move out from busy, polluted centres into suburbs, making one typical form of development a series of concentric rings around an over-developed old nucleus.[20] Although many towns grew

[15] For their methods of work, see Spring (1963), pp. 161–171.
[16] The Encumbered Estates Act (11 & 12 Vict., c. 48) allowed the mortgagee a power of sale by order of the Commissioners: see W. L. Burn (1948) 30 Tr. R. H. S. (4th Ser.) 61; P. G. Lane (1972) 3 Ec. and Soc. R. 413.
[17] Settled Estates Act 1856, 19 & 20 Vict., c. 120 (amended by 21 & 22 Vict., c. 77 and 27 & 28 Vict., c. 45). For difficulties in its passage, see F. M. L. Thompson, *Hampstead* (1974), p 172 ff. It gave no power to sanction mortgages. Note also 12 & 13 Vict., c. 26 and 13 & 14 Vict., c. 17, giving effect to certain leases that the life tenant lacked power to grant.
[18] Acts of 1870 and 1877 allowed the raising of money not only to build reservoirs but also to improve mansion houses. The latter was in the vain hope of drawing absentee landlords back to their Irish estates; but there, as Lord Dunsany remarked, fortification was already preferred to embellishment.
[19] Below, p. 168ff.
[20] As recent historical geography has shown, this pattern could be altered by natural features and by older patterns of land-holding: see, *e.g.*, R. Dennis, *English Industrial Cities of the Nineteenth Century* (1984).

to meet the labour demands of one major employer—factory or mineowner, shipbuilder, railway company—only a handful of paternal masters treated the provision of housing near their works as a co-ordinate part of the whole enterprise.[21] Elsewhere housing was left to independent investment and the lure of its regular profitability. What, it was said, was "as safe as houses"? Some of the largest landowners made very substantial investments in enclaves of villas or whole resorts.[22] But the owners of capital at every level were drawn to invest in the housing that they could afford, sometimes for their own occupation, but much more frequently as a source of income.[23]

To meet the new circumstances the techniques of property law required some adaptation. But the essential flexibility of concept, the large scope left for individuation by private contract, meant that owners and entrepreneurs could reach their goals without serious legal impediment.[24] Whether the ground-owner retained an interest by granting the builder only a lease, or whether he sold off the freehold, seems to have depended on local tradition. To some extent the tendency towards leasehold increased when the land had already been taken over by large estate-owners and let to agricultural tenants.[25] This factor could also determine the speed at which different parts of an area developed and the type of housing constructed. Long leasehold perhaps held some potential for producing better-quality building; its price reflected an investment over time by both builder-tenant and ground-landlord.[26] When the building was done, the great bulk of housing was not sold as freehold but let to domestic tenants, most of them on a weekly or monthly basis. The better developments were single family units, the poorer sank into sub-division and over-crowding.[27]

I. Trusts for Sale

In the process of urban development both the trust and the mortgage found vital employment. As we have seen, the trust was only a supportive element in the strict settlement of a landed estate: the first-born of each generation could not be expected to manage through the collaboration implied by legal ownership in the hands of others. Trusts secured the secondary and subsequent interests of the family and could be deployed over the whole estate when second-best conditions prevailed (where, for instance, an infant, female or wastrel was to inherit) or for unusual objects such as a long accumulation of

---

[21] Well-known instances included Sir Titus Salt at Saltire, and later Lever at Port Sunlight and the Cadburys at Bourneville.

[22] See esp. D. Cannadine, *Lords and Landlords* (1980).

[23] Even in the case of London, large landowner-developers were not able to exploit a monopoly position to push up the level of rents: Daunton (1983), pp. 73–84, 107–17.

[24] On the peculiar flexibility of English notions of property and their significance for capital developments, see O. Kahn-Freund, Introduction to K. Renner, *The Institutions of Private Law and their Social Functions* (1949), pp. 26–36.

[25] See Land Enquiry Committee, *The Land* (1914), II pp. 348–353, for a description of the land then exploited on the basis of freehold and leasehold.

[26] See Cannadine above, n. 22.

[27] See below, p. 150ff.

capital for the enhancement of the dynasty.[28] But where land was purely an investment other conditions prevailed; and for this case the conveyancers evolved the trust for sale, in which a whole capital, some perhaps in town leaseholds or freeholds, some lent on mortgage, some in government stock or even industrial or foreign holdings, was given over to trustees as legal owners. The trustees might well be the active managers, buying and selling in response to markets, collecting rents and dividends and paying them over to beneficiaries. The sharing among the family was not likely to adhere to the priorities of the strict settlement, especially as the device came to be used by the successful middle-classes. There could well be equal division among children and more flexible arrangements for special advancement to meet the crucial expenditures of life—the education and settling of sons in professions, the marrying of daughters. The settlor himself or those he might nominate (frequently the trustees themselves) could have a wide variety of powers to determine shares over time. So by the mid-nineteenth century emerged the discretionary trust. Equity courts were busy filling out the implications of these trusts and the powers by which they operated, where the deeds were ambiguous, contradictory or incomplete. They applied the limits of the perpetuities and accumulations rules to them and refused to allow them to become transparent dodges for outwitting creditors; otherwise they subjected them to no constraints in the name of public policy.[29]

II. Building Societies

The trust was coming to form a basis of business collaboration as well as of family sharing: it was "natural" to imply a trust when any owner transferred money or property for management by another; the more so when several were contributing to a common fund for an agreed purpose. This would include joint ventures into urban speculation and building trusts were a common phenomenon by 1800.[30]

One particular development was to have a lasting hold upon the institutions of the land industry: the building society first emerged in the late eighteenth century in a "terminable" form, one of the typical clubs by which the lower tradesmen and skilled workers joined together for protection or advancement. The aim of a building society was to provide capital enough for one member to acquire land and build premises, which would be mortgaged to the society; his repayments, together perhaps with further subscriptions, would allow the other members to buy and build in turn, until all had done so and any surplus could be redistributed. The managerial skills required

---

[28] For perpetuities, see above, p. 128, n. 24; the rule against accumulations was imposed by statute in 1800 (39 & 40 Geo. III, c. 98) as a reaction against Peter Thellusson's will which directed an accumulation of his fortune until the death of the last surviving male relative already then born: see J. H. C. Morris and W. B. Leach, *The Rule against Perpetuities* (3rd ed, 1962) Chap. 11.

[29] For the nature of the interests arising upon a trust for sale in historical perspective, see J. S. Anderson (1984) 100 L.Q.R. 86.

[30] For an instance, see R. S. Neale (1965) 7 Bus. Hist. 94.

for such an operation were complex: determining the order of preference, deciding what could be built, collecting dues and repayments,
organising additional borrowings and the investment of temporary
surplus, dividing up the ultimate cake.[31] When in the 1840s "permanent" societies began to develop, the Victorians could admire them
in earnest as evident aids to self-improvement and saving; but the
practical problems became even greater. Earlier building societies
had come under some of the political suspicion that attached to
friendly societies in general; and in 1836 the legislation regulating
the latter[32] was extended to building societies, which were placed
under the supervision of their own registrar.[33]

The first holder of the office, Tidd Pratt, brought an energy typical
of the new central supervisor to his task, encouraging in many ways
the standardisation of rules and the regularisation of financial and
other practice. As with so many other financial organisations of the
period, the recurrence of fraud and predation by administrators provided one motive for a desire to supervise. Because the institution
was so evidently valuable to the "industrious classes" a certain
measure of external direction by law was felt to be in order. One consequence was that the legislation of 1836, and the registrar's operations under it, were constantly being tested by important litigation.
There was, to take one instance, the question, could a society
increase its resources by borrowing? Or was this contrary to the Act
or to the judges' ideas of public policy? Ultimately rules were held
valid which allowed a society to borrow up to two-thirds of the
amounts secured to it by mortgages.[34] Gradually the societies worked
their way towards more precise legislation and fuller powers of management.[35] After 1874, special machinery involving incorporation
was made available to existing societies and compulsory for fresh
ones.[36] While there would continue to be collapses and scandals,[37]
the building societies took their place in the panoply of leading
financial institutions, their purpose being to raise a subscribed fund
for making advances to members upon mortgage security. In 1883,
Pollock saw them as a bulwark against land nationalisation, since
they had insured that "the artisans of the north country are already
in great part . . . . . . full owners of the homes they dwell in."[38]

---

[31] See Cleary (1965) Chap. 1. Note the attempt to attack the legality of one of these
societies under the Bubble Act, below, p. 251, n. 30.
[32] For which see below, pp. 295–296.
[33] 6 & 7 Will. IV, c. 32; for its passage and consequences, see Cleary (1965) Chap. 2.
[34] See esp. *Laing* v. *Reed* (1869) 39 L.J. Ch. 1; *cf. re National Building Soc.* (1869) L.R. 5
Ch.App. 309 (necessity for an express rule); *Re Victoria Building Soc.* (1870) 39 L.J. Ch.
628 (unlimited borrowing power ultra vires). See further, Cleary (1965), pp. 30–42.
[35] See Cleary (1965) Chaps. 5, 7.
[36] Building Societies Act 1874, following the Report of a Royal Commission (P.P. 1872
[C.514] XXVI) which noted the growth of middle-class institutions out of working-
class roots and refused to place the societies under the general companies legislation.
[37] The spectacular collapse of the Liberator Building Society in 1892 and of the Birkbeck in 1911 (with its popular banking business that turned out to be ultra vires)
certainly impeded the overall growth of the movement. Even so assets in 1920 were
three and a half times those of 1870: see Cleary (1965) Chaps. 8, 9, 11.
[38] Pollock (1883), p. 185.

III. RESTRICTIVE COVENANTS

The value of land turns not only on the uses to which it can be put: what can and cannot be done upon adjacent plots can affect market price and enjoyment quite as much. In rural conditions landowners and occupiers had come to rely upon the common law tort of nuisance[39] and property rights classified as easements and profits à prendre as ways of securing these external values. A nuisance action could terminate interferences of many kinds across boundaries— from plants, smoke, water, noise—imposing its discipline on all occupiers for the benefit of their neighbours.

By contrast easements and profits had to be created (either by grant or by some form of long usage) as limitations upon one piece of land for the benefit of another.[40] Rights of way and rights to bring water were typical easements; profits, such as rights to cut turf or to graze animals, were an intimate part of the division up of land yields that was traditional in many places.[41] Only two negative easements were recognised, both germane to the close conditions of village or town: the right to have a building supported by adjacent land and the right against obstruction to the light through particular windows. But the common law, wary of long-term inhibitions on the full potential of the burdened land, refused to extend these further, for instance, so as to give an easement to a view.[42] Indeed, in the nineteenth century, some judges would have drawn back from the right to light, had it not become so well-accepted as a legal entitlement.[43] When it came to urban development, the desire to maintain general standards of amenity was extremely strong. The owner of "good" property had one great fear, that it would lose value because the whole neighbourhood declined, the exclusive residences being subdivided, partly given over perhaps to business, the yards littered with pets and washing. For his purposes the law of easements was of very little service. If a housing development was offered as leasehold, extensive undertakings not to build, divide or disfigure could be covenanted; and thanks to the long-settled notion of "privity of estate," assignees of the lease and sub-lessees would be bound to observe the conditions. The obligations lay to the landlord and his successors in title who retained an interest in the very land and did not extend to the owners of adjacent properties. Even so this was machinery enough to make leasehold the preferred technique for such development.[44]

[39] As to which, see below, p. 154ff.
[40] Interference with an easement or profit was redressed by action for nuisance. For changing perceptions of the creation of these rights, see J. S. Anderson (1975) 38 M.L.R. 641.
[41] For the history, see Holdsworth, III pp. 153–157; VII pp. 321–342. Much of the detailed law was not worked out until after C. J. Gale's pioneering work on *Easements* had appeared in 1839. He filled lacunae with references to Roman law and other sources: Simpson (1986), pp. 261–264.
[42] Aristocratic land-owners who wanted to remove from their ancestral homes the sights of growing towns might be put to elaborate and expensive expedients: see T. R. Slater (1977) 2 Tr.Brit.Inst.Geog.(N.S.) 314.
[43] Eventually, the House of Lords settled that the interference must be serious enough to constitute a nuisance: *Colls* v. *Home and Colonial Stores* [1904] A.C. 179.
[44] For the development of doctrine, see Holdsworth, VII pp. 287–292; Simpson (1986), pp. 255–56.

Yet potential occupiers of respectable garden squares and villa-filled streets might well want freehold and here there were impediments of doctrine. If covenants between vendor and purchaser were to be judged by notions of contract, with the concept of privity confining obligations to the initial parties, they would be of little avail once plots changed hands. By common law, the benefit of a covenant was enforceable by those who claimed title from the covenantee (the vendor); but there was little authority for the view that the burden would likewise pass to the successors of the covenantor (the purchaser).[45] In 1834, Lord Brougham refused to accept that the burden would "run" at common law, and considered that equity should maintain the like position: the balance of utility did not favour permitting landowners to impose whatever idiosyncratic constraints they might choose on all subsequent owners.[46]

It became plain that this was seriously unsettling to standard conveyancing practice for the best sort of urban development.[47] By 1848, Lord Cottenham had decisively altered equity's course, holding, in the well-known decision of Tulk v. Moxhay,[48] that a successor of the covenantor who had notice of the covenant was thereby bound in conscience to honour it. That is a moral proposition that inevitably stands opposed to privity of contract. The quasi-economic grounds which Lord Cottenham employed for reinforcement carry no conviction. His decision was a way of supporting the established view that in such covenants, despite Brougham's scruples, lay market values meriting protection beyond the frame of contract. It was one of equity's last distinctive contributions to demands for the elevation of novel interests; and the lack of concern for its implications was, if nothing else, a measure of the determination to achieve the result.

As it was, the new doctrine was soon being extended in ways which seriously compromised the essence of contractual privity. A mortgagee of a ship was treated as bound by a prior charterparty of which he had notice[49]; covenants could impose trading restrictions of whatever kind, including, for instance, undertakings to sell only one brand of a product (such as beer) on the premises; indeed covenants could bind even if they involved the positive expenditure of money; the covenantee or some successor did not have to retain land that benefited from the covenant in order to be able to enforce it against any assignee of the original covenantor.[50] Here indeed was evidence of the dangers envisaged by Lord Brougham and in time the judges found reason to impose limits, drawing in particular on

---

[45] In *Keppell* v. *Bailey* (1834) 2 My. & K. 517, Lord Brougham reviewed the earlier case-law and distinguished covenants between lessor and lessee.

[46] *Keppell* v. *Bailey* (above n. 45), refusing to enforce a covenant requiring the covenantor's supply of limestone to be obtained from a particular quarry.

[47] *Cf.* the cases enforcing by injunction covenants not to build breweries on residential plots: *Whatman* v. *Gibson* (1838) 9 Sim. 196; *Mann* v. *Stephens* (1846) 15 Sim. 377.

[48] (1848) 2 Ph. 774.

[49] *De Mattos* v. *Gibson* (1855) 4 De G. & J. 276; followed in *The Strathcona* [1926] A.C. 108; and not finally rejected until *Port Line* v. *Ben Line* [1958] 2 Q.B. 146.

[50] Covenant to benefit trader rather than landowner: *Catt* v. *Tourle* (1869) L.R. 4 Ch.App. 654; *Luker* v. *Dennis* (1877) 7 Ch.D. 227; covenant to spend money: *Morland* v. *Cook* (1868) L.R. 6 Eq. 252 (maintaining sea-wall); *Cooke* v. *Chilcott* (1876) 3 Ch.D. 694 (supplying water).

analogies to covenants in leases and to easements: covenants had to be negative and they had to touch and concern the land (and not merely the trading upon it); and only a covenantee who retained land to be benefited could sue an assignee of the covenantor.[51]

Even within such a circumscribed framework, the long-term inconvenience of rights which bound all takers would come to be felt. Fluctuations in land prices and shifts in fashion could destroy exclusiveness in a way that restrictive covenants were not enough to withstand. The social pretensions of one generation could become a mere impediment to economic potential in the next. By the end of the century the judges were restive enough to be suggesting that, where the character of an estate had already changed, a restrictive covenant should no longer be enforced.[52] It would, however, need the profound alterations of the period before and after the First World War— and in particular the housing shortage to which the war contributed so drastically—before statute would furnish the courts with express power to lift covenants once they were judged to have lost their usefulness.[53]

PART 3: LAND AS AN INDUSTRIAL RESOURCE

The demands upon land imposed by industry, transport and towns entailed fundamental legal problems ranging far beyond those already considered. The first was the need to secure powers of compulsory acquisition for setting new ventures in motion—most notably in the establishment of roads, canals and railways. Secondly, the damage, inconvenience and personal danger that stemmed from many activities came in forms so varied that it would test the resources of the general law, particularly the criminal and tort law of nuisance, and call forth a long succession of statutes concerned with public health and environmental pollution. These formed prime material for mid-Victorian experiments in statehood. Amid high controversy, a significant balance was to be struck between central and local government, and also between the nominally executive and the nominally judicial, in the detailed execution of policies that in the most direct sense compromised the autonomy of private property.

I. Compulsory Acquisition

From the sixteenth century onwards, there were examples enough of cities and boroughs being granted power to acquire land compulsorily, for instance, for water supply and ports. In a typical passage Blackstone first announced the inviolability of private property even

---

[51] *Haywood* v. *Brunswick Building Soc.* (1881) 8 Ch.D. 403 (covenant to build houses etc. not enforceable against assignee); *LSWR* v. *Gomm* (1882) 20 Ch.D. 562 (covenant to reconvey not enforceable against assignee); *Allen* v. *LCC* [1914] 3 K.B. 42 (covenant not to build not enforceable by a local authority which held no local land).

[52] See *German* v. *Chapman* (1877) Ch.D. 271 at 279; *Knight* v. *Simmonds* [1896] 2 Ch. 294 at 298.

[53] Law of Property Act 1925, s.84(1).

against the general good of the community: "it would be dangerous to allow any private man, or even a public tribunal, to be the judge of this common good." Then came qualification: "The legislature above can, and indeed frequently does, interpose, and compel the individual to acquiesce"; but it acts only with caution and assures "full indemnification and equivalent."[54]

Blackstone could afford to play down the invasionary element in these arrangements. They occurred mainly in the mass of private acts dealing with transport. The eighteenth century's admixture of public obligation and personal interest led to the institution of turnpike trusts to take over sections of highway and maintain them out of tolls. In the movement away from control by the justices and compulsory labour by the whole community, which was the earlier system, large numbers of property owners in country and town were made trustees and the schemes were put to local ratepayers as means of shifting financial burdens onto the shoulders of road-users. The powers of compulsory purchase were mostly secondary, being for widenings and diversions which would bring the road to the estate of some major promoter.[55] In the case of canals, new routes dictated by the lie of the land made acquisition a more central issue. In the Duke of Bridgewater's first promotions, compulsion was a source of considerable opposition and subsequently he faced contests in Parliament from a determined estate owner. But in general, proprietors were content with compensation and proximity to the new cheap transport.[56]

In the case of the railways, the blow to landowners was softened by sums that totalled some 14 per cent of the companies' capital, a factor which helped to put their cost well beyond those of France, Germany and the United States. A burden of high freights was imposed that by the end of the century was to bear hard on British exporters. In the unique conditions of Britain's industrial dominance the railway promoters clamoured to pay despite the price. Here again, however, there were many landowners who realised the great enhancement that a railway would bring to the value of their remaining land and they were often among active promoters of extensions and branch lines.[57]

In the great years of railway building, Parliament laid down general rules about the emollient of compensation that were to last for three-quarters of a century. The Land Clauses Consolidation Act 1845 left the landowner with real opportunity to enhance his price upon a compulsory acquisition.[58] The Act was almost entirely concerned with procedures rather than with principles of assessment;

---

[54] *Commentaries*, I 139; see generally F. A. Mann (1955) 75 L.Q.R. 188.
[55] S. & B. Webb, *The Story of the King's Highway* (1913), p. 120.
[56] H. Malet, *Bridgewater: the Canal Duke* (1977), pp. 47–49, 121–29.
[57] H. Pollins (1952–53) 19 Economica 395; (1957) 3 J. Transp. Hist. 41, 103; S. Broadbridge, *Studies in Railway Expansion and the Capital Market* (1970).
[58] 8 & 9 Vict., c. 18. Other general Acts, as well as many private Acts, would rely upon its content: see *e.g.*, Railway Clauses Consolidation Act 1845 (8 & 9 Vict., c. 20). For their enactment, see O. C. Williams, *Historical Development of Private Bill Procedure* (1949), I p. 107.

the amount was a matter for the arbitrators, the juries (special or common) or the justices, to one or other of whom the assessment was entrusted.[59] What happened in consequence has yet to be studied in detail: landowners it seems, preferred to opt for an arbitrator-valuer. Certainly, railway representatives said that juries, (thinking perhaps of the eventual freights and passenger charges to their area), tended to prefer the railways' offer to the demands of landowners.[60] The courts showed little tendency to criticise generous awards, whichever kind of tribunal was responsible for them: the assessment might put a value upon a prospective use, however unlikely it might be that the land would ever have been given over to that use; this applied even where the acquirer was the only person ever likely to engage in the use of highest value.[61] In addition to this "market value" assessment, the owner was entitled to loss through damage to other land— loss of support, the deleterious consequences of severance and so forth[62]; and he was entitled to an added "solatium" for the indignity of compulsion—in 1845, a Lords Select Committee proposed that it should be at least 50 per cent.[63] Even at the outset of the next century, an Irish judge was uncertain whether an interest in possession merited an addition of as much as 20 per cent.[64]

Not until the last quarter of the century would this high respect for land-ownership come into conflict with the programmes of social reform aimed at slum clearance and the provision of working-class dwellings. As we shall see, the more egregious demands of slum landlords led to curbs upon their compensation claims.[65] But it would take until 1919, when the special aura of land-ownership had so noticeably dimmed, for basic principles and machinery to be open to review. The private arbitrators and juries were replaced by a panel of official arbitrators, forerunners of the present Lands Tribunal and a significant addition to the collection of administrative courts. A set of limiting principles, designed to keep compensation to realistic economic values, was imposed.[66] Perhaps most important of all, the generous rule of 1845 which gave the landowner his costs unless he got no more than had been offered him, and even then did not oblige him to pay the acquirer's own costs, was replaced by the normal indemnity rule of English litigation.[67] The official arbitrators were to be experts in land valuation. The only possibility of appeal lay in having the arbitrator state a case on a question of law to the High

---

[59] Two justices could determine claims up to £50; above that amount the claimant could choose an arbitrator (to whom another and an umpire could be added, if the other side so chose), or jury: 8 & 9 Vict., c. 18, ss.22, 23, 25–28. Under s.58, the parties could request justices to appoint a surveyor to the task.

[60] See the Lords Select Committee on Compensation for Land Compulsorily Taken for Railways, P.P. 1845 (420) X, evidence of Parker and Duncan.

[61] *Simpson* v. *South Staffs. Rly.* (1865) 13 W.R. 729.

[62] 8 & 9 Vict., c. 18, s.63.

[63] Report (above, n. 60), p. 1.

[64] *Re Athlone Rifle Range* [1902] 1 Ir. R. 433. 20 per cent. was too high for a mere rent-charge.

[65] Below, p. 182.

[66] Acquisition of Land (Assessment) Act 1919, s.2.

[67] 1845 Act, s.34; 1919 Act, s.5.

Court, whose decision was to be final.[68] Even so, it was a particular
turn in a more general movement that was to antagonise some of the
judiciary and it played a distinct part in their anti-bureaucratic alar-
ums of the late 1920s.[69]

II. Public Health and Amenity: The Common Law

"Every man should so use his own as not to damnify another" was
the simple prescription taken by Blackstone as the premise of the
common law of nuisance.[70] Under this rubric the conservers of local
conditions—the constables, justices, juries and Sewer Commissions—might seek the draining of water, the disposal of rubbish,
the upkeep of highways, rivers and bridges and the restriction of
polluting trades.[71] If individuals could be identified as responsible,
they could be indicted for public nuisance and required to abate it.
Alternatively, the Attorney-General might seek an injunction from
equity on the public's behalf. But equally, a private occupier or
owner who suffered a nuisance to his land might sue for personal
relief; this was possible if the cause arose either on private land or in
public (for instance on the highway) so as to cause him a larger
measure of injury than the public in general.[72]

As new techniques of production outstripped the methods of suppressing their undesirable side-effects, and as cities began to pour
out rubbish and sewage that were very hard to dispose of efficiently,
the courts had to decide whether to impede developments that
seemed essential to economic growth or to leave others to suffer.
They were obliged to apply old rules to conditions where the potential both for good and for evil was on a novel scale.[73] Given their deep
loyalty to the notion of private property which is evident in many of
their decisions, the tensions were considerable. But the problems
were increased by the absolute conception of property. Once a plaintiff was held to be suffering a nuisance he was normally entitled not
so much to damages at common law—which would have measured
the cost of continuing the nuisance—but rather to an injunction in
equity. The sufferer was to have all or nothing. There was little room
for intermediate compromise.

To some extent the courts could disguise the difficulty by tempor-

---

[68] They were to be appointed by a Reference Committee, consisting of the L.C.J., M.R.
and President of the Surveyors' Institution (for England), s.1. If the arbitrator
refused to state a case, the High Court might (in its discretion) compel him to do so:
s.6.

[69] See below, p. 191.

[70] *Commentaries*, III 217. How rigorously the maxim was enforced was largely a matter
for juries and much is now lost from view: *cf.* Brenner (1974). One apparent
defence—that a person could not complain if he "came to" an existing nuisance—
was abandoned in the 1830s: *Elliotson* v. *Feltham* (1835) 2 Bing N.C. 134; *Bliss* v. *Hall*
(1838) 4 Bing N.C. 783; But the notion of "zoning" survived: see below n. 84.

[71] See, *e.g.*, S. and B. Webb, *The Parish and the County* (1906), pp. 446–479; *The Story of
the King's Highway* (1913) Chap. 2.

[72] See F. H. Newark (1949) 65 L.Q.R. 480.

[73] The rule limiting private actions for public nuisance was one of the variables which
nineteenth century judges were to use to restrict the scope of the wrong: Brenner
(1974), pp. 420–424.

ising. During their Lord Chancellorships, Thurlow and Eldon each made it plain that interim injunctions were not to be had before the question whether there was a nuisance had been settled by a jury in a common law trial. The cautious Eldon refused interlocutory relief against a manufacturer of soap and black ash in Battersea—"a large trading concern composing property to a vast amount"—and he doubted his power even to impel a speedy trial at common law.[74] Cheap and rapid relief remained unlikely for at least the first half of the nineteenth century. But the procedural rapprochements of common law and equity in mid-century meant that slowness of process ceased to be so immediate a barrier to practical relief.[75] The injunction became more readily available in the very decades when the toll of industrialisation was becoming inescapably evident. As a counterweight, courts were empowered in their discretion to award damages "in lieu of, or in addition to, an injunction," and so were, if they chose, in a position to license (at a price) the continuance of a nuisance. They were to find the jurisdiction to a degree repellent but they refused to renounce it entirely.[76]

Beside questions of procedure stood issues of substantive rule. Traditionally juries had been instructed to concern themselves with the question whether the victim was really suffering a sufficient interference with the enjoyment and use of his land to amount to a nuisance. Twice at least, the courts toyed with the inviting possibility of abandoning this categorical approach, in favour of a balance in which the benefits of the activity—not only to the defendant, but also to his workforce and to trade in the neighbourhood and elsewhere—would be set against the inconvenience to the objector. But this would turn juries into felicific calculators, and the bulk of the judges could not contemplate the variable verdicts and the undermining of private property that would be the consequence. On the first occasion, when the issue was public nuisance, Lord Denman said: "in the infinite variety of active operation always going further in this industrious community, no greater evil can be conceived than the encouragement of capitalists and adventurers to interfere with known public rights, from motives of personal interest, on the speculation that the changes may be rendered lawful by ultimately being thought to supply the public with something better than what they actually enjoy."[77] On the second, Baron Bramwell showed his predeliction for a political economy grounded upon the sanctity of private property: "unless the defendant's profits be enough to compensate

---

[74] *Att.-Gen.* v. *Cleaver* (1811) 18 Ves. Jun. 212; and see *Weller* v. *Smeaton* (1784) 1 Cox 103; cf. the exceptional *Crowder* v. *Tinkler* (1816) 19 Ves. 617 (construction of gunpowder factory).

[75] The Chancery Procedure Act 1852 (15 & 16 Vict., c. 86), s.58, allowed interlocutory injunctions upon common law rights to be granted on the basis of affidavit evidence.

[76] Lord Cairns' Act (21 & 22 Vict., c. 27), s 2. This was inadvertently repealed by the Statute Law Revision Act 1883, which did not prevent the House of Lords from later giving it "customary" force: *Leeds Industrial* v. *Slack* [1924] A.C. 851.

[77] *R.* v. *Ward* (1836) 4 Ad. & E. 384, 404–05, disapproving Bayley J., *R.* v. *Russell* (1827) 6 B. & C. 566, 563; McLaren (1983), pp. 180–183.

[the loss to the plaintiff] I deny that it is for the public benefit he should do what he has done; if they are he should compensate."[78]

Nonetheless a way of compromising was found that typified both the techniques of the common law and prevailing currents of public opinion. A line that divided injury to property from personal discomfort was underscored. Those who suffered injury to their land continued to be protected with Blackstonian rigour. That is the essential significance of *Rylands* v. *Fletcher*,[79] a case which came subsequently to be treated as establishing its own category of liability. Negligence, in the sense of blameworthy default, was fast becoming the touchstone of most tortious liability for personal injury and had spread over into questions of damage to personal property.[80] So insidious was the attraction of fault liability that when Fletcher found his coal-mine flooded by Rylands' new reservoir,[81] counsel pleaded his case in negligence. The defendants established that the water had escaped down unknown shafts and (so it seemed) no blame could attach to their engineers.[82] Nonetheless the bulk of the judges were firmly of the view that, since the water had been artificially accumulated, liability was as strict as for private nuisances that were continuous and cumulative.

At just this juncture the House of Lords had also to decide whether Tipping, who owned a 13,000 acre estate in St. Helens, could recover damages for the air pollution from a neighbouring copper-smelting works. For the damage to the value of his land, which was found to have been rendered useless for agriculture, he was entitled to succeed; indeed he also secured an injunction against the operation. But for personal discomfort he could not even be compensated. In this his interest had to be subjugated to the "legitimate and free exercise of (the) trade in the neighbourhood."[83] Such a rule was not to be absolute and invariable, for both the degree of discomfort and the general nature of the neighbourhood were still to be brought into account.[84] But as far as industrial Lancashire was concerned, the dis-

---

[78] *Bamford* v. *Turnley* (1862) 3 B. & S. 66, 85, overruling *Hole* v. *Barlow* (1858) 4 C.B. (N.S.) 334; and see Brenner (1974), p. 410ff; McLaren (1983), pp. 169–79; and note P.S. Atiyah (1980) 23 J.L. & Ec. 191.

[79] (1865) L.R. 1 Ex. 265; (1968) L.R. 3 H.L. 330.

[80] Note the readiness to turn to negligence where an enterprise with statutory authority, such as a railway, caused an accident that injured land (fire damage), as well as things (causing horse to shy): *Vaughan* v. *Taff Vale Rly.* (1860) 5 H. & N. 679 (but note Bramwell B. *contra*, 3 H. & N. 743; L.R. 4 H.L. at 193–95); and see *R.* v. *Pease* (1832) 4 B. & Ad. 30.

[81] For the exceptional dangers posed by collapsing dams, and the relief of the two great Victorian disasters (Holmfirth (1852) by charitable subscription and Dale Dyke (1864) under the terms of the private Act, which imposed strict but limited liability), see A. W. B. Simpson (1984) 13 J. Leg. St. 209, 216–238.

[82] On the significance of negligence in fact and law, see Simpson (previous note), 238 ff.

[83] *St. Helens Smelting Co.* v. *Tipping* (1865) 11 H.L.C. 642; for the subsequent injunction to protect property; (1865) L.R. 1 Ch. 66.

[84] Thesiger L.J.'s well-known remark, "What would be a nuisance in Belgrave Square would not necessarily be one in Bermondsey" (*Sturges* v. *Bridgman* (1879) 11 Ch.D. 852 at 865) echoes earlier notions of "zoning" the decent residential from the polluted industrial: *R.* v. *Jordan* (1663) 2 Show. K.B. 327n.

tinction drawn by the Lords was overwhelming. A decade later, the Royal Commission on Noxious Vapours was to find that "persons whose houses are rendered almost uninhabitable by the stench of sulphuretted hydrogen from Widnes or St. Helens waste heaps appear to be practically without any remedy whatever."[85] Nor was the problem just that of the substantive rule. The Commission reported that even farmers who lost crops had great difficulty in pinpointing a culprit—an old problem, which arose equally with river pollution[86]—and they were met with procedural feints, such as removal from county to superior courts, which were too much for them.[87]

The cleft thus dug between property damage and personal inconvenience divided those who took all from those who got nothing from private nuisance actions. Contrast with the dismal lot of St. Helens townsfolk that of the owners of country estates who found their rivers turning foul and dead from the vain attempt of sanitary authorities in the towns to dispose of sewage. Following the procedural reforms of the 1850s, estate owners secured injunctions, despite the authorities' cries that there was no alternative open to them.[88] When the Birmingham Corporation pleaded the dire consequences of not being able to dispose of its sewage in the River Tame, Page Wood, V.-C. said "I am not sitting here as a committee of public safety, armed with an arbitrary power to prevent what, it is said, will be a great injury not to Birmingham only, but to the whole of England . . . My function is only to interpret what the legislature (the proper body to which all such arguments should be addressed) has considered necessary for the town of Birmingham."[89]

Parliament, however, was prone to lack of precision when it came to specifying who should have a claim for the deleterious consequences of acting under statute. The courts were left to wrest solutions from language that gave no real answers. Two crucial instances show a different aspect of the judicial process in mid-century. First there was the question whether compensation was payable to a trader such as a shopkeeper or publican who lost clientele during the course of construction works, because access became more cumbrous, but who did not suffer any permanent physical damage to his property. By the early sixties most of the judges were in favour of

---

[85] Royal Commission on Noxious Vapours, P.P. 1878 [C. 2159] XLIV, p. 14; and see McLaren (1983), pp. 194–205.

[86] Juries were not to convict unless satisfied that the defendant was perpetrating a nuisance, not merely contributing to it: see e.g., R. v. Medley (1833) 6 C. & P. 292.

[87] Report, n. 85, p. 34

[88] Sir Charles Adderley's success against the Birmingham Corporation (Att.-Gen. v. Birmingham (1858) 4 K. & J. 528) not only produced a crisis which lasted for 20 years, but set a precedent for similar actions; see, e.g., Spokes v. Banbury Local Board of Health (1865) 35 L.J. Ch. 105; Goldschmid v. Tunbridge Wells Improvement Commissioners (1866) 35 L.J. Ch. 382; Att.-Gen. v. Mayor of Leeds (1870) 39 L.J. Ch. 254; cf. Lilywhite v. Trimmer (1867) 36 L.J. Ch. 525, where an injunction was refused because the relatively slight level of the nuisance had to be balanced against concern for "the drainage of a not inconsiderable town" (Alton).

[89] Att.-Gen. v. Birmingham (above, n. 88); and see Senior v. Metropolitan Rly. (1863) 2 H. & C. 258; cf. R. v. London Dock Co. (1836) 5 Ad. & El. 163.

allowing such claims.[90] But when the issue was carried to the Lords, two of the three members of the House insisted on cutting back the rule; compensation required some exceptional hurt such as physical injury, not purely economic loss which resulted from a disturbance characterised as being no greater to the plaintiff than to other members of the public.[91]

As with enclosure, there was a level below which there was no need to pay elaborate respect to the interests of others, propertied or personal. That level was worked out by delineating rules such as those just mentioned. As the railways drove their "ventilating shafts" into the London metropolis and the other great cities, there were many below the reach of compensation who were simply displaced or discomforted without ceremony. The great mass of weekly tenants had no right which survived the "notice to treat" initiating a compulsory purchase. Even when Parliament began to insist that a company provide alternative housing, it would find no difficulty in buying off the tenants with a sovereign or two or remission of some back rent.[92]

Second came the question whether a person who suffered an admitted nuisance from the noise and dirt of a railway running by his premises had a claim to compensation: a question of obvious significance to the overall costs of railway operations. In 1869, a clear majority of the judges informed the Lords that they were in favour of liability: "if it were the law and practice to do individuals a damage for the benefit of the public without compensation, no one in particular could complain when it happened to him; . . . still such a law and practice would be highly inconvenient and dangerous."

Yet two members of a three-man House of Lords insisted that individuals must suffer for the greater good of all, since they could find nothing in the compensation provisions of the railway's Act which covered this category of sufferers.[93] Perhaps they had a keener feeling for the politically acceptable in an age hell-bent on progress. The railway interest kept the public aware of the high cost of such compensation as the companies did have to pay.[94] At any rate there was no significant movement to reverse the rules by new general legislation.

III. CONTROL OF LAND USE: STATUTORY AUTHORITIES

Nuisance proceedings, whether private or public, operated in a world of individual responsibilities, imposed mainly on landowners

---

[90] All three common law courts had come to the same conclusion: *Senior* v. *Metropolitan Rly.* (above, n. 89); *Cameron* v. *Charing Cross Rly.* (1864) 16 C.B.N.S. 430; *Ricket* v. *Metropolitan Rly.* (below, n. 91—but here a majority of the Exchequer Chamber disagreed).

[91] *Ricket* v. *Metropolitan Rly.* (1864) 5 B. & S. 149; (1867) L.R. 2 H.L. 175 (Lords Chelmsford and Cranworth; Westbury dissenting).

[92] See H. J. Dyos (1955) 2 J. Transp. Hist. 11, 90; (1957) 3 J. Transp. Hist. 23.

[93] *Hammersmith and City Rly.* v. *Brand* (1869) L.R. 4 H.L. 171 (Lords Chelmsford and Colonsay; Cairns dissenting); contrast *Duke of Buccleugh* v. *Metropolitan Board of Works* (1869) L.R. 4 H.L. 171, where the claimant was compensated for noise because he also had land appropriated (part of Montagu House taken for the Thames Embankment); see also P. S. Atiyah (above, n. 78).

[94] See Dyos (above, n. 92).

and occupiers. They were, moreover, a form of negative reaction to intolerable conditions. The first central authority to concern itself with public health problems, the Poor Law Commissioners, started off down much the same track[95]; they looked to ways in which the jumble of local authorities concerned with this or that aspect of the overall problem—borough corporations, improvement commissioners, highway trustees, commissioners of sewers—could be incited to root out those responsible for particular offences. The report of the three doctors, Southwood Smith, Kay and Arnott, which Chadwick set in motion after the London typhus epidemic in 1838, explored the relationship between filth and disease (and so destitution). Scientific explanations were as yet speculative and controversial since without a germ theory it was not known whether physical contact, or air, or water, was the chief means by which diseases passed. But there was evidence enough of some such links and clearly the dangers were increasing. The Report concerned itself primarily with the accumulation of rubbish, slops and sewage in individual dwellings of the city tenement areas.[96]

One of the results of this and of all the agitation which would follow was a series of Nuisance Removal Acts. Their chief purpose was to give to local authorities the power to inspect houses for the cause of reeking smells and other indicators of filth, and to obtain an order from the justices in petty sessions that the source be removed by the householder; or if he would not act, by the local authority, with recourse for the cost against the householder. The first Nuisance Removal Act completed the variegate web of local authorities responsible for public health in this rather limited sense; where there was no corporation or commission responsible, in countryside as well as town, the guardians of the poor became the authority.[97] The nuisances against which action might be taken would gradually be defined in more comprehensive fashion—smoke would, for instance be specially regulated by an Act of 1853.[98] But the main legislation required proof that the harmful activity be "injurious to health"; and this the courts tended to treat restrictively, requiring, as with common law nuisance, a definite disease, and not mere discomfort, to be the outcome.[99]

The doctors' report to the Poor Law Commission went one stage beyond this scheme imposing individual responsibility. As a measure of preventive planning, they advocated the introduction of building regulations which would require new houses to have at least a modicum of sanitation. Here was direct, though still regulatory, intervention in the private business of cheap housing and there was outcry soon enough from those who put it up and those who ran it. It would take until the last quarter of the century for much to be

---

[95] For the Commissioners, see below, p. 429ff.

[96] Poor Law Commissioners, Fourth Report, P.P. 1837–38 [147] XXVII App. A; Finer (1952), p. 156 ff; Lewis (1952), pp. 34–38.

[97] 9 & 10 Vict., c. 96, ss.1–2; renewed and extended by 11 & 12 Vict., c. 123; 18 & 19 Vict., c. 121; 23 & 24 Vict., c. 77; 26 & 27 Vict., c. 117.

[98] 16 & 17 Vict., c. 128 (and see 18 & 19 Vict., c. 120; 19 & 20 Vict., c. 107).

[99] See the Report of the Royal Commission on Noxious Vapours. P.P. 1878 [C.2159] XLIV, pp. 26–27; Brenner (1974), pp. 426–427.

done on this front.[1] Even so, this was limited vision compared with the panoramic plan which Chadwick himself evolved in his great Report on the Sanitary Condition of the Labouring Classes of Great Britain in 1842.[2] With a thoroughness wholly Benthamic, Chadwick saw, as the doctors had not, that the removal of festering rubbish and waste from the towns had to be carried out on a scale that could not be left to those responsible for individual dwellings. He seized upon an idea for which there was little precedent and no sure technique— an arterial drainage in which fast-running, continuous water supply would flush sewage and slops right away from conurbations, to be turned perhaps to use as manure in the same way as dung and compost were used in the country. While it was not impossible that complete drainage schemes of this order could be created by private enterprise,[3] Chadwick's first discussion of it, and much of the ensuing debate, assumed the issue to be about affirmative intervention by public bodies supported by local rates. It was the most uncompromising proposal of the mid-century years for collective governmental action and it attracted opposition of a fervour correspondingly unbridled.

In Chadwick's Report of 1842 the place of central authority was left in shadow. But as the case developed—through the two Reports of the ensuing Royal Commission[4] and the activities of the well-supported Health in Towns Association—a central office or commission emerged as a crucial source of energy in the design. In a handful of the largest industrial cities—Liverpool, Manchester, Leeds, Newcastle—leading figures on the corporations and other bodies set sewerage and related schemes in motion by securing local Acts.[5] The problems for them were already too exigent to await the emergence of any national planning; indeed the implementation of their arterial drainage schemes would be the first practical demonstration of the essential rightness of Chadwick's vision. He and his associates saw a central body as crucial not only to stimulate the second-order cities and towns into adequate action, but even more to tackle the largest problem of all, the drainage and cleansing of London, with its splay of 250 parish vestries, six Commissions of Sewers, and (ultimate bastion) the Commission for the City proper.[6]

The General Board of Health (G.B.H.) came into being in 1848 for an initial term carefully limited to five years.[7] It could intervene in a

---

[1] See below, p. 179ff.

[2] Published by the Poor Law Commission, but under Chadwick's own name and not as a Blue Book; its author, however, saw to its extensive promulgation (reprinted 1965); Finer (1952) Bk. 5, Chap. 1; Lewis (1952), pp. 38–40; O. MacDonagh (1975) 16 Hist. St. 507.

[3] Chadwick himself became involved in an ill-fated private venture to provide arterial drainage for London in 1847.

[4] State of Towns Commission, P.P. 1844 [572] XVII; 1845 [602] VXIII.

[5] For Liverpool, for instance, see 5 & 6 Vict., c. xliv, 9 & 10 Vict., c. cxxvii. The Towns Improvements Clauses Act and the Towns Police Clauses Act, both of 1847 (10 & 11 Vict., c. 34, 89) facilitated the obtaining of such local acts. See generally, B. Keith-Lucas (1954) 6 Ec. H.R. (2d) 290.

[6] For reform of the City's health provisions, see Lambert (1963) Chap. 4.

[7] 11 & 12 Vict., c. 63. For the extent to which opposition whittled down the original bill, see Lewis (1952) Chap. 8; Lambert (1963), pp. 65–70.

locality only upon a petition of one-tenth of the ratepayers or if the death rate per annum rose above 23 per thousand. Once brought in, the Board had considerable powers to require action (with the support of the rates) by establishing a local board of health. In boroughs this was the town council, in other areas a separate body elected by property owners and ratepayers. Many towns did seek the assistance of the G.B.H. in organising a sewerage and water system and the Board was able almost invariably to act by suggestion rather than compulsion. Despite this the Board would by 1851 have lost so much ground as to be fighting for its existence against virtually all the interest groups with any stake in public health questions: private water companies and cemetery companies (both of which saw a considerable profitability under threat), the plethora of local authorities, manufacturers, professional groups of doctors, engineers and lawyers (the last in the guise of Parliamentary agents who undertook the legislative business of the private interest).

The story of the Board's failure is complex. It was made so partly by Chadwick's inability to secure that the Board's ordinary powers extended to the London metropolis. This led him to a series of proxy measures towards the same end—a Royal Commission on Metropolitan Sewering, and attempts to take over the water supply and the burial of corpses as distinct interventions—all of which brought nothing but extreme bitterness. In addition the re-emergence of epidemic cholera in 1848–1849 had a distracting effect on the Board, since it then acquired quite separate emergency powers of intervention,[8] extending even to the London vestries and serving to screw their suspicions to a new pitch. Much of the failure had to do with personalities—above all, that of Chadwick, strong in self-belief and ready to war openly with the ignorance and self-interest which seemed around him on all sides. But it also taught a profound lesson about the way in which structures of government must be built so as to prevent clashes of personality from being the sole outcome of activity.

Two aspects of the lesson stand out. First, the form adopted for the new Board seemed, in the light of all the experience with the Poor Law Commissioners, to invite trouble.[9] The three Commissioners of the G.B.H. consisted of a cabinet minister and two civil servants, Chadwick and Ashley[10]; but the minister was given neither decisive authority nor ultimate responsibility. Once the first Cabinet member, Lord Morpeth, had been succeeded (in 1850) by the much less sympathetic Lord Seymour, it became plain that so highly contentious a subject must become both the responsibility and the charge of a Cabinet minister, if there was to be central direction at all; and that at the same time relations with the Treasury must be more clearly defined than had been the case.[11]

---

[8] These were conferred by the second Nuisances Removal Act (above, n. 97).

[9] See below, p. 432.

[10] The latter at least sat in the Commons until his elevation to the Earldom of Shaftesbury in 1851.

[11] Finer (1952), pp. 412–419 demonstrates how this was a crucial factor in the failure to deal with London's cemeteries. A fourth Commissioner, Southwood Smith, was added to bring in a medical expert.

Secondly, a Royal Commission, appointed by the Crown and not under Act of Parliament, ought not to become a device for decision-making. Such commissions had in the past been used to investigate problems and to adjudicate upon proposed solutions; some of them had been decidedly partisan in their recommendations and their membership. But the London Sewer Commission of 1847 was set up for the very purpose of planning an entire sewage system. As well as having a predominance of Chadwick's nominees, it also contained Morpeth, Ashley, Southwood Smith and Chadwick himself, who were soon to constitute the G.B.H. Morpeth felt it was necessary sop to local democracy that there should be four representatives of the London vestries. They were able to make such trouble for the Commission partly because of the antagonism that could be whipped up to its very constitution.[12] Toulmin Smith, a barrister with a roseate attachment to England's local institutions, was able to represent the true liberty of the subject as under uncompromising attack.[13]

In 1854, Seymour engineered the removal of Ashley and Chadwick as members of the G.B.H. (against the judgment of Palmerston and Russell); its control passed largely to one of their opponents, Sir Benjamin Hall. Under him, it continued to work with cooperative localities, but the tide of feeling against it swept it away at the end of its second term in 1858. Even so, what happened was to a degree cosmetic. The Board's officers were largely moved into a Local Government Act Office, which (significantly) was a branch of the Home Office.[14] They continued with much of the work that they had been doing. The Medical Officership, however, was attached to the Privy Council in pursuit of its work against epidemic diseases, and there grew notably in significance[15]

The Medical Officer appointed in 1855, Sir John Simon, was the second commanding figure of the public health movement, combining as he did a Chadwickian vision with an unacerbic temperament and great organisational flair.[16] Simon brought the bulk of local authorities to trust and, even more, to rely on the central services of his own Medical Department and of the Local Government Act Office.[17] This confidence enabled him to press for legislation which in the end would shape the whole range and administration of public health measures until 1936. In 1865 there was an Act on sewage utilisation which added the rural vestries to the labyrinth of sewerage authorities[18]; in the next year a Sanitary Act extended nuisance removal to the overcrowding of houses, insanitary places of work and industrial smoke. Then came an influential Royal Commission, mainly concerned with the structure of authorities, whose recommendations

---

[12] In 1849, Russell, the Prime Minister, would insist that both factions be replaced by new nominees: Finer (1952) Bk. 9, Chap. 1; Lewis (1952) Chap. 10.

[13] See esp. his *Centralisation or Representation?* (1848).

[14] Local Government Act, 21 & 22 Vict., c. 98. For the first time, by s.34, local authorities generally were empowered to stop the building of "back-to-back's."

[15] Public Health Act 1858, 21 & 22 Vict., c. 97; the Act was very nearly not made permanent in 1859: see Lambert (1963) Chap. 12 for the politics.

[16] See generally, Lambert (1963).

[17] Thanks to Simon's influence, the former absorbed the latter in 1870.

[18] Sewage Utilisation Act 1865.

were crucial to the root reorganisations of the 1870s.[19] In 1871, the liberals at last brought poor law and public health administrations together in a single government department,[20] the Local Government Board, with a President who was a Cabinet minister.[21] To this they annexed a reorganisation of relations between central and local health authorities, doing a good deal to eliminate overlaps and mutual restrictions among the latter.

It was under the Conservatives that the substantive powers were consolidated, rationalised and to some extent made more extensive.[22] At last public health had come to be seen as too embracing and too complex a question to be left to the vagaries of the market. The opportunities were too substantial for monopolising what was profitable (such as water supply) and ignoring what was not (such as rubbish removal). Equally, in a political frame where public health was to be paid for in the main by the land-owners and occupiers out of the rates for their immediate locality, it was for the local authorities to establish the main programme of action. But given the rapid advance of technical knowledge in most aspects of the subject, it was vital that central government should act as promulgator and point of reference for the most advanced information. To these prevailing conditions, Simon had adapted the new bureaucracy.

The inevitable tensions of public health could not, however, be dispelled by the enlightenment of Simon's Reports. The owners and occupiers who would have to pay were by no means converted to the intrusive and costly ideas of the second wave of bureaucrats. The planning of any health authority had accordingly to begin from the premise that against it stood a range of legal protections which the courts could be expected to uphold unless power to interfere had been granted by Parliament in quite unambiguous terms. In the classic test of the priority of rights, the Metropolitan Asylum District, acting under statutory power,[23] had erected a smallpox hospital in the pastoral suburb of Hampstead. The House of Lords, however, granted an injunction against receiving such patients because the danger of infection amounted to a nuisance of which surrounding occupiers could complain; and a mere power under statute (as distinct from a duty to act) did not license an invasion of the common law rights of others.[24] At the very least, provisions to compensate for the "injurious affection" would have been included, if Parliament had intended otherwise.[25]

Nonetheless the authorities were acquiring numerous powers and duties to act in ways which did indeed break in upon private rights. The general run of public health administration involved a mixture of fact-finding and evaluation that would in the end affect individ-

---

[19] Sanitary Commission, Second Report, P.P. 1871 [C. 281] XXXV.
[20] But other departments retained some oversight of health matters.
[21] Local Government Act 1871.
[22] Public Health Act 1875. One consequence of the amalgamation was that the poor law officials (headed by John Lambert) became dominant; this led to Simon's resignation in 1876.
[23] Metropolitan Poor Act 1867.
[24] *Metropolitan Asylum District* v. *Hill* (1881) 6 App. Cas. 193.
[25] As in *Hammersmith Rly.* v. *Brand* (see above, n. 93).

uals and so resemble much of the decision-making in courts. Issues were beginning to arise out of which an administrative law must needs evolve, however much common lawyers would seek to sap it of any independence meriting the name. Thus there were important questions of the proper procedures to be followed in reaching administrative decisions and of the extent to which the ordinary courts would supervise the process. London sewering authorities, for instance, had been given power, if a builder did not give them due notice in advance before starting to build, to pull down what had been built. The Court of Common Pleas, shocked by the extent to which private property might thus be invaded, held that, no matter how defiant or devious a particular builder might have been, the authority must give him the opportunity to be heard before ordering the demolition. Common law requirements of "natural justice" applied to the authority's decision, which was characterised as "judicial." Failure to comply made the authority liable in trespass.[26] The new machinery of government was bound at least to observe procedural "due process" in much of what it did.

Private interest became all the more powerful when it acquired a majority on a local authority and ensured a policy of masterly inactivity. Thus there carried over from Chadwick the ultimate question of how far central authority might force local action. While the legal powers of intervention given in 1848 had mostly been removed with the winding up of the General Board of Health a decade later, it was part of Simon's achievement gradually to revive the possibility. Nothing could be done as long as the local authorities were only given power to act and not placed under any duty. But a few duties, such as that of clearing streets of rubbish, had survived from 1848 and these were added to, for instance, in the Sanitary Act 1866, which imposed a duty regularly to inspect for nuisances and to take action against them.[27] To enforce such obligations, Simon himself looked to high judicial authority, turning to the traditional method of mandamus from Queen's Bench. The government, however, had sought to make the issue a local one; the justices of the peace were to have power to order that default in the provision of drainage, sewerage and water supply should be made good at a charge recoverable from the defaulting authority. But this so displeased local interests, that in the end any attempt at judicial interposition was abandoned and the power was conferred without demur on the Home Secretary.[28] For all the protestation of the previous twenty years, the executive had acquired a strategic new power in the complex business of seeing interventionist policies through into actual results.

By 1870, it was plain to all that public health control was a matter far beyond the resources of traditional judicial procedures and needed administration by doctors, architects, engineers, chemists and other new experts.[29] As we have seen, the courts, left to them-

---

[26] *Cooper* v. *Wandsworth Board of Works* (1863) 14 C.B. (N.S.) 180.

[27] Sanitary Act 1866, Pt. II.

[28] *Ibid.*, ss.16, 49; Lambert (1963), pp. 387–388; R. M. Gutchen, (1961) 6 Hist. J. 85.

[29] As is well-illustrated in the whole thrust of the Adderley Commission's Report (above n. 19) and in the series of investigations into river pollution (P.P. 1867 [3835, 3850] XIX; 1870 [C. 7, 37, 181] XL; 1874 [C. 951, 112] XXXII).

selves, would interfere only when a nuisance was truly serious; but they might then create an extremely difficult impasse. Administration, by contrast, might avoid such an upshot by stimulating preventive action.[30] Sewerage systems, for instance, had become a crucial safeguard in making urban housing less unhealthy. Under the Public Health Act 1875, local authorities would acquire new powers to impose minimum standards upon building and street lay-outs, aiming particularly to ensure some sufficiency of light and air.[31] From this point began the "bye-law era" of housing regulation which would leave so many British towns with long streets of uniform, single-fronted dwellings. Monotonous they mostly were, but a necessary improvement on much before.[32]

In other spheres it was sometimes possible to make rapid progress by the introduction of new techniques. By the time that the acid rain of west Lancashire had become a subject before the judicial House of Lords,[33] the political House had already stimulated action by central government.[34] Under an Act of 1863, a central inspectorate of alkali works, headed by the sanitary chemist, R.A. Smith, had begun work.[35] They were able to insist upon installation of a condensation process which liquified the discharge of hydrochloric acid. Moreover, what had until then been treated as a waste product in the production of sodium carbonate was found to have its own industrial uses. This surprising dispersion of a grave problem set in train an administrative system of careful collaboration between producers and inspectors, with the latter acting as engineering consultants rather than officious persecutors. Prosecutions were extremely rare, and remained so even as the Inspectorate turned its attention to the many other, less tractable problems of air pollution.[36] Much the same attitude would be engendered in the rivers inspectorate established in 1876,[37] as well as elsewhere in the regulation of economic activity.[38] It was a tradition which required reasonable expenditure when improved techniques evolved, but which responded readily to arguments that the only practicable means of reducing a danger would jeopardise the profitability of a business and hence the jobs of its workforce.[39] In working out this process of compromise, the various inspectorates generated an increasing mass of detailed regula-

---

[30] See above, p. 53ff.
[31] See ss.149–163. In the hope of persuading local authorities to act, the LGB published a first set of model bye-laws in 1877. The legislation was itself strengthened in 1890.
[32] See Burnett (1978), pp. 155–156; Daunton (1983) Chap. 3.
[33] *St. Helens Smelting* v. *Tipping*, above, n. 83.
[34] The Lords' Select Committee on the subject (P.P. 1862 (486) XIV) was the creature of northern landowners.
[35] Alkali Act 1863, 26 & 27 Vict., c. 124. For the whole development, see R. M. Macleod (1965) 9 Vict. St. 85.
[36] An attitude not unnaturally approved of by the producers, who both resisted the transference of supervision to local authorities and attacked an attempt by the LGB to take a firmer line. MacLeod (above, n. 35), pp. 103–04.
[37] Under the Rivers Pollution Prevention Act 1876.
[38] *Cf.* below, pp. 305ff., 605ff.
[39] This was explicitly acknowledged as proper by the Royal Commission on Noxious Vapours (above n. 85), p. 19; see Brenner (1974), p. 428.

tion,[40] but mostly they administered it in an accommodating spirit that provoked relatively few appeals against undue imposition. The common lawyers could rest undisturbed in their belief that they retained real control over the legality of administration, and that they could afford to exercise their power with a light hand.[41]

PART 4: A GRADUAL TRANSFORMATION: 1870–1950

I. ATTACK ON SETTLEMENTS

The amount of land in settlement at any time was never accurately known, let alone the degree of strictness that different settlements imposed. Thompson's estimate for the mid-nineteenth century is around one-half of the agricultural land in England and Wales,[42] and this is roughly confirmed by the "New Domesday Book" survey of 1873.[43] Radical opponents of settlements, however, pointed to various defects in the information gathered for the latter, and some of their pamphlets put the proportion of settled land as high as three-quarters.[44] By 1889, an experienced firm of estate agents could put it as low as a quarter.[45] On any reckoning the settlement system was central enough to the power of the landed class for it to be a prime object in any attack on their position.

After 1867, the "Land Question" became the subject of deep political feeling. It never acquired the vehemence that it attracted in Ireland, for its social roots were different. It was not the cry of a beleaguered tenantry against an economic subjugation imposed by absentee landlords and their grasping agents. It was a political challenge from a boisterously successful middle class—increasingly from radicals who were intellectual and professional by background.[46] Support from those most immediately affected—the tenant farmers— was hard to secure at any time before the agricultural depression of the latter seventies, and even afterwards not easy to sustain. While a good measure of the attack consisted simply of denunciation of the landed interest, it achieved its clearest focus in plans for change, and these very largely took the form of demands for more or less realistic law reform. The campaign illustrates the radical faith in Acts of Parliament as the means of shifting opinion in favour of social change, large or small. And indeed, in this case, at the end of the day there was a very substantial alteration in the organisation of land-holding, and in the social class of those who owned it. The great landowners

---

[40] Much of it sought to impose objective standards (for instance, maximum permitted levels of polluting discharge), but this was not always possible.

[41] See above, pp. 59–60.

[42] F. M. L. Thompson (1963), pp. 67–68.

[43] The "New Domesday" survey, by the Local Government Board (at the instance of the Earl of Derby), sought to deflate the more extreme assertions about the monopoly.

[44] See, e.g., G. C. Brodrick, *English Land and English Landlords* (1881) Chap. 3, and Perkin (1973).

[45] Thompson (1963), p. 68.

[46] For the background, see Perkin (1973).

were to shift much of their wealth away from their estates; and their own tenants and outsiders came in as full owners of the land and took upon themselves the whole financial risk of farming it.

In the classic sources of middle-class self-gratulation, there was ammunition enough against the system of settlement. Adam Smith had attacked entails for the political preferment that they helped to sustain and for the lack of economic incentive given to any life tenant to improve his estate; Smith's preference was for the yeoman with his forty-shilling freehold.[47] Even more basic was the prominence given by Ricardo to the notion of economic rent, the surplus profit which the large estate owner was able to extract from his monopoly over the ultimate resource for the sustenance of life. Yet Ricardo shared with Bentham and other utilitarians a preference for the large estate because of its economic efficiency. It was therefore difficult to find any thorough-going solution to the settlement problem; the philosophic radicals occupied themselves with the adjectival (conveyancing) or the purely symbolic (primogeniture).

The Benthamite conveyancer, James Humphreys, published an insider's critique in 1826 that aroused considerable controversy.[48] From it Brougham derived ammunition for his marathon speech of 1828, and likewise it engaged the attention of the Real Property Commissioners of 1829–1833. But while Humphreys was prepared to argue for a substantial increase in the powers of the tenant for life of settled land, not only to grant leases binding his successors but also to sell, exchange or partition the estate and use the proceeds (inter alia) to pay off encumbrances, the Real Property Commissioners remained much closer to the orthodoxies of the day. The land law, except in a few comparatively unimportant particulars, appeared to them to come almost as near to perfection as can be expected in human institutions.[49] The powers of settlement and testamentary disposition, when read with the rule against perpetuities, were compared favourably with the legal shackles imposed in some countries of European continent: "while capricious limitations are restrained, property is allowed to be moulded according to the circumstances and wants of every family."[50] The Commissioners contented themselves with criticisms of conveyancing procedures, which many considered to be outrageously cumbrous and defective.[51]

Between the two Reform Acts, the radicals in Parliament introduced a succession of bills to abolish primogeniture. They did so without expecting that this would in itself achieve anything of direct importance, since primogeniture, as a legal principle, operated only upon the intestacy of the owner of freehold land, and such a last

---

[47] *Wealth of Nations* Bk. 3, Chaps. 2, 4; and see Martin (1974).
[48] *Observations of the Actual State of the English Law of Real Property, with the Outlines of a Code* (1826); see also John Miller's *Inquiry into the Present State of the Civil Law of England* (1825). Sir Edward Sugden, subsequently Lord St. Leonards, leading expert in matters of property law and flinty defender of the status quo for the next forty years, responded in his *Letter to James Humphreys* (1826): "the strict settlement is free from all objection . . . whoever complained of the complex movements in a well finished watch?" (p. 14).
[49] First Report, P.P. 1829 (263) X, p. 6
[50] *Ibid.*, p. 7.
[51] See Holdsworth, XV pp. 168–181.

resort arose only occasionally. Accordingly their demand was a
purely political symbol.[52] Each bill signalled a joust between
attackers and defenders of the landed system—between those who
saw "feudal prejudice and error" as "much of what was monstrous in
the social and political condition of the country"[53] and those to
whom any concession was "incompatible with the existence of a
landed gentry," something tending to "republicanism."[54] At most
the abandonment of primogeniture was to its proponents the thin
end of a wedge that might eventually force out entails as contrary to
public policy.

The Anti-Corn Law enthusiasts who had massed popular support
for an attack on landed privilege, secured their object in 1846 with
disarming ease. The thorough-minded amongst them tried to sustain
the drive by turning it against the land law. Middle-class liberals
took up the reform of over-strict settlements, the laws of succession,
lack of either security or compensation for tenants, the game laws,
conveyancing.[55] A little was achieved: their pressure, for example,
contributed to the enactments increasing the power of the life tenant
under a settlement[56]; mortgaged land became the prime source from
which the money due was to be repaid by those administering the
debtor's assets[57]; agricultural tenants were given the right to remove
their "trade" farming fixtures.[58]

This new campaign, with "free trade in land" as its battle-cry,
became entwined with Cobden's plans for creeping democracy—the
county electorate was to be transformed by multiplying 40s. freeholds. But the freehold land movement gained ground only very
slowly and in any case tended to instal voters who regressed. Land
reform lost way in the Palmerston years alongside the whole movement for further political concession.

There was also a working-class interest in a return to "peasant"
farming, centred for a time in O'Connor's Chartist Land Company.
But after the founding of a few "colonies" this ended in financial collapse.[59] On the other remaining flank of Chartism, Bronterre O'Brien
developed ideas at a long remove from such re-adjustments of individual proprietorship: his plan for land nationalisation marked the
birth of state-directed socialism in the British political spectrum.[60]
Moreover, his plans were thorough-going enough to open a debate
about means that was to foment dissension among reformers in all
that followed. O'Brien himself wanted dominion in all land to be
vested in the state, which would determine the size of farms, the proportion of tillage to pasturage and so forth; land would be let at auc-

---

[52] F. M. L. Thompson (1964).
[53] William Ewart, in debating the first Primogeniture Bill in 1836; quoted by Thompson (1964), p. 26.
[54] Palmerston during the primogeniture debate of 1859, P.D.CLII 1154–1155.
[55] See F. M. L. Thompson (1964), pp. 36–39; Martin (1974), pp. 142–153.
[56] See above, p. 145.
[57] 17 & 18 Vict., c. 113 (Locke King's Act); and see 30 & 31 Vict., c. 69.
[58] 14 & 15 Vict., c. 25, s.3, which Act contained other improvements of the tenant's position: cf. above, p. 135. For the conveyancing reforms in this period, see below,
p. 174.
[59] See A. M. Hadfield, The Chartist Land Company (1970).
[60] See J. E. Barry, Nationalisation in British Politics (1965) 28–41.

tion to the highest bidder, thus allowing increased values to be reflected in rents.[61]

In the world re-ordered by the second Reform Act, the Land and Labour League preserved the O'Brienite inheritance, being among the first to appreciate its place in a Marxian analysis of capitalism. Somewhat uneasily by its side, the more middle-class Land Tenure Reform Association formed an alliance, concerned with the case either for land nationalisation or for taxation of the "unearned-increment" in the capital value of land.[62]

By contrast the main-stream of middle-class radicalism preserved a preference for private property, redistributed through the mechanism of the market—the Cobdenite demand for "free trade in land." The case was systematically organised: detailed proof was offered of the inefficiencies of an agricultural regime of landlords and tenant farmers, in contrast with the vigour and productiveness of the "peasant" ownership commonly found on the European continent.[63] For this the protagonists tended to blame differences of law, rather than differences in attitude and economic opportunity. Social customs could be denounced, but law could be reformed. So they continued the old grievances over conveyancing costs and lack of security for tenants[64]; and they proclaimed the virtues of compulsory partition of property upon death amongst all the children or remoter issue.[65] But more than anything, they demanded the abolition of the strict settlement, which rendered the death of any one life tenant of no significance to the passage of an estate down the line of first-born males. The evil of settlements was indeed the one cause upon which land reformers of every hue could agree.

An impending climax built up in the eighties, compounded by the British appearances of the American "single taxer," Henry George, in 1881–82.[66] He restated ideas about the re-appropriation of economic rent in uncompromising terms, demanding a capital tax on land that would remove the kernel and leave only the shell of landownership. At the same time, Joseph Chamberlain and his lieutenant, Jesse Collings, pushed the individualist cause to an extreme in the "Unauthorised Programme" for the 1885 election: they planned, so it seemed, to compel the repopulation of each three acres (plus cow) with peasants drawn from the best working-class stock of the teeming towns.[67] Collings used land reform to snuff Salisbury's new-lit government. But Irish Home Rule, which really sparked the politics of these years, also burnt out the fuel for land reform. The issue was postponed; and

[61] He argued, however, for acquisition only on the death of each private owner.
[62] J. S. Mill, Charles Dilke and Henry Fawcett were leading members of the latter. In 1881 the Land Nationalisation Society was formed, and in 1883 the Land Reform Union: see generally, Barry (above, n. 60) Chap. 2.
[63] J. W. Probyn (ed.) *Systems of Land Tenure* (1870, 1881).
[64] Sir J. Caird, *The Landed Interest* (1878); J. Kay, *Free Trade in Land* (1879); A. Arnold, *Free Land* (1880); O. Morgan, *Land Law Reform in England* (1880); G. C. Brodrick, *English Land and English Landlords* (1881); G. Shaw Lefevre, *English and Irish Land Questions* (1881); Pollock, (1883).
[65] For other proposals, see below, p. 182ff.
[66] His *Progress and Poverty* (1879) had a British edition in 1881. See esp. E. P. Lawrence, *Henry George in the British Isles* (1957).
[67] S. Maccoby, *English Radicalism 1853–86* (1938), pp. 301–302.

its counterpart—the confrontation between Lords and Commons—smouldered on for a generation.

Meanwhile the best advisers of the landed interest had already secured the one substantial amendment to the settlement system that was to be achieved. Cairns had prepared a Settled Land Bill for Disraeli's government, and in 1882 Selborne saw it through for Gladstone's.[68] It gave the incumbent tenant-for-life statutory powers to sell, mortgage, lease and improve the land which could not be excluded by the terms of the settlement and which he could not surrender by agreement with his father or anyone else. He could sell or mortgage the whole or any part of the estate, the consent of the court or the trustees of the settlement being needed only in the case of those ultimate symbols, the mansion house and the heirlooms. He could grant building leases up to 99 years, mining leases up to 60 years and other leases up to 21 years.[69] The interest of the other beneficiaries was translated from one in the land itself into one in the land or its proceeds. The tenant for life was required to pay to the trustees (or the court) the price of any sale for reinvestment in land or other suitable securities.[70] This "overreaching" gave the power of decision very largely to current head of the family, rather than to his trustees, who "would naturally take a languid and platonic view of the situation."

To some the Settled Land Act was "revolutionary." But its drafters intended to deflect more serious attacks. The land reformer, Arthur Arnold, tried to persuade his fellow Liberals that it was a life tenants' (i.e. a House of Lords') measure incompatible with their pledge to genuine reform of the land law. The Act wrote into all settlements the sort of power that (in one form or another) had been put into well-drawn settlements where the family was not thought to need special protection against the heir apparent. The Conservative Law Lord, Macnaghten, summarised the problem thus: "A period of agricultural depression, which shewed no sign of abatement, had given rise to a popular outcry against settlements. The problem was how to relieve settled land from the mischief which strict settlements undoubtedly did in some cases produce, without doing away altogether with the power of bringing land into settlement."[71] The judges had no difficulty in giving effect to the Act's policy of attaching paramount importance to "the well-being of the land,"[72] which was a way of saying that dynastic considerations had lost their overweening importance. To achieve this, legal interference with the free choice of settlors was necessary, but only in order to increase the freedom of each succeeding generation to act as it thought best.

Nonetheless the Act came at a time when it appeared to have dis-

---

[68] For its politics, see E. Spring (1977), pp. 52–54.

[69] Settled Land Act 1882, Parts III–V. The mansion house could be sold only with the court's permission; hence the application in the *Ailesbury* case (below, n. 71).

[70] *Ibid.*, Part VI.

[71] *Bruce* v. *Ailesbury (Marquess)* [1892] A.C. 356 at 364–365.

[72] *Ibid.* Significantly, the Court of Appeal and House of Lords showed an appreciation of the new attitudes by preferring the claims of the purchaser (the brewer, Guinness) to those of the Marquis' family, because the tenants and labourers on the estate would be better off: Spring (1977), p. 55.

tinct consequences. By 1890 there were enough owners of large estates seeking to escape the effects of depression by selling out for the market to be glutted, at least with estates being offered as a piece. By 1910 Lloyd George's threatening budget set off the movement for selling piece-meal, mainly to existing tenants. If it scarcely produced the social revolution demanded by the land reformers, it did at least effect a considerable change of ownership in land and prepare the country for a hectic bout of post-war selling, a shift without parallel since the dissolution of the monasteries and the confiscations of the civil war.[73] The Act of 1882 provided the power needed to make many of these sales. Its enactment even before the reform campaign of the eighties reached its height was a strategy at once of prudence and of positive desire.

Reform of the settlement system did not stand by itself. There came at the same time a clutch of alterations to conveyancing practice (which are discussed in the next section) and to the law of agricultural landlord and tenant. In Ireland, landlordism fired an inextinguishable rage and Gladstone, at least, saw concession as the only hope. He pushed through two reform acts, in 1870 and 1881, which provided a first measure of protection to tenants: to begin with, compensation for improvements; and then the truly substantial departures from "free contract"—fair rents, free sale and fixed tenures.[74] In England, the Irish Acts had repercussions, though in a less explosive atmosphere these were altogether more moderate in scope. To the earlier enactment allowing agricultural tenants to remove "trade" fixtures in certain circumstances,[75] there was at last added a right to compensation for improvements, notably drainage and manuring, which remained beneficial to the land after the termination of the tenancy. When first conceded in 1875, landlords were expressly allowed to "contract out" and many did so.[76] Gladstone's second government removed this possibility.[77] The landlord also lost his power to reserve the sporting rights exclusively to himself[78]; and the law of distress was significantly curtailed so as to put the landlord more in the position of the tenant farmer's other creditors, such as the seed merchant.[79]

The radical and urban elements in the Liberal party were able to carry the argument that these new, pre-emptive laws were not constraints upon freedom of contract. They were all to be seen as part of the underpinning provided by the state in enforcing contracts through its legal machinery. As such, the adjustments were necessary in order to enhance the economic freedom of the tenant to make

---

[73] In the period 1914–1927, about a quarter of the land passed into the hands of owner-occupiers: F. M. L. Thompson (1963), p. 332.

[74] See, e.g. J. P. D. Dunbabin, *Rural Discontent in Nineteenth Century Britain* (1974) Chap. 8; E. D. Steele *Irish Land and British Politics* (1974), Chap. 1; P. Bew in P. J. Drudy (ed.) *Ireland: Land, Politics People* (1982), Chap. 4

[75] Above, n. 58.

[76] Agricultural Holdings (England) Act 1875, esp. s.54.

[77] Agricultural Holdings (England) Act 1883, esp. s.55.

[78] Ground Game Act 1880 (esp. s.2), an Act made inevitable by evidence of the havoc to crops that rabbits and other game could wreak if the tenant was allowed no control.

[79] Agricultural Holdings (England) Act 1883, Pt. II.

the most of his opportunity. In an age of novel uncertainty over the future of domestic agriculture, the tenant was coming to be an object of real political concern.

II. THE ART OF CONVEYANCING

Any system of private property in land generates formal procedures for establishing title and interests. In England the art of conveyancing became peculiarly recondite, partly through the very sophistication that had been brought to dividing up interests and partly through the lack of any systematic public record of rights. As far the latter was concerned, copyholds and dealings in them did require to be entered in the manorial rolls. But for freehold and leasehold, the only surviving equivalents had been established in Middlesex and Yorkshire,[80] both commercially buoyant and relatively democratic counties, where registration of the deeds embodying land transactions was required.[81] But these registers failed to become a model for other local initiatives. In the result, as a chain of official investigations was to deplore, the state of many titles was most difficult to ascertain. Leading lawyers, even those who were otherwise unlikely to be inspired by a Benthamic zeal for reform, might espouse the case for public registration in one form or another. But progress was to prove highly elusive, thanks, in the first instance, to a stiff core of resistance from within the legal profession itself.

The attorneys and conveyancers were the first to see their livelihood threatened by plans for rationalisation. In 1804, the attorneys had secured, as a *quid pro quo* for Pitt's duties on legal practice, the exclusion from conveyancing (for reward) of those who did not pay the duty and were not members of an Inn of Court.[82] It was vital gain in the professional stakes and one to be guarded with the determined zeal typical of a modern profession. Yet so small and subservient a group could scarcely have stood their ground against their clients, the body of landowners, if the latter had been convinced of the case for economy. The traditional system of conveyancing was to cling to life because it was so closely intertwined with the great benefits that the landowners secured from the conveyancers—settlements and trusts by which to conserve the family wealth from generation to generation, which were a matter of private arrangement.

Certainly the steps involved in transferring a freehold were intricate and costly.[83] If there were a sale of the interest, the contract would first be recorded in the form of memorandum required by the Statute of Frauds 1677. The vendor had then to establish his title by showing that there was no one still within the time limit for ejecting him (a negative proof typical of common law method). Thanks to the

---

[80] Henry VIII's Statute of Enrolments 1536 (27 Hen. VIII, c. 16) had been side-stepped by the technique of lease and release; for which, see below, pp. 173–174.

[81] 2 & 3 Anne, c. 4; 7 & 8 Anne, c. 20; 8 Geo. II, c. 6. The Court of Chancery held that a conveyance of land in either county would bind a later purchaser who had notice of it: *Le Neve* v. *Le Neve* (1747) Amb.436.

[82] Above, pp. 46–47.

[83] See generally, Real Property Commissioners, 2nd Report, P.P. 1830 (575) XX; Pollock (1883) Chap. 7; de Villiers (1901) Chaps. 1, 2.

survival of the medieval "real" actions, the relevant periods of limitation were long indeed: conveyancers normally looked for documents of title going back sixty years, and not infrequently for a hundred. Some titles needed a private estate Act to clarify them. The vendor had to list the various transactions—settlements, mortgages, leases, rentcharges and so on—affecting the land since the title on which he relied. Against the danger that an intervening right would be overlooked or suppressed,[84] conveyancers had constructed a cumbersome and by no means efficient shield: long leases were granted to trustees for the sole purpose of satisfying some future purchaser that he need not have regard to transactions made subsequently to the lease.[85] These "attendant terms" had themselves to be investigated and they were by no means proof against all conflicting rights. Eventually, if these hurdles were surmounted the transaction would be rounded off with a conveyance that required further elaborate documentation involving the grant of a lease to the purchaser and then a release of the vendor's reversion under that lease as well as the appointment and assignment needed to deal with the "attendant terms." These contained, as did most such documents, an accumulation of traditional filigree that served no real function; but the conveyancers and their writing clerks charged by the folio and so the decorative transcription only burgeoned.

Equally elaborate forms accompanied the central rite of the strict settlement—barring the entail and resettling—the first step of which was achieved by common recovery or fine, which made use of court files as a safe place to set down a record. Even when freehold (again as distinct from leasehold) was to pass by will upon death, there were difficulties: the will had to be signed by the testator and attested by three witnesses; and it could apply only to land held at the date of signing.[86]

All of this struck the Real Property Commissioners as "exceedingly defective." As their most fundamental remedy they proposed a register of conveyances, drawing upon the Yorkshire and Middlesex precedents. Campbell, the chairman, and Brougham, the instigator of the Commission, were persistent presenters of bills to implement the recommendation.[87] The fate of the Bill of December 1831 illustrates why progress was difficult. Provincial solicitors—in an age before easy mails—feared that a register would place all the conveyancing business in the hands of their metropolitan brethren. They fomented criticism by suggesting to landowners that the registry proposal was a plot: it would provide the record on which to base a new land tax. Counter-petitions flooded the Commons and drowned the Bill.[88]

Instead, as so often, a modicum was done to strip the existing sys-

---

[84] On the possibilities of fraud, see the Real Property Commissioners, Second Report, P.P. 1830 (575) X, pp. 4–7. Special difficulties might be posed by rights of the owner, though mostly these were excluded; and by judgments in various ill-indexed court files.

[85] De Villiers (1901), pp. 4–6.

[86] Wills were increasingly the subject of artificial rules of construction, which made them the subject of contest and litigation.

[87] De Villiers (1901), pp. 15–16.

[88] See Royal Commission on Registration and Conveyancing, P.P. 1850 [1261] XXXII.

tem of its least justifiable extravagances. In the years after the Reform Act a number of the Real Property Commissioners' specific proposals were implemented: the back period for which the vendor of freehold had to prove his title was cut down by reducing the limitation period to twenty years,[89] and other difficulties in establishing a title, such as those raised by possible rights of dower,[90] were overcome; the conveyance of freehold was rid of its plethora of documents by abolishing "lease and release" and the "attendant terms" in favour of a single deed of grant[91]; the process of barring an entail was much simplified by dispensing with its fictitious actions,[92] wills of real and personal property were made subject to the same formalities and all realty owned at death was covered by a will made earlier[93]; the rules of inheritance of freehold on an intestacy were simplified in the interests of making title and transfer easier.[94] Brougham and others were responsible for an Act which aimed to eliminate much formal verbiage from conveyances by enacting short forms that would have the same effect[95]; but the Act was quietly ignored by conveyancers whose bills were calculated "by the yard."

There remained an "air of triviality" and "extreme caution" about all this legislation.[96] A new Royal Commission (1847–1850), which collected much evidence about foreign systems of registration, returned to the virtues of a register of deeds.[97] But Lord Campbell's attempt at implementation drew great hostility: the Incorporated Law Society claimed—against the radical case—that the register would increase the cost of conveying small properties, and—drawing on more established sympathy—that there would be a dangerous disclosure of family arrangements and settlements.[98] A Select Committee on a subsequent bill for the first time distinguished the concept of a titles register—i.e. a register which not merely recorded transactions so that anyone interested could make what they could of them, but one which stated and guaranteed the title and interests in the specified land.[99] Yet another Royal Commission (1854–1857) favoured the adoption of such a system, with a tri-partite register for fee simples, leases and charges (mortgages and other encumbrances);

---

[89] 3 & 4 Will. IV, c. 27, which also abolished most of the old "real" actions.

[90] 3 & 4 Will. IV, c. 105.

[91] 8 & 9 Vict., c. 106, 112. Until this legislation corporations had been obliged to convey by the medieval form of livery of seisin. 7 & 8 Vict., c. 76 (repeated in 8 & 9 Vict., c. 106, s.8) removed the need of trustees to preserve contingent remainders in settlements: see de Villiers (1901), pp. 17–18.

[92] 3 & 4 Will. IV, c. 74.

[93] 7 Will. IV. & 1 Vict., c. 26.

[94] 3 & 4 Will. IV, c. 106; and see 22 & 23 Will. IV, c. 35, ss.19, 20.

[95] 8 & 9 Vict., c. 119. Attorneys' conveyancing bills were subjected to taxation by the courts: 6 & 7 Vict., c. 73, s.37.

[96] Simpson (1986), p. 279.

[97] P.P. 1850 [1261] XXXII; and see the preceding Select Committee (H.L.), P.P. 1846 (411) VI, p. viii.

[98] The Society was at the point under considerable pressure from provincial attorneys. It was also conducting an inconclusive campaign against the certified conveyancers and conveyancing barristers.

[99] P.P. 1852–53 (889) XXXVI. The same idea had been presented to the Royal Commissioners of 1830 but was ignored by them: De Villiers (1901), p. 14.

equitable interests would be protectable only by caution or notice.[1] After attempts at implementation by both Cranworth and Cairns, Westbury succeeded with a Land Transfer Act of 1862.[2] Just as the highly successful Torrens title registries were beginning to be set up in the Australian colonies,[3] the case for public regulation in the mother country seemed also to have been won.

The Law Society Council appears if anything to have favoured the new Land Titles Registry, sensing perhaps that, however much the Act might admit a principle, its terms precluded much damage in practice. Nothing short of a truly sound title was registrable which made for expense and the rousing of sleeping defects. Westbury had moreover, been obliged to drop compulsion to register.[4] At all events, it was soon obvious that solicitors and clients between them had no interest in this means of removing the actual or possible defects in titles which were supposed to render them so expensive or difficult to deal with.[5] Certainly the reaction of solicitors (particularly in the provinces) was very different once this failure was investigated and first Selborne and then Cairns attempted to make registration compulsory upon the first change of ownership.[6] All Cairns managed was a new Act making registration possible without proof of an evidently indefeasible title and reducing limited interests, such as estates for life and in fee tail and short leases, to entitlements capable of protection by caveat.[7] But these amendments were irrelevant; even fewer titles were registered[8] and so the continuing failure of the scheme became an important strand in the Land Question of the eighties. Just as the Settled Land Act was passed before the "free trade" campaign reached its zenith, so also there came the one change in unregistered conveyancing practice that had for so long eluded the reformers. The practice of paying for documents according to length was at last put paid, but at the price of a scale of fees for conveyancing which were proportionate to the value of the transaction.[9] This solution had been actively promoted by the Law Society

[1] P.P. 1857 (ii) [2215] XXI. The fee simple owner would have an option of registering an indefeasible title guaranteed by the state.
[2] 25 & 26 Vict., c. 53. This was linked with 25 & 26 Vict., c. 42 which gave the Court of Chancery power to make declarations of title; these thereupon became registrable indefeasibly. In the wake of these developments there were also further improvements to unregistered conveyancing: e.g. Lord St Leonards' Act 1859 (22 & 23 Vict., c. 35—powers of appointment, trustees' powers); Lord Cranworth's Act 1860 (23 & 24 Vict., c. 145—trustees' and mortgagees' powers).
[3] The first was South Australia in 1858, where anti-lawyer feeling ran so high that the conveyancing monopoly was also extended to land agents. The system devised by Robert Torrens for that colony differed from the registration of title system that was to develop in England, above all in having a truly public register: see generally, the Select Committee, P.P. 1878–1879 (244) XI, p. vii and Evidence, 1752–1949.
[4] Kirk (1976) 139.
[5] In the period 1862–1868, original registrations totalled 416. A further Royal Commission explained this lack of use by pointing to defects in the structure of the 1862 Act: P.P. 1870 [C.20] XVIII, pp. xiv–xv, App. pp. 75–76.
[6] Kirk (1976) pp. 139–40.
[7] Land Registration Act 1875.
[8] In the first three years only 48 titles were registered: P.P. 1878–1879 (244) XI, p. iv.
[9] Solicitors' Remuneration Act 1881 (and Order thereunder of 1883, prescribing the scales set by a committee under the aegis of the Lord Chancellor): B. Abel Smith and R. B. Stevens, Lawyers and the Courts (1967), p. 198 ff; Offer (1981), pp. 36–40.

from 1870 onwards. It became, indeed, "the guarantee of the profession's prosperity until 1972."[10]

These economies in unregistered conveyancing slackened the pressure for a compulsory titles register, but the latter system stayed in operation. In Fortescue-Brickdale, Chief Land Registrar from 1900 to 1923, it acquired a determined champion. The introduction of scale fees for private conveyancing, if anything, served to sharpen the battle of the systems. The Registry "announced" that a purchaser of registered land acting for himself would pay an official fee that was between one-fifth and one-quarter of a solicitor's scale charge for unregistered land.[11] The Solicitors, moreover, did not help their case by soon beginning to press for the private scales to be increased.

Part of the argument turned on the continuing need to carry out complex investigations during the course of conveyancing. Yet the Settled Land Act, with its technique of "overreaching," implied that a purchaser from the life tenant under a settlement might ignore the interests of later beneficiaries. No great ingenuity was needed to devise means of putting other part interests "behind the curtain." As early as 1862, the conveyancer Wolstenholme, an opponent of any form of registration, had suggested the reduction of all legal estates in land to two—fee simple and leasehold—as a basis for securing that in conveyancing only a limited range of prior interests would need investigation. The future prospects of the Register also depended upon revamping the substantive law, as each investigation of its failure to attract much business made plain. But the registration system could be advanced by compulsion first, simplification later; while simplification must come first if private conveyancing was to remain in the competition. This was the fulcrum around which all the manoeuvring was to turn.

The Registry was in the fief of the Lord Chancellor and Lords Herschell and Halsbury in that office both tried their hand at achieving compulsory registration.[12] As the latter drew close to success, the Law Society adeptly secured, in his Land Transfer Act 1897,[13] the so-called "County veto." Compulsion was to be applied experimentally (following the legislative fashion of the day)[14] and only with the approval of the County Councils; through them the provincial solicitors could hope to exercise a less public sway. In the upshot, the County, and then the City, of London became the only district in

---

[10] Kirk (1976), p. 145. The Conveyancing Act 1881 prescribed short forms for standard clauses, such as covenants of title and covenants to produce deeds; others would be read into a conveyance unless explicitly excluded or varied. Once prolixity had no particular purpose, these short cuts could be adopted without regret.

[11] Hostility from the solicitors forced the withdrawal of the notes to users which the Registry had issued in 1889: Kirk (1976), p. 140.

[12] For their Bills and the background opposition by solicitors, Kirk (1976), pp. 140–141; Offer (1981), pp. 40–48.

[13] The Act provided the modern solution to difficulties over making good title: it allowed registration of titles as "absolute," "qualified" or "possessory," the defects in the last two being curable by effluxion of time. Even so, the courts compromised one of the basic guarantees of registration by allowing an unregistered transaction to be effective: *Capital and Counties Bank* v. *Rhodes*: [1903] 1 Ch. 631. This had to be corrected: Land Registration Act 1925, s.123(1).

[14] *Cf.* the Workmen's Compensation Act of the same year: below, p. 528ff.

which there had to be registration upon the first change of owner-ship. Solicitors kept up a barrage of criticism against a "land bur-eaucracy," with the intent of containing the spread of the new regime.[15]

The renewed attack on the landed interest, under Lloyd George's captaincy, brought conveyancing reform once more into prominence. Fortescue-Brickdale did not hesitate to seek support in the radical camp, asking for first registration to be made *gratis* in an extension of the compulsory areas, the expense to be met out of the proposed land increment tax.[16] This tax in its turn would be dependent on an accu-rate record of land-holding and land values, after the model of the German Cadaster, and for this the Register was the obvious basis. A Royal Commission under Lord St. Aldwyn listened with some sym-pathy to the case for extending registration, but ended inconclusively by accepting the need first to reform the substantive law.[17] The Liberals might have been expected to press on regardless. But Hal-dane, who moved to the Woolsack in 1912, emerged as the friend of a reformed system of private conveyancing.[18] For once, his Germano-philic instinct for bureaucratic solutions deserted him and leading conveyancers began drafting the elaborate legislation necessary.[19] The final solution was postponed by the war and it was delayed long enough afterwards for the forces of conservatism and professional interest to be able to claim a resounding victory. What Birkenhead, as Lord Chancellor, took up enthusiastically as a simplification of the substantive law, coupled with rapid extension of registration, was whittled down to the old experimental approach, so much favoured by the solicitors. The Law Society was able to hold back support until it had procured continuation of the "County veto" on compulsory registration—with the addition that, for the first ten years of the new scheme, central government would not even put up proposals to Councils for their approval.[20]

In the course of a century, the solicitors had risen steadily in power; to this their achievement in 1922 stands monument. Their direct representation in the Commons remained small, their tech-nique for protecting their principal source of income all the more masterful. They consolidated their achievement by securing a rise in

---

[15] The anathemas of Mr. J. S. Rubinstein, a solicitor with building society connections and a borough councillor, contrasted with the urbane negotiating of the Law Society council: Kirk (1976), p. 143; Offer (1977), p. 506 ff., (1981), pp. 70–74.

[16] See his evidence to the St. Aldwyn Commission, (below n. 17) First Report, Q.1454; Offer (1977), pp. 506–508.

[17] Royal Commission on the Land Transfer Acts, First Report, P.P. 1909 [Cd. 4509] XXVII; Second Report, P.P. 1911 [Cd. 5483] XXX.

[18] See Offer, (1977) who notes both Haldane's rivalry with Loreburn (an advocate of registration) and his Chancery background (though this had not told with a Lord Chancellor like Cairns).

[19] Chief amongst them was Sir Benjamin Cherry, who drafted both Haldane's unsuc-cessful Bills of 1913, and the eventual legislation for Birkenhead. Underhill also wrote influentially: his pamphlet, *The Line of Least Resistance*, was republished by the Scott Committee on Land Requisition and Valuation for Public Purposes (Min-istry of Reconstruction), Fourth Report, P.P. 1919 [Cmd. 424] XXXIX App. I. Offer (1977), pp. 511–513.

[20] Offer (1977), pp. 517–519.

the unregistered scales of one-third and in the registered scales of varying amounts, some in proportion very much greater.[21]

Conveyancing procedures were the crux of the matter. Once their future had been settled by compromise, the substantive law could be purged of archaisms and complexities.[22] This was done in a bill whose political neutrality was carefully affirmed on all sides.[23] Its basic plan had long been foreshadowed in discussions of reform: the number of legal estates was reduced to two—fee simple freeholds and leaseholds—in order that more limited interests and complex joint interests could be placed behind an equitable curtain; these were no longer of concern in conveying a legal interest because they were subject to the "overreaching" principle that (in somewhat different form) had been deployed in the Settled Land Act 1882.[24] Some interests in the land short of a legal estate did retain a binding effect on a purchaser,[25] but in order to acquire this quality many of these interests had now to be placed upon a register of charges. In the case of registered land, this was already part of the whole scheme; but for unregistered land, a Land Charges Register had to be specially created.[26] On it, the most important transactions to be recorded were various mortgages and other charges, estate contracts, and restrictive covenants.

At the same time, the transmission of property upon death was at last brought under a single regime. Marvellous as it would have seemed two generations before,[27] the heir-at-law lost his place as the direct inheritor of realty: primogeniture now stoppered an empty cask and it could be removed without offence. Upon an intestacy, the modern rules were laid down by which all property is divided amongst surviving spouse and/or children or certain remoter issue.[28] What ordinary people might expect to happen to their property became the governing consideration in dealing with the various contingencies. Order of birth ceased to be of significance, and likewise

[21] *Ibid.*, pp. 520–521.

[22] The ancient forms of tenure were standardised, an elaborate plan for the compulsory enfranchisement of copyhold tenure into freehold at last replacing the machinery that allowed this by agreement. The Statute of Uses and the Rule in Shelley's case— two sturdy obstacles to simplification with prominent places in the history of land law doctrine—were done away with. In place of the traditional, quite unreal form of mortgage at law more straightforward methods of mortgaging land were introduced, together with a more complete statutory code of the powers of the mortgagee to recover his debt out of the land. See Megarry and Wade, *Law of Real Property* (5th ed., 1984), pp. 123 ff, 915 ff.

[23] Drafted by Cherry, the Law of Property Bill 1922 was the longest on record. Sir Leslie Scott, Sol.-Gen., introduced it as "not a party Bill. It does not interfere between landlord and tenants. It leaves untouched the relations between the State and private owners." H.C. Deb. CLIV 89 (1922). Together with an amending Act of 1924, the 1922 Act and earlier legislation were codified in 1925 in a series of more manageable
' statutes: the Settled Land Act, Trustee Act, Law of Property Act, Land Registration Act, Land Charges Act and Administration of Estates Act. For the writing in explication, see J. S. Anderson (1984) 37 C.L.P. 63.

[24] See above, p. 170.

[25] *E.g.*, legal easements and any rights manifested by actual occupation of the premises.

[26] See Megarry and Wade (op cit., n. 24) pp. 133–136.

[27] See above, pp. 167–168.

[28] See Megarry and Wade, (op cit., n. 24) 539–566.

sex. Important to the simplification of conveyancing were the stan-
darised procedures for administering deceaseds' estates: realty as
well as personalty had now to be dealt with by executors acting
under a grant of probate or administrators upon letters of administration. But in all this nothing was done to interfere with freedom of
testation, any more than with the power of gift during life. One of the
most striking differences from the law of West European states survived unblemished. Only in 1938 was a measure of compulsion
introduced, bringing to heel the testator who tried to cut his dependant family out of his estate completely.[29]

III. Housing

(a) Local Authority Intervention

Public health touched no cognate issue more intimately than housing: the supply of water, the disposal of rubbish and excrement, the
building of rooms over privies, the provision of light and air, the
number of inhabitants per house or room—all these became focal
points in the campaigns of the experts and the fears of the populace
at large. It was the housing of the labouring poor that posed the
severest threat, above all in the cancerous sprawl of city slums. Traditionally in the countryside the lowest strata had provided their own
roof, throwing up hovels out of whatever stone, mud, timber, slate or
thatch could be had. But in the towns, and increasingly in the
country, house-building was becoming the work of the building
trades; and it was financed, apart from building commissioned by
owner-occupiers, by investors who looked for rent as their return.
House building and ownership for renting became a standard
investment among the propertied, from great landowners and
paternal industrialists to every variety of petty capitalist. Yet a speculative element was unavoidable. Every new builder hoped for the
best sector of the market that his capital would run to; his fears were
of neglectful, obstreperous tenants who would lose the neighbourhood its respectability, leading to a cycle in which rents could be
kept up only by dividing houses, floors or even rooms.[30] Out of the
whole process was to be generated the longest and most intense of all
the contests between individual self-reliance and the redistributive
protection of the state.

For the whole period to 1914, private investment for profit supplied the vast bulk of housing, supplemented only by a few subsidis-
ing employers, some charities concerned with one or other aspect of
the problem and the odd town council which was experimenting
with this form of municipal socialism. What statistics there are suggest that there was always a shortfall of housing, which stayed at
something like a constant figure; with the rise both in population
and provision it became proportionately smaller but it did not dis-

---

[29] Inheritance (Family Provision) Act 1938; for the present law, see, J. G. Miller, *Family
Property and Financial Provision* (2nd ed., 1984) Chap. 18.
[30] See Berry (1974); Burnett (1978) Chap. 2; Gauldie (1974) Chaps. 1, 3, 4.

appear.[31] What such statistics cannot begin to show is the decline of the worst-built, ill-maintained, ageing parts of the stock into degrading, tight-packed, disease-ridden slums. Their inhabitants struggled on in them, knowing no better or too exhausted by the business of staying alive for anything else.[32] Only when they were deprived of any roof at all, which could happen under programmes of clearance for highway improvements or railways, or even the removal of slums as such, was there a real likelihood of open revolt. But the respectable were coming to harbour a nagging, less specific unease about the social conditions of which the slums were a visible representation.

The housing question—as distinct from minimum building requirements, dictated by public health[33]—was thus whether the state, at the central or local level, should assume any responsibility itself for providing housing or at least for demolishing slums so that others might rebuild to a more acceptable standard. Throughout Victoria's reign and beyond, only very few would answer the question in any sense positively. The Diceyian image of a counter-current fits their position well, for their efforts all too evidently showed up the force of the mainstream. In Parliament, when new legislation was sought, and in the vestries and municipal councils when action was suggested, the proposals would be sure to meet an outraged barrage against so evident an infraction of economic principle. Fittingly, the novel movement was given its first impetus by the Earl of Shaftesbury, in Dicey's book that most unseeing of Tory philanthropists. In 1851, he actually steered through a Lodging Houses Act which gave local authorities the power, by rate or borrowing, to build or convert lodging houses and provide them at a rent neither too high for the labouring classes not so low as to amount to poor relief.[34] It contained an admission of principle, for those willing to see it as such, but no more. It was scarcely taken up anywhere, the exceptional case being Huddersfield, which quickly saw its new lodging houses swamped by the poor and homeless from the whole district around.[35]

The "scandal" of insanitary, overcrowded dwellings was a visible outwork of the entire system of urban production, in which unskilled labour abounded and wages were both very low and often intermittent. The successful and influential were beguiled by the belief that economic growth would bring its own solution to the problems of the poorest; they had only to be given a sense of their own moral capacity for work and thrift. A deterrent policy of poor relief was being pursued with the specific aim of eliminating any element of subsidy to wages; indeed its yardstick of "less eligibility" had to take as one measure the housing conditions of the world outside the workhouses.[36] There was little chance that municipal corporations and vestries would perceive any gap to be filled between the cheap-

---

[31] Gauldie, pp. 90–91, 145 ff.

[32] E.g., Gauldie, Chaps. 5, 6; Stedman Jones (1971) Chap. 8; Wohl (1977) Chap. 1.

[33] See above, p. 163.

[34] 14 & 15 Vict., c. 34.

[35] Gauldie (1974) Chap. 21, who shows that the contemporaneous Common Lodging Houses Acts (14 & 15 Vict., c. 28, 16 & 17 Vict., c. 41) gave the police powers of inspection, which were soon resented as intrusions onto private property.

[36] See below, p. 427ff.

est private rents and subsidised relief. It was at just this level of government that economic interest and political conviction coalesced into the strictest adherence to notions of non-interference. For all the efforts of Shaftesbury, and of the band of social reformers who kept the problem before the National Society for the Promotion of the Social Sciences (NAPSS) in the sixties, housing obstinately refused to be seen as a scandal for which there could be any remedy through law and state action, beyond regulation in the name of public health.[37]

The main test arose out of a scheme of the NAPSS and the Society of Medical Officers of Health that was put to Parliament in 1866 by their spokesman, McCullagh Torrens. It was a measure that put the issue squarely enough: not only were the vestries to be given powers to demolish insanitary buildings, purchase land and build dwellings for the labouring classes; the Home Secretary could demand that premises be inspected by medical officers and if necessary that demolition and rebuilding take place. The recipe of central direction without financial obligation had by this time a substantial, if chequered, history in social reform; it is no surprise to find Edwin Chadwick among the members of the NAPSS committee supporting it here. This and two succeeding bills suffered long and alarmed revision in committee until in 1868, Torrens finally secured legislation, the merest wraith of a robust original.[38] Vestries were left with power, on the report of a medical officer, to demolish or improve individual insanitary houses, but not whole streets. They had no power of compulsory purchase, and were in any case confined financially to a 2d. rate in the £ and such borrowing as they were prepared to shoulder.[39]

Here then was a template for legislation that would reflect dominant attitudes down to 1918. Enacted one year after the second Reform Act, it acknowledged the problems set in urban electorates by the worst housing and the consequent degradation of the whole environment; but its solution envisaged very little beyond some minor stimulants to the private market. Its design was open to limited adjustment, at least under Conservative government. In 1875, Disraeli's Home Secretary, Richard Cross, urged on by the purposeful voice of the Charity Organisation Society (COS), secured a second Act which allowed local authorities to clear whole areas of slums, if necessary by compulsory purchase.[40] Octavia Hill of the COS was the active proponent of what was unkindly labelled "5-per-cent phil-

---

[37] On the latter score, both the 1850s and 60s provided a stream of legislation. There were notable developments in London which affected housing, particularly the creation of the Metropolitan Board of Works to supervise building and the requirement that each metropolitan vestry appoint a medical officer of health: see 18 & 19 Vict., c. 55; 18 & 19 Vict., c. 120.

[38] Artizans and Labourers Dwellings Act 1868; Gauldie (1974), pp. 268–272; Wohl (1977), pp. 84–97. To be distinguished from the Labouring Classes Dwelling Houses Act 1866, a little-used statute permitting local authorities to borrow from the Public Works Loan Commissioners for housing: see Gauldie (1974), pp. 259–261.

[39] Gauldie (1974), pp. 265–272.

[40] Only if four neighbouring householders complained, the medical officer reported in favour of action and the local authority did nothing for three months, could central government take over: ss.12, 13. For the COS in general, see below, pp. 433–435.

anthropy": a programme in which local authorities would acquire
and clear slum sites, for selling or leasing to charities which would
rebuild and let at 5 per cent on investment. It belonged in turn to a
larger vision of progress: the middle and affluent working classes
were to move out of town centres into new suburbs; their place
would be filled by the least well-off, whose slums would be freed for
replacement. One of the conditions of the Cross Act, accordingly,
was an obligation on authorities who instituted clearance schemes to
secure the rehousing of those displaced, either through model dwelling trusts or, in the last resort and with central government approval,
by rebuilding themselves.[41] Both the Torrens and the Cross Acts,
which through their different procedures created alternative routes
to slum clearance, were amended in 1879 in the hope of improving
their use and eliminating their abuse.[42]

It was evident even in the seventies that the slum problem was
finding no solution either in the private market or through the first
timid steps in legislative tinkering. In the following decades, concern
began to intensify: the discoveries of the settlement movement, *The
Bitter Cry of Outcast London*, the demonstrations over unemployment
in 1886 and 1887, the Jack-the-Ripper murders, all contributed to a
growing unease. This found its most official expression before a
Select Committee in 1881–1882; and, once the Marquis of Salisbury
took it up as a proper cause for Tory concern, before a prestigious
Royal Commission.[43] The law was amended in 1882 and then twice
consolidated, with some extensions to take account of recommendations from the Commission and other pressures.[44] Nor were these
gradual alterations unimportant. The initial Acts were not merely
hopes rendered pious by lack of interest, or positive antagonism, in
the great bulk of vestries. They were undeniable examples of legislative intervention which made matters worse. The statutory procedures, after concessions to the demands of property, were so
complex that long delays occurred in the implementation of schemes.
Moreover the arrangements for compensation under the Cross Act,
which made use of arbitration by government nominees, followed
the usual pattern of generosity and rapidly led "house-knackers" to
stuff the worst properties with tenants in order to increase their
"value." This practice at least began to be curbed by amendment in
1879.[45] Even so, the intractable problem of rehousing loomed over
everything. Medical officers of health, whose reports were the first
step that would set the machinery of either Act in motion, were often
reluctant to take action, not because they were ignorant or had been
suborned, but because they saw all too plainly that a programme of
clearance and the inevitable delays before rebuilding would most

[41] Artizans and Labourers Dwellings Improvement Act 1875. The *Law Times* thought
the Cross Act and the Public Health Act marked "an abandonment of the let alone
policy and a return to the paternal system of government." See Gauldie, (1974),
pp. 274–281; Wohl (1977), pp. 97–105.
[42] By the Artizans' Dwelling Act (1868) Amendment Act and the Artizans' and
Labourers' Dwellings Improvement Act; see also the Artizans' Dwellings Act 1882.
[43] Select Committee Reports, P.P. 1881 (358) VII; 1882 (235) VII; Royal Commission on
the Housing of the Working Classes, First Report, P.P. 1884–1885 [C.4402] XXX.
[44] Housing of the Working Classes Acts 1885 and 1890, Public Health Act 1890.
[45] See above, n. 42.

likely lead to worse crowding in other adjacent areas. The same pattern would follow from action under the Acts as had occurred under
some of the town improvement schemes and with the inroads made
by railways.

According to the Royal Commission, it was not legislation that was
lacking but the political will to carry it out.[46] The verdict was comforting. Certainly the record of activity under the Torrens and Cross
Acts was derisory. Only Birmingham, led with skill and determination by Joseph Chamberlain, had adopted any large plan for the
removal of slums and had done so by moving both workers and
workplaces out into new suburbs. The small-workshop character of
much employment there had made this possible and Chamberlain
had secured special exemption from the statutory requirements to
rehouse on site, a success which led to changes in the legislation
itself.[47] Liverpool, long a leader in public health administration, had
used its local Acts to clear slums and build large estates of good quality, which were let at low rents.[48]

To turn these exceptions into norms, however, was not solely a
matter of local will. Central leadership might have attempted more,
applying the stick of compulsion or the carrot of grants-in-aid, both
of which would have needed new legisation. But it was precisely
such invasions of the private market that even those concerned with
the housing question—Tory philanthropists and "municipal socialists"—shied away from. Even so well-meaning a body as the Royal
Commission was left merely to ruminate upon the stoicism and
moral rectitude of the great bulk of slum dwellers.[49] Twenty years
later, the reforming Liberal government only moved tentatively on
housing. John Burns, who by the time he presided over the Local
Government Board had lost most of his early fire for the cause of the
working man, pushed through a Housing and Town Planning Act in
1909 which was grander in title than in achievement. It did increase
the rate of slum clearance. But on the housing front it went no further
than to abolish the requirement on local authorities to sell off what
they built and to increase somewhat the LGB's powers to stimulate
local activity.[50]

The hostility, the delaying tactics, the defeating amendments
which were the regular lot of legislative proposals of even this kind
manifested an unchanging attitude in Parliament. It was at the local

---

[46] Report (above, n. 43), pp. 27–29.
[47] The LGB had power to waive the re-housing clause under the Cross Act. By the
Housing of the Working Classes Act 1890 (following the Royal Commission), London Boroughs had still to re-house half of those displaced, but not authorities in the
provinces: Gauldie, pp. 279–280, 293–294.
[48] Gauldie (1974), pp. 299–300.
[49] " . . . while the evidence reveals an undoubtedly bad state of things, . . . the standard of morality among the inhabitants of these crowded quarters is higher than
might have been expected looking at the surroundings amid which their lives are
passed." (Report, above, n. 43, p. 13). One recommendation of the Royal Commission led to the Housing of the Working Classes Act 1885, o.12, which subjected
cheap housing on short leases to an automatic guarantee that it be fit for human
habitation at the outset and be kept in repair. Repeated in 1890 and 1909, the provision was held on a tight rein by the judges: J. I. Reynolds (1974) 37 M.L.R. 377.
[50] ss.40, 10, 11.

level that significant signs of modification occurred, as the propertied classes began to reconcile themselves both to democracy and to the limits of economic progress. One structural change was as significant as anything else. The creation of the county and county borough councils in 1888 gave the main public health and housing powers of local government to bodies elected on a wide franchise.[51] In some places this soon produced a substantial representation of labour. Cities such as Manchester, Sheffield and Bradford were drawn into the housing debate, their consciences stimulated by local pressure groups. Argument began to shift to the type of housing that should be provided—flats (the usual Tory view) or cottages (Lib/Lab). In the years 1890–1914, 179 authorities had loans sanctioned for house-building; in 1909–1914, 112 of them were drawing actively upon their entitlement. Even so, by 1914, philanthropy and municipal endeavour was supplying less than one per cent of the housing stock.[52]

(b) Rent Control

Various events swelled this trickle into a regular stream of local authority housing supported by state grant. They are partly the consequence of a war which put paid to regular house-building and contributed to a shortage of over 600,000 houses in the "land fit for heroes."[53] But the condition of the private sector over a longer term was equally significant. Three factors had accumulated, one upon the other. First, the late Victorian boom in house-building had exhausted itself by 1906; a marked depression of land values ensued which was to begin a reversal only in 1913.[54] Secondly (a contributing factor to the first), the cost of social programmes against poverty and ignorance was hurting property-owners by being paid for primarily out of rates. Landlords felt rate increases particularly because of the widespread practice of collecting rates from them, rather than from their tenant-occupiers under the compounding system (at a discount which local authorities kept trying to squeeze down).[55] Third, as the market showed signs of improvement, landlords were quick to alleviate their burdens by demanding rent increases.

All participants in the house-letting business had become familiar with collective action: societies of tenants, of landlords, and of financiers such as the building societies, were well-known interest groups who on occasion attacked or negotiated with one other or with indi-

---

[51] Local Government Act 1888, ss.17–19, provided for the appointment by county councils of medical officers of health and for execution of their reports.
[52] Daunton (1983), pp. 192–94.
[53] See the estimates of Bowley (1945) pp. 10–14 and Statistical Appendix.
[54] See Offer (1981) Chaps. 17, 18.
[55] Ironically, compounding remained common because its casual abolition by the Reform Act 1867, s.7, had provoked such *increasing* of rents that it had to be restored: Poor Rate Amendment and Collection Act 1869. For the story, see Englander (1983), Chap. 5; and for subsequent effects, Chap. 6.

viduals.[56] Owners could adopt the methods of the cartel by, for instance, agreeing to keep "empties" off the market, building societies could fix rates and conditions collectively. Solidarity would last until individuals succumbed to the temptation to steal a march. Tenants could do little save by breach of contract: usually by refusing to pay rent, sometimes by resisting distress or eviction. The language of industrial action was already used: rent strikes by groups of tenants had occurred but had disintegrated in the face of legal action, harassment or deception by landlords. The upturn of 1913, with its spate of rent increases, brought a renewal of such resistance. It was not, as Englander has shown, at the slum end of the market but among the respectable working class that the sense of outrage found effective organisation: in Wolverhampton, Birmingham, Leeds and Bradford, as well as in Glasgow, refusals to pay the increases were coupled with public meetings denouncing the behaviour of landlords.[57]

By the outbreak of war, rent strikes could no longer be dismissed as passing tests of landlords' resolve. The rapid movement of workers as well as servicemen soon added major opportunities for profiteering by landlords in the centres of war production. The courts were given extended powers to order the payment of overdue rent by instalments.[58] Agitation was already too advanced for tinkering of this order to suffice. Trade unionists, the Parliamentary Labour Party (and behind it the Workers National Committee), the Ministry of Munitions, all in differing ways were pressing for more. There was discussion of Fair Rent Courts, even by the Workers' National Committee. But suspicion of JPs, and to some degree of county court judges, as the natural associates of landlords, put paid to this arbitral idea (it would find no place until 1946).[59] The government were pushed—against every inclination—to a freezing of rents. The precipitating event developed in November 1915 from a rent strike in Glasgow: a massive demonstration of workers, and even more their wives, caused the Sheriff to adjourn the hearing of a set of eviction cases against non-payers.[60] The first of many Rent Acts, which was at once pushed through, froze the rents of unfurnished "dwelling houses" at their level at the declaration of war where the rateable value was below £35 in London, £26 in other parts of England and (signifcantly) £30 in Scotland.[61] It gave the tenant a statutory right to continue personally[62] in occupation after termination of the contrac-

---

[56] See Englander, Chap. 4 and Part 2; Cleary (1965) Chaps. 9, 10.

[57] Englander, Chaps. 7, 8, 10.

[58] Courts (Emergency Powers) Act 1914. Distress for rent was also made subject to a court order, a provision that was to be continued for rent-restricted property by the Rent Act 1920, s.6.

[59] This form of control was used when furnished lettings were subjected to regulation for the first time by the Furnished Houses (Rent Control) Act 1946.

[60] Englander, pp. 205–233; Melling (1980), pp. 91–101, 149–152.

[61] Increase of Rent and Mortgage Interest (War Restrictions) Act 1915, ss.1, 2(2). It was a criminal offence to extract a premium. For the legal evolution of rent restriction, see R. E. Megarry; The Rent Acts (10th ed., 1967), pp. 1–2.

[62] Extended by the 1920 Act, s.12(1), to include a surviving widow and occasionally other relatives, if they were living there on the tenant's death.

tual tenancy unless the landlord obtained a possession order on one
of a limited number of grounds[63]; and it protected landlords by limiting the extent to which their mortgagees could alter the rate of interest on variable mortgages.[64]

It was an emergency measure, due to expire six months after the
war's end. Laconic in character, it left the courts to determine such
important issues as what constituted a "dwelling house" and
whether overpayments of rent could be claimed back or withheld
from future rent.[65] It adjusted the positions of landlord and tenant in
a radical way and organisations such as Dan Rider's War Rents
League were besieged with requests for advice and legal aid. It could
not resolve all tensions: against a determined landlord the tenant
would need a court's protection; and a general mistrust of the law,
the known prejudice of some magistrates against tenants in arrears,
and the absence of any penalty against landlords who sought repossession without cause, meant that some rents still went up and
unjustifiable evictions still occurred.[66] The government found itself
obliged to limit even further the grounds for legitimate repossession,
first for munitions workers, then generally.[67] By the end of the war, it
became clear that the housing shortage was grave and the building
industry dispersed. The government was receiving advice from
influential quarters, including a Ministry of Reconstruction Committee,[68] to extend the duration of rent restriction for a limited
period. The rent strike became a tenants' tactic which was turned as
much against government departments and local authorities as
against private landlords.

As housing provider and rent-setter, government could not afford
to pursue an entirely selfish line, though it saw fast enough that rents
would have to rise since building costs were running at a quite new
level. Nor could it withdraw its war-time intervention in the rent
market for working-class housing as a whole. By 1919 it had settled
for a compromise that would prove irreversible. Rent restriction
would carry over until that future point (predicted with fervent optimism) when supply would again meet demand and market conditions could again prevail. Towards that end, and only as an
intermediate stepping-stone, central government would subsidise
house-building.

On the Rent Acts side of the equation, the extensions were short—

---

[63] These were: breach by the tenant; offer of alternative suitable accommodation;
    landlord's need of the premises for himself or defined relatives; any other reason
    deemed satisfactory by the court: s.1(3).
[64] ss.1(1), 1(4); for the effect on the market for mortgages, Daunton (1983), pp. 299–301.
[65] The Court of Appeal refused to allow the recovery of amounts overpaid from the
    commencement of the Act, since there was no express provision to permit it (as
    there was for premiums): Sharp & Knight v. Chant [1917] 1 K.B. 771. This strict insist-
    ence upon the need to find out one's rights before meeting a demand had to be
    altered hastily by the Courts (Emergency Powers) Act 1917. For the background, see
    Englander, pp. 257–259.
[66] Englander, pp. 256–257.
[67] Englander, pp. 242–251, 259–263; Defence of the Realm Regs. 2A; Rent (Amendment)
    Act 1918.
[68] P.P. 1918 [Cd.9235] XIII. Also influential was the Royal Commission on the Housing
    of the Industrial Population in Scotland, 1917–1918 [Cd. 8731] XIV.

initially to 1921, then 1923.[69] But they involved increases in the levels of rent protected—the 1915 limitations were doubled and then trebled by 1920; at the same time new scope for increasing them (up to 40 per cent.) was provided, mainly in the name of securing repairs and improvements. By 1923, the Conservative government found that to propose decontrol was enough to lose by-elections in its own safe seats.[70] Neville Chamberlain, who became Minister of Health, was obliged to continue control, though he made "creeping decontrol" possible: whenever a landlord recovered possession legitimately he could set whatever rent he liked upon re-letting.[71] By 1931 an eighth of all tenancies controlled in 1920 had been decontrolled.[72] Not till 1933 was the top bracket of housing—rateable values about £45 in London and Scotland and £35 elsewhere—taken out of the system; at the same time "creeping decontrol" was stopped in the bottom bracket—rateable values below £20 in London, £26.5s in Scotland and £13 elsewhere.[73] Complete deregulation remained the desideratum, at least among Conservatives. In 1938 another block was released—houses rated above £35 (London and Scotland) and £20, the rest being made subject to full control.[74] Dismantling might soon have been completed but for the renewal of war. This time it was at once clear that the cycle of shortages, rent increases and refusals to pay would have to be forestalled, the levels of rent restriction were put up to £100 and £75, there to stay until the modern adaptations of the system (if such it can be labelled) into one of fair rent assessment.[75]

(c) Building Subsidies

As for housing subsidisation, the once-for-all drive to provide the "homes fit for heroes" took both a public and a private course. On the public side, for the first time local authorities were placed under a legal duty to plan their housing provision and to execute their proposals once they had been approved by the Ministry of Health (suc-

---

[69] Rent Acts 1919, 1920, the latter following upon the Report of the Salisbury Departmental Committee, P.P. 1920 [Cmd. 658] XVIII. Thereafter the two-year extensions continued until 1927, when they became annual until 1933.

[70] One indication of the importance of protection to middle-class, as well as working-class, tenants: see F. W. Parish in F. G. Pennance, *The Verdict on Rent Control* (1972).

[71] Rent Act 1923; Report of the Onslow Departmental Committee, P.P. 1923 [Cmd. 1803] XII (Pt. 2). The temptation to landlords to get tenants out by threats, insidious pressure or trickery increased in consequence, as did the number of eviction proceedings. In Glasgow they became once more remarkably high: see Englander, pp. 307–310.

[72] The Marley Inter-Departmental Committee on the Rent Restriction Acts (P.P. 1930–31 [Cmd. 3911] XVII) found that controlled rents had on average risen 50 per cent. above their pre-war level, decontrolled rents some 85–90 per cent.—in the worst cases, much more. Some housing had thus become exorbitantly expensive—the more so since progress in slum clearance had been little more than token.

[73] Rent Act 1933.

[74] Increase of Rent Act 1938. Housing built since 1913 was not covered at any stage.

[75] Rent Act 1939, applying for the first time to post-1913 housing. The effect was to put 90 per cent. or more of all tenanted housing under control. For the subsequent history, see M. J. Barnett, *The Politics of Legislation* (1969); P. Beirne, *Fair Rent and Legal Fiction* (1977).

cessor to the LGB); and the expense of doing so was to fall upon them only to the extent of a penny rate—all further cost would come from the Treasury.[76] This financial formula was highly encouraging to local authorities but the scheme was pregnant with difficulties of application. So eager was the government to get ahead that it gave up its attempt to tie the councils to rents bringing in a specified return: they had only to procure the best rent "reasonably obtainable."[77] On the private side, builders of working-class housing which met Ministry specifications became entitled to a lump-sum subsidy working out at £150–160 per house (£15 millions being made available in total).[78] Much of this building was to altogether novel standards for working-class housing.[79] A Departmental Committee was soon to recommend that, as well as a host of administrative improvements in the scheme, local authorities should lose the protection of their financial ceiling and bear a proportionate part of the total cost.[80]

Some 170,000 houses were sanctioned for local authority building, and more than 40,000 for the private subsidy, before the economic collapse of 1921. "Geddes Axe" then ensured that the programme was wound down abruptly. Yet the housing shortage and the pressure on rents remained acute, even when the cost of building began to fall.[81] Chamberlain was obliged to act on this front as well. His "once-for-all" device adopted the opposite tack to the Addison scheme. It placed the ceiling on the Treasury contribution: £6 per annum was payable for 20 years on houses built by private builders or local authorities to specified standards[82]; but local authorities were to build only when they satisfied the Ministry that they would do it better than private enterprise. The houses had moreover to be completed within two years (by October 1925).[83]

The implication—that housing was once more about to become a market commodity—was averted by the arrival of the first, minority Labour government. Instead a highly significant intervention by the

---

[76] Housing, Town Planning, etc. Act 1919, esp. ss.1, 7. For a summary of the housing legislation, see Merrett (1979) App. 1.

[77] Local Authorities (Assisted Housing Schemes) Regs. 1919, Sched. B. This still contained the formula which the government had wished to make mandatory: that by March 1927 councils should charge an economic rent calculated as if the house had been completed by that date—it was taken as the point by which costs and supply would have returned to "normal." For earlier Ministry Memoranda on this formula (an interesting example of administrative technique), see Englander, p. 295.

[78] Housing (Additional Provisions) Act 1919—the two Acts were together the "Addison Acts," after the President of the LGB/Minister of Health who was chiefly responsible.

[79] This development drew upon the pre-war discussions of the form of local authority housing and the inspiration provided by the garden city movement. They were brought into focus by the Tudor Walters Report on Building Construction, P.P. 1918 [Cd. 9191] VII. See M. Swenarton, *Homes Fit for Heroes* (1981); Burnett (1978), pp. 218–221; and generally, M. J. Daunton (ed.) *Councillors and Tenants* (1984).

[80] Report on the High Cost of Building Working Class Dwellings P.P. 1921 [Cmd. 1447] XIII.

[81] The fall was considerable: building costs which had been over £1 per square foot in 1920 were down to under 10s. by 1922 and were to fall somewhat further: M. J. Elsas, *Housing Before the War and After* (1942), p. 17.

[82] The amounts could be compounded into a lump sum, which came to £75–100 per house.

[83] Housing Act 1923, s.1.

state was confirmed in post. Wheatley, the Health Minister, extended the Chamberlain subsidy for fifteen years (to 1939) and introduced a higher rate (£9 per annum for 40 years[84]) for housing that was to be let.[85] Local authorities had no longer to seek the imprimatur of the Ministry before they built for themselves.[86]

Yet beyond this basic step were wide areas for political division. In one direction lay the prospect of government provision of most working-class housing—a general take-over from the private builder and landlord. In another, state intervention would be a severely limited means of dealing with the abjectly poor who could never hope to pay a market price for endurable housing. The Conservatives, who soon replaced Labour, found the continuing post-war shortage still so pressing that they could move no further along the latter road than to reduce the subsidies in line with the falling costs of building.[87] The Labour government of 1929, by contrast, returned to the subject of slum clearance, so sadly neglected in the years of shortage. Since the main beneficiaries of central intervention had so far been the better-off working class, Arthur Greenwood, the Health Minister, applied the notion of central subsidy to slum clearance with a view to broadening the flow of assistance.[88] But economic and political turmoil intervened before the policy of increased spread had gone far. The National government soon adapted it: the new (Greenwood) attack on the most dilapidated, overcrowded housing was boistered, but the old (Wheatley) subsidy for working-class house-building in general was cut away.[89] Fostering the private building sector and encouraging owner-occupation of freehold houses became the main objectives. Had peace-time Conservative government continued, as with rent restriction the free market would have been progressively restored. Instead, the havoc brought by a second war made government support for massive housing programmes a necessary fact of post-war life. The inter-war period became a source of immediate experience that was to condition the nature and direction of modern developments.

The shifts of housing policy between the two world wars are too complex to admit of one-directional explanation.[90] Some of its initiation, and much of its maintenance in the face of reaction, found its source in that progressive liberalism which was to be taken over by the Labour party during its first experiences of government. Middle-class idealism and working-class self-interest had drawn from all the fervent discussion of a "land policy" an interventionary approach to the provision of working-class housing, urban and rural. The state was to play an increasing role in the refurbishing of housing stock

---

[84] In rural areas, £12.10s.

[85] He was able to secure a celebrated "gentlemen's agreement" with the building unions: manpower was built up in return for the guaranteed period of subsidy: Bowley (1945), p. 35.

[86] Housing (Financial Provisions) Act 1924, ss.1, 2.

[87] Bowley, p. 45.

[88] Housing Act 1930.

[89] Housing (Financial Provisions) Act 1933.

[90] Contrast the approaches of Bowley (1945), Burnett (1978) Pt. III, N. Merett (1979) and Daunton (1984) with the Marxist contributions to Melling (1980).

and the raising of living standards which depended so greatly upon it.

At the same time a much larger block of property-owning opinion was driven to accept some at least of these measures; they were a necessary concession if the essential characteristics of the old economic system were to be restored and maintained in an uneasy peacetime. As the historical evidence is accumulated, it is becoming plainer that the sense of outrage amongst tenants, expressed through their associations, their rent strikes and other threatening behaviour, was a vital part of the changes. The ferment was seized upon by revolutionary activists and others with wide-ranging radical sympathies. Lloyd George was able to play up a fear of revolution in order to get Addison's Bills through Cabinet. But the great bulk of the support came from working-class people who saw rents and landlords as causes unto themselves. The women who played so prominent a part in the most successful protests showed little of the same fervour even for their own suffrage. This begins to explain how politicians could muddle through by a series of hasty and reactive moves.

Those moves nonetheless encompass a considerable shift in the uses of law. A world in which terms of contract prevailed and landlords could look to the legal system in extracting their rents and forcing out bad tenants was, in the more "difficult" sectors, replaced by two mechanisms. The Rent Restriction Acts were crude curbs on rent increases and eviction in a relationship which was otherwise governed by private contract. Since the Acts were a response to shortage the price of housing just outside their limits shot up. The law demarcating their extent was accordingly a matter of acute controversy and was soon pitted with nice, not always consistent, interpretation.[91] They were an expedient which could not provide a permanent solution in the inter-war form.

The Housing Acts, however, with their base in social provision, demanded a wholly different structure. Planning and decision-making was undertaken at many levels by politicians and officers of central and local government. Once the broad lines of policy had been blocked in by legislation, rules and decisions were required to settle the types, numbers and location of houses. They would require allocation and the setting of rents which tenants could pay. Every stage of the process was potentially controversial; the difficulties of the private sector were not dissipated by a socialised system—inadequate supply of what tenants wanted, unduly high rents, reluctance to take on large families or tenants with bad rent records. But the combination of politics and legally-framed bureaucracy could prevent dissatisfaction from coming too closely into focus. The inter-war experience taught much about how this could be achieved. What was to be carried forward into the present era was an amalgam of policy and practice which left the new professionals of the business, the planners and architects, and those who would do the actual building (most often private contractors), with wide powers of decision that were insulated from effective monitoring or criticism.

[91] For a comparative survey of developments in the period, J. W. Willis (1950) 36 Cornell L.R. 54.

The courts, it is true, showed a distinct mistrust of programmes of intervention.[92] Slum landlords might not be the most attractive class of property-owners, but clearance schemes would oblige them to sur- render their land on compensation terms which had come to be strictly limited.[93] Lord Hewart C.J., soon after producing *The New Despotism*, gave a guarded reading to clearance powers in the Hous- ing Act 1925, Part II, which required that notice be given at the outset of the particular scheme of re-use of the cleared land; otherwise, the local authority would simply get an opportunity to re-sell or lease at the highest price.[94] But the House of Lords soon took a less critical attitude in a similar case where the authority was undoubtedly intending to re-house with the land reclaimed.[95] The malaise was not at this period long-lasting and it was confined to an insistence on procedural rectitude.[96] Certainly, the 1914 war and its aftermath con- firmed the general readiness to leave bureaucrats to the administra- tion of statutory schemes unmolested by common law standards of due process, let alone common law notions of reasonableness. This too would contribute to a post-war world where the constraints on experts were remote. Neither the old owners nor the new consumers would have much chance of objecting to what would be done in the name of superseding the one group and assisting the other.

(d) A Planned Environment?

A final factor would lead in the same direction. Visions of a world transformed by some form of land exploitation in the name of the community had held a wide appeal from the latter nineteenth cen- tury onwards. From them had evolved a new social responsibility

---

[92] Jennings (1936) traced the extent to which they showed a hostility to expropriation of private property: the record is patchy.

[93] See above, pp. 153–154.

[94] R. v. *Minister of Health, ex p. Davis* [1929] 1 K.B. 619 (a test case affecting most other improvement schemes: see Jennings (1936), p. 447). In dealing with the first case under the Housing Act 1930, where the court's powers of review were specially limited, Swift J. went out of his way (while deciding in favour of the particular local authority) to reiterate the rule of strict construction applying to statutes that expro- priated private property: Re *Bowman* [1932] 2 K.B. 621. Sir Carleton Allen supported him in articles published as *Bureaucracy Triumphant* (1931).

[95] R. v. *Minister of Health, ex p. Yaffe* [1931] A.C. 494; the Court of Appeal had been less accommodating: [1930] 2 K.B. 98. The case raised the effectiveness of the relatively novel device for excluding judicial review of vires—a provision stating that a minis- ter's order should have effect "as if enacted in this Act." This "Star Chamber clause" (Housing Act 1925, s.40(5)) had been specially condemned by Lord Hewart (*The New Despotism* (1929) p.246; see above, pp. 96–97). Both the Court of Appeal and the House of Lords held it ineffective to preclude their jurisdiction to review. The Housing Act 1930, s.11, had already changed the law before the appeal was com- pleted.

[96] In *Errington Minister of Health* [1935] 1 K.B. 249, the Court of Appeal applied to slum clearance procedure a rule of natural justice forbidding the Minister to consult the local authority without the knowledge of objectors, before confirming the clearance order. This suggested dissatisfaction with the House of Lords' earlier refusal to apply common law procedural standards to the determination of ministry policy (*LGB* v. *Arlidge*, above p. 96). Other judges found the new decision hard to apply: see *Frost* v. *Minister of Health* [1935] 1 K.B 286; Re *Manchester C.P.O.* (1935) 33 L.G.R. 314.

upon wealth in general expressed through increasing taxation. Large land-owning had been stripped of its sure profitability. The largest transference of land into the custody of communities had been through the programmes for working-class housing, and this had remained essentially piecemeal. The land that remained in private ownership had come to be subjected to a minimum level of responsibilities, such as the standards on new building in the name of public health and the various restrictions on the terms of leases in the name of tenants. The idea of an overall plan for the deployment of land remained ephemeral. Despite some passing good intentions the inter-war period provided little hard experience of such a regime in action.

Even before the first war, the prospects of a decently planned urban environment had grown from private middle-class developments to the idea of garden suburbs and cities.[97] The impress of this upon some of the more ambitious local authority projects had even led to a short section in Burns' 1909 Act which permitted a local authority (with LGB approval) to make a town planning scheme for land being developed so as to secure "proper sanitary conditions, amenity and convenience."[98] There was a procedure for consultation of interested parties. The slight use to which this section was put is a good measure of the limited progress of intervention in housing before 1914. A somewhat more adventurous provision in the 1919 Act introduced the prospect of eventual compulsion, but this was subsequently put off.[99] It was not until 1932, that the arrangements were extended to land in general, whether urban or rural and whether under development or not.[1] By the outbreak of war only three per cent of the country had become subject to operative schemes. However, a resolution by a local authority to adopt a plan had the effect of imposing "interim development control" and by 1937 about half the land was placed under this shadowy constraint. The bulk of builders felt no need to obtain the interim permission provided for in the Act before embarking on their schemes. Planning blight was still a rare disease.[2] The distortion of market values that restrictions on land use must produce had long been debated. Ideas of taxing the betterment conferred on those artificially advantaged had been a regular feature of radical programmes. Accordingly there were provisions in the first planning legislation for a levy by the local authority on those given planning permission: 50 per cent of the increased value, according to the 1909 Act, 72 per cent in the 1932 Act.[3] But the immense difficulties of assessment inherent in such schemes left them as stillborn as Lloyd George's general increment duty.[4]

---

[97] See M. Swenarton, *Homes Fit for Heroes* (1981) Chap. 1.
[98] Housing and Town Planning Act 1909, s.54(1), (4) and generally Part II. See Ashworth (1954) Chap. 1.
[99] The Housing, Town Planning & etc. Act 1919, Pt. II imposed a duty on local authorities for populations of over 20,000 to prepare plans by 1926, (s.46). This was extended to 1929 by the Housing etc. Act 1923, s.19.
[1] Town and Country Planning Act 1932. This Act dropped the compulsion to plan under the 1919 Act (see above, n. 99).
[2] Ashworth (1954), pp. 212–213
[3] *Ibid.*, pp. 107–109.
[4] See above, pp. 90–91.

These foreshadows of modern planning law were cast by an expanding expertise. The architects who in the early decades of the century had concentrated on the efficiency and comfort of houses for the masses, and had sought to bring a countrified grace to town estates, were coming to realise in the inter-war years that conditions for living depended on the organisation of the whole environment. There must be adequate road and rail connections, shops, schools and colleges, power supply, and facilities for leisure and culture. Above all else, industry and offices must be developed in proportion to the accommodation being built. And this in turn demanded analysis of natural resources, food supply, transport systems and economic demands of many kinds. There were a few demonstrations of what might be achieved, such as the satellite towns of Welwyn Garden City (north of London) and Wythenshawe (outside Manchester); and much urban sprawl, like the depressing estates which the London County Council was strewing across south Essex and other parts of the growing metropolis.[5]

With the bad so predominant, the good so occasional, the campaigners for a planned environment could attract increasing attention. In the Report of the Barlow Commission on the Distribution of the Industrial Population, they received definite, if somewhat mild, support.[6] Then, as in other areas of collective endeavour, the catastrophic dislocations of renewed war were to have their peculiar catalytic effect: the devastation of the cities by bombing presented opportunities on a massive scale. The primacy of the task led, even in 1943, to the creation of a Ministry of Town and Country Planning, which in the following year saw through an interim Act to encourage positive re-planning of blitzed and blighted town areas and two years later took charge of the development of new towns.[7] In 1947, the general responsibility for planning was placed on authorities at the county and county borough level. They were required to adopt a Development Plan for their entire area, which would designate the permitted use of each piece of land—for agriculture, industry, housing, education, open space, and so on.[8] The plan would be subject to five-yearly review. Moreover, most development of land within the designated use required permission from the local authority.[9] And the authority was to have greatly increased power over much else: slum clearance, the preservation of historic and meritorious buildings, the maintenance of waste lands, the retention of woodlands, the control of hoardings and the prevention of ribbon development.[10]

---

[5] See, generally, Ashworth (1954) Chap. 8; A. Sutcliffe, *Towards the Planned City* (1981) Chap. 3.

[6] P.P. 1939–1940 [Cmd. 6153] IV; G. M. Young (ed.) *Country and Town* (1943).

[7] Minister of Town and Country Planning Act 1943; Town and Country Planning (Interim Development) Act 1943; Town and Country Planning Act 1944; New Towns Act 1946; note also the Distribution of Industry Act 1945, controlling the siting of new industrial developments.

[8] Town and Country Planning Act 1947, Part II.

[9] 1947 Act, ss.12–25.

[10] ss.26–33. Between the wars, the stretching of housing out along the main roads, from towns was thought a sufficient problem for first restrictions to be imposed by an Act of 1932.

The object was a deployment of the land to the benefit of the whole community in a world which, so it was hoped, would be less fissured by the antagonism and inequalities of class. It did not adopt as its major premise the nationalisation of the land, which had enjoyed an active political platform since the days of O'Brien. Nor was the government intent on full-scale levy upon increments in the capital value of land in general, which the land taxers had long advocated, and which had been proposed during the War by the Uthwatt Committee.[11] Instead there was to be a development charge on the increased value which accrued when a developer was accorded planning permission—a tax which, as past efforts had already demonstrated, would prove difficult to assess and unpopular to impose.[12]

Nonetheless the programme was the most ambitious part of the whole social plan of the Attlee government, striving as it did to balance the needs to restore and develop the economy against claims to a decent living environment for the mass of ordinary people. The architects and planners, the economic and social analysts, were to supply the skills for informed choice. An exhausted country, eager for some new accommodation between the propertied and the labouring classes, was prepared to invest them with considerable power to get on with the job. The courts, reflecting this mood, refused to interfere when the Minister, Lewis Silkin, insisted upon putting through an order designating Stevenage as the first new town, despite the local objections put to an inquiry conducted on his behalf. Since the Minister was not under even a "quasi-judicial" duty, but was engaged in a political choice, he was only obliged to order the inquiry and consider the report; and he had done so.[13] This gave a fair wind to the new directors of land policy; central and local politicians with their planning bureaucrats, private developers with their contractors and professional advisers, could advance their views of social interest against the objections both of private property owners and of those who had environmental and other concerns in resisting development. In the result the new planning system was to become the focus of very considerable tension and constant adaptation.[14] But in the comparative innocence of the 1940s there were few to foresee it.

---

[11] Expert Committee on Compensation and Betterment; Young (above, n. 6).

[12] Accordingly it would be largely abandoned in 1954. By way of counter-balance, those who lost because the plan for their land imposed a fetter on its use were to be compensated: a government fund of £300 millions was established for the purpose, the government acquiring on payment the potential development value that might arise from a future change of use. But this too was highly complex and came to nothing.

[13] *Franklin* v. *Minister of Town and Country Planning* [1948] A.C. 87. Even before the New Towns Act had passed, the Minister had committed himself strongly to Stevenage as the first site; but this indiscretion was not enough to upset his subsequent "decision.".

[14] For the law and politics of modern planning, P. McAuslan, *The Ideologies of Planning Law* (1980); and, with reference to housing programmes, P. Dunleavy, *The Politics of Mass Housing in Britain, 1945–1975* (1981).

FURTHER READING

Land Law and Conveyancing Practice

Baker, J.H., *Introduction to English Legal History* (2nd ed., 1979), Pt. II.
de Villiers, J.E.R., *The History of the Legislation concerning Real and Personal Property during the Reign of Queen Victoria* (1901).
Holdsworth, Sir W., *A History of English Law*, Vol. III, pp. 3–275, Vol. VII, pp. 3–400, Vol. XV, pp. 167–92.
Kirk, H., *Portrait of a Profession* (1976).
Manchester, A.H., *Modern Legal History* (1980), Chap. 13.
Milsom, S.F.C., *Historical Foundations of the Common Law* (2nd ed., 1981) Chaps. 8, 9.
Offer, A., "The Origins of the Law of Property Acts 1910–25" (1977) 40 M.L.R. 505.
Offer, A. *Property and Politics 1870–1914* (1981).
Pollock, F., *The Land Laws* (1883).
Simpson, A.W.B., *A History of the Land Law* (2nd ed., 1986).
Underhill, Sir A., "Changes in the Law of Real Property" in Odgers, W.B., (ed.) *A Century of Law Reform* (1901) Chaps. 9, 10.

Deployment of Interests in Land and Housing

Beckett, J.V., "English Landownership in the later Seventeenth and Eighteenth Centuries: the Debate and the Problems" (1977) 30 Ec.H.R. (2d) 567.
Beckett, J.V., "The Pattern of Landownership in England and Wales, 1660–1880" (1984) 37 Ec.H.R. (2d) 1.
Bonfield, L., *Marriage Settlements 1601–1740* (1983).
Burnett, J., *A Social History of Housing 1815–1970* (1978).
Bowley, M., *Housing and the State* (1945).
Cannadine, D., *Lords and Landlords* (1980).
Chambers J.D. and Mingay G.I., *The Agricultural Revolution 1750–1880* (1966).
Clay, C., "Marriage, Inheritance and the Rise of the Great Estates in England, 1660–1815" (1968) 21 Ec.H.R. 503.
Clay, C., "The Price of Freehold Land in the later Seventeenth and Eighteenth Centuries" (1974) 27 Ec.H.R. 178.
Cleary, E.J., *The Building Society Movement* (1965).
Daunton, M.J., *House and Home in the Victorian City* (1983).
Douglas, R., *The Land, People and Politics* (1976).
Englander, D., *Landlord and Tenant in Urban Britain, 1838–1918* (1983).
English B. and Saville, J., *Strict Settlement* (1983).
Gauldie, E., *Cruel Habitations* (1974).
Griffith, J.A.G. "The Law of Property (Land)" in Ginsberg, M. (ed.) *Law and Opinion in England in the 20th Century* (1959) 116.
Habbakuk, Sir J., "English Landownership, 1680–1740" (1940) 10 Ec.H.R. 2.
Habbakuk, Sir J., "Marriage Settlements in the Eighteenth Century" (1949) 32 Tr.R.H.S. (4th) 15.

Melling, J., (ed.), *Housing, Social Policy and the State* (1980).

Merrett, S., *State Housing in Britain* (1979).

Martin, D., "Land Reform" in Hollis, P., *Pressure from Without in Early Victorian Britain* (1974) Chap. 6.

Perkin, H., "Land Reform and Class Conflict in Victorian Britain" in Butt, J., and Clark, I.F., *The Victorians and Social Protest* (1973) 177.

Spring D., *The English Landed Estate in the Eighteenth Century* (1963).

Spring, E., "The Settlement of Land in Nineteenth Century England" (1963) 8 Am.J.Leg.Hist. 209.

Spring, E., "Landowners, Lawyers and Land Law reform in Nineteenth Century England" (1977) 21 Am.J.Leg.Hist. 40.

Stedman Jones, G., *Outcast London* (1971).

Thompson, F.M.L., *English Landed Society in the Nineteenth Century* (1963).

Thompson, F.M.L., "Land and Politics in England in the Nineteenth Century" (1964) 47 Tr.R.H.S. (4th) 23.

Thompson, F.M.L., "The Social Distribution of Landed Property in England since the Sixteenth Century" (1966) 19 Ec.H.R. (2d) 505.

Thompson, F.M.L., "Landownership and Economic Growth in England and in the Eighteenth Century" in Jones, E.L., and Woolf, S.J., *Agrarian Change and Economic Development* (1969) Chap. 2.

Trumbach, R., *The Rise of the Egalitarian Family* (1978).

Control and Adaptation of Land Use

Ashworth, W., *The Genesis of Modern British Town Planning* (1954).

Brockington, C.F., *Public Health in the Nineteenth Century* (1965).

Brenner, J.F., "Nuisance Law and the Industrial Revolution" (1973) 3 J. Leg. St. 403.

Evans, E.J., *The Contentious Tithe* (1976).

Finer, S.E., *The Life and Times of Sir Edwin Chadwick* (1952).

Frazer, W.M., *The History of English Public Health* (1950).

Gonner, E.C.K., *Common Land and Enclosure* (1912).

Hammond, J.L. and B., *The Village Labourer* (1927), Chaps. 1–4.

Hennock, E.P., "Urban Sanitary Reform before Chadwick" (1957) 10 Ec.H.R. (2d) 113.

Jennings, W.I., "Courts and Administrative Law—the Experience of English Housing Legislation" (1936) 49 Harvard L.R. 426.

Jennings, W.I., "Judicial Process at its Worst" (1937) 1 M.L.R. 111.

Lambert, R.J., *Sir John Simon, 1816–1904, and English Social Administration* (1963).

Lewis, R.A., *Edwin Chadwick and the Public Health Movement* (1952).

MacDonagh, O., *Early Victorian Government 1830–1870* (1977) Chap. 8.

McLaren, J.P.S., "Nuisance Law and the Industrial Revolution— Some Lessons from Social History" (1983) 3 *Oxford J. Leg. St.* 155.

McLeod, R.M., "The Alkali Acts Administration" (1965) 9 Vict. St. 85.

Tate, W.E., *The English Village Community and the Enclosure Movements* (1967).

Turner, M.E., *Enclosure in Britain, 1750–1830* (1984).

Wohl, A.S., *Endangered Lives* (1983).

Chapter Three

COMMERCE AND INDUSTRY

In this Chapter attention shifts to the vast tide of capitalistic endeavour that drove industrialisation forward. Within it law has both a facilitative and a regulatory force: it affirmed private property against the predatory instincts of both sovereign and subject; it provided rules for making contracts and the machinery for enforcing them; it underwrote the assumption that the products of industry belonged to capital and that labour was entitled only to wages for work; it accorded special characteristics to the commercial bills and notes by which so much trade was financed; it elaborated the techniques for raising large sums of capital. Much of this underpinning had to be in position from the outset; some was a response to the demands of later, maturer stages of development.[1]

Trading in goods had been growing in significance since a handful of medieval communities had developed into substantial towns and more had become the focus of local economic activity, often with a periodic market to which merchants might travel considerable distances. One of the first demands of traders was for a jurisdiction which could dispose of their disputes swiftly and with understanding, so that they might get on with their real, ever-pressing business.[2] Special market courts—courts of piepowder[3]—were typically a part of the grant of market rights and they continued to function in some places into the eighteenth century. In the late Middle Ages, England also began to see enough of trade between the kingdoms and principalities of Europe to have some contact with the bodies of law merchant regulating the major trading routes. In the fourteenth century, the main commercial towns were granted Courts of Staple, in which merchants judged by their own customs, and these survived until the Tudor period.[4] The largest demand for such jurisdiction was always in London and there the court of the Admiral flourished in matters to do with ships as such and more generally with commercial transactions containing a foreign element.[5] The rise of the Council in the sixteenth century brought commercial suits before it, and for marine insurance a special court and register of transactions was created in 1601.[6] Equally the chartered companies

---

[1] On the long-range contribution of legal institutions to economic and financial growth in the period, see R. M. Hartwell, *The Industrial Revolution and Economic Growth* (1971) Chap. 11; B. L. Anderson in B. M. Ratcliffe (ed.) *Great Britain and her World 1750–1914* (1975) Chap. 5, and in F. Crouzet (ed.), *Capital Formation in the Industrial Revolution* (1972) Chap. 7; D. Sugarman and G. R. Rubin, *Law Economy and Society* (1984), pp. 3–13.

[2] For the early jurisdictions and mercantile law in general, see above, p. 29ff.; Holdsworth I, pp. 526–573; V, pp. 60–154; VIII, pp. 99 300.

[3] Probably, the *pieds poudrés* of the travellers.

[4] The culminating statute was 27 Edw. III, c. 2 (1353).

[5] In other ports there were local admiralty courts.

[6] 43 Eliz., c. 12.

for foreign trade, which increased in the same period, bred their own arbitral bodies. By then arbitration was a common technique—perhaps even the dominant mode—by which merchants settled their disputes.[7] Under the Tudors and Stuarts, the common law judges had issued prohibitions and other prerogative writs to curtail and control the jurisdiction of Admiralty, the Insurance Court and local courts. At the same time they had broadened their territorial jurisdiction over foreign dealings by a naked pleading fiction: if the plaintiff asserted his contract to have been made at (say) Paris in the Ward of Cheapside, the geographical solecism was not open to contradiction.[8] The financial incentive for this aggression was transparent, for the judges took their share of litigants' fees and the bar of their courts benefitted from an enlarged and wealthy clientele. But equally, there were wider political considerations in building the central courts into a bastion strong enough to withstand royal and other influence; and beyond even this, the absorption of law merchant into the common law reflects the pregnant attraction of capitalist adventure not merely for a discrete segment, but for a wide spectrum, of the propertied.

Even so, until the mid-eighteenth century, the common law courts were readier to exert their jurisdictional superiority than to evolve substantive rules for mercantile cases.[9] A great deal would be left to the verdict of juries on the particular facts. There is no denying that there were points at which the needs and customs of trading communities were very different from those of the landowning, agricultural world which had largely generated the common law of England. Merchants needed recognition of the negotiable character of bills of exchange and other notes promising to pay which would pass from hand to hand as financial instruments; and they needed the assurance that title to goods could in most circumstances be presumed from physical control over them. There was no room in the transitory world of trade dealings for the elaborate investigations that conveyancers made the rule for land or for the common law's insistence upon *nemo dat quod non habet*. Here were profound tensions which would take considerable time to resolve. But by the end of the seventeenth century the needs of the commercial community were becoming exigent enough for Lord Holt C.J. to make a vigorous start on the integration of mercantile custom. By the later eighteenth century Lord Mansfield would conduct a major offensive that would for the most part prove irreversible.[10] He combined his own wide learning—embracing Scots and continental systems as well as common law—with a readiness to consult the opinion of the City, both informally and through the special juries of merchants with whom he sat at the Guildhall.[11] As a result the bill of exchange and the promissory note, which under Lord Holt and other predecessors had been

---

[7] See above, p. 36ff.
[8] Blackstone, *Commentaries*, III p. 107.
[9] See J. H. Baker [1979] C.L.J. 295.
[10] Accordingly to be contrasted with Mansfield's moves to draw together common law and equity (*cf.* below, p. 215); and to supervise inferior jurisdiction by extending certiorari (see above, p. 32).
[11] See C. H. S. Fifoot, *Lord Mansfield* (1936) Chap. 4.

treated as transferable,[12] were accorded their prime modern characteristic of negotiability: the person who took the paper for consideration in the ordinary course of business acquired good title, despite earlier loss, theft or fraud.[13] Moreover it was accepted that no form of instrument might acquire this attribute once this was shown to be the accepted practice of the mercantile community. In the sphere of marine insurance, the many rules defining the rights and liabilities of insurer and assured began rapidly to take form, including the power of the insurer to avoid the insurance when relevant information was withheld by the assured.[14] There was also enough case law to begin on the principles of fire, life and other insurances, in many instances by adapting the rules of marine insurance.

All this and much else was of great importance to the City of London, where markets in bills and securities and in marine and other insurance were burgeoning.[15] But equally its impress extended outside, for the lending of money and dealings in bills and notes was leading to that volatile country banking which attorneys and landed estate agents did so much to foster. It is beyond the range of this chapter to explore the emergent rules affecting each of these types of transaction. We will be concerned with a series of root ideas that underlie the whole. We start with the articulation of general principles of Contract (Part I), which is a phenomenon of the industrial period and a process bearing ideological tensions that run throughout the chapter. From this we move to the sanctions which the businessman demands of the legal system in the hope of ensuring that his transactions progress towards successful execution. At the forefront, in our period, stands the enforcement of debts, for credit is a central factor in the insistent demand for capital. This leads to crucial questions about the debtor's insolvency, distributing his assets fairly among those creditors who rank equally and organising preferential treatment by way of security (Part II). Of this the obverse is the profound question, how far if at all, a debtor should be permitted in advance to limit his liabilities. The raising of capital and the limitation of liability are mainsprings in the evolution of the dominant form of business organisation under mature capitalism, the joint stock company (Part III). It in turn has allowed the emergence of business structures large enough to dominate markets and suppress competition within them. Accordingly the chapter ends with questions about market domination: how far should abuses of monopoly be controlled by law (Part IV); how far should developmental policies be pursued by the conferment of legal monopolies, taking as the prime instance, patents for inventions (Part V); and how far should

---

[12] This in itself ran counter to the common law's hostility to the assignment of debts (see below, p. 228). Holt had accepted the case for the bill of exchange but had drawn back in the case of the promissory note, accusing Lombard Street of attempting "to give laws to Westminster Hall" (*Clerk* v. *Martin* (1702) 2 Ld. Raym. 757). The result was reversed by statute (3 & 4 Ann., c. 9, 1704). The story illustrates the transitional state of the whole question: see generally, Holden (1955) Chaps. 3, 4.

[13] esp. *Miller* v. *Race* (1758) 1 Burr. 452; generally, Holden (1955) Chap. 6; Fifoot (above, n. 11), pp. 90–91.

[14] esp. *Carter* v. *Boehm* (1766) 3 Burr. 1905; R. Hasson (1969) 35 M.L.R. 615.

[15] For the development of marine underwriting within the ambience of Lloyd's Coffee House, D. E. W. Gibb, *Lloyd's of London* (1957) Chaps. 1–6.

the state take over the organisation of an industry which has come to be dominated by non-competing private interests (Part VI).

PART I. A WHOLE VIEW OF CONTRACT

By mid-eighteenth century, Contract was advancing as one of the great organising categories of liberal thought. The idiom of the social contract, descending from Thomas Hobbes and John Locke, provided a natural frame for a work such as Blackstone's *Commentaries*.[16] By his day, civilian countries, where the academic exposition of law was well embedded, had received general accounts of contract law. A high point in this tradition was the appearance in 1761–1764 of Robert Pothier's *Traité des Obligations*, a work which would in time have considerable influence even upon the common law world.[17]

Nonetheless Blackstone's account of contract law fell far short of that set of general principles which is implanted early in the mind of the modern law student. He acknowledged the rapidly increasing importance of contract as itself a form of property, placing it among his Rights of Things. He outlined the need of consideration to support an enforceable promise, and defined the circumstances in which the promisee must himself perform his side of the bargain before suing. He also described basic terms of a variety of contracts (notably those concerning the passing of property and risk in sales of goods).[18] In the next volume, he described the standard forms of action for enforcing contract: the writ of covenant for promises under seal in deeds; the form of the action on the case known as assumpsit ("he promised . . . ") for informal promises of all kinds.[19] Even so, assumpsit remained a rough heading under which to group more specific pleas,[20] many of them following the formulae of the "common counts."[21] Its condition resembled the modern law of torts. Only after Blackstone would a succession of writers, from Archdeacon Paley and Joseph Powell to Frederick Pollock and William Anson,[22] uncover a standard grammar beneath the work-a-day language of

---

[16] See Atiyah (1979), pp. 39–80.

[17] Especially after its translation as a *Treatise on the Law of Obligations* (by W. D. Evans, 1806).

[18] *Commentaries*, II Chap. 30.

[19] *Ibid.*, III Chap. 9. This division was taken from Sir Matthew Hale's *The Analysis of the Law* (1713, posthumous): Simpson (1979), pp. 545–546.

[20] Blackstone approved of the unmistakeably Darwinian evolution of assumpsit two centuries before, when it had supplanted the older writ of debt, as well as permitting action on promises that were not within debt: see S. F. C. Milsom, *Historical Foundations of the Common Law* (1981) Chap. 12; J. H. Baker, *Introduction to English Legal History* (1979), pp. 282–290; A. W. B. Simpson, *A History of the Common Law of Contract* (1975) Pt. II; S. J. Stoljar, *A History of Contract at Common Law* (1975) Chaps. 3–7.

[21] These formulae accommodated claims which would now be regarded as quasi-contractual, as well as contractual. See below, pp. 209–210.

[22] W. Paley, *Principles of Moral and Political Philosophy* (1785) Book II; J. J. Powell, *Essay upon the Law of Contracts and Agreements* (1790); F. Pollock, *Principles of Contract* (1876); W. Anson *Principles of the English Law of Contract* (1879). Simpson (1975) traces of the contribution to the evolution of basic doctrine of these and a number of works in between.

particular contracts which could be considered a general law of Contract.

As with other structuralist exercises, the true exposition of Contract would exert a fascination which all too readily excluded other matters from the range of worthwhile consideration. The process demanded a bold measure of induction from the writers: one or two equivocal cases were frequently made to stand for hard-edged general rules.[23] As an intellectual activity this evidently responded to deep-felt needs. The judges were searching for general principle in a rapidly expanding area of their business, and their small number constrained their own ability to generate precedent. In the past, much in the resolution of contract disputes had been left to the sense of juries. But many cases were becoming more complicated, and anyway juries could be prejudiced or cranky. Judges wanted rules by which to curb their excesses, just as lawyers and litigants wanted rules by which disputes could be settled without recourse to court.[24] In the latter nineteenth century, the introduction of systematic teaching and examination for entry into the professions, and even for university degrees, only added to the appeal of categorical doctrine.[25] But the profoundest appeal of Contract lay in the values which it came to embody. The generalisations evolved by text-writers and judges undoubtedly buttressed freedom of dealing and sanctity of bargain, the economic superiority of market-place pricing over government regulation, the moral righteousness of self-sufficiency and self-improvement. In this spirit, the new books would express contract in terms of Will Theory: an enforceable contract arose out of a meeting of minds—consensus ad idem.[26] This in turn would be analysed as a process of offer and acceptance. Even as these new concepts were emerging, however, it became clear that the subjective logic of Will Theory would not be allowed to overrule commercial good sense. Very largely it would be the objective manifestations of the parties' intentions which determined whether notionally they had been of one mind.[27]

The process of creating a general law of Contract can be presented as part of a larger ideological reorientation which accompanied the growth of industrial capitalism. That certainly is the position taken by Horwitz, writing primarily of the United States in the period after independence and finding then a "transformation" of contract (and other) doctrine into a capitalist instrument[28]; and by Atiyah, writing of England and finding a classical age of Contract in the century 1770–1870.[29] Both authors seek to identify two key shifts in the new formulation of contract: first, profits of an agreement are to be secured to a party who has bargained for them, the courts interven-

---

[23] For incisive demonstration of this process at work, see G. Gilmore, *The Death of Contract* (1974) Chaps. 1, 2.

[24] For this theme, see Atiyah (1979), pp. 345–358, 388–397.

[25] One purpose of Pollock's and Anson's books was to demonstrate that the common law was based upon principles and so worthy of the study in a university curriculum; see F. H. Lawson, *The Oxford Law School* (1968), pp. 37–41.

[26] The immediate source for this conception was Pothier's *Traité*.

[27] See below, p. 203ff.

[28] Horwitz (1977) Chap. 6.

[29] Atiyah (1979), Pt. II.

ing if necessary with an award of damages for expectation of loss; if there is a breach the law no longer merely restores property, money or the value of services transferred or given in execution by the victim of the breach. Secondly, the law gives up its earlier willingness to rectify elements of unfairness in bargains and instead insists on enforcing whatever terms have been agreed, and only those terms.

These hypotheses, and the detailed "proofs" offered in substantiation, are matters of high controversy, at no point more so than in the assumption behind them of a simple, agrarian eighteenth century still suspicious of entrepreneurial aggression and ready to stamp on its oppressive manifestations. As a view of England this perception underplays two centuries of manufacturing and trading, and of dealings through the substantial markets for many goods, not only in the metropolis but in a growing number of provincial centres. And in so far as it assumes a benignly paternal governance, it neglects the accumulating evidence of selfish, domineering, quarrelsome behaviour as a standard social pattern. Where it relies on the power of juries to do justice in a broad sense, it takes a romantic view of their ideal qualities, about which hard evidence is simply lacking.[30]

In a "line-by-line" refutation of Horwitz, Simpson has convincingly argued that the elements of a capitalistic contract law had been settled considerably earlier.[31] It was in the Tudor and early Stuart period, as assumpsit came to replace earlier forms of action, that mutual, executory promises became actionable and damages were used to make good profits lost through breach. Moreover the idea of a sustained evolution, from medieval beginnings, of supervision of the fairness of bargains amounts to a travesty of a law which was crudely severe on those who did not perform exactly what they promised, using as a prime weapon the threat of immediate imprisonment. Accordingly, the ideological commitments of the central courts on these fundamental issues operated over long time spans, without dramatic change at the onset of industrialisation: rather the nineteenth century brings a full flowering of ideas that had long been set in bud.

There is however a different ideological division—one not so much of time as of institutions within the system—which deserves more prominence than it has received in recent debate on the rise and fall of Contract. It will be argued that the courts of common law and equity inherited diverging attitudes to contract, which each continued to develop for a century after the advent of industrialisation. The common law would support a severely individualistic view of freedom and sanctity of contract. Equity, for all its fostering of landed, commercial and financial interests, would build up a protective jurisdiction of conscience as a refuge for those unfitted to a world of hard bargaining, or misled during their experience of it. Between these a peculiar balance was reached which depended on the structure of institutions, and which was therefore difficult to maintain under the "common" system introduced by the Judicature Acts. The contest between ideologies thus becomes most apparent in the

---

[30] *Cf.* Atiyah (1979), pp. 147, 169, with Simpson (1979), pp. 574–575.
[31] Simpson (1979); and in refutation of Atiyah, see Barton (1987).

period when the liberal hegemony of the mid-Victorian years is being threatened by a novel, democratic "collectivism." It is then that the predominance of the common law ideal would require uncompromising assertion and the legal system as a whole would carry forward basic ideas about the proper functioning of a capitalist economy which would remain in position throughout the first half of the twentieth century. In order to give detail to this picture, we will first sketch the development of essential precepts of Contract at common law, and then in equity, up to 1875, before passing to the age of their combined administration.

I. THE COMMON LAW BEFORE 1876

(a) Forming a Contract: Promise, Offer and Acceptance, Consideration

The action in assumpsit, as it evolved in the sixteenth century, called for a statement of the promise being sued upon, together with the consideration which would support it, *i.e.*, the "cause" or reason which sufficed to make it actionable.[32] But as contract litigation became more prominent in the common law courts, a certain refocussing occurred. In place of promise came the bi-partite steps of offer and acceptance. The shift had a natural place in a world where the typical contract was coming to be a bargain between two parties each promising some future performance[33]; and it was a necessary response to the increasing practice of contracting at a distance by post.[34] At the same time, consideration was more closely defined than before in order to restrict liability on informal promises to those which had this same element of bargain to them, as we shall see below.

But these changes were less than a radically new perspective. As noted, ideas about consensus ad idem were not allowed to under-

---

[32] See esp. Simpson (1975), pp. 257–263.
[33] Atiyah (1979) Chap. 7, argues that it was not until the period of industrialisation that the common law became much concerned with liability upon executory contracts. However, once it was accepted (around 1600) that assumpsit lay in respect of both executory and executed agreements, the law developed without any strategic distinction between the two. Certainly by the time of the Statute of Frauds 1677 the problems set by alleging executory contracts on oral evidence were such that the Statute's formal requirements (a memorandum in writing signed by the party to be charged with the contract) were applied to two types of contract when they had not been carried out: sales of goods over £10 (s.4) and contracts to transfer an interest in land (s.10). (The Statute did not apply to sales where there had been a deposit or delivery; and equity enforced informal land contracts which had been part performed on the basis that they were not intended to be caught by the Statute.) Failure to make this distinction in respect of the other kinds of contract within the Statute led to one of the long-standing tensions which plagued its whole history
[34] For the rise of the bilateral contract and the difficulties of fitting unilateral contracts—contracts where the performance by one side brings obligation into existence—into the prevailing analysis, see Simpson (1975), pp. 261–262; Atiyah (1979), pp. 441–443, 446–448.

mine the commercial convenience of judging intention by objective appearance.[35] The classic problem of the "ticket cases" provides a useful illustration. In the course of the eighteenth century the common law courts had come to impose strict liability upon carriers of goods to deliver them according to undertaking.[36] This treatment owed something to the public status of the "common carrier."[37] Equally what was happening seems typically "contractualist." By 1784, Lord Mansfield could explain that the basic liability need admit of exceptions only for extreme cases (acts of God and the King's enemies[38]) because it was open to the carrier to accept the goods only on terms which limited his liability for loss or damage.[39] Evidently this had become standard practice, carriers using advertisements in newspapers, displays at their premises, invoices and receipts for the purpose. The practice was to limit liability to a value of (say) £5 unless the goods' owner notified a higher value and paid an extra premium.[40] But by the end of the century, terms excluding liability entirely were coming to be noticed in the case-law, and with no ready approval.[41] The judges in their turn began to insist that the excluding term be "brought home" to the goods owner, using to this end the new language of offer and acceptance.[42] Lord Tenterden went so far as to hold that written notice to a person who could not read would not suffice,[43] but that seems soon to have been regarded as too scrupulous: it was enough to include the term on a receipt given when the goods were handed in, without proof that it had been read

---

[35] Offer and acceptance make their appearance in *Payne* v. *Cave* (1789) 3 T.R. 148 and *Cooke* v. *Oxley* (1790) 3 T.R. 653. By *Adams* v. *Linsell* (1808) 1 B. & Ald. 681, the objective notion is creeping in that the offeror must be presumed to continue intending his offer during its course in the post, unless a withdrawal is received before acceptance.

[36] For the evolution of this duty from less severe seventeenth century rules, notably in Admiralty law for the carriage of goods by sea, see E. G. M. Fletcher *The Carrier's Liability* (1932), pp. 152–174; J. N. Adams, in E. W. Ives and A. H. Manchester (eds.) *Law Litigants and the Legal Profession* (1983), p. 39.

[37] In his classic judgment on the duties of care owed by a bailee in *Coggs* v. *Barnard* (1703) 2 Ld. Raym. 909, Lord Holt had imposed a high standard on all bailees in public employment, but this idea would survive only in relation to common carriers and innkeepers.

[38] It was by confining the scope of these exceptions that the duty of care was made increasingly absolute: see esp. *Proprietors of Trent Navigation* v. *Wood* (1785) 3 Esp. 127; *Forward* v. *Pittard* (1785) 1 T.R. 27; C. Abbott, *Merchant Shipping* (1st ed., 1802) p. 203. The shipping interest had been able to protect itself against liability for loss of valuables through the embezzlement of their masters and crew beyond the value of the vessel, appurtenances and freight: 7 Geo. II, c. 15 (1734), later extended by 26 Geo III, c. 86 (1786) and 53 Geo. III, c. 159 (1813); Fletcher (above, n. 36), pp. 175–177.

[39] *Barclay* v. *Cuculla y Gana* (1784) 3 Doug. 389 at 390.

[40] First noticed in *Gibbon* v. *Paynton* (1769) 4 Burr. 2298, it was treated as standard practice in such cases as *Kirkman* v. *Shawcross* (1794) 6 T.R. 14 at 18 (Lord Kenyon) and *Nicholson* v. *Willan* (1804) 4 East 507 at 513 (Lord Ellenborough). See generally, Fletcher (above, n. 36), pp. 175–196.

[41] See *Maving* v. *Todd* (1815) 1 Stark. 72 at 73; *Leeson* v. *Holt* (1816) 1 Stark. 186 (both Lord Ellenborough). The courts did require that notice of complete exclusion be specifically pleaded: see, *e.g.*, *Latham* v. *Rutley* (1823) 2 B. & C. 20.

[42] *Leeson* v. *Holt* (above, n. 41)—notice in paper inadequate without proof that the plaintiff took the paper.

[43] *Davis* v. *Willan* (1817) 2 Stark. 279.

and understood.[44] Thus the courts arrived at a sufficient "meeting of minds" which allowed enterprises to establish an operable system (from their perspective) for the incorporation of "small print" limitations and exclusions.[45] On this foundation, the judges of mid-century would insist that the clauses must be interpreted as they stood[46]; there was very little scope for overriding considerations of public policy,[47] expressed either in direct terms or by hostile readings of the clauses *contra proferentem*.[48] This was one of the most striking outworks of Contract, one that would still loom quite as large in the 1930's.[49] Not until the 1950s and 1960s would the courts feel it their particular mission to take the consumer's part against the protections of the enterprise that were always built into "adhesion contracts."[50]

In other respects, the objective view of contract formation served to concentrate attention on the terms of offer and acceptance. As we shall note later, misrepresentations made in the course of negotiations might be without legal effect if they were not turned into guarantees by the actual terms.[51] The tendency was thus to treat every transaction as if it embodied the mutual suspicions of an art sale, the seller fearing that he had overlooked a masterpiece, the buyer concerned for the authenticity of the work. Yet caveat venditor, caveat emptor never became the one categorical imperative. Mainly by the technique of implying warranties the judges were able to give some place to the basic assumptions common to the bulk of sales and similar dealings, even where they were not made explicit. In sales of land,

[44] *Cf.* Lord Ellenborough, *Kerr* v. *Willan* (1817) 2 Stark. 53; *Rowley* v. *Horne* (1825) 3 Bing. 2. In 1830, land carriers won special statutory protection against loss or damage to valuables (as defined) unless they were expressly notified by the sender, or a servant was guilty of felony or the carrier was guilty of personal neglect or misconduct (11 Geo. IV & 1 Will. IV, c. 68). See Fletcher (above, n. 36), pp. 201–206.

[45] By mid-century, railway passengers were expected to have read the conditions on timetables: *Hurst* v. *G.W.R.* (1865) 19 C.B.N.S. 310; and other notices to which they were referred by receipts or tickets: *Watkins* v. *Rymill* (1883) 10 Q.B.D. 178; *Parker* v. *S.E.R.* (1877) 2 C.P.D. 416.

[46] See, *e.g. Carr* v. *Lancashire etc. Ry.* (1852) 7 Ex. 707; *Peek* v. *North Staffordshire Ry.* (1863) 10 H.L.C. 473; *McCawley* v. *Furness Ry.* (1872) L.R. 8 Q.B. 57. Note also the Railway and Canal Traffic Act 1854, 17 & 18 Vict., c. 31, s.7, requiring exemption clauses to be "just and reasonable," which found little liking among the judges: see *Manchester etc. Rly* v. *Brown* (1883) 6 A.C. 703; J. H. Baker (1971) 24 C.L.P. 53 at 73–76.

[47] Carriers of goods were still considered unable to exempt themselves from their own gross negligence in the 1820s (see, *e.g., Batson* v. *Donovan* (1820) 4 B. & Ald. 21—an idea which had associations with the public responsibilities of the "common carrier"). But by *Austin* v. *Manchester etc. Ry.* (1852) 10 C.B. 454, it was plain that nothing of this remained. Exemptions from liability for personal injury were, however, thought to be ineffective for another decade or so: see below, pp. 513–515; and, even afterwards, the courts tended to be strict over what was sufficient notice: see, *e.g. Stevenson* v. *Henderson* (1875) L.R. 2 H.L. Sc.App. 471; *Richardson* v. *Rowntree* [1894] A.C. 217.

[48] Typically, the watchword was Parke B.'s: "It is not for us to fritter away the true sense and meaning of these contracts, merely with a view to make men careful": *Carr's* case (above n. 46) at 505.

[49] Furnishing the severe decisions in *Thompson* v. *L.M.S.* [1930] 1 K.B. 41 and *L'Estrange* v. *Graucob* [1934] 2 K.B. 394.

[50] The decisions, in which Lord Denning M.R. played a catalytic role, would in turn lead to the Unfair Contract Terms Act 1978.

[51] See below, p. 221ff.

and later of goods, an implied warranty of good title had been established.[52] To this nineteenth century courts began to add, in sales of goods by traders, warranties that the goods would at least be of merchantable quality in circumstances where the buyer had no chance to inspect for himself.[53] This development was certainly not without tension: in the 1840s and 1850s the Court of Exchequer, the severest advocate of high Contract, sought to insist upon guarantees being expressly extracted.[54] But it failed to persuade the other common law courts and made no permanent inroad on the developing law.[55] Chalmers, in his codification which became the Sale of Goods Act 1893, was able to distill from the case law implied conditions concerning title, quiet possession, sale by description and sale by sample; and, where a seller traded in the goods, implied conditions of fitness for purpose and merchantable quality.[56] These would survive into modern times by a process of gradual evolution through interpretation, much as before. The implied term accordingly stands as the common law's chief device for a cautious and circumspect alignment of individual contracts with general expectations. So far as England is concerned, there is no real evidence for the argument that the implied warranty had, in the eighteenth century, been erected into an insurance of the buyer's "sound price," only to be dismantled by the advance of capitalistic ideals.[57]

The same is true of the allied claim that consideration—the essential requirement beside promise in assumpsit—was used to insist upon a just price for a thing of sound value.[58] But that does not end the fascination of "consideration," since its abstract character made

---

[52] The warranty was for long treated as actionable for the reliance placed upon it; only in the eighteenth century did it come to be thought of as a promise actionable in assumpsit: see S. F. C. Milsom, *Historical Foundations of the Common Law* (2nd ed., 1981), pp. 320–322, 364–366.

[53] Equally, goods sold by sample or by description were impliedly warranted to answer to the sample or description: see esp. *Gardiner* v. *Gray* (1815) 4 Camp. 144 (the fact that a sample of the waste silk in question had been supplied was ignored); *Jones* v. *Bright* (1829) 5 Bing. 533 (purchaser of copper to sheath a ship found to be reliant on the seller's knowledge of its quality); *cf. Parkinson* v. *Lee* (1802) 2 East 314 (opportunity to inspect the rotten hops sold). See generally S. J. Stoljar (1952) 15 M.L.R. 425, (1953) 16 M.L.R. 174.

[54] Especially in cases where the sale was characterised as being of "specific goods": *Barry* v. *Gibson* (1838) 4 M. & W. 399 (sale of ship for £4,200, when through wrecking it was only worth £10); *Chanter* v. *Hopkins* (1837) 3 M. & W. 390; *Emmerton* v. *Matthews* (1862) 7 H. & N. 586.

[55] Common Pleas and Queen's Bench placed considerable reliance on implied warranties that goods sold by description would meet it (see, *e.g.*, *Wieler* v. *Schilizzi* (1856) 17 C.B. 619; *Josling* v. *Kingsford* (1863) 13 C.B.N.S. 447; *Biggs* v. *Parkinson* (1862) 7 H. & N. 955; *Jones* v. *Just* (1868) L.R. 3 Q.B. 197); or that goods would be fit for a disclosed purpose (*Shepherd* v. *Pybus* (1842) 3 M. & G. 868; *Ollivant* v. *Bailey* (1843) 5 Q.B. 288).

[56] See Sale of Goods Act 1893, ss.12–15. Within a regime of freedom of contract, the terms could be expressly excluded and often were by standard exemption clauses.

[57] Atiyah (1979) musters practically no evidence for the first part of the proposition (pp. 178–180) and admits that there was in the nineteenth century only "a brief flirtation" with caveat emptor (pp. 464–479). In the United States attraction was rather more substantial; but *cf.* Horwitz (1977), pp. 167, 180 with Simpson (1979), pp. 580–585.

[58] Again, *cf.* Horwitz, pp. 165–167 with Simpson, pp. 573–580; and note also Atiyah, pp. 167–177, mainly concerned with equity rather than common law.

it a useful device for expressing ideas about what promises should be enforceable; and, as is well-known, there were expansive notions of consideration which by 1840 had been firmly rejected. In the nineteenth century, consideration contributed vitally to the conception of contract as a reciprocal bargain affecting only the parties to it: a promisee alleging an enforceable promise had to show some countervailing benefit to the promisor or a detriment "moving from" himself in return.

Certainly from the emergence of assumpsit onwards, this sort of benefit-or-detriment consideration had been recognised as a sufficient ground for enforcing a promise. But there had been other possibilities. These had given "consideration" its signification of any sufficient reason for enforcement. Lord Mansfield's celebrated suggestions that commercial promises might be enforceable merely because they were in writing, and that promises of gifts to family members might be supported by the "good" consideration of natural love and affection,[59] were not some Scoto-civilian heresy, but amplifications of common law thought.

The first suggestion proved too unorthodox for Mansfield's own brethren.[60] The second suggestion, however, would not be definitively rejected until 1840.[61] It unmistakably addresses the acceptability of arrangements for limiting liability and so touches a fundamental issue for law under capitalism—one that recurs frequently in the subsequent sections of this chapter. The desire of traders to protect their assets from the demands of creditors is as old as trade itself and some of their crude shifts had long been legally ineffectual. Elizabethan legislation had condemned the transfer of a person's assets to some relation or friend on (say) the eve of his insolvency: this was conveyance to defraud creditors and the latter were entitled to recover the things or money back for the purpose of satisfying their claims.[62] But a conveyance away at some earlier stage might lack any intent to defraud and so be allowed to stand.

What then of promises to make gifts to family members? If they were readily enforceable and proveable even by oral evidence, the law against fraudulent conveyances and preferences would have to bear a heavy weight indeed. Yet it was just in this direction that Mansfield's view of "good" consideration pressed, as Blackstone plainly recognised.[63] One consequence could be seen in bankruptcy proceedings, where family members were said to compete in the distribution of assets, asserting promises of many sorts which the trade creditors might regard with heavy suspicion but be hard put to upset. By the 1830s complaints about the problem were constant;[64] yet at the same time, the old, crude remedies for recovering debts were also being seriously questioned. As we shall see, it was a moment when the creditor's position was peculiarly in flux and the

---

[59] *Pillans* v. *Van Mierop* (1765) 3 Burr. 1663; *Hawkes* v. *Saunders* (1782) 1 Cowp. 289.
[60] *Rann* v. *Hughes* (1778) 7 T.R. 350n.
[61] See below, n. 66. But the idea had come under severe criticism in the reporters' note to *Wennall* v. *Adney* (1802) 3 Bos. & Pul. 248.
[62] 13 Eliz., c. 5; see Holdsworth IV, pp. 480–482.
[63] *Commentaries*, II, p. 244.
[64] See Welbourne (1932), pp. 57–58, 60–61.

future extent of legal support for his claims was anything but predictable.[65] In finally ruling that the "good" consideration of natural love and affection was not enough to support an informal promise of a family gift, the Court of Queen's Bench spelled out the "mischievous consequences for society" of holding them enforceable: "the frequent preference of voluntary undertakings to claims for just debts. Suits would thereby be multiplied, and voluntary undertakings would also be multiplied, to the prejudice of real creditors."[66]

Consideration was accordingly about factors of policy other than a sufficient intention to be bound by a promise. This became equally clear of other detailed aspects of the doctrine, to which we come later.[67] Here we should mention a general resonance of the proposition that a person must provide consideration for a promise in order to be able to sue upon it: that an outside third party could neither receive rights nor be subject to liability under it. That this notion of privity should be applied as much to benefits as to burdens for third parties marks it as an categorical expression of a liberal ideal: a wariness of private treaty creating rights and duties in any portion of the world beyond its parties. Yet it was a rule not merely for commercial dealing: its classic expression was reached in the context of marriage. If the fathers of bride and groom agreed together to settle property on the pair, the groom gained no right to sue his father-in-law on the latter's promise.[68] The cases where private transactions had an effect on the world outside were confined to conditions defined in terms of property rights. Common law might recognise new instances of "property," but this was always a gradual process. If privity of contract were to be compromised, private individuals would have the power to blur the distinction between rights *in personam* and *in rem*, and this could not be allowed.

What individuals could not achieve, the courts were equally reluctant to bring about by liability imposed from outside. Most immediately in point was the action on the case for deceit. If a misstatement by one person to another led to a contract between them, this action might provide relief even in the absence of a term guaranteeing the truth of the information misstated; if it did not lead to a contract between the two, the action would be a form of personal liability that was distinctively tortious. In *Pasley* v. *Freeman*,[69] King's Bench

---

[65] Below p. 229. The Royal Commission on Bankruptcy and Insolvency (P.P. 1840 [274] XVI) argued that, following the abolition of arrest on mesne process in 1838, it was essential to introduce a summary process for examining a debtor about his assets. "At present, a debtor who is insolvent and wishes to give preferences resists the hostile creditor's just claim in order to prefer the favoured creditors; and it frequently happens that from preferences and other frauds, the hostile creditor receives no satisfaction and is burdened with heavy costs" (pp. x–xi).

[66] *Eastwood* v. *Kenyon* (1840) 11 Ad. & E. 38. The elimination of good consideration of this kind did not put paid to difficulties about family promises, since they might be under seal or supported by a nominal money consideration. But such things at least required organising in advance; cf. Simpson (1975), at pp. 262–263. For Holdsworth's view that the change of doctrine flowed from the more precise requirements of pleading ushered in by the Hilary Rules of 1834, see (1932) 1 C.L.J. 273.

[67] See below, p. 212.

[68] *Tweddle* v. *Atkinson* (1861) 1 B. & S. 393; and for an earlier categoric statement, *Price* v. *Easton* (1833) 4 B. & Ad. 433.

[69] (1789) 3 T.R. 51.

accepted that the second, tortious form did exist, as well as the first: a defendant who incorrectly told a plaintiff that a third person's credit was good was liable for the plaintiff's loss if in consequence he entered a damaging contract with the third party; but at the same time the Court imposed the highly significant limitation—that the defendant had to be deliberately lying—a negligent mistake on his part was not enough. Thus even in the late eighteenth century liability for misrepresentations was being generally confined to cases of dishonesty or express guarantee. A foundation was being laid which would constrict other developments of tortious liability for economic injury, as they came to be examined through the nineteenth century.[70]

Nor was the threat to be couched only in terms of tortious wrong. As Atiyah has shown so fully,[71] the common law courts were increasingly reluctant to accept that civil obligation, however classified, could stem either from the mere receipt of benefit or from mere action in reliance upon another's stated intention. Certainly, seventeenth and eighteenth century courts had countenanced forms of assumpsit where money, other property, or even the saving from liability, had benefited a defendant at the plaintiff's expense without there being any contract. This was recognised under common counts for money had and received (by the defendant to the plaintiff's use), for money paid (to a third party) and for *quantum meruit* and *quantum valebant* (for the value of services and goods).[72] These types of claim were developed furthest where the benefit consisted of money, since as the medium of exchange its value was fixed and capable of direct recompense. Lord Mansfield, in a celebrated excursion, characterised the action for money had and received as one arising under an obligation, from the ties of natural justice.[73] But where the benefit consisted in goods received or services rendered without agreement to pay for them, to impose liability would have seared the most tender susceptibilities of the Victorian individualist. As Pollock C.B. put it: "one cleans another shoes. What can the other do but put them on?"[74] Accordingly, through a long series of decisions, the tendency of eighteenth century courts to expand the range of "quasi-contracts"

---

[70] Accordingly, the attempt to expand the old tort of enticing away of servants into a tort of inducing breach of contract in other circumstances took hold only gradually, and in the end out of a determination to deal with industrial action by labour: see below pp. 287, 330.

[71] Atiyah (1979), pp. 181–189, 455–450.

[72] These were classified by Blackstone (*Commentaries*, III pp. 158–163) as contracts implied by law, and for a century most writers would follow him, until Leake popularised the Romanistic term quasi-contract. For this development in relation to the modern law, see Lord Goff and G. H. Jones *The Law of Restitution* (3rd ed., 1986) Chap. 1.

[73] *Moses* v. *McFerlan* (1760) 2 Burr. 1005 at 1008, where Mansfield used the action to review the judgment of an inferior tribunal—one of his favourite endeavours. The formula was: money had and received *to the plaintiff's use*: the phrase epitomises the attractive power that equitable notions of trust had for common lawyers in the period.

[74] *Taylor* v. *Laird* (1856) 2 L.J. Ex. 329 at 332; later to be echoed in Bowen L.J.'s dictum: "liabilities are not to be forced on people behind their backs any more than you can confer a benefit on a man against his will" (*Falcke* v. *Scottish Imperial Insurance* (1886) 34 Ch.D. 234 at 248).

was slowly reversed: a person, for instance, who made a payment mistakenly to another, could recover it only if his mistake led him to believe that he was liable to that other; a man who discharged another's debt without the latter's authority could have reimbursement only where he was subject to a common demand for it.[75]

It was a position which required careful protection not only from the undue expansion of rights of action but also from the "evidential" principle of estoppel—the concept which debarred assertions in litigation that were contrary to apparent truth. Estoppels had long been known in the common law as arising from the records of litigation and for public acts relating to titles in land.[76] As trials became a matter of evidence, the underlying notion was gradually extended: a person should not be permitted to lead another to act upon a given supposition and then to turn round and deny it.[77] This had increasing application in a world of commerce, where bills of exchange and documents of title to goods in transit had to be taken as face value.[78] By 1837, any representation, by words or conduct, was in principle capable of giving rise to an estoppel, which stood accordingly as some common law equivalent to equitable ideas of reliance and trust.[79] But the concept had only to be given general form for it at once to acquire modifications which would prevent it from destroying the careful balance set in cases such as *Pasley* v. *Freeman*. The two main qualifications were that estoppels could be raised only in defence to claims by those who sought to go behind their earlier representations[80]; and they could relate only to representations of fact and not to statements of future intention akin to promises.[81] Both limitations became conditions of some complexity; but their joint thrust was undoubtedly to stop civil obligation spreading to circumstances where there was no bargain supported by legally recognised consideration.[82]

(b) Justifications for Non-Enforcement: Mistake and Improper Pressure

It had long been recognised that certain categories of people must be protected by law from the full rigours of contractual liability. The best-established case was that of infants—those under twenty-one,

---

[75] See Goff and Jones (above, n. 72), pp. 87ff; 310ff.

[76] See Holdsworth, IX pp. 144–163;

[77] Lord Mansfield's decision in *Montefiori* v. *Montefiori* (1762) 1 W.Bl. 363 marked an important advance.

[78] As to bills, see above p. 199; as to factors, see below p. 238.

[79] *Pickard* v. *Sears* (1837) 6 Ad. & E. 469 at 474 (Lord Denman C.J.).

[80] The emergence of this "shield-not-sword" limitation was gradual, but was clearly spelled out by Bowen L.J. in *Low* v. *Bouverie* [1891] 3 Chap. 82 at 105; see generally D. C. Jackson (1965) 81 L.Q.R. 84, 223.

[81] *Jorden* v. *Money* (1854) 5 H.L.C. 185, where in the House of Lords, Lords Cranworth and Brougham (both common lawyers) refused to allow estoppel to circumvent the requirement of the Statute of Frauds 1677 that a contract in consideration of marriage must be evidenced in writing; the Chancery member of the House, Lord St. Leonards, was in favour of using the promisee's reliance on the promise to create a new (equitable) exception to the Statute; see also P. S. Atiyah, *Consideration in Contracts* (1971), pp. 53–58.

[82] But *cf.* below, pp. 221–222.

the gentlemanly age of majority—who might avoid liability during infancy, save for the receipt of necessaries.[83] There were also rules protecting lunatics and drunkards. But here the nineteenth-century preference for the objective assessment of contractual intention was used to limit the exception severely: a contract could be avoided only if the other side knew that the lunatic or drunkard was at the time incapable of forming an intention to contract.[84]

Apart from this, adults were to be treated without discrimination as responsible for the consequences of entering any contract that was not illegal. The very considerable hostility towards excusal on grounds of unfair pressure or mistake, provides the most distinctive manifestation of contractual sanctity in the common law canon. Very occasionally, some fundamental mistake—something which altered the whole basis of the contract—might suffice to render an agreement void[85]: sales of non-existent goods or things that turned out already to belong to the buyer, became established instances.[86] The same result might be expressed in terms of an implied condition precedent: life assurance, for instance, was taken subject to the pre-condition that the "life" was not already deceased.[87] In addition, implied terms in sale and similar contracts wrote in "standard" terms of guarantee.[88] But beyond this, there was a steady refusal to take any account of mistakes about the quality of goods or services, however much they had in consequence been overpriced or undervalued.[89]

As for improper pressure, it was said that the common law would avoid a contract for "duress" only if there had been a threat to life, liberty or personal freedom. No matter that, according to eighteenth century courts, money paid under "duress of goods" was recoverable.[90] If instead there had been a new contract after an unjustified threat to seize or retain goods, it was binding; a man of ordinary

---

[83] The law relating to infant's contracts already had a long and complex history. The tendency of shopkeeper juries to find against infants by deciding that what was supplied to them were necessaries created a minor scandal in the 1870s. In consequence the judges took power to decide what was capable in law of being necessary (*Ryder* v. *Wombwell* (1868) L.R. 4 Ex. 32); and Parliament enacted the confusing Infants Relief Act 1874.

[84] See, *e.g. Molton* v. *Camroux* (1848) 2 Ex. 487.

[85] The theory of contract formation—in terms of objectively corresponding offer and acceptance—was used to eliminate most opportunities for arguing that one party or even both actually thought the agreement to be about something different: the most notable instance was *Smith* v. *Hughes* (1871) L.R. 6 Q.B. 597 (did the buyer *contract* to buy "old oats" or only "oats"?). For the curious case of *Raffles* v. *Wichelhaus* (1864) 2 H. & C. 906 and the attempts of commentators to fit it within the theory of objective intention, see Gilmore (1974), pp. 35–43.

[86] Drawing on *Couturier* v. *Hastie* (1856) 5 H.L.C. 673; and *Cooper* v. *Phibbs* (1867) L.R. 2 H.L. 149 (a case in equity).

[87] *Strickland* v. *Turner* (1852) 7 Ex. 208.

[88] See above, p. 206.

[89] See further below p. 224. The issues of proof in mistake became acute after the parties became entitled to give evidence on their own behalf (in 1851: 15 & 16 Vict., c.99, s.2); see Barton (1987), p. 129.

[90] The classic authority was *Astley* v. *Reynolds* (1741) 2 Strange 915, an instance of a common count in assumpsit which would fall to be classified as "quasi-contractual." Like tort, quasi-contract would certainly seem to nineteenth-century common lawyers a form of relief *ab extra* which might undermine contract if it were not strictly controlled.

firmness ought to have resisted the threat instead of submitting to the agreement.[91] Contract was of a higher order than a mere payment.

This was a rigidly severe view and one which required some qualification even at common law, particularly where threats were made to pursue unfounded claims or to break existing obligations. However, the judges resorted to technical rules about consideration, in order strictly to confine their intervention. To be without consideration, and so unenforceable, the compromise of a disputed claim must have been procured in bad faith, that is, in the knowledge that the claim itself was without foundation.[92] Where a threatened breach of contract was compromised, only in the case where the person threatening not to carry out his obligation merely promised the same person that after all he would perform would there be no consideration; if he undertook to do something more, or to do something for someone else, there would be a new, binding agreement.[93] The thrust even of these rules was, save in extreme cases, to oblige a person to act with reasonable firmness. If he chose not to fight a claim or a threatened breach, but instead to compromise, in most cases he would have to stand by the consequences.

(c) Execution of the Contract: "Frustration," Breach and Damages

Quite as severe was the view that emerged of changes in circumstances between the making of a contract and its performance. Whatever the scope of "fault" as a basis for the imposed liabilities of tort law, the assumed responsibilities of contract were held to require strict adherence to obligation; even accident or inevitable necessity were said to make no difference, unless an explicit term made them into an escape route. The view that express conditions alone could qualify an "absolute" contract enjoyed a half-century of popularity after its appearance in Williams' 1802 edition of *Saunders*.[94] Only after mid-century did it begin to be qualified by the implied term device—used in cases of accidental destruction of the subject-matter—and the slightly broader notion of "frustration of venture"— limiting the scope of charterparties and other maritime contracts where untoward impediments had supervened.[95] Here were threads

---

[91] See esp. Parke B., *Attlee* v. *Backhouse* (1838) 3 M. & W. 633; Denman C.J., *Skeate* v. *Beale* (1840) 11 Ad. & E. 983. Remarkably this statement would continue to be repeated in textbooks until the 1960s, despite various signs that it ought to be qualified.

[92] *e.g.* Mariott v. *Hampton* (1797) 7 T.R. 269; *Wade* v. *Simeon* (1846) 2 C.B. 548; *Cook* v. *Wright* (1861) 1 B. & S. 559; *Callisher* v. *Bischoffsheim* (1870) L.R. 5 Q.B. 449.

[93] A rule concocted by the texts out of *Stilk* v. *Myrick* (1809) 2 Camp. 317 and *Hartley* v. *Ponsonby* (1857) 7 E. & B. 872—on which process, see Gilmore (1974), pp. 21–34. A *fortiori*, compromises to meet a debt only in part could not logically form consideration, and so the House of Lords held, reiterating an old rule, in *Foakes* v. *Beer* (1884) 9 A.C. 605: this cast doubt on earlier decisions such as *Sibree* v. *Tripp* (1846) 15 M. & W. 22 which had found ways of side-stepping that result.

[94] A quite unjustified generalisation of the rule in *Paradine* v. *Jane* (1647) Aleyn 26, Style 47: see Gilmore (1974), pp. 44–48.

[95] On the emergence of these qualifications from such cases as *Taylor* v. *Caldwell* (1863) and *Freeman* v. *Taylor* (1831) 5 Bing. 124, see Simpson (1975), pp. 269–272.

from which the doctrine of frustration of contract would eventually be woven; but even so its emergence was to be gradual, its place confined to the very fringes[96]

Enmeshed in the reluctance to excuse for "frustration" was a disapproval of contracting parties who did not make explicit provision for the event, through insurance or express condition in the agreement. Where, on the other hand, terms were built into the contract in the hope of securing correct, prompt performance without having to resort to litigation, they generally found support from the judges. The long-received notion that one party to a contract might make his own performance conditional upon performance by the other side was underpinned by case-law which showed considerable enthusiasm for the whole idea. Pre-conditions came to be read, unless clearly expressed to the contrary, as being "indivisible."[97] The builder who left a house half built could claim nothing for the work done, unless there were arrangements for payment by instalments.[98] In commercial transactions, a seller, likewise, was obliged to provide exactly what he had agreed—any deviation in quality, quantity, time of delivery or method of shipment absolved the buyer from paying, whether or not he was in any degree prejudiced.[99] It was an attitude which encouraged the nicest attention to the details of responsibility, but it would with time come to seem unduly burdensome. Given a regime of strict liability, contracts could be broken for a host of reasons—from outright dishonesty to quite unpredictable misfortune. The rule for indivisible contracts began to be qualified by specific statute[1] and eventually by the rule that "substantial" performance would suffice to restrict the other side's position to a claim in damages.[2] Obligations of sellers and other parties came to be classified merely as warranties, giving the buyer the right to damages but not to refuse himself to perform.[3] These, however, were exceptions; the rule still showed what the basic preference was.

In numerous respects the law of contractual breach acquired structure as the nineteenth century progressed.[4] It became settled that for breach of a condition, the party not in breach had the right to terminate the contract even in advance of the date when performance would have been due, and to claim damages for his outgoings or expec-

[96] *Ibid.*, pp. 272–273; Gilmore (1974), pp. 77–79.

[97] The doctrine of the indivisible contract was distilled from *Cutter* v. *Powell* (1795) 6 T.R. 320, in which, however, a mate contracted to perform a voyage for some four times the going rate on condition that he would be paid only on completion: clearly a special assumption of risk: see Goff and Jones (above, n. 72), pp. 452–453.

[98] *Appleby* v. *Myers* (1867) L.R. 2 C.P. 65.

[99] *Bowes* v. *Shand* (1877) 2 A.C. 455.

[1] Notably, the Apportionment Act 1870.

[2] Not till *Dakin* v. *Lee* [1916] 1 K.B. 566 would this be made explicit, though there were much earlier precursors—*e.g.*, *Boone* v. *Eyre* (1779) 1 H.Bl. 273; *Broom* v. *Davis* (1794) 7 East 480n.

[3] The "contractualist" theory, that the initial terms of obligation should determine whether a breach could lead to determination of the contract or only to damages, seems to have been advanced by the conception of Pollock's *Principles of Contract* which was devoted to questions of formation; the distinction was then affirmed in the implied terms of the Sale of Goods Act 1893.

[4] For the view that the emergence of these rules demonstrated a fundamental shift in perception of contractual liability, see Atiyah (1979), pp. 424–434.

tations.[5] Where there has been failure to perform, or mis-performance, the victim of the breach would be expected to take reasonable steps to mitigate the damage that would otherwise flow.[6] These rules were important in defining in advance the choices open to the victim, factors which otherwise might have to await the judgment of a jury for determination.

The best-known limitation on the discretion of juries, however, was the rule subjecting the estimation of damages to expectations that were reasonably foreseeable by the parties at the time of contracting. The case in which the rule was first unequivocally adopted—the celebrated *Hadley* v. *Baxendale*[7]—concerned a carrier firm's delay in transporting the engine shaft for a flour mill to its maker for repairs, thus causing the mill itself to stand idle for an unnecessary period. Despite the carrier's clerk having been told things which suggested that delay would mean the loss of operating profits, the Court of Exchequer, applying the new rule, held that the jury should have been instructed to award nothing for such loss.[8] The restrictive tenor of the decision laid a foundation for later cases establishing that business organisations were not to be tied to special risks unless employees who were told of them by customers had authority to accept additional responsibilities—for instance, by having special terms available.[9] Save for those who consider expectation damages to be a nineteenth century innovation, the rule probably introduced no startling change over earlier, looser practice.[10] Nor is it properly to be regarded as imposing a drastic constriction on earlier generosity with a view to protecting emergent industry; it is scarcely to be ranked with the "implied contract" that protected employers from vicarious liability for accidents arising in "common employment."[11] Nor did it have the extreme quality of the rule protecting vendors of land who proved unable to show good title: they were liable only for the purchaser's expenses to completion and not for his consequential losses (a rule which had its point, given the vagaries of eighteenth-century conveyancing).[12] But the use of

---

[5] *Cort* v. *Ambergate* (1851) 17 Q.B. 127; *Hochster* v. *De la Tour* (1853) 2 El. & B. 678.

[6] See esp. *Gainsford* v. *Carroll* (1824) 2 B. & C. 624.

[7] (1854) 9 Ex. 341 Alderson B.'s statement of the rule had two "branches," referring both to damages arising "naturally, *i.e.* according to the usual course of things"; and damages "reasonably supposed to have been in the contemplation of both parties at the time they made the contract, as the probable result of the breach of it."

[8] For this crucial aspect of the case at trial and at Westminster, see R. Danzig (1975) 4 J. Leg.St. 249, esp. 261–62.

[9] *British Columbia Saw Mill* v. *Nettleship* (1868) L.R. 3 C.P. 499; *Horne* v. *Midland Ry.* (1873) L.R. 8 C.P. 131.

[10] It was to be found in Pothier (see Simpson (1975), p. 275) and made its way to England via the United States and the considerable learning of Willes, counsel for the plaintiff (see Danzig (above, n. 8), pp. 257–258, pp. 274–276). The view that contract damages should be limited to the value received by the party in breach was occasionally encountered but made no headway: Simpson (1975), p. 277.

[11] See below, p. 496ff.

[12] The rule, settled by the House of Lords in 1776 (*Flureau* v. *Thornhill* (1776) 2 W.Bl. 1078), has been claimed as evidence of a general refusal to award expectation damages (Horwitz (1977), pp. 163; Atiyah (1979), pp. 200, 427–428), but was surely exceptional (Simpson (1979), pp. 552–553). It was criticised and limited in a number of decisions but upheld with regret in *Bain* v. *Fothergill* (1874) L.R. 7 H.L. 158.

reasonable foresight as the touchstone for the general rule on remoteness of damage is characteristic of the common law milieu of the 1850s, as of later periods.

To conclude, in the century before the Judicature Acts, the common law evolved a conspectus of Contract in general which viewed bargaining as a robust commercial activity. The individual must be left to watch out for himself and to shoulder the consequences of his unguarded risks. There would be exceptions and qualifications, where ordinary business expectation justified it, but the instinct was always to confine the courts' role first, to defining the requisite characteristics of a bargain and then to insisting that the agreement be made good.[13] It was not for the state (through the courts), save in a few well-defined situations, to constrain contractual freedom, any more than it was for legislatures and bureaucracies to interfere with free markets for goods, services and labour. In particular the courts were reluctant to treat bargains as illegal and void on grounds of immorality or public policy. The Jacobean view of public policy as an "unruly horse"[14] was for Victorian judges a telling image; indeed they wanted to declare that it was not for them to create new heads for this form of interfering regulation. In the great test of this issue, *Egerton* v. *Brownlow*,[15] the House of Lords, after taking the judges' advice, refused to adopt so categoric a self-denial; but it was clear that public policy had become a weapon to be used only with the nicest discrimination.[16]

II. EQUITY BEFORE 1876

In the seventeenth and eighteenth centuries, courts of equity, besides making a signal contribution to the mesh of property rights in land, lent their support to the growing exploitation of capital: the mortgage was re-interpreted so as to make it a flexible and workable loan transaction, a way was found to render debts assignable and so to convert them into an important species of property, a combination of partnership and trust allowed the evolution of the deed-of-settlement company.[17] This friendliness towards new deployments of wealth helps to explain Lord Mansfield's interest not only in mercantile law, but also in equity, as a means of vitalising the common law. On their side judges in Chancery showed a decent respect for sanc-

[13] Given Atiyah's insistence upon the dominant force of freedom of contract in the century before 1870, it is curious to find him belittling the sway of more general ideas of laissez-faire: Atiyah (1979), pp. 231–237, *cf.* above, p. 64.
[14] The phrase was attributed to Hobart C.J. by Burrough J. in *Richardson* v. *Mellish* (1824) 2 Bing. 229 at 242; for the earlier history see P. H. Winfield (1928) 42 Harv. L.R. 76; *cf.* W. S. M. Knight (1922) 38 L.Q.R. 207.
[15] (1853) 4 H.L.C. 1. The issue was of the highest sensitivity: could the gift of a great estate be subject to the condition that the donee have a named peerage conferred upon him by Her Majesty? The Lords, *pace* the judges, felt it essential to rule against the condition.
[16] See also below, p. 269.
[17] See above and below, pp. 127–128, 250ff.

tity of contract.[18] "Equity," it was said, "mends no man's bargain," and pronouncements of this kind gathered a certain momentum.[19] But they did not, as in the common law courts, become the directing force; rather they acted as a brake on very different ideas.

(a) Creating Obligation

The moral premise which most often sustained equitable intervention was the need to honour trust. It was an capacious idea which had been given particular substance by according equitable property interests to the beneficiaries under "a trust." But as well as this, there could be an equitable obligation (not necessarily conceived as a property right) in various circumstances where there had been reliance upon the word of another, a reposing of confidence, an expectation of good faith.[20]

Equity's acquaintance with contract was traditionally in dealings with land and family wealth, rather than with goods and services in trade. In the former context ideas of good faith flourished in ways that were foreign to the harsh ethics of commerce. Chancery could echo common law in insisting that there was "no equity to perfect an imperfect gift."[21] But, particularly in the high family politics of a marriage alliance, promises of gift were taken to have legal effect in various circumstances. Terms of the marriage settlement such as covenants to settle after-acquired property were enforceable not only by the actual parties: the two fathers, trustees and perhaps the husband, but also others "within the consideration"—children of the marriage and even grandchildren, provided that they were named as beneficiaries.[22] Other promises that were not part of the formal settlement had equally to be made good if they were specific representations which had been followed by the marriage.[23] The same was true of reliance on other promises in a family context: the father who induced his son to build on land by seeking (ineffectively) to transfer

---

[18] By mid-eighteenth century, there was a net of relations between the two jurisdictions rather than any major rift. The Court of Exchequer was, moreover, a court of equity as well as of common law until 1841—significantly a date at which its members were leading the drive towards common law objectives.

[19] e.g. Lord Mansfield, Howe v. Peers (1768) 4 Burr. 2225 at 2228.

[20] Thus an injunction to restrain breaches of confidence became available—Lord Eldon allowing it for the unauthorised publication of a surgeon's lectures (Abernethy v. Hutchinson (1825) H. & Tw. 28), Lord Cottenham for listing the titles of Queen Victoria's private sketches (Prince Albert v. Strange (1848) De. G. & Sm. 652). It would blossom into an important industrial and commercial jurisdiction in modern times.

[21] Turner L.J. Milroy v. Lord (1862) 4 De. G. F. & J. 264 at 274; and for the constitution of trusts, Lord Eldon, Ellison v. Ellison (1802) 6 Ves. 656 at 662.

[22] The rule was not settled in this form until the 1890s (see, e.g. MacDonald v. Scott [1893] A.C. 642). Occasionally the ambit had been somewhat wider in earlier cases (e.g. Clark v. Wright (1861) 6 H. & N. 849).

[23] E.g., Hammersley v. De Biel (1845) 12 Cl. & F. 45. At first instance, Lord Cottenham had expressed the principle very broadly; in the Lords, Lyndhurst, Brougham and Campbell echoed him—all common lawyers with Chancery experience. For the subsequent importance of this decision (despite Jorden v. Money, above, n. 81), see, e.g. Prole v. Soady (1861) 2 Giff. 1 (Stuart V.-C.). It was not easy to fit these cases within the frame of common law consideration, since the recipient of the gift was already engaged to marry. But when Common Pleas managed to find consideration, the case became a leading authority in the texts: Shadwell v. Shadwell (1860) 9 C.B.(N.S.) 159.

it to him by deed poll[24]; the niece who kept house for her uncle upon an oral promise that she would have a life interest in houses by his will.[25] The desire to protect conduct in reliance reached out beyond family arrangements: a promise to a tenant that he might have a long lease if he built upon a piece of land, was, according to Lord Kingsdown, enforceable once the building was done[26]; a government's encouragement to a licensee to spend large sums on building a jetty on its land would lead to the licence becoming irrevocable.[27]

The same approach carried through to the course of execution of a contract: if the purchaser of land gave the vendor more time than the contract allowed in order show good title, he would not be entitled to go back to the original date[28]; likewise if a landlord led his tenant to suppose that he would not insist strictly on the time limit for carrying out repairs.[29] In equity there was no need to show a contract of variation which was supported by common law consideration and met Statute of Frauds formalities. What equity would require in order that the promise be made good varied with the circumstances, for it was characteristic of the whole jurisdiction that remedies should be shaped in the court's discretion in order to achieve substantial justice. But the cases included orders to convey a promised freehold and money judgments for a promised sum or even some other promised benefit. Once this point was reached, equity was approaching a compensatory remedy for failing to make representations good,[30] and this accorded ill with the scruples of common law which stemmed from *Pasley* v. *Freeman*.[31] What is so striking is that this direction was being given to equity in the middle decades of the nineteenth century, just as common law ideas of consideration and privity were in converse movement.

(b) Justifying Non-Enforcement

Equity also intervened against the unfairness of bargains on a not inconsiderable scale, refusing specific performance of executory obli-

---

[24] *Dillwyn* v. *Llewellyn* (1862) 4 De. G.F. & J. 517.

[25] *Loffus* v. *Maw* (1862) 3 Giff. 592 (Stuart V.C.); and see below, p. 222.

[26] *Ramsden* v. *Dyson* (1866) L.R. 1 H.L. 129 at 170; but the great equity practitioner failed to persuade his fellows even with a preliminary written memorandum: Lord Cranworth firmly restricted any interference to mistakes about existing rights, which were deliberately acquiesced in.

[27] *Plimmer* v. *Mayor of Wellington* (1884) 9 App.Cas. 699.

[28] A long line of cases is reviewed by Lord Cranworth V.C. in *Parker* v. *Thorold* (1852) 2 Sim. N.S. 1; as a common lawyer sitting in equity he thought the cases went so far as "to have made a new contract for the parties"; but for the basic rule he had the authority of Lord Eldon (*Seton* v. *Slade* (1802) 7 Ves.Jun. 265).

[29] *Hughes* v. *Metropolitan Ry.* (1877) 2 A.C. 439; and see *Birmingham and District Land* v. *L.N.W.R.* (1888) 40 Ch.D. 268; and below, p. 222.

[30] Sheridan (1957), pp. 29–33, deals with the line of equity cases after *Pasley* in which representations were to be made good on grounds of "gross negligence, forgetfulness, failure to know what one ought, and absence of reasonable grounds for belief." See esp. *Pulsford* v. *Richards* (1853) 17 Beav. 87; *Jennings* v. *Broughton* (1854) 5 De G.M. & G. 126; *Slim* v. *Goucher* (1860) 1 De G.F. & J. 518; *Higgins* v. *Samuels* (1862) 2 J. & H. 460.

[31] (1789) 3 T.R. 51.

gations and ordering rescission of executed transactions.[32] This tradition, moreover, was quite as forcefully implemented in the nineteenth as in the eighteenth century, at least so long as the Court of Chancery retained its separate identity.

The harsh realities of bargaining in the medieval and early modern period were marked by the extensive use of penal bonds as a guarantee of due and exact performance of an undertaking.[33] As early as the seventeenth century, the Chancellor had evolved a jurisdiction for granting relief against penalties, larger amounts or other increased burdens imposed upon a person who failed to meet his liability.[34] This would in time extend to equitable relief against forfeitures (so that a lessee late with his rent would be given time to pay without suffering termination of the lease)[35]; and to so-called "clogs" on a mortgagor's equity of redemption—time clauses and additional obligations qualifying his entitlement to discharge the mortgage by repayment of the loan plus interest.[36]

The equitable conception of undue influence, like its cousin, the good faith required of a fiduciary,[37] was carried forward from the eighteenth to the nineteenth century in ways which gradually reinforced its impact.[38] If one person was able to govern the thinking of another so as to leave him no real ability to choose freely whether to make a gift or a contract, equity would rescind it.[39] Undue influence came to be presumed where a parent secured a benefit from a child, a solicitor from a client, a doctor from a patient, a mother superior from a nun. Equally the presumption of influence might be raised from proof of particular circumstances, as typically where a wily or domineering companion took over the affairs of an elderly or sick person and extracted a personal advantage. Once the influence was shown or presumed, the court would treat with great suspicion any gift or

---

[32] The long-established order for specific performance is a vital clue to the very conception of contractual obligation, for there could be no more positive way of insisting that a party should have what he bargained for, and not merely what was needed to put him back in his original position: see Simpson (1979), pp. 547–549. Specific performance was granted only in discretion, the principal limiting factor coming to be that damage at common law should not be an adequate remedy. But in sales of land the remedy was normally available: see, generally, Sir E. Fry, *Specific Performance* (1st ed. 1858), Pt. I.

[33] See A. W. B. Simpson (1966) 82 L.Q.R. 392 and Simpson *A History of the Common Law of Contract* (1975), pp. 88–126.

[34] See Holdsworth, I pp. 457–458. Under Lord Mansfield, common law began to accept a similar rule permitting juries to return verdicts for the actual loss suffered: *Lowe* v. *Peers* (1768) 4 Burr. 2225.

[35] Lord Eldon was however responsible for preventing the expansion of this jurisdiction from money payments to other obligations, such as the repair of buildings; he found it difficult in such cases to take account of any consequential disadvantage to the landlord and he showed himself generally uneasy about interfering with plain terms of agreement: see *Hill* v. *Barclay* (1811) 18 Ves. 56; *cf. Sanders* v. *Pope* (1806) 12 Ves. 282 (Erskine L.C.).

[36] See below, p. 225.

[37] For which, see below, p. 263ff.

[38] Lord Hardwicke's embracing view of equitable fraud encompassed: actual fraud, fraud apparent from the senseless nature of the bargain, fraud from the condition of the parties, fraud by imposition on non-parties and the fraud in catching bargains with expectants: *Chesterfield* v. *Janssen* (1751) 2 Ves. Sen. 125 at 155–57.

[39] Lord Eldon provided classic authority in *Huguenin* v. *Baseley* (1807) 14 Ves. 273. For the flow of case-law from the eighteenth century on, see Sheridan (1957) Chap. 5.

transaction at an undervalue that had not been preceded by fully independent advice. It was not enough to show that a fair price was being paid: by 1860, Romilly M.R. can be found insisting upon proof "that by no possibility could more be obtained."[40]

Equity did not confine its attention to relationships which had built up over time, but would also interfere in bargains between "strangers," if they were unconscionable; and the starting point for such an allegation was an element of undervalue in the transaction—generally "gross," rather than "mere," undervalue.[41] The jurisdiction was still of uncertain scope in the eighteenth century, though there were clear indications that something more than just a hard bargain must be shown.[42] The nineteenth century settled upon the proposition that the Court would be "astute . . . to infer fraud from inadequacy,"[43] particularly if there were some additional element—humble station in life, sickness, youth, age, poverty, lack of understanding of the transaction or other "ignorance." A regular flow of such cases continued to come before mid-century judges: Romilly M.R., Knight Bruce L.J. and Page Wood V.C. all made important statements about the doctrine.[44]

The equitable requirement of conscionability was used to attack two kinds of transactions with moneylenders.[45] In the *post obit* bond, the loan was on terms of repayment of a larger sum at a future date, typically the date on which the borrower came into an inheritance through the death of a relation, subject to the condition that the borrower was still then alive. If the difference between the two amounts was considerable, Chancery would in effect ignore the added gamble of the borrower's premature death and would rescind the original terms, on payment of the amount lent plus a moderate interest.

Even more significantly, where the heir to an estate, or some other person entitled to an expectancy, sold his whole interest for less than its value, the transaction would be set aside, and nineteenth century judges began to insist that any undervalue would justify their interference. In this they were assisted both by the emergence of actuarial science (with its calculation of life expectancies for the insurance industry) and by the growth of regular markets in expectant interests. The former tended to be higher in value and appealed to Lord Eldon, who was hostile to the very transaction; but other judges were not, and the House of Lords in the end preferred the latter.[46] But the

---

[40] *Grosvenor* v. *Sherratt* (1860) 28 Beav. 659 at 662.
[41] The question often took the form, should the court refuse to order specific performance of a contract to transfer land or other property where the consideration was much too large or small? Barton's recent review of the cases (which include a striking batch decided in the aftermath of the South Sea Bubble) shows that there must have been some additional element to inequality for the relief to be accorded: Barton (1987), pp. 123–130.
[42] See Sheridan (1957) Chaps. 4, 7.
[43] Lord Eldon in *Underhill* v. *Horwood* (1804) 10 Ves. 209 at 219; *Stilwell* v. *Wilkins* (1821) Jac. 280 at 282.
[44] See *Harrod* v. *Harrod* (1854) 1 K. & J. 4; *Clark* v. *Malpas* (1862) 4 De G.F. & J. 401; *Summers* v. *Griffiths* (1866) 33 Beav. 27.
[45] See Sheridan (1957) Chap. 8; Barton (1987), pp. 132–143.
[46] *Aldeborough* (*Earl*) v. *Trye* (1840) 7 Cl. & F. 436: otherwise it was feared that the expectancy would be quite unsaleable.

mid-century judges continued to insist on proof by the purchaser that he had given the full market value.[47] Parliament indeed imposed some restraint on this enthusiasm: the Sale of Reversions Act 1867 prescribed that bona fide transactions of this kind were not to "be opened or set aside merely on the Ground of Undervalue." But soon enough, Selborne L.C. was reasserting the equitable power to prevent "fraud" in the broad sense of "any unconscientious use of the power arising out of circumstances and conditions," such as "weakness on one side, usury on the other, or extortion, or advantage taken of that weakness."[48]

(c) Execution of Agreements.

In matters of contract, the focus of common law's attention was increasingly upon the moment of consensus, when minds met in a bargained exchange. Equity retained a longer vision of the relationship. The special character of the jurisdiction—a resort where common or special law could not achieve justice—and, as a consequence, the discretionary character of its remedies, strengthened the tendency to bring into account all the circumstances from the first negotiations to the date of decision. Thus, as already noted, equity might disregard terms making time of the essence and it refused to enforce oppressive bonds under seal imposing, for instance, a penalty for late performance.[49] Yet plainly an agreement to pay a fixed sum for a contractual breach could bring the consequences of breach into focus, sharpening perceptions in a manner in which judges were likely within limits to approve. Accordingly, in equity as well as at common law, there was some considerable readiness to uphold, as "genuine pre-estimates of damage," terms which prescribed a sum per acre for ploughing land or cutting timber contrary to a lease, or an amount payable for breach of a non-completion clause in the sale of a business or termination of a partnership.[50] Here the tendency of both systems was to arrive at a common point of balance.

III. After the Judicature Acts

By the late nineteenth century, the jurisdictions of common law and equity had operated in loose tandem for long enough to have few rules that were directly irreconcilable. Accordingly there was little scope for the Judicature Act's directive giving preference to the rules of equity.[51] The real differences of focus operated at one remove from simple conflict. Because of this, and because in both the High Court

---

[47] See, *e.g. Bromley* v. *Smith* (1859) 26 Beav. 644 (Romilly M.R.); *Talbot* v. *Staniforth* (1861) 1 J. & H. 484 (Page Wood V.C.).

[48] *Aylesford (Earl)* v. *Morris* (1873) L.R. 8 Ch.App. 484 at 490–491—the case was not within the Statute but proved for a time influential: see *O'Rorke* v. *Bolingbroke* (1877) 2 A.C. 814; *Fry* v. *Lane* (1888) 40 Ch.D. 312.

[49] See above, p. 218.

[50] *Kemble* v. *Farren* (1829) 6 Bing. 141; *Webster* v. *Bosanquet* [1912] A.C. 394.

[51] Judicature Act 1873, s.25, which dealt with a number of conflicts of detail by specific ordinance.

and the appellate courts there were substantially more common law-yers than Chancery men, common law ideology had a real chance to extend its domain. And that accretive process is the dominant characteristic of the period to 1950.

(a) The Elements of Contract

The most forceful re-assertion of common law values came in 1889. In *Derry* v. *Peek*,[52] a House of Lords composed of common lawyers reiterated uncompromisingly the position of *Pasley* v. *Freeman*: mis-representations which led others into contracts gave rise to a claim for damages for consequential loss only if there had been deceit in the common law sense. The tendency of equity decisions to allow a money bill (*i.e.* damages) as a way of making good negligent mis-statements were treated as heretical—something that, according to Lord Bramwell, would cause "mercantile men . . . to cry out."[53] The decision was quite uncompromising. It concerned misstatements in a company prospectus—a situation which many felt to call for par-ticular protection.[54] Equity was in future permitted only to grant rescission of contracts induced by innocent misrepresentations;[55] and the House of Lords affirmed that other common law barrier to wider liability: representations made in the course of negotiations were not terms of the contract unless they had clearly been made so.[56] *Derry* v. *Peek* was ill-received among Chancery lawyers,[57] and later an equity-dominated House of Lords would create an exception where there was a "special relationship" between the misrepresentor and the person misled.[58] But for another half-century this would be thought a narrow, uncertain category.[59]

If the plainest case of misplaced reliance was to give rise to redress only in strictly limited measure, equally there was a steady playing down of equity's instinct in other circumstances to honour state-ments and promises relied on. Equity had been prepared, sometimes with alacrity, to override the requirements of the Statute of Frauds where the part performance of a contract provided a basis for infor-mal proof of its terms. But in *Britain* v. *Rossiter*, the doctrine of part performance was confined to contracts for the transfer of interests in

---

[52] (1889) 14 App.Cas. 337; for its context see below, p. 265.
[53] *Ibid.* at 349; *cf.* above, p. 217. The case was at once reaffirmed in *Low* v. *Bouverie* [1891] 3 Ch. 82 and *Le Lievre* v. *Gould* [1893] 1 Q.B. 491 (and see below, pp. 510–512).
[54] Thus Anson had argued that the company owed a duty of utmost good faith to dis-close all relevant facts in its prospectus (*Principles of Contract* (1st ed., 1879), pp. 142–143) and the question remained unsettled for a long period.
[55] Damages were not to be awarded in the guise of payments to put a party into his original position: *Whittington* v. *Seal-Hayne* (1900) 82 L.T. 49.
[56] *Heilbut Symons* v. *Buckleton* [1913] A.C. 30—a very rigid application of the distinc-tion.
[57] As reported by Pollock: see M. de W. Howe, *Holmes-Pollock Letters* (1963), p. 322.
[58] *Nocton* v. *Ashburton (Lord)* [1914] 2 A.C. 932.
[59] The trend was not reversed until *Hedley Byrne* v. *Heller* [1964] A.C. 465; see R. B. Stevens (1964) 27 M.L.R. 121.

land[60]; and in *Maddison* v. *Alderson*, it was insisted that the acts of part performance be unequivocally referrable to the type of contract in question and not be capable of some alternative explanation, such as an intended gift.[61]

The textbooks of the period mark the demotion of other equitable ideas of reliance. Contractual liability was held to require benefit-or-detriment consideration, as much for the variation of existing rights as for the initiation of a new relationship. *Hughes* v. *Metropolitan Ry.* appeared to offer no general qualification of this.[62] The House of Lords' dogmatic insistence that English law knew no *ius quaesitum tertio*[63] provided definitive reinforcement. It was open to contracting parties to act for others as agents or to confer property rights on others by declaring trusts: but the courts would not use these techniques by implication as a means of neutralising the rule of privity.[64] Equity's concepts of implied and constructive trusts were held to arise only in limited and defined circumstances.[65] When the House of Lords felt it necessary to resolve complex issues in the winding up of the Birkbeck Building Society by resorting to extensive notions of "tracing" property in equity, it was careful to find that the claimants of the property in question (depositors in an ultra vires bank carried on by the building society) had in reality kept title to their money all through.[66] This wrapped in exceptional mystery the court's evident feeling that a constructive trust or similar equity should be imposed to the extent that would do justice in the circumstances.

Clearly the judges, whatever their background, could conceive no extensive basis for civil liability in the receipt of benefit without consideration or gift. On the common law side, the "quasi-contractual"

---

[60] (1879) 11 Q.B.D. 123. This left a difficulty where the contract was for the consideration of marriage, where it was not to be performed within a year and where it was of guarantee. One "common law" court was driven to implying a contract in place of the unenforceable express contract: *Scott* v. *Pattison* [1923] 2 K.B. 723.

[61] (1883) 8 App.Cas. 467. Lord Blackburn could make no sense of the various decisions in equity; Lord Selborne L.C. agreed that the limit must be imposed. The Court also refused to treat the oral contract part performed as a representation relied upon; the view in *Jorden* v. *Money* that an estoppel could arise only in respect of a misrepresentation of fact was now treated as the defining limit (*Prole* v. *Soady* (above, n. 23) *Loffus* v. *Maw* (above, n. 24) were overruled). To this would soon be added the view that an estoppel could not ground a cause of action (see above, p. 210).

[62] The line of cases of which it was a late and striking example (see above, p. 217) was not to be found in, *e.g.* Salmond and Winfield's *Principles of the Law of Contracts* (1927) or Pollock's *Contract* (10th ed. 1936). The latter, following *Maddison's* case (above, n. 61) describes as "equitable estoppel" the liability to make good representations of *fact* (see p. 501 and generally Chap. 13—Agreements of Imperfect Obligation—a curious, recondite assortment).

[63] *Dunlop* v. *Selfridge* 1915 A.C. 847; and see below, p. 272.

[64] This limited the potential of equity decisions such as *Lloyd's* v. *Harper* (1880) 16 Ch.D. 290 and *Re Flavell* (1883) 25 Ch.D. 89.

[65] The growing literature on equity and trusts accordingly contributed to the new evolution as well as that on contract, and often in the same direction. F. W. Maitland, for instance, said: "At one time certain judges in the Court of Chancery had almost succeeded in inventing a doctrine that equity would compel a person to 'make good his representations' and would thus go beyond the law of contract. But the wholesome influence of the Judicature Act, and the decision in *Maddison* v. *Alderson*, seem to have given the death blow to this loose doctrine." (*Lectures on Equity* (1st ed. 1909), pp. 306–307).

[66] *Sinclair* v. *Brougham* [1914] A.C. 398.

emanations of assumpsit formed an embarrassing historical residue. The existing cases came to be explained rather desperately as based upon "implied contract": they were essentially anomalous and certainly not to be generalised.[67] Thus it remained possible to insist that, in place of the forms of action, civil liability at common law arose either in contract or in tort. Any attempt to stray beyond their confines towards obligations arising from "the ties of natural justice"[68] was labelled "well-meaning sloppiness of thought."[69]

(b) Excusal from liability

One resonance of *Derry* v. *Peek* sounded against any broad scope of equitable "fraud." The texts now placed equity's jurisdiction to relieve the poor, aged and ignorant from oppressive bargains under the heading of undue influence.[70] Discussion was largely directed to defining the circumstances in which a finding of such influence could be justified, either from a presumption or actual demonstration that one person had so dominated the thinking of another that he could not choose what to do for himself. As we have seen, one underlying animus which had earlier given force to the jurisdiction was the fear of moneylenders. Now changes in the forms of wealth-holding within families, the growth of careers for the children of the wealthy and the expansion of respectable sources open even to those in desperate need of money were limiting the crushing demands which moneylenders were wont to impose. Equally Parliament was now prepared to curb what it regarded as their excesses. In 1882, as we shall see, it severely impeded the use of bills of sale as security for personal loans.[71] And with that experiment for precedent, in 1900 it passed a Moneylenders Act which divided the bad from the good by distinguishing the moneylender from, in particular, the banker.[72] The former came under an obligation to register; he was obliged to put his transactions in written form and to keep proper records under threat that otherwise the entire loan (not merely the interest) would prove irrecoverable; and the county courts and High Court were given power to reduce excessive rates of interest.[73]

The burden of relieving against unfair loans and other money-raising transactions, which had lain entirely in equity's province

---

[67] This "theory," the standard view in the first half of the twentieth century, had its apotheosis in *Sinclair* v. *Brougham* (above, n. 66) For the gradual resilement in modern law see Lord Goff and G. H. Jones *Law of Restitution* (3rd ed., 1986), Chap. 1.

[68] This characterisation of the action for money had and received by Lord Mansfield aroused the disdain in particular of Lord Sumner (*Baylis* v. *London* (*Bishop*) [1913] 1 Ch. 127 at 140 and *Sinclair* v. *Brougham* at 454).

[69] By Scrutton L.J. in *Holt* v. *Markham* [1923] 1 K.B. 504 at 513.

[70] See, *e.g.* W. R. Anson, *English Law of Contract* (1st ed., 1879), pp. 156–163.

[71] Below, pp. 241–242.

[72] The cast of public enemies was led by Isaac Gordon of Birmingham, who defended loans at 3,000 per cent. interest before a S.C. on Moneylending (P.P. 1897 (364) XI; and see 1898 (260) X) and faced a nakedly hostile Court of Appeal in *Gordon* v. *Street* [1899] 2 Q.B. 641; Atiyah (1979), pp. 711–713.

[73] This was a generalisation of the established jurisdiction in equity: see P.P. 1898 (260) X at VI. In 1927 it would be prescribed that a loan at a rate of more than 48 per cent. per annum would be presumed harsh and unconscionable: Moneylenders Act, s.10.

since the Usury Laws had been repealed in 1854, now seemed to pass primarily to legislation. The rules of equity for sales of reversions, post obit bonds and other oppressive transactions could be relegated to footnotes as mysterious atavism.

As for mistake, the common law remained antagonistic to any undermining of apparent consensus ad idem: it would take account of a misunderstanding shared by the parties only if it undermined a "foundation essential to the existence of the contract."[74] The possibility that equity took a more flexible view of the matter could be discounted without serious consideration.[75] In perhaps the last great exposition of contractual sanctity, Lord Atkin concluded that mistakes about quality were no more than risks run: "it is of paramount importance that contracts should be observed, and that if parties honestly comply with the essentials of the formation of contracts— i.e., agree in the same terms on the same subject-matter—they are bound, and must rely on the stipulations of the contract for protection from the effect of facts unknown to them."[76]

(c) Execution of the Contract

As we have already noted, the common law rules imposing strict obligations to fulfil contractual obligations were in some measure modified: by admitting the concept of frustration and by such rules as that concerning substantial performance of an indivisible contract.[77] In the opposite direction, common law, having absorbed equity's refusal to give effect to a penal stipulation, continued to ensure that there was no undue inhibition of the power to build "genuine pre-estimates of damage" into the contract. In the culminating case, the House of Lords allowed a clause to stand which laid down a standard payment for each failure to respect a minimum resale price, even though the actual injury might vary from instance to instance.[78]

In similar vein, equity's old protectiveness towards mortgagors and against mortgagees had implanted the rule that, after the initial date for repayment, the borrower's equitable right to recover the secured land upon repayment of the sum borrowed and the prescribed interest must not be impeded by any other "clogging" obligation.[79] The origins of the rule probably lay with the particular form of the mortgage transaction; but over time it developed partly in order to prevent the Usury Laws from being side-stepped by dressing extra interest up as capital premiums. Once those laws were

---

[74] See esp. *Bell* v. *Lever Bros.* [1932] A.C. 161. This extremely limited basis for interfering with contracts was used to define the scope of frustration; and at one stage, Blackburn J. had sought to make it the test even of misrepresentation (*Kennedy* v. *Panama Mail* (1867) L.R. 2 Q.B. 580).

[75] e.g., *Bell's* case (above, n. 74) at 218. Lord Denning would later take a different view of equity's potential (in *Solle* v. *Butcher* [1950] 1 K.B. 671 and later cases).

[76] *Ibid.*, at 224.

[77] Above, pp. 212–214.

[78] *Dunlop* v. *New Garage* [1915] A.C. 79; for resale price maintenance see below, pp. 272–273.

[79] For the evolution of the rule, see Holdsworth, VI 664–665; R. W. Turner, *The Equity of Redemption* (1913), pp. 175–183.

finally repealed in 1854, the rule against clogs had once more to be seen as part of equity's refusal to support unconscionable bargains; and that meant overriding what the parties had chosen to agree on a scale far too indiscriminate for common law minds. Lord Bramwell expressed the incomprehension of Economic Man over the rule of equity, but could not at once secure its abrogation.[80] Two leading Chancery figures, however—Lord Lindley and then Lord Parker— saw that the equity needed remoulding so as to strike only against clogs that were not reasonable commercial bargains, and by 1914 this curbing of earlier enthusiasm had to a considerable degree been achieved.[81] Sanctity of contract had become the bedrock of the whole judicial edifice.

It is not easy for today's student to perceive the harsh uniformity of contract as it was purveyed by judges and texts in the 1930s and 1940s, for it has since been subjected to a metamorphosis: judges have rediscovered equitable ideas that had appeared defunct, and Parliaments intent on protecting the consumer have insisted on redirection through enactments specific and general. In an account which brings the story through to 1950 it has accordingly been important to emphasise both the long period, which included the first century of industrialisation, in which distinctive attitudes towards contracting were maintained at common law and in Chancery; and the succeeding stage, lasting almost as long again, in which the common law's rules moved from being the standard answer for the general run of cases to become the dominant principle for all.

That an equitable tradition quite distinct in emphasis from that of the common law could survive for much of the nineteenth century is a striking illustration of the tenacity of competing ideologies in societies that are both complex and relatively liberal. Equally in such societies the tension between the desire to encourage independence and the desire to protect the weak and unfortunate will be difficult to resolve: both individuals and social groups will have to reconcile somehow their instincts for self-help and for charity, for laissez-faire and for social welfare. For a significant period, the two groups which had emerged as the dominant elements of the legal system seemed to keep apart (despite the endeavours of Lord Mansfield) so that, in conceptions of contractual obligation, each could remain at its pole. In all this there seems to be some association with the ideological positions of the two emerging classes of property-owners, though, since the courts derived considerable strength from the fact that they were not the resort of a single estate, the relationship is somewhat indirect and blurred. When Chancery went so far to undo the sales of reversions at less than full market value it had the young heir of a landed estate in the centre of its vision; more generally its rules were in considerable measure bred for a world of landed property and familial alliance; whereas the common law's drive grew around commercial litigation of large and medium-sized business—the entrepre-

---

[80] *Salt* v. *Northampton (Marquess)* [1892] A.C. 1 at 18–19.
[81] Lindley's attack (*Santley* v. *Wilde* [1899] 2 Ch. 474) at first provoked defence (*Noakes* v. *Rice* [1902] A.C. 24; *Bradley* v. *Carritt* [1903] A.C. 253); Parker largely carried the day in *Kreglinger* v. *New Patagonia Meat and Cold Storage Co.* [1914] A.C. 24, but the precise dividing line has never been clearly delineated.

neurial middle class which became so energetic a force in the first half of the nineteenth century.

Of the many motives which contributed finally to the Judicature Acts, the feeling that the two jurisdictions pulled too evidently in different directions was undoubtedly one. It is certainly tempting to view the consequent moulding of contract according to common law forms as a legal analogue of that drawing together of landed and commercial wealth which was obliterating boundaries between upper and middle classes. To label the state of contract law in this period "stagnant," or to deride judicial decisions as "formalistic," does not comprehend what was happening. Certainly by 1900 there had been a long evolution of rules about Contract, in general and in particular, and cases could frequently be disposed of simply by reciting them as categoric determinants. But this was not simply a conservatism rendered blind by the constraints of the past. It was the reiteration of severely liberal values in the face of novel, democratic questioning. The ideals on which the greatest nation of the nineteenth century had been built were facing the challenges of a highly uncertain future: from abroad, came increasing competition and recurrent war-mongering; at home labour was acquiring economic and political power of a quite new order. There might come to be a common law seriously at odds with the dictates of collectivist government expressed through apparently paramount legislation. However remote that prospect, it was at least important to define fundamental premises without equivocation.

PART 2: DEBT, BANKRUPTCY, INSOLVENCY

I. ENFORCING DEBTS

As the money economy grew, as wealth spread from land to movables and services, as the true possibilities of capitalist venture began to dawn, the range of dealings on credit multiplied. Already in the buoyant commercialism of the eighteenth century, courts were expected, as a prime function, to discipline the repayment of debt. In the towns local courts were revived or created afresh as courts of requests—traders' tribunals for the traders' great problem; and in the prisons, the number of debtors grew until they could no longer be easily handled.

To some degree, there were forms of self-help in the matter of credit, particularly through the taking of security by devices such as mortgages, encumbrances, and charges—and to these we will come.[82] But much credit was unsecured. In a world where income was often seasonal or spasmodic, where currency could still be hard to find, where sources for borrowing were limited, credit was an inevitable aspect of daily living at every level, as well as of agriculture, industry and commerce. Debt is a complex relationship, which we perceive today through economic and legal assumptions about market forces and consumer protection, methods of recovery, rules

[82] Below, pp. 237ff.

for bankruptcy and winding up, means of granting security and acting under limited liability. But it is also a relationship with a long ancestry which can be retraced only by cutting away these preconceptions.

Even at the beginning of the industrial period, debt was still coloured by two ideas that are not easy now to appreciate. The first was the survival of hostility towards usury. The medieval church had taught that all lending at interest was sinful, though with the growth of trade it was even then becoming an inevitable need. The tension this generated contributed much to the harsh history of European Jewry. The basic instinct of the capitalist was an understanding of the value of wealth over time and in Tudor England it became clear that some new compromise was emerging.[83] A series of post-Reformation Usury Laws set maximum rates of legal interest for moneylending, which in 1713 finally settled at 5 per cent.[84] Various types of transaction involving some element of credit were by then defined as not usurious: to this end leases of land, partnerships and annuities (payments during life) were being used to dress up what were effectively loans at interest.[85] The real objection to usury had probably always been to the oppressive extraction of harsh interest from those desperate to borrow who could find no other source; now it was being acknowledged that borrowing without pressure had economic and social advantages. Yet the limitation on interest, for all the uncertainties of its scope, was to remain operative throughout the early industrial period, being finally abandoned only in 1854. A loan which fell foul of the Usury Law was unlawful and so unenforceable by the lender. Adam Smith did not consider that free market notions justified the lifting of this prudent fetter on cupidity, and there were many in the ruling class who believed their ability to find low-rate mortgages depended upon the 5 per cent. ceiling.[86] However, Bentham achieved a distinct success by arguing against any regulation, thus out-Smithing Smith[87]; and there were always financiers and bankers ready to put the same case. In 1818 a Select Committee listened attentively to Ricardo and recommended repeal[88]; in 1837 there was an important exemption of bills of exchange payable in under twelve-months; and finally abandonment, after a long period of low interest rates which had made the ceiling seem high, at least for mortgages and other well-secured loans.[89]

---

[83] It was, however, a long and uncertain struggle: see R. H. Tawney (ed.), *Wilson on Usury* (1925): Introduction; A. W. B. Simpson, *A History of the Common Law of Contract* (1975), pp. 510–518.

[84] See esp. 37 Hen. VIII, c. 9 (1545)—maximum of 10 per cent.—repealed in 1551–1552); 13 Eliz., c. 8 (1571—10 per cent.); 21 J. I, c. 17 (1623—8 per cent. interest being formally recoverable for the first time); 12 Ch. II c. 12 (1660 6 per cent.); 12 Anne St. 2, c. 16.

[85] Holdsworth VIII, pp. 104–106 (and generally, pp. 100–113).

[86] *Wealth of Nations* (1976 ed.), pp. 356–358; see generally Atiyah (1979), pp. 550–551.

[87] *Defence of Usury* (1787, reprinted 1816); the later classical economists mostly followed him.

[88] P.P. 1818 (376) VI; and see 1821 (410) IV.

[89] 7 Will. IV & 1 Vict., c. 80; 17 & 18 Vict., c. 90. Byles J., Atiyah's paternalist survivor on the bench, wrote a tract against repeal (*Observations on the Usury Laws* (1845)); but he seems by then to have been a lone voice: *cf.* the Select Committee, P.P. 1845 (611) XII.

The second ancient perception of debt was that the relationship placed the debtor in bond to his creditor. Many early societies reduced debtors to servitude in order to enforce repayment through labour. In medieval England a derivative of this notion survived.[90] The courts of common law, mainly through early statutes, acquired power to arrest defendants before their trial for debt, as for other causes, so as to ensure their presence at the trial (arrest on mesne process); and equally to enforce judgments against them (arrest on final process). If this did nothing to make the debtor work off his liability, it could act as a stringent incentive to find some source for the money due. A more direct way of extracting payment of a debt from a judgment debtor could be to seize and realise his assets in satisfaction and such procedures were certainly available: writs might issue directing the sheriff to seize and realize chattels[91] or ordering that the judgment creditor be given possession of land.[92] But land itself was too sacrosanct to be the subject of an enforced sale; and in the eighteenth century there was still no means of proceeding against the newer forms of wealth: bank accounts, negotiable instruments, annuities and similar choses in action. Accordingly, the danger of being thrown into a debtor's prison loomed over all credit transactions, keeping the relationship personal and thus impeding the commercial desire to treat debts as negotiable property, transferrable to others at a discount.[93]

Arrest on mesne process was a creditor's weapon of variable impact. Some appreciation of its dangers appeared from successive statutes which required that the alleged debt be at least £2 (1725), then £10 (1779), then £20 (1827).[94] Even so, since it operated merely upon the issue by the creditor of a writ, it could have an effect, removing the defendant from his daily existence and cutting him off from such means of earning as he might have. If he had some substance, he might seek and be granted bail, since the whole purpose was only to ensure his appearance at trial. The well-organised and the canny might accordingly find little to terrorise them in the process. One way was to resort to rescue by a bail-broker. "Bail, as is well known, may always be procured at a premium proportionate to the risk."[95] But that might only be to fall prey to a truly voracious creditor.

After 1813, there were permanent arrangements of a sort, where a debtor was prepared to surrender his available assets to his creditors, for getting him out of prison.[96] Even so, there was a growing feeling that a system which sent 10,000 or so debtors into the prisons each

---

[90] See Holdsworth, VII pp. 229–233.
[91] *Fieri facias* was the normal form by the eighteenth century. If it proved inadequate it might be followed by arrest of the debtor, but *fi. fa.* was not permitted after arrest: see Blackstone, *Commentaries*, III Chap. 26.
[92] The writ of *elegit* entitled the creditor to possession of one half of the debtor's freeholds; but arrest of the debtor was thereafter precluded.
[93] The fear that a man's enemy might become his creditor had real meaning even at the end of the eighteenth century: see, *e.g.*, Lord Kenyon, *Exall v. Partridge* (1799) 8 T.R. 308, p. 311.
[94] 12 Geo. I, c. 29 (for superior courts already £10); 19 Geo. III, c. 70; 7 & 8 Geo. IV, c. 71.
[95] Common Law Commissioners, Fourth Report, P.P. 1831–32 (239) XXV, p. 8.
[96] See below, p. 234.

year (a quarter or more on mesne process)[97] was too expensive, too indiscriminate, too open to abuse and overweaning pressure.[98] Reform of the sanctions for debt became one part of the Benthamite campaign for a restructured system of debt courts; one argument for putting these courts in the charge of lawyers was that tradesmen could not be expected to control abuse of the enforcement process.[99] The new county courts—a country-wide system replacing the plethora of local and request jurisdictions—would be introduced in 1846 to deal with small debts; and the processes of the higher courts would eventually become less cumbersome, notably by providing a rapid summary procedure against those who did not contest the claim.[1]

But this was achieved only after changes in enforcement rules. In 1832, a majority of the Common Law Commissioners recommended restricting imprisonment for debt to cases of fraud, deliberate removal of assets and refusal after judgment to surrender assets towards payment.[2] This did at least lead to the abolition of arrest on mesne process in 1838.[3] At the same time the courts seem to have grown chary of sending judgment debtors to prison and the numbers finding their way there decreased very substantially.[4] There was a sharp anxiety among traders which provoked inquiries into insolvency, bankruptcy and the enforcement of judgment debts.[5] But the radical campaigners continued to press for abolition of imprisonment. In 1844 an Act excluded it even after judgment for debts less than £20, save where there was fraud or equivalent misconduct.[6] This was indeed legislation to test the balance of "public opinion." At once came an immense commercial outcry and rapid modification. In 1845, for debts less than £20, imprisonment for up to 40 days might be ordered on a number of grounds, including failure to pay (by instalments or otherwise) when the debtor apparently had means to do so[7]; thus began an open discrimination against the small debtor which would last until 1970.

The County Courts, finally instigated amid all this agitation in 1846, were given jurisdiction over debts under £20 and equivalent powers of imprisonment.[8] The county court judges were thus put to administering consumer credit as it affected, in the main, the work-

---

[97] See the Return for 1830–1834, P.P. 1835 (199) XLIV.

[98] See esp. the views of the Common Law Commissioners: above, n. 95.

[99] The Common Law Commissioners were in large measure hostile to them, contrasting them with the lawyer-run Palace Court of Westminster: Fifth Report, P.P. 1833 (247) XXII. But the extravagant fees extracted by its officers and attorneys led to its demise twenty years later: see T. Mathew, *For Lawyers and Others* (1937), p. 37.

[1] See the Common Law Procedure Act 1852 (15 & 16 Vict., c. 76, ss.27–28).

[2] Above, n. 95.

[3] 1 & 2 Vict., c. 100. The same Act allowed final process against debts, bills and other intangible assets of the debtor; and it allowed the judgment creditor possession of all the debtor's land by *elegit*: see Holdsworth, XV pp. 114–115.

[4] See the Return of Persons Confined for Debt, P.P. 1844 (292) XXXVIII.

[5] Notably the Royal Commission chaired by Erskine J.: P.P. 1840 [174] XVI.

[6] 7 & 8 Vict., c. 96.

[7] 8 & 9 Vict., c. 127; other grounds included contracting the debt without reasonable prospect of repaying.

[8] 9 & 10 Vict., c. 95, ss.9, 99. The judges had power to imprison merely for failure to answer the summons.

ing-class debtor. Some of them disliked the creditors who most regularly pressed the system to its extreme—small-scale moneylenders and the tallymen who hawked finery and household articles and collected payments by regular calls.[9] Often enough these people preyed upon acquisitive instinct or desperate misfortune; a judge might mark his distaste by ordering repayment in derisory instalments. But in the general run of affairs, the process was much more likely to work summarily against the debtor, without any real inquiry into his or her predicament; the courts were prone to accept on scant evidence that the debtor probably had means to pay and ordered imprisonment as a deterrent both specific and general. Inevitably, the cunning managed to scrape up what was necessary when the sheriff arrived, while the hopelessly down-trodden became the sacrificial lambs.

In the 1860s there was once more a campaign for abolition of imprisonment for debt and a Select Committee on Bankruptcy made this its first recommendation.[10] An Act of 1869 proudly announced the abolition; but at the behest of commercial interests, it added an exception allowing imprisonment for debts under £50 for up to six weeks, where the debtor, having apparent means to do so, failed to pay.[11] As the Spencer Walpole Committee was soon to find, there had been no change of significance.[12] In the decade 1871–1880, 5 per cent. of county court judgments would lead to orders of imprisonment, and 1 per cent. to actual imprisonment, giving an annual average of nearly 6,000 going to prison. Though the proportions would thereafter decline, the annual totals would rise until they were an average of nearly 10,000 for 1901–1910. Only after that would war and economic difficulties reduce the numbers considerably. Then the problem could be submerged for decades.[13]

II. BANKRUPTCY AND INSOLVENCY

In the relation between individual creditor and debtor, competition between creditors has long cast a dark shadow, compounded of legal complexity, duplicit conduct, and fearful watchfulness. To understand its influence requires an account, first, of the procedures—bankruptcy, insolvency, mutual agreement—that evolved to achieve a composition among the creditors out of whatever assets the debtor had; then of the machinery which could be used by one creditor to

---

[9] See G. R. Rubin in Rubin and D. Sugarman, *Law Economy and Society* (1984), pp. 241, 321; and evidence to the Spencer Walpole Committee (below, n. 12).

[10] P.P. 1865 (144) XII.

[11] Debtors Act 1869, s.5.

[12] P.P. 1873 (348) XV. The attempt to ameliorate the lot of the lower-class debtor (owing less than £50 in toto) by a simple administration of assets in the County Courts (Bankruptcy Act 1883, s.122) proved a failure; but some County Court judges achieved a rough division in their debt judgments: see Committee on Enforcement of Judgment Debts, P.P. 1969 [Cmnd. 3909] XXXVI, paras. 737–742.

[13] Not till the lifting of wartime credit restrictions in the late 1950s would the annual average rise again to 6,000 and above. The unease would lead to a substantial investigation by the Payne Committee (see above, n. 12) and considerable, though by no means complete, curtailment of imprisonment for debt. For the comparative figures, see the Committee's Report, App. 14.

secure priority over others; and finally of the techniques by which an investor could limit his liability for debt and other obligations through joint stock incorporation. It is to each of these subjects that chapter next turns.

Bankruptcy is the legal concept which perhaps most clearly registers the changing ideology of credit. From its early manifestations in Tudor England bankruptcy has been complicated by the pressures from three forces: the desire to punish the bankrupt by public censure, the wish to organise an administration of his assets so that competitors are treated fairly and efficiently, and the hope that the process could absolve the bankrupt of his liabilities and allow him to rehabilitate himself. In the early stages, the third of these remained a much less powerful motivation than the first two. So long as the creditor's basic remedies were as much against the debtor's person as his possessions, bankruptcy was an additional deterrent aimed at those who failed to submit to these ordinary processes. A response to demands of the mercantile community, it was available only against a "trader," and was a special threat to those for whom credit was essential to business, not a privilege of those who had gambled and lost.[14]

Bankruptcy had become a procedure conducted by commissioners (mainly lawyers) appointed by the Lord Chancellor. For a commission to issue, the trader had to be shown to have committed an act of bankruptcy: he must have put either his person or his property out of circulation in one of the defined ways—by keeping to his house, departing from it, seeking sanctuary, going to prison, or leaving the country, making a fraudulent conveyance of his land or goods, allowing goods to be attached, or offering preferential treatment to a creditor who threatened a petition in bankruptcy.[15] This led to the public humiliation of the commissioners' examination to discover assets. In bankruptcy the seizure of assets could even include land, property conveyed to others by way of gift, property transferred after the act of a bankruptcy and the property of others (such as stock-in-trade) which was on the bankrupt's premises in his "reputed ownership."[16] If necessary, there could be forced entry to the premises in order to effect the seizure. The available assets were to be rateably distributed among creditors. There was a splay of criminal offences which a bankrupt who failed to cooperate in this process might commit, and eighteenth century Parliaments were active in turning the most heinous into capital crimes (with the consequence that they were rarely employed).[17]

Under the Tudors the prospect of the honest trader being absolved from his liabilities at the end of the day was not entirely forgotten, since the Council could sometimes be persuaded to grant a discharge

---

[14] For the early history in England, see Holdsworth, VIII pp. 229–245, IX pp. 245–247; Cohen (1982).

[15] The concept was broadened through a series of statutes: see esp. 13 Eliz., c. 7; 1 Jac. I, c. 15; 21 Jac. I, c. 19; 10 Ann., c. 15; 5 Geo. II, c. 30; for the obscurities about the debtor's state of mind, see below, p. 232.

[16] Cf. the limitations on the execution of judgment debts, above, p. 228.

[17] See, e.g., 4 Ann., c. 5 (refusing to surrender person or property within 30 days of notice); 5 Ann., c. 22 (embezzling with intent to defraud creditors).

from existing liabilities to the person who cooperated to the best of his ability; after the Restoration, however, the only equivalent power lay with Parliament through a private Act or a temporary absolution of debtors; apart from this, any excusal was left to individual creditors. In the reign of Anne, there was an attempt to improve the bankrupt's lot by an Act allowing the Commissioners to discharge him from debts extant at the date of bankruptcy, if he had complied with the requirement to surrender up assets and undergo examination.[18] But this was too much for mercantile opinion. In the following year, discharge was restricted to those who obtained the assents of four-fifths of the creditors (reckoned both by number and by value), the commissioners and the Lord Chancellor.[19]

Even though the bankrupt's chance of securing absolution lay with others, the very possibility became a deeply attractive appendage of the system. Blackstone, for instance, presented bankruptcy as above all a privilege offered to the honest trader, and justified reserving it to traders by the special economic value of their risk-taking[20]—in a sense the ultimate appreciation of capitalist adventure. Yet if the entrepreneurial instinct was specially to be prized, those who exhibited it could wreak particular havoc by abusing the system of credit. Bankruptcy continued, without much hope of consistency, to be an added sanction against trader-debtors who sought to escape ordinary debt-enforcement. It came accordingly under a growing volley of criticism, which could only be aggravated by the fact that both its subject and its procedures laid it open to the eighteenth-century penchant for malign administration.[21]

In 1800 there were some 700 bankruptcy commissioners for 140 courts around the country, each paid by the sitting.[22] The proceedings in London were described by a commissioner as, "the worst constituted court of justice that can be imagined": the panels of commissioners might change as a case progressed, and creditors competed to attract attention in intolerable noise and confusion; the very rules were likely to be bent at the whim of the bench and the right of appeal to the Lord Chancellor became so protracted as to afford more opportunity for abuse than anything else.[23]

The active creditors could manipulate the system in myriad ways. The commissioners did not themselves administer the assets but would appoint one or more creditors as treasurers under their supposed supervision. It was easy for these assignees to make off with the available assets; a fictitious creditor could be hired, replete with forged bills, if that was the object. Equally, a substantial creditor might press for some fraudulent preference as a condition of signing the bankrupt's certificate of discharge.

---

[18] 4 Ann., c. 17, s.7; the same statute allowed the responsible bankrupt who paid at least 8s. in the £ an award out of the assets of 5 per cent. up to £200; this small help towards a new start would survive in later legislation.

[19] 5 Ann., c. 22, s.2. The three assents remained quite distinct: mandamus would not lie against the commissioners.

[20] Commentaries, II Chap. 31.

[21] See in general, Welbourne (1932); Cohen (1982).

[22] Many country commissioners had very little work.

[23] See the case mounted against the existing morass before the Select Committee on Bankruptcy Laws, P.P. 1818 (276) VI.

The catalogue of abuses open to debtors was even longer. A trader could try to shelter behind a more-or-less sham bankruptcy. He could hide away his assets, or get them into the hands of family or friends. He might organise large debts or annuities which his relatives could afterwards prove. Then he could arrange an act of bankruptcy on which a compliant or fictitious creditor would issue a fiat against him. He might use the laborious opening stages of bankruptcy to secure respite from genuine demands. And he could at any time counter-attack a petitioning creditor by requiring proof afresh of the act of bankruptcy. The unscrupulous and the unfortunate became admixed in a procedure that left the judges struggling vainly to exert some kind of authority.[24]

Because of its harshness and the opportunities for abuse, they were inclined to emphasise the quasi-criminal character of the process. A well-meaning debtor might be preserved from surrender of all assets or from forcible entry by a finding that, since he had not acted with intent to defraud creditors, he had committed no act of bankruptcy,[25] or by a refusal to treat an arranged bankruptcy as properly based.[26] Accordingly, on a range of fronts, bankruptcy was an evident target for reform, though it was still far from clear in which direction and by what means the campaign should proceed. Sir Samuel Romilly became a leader of this, as so many other, attempts to re-shape judicial administration and piloted through bills in 1809 and 1813 containing sundry interstitial modifications. These included a reduction in the proportion of creditors needed to assent to the certificate of discharge from four-fifths to three-fifths.[27]

Most proposals from merchants and reforming lawyers were for making bankruptcy a regular process of absolution.[28] The Select Committee of 1818 recommended that a trader should be able to place himself in bankruptcy by his own nomination and this indeed became the law in 1824, thus avoiding the pretence that even the most well-intentioned trader had perpetrated an exceptional wrong.[29] But the Select Committee, which was attentive to voices from the business community, wanted to revert to a four-fifths majority of creditors for certifying discharge, and would countenance

---

[24] Although, from the general Act of 1732 (5 Geo. II, c. 30, s.24), the Lord Chancellor had supervision of the commissioners, the actions of creditors, assignees and others might well be challenged by a collateral action at common law. This did not aid consistent interpretation of the law.

[25] Despite the ambiguity of a number of earlier decisions, Lord Kenyon insisted that the criminal law requirement of mens rea was essential to an act of bankruptcy: *Fowler* v. *Paget* (1798) 7 T.R. 509.

[26] Thus Lord Mansfield refused to treat a bankruptcy arranged between debtor and creditors as "the crime of denying oneself to another," (*Hooper* v. *Smith* (1763) 1 Black 441). Lord Kenyon initially showed some sympathy for the opposite persuasion (*Roberts* v. *Teasdale* (1790) Peake N.P. 38), but later refused to make the new departure (*Stewart* v. *Richman* (1794) 1 Esp. 108).

[27] 49 Geo. III, c. 121 (for the certificate, s.18); 53 Geo. III, c. 102.

[28] This pressure for reform deserves comparison with that which would bear upon divorce law in the twentieth century: see below, p. 396ff.

[29] Select Committee Report (above, n. 23, p. xii); 5 Geo. IV, c. 98, s.6. It soon proved to be an easy source of duplicity and in 1842 the bankrupt was required to show that he would pay at least 5s. in the £ (5 & 6 Vict., c. 122, s.44); but this in turn proved unduly stringent.

handing over the decision to a tribunal only in exceptional circumstances. A very limited power to override a single intransigent creditor was indeed introduced in 1824; but even this proved too much and it was repealed in the following year.[30] Not until Brougham ascended the Woolsack was anything done to alter the administrative structure. His Act of 1831 replaced the 70 Commissioners in London with a body of four judges and six commissioners.[31] There was also an intermediate Court of Review comprising three of the new judges. In turn, however, it would come in for heavy criticism and would be abolished in 1847.[32]

Dissatisfaction even with such a change was merely one instance of a deeper malaise. A search for some more satisfactory mode of coping with insolvencies would run unrelentingly until at least the 1880s. One element of tension was the continuing confinement of bankruptcy to traders.[33] Eighteenth-century Parliaments had from time to time absolved debtors from prison (whether or not they were bankrupts) upon cession of their available assets and this was made a regular and permanent system in 1813.[34] The pressure on gaol space was in places grave and the wastefulness and public expense of permanently incarcerating a debtor had become increasingly apparent. The creditor was supposed to help support the debtor, but the latter might slide into permanent incarceration with a modicum of support from relatives, friends or the county rate. The 1813 Act appointed an Insolvent Debtors Court for London but in the provinces left the task of examining debtors, as under the earlier statutes, to the justices. Later the London insolvency commissioners would be sent out on circuit to do the work.[35] Once they were satisfied that a debtor had done what he could towards satisfying his creditors, he would be released and the creditors could only look to such future assets as he might acquire. The process, however, contained no mechanism for wiping out the debts; only a compromise with each creditor would achieve that. It became clear to the Erskine Commission in 1840 that this insolvency process was being frequently used for small traders—those who did not owe enough to seek or be brought into bankruptcy.[36] They accordingly recommended that bankruptcy should become available against traders and non-traders alike.[37] This, however, was not to be until 1861, when finally the separate scheme for insolvent debtors was abandoned.[38]

---

[30] 5 Geo. IV, c. 98, s.122; cf. 6 Geo. IV, c. 16, s.122. Only in 1849, was the decision given over to the commissioner (see below, n. 42).

[31] 1 & 2 Will. IV, c. 56. Lord Eldon had stood in the way of earlier reform; see e.g., the Chancery Commission Report (under his chairmanship), P.P. 1826 (143) XV, pp. 35–37.

[32] 10 & 11 Vict., c. 102. Its place was taken, first, by a Vice-Chancellor, and then by the Lords Justices in Chancery.

[33] There was much law on who counted as a trader. Not only did it exclude the higher ranks, but also, in most circumstances, farmers, builders, miners, brickmakers: see Welbourne (1932), pp. 55–57; Cohen (1982), pp. 160–161.

[34] 53 Geo. III, c. 28; for the last temporary Act, see 52 Geo. III, c. 165; and see Holdsworth XIII, pp. 277–278; Cohen (1982), pp. 153, 157–159, 162–164.

[35] 5 Geo. IV, c. 61.

[36] Two-thirds of the 3,691 before the Insolvent Debtors Court in 1839 were traders: P.P. 1840 [274] XVI, p. 14.

[37] Ibid., pp. 23 ff.

[38] 24 & 25 Vict., c. 134.

The more immediate outcome of the Erskine Commission, amid the various moves on the procedures and sanctions of debt enforcement by individual creditors,[39] was the institution of a new regime of bankruptcy administration. The judges and commissioners were given greater powers and official assignees were introduced to administer the bankrupt's assets from the outset and act as a check on creditors' assignees.[40] They proved in the event to be an expensive encumbrance, lacking both experience and probity. At the same time minor officers of the court continued to exercise an "occult influence over practitioners," particularly in the matter of unnecessary fees. Some of the commissioners were disgracefully slack and partisan.[41] More generally there was dissatisfaction with the way they exercised their increased power to grant discharge.[42]

The reaction against the first set of bankruptcy reforms, typical of its period, sought to leave the bankrupt and his creditors substantially free of official interference, following the Scottish model.[43] In 1869 the Official Assignee disappeared and the trustee in bankruptcy (frequently a solicitor) was placed under the supervision of a creditors' committee of inspection, with reference to the court as a last resort.[44] But banishing greedy officials only allowed greater licence to unscrupulous debtors and creditors. The 1869 Act was soon being denounced as not having, "in its working, satisfied the expectations of the public inasmuch as it affords great facilities for a debtor to relieve himself of his liabilities, while there is great extravagance in administering and long delay in winding up estates."[45]

Either the bankrupt (in collusion with friendly creditors), or unfriendly creditors, could dominate proceedings by obtaining proxies from other creditors to vote at creditors' meetings: "It happens, not occasionally, but so frequently as almost to form the rule, that a stranger, so far as appears upon the face of the proceedings, is enabled by the proxies he has obtained, to vote himself trustee, to fix his own remuneration, to nominate the committee of inspection, to order the payment of his costs, and finally to vote, in liquidation cases, the debtor's discharge."[46]

The only feasible reform was to move back in the direction of official supervision. The Bankruptcy Act 1883 reincarnated the Official Assignees in the form of Official Receivers. It curbed the manipulation of the system by severely limiting the conditions upon which proxy powers could be given and by allowing the court once

---

[39] The virtual abandonment of arrest on mesne process in 1838 removed the simplest course for establishing an act of bankruptcy (*i.e.* remaining under arrest for debt for 21 days).

[40] 5 & 6 Vict., c. 122, ss.48–57, 92.

[41] See esp. Royal Commission on the Court of Bankruptcy, P.P. 1854 [1770] XXIII; Select Committee on the Bankruptcy Act 1861, P.P. 1865 (144) XII.

[42] Acquired in 1849 (see above, n. 30), this was complicated by allowing the certificate to be of various kinds, depending on the behaviour of the bankrupt before and during his bankruptcy.

[43] Bankruptcy Acts 1861 and 1869.

[44] Bankruptcy Act 1869, ss.14–20.

[45] Lord Chancellor's Committee on the Bankruptcy Act 1869, P.P. 1877 (152) LXIX.

[46] *Ibid.*, at pp. 1–2.

more to decide whether, and upon what terms, the bankrupt should be granted his discharge.

There did finally emerge a system that was at least moderately workable. The official receivers of 1883 brought in a degree of scrupulousness and cost-consciousness that had been so lacking in the official assignees and other court officers of the 1830s and 1840s. At last it could be claimed that bankruptcy was no longer "that state of things which exists when, a man being unable to pay his debts, his solicitor, and an accountant, divide all his property between them."[47]

In 1908 the Muir McKenzie Committee could report:

"the evidence and documents placed before us do not disclose any dissatisfaction on the part of the commercial community with the main features of the existing law and procedure; while evidence and statistics from official sources show that there has been a large reduction in the amount of insolvency throughout the country since the present system came into force."[48]

Even so, this belated onset of Victorian propriety can scarcely have been the cause of the apparent reduction in insolvency. A more complex shift was at work. It is in the last quarter of the nineteenth century that debtors acquired a novel and remarkable weapon in the taking of business risks. Increasingly, small businesses as well as large were becoming the property of registered companies and through this mechanism the individual trader could not only shelter behind liability limited to the assets of the company but could even, if he planned carefully, secure for himself a preferential interest in whatever assets there might be on winding up. This opportunity, accepted as legally effective by the House of Lords in 1897, was the outcome of a series of parallel developments, some of which we have still to review.[49] But among them undoubtedly was the ever-shifting, deeply unsatisfactory experience of bankruptcy. It had led over time to acceptance of the notion that all those (not just traders) who had been brought to insolvency, unless they were irredeemably unscrupulous, should be absolved from their debts after administration of their assets and this had undoubtedly contributed to acceptance of limited liability. But so equally had the dispiriting search for a system of bankruptcy administration which was proof against manipulation by the greedy and disreputable.

In practice, a new distinction between traders and others were emerging, since non-traders rarely formed companies for their affairs. Ironically, bankruptcy was becoming the likely fate only of those who had been excluded from it until its Victorian transformation—minor traders and private individuals. Even so, among these some would have debts and assets on so small a scale that a formal

---

[47] W. B. Odgers, A. Century of Law Reform (1901), p. 14.
[48] Board of Trade Committee on Bankruptcy Law, P.P. 1908 [Cd. 4068] XXXIV, para. 12.
[49] See below pp. 261–262.

administration would not be economic. Typically they formed the category against whom creditors continued to demand the sanction of imprisonment for debt.

III. Secured Credit

The processes of bankruptcy and insolvency, and equally the winding up of partnerships and companies, were all in a sense collectivist: they posited that, where a debtor did not have the resources to meet all his creditors, it was fairer and more orderly to provide for each a rateable share out of a common pool. However, the ferment of competition among creditors built up individualistic counter-pressures; new methods were constantly surfacing by which one creditor would seek to obtain preferential treatment ahead of the general run.[50] Mostly this was achieved by the assertion of ownership or a secured interest in some part of the debtor's possessions or other assets. The common law tended to treat novel ways of gaining security with hesitancy; but if a reasonably powerful commercial group determined to press for a particular transaction, sooner or later it was likely to receive legal recognition. The case was always that, if a provider of credit could not deal on the preferential terms, he would not do so at all, or only at a price which would remove all hope of profit from the debtor's own activity. It was a beguiling argument which could only gain in allure alongside the growth of credit.

The common law provided various conceptual mechanisms for the creation of security—in particular through ownership, bailment and lien. The mortgage of land, in its most formal version, had come to operate through the first of these, the borrower transferring his interest in the land (fee simple, copyhold, etc.) to the lender for the duration of the loan, even though, in the first instance, the borrower would remain in possession.[51] As we shall see, a form of chattel mortgage with essentially similar characteristics would develop as the bill of sale. The lesser rights of possession—the interests held by warehousemen, factors, repairers, carriers, pawn-brokers and others—had come to be grouped as bailments, each being fleshed out with detailed rules embodying the intention behind the particular transaction.[52] Thus the pledge granted to a pawnbroker gave him the right to retain the goods until he was repaid as agreed and to sell up if he was not paid. A granting of credit, sometimes by the bailor, sometimes by the bailee, was a likely part of many other bailments and some form of preferential treatment was generally sought as a condition. In recognition of this desire on the part of the creditor, trade practice came to justify what was often accorded the status of a lien.

---

[50] Witness the considerable variety of transactions that would rank as bills of sale: below, pp. 240–241.
[51] Above, p. 74.
[52] The generalisation of bailment law received particular stimulus from *Coggs v. Bernard* (1703) 2 Ld. Raym. 909 (Lord Holt on the duties of care of different types of bailee); and from Sir William Jones' scholarly *Essay on the Law of Bailments* (1781).

At common law, a lien was generally the right to retain possession of an object until due payment was made, but not to sell it off.[53] The repairer, carrier, innkeeper and factor, each came to have a common law lien for his services; the vendor of goods a lien for their price.[54]

But where goods were to be moved over long distances, the problem was to provide protected credit during the course of their transit. A producer or distributor with goods on his hands might be willing enough to accept payment at a later date. The growing range of negotiable instruments had helped to facilitate this financing. But he needed more, and in seventeenth century bankruptcy law an extension of the lien concept had given him the right to stop goods while still in transit to the buyer.[55]

On the other hand, the production of goods might be stimulated by an advance of finance, as where the goods were to be made abroad to the order of a British merchant, given perhaps by his local factor. The merchant might in turn sell them for an advance to a consignee, so beginning a passage down a commercial chain in the home market. Here the need was for a title or secured interest in advance of actual possession.[56] Yet the common law courts were reluctant to depart from their basic premise that only a person with sufficient title or authority could grant a secured interest in property. In 1823, Parliament was persuaded to intervene.[57] Factors would be taken to have the authority with which they were apparently clothed by being in possession (say) of the bill of lading or warehouseman's warrant for goods.[58] A series of Factors Acts thereafter added further limits on the ability of a principal secretly to restrict his agent's authority.[59] As we shall see, it was a progression that would come to disturb not only mercantile credit, but also consumer credit in the form of hire-purchase.[60]

However, before we reach that relatively modern phenomenon, we must contrast the development of two widespread practices—pawnbroking and money-lending upon bill of sale.

---

[53] Equity adopted the term for a different institution—a charge over property which did not depend upon possession and allowed sale in order to realize the interest: see generally Holdsworth, VII pp. 511–513.

[54] Equally the vendor of land who had not been paid the full purchase price had acquired a charge over the land for the balance owing.

[55] Holdsworth, VIII p. 243.

[56] The oldest exception to *nemo dat quod non habet* at common law had covered sales in market overt. By the nineteenth century, however, such simple protection was of little relevance to the mercantile community, and there were recommendations to remove it (*e.g.* Mercantile Law Commission, Second Report, P.P. 1854–1855 [1977] XVIII at p. 6; and P.P. 1893–1894 (374) XV at p. 11.) But it survived and was codified in the Sales of Goods Act 1893, s.22.

[57] A Select Committee of the Commons rehearsed the dissatisfaction and alarm of the mercantile community at the common law's requirement to investigate the true title to goods in the course of trade: P.P. 1823 (452) IV.

[58] 4 Geo. IV, c. 84; 6 Geo. IV, c. 94. The Acts partly confirmed common law notions of agency by estoppel; even so they were restrictively interpreted, making later statutory intervention necessary.

[59] 5 & 6 Vict., c. 39; Factors Acts, 1877 and 1889; see generally, Holdsworth, XIII pp. 379–384, XV pp. 93–94.

[60] Below, pp. 243–244.

(a) Pawnbroking

Pawnshops—and their even dingier relations, the "dolly-shops"— were institutions of crucial significance to lower-class life in the growing towns. By 1860, in Liverpool alone, there were said to be nearly 10 million pawn transactions a year. The articles pawned ranged from quite valuable furniture and jewellery to extremely humble clothing and bedding. Sunday best might be put in from Monday to pay-day. Laundresses might pawn each day's washload in order to redeem the previous day's, so that it could be laundered and returned.[61] The pawnbroker provided a regular recourse that could keep tottering domestic economies from total collapse. An essentially urban phenomenon, pawning was already receiving attention from municipal authorities in Tudor times. While there would thereafter be a growing body of regulation, public and charitable institutions to lend by pawn did not take hold to the extent that occurred in some European cities.[62] The English trade was private and ran from the respectable to the extremely seedy.

By the end of the eighteenth century, the regime of "police" covering pawnbrokers was given over to the justices of the peace. It was not a control which would develop nineteenth-century attributes, such as a special inspectorate or central supervision; but equally it was never suppressed, despite all the demands for the trade to enjoy the freedom of other moneylenders and traders. Perhaps because it runs so counter to the Diceyian picture of laissez-faire, pawnbroking has until recently received no adequate history.[63] Yet its prevalence means that it cannot be dismissed an an unrepresentative quirk.

Initially, interference had sprung from the self-interest of the propertied, for the pawnshop was an obvious place for the dishonest servant or petty thief to raise something on what he or she had taken. To this end, pawnbrokers were forbidden to take military items and property of the poor law authorities as pledges; they were obliged to keep proper books of their transactions; and in 1785 they were required to register.[64] But other objectives grew out of this first impetus, more apparently concerned with the lot of the borrower. Pawnbrokers were required to keep unredeemed pledges for a considerable period, to sell them (in many cases) at public auction and to keep any surplus over the sum due for payment back to the borrower.[65]

Above all, rates of interest had come to be controlled by special rules. The 5 per cent. limit of the usury laws was lifted in 1757 but in 1784 loans up to £10 were confined to $\frac{1}{2}$d per 2s. 6d per month

[61] Much social information about the practice and significance of pawning can now be found in Hudson (1982), esp. Chaps. 3–6; Tebbutt (1983) Chaps. 1–4; J. H. Treble, *Poverty and the Urban Labour Market* (1979), pp. 130–139.

[62] The Charitable Corporation, founded in 1707, was intended for such a role, but after years of mismanagement it collapsed in 1731; see (1742) 3 Atk. 400.

[63] But see now the books referred to in n. 61 above.

[64] Their annual licence fee was set at £10 in London and Edinburgh, £5 elsewhere: 25 Geo. III, c. 48, s.1.

[65] See 24 Geo. III (ii), c. 42, ss.6, 7. For loans above 2s. the pawnbroker was required to give a duplicate ticket recording the details: ss.3–5. For very small loans, this ticket could not be the subject of a separate charge until 1860: 23 & 24 Vict., c. 21.

(equivalent to 20 per cent. per annum if the full amount were lent for the full period—otherwise more)[66]; in 1796 this was reduced to 15 per cent. for loans of £2 to £10.[67] It was said in justification that juries had become prone to award only a very low amount of interest on moneylender loans, marking their abhorrence of the extortionate terms.

This was an attempt to define a reasonable maximum. A consolidating measure of 1800[68] set a legal frame that would survive the advances of economic liberalism in the money market, and in particular the abandonment of the usury laws in 1854. Its effect was undoubtedly patchy, for in the poorest districts there were thousands of pawnbrokers who did not even register, let alone conform to the law's conditions.[69] Only if a private informer, incited by the prospect of sharing in the fine, took action would anything happen.[70] This would contribute, as in so many businesses and professions, to a growing gulf between the respectable top—discreet lenders to the middle classes in times of hardship—and the unscrupulous bottom. When eventually there was a campaign to lift the system of regulation, it was the best-established pawnbrokers who promoted the case for greater freedom in substantial transactions, but greater supervision for the small.[71] Here as elsewhere, competitors were ready to espouse the cause of consumer protection to their own ends.[72] An act of 1872—essentially the law until 1974—increased the permissible rates to equivalents of 25 per cent. per annum for loans up to £2; and 20 per cent. for £2–10, with exemption where a "special contract" procedure was followed.[73]

(b) Bills of Sale

A system of credit which was generous in its allowable forms of security came under proportionate pressure to provide some means by which each new creditor could inform himself about the preferences already given by his debtor. The idea of a specified form of notice had a strong appeal in a world so taken with self-reliance. The issue grew in significance with the practice of organising a chattel mortgage in the form of a bill of sale—a transaction in which (typically) money was lent on goods by assigning title in them to the

---

[6] If the ½d. was charged on 3d. lent for a week, the rate of interest was over 800 per cent. per annum.

[67] 24 Geo. III (ii), c. 42, s.1; 36 Geo. III, c. 87.

[68] 39 & 40 Geo. III, c. 99. The prevous Acts had been temporary.

[69] Tebbutt (1983), p. 127. In 1856 an Act against "dollyshops" somewhat increased the level of registration (19 & 20 Vict., c. 27).

[70] This happened from time to time and might well be used by the trade to snuff out a newcomer. Magistrates were given power to reduce the statutory penalty payable to informers whose conduct they disapproved of, first in London (2 & 3 Vict., ss.32–35); and then, after a bad case in Staffordshire, generally (22 & 23 Vict., c. 14).

[71] See Tebbutt (1983), pp. 126–130; the phenomenon was by no means novel: leading pawnbrokers were behind the efforts in the 1740s which led eventually to the Act of 1757; Hudson (1982), p. 35.

[72] See Select Committee on Pawbrokers P.P. 1871 (419) XII; A. L. Minkes (1953) 20 Economica (N.S.) 10.

[73] Pawnbrokers Act 1872, ss.10, 31, Sched. 4.

lender while leaving them in the possession of the borrower.[74] Such an arrangement was inherently likely to mislead third parties, though in the bankruptcy of a trader-borrower the lender was likely to find that the assets in question were treated as in the former's reputed ownership and so part of his estate.[75] In 1854, just as the credit market was being freed of the last fetters against usury, bills of sale were required, in order to affect third parties, to be registered with the Court of Queen's Bench: if they were, the goods were good against execution creditors, save to the extent that the goods were not actually seized in distress (e.g. by a landlord for rent) or brought into bankruptcy under the reputed ownership provision.[76]

This manifestation of the notice principle, typical of its time, established a certain balance among the different categories of creditor which lasted for a quarter-century. But in 1878 it was upset: in the course of revising and expanding the bills of sale legislation, goods covered by a duly registered bill were excluded from the reputed ownership rule in the bankruptcy of a trader.[77] This significant readjustment produced unexpected consequences. Previously, moneylenders had chosen not to register many of their bills of sale—because of the inconvenience and expense, but even more because the publicity might provoke doubts about the debtor's solvency and a rush to get at his assets. Bills of sale were considered last-ditch resorts adding to likely ruin by their own harsh terms. Once there was a distinct advantage in bankruptcy for a registered bill, not only were more traders' bills registered, but a much higher proportion of small loans began to be similarly treated, even though they would not benefit in the same way.[78] This in turn provoked an outcry against the "Shylockian propensities" of moneylenders (which had not changed) and the march that they were now able to steal (which had, to some extent). From many quarters—the trading community, and professionals like county court judges, solicitors and accountants—there were proposals to make lending on bills of sale much less easy to effect: the fraudulent debtor should be prevented from deploying fictitious bills to hide away his property; the bona fide debtor should be stopped from signing a moneylender's bill when he ought to be submitting to bankruptcy; the trader should be prevented from making a hostage of all his means by signing a floating bill over whatever assets (including stock and plant) he held from time to time.[79] Atiyah has seen in this upsurge of protest, and the restrictive

[74] In this, the bill of sale followed the technique of the common law mortgage of land: see above, pp. 127–128. But with land, the documents of title formed the basis of conveyancing practice which served to reduce (if certainly not to eliminate) the likelihood of an innocent purchaser acquiring title without knowledge of a prior mortgage. With chattels the matter was even less secure.
[75] See above, p. 231. Trade practice would determine the circumstances in which a trader was taken to have reputed ownership of things that were not his.
[76] 17 & 18 Vict., c. 36. For the priority of the bankruptcy rule, see ex p. Harding (1873) L.R. 15 Eq. 223; F. C. J. Millar and J. R. Collier, Bills of Sale (2nd ed. 1860), pp. 181–216.
[77] Bills of Sale Act 1878, ss.8, 20.
[78] Registrations in 1875, 11,814 for £2,123,000; in 1880, 56,828 for £4,333,000.
[79] See Evidence to the Select Committee on the Bills of Sale Act (1878) Amendments Bill, P.P. 1881 (341) VIII (some from moneylenders); and the Circulars to County Court Judges, P.P. 1881 [C. 2859] LXXVI.

Act of 1882 which followed, a novel, neo-liberal concern for the plight of the consumer.[80] Certainly there was a deal of talk about those too foolish or too desperate to be able to organise their affairs adequately under the regime of "free" choice. But this was scarcely new: it belongs to that line of paternalism which had never allowed money-lending by pawnbrokers to be deregulated and which had continued, through the courts of equity, to supervise credit and other transactions against unfairness.

The interest which was strong enough to procure legislative reaction was that of creditors, not borrowers. The Act of 1878 did not stimulate lending on bills of sale so much as registration of bills. Its partial enhancement of the moneylenders' position touched a highly sensitive commercial nerve. Landlords and trade creditors felt that their positions were being undermined and there was much talk of fraudulent preferences and debtors' others tricks. The Act of 1882 was, indeed a severe piece of regulatory machinery. Failure to comply strictly with its formalities and registration procedure in many cases rendered the loan itself void[81]; and floating charges were effective only if a cumbersome procedure of listing the assets was followed.[82] The bill of sale in consequence lost its commercial attraction, at least in dealings with individuals.[83] Lending could be organized in other ways, though doubtless at some price. Parliament, in a confused upsurge of feeling against a traditional enemy of the respectable, was willing to accept this consequence. Indeed by letting in the extreme sanction of non-recovery of the debt itself, it laid the crucial precedent for the legislation which in 1900 would constrain moneylenders *eo nomine*.[84]

(c) Hire purchase

There were other transactions, none too distant from bills of sale, which were coming to play an increasing role in the provision of both trade stock and domestic goods. The instalment credit transaction, which in the latter nineteenth century became "hire-purchase," had antecedents in the 1840s. Symbols of domestic gentility, such as pianos, began to be offered on terms that the purchaser would pay by instalment and would take the goods on hire until he had completed. It was used from the 1860s by mining companies to acquire rolling stock.[85] This became the great sales device of the Singer company for its sewing machines, both to domestic and to trade buyers.[86]

---

[80] Atiyah (1979), pp. 708–713.
[81] Courts could, however, strive to escape this draconian result: see *Davies* v. *Rees* (1886) 17 Q.B.D. 408. The Act required the lender to give five days notice of his intention to remove or sell the goods (s.13), a provision which might well leave the advantage with a landlord or judgment creditor.
[82] Ss.5, 6, 9.
[83] Loans to "incorporated companies" were explicitly excluded: s.17; see below, p. 262.
[84] See above. pp. 223–224.
[85] For the early uses of hire purchase in Britain, R. Harris *et al*, *Hire Purchase in a Free Society* (1961), pp. 19–23.
[86] Thus bringing American practice to Britain: R. A. Lynn (1957) 31 Bus. Hist. R. 414.

Independent financial intermediaries made an early appearance on the scene, buying from the original seller and re-selling to the original purchaser on hire-purchase terms, essentially in the manner of the modern finance house. Sales by instalment became another outlet for the lender of money; one, moreover, that provided a reasonably secure form of priority over the goods, but which could be on such terms as the two sides "agreed." There were often long and complex standard forms, which could subject a defaulting purchaser to immediate re-seizure, loss of everything so far paid and even the liability to pay further "compensation."

The typical hire-purchase differed from moneylending upon bill of sale in one vital particular: the goods forming the security would initially be owned by the vendor, not the borrower of the money. It was of course possible to dress up money borrowing as hire-purchase of goods by having the borrower first transfer his own goods to the lender (the amount lent being the price), in order to buy them back by instalments which reflected the repayments on the loan.[87] But apart from devices such as this, the courts proved willing to hold that hire-purchase fell outside the constraints of the Bills of Sales Acts,[88] and the transaction flourished without even such safeguards as obligatory formalities or registration of the creditor's interest.

The serious threat to the financier's position came from another quarter. In 1889 the Factors Acts, as well as being consolidated, were extended in a vital particular. A person who had bought or agreed to buy goods could, if he were put in possession of them before becoming their owner, transfer a title good against the seller to his own purchaser or pledgee, if the latter acted in good faith.[89] Arguably, the person who took goods on hire-purchase had "agreed to buy" them and could therefore give a good title even if he resold before completing his instalments. If he could, the vendor's or financier's security would be in jeopardy. The Court of Appeal indeed held this to be so, if the person taking the goods was under an obligation to buy them on paying the last hire instalment.[90] But two years later, the House of Lords was persuaded that, provided that there was no obligation to buy the goods but only an option to do so, the hire-purchaser had not "agreed to buy." It would, however, be a strange case where he would not do so, after paying all the instalments.[91] But for this benign casuistry, legislative correction would doubtless have been sought, since instalment selling was a rapidly developing practice;

---

[87] For the case-law attempting to settle which transactions remain caught by the Bills of Sale Acts, see H. G. Hanbury and H. Waldock, *Law of Mortgages* (1st ed., 1938), Chap. 7.

[88] See esp. *McEntire* v. *Crossley* [1895] A.C. 457.

[89] s.9—subsequently Sale of Goods Act 1893, s.25(2). It replaced a provision of 1877 which operated only when the buyer in possession had documents of title; this normally applied only to a trade sale.

[90] *Lee* v. *Butler* [1895] 2 Q.B. 318.

[91] *Helby* v. *Matthews* [1895] A.C. 471, where the option was found in the hirer's entitlement at any time to end the hiring, though this did not in the particular case have onerous financial consequences (as later became common).

but it might have been obtained only with a measure of limitation on the most aggressive tactics.[92]

The first great age of hire-purchase really began with the motor-car, and was later augmented by the growth of a wide range of expensive household goods, many of them electrical. Instalment credit put these things within reach of lower middle-class and upper working-class households; and it proved a real incentive to industrial and agricultural investment. The pattern of hire-purchasing arrangements did not change much from that settled by 1895. The finance companies involved were either subsidiaries of manufacturers or independent institutions. The banks, however, mostly remained aloof. The middle-classes still derided the "never-never," however much they might resort to it on the quiet. The largest finance house of the inter-war period, the United Dominions Trust, was sponsored from New York. It became so important that at the beginning of the depression in 1929, the Governor of the Bank of England found it expedient to recognise its value in maintaining demand and therefore jobs, by purchasing £500,000 preference shares.[93] This growth of respectability out of dependence helps to explain why hire-purchase came to be accepted by courts and legislature.

Pawnbrokers and moneylenders had fallen under the increasing suspicion of post-1867 Parliaments, but those who financed "ordinary" hire-purchase were left without any obligation to obtain a licence or to put their dealings into a given form, or to keep them open for inspection. Nor were they obliged to register their interest in order to secure priority against other creditors. Innocent consumers who had little or no idea of their obligations had no chance to withdraw once the agreement was signed; nor could they resist forfeiture clauses which permitted instant re-possession even when most of the price had been paid and the goods retained a substantial proportion of their initial value.[94] In the inter-war years the most oppressive cases frequently concerned door-to-door salesmen, who were themselves squeezing a living from their slender commissions on sales.[95] Apart from deceptions over price, terms and the quality of goods, a common fraud was to lead the purchaser into thinking that he or she was taking the goods on temporary approval when in fact a binding hire-purchase agreement was being signed. Physical violence was often used to extract payment of the instalments, finance companies or their collecting agents employing "bruisers" for the purpose. The "snatch-back" was more in evidence than ever, some lenders deliberately encouraging default at a late stage. It was common to link successive agreements for different goods together so

---

[92] A 1912 bill to reverse *Helby* v. *Matthews*, so far as innocent purchasers of the goods were concerned, made no progress.

[93] Harris *et al* (above, n. 85), p. 29.

[94] *Cramer* v. *Giles* (1883) 1 Cab. & El. 151, (affd. 1884) was just such a case. It well illustrated the process by which equity was sapped of vitality, particularly after the Judicature Acts. In the Court of Appeal, Fry L.J. (continuing a train of thought set up by Lord Eldon—see above, p. 218) held it an inappropriate case for equitable relief allowing more time to pay, since it concerned chattel hire and not the lease of land.

[95] They were a new variety of the itinerant packmen and tally-men who had long made good business out of working-class women: see above, p. 230.

that default in respect of any one of them gave the right to foreclose on all.[96] One MP estimated that there were "on average 600 seizures a day due to arrears of payment."[97]

The corrective Act of 1938 contained protection only for small transactions,[98] but for these it made significant inroads into the freedom of finance companies to impose whatever terms suited them best.[99] The hirer had to sign the contract and be given a copy of it, which had to set out the essential terms of the transaction, such as the retail cash price, the hire purchase price, and the terms for repayment; otherwise it could not be enforced.[1] The implied terms by which the owner guaranteed good title, fitness for purpose and merchantability could not be eliminated by an express term to the contrary.[2] The Act also limited "snatch backs." If the hirer had paid one-third of the hire-purchase price and did not voluntarily terminate the agreement, the owner had to obtain an order from a county court giving repossession and the judge was invested with a wide power instead to order that the outstanding sums be paid off on fair terms.[3] The hirer who chose to terminate—trying perhaps to do the right thing after losing a job or some other misfortune—had to pay half the hire-purchase price (but not more) if the agreement so provided.[4] This could operate harshly but the courts were not empowered to intervene where this produced an evident profit for the finance organisation.[5] The War taught governments a different lesson. The urgent need to stop profiteering required not only price controls but controls on the amount and rate of credit. From this detailed legislation, which was to last until 1958,[6] it was appreciated that the amount lent could be curtailed by prescribing a minimum deposit and a maximum period for repayments. Such tactics would become a major form of manipulation, as post-war governments turned to

---

[96] P.D. 1937–1938 CCCXXX 729–770.

[97] J. R. Leslie, *ibid.*, p. 740.

[98] The original monetary limit on the "hire purchase price" was £100 (£500 for livestock, but only £50 for motor vehicles and rolling stock). These would be raised on a number of occasions, starting in 1954.

[99] A Working Party chaired by Dr. Morgan, Warden of Toynbee Hall in the East End of London, drew representatives of the finance houses into the process of formulating detailed proposals. Social workers and county court judges were among those lending influential support to the measure. In the course of the Bill, when its sponsor, Ellen Wilkinson, sought amendments going beyond the concordat with commercial interests, she was publicly rebuked by the Acting President of the Hire-Purchase Trade Association: see J. J. MacManus (1978) 5 Br.J. Law and Soc. 185.

[1] Hire Purchase Act 1938, ss.2, 6.

[2] s.8.

[3] ss.11, 12.

[4] s.4.

[5] Before the Act, and for the many cases outside its financial limits, there was no effective control over the minimum part of the price which could be demanded, either for breach or upon termination permitted by the agreement. The weakening of equity's jurisdiction to give relief against penalties (see above, p. 224) meant that the judges upheld terms of this kind, treating them as genuine pre-estimates of damage: the leading case, *Roadways Transport Development* v. *Browne and Gray* (1927) Jones and Proudfoot, *Notes on Hire Purchase Law* 118 and other decisions are reviewed in *Cooden Engineering* v. *Stanford* [1953] 1 Q.B. 86, where, in the post-war atmosphere, they were reversed.

[6] Goods and Services (Price Control) Act 1941 and the various orders made under it. Minimum deposit requirements and other controls were to be reintroduced in 1960.

Keynesian regulation by stoking and damping demand: and so widespread would hire-purchase for a time become that it was primarily to this form of transaction that the "stop-go" controls would be applied.

Through most of our period, legal regulation was imposed upon credit when money was borrowed, but not when goods or services were supplied against later payment. The social experience of the two forms of credit had been essentially different. Hire-purchase fell between the two stools, since it was a method of purchasing goods in which a charge for the time value of money was built into the price. When eventually it was accepted that there must be control of rapacious hire-purchase financiers in the interests of ignorant and gullible buyers, it had to take the form of statutory intervention, for the constriction on notions of good faith in the general law of contract left the judges without power or inclination to act by themselves.[7] The 1938 Act had the advantage of being carefully thought through and so was able to define with some clarity the circumstances which would constitute unfair practice.[8] It was undoubtedly a signal that "consumerism" was acquiring a distinct voice, which in the postwar period, would be raised to demand legal regulation as a guarantee of basic fairness in general trading. However it was little heard until the economic recovery that foreshadowed further war. And that is one further measure of the sway of free bargaining ideals among those who for so long dominated the processes of essential trade and commerce.

PART 3: THE LIMITED LIABILITY COMPANY

I. Evolution of the Joint Stock Company

The business corporation of modern times acquired its essential attributes in the mid-Victorian years, in a form which was claimed peculiarly to embrace the virtues of *laissez-faire*. The result was a legal skeleton on which the flesh of big business organisation could be engrafted: not only could the registered company with limited liability determine the capital structure of an enterprise, but it could provide the authority to whom managerial responsibility was owed and the entity which would deal with the outside world and would employ staff and labour. At the same time it would furnish smaller, essentially private, business with a protective shell against full personal liability. The corporate form would in the twentieth century become usual and acceptable at all points on the scale of business size; indeed it would provide a model for the organisation of state enterprise, with the public corporations that were established to run the nationalised industries after the second world war.[9]

For much of the nineteenth century, however, corporate form was an object of suspicion—a likely means of deception, a creature of

---

[7] See, *e.g.*, the instance in n. 94 above.
[8] Even the revisions of 1965 built upon its foundations.
[9] See below, pp. 274–275; and Gower (1979) 63–66.

wild and evanescent schemes, the antithesis of the solid and respectable. The legal developments of 1855–1862 were accordingly the outcome of a long, slow evolution against which there had been sustained resistance. Adam Smith had not seen the joint stock company with limited liability as a natural or necessary part of flourishing capitalist markets. On the contrary, the formula allowed the investor to lay out his money for management by others, who would all too readily use it negligently and profusely.[10] To Smith, as to many of like mind, full personal responsibility was a precondition of the proper functioning of a free economy, the duty of the legal system being to enforce that responsibility, not to provide machinery for securing exemption from it.

Yet eventually the corporate form became available as of right because of three insistent pressures. First there was the need to amass large amounts of capital for some extensive projects, notably for the transport systems of canal and rail and for financing through banks and insurance. Indeed, Smith had recognised such cases as legitimate and, with his usual pragmatism, had approved of their organisation by joint stock companies because, he said, their management could be reduced to strict rule.[11] Secondly, there was the ever-bubbling desire to live by financial gambling, which could be all too easily accommodated by markets in stocks and shares. The raising of government loans through Bank of England stock[12] had fostered these prospects to such an extent that, by the beginning of the nineteenth century, the London Stock Exchange could be formed as a regularising institution, with its own rules and procedures for buying and selling against future values.[13]

Thirdly, there was the desire to be able to risk capital without exposing entire personal fortunes. Other procedures helped in this sort of conservation. As we have seen, the strict settlement of land prevented the incumbent head of the family from risking all its value in any generation[14]; lending transactions did not carry with them responsibility for the failure of the borrower's enterprise (unless, at least, the creditor chose to take a share of profits as the measure of interest[15]); bankruptcy was coming to provide a means by which honest debtors could wipe their slate of indebtedness clean for the future.[16] The joint stock enterprise, however, seemed capable of far simpler and more flexible application to this same end, if only it could be made to carry limitations of liability that would be good against outside creditors.

---

[10] *Wealth of Nations* (1976 ed.) pp. 733–758.

[11] *Ibid.*, pp. 756–758.

[12] See generally, E. V. Morgan and W. A. Thomas, *The Stock Exchange* (1962), Chap. 3; for the use of lotteries to attract investors in the period 1720–1784, p. 45.

[13] There had been an attempt to forbid forms of gambling on future prices as illegal stock-jobbing under Barnard's Act 1733, 7 Geo. II, c. 18. The Stock Exchange would come to regulate time bargains under the "contango" system: a purchaser or seller who wished to hold off completion from one accounting period to the next could do so on payment of a rate which varied with the number of similar cases: Morgan and Thomas (above n. 12), pp. 59–64, 147–151.

[14] See above, p. 128ff.

[15] See below, p. 256.

[16] See above, p. 232ff.

The idea of conferring legal personality upon an entity distinct from human individuals had medieval roots.[17] The corporation sole had been the means for holding and organising the property of public and ecclesiastical offices through a perpetual succession of incumbents—the Crown, bishoprics, benefices. The corporation aggregate had given similar structure to boroughs, institutions of learning and guilds of merchants. Once the idea was turned to commercial organisation its functions began to grow. Guilds regulated trade in myriad ways and could provide an outlet through which goods were required to be distributed. The same variety of purpose became manifest when incorporation was granted to the foreign trading companies of the early modern period—the Levant and Russia Companies (1551, 1553), the East India Company (1612) and numerous others. Politically these companies strove for friendly relations with local tribes and leaders; economically they set up trading posts and colonies, and provided mutual protection against pirates and hostile natives, as well as keeping out interlopers, British or foreign. Eventually they might set up trading ventures, for particular occasions or over time, rather than leave the risk-taking entirely to individuals. At this juncture they became true precursors of the modern trading company.

This experience affirmed that corporate personality could be acquired only by grant—by Crown charter or Act of Parliament. Some of the legal relationships between the corporation and those who acted in its name would be defined in the authorising document; others came to be determined by rules of common law. By the end of the eighteenth century, the law of corporations was the law governing such bodies, internally and in relation to the outside world. Its thrust was public rather than private and its concern as much with exclusive privilege as with joint responsibility.[18] Until the late seventeenth century, however, joint ventures in domestic trade rarely used the corporate form. In the middle ages the common law had come to accept the form of partnership known to Roman law as *societas*, in which each partner shared profits and losses in proportion to his agreed or contributed share, but without any limitation of personal liability to outsiders. The form, *commenda*, in which managing partners bore full personal responsibility, but "sleeping" contributors of capital were liable only in the amount of their contribution, did not take lasting root in England; indeed its central conception would be resisted long after other trading states began to give it modern form.[19]

The English version of *societas* continued to be used, because it was the legal formula available to meet an ever-growing demand. But it became beset by problems of enforcement. In actions by or against the partnership, either at common law or in equity, all the partners

---

[17] See generally Holdsworth, VIII pp. 192–222; W. R. Scott, *Joint Stock Companies to 1720* (1909), I Chap. 1.

[18] Thus S. Kyd's *Law of Corporations* (1794) is largely concerned with borough corporations and similar bodies. Adam Smith's account of trading corporations (above n. 10) gives most prominence to those with monopoly privileges. A good instance was that of marine assurance: see below, n. 22.

[19] See below, pp. 253–254.

had to be joined; and error meant that proceedings must begin afresh. Disputes between partners (which went mainly to Chancery because that court had procedures for taking accounts) could often be resolved only upon a dissolution of the partnership—a rule which gave a disgruntled partner considerable bargaining power.[20] The lack of a readily defined, unchanging entity which could contract, own property, sue and be sued, could mean that a joint venture would not command business confidence, quite apart from the question of individual responsibility. The notion of joint stock in a corporation accordingly seemed to answer a range of legal difficulties that stood as barriers to commercial viability.

However, against the ready development of any such idea stood the spectre of the South Sea Bubble.[21] At the end of the seventeenth century—particularly after the formation of the Bank of England in 1694—private ventures had begun to raise capital by offering joint stock to subscribers. Mostly they did so under Crown charter, though they might well be departing from the original purpose of the grant, and in some cases the claimed charter did not exist. Combining this new attraction with older ideas of foreign trading monopoly, the South Sea Company had proposed a grandiose scheme for securing the trade with South America and beyond from the government, partly for cash and partly by taking over almost the entire national debt. In 1720 all sight of the viability of the proposal was lost in hectic trade in the Company's shares, and equally in other joint stock. The bubble was soon enough pricked, leaving the government in disgrace for its embroilment, some major investors ruined and many leading families ensnared in long-term debt. The fearsome capacity of joint stock to stoke the speculative instinct had all too soon built an unmanageable head of steam.

It was an event that would remain in the collective memory of the ruling class for generations, lending support, for instance, to Adam Smith's views on the matter. The Crown remained most reluctant to grant new charters, Parliament rarely passed private bills of incorporation. In terms of general law, 1720 left on the statute book the Bubble Act.[22] Enacted as the share market was still accellerating, and designed to protect the South Sea venture from the indiscriminate offers of other stock, it sought to strike hard and wide. It rendered a number of acts indictable as public nuisances, the subject of treble damages and even of praemunire[23]: acting as a corporate body; raising transferable stock or transferring such stock without the authority of Parliament or a charter; and acting or claiming to act under an obsolete charter.[24]

---

20 See below, n. 27.
21 The classic account is W. R. Scott, (above, n. 17) Chaps. 20, 21; see also Cooke (1950), pp. 80–83; L. C. B. Gower (1952) 68 L.Q.R. 214.
22 6 Geo. I, c. 18, s.18 ff. The first part of the Act, however, granted exclusive corporate privileges in marine insurance to the Royal Exchange and London Assurance Companies: see G. Clayton, *British Insurance* (1971), pp. 53–54.
23 In principle, this ancient penalty could lead to forfeiture of life and goods.
24 Holdsworth, VIII pp. 219–220, in an acute attack of hindsight, blames Parliament for constraining what should have been made freely available.

A few traces remain of actual enforcement of the Act in the 1720s, but in succeeding decades it was left as a passive admonition.[25] Since the public authorities would rarely sanction joint stock, the lawyers met an irrepressible demand with a device—the "deed of settlement" company—which crossed the concept of partnership with that of trust. As their experiments evolved into a standard type, the formation document—the deed of settlement—came to provide for membership of the company to be divided into subscribers' shares, for the assets to be vested in trustees and for the management of the business to be by a body of directors. The shareholders subscribed the deed and so became partners, with such rights to terminate their interest and transfer the shares as the deed might prescribe. The structure was not without its inherent difficulties. The trustees, as legal owners, could sue and be sued in some matters of property.[26] But many other questions, including those of internal financial arrangement, were at the mercy of a restrictive partnership law that resisted adaptation to the new type of venture. In particular, all the subscribers, as partners, might have to be joined in any suit and served with copies of the papers.[27]

Moreover, the closer the draftsman of the deed came to specifying that the shares were to be transferable, that rights and liabilities were to end with such a transfer, or that liability was to be limited to the nominal value of the shares, the more he approached the forbidden territory of the Bubble Act. Certainly in the decades after 1720, there was thought to be particular danger in providing for transferability. But as the century wore on, and joint stock was used for mining ventures, overseas trade, non-marine insurance and canals, a modus vivendi emerged which was reflected in the practice of the Law Officers. They advised against petitions to the Crown for charters on the ground that voluntary "partnerships" were an adequate form. Accordingly, any question of their enforcing the Bubble Act receded. The difficulties that these joint stock associations faced in mounting litigation were mostly avoided by the standard resort of the business community—arbitration. It was this balance of competing demands and suspicions which Lord Eldon could still in 1825 reflect, when he remarked of deed-of-settlement companies: "they do not come into courts of justice; they act as a mutual understanding and a kind of moral rule; and I believe that, in that way they manage their affairs very well."[28]

However much the conservative instinct may have been to leave companies to their own devices outside the legal order, by that time the question could no longer be so simply dismissed. Periodically,

---

[25] On the continuing influence of the Bubble Act over eighteenth-century practice, see Dubois (1938) Chaps. 1, 3.

[26] See, e.g., Metcalf v. Bruin (1810) 12 East 400.

[27] Lord Eldon would make this very plain in Van Sandau v. Moore (1826) 1 Russ. 441— an attempt by one of some 300 shareholders to have company dissolved on discovery that the deed of settlement differed from the prospectus; the plaintiff abandoned his action on being required to proceed against all the others and take copies of their answers.

[28] Ibid., p. 471.

short-lived "bull" markets in stock trading were beginning to recur. If not on the scale of 1720, they were frightening enough to politicians and to all who had a stake in the financial stability of the country. A first reminder of the effect had come in the mid-1790s and was repeated more forcibly a decade later and then in the mid-1820s. In 1806–1807, the war-time economy stimulated the sudden promotion of some forty companies, most of them flimsy, some downright fraudulent.[29] In the aftermath, the Bubble Act was revived for use against companies whose deeds of settlement provided for free transferability of shares and limited liability of shareholders. Lord Ellenborough led the judges in upholding this attack; he labelled the attempts at limited liability "a mischievous delusion to ensnare the unwary public."[30]

In 1824–25, in "a veritable avalanche of extravagant promotions and general speculation," some 624 companies were floated, many upon the promise that a statute or charter would be obtained; only 127 would survive to 1827, 74 of them in mining, gas and insurance.[31] Again the courts were to mark the agitated concern of those in authority. Abbott C.J. declared the Equitable Loan Bank to be illegal under the Bubble Act for providing transferable shares in its deed.[32] And Lord Eldon, after first threatening further legislation, lent all his authority to the view that already such formations were unlawful, both under the Bubble Act and (a novel addition) at common law.[33] The position that deed-of-settlement companies were to be ignored by the law, except occasionally when hectic stock dealing had to be suppressed, could scarcely be sustained. Ephemeral ventures in this form might be an easy catch for the gullible, but the company was also beginning to be used by more substantial concerns in the great expansion of industrial and commercial capital.[34] Despite the diatribes of Eldon and other judges, Peel and Huskisson listened to the City of London and saw to repeal of the obscure and absurdly severe Bubble Act, even before the 1825 session was out.[35]

---

[29] See Hunt (1938), pp. 14–16, 30–34, 60–61.

[30] *R. v. Dodd* (1808) 9 East 516, in which prosecution was left to the Attorney-General *ex officio*; then followed *Buck v. Buck* (1808) 1 Camp. 547; *R. v. Stratton* (1809) 1 Camp. 549n.; *R. v. Webb* (1811) 14 East 406; *cf. Brown v. Holt* (1812) 3 Taunt. 587; *Pratt v. Hutchinson* (1813) 15 East 510 (a building society); *Ellison v. Bignold* (1821) 2 J. & W. 503.

[31] H. English, *A Complete View of Joint Stock Companies Formed in 1824 and 1825* (1827).

[32] *Josephs v. Pebrer* (1825) 3 B. & C. 639: "every one must observe that the signs of the times require us to declare it without delay."

[33] P.D. 1825 XII 31, 127; *Van Sandau v. Moore* (above, n. 27); *Kinder v. Taylor* (1825) 3 L.J. Ch. 68 at 81; Hunt (1938), pp. 34, 38–40.

[34] The Rothschilds and Barings were using the boom very successfully to promote their Alliance Insurance companies: Hunt (1938), p. 32.

[35] 6 Geo. IV, c. 91. Occasionally judges would revert to Eldon's proposition that acting as a corporation was contrary to common law, particularly when the enterprise looked suspicious. Thus, Best C.J. (*Duvergier v. Fellows* (1828) 5 Bing. 248, 267—company evading restriction on number of assignees of an invention patent); and Shadwell V.C. (*Blundell v. Winsor* (1837) 8 Sim. 601—"imaginary" gold-mining venture). In less unsympathetic cases, the opposite view was espoused (Brougham L.C., *Walburn v. Ingilby* (1833) 1 My. & K. 61); and on the eve of Gladstone's general Act, this was accepted as the law: *Garrad v. Hardy* (1843) 5 M. & G. 471; *Harrison v. Heathorn* (1843) 6 M. & G. 81.

II. After the Repeal of the Bubble Act

Thus opened the second phase in the gradual shift of opinion towards incorporation with limited liability as of right, during which the contradictions of the preceding years would only intensify. Periods of speculative fever would recur, with their clouds of fly-by-night promotions: a first boom stimulated by railway investment came in 1834–1836, the great "Railway Mania" in 1845–1847. The question of joint stock was constantly in issue, the outcome anything but apparent. But there were a number of pointers.

First of all, there were signs that joint stock might be more regularly available through the channels of special statute or Crown charter. For more than a half-century a private Act had been in any case needed for ventures, such as canals, which would have to be equipped with powers of compulsory purchase, and this necessity was about to spread into railway promotions.[36] The large initial capital for all such enterprise made its own case for joint stock. But against this stood the argument that passing the bill (or equally, granting the Crown charter) would set an official imprimatur on a commercial risk. In 1825, Parliament was pressed from many quarters with private Bill promotions and the blockage brought to prominence one legal difficulty over the alternative of a charter: it was highly uncertain that the shareholders in a chartered corporation could be made to bear *any* personal responsibility for its liabilities.[37] In consequence, the Crown was given statutory authority to attach such responsibility to shareholding and indeed to determine whether there should be limits to personal liability.[38] But this proved to be only the first of a series of inducements to the Board of Trade (which exercised the Crown's power in the matter) to be more liberal, all of which were to have little effect, for "Adam Smith's ghost still stalked in Whitehall among the King's advisers."[39]

Secondly, the practical difficulties of a deed-of-settlement company in suing or being sued, raised by Lord Eldon to a form of art, could nevertheless be overcome, if the association were empowered to sue and be sued in the name of an officer. Eighteenth-century Parliaments had not been wholly adverse to this limited form of aid, if sought by means of a private bill, and had even given such a power to friendly societies which registered under the Act of 1793.[40] Parliament's next attempt after 1825 to encourage the Board of Trade had the grant of power to sue and be sued particularly in mind: in 1834,

---

[36] Dubois (1938), pp. 93–104 gives instances of private Act provisions imposing unlimited liability, limited liability and (by implication) no personal liability at all. By 1845, the statutory form had become so regularly employed that standard provisions were enacted in the Companies Clauses Act and Railway Clauses Act (8 & 9 Vict., cs. 16, 20).

[37] The Attorney-General took the view that there was no such liability: P.D. 1826 XIII 1020 (and see *Elve* v. *Boyton* [1891] 1 Ch. 501). The contrary view, espoused by a number of legal historians, has been exploded by D. Jenkins, *Skinning the Pantomime Horse* (1974).

[38] Limited liability was granted to the Nova Scotia Mining Company: Hunt (1938), pp. 58–59.

[39] Hunt (1938), pp. 57–58, *cf.* Cooke (1950), pp. 130–131.

[40] 33 Geo. III, c. 54, s.11; Dubois (1938), p. 231.

the Crown was authorised to grant by letters patent (rather than a full charter) "some of the privileges of and incident to corporations."[41] But, with this and a succeeding statute of similar nature,[42] the Board continued its cautious examination of the merits of each proposal for which special privileges were sought.[43]

Thirdly, there was the special case of banking. One survival of older monopoly ideas was the protection afforded to the Bank of England by the prohibition of banking partnerships of more than six people anywhere in England and Wales.[44] The wealthy private banks of the City of London had shown little interest in provincial business and small country banks had proliferated, many of them issuing their own banknotes. Their inability to build a capital base through partners or joint stock made them sensitive to financial frosts such as the ending of the 1825 boom.[45] A campaign mounted by Thomas Joplin of Newcastle, with Ricardo's support, insisted on the urgency of removing the legal fetter upon a fundamental financial activity. In 1826 banks operating more than sixty-five miles from London were allowed unlimited numbers of share-partners and were given the right to sue and be sued in the name of a public officer.[46] In 1833 Joplin secured an extension of the same right within the sixty-five mile radius to any bank which forswore the entitlement to issue its own notes.[47] Banking came, from a position of special constraint, to be the first field in which deed-of-settlement companies with particular advantages could be formed without official approval. It was a telling precedent.

Fourthly, came a resurgence of interest in the limited partnership idea. The old civilian conception of a *société en commandite*, in which active partners were personally responsible in full but investing partners were liable only to the extent of their agreed share, had been given modern form in France, the state of New York and elsewhere; a somewhat different version had even been granted for Ireland as early as 1782.[48] A report to the government by Bellenden Ker recounted the arguments of the banker, Francis Baring, and the economist, Nassau Senior, that industrial progress had been advanced in those places by this instrument of capital formation; but Ker found majority opinion still to be against and so refused to recommend changing the law.[49] At the same time, the judges were berated for failing to allow access to law against deed-of-settlement companies under existing partnership law: with the result that rash and fraudu-

---

[41] 4 & 5 Will. IV, c. 94.
[42] Will. IV & 1 Vict., c. 73 (1837)—the immediate product of Bellenden Ker's Report—for which, see below, n. 49. For an attempt to get through more general legislation in the following year—defeated by Brougham—see Hunt (1938), pp. 83–87.
[43] Cooke (1950), pp. 130–131.
[44] 6 Ann., c. 22, s.9.
[45] For their growth, see L. S. Pressnell, *Country Banking in the Industrial Revolution* (1956).
[46] 7 Geo. IV, c. 46. They had to make a return of members, thus anticipating the general scheme of 1844
[47] 3 & 4 Will. IV, c. 98; Hunt (1938), pp. 64–67; Cooke (1950), pp. 122–123.
[48] An article by John Austin (Parl. Hist. and Rev., 1825, 711) had done much to revive interest in the idea; and see Ker's Report (n. 49, below) for the comparisons.
[49] P.P. 1837 (530) LXIV, pp. 19–23.

lent promoters were in practice immune from redress. Ker's solution to this was a system of registration for large partnerships, which would carry with it the right to sue and be sued in the name of an officer. Failure to register would render the transfer of shares illegal.[50]

III. REGISTRATION AS OF RIGHT: 1844–1862

Ker's conclusions represented the balance of respectable opinion over the ensuing decade. Around 1840 an outcrop of scandals over insurance companies only served to enhance the case that deed-of-settlement partnerships must be brought within some framework of legal responsibility. The young Gladstone, as Peel's President of the Board of Trade, took up Ker's main proposal[51] and in 1844 secured crucial new legislation.[52] Partnerships of more than twenty-five members, insurance companies and insuring friendly societies, and partnerships with shares transferable without the consent of co-partners, were obliged to register with the Board of Trade.[53] No longer, however, was there to be any official assessment of the merits of the venture; registration was to act merely as a notification to the public. The market for joint stock investment would be liberated. Only the procedure of formation would be constrained by a two-stage process of notification, designed to give some warning about new promotions: a company seeking the initial capital for formation could secure "provisional registration," upon filing the prospectus, and the names of promoters and those of the "provisional committee." After the deed of settlement had actually been signed[54] and a copy filed with information about the objects, capital structure, directors, members and other matters, "complete registration" could be secured. Fraudulent promotions which got no further than relieving the first investors of their capital had certainly become an increasing nuisance. In the heated months of the "railway mania" they were to swarm, and it was soon apparent that two-stage registration did little to improve the judgment of those gambling on quick returns: a large proportion of the flotations never reached complete registration.[55]

The collapse of 1847–1848 imposed inordinate strain on the machinery for winding companies up. A registered company under the 1844 Act was still a partnership: a shareholder-partner was liable to be sued individually for "corporate" debts, since they were not

---

[50] *Ibid.*, pp. 4–19. He thought registration should apply to partnerships of more than fifteen.

[51] In 1843 he put some vigour into a Select Committee that had been in existence since 1841: P.P. 1844 (119) VII.

[52] 7 & 8 Vict., c. 110. In the same year Gladstone saw through Acts on railway regulation (c. 85), company winding up (c. 111—below, n. 57) and joint stock banks (c. 113); to be followed next year by the "clauses" Acts (above, n. 36).

[53] There were various exclusions: see Cooke (1950), pp. 136–137.

[54] It had to be signed by a quarter of the potential subscribers for at least a quarter of the shares.

[55] For a contemporary account, see D. Morier Evans, *The Commercial Crisis, 1847–48* (1848).

owed by a legally distinct *persona*.[56] The shareholder might in response seek an account in chancery, winding up the partnership in the hope of seeing the available assets used in satisfaction and a rateable call made on all the holders of stock for any deficit. Gladstone had improved matters with a separate Act in 1844 allowing creditors to issue a fiat in bankruptcy against the company itself; if assets could not meet liabilities, the Court of Bankruptcy would request the Court of Chancery to institute a call upon shareholders for the shortfall. Upon Chancery appointing a receiver for this purpose, shareholders would cease to be exposed to individual liability.[57] To this was added, in 1848, a procedure by which a shareholder who had reason to suppose that the company might be failing could institute winding up proceedings in Chancery; this could not lift his own liabilities to creditors, but it might stop them mounting further.[58] Such an interlacing of jurisdictions could only lead to complications and the insolvency of companies became as much prey to the hectic competition between creditors, the duplicity of those liable and the greed of administrators, as were individual bankruptcies. The danger to a shareholder of exposing his whole fortune to the predations of these processes was clearly a disincentive to taking deed-of-settlement stock.

Yet in Britain the economic case for limited liability was scarcely powerful. Other countries might be beginning to examine the potential of joint stock as a vehicle for industrial advancement. Britain had already outstripped them by businesses built upon individual capital—the profits of agriculture or other enterprise, straightforward borrowing (under mortgage or otherwise), the clubbing together of families or a few active partners. The process of growth had been relatively slow by comparison with what was about to happen in the United States and Germany and capital had rarely been in short supply for extended periods: low interest rates continued to predominate.[59]

A history which said much for the virtues of individual effort, yet also disclosed a growing social division between classes, produced one new element in the arguments about limited liability.[60] One strain of idealistic radicalism was directed, particularly by J. S. Mill and the Christian Socialist, Slaney, towards the need to link the technical resourcefulness of the working-class with middle-class capital—the ever-growing savings of the decently comfortable. The inventive machine-worker needed capital to develop his own ideas, the respectable investor needed limited liability if he were to join in this sort of venture, and a range of joint stock if he were to spread his

---

[56] An increasing number of companies were providing for limited liability in their deeds-of-settlement, to be arranged through the mechanism of contracts with outsiders. The Court of Chancery, however, in the end decided that only parties to such contracts could be affected by the limitation, in accordance with the notion of privity: *Greenwood's Case*, (1854) 3 De G.M. & G. 459 at 475.

[57] 7 & 8 Vict., c. 111, ss.10, 20; Cooke (1950), pp. 147–149.

[58] 11 & 12 Vict., c. 45.

[59] See P. Deane and W. A. Cole, *British Economic Growth 1688–1959* (2nd ed., 1978), Chap. 8.

[60] See J. Saville (1956) 7 Ec.Hist.R. (2d) 418; and generally for the next stage, Hunt (1938) Chap. 6; Cooke (1950), pp. 151–168, Jefferys (1977) Chap. 1.

risk.[61] Under the existing law, an investor could not even lend at interest varying with profits without being treated as a partner, thus becoming jointly liable for all debts and other amounts due from the business[62] and legislation to avoid this was one positive recommendation of a Select Committee on Partnership in 1852.[63]

Neither this Committee nor an ensuing Royal Commission on Mercantile Laws[64] could bring itself to accept that limited liability should change from being a privilege for a registered company into an entitlement. But the counter-argument was beginning to flow, and was given impetus by the dissenting opinion of Bramwell Q.C. and others on the Royal Commission.[65] A Commons debate then lent considerable support[66] and the Board of Trade took it up in preference to proposals for amending partnership law so as to restrict the liability of lenders.[67] It was a time, amid the anxieties of the Crimean war, when Palmerston's government wished to appear active, and Lord Stanley of Alderney claimed it to be a measure of "peculiar urgency."[68] It is hard to doubt that financial interests quietly pushed the government into its particular course on limited liability; not for nothing was the City in the 1850s, "Whig to a man."[69]

Certainly the legislation was of a piece with the abolition of the Usury Laws and the regulation of bills of sale in accordance with the principle of notice.[70] Public notification became a *leitmotif* of the new company legislation. In 1855 a short amendment to the Act of 1844 allowed shareholders' liability to be limited to calls for the unpaid portion of the nominal value of their shares, once complete registration of the deed of settlement was effected; the Lords, however, still insisted that at least twenty-five members holding at least £10 shares paid up to 20 per cent., should have subscribed for three-quarters of the nominal capital or more.[71]

Led by the assiduous arch-liberal, Robert Lowe, Vice-President of the Board of Trade, even such vestigial protections were purged in the following year, when provisional registration was eliminated, the number of incorporators was reduced to seven, and limited liability

---

[61] This was a principal theme of the Select Committee on Investments for the Savings of the Middle and Working Classes, P.P. 1850 (508) XIX; Hunt (1938) Chap. 6. The savings of working class collecting societies were further protected by the Industrial and Provident Societies Acts of 1852, 1854 and 1856. Building and friendly societies were already regulated.

[62] *Grace* v. *Smith* (1775) Black W. 997—the arrangement was accordingly held not to offend the Usury Laws.

[63] P.P. 1851 (509) XVIII.

[64] P.P. 1854 [1791] XXVII.

[65] *Ibid.*, pp. 23–29; there were four other dissents.

[66] See P.D. 1854 CXXXIV 752–800.

[67] Limited partnership bills were introduced in 1855 and 1856, but allowed to lapse. The joint stock company at the period was conceived to be about a "real" institution: see P. Ireland in J. N. Adams (ed.) *Essays for Clive Schmithoff* (1981), p. 29.

[68] See Cooke (1950), p. 156; and also for the hostility of the Manchester Chamber of Commerce, stirred mainly by John Bright. For other protests, legal and industrial, see Formoy (1923), pp. 120–122.

[69] See H. Perkin in J. Butt and I. F. Clark. *The Victorians and Social Protest* (1973), p. 208ff.

[70] See above, XXX, p. 241; 18 & 19 Vict., c. 133, s.1.

[71] The Lords' did not, however, insist upon a proposal that the nominal capital should be at least £50,000.

made available on whatever terms were specified in the memorandum and articles of the company filed on the public record.[72] Lowe was categorical:

> "The principle is the freedom of contract, and the right of unlimited association—the right of people to make what contracts they please on behalf of themselves, whether those contracts may appear to the Legislature beneficial or not, as long as they do not commit fraud, or otherwise act contrary to the general policy of the law . . ."[73]

The tide continued to run: joint stock banks were placed under the same essential regime in 1858[74] and insurance companies in 1862.[75] The Companies Act of that year gave the Victorian legislation a final form which would last with relatively minor modifications until 1948.[76]

IV. Deployment of Registered Companies

A quarter-century later, Lord Bramwell confirmed with pride that the legislation had been passed strictly without regard to the use that might be made of it.[77] Lowe even claimed that to build in protective devices would only lull investors to sleep, "depriving them of the safeguard which Providence intended for them, and helping fraudulent men to mislead and delude them."[78] As it was the promoters of ephemeral ventures continued to find the device of incorporation remarkably handy. Shannon estimated that between 1856 and 1865, 30–40 per cent. of the 5,420 registrations were entirely abortive and that over 60 per cent. had disappeared within ten years; McGregor found the proportion of abortive companies in 1880 still to be about a quarter.[79] In 1866 the new institution faced its first crisis. Overend Gurney, the City of London's largest discount house, had turned itself into a public company in the previous year. The prospectus had been less than candid about certain long-term loans. However, the flotation had been highly successful, and the collapse into liqui-

---

[72] 19 & 20 Vict. c. 47. Under this Act, the model deed-of-settlement, which had been attached to the Act of 1844, became Table B (in 1862, Table A)—a set of articles of association which would apply in default of any specific provision.

[73] P.D. 1856 CXL 129.

[74] 21 & 22 Vict., c. 91; and note 20 & 21 Vict., c. 49, assimilating banks to other companies in other respects; Cooke (1950), pp. 163–166.

[75] In the general legislation of that year: see Cooke (1950), pp. 166–168.

[76] 25 & 26 Vict., c. 62; Cooke (1950) Ch. 11. The major amendments would come in 1900, 1907 and 1929.

[77] (1888) 9 J.Inst. Bankers 382.

[78] P.D. 1856 CXL 138.

[79] H. A. Shannon (1932) Ec.Hist.Supp., Ec.J., II, 396; D. H. McGregor (1929) 39 Ec.J. 496. As Shannon shows, the years after 1863 produced a growing flurry of speculation, itself a precursor of the crash of 1866.

dation caused a financial panic in which many other companies failed.[80] Because the Overend company had followed the standard practice of issuing shares on which only a minor proportion of the nominal amount had been paid, the shareholders remained good for more than the outstanding debts and the limitation of liability was of no consequence. Other, perfectly sound, companies found that the possibility of calls on their shares rendered them for a time unsaleable. Since the legislation did not allow for any reduction of nominal capital, a voluntary liquidation, followed by the formation of a new company, was the sole, cumbersome cure.

In the ensuing Parliamentary enquiry, Lord Romilly M.R. and Page Wood V.C., who were grappling with overloaded lists for winding up in Chancery, demanded more surveillance from the law: "it is not sufficient to say that because a man is a foolish person, therefore he must be allowed to ruin himself in his own way."[81] But Lowe was a prominent member of the Select Committee and saw to it that nothing came of Romilly's plea for imposing greater liabilities on director-shareholders. In the ensuing legislation, a procedure was instituted for reducing a company's capital by applying to the court. Companies were also enabled to be formed with unlimited liability imposed on directors alone, thus providing some equivalent for a *société en commandite*; but it was a mere alternative and acquired no popularity whatsoever.[82]

Ten years later, another Select Committee could be so far moved as to recommend the re-introduction of provisional registration, the instigation of a minimum nominal value for shares and a minimum subscription before allotment. At the same time it accepted a motion from Lowe that "No safeguard . . . against loss in any business can be effectual unless a man, before he parts with his money or pledges his credit, carefully inquires into the nature of the undertaking, and the character and credit, pecuniarily and morally, of those with whom he is to be associated."[83] The law was left unchanged, the London Stock Exchange showing itself nakedly hostile to any attempt from outside to impose requirements for disclosure in new pro-

---

[80] Despite the misleading nature of the prospectus, attempts by shareholders to avoid their liabilities on liquidation succeeded only to a limited extent: see *Oakes* v. *Turquand* (1872) L.R. 2 H.L. 325; *Overend & Gurney Co.* v. *Gibb* (1872) L.R. 5 H.L. 480; *Peek* v. *Gurney* (1873) L.R. 6 H.L. 377.

[81] Select Committee on the Limited Liability Acts, P.P. 1867 (329) X, Q. 1394.

[82] Companies (Amendment) Act 1867; for the six instances, see P.P. 1895 [C. 7779] LXXXVIII, p. 64. The belief persisted that *en commandite* partnerships would unlock capital for small businesses in a way that could not be achieved otherwise, even as it became clear that the registered company could accommodate "one-man" businesses. The great concern of 1850 that lenders on profit terms should not be deemed partners was given effect by case-law in 1860 (*Cox* v. *Hickman* (1860) 8 H.L.C. 268); and subsequent legislation (28 & 29 Vict., c. 86—inaccurately christened "Bovill's Act") was held to have achieved no further liberalisation (see *Syers* v. *Syers* (1876) 1 App.Cas. 174; *Pooley* v. *Driver* (1876) 5 Ch D. 458). Sir Frederick Pollock's proposal to include the *en commandite* form in his draft codification of partnership law was dropped from the actual enactment of 1890. Finally, but again to no practical effect, a Limited Partnerships Act was put through in 1907 after encouragement from the Reid Committee (below, n. 5), para. 89.

[83] P.P. 1877 (365) VIII.

motions.[84] Even in the 1890s, when it was pointed out to the Davey Committee on Company Law Amendment that some countries did exert some control by limiting the types of capitalisation, the Committee was ready with the answer: the British had attracted far greater investment through their unfettered type of limited liability company.[85]

V. Interpretation by the Courts

By 1890, with three decades of experience and more, some 2,500 limited liability companies were being formed each year in England, and by the end of the decade that figure had well-nigh doubled. Among these were a growing number of substantial British businesses, hoping to attract new capital through shareholdings protected against full personal liability. This attraction had been increased by the devisings of financial entrepreneurs and their lawyers. In the wake of the Overend Gurney debacle, shares of small denomination—£1 or even 1s. or 1d, fully paid from the outset—began to take the place of £10, £20 or £50 part-paid shares.[86] With this, in some companies, the holdings spread from a few participants, more or less closely involved in management as well as ownership, to a diverse group of mainly passive investors.

In the 1880s two differential devices were popularised. The preference share carried a fixed rate of interest rather than an entitlement to dividends determined periodically, and a prior right over ordinary shareholders to the residue of assets on a winding up. The debenture was a loan, which frequently gave a charge over company assets by way of security and thus conferred high priority in a winding up—in advance even of the ordinary creditors of the company.[87] That highly convenient device, the floating charge over the stock-in-trade and other assets of a business from time to time, continued to be attached to debentures even when the 1882 legislation curbing the deployments of bills of sale impeded this form of security in respect of loans to individuals.[88]

At the same time as these practical demonstrations of the great potential of a liberal company regime, the courts were having to deal with a host of uncertainties about which the legislation gave no clear guidance. In the main, they showed themselves perfectly willing to work from the same premises as the draftsmen of the Acts: the entitlement to register carried with it simply the obligation to give public notice of the purpose, structure, powers and managerial arrangements. The judges were obliged to spell out the logic of the notice principle: the public statement of the capital structure meant that it could be neither increased nor decreased save through the

---

[84] E. V. Morgan and W. A. Thomas, *The Stock Exchange* (1962), pp. 147–148; and note the criticism of time-bargain practice on the Exchange by the Select Committee on Foreign Loans (P.P. 1875 (152) XI, pp. xlvi–xlviii).

[85] P.P. 1895 [C. 7779] LXVIII, p. xiii; and see Horn in Horn and Kocka (1979), p. 123.

[86] For details of the growing use of small shares, beginning with mining and cotton, see Jefferys (1977) Chap. 4.

[87] *Cf.* above, pp. 237ff. For these developments, Jefferys (1977) Chaps. 5, 6.

[88] See above, p. 242 and below, p. 262.

procedure before the court which the legislation provided[89]; a decrease was not to be secretly effected by the company buying its own shares.[90]

The House of Lords also concluded that the requirement to state the company's objects in the memorandum was pre-emptive. Contracts made for other purposes would be ultra vires and of no effect; even a unanimous resolution of the shareholders could not make it otherwise.[91] The public notification was not merely for their benefit, but also for that of creditors and future investors.[92] It was by no means a foregone conclusion that the courts would press matters so far. There were divergent precedents for them to consider: chartered corporations were, so it seemed, bound by their contracts, even if outside the objects stated in the charter.[93] On the other hand, the ultra vires rule had been applied with fair stringency to statutory corporations, notably railways; their compulsory purchase powers and monopoly potential had marked them out for supervision to ensure that the public interest behind the exceptional powers was respected.[94] However, the two great commercial judges, Willes and Blackburn JJ., both sought to reduce the rule to one protecting shareholders only, and not the public in general: ultra vires would become an objection that a shareholder alone could raise and then only before execution of the contract.[95] This did not attract a majority of the bench, either in relation to statutory corporations, or subsequently, in respect of registered companies.[96] But eventually the commercial view—that sanctity of corporate contracts counted for more than public notification of the company's objects—was after all permitted in large measure to prevail. The effect of the strict rule was to lead lawyers to draft very wide objects clauses; and their intentions were much assisted by the House of Lords' approval of a sub-

---

[89] Increases in capital had been provided for in 1862, but decreases had to be specially dealt with in 1867; see above, n. 82.

[90] *Trevor* v. *Whitworth* (1887) 12 App.Cas. 409 (it made no difference that the memorandum allowed the purchase); *Ooregum Gold Mining* v. *Roper* [1892] A.C. 125 (shares could not be issued as fully paid up when they were not).

[91] There was no provision equivalent to that in the 1844 Act (7 & 8 Vict., c. 110, s.10) allowing shareholders in a deed-of-settlement company to consent to a new deed and register it.

[92] *Ashbury Carriage Co.* v. *Riche* (1874) L.R. 7 H.L. 653, see esp. p. 687, *per* Lord Hatherley. For the controversy, see C. H. S. Fifoot, *Judge and Jurist in the Reign of Queen Victoria* (1959), pp. 57–75.

[93] They might however lose their charter in *scire facias* proceedings if they acted beyond their powers: *Eastern Archipelago Co.* v. *R.* (1853) 2 El. & Rl. 856.

[94] See, *e.g.*, *Colman* v. *Eastern Counties Rly.* (1846) 10 Beav. 1 (two railways not permitted to establish steam-packet company from Harwich); *East Anglian Rly.* v. *Eastern Counties Rly.* (1851) 11 C.B. 775 (public interest ordained that railway could itself avoid liability on its ultra vires contracts; approval by shareholders made no difference). For a technique of *conditionally* promising landowners compensation for an extension of line, if they would not oppose the bill giving power to acquire the necessary land, see *Eastern Counties* v. *Hawkes* (1855) 5 H.L.C. 331.

[95] Their starting point was Coke's theory that at common law a corporation had the powers of a natural person: see esp. their dissenting judgments in *Taylor* v. *Chichester & Midhurst Rly.* (1867) 2 Ex. 356.

[96] *Ashbury* case (above, n. 92)—and for Blackburn J.'s dissent in the Exchequer Chamber, see (1874) 9 Ex. at 264; for statutory corporations, see ultimately *A.-G.* v. *Great Eastern Rly.* (1880) 5 App.Cas. 473.

clause which stated that each object was to be construed as independent of the others.[97] This averted the danger that a purpose such as
borrowing or investing would be construed as purely ancillary to the
main objects. The ultra vires rule was to linger,[98] but only as an occasional trap for the unwary. The ultimate freedom, in company consti-
tutions as in contracts generally, was that the courts would give legal
efficacy to whatever was clearly expressed, rather than seek to constrain action by rules of interpretation, arcane or nakedly hostile.

Of all the issues that came to surround the registered company,
none more plainly evidenced the ideological thrust of the schema
than the view taken of the "one-man" company—a view which, at
the same time would ensure that corporate form would become a
ubiquitous feature of mature capitalism. As the Davey Committee
found, the bulk of company formations were for small businesses;
and the degree of protection available to their owners, by making use
of the ingenuities of the 1880s, became manifest in the House of
Lords' positivistic decision, *Salomon* v. *A. Salomon & Co. Ltd.*[99] After
building up a reasonably successful leather and shoe business, Aron
Salomon had sold it to a company, whose shares were almost all
owned by himself.[1] The price of £39,000—unquestionably an over-
valuation—was received by Salomon partly in shares and cash, but
as to £10,000 by way of debenture secured by floating charge over the
company's assets. Within a year the company was insolvent and had
to be wound up.[2] The Court of Appeal found the arrangement, which
left the original business owner as preferred creditor, deeply offensive, labelling it "a device to defraud creditors."[3] But the House of
Lords refused to agree that the preference should be disallowed,
reading the Companies Act with an apparently severe logic: the company was a distinct legal entity, not an "alias" for Salomon, and its
purchase of the business had involved no prejudice to creditors at
the time[4] (they were all paid by Salomon from the cash portion of his
price). Whatever might be the case for change, there was nothing
impermissible in what had been done under the existing law and
therefore nothing which could undermine its consequences.

The Lords' decision came as company law was undergoing political review, for the Davey Committee had just reported[5] and the

[97] *Cotman* v. *Brougham* [1918] A.C. 514. The Wrenbury Committee (P.P. 1918 [Cd. 9138]
  VII) sought to modify this development by dividing powers from objects. But the
  City resisted and the Greene Committee (P.P. 1926 [Cmd. 2657] IX) drew back.
[98] For its current shadowy form, see Gower (1979) Chap. 8.
[99] [1897] A.C. 22. For the family and business background, see G. R. Rubin in J. N.
  Adams (ed.) *Essays for Clive Schmitthoff* (1981), p. 99.
[1] Seven corporators were at that stage required: Salomon held 20,001 of the issued
  shares, the other six associates held one each (possibly on trust for him).
[2] Government contracts, a considerable part of the business, were not renewed.
[3] [1895] 2 Ch. 323; at first instance, Vaughan Williams J. reached the same result by
  treating the company as Salomon's agent.
[4] Later creditors who failed to inquire about debentures had, according to Lord
  Watson, to "bear the consequences of their own negligence": *ibid.*, p. 40.
[5] The Committee, of which Vaughan Williams J. was a member, approved of the
  Court of Appeal's view of the matter and proposed additional grounds for winding
  up in such cases: P.P. 1895 [C. 7779] LXXXIII, pp. viii–ix. On the later Reid Committee, only a minority were in favour of eliminating the floating charge: P.P. 1906
  [Cd. 3052] XCVII, pp. 14–16, 27–29.

government was considering its options. In 1900, the very year in which it placed novel constraints on moneylenders,[6] Parliament chose only to reinforce the requirements of public notice in the law of company structure. It insisted on registration of debentures and other charges with the Registrar (and not merely with the company itself).[7] But it did not require secured loans to the company to comply with formalities such as those which made bills of sale over an individual's property so difficult to grant. It did not limit the use of floating charges by calling for a complete listing of items as they came to be covered.[8] The winding up laws were not made to include the "reputed ownership" rule that could swell the assets of individual traders in bankruptcy.[9] The "Salomon company" was shown to be acceptable in other ways: for the first time since 1856, companies were required by the 1900 Act to have an annual audit of accounts[10]; but when it was added that these accounts must be filed in the companies registry, this was not extended to private companies whose shares were not open to public subscription.[11]

A complex re-adjustment was being completed by which, in large measure, the trading entity was to be distinguished from the private individual (as in early bankruptcy law). The new distinction depended upon the entrepreneur taking steps in good time to form a company and so to procure in advance limited liability and other advantages such as preferences through debentures. Bankruptcy could thus be left as a catch-net for traders who did not take such precautions, and for individuals who did not trade. Individuals were also to have some measure of legal help against the long-feared rapacities of moneylenders. But protective laws about borrowing would not be allowed to cramp the style of companies. Instead, sanctity of contract in dealings with them was subject to a new type of risk-spreading device. Those who dealt with a company on credit terms ran the danger, in the competition among creditors, that, thanks to limited liability, there might be nothing worth competing for. They might agree initial terms without legal constraints after such inquiries as they deemed prudent. Beyond that, they could spread the risks of non-recovery by allowing a large number of customers to run up small debts, rather than the converse. A good segment of financial, legal and political opinion had come, perhaps wearily, to consider such a discipline upon creditors by no means unhealthy. It was more acceptable for the state to mark the limits of its support for credit by this machinery than for it to police any more completely the moral virtue of meeting debts to the full.

---

[6] See above, pp. 223–224.
[7] Which was all that the 1862 Act, s.43, required; there was no right of public inspection.
[8] For these constraints upon bills of sale, see above, p. 242.
[9] See above, p. 231.
[10] s.21. For the history of the statutory accounting requirements, see H. C. Edey and P. Panitpakdi in A. C. Littleton and B. S. Yamey (eds.), *Studies in the History of Accounting* (1956), p. 356.
[11] Companies Act 1907, s.21; and similarly for the directors' annual report, s.22. The exempted companies had also to have restrictions on transferability of shares and to limit members to fifty, s.37.

VI. Managers: Competence and Honesty

One clue to the acceptance of the "one-man" company lay in the continuing predominance of management by the owners of businesses. Even where the corporate form was being adopted, those who held the bulk of the shares tended to remain in charge. The "one-man" company accordingly differed in degree rather than in kind even from public companies with stock exchange listings.[12] This phenomenon had many consequences for the shaping of company law in its details. The relations of shareholders as owners to directors as managers would be defined in provisions of the memorandum and articles concerning voting rights in shareholders' meetings, the conferment of powers on directors to act for the company and the like. It was normal to provide that decisions at shareholders' meetings should be taken by majority vote (though special matters might require some higher proportion). The courts proved extremely reluctant to impose external limitations which would allow a minority to challenge a decision put through by the majority, even where the majority stood to gain and the minority to lose in a quantifiable measure. Only in extreme cases of "fraud" did exception creep in.[13]

As part of this attitude, it was held that a director owed no duties to individual shareholders, only to the company.[14] Directors, moreover, were to be treated as ordinary businessmen, not as in any sense measuring up to some professional standard of competence. The attraction of solid, titled names onto boards, on the understanding that their bearers might attend board meetings as it suited them, was too standard a practice to permit of any other conclusion. The Overend Gurney directors escaped any personal liability for the risky loans which had led to downfall because it could not be said that "no men with any ordinary degree of prudence, acting on their own behalf, would have entered into such a transaction."[15] Lord Hatherley, in so deciding, regarded corporate ventures as inherently hazardous and refused to impose on directors the duty of caution which he would expect of trustees in holding property for beneficiaries.

---

[12] In 1914, four-fifths of the 62,672 active companies were private. So far as industrial companies were concerned this reflected the local and regional basis of their financing: Jefferys (1977) pp. 129–130; P. L. Payne (1967) 20 Ec.H.R. 519.

[13] K. W. Wedderburn has shown that the Court of Chancery settled on abiding by majority rule, just as it was moving away from Lord Eldon's refusal to allow an account between partners in a continuing partnership: see [1957] C.L.J. 194, pp. 196–199. *Foss* v. *Harbottle* (1843) 2 Hare 461)—the decisive case for companies—held that minority shareholders could not object to the company buying land from one of its directors, however much this might be to the latter's advantage; and later it was held that the benefiting director in such a case might use his rights as a shareholder to secure majority approval: *East Pant Du* v. *Merryweather* (1864) 2 H. & M. 254; *North-West Transportation* v. *Beatty* (1887) 12 App.Cas. 589. But subsequent proceedings in the *East Pant Du* case ((1867) L.R. 5 Eq. 464n) showed that there might be fraud, entitling a member of the minority to bring a representative action on behalf of them all, where the payment had included a "kick-back" to another director; and so began the exception, which nevertheless was treated with an uneasy reticence. For the present law, see Gower (1979) Chap. 26.

[14] *Percival* v. *Wright* [1902] 2 Ch. 421.

[15] *Overend Gurney* v. *Gibb* (above, n. 80), p. 509.

There was however, one matter which the judges saw as going to honesty rather than competence: the obligation not to take personal advantage of the position of director. Here indeed the equitable principles generated to deal with trustees were transferred equally to directors and indeed to other fiduciaries; and in the process they were progressively hardened.[16] In the eighteenth century, Lord Chancellor King had settled that a trustee who personally took the renewal of a trust lease must hold it for the trust.[17] Lord Eldon had applied the same principle, for instance, to purchases by the trustee of trust property and by mid-century, Lord Cranworth could say, in words much repeated, that no trustee or director "shall be allowed to enter into engagements in which he has, or can have, a personal interest conflicting, or which possibly may conflict, with the interests of those whom he is bound to protect."[18] The categorical nature of the rule was said to be necessary because of the judges' inability to investigate whether in particular circumstances there was an actual conflict of interest and duty. They felt that they would be too much at the mercy of plausible fiduciaries; it was better to insist that any fiduciary who wanted to pursue his own advantage should obtain the informed consent of the beneficiaries or the company. As regards company promoters and directors, the rule was strengthened in the decades after the Judicature Acts. When it came to this form of discipline, the common law did not strive to curtail equity. Where, for instance, promoters secured respectable names for the board by making secret payments to them, the courts had held the directors liable to repay if the money came from the capital subscribed by shareholders.[19] In 1862 Lord Chelmsford hesitated to order the same if the money had come from the promoters alone.[20] But by the 1880s the judges had extended the liability to this case as well and it was said that a bribe or commission to a fiduciary was repayable by action at common law as well as in equity.[21]

Dicey saw in this an unreal probity: "The Courts maintain, or attempt to maintain, rules as to the duty of an agent towards his employer which are admitted by every conscientious man to be morally sound, but which are violated every day by tradesmen, merchants, and professional men, who make no scruple at giving or accepting secret commissions; and these rules Parliament hesitates

---

[16] See, esp., L. S. Sealy [1962] C.L.J. 69; [1963] C.L.J. 119.

[17] *Keech* v. *Sandford* (1726) Sel.Cas.T. King 61—the case would give its name to the whole doctrine. Since ecclesiastical and charitable bodies were forbidden by statute (or custom) to take leases for more than certain periods, options in their favour could not have legal force; but it was peculiarly invidious for a trustee to take a personal renewal in their place and this was a common circumstance for application of the principle: see S. Cretney (1970) 33 Conv. (N.S.) 61.

[18] *Aberdeen Rly.* v. *Blaikie* (1854) 1 Macq. 461 at 471.

[19] *e.g., Cornell* v. *Hay* (1873) L.R. 8 C.P. 328.

[20] *Tyrell* v. *Bank of London* (1862) 10 H.L.C. 26 at 60–61.

[21] *Metropolitan Bank* v. *Heiron* (1880) 5 Ex.D. 319; and it made no difference that the principal could not itself have made the profit: *Boston Deep Sea Fishing* v. *Ansell* (1888) 39 Ch.D. 339. It was even suggested that a bribe was recoverable twice—from the fiduciary and the person bribed—though this never became clear law: see Gower (1979), p. 611.

or refuses to enforce by statute."[22] There have since been numerous opportunities to turn towards less indiscriminate condemnation, but almost always they have been resisted.[23] The point at which the equitable tradition of intervention kept its evident meaning for the bulk of the judiciary was on this issue of honesty. The courts might demand little by way of judgment or skill, but they would not countenance the taking of personal advantage. Those who were caught doing so—however slight the chance—must transfer back assets or repay profits.

The rule restraining the making of personal profits was applied not only to directors but equally to promoters of companies.[24] As the long history of abuses in company formation stood witness, the public flotation of a company was a prime opportunity for the downright fraudulent, as for the incurably optimistic. Promoters face an inevitable temptation to colour in the good points in a prospectus and blank out the bad. The gap between their state of knowledge of the opportunity on offer and that of potential investors is frequently wide. Some judges and writers supported the view that an obligation of good faith was owed, requiring promoters positively to state all material facts, as in an insurance proposal, or risk the allotment of shares being set aside.[25] The decision in *Derry* v. *Peek* that promoters and directors were not liable to pay damages for including actual misstatements in their prospectus, in the absence of deliberate fraud, was accordingly a particularly unbending re-assertion of common law attitudes.[26] Its harshness did more than offend Chancery lawyers: Parliament immediately intervened to impose the duty which the House of Lords had refused to find.[27] Then, a long list of requirements for any prospectus was prescribed in 1900; and (to prevent avoidance of this) the requirement of a statement in lieu of prospectus was added in 1908.[28] Later again, the novel phenomenon of door-to-door hawking of shares was thought dubious and oppressive enough to warrant making the practice criminal.[29] In the first half of the twentieth century, the general law relating to companies was improved in detail by amendments of this sort, notably in 1929 and 1948.[30] The thrust of what was being done was to reduce the opportunities for abusing the mechanism of incorporation. But the fine tuning was undertaken with an acute awareness that the adaptability

---

[22] *Law and Public Opinion in England* (2nd ed., 1914), p. 368.
[23] For more recent developments, primarily in relations to directors, see, *e.g.*, Gower (1979), pp. 583–601.
[24] Esp. *Gluckstein* v. *Barnes* [1900] A.C. 248. For changes in promotion techniques see, Jefferys (1977) Chap. 7.
[25] Above, p. 223, n. 70.
[26] Above, pp. 221, 223.
[27] Directors' Liability Act 1890.
[28] Companies Acts, 1900, ss.9, 10; 1907, ss.1, 2; 1908, ss.80–84; and see the Davey Committee (above, n. 5), p. vi; Loreburn Committee (above, n. 5), pp. 6–10.
[29] Prevention of Fraud (Investments) Act 1939; implementing the Bodkin Committee on Share-Pushing, P.P. 1937 [Cmd. 5537] IX; and the Anderson Committee on Unit Trusts, P.P. 1936 [Cmd. 5259] X.
[30] Preceded by the inquiries of the Greene Committee (P.P. 1926 [Cmd. 2657] IX) and the Cohen Committee (P.P. 1944–1945 [Cmd. 6659] IV) respectively.

of the device should never be prejudiced unless the results would be an unequivocal gain.

VII. The Corporate Economy

The registered company finally acquired its central economic significance when it became the standard form not only for small businesses, but also for the major firms of British industry. In 1885, there were still only 60 companies in home production and distribution quoted on the London stock exchange; but by 1907 the number had grown to 569 and by 1939 it would reach 1712.[31] On the provincial exchanges similar opportunities for investment would burgeon.

One impetus for this major change was undoubtedly that the exchanges were proving an efficient source for raising new capital. A threshold of mutual confidence was being crossed. Investors were becoming less chary of investing outside the range of government stock and railway shares as solid enterprises in cotton, engineering, shipbuilding and the like appeared on the exchanges. The appeal to the public for capital had a necessary tendency to divide ownership from management, a departure from the pattern in the earlier industrial companies. But it was a change that admitted of many degrees, for the old family interests which had made up a business often continued after flotation to occupy a commanding position by retaining large shareholdings and using both their voting power and the fact that they had always managed the concern to stay on the board of directors in executive positions. Nevertheless the size that some companies were beginning to achieve would make management a complex strategy. It opened organisational fronts which called for varied expertise: financial control, demand prediction, management of personnel, marketing and distribution were each acquiring a sophistication that called for much higher skills of coordination and judgment from those directly responsible to the board. It was not a development which meshed easily with family control, generation upon generation; the more so, given the unchanging tendency of the successful middle-classes to acquire the education and imitate the breeding of the landed leaders of society. Yet from the 1890s onwards, there was no denying the immense success of large-scale business in the United States, and of the cartels and dominant firms which were so encouraged in Germany. The corporate form of enterprise, particularly in the liberal version that had been pioneered in Britain, left it open for industry and commerce there to grow in equivalent ways, by the reinvestment of profits and the attraction of new capital, as by the amalgamation or collaboration of enterprises. Rationalisation of resources was increasingly to become an acceptable objective, even among those British who had been taught to revere free trade and the efficiency of entrepreneurial competition. It is with the consequences of this change that the final Parts of this Chapter are concerned.

[31] See Hannah (1983), Chap. 2.

PART 4: LEGAL CONTROL OF ANTI-COMPETITIVE
ACTIVITY

By the 1870s Britain may well have come closer to textbook conditions of free competition—its market-places jostling with suppliers—than any industrialised state has since managed. It was a
domestic condition which, combined with a dominance in many
international markets, helped to prolong the faith in free trade, when
the emerging rivals—with the United States, Germany and France at
their head—were turning back to a protectionism which would
secure their home industries against foreign intrusion. In such an
ambience, the British would prove slow to follow American example
in building up truly large enterprises, which, by organising the
whole of production and distribution within an industry, could
become dominant within it, either single-handed or through market-
sharing with a few other firms of comparable size and efficiency.
Around 1900 there was some flurry of merger activity in a few British
industries, but without notable success. Only in the disturbed conditions of the 1920s would much of a movement for "rationalisation"
set in.[32]

For most of our period, the fear in Britain was of too much competition rather than too little. The question whether the state should
intervene to inhibit anti-competitive activities among the leading
firms of an industry could accordingly be left to one side. Certainly
there was no public feeling to equal the outcry which had led the
United States to enact the Sherman Act of 1890 against the restrictive
practices and the monopolising activities of the first big business
"trusts" there—in petroleum, meat, sugar, whisky and so on.[33]

Yet the instinct to monopolise is as old as trade itself. To be able to
restrict the supply of a commodity so as to raise its price to the level
which, after taking into account demand and costs, allows the maximum exaction of profits is a heady stimulant to entrepreneurial
endeavour and capitalist risk-taking. The middle ages has feared
engrossers, badgers, forestallers and regraters who in various ways
cornered corn and other supplies before or as they reached market,
and a succession of statutes made their activities criminal.[34] The
addictive tendency of Elizabeth and her Stuart successors to reward
favourites by granting them patent monopolies over particular trades
had attracted the growing resentment of the Commons and the
hostility of the common law judges. The latter, led by Coke C.J., had
been prepared to pronounce monopoly illegal and so to foster a

---

[32] See above, p. 80.
[33] The contrast was the more striking because of the common legal heritage: the Sherman Act claimed parentage in the common law's antipathy to monopoly and
restraint of trade (for which see the next paragraph): see W. L. Letwin, *Law and
Economic Policy in America* (1965); and for a comparison of the position in the U.S.
with that of England, Germany and France, W. R. Cornish in Horn and Kocka (1979),
p. 280. The "trust" was used in the U.S. until (from 1889) companies began to be
permitted to own shares in other companies. In Britain the practice seems to have
crept in at an earlier stage.
[34] See W. Herbruck (1929) 27 Michigan L.R. 365; D. Dewey (1957) 41 Virginia L.R. 759.

distinctively liberal and individualist strain in common law thought.[35] The principle would be used to declare against unwarranted attempts to impose local guild and similar restraints and would meld into a broader doctrine against "general" restraints of trade. This might be used against masters or journeymen who sought to exclude un-apprenticed workmen from their trade, or against an anti-competition clause in a contract of service or the sale of a business. It was an open-ended conception capable of adaptation against novel threats to the freedom of capital and trade, and its potential as a weapon against the collective action of labour would prove daunting.[36]

I. The End of Mercantilist Regulation

In the economic conditions of the later eighteenth century there was a shift in attitudes as markets developed on a larger scale and it became possible to hope that competitors would always emerge to challenge the combination of traders intent on dividing up or shar-ing out markets. The very fact of wholesale trading made the old laws against engrossing and the like appear anomalous. In 1772 Parlia-ment was persuaded to repeal the chief statutes against these prac-tices.[37] But the country was not entirely ready for such progressive ideas. Sharp inflations of food prices, particularly in the war disrup-tions of the 1790s, brought panic buying and deep suspicion of profi-teering. In 1800 Lord Kenyon, in tones richly paternal, led King's Bench to hold that at common law engrossing and regrating remained criminal.[38] Convictions of merchants for these offences were greeted with wild enthusiasm. It would not be until 1844, that this residual form of criminal liability was lifted by statute, though there is no evidence of positive application of the law in the interim.[39]

This indicates the long term trend, which is also marked in civil litigation. Adam Smith had noted with some unease the instinctive tendency of merchants to collaborate on prices, wages, supplies and so on, to the disadvantage of consumers or workers; but in general he was prepared to trust to the sovereign remedy of competition from outsiders or from insiders, duplicit or weary of the game.[40] From 1815, the common law judges showed little willingness to treat market-sharing arrangements between traders as anything other than

---

[35] See below, p. 293.

[36] See below, pp. 296ff., 312ff., 328ff.

[37] 12 Geo. III, c. 71; a turn strongly approved by Adam Smith: *Wealth of Nations* (1976 ed.), p. 534.

[38] R. v. *Waddington* (1800) 1 East 143 and 167 (and for other disputes about the law, see *ibid.*, p. 150); R. v. *Rusby* (1800) Peake Add.Cas. 189.

[39] However, in 1807—still under war conditions—Lord Eldon refused to allow a bill in equity designed to reveal the true circumstances of a deal between a powerful "Fruit Club" and another trader over a particular cargo. He denounced the Club's activi-ties as "a conspiracy against the vendors: next a conspiracy against the world at large": *Cousins* v. *Smith* (1807) 13 Ves. 542. It has been said (see, *e.g.* Bowen L.J. in the *Mogul* case (below, n. 46, p. 619)) to treat this as outdated conservatism; but for very similar attitudes during World War I, see below, p. 272.

[40] But he opposed the protectionist legislation of mercantilism: *Wealth of Nations* (1976 ed.), pp. 462, 493.

enforceable contracts. A restraint of trade there might be; but, as Jessel M.R. would later express it:

" . . . you are not to extend arbitrarily those rules which say that a given contract is void as being against public policy, because if there is one thing more than another that public policy requires it is that men of full age and competent understanding shall have the utmost liberty of contracting, and that their contracts when entered into freely and voluntarily shall be held sacred and shall be enforced by courts of justice."[41]

An agreement between two coachmakers to fix prices and divide services; an agreement between three Oxford box-makers to divide the country between them; an agreement between builders to refrain from tendering for work so that all would share in the profits of a single high bid by one of them; an agreement among dock firms to share work and profits—all these were held enforceable.[42] The obvious capacity of railways to behave as monopolists would provoke curbing legislation on some fronts—notably the control which began in 1854 over their freight rates.[43] But other mutually supportive arrangements were allowed to continue—notably those which eliminated competition over fares and freights between various destinations. Disputes between participants went to arbitration, on occasion before the prestigious figure of Gladstone.[44] Only when it came to labour relations would the reaction be different. In *Hilton v. Eckersley*, a combination among masters to fix wages and conditions of employment was held void as an illegal restraint of trade; otherwise, by simple reciprocity, the courts would have to entertain questions of trade union agreement, and even, according to Lord Campbell, the "fantastic and mischievous notion of a 'Labour Parliament.' "[45]

II. THE COURTS AND "UNFAIR" COMPETITION

"Loose-knit combinations" of traders—going by such names as trade associations, marketing pools, cartels, conferences, rings—were a

---

[41] *Printing and Numerical Registering* v. *Sampson* (1875) L.R. 19 Eq. 462, p. 455 (unsuccessful attempt by assignor of an invention patent to escape obligation to assign rights in improvements).

[42] *Hearn* v. *Griffin* (1815) 2 Chitty 407; *Wickens* v. *Evans* (1829) 3 Y. & T. 318; *Jones* v. *North* (1875) L.R. 19 Eq. 426; *Collins* v. *Locke* (1879) 4 App.Cas. 674.

[43] The Railway and Canal Traffic Act 1854, 17 & 18 Vict., c. 31, ss.2–4, conferred jurisdiction on the Court of Common Pleas. It was a task inimical to the judges and was given to Railway Commissioners by the Regulation of Railways Act 1873.

[44] See P. S. Bagwell, *The Railway Clearing House in the British Economy* (1968), Ch. 9. Companies which sought to escape liability under pooling arrangements by pleading that their actions were ultra vires the powers given them by statute found no sympathy in the courts: see *Shrewsbury & Birmingham Rly.* v. *L.N.W.R.* (1851) 21 L.J.Q.B. 89; *Hare* v. *L.N.W.R.* (1861) 2 J. & H. 80; cf. *Midland Rly.* v. *L.N.W.R.* (1866) L.R. 2 Eq. 524.

[45] (1855) 8 E. & B. 47 at 66. Ernest Jones had begun to campaign for a Labour Parliament during the Preston textile strike of 1853: J. Saville, *Ernest Jones, Chartist* (1952), pp. 53–55, 264–274.

growing feature of the late Victorian economy, a response more commonly to conditions of depression than expansion, a tool of defence until trade improved rather than an instrument of monopolistic aggression. A pooling arrangement typically strove (through the administration of a trusted secretary) to determine the existing market shares of the collaborating traders, so as to allow them thereafter only the same proportion of total sales of the pool. The Secretary would organise payments into the pool for excess sales and rebate out of the pool for sales below allotment. The system might save the least competitive from going under during stretches of slack trade, thus preserving capacity for the livelier times of the next turn in the cycle.

Although disputes between such collaborators were commonly referred to arbitration, some still found their way to court. It became plain that the judges would only re-affirm their earlier attitude. They would not treat common law as a positive means of promoting competition: "to draw the line between fair and unfair competition, between what is reasonable and unreasonable, passes the power of the courts."[46] This abnegation came first in answer to a novel attempt at "strong" legal redress. In the *Mogul* case, a ring of shippers had succeeded in excluding an outsider from shipping the annual China tea harvest to Britain by such tactics as threatening the consignors of the tea with no transport for the bulk of their cargo if they dealt with the outsider. This the outsider claimed to be a tortious conspiracy to cause trade injury which sounded in damages. But the judges found nothing actionable in conduct undertaken in the selfish pursuit of "legitimate" business interest: for nothing had been done which by itself was in any sense unlawful.[47]

True, most of the judges said or assumed that the agreement of the shippers' "conference" against any one of their number would not have been enforceable because it was in undue restraint of trade. Soon afterwards, in the different context of a restrictive covenant not to compete, which had been given by the seller of an arms business to the purchaser, the House of Lords restated the restraint of trade doctrine so as to require the courts primarily to consider whether the restraint was reasonable in the interests of the parties to it and only secondarily (and as it would prove, to a shadowy extent) in the interests of the public.[48] This *Nordenfeldt* rule would be applied with some severity in order to guarantee to an individual employee the right to take his labour where he wished (itself one reaction against collective restraints upon labour).[49] But when it came to mercantile agreements such as the sale of a business, a much more benign attitude prevailed towards upholding non-competition clauses.[50]

So equally, with mutual restraints on business competition, horizontally between manufacturers or distributors or vertically down the distribution chain, in the many forms of restrictive practice that

---

[46] Fry L.J., *Mogul S.S.* v. *McGregor Gow* (1889) 23 Q.B.D. 598 at 625–626.

[47] *Mogul S.S.* v. *McGregor Gow* [1892] A.C. 25.

[48] *Nordenfeldt* v. *Maxim Nordenfeldt* [1894] A.C. 535.

[49] See *Mason* v. *Provident Clothing* [1913] A.C. 724; *Morris* v. *Saxelby* [1916] 1 A.C. 688. Severance of part of the clause was unlikely to be allowed in an employment case.

[50] In addition to the *Nordenfeldt* case itself, see, *e.g.*, *Vancouver Malt* v. *Vancouver Breweries* [1934] A.C. 181.

were burgeoning. The Privy Council upheld the standard tying
agreements by which the United Shoe Machinery of Boston and its
various national subsidiaries leased their machines to shoe manufacturers and so acquired a dominant position in the industry as a
whole in various countries. Nothing had deprived the manufacturer-
lessees of their freedom to decide whether to enter the agreements in
the first place and any evil, according to the Conservative Lord
Atkinson, "may be capable of cure by legislation or by competition,
but . . . not by litigation."[51] An Australian version of the United
States Sherman Act, couched in rather more limited terms, was held
by the Privy Council not to apply to a combination among coal-ship-
pers intended to restrain an impending downturn in freight rates.
Lord Parker insisted, in applying the *Nordenfeldt* principle, that, once
the agreement was found to be in the interests of the parties (which
was a natural inference from their entering into it), there was a heavy
onus in showing that nevertheless it was against public interest.[52]
The House of Lords could find no sympathy for a salt manufacturer
who sought to escape liability under an agreement with an amalgamation of salt manufacturers designed to maintain prices. Because
the restraint of trade had not been pleaded, no evidence had been
introduced upon which to substantiate the claim that the restrictive
agreement injured the public. The Liberal Lord Chancellor, Haldane,
speculated that too much competition might lower wages and cause
unemployment and labour disturbance; Lord Sumner approved the
term by which the parties agreed not to open new salt-bearing
ground, for its tendency to conserve resources.[53]

III. SHIFTING PERCEPTIONS

War conditions, however, produce sudden demands and unexpected
scarcities and so create immense opportunities for profiteering. In
Britain the effect was evident enough after 1914, but it took official
investigations in the United States of the predatory activities of the
"Meat trust" for it to be realised just how serious the problem might
be. The trust had come to control a substantial part of the world's
meat supply and was deriving a large part of its immense profits
from Britain. In 1918–19 a Ministry of Reconstruction Committee on
Trusts heard much from industry on the need for the organisation of
consortia and cartels if British business was to survive the rigours of
international competition.[54] Into this case was woven the demand
that home and colonial markets be at last protected by tariff preferences; the profits of this preferment would allow them to go price-
cutting in foreign markets. This was the language of rationalisation,
but the Committee remained suspicious. It recommended arming the
Board of Trade with powers of investigation into restrictive practices
and monopolistic action and the setting up of a Tribunal to which the

---

[51] *USM Canada* v. *Brunot* [1909] A.C. 330; and see *BUSM* v. *Somervell* (1906) 95 L.T. 711;
P.D. 190 CLXXI 686.
[52] *A.-G. for the Commonwealth* v. *Adelaide Steamship* [1913] A.C. 790.
[53] *North-Western Salt* v. *Electrolytic Alkali* [1914] A.C. 461.
[54] See Committee on Trusts, P.P. 1918 [Cd. 9236] XIII.

Board might refer cases for a decision on whether the activities were contrary to the public interest. At the end of this process, however, only political action was envisaged: the American armoury of criminal prosecutions and civil remedies was not to be copied. A Standing Committee on Trusts was indeed created and delivered fifty-seven reports on pricing, some of them unequivocally critical.[55]

In line with this mistrust, a pooling association of cased-tube manufacturers was held by the courts to be in unreasonable restraint of trade; a participant could therefore not sue on the contract to claim a rebate due to him for not filling his quota.[56] An attempt to hold an Irish milk-producer to an indeterminate contract to supply all his production to a cooperative dairy was similarly held to be contrary to the public interest.[57]

Yet the post-war boom was short-lived enough, collapsing by 1921 into slump and the edgy uncertainties which were to follow. On the political front, the Standing Committee on Trusts was abandoned in May 1921. Occasional arguments subsequently for its resurrection attracted no serious support. Even the Labour Party was unable to make progress on a Consumers' Council against monopoly pricing and other practices.[58]

The courts also reverted to their old line. In 1928, a joint marketing organisation set-up by hop-growers was judged proper since the parties had joined it in pursuit of their own interests—questions of public interest in the arrangement were not even raised.[59] Resale price maintenance was looked upon in similar light. The practice, which aimed to protect smaller distributors against the price-cutting efficiencies of chain-stores and large outlets,[60] had before the war run against a strict application of privity of contract: the manufacturer who had agreed to impose the standard resale price could not enforce it against retailers who bought only from an intermediate wholesaler.[61] But techniques evolved for side-stepping this barrier: wholesalers were obliged to sue indirect retailers; manufacturers organised "stop-lists" among themselves collectively so that defaulting retailers would be unable to obtain supplies; and they offered "offenders" the more lenient alternative of a penalty to keep their names off the list. The irascible Lord Hewart C.J. led the Court of Criminal Appeal to denounce this last practice as blackmail (demanding with menaces).[62] But with equal determination—and more opportunity—the civil courts refused to accept that the practice amounted to this crime, since the pursuit of "legitimate trading interest" provided the

---

[55] The Standing Committee on Trusts was established under the Profiteering Act 1919. See generally, Hannah (1983), Chap. 4.
[56] *Evans* v. *Heathcote* [1918] 1 K.B. 418.
[57] *McEllistrim* v. *Ballymacelligott Cooperative* [1919] A.C. 848.
[58] See Hannah (1983), p. 47.
[59] *English Hop Growers* v. *Dering* [1928] 2 K.B. 174.
[60] For its emergence from chemists' goods in the 1890s to books, periodicals, photographic materials, records confectionery and cars—see B. S. Yamey (1952) Econ.J. 522; *Resale Price Maintenance* (1966), pp. 251–254.
[61] See *Taddy* v. *Sterious* [1904] 1 Ch. 534 (tobacco); *McGruth* v. *Pitcher* [1906] 2 Ch. 443 (shoe rubbers); and especially *Dunlop* v. *Selfridge* [1915] A.C. 847 (tyres).
[62] *R.* v. *Denyer* [1926] 2 K.B. 258.

defence of reasonable cause; equally it prevented there being any tortious conspiracy.[63]

Once again the judiciary had sensed the economic atmosphere of the moment. The catastrophic depression in world trade made rationalisation an urgent necessity in preserving the existing structures of capital. If the relatively stable twenties saw a particular drive towards merger, the thirties turned rather to cartelisation and restrictive agreements.[64] Some agricultural producers secured political backing in the form of statutory marketing boards, which were run by their representatives and designed to match production to demand.[65] Certainly the state provided a major buttress against foreign competition when finally in 1932 it abandoned free trade and instituted the protective tariffs which allowed for imperial preference.[66] Beyond this, the taxation system was used to some extent to encourage the reduction of surplus plant and re-location in units of larger, more efficient size.[67]

While these interventions were in the main indirect, their effect was unquestionably significant. The essentially private arrangements acquired a greater stability than ever before: it became worthwhile for market leaders to abide by their agreed rules, rather than backsliding into surreptitious breaches. And the reversion soon enough to war conditions greatly enhanced the process. A government needing to direct production as never before turned to the trade asssociations and groupings for help that could not wait upon bureaucratic manoeuvrings.

Partly because governmental controls were so much more complete in the second world war, its aftermath did not produce the same ferment against profiteering that followed the first war. The Labour Government was sufficiently uneasy with a private industrial sector largely characterised by "imperfect competition" to set up a Monopolies and Restrictive Practices Commission in 1948.[68] This followed the pattern established by the Standing Committee on Trusts a quarter-century before: the new machine was to be for investigation and report, not for legal condemnation. If its reports were unfavourable, they would have to be followed by political intervention.[69] For the time being, the country was preoccupied not with the aggression of dominant firms but with the need to rebuild industries able to compete in the reviving markets of the world. Much attention was

---

[63] See esp. *Hardie & Lane* v. *Chilton* [1928] 2 K.B. 306; *Thorne* v. *Motor Trade Association* [1937] A.C. 797.

[64] See Hannah (1983), Chaps. 7–9.

[65] Boards were created for milk, bacon, potatoes and hops under the Agricultural Marketing Acts 1931 and 1933; *cf.* the subsidy arrangements of the Wheat Act 1932 and the Sugar Industry (Reorganisation) Act 1936. The coal mining industry adopted a system of quotas administered by a central council under the Coal Mines Act 1930 Part I. Part II created a Commission for amalgamation of collieries which laboured to little effect.

[66] See above, p. 79ff.

[67] Hannah (1983), p. 136.

[68] Monopolies and Restrictive Practices (Inquiry and Control) Act 1948.

[69] By 1956, recovery would be sufficient for it to be felt necessary by the Eden government to set up a Restrictive Trade Practices Registry and Court to deal with some cartel-like activity: see R. B. Stevens and B. S. Yamey, *The Restrictive Practices Court* (1965).

focused on the state's role in promoting enterprises large and efficient enough to survive an unpredictable future. The Labour government saw the rationalisation movement of the inter-war period as an intermediate stage in a progress towards nationalisation of whole industries; and within the business community there was undoubtedly support for greater public and private collaboration.[70] The main arguments were over the extent to which the process should be carried and degree of socialisation to be achieved.

Consensus was strongest over the utility services of transport and power, where already there had been a considerable measure of public intervention—by local authorities in pursuit of "municipal socialism"; in the Metropolis by the creation of the Port of London Authority (1908) and the London Passenger Transport Board (1932)[71]; at national level, by the Post Office, the BBC and, on the eve of war, the conversion of Imperial Airways into BOAC. Attlee's government brought in legislation nationalising gas and electricity, thus replacing a patchwork of local authorities and commercial enterprises over-sewn with statutory regulation; allied to this the coal industry was nationalised since it provided the chief energy source for both types of power. The government's largest creation was the scheme nationalising the railways, canals and inland waterways, road haulage, the London transport system and (in anticipation) the main harbours and passenger road services, all under a British Transport Commission. The one staple production industry which was similarly treated was iron and steel.[72]

This last case would provide the great post-war cause between those whose goal was social ownership and political planning and those who sought only to prop up an essentially private system by public intervention at necessary points. Churchill's government moved soon enough to de-nationalise (or in today's jargon, privatise) the steel industry, perceiving that its potential profitability was considerable and that it accordingly fell outside the compass of "lame duck" enterprises which national interest obliged the state to maintain. The other major nationalisations, however, the Conservatives would keep and seek to improve.

In creating the new state monopolies, the Labour government adhered in form to the public corporation. Amongst other advantages this demonstrated to doubters that authority would lie primarily with managerial experts, rather than with political amateurs. The new Boards and Authorities were a revival of the pre-industrial semi-public corporations and trusts, rather than an evolution from the joint stock business company. Their object was to provide a public benefit which was not directly tested by market confidence, since there was no share capital and investment was sought through loans that were buttressed by Treasury guarantee. Instead of being concerned with shareholders and debenture-holders, the boards and

---

[70] See above, pp. 116–117.

[71] The P.L.A. had been the one significant instance of transfer to public ownership before the First War; for the L.P.T.B., see above, p. 116.

[72] The details of the various schemes are beyond the scope of this book: see W. A. Robson, *Nationalized Industry and Public Ownership* (1960); E. E. Barry, *Nationalisation in British Politics* (1965) Chap. 15.

chief executives were answerable to the relevant Minister who in turn bore political responsibility before Parliament and the electorate. To turn this form of responsibility into reasonably effective supervision was the great challenge of the new dispensation. On the one hand, the management must be allowed freedom to react swiftly and with purposeful initiative. On the other, there needed to be some continuing pressure against comfortable resistance to change, rosy-eyed experimentalism, refusal to consider the consumer's interest in cost-cutting and the tendency towards favouritism or downright dishonesty.

Yet as the new national corporations took up the reins, they could rely on a considerable measure of goodwill—in the press, the political parties and elsewhere. There was, after all, a pattern of behaviour among those who organised and managed so much of British life, in which a paternal concern for the welfare of others was welded to rooted convictions about how their lot could best be improved. From the management of the established church and the landed estate, this spirit had spread to the organisation of social services, education, cultural affairs, sports and other pastimes, as well as to the great British service of Empire. Now that it was to be applied to the monetary system and the planned development of macro-economy, there was equal hope that the management of individual businesses within industries could become the subject of attitudes which placed efficiency and self-interest in balance with a larger objectivity and altruism—an approach often summed up by the label "professional." In such a world, fears of the greed and complacency of market domination could for the moment be held in abeyance.

PART 5: TECHNOLOGICAL ADVANCE AND THE PATENT SYSTEM

I. Early Industrialisation

A legal system which gives its ultimate allegiance to sanctity of contract rather than to freedom of trade provides an environment in which competition may wane just as it may wax. But it is one thing for the law to adopt a neutral attitude to the agreements that it will enforce, taking no account of whether they promote or restrain trade. It is another deliberately to confer monopolistic opportunities in the market-place. In our period, which, even at its close, knew little enough of state licensing and planning of economic activity, this latter course remained a rarity. One notable exception to this—the patent for invention—stands sufficiently in the van of industrial progress to make a final subject for this chapter.

Exactly what significance should be accorded to invention in accounting for the emergence of industrialisation has divided economic historians, as, in a smaller way, has the question of the patent system's contribution to the fostering of invention. The emphasis in Sir John Clapham's generation was upon such factors as the relative cost of labour and machinery in accounting for the great breakthrough. But more recent historians have accorded equivalent status to the discovery and perfecting of machines and processes.[73] Likewise an earlier generation treated the contribution of the patent system towards industrialisation as obscure and peripheral. But, as it is coming to be realised that the introduction of new technology was always hazardous and sometimes long-delayed, that view is beginning to be challenged.[74]

The Statute of Monopolies 1624 had been Parliament's most determined effort to stop James I from indiscriminately granting monopoly privileges in trade.[75] But the Act contained an express exception for inventions comprising a "manner of new manufacture" in the Kingdom: patents to introduce them were limited to fourteen years.[76] For this one case, what had begun as a matter of royal grace and favour assumed the character of a legal entitlement.[77]

The British were not the first to take this step, but theirs became the prototype which would survive to the period of industrialisation. It was adopted as an instrument for economic development by a country which had sensed that it was backward in its technical knowledge and achievements—in comparison with France and the Low Countries—yet was beginning to understand the immense possibilities inherent in catching up. In seventeenth century usage, an inventor included in particular one who brought a foreign technique into the country and established a manufactory which had not previously been known there.[78] The same motivation has since proved a powerful incentive in leading other "developing" countries to adopt (or retain) a patent system.[79]

The early administration of this British system became entangled in the jungle of eighteenth century "place," but still it characterises the determination in the early modern period to secure an economic

---

[73] See J. H. Clapham, *Economic History of Modern Britain: the Early Railway Age* (1939), p. 143; but *cf.* D. Landes, *The Unbound Prometheus* (1969), Chap. 2.

[74] See esp. Dutton (1984), Chaps. 6–8.

[75] 21 J. I, c. 3. See above, pp. 267–268.

[76] For the emergence of the patent system, see W. H. Price, *The English Patents of Monopoly* (1913); H. G. Fox, *Monopolies and Patents* (1947) Chaps. 4–6.

[77] Until 1753, the validity of patents remained a matter for the Privy Council, but thereafter both validity and infringement became matters for the courts.

[78] Fox (above, n. 76), pp. 214–232, W. D. Hulme (1900) 16 L.Q.R. 55. The concept of the importation-inventor would survive in law until 1977; but at least in later law the person who "stole" the idea from abroad or who was breaking confidence in trying to obtain a patent for himself could be prevented from doing so.

[79] This is one of the root contrasts with copyright—the other most wide-spread form of intangible property right in ideas. Copyright, which protects the stuff of culture, education, entertainment and business systems, also acquired its modern form first in Britain: once Tudor and Stuart censorship of printing gave way before notions of free speech, an Act of 1709 (8 Ann., c. 19) gave authors (and their publishers) the right for a limited term to prevent the *copying* of their published works. Countries have rarely been ready to adopt such a sytem and give protection under it to foreigners until they are convinced that the economic advantages of doing so outweigh the gain from cheaper piratical production. The history of the copyright system (and of lesser forms of intellectual property, such as registered designs) cannot be treated in this book but can be found in T. E. Scrutton, *Law of Copyright* (4th ed., 1903) Chap. 1; A Birrell, *Seven Lectures on Copyright* (1889); Holdsworth, VI pp. 360–379; W. R. Cornish, *Intellectual Property* (1981), pp. 293–308.

underpinning for European leadership and to do so by individual initiative, saved as far as possible from the vagaries of bureaucratic discretion and interference. The right to a patent, defined (at least in principle) by legal rules, had come much earlier than, for example, the right to incorporate. Once it was accepted that there must be some special incentive in order to get new technologies launched, the method was true to liberal premises. The patent gave the right to prevent any competitor from using or selling the protected invention for the duration of the monopoly. The incentive to make technical discoveries, and even more to work them up into a saleable process, product or apparatus, lay in the chance of commercial success free from direct competition. Patents came to be spoken of as private property; and this encoded the message that, as with tangible things, inventions would have their potential most effectively realised if an owner had an exclusive, legally protected right of exploitation, which he would be left to develop as he found most profitable. The small trickle of invention patents before 1760 proved enough to keep the system from atrophying, if not much else. But from that date the number of applications would grow and many patents would cover home-developed techniques rather than importations from abroad.[80] The annual total would fluctuate somewhat, following pretty closely the pattern of the trade cycle, until 1852, when—very tardily—the procedure for procuring a patent would be made less costly and time-consuming. The numbers granted would then rise from hundreds to thousands each year; and for the first time there would be real public debate about the need for a patent system, which was undeniably a state-backed monopoly and so needed very considerable advocacy amid the intense admiration of competition.

The growth in numbers of patents represented a triumph over adversities. The granting process, originating from the Clerks Act 1536,[81] involved the preparation of a medley of petitions, warrants and bills for presentation at some ten different offices.[82] Separate grants had to be sought for England and Wales, Ireland and Scotland. For a purely English patent, the cost in official fees alone was £100–120.[83] Until after 1800 there seem to have been no agents regularly available to guide an inventor or his sponsors through the labyrinth; the growth of the distinct profession of patent agent originates from this period, through an initiative of clerks from the offices dealing with patents.[84]

The risks inherent in patent protection were heightened by attitudes among the judges. The law which determined what was patentable was still primitive and liable to change. While it was clear that a patent could be had for a new machine or article, there were doubts, not entirely put aside until 1842, about novel processes of

---

[80] For the annual figures 1750–1852, see Dutton (1984), p. 2. Still in the decade 1750–59, the annual average was 9; but in 1760–69 it was 21, by 1801–09 it was 112 and by 1840–49 had become 458.

[81] 27 Hen. VIII, c. 11.

[82] Eventually ridiculed by Dickens in *Little Dorrit* and *The Poor Man's Tale of a Patent*.

[83] For all three, about £400: Dutton (1984), p. 35.

[84] See Dutton (1984) Chap. 5.

production, and new ways of using old machines.[85] There had been some shift over the requirement that the "manner of manufacture" be "new": originally, it appears that a patent could be defeated only by showing that the invention had already been in use in the country, an idea associated with the policy of attracting foreign technology. But, at least by the 1770s, publication of the idea in the country was being treated as enough to anticipate and defeat the patent.[86] But the most persistent difficulty arose from a fundamental conflict of objectives. As inventiveness began to exhibit its potential, a protectionist desire surfaced which sought to stop any flow abroad of new techniques. In a series of statutes, mainly between 1750 and 1786, Parliament prohibited the export of machines and tools.[87]

The courts, however, had as their task to determine whether a patent was infringed and, after 1753, whether the grant was itself valid. Accordingly, they needed to know what the alleged invention was and felt that competitors should have some way of finding out in advance what ideas were the subject of monopoly rights. The practice of enrolling a specification of the patented invention in Chancery began in the early eighteenth century, possibly as a move by patentees to lay a securer foundation for their own protection.[88] The letters patent began to call for an enrolled specification and for this the "contractualist" explanation came to be offered that the monopoly was given only in consideration of an adequate description of the invention. Where a patentee was suspected of grasping tactics—as was Arkwright over his wool-carding patents—the judges might insist on a high measure of clarity in the description.[89] Caught in this dilemma, Arkwright ruefully threatened, "as they *would* have his machinery made public, to publish descriptions and copper plates of all the parts, that it might be known to foreign nations as well as our own." From this Josiah Wedgwood sought to dissuade him, arguing that "his opponents were few indeed in comparison with the great body of people who would be benefited by having his admirable inventions confined to ourselves."[90]

There could be no resolution of this tension until the British were confident enough to accept free trade even in technical ideas. The laws against machine exports would not finally be lifted until 1841. Then it became possible to treat the patent system as a real source of

[85] The apprehension was that a monopoly might be granted in a general scientific principle: see esp. *Boulton & Watt* v. *Bull* (1795) 2 H.Bl. 463; and for the resolution: *Crane* v. *Price* (1842) 4 B. & G. 580; W. M. Hindmarch, *Law of Patents* (1846) Chap. 5.

[86] Accepted, *e.g.*, in *Liardet* v. *Johnson* (1778), for which see W. D. Hulme (1902) 18 L.Q.R. 280—but the decision was less influential than Hulme suggests—see J. N. Adams and G. Averley (1986) 7 J.Leg.Hist. 156; and see Adams (1987) 8 J.Leg.Hist. 18.

[87] For details of the legislation see the Select Committee on Export of Tools and Machinery, P.P. 1825 (504) V, pp. 6–9.

[88] This was the explanation of the first known instance, Naismith's patent (1711) by W. D. Hulme (1897) 13 L.Q.R. 313, p. 317; but it has been doubted by D. S. Davies (1934) 50 L.Q.R. 86, p. 91, and more emphatically by Adams and Averley (above, n. 86).

[89] See *R.* v. *Arkwright* (1785) Webster's P.C. 64.

[90] See R. S. Fritton and A. P. Wadsworth, *The Strutts and the Arkwrights* (1958), p. 88. A bill to enable the specification to be kept secret during the patent's life came to nothing (see J.H.C., May 9, 1793); but later the registered design system would introduce just this form of secrecy.

technical information. The Patent Office, which began to assume its modern form in 1852, was given the responsibility of publishing specifications at grant.[91]

By the beginning of the nineteenth century a considerable number of invention patents were being granted and only a small proportion of them were the subject of formal litigation.[92] But the inherent difficulties of the system were by no means all to the disadvantage of the patentee. Faced with a determined competitor a patentee would have no alternative but to sue or give up any claim, because his right was in one sense peculiarly dependent on the machinery of court orders: for a decision that the patent was infringed and for damages he would have to look to the common law courts, for an injunction to Chancery. Yet the complexity and costs of patent proceedings were already notorious (and so they have since remained). The weaker-willed, particularly if offered the chance to buy peace by taking a licence from the patentee, might well succumb. Dutton, in his recent examination of the available evidence, concludes that there was a very real appreciation of the risks of seeking to establish a new technique in place of standard practices. Cases were common enough of failed endeavour and of inventions which languished for want of entrepreneurial drive. Inventors, and those who might be persuaded to back them financially, needed the imperfect device of the invention patent. In many cases, they were at least able to use their grant as an item of window-dressing which would help in launching the show. Whether more inventions were exploited, whether introduction came faster than if there had been no such incentive, can only be guessed at; but it looks from his evidence that patents played a more significant part than was previously appreciated.[93]

II. PATENTS: REFORM OR ABOLITION?

As to why the granting system was allowed for so long to remain a remote haven of sinecure, there are some clues in the attitudes of those who had to do with patents. The unfavourable decisions of the judges, as well as statements of inventors and men of commerce, show a ready appreciation that patents were dangerous things and should accordingly be reserved for those with unquestionable inventions; to make them more easily available would lead the unscrupulous to assert all sorts of claims which it would be very time-consuming and expensive to dispose of. When, after various attempts to get the system reviewed, a Select Committee met to receive evidence in 1829, the preponderant complaint before it was of the obscurity and impenetrability of specifications; but there was little agreement on how matters might be improved. Symptomatically the Committee did not continue long enough to report.[94] But it was said by

[91] After 1825, the Treasury had power to permit exporting under licence and the control had become largely illusory: Select Committee on Exportation of Machinery, P.P. 1841 (201) VII.
[92] Dutton (1984), pp. 71–72, working on incomplete data, suggests that the proportion of patents litigated rose slightly after 1840.
[93] Dutton (1984) Chaps. 7–9.
[94] P.P. 1829 (332) III; Dutton (1984), pp. 41–46.

witnesses (and repeated subsequently) that, if the granting regime were to be liberalised, it might be necessary (following French and American precedents) to refer petitions initially to a Committee of scientific experts for a view on the merits of the case. At the same period, the root value of the great inventions was coming at last to be more widely appreciated among the influential—a distinctive strand in a broader political canvas. The judges, for instance, became noticeably more friendly towards invention patents and there was increasing discussion of how the system might be improved.[95] Brougham took an interest and pushed through some minor amendments, including an arrangement by which the Privy Council could extend the patent term in exceptional cases where it had taken a long time to secure a commercial return. Previously this could have been achieved only by private Act.[96]

The changes of 1852, when they at last came, were spurred by the reconciliatory movement to foster the ingenuity of working men by middle-class financial backing.[97] Although opponents of the whole system were beginning to appear even at this point, the running was made by those who wanted to see it more readily available and easily enforced.[98] The old convoluted system of application was replaced by what was in effect a simple process of registration at the new Patent Office, the patent being a single grant for the whole United Kingdom.[99] The official fees, though in the end greater than previously for an English patent, were spread over three stages; initially the cost was reduced to £25.[1] The applicant might file a provisional specification and then take a year in which to put in his complete version. Since it was now well settled that the first among rival inventors to get to the patent office would have the better entitlement, this system allowed some valuable leeway in the business of working out technical details and refinements.

The fear that greater liberality would induce licence seemed soon enough to be realised.[2] Even transparently bad patents had to be resisted before a judge and jury and that remained an expensive and problematic business. While support for the system continued among many technicians and businessmen, and it was assiduously advanced by patents agents and specialist lawyers,[3] severe liberals—economists, journalists, politicians and others—began to urge the wastefulness of the patent monopoly in a world of free and expand-

---

[95] See Dutton (1984), pp. 46–49, 77–81.
[96] 5 & 6 Will. IV, c. 83.
[97] See above, pp. 255–256; for other references, see Dutton (1984) Chap. 3.
[98] See Lords Select Committee on Two Bills to amend the Patent Law, P.P. 1851 (486) XVIII; interestingly the Chairman, Lord Granville, was an anti-patenteer.
[99] 15 & 16 Vict., c. 83. The new administration, typically for its time, came under the supervision of Lords Commissioners ex officio.
[1] Ibid., ss. 6–9.
[2] The numbers of patents granted rose immediately to some 2,000 a year; two-thirds of them would lapse within three years: see Royal Commission on Patents for Invention, P.P. 1864 [3419] XXIX, p. 6.
[3] Agents who undertook the work of procuring patents had begun to appear early in the century, at first from within the bureaucracy. They would grow into a distinct specialist profession, given statutory status in 1883: see Dutton (1984) Chap. 5.

ing trade.[4] Against moral arguments that an inventor deserved reward, the anti-patent school urged that the ability to innovate came largely from the state of technical knowledge of the whole industry—witness the frequency with which several inventors would come to the same discovery at much the same time. Nor was it any longer accepted that the making and application of inventions needed the special incentive of limited monopoly; competition was arguably as effective a goad, for the first inventor would always have his "lead-time." These ideas had a striking impact in some countries which had yet to achieve much in the way of industrialisation: in Switzerland and Holland the patent systems were abandoned for decades. Indeed, it needed both the great depression of world trade after 1873, and a propaganda campaign "quite remarkable for the time," to reverse the current.[5]

In Britain the anti-patent feeling was caught up not only in concern over the growing number of grants that were of dubious validity but also over the disruptive effect that lengthy patent litigation might have on a major industry.[6] In the late 1860s a number of leading public figures despaired of ever finding a workable system and a Royal Commission reported in favour of halving the patent term, subjecting applications to strict examination, forfeiting the patent for failure to work in Britain within two years and compulsory licensing. A Bill to this effect was passed by the Lords in 1874, though abandoned in the Commons.[7]

Three years later, however, the international balance was tipped the other way when Germany enacted a patent law for the whole Reich—one of the first marks of her commitment to catching up on industrial strength by a determined protectionism. By 1883 the leading patent countries, including the United Kingdom, were joining together in the Paris Convention, which established a principle of equal treatment for the nationals of all participant countries and aided the process of applying for patents in a number of countries by a system of priority dating. It also curbed the enthusiasm for invalidating patents if they were not at once used for production in the particular country.[8]

The flood of societies, pamphlets, meetings and lobbying behind this shift saved the British patent system from any drastic foreshortening or cutting down, but in the end it was substantially modified so as to restrain some of the excesses identified by the Royal Commission. A Committee in 1901 acknowledged that perhaps a half of all patents being granted lacked novelty when read against earlier

---

[4] For this anti-patent movement in Britain and Europe, see F. Machlup and E. Penrose, (1950) 10 J.Econ.Hist. 1; for the main political expression of criticism in Britain, see Royal Commission on Patent Laws, P.P. 1864 [3419] XXIX; Select Committee on Letters Patent, P.P. 1872 (193) XI.

[5] Machlup and Penrose (above, n. 4), p. 5. For the Dutch and Swiss experience, see E. Schiff, *Industrialization without National Patents* (1971).

[6] See L. F. Haber, *The Chemical Industry during the Nineteenth Century* (1971), pp. 167, 198–199, for the view that the strategic German advances in dye-stuffs were possible without the distracting litigation which affected the British chemical industry.

[7] Machlup and Penrose (above, n. 4), pp. 3–4.

[8] On the Convention, see S. P. Ladas, *International Protection of Industrial Property* (1930): E. Penrose, *The Economics of the International Patent System* (1951), Chap. 3.

British specifications and a search through this material and consequent examination by the Patent Office was instituted in 1905.[9] The fear that foreigners—in particular the German chemical industry— might acquire British patents purely for the purpose of protecting their import trade into the country led in 1883 to the first tentative provisions for compulsory licensing on this and related grounds.[10]

As far as enforcement was concerned, a practice had been developing of ending the specification with a claim or claims to invention monopolised. This became a positive requirement of the system in 1883.[11] It seemed to offer some solution to the old dilemma of how to give the patentee coverage of alternative versions of the invention without letting him annexe ideas that were essentially different or belonged to territory not yet explored.

As a counterpart, juries might be waived by either party in an infringement action and frequently were.[12] The judges, as sole arbiters of patent issues, began to exhibit something of the hostile scrupulousness towards specifications which had characterised the period up to 1830. Claims were treated as marking out monopoly territory and were accordingly construed against the patentee where there was ambiguity. The game of determining their meaning was played by the standards of the best Chancery minds[13] and that certainly left the patentee with an unfavourable handicap.

In the first half of the twentieth century, the essential rules would remain very much in this condition, the periodic investigations and legislation being concerned with minor adjustments.[14] The paradox of the history accordingly is that an evidently restrictive device should have had its most free deployment in the high age of liberalism. Partly it did so because, if there had to be incentives to stimulate the introduction of new techniques, then the patent system came closer to minimal intervention than direct subsidies, or actual conduct of research, by the state. The motivating force behind the Act of 1852 was the desire to make the market-opportunity monopoly of a patent available to the small innovator as well as the established industrialist. Its disturbing effects greatly advanced the case for abandoning the whole system; but it also provoked a conservative reaction, led by the larger, better-established users, for the re-erection of more substantial barriers to acquiring and exploiting patents.

In the twentieth century movement to "rationalise" private industry, patents could be used for shoring up the position of the reigning firm or cartel, particularly if the rights were shared together in a pool which contained all the advanced technology of the moment. This might, of course be viewed as an unjustified expansion of the power intended by the patent grant. But even in the 1950s the issue was

---

[9] See, P.P. 1901 [Cd. 506, 530] XXIII: Patents Act 1902.

[10] Patents Designs and Trade Marks Act 1883, s.22. A strengthening of the provision in 1907 was given a limited reading in *Hatschek's Patent* (1909) 26 R.P.C. 228: see Haber (above, n. 6), pp. 199–200. The 1907 Act, s.38, also sought to outlaw certain contractual clauses which were considered to "extend" the monopoly.

[11] 1883 Act, s.5(5).

[12] Judicature Act 1873, s.57.

[13] As in *Nobel* v. *Anderson* (1895) 12 R.P.C. 164.

[14] See T. A. Blanco White, *Patents for Inventions* (4th ed., 1974), pp. 26–31; W. R. Cornish, *Intellectual Property* (1981), pp. 83–84.

rarely raised in the public arena.[15] This is at first glance surprising, for in post-war conditions the dominant groupings of an international industry were as likely to be foreign as British. In the past, it has been the deployment of the patent system by outsiders which had most readily raised the cry of "monopolistic abuse" and led to attempts at curbing, such as compulsory licensing and provisions against "tie-ins." That there was so little concern over patent pools once more underscores the preoccupations of the recovery period where we leave this history. What was most vital was to find a legal and political framework which would allow British industry—some of it now nationalised—an adequate place in world markets. If the price was a degree of monopolistic behaviour by the most successful, this was something which, for the moment, the consumer would have to shoulder.

FURTHER READING

Atiyah, P. S., *The Rise and Fall of Freedom of Contract* (1979).
Barton, J. L., "The Enforcement of Hard Bargains" (1987) 103 L.Q.R. 118.
Cohen, J., "The History of Imprisonment for Debt and its Relation to the Development of Discharge in Bankruptcy." (1982) 3 J. Leg. Hist
Cooke, C. A., *Corporation, Trust and Company* (1950).
Dubois, A. B., *The English Business Company after the Bubble Act, 1720–1800* (1938).
Dutton, H., *The Patent System and Inventive Activity during the Industrial Revolution* (1984).
Formoy, R. R., *The Historical Foundations of Modern Company Law* (1923).
Gilmore, G., *The Death of Contract* (1974).
Gower, L. C. B., *Modern Company Law* (4th ed., 1979), Chaps. 2, 3.
Hannah, L., *The Rise of the Corporate Economy* (2nd ed., 1983).
Holden, J. M., *The History of Negotiable Instruments in English Law* (1955).
Horwitz, M. J., "The Triumph of Contract" in *The Transformation of American Law* (1977) Chap. 6.
Hudson, K., *Pawnbroking* (1982).
Hunt, B. C., *The Development of the Business Corporation in England, 1800–1867* (1936).
Jefferys, J. B., *Business Organisation in Great Britain 1856–1914* (1977).
Simpson, A. W. B., "Innovation in Nineteenth Century Contract Law" (1975) 91 L.Q.R. 247.
Simpson, A. W. B., "The Horwitz Thesis and the History of Contracts" (1979) 46 U.Chic.L.R. 533.
Tebbutt, M., *Making Ends Meet: Pawnbroking and Working-Class Credit* (1983).
Welbourne, E., "Bankruptcy before the Era of Victorian Reform" (1932) 16 Camb.Hist.J. 51.

---

[15] Not until the Fair Trading Act 1973, s.101, would patent pools be brought unequivocally within the embargoes of the legislation against restrictive trading practices.

Chapter Four

LABOUR RELATIONS

At the beginning of our period the need to work long and hard dominated the lives of the great bulk of the population. Only members of the landed class could expect sufficient provision without personal effort. As the economy grew, the numbers not directly engaged in income-producing labour would increase, and would spread somewhat further down the social class structure. Among men, some of the elderly might be able to enjoy a retirement not forced on them by physical deterioration. Among women, marriage increasingly brought a change from domestic, agricultural or cottage industry to the labour of child-bearing and house-running, a practice intimately linked to late marriage and the whole pattern of family size and routine.[1]

Children were pushed into work from low ages, when it was available, boys into agriculture and textiles, girls into textiles and domestic service. The extent of child employment in the eighteenth and early nineteenth century can only be guessed at, but it was commonplace. It did not begin to decline until the third quarter of the nineteenth century, when a general rise in real wages (including in agriculture), combined with an increasing degree of mechanisation and regulatory legislation to make it possible to insist upon schooling to the age of thirteen.[2]

The relationships of labour have a relevance to every chapter of this book. Here we are concerned essentially with the contract to provide labour to others for their undertakings, as distinct from labour which leads to the sale of products or to the supply of services on an independent basis. It is a root element in capitalist enterprise, giving legal form to its divisions of labour. With the increase in large farms and the organisation of industry on a factory and workshop basis there was a significant process of change from the latter eighteenth century on. It would eventually bring in its train the modern contract of employment—typically a relationship of some permanence, for a money wage or salary on a full-time basis, with social security payments, PAYE tax deductions, fringe benefits and legal protection against redundancy and unfair dismissal. However, at the beginnings of industrialisation, there was a considerable range of rela-

---

[1] See below, p. 357. In 1851 the census recorded women as 30 per cent. of the whole workforce, only a small proportion of them married. Of this 2.7 million, one million were in domestic service, that immense consumer of Victorian labour. See also, Hunt (1982), pp. 17–25; I. Pinchbeck, *Women Workers in the Industrial Revolution* (1930), esp. App. pp. 317–321; M. Hewitt, *Wives and Mothers in Victorian Industry* (1958), esp. Chaps. 12–14; and, for the later period, J. Lewis, *Women in England 1870–1950* (1984) Chaps. 4, 5.

[2] See below, p. 438ff. The beginnings of the decline in the birth-rate aided the process. See generally, Hunt (1982), pp. 9–17; O. J. Dunlop and R. D. Denman, *English Apprenticeship and Child Labour* (1912) Chaps. 27–28; I. Pinchbeck and M. Hewitt, *Children in English Society* (1969), II 650–56; M. Cruikshank, *Children and Industry* (1981).

tionships for the provision of labour. The temptation to treat any one of them as the norm by virtue of today's familiarities needs to be resisted.

By about 1875 the old forms of service had moved some distance towards modern conceptions of employment. That year also marks a culmination in the legislative recognition of trade unions. It is accordingly at that point that the two Parts of the Chapter divide.

PART 1: SERVICE AND ITS REGULATION 1760–1875

I. LABOUR IN COUNTRY AND TOWN

At the end of the eighteenth century, agriculture still absorbed the energies of a third of the British workforce, a figure which would fall to just over a fifth in 1851 and to a twelfth by 1911.[3] As we have seen, the direction of change was already towards the large units of farming that would supply adequate rents for estate owners and good livelihoods for substantial tenants.[4] Population pressure pushed up demand for food and awakened the acquisitive to the possibilities of land purchase, rationalisation of holdings and enclosure. The effect on agricultural labour was to increase the proportion of those who worked for others, either as "servants" in an old and specific sense, or as casual labourers. The servant in husbandry was normally hired from year to year, initially at a hiring fair. He received for his work, lodging and provision mainly in kind, the only money being a terminating "wage" which stood as a bond for good and faithful service. So long-standing was this form, that the common law presumed a hiring to be by the year until the contrary was shown.[5] This meant that neither side, in the absence of a breach, had any right to terminate the contract by earlier notice; and to prevent it from running into a new term, each had to give a quarter's notice before the annual expiry date.[6]

The relationship was familial, placing the servant under the master's dominance, as with his own wife and children, and domestic servants strictly of the household. This meant that the master had the right to order the servant to work at any time of the day or night.[7]

---

[3] In mid-nineteenth century, agriculture would still be the single largest industry. By 1911, it would be among a number of industries with one to two million workers: others were metal manufacture, building, transport and mining. Domestic service (mainly by women) was larger than any.

[4] Above, p. 136ff.

[5] See, *e.g.* Blackstone, *Commentaries*, I p. 425, referring to the "natural equity" that the master should maintain the servant "throughout the revolutions of the respective seasons; as well when there is work to be done, as when there is not." The presumption would remain law until 1969.

[6] The quarter's notice was standard in agricultural hirings. But domestic servants (in a strict sense) were covered by only one month's notice; this short period was certainly inappropriate to a skilled servant such as an army agent's clerk: *Beeston* v. *Collyer* (1827) 4 Bing. 309: "it would be extraordinary if a party in his station in life could be turned off, like a cook or scullion" (*per* Best C.J.).

[7] Hence the distinction of "exceptive hirings," for poor law purposes, where the labour was "only" for the twelve hours that a factory was running: see below, p. 420; and O. Kahn-Freund (1977) 93 L.Q.R., pp. 521–522.

The farm servant who refused to go on a journey without first having his dinner,[8] the maid who absented herself to visit her dying mother,[9] any servant guilty of an act of insubordination or dereliction of duty, might be punished (physically beaten, if under age[10]) or summarily dismissed.[11] It was not an unanswerable authority: excessive punishment and cruelty might lead to criminal conviction of the master or an order to pay damages—such disputes were not uncommon at quarter sessions or before individual justices or in a local court; occasionally they even reached the rare world of the royal courts.[12] Moreover, the master (at least in some ideal view) took responsibility for the servant's physical and moral condition. He was expected to provide during sickness, and even perhaps to call in medical assistance.[13] Nonetheless, eighteenth century judges had no more difficulty than those four centuries before in seeing the servant, like a wife or child, as the property of the master, so that he might sue for damages if another enticed the servant away.[14] Lord Kenyon was willing to extend this liability to include even the employer who took on another's servant without initially knowing of the broken relationship.[15] As a form of paternalism it was highly possessive.[16]

In-service in agriculture was typically the experience of the young, as they moved away from their own families. Casual labouring on a daily or weekly basis, was a condition to which the agricultural worker graduated with time, as he married and was allowed a cottage,

---

[8] *Spain* v. *Arnott* (1817) 2 Stark. 256.

[9] *Turner* v. *Mason* (1845) 14 M. & W. 112.

[10] The beating had to be "with moderation." If the servant died in the process, it would be death by misadventure unless "so barbarous as to exceed all bounds." The servant who ran away would be imprisoned by the justices for up to a year, unless he returned; but he could not be kept by a master as a prisoner: see *Burn's Justice of the Peace* (ed. of 1805), pp. 190–191.

[11] The Statute of Artificers required a summary dismissal to be approved by the justices (s.5) and Lord Mansfield insisted that this be done: *Temple* v. *Prescott* (1773) Cald. 14n.; but other judges of the King's Bench considered that a master could sack a maid without ceremony on discovering her pregnancy: *R.* v. *Brampton* (*Inhabitants*) (1777) Cald. 11.

[12] See, *e.g.* the decisions in n. 9 and 10 above.

[13] At common law, this appeared to give the servant no more direct right of action than a wife or child (see below, p. 370). But as late as 1795, Lord Kenyon was prepared to recognise that an apothecary might sue the master upon an implied undertaking to pay for attention to a servant while under the master's roof: *Scarman* v. *Castell* (1795) 1 Esp. 270. But this was not the case for a servant in husbandry if he was elsewhere (*Luby* v. *Wiltshire*, see *ibid.*, at 271, Lord Mansfield C.J.); it was soon excluded for a weekly servant (*Simmons* v. *Wilmot* (1799) 3 Esp. N.P. 91, Lord Eldon), and then more generally, in order not to overburden "many persons who are obliged for purposes of their trade, to keep a number of servants": *Wennall* v. *Adney* (1802) 3 B. & P. 247 (where a counsel sought to put liability upon Lord Mansfield's notion of a consideration growing from "natural love and affection"—see above, p. 207; this provoked the reporters into a celebrated note attacking the Mansfieldian heterodoxy). In effect, any responsibility for medical attention was left to the overseers of the poor.

[14] The action for seduction or enticement, *per quod servitium amisit*, first appeared as a judicial extension of the Statute of Labourers 1349: Holdsworth, IV pp. 383–385.

[15] *Blake* v. *Lanyon* (1795) 6 T.R. 221, an important stepping stone in the evolution of the tort of inducing breach of contract: see below, pp. 329–330.

[16] See generally, Fox (1985), pp. 2–5, 44–47.

with perhaps a plot and some grazing animals.[17] Practices varied between localities but the long-run movement was to increase the proportion of casual workers to in-servants. Apart from the cottage, the day labourer tended to be paid in money, though part might still come in kind. The labourer's earnings accordingly fluctuated with the seasons; and in years of poor harvest he and his family would be afflicted with longer periods of under-employment than usual. A general over-supply of such labour settled as an endemic blight upon the southern counties in late eighteenth century, keeping earnings from labouring wages very low and forcing communities to adopt expedients to supplement them, mainly through the machinery of the poor law.[18] It was an imbalance that the progress of industry would not re-adjust for a half-century.

The medieval towns had fostered numerous crafts; cloth-making, clothing and leather-work, milling, baking and brewing, saddlery and bow-making are among those listed in the Elizabethan Statute of Artificers 1563. They carried forward the old guild structure by which an entrant progressed from apprentice to journeyman and thence to master craftsman. This imported a two-fold division of service, providing an urban counterpart to agricultural labour. The apprentice, whose family generally paid a premium for his induction into the mysteries of the craft, was taken into the master's family and subjugated to his will (and his wife's). Lasting mostly for seven years, it was a long and often difficult relationship which could collapse amid recriminatory litigation.[19] Once it was complete, the fledged craftsman would continue to work for a master, with a journeyman's independence and in general for a money wage. This might be calculated by time (in which case the difficulty was to secure hard work) or by the piece (when attention shifted to shoddy workmanship).[20]

Many of these trades had, through local bye-laws or charters, or through general legislation,[21] succeeded in making apprenticeship a condition of entry. While this type of restriction was becoming increasingly hard to enforce in the eighteenth century, equally it might survive until mechanisation induced capitalist production on a large scale. This would finally put an end to the journeyman's hope that, by a little saving and a degree of luck, he would be able eventually to set up on his own. He became perforce a skilled wage-worker for life.

The organisation of production by investment of considerable capital and the employment of substantial labour had been building sporadically before the appearance of the cotton factories with their powered machines for spinning and weaving. In textiles particularly, there had been the growth of cottage industry in which the

[17] But to get this labouring force to live in a neighbouring parish would keep down the poor rate: see below, p. 426. So there was an undoubted tendency for the better organised, less paternal estate owners and farmers to reduce their own supply of agricultural cottages; sometimes they knocked them down.
[18] See below, p. 425ff.
[19] See Dunlop and Denman (above n. 2) Chap. 11; Rule (1981), pp. 95–101.
[20] On the growth of skilled work in eighteenth century manufacture and mining, see Rule (1981) Chap. 1, M. Berg et al. (ed.) *Manufacture in Town and Country before the Factory* (1983), Chaps. 1, 2.
[21] Discussed below, p. 289ff.

outworker took the material and hired the frame or other tooling from the entrepreneur. Payment was normally by the piece for completed work. It was a form of enterprise for unmechanised weaving (notably in the woollen manufacture of the south-west), lace-making and some types of metal-work, with which it proved difficult for independent worker-craftsmen to compete. Typically it spread from a manufacturing town into the surrounding villages, where it took hold as work for those members of a family not immediately engaged in agriculture. It provided the precedent from which the cotton factories of the north-west grew.

In addition there were proto-industries of more integral character: mines for coal, iron, tin and copper, ironworks, glassworks, potteries and dockyards required substantial capital and the employment of labour forces of a hundred or more, rather than the workshop of a dozen or so, which counted as a large unit for the older trades.[22] These carried farthest the division of labour which separated the worker from any responsibility or profit in the thing produced; he did not make or purchase the starting material, he neither owned nor ran commercial risks in the product. His risk centred around the "wage," however precisely it was made up, and to earning it he devoted a large part of his waking hours. It was for the master primarily to choose how substantial that risk would be. In some of the early manufactures such as glass, the need to conserve a trained workforce meant that contracts might be for several years.[23] But the movement was towards short service in which the labourer bore his own risks and could look only to charity or the poor law to save him from starvation once work dried up. The turning of employment from a serflike status, with fixed and subjugate conditions, into a "free" contractual relationship—Maine's celebrated indicator of a progressive society[24]—was not something which had to be demanded by industrial capitalism. Several centuries of experimentation put the causative thrust the other way. In allowing the capitalist to organise his labour on terms not dictated by outside practice, the law fulfilled an important precondition of the coming industrialisation.

II. The Old Controls

(a) The Statute of Artificers

In 1800 there were still numerous statutory controls over the various forms of labour, chief among them being the Statute of Artificers 1563. This Act, part of the wide Tudor fear of landless, marauding

---

[22] See, e.g., W. H. B. Court, *The Rise of the Midland Industries* (1938), p. 177 ff.; D. Bythell, *The Handloom Weavers* (1969); M. I. Thomis, *The Town Labourer and the Industrial Revolution* (1974) Chap. 5; Fox (1985), pp. 61–67.

[23] The silkworker pauper who was the subject of the *Devizes* case (below, n. 54) was bound for a period of four years.

[24] *Ancient Law* (1861) Chap. 5. On attitudes to wage labour in the early modern period, see C. Hill in C. H. Feinstein, *Socialism, Capitalism and Economic Growth* (1969), p. 338.

vagrants, had struck out in three main directions. First, it had required justices at sessions annually to set wages, both the money wages of town labour and the mixed provisions of the country.[25] The measure was primarily to curb higher demands, the main penalties being against those who paid and received more than the rate set.[26] As a system, its application seems always to have been patchy. Certainly in the eighteenth century, it was increasingly ignored. In some counties the old rates were re-set as a matter of form, because prices changed little and the main stimulus for altering wages was missing. But, as we shall see, wage-fixing was by no means wholly moribund.[27]

Secondly, the Statute imposed seven-year apprenticeships on all those entering any "craft now used within the realm"[28]—a period far longer than was needed to teach the skills of most trades and accordingly intended to impose a close, domestic control over an otherwise unruly element in the towns.[29] Thirdly, the justices were empowered to compel into yearly contracts of service those who had a trade but no employment and those who were without work on the land.[30] But to do this, required willing employers, and the hope of turning the justices into directive labour exchanges was unreal; nine years later the parishes were obliged to assume responsibility for the destitute through a public poor law.[31] For all the fears of roving marauders, there was a need to procure mobility of labour. The means of watching over that movement would be procured by the rules of settlement, removal and certification of the poor law, rather than through masters' testimonials as envisaged by the 1563 Act. By contrast a section of the Act sought to impose discipline on piece-workers by requiring them, on pain of a month's imprisonment or a £5 fine, to complete work undertaken.[32] This, with its re-enactments and extensions in Master and Servant Acts, would remain a regular weapon in work-force control during the first century of industrialisation.[33]

(b) The Fate of Tudor Regulation

In pre-industrial as in industrial conditions, work was often harsh and exhausting; sometimes it was dangerous and unhealthy. But those who laboured were not all reduced by it to a condition of abject submission, any more than they all went to work in smiling cooperation. There is considerable evidence that, in line with human relationships generally, in-servants and wage-labourers treated their

[25] 5 Eliz., c. 4, ss.15–19.
[26] But a later statute (1 Jac. I, c. 6) made it an offence for clothiers to pay their workers less than the rate.
[27] See generally, W. E. Minchinton (ed.), *Wage Regulation in Pre-Industrial England* (1972), Intro. and pp. 34–91 (R. H. Tawney).
[28] 5 Eliz. I, c. 4, s.26.
[29] Adam Smith (*Wealth of Nations* (1976 ed.), pp. 135–140) made a strong case against undue protection through apprenticeship, which was much repeated.
[30] 5 Eliz. I, c. 4, ss.3–7. The justices could direct labour to get in the harvest: see ss.22–23.
[31] See below, p. 417ff.
[32] 5 Eliz. I, c. 4, s.13.
[33] See below, pp. 294–295.

employers argumentatively, aggressively, truculently.[34] This helps to explain the severity of the master's legal powers of command and control. Deference and obedience were demanded without any natural expectation that they would be accorded; the vertical lines of place seem often to have needed harsh assertion if they were to remain at all firm.

It also suggests why ordinary workers joined together periodically in protest against their conditions and in the hope of extracting some amelioration. Collective action, as recent studies have made clear,[35] was a regular phenomenon of working relations in the town trades, especially when a shortage of particular skills or legal protection against interlopers gave strength to the cause. Masters, as much as journeymen, found mutual agreement preferable to competition with each other. On the workers' side, the strike was a not uncommon weapon. These "combinations" or "conspiracies" (as they were labelled) could occur without the continuing organisation that would later be provided by trade unions. But just as it was among employees with craft skills that the union idea was gradually bred, so it was with them that the hope of retaining and re-enforcing parts of the Statute of Artificers still remained alive. Against their masters they wanted improved conditions and security; against the rest of the world—in particular the organisers of new, mechanised efficiencies—they needed even more basic protection.

The wage-fixing power of the justices was, as already noted, no regular institution of eighteenth-century life, rural or urban. But still it had a place, not so much as law imposed from above, but rather as law to make firm and general the results of confrontation and negotiation. Between masters and journeymen there are numerous instances of wage and other demands, accompanied by strikes, mob processions and destruction of work—aggressive tactics, which resulted in a compromise brought before justices: their fixing of a wage rate then gave security that the bargain would be observed and could be imposed on any minority of masters who could not be brought in by agreement. A few trades that were prone to conflict had, in the course of particular settlements, acquired more modern statutes that provided for wage-rate fixing by the justices. The London tailors had been embroiled in a large strike in 1720 which led to an actual prescription of a wage and hours in the Act itself, as well as a power for the justices to alter the levels.[36] Occasionally, masters reacted against this process: in 1757, the West country clothiers even secured the repeal of special wage-fixing arrangements for their piece-work which had been enacted only in the previous year.[37]

The Act of Elizabeth, however, continued in place and was thought of by both masters and journeymen in established trades as an

---

[34] On the constant complaint of the upper classes against the insolence of servants, see J. J. Hecht, *The Domestic Servant Class in Eighteenth Century England* (1956) Chap. 3; P. Horn, *The Rise and Fall of the Victorian Servant* (1975) Chap. 7.

[35] See below, p. 295ff.

[36] 7 Geo. I, c. 13; revised by 8 Geo. III, c. 17.

[37] 29 Geo. II, c. 33, 30 Geo. II, c. 12. A well-known later example of special machinery was that for the Spitalfields silk weavers: 13 Geo. III, c. 68; 32 Geo. III, c. 44; A. Plummer, *The London Weavers' Company* (1970), pp. 315–339.

ultimate point of recourse, if negotiation or informal arbitration proved ineffective. Certainly, magistrates regarded intervention in serious labour disputes as a normal role, indeed one of their peace-keeping functions in a world where social tensions easily disintegrated into threats and violence. In London, the blind Sir John Fielding, who assiduously built up the special position of the Bow Street magistracy, was regularly involved as an intermediary; but this was the case with any justice who could command a measure of respect from both sides.[38] One of the major strains upon the magisterial system when applied to the coming industrial districts would be its inability to produce such figures of trust.

Already, by the time of the wars with France, however, there was an undoubted shift in perceptions. Between 1800 and 1804, for instance, London tailors, carpenters and shoemakers all procured wage rises from Quarter Sessions.[39] Then in 1811 journeymen millers in Kent sought and procured a mandamus from King's Bench to their sessions to consider a case under the statute; but Lord Ellenborough pointedly left it to the discretion of the Sessions whether or not to set a rate. In due course, they refrained.[40] The prevailing mood of the Commons was displayed by a Select Committee which pronounced that

> "no interference of the legislature with the freedom of trade, or with the perfect liberty of every individual to dispose of his time and of his labour in the way and on the terms which he may judge most conducive to his own interest, can take place without violating general principles of the first importance to the prosperity and happiness of the community . . . "[41]

In 1813, the wage-fixing provisions of the Statute of Artificers were accordingly repealed.[42] But that of itself was by no means sufficient to atomise labour markets so that neither masters or men in future sought to act in concert. It was merely one step in the movement to control "combination," and to that we return below.

The Elizabethan regulation of apprenticeship retained its staying power as long as it functioned as part of the whole system of guild regulation, by which only the craftsmen who had freedom of the borough or corporation could practise independently within its bounds. The guild might well prescribe the number of apprentices a master could have and provide machinery for wage and other negotiations with the journeymen. The seven-year term was likely to enhance restrictions of trade to the benefit of all within it. It could prove a real barrier in particular to capitalists with new methods who wanted to set up business with numbers of workers paid at less than journeymen rates.

In the course of the eighteenth century, guild restrictions came

---

[38] See Dobson (1980) Chap. 6.
[39] I. Prothero, *Artisans and Politics in Early Nineteenth Century London* (1979), pp. 38–39.
[40] *R.* v. *Kent (Justices)* (1811) 14 East 395.
[41] Report on Weavers' Petition P.P. 1810–11 (232) II, p. 1; see likewise the Select Committee on Woollen Manufacture, P.P. 1806 (268) III.
[42] A few special cases, such as the Spitalfields Acts, would survive a little longer.

under increasing attack, not least from the common law courts, which from the previous century had begun to destroy the more egregious guild rules as being unreasonable restraints of trade[43]; in so doing they would frequently create (and win) a conflict of law with borough or corporate tribunals which existed to police the trade of the town and drive away intruders.[44] In the same spirit, the common law courts confined the apprenticeship requirement of 1563 to its literal terms, allowing it to cover no trade which had developed since, and in other ways restricting its scope.[45]

As small-scale industry spread from established towns to rising villages, there might be no one with the interest and persistence to enforce the apprenticeship requirement where it did apply. In many trades it succumbed.[46] Sometimes it was subverted by masters, who, expecting a growth in business over a long term, took on shop-fuls of "false" apprentices. In the disturbed conditions of the Napoleonic wars, journeymen in numerous trades and places began to organise against undercuttings of the old system where it remained. The "Luddite" machine-breaking in the Midlands in 1811–12 was directed against framework-knitting masters who were using untrained labour to produce inferior goods.[47] In London, the great centre of many crafts, a series of prosecutions to enforce the law was launched using the same attorney, Chippendale.[48] Then in 1812 the "mechanics of the metropolis" petitioned Parliament for restatement and extension of the legal prohibition. They were countered by masters who rallied fears that this would constitute a first victory for workmen intent on collective enforcement of all sorts of terms and conditions. A year after the abolition of wage-fixing, Sergeant Onslow's Bill to repeal the remaining sections of the 1563 Act was easily carried, amid rhetoric which showed how thoroughly Adam Smith's arguments had been transmuted into simple cries of *laissez-faire*.[49]

Blackstone's account of master and servant law underscored its serf-like elements. Although he distinguished between in-service, apprenticeship and day labour, he placed his description among the personal relationships, preceding those of husband and wife, parent and child, guardian and ward; only a passing reference was to be

---

[43] See above, pp. 267–268. On apprenticeship generally, see Dunlop and Denman (above, n. 2); Rule (1981), Chap. 4.

[44] Notably in Coke C.J.'s famous decision against the tailors of Ipswich for requiring a qualified tailor to seek their licence before working there: (1615) 11 Co. Rep. 53a.

[45] In *Raynard* v. *Chase* (1756) 1 Burr. 2, Lord Mansfield castigated the statute as penal, in restraint of natural right, contrary to the common law in general and of doubtful policy. He approved of cases confining it strictly to the trades it listed; mentioned the limitation that a person duly apprenticed to one trade could thereafter practise another; and held that a sleeping partner did not have to be qualified if the active partner was.

[46] When the tailors of Bath were deprived of their enforcement power in 1765, apprenticeships disappeared in all trades: R. S. Neale, *Bath* (1981), pp. 63–69. For London, see J. R. Kellett (1958) 10 Ec.H.R. (2d) 381.

[47] M. I. Thomis, *The Luddites* (1970).

[48] For details, see Prothero (above, n. 39) Chap. 3; T. K. Derry (1931) 3 Ec. H.R. 67 discusses conflicts among calico printers (1803–04), woollen workers (1802–06), cotton weavers (1808) and silk weavers (1811), mostly in country districts.

[49] Derry, above n. 48.

found in his discussion of contract.[50] Equally he gave somewhat anachronistic prominence to the various regulations of the Statute of Artificers.[51] Yet wage-fixing and compulsory apprenticeship were already sporadic and would fail entirely when workers sought to give them new effect. For the growing number of capitalist employers, facing the organisation of labour on scarcely precedented scale, the power to set terms without legal preconception was vital and accordingly they pushed towards the contractual, variable possibilities in the earlier forms.

As mechanised cotton mills began to take over cotton production they were worked partly by parish apprentices and partly by families drawn in from surrounding agriculture, cottage work and, soon enough, from their own first generations. The apprentices might still be bound for long periods, but the older workers were mostly taken on piece-work rates, or daily, weekly or even hourly terms, often bringing in family members to help them, as in domestic manufacture. The employer thus had a force which could be set to such work as he had, running his machines for fourteen, sixteen or even more hours a day to meet peak production, putting onto short time in slack. He could impose discipline in all sorts of matters if he chose. Already in the early eighteenth century, the great Crawley ironworks in County Durham had operated to a Lawbook. Here were prescribed numerous offences which might result in fines (from wages) of a few pence to forty shillings, demotion and ultimately dismissal.[52] At his Etruria pottery, Josiah Wedgwood laid down a moral, paternal regime in great detail; there were, for instance, fines for leaving a fire at night and playing fives near windows; to strike an overseer or abuse him courted dismissal.[53] Masters who did not commit themselves to explicit rules could claim a large discretion over what was to be done and not done. In 1829 a silk factory foreman gave evidence that the rules "existed only in the breast of the master but were known and acted on by the work people."[54] So it must often have been.

While the ascendant manufacturing interest had no difficulty in removing legal fetters which got in the way of its needs, equally it was able to secure law that it deemed a necessary supplement to internal discipline. When domestic outwork was reaching its height, an Act of 1777 refurbished older provisions against failing to complete piece-work: it became an offence to neglect the working up of materials for eight consecutive days, punishable with up to three months in a house of correction or prison.[55] Then in 1823 the Master and Servant Act rendered virtually any breach of an employment contract by a servant a summary crime, again with a maximum of

---

[50] *Commentaries*, I Chap. 14, III Chap. 9. O. Kahn-Freund ((1977) 93 L.Q.R. 508) notes, as a remarkable illustration of Blackstone's impress, that master and servant was still an aspect of textbooks on domestic relations law appearing in the 1950s.

[51] Equally so in much-used compendia such as *Burn's Justice of the Peace* (tit. Servants).

[52] *The Lawbook of the Crawley Ironworks* (ed. M. W. Flinn, 1957).

[53] N. McKendrick (1961) 4 Hist. J. 30.

[54] *R. v. St John, Devizes* (1827) 9 B. & C. 396.

[55] 17 Geo. III, c. 56, s.8; and see 6 Geo. III, c. 25, on failure to complete a contract of service.

three months' imprisonment.[56] As a penal contract, employment thus became nakedly one-sided, for a master in breach could only be sued for damages.[57]

(c) Conspiracy and Combination

Adam Smith accepted as a commonplace that wage-labour would breed collective action, the workmen combining to raise wages, the masters to lower them.[58] Dobson has traced accounts of 383 British labour disputes between 1717 and 1800. Nearly three-quarters of the issues were over wages or hours, many of the rest over breaches in established practices of apprenticeship or working methods—the factors which set a craft apart from the competition of the unskilled. The disputes occurred with somewhat increasing frequency as the century progressed, particularly in the early 1790s, though there had been bad years in the 1730s and the Wilkesite disturbances of 1768 had brought a rash of strikes in their train. London, with a sixth of the population, had rather more than its share of disputes, for the concentration of workers and the capitalising tendency of the masters gave a cutting edge to its labour conflicts. Other areas of recurrent trouble were the south-west with its woollen-cloth trades and the north-west, where hatmakers, carpenters, coalmen, weavers and cotton-workers were all recorded as having struck. A similar variety of trades were embroiled at one time or another in different parts of the kingdom, and very occasionally even some segment of the agricultural work-force.[59] There were aspects of life within the craft trades which made joint action on demands a natural feature of life. In London, in particular, the supply of workmen was secured through houses of call—public houses at which became recognised collecting points. Without any elaborate organisation the journeymen at a house might evolve a standard set of rules which they presented to masters for acceptance and they might well link with the other houses when larger-scale action was called for.[60] Wages were often paid at the houses and a box club might be run there, offering, for small weekly contributions, some security against illness, incapacity, burial and widowhood. In such an environment, close-knit associations of workmen could flourish effectively, working within a tradition which acknowledged both journeyman and master and allowed for the one eventually to become the other. It was a condition that lacked the formal relationships of modern trade unionism, through some tendency to settle upon written rules and the election of distinct officers became apparent with time. The box club, in particular, often evolved into a form

---

[56] 4 Geo. IV, c. 34; D. Simon in J. Saville (ed.) *Democracy and the Labour Movement* (1954) 160; T. R. Tholfsen, *Working-Class Radicalism in Mid-Victorian England* (1976), pp. 180–186.
[57] 4 Geo. IV, c. 34, ss.1, 2.
[58] *Wealth of Nations* (1976 ed.), pp. 83–85.
[59] Dobson (1980), esp. Chap. 1 and App.; and see Rule (1979) Chaps. 7, 8; Webb (1920), pp. 19–47.
[60] Dobson (1980) Chap. 3.

of friendly society, and might receive both protection and inspection by Quarter Sessions under an Act of 1793.[61]

For the most part, as the Webbs chose to underscore, this was a stage before the emergence of modern trade unionism. But its informality and occasional character should not be taken, as they implied, to demonstrate ineffectiveness, a condition from which evolution was inherently desirable. It was a response of its own time, when trade and labour recruitment remained largely local, and masters and servants still enjoyed a symbiosis that capitalist organisation would sever. It embraced only a small, relatively privileged sector of those who lived by manual labour.[62]

The calls for re-instigation of the Elizabethan statutory machinery were not the only signs of increased demands from labour under the disturbed conditions of war and economic fluctuation. Craftsmen were beginning to coordinate between localities and even between different parts of the country. Their use of lawyers in pursuit of their campaigns showed their ability to raise funds towards sustaining their position.[63] Justices and government alike were becoming alarmed that organisation was being coordinated between localities and even different parts of the country. The hot Jacobin talk of the corresponding societies might spread, so they feared, to the craft clubs and lead them from their legitimate pursuits to revolutionary aspirations.[64] In a nervous atmosphere, when there had already been much indictment against treason and sedition and a variety of new laws against illegal oath-taking and unlawful meeting, the Combination Act of 1799 was passed, to be replaced by a somewhat modified version in 1800.

Both the Webbs and the Hammonds wrote of these Acts as initiating a quarter-century of repression against incipient trade unionism.[65] Dorothy George challenged this on two fronts: first, because these Combination Acts were merely the end-point of an eighteenth century tradition rendering strike activities and similar "combinations" illegal under the common law and through statutes directed to particular trades; and secondly because the Acts were in practice not much resorted to.[66] As to the prior history, she overstated her objection in some degree. All these historians, and others, have repeated, apparently without investigation, that there were forty-odd statutes against combinations already on the statute book, because this had been Whitbread's rather indiscriminate estimate in

---

[61] 33 Geo. III, c. 54. Twenty years after its enactment, the Manchester magistrates were much disturbed that they had passed as friendly societies clubs which they had come to fear as dangerous combinations of journeymen; and they petitioned the Home Secretary for new legal protection: see Aspinall (1949), pp. 156–158.

[62] But informal relations could be of great significance even in new trades such as cotton weaving: H. A. Turner, *Trade Union Growth, Structure and Policy* (1962) Pt. II.

[63] In *R. v. Nield* (below, n. 78), for instance, the unionists were able to instruct five counsel, led by the celebrated Thomas Erskine.

[64] For indications of these fears, see Aspinall (1949) Chap. 2; Thompson (1968), pp. 544–558; *cf.* Dobson (1980), p. 122.

[65] Webb (1920), pp. 71–72; Hammond (1925), p. 129; and see Fox (1985), pp. 73–91; J. V. Orth (1987) 5 Leg. Hist. H.R. 175.

[66] (1927) 1 Ec. Hist. R. 214 (and also (1936) 6 Ec. Hist. R. 172); but *cf.* Orth (above, n. 65).

1800.[67] There were certainly a few instances, including a venerable Act of 1548 against price-fixing as well as improper wage-demands;[68] but most of the specific trade statutes said no more about illegal collective action than about statutory wage-fixing by the justices.[69] What had become settled in the course of the eighteenth century was that the common law crime of conspiracy extended to collective action by workers to procure or sustain demands. The journeymen tailors of Cambridge had been successfully prosecuted for this offence in 1721[70]; for the rest of the century Dobson has traced some thirty instances of similar proceedings, or attempts at them.[71] The range of common law conspiracy was far from clear, but it was an indictable misdemeanour requiring the solemnities of presentation by grand jury and conviction by trial jury. What the Combination Acts brought—as had the occasional precedent covering, for instance, the London tailors, the silkworkers, the hatters, the paper-makers[72]—was the chance of a rapid disposal of the question of criminality, together with a brief sentence. In a world where the magistracy had to maintain an active watch and bring a peaceful conclusion if they could to arguments which mostly had some justification on each side, summary discipline added a distinctive weapon. In particular, it might enable the leading spirits in a journeyman's club or union to be picked off by prosecution before the general run of their fellows had been persuaded into striking. At that point, a short spell in prison with little ado might be a deflection, while if it was delayed until the dispute was truly under way, it could become a cause of its own and multiply the difficulties facing conciliators.

The 1799 Act was passed rather casually on a petition from the master millwrights,[73] who sought means of nipping "conspiracies" of their workmen in the bud. Turned by the government, on Wilberforce's suggestion, into a statute of general effect, it represented the perennial, simplistic hope that strikes can be eliminated by repression. It treated contracts and combinations between workmen as illegal if they were for obtaining any advance of wages, for reducing or altering hours of work, for decreasing the quantity of work, for

---

[67] Parl. Reg. LV, 469.

[68] 2 & 3 Edw. VI, c. 15; Hedges and Winterbottom (1930), p. 12. It was occasionally resurrected in the eighteenth century: Rule (1979), p. 175. Trades which did have enactments outlawing combination were the London tailors (see above, n. 36) and the papermakers (36 Geo. III, c. 111—the precedent for 1799).

[69] Despite announcing that they were intended to put down unlawful combination, they often concentrated upon providing against embezzlement of work materials and payment of wages by truck—clearly grievances which had led to disturbances and thence to the enactment.

[70] (1721) 8 Mod. 10 ill reported, but apparently accepted in R. v. Eccles (1783) 1 Leach 274 and R. v. Mawbey (1796) 6 T.R. 619 at 636; see R. S. Wright, Law of Criminal Conspiracies (1872), pp. 52–53; Hedges and Winterbottom (1930) Chap. 2.

[71] Dobson (1980), Chap. 9, esp., pp. 127–129. The sentences, when the proceedings were actually carried to conviction, were mostly for a month or two in prison, though in one or two cases the period was two years. Even these, however, were mild punishments in the age of the "Bloody Code" against property crimes.

[72] See 7 Geo. I, c. 13 and 8 Geo. III, c. 17; 32 Geo. III, c. 44; 22 Geo. II, c. 27 and 17 Geo. III, c. 55; 36 Geo. III, c. 111.

[73] i.e. significantly, the engineers of the new mechanised industry. For the Parliamentary course, see Hammond (1925), pp. 115–124.

preventing any person from employing whomsoever he should think proper, or for "controlling or in any way affecting any person carrying on manufacture, trade or business, in the conduct or management thereof."[74] The revised version in the following year, which originated from a group of radicals, including the playwright, Sheridan, adhered to this embracing formulation; but it also made masters' combinations void and subject to a £20 fine, a provision that proved to be not entirely cosmetic.[75] More importantly it required two justices to hear the charge, rather than one, and gave a right of appeal to quarter sessions—a significant counter-response for those accused.[76] In addition, there were provisions for the compulsory arbitration of disputes by nominated arbitrators or, if necessary, by a single justice (and above him quarter sessions).[77] This last indicated that the prohibition against contracts and combinations, broad as it appeared to be, could scarcely cover every meeting of workmen to submit a claim. The judges indeed required proof of an agreement to pursue the claim by withdrawal of labour, picketing, violence or similar pressure.[78] Even so, some clubs took the precaution of adopting the form of friendly societies,[79] or of avoiding rules requiring members to support positive action (unless it was to seek amendment of the law by Parliament, which remained outside the Act).

As to the extent to which the Act was actually deployed, the history remains clouded, for there are no statistics and such reports as have been recovered (mainly from newspapers) tend to be imprecise about the basis of the prosecution. In 1824, when Francis Place orchestrated his campaign for repeal, it was argued both that the 1800 Act was unused and that it forced unions of men into secret and violent conspiracies.[80] Clearly it was employed patchily and not as part of some unrelenting campaign to stamp out labour organisation wherever it reared its head. This was so not only because the criminal law as a whole was in amateur hands, but because the economic complexities of labour relations, then as now, made prosecution a twin-edged weapon.

At the present stage of knowledge, the Webbs remain the best guide. On their evidence, the Act had only a small role in established crafts. In Nottingham, for instance, with some fifty craft unions in this period, only five prosecutions were known.[81] On the other hand,

---

[74] 39 Geo. III, c. 81. For the two acts, see Hedges and Winterbottom (1930) Chap. 3.

[75] 39 & 40 Geo. III, c. 106, ss.1, 17.

[76] *Ibid.*, ss.2, 23. No justice could sit if he were a master in the trade in question—a problem in the new industrial districts in particular: s.16.

[77] *Ibid.*, ss.18–22. Though no evidence has been found of actual reliance on these provisions, their existence may well have induced the two sides to a dispute to use a conciliator or voluntary arbitrator. These, after all, were not infrequently resorted to.

[78] See *R. v. Nield* (1805) 6 East 417; "If workmen could have borne the cost of appeals, it seems probable that many of the dubious convictions might have been quashed in this way" (Hedges & Winterbottom (1930), p. 30); but certiorari was notoriously expensive. Note s.9 of the Act which obliged a conspirator to give evidence for the Crown, with the advantage of indemnity from prosecution himself.

[79] Following the registration procedure under the Act of 1793; see above, p. 61.

[80] See below, p. 299.

[81] M. I. Thomis, *The Town Labourer and the Industrial Revolution* (1974), p. 138. Even so a determined employer might resort to the courts, as did the proprietor of *The Times* against his printers in 1810: Webb (1920), pp. 78–79.

it was used, amid magisterial denunciations, to put down strikes in the new industries of the north, notably cotton: the Scottish weavers in 1812, the Bolton weavers in 1817, the Manchester spinners in 1818 were all dealt with in peremptory style which contributed to "an abundant record of judicial barbarities."[82]

The real novelty lay not so much in the Combination Acts themselves as in the emerging forms of industrial employment and the new basis of labour relations which they entailed. The old and complex linkages between masters and journeymen were being replaced by the structural divide between capitalist mill-owners and their hands. "Combination" in these conditions was acquiring a new fearfulness. Employers might band together to resist workers' demands, or assert their own, just as they commonly combined against customers to set prices, divide markets and limit supplies. Even so there were plenty among them who expected direct state support against defiance by those they employed: the criminal law would continue for the first three-quarters of the new century to be a weapon in their hands but one that could rarely be turned against them—a class instrument in a world coming to be defined by class divisions.

The Act of 1800, together with the prohibitions against combination in particular trades, the common law of conspiracy and the master and servant laws, survived through the years when wage-fixing by the justices and compulsory apprenticeship lost their lives, repeals which could only increase the tendency to group action by labour. While there were those, such as the framework-knitter, Gravener Henson, who stressed the superfluity of the anti-combination laws[83]; the tailor, Francis Place, the undoubted leader of the campaign to secure their repeal, made much more of their distortive effect upon the functioning of orthodox market principles.[84] The laws, he argued, drove journeymen and operatives into secret conclave and violent, destructive action. Freed of these constraints, workers would appreciate the real prospects of wage and other demands and would allow the market to determine whether or not they were in a position to succeed against their masters. Accordingly he found support among radicals in Parliament—notably Joseph Hume—and even some manufacturers. A carefully organised Select Committee was led to recommend repeal[85] and the ensuing Act went a considerable way: those (workmen or masters) who entered agreements of the type listed in the Act of 1800 should not be liable to prosecution under it or "any other Criminal Information or Punishment whatever, under the Common or Statute Law."[86] There was also an explicit entitlement to engage in peaceful picketing; but violent or threatening behaviour of various kinds remained unlawful.

The following months brought an upturn in trade, a rise in food prices and with them a run of wage demands supported by strikes.

[82] Webb (1920), pp. 81–83.
[83] For Henson's part, see M. D. George (1927) 1 Ec. Hist. R. 214, 215; Prothero (above, n. 39), p. 175.
[84] For Place's campaign and the evidence to Hume's Committee, see Webb (1920), pp. 96–105; Pelling (1976), pp. 20–23; Prothero (above, n. 39) Chap. 9.
[85] Report, P.P. 1824 (51) V.
[86] 5 Geo. IV, c. 95; Hedges and Winterbottom (1930), pp. 36–38.

Many manufacturers were not prepared to countenance such disruption and organised a Select Committee to counter what had been done.[87] The government looked nervously at signs of co-ordination between different trades and different parts of the country in support of the strikes. Against the threat of reversing legislation, unions organised massive petitions and the government secured a compromise measure which contained no flat prohibition of combination as such but which restated more broadly the prohibitions which had been kept in the 1824 Act.[88]

On the one hand, by section 4, no one was to be liable to prosecution for taking part in a combination, if wages, prices and hours alone were discussed, and the wages and hours in question were those of the persons actually present in a meeting at any one time. On the other, section 3 specified particular acts which would expose "every person so offending, aiding, abetting or assisting therein" to a term of three months in prison with or without hard labour. These included:

  (i) forcing any workman to depart from his hiring, or to return his work before it was finished; or preventing any workman from entering into any employment;
 (ii) forcing or inducing any person to belong to any club or association or to contribute to any funds or pay any fines; or
(iii) forcing any manufacturer, or person carrying on any trade or business, to make any alteration in his mode of conducting it or to limit the number of his apprentices or the number or description of his workmen.

But in each case, to constitute the offence under this section the act in question had to be done "by violence to the person or property of another, or by threats or intimidation, or by molesting or in any way obstructing another."

Ill-defined as the boundary between these provisions was, they provided fundamental texts for a highly contentious debate over half a century. Certainly, the limited scope of section 4 put the organisation of a regional or national union outside its terms; this had been a major objective of the government and would continue to be something truly frightening to those in authority. Apart from this, the Act left it open for argument (the Act of 1824 having been repealed) that activity directed against "black-leg" labour was a criminal conspiracy at common law because it was in restraint of trade. In the course of debate upon this omission, Lord Eldon conceded that such proceedings were not contemplated by the Act, and would not be permitted.[89] But this was a purely political undertaking. Within a few years, Patteson J. was telling a jury that the Act of 1825 was "never meant to empower workmen to meet and combine for the purpose of dictating to a master whom he should employ"; to do so was to over-

---

[87] P.P. 1825 (437) IV.

[88] 6 Geo. IV, c. 129; Hedges and Winterbottom (1930), pp. 38–51; J. V. Orth (1981) 2 J. Leg. Hist. 238.

[89] G. Wallas, *Life of Francis Place* (1918 ed.) 239; *cf.* Hedges and Winterbottom's view that the contrary was the common assumption of the time: pp. 39, 42.

step the bounds of section 4, which amounted to a conspiracy at common law.[90]

III. Factory Regulation

(a) The First Attempts

The creation of the mechanised factory did bring in its train a
modest measure of external regulation on novel lines, notably in the
acts restricting the hours of children and women and imposing certain other conditions in textile factories, and mines and other industrial employment. The starting point was an Act promoted by the
elder Robert Peel, Tamworth mill-owner and ultimately a reasonably
dispassionate observer of the factory phenomenon.[91] The Act would
have no practical impact but it demonstrated two crucial factors in
what was to follow. First, paternal control would remain permissible
in favour of people who could not sensibly be treated as free agents.
Secondly, the more enlightened manufacturers might positively support external regulation if it would enable them to adopt reasonable
standards without being undercut by meaner competitors; indeed, it
might help more generally in preserving their share in the market
and allow them to survive the chills of trade depression better than
less established rivals.

The early cotton mills were mostly at remote sources of water-
power and the need to move up a labour force made pauper-children
(many from London) a necessary source, for all that they had to be
clothed, fed and housed. This bastard form of apprenticeship had
nothing of the personal relationship of the craft-shop and revelations
of the dreadful, destructive conditions in many mills helped to make
Peel's case for some limitation. His Act required all apprentices in
textile mills to work for no more than twelve hours a day (excluding
meal-times), and to be provided with clothing, instruction and separate sleeping for the sexes.[92] There were also some basic sanitary
provisions that affected all factories and mills, whether or not they
contained apprentices.[93] Enforcement was supposed to be secured
through inspection by two nominees of quarter sessions,[94] since
most of the labour had come from poor law authorities. But there
were only a few trial runs at investigation and the Act was ignored.

In any case, its world was being replaced by the conditions of
steam power. New factories were built in industrial towns and the
men given charge of machines became the employers of children—

---

[90] *R. v. Bykerdike* (1832) 1 M. & Rob. 179. For the further history, see below, p. 312.
[91] But it was his own mill at Ratcliff Bridge that first aroused the concern of Dr. Percival
and his fellows on their Manchester Board of Health. For their Report of 1796 and its
effect on Peel, see Hutchins and Harrison (1926), pp. 7–13; Thomas (1948), pp. 8–13.
Even earlier there had been an ineffective attempt to regulate pauper chimney boys
by an Act of 1788: see B. Inglis, *Poverty and the Industrial Revolution* (1971), pp.
30–32; and also, pp. 132–138, 167–169.
[92] 42 Geo. III, c. 73, ss.3–4, 6–8.
[93] *Ibid.*, s.2 (whitewashing and ventilation); s.10 (infectious disease).
[94] *Ibid.*, ss.9, 11–14.

their own or their neighbour's—under forms of sub-contracting. The children were needed to crawl into confined spaces under the machines and they had to be kept at work (often by flogging) for the twelve hours or more that the factory ran. Robert Owen, as manager of one of the earliest experiments in paternal factory planning—the New Lanark Mills, with their own village and school—had excluded children under ten from work and had kept hours to twelve including meals and yet had maintained a very profitable business. His ideas caught the attention of those shocked by the inhuman possibilities of factory organisation and disturbed by the manufacturers as a new social and political presence.[95]

The elder Peel was moved to seek new legislation and between 1815 and 1819 became engaged, with Owen, in a series of Parliamentary tussles against the mill-owners and their supporters.[96] In the end an Act of 1819 emerged, much reduced in scope on the original proposals. It applied only to cotton factories from which it entirely excluded children under nine (not ten), while imposing maximum hours for those under sixteen (not eighteen) to twelve, including $1\frac{1}{2}$ hours for meals (without any provision for schooling).[97] Enforcement was left to rewarded informers, a requirement that sessions appoint a paid inspector having fallen to a particularly hostile counter-attack. Again, this meant that the Act was nugatory in effect; apart from other things, there were grave difficulties in proving a child's age or the hours he or she actually worked.[98] Nevertheless at the time when the tide of free market ideas was in full race, it established that the employment of children as a whole, within a given industry, might be regulated and that the mill-owner could be made the responsible party even if he was only the head-contractor in a sub-divided empire.

(b) The Act of 1833 and its Aftermath

The question of children's hours accordingly refused to die. Its vitality derived from a cross-fertilisation of motives. Genuine concern for the health and life expectation of factory children remained a political rallying point, particularly among humanitarian Tories, who saw brute self-interest in demands for free contract and wanted the chance to impose fundamental decencies by way of regulated, "fair" competition. By their side came that growth in political awareness in parts of the work-force itself which would build upon demands for education, political rights and trade unions. Workers' leaders saw in

[95] Owen's first work, *A New View of Society*, began to appear in 1813. His evidence to Peel's Committee of 1816 gave considerable publicity to his ideas and for a time he enjoyed some success with fashionable society: G. D. H. Cole, *Life of Robert Owen* (1926).

[96] For details, see Thomas (1948), pp. 17–26.

[97] 59 Geo. III, c. 66, ss.1–7. Protected children were excluded from night-work (9 p.m.– 5 a.m.) and dinner hours were regulated.

[98] In 1825 and then in 1831, Sir John Cam Hobhouse was able to press through amending Acts (6 Geo. IV, c. 63, 1 & 2 Will. IV, c. 39) which nominally added to the obligations on mill-owners. The second even increased to the age of 18 the limit of 69 hours a week (for details, see Thomas (1948), pp. 28–32). They too went largely unenforced.

a ten-hour day for factory children the chance to limit the hours of the whole factory, since they played an essential part in running the machines.[99] On the other side, most mill-owners conceded that there was no escaping some regulation of their child-workers and they were obliged to argue for solutions that would not impede free bargaining by adults. This led them back to Owen's notion of a "relay" of children working shorter hours in shifts beside the adults.

In 1830, Richard Oastler's rousing articles in the *Leeds Mercury* on "Yorkshire Slavery" triggered mass demonstrations by operatives for a ten-hour day, ostensibly for young workers. His friend, Michael Sadler, introduced a bill to this end in December 1831 and had it referred to a Select Committee under his own chairmanship. Shortly after the passing of the Reform Act, the Committee published a barrage of evidence demonstrating the depths to which ill-treatment of factory children might sink.[1] Sadler had just lost his seat in the new elections and leadership of the ten-hours movement was taken over by Ashley, who introduced his own Bill on the lines of Sadler's, but with severer penalties than before.[2]

The masters just succeeded in procuring the appointment of a Royal Commission to disprove the "utterly unjustifiable" imputations against them. As Commissioners, the government put in the Benthamite team of the young Edwin Chadwick, Thomas Tooke and Dr. Southwood Smith. Though the assistants that they sent out for information were spurned by the Short-Time Committees as the merest lackeys of the mill-owners, the Commissioners' first Report was critical in tone, finding many textile-factory children to "suffer the immediate effects of fatigue, sleepiness and pain" and the remote effects of "deterioration of the physical constitution, deformity, disease, and deficient mental instruction and moral culture."[3] Accordingly, in terms unmistakeably Chadwick's, the Report recommended that children under nine should not be employed at all in factories, while those under fourteen should work a maximum of eight hours a day. The restriction to eight hours left adults to be worked as "free agents" for double a child's shift: Chadwick never abandoned the central yardstick of the classical economists that the conditions of adult labour must be settled by bargaining.[4] Instead the children were to be better fitted for this adult position by the great Benthamic solution, education: a ticket system would ensure that factory children attended school in the other half of their day.[5] And something of his penchant for self-executing remedies appeared in proposals for preventing accidents by imposing strict liability on employers to compensate victims.[6]

A bill, drafted by Chadwick and modelled on the report,[7] was

[99] For the beginnings of the ten-hours movement, see Thomas (1948) Chap. 3.
[1] P.P. 1831–32 (706) XV.
[2] See Thomas (1948), p. 44.
[3] P.P. 1833 (45) XX, pp. 29, 33. For their subsequent reports, 1833 (519) XXI, 1834 (167) XIX, XX.
[4] See, generally, S. E. Finer, *The Life and Times of Sir Edwin Chadwick* (1952), pp. 19–27.
[5] For the role of factory regulation in the provision of working-class education, see below, pp. 440–441.
[6] See below, p. 515.
[7] Thomas (1948), pp. 64–65.

rapidly passed into law in order to outpace Ashley's ten-hours bill.[8] It applied to most kinds of textile factory, though not to lace or (for the most part) silk manufacture. Children under nine were not to be employed at all; those under thirteen were to work no more than a nine-hour day and forty-eight hour week; young persons under eighteen were restricted to a twelve-hour day and sixty-nine hour week.[9] For any offence the fine was a mere £1, and only one fine per day could be imposed for a particular type of offence. While this allowed for the relay policy, it was otherwise no more than an extension of the 1819 Act; the education provisions were rendered of no account by Lords' amendments and the safety provisions disappeared. The best-known novelty—showing Chadwick's respect for his master, Bentham—was the creation, under the Home Office, of the factory inspectorate of four, with provision for sub-inspectorships to give local assistance.[10] Private enterprise was to be policed by central government, a striking development at the very time when mistrust of the "new police" was running so high. The inspectors were made magistrates and were vested with powers not merely executive, but also legislative and judicial, going well beyond the amalgam of power conferred on justices in general. The Inspectors could make regulations for their districts without even submitting them to Parliament, and they could hold summary proceedings on view and convict in the very cases that they were investigating.[11]

The offences were, moreover, a prototype of administrative criminal law: the factory occupier was made liable whether or not he knew that children were being improperly employed.[12] The inspector prosecuting would have many factual difficulties in his path,[13] but he would at least be freed of the obligation to show the occupier's mens rea.[14] In face of such determination to make the law bite, the inspectors' power to act as judges in their own cause became a focal point in a cry for separation of powers. Russell, as Home Secretary, drew the inspectors back and the Act of 1844 confirmed the new scrupulousness by confining them to their executive role. Jurisdiction was for the magistrates; and they would sometimes demonstrate hostility

---

[8] The Commission had carried through its First Report in the 2½ months that the government had before Ashley's bill came up for second reading. Cf. W. G. Carson in R. Hood (ed.) *Crime, Criminology and Public Policy* (1974), p. 107.

[9] 3 & 4 Will. IV, c. 103, esp. ss.1, 2, 8; Thomas (1948), pp. 65–70; U. R. Q. Henriques, *The Early Factory Acts and their Enforcement* (1972); O. MacDonagh, *Early Victorian Government* (1977) Chap. 3.

[10] Chadwick's original proposal was to give the JPs a concurrent power of inspection, so that, where they were unbiased, the workforce could go to them: Finer (above, n. 4), p. 66.

[11] *Ibid.* ss.17–19, 33. The sub-inspectors, however, had no power to compel the appearance of witnesses.

[12] The court was, however, empowered to mitigate even the £1 minimum fine, if the offence was not wilful or grossly negligent: s.32.

[13] The chief witnesses might be hands who feared for their jobs. The continuing difficulties over children's ages made Chadwick an eager advocate of birth registration: see below p. 364.

[14] *Cf.* W. G. Carson (1970) 10 Br. J. Crim. 383; (1979) 7 Int. J. Soc. Law 37; (1980) 8 *ibid.* 187, with P. W. J. Bartrip and P. T. Fenn (1980) *ibid.* 175; (1983) 10 J. Law & Soc. 201. See also, below, p. 605ff.

towards the efforts of the inspectors to put the legislative machinery into operation.[15] The 1833 Act was in any case greeted by both manufacturers and operatives with a contemptuous fury. The ten-hours movement still demanded legislation which now would have the effect of *adding* hours to the factory child's day. Some manufacturers, on the other hand, convinced the inspectors and then the government that the relay arrangement was unworkable. The latter's nerve failed to the extent of promoting a bill to repeal this all-important part of the 1833 Act. It was Ashley, who saw the foolhardiness of conceding so much ground to masters determined to drive out all legislative interference, and his opposition prevented the government from completing its *volte face.*[16]

Gradually, the inspectors were able to set about enforcing the Act,[17] somewhat waveringly supported by Whig, then Tory governments. As many administrative defects appeared the inspectors pressed for legislative improvements of their own devising: the self-generative processes of bureaucracy became conspicuous. Reform was not easily achieved against the opposition of the manufacturers. Only after Bills had been lost on three occasions did the Act of 1844 become law. This gave the inspectors better control over such persistent problems as the certification of children's ages by extensions of hours to make up for time unavoidably lost and it introduced requirements for schooling and the fencing of machinery that had a certain effect.[18]

But the question of hours remained unavoidable. The short-time movement remained completely opposed to the "relay" policy of the 1833 Act, though for a time the case for the ten-hour day could not be pushed. Instead there was some concentration on extending the range of trades covered by the legislation. Ashley's Children's Employment Committee of 1840 exposed the dreadful conditions to which women and children were subjected in many mines and a wave of sympathy swept through an Act keeping not only boys under ten but also women of any age out of the pits.[19] Opposition from the colliery owners, however, was powerfully organised and only token implementation of the provision for inspection now allowed for several years.[20]

At the same period Ashley also procured a committee of inquiry

---

[15] How frequently is now disputed: *cf.* A. E. Peacock (1984) 37 Ec. H.R. (2d) 197; (1985) 38 *ibid.* 431, discounting the resistance, with Bartrip 38 *ibid.* 423, taking the traditional view. Note also the suggestion that the high conviction rate under the 1833 Act may have been an attack by steam-mill owners on water-mill owners: H. P. Shovel (1977) 20 J. Law Econs. 379; C. Nardinelli (1985) 38 Ec. H.R. 428.

[16] Hutchins and Harrison (1926) Chap. 4; Thomas (1948) Chap. 6; Henriques (above, n. 9).

[17] The most courageous was the radical, Leonard Horner (for whom, see B. Martin (1969) 14 Int.J.Soc.Hist. 424). For the background of the inspectorate generally see D. Roberts, *Victorian Origins of the Welfare State* (1962), pp. 177–178; and for their development, T. K. Djang, *Factory Inspection in Great Britain* (1942), pp. 31–41; H. W. Arthurs, *Without the Law* (1985), pp. 102–107, 114–115.

[18] 7 & 8 Vict., c. 15; Thomas (1948) Chaps. 10, 13, 14; and see below, pp. 440–441.

[19] P.P. 1840 (various) X; 5 & 6 Vict., c. 99, and note the Commission's Report, P.P. 1842 [380–82] XV–XVII.

[20] See O. MacDonagh in R. Robson (ed.) *Ideas and Institutions of Victorian Britain* (1967) Chap. 3; R. K. Webb (1955) 27 J. Mod. Hist. 352; Arthurs (above, n. 17), pp. 107–13.

into trades outside the range of the 1833 Act, which had much disturbing to report of the hours and conditions of children, first in lace
and silk making, and then in the fabric-processing, clothing, glass,
pottery, metal, paper, printing and similar manufactures.[21] All that
came of this was an Act, applying a mild measure of regulation to
children's employment in calico printing.[22] It was to take another two
decades before the factory legislation was extended in any real
degree to the non-textile trades.

In 1844, Ashley returned to Parliamentary activism for ten hours,
now seeking to use the case of young persons and all women as the
basis for general regulation. In its own textile Factory Bill even the
government felt obliged to bring all women within the twelve-hour
day prescribed for those under eighteen, even though this would
breach the sacred freedom of adults to contract as they would. Ashley
almost succeeded in reducing their hours to ten. The arguments had
become more specific, even if, in terms of economic theory, they
scarcely rose above the commonplace. Less was heard of "free
agency," more of the effect that limited hours would have on wages,
profits and level of employment of those affected.[23] In 1837, Nassau
Senior had produced his notorious calculation purporting to demonstrate that profits could be made only in the last hour of an $11\frac{1}{2}$-hour
day, and of this much was heard in the debates.[24]

Nonetheless all the fact-finding about the long hours often worked
by the notionally "free," and the disastrous effects that such work
could have on health and constitution, was beginning to tell. So also
was the fact that the administration of the existing laws had proved
possible under the aegis of the inspectors who themselves had
become an important influence for further intervention. In 1847, in
the midst of a downturn in trade, Fielden succeeded with a bill limiting young persons' and women's hours in textile factories to ten per
day and fifty-eight per week.[25] It was a crucial achievement, one
treated by Dicey as showing how legal change in a collectivist direction might work upon public opinion more generally.[26] In a political
world which turned its face against direct democratic concessions to
the working class, but which had conceded the case for a market
economy in bread, there was added at least a small guarantee against
conditions of labour which sapped life of other significance.

This early history of legislative interference with contracts of
employment emphasises the incapacity of the common law, by technique or temperament, to perform an equivalent function. The
judges, indeed, were furnished with little opportunity to influence

---

[21] P.P. 1843 [430] XIII. As the Committee emphasised, in the worst places of work it
was the operatives who were left to employ the children.

[22] 8 & 9 Vict., c. 29; Hutchins and Harrison (1926), pp. 120–131; Thomas (1948) Chap.
17.

[23] M. Blaug ((1956) 72 Q. J. Econs 211) shows that the leading economists, far from
being supporters of the legislation (as claimed by Robbins and others), provided the
main arguments against each extension of protection; they were, however, prepared
to acquiesce *ex post facto* in the degree of regulation already achieved—a significant
example of the power of law to mould influential opinion.

[24] *Letters on the Factory Act* (1837), pp. 12–13.

[25] 10 & 11 Vict., c. 29.; Thomas (1948) Chap. 18.

[26] *Law and Public Opinion in England* (2nd ed., 1914), p. 239.

the development of the Factory Acts until after 1847, when some manufacturers sought to prevent the working time of their factory from being cut down to the prescribed hours for the employment of women or young persons by staggering their hours (a scheme accordingly labelled "false relay," to distinguish Chadwickian half-time relays). The inspectors denied the legality of this practice. A test case in 1850 showed the general dislike harboured by the judges for such legislative interference with contractual "freedom."[27] The crucial statutory provision, being penal, was construed strictly by the Court of Exchequer. Nowhere could the court find a statement sufficiently plain to prevent regulated workers from agreeing to "any intervals of leisure that may be thought convenient."[28] This acceptance of the "false relay" made it once more very difficult for the inspectors to determine whether the Act of 1847 was being observed. But such was the lingering antagonism to the Act that it took two further statutes, and the concession of two extra working hours in the week, to outlaw the practice of staggered working.[29]

There were to be many further battles over maximum hours in the various forms of manual employment, in which economic liberals argued the virtues of freedom of choice against the advocates of a minimum standard defined by legislation. In 1864, in particular, an act was finally passed to restrict children's hours in a number of trades where immensely long hours were still common.[30] In 1872–74 the textile operatives would once more use the case of women and children to secure a small reduction in the working week.[31] The notion that an outside limit should be imposed upon the work of the adult male remained anathema and altogether the regulation of hours ceased to be a matter for statute, despite periodic demands from unions.

Parliamentary intervention was good only for outlawing the most oppressive or dangerous of conditions. The prescribing of maximum hours in textiles only followed the lines already laid by the leading artisans. By the beginning of the nineteenth century, the London trades had reached a norm, it seems, of $10\frac{1}{2}$ working hours a day (12 with meals). By the 1830s they were moving to 10 hours and in the 1860s to 9 hours ($9\frac{1}{2}$ during the week, with a short Saturday). Not till the 1890s would the eight-hour day make headway, being accepted,

[27] *Ryder* v. *Mills* (1850) 3 Ex. 853. Only by the parties agreeing to the imposition of a fine above the statutory maximum was it possible to bring the appellate machinery into operation.

[28] Per Parke B., *ibid.* at 872. He also remarked that, "though the immediate question in this case did relate to adult females, who are more capable of taking care of themselves, and of continued labour, than children, and consequently need less protection, and on whom the restriction from employing themselves as they think best appears more of a hardship, the point to be decided is the same as if we were considering the case of children and young persons only."

[29] 13 & 14 Vict., c. 54 (1850); 16 & 17 Vict., c. 104 (1853). Ashley incurred the odium of the Short-time Committees by urging that the extra time provided a workable compromise: Thomas (1948), pp. 316–327.

[30] For this and similar legislation, see Hutchins and Harrison (1926) Chaps. 7, 8.

[31] By the Factory Act 1874. The complex law was consolidated and extended by the Factory and Workshop Act 1878. For the view that this regulation stimulated a move towards workshops and sweating, J. Schmiechen (1975) 28 Ec. H.R. (2d) 413; but *cf.* J. Morris (1982) 35 Ec. H.R. (2d) 292.

for instance, in government and municipal works.[32] All this was a gradual accretion by bargaining. In its course the number of hours ceased to be a measure of what was bearable in itself and became a standard for calculating wages beyond which overtime would be payable.

(c) Truck under Industrial Conditions

The abandonment of wage-fixing by justices in 1813 set a course from which there was to be no direct deviation for the remainder of the century, even for the special groups whose hours might be limited. But the manner of paying wages did not fall quite under the same ordinance. Truck—payment in kind rather than in money— was an old phenomenon and one not necessarily pernicious in a world where coin was not always available, and arrangements for giving credit were crude.[33] A long history of legislative attempts to regulate truck[34] stood witness, however, to the uncertainties of value involved where goods were given in return for work and to the ease with which the practice disintegrated into deception.[35] The Truck Act 1831, passed mainly on the initiative of large employers who were in direct competition with truck-masters,[36] up-dated the earlier legislation and made it more general.

The Act was, for its time, of considerable breadth, since it applied to all "artificers"—including adult males. The only sustained objection to it came from a small knot of Ricardian theorists, headed by Joseph Hume. They argued that truck was a device employed mainly by smaller employers in times of depressed trade and monetary shortage to avoid going out of business; the new legislation would simply increase unemployment; only an inflationary policy, including remission of taxation, would produce a real benefit.[37]

The Act contained elaborate provisions requiring the payment of wages in current coin of the realm, on pain inter alia of summary prosecution. The initial enthusiasm generated by the legislative campaign led to the institution of a few prosecutions in the early years. But employees, who if they could have found non-truck employment would have preferred it, showed little interest in taking proceedings themselves. Down-turns in some trades continued to induce small employers to resort to truck as a method of effecting cuts in agreed

---

[32] For this, see S. & B. Webb, Industrial Democracy (1898), pp. 352–353.

[33] Truck might amount to outright compulsion to buy goods or might consist of supplying goods on the credit of wages due but not yet paid. See on this, and generally, Hilton (1960).

[34] For these statutes, stretching back to 1465, see Hilton (1960), p. 7.

[35] As Hilton (p. 4) points out, "fraud" is a word sometimes used by historians pejoratively of truck in itself.

[36] 1 & 2 Will. IV, c. 36. The progenitor of the Bill, Edward Littleton, was a large employer in Staffordshire, the area where truck was most rife. He had also sponsored an Act in 1820 intended to breathe life into the earlier legislation: 1 Geo. IV, c. 93. It had been opposed by Ricardo and Hume, who succeeded in securing its non-renewal three years later: Hilton (1960), pp. 98–100.

[37] See Hilton (1960), pp. 107–108.

rates of pay.[38] Each decade brought a campaign for further legislative intervention,[39] aimed mainly at practices equivalent to truck.[40] But it was not until 1887, when the evil itself had largely abated under the general rise in wages, the effects of trade union pressure and changes in manufacturing organisation, that the inspectors of factories and mines were given supervisory power over truck itself.[41]

The Act of 1831 did not prove to be the beginning of an administrative momentum of the MacDonagh type: truck created no persistent sense of real scandal, of the kind that Oastler and Ashley could conjure over the employment of women and children. The "morality" of the practice was too liable to seem ambiguous; preclusion of it by law and bureaucratic inspection encroached too nearly on the central "freedom" of the labour contract.

IV. TRADE UNIONS AND LEGALITY

(a) The Fortunes of the Unions

In the period after 1825, two fairly distinct directions were taken by unions of labour. Robert Owen's cooperative ideas found a receptive audience among artisans and mechanics eager for education and improvement. From this sprang a succession of attempts to form large, cross-craft unions—among engineers, among building workers, among clothiers. The cotton spinner, John Doherty, became a prominent leader, particularly with his National Association of United Trades for the Protection of Labour (1831–32), which sought to provide a federal umbrella uniting all trades. Then the Grand National Consolidated Trades Union (1834), with which Owen was directly associated, held great conferences and claimed a membership of 800,000 (though subscribers totalled no more than 16,000). The spread of this last to remote Dorset caused panic among the squires and the notorious prosecution of the seven agricultural

---

[38] The degree to which truck persisted until 1870 is detailed in the Report of two royal commissioners (one of them Charles (later Lord) Bowen) on the Truck System, P.P. 1871 [C. 326, 327] XXXVI.

[39] Hilton, Chap. 6.

[40] In 1860, unionised miners succeeded in procuring the first legislation on check-weighmen (the Inspections (Mine Regulation) Act) allowing the men to appoint their own official to ensure that the weighing of ore (on which wages depended) was done without cheating. The charging of excessive rents to frame-knitters for the hiring of frames was controlled by the Hosiery Manufacture (Wages) Act 1874. Eventually, too, the practice of fining for poor workmanship and misbehaviour, which had been used in some industries largely as a wage-cutting device, was placed under certain rather ineffectual limits by the Truck Act 1896. The pious hope that truck could bring the benefits of labour to the whole family, whereas money wages too often disappeared in drink, sometimes figured as a reason for opposing the legislative curtailment of truck. Certainly the payment of wages in public houses was prohibited in mining in 1842 (5 & 6 Vict., c. 99, ss.10–12—after a Committee chaired by Ashley) and generally in 1883 (Payment of Wages in Public Houses (Prohibition) Act). See F. Tillyard, The Worker and the State (1923), Chaps. 2, 3.

[41] Truck Act 1887, passed partly on the initiative of Charles Bradlaugh. (It also extended the scope of the 1831 Act to all manual workmen except domestic servants.) The inspectors scarcely made use of their new powers: Hilton (1960), pp. 142–146.

labourers of Tolpuddle. The outrage that the proceedings engendered allowed the GNCTU to organise highly indignant protests, but within months the organisation had collapsed. As with the others, sectional interest outweighed common purpose and no financial basis for survival could be established.[42]

These efforts at "general union," however, were symptomatic of a distinct consciousness of a working-class opposed in particular to a middle-class of capitalist employers, which had various other expressions: in the fervour for Parliamentary reform and the disappointments bred by 1832; in the programmes for workers' education through mechanics institutes and day schools; in the fear of the new London and municipal police and suspicion of the "new" poor law of 1834; and, most closely, in the support for the ten-hour day in the textile factories. In the succeeding years it would mostly be channelled into political protest under the Chartist banner and then into the campaign against the Corn Laws, which proved an effective distraction from Chartism. It was a period of recurrent tensions, when the propertied did not sleep altogether calmly in their beds.[43]

The other path for trade unionism was the traditional course of the craft clubs and houses of call. Where they were not outpaced by technical change, skilled manual workers would strive to restrict entry so as to maintain their higher wages and security of work. These "aristocrats of labour" were often as well-off as the lower middle-classes; their children not infrequently moved or married into the white-collar ranks of clerks and supervisors.[44] In all this, the union provided the security of a benefit society and the strength needed for negotiations with employers. When engaging in the latter, the union might well put itself forward as collaborator rather than as antagonist, in common cause against the purchasing public. There were many signs that these local craft unions looked askance at the millenial aspirations of the general unions and the Chartists.[45]

Yet there was also common ground between the two paths. Not all established unions saw the virtues of harmonious collaboration: there were long and bitter strikes. Not all could sustain their privileged position against less skilled, cheaper labour and would find it hard to survive downturns in trade: this was the fate, for instance, of the Miners Association of Great Britain in 1848.[46] Many came to see virtues of collaboration between different crafts: trades councils of workers began to be formed in counterpoise to chambers of commerce in the business community.

Then in the 1850s appeared the first of the "new model" unions (to use the Webbs' terminology)—federations of local craft unions in particular trades which were able to sustain a central office that could promote the union's position on a national and regional level. The Amalgamated Society of Engineers was formed in 1851 and proved

---

[42] For these developments, see G. D. H. Cole, *Attempts at General Union* (1953); Hunt (1982) Chap. 6; Pelling (1976), pp. 28–34; Fox (1985), pp. 91–96.

[43] See, Hunt (1982) Chap. 7; Fox (1985), pp. 96–102.

[44] G. Crossick, *An Artisan Elite in Victorian Society: Kentish London 1840–1880* (1978); T. R. Tholfsen, *Working Class Radicalism in Mid-Victorian England* (1976), Chap. 9.

[45] Musson (1972).

[46] A. J. Taylor, (1955) 22 Economica 45; Pelling (1976), pp. 37–38.

itself strong enough to survive a three-month strike next year; the Amalgamated Society of Carpenters and Joiners in 1860, in the wake of a long dispute in the London building trades. There was much in their structure (for all the independence that the local branches retained) which would push these new associations in the direction of moderation and caution. The decision to strike was given to the central committee and this allowed for second thoughts and a careful eye to conserving funds.[47]

Accordingly the mid-nineteenth century does not divide neatly into a period of revolutionary hostility, succeeded by one of calculating collaboration, which was the Webbs' view of the overall pattern. Both periods contained the steady rumble of sectarian activity as well as occasional outbursts that were class-wide and militant in intent. But the unions which had grown into enduring institutions derived from eighteenth-century roots in the skilled crafts and retained a good deal of the inherent exclusiveness of their origins.

After 1825, the law continued to impose criminal prohibitions upon strikes and associated acts which were anything more than the simple withdrawal of labour in protection of wages or hours.[48] In the years of the efforts at "general union" there seems to have been comparatively little resort to this form of discipline.[49] The Martyrs of Tolpuddle, who had done no more than partake in secret rites of initiation into the GNCTU, were prosecuted under a law against illegal oath-taking which had been passed in the wake of the Mutinies at Spithead and the Nore.[50] The flamboyant Baron Williams first directed the jury that such conduct was indeed within the scope of the Act[51] and then imposed the maximum sentence of seven years' transportation.[52] In the upshot the government learned the dangers of indulging in such show-trial savagery and granted pardons.[53] Other situations, such as the agricultural uprisings in the winter of 1830, led to arson, machine-breaking and personal violence and could be dealt with as such by the special Commissions which descended to mete out retribution.[54] The Master and Servant Act continued to be used to move against those actually on strike without completing work or giving due notice.[55] Large employers in any case often had other weapons for the business of strike-breaking: in 1844 Lord Londonderry led a victory against the Northumberland and

---

[47] See Webb (1920) Chap. 4; Pelling (1976), pp. 41–44; Hunt (1982), pp. 250–264. But the "new model" had evident antecedents; see Fox (1985), pp. 134–135.

[48] See above, pp. 300–301.

[49] But note the case of *Bykerdike,* above, n. 90.

[50] 37 Geo. III, c. 123.

[51] Lord Ellenborough had once so held (*R. v. Marks* (1802) 3 East 157). But by 1834, the Law Officers, mindful of such respectful ceremonies as those of the freemasons, were very doubtful: W. H. Oliver (1966) 10 Lab. Hist. 572.

[52] *R. v. Loveless* (1834) 6 C. & P. 596; for a curious rousing of the spectre of the 1797 Act, see *Luby* v. *Warwickshire Miners' Assoc.* [1912] 2 Ch. 371.

[53] See generally, J. Marlow, *The Tolpuddle Martyrs* (1972) (for the failure of subsequent prosecutions at Exeter and Oxford, see pp. 113–114, 160–161); R. Dickson (1986) 7 J. Leg. Hist. 178.

[54] See E. J. Hobsbawm and G. Rudé, *Captain Swing* (1969), esp. Chaps. 13, 14.

[55] See above, pp. 294–295.

Durham Miners Union by evictions from houses and pressure on local tradesmen not to supply strikers.[56]

(b) Judicial Views in Mid-Century

It was not until the 1850s, when the established local unions began to show signs of larger organisation and cross-help that range of the criminal law against strikes came once more to the fore. The leading cases of *Rowlands* and *Duffield*,[57] which did much to demonstrate the reach of section 3 of the 1825 Act, arose out of a single strike. The Wolverhampton tinplate-workers society had called in organisers from a National Association of United Trades to run the strike, which was an attempt to secure from two manufacturers the same rate of wages as the other employers were already paying at a time of great demand. One parry by the masters was to put men onto long-term contracts, so that any rapid strike would be criminal under the Master and Servant Act 1823. The unionists nevertheless not only withdrew their labour but persuaded other workers to do the same. The employers scoured the Midlands for substitutes and even went as far afield as France and Germany. These blacklegs were effectively discouraged: mostly they were given enough to drink and put on a train home. The jury refused to accept the little evidence that was offered of violence by the pickets who organised this riposte. However, Erle J., the trial judge, led the jury to convict the defendants on a wide variety of conspiracy counts which did not allege violence. His directions to them make clear his general view of the 1825 legislation: that section 4, in allowing workmen to combine (without breaking their contracts) to raise *their own* wages, set a boundary. Beyond it they could not interfere with the freedom of employers to conduct business, or of other workers to dispose of their labour, as they chose. Whether a strike which overstepped this limit constituted a conspiracy at common law or a conspiracy to offend section 3 of the Act seemed scarcely to matter; each left the question of fine or imprisonment to the court's discretion.[58] Some activities of the strikers clearly fell within the specific list in that section, and it was held that, despite the absence of violence, the activities had involved "threatening," "molesting" or "obstructing" the employers or their workmen. This construction ran directly counter to the narrower view, laid down four years previously by Rolfe B. in a very similar prosecution against picketers[59]; but Erle's position was largely upheld by the full Queen's Bench and became the dominant judicial view in the ensuing years. Only in the case of three of the most vaguely worded counts, which bore no close resemblance to the specific prohibitions

---

[56] Webb (1920), pp. 100–101, 168.

[57] (1851) 5 Cox 404, 436, 466. On the 1825 Act, see Hedges and Winterbottom (1930), pp. 42–51.

[58] Conviction for conspiracy to commit a summary offence could result in punishment greater than for that offence itself. On a conspiracy charge, evidence against one co-defendant was admissible against others; and the conspiracy might be inferred from the fact that several defendants individually had done acts which tended towards a common purpose: see, *e.g.*, *R. v. Druitt* (1867) 10 Cox at 602.

[59] *R. v. Selsby* (1847) 5 Cox 495n.

of section 3, did the court, without finally ruling on the question, consider it advisable that the prosecution should withdraw.

Employers thus secured a wide interpretation of section 3 which could be applied in summary proceedings up and down the country. In the following years the higher courts proceeded to rule that various forms of union pressure were illegal, directly under section 3 or by common law operating in the no man's land of the 1825 Act. A strike was illegal if it was to secure the dismissal of the disobedient union member.[60] A member who refused to collaborate in a demarcation dispute could not be threatened with being sent to Coventry or with expulsion from the union.[61] A closed shop could not be enforced by threatening to strike, however politely or regretfully the proposed withdrawal of labour was worded.[62] In these cases, the judges saw their public duty to proffer tremendous homilies upon the orthodoxies of political economy, as enshrined in the text of 1825. Lord Campbell's pronouncement in the union discipline case ("one of the most important cases ever brought before a British jury") is typical:

"By law every man's labour is his own property, and he may make what bargain he pleases for his own employment; not only so— masters and men may associate together; but they must not by their association violate the law; they must not injure their neighbour; they must not do what would prejudice another man . . . If this were permitted, not only would the manufacturers of the land be injured, but it would lead to the most melancholy consequences to the working classes."[63]

Above all, there was to be no alleviation of the judicial aversion to picketing. The National Association of United Trades, though effectively broken by the proceedings arising out of the Wolverhampton tin-makers strike, continued a small committee which in 1859 procured the Molestation of Workmen Act.[64] The somewhat surprising concessions of this statute suggest a greater fluidity of opinion on the subject in Parliament than on the bench. Attempts "peaceably and in a reasonable manner, without threat or intimidation, direct or indir-

---

[60] R. v. Hewitt (1851) 5 Cox 162.

[61] O'Neill v. Longman (1863) 4 B. & S. 376.

[62] Walsby v. Anley (1861) 3 E. & E. 516; Shelbourne v. Liver (1866) 13 L.T. (N.S.) 630; Skinner v. Kitch (1867) 10 Cox 493.

[63] R. v. Hewitt (1851) 5 Cox at 163.

[64] 22 Vict., c. 34; Webb (1920), p. 277; J. V. Orth (1982) 3 J. Leg. Hist. 238. On the bench, however, there was some measurable difference of opinion. At one extreme, Crompton J. maintained the old opinion that at common law labour combinations were criminal conspiracies, and that section 4 of the 1825 Act conferred a strictly limited exemption from penal consequences: see Hilton v. Eckersley (1856, discussed above, p. 269). At the other, Erle C.J. and Cockburn C.J. required, for an indictable conspiracy, that the collaborators must contemplate at least the violation of a private right, or of a public right with particular damage to an individual; a strike or a threat to strike would not per se be unlawful. In Wood v. Bowron, (1867) 2 Q.B. 21, Cockburn said: "Large numbers of men, who have not the advantages of wealth, very often can protect their own interests only by means of association and co-operation, and we ought not to strain the law against men who have only their own labour and their association by which they can act in the assistance of one another." See also R. v. Stainer (1870) 11 Cox 483.

ect, to persuade others to cease or abstain from work" were not to fall within section 3 of the 1825 Act.[65] But soon enough this was shown to give little protection: in *R. v. Druitt*[66] a lock-out and strike grew out of a wages dispute in the London tailoring trade. The organising sub-committee of the workers had given careful instructions to their many pickets to keep to peaceful and reasonable communication of their case, though (inevitably) there were some incidents in which these instructions were exceeded. Irrespective of this, and despite the new legislation, Bramwell B. is reported to have summed up:

> "Even if the jury should be of opinion that the picket did nothing more than his duty as a picket, and if that duty did not extend to abusive language and gestures such as had been described, still if that was calculated to have a deterring effect on the minds of ordinary persons, by exposing them to have their motions watched, and to encounter black looks, that would not be permitted by the law of the land . . . If the jury were satisfied that this system, though not carried beyond watching and observation, was still so serious a molestation and obstruction as to have an effect upon the minds of workpeople, then they ought to find these three men guilty."[67]

And so, to be legal, picketing had to be quite innocuous. To overstep the mark was to risk not only a prosecution, but also, as Malins V.C. held in 1868,[68] an injunction, to which attached the roving sanction of contempt of court. Thus did a new, more terrible, dragon for the unions—the prospect of civil proceedings against dispute activity—make its appearance on the horizon.

(c) The Royal Commission

In theory, as the century progressed, the law against union combinations became less severe, and so it is often pictured. But the portrait is scarcely true to life: not until the unions became firmly and broadly organised was the full potential of the criminal law against their activities explored. Unionists responded to this growing pressure by joining the bid for greater political power. The years before and after the Second Reform Act were a moment not only of great opportunity but of considerable danger. Alongside the judicial hostility against picketing displayed in such judgments as *Druitt*, there were two other disturbing portents. First, in the autumn of 1866, a serious explosion occurred in Sheffield which was said (and eventually found) to have been an act of union retaliation against an ex-member.[69] In the press and Parliament a feeling of outrage erupted.

---

[65] The Act also broadened section 4 of the 1825 Act by providing that no person should be prosecuted for conspiracy by entering an agreement to fix rates of wages, even if he himself was not in the employment in question. This gave new protection to union officers.

[66] (1867) 10 Cox 592.

[67] *Ibid.* at 601.

[68] *Springhead Spinning* v. *Riley* (1868) L.R. 6 Eq. 551.

[69] See generally, S. Pollard, *The Sheffield Outrages* (1971); and for violence among Manchester bricklayers, R. N. Price (1975) 66 P. & P. 110.

Even the moderate *Daily News* could insist that "the unions must be stamped out as a public nuisance."

Secondly, as if in answer, the courts delivered a further legal blow to union stability. Like other benefit societies of the period the unions had to face the problem of financial administration by inexperienced treasurers. In some cases, incompetence turned into deliberate depredation. Against this the general criminal law was unhelpful, for one of its historical encumbrances was the rule that one joint owner could not steal from another. Accordingly, the friendly societies had secured special legislation, which provided a summary offence against a defaulting officer or member, and gave the magistrates the power, in the same proceedings, to order reimbursement to the society.[70] This was the provision under which unions sought to shelter by securing its application to any "friendly society established . . . for any purpose which is not illegal," provided that it had deposited its rules with the Registrar of Friendly Societies.[71] Several of the larger unions had accordingly done so.

In *Hornby* v. *Close*,[72] the Boilermakers Society sought to proceed against a defaulting official under this provision. But the Court of Queen's Bench held, on the strength of the union's rules against accepting piece-work or work in a shop under strike, that it was established in unlawful restraint of trade—an "illegal" purpose as far as the Friendly Societies Act was concerned. This could be said to follow logically from the earlier decisions on the unenforceability of industrial combinations and the criminality of strike action beyond the confines of the 1825 Act. But its practical consequence was to deprive unions of protection for their respectable benefit activities.

While the decision itself exposed the movement considerably, it also provided the leaders with a cause for sympathy that might be placed in balance against the events in Sheffield.[73] In February 1867, Derby's government set up a Royal Commission with wide powers to enquire into the organisation and rules of the unions, their effect on workmen, employers, industrial relations and trade and industry;

---

[70] 18 & 19 Vict., c. 63, s.24.

[71] *Ibid.*, s.44.

[72] (1867) L.R. 2 Q.B. 153.

[73] There are various legal indications of sympathy for the unions on the question. In 1868, Russell Gurney secured an act (31 & 32 Vict., c. 116) which amended the law of larceny and embezzlement so as to permit prosecutions against a joint-owner. This was immediately and successfully used against an official of the London Operative Bricklayers (*R.* v. *Blackburn* (1868) 11 Cox 157), the Common Sergeant emphasising that "a trade union consists of poor men laying by a portion of their wages against the necessities of their deserving brethren who by reason of loss of work, sickness or accident were compelled to seek assistance." Nothing was heard of the impropriety of strike rules as an objection to the prosecution, despite the precedent of *R.* v. *Hunt* (1838) 8 C. & P. 642.

In 1869, the carefully drawn rules of the Amalgamated Society of Carpenters and Joiners, which imposed no directly restrictive obligations on members, were treated in the same way as those in *Hornby* v. *Close* (*Farrer* v. *Close* L.R. 4 Q.B. 602—a different defendant). But two members of the Court dissented, insisting on the clearest proof that the society did operate against the public interest. One of them, Hannen J., remarked that, in holding acts done in furtherance of strikes to be illegal, "we should be basing our judgment, not on recognised legal principles, but on the opinion of one of the contending schools of political economy."

and to suggest improvements in the law.[74] On the very eve of political reform, the trade unions were placed on trial.

The Royal Commission was chaired by Sir William Erle. The precarious position of the unions was emphasised by the absence of any working man on the Commission, though after substantial protests the government added Frederick Harrison—Comteian positivist, liberal and close associate (with Professor Beesly) of the "Junta" of "new model" union leaders.[75]

Through the summer of 1867 the sub-commission investigating in Sheffield secured revelations of guerilla activities in various small unions of grinders, including "rattening" (the temporary removal of tools), and personal violence. Dramatic though these revelations were, they concerned only a few small and backward societies, the vestiges of an older, cruder industrial condition.[76] If anything, they strengthened the arguments of the sober and respectable leaders of the new, large unions of the most important skilled workers, presented to the Commission with particular effect by Robert Applegarth, Secretary of the Amalgamated Society of Carpenters and Joiners and a central figure in the "Junta." In the end he and his fellows found that they had the sympathy of a minority of three on the Commission,[77] whose report, in a changing political atmosphere, was to have great significance.

The majority, however, while avoiding shrill vehemence, took a conservative position which allowed little concession on the question of the legal regulation of unions.[78] Industrial activism that stepped beyond the confines of the 1825 Act was to remain penal—in particular, picketing against strike-breakers. In addition, "many of the Rules and Bye-laws of some of the trade unions are framed in defiance of well-established principles of economical science, and tend to restrict the free action of those principles on which depend the well-being and progress of society"—rules limiting the numbers of apprentices and the introduction of machines, rules enforcing a closed shop, rules against sub-contracting and piece-work and arrangements for the support of other unions on strike. Unions with such objects, were (as in *Hornby* v. *Close*) to be treated as lacking legality.[79] However the majority approved of voluntary arbitration and the benevolent funds organised by unions. They would have

---

[74] In order to get at the truth about the outrages, the Commission was given special powers of investigation, including the power to offer witnesses indemnity against prosecution.

[75] The "Junta" label was given by the Webbs to the group centring around Applegarth (ASCJ), Allan (ASE), Guile (ironfounders), Coulson (bricklayers) and Odger (shoemakers). For the Positivists and their high-minded hopes for the working-class as a moral influence, see R. Harrison, *Before the Socialists* (1965) Chap. 6; and above, p. 111; and for attitudes towards political economy, E. F. Biagini (1987) 4 Hist. J. 811.

[76] Reports of Examiners, P.P. 1867 [3952–I] XXXII; 1867–68 [3980] XXXIX.

[77] In addition to Harrison, these were the radicals, Thomas Hughes M.P. and the Earl of Lichfield.

[78] Eleventh and Final Report of the Trades Unions Commission, P.P. 1868–69 [4123] XXXI, esp. paras. 60–75, 78–91. On the Commission and its consequences, see Pelling (1976) Chap. 4; Hunt (1982), pp. 267–271; Fox (1985), pp. 149–160.

[79] On the other hand, unions which did not have such objects would be permitted to register with the Registrar of Friendly Societies and thus to enjoy a "capacity for rights and duties resembling in some degree that of corporations." (paras. 80–83).

liked to see benefit and trade activities conducted by different societies but thought it feasible only to recommend that the funds for the two activities be kept separate.[80]

It was the belief of the minority that trade unionism brought great and deserved benefits to the working class.[81] Freedom to pursue industrial action, so long as it did not offend the general law, must be conceded, in order to give the unions bargaining power comparable to the combinations of capitalists, which in such practices as blacklisting and wage-fixing, operated beyond the bounds of any legal regulation. None of the union practices so repugnant to the majority—not even closed shop demands and sympathetic payments to strikers in other unions—were considered by the minority to have produced seriously deleterious effects on industry or on workingmen themselves. Accordingly the minority proposed removing the combined fetters of the common law of conspiracy and the 1825 Act on industrial action; and the civil position of unions should no longer be affected by the restraint of trade doctrine. Instead certain agreements should not be directly enforceable in law, for here the minority accepted the unionists' suspicion of the courts and how they might behave if empowered to meddle in internal affairs. In addition, unions which registered with the Registrar of Friendly Societies would acquire certain legal advantages in the management of this property similar to those already given to friendly societies. And the Minority poured scorn on the Majority's proposal to separate trade and benefit funds as "an arbitrary interference with the liberty of association."[82]

(d) The Liberals' Response

Both political parties appreciated that they must give a measure of attention to the Minority as well as to the Majority Report of the Commission. First the Liberals, after some prevarication,[83] insisted on maintaining a mid-way position. In the Trade Union Act 1871, the view of the Minority was implemented as far as the civil status of trade unions were concerned. The mere fact that the purposes of a trade union constituted a restraint of trade no longer rendered them unlawful, either so as to render a member liable to criminal prosecution for conspiracy or otherwise, or so as to render void or voidable any agreement or trust.[84] In addition, certain legal proceedings could not be entertained: those "instituted with the object of directly enforcing or recovering damages for the breach of an agreement

(1) between members of a trade union as such, concerning the

---

[80] Some employers chose to attack the financial stability of the benefit funds of the largest amalgamations. But the Majority Report refused to accept actuarial criticisms, pointing to the unions' unlimited power to raise funds by special levies should the need arise: paras. 85–91.

[81] See the dissent of Harrison, Hughes and Lichfield in P.P. 1868–69 [4123] XXXI and the ensuing statement of reasons to which Lichfield did not feel able to subscribe.

[82] *Ibid.*, at pp. lx–lxi.

[83] They gave the unions temporary protection against *Hornby* v. *Close* by the Trades Unions Protection Act 1869.

[84] Ss.2, 3; Hedges and Winterbottom (1930) Pt. II, Chap. 1.

> conditions on which members for the time being . . . shall or
> shall not sell their goods, transact business, employ or be
> employed;
>
> (2) for the payment of any subscription or penalty to a . . . union;
> (3) for the application of [union] funds
>   (a) to provide benefits to members; or
>   (b) to furnish contributions to any non-member employer or
>   workman in consideration of such person acting in con-
>   formity with union rules or resolutions; or
>   (c) to discharge any fine imposed by a court;
> (4) between one trade union and another."[85]

Other sections carried out the proposals for registration and consequent protection of property.[86]

But when the government's bill was first presented it also contained clause 3, which very largely reproduced section 3 of 1825.
While "threats" and "intimidation" were now defined only to cover
threats of physical violence, there was no knowing whether the
clause as a whole would be treated in this spirit. The Molestation of
Workmen Act 1859 was to be repealed and its assurance (for what it
was worth) of the lawfulness of peaceful picketing was not repeated.
Protest against the clause was principally organised through the
third national Trades Union Congress. This brought together the
northern originators of the Congress and the London "Junta" in a
united front from which the T.U.C.'s influential Parliamentary Committee would develop. The government's determination to keep the
core of the criminal labour laws remained unshaken. Its sole "concession" was to put clause 3 into a separate bill, which, after some
confused amendments, became the Criminal Law Amendment Act
1871.[87] Offences concerned with threats and intimidation had now to
involve a breach of the peace. Much wider were the offences involving molestation and obstruction of a person with a view to coercing
him in various ways in his trade or business: they could be constituted by watching or besetting the house or other place where the
person resided, worked, carried on business or happened to be. In
the eyes of an unsympathetic judge, this might apply to picketing,
however peaceful.

The unions soon learnt how little their legal position had changed
in regard to industrial action. 1872 brought an upturn in trade which
was accompanied both by substantial strikes and a novel, though
temporary, outbreak of unionism amongst agricultural workers.
There were a great many prosecutions of strikers and their supporters, under the Master and Servant Acts and the Criminal Law
Amendment Act, particularly before justices. Even *The Times* felt
uneasy over the brief imprisonments the wives of farm labourers in
Oxfordshire when they had only shouted at black-leg labour.[88]

---

[85] S.4; Hedges and Winterbottom (1930) Pt. II, Chap. 2.
[86] See C. Grunfeld, *Modern Trade Union Law* (1966) Chap. 6.
[87] Hedges and Winterbottom (1930), pp. 111–118.
[88] *The Times*, May 23–June 23, 1873. This was the Chipping Norton bench's reaction to
the spread of Joseph Arch's National Agricultural Labourers' Union, short-lived
though it proved.

Details of these and great many other cases were assiduously collected for the Parliamentary Committee by George Howell, a prominent member of the Junta.[89]

Most damaging of all, in November 1872, members of the newly-
formed Amalgamated Gas Stokers' Society went in a large body to
demand that the superintendent of the Beckton gasworks reinstate
one of their members, who had been dismissed for union activities.
The leaders were prosecuted and convicted of conspiracy to secure
simultaneous breaches of contract (contrary to the Master and Servant Acts). There were also counts charging a common law conspiracy to interfere with the free will of another by threats and
intimidation, almost exactly as in *Druitt's* case. Brett J. instructed the
jury:

> "there is improper molestation if there is anything done with an
> improper intent, which you shall think is annoyance or an unjusti-
> fiable interference, and which in your judgment would have the
> effect of annoying or interfering with the minds of the persons
> carrying on such a business as this Gas Company was conduct-
> ing."[90]

The Criminal Law Amendment Act had stated that no person
should be liable to punishment for doing or conspiring to do any act,
on the ground that such act restrained or tended to restrain the free
course of trade, unless such act fell within the express prohibitions of
the Act itself. But Brett J. held this to have no effect on common law
offences when (at least nominally) they were not founded upon
"restraint of trade" but upon "improper molestation."[91] On the evidence, the jury refused to find against the defendants on these
counts. Soon afterwards the statutory proviso was robbed of any
residual value by the pronouncement of Cleasby B. that "if watching
and besetting is carried on to such a length and to such an extent that
it occasions a dread of loss, it would be unlawful" under the 1871 Act
itself.[92]

(e) Conservative Concessions

The steady rain of punishments upon the heads of union activists
at least gave their leaders abundant material with which to keep up a
fusilade against the compromise of 1871. Gladstone took little interest in the whole question and this contributed to the decline of his
first ministry. Disraeli's pledges of social reform, which included

[89] Later summarised in his *Labour Legislation, Labour Movements and Labour Leaders*
(1905), II. In 1874, a Sheffield firm demonstrated the full range of the Master and Servant Acts (even after their amendment in 1867) by obtaining against a worker an
order for repayment of their loss of profits during a strike and three months'
imprisonment for failing to return to work; then they saw to it that he got no work
elsewhere in the town: TUC Circular, June, 1874.
[90] *R.* v. *Bunn* (1872) 12 Cox 316 at 339–340; K. D. Brown in Wrigley (1982), p. 118.
[91] Although in 1873, Lush J. directed a jury in a contrary sense, it was Brett J.'s view
that was generally applied: see Royal Commission on the Labour Laws, below,
n. 26, 104, 106.
[92] *R.* v. *Hibbert* (1875) 13 Cox 82, 87.

promises to improve the legal position of trade unions,[93] fell to be
redeemed after his electoral success in 1874. The cabinet's first move
was to push the industrial disputes issue off onto another Royal
Commission, this time headed by Cockburn C.J. It duly reported in
favour of minor ameliorations, particularly in regard to the crime of
conspiracy.[94] But by now the political organisation of the union
movement had passed its adolescence: the leaders all but ignored the
Commission[95] and insisted to the government that the recommendations were pusillanimous. In 1875, the Home Secretary, Sir Richard
Cross, who introduced so much of the social legislation of his
government, put through two bills fundamentally affecting trade
union law. The first replaced the criminal penalties of the Master and
Servant Acts entirely by civil remedies; the second in essence
espoused the proposition in the Minority Report of 1869, that the
general law alone should determine the extent of criminal liability for
industrial action.

The Employers and Workmen Act 1875 gave the new civil jurisdiction over employment contracts to the County Courts, if the sum
claimed exceeded £10, and to the Magistrates' Courts, if it did not.
The old power to order a servant back to work on pain of imprisonment gave place to a power, if both parties agreed, to waive damages
and take security for future performance of the contract.[96] Although
this was couched in neutral terms, it is clear from the Parliamentary
debates that it was conceived as a method of impelling a man back to
work, rather than a technique for securing his reinstatement when
wrongfully dismissed.[97]

The Conspiracy and Protection of Property Act 1875, sought to end
charges of criminal conspiracy to commit ill-defined abuses during
the course of trade disputes: "an agreement or combination by two
or more persons to do or procure to be done any act *in contemplation
or furtherance of a trade dispute between employers or workmen*[98] shall
not be indictable as a conspiracy if such act committed by one person
would not be punishable as a crime."[99] Memories of recent strikes
were too strong for all special criminal statutes to be repealed.
Indeed, the threat to a vital supply presented by the gas stokers'
strike of 1872 led to the introduction of criminal penalties against gas
or water employees who "wilfully and maliciously broke their contracts in the knowledge that they would probably deprive inhabi-

---

[93] The T.U.C. Parliamentary Committee had sought appropriate pledges from all candidates.

[94] P.P. 1875 [C. 1157] XXX.

[95] The miner-M.P., Alexander Macdonald, was persuaded to serve as a member; he
dissented.

[96] In the controversial atmosphere of 1867, the Abdullamite Conservative, Lord Elcho,
then a promoter, with the miner-unionist, Macdonald, of non-militant unionism,
had secured a partial amelioration of the Master and Servant Act; but the power to
fine, and to punish "aggravated" cases had remained: see C. J. Kauffman in Brown
(1974) Chap. 8; Fox (1985), pp. 139–140.

[97] See, *e.g.* P.D. CCXXIV 1677–78.

[98] The words "between employers or workmen" were subsequently repealed by the
Trade Disputes Act 1906, s.1.

[99] In addition conspiracy to commit a summary criminal offence in contemplation or
furtherance of a trade dispute was to carry no sentence of imprisonment greater
than that permitted for the summary offence itself: s.3.

tants to a great extent of their supply."[1] A broader section made similar provision against employees whose breach of contract would probably "endanger human life, or cause serious bodily injury, or . . . expose valuable property . . . to destruction or serious injury."[2] And section 7 retained a version of the 1871 section aimed at oppressive tactics against opponents during industrial action. But now the crucial provision was qualified: "attending at or near a house or place . . . in order merely to obtain or to communicate information shall not be deemed a watching or besetting." This concession was procured by the TUC Parliamentary Committee at a late stage of the Bill's progress, and even in this form it did not go as far as the Act of 1859, for it did not admit "persuasion," however peaceful. Narrow though it was, the difference provided a legal trapdoor manipulable by any court unsympathetic to picketing.

Altogether the Bills acknowledged the new-found strength of a union movement fortified by the Parliamentary franchise. The admission of principle was larger than in any other social legislation enacted in the last quarter of the century. To a significantly greater degree it was to be legitimate to use collective power, even where the result was to interfere with the freedom of others to dispose of their capital or labour as they saw fit. To liberals of Dicey's stamp this was the foremost, and least admissible, concession and it explains why they regarded "collectivism" rather than "socialism" as the evil of the hour. Most union leaders of this period were content to remain within the fold of capitalist production, but they sought a new structure of power within which to conduct their arguments with employers. The ability to bargain collectively, with the ultimate threat of a legitimate withdrawal of labour, was substantially secured in 1875, and would last without serious challenge for twenty years. And law, as a protection for the employee, was henceforth to be used primarily to assist the weak, who were not able to look to a union to fight their battles for them.

From mid-century onwards there had been a noticeable growth in regular, relatively formal institutions for labour bargaining. The results were well publicised before the Royal Commission of 1867–69 and they were taken as an earnest of good faith, responsibility and collaboration from the union movement of the future; without this development the political and legal history of 1871–75 might have been very different. As we have seen, the older craft unions had long negotiated with the masters of their locality from time to time. They had often resorted to "honest brokers," men trusted by both sides to act as conciliators and, if necessary, arbitrators, in resolving disputes over wages, hours, exclusive rights and other conditions of work. As the industrial trades began to be unionised, employers would pass the point where they could hope to ignore and suppress and, often after much further struggle, might accept that dealings with the new collectivities were best conducted by established procedures. This might at least reduce explosions of violent fury (of the Sheffield variety) and it could help in maintaining any deal that was struck.

---

[1] Ss.4, 5, extended in 1919 to electricity supply workers.
[2] S.6. See generally Hedges and Winterbottom (1930), pp. 117–118.

The union leaders, for their part, liked the enhanced status and the improved recruitment of members that this would bring.

Two experiments demonstrated how conciliation machinery might induce employers to move on from embattled intransigence.[3] In 1860, an impending dispute in the Nottingham hosiery trade was headed off by the sympathetic and influential employer, A. J. Mundella, who secured a settlement on terms that "a board of arbitration and conciliation should be formed." He became its chairman himself. While it was empowered to act as an arbitral body, the chairman having a casting vote, Mundella saw the advantages of securing agreed results and scarcely ever used his power to impose an outcome.

Four years later, also in face of an impending strike, Judge Rupert Kettle of the Worcestershire County Court was invited to preside over a board of six arbitrators drawn from the carpenters of Wolverhampton and their employers. This he moulded into a permanent body, taking care, with professional scruple, to have the agreement incorporated into the contracts of employment of individual employees.[4] In the process of implementing these rules, moreover, he did not hesitate to have recourse to the laws of political economy. The price of products was treated as supplying the fund for wages: if the one fell so should the other, without reference to the question of profits. Despite form and formulae, however, the negotiations before Kettle were, like Mundella's, conciliatory rather than arbitral.

By the late sixties, the success of these ventures was leading to their adoption in other trades, such as lace, pottery and, in 1869, iron and steel. Early in 1867, Lord St. Leonards, at the request of "thousands of operatives," was able to pilot through a bill giving the Crown power to license a conciliation board, upon the petition of both sides of an industry. Though this particular mechanism was to be ignored, as had the earlier attempts at compulsory arbitration,[5] it was part nonetheless of that current of hope for industrial relations which, in the very year of political reform, was flowing strongly.

Judge Kettle's care in incorporating the results of collective bargaining into individual contracts was carried a considerable distance, since he saw to the inclusion not only of the final outcome but also of the agreement to submit the dispute to arbitration. It was a lawyer's appreciation that the procedural was quite as significant as the substantive in defusing a charged atmosphere. What was being established was not merely that there would be discussions if and when issues arose but that there would be regular meetings or other procedures to deal with defined issues by reference to settled types of information and calculation. This was no novelty, but related back to the old craft practices of negotiating and recording the outcome with Quarter Sessions or by some other formality. In some industries— notably coal and iron and steel—the formula of tying wages to prices became a regular sliding scale, and in some cases, where the unions

---

[3] See J. R. Hicks (1930) 10 Economica 25; V. L. Allen (1964) 9 Int. Rev. Soc. Hist. 237.
[4] Mainly by the technique of posting the terms in prominent positions in the works: Royal Commission on Trade Unions, 4th Report, see P.P. 1867 [3952] XXXII at 26.
[5] See above. p. 298.

were weak or non-existent, it was imposed by employees to their evident disadvantage.[6]

Kettle's scrupulousness may also perhaps have stemmed from an appreciation that the collective bargain of itself might have no legal effect. Before 1871, the collective agreement might have offended the common law policy against restraints of trade; after the Trade Union Act of that year, in many cases the agreement would not have been directly enforceable in court because it would have been an agreement between one trade union and another; "trade union" was defined to include not only associations of workmen but associations of masters for imposing restrictive conditions on the conduct of any trade or business,[7] and given that much collective bargaining was for a whole trade in a given locality, the preclusion of the 1871 Act would apply.

The question, however, seems largely to have been ignored over a long period. It was a prime illustration of how the business community, in its labour relations as in so much else, operated by norms that were not considered to be within the range of the general law. Ultimately it would be said that a collective bargain was not normally to be understood as intended to create legal relations. But that was very much a lawyers' rationalisation *ex post facto*.[8] The essential relationship of management and labour, as it had emerged by 1875, was set apart from legal discipline by the practices which Britain's unique condition, industrially and politically, allowed to emerge. But "collective laissez-faire" would not be complete, so far as the unions were concerned, if their ability to take industrial action in support of claims was to be legally fettered. It was by no means so clear that the advances on this front, contained in the Conspiracy and Protection of Property Act 1875, were firmly founded.

PART 2: EMPLOYMENT 1875–1950

I. The Emergence of the New Unionism

(a) Labour Conditions

The fall in prices of 1874 pushed the economy into that passage of sporadic difficulties and unsettling changes which has been labelled the "great depression." It brought with it the phenomenon of persistent unemployment and underemployment, for the first time in industrial conditions.[9] The respectable were exposed to the plight of

---

[6] For instance in the South Wales coal mines: see K. Burgess, *The Origins of British Industrial Relations* (1975) Chap. 3.

[7] s.23, amended somewhat in 1876: see Hedges and Winterbottom (1930), p. 92.

[8] The perception of the issue would be much raised by Kahn-Freund, see esp. his essay in A. Flanders and H. Clegg, *The British System of Industrial Relations* (1956) Chap. 2.

[9] The percentage unemployed began in these years to move between 2 and 11 per cent. It was only a hint of the conditions that would prevail after 1929.

the poorest; in 1886 and 1887 London demonstrations by the unemployed took an ugly turn.[10]

At the bottom of the labour market, unskilled and semi-skilled workers engaged in "almost ceaseless toil, hard and often unhealthy," for extremely low wages.[11] A Lords Select Committee could only look to moral suasion for a remedy.[12] Law could not be used to impose wages levels, restrict hours and prevent home-work or sub-contracting. It was hoped, however, that in making supply contracts, central and local government would insist on such guarantees as minimum wages and employment only in factories.[13] The new London County Council and other local authorities adopted resolutions on fair conditions. And in 1891, Sidney Buxton persuaded the House of Commons to adopt its own "Fair Wages Resolution," a declaration that the Government in its contracts would "insert such conditions as may prevent the abuses arising from subletting, and make every effort to secure the payment of the rates of wages generally accepted as current for a competent workman in his trade."[14] While not explicitly saying so, it was intended to submit contractors to the threat of removal from the list of tenderers if they did not comply. Discreetly and cautiously, government took its place at the head of the forces for decent employment. As in the private sphere, the norms were to be supported by sanctions that were economic, but not legal.

These were years in which the trade union movement remained largely within its earlier mould, concerned to preserve the privileges and differentials of skilled work, collaborating with employers and concentrating on the insurance and saving functions of benefit funds. In the political arena, men such as Henry Broadhurst, Thomas Burt and George Howell kept the Parliamentary Committee of the TUC in a "Lib-Lab" conjunction with radical employers such as Mundella and Thomas Brassey. Their objectives were strictly limited, and they became much preoccupied with questions of safety and accident compensation.[15]

To these men, as to employers and the world outside, the sudden

[10] See below, p. 597.

[11] Select Committee on the Sweating System, Fifth Report P.P. 1890 (169) XVII. It did recommend some extensions of the Factories and Workshops Act and stricter enforcement. See generally D. Bythell, *The Sweated Trades* (1978); J. Rickard (1979) 18 Hist. St. 582; J. A. Schmiechen, *Sweated Industries and Sweated Labour* (1984).

[12] Growing pressure for such a move had begun some years before in the London Society of Compositors: Webb (1920), pp. 384–386. In a number of the low-wage trades government authorities were important customers.

[13] The Conservative leadership would, however, only agree to a diluted version of Buxton's original resolution: P.D. CCCL. 616–647, esp. 626, 642; and see generally, Sir R. D. Denman (1947) 18 Pol. Q. 161. While the resolution referred to the Lords Committee's revelations concerning the sweated trades, its scope was not confined to them; in the sweated trades, indeed, union power was weak and so the reference to "current" wages (*i.e.* union rates) can have had little meaning in those fields. See O. Kahn-Freund (1948) 11 M.L.R. 270 at 275.

[14] If the necessary terms were written into the supply contract, they would be legally enforceable; this was later required: see Kahn-Freund (above, n. 13), pp. 274–275.

[15] For this the "Front Bench" were wigged by the Webbs; but some historians have greater sympathy for their scepticism of land resettlement, municipal enterprise and nationalisation as an answer to the besetting problem of urban unemployment: Webb (1920), Chap. 7; Clegg *et al.* (1964), pp. 51–54.

spread of militant unionism that accompanied the upturn in trade of 1888–89 came as a considerable shock.[16] The burst of demands was dramatic: the remarkable strike of East End matchgirls, the succession of short strikes by seamen organised within Havelock Wilson's new national federation, the major concessions secured by Will Thorne's gas-stokers from the London companies, and finally the great London dock strike, which secured a wage of 6d. an hour—"the docker's tanner." All of a sudden it seemed that trade unions for the great mass of semi-skilled and unskilled workmen might succeed to an unimagined degree. By 1890, perhaps 350,000 had joined the nine largest of the new societies.

The phenomenon was a complex one, beginning too rapidly and feeding upon enthusiasms too various to establish any coherent pattern. Hyndman's Social Democratic Federation and other socialist organisations provided an intellectual stimulus for the new leaders, such as Tillett, Burns and Mann, who led the Dock Strike. But the major reconstructions demanded by Socialists aroused suspicion in many supporters of the new industrial militancy, and often the attraction of leaders lay more in their personal vigour than their political beliefs. Moreover the early successes could not be sustained, as the demand for labour tailed off and employers began to organise resistance. Those unions that survived did so in many instances because they were alliances of closed-shop, regularly employed workers, who found that recognition of their organisations by employers led them into the paths of collaboration.[17] Equally, the impact of the new movement produced a greater readiness on the part of some established unions to recruit upon a wider basis.[18] Despite the acrimonious debates between the "old" and "new" unionists in the nineties, there could be no simple division into two categories, the old craft and the new general unions.

Whatever the myths, the sudden growth of unionism amongst new categories of worker was real and to an important degree sustained.[19] Lower-paid workers could not pay substantial contributions to benefit funds, but could at most build a strike fund in the hope of securing immediate concessions from employers. Militant confrontation on a large scale was a necessity. And since employers had the option—often not available against skilled workers—of bringing in unskilled blackleg labour by way of retaliation, the struggle could be long and hard.[20] As early as December 1889, the gasworkers of the South Metropolitan Gas Company proved unable to maintain their earlier victory: 2,000 struck, only to find 4,000 replacements already engaged by the Company. Organisers appeared who were able systematically

---

[16] For what follows, see in particular, Phelps Brown (1959); Clegg et al. (1964) Chap. 2; Pelling (1976) Chap. 6; R. Price, *Masters Unions and Men* (1980) Chap. 6.
[17] E. J. Hobsbawm (1964), Essays 9–11.
[18] A significant example was the Amalgamated Society of Engineers, which in 1892 began to recruit semi-skilled machine-men.
[19] Both the Transport and General Workers Union and the National Union of General and Municipal Workers have their origins in this period. For the incidence and effect of the "new unionism" generally, see Clegg et al. (1964), pp. 82–96.
[20] For the incidence of strikes in the late nineteenth century, see M. J. Haynes in J. Benson (ed.) *The Working Class in England 1875–1914* (1985) Chap. 4; J. Cronin, *Industrial Conflict in Modern Britain* (1979); and in Wrigley (1982) Chap. 4.

to recruit "free" labour.[21] William Collison's National Free Labour Association, established in 1893, was the best-known and respectable, achieving in 1898 a link with the Employers' Federation and its Parliamentary Council.[22]

Confrontations between unionists and "free labour" men might turn ugly. Blacklegs were sometimes threatened with physical violence.[23] On the other side, the police (often relying on support from the magistracy) openly took the strike-breakers' part.[24] From such clashes, a press that mostly supported the employers could whip up fears of "organised terrorism."[25] In fact there remained overall a high degree of respect for law; civil disorder in any serious degree remained a rarity.

(b) The Royal Commission on Labour

In addition to industrial counter-moves, the new unionism provoked a significant political response and an even more decisive legal reaction. By 1891, Salisbury's government had appointed a Royal Commission, under the Duke of Devonshire, to inquire into labour relations and "to report whether legislation can with advantage be directed to the remedy of any ills that may be disclosed, and, if so, in what manner." A quarter of the members were unionists; and of these, four were avowed socialists, as their Minority Report was to show.

The Commission assembled a remarkable picture of labour relations in every section of British industry from the great staples to the mean sweated trades.[26] The reports depicted the wide variety of practices by which wages and other conditions were either agreed or imposed. The Majority were persuaded that "many of the evils . . . cannot be remedied by legislation, but we may look with confidence to the gradual amendment by natural forces now in operation which tend to substitute a state of industrial peace for one of industrial division and conflict."[27] Accordingly, their Report swept aside any prospect of compulsory arbitration. Regarding disputes over future terms and conditions and over bargaining procedures, it would go no further than to adopt Mundella's Bill of 1893.[28] This gave the Department of Labour statutory authority to maintain the conciliation service which had already begun to form around the Department's activities in collecting labour statistics. Even as regards disputes over existing rights, where the model of the French conseils de prud'hommes was examined as it had been in the past, it could find

---

[21] J. Saville in Briggs and Saville (1960), p. 322; Fox (1985), pp. 186–199.

[22] By its side, the Free Labour Protection Association was formed in 1897, with the Earl of Wemyss (formerly Lord Elcho) as chairman. He brought to it the rampant individualism of the Liberty and Property Defence League.

[23] Lord Askwith, Industrial Problems and Disputes (1920), p. 295.

[24] For an example, see Clegg et al. (1964), p. 68.

[25] The Times, December 20, 1903 (editorial on the Taff Vale trial).

[26] This evidence is summarised in Part II of the Fifth and Final Report of the Royal Commission on Labour, P.P. 1894 [C. 7421] XXXV. A considerable quantity of comparative material was also amassed.

[27] Ibid, para. 363.

[28] This emerged as the Conciliation Act 1896.

no sufficient case for legislation. At most, local authorities were to be empowered to create special bodies to meet particular difficulties.[29]

The Socialist Minority gave a pungent diagnosis of the evils of industrial society and listed the legislative changes which they demanded by way of remedy: a general Eight Hours Act[30]; extension and real enforcement of the Factories Acts; proper housing for the working man and "honourable maintenance" in old age; the payment of standard union rates by all government departments and local authorities; the extension of joint industrial boards at least to disputes over the interpretation of existing agreements; and most fundamentally, the substitution for private capital of national or municipal enterprise wherever possible, and "where this substitution is not yet practicable . . . the strict and detailed regulation of all industrial operations so as to secure to every worker the conditions of efficient citizenship."

The Fabian accent is unmistakeable. Labour relations were to progress with social improvement step by step, and the method of improvement was to be legislation.[31] Strangely, it was over the question of means that the socialists came closest to their most vigorous opponents on the Commission. For a group of eight among the majority appended observations which suggested that, far from wholeheartedly accepting the voluntarist thesis, they hoped eventually for a shift of opinion towards the legal enforceability of collective agreements; and this they assumed would follow from allowing unions and employers' associations to acquire separate legal personality. In that event, if "a body had agreed to submit future disputes . . . to arbitration, and subsequently refused to do so and resorted to a strike or lock-out," it might be sued for damages.[32] Inevitably those who strove for dominance in labour relations should look to a legal framework that would buttress their particular position. In both the United States, where comparatively the unions were weak, and in Australia, where comparatively they were strong, movements of opinion were in progress which would introduce compulsory legal techniques for the resolution of disputes both of interest and of right.[33] In Britain, the unique balance of power between the two sides of industry, together with special experience of early industrialisation, was to mean the retention of "collective laissez-faire" to a unique degree.[34]

---

[29] Above, n. 26, paras. 292–315.

[30] The eight-hour day had become the most immediate of socialist demands, being proposed partly as a remedy for unemployment. By 1890 the TUC was persuaded to adopt a motion in favour of the principle, though some workers (such as the Durham and Northumberland miners) feared that they would lose their already more favourable position. Numerous eight-hour bills were introduced, but in the end none succeeded.

[31] Sidney Webb played a large part in drafting the Minority Report: B. Webb, *Our Partnership* (1975 ed.), pp. 40–41.

[32] Observations, para. 23. The signatories included several of the employer-members and the principal lawyer, Sir Frederick Pollock, Professor of Jurisprudence at Oxford.

[33] New Zealand introduced compulsory arbitration in 1894, just as the Royal Commission was reporting (*cf.* Appendix V of its Final Report).

[34] Kahn-Freund (1959), p. 215.

One assumption was taken as a constant in these debates: a trade union could not be sued, and so collective agreements were incapable of enforcement by legal process.[35] The point is driven home by a special arrangement reached in the footwear industry. In 1895 there was added to the annual conciliation procedure an agreement to submit irreconcilable differences to arbitration. A document, executed with the full solemnity of a deed under seal, set up a trust fund to which both sides made contributions. Out of this fund, the arbitrator might award penalties to be paid for breach of agreement.[36] That an important industry should take such pains to construct an edifice of private norms appeared to some to be one harbinger of enforcement through the general law. Such was the strength of the counter-tradition that this was not to be. Indeed, as we shall see, the assumption that collective bargains as a rule created no legal obligations was to outlive the premise upon which it was built: that unions were incapable of suit.

(c) Judicial Activism

The determination of hostile employers to find some legal means of breaking strikes led them to turn attention from criminal to civil remedies. For this, there were a number of reasons, partly substantive, partly procedural. In 1891, the Lord Chief Justice, Coleridge, led a Divisional Court in limiting the scope of the crucial part of the Conspiracy and Protection of Property Act 1875.[37] The Court read "intimidates," in the phrase "uses violence to or intimidates another person," to encompass nothing beyond a threat to use violence to person or property. The court refused to accept that "strikes and combinations expressly legalised by statute may yet be treated as indictable conspiracies at common law."[38]

In any case, there were definite procedural advantages to be had from civil process. When a civil case came to trial, the employer might have a special jury.[39] A verdict against strikers and union organisers might result in substantial damages representing the employer's lost profits during the strike.[40] If a way could be found to

---

[35] See above, p. 323.

[36] A. Fox, *History of the National Union of Boot and Shoe Operatives* (1958), p. 148.

[37] *Gibson* v. *Lawson; Curran* v. *Treleavan* [1891] 2 Q.B. 545. In the preceding years there had been a few prosecutions of picketers (*e.g. R.* v. *Bauld* (1876) 13 Cox C.C. 282). Here, five judges sat in order to clarify the scope of the law.

[38] *Ibid.,* p. 560, disapproving the well-known views of Bramwell (in *Druitt*, above, p. 319) and Esher (Brett) (in *Bunn*, above, p. 314) and relying instead on Wright J.'s lucid *Law of Criminal Conspiracies* (1872), pp. 50–59. The new view against criminal conspiracy at common law was criticised by such trenchant conservatives as Halsbury (see the *Mogul* case [1892] A.C. at 38), just as Lindley reserved his opinion on the interpretation of "intimidation": *Lyons* v. *Wilkins* (*No. 1*) [1896] 2 Ch. at 824; for which very different decision, see below, p. 331.

[39] By this time, special jurors were chiefly selected by reference to a property qualification (occupation of a dwelling) higher than that for common jurors. A century before special juries had also been used in criminal prosecutions, notably for sedition; but in such cases they were too openly partisan to have survived. How they could behave in a civil action against a trade union is well-illustrated by *Trollope* v. *London Building Trades Federation* (1896) 12 T.L.R. 373.

[40] But against such individuals, the judgment might prove valueless.

attach union funds in satisfaction of the judgment, a quite new method of crippling collective action by labour would become available. Moreover, long before any trial a civil court might impose an interlocutory injunction on the strike organisers, ordering them to refrain from further activity until the issue between management and men could be tried. All that was needed was to show a *prima facie* case that legally wrongful injury would result. To disobey such an order would then be contempt of court, and this could be punished by fine or imprisonment entirely at the court's discretion. Any move required a civil cause of action to lie and in that direction lawyers began active exploration.

The search was to take place at a time when they were testing the range of law of torts in other spheres of economic activity. In the main, the courts were insisting that, in the hard world of competition for customers and scarce resources, the common law would not hold activities to be wrongful merely because they must injure others. In *Mayor of Bradford* v. *Pickles*,[41] the House of Lords held that a man might exercise his freedom in law to extract subterranean water from beneath his land even though his only purpose was to make a local authority pay him to stop: a "malicious" motive (if so it could be described) could not turn a lawful act into a tort. Equally in point, in the *Mogul* case,[42] the House affirmed that a trading ring might combine to exclude a competitor by offering price-cutting inducements to clients who refrained from dealing with the competitor. In this there was no actionable conspiracy, provided that the ring did nothing in itself unlawful, and (here came a rub) provided that their motive was to advance their own selfish interests rather than to injure the competitor.

Very different was the approach of many of the senior judges to industrial disputes. The lead came in *Temperton* v. *Russell*,[43] a case of secondary boycott. The defendants, officials of three building unions in Hull, were seeking to secure observance of agreed "working rules" (directed against "labour-only" and other sub-contracting) by a non-compliant firm. The plaintiff, a master mason, had been supplying building materials to this firm and refused to stop doing so. In order to put effective pressure on the latter, the unions instructed members not to work on any materials supplied by the plaintiff to anyone. The Court of Appeal upheld the special jury's verdict of £250 in his favour on three grounds. First, so far as the union pressure induced other builders to break existing contracts with the plaintiff, so far as workers were induced to break existing contracts with the plaintiff, and so far as workers were induced to break their contracts of employment with him, the tort of inducing breach of contract had been committed. The notion of such a tort had emerged in *Lumley* v. *Gye*,[44] but it had scarcely flourished in face of the disapprobation of

---

[41] [1895] A.C. 587; *cf.* also the scrupulous limitation of liability for mis-statements (*Derry* v. *Peek*, above, p. 221) and for unfair advertising practices (*White* v. *Mellin* [1895] A.C. 154).
[42] *Mogul Steamship Co.* v. *McGregor, Gow* [1892] A.C. 25, above, p. 270.
[43] [1893] 1 Q.B. 715.
[44] (1853) 2 El. & Bl. 216.

Willes J. and several other judges.[45] Now it was accepted within the canon of common-law torts, whether the contracts in question were commercial or for labour.

The second and third grounds of liability[46] related to the situations where traders or workers were induced not to *enter* contracts with the plaintiff, a choice that was in law perfectly open to them. This was held wrongful, either because it was "malicious," or because (despite the *Mogul* case) it amounted to a "malicious" conspiracy to injure. The validity of both these contentions was to be hotly contested by the unions in subsequent cases. The first alternative ran counter to a general principle that was to be affirmed within months by *Mayor of Bradford* v. *Pickles*. And subsequently in *Allen* v. *Flood*,[47] the House of Lords concluded that no exception to this principle was to be admitted. Malice, even on the part of trade unionists, could not transform what was legally permissible into actionable wrong. But it was a near-run thing, a victory for the Liberal, Herschell, who carried a majority of the House against the advisory opinions of six of the eight judges specially summoned for the occasion; and it left the law affecting industrial disputes in a condition of great confusion.

Allen v. *Flood*, a demarcation dispute in the London docks, was argued as a case in which an official had procured the discharge of workers competing with his own union: the effect of combined action as a conspiracy was not explored. Within four years, it was held by the House that this very fact might make all the difference. The *Mogul* case had allowed that a conspiracy to act in a manner entirely lawful could itself be tortious if the motive for action was a malicious intention to cause injury to another; the *Temperton* case had shown that a jury might find such malice in secondary boycott activities of a union. In *Quinn* v. *Leathem*[48] the boycott did not persuade suppliers or employees to do anything that amounted even to breach of contract, let alone a crime or distinct tort; but still the House were unanimous that this "wide" form of tortious conspiracy had been committed. Lord Halsbury set the tone by his peremptory dismissal of the argument that such a result would be inconsistent with *Mogul* and *Allen*: "Such mode of reasoning assumes that the law is necessarily a logical code, whereas every lawyer must acknowledge that the law is not always logical at all."[49] And, indeed, whatever might be thought of the differentiation of joint from individual action, it remained an utter puzzlement to many that "malicious" secondary pressure when practised by a union became for a business cartel the pursuit of legitimate self-interest. Never was the law more nakedly the partisan of masters against men.

Beside these means of finding that pressures exerted on employers

---

[45] The doctrine had some roots in the old action for seduction of servants: see above, p. 287. But the new extension, depending on malicious inducement, was distinct in a number of respects. Those who objected to it, felt it to be an erosion of the privity doctrine that contracts created obligations only for the parties to them: see, *e.g.* Coleridge J., dissenting in *Lumley* v. *Gye* (above, n. 44).

[46] The importance of these heads in the action was that the jury allotted four-fifths of the damages to them.

[47] [1898] A.C. 1; for personalities, see R. F. V. Heuston (1986) 102 L.Q.R. 90.

[18] [1901] A.C. 495.

[49] *Ibid.*, 506.

and their customers were tortious, the courts also launched an attack on non-violent picketing. In *Lyons* v. *Wilkins*,[50] an interlocutory injunction was granted on the loose principle that a likely case of criminal behaviour had been made out, the supposed crime being "watching and besetting" the employer's premises.[51] But the Act of 1875 had the specific proviso excluding from illegality "attending at or near the . . . place where a person . . . carries on business . . . in order merely to communicate information."[52] Since the union had been careful to post only two pickets at a time, and had them merely hand out cards requesting non-union workers to stay away from the firm as soon as they were free in law to do so, the case was far from obvious. Yet the Court of Appeal was prepared to distinguish between communicating information *simpliciter*, and doing so when "the object and effect [is] to compel the person so picketed not to do that which he has a perfect right to do."[53] As Lindley L.J. remarked, "You cannot make a strike effective without doing more than is lawful."[54] The case was then taken to full trial, and judgment was reserved until the House of Lords had pronounced its opinion in *Allen* v. *Flood*. But the Court of Appeal hearing *Lyons* found nothing relevant in the *Allen* decision and took the opportunity to reiterate its casuistic distinction between picketing to inform and to persuade.[55]

Thus the intumescence of the substantive law. But there were growths just as significant in adjectival matters—three in particular. First, could all the members of a trade union be made subject to a judgment by suing one or two of them in a representative action? Second, could a trade union itself, despite its lack of corporate status, be made party to an action, at least if it was registered under the Act of 1871? Third, if it could, it must, like a corporation, be treated as acting through its agents; in what circumstances, then, did it authorise action on its behalf?

Since the Judicature Acts, equity's device of a representative action had been available in proceedings concerning common law rights and there were a number of possible spheres for its application by or against unincorporated groups. But the courts proved reluctant to sanction its employment in new ways, fearing to give judgment against persons who had had no chance to show that their interest differed from that of their representative. Even against the members of trade unions, the Court of Appeal in *Temperton* v. *Russell* ruled that no representative action could be constituted.[56] This might have ended the question, but in *Taff Vale Railway* v. *ASRS* Lords Mac-

---

[50] [1896] 1 Ch. 811.
[51] The interlocutory injunction also issued against secondary boycott activities, on the strength of the broader grounds in *Temperton* v. *Russell*.
[52] Conspiracy and Protection of Property Act 1875, s.7(4).
[53] Lindley L.J., [1896] 1 Ch. at 826.
[54] *Ibid.* 820; echoing Bramwell B., *R.* v. *Bailey* (1867) 16 L.T. (N.S.) 859.
[55] [1899] 1 Ch. 255. On this second occasion the Court of Appeal gave more thought to the principle that injunctions are granted to prevent wrongful infraction of private rights, not mere criminal offences. Invasion of private right was held either to follow by implication from the prohibitions of the 1875 Act, or else because the picketing constituted an actionable nuisance—in the circumstances, a decidedly strained view.
[56] [1893] 1 Q.B. 435.

naghten and Lindley strove in the most vigorous terms to assert that this formula could be used to sue trade unions, registered or unregistered, so as to render union funds liable for damages and costs.[57]

The second question received the House of Lords' answer also in the *Taff Vale* case,[58] decided a fortnight before *Quinn* v. *Leathem*. The dispute in question, typical of labour relations in the railways at the time, had begun as a long-standing wage claim and had disintegrated into a strike over the alleged victimisation of a union spokesman. The railway, led by its pugnacious general manager, Ammon Beasley, brought in "free labour," and the strikers responded with "persuasion" a good deal less circumspect than in *Lyons* v. *Wilkins*. Farwell J. granted an interim order against two union officials[59] enjoining "watching and besetting." And after the strike was over he went on to rule that his order might extend to the union itself, since it had been registered under the 1871 Act. That Act he held to invest trade unions with the "essential qualities of a corporation" and accordingly to render them suable in tort. Parliament could not be taken to have legalised "irresponsible bodies with such wide capacities for evil."[60]

A unanimous House of Lords also reasoned in essentially similar terms.[61] Lurking behind the argument, though enshadowed by the 1871 Act and its registration procedure, was the jurisprudential notion that large and powerful collectivities should be treated as legal persons by the courts: in terms of contemporary German theory, all corporations were "real" persons and not fictitious projections of the law.[62] The contrary case—that in withholding corporate status in 1871, Parliament had kept back any ability to sue or be sued—found the support of a unanimous Court of Appeal.[63] The historical evidence almost entirely pointed to this view of Parliament's intention

---

[57] [1901] A.C. 426 at 438–439, 444. Lord Macnaghten chose to explain away *Temperton* as a case where the selection of representatives was inappropriate.

[58] [1901] A.C. 426. The question had been aired on several occasions in the 1890s, the weight of judicial opinion apparently being against allowing the union to be sued: cf. *Pink* v. *Federation of Shipping Unions* (1892) 67 L.T. 258; *Trollope* v. *London Building Trades Federation* (1895) 72 L.T. 342; *Warnham* v. *Stone* (1896), unreported; see Webb, *Industrial Democracy* (1898) 858; *Lyons* v. *Wilkins* [1899] 1 Ch. at 259. *Temperton* v. *Russell* [1893] 1 Q.B. 435 makes the same assumption.

[59] These were James Holmes, West of England organiser, who started the strike unofficially, and Richard Bell, the union's secretary and soon to be a Labour Representation Committee M.P., who was impelled to give financial support. See below, n. 77.

[60] [1901] A.C. at 430.

[61] The substance of Lord Halsbury's speech was confined to a single sentence: "If the Legislature has created a thing which can own property, which can employ servants and which can inflict injury, it must be taken, I think, to have impliedly given the power to make it suable in a Court of Law for injuries purposely done by its authority and procurement": *ibid* at 436.

[62] For Maitland's interest in this theory, see above, p. 114; and for his impact, W. M. Geldart (1910) 27 L.Q.R. 90. Pollock, on the other hand, espoused a sceptical positivism on the matter: corporations, if not truly fictitious, at least acquired their legal capacities solely from Parliamentary enactment or Crown grant: (1911) 27 L.Q.R. 219.

[63] [1901] 1 Q.B. 170. The 1871 Act (s.9) had specifically given to *trustees* the power to bring and defend actions touching the property of a registered union. "A most remarkable section," said A. L. Smith M.R., "if . . . the purview of the Act is that a trade union can be sued in its registered name": (p. 176).

in 1871[64]; but the rule that Parliamentary debates are not an admissible aid to the interpretation of statutes kept this out of direct argument.[65]

The proceedings which reached the House of Lords in 1901 were interlocutory; and so long as the resulting injunction was obeyed it mattered little whether the order bound the union or only its officials, since they would be its active agents in any event. But Beasley insisted on pressing the case to trial for an award of damages,[66] and it was in January, 1903, when the railway agreed to settle for a sum of £23,000, that both sides of industry were finally shown the immense significance of the House of Lords' decision. Any strike which involved either a withdrawal of labour in breach of contract, or "watching and besetting" in the sense of picketing to persuade, would be tortious; and if ordered by union officials, the resultant damage to the employer might be recovered from union funds. In the labour conditions of the time, the confines of legitimate action had become narrow indeed.

Other employers took to litigating under the new dispensation. In 1902 the weavers of Blackburn were held liable for wrongful picketing and libel, the cost to their union being some £11,000.[67] In 1905, the South Wales Miners Federation were obliged to pay damages in the region of £60,000 after the House of Lords upheld a finding of inducing breach of contract; the Federation had ordered a series of one-day stoppages in the hope of protecting sliding-scale wages. The stoppages were directed not at the employers but at the middlemen dealers in coal; but that was not treated as amounting to any justification.[68]

Only in the months after the Liberal victory of 1906, when new legislation on industrial action was under scrutiny, was there a noticeable onset of judicial caution. In February, the Operative Printers' Assistants Society escaped liability for picketing, when the Court of Appeal insisted that the activities must be shown to constitute a civil

---

[64] It is true, however, that the *tortious* liability of unions was not an issue in the debates of the sixties and seventies: see Report of the Royal Commission on Trade Disputes, P.P. 1906 [Cd. 2825] LVI, para. 22. But the need for special protection had been impressed by the Positivists on some of the less sophisticated unionists: see R. Harrison, *Before the Socialists* (1965), p. 287; and generally, for the feeling that the law was weighted against them, H. Pelling, *Popular Politics and Society in Late Victorian Britain* (1979) Chap. 4.

[65] Haldane, leading for the union, did succeed in referring to the Minority Report of 1869, as the basis of the 1871 Act; and this was taken up by Lord Macnaghten to his own ends: see [1901] A.C. 426 at 435, 438; *cf. Citrine's Trade Union Law* (3rd. ed., 1967), p. 182, n. 76.

[66] The special jury found the defendants to have molested by unlawful means and to have induced breaches of contract. The verdict was reached in ten minutes without leaving court: *The Times*, December 20, 1902.

[67] Clegg *et al.* (1964), pp. 323–324.

[68] *Glamorgan Coal Co.* v. *South Wales Miners Federation* [1905] A.C. 239 (hearings had been spread over nearly three years). Other cases that added to the legal pressure on the unions were *Giblan* v. *National Amalgamated Labourers' Union* [1903] 2 K.B. 600 (civil conspiracy arising out of an attempt to secure payment of debt by member to union); *Read* v. *Friendly Society of Operative Stonemasons* [1902] 2 K.B. 732 (union pressure for dismissal of an apprentice; held to make it liable for inducing breach of contract).

wrong such as a common law nuisance and that the 1875 Act had done nothing to extend the scope of what was "wrongful"[69] (an attitude very different from that in *Lyons* v. *Wilkins*[70]). In May, the House of Lords held the Yorkshire Miners Association not liable for a strike called by two of its branches, because they had acted beyond their power under the rules[71]; this was so even though the union had supported the strikers for several months with benefits.[72] By then, as we shall see, the political balance was nicely poised.

(d) Reactions to Taff Vale

The intervention of the judges in *Taff Vale* and the surrounding cases gave them a unique chance to re-weight the scales of social conflict. In industrial terms, the consequences of the decision are not easily calculated.[73] In the years 1902–05, the number of stoppages and workers involved in them was much reduced.[74] Doubtless the new liabilities of unions and officials had a dampening effect. But equally the trend was beginning to show before the *Taff Vale* judgment made a real impact (*i.e.* with the award of damages in 1903)[75] and this reflected the beginnings of the fall in real wages which in the pre-war period would eventually reach 10 per cent.[76]

Politically, however, the consequences were more evident: the judicial attack on the "right to strike" became part of the growing disgruntlement with Conservative rule, giving the Liberals a radical cause and sustaining the Labour Representation Committee in its struggle to establish an independent working-class voice. Both would draw distinct benefits from it in the election of 1905, with its Liberal landslide and the return of 29 LRC candidates. But both before and after that result it was far from clear what would be done in re-adjustment. Certainly among unionists and sympathisers there were those who thought legal restraints were necessary for a disciplined and responsible movement: they included the Secretary of the Railway Servants Union itself, Richard Bell,[77] and the Webbs in a

---

[69] *Ward Lock & Co.* v. *Operative Printers' Assistants' Society* (1906) 22 T.L.R. 327. At the trial the jury had found the small level of picketing to be injurious and to have involved attempts to persuade non-union labour to break contracts of employment: the Court of Appeal could see no sufficient evidence on either point.

[70] Above, p. 331.

[71] *Denaby and Cadeby Main Collieries* v. *Yorkshire Miners' Association* [1905] A.C. 384 (the Court of Appeal had already taken the same view before the election).

[72] But separate proceedings (*Yorkshire Miners Assoc.* v. *Howden* [1905] A.C. 256) determined that the payments were unauthorised. The set of circumstances was highly complicated.

[73] Clegg *et al.* (1964) Chap. 9; and see Phelps Brown (1959) Chap. 2; F. Fealey and H. Pelling, *Labour and Politics 1900–1906* (1958) Chaps. 3, 4. In comparison with 1899–1902, the number of days lost through stoppages was reduced by nearly two-thirds: *ibid.*, p. 329.

[74] The trend is perceptible from 1899 onwards.

[75] With costs the total bill was £42,000: Webb (1920), pp. 601–602.

[76] A definite rise once more in the period 1906–1909 can be related both to the new legal immunities provided in 1906 and to increasing evidence that profits were rising while wages were falling.

[77] Bell saw the judgments as necessary to curb the enthusiasms of "the younger bloods."

new edition of their *Industrial Democracy*.[78] Beyond them, there were many who, following Dicey, considered that special immunities from legal liability, such as Parliament had apparently intended to confer in 1871–76, to be a constitutional solecism stultifying the rule of law at its base. In 1905, the Parliamentary Committee of the TUC consulted the Liberals, who were much under the guidance of the lawyers, Asquith and Haldane. Together they sponsored a Bill which, in addition to moderate ameliorations of the crime of picketing and the tort of conspiracy, would have exempted unions from damages unless it could be proved that the members in question had "acted with the directly expressed sanction and authority of the rules." Even to this the Government responded with the tactic of another Royal Commission, and opinion in the TUC rapidly hardened.[79] No unionist was included on the Commission and it was boycotted by the movement.[80] Congress now decisively favoured complete immunity of union funds from damage awards and turned for help to Sir Charles Dilke.

In the campaign for the 1905 election this became an effective and uncompromising lobby. Campbell-Bannerman pledged the Liberal party in support, and many individual candidates gave the same undertaking. The Parliamentary Committee's Bill was introduced before the new Parliament was two months old. But in the meantime, Campbell-Bannerman had published the Royal Commission's Report showing a bare majority in favour of moderate compromise.[81] Since Haldane and the Government's Law Officers were bitterly opposed to the "legal monstrosity" of complete immunity, the Government introduced its own Bill on Royal Commission lines.[82] But pressure from the unions' supporters forced the introduction of a crucial amendment conceding the Parliamentary Committee's demand to the extent of excluding a union's liability (in all circumstances, not merely in trade disputes) "for the recovery of damages in respect of any tortious act alleged to have been committed by or on behalf of the trade union." This clause continued to be the subject of hard bargaining. After various additional amendments a final settlement was reached, at a private meeting with the Attorney-General. The limiting words "for the recovery of damages" were removed, so that the clause appeared also to give exemption from the grant of injunctions.[83]

[78] 2nd ed. 1902, pp. xxxiii–iv (with very limited draft Bill); Clegg *et al.* (1964), pp. 317–320.
[79] For details of the ensuing political campaigns, Clegg *et al.* (1964), pp. 320–325, 369–370; Webb (1920), pp. 604–608; Fox (1985), pp. 179–186.
[80] The Commission consisted of two conventional lawyers (Viscount Dunedin (Chairman) and Arthur Cohen, K.C.), an industrial arch-foe (Sir William Lewis), a fair-minded civil servant (Sir Godfrey Lushington), and Sidney Webb.
[81] Report on the Royal Commission on Trade Disputes and Trade Combinations, P.P. 1906 [Cd. 2825] LVI. Lewis and Lushington, in differing degrees, wanted fewer concessions to the unions. Webb was one of the majority but added a rider favouring compulsory arbitration on the Australasian model. See W. M. Geldart (1906) 16 Econ. J. 189.
[82] For the Parliamentary career of the Bills, Clegg *et al* (1964), pp 393–395· see also Phelps Brown (1959) Chap. 3.
[83] This became section 4 of the Act. It contained two additional points: the device of the representative action, the use of which had been encouraged in *Taff Vale*, was excluded; but it was declared that the section did not affect the liability of union

In addition, in its final version the first three sections of the Bill conferred immunities from suit upon *individuals* (such as union officers and members) where their actions were "in contemplation or furtherance of a trade dispute." The first gave immunity from that form of the tort of conspiracy which covered agreements to do lawful acts for the predominant motive of injuring others; this was intended to undo the main basis of *Quinn* v. *Leathem*. The second gave immunity to picketing which involved "peacefully persuading any person to work or abstain from working"; this was to reverse *Lyons* v. *Wilkins*. The third rendered non-tortious the acts of inducing breach of contract of employment,[84] and of interfering with the trade, business or employment of any other or with his right freely to dispose of his capital or labour; this annulled *Taff Vale* and certain broader pronouncements in *Quinn* v. *Leathem*. And while each immunity was confined to the circumstances of a trade dispute, this was defined broadly enough to cover "any dispute between employers and workmen, or *workmen and workmen*, which is connected with the employment or non-employment or the terms of employment, or the conditions of labour, of *any person*."[85]

In these terms, in December 1906, the Bill became law, excluding the possibility of legal redress, save in peripheral areas, against union officers and members personally. The circumstances still courting legal liability included inducing breaches of contracts that were not for employment (for instance, in secondary boycotts), and indulging in or threatening violent picketing. Equally, to overstep that ill-defined boundary between trade disputes and political action would be to move into territory governed by the general law of torts, unfettered by the special provisions of the Act. The growing participation of government in the economy would serve to render an uncertain distinction even less determinate.

II. STATE UNDERPINNING: TRADE BOARDS

After 1906 the Liberals, casting around for a social programme that would retain them a sizeable working-class allegiance, continued to listen to their radical wing and to eye the plans of the emergent Labour Party. In the Lib-Lab coalition of the previous decades, the "method of legal enactment" had found a strictly limited application. The Labour Department of the Board of Trade had fostered voluntary negotiation but had not sought to impose the government's will upon central questions of labour contracts. That was a maintainable position in the relative quiescence of the early Edwardian years, but it was not a permanent possibility. The basic guarantees which in the end were the crux of the Liberals' solution comprised the state-run benefits for sickness and unemployment, for which a person qualified through his own and his employer's contributions at work. This

---

trustees to be sued in respect of misuse of union funds. The latter was included at the behest of Osborne, who was already contemplating his attack on the "Labour-pledge" rule of the ASRS: see p. 341ff. below.

[84] Another hotly contested provision, it was inserted at Dilke's behest only at the Committee stage.

[85] Italics added.

was traditional ground for the benefit activities of unions, and, as will be seen, the state sickness scheme had to be cast in forms which gave unions an administrative role and the opportunity to provide somewhat enhanced payments to their members.[86]

Beyond this, and despite considerable misgivings from the labour movement, the government in 1909 created a national network of labour exchanges, aimed at facilitating the movement of labour into new jobs and so ameliorating where possible the effects of unemployment.[87] Closest of all to the essential trade union function, however, was the creation, in the same year, of trade boards. The problem of sweated labour, previously mourned as shocking but inevitable,[88] was to be tackled by the boards. The possibility of legislative intervention had never been wholly forgotten, thanks to the persistence of radicals such as Sir Charles Dilke, but it was only in the atmosphere after 1906, that he gained such useful support as a press campaign run by *The Daily Mail*. Very low wages were coming to be seen as a crucial evil, requiring the creation of statutory boards with the sole function of fixing minima in the worst trades where voluntary negotiating machinery did not exist. An equal number of representatives from each side of the industry would sit together with independent "additional members." The independent members were to be both conciliators and (if unsuccessful) arbitrators—a combination of functions which, in the circumstances, was potentially incompatible.[89]

The Trade Boards Bill became law in 1909 partly by virtue of its pragmatic nature. In the first instance, boards were created for only four trades—bespoke tailoring and the making of paper boxes, lace and chains.[90] Equally its passage was assisted by the fact that it was not the government that was directly fixing a minimum necessary to subsistence—a level below which positive harm would be done to the nation's stock of labour. The boards were independent entities and might indeed be viewed as a major step towards voluntary negotiating machinery. But the Department of Labour might initiate the creation of new Boards.[91] It was responsible for nominating the all-important "independent members," and, at least initially, it was likely to be involved in the choice of workers' members. The trade board scheme for minimum wages, while it might ultimately reduce the number of jobs at the bottom end of the employment scale, worked primarily as a discipline upon the employers. Accordingly it was the representatives of capital who protested most vigorously against this novel invasion of the free market in labour. They argued

---

[86] See below, pp. 454–455.

[87] Below, pp. 450–451.

[88] See above, p. 324.

[89] A model had been provided by the Australian state of Victoria. See above, p. 327, and also E. Halévy, *A History of the English People in the Nineteenth Century* (1961 ed.), VI pp. 244–253; Lord Amulree, *Industrial Arbitration in Great Britain* (1929) Chap. 18; F. J. Bayliss, *British Wages Councils* (1962) Chap. 1.

[90] All trades with bad reputations for exploiting women home-workers. Some 400,000 workers in all were covered. Chain-making was a late substitute for blouse-making. A number of other trades were added in 1913.

[91] For the Department's role, see R. Davidson in G. Sutherland (ed.) *Studies in the Growth of Nineteenth Century Government* (1972), p. 227; and *The Labour Problem in late Victorian and Edwardian England* (1985), pp. 85–98.

that any attempt artificially to raise the level of wages would turn the sweated into unemployed, particularly since the prime targets (while free trade remained unbreachable) were products easily attacked by foreign competitors. But all they secured was a brake on with speed with which orders could become binding upon them.

At the same time their malaise was increased by other pressures reflected in legislation. In 1908, the miners at last won their campaign for an eight-hour day.[92] Their case could be founded on the peculiarly harsh nature of the work.[93] But its success came partly from the special parliamentary strength of the miners. In the unprecedented wave of strikes, which ran for two years from 1910 and mirrored the constitutional challenge of Lords to government, the miners again played a part crucial enough to secure special legislation.[94] In October 1910, a riotous attack by the men on the pithead at Tonypandy was the first reminder to the country that the government could be obliged to use troops if industrial violence threatened or broke out. But even more important was the miners' strike of March 1912. The successes of mass action amongst the seamen, railway workers, Manchester carters and Liverpool dockers during the febrile summer of the previous year was reflected in an amendment to the rules of the Miners' Federation of Great Britain: this made it possible for the union to call a general strike. As with the earlier threats to nationally vital industries, the government became directly involved in seeking a settlement. But it was only upon Asquith's proposal of legislation to create minimum wage boards that would fix rates for the different mining districts that the strike was called off.[95] Statutory intervention had thus been admitted not just at the very bottom of the labour market[96]; and while, as events came about, the miners were not afterwards much concerned with minima, the principle of thus protecting basic levels of pay had nevertheless been conceded as part of the new, cautious collectivism.

III. Internal Union Affairs

Who and what had been defeated by the events leading to the Trade Disputes Act? The lawyers, almost to a man, felt that, in setting the unions beyond responsibility in matters of tort, a constitutional

---

[92] Coal Mines Regulation Act 1908.

[93] When shop assistants sought a limit on their very long hours they only secured "early closing" and a half day once a week. For the inter-war history, R. Lowe (1982) 35 Ec. H.R. (2d) 254.

[94] For contrasting views of the degree to which there was any interrelation between these events, H. Pelling, *Popular Politics and Society in late Victorian Britain* (1979 ed.), pp. 147–149; J. White in J. E. Cronin and J. Schneer, *Social Conflict and Political Order in Modern Britain* (1982), pp. 73–75; R. Church (1987) 30 Hist. J. 841.

[95] The government's Industrial Council, founded in 1911 to enquire into disputes referred to it, demonstrated its ineffectiveness by producing no proposals: Amulree (above, n. 89), p. 115; Fox (1985), pp. 260–262.

[96] Coal Mines (Minimum Wage) Act 1912; which would after a decade be replaced by collective negotiation: see Kahn-Freund (1959), p. 234.

outrage had been perpetrated.[97] So equally, in political circles beyond the confines of the labour movement.[98] Within the unions there were many whose political loyalties remained with the major parties and who regarded with dismay the emergence of a functioning Labour Party, to which socialist majorities were voting financial support. From these tensions was to emerge the first *Osborne* case, which for notoriety gives place only to *Taff Vale*. In its wake it was to bring a spate of similar actions.[99] They stem from dissenting unionists, the support of outside antagonists of the unions and a sympathetic legal response from the judges.

Before we examine them, however, we must look at two related issues of law. These arose from the legislative forms devised to meet the situation of 1871. The first object of the Trade Union Act of that year had been to prevent unions from being treated as illegal merely because they pursued policies in restraint of trade. This was declared by section 3. There were two consequences: the provisions for registration; and, following the Minority Report of the preceding Royal Commission, the declaration in section 4 that unions thus rescued from illegality nonetheless, for certain purposes, were suspended in a legal limbo: the courts were not to entertain "any legal proceeding instituted with the object of directly enforcing or recovering damages for the breach of" the five particular types of agreement mentioned above.[1]

In the main these concerned the internal relations of members, including mutual restrictive agreements concerning trade and labour, union dues and fines, and the application of disbursements of funds for members' benefits, the purchasing of outsiders' co-operation and the discharge of court fines. The first question which stemmed from the particular form of the Act arose as follows. A society of workers purely for mutual insurance against sickness or old age would not have been illegal before 1871; nor would a trades council which existed for exchanging information and discussing common interests. Because neither, therefore, needed the dispensation of section 3, it followed that the concession secured in section 4 was not open to them. The contracts of such bodies were enforceable under the general law. Accordingly, a member who sought a union benefit must argue that the union had all along been lawful, while the union must seek to demonstrate its illegality by common law standards. Until 1889 there was little discussion of the criteria for determining whether associations had always been lawful. But in that year the Bradford Power-Loom Overlookers' Friendly Society

---

[97] G. R. Askwith, *Lord James of Hereford* (1930), pp. 294–295. The *Law Times* of December 15, 1906, gave voice to this hostility, while the *Solicitors' Journal* (November 17, 1906), adopted a more neutral tone. Dicey, *Law and Public Opinion in England* (2nd Ed. 1914), pp. xliv–xlvii is representative of academic opinion.

[98] But note Clegg *et al.* (1964): " . . . class feeling rose nowhere near the pitch to which it had been aroused by the 'new unionism' and the engineers' lock-out in the nineties, or to which it was again aroused after 1909, especially during the Labour unrest of 1911 and 1912." (p. 415).

[99] See below, p. 344.

[1] Above, pp. 317–318.

was held lawful because it was first and foremost a benefit society.[2] Accordingly a member could sue for an accident benefit provided in its rules. The society, it is true, did have "trade" rules, but these the court felt able to dismiss as "incidental." Subsequently the courts were to make the similar but distinct point that the trade rules were "severable" if trade and benefit funds were kept separate.[3]

The Bristol Trade and Provident Society, a case in point, was unusual in being a union which drew its members from a variety of trades. It did not engage in collective bargaining and, while it might support strikes from its trade fund, it did not organise strikes. In this the Court of Appeal found further reason for treating the society as legal, and allowing a member to recover a fine improperly deducted from sickness benefit.[4]

> "Strikes per se are combinations neither for accomplishing an unlawful end nor for accomplishing a lawful end by unlawful means, and I therefore come unhesitatingly to the conclusion that the fact that the arrangements for giving strike pay do in a sense facilitate strikes is quite immaterial for the purposes of our decision. . . . "[5]

Yet this friendly characterisation of strike action was something of a Trojan horse; for it might end in the courts asserting full power to adjudicate upon the internal affairs of many unions.

The new determination to impose legal responsibilities upon unions is very evident in this issue, which we may call the question of *legality*. So it is, in a parallel development of the question of *enforceability*, arising from the interpretation of section 4. This assumes the union in question to be illegal at common law and therefore to fall within the ambit of the section 3. There were two recurrent difficulties: the member who sued to stop wrongful expenditure in favour of other people, and the member who claimed that he had been wrongfully expelled and so excluded from his entitlements. Did their claims involve *direct enforcement* of the various agreements covered by the section?

One approach favoured a broad view of what was excluded. In particular, in *Rigby* v. *Connol*, Jessel M.R. refused to allow an action by an expelled member of the Journeyman Hatters' Fair Trade Union: "if I decide in favour of the plaintiff, I directly enforce [the agreement contained in the rules,] because I declare him entitled to participate in the property of the union."[6] But soon decisions on improper

---

[2] s.4 was treated as a bar in Scotland, (*McKernan* v. *United Operative Masons' Association* (1874) 1 R. 453) and again in England (*Old* v. *Robson* (1890) 64 L.T. 282; *cf. R.* v. *Registrar of Friendly Societies* (1872) L.R. 7 Q.B. 741).

The seeds of difference were already implanted in the case-law, however; against the conservative view that "trade" objectives created unlawful restraints, could be set the more favourable view of withdrawals of labour taken by Hannen and Hayes JJ. in *Farrer* v. *Close* (above, p. 315).

[3] *Swaine* v. *Wilson* (1889) 24 Q.B.D. 252.

[4] *Gozney* v. *Bristol etc. Trade Provident Society* (1909) 1 K.B. 901. The notion of "severance" was also being used as a device for distinguishing degrees of heinousness in other aspects of restraint of trade; above p. 270.

[5] *Ibid., per* Fletcher Moulton L.J., pp. 921–923; *cf.* O. Kahn-Freund (1944) 7 M.L.R. 192, 200.

[6] (1880) 14 Ch.D. 482, 490–491; see also *Duke* v. *Littleboy* (1880) 43 L.T. 216.

expenditure were pointing in a different direction. In *Wolfe* v. *Matthews*, Fry L.J. enjoined union officers from carrying out a merger which did not satisfy the requirements of the Trade Union Acts. "All that is sought here is to prevent the payment of monies to somebody else. Either that is no enforcement of an agreement at all, or it is an indirect enforcement."[7] When in the Yorkshire Miners strike of 1902–1903 a dissentient member sued to stop payments to strikers as being impermissible disbursements, the House of Lords accepted that this was the proper interpretation of section 4 and the correctness of *Rigby* v. *Connol* fell open to question.[8]

At this point in the history, the first *Osborne* case was carried to the House of Lords. Whether or not the Amalgamated Society of Railway Servants was illegal at common law, the issue concerned improper expenditure and so, following the *Yorkshire Miners'* case, the action could be brought. In this dispute, section 4 was to acquire a different significance. In the wake of its *Taff Vale* defeat, the union revised its rules.[9] A rule was adopted permitting the use of union funds for the support of Parliamentary candidates and members provided that they stood for the Labour Party and accepted its whip. A substantial minority of the union objected to this association with the Labour Party, amongst them W. V. Osborne—head porter, secretary of the Walthamstow branch and a liberal of the old trade union school.[10] His intention was to attack not political expenditure *per se* but its application in the socialist cause.[11] The argument was developed on two lines, the separate issues of *constitutionality* and *vires*. The constitutional question, for all its political immediacy, only attacked those rules of the society which required acceptance of the Labour Party whip and so (it was alleged) fettered the member of parliament's freedom of individual conscience. For this reason the rule was said to be contrary to general public policy. The question of vires, applying the principle that a body existing under statutory authority might exercise only those powers allowed it by its enabling act, had a technical, non-political colour. But if it succeeded its consequences would reach much farther, for it might prevent all political support and indeed, other activities in which unions then engaged.

---

[7] (1881) 21 Ch.D. 194.

[8] *Yorkshire Miners' Association* v. *Howden* [1905] A.C. 256.

[9] Sir Robert Reid, in a joint opinion with Sir Edward Clarke, had advised the union that a rule properly passed at the A.G.M. might provide for a compulsory political levy. Accordingly, as Lord Loreburn, he was precluded from sitting on the *Osborne* appeal: P. Bagwell, *The Railwaymen*, (1963), pp. 245–246. The same view of the law was apparently taken by the Chief Registrar of Friendly Societies, who refused Osborne's application to disallow the rule in its final form, *ibid.* 246. And so also, a Divisional Court: *Steele* v. *South Wales Miners' Federation* [1907] 1 K.B. 361.

[10] See G. W. Alcock, *Fifty Years of Railway Trade Unionism* (1922), pp. 338–340, and Osborne's own version of the affair, *My Case* (1910). For the two cases in general, *cf.* Webb (1920), pp. 615–631; P. S. Bagwell, *The Railwaymen* (1963) Chap. 9; Clegg *et al.* (1964), pp. 413–420.

[11] The vision of a socialist party stuffing its war coffers with the proceeds of union levies was vigorously denounced by the *Daily Mail* and *Daily Express*. Whether Osborne benefited by financial as well as moral support from non-unionists in his litigious forays is not known, though often alleged by his opponents: see Bagwell (above, n. 10), pp. 253–254.

Both the Court of Appeal and the House of Lords found against the union. In the lower court, two judges very much of a mind to foster legal intervention of union affairs, waxed eloquent on the constitutional audacities of the rules in question.[12] In the House of Lords Lord James, rather apologetically, and Lord Shaw, in grander terms, took the same line.[13] But the other three members, staunch Conservatives all,[14] deliberately disavowed any intention of taking up the constitutional question. Instead they insisted that trade unions were the subject of the *ultra vires* rule, well-known in its application to municipal and commercial corporations; and that the Trade Unions Acts 1871 and 1876, in defining the expression "trade union" and in delineating the agreements covered by section 4 of the former act, laid down the list of permissible powers.[15] Nothing in these Acts gave a power of expenditure to support any candidate or member of parliament.

Both justifications for the decision suggest a high measure of tendentiousness. Of the constitutional argument, Heuston has remarked, "it is difficult for anyone not brought up in England to understand how three men, two of whom had been in their time members of Parliament, and thus had practical experience of the working of the party machine, should have committed themselves to statements so out of keeping with the nature of English constitution in the twentieth century."[16] Nothing in British parliamentary tradition obliged members to foreswear financial support from outside organisations and many directors of railway companies and major industries had anchored themselves to the Conservative and Liberal benches.

But the *vires* point appears equally strained. The analogy was to corporate status which the Trade Union Acts had deliberately refrained from conferring. The *ultra vires* doctrine had been applied to registered companies in general as a necessary implication from the terms of the Companies Act; but that Act permitted those promoting the company to select for themselves the objects desired.[17] In essence the same applied to companies incorporated by special act.[18] The analogy was perhaps strongest to municipal corporations since

---

[12] Fletcher Moulton and Farwell L.JJ., *Osborne* v. *Amalgamated Society of Railway Servants* [1909] 1 Ch. 163, 186–187, 196–198.

[13] *A.S.R.S.* v. *Osborne* [1910] A.C. 89, 99, 107–115.

[14] Lords Halsbury, Macnaghten and Atkinson, *ibid.*, 91–97, 101–105.

[15] "Trade Union" was defined in the two Acts principally in order to determine what bodies should qualify for the privilege of registration conferred by them in 1871. The definition was limited to bodies illegal at common law. The unfortunate discrimination that this invoked against "legal" unions was remedied in 1876 (s.16). Thereafter the operative part of the definition was contained in the following brief phrases: "Any combination, whether temporary or permanent, for regulating the relations between workmen and workmen or between masters and masters, or for imposing restrictive conditions on the conduct of any trade or business . . . " While Lords Macnaghten and Atkinson laid most stress on this definition, Lord Halsbury's emphasis is on the agreements listed in section 4 of the 1871 Act.

[16] R. F. V. Heuston, *Lives of the Lord Chancellors* (1964), pp. 163–164; see also R. B. Stevens, *Law and Politics* (1978), pp. 247–248.

[17] Above pp. 260–261.

[18] *Ibid.*

their objects were defined by the terms of a general statute.[19] But even here, Parliament's intention to delimit the range of powers was reasonably clear, whereas it requires the most oddly focused vision to see any similar intention in the Trade Union Acts. This legislative amputation was particularly infuriating to the Webbs.[20] Their analysis of union development towards a central and responsible role in the modern state showed how closely the "method of legal enactment" had been allied to the "method of mutual insurance" and the "method of collective bargaining."[21] The earlier decisions on "legality" under section 4 had seen virtue in a union pursuing both mutual insurance and collective bargaining by keeping benefit and strike funds apart. Now the law appeared to be insisting that the first technique—the seeking of new legislation—was simply not open to the unions at all, since they were debarred from spending anything in its pursuit.

There was, moreover, an immediate sequel to be taken into account. Osborne was expelled from the Union under a rule permitting expulsion of a member "found guilty of attempting to injure the Society or to break it up otherwise than as allowed by these rules, and the same being proved to the satisfaction of the Committee." Osborne proceeded to a second action to negate his expulsion and so brought forward once more the *legality* and *enforceability* issues inherent in section 4. The Court of Appeal, in finding in Osborne's favour, used both these as alternative justifications.[22] It was held, building upon one rationale of the *Bristol Trade Society* case,[23] that since the rules only gave the A.S.R.S. power to *sanction* a strike rather than to *order* one, the union was not unlawful at common law; on this view, section 4 had no limiting effect. If on the other hand, the union was unlawful at common law, an action over expulsion was not directly enforcing a section 4 agreement and so could be brought. *Rigby* v. *Connol*[24] was effectively overruled.

An expulsion for daring to litigate was likely to provide a particularly firm response from the courts. The first reason given for the decision had its ironies. The actual distinction between sanctioning and ordering a strike was a confection of the court-room, but the desire to extend union legality that lay behind it was realistic enough. For it stemmed from a true appreciation of the Webbian perspective that unions, by building benefit funds and using the strike weapon as a last resort, could have the practical power to pursue collective bargaining and secure legislative support for it. In this the court ran quite counter to the philosophy of the majority of the first *Osborne* case. Indeed, at a technical level their view might also be seen as undercutting those judgments. For if a union is legal at common law how can it be said that it "places itself under [an act of parliament] and by so doing obtains some statutory immunity or

---

[19] Above pp. 58, 85–86.
[20] Their denunciations are summarised in their *History* (1920), pp. 615–616; *cf.* Bagwell (above, n. 10), p. 259; Clegg *et al.* (1964), pp. 414–415, II. Pelling (1982) 25 Hist. J. 889.
[21] *Industrial Democracy* (1898), Part II.
[22] *Osborne* v. *A.S.R.S.* (*No. 2*) [1911] 1 Ch. 540.
[23] Above, n. 4.
[24] Above, n. 6.

privilege?"[25] It is no surprise, therefore, to find that a year later, the House of Lords quietly disapproved of the wide view of the legality of unions.[26] For the future, the scope of section 4 was to be judged by the *enforceability* test.

Direct enforcement was to be understood in that limited sense which left the courts free to examine allegations of improper expenditure and wrongful expulsion. In the months after the Lords' judgment in the first *Osborne* case, a long succession of actions were organised to stop Labour party support by other unions.[27] The common form of injunction included a prohibition against distributing moneys for any purpose other than the purposes of section 16 of the Act of 1876 and in particular from making any payments for the purpose of securing or maintaining Parliamentary or municipal representation. From the generality of this formula it seemed to follow that expenditure on, for instance, education, journalism, law reform and assurance benefits for widows and children would be impermissible.[28]

The joint TUC-LRC Board pressed for legislation completely to restore the pre-*Osborne* position, but the Government, already engrossed in its constitutional match with the House of Lords, was in no mood to revive the strength of the stricken challenger on the sidelines. In 1911, it sought to dispose of the matter by conceding salaries of £400 per annum to members of parliament.[29] But it was plain that much wider issues were involved. The eruption of major strikes, first on the railways and then in the mines and docks, placed the government in the role of conciliator to a degree never previously experienced, and so the claim for further legislation was kept to the fore.

Eventually, the Trade Union Act 1913 gave the unions not their whole demand, as in 1906, but the practical freedom to make payments without regard to any statutory limitation of objects.[30] The legitimacy of expenditure would in future be a matter for the rulebook and resolutions passed in accordance with its procedure. However, the sensitive question of political levies produced an elaborate compromise. Before there could be expenditure on political objects, there had to be a ballot in favour of a separate political fund; the Registrar of Friendly Societies had to approve the rules for this fund.

---

[25] Thus had Lord Macnaghten phrased the precondition for application of the ultra vires rule: [1910] A.C. at 94.

[26] *Amalgamated Society of Carpenters and Joiners* v. *Russell* [1912] A.C. 421.

[27] For references, *Citrine's Trade Union Law* (3rd ed. 1967), pp. 18–19. According to the Webbs ((1920), p. 631): "discontented or venal Trade Unionists were sought out by solicitors and others acting for the employers, and induced to lend their names to proceedings for injunctions. . . . " and in some of the cases the union tried to make outside fermentation an issue (without success—see *Thurlowary* v. *Amalgamated Union of Shop Assistants Warehousemen and Clerks, The Times,* December 9, 1910, *Parr* v. *Lancashire and Cheshire Miners' Fed., The Times,* January 29 and 30, 1913). But how far outside support extended beyond the moral to the financial remains conjectural. Clegg *et al.* (1964), p. 418, note that after the introduction of the new rules for political levies in 1913, very substantial minorities elected to "contract out"; in the case of the miners, 43 per cent.

[28] Injunctions covered subscribing to educational classes and taking shares in a "Labour" newspaper: Webb (1920), p. 631.

[29] See Erskine May, *Treatise on the Law . . . of Parliament* (17th ed., 1964), p. 18.

[30] s.1(1) (redefining "trade union").

Contributions to the fund had to be separately levied; and any member not wishing to participate must be given the opportunity to contract out by simple notice addressed to the union.[31] But for this purpose, only a very limited, positively English, set of activities counted as "political": the payment of electoral expenses and members salaries which had been the nub of Osborne's attack. Supporting the causes of the Labour movement—for instance, by running a newspaper—was not in the list.[32]

IV. Labour in the World War Era

The first World War saw major intervention by the state to put the economy on a war footing. The effect on industrial relations was considerable, and not only for the period of hostilities.[33] The proportion of the civilian workforce in trade unions rose from 13.4 per cent. in 1910 to 34.9 in 1920.[34] One domestic consequence of war conditions was an average rise in the cost of living of 27 per cent. per annum. The government was pushed into controlling rents at the lower end of the market, and then price controls and some food rationing, but wages had still not returned to their 1913 real-term level by the war's end. Beyond this, labour shortages meant the introduction of women and young workers into skilled and semi-skilled jobs; inevitably there were anxieties over the long-term effects of this dilution, particularly once peace returned.

During the war the syndicalist ideas which had taken root in the pre-war confrontations fostered the growth of a shop stewards movement, in which union activity centred on shop floor organisation in each plant. To a novel degree this was freed from the control of national or regional officers and it expressed sometimes a strong anti-military ideal, and sometimes a special fear for old demarcations of skills.[35] Accompanying this rise in industrial activity came the growth in Labour Party support. The party itself found great difficulty in coming to terms with the war, a majority of leaders and members surrendering their pre-war commitment to the pacificism of the second International and joining the war effort, the left wing continuing to denounce the war as an ultimate struggle in the crisis of capitalism. Yet the Party survived these strains. It began to feel that it might draw the democratic allegiance of the people so as to use

---

[31] s.3 The Registrar applied his discretion by publishing model rules and requiring fairly close adherence to them.

[32] The Registrar, who was given jurisdiction over breaches of the political fund rules, had eventually to decide whether a union's contributions to TUC funds, which were then used partly to maintain *The Daily Herald*, were improper. In a witty judgment, he held not: see his report for 1925, and *cf. Forster* v. *National Union of Shop Assistants, etc.* [1927] 1 Ch. 539.

[33] See generally, M. B. Hammond, *British Labour Conditions and Legislation during the War* (1919); G. D. H. Cole, *Labour in Wartime* (1915); W. Hannington, *Industrial History in Wartime* (1940); Pelling (1976), pp. 143–158; Fox (1985), pp. 280–300; Rubin (1987).

[34] It would fall back from a third to a quarter during the depression, and make another jump only during the next war. By 1950, the proportion was 44.3 per cent.

[35] See J. Hinton, *The First Shop Stewards' Movement* (1973); J. B. Jefferys, *The Story of the Engineers* (1945).

the parliamentary system to govern; equally the new measure of government intervention and regulation might be carried over to a peace-time condition of state economic management.

The trade union and Labour Party leaders who were prepared to collaborate in the war effort made very substantial concessions towards controlling the course of labour disputes. Many of these limitations were embodied in the Treasury Agreements of March 1915, which set aside established union rights and customs for the duration of the war.[36] In addition, Asquith's coalition government pushed through the Munitions of War Act 1915 imposing on munitions workers (and workers in other war industries to which it was extended by proclamation) the compulsory arbitration of labour disputes by a Board of Trade appointee or court; and making it a criminal offence to strike or take part in a lock-out while the arbitration was pending. In "controlled establishments" it became an offence to disobey factory regulations. Munitions workers required their employer's certificate if they were to seek fresh employment. In the first nine months of operation, there were over 1,000 convictions of strikers and 10,645 convictions for other breaches of the Act.[37] Even so, it proved inoperable against the wages strike of the South Wales coal fields, shortly after it took effect; and numerous other strikes occurred despite its existence.[38] Nonetheless, in conjunction with the Defence of the Realm Regulations, the government had novel whips for use when legal goads or threats seemed likely to profit it.[39]

With the ending of the war a host of questions required answer. The labour movement, excited by developments in Russia, would have no truck with belligerent threats against the new Communist government there; when some of the Tories in the Coalition Cabinet tried to press LLoyd George into action he was able to use the strike threats of the trade unions to side-step them.[40] The threat to strike in order to prevent the country joining another war did indeed have a political rather than an industrial objective, though at the time there was little discussion of its legality. It makes, however, a decided contrast with the issues that were to precipitate the General Strike six years later.[41]

The government's own plans for the economy wavered. Government direction of railways and coal-mining during the war pointed towards their nationalisation in peace-time. In 1919 a miners' strike could be averted only by setting up a Royal Commission under Sankey J. on the future of the industry, the Government undertaking to abide by its conclusions. But when the Commission recommended

---

[36] Labour Yearbook 1916, pp. 60–61.

[37] Hannington (above, n. 33), p. 63; thereafter, there were no official statistics—part of a widespread clamp-down on information.

[38] Of the 3,099 strikes recorded during the war, four-fifths were in Munitions Act industries: I. D. Sharp, *Industrial Conciliation and Arbitration in Great Britain* (1950), p. 317.

[39] See Rubin (1987) Chaps. 2–4; Phelps Brown (1983) Chap. 4.

[40] A. J. P. Taylor, *English History 1914–1945* (1965), p. 143.

[41] The events which did cause constitutional jitters surrounded the emergence of militant trade unionism in the police forces. A strike in 1918 before the war's end led to an immediate pay rise but no recognition of the police union: see below, p. 615.

first a wage increase and then, by bare majority, state ownership, the government simply prevaricated. Later in the year, the railwaymen actually went on strike and secured most of their wage and other demands; but again on the question of ownership the government temporised and eventually got an agreement to the rationalisation of the companies into four groups, still privately owned. A number of other temporary measures—an extension of rent control, introduction of an "Out-of-Work Donation" for unemployed ex-servicemen, controls on profiteering—were instituted alongside social improvements such as the Fisher Education Act and the Addison Housing Act.

There had indeed been considerable planning for "reconstruction" during the latter stages of the war. In the field of labour relations, the Whitley Committee made five reports, proposing for each industry, at least as an ultimate ideal, a national joint council, district joint councils and works committees.[42] As an interim measure in unorganised industries, the Ministry would set up Trade Boards; they would no longer be confined to eliminating "sweated" wages, becoming instead a major force in the movement towards the Webbs' "national minimum" for all.[43]

The joint industrial councils would deal not only with wages, hours and related questions but also with conditions of work, technical education, research and development and proposed legislation affecting the industry; but beyond this the traditional preserves of management would not be entered. In the event, little of this eventuated save in the field where government least expected or welcomed it. "Whitley Councils" became regular features of employment by central and local government.[44] The arbitral service offered by the Department of Labour, which had been regularly available since 1908 to those who wanted it, was given over to an Industrial Court. Despite its name, it continued to be a voluntary service, whose awards had no more legally binding force than a collective agreement.[45] Behind these developments lay the assumption that peace would restore an economy of private enterprise, still primarily unregulated, but with a modest degree of state underpinning. In matters of the health, unemployment, pensions and housing of employees, and education of their children, the pre-war beginnings would be built upon, in order to contain the discontents of a democratised working class and to ensure the survival of a viable labour force.

---

[42] J. H. Whitley, later Speaker of the Commons, chaired the Committee for the Ministry of Reconstruction: see esp. its First Report, (P.P. 1917–18 [Cd. 8606] XVIII) and the Ministry's own Memorandum (P.P. 1918 [Cd. 9085] XXII); Fox (1985), pp. 293–298.

[43] The Trade Boards Act 1918 led to the creation of some 35 new boards, in, for instance, shoe-making, tobacco, milk distribution, jute and flax and laundries; see further below, at n. 49. A special system evolved for agriculture, which until the second war would operate primarily through local committees on the trade board model.

[44] See Pelling (1976), pp. 160–161; Fox (1985), pp. 293–298.

[45] It would continue in operation, accumulating a number of extra functions, until being replaced by the Central Arbitration Committee in 1976.

This assumption could certainly not be taken for granted at the immediate end of the war and the drive towards restoring the essentials of the capitalist economy continued to be a hazardous one. In 1920 the miners, incensed by the government's duplicity over the Sankey Commission, came out on strike and the possibility of triple alliance support from dockers and railway workers was averted only by the government making some significant (but temporary) concessions on wages and on continuation of the war-time regulation of the industry. At the same time it pushed through the Emergency Powers Act 1920,[46] giving itself, if necessary, immensely wide legal authority to take over economic functioning and to restrain individual liberties—a peace-time version of the Defence of the Realm Act 1914. Hasty as the progress of the bill was, the government had still to accept provisos that it would not by regulation introduce military conscription or make it criminal to participate in a strike or peaceful picketing accompanying one.[47]

Six months later the miners came to the verge of striking, this time with votes from their allies to come out in support. The government, determined not to concede in a fight which appeared revolutionary, invoked the Act. It became one element, together with the rapidly deteriorating economic condition of the country—the disappearance of profits, the rise in unemployment, the demands for wage cuts—which tested the true resolve of the alliance and found it wanting. On "Black Friday" the railwaymen's leader, J. H. Thomas, brought about a reversal of position from within and the government was able to proceed with its plans to decontrol the mining industry, returning its labour negotiations from the national to the district level, and thus forcing the Miners' Federation once more to deal with individual owners. Effective union militancy was for the moment at an end.[48] As an echo in the non-organised sphere, the Trade Boards were denounced by employers as instruments which retarded the necessary fall in wages. Their effectiveness was much reduced by action within the Ministry of Labour; no further Boards would be created until 1931.[49]

It was the intractable antipathies of the mining industry which would once again turn the government to deploying the Emergency Powers Act, this time in conjunction with a body of middle-class volunteers, the Organisation for the Maintenance of Supplies. The General Strike of May 2–11, 1926[50] was preceded by nine months of direct threat from the Triple Alliance and other unions that this time

---

[46] See above, p. 81.

[47] s.2.

[48] In 1921, the Railways Act rationalised the railways into four amalgamations but put them in private hands. A National Wage Board for Railways was established but workers acquired no place in management.

[49] The Cave Committee (Second Report, P.P. 1922 [Cmd. 1645] X) strongly favoured this retrenchment: see Bayliss British Wages Councils (1962) Chap. 2.

[50] See generally, G. A. Hutt, Post-war History of the British Working Class (1937) Chaps. 5, 6; J. Symons, The General Strike (1957); A. Mason (1969) 14 I.R. Soc. Hist. 1; J. Skelley (ed.), The General Strike 1926 (1976); Pelling (1976), pp. 159–180; Fox (1985), pp. 327–336.

the country's workers would stand by their beleaguered comrades.[51] Their determination was strengthened by fears for themselves: Baldwin had made it clear that, so far as the government was concerned, the whole workforce must take a reduction in wages. The issue in the General Strike thus lay at the heart of the labour relationship; it did not demand a restructuring of politics or seek to influence government policy in foreign affairs or any other non-industrial matter.

Before the strike finally precipitated, the government had again conceded a temporary subsidy to the mining industry for the duration of another Royal Commission, this time chaired by the Liberal, Sir Herbert Samuel. The leaders of both sides hoped that this might engineer a compromise, but the report upheld the need for wage-cuts and contained only vague suggestions about restructuring for future prosperity. The TUC's leaders were eventually moved to call the workers in most essential industries out on indefinite strike. The government talked loudly of insurrection, particularly in its *British Gazette* (organised by Churchill). It saw to the maintenance of transport and power through the military and OMS volunteers and it watched the ebbing morale of the insecure TUC leaders. Their capitulation after nine days came as a deep shock to the strikers, who had enjoyed their solidarity and expected major concessions as part of any deal. Instead they were left with nothing and had often to sign humiliating admissions of their wrongdoing as a condition of getting their jobs back.[52]

In this most dramatic of all labour confrontations, the law played a lively role on the sidelines. Through the Emergency Powers Act, it authorised the machinery of economic organisation and at the same time imposed novel discipline on a range of support for the strike— from distributing, or even possessing, strike bulletins to throwing orange peel at a bus: some 2,500 prosecutions were brought for the period, and magistrates did not hesitate to use the bench as a pulpit.[53]

More fundamentally, the strike itself was declared to be "utterly illegal," making it "unlawful" for leaders to order the withdrawal of labour and for workers to comply. This controversial anathema was first pronounced in the Commons by the right-wing Liberal Q.C., Sir John Simon (on the third day[54]) and then echoed on the bench by Astbury J. (on the ninth day[55]). Simon drew from his major premise the conclusions: (a) that the immunities of the 1906 Act were inapplicable—this despite the express recognition in section 5 that they covered sympathetic strikes; and (b) that a dissident non-striker

---

[51] In the autumn of 1925, the government showed its nervousness by prosecuting twelve leading Communist Party members for sedition and under the Incitement to Mutiny Act 1797. They were sentenced to terms of imprisonment after refusing Swift J.'s curious offer to let some of them off if they renounced their opinions. It was a sorry relapse into a dangerous style of political censoring. For details, J. Klugmann, *History of the Communist Party of Great Britain* (1969), II, pp. 67–69.

[52] Sir J. Simon, *The General Strike* (1926), p. xxii, gives the terms required by the railway companies.

[53] For startling examples, see Hutt (above, n. 50), pp. 162–163; Klugmann (above, n. 51), pp. 163–169.

[54] Simon (above, n. 52), pp. 5–7.

[55] *National Sailors' and Firemen's Union v. Reed* [1926] Ch. 536.

could have an injunction to prevent his union from depriving him of union benefits—this despite the embargo on "direct enforcement" of union rule-books by the 1871 Act. Astbury J. supported all this in a wide-ranging judgment which by injunction informed a branch of the National Union of Seamen that it could not lawfully call members out, award them strike pay or refuse benefits to members who remained at work.[56]

Among the strikers, this seems mostly to have been taken as a partisan annexation of the legal system in the cause of propaganda—so at least the strikers' newsheets treated it. But at the TUC it probably heightened the strain upon men who had called the strike without the least intention of making any fundamental challenge to the political authority of the country, yet found themselves apparently at the junction between revolution and capitulation.[57]

Yet the case for regarding the strike as "unlawful" was extremely thin and Astbury J. made no detailed attempt to deal with the technical arguments. The strike was clearly in support of the miners' wage and other claims and so "in contemplation or furtherance of a trade dispute"—the characteristic which imported the special protections of the Conspiracy and Protection of Property Act 1876 and the immunities given to individuals by the 1906 Act. Because the strike was so widely supported, the element of illegality did not arise through violence and threats towards blacklegs or outside suppliers and there was nothing that could amount to the political offences of sedition or treason. A year later, Goodhart could find no legal basis on which such a strike could be "unlawful" merely through its effective pressure on the mineowners and the government. He felt compelled to this conclusion, while calling for an alteration in the law which would allow legal action against a strike which produced such a result.[58]

The government was not slow in responding to such calls. Its Trade Disputes and Trade Unions Act 1927[59] rendered illegal any strike which in addition to its trade objective was "designed or calculated to coerce the Government either directly or by inflicting hardship upon the community."[60] Despite repeated declarations, during the course of the Bill, that this was intended only to deal with a general strike, the indefinite terms could undoubtedly cover circumstances that were not so all-embracing. This provision and the specific crimi-

---

[56] In the *Reed* case, the Seamen's union president, Havelock Wilson, had refused to allow it to join in the General Strike. When a London branch disobeyed this, he brought proceedings to enjoin it, thus providing Astbury J. with an admirable opportunity to air his view.

[57] Simon and Astbury each claimed a major role in putting the strike down. "How many countries are there in the world," Kahn-Freund once remarked ((1959), p. 227) "in which, in a national crisis of this kind, public opinion could be influenced by the utterances of a lawyer-politician and a judge?"

[58] A. L. Goodhart (1927) 36 Yale L.J. 464; for more extreme calls on the employers' side, see W. A. Garside in B. Supple (ed.) *Essays in British Business History* (1977), p. 244.

[59] The government was forced to use the closure to get it through. On the Labour side, Macdonald sought to muzzle Henry Slesser, the lawyer best able to deal with it in his ranks: see Slesser's *Judgment Reserved* (1941), p. 204.

[60] S.1. The government disdainfully extended the Act to employers' lock-outs, when attacked by the Labour party on the matter. A proviso was also added excepting the mere act of coming out on strike.

nal sanctions attached to it were enacted as a "declaration" of the law. Nothing so disingenuous was attempted for the other provision arising directly out of the General Strike: this gave a dissident member the right to claim damages or reinstatement if he was expelled or penalised for refusing to take part in an "illegal" strike; the provision was simply made retrospective to May 1, 1926.[61]

The opportunity was taken to revise the general law against picketing, so as to bring it once more to Lindley L.J.'s position: that no effective picketing could be legal. For now it was to be an offence to picket so as to "intimidate"—and intimidating could include causing reasonable apprehension of "injury," including "injury to a person in respect of his business, occupation, employment or other source of income . . . "[62] Civil servants were forbidden to join TUC-affiliated unions or unions with non-civil servant members; and local and public authorities were not allowed to insist (as some Labour boroughs were doing) upon union membership as a condition of employment. Finally, the contracting-out rule for union political funds under the 1913 Act was changed to a rule requiring a "contract in"; the effect initially to reduce union contributions to the Labour Party by more than a third.[63] When the Labour government of 1946 saw to the restoration of the 1913 presumption, the contributions rose at once by two-thirds.[64]

The Labour government of 1929 naturally explored the possibility of repealing the whole 1927 Act, but they were not able to persuade their Liberal allies to support the move. It therefore remained in effect until its simple abnegation by the Attlee government in 1946. The 1927 Act was to operate during a period of undoubted industrial peace and to this it perhaps made a shadowy contribution. But as an act of revenge it was carefully muted by Baldwin. It did not reverse the immunities of the 1906 Act which protected individual unionists and union funds from liabilities in tort for industrial action. The General Strike had lessons not only for labour. Industrialists were among those who realised that their own future lay in an accommodation with the moderate forces on the labour side. In 1928, Sir Alfred Mond, head of Imperial Chemical Industries, was able to re-establish talks with the TUC, led by Ben Turner and Ernest Bevin. They boosted the chance of cooperation over essentials, a workable truce that would leave industry and commerce mostly in private hands, without the concession to labour of any real part in management.[65] In the event, it was Ramsay Macdonald's minority government which would have to grapple with the severest constraint upon the hopes of labour—the descent into the abyss of world recession and massive unemployment. Here more than anything was the force which kept the National Minority Movement and other uncom-

---

[61] s.2.
[62] s.3. This would apply to the Conspiracy and Protection of Property Act, s.7 and so overrule *Gibson* v. *Lawson*: see above, p. 328.
[63] Contributions fell from nearly £39,000 to just over £25,000; but they grew again as new members were signed on—it was easier to get "contracting in" at the outset.
[64] From some £55,000 to just over £91,000.
[65] See Fox (1985), pp. 325–327, 336–340.

promising antagonists of capitalism in isolation on or beyond the left-fringe of the Labour Party.

For the Second World War, the government had available the template cut during the First War. Acting under Defence Regulation powers,[66] the Minister of Labour made the Conditions of Employment and National Arbitration Order 1940—Order 1305. A National Arbitration Tribunal was created with the usual tri-partite structure; it was chaired until 1944 by the redoubtable Simonds J. A trade dispute was to be referred to the Minister, who, if he could not himself secure a settlement, would refer it to the Tribunal. This compulsory arbitration award became binding on employers and workers to whom it related, as an implied term of individual contracts of employment.[67] There was a procedure for making a recalcitrant employer adhere to the terms of a collective agreement or award affecting his industry: the matter would be referred to the Minister and, if necessary, the Tribunal.[68] To participate in a strike (or lockout) became an offence. Prosecutions would occur on 111 occasions involving 2,681 workers and two employers.[69] As in the first war, this criminal law sanction could not be used effectively against a determined and united workforce, as a strike at the Betteshanger colliery, Kent, in 1941 was to demonstrate: the imprisoned leaders had to be let out on a pretext, as there was no one else with whom to negotiate a return to work.[70]

The First War had seen the initiation on both of military conscription and compulsion to stay in essential civilian work (through the system of leaving certificates). By 1939, conscription was accepted as a necessary reality, and as a counterpart, the direction of civilian labour was carried further. A series of Essential Work Orders[71] fashioned a system directed by National Service Officers: in the many industries deemed crucial to the war effort their sanction was needed both for an employee to leave and for an employer to dismiss. At most the employer was entitled to issue a provisional dismissal to an employee alleging him to be guilty of serious misconduct. This, however, was subject to the employee's right to proceed before a Local Appeal Board which would reach a finding on the allegation[72]; in consequence the National Insurance Officer would either allow the dismissal or order reinstatement. Failure to comply with directions of Officers was a criminal offence for which a fine and imprisonment were penalties: employers seem only to have been fined but workers were sometimes imprisoned and then expected to comply with the original direction to them.

Compulsory labour in peace-time had disappeared in 1875 with the abandonment of the Master and Servant Acts. Its re-introduction

---

[66] Defence Regulation 58A, 1940.

[67] Part I.

[68] Part II.

[69] Maximum penalties were a fine of £100 or three months' imprisonment.

[70] See H. Emerson in Royal Commission on Trade Unions, P.P. 1968, [Cmnd. 3623] XXXII, App. 6, p. 340.

[71] Consolidated in the Essential Work (No. 2) Order 1942.

[72] During this period the dismissal was treated as ineffective and the worker was entitled to his wages.

was admissible only in the extraordinary circumstances of war. The Essential Work Orders were repealed at its end—before the reinstatement of pre-war industrial practices which the unions had agreed to suspend[73]; and well before the termination of compulsory arbitration and the ban on strikes under Order 1305.

The last fact is at first glance surprising, given that the return to peace was this time in charge of a Labour government, much occupied with plans for a more egalitarian society under political direction. But the government were struggling with many things: with the creation of a universal health service, with national insurance and allied schemes on the Beveridge model which relied considerably on employer-employee contributions, on the nationalisation of mines, docks, railways, gas and electricity, iron and steel. A considerable deflation was expected, as after 1918, and the government was deeply anxious about how to manage the necessary wage reductions. Even in war-time the power to prescribe maximum wages had not been assumed in Britain (unlike in the United States) and certainly could not be contemplated as a tool of peace-time management. The anti-strike machinery of Order 1305 was kept in position during the hard years of 1946–48 and actually put to use as new room for manoeuvre appeared: leaders of dock and gas unions were prosecuted in 1950 and 1951. This the unions considered intolerable and Order 1305 had its teeth pulled.[74]

In the end, accordingly, labour relations resumed the patterns of the Edwardian settlement. In the general run, rights enforceable in law existed only in the individual worker's contract with his employer. To this the courts had insisted on annexing conditions which guaranteed liberal virtues: no employee could be compelled to serve, no employer to keep in service; if either broke the contract, the remedy was not an injunction but only damages.[75] Neither was entitled to substitute a third party for himself (by assignment of his interest) without the consent of the other. The employee's right to choose his employer—even a remote, abstract corporation—was said by Lord Atkin to constitute "the main difference between a servant and a serf."[76] More importantly, the courts used their carefully guarded weapon of public policy to insist that an employee should not (save in limited cases) be tied to his present employer by clauses preventing him from leaving to join a competitor or to set up in competition himself; on this the House of Lords had placed new emphasis in the very years when it was most vigorously attacking the effects of collective labour action.[77] It was perhaps the common law's

---

[73] By 1947, the EWO, which had applied to 8½ millions, only affected 185,000 and was soon to be ended entirely. See also the Restoration of Pre-war Trade Practices Acts 1942 and 1950.

[74] It was replaced, until 1958, with the Industrial Disputes Order (O. 1371), which sought to maintain compulsory arbitration without criminal sanctions.

[75] Because "no court of law or equity has ever considered it had power to grant" reinstatement, the King's Bench Division refused to accept that the National Arbitration Tribunal had been impliedly given such a power under O. 1305: *ex p. Herbert Crowthier* [1948] 1 K.B. 424.

[76] *Nokes* v. *Doncaster Amalgamated Collieries* [1940] A.C. 1014 at 1026.

[77] The principles of the *Nordenfeldt* case were applied only with caution to employment contracts: see above, p. 270.

most significant contribution to the processes of competition, for it
was in consequence very difficult to prevent business and technical
information from leaking to rivals.[78]

More generally, the courts treated the individual contract as a business deal, giving its explicit terms effect over contrary customs or
understandings (even if they had been settled by collective agreement); and they were in general reluctant to add terms into the agreement by way of implication if the argument for doing so was put
upon general business efficacy.[79] But where the employee was
intended to be covered by a collective agreement and his individual
terms were silent, it was only realistic to assume that express terms of
the former had been "incorporated into" the latter.[80]

The whole tradition, as we have seen, was to accord no legal status
beyond this to collective agreements or arbitration awards, unless
quite exceptional steps had been taken.[81] The long antipathy towards
court processes or the unions' side made them prefer to submit disputes over the content or procedures of collective agreements to a
fresh negotiation.[82] This position was maintainable because, by and
large, the unions had won their right to negotiate (often after decades
of hostility) out of their membership size and industrial strength.[83]
On the whole, they had not sought legislation in order to oblige
employers to treat with them.[84] They had managed by their own
strength to eliminate "the document"—an employer's requirement
that his employees forswear union membership.[85] In various places
and trades they had established closed shops, but they had not succeeded in imposing them through legislative backing.[86]

---

[78] Specific technical and other secrets were protectable by restrictive covenants (if they
were no wider than was reasonable) and also under implied obligations to preserve
confidence; but often these obligations proved difficult to enforce. Not until after
the Second War did the courts show much inclination to develop the scope of the
action for breach of confidence: see, e.g., Saltman Engineering v. Campbell (1948) 65
R.P.C. 203; but it was suddenly extended against "moonlighting" technicians:
Hivac v. Park Royal [1946] 1 All E.R. 350.

[79] An approach which would reach its apotheosis only in Lister v. Romford Ice [1957]
A.C. 555 (an employer does not impliedly undertake not to seek indemnity from the
employee, when the latter negligently causes an accident for which the employer is
also (vicariously) liable—despite the common practice of the employer insuring
against liability).

[80] In an increasing number of industries, there had, since the mid-nineteenth century,
been a statutory obligation on the employer to give a written "ticket" or other notification of at least the wages or the precise work to be done: this began with the
hosiery and silk industries in 1845 and was extended to all textiles in 1891: see F. W.
Tillyard, The Worker and the State (3rd ed., 1948), pp. 80–82, 86–90.

[81] See above, p. 323.

[82] For this characteristic tendency to turn disputes of right into disputes of interest, see
Kahn-Freund (1959), pp. 234–235.

[83] For the earlier hostility, it should be recalled that until after the large strike of 1911,
most railway companies were able to resist negotiating with rail unions.

[84] In the post-war nationalisations, the new employing authorities were in two cases
placed under a statutory obligation to seek or enter negotiations: Coal Industry
Nationalisation Act 1946, s.46; Transport Act 1947, s.95.

[85] In isolated instances, however, forswearing union membership continued to be
insisted on—the Scottish printing firm, D. C. Thompson, did so from the General
Strike onwards until the 1950s: see P.P. 1951–52 [Cmd. 8607] XV and Thompson v.
Deakin [1952] 2 All E.R. 361.

[86] See Kahn-Freund (1959), pp. 231–232.

Union strength in turn depended on the ability to withdraw labour in a disciplined way. The first important victory in the battle for the "right to strike" had been as early as 1824 and the period to 1906 had seen a succession of advances and retreats in the lifting of criminal and then civil liability from activity in trade disputes, including peaceful picketing. The Act of 1906 established its *cordon sanitaire* and the ensuing conflict over the scope of trade union objects led in the end to constraints on how the unions organised political funding. They were left free to adopt rules about decisions to strike as they chose; in particular, they came under no legal obligation to ballot members before acting. Even the revivals of this trend in the Act of 1927, following the General Strike, were limited in scope; they could be repealed by Labour in 1945 in a way which presented the pre-1914 settlement as the norm.

In the years after 1918, the courts had adopted a more conciliatory attitude to trade union activity. Goddard L.J., for instance, acknowledged collective bargaining as "the great benefit of a trade union"[87]; and the House of Lords refused any longer to regard the organisation of a strike or boycott as necessarily involving "malicious intent"[88]; yet this had been the element in *Quinn* v. *Leathem* which had converted joint action into tortious conspiracy. "English law" said Lord Wright " . . . has for better or worse adopted the test of self-interest or selfishness as being capable of justifying the deliberate doing of lawful acts which inflict harm, so long as the means employed are not wrongful . . . "[89] The events of 1900–1920 had led the judges, however wearily, to apply this test to the collective organisation of labour as they already did to business cartels.

This acknowledgment of the position of labour in a plural, democratic world would continue to inform the whole character of modern labour relations in Britain. The restoration of legal freedom of organisation and action after 1951 was in its way deeply conservative, the recognition of values evolved through a long historical experience. Embedded within it was an understanding that, by and large, British trade unionism had not been so much about utopian challenges to the entire capitalist system, as about a narrower, often sectional, protection. The coming of industrial organisation had not made daily existence less predatory than it had been when the first journeymen's clubs began to negotiate with masters. The great span of political opinion had, however, come to accept that their successors should be reasonably free to fight for their place in a world that remained hard, for all its increasing comfort.

V. FURTHER READING

Aspinall, A., *The Early English Trade Unions* (1949).
Briggs A., and Saville J., (eds.) *Essays in Labour History*: I (1960); II (1971).

---

[87] *Evans* v. *National Union of Printing Workers* [1938] 4 All E.R. 51 at 54.
[88] *Reynolds* v. *Shipping Federation* [1924] 1 Ch. 28; *Crofter Harris Tweed* v *Veitch* [1942] A.C. 435; see also *Sorrell* v. *Smith* [1925] A.C. 700.
[89] *Crofter* case (above, n. 88) at 472.

Brown, K. D., (ed.) *Essays in Anti-Labour History* (1974).

Clegg, H., Fox A., and Thompson, A., *A History of British Trade Unions since 1889* (1964).

Dobson, C. R., *Masters and Journeymen* (1980).

Fox, A., *History and Heritage* (1985).

Gray, R. Q., *The Aristocracy of Labour in Nineteenth-Century Britain* (1981).

Hammond, J. L. and B., *The Town Labourer* (2nd ed., 1925).

Hedges, R. Y. and Winterbottom, A. *The Legal History of Trade Unionism* (1930).

Hobsbawm, E. J., *Labouring Men* (1964).

Hobsbawm, E. J., *Worlds of Labour* (1984).

Hilton, G. W., *The Truck System* (1960).

Hunt, E. H., *British Labour History 1815–1914* (1981).

Hutchins, B. L., and Harrison, A., *A History of Factory Legislation* (3rd ed., 1926).

Musson, A. E., *British Trade Unions 1800–1875* (1972).

Kahn-Freund, O., "Labour Law" in Ginsberg, M., (ed.), *Law and Opinion in England in the 20th Century* (1959), pp. 215–263.

Manchester, A. H., *Modern Legal History of England and Wales* (1980), pp. 327–346.

Pelling, H., *A History of British Trade Unionism* (3rd ed., 1976).

Phelps Brown, H., *The Growth of British Industrial Relations* (1959).

Rubin, G. R., *War, Law and Labour* (1987).

Rule, J., *The Experience of Labour in Eighteenth-Century Industry* (1981).

Thomas, M. W., *The Early Factory Legislation* (1948).

Thompson, E. P., *The Making of the English Working Class* (rev. ed., 1968).

Wrigley, C. J., (ed.) *A History of British Industrial Relations, 1875–1914* (1982).

Chapter Five

THE FAMILY

The family, that most basic and close-binding of social groups, is an institution rooted in economic circumstance and shaped by moral belief and social practice. As such it is now in the forefront of social history, for it is an integral part of the history of populations, of relations between the sexes, of labour, of ways of providing for the young, the old and the sick.[1] The extensive recent work on historical demography has made an understanding of the English family over time more complete than in most countries; and this despite the lack of any national system until the nineteenth century of recording fundamental events such as births, deaths and marriages. From parish records and other more occasional listings by local inhabitants it is possible to piece together the essential first stages of the picture.[2] Here can be found some confirmation, at the beginning of our period, of the long movement towards the individual and away from the communal, whether that community was the village, the manor or the family in its wider connotations.

In England, as in most of North-western Europe, the nuclear family had long predominated over the extended family. Father, mother and children expected to live and subsist apart from grandparents and collateral relatives, as appears from the small size of the average family. These units were formed (generally by some type of "marriage") at a relatively late age, some ten years or longer after puberty, the husband and wife being relatively close in age and social rank. If they treated marriage as a permanency, they would expect to live together for fifteen or twenty years before one of them died. During this time they would themselves nurture such of their children as survived birth: the rate of child mortality was very high. In terms of averages, then, families were transitory groupings in which death was a constant presence at every age and every social level.[3]

One aspect of economic patterning which accounts for the lateness of family formation in pre-industrial conditions is service. Only in the upper levels of society did a family allow time for more than rudimentary steps towards education, though the eighteenth century saw some spreading downwards of elementary schools. For most of the population, the young were expected to learn what they could for use in life by entering service of another family, often of somewhat higher position. Whether this led to an apprenticeship in a trade, or

---

[1] For the future of family history, see L. Stone (1981) 12 J. Interdisc. Hist. 51; D. Levine (1985) 107 P. & P. 168.

[2] The work of two decades is authoritatively summarised in E. A. Wrigley and R. S. Scofield, *The Population History of England 1541–1871* (1981); and see R. Wall, *Family Forms in Historic Europe* (1983), esp. Chaps. 2, 16.

[3] See P. Laslett, *Family Life and Illicit Love in Earlier Generations* (1977) Chap. 1; M. Mitterauer and R. Seider, *The European Family* (1982) Chaps. 1, 2.

an early hiring for agricultural or household work, it would occupy a substantial proportion of life—through adolescence to adulthood. Only then would the setting up of a new family become practicable and even then might be delayed until some precipitating event, like the woman's pregnancy or death of a parent. The new unit would survive on the husband's work or trade with as much help as his wife could give alongside the demands of birth and babyhood. It was this pattern that was adapted by the coming of factory labour. In its early manifestations the factory used the whole family to work as far as this was physically possible; later it made the husband the wage-earner and led the wife away from her pre-marriage work to the care of children and home, with such casual jobs as she could fit into this routine.[4] At higher social levels, the growth of cities would mean that men worked apart in offices, leaving their wives to the genteel supervision of servants in a home that would cease to be in the city centre, becoming instead a train or tram ride away in a respectable suburb.

Beyond the statistical and the economic lies the emotional, the most intriguing of all aspects of family history and the hardest to recapture. One pervasive source is the literature of advice, some high-minded, more homely, which came in unending current for the benefit of the literate, together with more reflective or descriptive writings which are perhaps less pre-occupied with highly idealized desiderata. The family had undoubtedly become a central representation of social values. At no period are these values wholly uniform but there do appear to be shifting tendencies, at one moment towards a pole of censoriousness, at another to a pole of permissiveness.

In the English world of predominantly nuclear families, the censorious pole treated the husband and father as a dominant, patriarchal figure, who would expect submissive obedience alike from wife, children and servants. He would enforce his word by beatings and other physical repression. At least among the propertied, as a devolution from older forms of arranged marriage, his own choice of spouse would pay as much attention to dowry and inheritance as to compatability of temperaments. A repressive attitude to sexuality would inhibit opportunities for courtship and intimacies before marriage; and even in marriage sexual intercourse was the necessary cause for procreation rather than a means of gratification. Once children were old enough to be reasoned with they were to be lectured and disciplined into a cooperation based on fear. By contrast, at the permissive pole marriage was treated as a partnership of something approaching equality, in which mutual affection and pride in sexuality were high values; so both husbands and wives could engage in adulterous liaisons without courting much in the way of disapproval. Children were to be loved and encouraged, provided with education and helped in other ways towards adult fulfilment.

[4] See M. Hewitt, *Wives and Mothers in Victorian Industry* (1958), pp. 29–30 (sample showing some 30 per cent. of married women in cotton districts to be employed in 1850); pp. 35–47 (challenging the view that employment of women led to younger marriages); D. Levine, *Proletarianization and Family History* (1985) Chap. 1.

There is certainly a case—it has been made with great lucidity and detail by Lawrence Stone[5]—that, in the higher reaches of English society, there was a flux over time between these two poles which took the form of a wave rather than a single line. Attitudes to family relationships accordingly follow their own path of fashion; they are not to be explained by any single movement towards modernisation, nor by the economic changes which accompanied industrial capitalism. In Stone's analysis, the prescriptive and descriptive literature in the seventeenth century was predominantly censorious in tone; this was gradually superseded in the eighteenth century by a movement towards the permissive, which was certainly underpinned by increasingly easy attitudes among the aristocracy towards living and loving; but from the beginning of the nineteenth century there was a marked reversion to the censorious, which in many respects was to last through the rest of our period, giving place only in the years after 1945 to the widespread permissiveness of the present.

Stone has himself accepted criticism that what pertained to the literate and propertied proves little about family life for the bottom four-fifths of the populace.[6] In their struggle for existence, harsh economic reality dictated much of how husbands treated wives, and parents treated children. Drink might well have the first call on the husband's earnings, ready violence was the lot of his wife and children, all had to work when they could, and as soon as they were able. But there is no evidence that the position varied much from 1650 to 1750 or 1850. Only the gradual rise in earning power that worked its way downwards in the latter nineteenth century would begin to leave room for refinements of the kind that had come so fiercely to concern the middling and upper classes.

Stone's perceptions seem particularly germane to the subject-matter of this chapter. For we are not primarily concerned here with the "public" law of the family—the provisions through the poor law and charity doles for families which could not sustain themselves, and for the young, the sick and the aged who had no real family.[7] This chapter gravitates round the "private" law which was generated for those with sufficient means to be concerned with family property and with responsibilities for maintenance while the family continued as a unit or when it split apart in a breakdown of relationships. One sign of the slowly improving position of the working population is the creation in 1878–1895 of a "private" jurisdiction in the magistrates' courts, carefully tempered to meet what were deemed their appropriate needs.[8]

Our account of developments in family law is accordingly in two parts. The first concentrates upon shifts in the century after 1750, the second with the later Victorian, Edwardian and World War periods.

---

[5] Stone (1977; 1979); Bonfield (1983) cf. Macfarlane (1986), Part III.
[6] Stone (1979 abridgment); and see M. Anderson, *Family Structure in Nineteenth Century Lancashire* (1972); D. Vincent (1980) 5 Soc. Hist. 223; Gillis (1985), p. 14.
[7] For an historical distinction between public and private family law, see J. ten Broek (1964) 16 Stanford L.R. 257 (Part I).
[8] See below, pp. 391–392.

PART 1: PRIVATE FAMILY LAW 1750–1850

I. Forming a Family: Marriage[9]

The nuclear family, according to Christian orthodoxy, was founded upon the union by marriage of one man and one woman for their joint lives to the exclusion of all others.[10] Over time, as the units within the larger family grew more distinct, the marital relationship increased in significance and alternatives to it were more forcibly disapproved. In England the Tudors had enacted criminal legislation against abduction of women and the sexual violation of girls under ten.[11] In the succeeding century the church courts turned the repressive severity of their times against adulterers and fornicators. These official attitudes were replicated in expressions of popular disapproval; adultery and other departures from rigid propriety could be visited with "rough music"—boisterous mockery or worse and such practices survived on into later periods.[12]

The very act of marriage had gradually acquired a greater solemnity. In 1439 the Church of Rome had elevated it to the level of a sacrament, and the protestant churches, if they would not go so far, would grant it a "holy estate." Medieval practice had varied in its attention to the niceties of form. Marriageable age had been set at or below puberty (14 for men, 12 for women).[13] The church courts had recognised as sufficient ceremonies not only those by church rite but also informal exchanges of vows, either to marry at once (*per verba de praesenti*), or to marry in the future if this was consolidated by sexual union (*per verba de futuro*). The rules for a priestly marriage demanded: the proclamation of banns in the parish of residence or else a special licence; marriage in church in the morning hours; and paternal consent in the case of a groom or bride under twenty-one.[14] One part of the orthodoxy which James I had sought to fix upon his Established Church had been an attempt to impose these stricter requirements for marriage.[15]

While it became an ecclesiastical offence for priests to participate in ceremonies outside the prescribed procedures, the ecclesiastical courts did not alter their view of the efficacy of informal marriage; and even common law would not treat a lack of banns or parental consent as a defect after the event.[16] Any more exigent claim would have confronted age-old community practices which themselves

---

[9] See T. E. James in Graveson and Crane (1957), Chap. 2..
[10] And so in law: *Hyde* v. *Hyde* (1866) L.R. 1 P.D. 130 (polygamy among Brigham Young's Mormons not recognised as marriage).
[11] See G. E. Parker (1983) 21 Osgoode Hall L.J. 187.
[12] E. P. Thompson (1972) Annales 27.
[13] There it would remain until raised to 16 in 1929 (Age of Marriage Act), in acknowledgment of a League of Nations campaign against child marriages.
[14] By Rubric in the Book of Common Prayer.
[15] At the same time, bigamy was made an offence at common law: 1 Jac. I, c. 11.
[16] The common law position is reviewed at length in *R.* v. *Millis* (1844) 10 Cl. & F. 534.

imposed due solemnity upon a deeply serious commitment. Gillis has shown that among the peasants and artisans who made up the substantial middle of the population, there existed elaborate rituals for seeking and courting a bride.[17] These would reach a first culmination in the exchange of vows—the *verba de praesentes* or *de futuro* of the ecclesiastical law. Later might come a church wedding and removal to a separate home, each surrounded by "big wedding" ceremonial, and each amounting to one act in "a social drama involving family, peers and neighbors in a collective process aimed at making things right economically, socially and psychologically, as well as legally."[18] In this measured procedure, as in the "little weddings" which evolved for more transitory, non-landed sectors of the dividing economy, there remained room for trial-and-error, so that before any confirmation by church ceremony, and sometimes even later, a partner could withdraw into bachelordom or spinsterhood.[19] In the history of marriage and its ending, control by church and state accordingly arrives only as our period begins, and even then has considerable headway still to make.

Nonetheless, pressures towards that end continued throughout the seventeenth and early eighteenth centuries, which had to do with an aristocracy and gentry increasingly devoted to a severe primogeniture. While for them the early and fruitful alliance of the first-born male was an obvious desideratum, this was scarcely so for the younger brothers. They would have only their portions on which to make their way, unless they could marry an heiress. Since the chance, even at these elite levels, of children surviving to adulthood rather declined as the century progressed, heiresses were by no means uncommon[20] and their captivation became fair game for young bloods. Secretive ceremonies, kept in particular from the bride's family, were common not only in the higher levels where there were expectations of substantial property, but lower down the social scale. In a world where parents often discouraged early marriage and sought to restrict the chances of sexually awakening contact between young people, defiant running away was an all-too-likely counter-thrust. In the early eighteenth century, London had its centres for clandestine marriage in Mayfair and the Fleet prison. Equally there were places throughout the country where privy ceremonies were readily available, and areas also where pure folk-practices, (such as the Welsh and Shropshire besom-jump wedding) were widespread.[21]

The landed class had brought upon themselves the deep tensions that surrounded clandestine marriages. On repeated occasions, the House of Lords had promoted bills to render them insufficient for all purposes; but the Commons (where younger sons were placed) had

---

[17] Gillis (1985), Chap. 1.
[18] *Ibid.*, p. 17; and for the various rituals and their symbolism, Chap. 2.
[19] Chap. 3; for the significance of breach of promise suits, in the civil and church courts, p. 50–51.
[20] See above, p. 131.
[21] See below, nn. 27, 46.

as regularly refused to accede.[22] Eventually—in 1753—Lord Hardwicke pushed through a bill requiring observance of the rules for a
formal church wedding (including parental consent up to the age of
twenty-one).[23] Marriages which did not follow these prescribed
forms were void. Clergy who knowingly broke the rules became
liable to transportation for 14 years.[24] The Act, which at first sight
seems a victory for parental control and the conservation of family
property, had more complex motives to it.[25] Some at least of the
speeches on the bill paraded a concern for marriage as a condition of
enduring affection. The need for conjugal love, for mutual com-
panionship, for a compatibility of temperaments to sustain whatever
fortune might befall, was unlikely to be the paramount concern of the
fortune-hunter. On a different tack, there was a certain unease at the
notion of a statute redirecting so fundamental a social practice at all
levels. But those who could not afford or could not accept a Church
wedding, with the exception of Quakers and Jews,[26] were left without other recourse. The Act displayed a myopic preoccupation with
the affairs of those who passed it.

Gillis has shown how, even though the Act withdrew the clergy
from their previous involvement in clandestine ceremonies, such
practices remained widespread.[27] The moneyed could resort to
Gretna Green and other cross-border towns where a Scots marriage
could be had with the old informality[28]; miners and labourers in the
north seem equally to have followed this route. But up and down the
country, and particularly in its less conspicuous corners, there were
people who resorted to folk ceremonies—exchange of rings, broom-
jumping and the like—to notarise their arrangements. Some were
simply too poor to meet the Church's fees.[29] More were overstepping
social propriety and so wanted both privacy and the imprimatur of a
ceremony: pregnant women and their lovers, fortune hunters,
widows and widowers re-marrying too hastily, those whose age,
social status or religion were unacceptably different, bigamists,
bankrupts, even the odd pair of homosexuals. A few communities
developed their own rules because full Christian marriage was
impracticable: groups perhaps where males would have to move on
from time to time to find work; or where, because the larger family
would live together, a trial period was a good precaution.[30] These
practices mark at once how important to social acceptability some

---

[22] Stone (1977), p. 43.
[23] 26 Geo. II, c. 33; for its enactment, Gillis (1985), pp. 140–142.
[24] The Act was also important in requiring parish clergy to keep regular records of
marriages.
[25] See Trumbach (1978), pp. 107–109; Stone (1977), pp. 35–37.
[26] They were granted exemption to follow their own rites.
[27] Gillis (1985), Chap. 7.
[28] Or the Channel Islands, the Isle of Man or the Continent. For Lord Hardwicke's horror at the allurement away of an 18-year-old heir to a marriage at Antwerp, and his
readiness to intervene against the scheming wife, see *Butler* v. *Freeman* (1756) Amb.
301. Scotland became a less easy resort for eloping couples after an Act of 1856 (19 &
20 Vict., c. 96), promoted by Brougham, required residence there for 21 days.
[29] Gillis (1985), pp. 196–206; O. Anderson (1975).
[30] Gillis (1985), pp. 192–196.

form of marriage was, and how little consequence attached to compliance with the Church's procedures in their post-1753 form. For those whom the Hardwicke Act did affect, failure to meet its requirements meant that the marriage was void. If this could subsequently be established, children would be rendered illegitimate and entitlement to property might be defeated. But above all, each partner would be free to marry someone else, so that one consequence of the Act's severity was to provide one way of dealing with marriage breakdown, in which context we shall return to it.[31] In 1822, however, the hard cases that could result ultimately persuaded Parliament that absence of parental consent or lack of due form in banns or licence should no longer invalidate the marriage.[32]

Equally important to the demand for nullification were the substantive embargoes on marriages within the rules of consanguinity and affinity, and to these likewise we shall return.[33] But there were factors apart from the freedom to re-marry which affected the prohibited relationships. The post-reformation rules on the subject, deriving in the main from biblical authority,[34] had placed marriages between first cousins outside the prohibited degrees.[35] They had the particular advantage that estates descending to an heiress could be kept within the family by finding her a cousin-husband.[36] On the other hand, the rules of affinity kept stubbornly to the prohibition of a man's marriage with his deceased wife's sister, even as most other European countries came to admit it.[37] This rule perhaps expressed a deep-felt attitude among the aristocracy, which gave a distinctive place to the brother-sister relationships of a man not only to his own siblings but to those of his wife.[38] Re-marriage with a wife's sister was certainly treated by great men, ecclesiastical authorities and judges with revulsion and labelled incestuous. In 1835, Lord Lyndhurst sponsored an Act which turned marriages within the prohibited degrees from being voidable at the instance of one or other party (while both lived) to being wholly void.[39] The object was dissuasion, particularly of marriage with deceased wife's sister. Yet a confidential survey in 1846 revealed that a not insignificant number of marriages had since taken place between respectable men and their sisters-in-law who evidently felt the relationship to be one of comfort and mutual help, rather than of illicit passion.[40] Despite con-

---

[31] Below, pp. 375–376.
[32] 3 Geo. IV, c. 75; amended by 4 Geo. IV, c. 17 and 76, the latter retaining the penalty of nullity for wilfully entering the ceremony without the requisite banns or licence.
[33] Below, p. 375.
[34] Leviticus c. 18, given force by 25 Hen. VIII, c. 22, 28 Hen. VIII, c. 7.
[35] Provided specifically by 32 Hen. VIII, c. 38.
[36] For this process of familial inheritance, see Trumbach (1978), pp. 19–21; Stone (1984) Chap. 4; above, p. 128ff.
[37] Hill v. Good (1674) Vaughan 302. For the rule, see Trumbach (1978), pp. 26–33; C. F. Behrman (1968) 11 Vict. St. 483.
[38] Also illustrated by the rule that siblings inherited from each other, rather than the property going to grandparents, who were also related in the second degree: Evelyn v. Evelyn (1754) 3 Atk. 762.
[39] 5 & 6 Will. IV, c. 54; tested in Ray v. Sherwood (1836) 1 Curteis 173.
[40] P.P. 1847–48 [973] XXVIII.

stant attempts after this to change the law,[41] it would take until 1907 to overcome old prejudices.[42]

From 1753 onwards, Dissenters and Catholics alike needed the procedures of the established Church in order to contract legally binding marriages. It says much about the dependent character of the new Methodist dissent that the Church's monopoly could survive so long.[43] When change came in 1836, it was as much a concession to the utilitarian spirit of social inquiry as to religious toleration.[44] As an adjunct of the new, national system for registering births, deaths and marriages,[45] the registrars became responsible for celebrating entirely secular ceremonies of marriage.[46] Only as a corollary of this power could dissenting sects provide equivalent services: by having their chapels registered for the purpose and having the civil registrar present to validate the proceedings.[47] Indeed the form of the law betrays an equal concern with the continuing practices of informal "marriage." Certainly the statistical effects are suggestive. The established Church gradually lost its dominance (its marriages falling from about 90 per cent. in 1800 to about two-thirds of the total in 1910). Of the corresponding rise in other forms, about two-thirds consisted of civil marriages and only one-third dissenting and other religious forms. In the early stages, the relatively small proportion of dissenting marriages (in relation to the numbers of dissenters in the population) may partly be explained by the administrative complications and extra cost of organising a chapel marriage.[48] But Olive Anderson has argued persuasively that older, less mundane factors were at work. In particular, the global statistics disguise the existence of pockets of the country where civil marriage was the norm, just as previously there had been places which stuck to old folk practices.[49] The registration system enabled a persistent heterodoxy to be drawn within the net of state supervision, legal responsibility and statistical calculation. The number of marriages in the formal legal sense would begin to rise, even though it would not be until the twentieth century

---

[41] See Marriage Law Reform Association, *Debates on the Deceased Wife's Sister Bill* (1895). Gilbert got a good rhyme out of attempts "to prick that annual blister.".

[42] Deceased Wife's Sister's Marriage Act 1907. Marriage with deceased husband's brother, never a prominent concern, was not admitted until 1960.

[43] Methodists continued willing to use the Church for occasional services for much of the nineteenth century: W. O. Chadwick, *The Victorian Church* (1970), II pp. 143–145; and see O. Anderson (1979), pp. 155–156.

[44] The Church admitted that the collection of demographic information through the parish register system was hopelessly inefficient: Chadwick (n. 43 above), pp. 145–146.

[45] 6 & 7 Will. IV, c. 86. Edwin Chadwick, though not the Act's progenitor, made important suggestions for improving the statistics that would result. The Tories stopped the Whigs from getting a central power to appoint the local registrars by putting it in the hands of the local Boards of Guardians: S.E. Finer, *Sir Edwin Chadwick* (1952), pp. 124–126, 143, 154–155.

[46] O. Anderson (1975); and see generally, Royal Commission on the Laws of Marriage P.P. 1867–68 [4059] XXXII.

[47] Until 1856, the equivalent of banns had to be read at meetings of the poor law guardians, making it initially a "lower caste mode of alliance": see O. Anderson (1975), pp. 63–66.

[48] See on this, R. Floud and P. Thane (1979) 84 P. & P. 146.

[49] O. Anderson (1979) *ibid.* 155.

that the average age on marriage became noticeably lower than it had been.

II. Sustaining the Family: Property

(a) The Husband's Property

In a world where men organised most economic activity, the property that a husband brought to a marriage, from his family or through his earning capacity, was likely to be more significant than that coming from the wife. For those whose wealth grew from land-ownership, the organisation of interests between the generations had, as we have seen, come to centre in the system of settlements.[50] For the first-born inheritor of the main estate, the succession would be organised at his majority or marriage, with the portions of his younger brothers and the dowries of his sisters being determined as part of the process. For a younger son, marriage would likely bring its own settlement between himself or his family and his bride's family. These arrangements at the time of marriage—the estate planning that was brought to such sophistication by 1750—settled the new family's property from the outset, laying out the succession in the generation to come; providing the wife with her personal spending allowance (pin-money) and a jointure or other arrangement on her husband's death[51]; disposing of the dowry which she brought into the marriage so as to preserve her a separate interest (with perhaps an ultimate reversion to her own family)[52]; obliging each partner to bring later inheritances and other gifts into the settlement. For the upper stratum affected by settlements, the distribution of property on death under the terms of wills was proportionately of less significance.[53]

For middling people with a modicum of wealth, the law's tuning was much less fine, though its resonances are now less easy to recapture.[54] There are signs of that long movement from simple, imposed solutions, which gave primacy to the family community, towards a greater freedom of individual choice. But it is a fitful shift much varied by local traditions. As we have already noted, the ability to dispose of freehold land during life preceded the freedom to do so by will. This may have reflected a nascent commercialism; but equally it met the desire of parents to decide for themselves how the land should pass to the next generation as their children reached adulthood and they faced old age.

Certainly if the matter was left until the death of the husband and

---

[50] Above, p. 123ff.

[51] The jointure was one technique for displacing the older, common law right of dower, discussed in the next paragraph but one.

[52] See further, below, p. 367ff.

[53] At this level, failure to make a will, so that the rules of inheritance (realty) and intestacy (personalty) took effect, was no more than an occasional accident.

[54] On patterns of expectation about inheritance ("grids"), see E. P. Thompson in J. Goody *et al.*, *Family and Inheritance*, (1978) Chap. 9, *cf.* also J. P. Cooper, *ibid.*, Chap. 8; Horwitz (below, n. 57).

father, there survived even into the period when land could be left by will rules giving the widow an overriding interest in the family lands. If the land was freehold, at common law her dower gave her a life interest in one-third of all lands owned by the husband at any time during the marriage. Since this attached even to lands that had in the interim been sold, it was antagonistic to the notion of land merely as an asset. It is not surprising to find that a batch of practices had developed to displace the operation of dower. Not only could this be achieved by a marriage settlement giving the widow a jointure instead; other conveyancing devices came to suffice. However, the best-known reached perfection only at the end of the eighteenth century.[55] If the land was copyhold, the widow might, by the custom of the manor, have free-bench in it—the right to occupy a third or a half, or to receive a third or a half of rents and profits, either for her life or so long as she kept from adultery or re-marriage. Here too an occasional record suggests that sometimes procedures evolved by which the husband could displace his wife's entitlement in advance of her widowhood, so as to render the copyhold alienable to children or strangers.

Likewise with chattels and other personal property. As late as Tudor times the common law seems to have allowed a widow and children a fixed proportion of the deceased husband's personalty, of which he could not deprive them by will.[56] By the later seventeenth century, however, this had been reduced to a local (though widespread) custom of the Province of York (excluding Chester), Wales and the City of London.[57] At that point statutes had cut it back further, making the share of widow and children merely a more favourable variant of the "general" rules of intestacy (i.e. those of the Province of Canterbury).[58] In eighteenth and nineteenth century England, no notion of any community of property at death survived to qualify the power of the husband and father to disown members of his immediate family by his will. No rule associates more clearly the deep-felt attachment to patriarchy and individuality of property rights. The power to cut off without a penny was the ultimate sanction of Victorian respectability.[59] There would be no qualification of free testamentary capacity until 1938.

---

[55] Fearne's technique (*Essay on Contingent Remainders* (1791)) involved three conveyances, leaving the husband with a life interest and an ultimate remainder (neither of which were liable to dower), between which was sandwiched an extremely contingent remainder to trustees. Not surprisingly, the Land Law Commissioners recommended a simple procedure for barring dower (First Report, P.P. 1829 (263), X, pp. 16–20). This was given effect by 3 & 4 Will. IV, c. 105.

[56] Kenny (1879), pp. 66–67. The widow's right to keep her paraphernalia (clothes, and in some instances, jewels, bed and bedroom furnishings) survived longer.

[57] 4 & 5 Will., c. 2; 7 & 8 Will. III, c. 38; 3 Ann., c. 5; for the custom of London, which survived until 1725, see H. Horwitz (1984) 2 L. & Hist. R. 223.

[58] The Canterbury rules were applied to the whole jurisdiction in 1856: 19 & 20 Vict., c. 94.

[59] The testator's power was enhanced by the developing law of secret trusts: he might leave property to a person (named or not named as a trustee) for distribution in accordance with private instructions. He thus had the freedom to prefer favourites, assuage conscience or pursue any other motive without showing his relations or the world.

(b) The Wife's Property

What then of the property which a wife brought into a marriage—through her personal fortune as an heiress, her dowry or what she herself could earn? The common law had developed ground rules with a strongly patriarchal core to them: by the eighteenth century in law husband and wife were one, it being the wife's personality that was merged into that of the husband. She was therefore deprived during "coverture" of civil capacity to sue or be sued in her own name or to be regarded as the legal owner of property.[60] Accordingly, the chattels and money that she brought to the marriage became her husband's. So complete an annexation, however, was not the invariable approach. The common law itself varied the rule when it came to interests in land. In her freehold he acquired a right to manage and to take the income during their joint lives, and as a tenant by curtesy he obtained an interest during any period in which he survived her, provided that there had been at least one child of the marriage.[61] By these provisions the capital value of the land was kept from the husband and his creditors and it would pass to her heir-at-law rather than her husband's. The rules clearly reflected the due claims of her own kin in their lands. Leasehold remained the wife's: however, the husband acquired not only the right to rents and profits but the right to sell the lease during their joint lives and to sole entitlement if he survived her.[62]

The common law's typology treated the husband as the single focus of both rights and duties for the household. While he owned or controlled the family assets, including the property brought in by his wife, he became responsible for her pre- and post-marriage debts, torts and other liabilities. Outsiders had only to consider the husband's creditworthiness. They looked to him for payment of family bills. They could treat the wife as his agent for necessary goods and services without needing his express authority; his implied authority could only be withdrawn by adequate notice to the contrary,[63] and even notice was of no avail when he had deserted her without cause.[64] The rules doubtless remained because of a preponderance of households in which the wife's role was essentially subordinate—entirely domestic or at most an assistant in family farming, trade or business. They did not suffice when women conducted quite separ-

---

[60] Blackstone (*Commentaries*, I Chap. 15, s.3) represented this as ineluctable common law, and underplayed, even for his time, the developments in equity discussed below: see M. Beard, *Women as Force in History* (1946) Chap. 4. For details of the common law position, see Roper (1826) Chaps. 1–6; Kenny (1879) Pts. II, III.

[61] Roper (1826) Chap. 1; the interest arose in copyhold only by special custom of the manor.

[62] These rules were developed by analogy to those for the wife's choses-in-action (rights to sue for debt, etc.): on these the husband had to sue during coverture, in order to make himself owner of the proceeds.

[63] Kenny (1879), pp. 96–98.

[64] These forms of implied authority were the one practical means in law by which to oblige the husband to maintain his wife; they would survive until 1970. But the adulterous wife, however much provoked, had nothing but the ability to contract as a feme sole: see *Govier* v. *Hancock* (1796) 6 T.R. 603; *Cox* v. *Kitchin* (1798) 1 Bos. & Pul. 338; *cf. Norton* v. *Fazan* (1798) 1 Bos. & Pul. 228. For details, see Shelford (1841) Chap. 3, Macqueen (1849) Chap. 4.

ate businesses or where they brought in such wealth of their own as to stake a real claim to independence. In these cases patriarchal notions did not invariably dominate; both local custom and rules of equity were used to achieve variations.[65] Women were more likely to have distinct businesses in urban conditions and it was well-settled in the customs of London that wives were treated as principals for such trading purposes, just as if they were unmarried, so long as their husbands continued to agree to the arrangements.[66] How far this is merely an instance of a wider phenomenon, allowing women to assert separate property by local custom in other circumstances is a matter that has yet to be explored.[67]

What is well-known is that equity, which provided the wealthy with their own code of customary practices, came to offer a certain independence to propertied brides through the device of the trust.[68] It would accept that property given by a marriage settlement to trustees (who would likely include confidants, normally male, of the bride's own family) for her "separate use" made her, rather than her husband, the beneficiary; and if she, for instance, contracted in respect of this separate property, she could be sued through her trustees for satisfaction. Once an adult, she could override the restraining guidance of the trustees. But under Lord Thurlow, Lord Alvanley and Lord Eldon, the trustees' position was much strengthened where her interest was declared to be "not by anticipation."[69] This simple "restraint on alienation" confined her entitlement to income of the property during the marriage. Only when her husband pre-deceased her did she gain the power of alienation. The first object of the device was to prevent the husband from later "kissing or kicking" the property out of his wife. It naturally appealed to any bride's father who wanted his contribution to the marriage to have some permanence and to pass to the next generation or, if there were none, then back to such successors as his daughter might choose, rather than to his son-in-law.

In the eighteenth century the Court of Chancery developed these ideas with a degree of enthusiasm. It would accept any clear expression of intent that a wife was to receive property of her own as enough to give rise to a separate use[70]; and if no trustees were appointed, the court would deem the husband, as the owner at common law, to be the trustee.[71] Where substantial property became due

[65] See generally, Kenny (1879) Chap. 4.

[66] See, e.g., A. Pulling, The Laws and Customs of the City of London (1844), pp. 179–180, 484–485; Roper (1826) Chap. 16, s.5.

[67] Selden Society, 1904, Borough Customs, includes a number of custumals, mainly fifteenth century, showing that a wife could sue and be sued as a trader.

[68] For details, see esp. Roper (1826) Chaps. 18–21; J. P. Peachey, Law of Marriage Settlements (1860) Chaps. 6, 9; Kenny (1879), pp. 88–93.

[69] The device was one variety of "spendthrift trust." It is thought to have originated with Lord Thurlow, who was dismayed at the prospect of a wife making over her settled property to her husband "while the wax was yet warm on the deed" (Pybus v. Smith (1791) 3 Bro C.C. 340). He accordingly included the new phrase in the settlement of a Miss Watson, to whom he was trustee (see Parkes v. White (1805) 11 Ves. 221).

[70] A wife who died during coverture could leave only this separate property by will: see Kenny (1879), pp. 109–110, 144–145.

[71] Bennet v. Davis (1725) 2 P. Wms. 316.

to him through his wife, and he needed the assistance of equity to recover it,[72] he would be obliged to hold a proportion on trust for her separate use and that of their children (often a half, but all the circumstances would be examined).[73] Moreover, where the husband agreed to his wife's carrying on a separate business, it would be treated as hers—certainly if the assets of the business were transferred to trustees for the purpose, and probably even where they were not.[74]

In the industrial age, England never acquired a codified set of matrimonial property regimes such as was laid out in the Code Napoléon for French spouses and their families to choose between. But in the developments of local custom and equity there was a striving towards some comparable result: first a presumptive solution at common law, giving the husband prime position even to the extent of the freedom at his death to dispose of the family assets as he chose. But (for those who penetrated the mysteries of the law far enough) he might consent to a variation which allowed his wife to trade separately; and variation was possible primarily at the instance of the wife's family, to set her up with an independent inheritance.

The central notion of securing the wife a measure of independence through property was necessarily at variance with any simple, invariate notion of patriarchal dominance, and the vigour with which eighteenth-century courts developed the idea (as we shall see further illustrated when we come to the subject of matrimonial breakdown) seems a clear indication of a shift towards a somewhat more equal conception of the relations of husband and wife. The basic principles were so clearly established that the judges of the turn of the century would make no serious inroads upon them. But they displayed a distinct reluctance to develop the law further down the same track—leaving exactly this course to be pursued in the legislation of 1870–1882.[75] Certainly, their own prime contribution—the restraint upon alienation—should not be regarded as a further step in some unwavering progress towards emancipation. While its first object was to erect a barrier against the wiles of the husband, it equally placed restraints upon the wife herself in the interests of her own kin.[76] It limited her interest to the income on the capital during the husband's life, and more generally it placed her under the advisory surveillance of trustees who could be expected to be alive to her family's interests as a whole.

III. Sustaining the Family: Children

In the upper levels of eighteenth century society, children were becoming the subject of a new awareness. They were ceasing to be mere adults in miniature; their emotional and educational needs

---

[72] As, for instance, where it was a trust interest or a mortgage requiring foreclosure.
[73] See, e.g., Beresford v. Hobson (1816) 1 Mad. 373 (personalty); Sturgis v. Champneys (1839) 5 My. & Cr. 97 (realty). The property had to be more than £200 in value for a division to be made.
[74] See Roper (1826) Chap. 18, s.4.
[75] See below, p. 398ff.
[76] See esp., Kahn-Freund (1955), pp. 273–275.

were coming to be perceived as something apart.[77] Parents were encouraged to be less harshly repressive, to express their feelings of love, to be understanding of everything, from insubordination to sexual discovery. Yet it was a patchy change. For instance, as older patterns of service began to be replaced with education in boarding schools, there seems to have been little enough concern with the cruel and vicious conditions prevailing in many of them. There are also signs of a subsequent revulsion against this gradual penetration of a kindlier concern. Severe discipline was an essential part of the Victorian patriarchal ideal. While attitudes were by no means uniform, on everything from breast-feeding and cold baths to masturbation and the Bowdlerisation of Shakespeare, came a mountain of recommendation for the formation of dutiful character—anxious, active, devoted to Christian service.

Something of these shifts in attitude is reflected in legal developments, but only to a limited degree. For a start, the eighteenth century made no substantial infraction into the medieval distinction of legitimate from illegitimate children. Here was the fundamental premise of the succession to titles and to property and it was unlikely to be reviewed in a world built upon a strict notion of primogeniture. A father could not even legitimate his child by subsequently marrying its mother, and no notion existed of adoption, by which family relationships could be transmuted.[78] The only obligations that could be imposed upon the father of a bastard child arose from the crude rate-savings of the public poor law.

Even in relation to his legitimate children, the father assumed nothing by way of substantial responsibility in private law: in proclaiming him to be under the duty to maintain, protect and educate his children, Blackstone had to admit that this was a moral rather than a legal obligation.[79] The father was left free to discipline them as he chose, subject only to the ultimate sanctions of the criminal law against homicide and serious assaults, sexual and otherwise. Private law was mainly concerned with rights of custody and access, both in cases where the parents were alive and those where a guardian had instead been appointed. It was often enough one factor in the difficulties of family breakdown, and must be considered again in that context.

The basic premise of both law and equity in custody disputes over legitimate children was one of strict patriarchy—"the sacred right of the father over his own children."[80] He could even rule from the grave, since the decisions of any guardian appointed by him would

---

[77] On this development in a European context, see P. Aries, *Centuries of Childhood* (1965); and J. H. Plumb (1975) 67 P. & P. 64; Stone (1977), Chap. 9.

[78] Legitimation *per subsequens matrimonium*, however, might be permitted by manorial custom, which in some places survived until the nineteenth century: Gillis (1985), p. 19.

[79] *Commentaries*, I p. 451. A child could not pledge his or her father's credit for necessaries without express authority: *Mortimore v. Wright* (1840) 6 M. & W. 482; but the wife might do so on the child's behalf if she was keeping it: *Bazeley v. Forde* (1868) L.R. 3 Q.B. 559.

[80] See generally, P. H. Pettit in Graveson and Crane (1957) Chap. 4. When it came to disputes over children, the ecclesiastical courts were allowed no place, the question being one for common law or equity.

override the wishes of his widow.[81] If the father already held the children, it was unlikely that anyone else, even the mother of very young children, could recover them from him by habeas corpus or by wardship proceedings in Chancery.[82] If he was bringing the proceedings to get the children back, the Court of King's Bench, led by Lord Mansfield, showed a readiness to be flexible, holding that each case should be decided on its own circumstances. The court refused to order that a father who had ill-treated his family and had gone bankrupt should have a six-year-old girl back from her mother, even though the "natural right" was with him.[83] Equity's movement in the same direction is marked most particularly by a new readiness to take jurisdiction over children in danger, using the King's power as *parens patriae* to make them wards of the court, and appointing a trustworthy guardian for them.[84]

But so broad a discretion, which gave some place to the wishes of the child (if he or she was old enough to be asked), was not acceptable to the next generation of judges. The presumption in favour of the husband was re-asserted as regards children who were not old enough to fend for themselves.[85] Only if it was "essential to their safety or their welfare, in some serious and important respect" would his power of decision be treated as lost or suspended.[86] Immorality, cruelty or bad character had to be extreme to justify such an intervention,[87] though denial of religious principles would bring readier condemnation.[88] The courts would not treat a father as surrendering his rights just because he could not maintain his family or because he was living in adultery.[89] Only if he allowed the children to be brought up in a superior social position, because some other relation

---

[81] The last traces of the notion that the wife had guardianship over the younger sons and daughters seems to have gone in the seventeenth century with the disappearance of feudal obligation.

[82] Habeas corpus proceedings could be brought not only in King's Bench but in the other common law courts and, in some circumstances, in Chancery; but in the last, wardship proceedings became the common process from mid-eighteenth century (see below, n. 84). A precondition of Chancery's intervention was that the child had property settled on it (at least notionally): *Wellesley* v. *Beaufort* (1827) 2 Russ. 1 at 26; cf. *Re Spence* (1847) 2 Ph. 247.

[83] *Blisset's Case* (1767) Lofft. 748. And see *R.* v. *Delaval* (1763) 2 Burr. 1434, where the court, fearing the father's complicity in putting an 18-year-old girl out as mistress to Sir Francis Blake Delaval, ordered the latter to set her free to go where she would without interference from anyone.

[84] For the decisions of Lord Hardwicke and Lord Thurlow, see *Butler* v. *Freeman* (1756) Amb. 301; *Powel* v. *Cleaver* (1789) 2 Bro. C.C. 500; *Creuze* v. *Hunter* (1790) 2 Cox 242.

[85] Since parental rights were considered to survive to the aristocratic age of majority—twenty-one—it was possible to confine the discretionary element in the earlier cases to the upper bracket.

[86] So Lord Ellenborough ordered the mother to surrender a child still being breast-fed to the father in *R.* v. *De Manneville* (1804) 5 East 221; a view shared by Lord Eldon in Chancery, despite evidence of the father's Jacobin sympathies (which led him to order that the child should not be taken out of the country): *De Manneville* v. *De Manneville* (1804) 10 Ves.Jun. 52.

[87] As in *Wellesley* v. *Beaufort* (1827) 2 Russ. 1, where the heir to a peerage had taken his family to France on his wife's pin-money in order to escape his creditors and had there set about inculcating immoral habits in his children.

[88] So suffered the poet, Shelley (*Shelley* v. *Westbrooke* (1817) Jac. 266).

[89] Provided that he kept his mistress away from the children: *Ball* v. *Ball* (1827) 2 Sim. 35; *R.* v. *Greenhill* (1836) 4 Ad. & E. 627.

or benefactor had settled property on them, would he not be allowed to revoke the arrangement to the disappointment of their expectations.[90]

If the wife were living apart from the husband she could not even expect an order of access to visit, save in exceptional circumstances. Though he felt obliged to apply this rule against a mother, Hart V.C. was discomforted: "If any [alternative] could be found, I would gladly adopt it; for, in a moral point of view, I know of no act more harsh or cruel than depriving the mother of proper intercourse with her child."[91] Some years later, Sergeant Talfourd appeared for a mother who had been imprisoned for refusing to comply with a habeas corpus order to hand her children over to their adulterous father[92] and he undertook to secure amending legislation. In this campaign he was helped by the authoress, Mrs. Caroline Norton, at that stage locked in combat with her own husband over access to her children.[93] Talfourd did eventually succeed[94]; but only to a modest degree. The Custody of Infants Act 1839 allowed the Court a discretion to award custody to a wife innocent of adultery where the children were under seven, and empowered it to grant access if they were older.[95]

According to parish records the rate of illegitimate births was increasing noticeably in the late eighteenth century,[96] though why is not clear. It may have had to do with the new formalities for marriage and with a less severe attitude toward non-marital relationships, which allowed the births to occur and to be acknowledged.[97] The position of the illegitimate child even surfaced occasionally in the superior courts. In private law, it was deemed a *filius nullius*, with no rights arising by virtue of its relationship to either parent; it could not therefore take under a will bequeathing property to the father or mother's "children."[98] The father could assert no superior right to custody; if there were a dispute on the subject with the mother, she would usually be preferred, at least until the child reached seven.[99]

---

[90] Lord Eldon chose to justify this by premising the father's right upon his duty to maintain: *Lyons* v. *Blenkin* (1821) Jac. 246 (where earlier case-law is discussed).

[91] *Ball* v. *Ball* (above, n. 89).

[92] *R.* v. *Greenhill* (above, n. 89).

[93] As Pierce Stevenson, she published her *Plain Letter to the Lord Chancellor* (1837) on the subject, and circulated it to MPs; for the Nortons, see A. Acland, *Caroline Norton* (1948) and below, p. 399.

[94] He was helped by Lord Lyndhurst, a consistent supporter of family law reforms, and by Lord Denman C.J., who had become disturbed by his own decision in *Greenhill*.

[95] 2 & 3 Vict., c. 54.

[96] See P. Laslett, *Family Life and Illicit Love in Earlier Generations* (1977), Chap. 3.

[97] Deliberate killing and abandonment of new-born children were continuing social problems in a world which in any case was used to still-births and the death of babies through illness. See further below, p. 578.

[98] Neither would the parents inherit upon the child's intestacy: Blackstone *Commentaries*, II pp. 505–506. Note Finer and McGregor's suggestion that the middle-class preference for partible inheritance over primogeniture became a new reason for condemning illegitimacy: (1974) p. 117.

[99] But, as ever, property could make a difference for Lord Eldon, who held that a substantial settlement on natural children gave the father the right to appoint a guardian: *Curtois* v. *Vincent* (1820) Jac. 268.

The status of illegitimacy, moreover, was one which only Parliament could alter, and it appears to have been highly reluctant to do so.[1]

When it came to the poor law, which alone affected the great bulk of bastard children, the lack of legal relationship between the child and its putative father had been overriden by the determination to make him provide if at all possible.[2] The old Poor Law allowed a pregnant single woman to name a man as father to the overseers of the poor or to any substantial householder. She might then have a justice of the peace arrest the man. He would be committed to prison unless he could give security, or enter recognisances to indemnify the parish for having to maintain the child. The Poor Law Commissioners of 1833–34, by a nice amalgam of religious prescription and utilitarian calculation, found this procedure wanting.[3] Unmarried women could use their pregnancy as a path to support and marriage by an accusation easily made and difficult to refute. "All punishment of the father is useless," since "Providence appears to have ordained that [the bastard] should be a burthen on its mother, and where she cannot maintain it, on her parents." The Poor Law Amendment Act 1834, allowed a putative father to be pursued for maintenance only at Quarter Sessions; corroborative evidence of paternity was required; the maintenance order should go only to the cost of supporting the child up to seven, and not the mother.[4] So substantial a change left the payment of maintenance most often on the parish, but it placed the obloquy directly on the shoulders of the mother.

Those who objected to the apparatus of the new poor law as a whole were able to find special reasons for disliking the new bastardy provisions. Philpotts, Bishop of Exeter, in high Tory manner, pronounced the transfer of blame to the mother to be contrary to natural law and equal justice. More interesting was the ill-feeling that the change produced in communities where the social expectation had been that impregnation obliged a man to marry the woman before the birth. Thus the Rebecca Riot Commissioners reported that subsequent marriages were becoming rarer, women were tempted into a life of vice, while "the man evades or defies the law, with a confidence which has outraged the moral feeling of the people to a degree that can hardly be described."[5]

By 1844, the Poor Law Commissioners felt that the new purity on which the Act tried to insist could not be enforced against pressure of such an opposed morality. The unmarried mother was given back her right to seek maintenance from the father by applying to petty sessions, but subject to a requirement of corroborative evidence of

---

[1] The subject finds no place in F. Clifford, *A History of Private Bill Legislation* (1885–1887).
[2] See generally U.R.Q. Henriques (1967) 37 P. & P. 103; H. Elisofon (1974) 2 Anglo-Am. L.R. 306; I. Pinchbeck and M. Hewitt, *Children in English Society* (1973), II pp. 583–587; Finer and McGregor (1974), pp. 115–121.
[3] See their Report, P.P. 1834 (44) XXVII, pp. 92, 197–198.
[4] 4 & 5 Will. IV, c. 76, ss.69–76.
[5] Henriques (above, n. 2), p. 118.

paternity.[6] Not till 1868, did the poor law authorities re-acquire the power to recover from the father the cost of relieving a bastard child.[7]

At all stages, paternity proceedings operated at the margin of the poor law, striving to keep mother and child out of the workhouse and off the rates. Even less fortunate were children who did not belong to the weakest of families—the foundlings, orphans and runaways for whom there was no other hope. Many poor-house children went off to the servile drudgery of the water-powered mills, the mines, the ships. There were a few charities which sought to rescue "waifs and strays"; more were founded as the urban condition showed how children too readily sank to the prison, the transport ship or even the gallows. Eventually the central state would add its set of institutions—the reformatory and industrial schools—to the mixed array of local and philanthropic effort. But that was to be a relatively late step in the movement for institutions. It belongs, like state intervention in the name of education, very largely to our later period.

IV. ENDING THE FAMILY: MARRIAGE BREAKDOWN

(a) Ecclesiastical Jurisdiction

The sacramental and indissoluble nature of marriage, of which the Church of Rome had become convinced by the end of the Middle Ages, was a matter of high controversy in the Reformation. Luther had declared marriage to be no more than a civil contract and claimed biblical authority for its dissolution in favour of one party upon the adultery of the other. Calvin had followed him in this and John Knox had carried the doctrine to Scotland, where the law came to allow full divorce (with the ability to marry another) upon proof of adultery or four years' desertion. In England the newly-established Church had vacillated, and on occasion divorces *a vinculo matrimonii* had been pronounced. But in the seventeenth century, opinion had hardened in favour of treating marriage as indissoluble, if not sacramental.[8]

This position fell to be supported by the ecclesiastical courts in the matrimonial relief available from them to spouses in conflict. They would grant an order for the restitution of conjugal rights against an errant husband or wife, which would seek to enforce the central obligation in matrimony—co-habitation.[9] There might, however, be faults or offences in matrimony too grave for this obligation to be insisted upon. The courts could not treat these wrongs as justifying termination of the marriage entirely but they would order a suspension of the obligation to cohabit: a divorce *a mensa et thoro* (from bed and board) could be granted against either husband or wife on the

---

[6] 7 & 8 Vict., c. 101, s.1–9; the maximum was 2s. 6d. a week until the child reached 13 (increased to 5s. until 16 in 1872 and to £1 a week in 1925).

[7] Poor Law Amendment Act 1868, s.41.

[8] McGregor (1957), pp. 5–10; Finer and McGregor (1974), pp. 85–88.

[9] No order more evidently demonstrated the weakness of the ecclesiastical courts in securing respect for their decrees.

ground of his or her cruelty, adultery or unnatural sexual indulgence. The order was (in principle) available only to a spouse who was truly aggrieved, and so not to one who had connived at the adultery initially, had condoned it subsequently, had colluded in getting up a faked case or had been equally guilty of a matrimonial wrong.[10]

This was the fore-runner of the modern degree of judicial separation and its principal effects were upon the duty of the husband to maintain his wife.[11] If the husband was the guilty party, he would normally be ordered to pay her alimony, which was commonly reckoned at about a third of his income, or even a half if his conduct had been peculiarly offensive and the wife had brought considerable wealth.[12] If the wife was guilty, she would be left without recourse against the husband. Accordingly the procedure would be valueless to her unless she could look to a lover, separate property, or her own earning capacity.

If the courts could not fully divorce those who had married, they were inevitably under pressure to find that no valid marriage had occurred in the first place. The medieval church, for all its veneration of indissolubility, had lavished invention upon notions for nullifying the tie: precontract and relationships of consanguinity and affinity between the parties could exist in so many conditions that they sufficed for many of the powerful and propertied who wanted the freedom to marry elsewhere.[13] This extraordinary contrast was one source of Luther's contempt and the reformed church in England had at once stripped the substantial causes of nullity back to the Levitical degrees of relationship, together with a number of occasional grounds: lack of age, force, fraud, idiocy, lunacy, and impotence.[14] In the eighteenth century, it accordingly became the procedural defects in marriage which provided the readiest path to annulment. The requirements of Hardwicke's Act—banns or licence, ecclesiastical ceremony, parental consent—were strict. Failure to comply made the marriage void (and bastardised the children). Defects could be unearthed years later to justify a declaration of the nullity by an ecclesiastical court and with it the freedom to marry another. To some, such as the civilian lawyer, Dr. Phillimore, this could cause scandalous injustice, and he finally succeeded in 1822 in preventing formal defects from having a nullifying effect when the flouting of the marriage law had not been wilful.[15] But others thought of this type of nullity as a surrogate for judicial divorce *a vinculo*, carefully preserved from undue use by the sleight-of-hand involved.[16] Philli-

---

[10] For nineteenth century practice, see, *e.g.* Shelford (1841), pp. 386–458.

[11] The Court of Common Pleas eventually refused to hold that the sentence turned the wife into a feme sole: *Lewis* v. *Lee* (1824) 3 B. & C. 291.

[12] *e.g.* Shelford, pp. 586–607. Only ecclesiastical penalties lay to enforce payment until 1813, when imprisonment became available (53 Geo. III, c. 127, s.1).

[13] For evidence that such suits were in fact rare, see R. H. Helmholz, *Marriage Litigation in Medieval England* (1974), pp. 77–87.

[14] See above, p. 363.

[15] For his Act and its amendments, see above, *ibid*. He had previously met resistance from the House of Lords: P.D. 1822 VI 1330; VII 1132, 1635.

[16] When he could be heard, this was the position taken by the elderly Lord Stowell: P.D. 1822 VII 1452–53.

more's success against this older, more cynical view is one mark of a
severer morality at work.

(b) Separations by Negotiation

As mutual affection acquired a more central stake in propertied
marriage, among possible corollaries were that sexual partiality could
properly shift over time, and that if passion had turned to hatred or
indifference it might be better for the couple to part. Certainly the
moral perceptions of the Georgian aristocracy made separations common enough, in every variety from the passing to the irrevocable.
The dynastic ambitions of parents could all too easily result in bitter
mis-matching. But the conflict could be resolved with relative ease
when the couple had more than one house to live in and the wife's
position was secured by her separate property in equity. The great
world lowered its disapproval of lovers and their mistresses.

In this climate, the courts, despite their acquaintance with some of
the least aimiable consequences, began to adapt. In principle the
ecclesiastical courts did not grant a husband a divorce *a mensa* from
his adulterous wife if he had himself connived at the adultery, or had
condoned it by having her back, or had colluded in getting up the
divorce proceedings. Yet in the years up to 1790, it seems that cases
in which such a defence succeeded were a rarity in the London Consistory Court.[17] Moreover, if the couple reached a separation agreement, prescribing the terms as to property and maintenance on
which they were to part, both Common Law and Chancery would
assist the arrangement.[18] Just as Chancery had used its trust device to
give the wife and her family a separate property, so on separation it
became possible to have trustees secure her a separate position on
whatever terms the husband would admit: his promise to pay or provide maintenance might be conditioned upon her remaining
chaste[19]; the trustees might undertake to indemnify the husband for
debts incurred by her (for which, at common law, he alone would be
liable),[20] property in the marriage settlement might be re-distri-
buted, if there was power to do so.[21] In *Lord Rodney* v. *Chambers*,[22]
King's Bench found that such contracts were "inveterate in the law"
and so enforceable, however undesirable the consequences as a
matter of policy. This was so even where the parties had fallen out
once and been brought to a reconciliation on terms that, should the

---

[17] Sir William Wynne could recall only the case of the actor, Colley Cibber, in which
connivance had been made out: *Hodges* v. *Hodges* (1795) 3 Hagg. Ecc. 118.

[18] See Roper (1826) Chap. 22.

[19] But if he did not so prescribe, the court would not imply it: see *Seagrave* v. *Seagrave*
(1807) 13 Ves Jun. 439; *Jee* v. *Thurlow* (1824) 2 B. & C. 547.

[20] This was necessary, if the maintenance agreement was to affect his creditors: *Wor-
rall* v. *Jacob* (1817) 3 Mer. 256; Roper (1826) Chap. 22, s.2.

[21] Chancery might help in adjustments that reflected the spirit of property transactions: in one case (*Ball* v. *Montgomery* (1793) 2 Ves. J. 191) the husband had a life
interest under a marriage settlement. Upon separation, Lord Loughborough refused
to order that the interest on the settled property should be paid to him until he
agreed to a proper separation arrangement, because the property had originally
been the wife's and had been intended partly to support her.

[22] (1802) 2 East 283—the note of regret was, however, pronounced.

wife in future have cause to leave once more, the husband should pay her an annuity. In the arrangement before the court, the trustees were treated as a domestic forum in place of the ecclesiastical court, "erected to consider whether she should live separately from her husband, and have a separate maintenance. That was some check upon her and intended to operate as such."[23]

Under the common law rules, a simple contract between husband and wife would be meaningless, since they were regarded as one. Hence the need for trustees and the intervention of equity before she personally could claim under the agreement. Yet in 1792, in equity, Pepper Arden M.R. went so far as to decree, simply at the wife's instigation, specific performance of a separation agreement. Her estranged husband was to pay her the £100 per annum to which he had agreed; both were German and she had honoured her undertaking to remain living abroad.[24] By this point some movement in the wife's favour had also occurred on the common law side. Lord Mansfield and Buller J. had led the King's Bench into the view that when husband and wife had separated it did not necessarily follow that she lacked all capacity to contract. At least if the husband were living out of England, or if the wife had separate property, she might pledge her own credit with traders and be made liable to them.[25]

Yet about 1790, a sterner, less accommodating attitude began to make itself felt. Matrimonial re-arrangements were good material for the spirit of the Proclamation Society, the rectitude of the Clapham Sect, to work upon. Its presence could be felt in the ecclesiastical jurisdiction, particularly in the judgments of Eldon's brother, Stowell. For instance, he insisted that a divorce *a mensa* for the husband's cruelty must, in all save exceptional cases, involve physical harm and not just mental affliction: "When the principle is understood that they must live together, except for a very few reasons known to the law, they learn to soften by mutual accommodation that yoke which they know they cannot shake off; they become good husbands and wives from the necessity of remaining husbands and wives; for necessity is a . . . master in teaching the duties it imposes."[26] The defence of connivance, moreover, acquired new force. An adulterous wife might resist a decree against her (which would release her husband from maintaining her) by showing his "extreme negligence to the condition of his wife," or that he had let "the licentiousness of the wife take its full scope."[27]

The new spirit found its way into common law. With unusual solemnity the three benches sat en bloc to overrule Lord Mansfield's heresy of treating a wife who had separated voluntarily as a *feme*

---

[23] Per Lawrence J., (1802) 2 East at 196.

[24] *Guth* v. *Guth* (1792) 3 Bro. C.C. 614.

[25] *Ringstead* v. *Lady Lanesborough* (1783) 3 Doug. 197; *Barwell* v. *Brooks* (1784) 3 Doug. 373; *Corbett* v. *Poelnitz* (1785) 1 T.R. 5; and see *Cox* v. *Kitchin* (1798) 1 Bos. & Pul. 338.

[26] *Evans* v. *Evans* (1790) 1 Hagg. Con. 35 at 36–37

[27] *Lovering* v. *Lovering* (1792) 3 Hagg. Ecc. 85; *Moorsom* v. *Moorsom* (1792) *ibid.*, 87; *Timmings* v. *Timmings* (1792) *ibid.*, 76; followed by Sir William Wynne in *Gilpin* v. *Gilpin* (1804) *ibid.*, 150, where the expressions quoted were used; and in *Hodges* v. *Hodges* (above, n. 17); *cf. Crewe* v. *Crewe* (1800) 3 Hagg. Ecc. 123.

sole.[28] Likewise, in Chancery doubts about the wisdom of the eighteenth century direction were expressed at length, above all by Eldon. He lingered over his regrets that agreements for separate maintenance had been treated as valid[29] and was restrained only by his sense that dicta and decision had too clearly settled the law for him now to reverse it.[30] He followed Lord Loughborough in insisting that equity would intervene over separation agreements only where there were "special" circumstances (*i.e.* where there was a trust or the wife acquired a fortune after separation) and agreed with him in disapproving Pepper Arden's order to a husband to pay maintenance to his wife at her suit.[31] He refused to countenance any suit upon an arrangement for future separation, common as this was in settling the terms of a reconciliation. He thus turned away from the recent trend in the King's Bench: "people should understand that they should not enter into these fluctuating contracts; and after that sacred contract [*i.e.* the marriage itself] they should feel it to be their mutual interest to improve their tempers."[32] And soon enough this also became the rule of the common law.[33]

Yet the judges even of Eldon's generation felt obliged to stick to middle ground. They did not insist upon proof of adultery or cruelty sufficient for an ecclesiastical divorce before upholding a private separation deed[34]; at most, it seems that they expected some indication in it that the arrangement was a compromise of a potential suit for divorce *a mensa.*[35] In the end, the House of Lords held that a promise not to proceed further in the ecclesiastical courts was itself consideration upon which equity would decree specific performance of the articles of separation; the court would not inquire into the cause.[36]

Separation agreements might have become undeniable necessities of life, but the same submissiveness was not to be shown to a father's agreement to surrender custody of his children, whether to his wife,

---

[28] *Marshall* v. *Rutton* (1800) 8 T.R. 545; the case was argued twice, Buller J.'s absence on the second occasion giving "occasion to lament." Even the wife's customary right in the City of London, was confined to actions in the City Courts rather than at common law: *Beard* v. *Webb* (1800) 2 Bos. & Pul. 93.

[29] But effective they were, as appeared from the remarkable *Bateman* v. *Olivia, Countess of Ross* (1813) 1 Dow. 235.

[30] *St. John* v. *St. John* (1805) 11 Ves. Jun. 526. He also refused to order that moneys be paid over to a separated wife from her separate estate without an ecclesiastical decree of alimony: Roper (1826) Chap. 22.

[31] *Lezard* v. *Johnson* (1797) 3 Ves. Jun. 352; and see above, n. 24.

[32] *St. John* v. *St. John* (above, n. 30) at 530; and see, *e.g.*, *Westmeath* (*Marquess*) v. *Salisbury* (*Marquess*) (1831) 5 Bligh N.S. 339.

[33] *Durant* v. *Titley* (1819) 7 Price 577—though the notion survived of setting up a "family tribunal" to determine whether there had been a matrimonial offence: *Jee* v. *Thurlow* (1824) 2 B. & C. 547 at 552, per Bayley J.

[34] Lord Stowell insisted that the ecclesiastical courts would have nothing to do with private arrangements (*Mortimer* v. *Mortimer* (1820) 2 Hagg. Con. 318); but the position there was not of prime importance.

[35] According to Macqueen (1849), pp. 332–333, judges differed in the attention they paid to the matter; he advised saying something stronger than that "unhappy differences" had arisen.

[36] *Wilson* v. *Wilson* (1848) 1 H.L.C. 538. This left for later times the question whether matrimonial courts could re-open the terms upon which separation had been reached: Victorian courts tended against, but eventually the House of Lords favoured doing so: *Hyman* v. *Hyman* [1929] A.C. 601.

to grandparents or to anyone else. Lord Eldon set in train a refusal to treat custody agreements as binding that was to have a long endurance.[37] The father could lose custody only by intervention of Chancery itself and it would require proof against him of peculiar neglect or viciousness. Mother and children could never rely upon his mere word. Not until 1873 would Parliament attempt a moderating intervention and even that, as we shall see,[38] did little to alter the older assumption of the courts, which had a root both deep and tough.

(c) Divorce Extraordinary: Private Acts and Wife-sales

As earlier routes to the ending of marriages became barred, the most powerful saw to it that there could still be some ultimate means of escape.[39] In the decade of the Restoration, just as it became clear beyond question that no court had the ability to grant a divorce *a vinculo*, Lord Roos secured for himself a full divorce by Act of Parliament. There were high protestations but he met them with the most urgent of reasons, the need to replace his adulterous wife with one who might secure his line. By 1700 a trickle of imitations was beginning. As we shall see, the dynastic concern behind them was long to justify a double standard: as adultery came to be the sole ground for a private divorce Act—and after 1857 for a judicial divorce—a wife would succeed only if her husband's adultery was "aggravated" by bigamy, incest or unnatural vice. Short of this, she suffered no "very material injury" and she ought not to resent her husband's unfaithfulness; so many lesser men repeated after Dr. Johnson.[40] In the period to 1857, only four women would ever succeed in securing a divorce Act[41]; whereas after 1750, about 15 men succeeded in each decade, a figure which then rose in fits until it reached 53 in the decade 1841–50, making a total of 318 for the period to 1857.[42]

The course for such an Act, which became increasingly standardised in the eighteenth century, was designedly elaborate.[43] Normally the petitioning husband was expected first to establish his wife's guilt in an action at common law against the adulterer for criminal conversation (thus proving the matter to the satisfaction of a jury). Then there had to be an ecclesiastical divorce *a mensa* (follow-

---

[37] Once he put it in terms of the father's *duties*, "given him by God and nature," the result was inescapable: *Westmeath* v. *Westmeath* (1819) Jac. 251; and see also the *de Manneville* and *St. John* cases (above, n. 86, 30). For the position—essentially unchanged—in mid-century, see *Vansittart* v. *Vansittart* (1858) 4 K. & J. 62.

[38] Below, pp. 403–404.

[39] The post-Reformation history of the subject was treated in detail (thanks to the Secretary, Macqueen) in the Campbell Commission Report P.P. 1852–53 [1604] XL, pp. 1–11. For modern accounts, see S. Anderson (1984), Horstman (1985) Chaps. 1, 2.

[40] See generally, K. Thomas (1959) 20 J. Hist. Ideas 195.

[41] Seven tried; more obtained divorces *a mensa*: see, *e.g.*, the list in the Campbell Report, pp. 29–31.

[42] Another 92 failed, or did not proceed; see S. Anderson (1984), p. 415ff.

[43] A succession of Bills after 1770 sought to remove the right of the couple to re-marry after the Divorce Act (witness, *e.g.*, Lord Auckland's optimistic Adultery Prevention Bill 1800). These were one expression of the severer morality which attracted the judges, but they never commanded a Parliamentary majority: see S. Anderson (1984), pp. 423–424.

ing the largely documentary process of the civilians that drew such
common law disdain). The records of both proceedings then went
with the Bill, first to the Lords, then to the Commons and back. Given
the main object at stake, this became a use of private legislation that
was peculiarly "judicial," regularised by precedent into a normative
regimen.[44] Even so, there remained a residue of discretion natural to
a legislative process.[45] Certainly there was a flux in attitude that was,
if anything, more marked than that relating to separation arrangements and the like. Anderson has suggested that the dominant role
played by the Lord Chancellor in the Lords made his personal prede-
lictions a crucial factor in the outcome of petitions. Under Thurlow in
the 1780s, under Eldon (for the first quarter of the next century) and
later under Brougham, Parliamentary divorce was made difficult by
an insistence not only on the clearest proof of the adultery but also
that the husband be truly aggrieved; he must in no way have colluded in the proceedings or allowed his wife's liaison to carry on
without unrelenting protest.[46]

Even in the 1840s Parliamentary divorce was a highly unusual remedy for matrimonial breakdown and was by then coming to be
attacked as a class privilege reserved for aristocrats with an entry into
legislative circles. In fact, while this had largely been the case a century before, when the possibility was still novel, it had ceased to be
so by 1800, when there were applications from the service, professional, merchant and even lower ranks.[47] Nor was the common
claim justified (for all that it was to be repeated by the Campbell
Royal Commission in 1853) that even an undefended process would
cost in the order of £700–800, with the amount running into thousands if the wife or co-respondent resisted at any stage. As typical
figures, these amounts were some exaggeration and in any case failed
to distinguish the cases where the husband was left to pay everything from those in which the criminal conversation damages against
the co-respondent would shift some or all the burden to him.[48] Parliamentary divorce depended not so much on absolute wealth
(though it certainly needed some resources) as upon resilient determination.[49]

At a lower social level, the practice of wife-selling was sometimes
used to signify the end of a marriage, and the start of a new liaison.
The sale itself was the crudest expression of male superiority, the
woman often being led to a market, exhibited in a halter and knocked
down for a price, sometimes pre-arranged and sometimes competi-

---

[44] The foundation became Lord Loughborough's Standing Orders of 1798 (for the
Lords) under which the petitioner could be required to attend for examination; in
the Commons Labouchere's motion of 1840 secured a hearing before a Committee
instead of the whole House, so increasing the "judicial" character. In the Commons
also, one member would act as "Ladies' Friend" to ensure that, for all their guilt,
wives were given a moderate provision for their support: Macqueen (1849), p. 213.
See generally, F. Clifford, *History of Private Bill Legislation* (1885), I Chap. 5.

[45] *cf*. Dr. Lushington, Campbell Commission Report (above, n. 39), pp. 37–38.

[46] S. Anderson (1984) p. 424ff.

[47] *Ibid. passim.*

[48] *Ibid.*, pp. 436–442.

[49] See further below, pp. 386–387.

tive, just as if she were a prize cow.[50] The use of such "legal" formality seemed to express a deep-seated desire for a certain propriety and finality in sexual relations. Participants and observers presumably took the procedure to effect the necessary changes of status, without concern for the fact that it flew in the face of the established law of marriage.[51]

Some wife sales seem to have been the regularisation of an established relationship between a wife and her lover, putting into documentary form (in which an attorney likely had a hand) terms by which the husband would undertake not to apply for restitution of conjugal rights and would at the same time be declared free from liability to meet his wife's debts. As such they are no great remove from the separation agreements of the propertied. But the instances that shocked the respectable were a part of the rowdy, drink-sodden, sexually charged end of hiring and agricultural fairs[52] and went with rough music, cruel sports and "friendly" demands for money. They might not only be denounced in newspapers but could lead to prosecution of both husband and purchaser for conspiring to corrupt public morals.[53] But this was intermittent. In the social upheavals of the French Wars, there was little effort to stamp out the wife-sales at Smithfield Market. They were probably too useful to be gainsaid.

It is in the century after 1750 that most reports survive of wife-selling, since they made good fodder for an expanding press. Yet even an assiduous cull of newspapers and other sources suggests that the practice was never very widespread[54]—to be compared indeed with the sparse incidence of Parliamentary divorces through just the same period. Both were exceptional.

We have no figures, but we can be sure that a considerable number of marriages came wholly adrift each year. Many of these involved nothing more than the departure of one or other partner. Much of this splitting was part of the constant mobility among the poor in search of work, rather than simple incompatability or switch of affections. In some areas, at the lower social levels, this was part of an accepted code, marked perhaps by a simple act such as returning a ring or re-jumping the broom. The folk-customs of "divorce" perhaps survived longest in isolated communities because the neighbourship was so close.[55] Elsewhere, particularly in towns, those who found new partners, if they bothered with more than cohabitation, could marry bigamously with little risk. Even with the requirement of banns, there were anonymous places, such as the collegiate

[50] To the French, this was a standard instance of English barbarity.
[51] Menefee (1981) Chap. 6 tries to assess the meaning of the various stages to those involved.
[52] This makes more credible the pivotal event in Hardy's *Mayor of Casterbridge*.
[53] In *R. v. Delaval* (above, n. 83), Lord Mansfield gave wife-selling as an instance of this flexible crime, which he insisted King's Bench would enforce as part of its "superintendency of offences *contra bonos mores*" (at 1438–1439).
[54] Menefee (1981), Appendix, identifies 387 instances for which records survive, the bulk occurring in the period 1750–1850. For Smithfield cases, see instances 80, 83, 84, 86.
[55] See Gillis (1983), pp. 271–273; but note Henry Mayhew's evidence of similar practices among costermongers, dust collectors and chimney-sweeps in London: cited, *ibid.* at p. 273.

churches of the great cities, where hundreds of names were read to
an undiscriminating congregation.[56]

PART 2: NEW PRESSURES ON FAMILY LAW: 1850–1950

In the second half of the nineteenth century, legislation introduced
judicial divorce and a distinct legal status for married women. These
were changes which inured mainly to the benefit of the propertied
middle of the population. But the demand for them can scarcely be
labelled "middle class" for both were essentially destructive of the
stable, united family, ruled with a just severity by the husband and
father. As we shall see, there are many indications in the way in
which these reforms were carried out, to show how conventional this
view of the Victorian family was. The root significance of the changes
is that, as always, there existed challenges to the current orthodoxy
about the family. It was possible, in an age where statutory reform
had become the stuff of radical endeavour, for pressure groups to
organise successfully against a widespread, but rather amorphous,
conservatism. But rewriting the statute book provided no necessary
passport to a truly altered world.

Beyond these limited concessions in the sphere of private law
comes the development of a matrimonial jurisdiction at the magistrates' level, private in form though often public in effect, which
would at last bring legal machinery into the resolution of family
breakdowns at working-class level. At the same period, the law
affecting children, in both its private and public aspects, becomes
more elaborate and in some measure more flexible. Through these
developments and their sequels in the period to 1950, we can gain
some measure of attitudes to the family as they were reflected in law.
Change on most fronts came only after sustained attack against
strongly marshalled resistance. The central Victorian vision would
prove highly resilient.

I. The Movement for Judicial Divorce

The disparity between parliamentary divorce in England and judicial
divorce in Scotland attracted few criticisms in the early nineteenth
century. In the utilitarian precepts developed by Bentham and his
associates, marriage could be nothing more than a consensual transaction. It followed that divorce should be also, but Bentham wished
to deter "caprice" by a procedure that allowed sufficient time for
reflection; and he wanted to deter ill-treatment in marriage by allowing only the suffering spouse the power to remarry.[57] Sir Samuel
Romilly included arrangements in his draft for a Civil Code which
would allow the poor to divorce, though on less radical principles.[58]
Both drew inspiration in particular from revolutionary France where

---

[56] *Ibid.*, at pp. 193–194.
[57] *Principles of the Civil Code, Works* (Bowring ed., 1843), I pp. 352–355; *Theory of Legislation* (7th ed., 1891), p. 207.
[58] *Memoirs* (1840), III p. 372.

divorce had been introduced for various matrimonial offences and even by mutual consent.[59]

Divorce reform also became a secondary theme in the Church-and-State question of the future of the ecclesiastical courts. From within those courts leading civilians argued that full divorce was on occasion socially necessary and should be made available through a simpler procedure than by Act of Parliament. Dr. Phillimore promoted a general Bill for judicial divorce after the scandal of the second Lord Ellenborough's own private divorce Act in 1830.[60] Dr. Lushington added his Benthamic voice on a number of occasions. But once the ecclesiastical courts survived investigation in 1832,[61] the issue receded in favour of marriage reform.[62] In the 1840s it revived, particularly under the championship of Brougham's Society for the Promotion of Amendment of the Law. The radically-minded lawyers who were its mainstay insisted that parliamentary divorce was a special privilege of the very rich who were able and willing to lay out several hundred pounds, or perhaps thousands.[63] The matter was epitomised by Mr. Justice Maule on Assize in 1845. Pronouncing sentence on a bigamist, Thomas Hall, who had misled his second "wife" to the altar, he enumerated the proper steps that the prisoner should have taken to rid himself of his first, adulterous wife by private Act. He "might perhaps object to this that he had not the money to pay the expenses, which would amount to about £500 or £600—perhaps he had not so many pence—but this did not exempt him from paying the penalty of committing a felony."[64]

The press, led by *The Times*, took up the reformist cause.[65] In 1850 Russell's government, responsive to the Low-church Whiggery which sort to sever Church from State, was moved to appoint a Royal Commission under the chairmanship of Lord Campbell. Thanks to its membership the Commission built a case against Parliamentary divorce as an occasional privilege reserved by its expense and complexity for the uppermost class.[66] It proposed to transfer the procedure to a single new tribunal, consisting of a Chancery judge, a

---

[59] On the restoration of the monarchy in 1816, the divorce provisions of the Code were repealed. Their effect during their currency became a matter of constant dispute between divorce reformers and opponents everywhere.

[60] Ellenborough's proceedings succeeded despite the evident taint of connivance and collusion. Phillimore, a leading advocate of Doctor's Commons, favoured transfer of divorce from Parliament to Chancery.

[61] Above, p. 29.

[62] Above, p. 364.

[63] Above, p. 380.

[64] *The Times*, April 3, 1845, where it is said that Hall was sentenced to four months imprisonment with hard labour for the deception of his intended wife. Versions such as those given by O. R. McGregor, *Divorce in England* (1957), pp. 15–17 and R. E. Megarry, *Miscellany-at-Law* (1955), pp. 116–117 proceed to a more scathing denouncement; and see Mueller (1957) at p. 549, n. 15 for other sources.

[65] Legal protagonists kept up their fire: see esp. the report of the Society for the Promotion of Amendment of the Law (1848) 8 Law Rev. 347; Brougham's speech on law reform, P.D. 1848 CXVIII 899.

[66] Much of the evidence was a republication of that given to the Lords Committee on Brougham's Bill of 1844. The Lord Advocate's evidence showed that, of 95 decrees of divorce *a vinculo matrimonii* granted in the Scots Court of Session between 1836 and 1841, almost every case involved small tradesmen or wage-earners; and about a third of the cases were brought by the wife.

common law judge and a judge of the ecclesiastical courts. This new body would follow common-law procedure, with oral evidence rather than dispositions. The "double standard" would continue in exaggerated form: husbands might use the court to divorce their wives for adultery, but save in cases of "incest, bigamy and the like," wives must continue to resort to Parliament and show exceptional aggravation.[67] The one High-Church figure on the Commission, Lord Redesdale, would have preferred to abandon even Parliamentary divorce. He feared the avalanche implicit in the majority's proposals:

> "These Divorces will thus be open to another and numerous class, but a still more numerous class will equally be excluded as at present. Once create an appetite for such licence by the proposed change and the demand to be permitted to satisfy it will become irresistible. The cry for cheap law has of late been universally attended to . . . and it must ultimately lead to extreme facility in obtaining such divorces."[68]

The majority's moderation nonetheless appealed to influential lawyers of a generally conservative bias. Lord Cranworth's Bill of 1854 followed the proposals, but it failed, partly because it sought to transfer the jurisdiction simply to the unpopular Court of Chancery. Lord Lyndhurst indicated his intention to introduce a divorce system on Scots lines into England; and when Cranworth tried another, very narrow Bill in 1856, Lyndhurst sought to broaden the grounds for divorce included in it.[69] After Palmerston's electoral victory in 1857, he found in divorce a "practical reform" which would head the livelier spirits in his large majority from the fundamental radicalism of a franchise extension.[70] The processing of the Government's Bill proved laborious because Gladstone's conscience demanded that he oppose the measure clause by clause; and in the Lords the energetic Bishop of Oxford, Samuel Wilberforce, did likewise.[71]

Dicey considered the divorce legislation of 1857 to be Benthamic in inspiration,[72] but it was far from the root-and-branch reappraisal proposed by Bentham himself. Those who spoke in Parliament were almost exclusively concerned with the spiritual justification for, and the wisdom of, extending divorce to a limited new class. It was taken that the basis for a new jurisdiction would be much the same as in Parliament and the ecclesiastical courts. As the Attorney-General, Bethell, said in introducing the measure, it was essentially procedural.[73]

---

[67] P.P. 1852–53 [1604] XL, pp. 12–22.

[68] *Ibid.*, p. 26.

[69] Horstmann (1985), pp. 72–73.

[70] For this period, see J. F. Macqueen, *Divorce and Matrimonial Jurisdiction* (1858), pp. 33–35; S. Maccoby, *English Radicalism 1853–1886* (1938), pp. 61–66.

[71] For the religious background, see Horstmann (1985) Chap. 3; and for debates, Woodhouse (1959).

[72] *Law and Public Opinion in England* (2nd ed., 1914), p. 184; followed, for instance, by R. H. Graveson in Keeton and Schwarzenberger (eds.) *Jeremy Bentham and the Law* (1948), p. 115.

[73] For the enactment in general, see R. H. Graveson in Graveson and Crane (1957), pp. 6–14; Horstmann (1985) Chap. 5; M. L. Shanley (1982) 25 Vict. St. 355.

Adultery alone was to ground relief; Lyndhurst's attempt to introduce the Scottish notion of desertion for a period of years found few
supporters.[74] Moreover, the double standard of the patriarchal
dynasty was to continue; simple adultery would be a matrimonial
offence by the wife, but "accidental adultery" by the husband would
not count.[75] Lyndhurst, and even Gladstone, inveighed against the
injustice of this proposal but did not prevail. Instead the petitioning
wife was left to prove her husband's rape, incest, bigamy, cruelty or
desertion for two years, as factors "aggravating" his adultery, or el e
his commission of an unnatural offence.[76]

One line of utilitarian argument came to nought. The Archbishop
of Canterbury was amongst those who sought to prevent the "guilty"
from having the right to re-marry. "Could any stronger inducement
be offered to an incipient passion than the prospect that in the end it
might legitimately be indulged"?[77] The answer was, however, to
hand: there were "dissolute and depraved men," who were in any
case "exulting over the licence which they expect to receive at the
hands of the legislature"; nothing could please them better than that
they could not be compelled by their mistresses to marry again. The
matter was accordingly dropped.[78]

So also was a proposal that there be substituted for the action of
criminal conversation against the wife's lover a criminal sanction.
The Lords did pass an amendment, strongly supported by Bishop
Wilberforce, giving the divorce judge a discretion to fine or imprison
a (male) co-respondent.[79] But in the end the essence of "crim. con."
was preserved instead: the husband was given the right (either as
part of, or even independently of, divorce proceedings) to claim
damages from the wife's seducer.[80] As before, these would take
account of her economic value, the injury to the husband's feelings
and the means and conduct of the co-respondent—a curious amalgam of compensation, consolation and condemnation, and one only
to be contemplated between men.[81]

The Church and State question was settled in favour of a new secular tribunal, the Divorce Court. The ecclesiastical courts were at last
to be stripped of all their lay jurisdiction; the civilian lawyers of

[74] For the debate over the scriptural authority for this, see W. O. Chadwick, *The Victorian Church* (1966, 1970), I pp. 482–483; II pp. 438–439.

[75] Above p. 379. Despite this, about 40 per cent. of petitions would be by wives, rising
to some 45 per cent. before the First World War. During the war the proportion
would fall as low as 20 per cent.; after the 1923 Act (below, pp. 396–397) it would rise
to 50–60 per cent.: Rowntree and Carrier (1958), p. 201.

[76] Reference to unnatural offences was originally omitted, since, said Lord St.
Leonards, the Act "would be in the hands of the purest women in England": P.D.
1857 CXLVII 2029. For the grounds of divorce see the Matrimonial Causes Act, 1857,
s.27.

[77] P.D. 1857 CXLV 828.

[78] The same arguments had been rehearsed over Lord Auckland's Bill of 1800; see
above, n. 43.

[79] Again the proposal was by no means novel. Lord Auckland's Bill (see n. 43) had at
one stage contained the same proposal. And in 1841 the *Law Magazine* had argued
that adultery was already indictable as a common law conspiracy.

[80] See Matrimonial Causes Act 1857, ss.33, 34. The action was to survive until 1970.

[81] *Ibid.*, s.33. The ecclesiastical jurisdiction to grant divorce *a mensa et thoro* became the
modern order of judicial separation: s.16.

Doctors' Commons were to share rights of audience with their common law rivals in both matrimonial and testamentary matters.[82] Clergy of the established church, who had not in the past shown any noticeable disinclination to re-marry those divorced by Parliament, now found their consciences sorely troubled, a condition exacerbated by their legal obligation to marry any couple not subject to a known incapacity. Their scruples were respected, after long argument: they were excused from having themselves to marry the guilty parties to divorce suits, but they could not object to the use of their churches for ceremonies performed by others.[83] The compromise was symptomatic of a deeper uncertainty. The Church had been able to find no united conviction upon the acceptability or otherwise of divorce. So it temporised and hoped that the measure would in practice prove restricted in its effect. Even Bishop Wilberforce, who first attacked the Bill as "giving to the lower classes disastrous disadvantages to which the higher classes only have hitherto been exposed," came to think that it would be "a law for the rich; it was an immunity for the adulterers and adulteresses in the high places of England."[84]

II. Divorce by Judicial Decree

Despite the Act of 1857, the notion of divorce remained deeply unpalatable to much of the middle and upper classes and long would remain so. Lord Redesdale's fears of a popular deluge were exaggerated simply because so many pressures ensured that judicial divorce would be a difficult, and in some respects perilous, course. Most formidable was the great wall of social displeasure. A divorced man, and even more a divorced woman, had to reckon with total or virtual ostracism from drawing-rooms and dinner-tables. So direct a flouting of family and marriage provoked a narrow and undiscriminating hostility from the respectable. Parliament had underscored this moral antipathy by continuing the pre-condition of a "matrimonial offence" involving (at least) a breach of sexual fidelity. There would be an equalising of the grounds for divorce in 1923 but no significant extension until 1937.[85]

In procedural matters, the new Act was equally severe. Proceedings had to be launched before the Divorce Court in London, with all the formality and expense that this entailed.[86] The cost was some £40–£45 if undefended and £70–£500 if defended. The ordinary working man or woman could pay for such a privilege only by considerable saving for long periods. Very occasionally the poor person's

---

[82] Above, p. 42.

[83] Matrimonial Causes Act 1857, ss.57, 58. 6,000 clergy had petitioned in order to extract even this concession; and it was hoped that no priest would ever be persuaded to use another's church for so debased a ceremony: W. O. Chadwick, *The Victorian Church* (1966), I pp. 483–484.

[84] P.D. 1857 CXLII 1982; CXLVI 227.

[85] See generally, Horstman (1985) Chap. 5.

[86] Initially the Divorce Court had to comprise three judges to hear divorce petitions, one being the Judge Ordinary, specially appointed to preside over this and the new Probate Court, and the others being drawn from a pool of superior judges. This proved too cumbersome, and the Judge Ordinary was given sole jurisdiction in 1860. In contested cases, juries were quite commonly used.

procedure was open to a divorce petitioner. But until 1882, it was necessary for an applicant to show that his capital assets were worth no more than £5 (in that year the sum was raised to £25).[87] The number of divorces did progressively increase. But the rise was gradual and even in 1900 less than 600 petitions would succeed each year.[88]

Inevitably a great deal was left to be worked out by the Divorce Court. To a considerable extent the judges adapted the civilian law of divorce *a mensa*, generally following the severer approaches that had emerged after 1790, as for instance, on the question of cruelty (now an aggravation of adultery on which a petitioning wife might rely). Following Lord Stowell's hostility to any extended notion of the subject,[89] "mental cruelty" was admitted only where abusive, threatening, or dictatorial conduct was so gross as to endanger the other partner's health of mind.[90] By this test, Earl Russell failed to secure a decree of judicial separation from a wife who continued publicly to accuse him of unnatural offences long after she must have known that her tales were baseless.[91] In England cruelty was not to become "one of the dazzling success stories of family law," as it did in much of the United States.[92]

The new Court was able to follow similar precedents in interpreting the bars to relief in the 1857 Act. Connivance, by consenting to or acquiescing in adultery before it took place, had an enduring effect, no matter how often the guilty party indulged him- or herself again with the same or another person. "It would be a disgrace to the law," said Lord Westbury in 1864, "to suppose that a husband may connive at the adultery of his wife on Monday, and yet be at liberty to complain of a repetition of the adultery on Tuesday."[93] Condonation of adultery after the event, by reinstating the guilty spouse with an intention to forgive, would also wipe the slate clean, though in this case only *pro tempore*.[94] As regards collusion, the civilian notion was confined to the agreed faking of evidence. Where one spouse arranged to commit adultery in order to provide the other with the evidence to obtain a remedy, the collaboration amounted to conniv-

---

[87] Even after 1883, the procedure was so cumbersome as to be "almost inoperative," being subject to well-nigh prohibitive conditions: R. Egerton, *Legal Aid* (1946), pp. 8–9.

[88] See Rowntree and Carrier (1956), p. 200ff.

[89] Above, p. 377.

[90] An instance of this was *Kelly* v. *Kelly* (1869) 2 P. & D. 31; *cf. Smallwood* v. *Smallwood* (1861) 2 Sw. & Tr. 397, disregarding a single act of cruelty. In an 1859 amendment, wives were made competent witnesses against their husbands in divorce proceedings, thus allowing proof of cruelty otherwise impossible: 22 & 23 Vict., c. 61, s.6.

[91] *Russell* v. *Russell* [1897] A.C. 395; and see below, p. 393.

[92] L. M. Friedman and R. V. Percival, (1976) 5 Jo. Leg. St. 61. In 1884, refusal to comply with a decree of restitution of conjugal rights was made a separate "aggravation" of the husband's adultery. In consequence, this order gained a temporary popularity.

[93] *Gipps* v. *Gipps* (1864) 11 H.L.C. 1, 14. See above, pp. 375–376.

[94] Here at least the subjugate position of the wife was allowed to her advantage. Resumption of sexual intercourse was taken as conclusive proof of condonation by the innocent husband, but not by the innocent wife, because she "is hardly her own mistress; she may not have the option of going away; she may have no place to go; no person to receive her; no funds to support her . . . " *Keats* v. *Keats* (1859) 1 Sw. & Tr. 334, 337.

ance and was so treated.[95] But now the Divorce Court might hold that there was collusion in any agreement to initiate or continue a suit in return for some benefit, such as an undertaking to pay the petitioner's costs or to provide evidence of adultery in return for not enforcing a judgment for damages against a co-respondent. By 1895, it was settled that such financial agreements about divorce proceedings, even if openly declared to the court, barred the decree.[96]

After 1857, antipathy to the whole idea of divorce was expressed as a fear of collusive arrangements.[97] Yet from the outset many divorce proceedings went undefended or were not seriously contested, either from supine acquiescence or positive encouragement to petition. So in 1860, in order to stem any flood of collusive divorces, the two stages of decree nisi and decree absolute were introduced. The period in between[98] was to allow an officer of the court, the Queen's Proctor, to investigate collusion or the other bars, and consider whether there were points of law to be raised against undefended petitions.[99]

In addition to the absolute bars, the court in its discretion might refuse a divorce either because the petitioner had been guilty of adultery, cruelty, desertion, or neglect or misconduct conducive to the respondent's adultery; or because the presentation of the petition had been unduly delayed. At least since Lord Stowell, the ecclesiastical courts had not wavered in their condemnation of an adulterous petitioner.[1] Equally, under the new dispensation, the petitioner would find his case rejected whether he tried to conceal his own turpitude or frankly admitted it in court.[2] Only if he remarried believing the first spouse to be dead, or if a wife-petitioner had been forced by her husband to live as a prostitute, was any distinct exception admitted.[3]

The largest opportunities to emphasise the punitive, quasi-criminal aspects of the new divorce came with the consequential issues of alimony and rights over children. As we have seen, the ecclesiastical courts would award an innocent wife substantial alimony on a divorce *a mensa et thoro*, but would give a guilty woman nothing. Parliament, through the discreet offices of the "Lady's Friend," had taken a

---

[95] *Crewe* v. *Crewe* (1800) 3 Hag. Ecc. 123.

[96] *Churchward* v. *Churchward* [1895] P. 7, where the earlier law is reviewed.

[97] Remarking on the "fearful amount of collusion" in the Divorce Court, Sir George Bowyer MP., called it an "Encumbered Estates Court for the transfer of women": P.D. 1860 CLX 1746.

[98] Originally three months, it was enlarged to six months in 1866.

[99] Matrimonial Causes Act 1860, s.7. Very different views were expressed in the debates about the extent of collusion: see P.D. 1858 CL 2194ff.; 1859 CLIV 559ff.; CLV 141ff.; 516ff.; 1860 CLVI 232; CLVII 1873; CLX 1628.

[1] Lord Stowell's cold comfort had been that "the parties may live together and find sources of mutual forgiveness in the humiliation of mutual guilt": *Beeby* v. *Beeby* (1799) 1 Hag. Ecc. 789, 790.

[2] See, *e.g.*, *Latour* v. *Latour* (1864) 33 L.J. (P.M. & A.) 89 (attempt to conceal petitioner's *de facto* union with another woman since 1838 after divorce *a mensa et thoro*); *Clarke* v. *Clarke* (1865) 34 L.J. (P.M. & A.) 94 (frank confession of single act of adultery after wife ran away with petitioner's brother).

[3] More doubtfully, condonation of the petitioner's adultery might render it excusable: *Morgan* v. *Morgan* (1869) L.R. 1 P. & D. 644.

less censorious attitude.[4] The new Divorce Court was initially given powers in the matter of maintenance which reflected rather narrowly the social position of those involved in Parliamentary and ecclesiastical divorce: it might require a husband to secure to the wife such capital sum or annual payment "as, having regard to her fortune (if any), to the ability of the husband, and to the conduct of the parties, it shall deem reasonable."[5] When it became apparent that the court was also having to deal with husbands whose resources could not provide capital or annual sums, weekly or monthly payments without security had to be permitted; and the court had also to be allowed to modify or suspend its order temporarily if the husband should be unable to comply with it.[6]

How, then, was this power to be exercised against "guilty" and "innocent" husbands? In favour of innocent wives the first judge of the Divorce Court, Sir Cresswell Cresswell, adopted a policy of awarding no more than a bare maintenance.[7] This, his successor disparaged as "starving a wife into preferring judicial separation to divorce," and a principle which gave the guilty husband "a pecuniary interest in adding cruelty and desertion to his adultery."[8] Thereafter, the petitioning wife would usually be awarded maintenance equivalent to a third of her husband's income, thus following the former practice of the ecclesiastical courts.[9]

Towards "guilty" wives no mercy was to be shown.[10] The practice, as counsel informed the Court of Appeal in 1883,[11] was to refuse her any maintenance at all unless there were special circumstances.[12] "I am sorry to hear it," interposed Sir George Jessel, "it was not intended that a guilty wife should be turned out into the streets to starve." But if moral judgment was not in future to be passed by this means, social circumstances were to be considered instead:

"When a working man who has married a washerwoman obtains a divorce, she can very well go back to washing again. That is a quite different case from that of the gentleman of large means who obtains the special privilege by Act of Parliament."

Though it seems that this judgment only led to guilty wives being awarded some slight modicum, it did point in a new direction.[13] The

---

[4] Above, n. 44.
[5] Matrimonial Causes Act 1857, s.32.
[6] Divorce and Matrimonial Causes Act 1866.
[7] *Fisher* v. *Fisher* (1861) 2 Sw. & Tr. 410.
[8] Sir James Wilde (later Lord Penzance), *Sidney* v. *Sidney* (1865) 4 Sw. & Tr. 178.
[9] This rule of thumb did not begin to be abandoned until the inter-war years; and it has shown a tendency to revive from time to time ever since: see J. L. Barton in Graveson and Crane (1957), p. 361.
[10] The court was positively empowered to re-write the marriage settlement of a guilty wife for the benefit of her husband and children: Matrimonial Causes Act 1857, s.45.
[11] *Robinson* v. *Robinson* (1883) 8 P D 94
[12] The most she could hope for would be that damages recovered from a co-respondent would be settled on her, under the Matrimonial Causes Act 1857, s.33.
[13] For the impossibility of "guilty" wives seeking maintenance before summary tribunals, see below, p. 392.

law was just beginning to turn from condemnation of the past towards provision for the future, a revolution that would take many decades to complete.

Over children, the attitude of the courts changed even more gradually. Established principles gave predominance to the wishes of the father, save in cases of extreme misconduct, when the welfare of the child categorically dictated some other course.[14] Full divorce was thought to raise new considerations, and the Act of 1857 gave the courts a general discretion to make "just and proper" provision for the custody, maintenance and education of children of the marriage being terminated.[15] In the event custody went almost invariably to the innocent party; and "guilty" wives, though not always "guilty" husbands, were deprived even of a right of access. As Cresswell J. announced soon enough:

> "It will probably have a salutary effect on the interests of public morality, that it should be known that a woman, if found guilty of adultery, will forfeit, as far as this court is concerned, all rights to the custody of or access to her children."[16]

Occasionally the child's own well-being was emphasised.[17] The Guardianship of Infants Act 1886, indeed, enjoined courts to adopt this as the prime consideration in all matters relating (amongst other things) to the custody or upbringing of an infant.[18] But this was scarcely allowed to produce much variation. Even in 1910 grave severity marked the attitude of the first-instance judge in *Mozley Stark* v. *Mozley Stark*. A husband had divorced his wife and had been awarded custody of his twelve-year-old daughter. Four years later the daughter telegraphed her mother, who had remarried, saying that she was arriving penniless at a certain railway station. For meeting her and taking her home, Bargrave Deane J. declared the mother to be in contempt of court and awarded costs against her present husband. Fortunately the Court of Appeal discharged these orders, declaring that "the matrimonial offence which justified the divorce ought not to be regarded for all time and under all circumstances as sufficient to disentitle the mother to access to her daughter or even to custody."[19] Yet in the inter-war years judges of the Divorce Division were still refusing access to mothers in cases where there was substantial reason for taking a more sympathetic attitude towards their claims.[20]

---

[14] See above, p. 370ff.

[15] Matrimonial Causes Act 1857, s.35.

[16] *Seddon* v. *Seddon and Doyle* (1862) 2 Sw. & Tr. at 640.

[17] See in particular, Lord Cairns in *Symmington* v. *Symmington* (1875) L.R. 2 H.L. (Sc.) 415, who stressed the importance of affording access to both parents where other circumstances allowed.

[18] It was inevitably relevant to divorce proceedings: *Handley* v. *Handley* [1891] P. 124; *Re A and B* [1897] 1 Ch. 786.

[19] [1910] P. 190.

[20] See, *e.g.*, the decisions of Duke J. (later Lord Merivale P.) in *B.* v. *B. and T.* (1921) 37 T.L.R. 868; *B.* v. *B.* [1924] P. 176 (where Duke was reversed by the Court of Appeal).

III. Protecting the Working-class Wife

Violence remained an invariate factor in much family life. Indeed from those who looked for true order in a rigid patriarchy it earned a guarded approval.[21] There would remain in the law, for instance, a certain penchant for the idea that a husband might subject a wife to "reasonable" chastisement and even, if necessary, to restraint.[22] The courts had, of course, to do with the cases of wife-beating, child-beating, and lockings-up which were quite beyond reason. The justices might then use their power to bind the husband to keep the peace, with its threat of fines and imprisonment for disobedience. In 1828 and 1853, they were given added powers to try summary assaults.[23] The most serious attacks could be sent for trial on indictment at quarter sessions or assizes. The wife was, by way of exception to the common law's normal rule, permitted to give evidence against her husband. Even so, it required great courage for most wives to do so, and many proceedings faltered.[24]

When the refined issue of married women's property began to be lobbied in the 1850's the leaders were somewhat non-plussed by the appeals of wives pre-occupied with the simple fact of physical safety.[25] As a matter of public concern, however, wife-battering was perceived as a danger for the working-classes. The will to interfere, which received a political fillip in 1867, was buttressed by a steady flow of scandalous revelations, both about vicious assaults on women and deadly neglect of children. Judges, stirred by old ideas of military discipline, advocated the rugged tit-for-tat of flogging.[26]

In 1878, Lord Penzance, aided by Francis Power Cobbe's telling pamphlet, *The Truth about Wife Torture*, proposed legislation on a different line. To a bill concerned with costs for the Queen's Proctor, he tacked on a clause giving a wife power to obtain from a magistrates' court a separation order, once her husband had been convicted of aggravated assault on her. The court might, moreover, require him to pay her a weekly sum of maintenance.[27] Conceived primarily as a

---

[21] A husband who forced his attentions on his wife would not be guilty of rape: *R. v. Clarence* (1889) 22 Q.B.D. 23 at 51, *per* Hawkins J.—a proposition which, however, was by that period beginning to be modified. Likewise the wife who killed her husband ceased in 1848 to be guilty of *petit treason* and became an ordinary murderess.

[22] Blackstone (*Commentaries*, I 445) suggested that the power of correction had come to be doubted, but that the right to restrain for "gross misbehaviour" remained, an opinion followed in *R. v. Cochrane* (1840) 8 Dowl. 630 (*cf. R. v. Leggatt* (1852) 18 Q.B. 781). When finally it was denied in *R. v. Jackson* (1891) 1 Q.B. 671, there were expressions of astonishment: see, *e.g.*, Lynn Linton (1891) 29 Nineteenth Century 691.

[23] 8 Geo. IV, c. 31, s.27; 16 & 17 Vict., c. 30.

[24] Nonetheless police returns showed a considerable number of convictions: see, *e.g.*, P.P. 1857–58 (107) XLVII 355.

[25] The debates on Fitzroy's Bill of 1853 (above, n. 23) and regular newspaper reports added to the cause; "wife-beating," according to the *Westminster Review*, had become "a new compound noun."

[26] See Reports on the Law Relating to Brutal Assaults, P.P. 1875 [C.1138] LX 15–21; O. R. McGregor *et al.*, *Separated Spouses* (1970) 12ff. For the "baby-farming" scandals, see below, p. 405.

[27] Matrimonial Causes Act 1878.

legal means of helping the wife to secure physical protection, the financial provision in the Act soon began to develop its own function. By an Act of 1886, a husband who wilfully refused or neglected to maintain his wife and children, and deserted her, might be ordered to pay maintenance (of up to £2 per week).[28] By 1895 it was possible to consolidate and broaden these different provisions by allowing orders for separation, custody of children or limited maintenance, which were to be made on a number of grounds: conviction of aggravated assault, desertion, persistent cruelty or wilful neglect to maintain.[29] This was the poor wife's judicial separation, and it applied with an unbending moral rigour; no husband could be obliged to maintain a wife who had already committed adultery or did so subsequently.[30]

The respectable classes who could raise the money and face the social hostilities of a decree of divorce could bring their marriages completely to an end. But, as was well-understood at the time, the mass of people now had a second-class system which could at most condemn them to the "living death" of a separation.[31] Deserted, battered and neglected wives no longer had the poor-law authorities as their only recourse, leaving it to the public system to seek reimbursement from the husband. Instead they might, to a limited extent, act for themselves like their betters. Many of them did so: even in 1893 there were 3,482 applications, which by 1900 had grown to 9,553 and in the period 1910–13 averaged 10,765 a year (about 70 per cent. succeeding against the husband).[32]

Why they chose to go to the magistrates and what they hoped to achieve is more obscure. The question is linked with the variations and confusions in the whole administration of the poor law.[33] Many Boards of Guardians were obsessed with the spectre of improper claims and were ready to suspect that desertions were collusive. Some, accordingly, would refuse relief outside the confines of the workhouse. Others required the wife to secure a maintenance order for herself as a condition of outdoor relief, making the new "private" procedure a mere appendage of the public system. Others again gave outdoor relief and continued the practice of pursuing husbands themselves where possible. In the years 1900–1913, the annual total of applications by them for orders against husbands approached 5,000 (of which about 90 per cent. succeeded).[34]

---

[28] Married Women (Maintenance in Case of Desertion) Act 1886. The £2 limit was to remain until 1949; the possibility of claiming an additional 10s. per week for each child under 16 was added by the Maintenance Orders (Facilities for Enforcement) Act 1920.

[29] Summary Jurisdiction (Married Women) Act 1895. These grounds were somewhat extended in the Licensing Act 1902, the Summary Jurisdiction (Separation and Maintenance) Act 1925 and the Matrimonial Causes Act 1937 (which at last added adultery).

[30] Summary Jurisdiction (Married Women) Act 1895, ss.6, 7. Only condonation would excuse her.

[31] So described to the Gorell Commission (below, n. 47) para. 228, by the divorce judge, Bargrave Deane J.

[32] For full statistics see McGregor et al, (above, n. 26), p. 33.

[33] See below, p. 432ff.

[34] McGregor et al, (above, n. 26), p. 33.

IV. DIVORCE FOR ALL?

By the beginning of the twentieth century, the Victorian compromises on divorce and separation were attracting a new measure of dissatisfaction. Impatient intellectuals ridiculed the bondage that the existing law made of marriages. William Morris imagined an England where marital unions lasted no longer than inclination and the Divorce Court dealt only with matters of property. H. G. Wells attacked the "proprietary" rights of the pater familias, which under socialism would disappear together with other forms of private ownership. Bernard Shaw denounced the "inhuman and unreasonable" marriage law as a stimulus to "anarchical experiments."[35] At a deeper level the psychology of Havelock Ellis and Freud presaged a new scientific attempt to understand sexual relations and their bearing on marital discord.[36]

Meanwhile the second Earl Russell[37] was convicted of bigamy after obtaining a Nevada divorce and remarrying.[38] Thereafter he took up the cause of radical reform, advocating not only divorce after three years' separation but also divorce after only one year's separation if both parties agreed. His bill of 1902 proposing this latter ground was intended, said the outraged Lord Halsbury, "for the abolition of the institution of marriage."[39]

If these were unacceptable extremes, others were prepared to seek less radical changes. In 1892 a Scots back-bencher, W.A. Hunter, secured a second-reading debate on the desirability of extending the grounds of divorce in England to those available in Scotland: adultery alone in the case of husband as well as wife, and desertion for four years.[40] His bill was defeated, but unorthodox opinion on the matter could not be stifled. In 1906 a Divorce Law Reform Union was set up, with members who included Sir Arthur Conan Doyle, Gilbert Murray and F. E. Smith.[41]

In that year also, Gorell Barnes J. found the magistrates' jurisdiction, as re-formulated in the Summary Jurisdication (Married Women) Act 1895, to pose a serious impediment in the working of the divorce laws. In *Dodd* v. *Dodd*,[42] he held that a wife who secured a

---

[35] Morris, *News from Nowhere* (1890), Wells, *Socialism and the Family* (1906), Shaw, *Getting Married* (1908).

[36] The first volume of Ellis' *Studies in the Psychology of Sex* appeared in 1897, Freud's *Interpretation of Dreams* in 1900.

[37] For his first matrimonial difficulties, see above, n. 91.

[38] [1901] A.C. 446. The question of when English courts should recognise foreign divorces, which lay behind this prosecution, was becoming more difficult with the introduction of "easy" divorce in certain jurisdictions. In 1895, the Privy Council held that divorce could be granted only in the jurisdiction where the husband (and therefore the wife) was domiciled, in the strict sense of that term: *Le Mesurier* v. *Le Mesurier* [1895] A.C. 517.

[39] P.D. 1902 CVII 408. Russell tried again in 1903 and 1908, as did Horatio Bottomley in the latter year, without any real hope of success.

[40] P.D. 1892 LII 1437–49.

[41] See E.S.P. Haynes, *Divorce Problems of Today* (1910); for a comparison with France, G. L. Savage (1982) 16 J. Soc. Hist. 103.

[42] [1906] P. 189.

separation order from the magistrates thereby brought to an end any desertion by her husband that would otherwise accumulate (if the husband was also adulterous) towards a divorce. Barnes' judgment set out deliberately to emphasise all the "inconsistencies, anomalies, and inequalities almost amounting to absurdities," in the current law of divorce and separation—a judicial impetus for reform which has few modern parallels.[43]

In 1908, as chairman of a Committee to examine the distribution of business between High Court and County Courts, Gorell Barnes ensured a recommendation that selected County Courts should be given a divorce jurisdiction, where the petitioner's assets did not exceed £50 and the joint income of the spouses did not exceed £150. This put in issue the exclusive right of audience of the Bar. In the Committee's view the seriousness of divorce and the need to ferret out collusion, required the exclusion of solicitors as advocates in the proposed County Court proceedings.[44] But this special compromise was needed because there was "a practical denial of justice [to] people who belong to ranks in life in which the relief obtained under the Divorce Acts is probably more necessary than in ranks above them."[45] Barnes (ennobled as Lord Gorell) proceeded to raise these proposals in the Lords. The government replied by instituting a Royal Commission on Divorce, and he was appointed chairman of it.

The Gorell Commission's Report in 1912 was "of remarkable clarity and intellectual distinction."[46] The voluminous evidence made plain how directly the Commission's writ went to the role of the state in the maintenance of family morality. As the Majority Report of the Commission set out with admirable objectivity, most of community derived its beliefs about divorce from the teaching of the different Christian churches; and these had long given rise to keen disputation, as well as to important legal variations between different parts of the kingdom. There was indeed support for the propositions that either all marriages or all Christian marriages were indissoluble; or that marriages were dissoluble for adultery alone, for adultery and desertion, or for these and other serious grounds based upon the necessities of human life.[47] But there was also a great deal of utilitarian evidence. The Women's Cooperative Guild[48] attacked anomalies and hardships in the law by reference to individual cases: thousands of women were said to endure bad marriages because they had no reliable means of securing maintenance for themselves and their

---

[43] Subsequently endorsed by the Court of Appeal: *Harriman* v. *Harriman* [1909] P. 123.
[44] See the Report of the Committee on County Court Procedure, P.P. 1909 (71) LXXII.
[45] *Ibid.*, p. 23.
[46] McGregor (1957), p. 26.
[47] Report of the Royal Commission on Divorce and Matrimonial Causes, P.P. 1912–13 [Cd. 6478] XVIII, para. 40, where summaries of individual evidence are set out.
[48] The Guild, an off-shoot of the co-operative movement, had nearly 25,000 members. Its views were singled out for attack by the Minority, which accused members of the Majority of undervaluing evidence of that other large organisation of women, the Mothers Union (see pp. 171–177). The latter, a powerful organisation, operating largely under the auspices of the established church, had as its primary object "to uphold the sanctity of marriage" and had been a vociferous opponent of extensions to the divorce laws: see W. O. Chadwick, *The Victorian Church* (1970), II pp. 192–193.

children if they left their husbands. Accordingly the Guild supported a radical extension of divorce to include the grounds of persistent refusal to maintain, mutual consent and incompatability.[49]

The Commission itself contained no member who sought to advocate the elimination of divorce and there was agreement that there should be some extension of the grounds on which a marriage could be annulled.[50] But on the central issue there was division. The majority took the temperate position that "the State must deal with all its citizens, whether Christian, nominally Christian, or non-Christian" and accordingly proceeded "to recommend the legislature to act upon an unfettered consideration of what is best for the interest of the state, society, and morality, and for that of the parties to suits and their families." In their view, the grounds for divorce should be moderately extended to include desertion for more than three years, cruelty, insanity, incurable drunkenness, and imprisonment under commuted death sentence.[51]

The Commission had among its members three who espoused the view of the upper ranks of the Anglican church and so dissented.[52] Divorce, if not totally avoidable, was highly undesirable. If it were allowed to spread amongst the lower orders there would be a disintegration of family life such as was said to characterise France, the United States and Japan. This minority opposed any extension of the grounds for divorce and proposed some restrictions. They would concede only that very few local courts ought to have divorce jurisdiction and that the "wholesale facilities" proposed by the Majority would be "likely to have a gravely unsettling influence on large classes of the people who would otherwise never contemplate, and who ought not to contemplate, divorce."[53]

On its appearance, the Majority report excited considerable hostility among the influential.[54] The faltering Liberal government could afford to do nothing and the cause of reform suffered a substantial set-back by the death of Lord Gorell in 1913.[55] However in 1914, the limits on aid under the Poor Persons Procedure were increased so as to encompass anyone with capital of less than £100.[56]

The war provided a respite in the twin campaigns of the reformers for more accessible divorce courts, and for broader grounds of relief. But war on such a scale brought great upheaval to family ties and put

[49] The Guild also wanted the doctrine of recrimination to end (see above, p. 388), custody of children to be governed by their best interests, and proceedings to be in County Courts in camera.

[50] So also on the presumption of death: Report (above n. 47), paras. 350–364.

[51] Ibid., paras. 50, 236–329.

[52] Cosmo Lang, Archbishop of York; Sir William Anson, law don and staunch conservative; and Sir Lewis Dibdin, Dean of Arches.

[53] Report, pp. 189–190.

[54] The Times, for instance, printed the Minority Report in full.

[55] His son promoted a Bill covering the minor, non-controversial recommendations of the Commission, but even this made no progress.

[56] Poor Persons Rules 1913–1914, confirmed by the Administration of Justice Act 1920, with the addition of an earnings limit of £4 a week. The aid was administered by a Department of the Supreme Court, but suffered from a lack of volunteer barristers and solicitors: Gibson (1970), pp. 92–93.

very considerable pressure upon such legal provision as there was for legitimating changes of partner.[57] Indeed, it was the sheer problem of access to courts that seemed the greater difficulty in the years immediately after the war. One or other of the pre-war plans to make divorces available in assize or in county courts, or else further to extend the poor person's procedure, had to be conceded. The professional organizations argued for solutions that would be to their own advantage. In 1920, Lord Birkenhead promoted a successful bill to give effect to the compromise formula accepted by the Gorell Commission. Divorce would be available at a limited number of assize towns (ten were scheduled in 1922).[58] The preliminary stages, however, continued to be handled by the London registry, to the advantage of metropolitan solicitors. This scarcely eliminated the need for poor persons' assistance and the existing scheme was distended grossly by applicants for divorce. The Law Society, disturbed already by the Poor Persons Department of the Supreme Court,[59] persuaded a Committee under Lawrence J. that it should organise a revised scheme of voluntary aid.[60] In return, it sought county court divorce but secured only an increase in the assize towns for hearing poor persons' divorces.[61] The effort that maintaining this scheme cost the solicitors was intense and detracted from other legal services to the poor, such as advice and criminal legal aid. But in this one field, where access to civil courts was vital to secure a financially viable change of matrimonial relationships, the system was at last made somewhat more open.

As the first world war came to a close, the Divorce Law Reform Union began once more to press the views of the Gorell Majority, finding a Parliamentary champion in Lord Buckmaster. From 1918 on he presented a series of bills which more or less completely adopted the Majority solution. But on each occasion he had to meet the total opposition of Catholic spokesmen, antagonism from the Anglican bishops, who were at least agreed that there should be no move beyond the Minority compromise, and the hostility of such well-supported organisations as the Marriage Defence League, whose President, the Duke of Northumberland, at one point remarked "To get rid of Christianity between tea and dinner on an afternoon in the spring is no light matter."[62] Governments refused to supply Commons time and so killed each bill.

By 1923, the persistent Buckmaster was reduced to introducing a single-clause bill allowing wives, like husbands, to divorce for adul-

---

[57] Rowntree and Carrier (1958), p. 205, estimate that the 90 per cent. increase in the divorce rate between 1913 and 1922 was due to the war and the improved Poor Persons' Procedure in roughly equal proportions.

[58] For details, see Abel Smith and Stevens (1967), pp. 142–148; Gibson (1970), pp. 93–95.

[59] See above, p. 104.

[60] But with administrative expenses met by the Treasury: Report of the Poor Persons' Rules Committee P.P. 1924–1925 [Cmd. 2358] XV.

[61] Supreme Court (Poor Persons) Order 1925. District registries for divorce were also established.

[62] P.D. (Lords) 1920 XXXIX 860. But in 1921 the League disgraced itself by issuing demonstrably false propaganda.

tery alone.[63] So, in an age which was doing a good deal formally to give women equality with men, there passed away the notion of the husband's "accidental adultery" and with it the most egregious application of the double standard. Buckmaster's friends feared that the good would indeed be the enemy of the best, and so it proved.[64] He tried once more to secure a wider bill but without success. The only other achievement of reformers in the period was the severe curtailment of press reports of divorce hearings,[65] thus suppressing chronicles which Queen Victoria, for one, had supposed to be more "pernicious to the public morals of the country" than "the worst French novels."[66]

In the thirties, informed opinion was affected to some extent by historical and sociological studies which suggested that the Victorian divorce law had no claim to unalterable validity.[67] But here again a single, deft publicist did more than anyone to procure legal change. A. P. Herbert not only wrote a series of *Misleading Cases* and a novel, *Holy Deadlock*, to demonstrate the duplicity provoked by the law, under which so many consensual divorces were arranged by proof of "hotel adultery"[68]; he also steered through an Act which he introduced as a novice, non-party member of parliament, and which embodied most of the proposals of the Gorell Commission majority, twenty-five years after their publication.[69]

In consequence, divorce became available on three main grounds: adultery, three years' desertion and cruelty.[70] The number of divorces at once rose sharply. But before time could elapse which would have shown how far the Act's effect was only temporary, another war intervened. The demand for the dissolution of marriages accelerated far more rapidly than ever before, prejudicing "the morale of the fighting Forces, which was severely affected, as was that of civilians by anxiety over their personal affairs."[71] The armed services were obliged to set up their own legal aid scheme for divorce, which was run for them by Law Society staff, thanks to a Treasury grant. Aid

---

[63] Matrimonial Causes Act 1923. The old order kept its sentimental defenders: witness Sir Henry Craik, member for the Scottish Universities:"Chastity in women is a star that has guided human nature since the world began, and that points far higher and teaches us of the other sex things which we could not otherwise know . . . But I do not think that any mere man would thank us for enshrining him in such a halo." (P.D. 1923 CLX 2374). And opponents secured an amendment which prevented past adulteries from counting. On this period, see Stenton (1982) Chap. 3.

[64] The Act appears to have increased the rate of divorce by 20–25 per cent.: Rowntree and Carrier (1958), pp. 225–308.

[65] Judicial Proceedings (Regulation of Reports) Act 1925. In 1913 the House of Lords had preferred the interests of the public to the feelings of the parties in holding that there was no inherent power to order that divorce proceedings be heard *in camera*; *Scott* v. *Scott* [1913] A.C. 417.

[66] *Letters*, III p. 482.

[67] *e.g.* R. S. Briffault, *The Mothers* (1927).

[68] Evidence from a maid or someone else that she had discovered the lovers abed was necessary because of the requirement, running back to the practice of the ecclesiastical courts, of corroboration.

[69] Matrimonial Causes Act 1937.

[70] *Ibid.*, s.2; the other grounds were incurable insanity (new), bestiality and sodomy (old). The grounds of nullity were extended to include wilful refusal to consummate the marriage (s.7), though it was rarely relied upon.

[71] R. Egerton, *Legal Aid* (1945), p. 18.

was afforded to many outside the poor persons' procedure and it would have been extremely difficult to go back to former parsimony once peace was restored. Instead, as the Rushcliffe report presaged,[72] the positions which both the Bar and the solicitors had done so much to cement during the inter-war period would be enhanced. Having won its right to administer a voluntary scheme, mainly for divorce, the Law Society would now, through its central office and local committees, run a Government-funded scheme in which professional legal aid (and advice) would be paid for at something approaching private rates.[73] The Bar, as well as sharing in this new opportunity, would retain its exclusive right of audience in divorce matters since retaining the jurisdiction would remain in the High Court. To provide the judicial manpower, special commissioners would be brought in, most of them county court judges changing gowns for the day.[74]

Divorce was in demand as never before, partly because formal marriage itself had become more popular. Couples married younger as they acquired greater independence. At the same time an increasing life expectancy added to the prospect of a marriage lasting beyond the growing up of the children. The professions were able to maintain their positions in divorce administration partly because of a wider determination to conserve the dam against flood.[75] Thus the Archbishop of Canterbury would join the President of the Probate Divorce and Admiralty Division in insisting that due High Court solemnity must continue to surround the process of accusation and award, and that only the professional rectitude of the Bar could withstand a deluge of trumped-up cases.[76] It was a powerful resistance that was to hold through the 1950s.[77] It would put off until 1970 the decisive shifts that are embodied in the relatively open divorce law of the present.

V. MARRIED WOMEN'S PROPERTY

Despite the imaginative deviations of eighteenth-century equity, the presumptive rules governing a married woman's property remained those of the common law: the husband acquired ownership or effective control of it, at the same time assuming both rights and responsibilities in contract and tort on her behalf.[78] Eve, the rib of Adam, was an image that suited the swelling patriarchy, whether in the world of the propertied great (whose position allowed them the special advantages of equity) or in the middling ranks (whose

---

[72] See above, p. 104.
[73] On the evolution of the Legal Aid and Advice Act 1949, see R. Egerton, (above, n. 71) Chaps. 3, 15; Abel-Smith and Stevens (1967) Chap. 12.
[74] The Denning Committee at this juncture proposed some moderate stream-lining of divorce procedure, P.P. 1945–46 [Cmd. 6881, 6945] XIII.
[75] Even as it was, the post-war peak was 48,501 petitions in 1947 and this would settle to a figure of just under 30,000 a year in the early 50s. The bumper year of 1938 had produced only 10,233: Rowntree and Carrier (1957), pp. 201–202.
[76] Abel-Smith and Stevens (1967), pp. 323–25.
[77] Fortified by the Report of the Morton Royal Commission of 1956 [Cmnd. 9678]; for which see esp. McGregor (1957), Chaps. 5, 6.
[78] Above, p. 367ff.

modest wealth might preclude any aspiration of marrying by settlement). It was a vision in comfortable harmony with the wider idealisation of woman in her separate sphere: pure, ladylike, adorable—and in consequence unfitted to the affairs of the world, the management of wealth or the life of the mind.[79] Yet with a Queen once more on the throne—and married—a very different vision of female abilities and roles was beginning to surface. In radical and literary circles, the possibilities of marriage as a partnership, education in the universities, entry into closed professions were all explored. Tennyson's *The Princess* (1847) dignified the cause by its fervent rhetoric.[80]

By 1854, Barbara Leigh-Smith could take the reform of married women's property law as the representative issue on which to stage a first political fight. Her own sympathies were drawn to the subject by a vitriolic encounter between Caroline Norton and her husband in the Westminster County Court (over his liability to pay for repairs to her coach).[81] With an active committee and some famous support she organised a widespread campaign in 1855, which drew the attention among others of the Law Amendment Society.[82] This connection would provide Parliamentary advocacy from Brougham, Sir Erskine Perry and Matthew Davenport Hill.

When Perry introduced a Commons motion on the subject in 1856, he provoked an outraged astonishment: "If a woman had not full confidence in a man" pronounced Malins Q.C., "let her refrain from marrying him."[83] But next year, just as the government's Matrimonial Causes Bill was making its way, Perry introduced a Bill which did pass its second reading.[84] It sought to declare a married woman capable of "holding, acquiring, alienating, devising and bequeathing Real and Personal Estate and of suing and being sued as if she were a Feme Sole."[85]

Opponents were ready to suggest the "discomfort and dissension" in families that would follow, the general improvidence of women, their likely tendency to favour one child at the expense of another. Lord St. Leonards blew cold upon a scheme that would "give a wife all the distinct rights of citizenship." But it was he who proposed a compromise, in the form of an amendment to the Matrimonial Causes Bill, to meet the most telling complaint on the score of married women's property. As this finally emerged, a deserted wife was entitled to apply to the Divorce Court, a Justice of the Peace or a Police Magistrate (each according to her station) for an order to pro-

---

[79] For "the Perfect Wife" and the accompanying "spread of gentility" see J. A. and O. Banks, *Feminism and Family Planning* (1964) Chaps. 5, 6; N. St. John-Stevas in Graveson and Crane (1957), pp. 257–259.

[80] But it still received the guy direct in Gilbert's *Princess Ida* (1884).

[81] See *The Times*, August 19, 20, 1853; Mrs. Norton, *English Laws for Women* (1854) and *A Letter to the Queen on Lord Cranworth's Marriage and Divorce Bill* (1855); Barbara Leigh-Smith (later Bodichon), *The Most Important Laws concerning Women* (1854); Stenton (1982) Chap. 1; Holcombe (1983), pp. 50–58.

[82] But see above, p. 391.

[83] P.D. 1856 CXLII 1278.

[84] It was preceded by one introduced by Brougham.

[85] For the debates, see E. S. Turner, *Roads to Ruin* (1966) Chap. 6; V. Ullrich (1977) V.U. of Wellington L.R. 13; Holcombe (1983) Chap. 5.

tect her earnings and property from seizure by her husband. Only on proof of definite matrimonial breakdown through the husband's fault was there to be any departure from the patriarchal norm inherent in the common law rules.[86]

However, the band of clever, independent women who could not accept for themselves the self-effacing routine of middle-class family life, refused to treat this as the end.[87] Their case for Parliamentary franchise was put by J. S. Mill in the Reform Bill Debates of 1867 and, though it did not succeed, the borough franchise went to female householders in 1869.[88] A new Married Women's Property Bill, introduced by Shaw-Lefevre in the previous session, was referred to a Select Committee which, in the changed political atmosphere, heard a great deal about working-class conditions. On the one hand, there were the lazy, drunken and dissolute husbands who were said to live on the earnings of their wives, and yet had well-nigh absolute power to drive them from house and home. On the other, the Rochdale Equitable Pioneer Co-operative Society, doyen of the great distribution co-operatives, said that it always treated a wife's account as separate and would not allow her husband to draw on it without her consent. In the Committee's view, this practice had to be treated as of "doubtful legality"; but, if so, the law was in need of amendment, for disaster would strike the town if the wives' savings were open to predation by their husbands.[89]

Nothing was achieved until the session of 1870, when a similar bill was introduced by Russell Gurney, Recorder of London.[90] It was emasculated during its passage by Lords' amendments, but did in a fashion reach the statute book.[91] It did not adopt the simple principle of treating a married woman as if unmarried; instead certain of her property would be treated as if settled to her separate use within the technical meaning of equity: earnings, personal property and income from real property coming to her on an intestacy, legacies up to £200, and, if she so requested, certain investments.[92] This limited and notional expansion of separate property in equity was a conservative ploy to concede only a minimum of ground. Possibly as a counterweight, a husband was no longer to be liable for his wife's antenuptial debts, her own separate property becoming the only source from which satisfaction might be secured. But in the absence of a settlement, much of the wife's property on marriage still passed to her husband. On the anguished plea of traders that women had only to marry in order in effect to cancel their debts, the new law was

---

[86] 20 & 21 Vict., c. 85, s.25–26; M. L. Shanley (1982) 25 Vict. St. 355.
[87] Holcombe (1983) Chap. 6.
[88] Above, p. 17.
[89] Report, P.P. 1867–68 (441) VII; Holcombe (1983) Chap. 7.
[90] He had introduced a similar bill in the previous year.
[91] In the end it went little further than the truly conservative counter-Bill, promoted by Henry Raikes. See generally, Ullrich (above, n. 85); Holcombe (1983) Chap. 8; and for the comforting elements of legal continuity in the Act of 1870, Dicey (1914), pp. 371–398.
[92] Married Women's Property Act 1870, ss.1–8. By s.9 (now s.17 of the 1882 Act) was created the summary procedure for matrimonial disputes over property, that had been included in Sir Erskine Perry's Bill of 1857 (see n. 84 above).

amended to make the husband liable for pre-nuptial debts to the extent that he received her property.[93] The reformers' campaign, with its Millian call for personal individuation, epitomised the potentialities of late Victorian radicalism. On Gladstone's next return to office, the lobby, with a quarter-century's experience, achieved its decisive thrust.[94] In 1882, a married woman was given complete power to acquire and dispose of all kinds of property "as if she were a *feme sole* without the intervention of any trustee."[95] At the same time express settlements continued to have their old effects and restraints on alienation could still put in trustees of the wife's family as protectors. The Act failed to treat married women as wholly independent persons.[96]

The Act bound a married woman to a contract entered into by her "in respect of and to the extent of, her separate property," including property acquired after the contract was made. The courts refused to treat her as liable, for instance, to imprisonment for wilfully failing to pay a debt under £50[97]; and insisted that she have sufficient separate property at the contract date to show that she did intend to enter the particular contract with reference to it. So complex a requirement could render the enforceability of married women's contracts a thing of chance. Again at the behest of traders, Parliament intervened in 1893 to remove these refinements.[98]

In tort, the Act relieved the husband of liability for his wife's antenuptial wrongs but was less explicit concerning her torts after marriage. The judges struggled to decide whether her separate property placed tort liability exclusively on the wife's shoulders, whether the separate property made her primarily, and the husband secondarily, liable, or whether the old responsibility of the husband survived. In the end the House of Lords, by a bare majority, held fast to this last solution.[99] Only in 1935, following the recommendation of the newly-formed Law Revision Committee, did a wife acquire complete individuality in matters of contract and tort.[1]

Even this Act left untouched one practical consequence of the old fictional amalgamation of husband and wife: that one could not sue

---

[93] Married Women's Property Act (1870) Amendment Act 1874; Holcombe (1983), pp. 156–191; Stetson (1982) Chap. 3.

[94] Holcombe (1983), pp. 195–205.

[95] Married Women's Property Act 1882, s.1.

[96] While the wife could now leave her property by will, the position on her intestacy was not altered: see R. Crane in Graveson and Crane (1957), pp. 245–248.

[97] *Scott* v. *Morley* (1887) 20 Q.B.D. 120; Dicey, (1914), pp. 392–393.

[98] Married Women's Property Act 1893. Once the wife acquired some capacity to purchase, she might buy the household assets from her husband, and the courts held that such a transaction did not require the receipt for the purchase money to be registered as a bill of sale, despite the fact that creditors would commonly think that the goods remained the husband's: *Ramsay* v. *Margrett* [1894] 2 Q.B. 18; *French* v. *Gething* [1922] 1 K.B. 236. A gift, however, would not serve this purpose, unless there was "delivery": 1882 Act, s.10; *Cochrane* v. *Moore* (1890) 15 Q.B.D. 57. Executory agreements between husband and wife would not be enforceable if they were "not intended to create legal relations": *Balfour* v. *Balfour* [1919] 2 K.B. 571.

[99] *Edwards* v. *Porter* [1925] A.C. 1.

[1] Law Reform (Married Women and Tortfeasors) Act 1935. The wife's powers, in the interests of the household, to pledge her husband's credit (above, p. 370) continued unchanged (until 1970).

the other in tort. The artificiality that this might produce became more apparent with the advent of the family car and its propensity to injure. The judges adhered to the rule that a wife could not sue her negligent husband, even though he would normally be indemnified against any liability by his insurers.[2] To some extent, insurance policies were revised to take account of this legal hiatus; but the principle itself would not be altered until 1962.

The campaign to secure independent private rights for married women stood surrogate for the claim of all women to political, professional and educational rights. As property ownership was fragmented within the family it ceased to be so evident that the head of household should be the sole bearer of the franchise; indeed as property lost its paternal attribution, its entire abandonment as a necessary condition for the Parliamentary vote was presaged. 1918 would bring votes, not just for women, but for adult men still at home and for lodgers. But the concession of separate private rights to married women, as with the admission of women to universities and professions, was a victory more symbolic than real. The wife who remained at home and depended on her husband for the family's upkeep, or whose own earnings were absorbed into the cost of day-to-day living, would have nothing that she could call her own. Even her savings out of housekeeping provided by the husband in law belonged to him. The separation achieved by the Married Women's Property legislation was a crude device for an institution that, so long as it survived, was inherently communal. If the main assets of the household were clearly placed in joint ownership, then the wife might look forward to her equal share upon a parting or her husband's death. In the growing desire for home ownership, associated between the wars with the advance of the building societies, the practice of conveying the house into their joint names became regular. In less clear circumstances, the wife might have the help of a court under the Married Women's Property Act 1882, s.17. But if the property remained the husband's, her only protection against his whim, his dislike or his revenge came in 1938: if he used his will to cut her out of any share in his estate on his death, the courts were given power to override his freedom of testation.[1a]

VI. CHILDREN: PRIVATE RIGHTS

Determining the custody of children upon a divorce or judicial separation was not the only occasion upon which parents might seek the aid of courts of law over the custody, education or religion of their children, or access to them. Conflicts might arise between couples who were living apart, or who had religious differences incapable of compromise. Equally there were conflicts between a parent and other relatives, and between persons neither of whom were parents. In such tussles one or other parent might be clearly in the wrong, or neither might be definitely to blame. In the general jurisdiction of Chancery as *parens patriae* the conflict was rarely between wrongdoer

---

[1a] Above, p. 179.

[2] The rule was even extended to the case where the pair married only after the accident: *Gottliffe* v. *Edelston* [1930] 2 K.B. 138.

and victim, as was the assumption in divorce. As we have seen, the views of the father were to prevail unless there were the strongest reasons for displacing them.[3] Here also the law was gradually changed so as to give more importance to the likely happiness of the child in future. As so often this utilitarian aim was borne in upon an *a priori* claim: that the wife should be treated as having a right to custody equal to that of her husband. To the campaigners for women's rights, and to liberals generally, there seemed nothing untoward in this argument. The judges, however, showed little inclination to vary their established position on the matter.[4] Accordingly a series of statutes attempted to induce the change. Lord Penzance took charge of a bill in 1873 which broadened Talfourd's Act of 1839 by allowing a court to award the mother custody of, or access to, any child under sixteen.[5]

In 1886, another Act stated that orders of custody and access were to be determined by "having regard to the welfare of the infant and to the conduct of the parents and to the wishes as well of the mother as of the father." The wife was also given certain limited and provisional powers to appoint a testamentary guardian on her death.[6] The Act, directed towards conflicts between spouses rather than with strangers, produced a somewhat uncertain weakening of the earlier robust preference shown by the courts for the father's wishes.[7]

It was not, however, until 1925 that, in all proceedings involving custody or upbringing, or in administering trust property for an infant, the court was obliged to treat "as the first and paramount consideration" the welfare of the child; and the father's claim was not to be regarded as superior to the mother's. Each parent was to have an equal right in the appointment of testamentary guardians and in consenting to the marriage of an infant.[8] Yet even so, there were ways in which judges could express a preference for the "innocent" spouse and for parents against non-parents. Since the rule, said Eve J., "does not state that the welfare of the infant is to be the sole consideration but the paramount consideration, it necessarily contemplates the existence of other conditions, and amongst these the

---

[3] Above, p. 370ff. But the acknowledgment that the benefit to the child should be considered made the rule of equity at least in form less strict than at common law. In the resolution of conflicting rules under the Judicature Act 1873 (s.25(10)), it was expressly provided that equity's principle should prevail: see, *e.g. Thomasset* v. *Thomasset* [1894] P. 295, 300.

[4] See, *e.g. Re Agar-Ellis* (1883) 24 Ch.D. 317, described by Lord Upjohn as a "dreadful" case, "where the Court of Appeal permitted a monstrously unreasonable father to impose on his daughter of 17 much unnecessary hardship in the name of his religious faith" (see [1969] 1 All E.R. at 829).

[5] Custody of Infants Act 1873. The wife's adultery ceased to be an automatic bar to entitlement. The Act also overrode equity's former refusal to treat as binding a husband's undertaking in a separation deed to surrender custody of children to his wife. But the courts were left with an ultimate discretion, as that radical in sexual matters, Mrs. Annie Besant, found to her cost: *Re Besant* (1878) 11 Ch.D. 508.

[6] Guardianship of Infants Act 1886.

[7] *cf., e.g., Re McGrath (Infants)* [1895] 1 Ch. 43; *Re A. and B. (Infants)* [1897] 1 Ch. 786; *R. v. New* (1904) 20 T.L.R. 583.

[8] Guardianship of Infants Act 1925. The Act also extended jurisdiction in guardianship to magistrates' courts.

wishes of an unimpeachable parent undoubtedly stand first."[9] That
there were still judges prepared to use such ideas to subvert the principle of the infant's welfare, however "paramount," was demonstrated by a majority of the Court of Appeal (overruling two courts
below) in Re Carroll (No. 2). The court refused to consider anything
but the wishes of an unmarried mother who wanted her child placed
in a Catholic institution; accordingly the child was removed from a
Protestant couple who wished to adopt it. The only exception,
according to Scrutton L.J., arose where "the mother is of so bad a
character that her wishes as to religion and education may be disregarded."[10]

In conflicts between parents, to abandon any presumption in
favour of the father was to ask the courts to show a Solomonic wisdom. With time, presumptions drawing on the current nostrums of
child psychology began to ease the task of decision. In particular,
upon divorce, the custody of young girls would normally be given to
the mother and older boys to the father. These practices even came
for a time to be regarded as "principles." But so long as divorce
turned upon accusation, courts would find it hard not to show some
preference for the "injured" parent.

VII. CHILDREN: THE UNDERPRIVILEGED

The history of communal help for poor and deprived children is a
drab, slow-moving tale. From the late eighteenth century, the propertied had come to recognise that juvenile delinquency posed its
special threat to the condition of the towns. By mid-nineteenth century, experimentation in the treatment of criminal adolescents could
be fashioned into a system of reformatories for the convicted and
industrial schools for the refractory. Once the poor law began to be
institutionalised with the spread of workhouses, the guardians of the
poor were likewise obliged to face the problems of bringing up their
young charges with rather more attention than a rapid despatch into
some murky corner of the labour market.[11] After 1870, the schooling
of pauper children became part of a larger responsibility, as governments promoted a modicum of education for all.[12]

The dangers for children in the lowest social strata were constant.
They were born to mothers who knew nothing of contraception and
little enough of abortion, an ignorance which their betters thought it
right to conserve. Many died at birth or within their earliest weeks of
natural causes. But, while the extent is immeasurable, it is clear that
many pregnancies were kept secret so that the babies could be killed
or allowed to die through neglect. Shame and economic necessity

---

[9] [1926] Ch. 676 at 684.
[10] [1931] 1 K.B. 317 at 335.
[11] See above, pp. 301–302 and below pp. 430, 585–587.
[12] See esp. the Report of the Departmental Committee (chaired by A. J. Mundella) on
the Maintenance and Education of Pauper Children in the Metropolis, P.P. 1896 [C.
8027] XLIII.

drove many to such a course—but particularly unmarried mothers—and the criminal law in practice provided only perfunctory redress.[13]

If there was a little money, a child might be dealt with by leaving it with a "baby-farmer." In some instances, the "farmer" acted as agent in finding the baby a new home in a world that knew no system of legal adoption. But it appears from the chilling evidence given to the official inquiry of 1871 that most of these children met an early death through abandonment, neglect, underfeeding, lack of natural milk and opiates. It was estimated that between 70 and 90 per cent. of "farmed" children in the big towns died, as compared with a national death rate among children of about 16 per cent. But any statistical assessment was a guess since "nobody except the owners of these houses knows anything more about them; their births are not registered, nor are their deaths; some are buried as stillborn children, some are secretly disposed of, many are dropped about the streets."[14] The inquiry was stimulated by cases such as the conviction and hanging of Margaret Waters for the murder of five children that she allowed to waste to death. The Committee considered that the largest number of cases where there was criminal disregard for children's lives occurred in the Metropolis and some of the larger Scottish towns; in Yorkshire and Lancashire "carelessness, and not crime" was the principal cause of mortality.[15]

Even in 1872, when faced with scandal, Parliament did no more than require persons receiving children for reward, if any were under seven, to register and secure a licence.[16] The provision seems to have been largely ineffective, the registered "farmers" simply passing their charges on to the unregistered and untraceable. Tales of horror still burst forth from time to time. It was not until 1897 that local authorities were obliged either to appoint inspectors of baby-farms or to make use of voluntary women visitors.[17] Further convictions of baby-farmers, some for murder, were in part responsible for the provisions of the Liberals' Children Act 1908, the so-called "Children's Charter."[18]

The main attempt to help neglected and maltreated children came through voluntary effort, partly by uncovering and preventing cruelty, and partly by setting up orphanages and other homes, in parallel with the reformatories and industrial schools and the poor law institutions, where positive programmes of rehabilitation and education could be pursued in relatively "uncontaminated" surroundings. In 1884, the aged Lord Shaftesbury presided over the inaugural meeting of the London Society for the Prevention of Cruelty to Children, which five years later could be converted into the present National Society (NSPCC). In 1889, the Society con-

---

[13] There were some 40 prosecutions each year for concealing births in the years 1834–37: see Criminal Tables, P.P. 1838 [115] XLIII p. 116.

[14] Select Committee on the Protection of Infant Life, P.P. 1871 (372) VII, p. iv.

[15] *Ibid.*, p. iii.

[16] Infant Life Preservation Act 1872. The practice of insuring the lives of such children was restricted by the Friendly Societies Act 1875, s.28.

[17] Infant Life Protection Act 1897.

[18] For information about ill-treatment, see the Report of the Select Committee on Infant Life Protection, P.P. 1908 (99) IX; esp. the evidence of R. J. Parr, Director of the NSPCC, Q. 184 ff.

vinced Parliament that their kind of work could only be carried on with much broader powers of intervention. An Act of the same year made it an offence wilfully to ill-treat, neglect, abandon or expose a child in a manner likely to cause it suffering or injury to health. Constables were given powers to arrest people charged with these offences and magistrates could place their child victims with a "fit person" (if possible of the same religious persuasion). To a limited extent also, the use of children in a variety of employments was forbidden.[19]

Even earlier than this Dr. Barnardo had opened his first Home, also with Shaftesbury's support, and he had proceeded to build up a network of institutions designed to equip rescued children with the training to lead a successful adult life, in England or abroad. One problem for all organisations which took over the upbringing of children was that, when they came of economic age, neglectful parents might suddenly wish to reclaim them. There had been at least token modification of the old preferences of the private law system to give custody to the father of legitimate children and of illegitimate children to the mother. But children's homes could still find it extremely difficult to fight off such parents. Barnardo tried to have them sign away their rights at the outset (an arrangement without legal effect); and if this did not work he sometimes met them with open or surreptitious defiance. His skirmishes moreover were not without inter-denominational bigotry: as a Protestant Irishman he did not care to surrender his charges into the arms of a Catholic church, which in his view did precious little to rescue neglected children. In consequence, on two much publicised occasions, he was ordered in habeas corpus proceedings to return a child to its mother.[20]

His defiance of the law extracted a measure of admiration even from some of the judges who ruled against him. The affairs were a significant illustration of the potential of a court-room to air scandal and so change public attitudes. The Custody of Children Act 1891 was passed to give Barnardo the kind of protection that he had already claimed. Courts were empowered to refuse custody to a parent who had abandoned or deserted a child, or had "otherwise so conducted himself that the court should refuse"; and a parent who had allowed the child to be brought up by another person at that other's expense, "for such length of time and under such circumstances as to satisfy the court that the parent was unmindful of his parental duties", might not secure custody unless the court was satisfied of his fitness. The law thus allowed not only private institutions and poor law guardians, but also foster-parents and "adopters," some chance of keeping children away from the least desirable parents.

It was not until the mid-1920s that the modern law of adoption would establish its first roots. It did so as part of the realignment of property law that ended the special status of the old landed order. After a half-century of resistance, primogeniture—the great banner—

---

[19] Prevention of Cruelty to, and Better Protection of, Children Act 1889.
[20] See *R.* v. *Barnardo* (1889) 24 Q.B.D. 283; *Barnardo* v. *McHugh* [1891] A.C. 388; J. W. Bready, *Doctor Barnardo* (1930) Chap. 12.

was surrendered up: real property was to pass upon intestacy in a partible succession just as did personalty.[21] With such an ultimate admission, the old mystery attaching to the legitimate line lost its wonder. The Legitimation Act 1926 permitted the stigma of bastardy to be lifted by the parents' subsequent marriage.

At the same time, an Adoption Act was passed after a short but heated campaign. The practice of taking children into propertied families—from poor or deceased relations, or servants, or through other connections—had a long history, which had once been part of the ubiquitous practice of service. Boisterous Tom Jones and demure Fanny Price led a phalanx of literary examples. Such children might be given property expressly (and perhaps obliged, as a condition, to adopt the name and arms of the benefactor, if he or she was intent on securing a successor).[22] The quasi-parental relationship might be recognised by the law in a number of secondary ways.[23] But there was no serious question of setting up legal machinery to effect an adoptive relationship of parent and child in a full sense.

At the lower social levels, the nineteenth century Children's Societies—Dr. Barnardo's and the Church of England's Waifs and Strays, for instance—had been content to place children out in families upon an informal basis of fostering. This left the society with a continuing interest which was often pursued by supervision against maltreatment and payment in support. Only in the second decade of the new century did charitable agencies develop which sought to place illegitimate and abandoned children with adopting parents who would assume full responsibility for their upbringing.[24] It quickly became clear that there was a demand to adopt, particularly from middle-class, childless couples who were ready to support pressure for legal reform; indeed this proved so lively that its failure to appear earlier—at a period when adoption laws were being introduced in parts of the colonies and the United States—must depend upon social attitudes pitted with class division. These were put clearly enough in the opposition that was raised to the idea during two Select Committees and a succession of Bills in Parliament between 1920 and 1926. The stigma of illegitimacy was, to many among the respectable, a necessary visitation in the interests of discouraging extra-marital intercourse, particularly among the poor. The notion of wiping it away by substituting an artificial parentage remained deeply disturbing, the more so if a child would thereby move into a class for which genetically it was assumed to be unfit.

Indeed, the ultimate Act of 1926, which was built upon the positive

---

[21] Administration of Estates Act 1925; see above, pp. 178–179

[22] It was to such adult arrangements that the Roman Law (and its modern successors) had applied a notion of adoption.

[23] Thus advancements that would create no resulting trust might be made by a person *in loco parentis*. The "parent" could also sue for loss of the child's services by the *actio per quod servitium amisit*.

[24] The displacement and orphaning of children during the World War was one incentive for the formation of the National Adoption Society (1917) and the National Children's Adoption Association. Equally it was a by-product of the suffrage movement for women: M. Kornitzer, *Child Adoption in the Modern World* (1952), pp. 60–62, 348–349.

recommendations for change of the two Select Committees,[25] none-theless took account of the counter-arguments: the adoptive parents assumed the duties of the parents of legitimate children for "custody, maintenance and education"; their new child did not inherit from them upon an intestacy[26]; they were not prohibited from marrying with the child under the ordinary law of marriage, any more than a guardian would be. The adoption process required the intervention of a court, which would normally act only with the consent of the parent, parents or guardian with rights of custody.[27] The child's own interests would be represented by a guardian ad litem, who would generally be a local authority worker, concerned with social circum-stances rather than legal pre-conditions.[28] The foundations thus laid would gradually reduce casual adoption, where the first concern of the natural mother and her family was to dispose of the object of shame, and the main motive of the recipients was pecuniary.[29] In 1937, the Horsburgh Committee found that not all adoption societies and agencies (which were involved in about 10 per cent. of all adop-tions) carried out much investigation of the circumstances of the adopters.[30] As a result new legislation required them to take up refer-ences, conduct a personal interview and home visit, and to follow up the adoption during a three-months probation.[31]

Adoption proved to be a useful machinery for regularising the re-organisation of families—after death or divorce—and in a substantial proportion of cases a natural parent was one of the adopters. But in rather more instances the child went to unrelated adopters and the societies found that there was a regular flow of couples, many of them childless, who were eager to adopt—more than there were chil-dren who were regarded as suitable for placement. A total of under 3,000 adoptions in 1927 would swell steadily until it reached a post-war peak of 23,564 in 1946.[32] Formal machinery, supported by an increasing number of well-intentioned, disinterested organisations was strengthening the chances of some of the country's least-wanted children.

In one sense, a formal procedure for adoption represented a break with the past: the judicial system of the state, aided by the investiga-tory abilities of local authorities, had acquired power to transfer a familial relationship from natural to adoptive parents. There had

[25] Hopkinson Committee, P.P. 1921 [Cmd. 1254] IX; Tomlin Committee, P.P. 1924–1925 [Cmd. 2401, 2469] IX; six private members' bills were presented altogether.
[26] Adoption of Children Act 1926, s.5(2), following recommendations of the Tomlin Committee favouring caution. The change came with the Adoption Act 1950.
[27] s.3, also requiring that the adopter receive no payment for adopting; the same was required of adoption societies by the Adoption of Children (Regulation) Act 1939.
[28] s.8(3).
[29] With luck the child would be paid for at a profitable rate and would then turn itself into a form of cheap labour.
[30] Departmental Committee on Adoption Societies and Agencies, P.P. 1936–1937 (Cmd. 5499, 1937) IX.
[31] Adoption of Children (Regulation) Act 1939, in operation in 1943. The counties and county boroughs, which were the poor law authorities after 1929, became involved informally in organising adoptions but only acquired power to act as agencies in 1950.
[32] For the statistics, see Report of the Houghton Committee on the Adoption of Chil-dren, P.P. 1971–172 [Cmnd. 5107] XXXVIII, App. B.

been no such departure previously from the pattern dictated by reproductive capacity. Yet from another, and probably more significant, perspective, adoption is only a further point along a line of intervention by which the state has increased its power to regulate the creation, maintenance and dissolution of families. This Chapter has traced how, over the preceding two centuries, it had come to determine what should constitute marriage, and what should be the consequences in terms of property rights and other obligations—between husband and wife and in their relation with their children. The introduction of adoption coincided with a period in which divorce was becoming rather more usual. But both still operated within a frame of thought set by the standard Victorian perception of the family—that it would be established by legally effective, heterosexual marriage and would function under conditions in which the husband and father, the sole or primary breadwinner in many cases, would be the centre of power and authority within each nucleus. The relationships, in accordance with Christian teaching, were to be permanent—between the couple until the parting of death, with the children until adulthood. Not conforming to this pattern was liable to be adjudged a moral failure, an attitude supported at various points by the law—for instance in the grounds for, and consequences of, divorce and in questions over the custody, maintenance and education of children. In 1950, as we leave the story, we are looking at a conformist world, distanced from a present in which the freedom to enter, maintain and sever personal relationships has advanced to the status of a prime virtue.

Further Reading

Anderson, O., "The Incidence of Civil marriage in Victorian England and Wales" (1975) 69 P. & P. 50.

Anderson, S., "Legislative Divorce: Law for the Aristocracy ?" in Rubin, G. R., and Sugarman, D., *Law Economy and Society* (1984), p. 412.

Bonfield, L., "Marriage, Property and the 'Affective Family' " (1983) 1 Law & Hist. R. 297.

Dicey, A. V., *Law and Opinion in England in the Nineteenth Century* (2nd ed., 1914), pp. 371–398.

Finer, M., and McGregor, O. R., "The History of the Obligation to Maintain" in Report of the Committee on One-Parent Families, P.P. 1974 [Cmnd. 5629] XVI, App. 4.

Gillis, J. R., *For Better, For Worse* (1985).

Gibson, C., "The Effect of Legal Aid on Divorce in England, Part I: Before 1950" (1971) 1 Fam.L. 90.

Graveson, R., and Crane, F. R., (eds.), *A Century of Family Law* (1957).

Holcombe, L., *Wives and Property* (1983).

Horstman, A., *Victorian Divorce* (1985).

Kahn-Freund, O., "Matrimonial Property in England" in Friedmann, W., (ed.) *Matrimonial Property Law* (1955).

Karminski, Sir S., "Family Law" in Ginsberg M. (ed.) *Law and Opinion in England in the 20th Century* (1959), pp. 286–295.

Kenny, C. S., *History of the Law of England as to the Effects of Marriage on Property* (1879).

Macfarlane, A., *Marriage and Love in England* (1986).

McGregor, O. R., *Divorce in England* (1957).

Macqueen, J. F., *The Rights and Liabilities of Husband and Wife at Law and in Equity, as Affected by Modern Statutes and Decisions* (1848).

Manchester, A. H., *Modern Legal History of England and Wales 1750–1950* (1980) Chap. 15.

Mueller, G. O. W., "Inquiry into the State of a Divorceless Society" (1957) 18 Pittsburgh L.R. 545.

Roper, R. S. D., *Treatise of the Law of Property arising from the Relation between Husband and Wife* (2nd ed., by Jacob, E., 1826).

Rowntree, G., and Carrier, N. H., "The Resort to Divorce in England and Wales, 1858–1957" (1958) 11 Pop.St. 188.

Shelford, L., *A Practical Treatise of the Law of Marriage and Divorce and Registration, as altered by the Recent Statutes* (1841).

Stetson, D. M., *A Woman's Issue* (1982).

Stone, L., *The Family, Sex and Marriage in England, 1500–1800* (1977; abridged ed., 1979).

Trumbach, R., *The Rise of the Egalitarian Family* (1978).

Walvin, J., *A Child's World* (1982) Chap. 11.

Woodhouse, M. K., "The Marriage and Divorce Bill of 1857" (1959) 3 Am.J.Leg.Hist. 273.

Chapter Six

POVERTY AND EDUCATION

In any community prevailing ideologies stamp a deep impress on the organisation of social provision. For Britain this is quite as true of the Victorian period, which strained to underscore the liberal virtue of self-sufficiency, as for the succeeding century with its growing acceptance that the rudiments of decent existence must be collectively guaranteed. But the modern "welfare state" began to approach completeness only in the aftermath of the Second World War. A world of social security, supplementary benefit, national health, compulsory education to secondary level, and support services for a range of other needs, has its own labyrinths, but we shall see only their initial lines being laid in law, political direction and administrative practice. Law, however, is as much part of the less ambitious schemes of support which were found from the middle ages onwards. As such it records shifts in social attitudes. But equally it provides a vital source of continuity and so it is easy to invest its place in the history with an undue "progressivism." Because, for instance, the state has come to be the prime mover in welfare provision and education, it is tempting to focus upon the evolution of its role and on accompanying modernisms such as entitlement to benefits and administration by experts. These are the product not only of democratic government but of overwhelmingly urban, often rootless, living to ages of 60, 70 or more. We begin, however, with a close-knit, mainly agricultural society in which the great bulk of people survived short lives on a bare subsistence; and even with the coming of industrial town-life, the very poor would continue to form a large pool at mortal risk. However close or diffuse the local community, it would fall to its propertied strata to decide what should be done to alleviate the worst destitution and ignorance. This might be left to their private benevolence or involve some communal arrangement, possibly even under central supervision. Whatever course was followed, it would remain essentially their action. The modern divide between state provision and private philanthropy accordingly has no prior history.

Our account of legal provisions must encompass, first, the operation of charities, which start from individual benevolence but soon approximate to communal resources, managed by delegates of the respectable; and, secondly, the gradual supplementation of such benevolence with direct community action, again managed by the propertied. We shall be concerned with two main fields of provision—the relief of poverty and the giving of education, the one a relentless round, the other an emergent panacea for social improvement and economic progress. Our prime focus is upon the types and ranges of solution that were adopted across our period, outcomes amounting always to a compromise between those who urged greater assistance to better the chances of the less fortunate and raise

411

a hedge against social discontent, and those who feared that generosity would only stir new longings and supply the energy for seeking
their fulfilment. There are two other related themes. One is the tendency of the relatively well-off to appropriate the resources of "welfare" to their own ends. This becomes a crucial aspect in the
development of the education system but is not confined to that
alone. The other is the close link between welfare measures and
social control. For much of our period the marshalling of vagrants
and work-searchers was a major "police" function to which criminal
prosecution formed only an ultimate adjunct. Equally, the cause of
popular education advanced not so much for the economically useful
skills that it would provide as for its chance to inculcate a true sense
of religious and moral obligation in a world of increasing expectation.

In its first two Parts, the Chapter surveys provision for the relief of
destitution, and then for education, in the period to 1890. The latter
two Parts deal with those subjects in the years, 1890–1950.

PART 1: DESTITUTION IN COUNTRY AND TOWN 1750–1890

I. The Inherited Structure

The medieval church was the one general provider of succour for the
needy,[1] just as it was the main source of teaching. The tithes on land
were originally intended for the care of the aged, sick and destitute as
well as for the upkeep of the priest and the church.[2] The disintegration of this function of tithe proved to be an important factor in
the break-up of the church, and the Tudor state set about building
some form of provision afresh in the post-Reformation world. The
new church was an active propagandist for benevolence as a Christian virtue, and indeed a considerable flow of charitable giving
established poor-houses, pauper doles, schools for poor children and
a range of other religious and public objects.[3] In support of this, a
secular law of charities became centred upon the Lord Chancellor's
enforcement of endowed trusts. At the same time much was done to
keep a check on the rootless poor and even to revive communal obligations formerly met through the tithe (which had irretrievably
become a right of private property) by the institution, in 1572, of a
public poor law. At the end of Elizabeth's reign, a system of reviewing parish charities was established by statute alongside a restatement of poor law obligations. This is the bi-polar construct which
would form the main inheritance of Georgian England.

---

[1] To some extent, the manor also assisted, and, in the towns and boroughs, the guilds.
[2] See above p. 141.
[3] The leading historian, W. K. Jordan (esp. *Philanthropy in England 1480–1660* (1978))
paints an over-coloured view of its extent: see Chesterman (1979), p. 17.

(a) Endowed Charities: the Legal Frame

For charitable giving, law was needed primarily to facilitate, and only secondarily to energise and to curb. Where the gift was simple and immediate—food for a beggar, largesse to the crowd—it was enough to be able to decide whether a gift had been made and to control any contest among recipients.[4] But where there was an element of permanence—and in particular if there was to be an endowment of land or a fund so that only its income would be used for the object—much greater sophistication was called for. The medieval church had long received endowments for the maintenance of fabric and the conduct of religious office, as well as for the material needs of its people, and over this the ecclesiastical courts had provided a measure of supervision. Equally the Court of Chancery had come to recognise and enforce gifts upon charitable "uses."[5] By the end of the sixteenth century its authority over charitable "trusts" (as they were coming to be called) was established as the significant source of legal regulation, for all endowments save those which had their own visitor.[6]

In the century following the break-up of the medieval church, the cause of charity was reflected in its treatment by the Lord Chancellor. Much of what he did could draw upon the older practice of the ecclesiastical courts. Both accepted that charity was entitled to the fundaments of an endowment: first, that no objection would lie to the perpetual dedication of property to its purpose; and second, that the beneficiaries might be left for selection by the trustees from time to time. It was the very permanence of a foundation and its ability to meet need as it recurred in each generation that secured charity a position which was not allowed to trusts for private beneficiaries. If the specified purpose should for any reason fail, Chancery would assist by directing an application cy-pres—to another similar purpose.[7] And beyond this, the court, sustained at some points by statutory provisions, would rectify defects in conveyancing and other matters, in order to ensure that charitable trusts were not lost through formal errors.[8]

Royal government, moreover, strove to see that charity trustees were active in pursuing the prescribed objects of their trust. The Statutes of Charitable Uses 1597 and 1601 provided for investigations

---

[4] There could be questions of considerable sensitivity even here: the rounds of the poor to collect alms at given seasons was a folk-custom that could seem threatening to those who thought it had gone too far: in the context of the agricultural riots of 1830, see E. Hobsbawm and G. Rudé, *Captain Swing* (1969), pp. 60–61.

[5] Charitable uses were not affected by the Statute of Uses 1535, since there were no specific beneficiaries in whose favour that statute could transfer the legal estate in question. This was one crucial factor in fostering the concept of a distinct estate in equity for the beneficiaries of a trust.

[6] Visitors were appointed to charities of particular splendour, such as schools and colleges of royal or noble foundation.

[7] For the emergence of this doctrine, see Jones (1969), pp. 72–75; L. A. Sheridan and V. T. H. Delany, *The Cy-Pres Doctrine* (1959), pp. 5–10; E. L. Fisch (1953) 51 Mich. L.R. 375; H. Gray (1953) 33 Boston U.L.R. 30.

[8] See Jones (1969), pp. 59–72; Chesterman (1979), pp. 22–24.

into the charitable holdings of parishes for the poor, the sick and others in need.[9] These were to be instigated by Chancery through commissions to the bishop, and could lead to wide-ranging orders to rectify maladministration, loss of property and other neglect.[10] They began with a spate—over a thousand commissioners' decrees being recorded in the period to 1625—and the flow continued until 1688.[11] After that, however, a new procedure became more frequent, one which reflected a general slackening in the urge towards charitable endeavour. On behalf of the Crown, in its role as protector of the people, the Attorney-General began to bring Chancery informations to secure the due enforcement of charitable trusts; but he acted only upon the instigation of an individual relator, who bore the risk of costs. This was unquestionably a significant development in the legal supervision of public affairs, and so far as concerned charities it had a directness about it in getting at real cases of neglect and dishonesty. But occasional informations were no substitute for the periodic survey of the range of available charities, which the commissions had provided.[12] In the course of the eighteenth century, many charities would simply be lost, others would be transferred to doubtful ends (such as simply reducing the poor rate), and others again would be milked by trustees and their friends for their own benefit.

Another indication of changing attitudes came over the question of perpetuity, which bore so fundamentally upon the balance of power within the landed interest. The freedom to tie up land in a charitable endowment received a sharp check with Jekyll's Mortmain Act 1736.[13] Devises of land by will upon charitable trusts were declared invalid, as were settlements inter vivos to the same end if made within twelve months of death. Other gifts during life were permissible but required enrolment in Chancery within six months.[14] In the eye of those who passed the act with such apparent unconcern lay the Church of England's major instrument of landholding, Queen Anne's Bounty; without some check it might indeed have grown to a size truly monopolistic. Surrounding this was a not wholly disinterested distaste for death-bed benevolence; and also keen feeling against the more egregious opportunities for disinherit-

---

[9] 3 Eliz. I, c. 6; 43 Eliz. I, c. 4. The preamble to the 1601 Act contained an extensive list of the types of charity to which it applied, which would later be used as a focus for defining "charity" for all purposes: see below, n. 22.

[10] For the scope of the Statutes and legal powers of the commissions, see Jones (1969), Chap. 4.

[11] Jones (1969), App. 1, lists the number by county.

[12] Commissions did not entirely die out until the late eighteenth century, the last being established in 1787: Jones (1969), p. 52 and App. I.

[13] 9 Geo. II, c. 36. The medieval use of the term "mortmain" had been for the prohibition upon transfers of land without royal licence to corporations (including the corporations sole of ecclesiastical office); their perpetual existence undermined the feudal obligations arising on succession. Now the term was being fitted to a hazard of a more commercial age.

[14] There were about 30 enrolments per annum during the rest of the eighteenth century, a figure which would increase with the flood of Victorian benefaction to over 1,200 per annum in 1857–1865; Tompson (1979), p. 58. Oxford, Cambridge, Eton, Westminster and Winchester were exempted from the Act; Queen Anne's Bounty was not.

ing an heir provided by a wholly individualistic law of wills.[15] The Act was not just the product of its aggressively selfish time.[16] Its objectives clearly appealed to judges in later generations, who proved ready to advance its nullifying effect by an extensive conception of what was a charitable object[17] and by a liberal definition of what constituted a devise of land.[18] Their approach would scarcely waver even as deserving exceptions came to be admitted, particularly by private Act. But equally Parliament could not be prevailed upon to give up the basic rule of 1736.[19] It would remain until the power and sanctity of land was truly on the wane.[20]

The Statute of 1601 had listed in its preamble a miscellany of objects which its scheme for commissions might cover and these placed a strong, but not exclusive, emphasis on providing the needy with subsistence, financial support and education. Eighteenth century Chancellors, referring sometimes to its "spirit and intendment," were content to treat any "gift to a general public use, which extends to the poor as well as the rich" as attracting the advantages in equity of a charity.[21] Not only could this further the range of Mortmain, but it could bring aid to ratepayers in paying for local services and in allowing them their own benefits such as schools for their children. Later, particularly under Lord Eldon, there would be signs of retrenchment on this, as on other aspects of charity law. He refused to uphold a bequest on trust to the Bishop of Durham for "such objects of benevolence and liberality as he should most approve of."[22] But still it was accepted, following Sir Samuel Romilly's argument in the case, that charity encompassed a broad range of four objects: "the relief of the indigent; . . . the advancement of learning; . . . the advancement of religion; and . . . the advancement of objects of general public utility." Arden M.R. also took a scrupulous

---

[15] See C. S. Kenny, *The True Principles of Legislation with regard to Charitable Uses* (1880), pp. 59–69; Owen (1960), pp. 87–88; Jones (1969), pp. 107–113; A. H. Oosterhoff (1977) 27 U. Toronto L.J. 257 at 277–288.

[16] Jones (1969), pp. 113–119 shows that the Act was interpreted with a certain circumspection by one of its progenitors, Lord Hardwicke L.C.; but that during the regime of his successor, Lord Northington, it became the instrument of a veritable witch-hunt against charity.

[17] *e.g., Thornton* v. *Howe* (1862) 31 Beav. 14, where a trust to propagate the eccentric Messianism of Joanna Southcote was held charitable, as being for the advancement of religion, only to strike it down as void; see generally Jones (1969) Chap. 9; Chesterman (1979), pp. 55–56.

[18] Thus gifts of money to purchase land, railway and canal shares, mortgages of turnpike trust shares and land held upon trust for sale were all brought within the purview of the Act: *Giblett* v. *Hobson* (1834) 3 My. & K. 517; *Att.-Gen.* v. *Wilson* (1838) 2 Keen 680; *Att.-Gen.* v. *Ackland* (1830) 1 Russ. & My. 243; *Harrison* v. *Harrison* (1829) 1 Russ. & My. 72; Jones (1969), pp. 118–119.

[19] A bill in 1773 had attempted to divert charitable investment from land by creating a "mortmain" fund: Tompson (1979), p. 58, n. 2. One Select Committee (P.P. 1844 (536) X) could find little point in the law, but another saw abolition as offering too ready a hostage to papal aggression (P.P. 1852 (493) XIII): Owen (1964), p. 319.

[20] The complex law on the subject was consolidated in 1888 and somewhat relaxed in 1891; but it would not be until the Charities Act 1960, s.38, that it finally disappeared: Chesterman (1979), p. 62.

[21] Lord Camden L.C., *Jones* v. *Williams* (1767) Amb. 651.

[22] *Morice* v. *Bishop of Durham* (1804) 9 Ves. 399—the case concerned a bequest of personalty and so avoided mortmain.

view of the cy-pres jurisdiction to re-direct charitable trusts whose purposes were outmoded. If the difficulty arose at the outset, the court was to intervene only if some intention to make a charitable benefaction generally could be discerned in addition to the nominated purpose; otherwise the gift failed and the donor or his estate kept the property.[23] Where the trust had been in effect it was not enough that its given purposes were becoming obsolescent through changes in need or an increase in income. "If the Legislature thinks proper to give the power of leaving property to charitable purposes, recognised by law as such, however prejudicial, the Court must administer it"; and so the Jarvis Charity—£100,000 invested for the poor of three small parishes—remained unalterable.[24]

Even when a new scheme was necessary because of impossibility, it had to be for the "next nearest" purpose, not for some appropriate local need. Every possible attention was to be paid to the "dead hand" of the original founder.[25] The vagaries of individual choice were rarely to be trimmed to meet larger policies aiming at overall efficacy. This was an important, long-surviving attitude in the court, but its debilitating effects were probably minor compared with the increasing cost and slowness of applying to Chancery for any form of assistance in administration. Because of their indefinite duration endowments might need periodic help—to appoint new trustees,[26] to protect property and to direct its investment, as well as to revise its purposes cy-pres. Chancery was ready enough to put trust funds under its own cumbrous administration,[27] but that process, as everything else before the court by Eldon's time, had become debilitating.[28] Many charities remained effective by ignoring the requirements of the law[29]; others, of course, were mismanaged with impunity.

In the eighteenth century there was only one real attempt to assess nationally what charitable resources were available for poor relief. Thomas Gilbert, the well-known poor law reformer, finally persuaded Parliament in 1786 to institute an inquiry in each parish into donations for the benefit of the poor. Incomplete as the Returns were (even after 4,000 supplementary inquiries), they indicated that charity income at least equalled that being expended on the poor law and also that a considerable measure of abuse lay ill-concealed. But the information was to be left unconsidered for another quarter-

---

[23] *Corbyn* v. *French* (1799) 4 Ves. 418; the rule grew out of attempts to avoid the Mortmain Act: *e.g.*, *A.G.* v. *Goulding* (1786) 2 Bro. C.C. 430.

[24] *Bishop of Hereford* v. *Adams* (1805) 7 Ves. Jan. 324; and see below, pp. 424, 433.

[25] Kenny (above, n. 15), p. 213.

[26] One of the earliest applications of incorporation—for bishoprics and other ecclesiastical holdings, bodies such as Oxford and Cambridge colleges, livery companies and boroughs—was to provide a legal entity in which property could be perpetually vested for charitable and like purposes, thus avoiding the need for regular transfers to new trustees.

[27] Tompson (1979), pp. 67–68.

[28] In the late eighteenth and early nineteenth century, the Attorney-General instituted an average 18 suits to protect charities each year. There were two or three private Acts a year to resolve charity problems: Tompson (1979), pp. 59–68.

[29] On "self-help" by trustees, see Tompson (1979), pp. 72–77.

century.[30] There are indications that at this period new benevolence was swelling considerably, a reflex of growing concern over the misery of the poor and the straits to which they might be driven. In years of bad harvest and high prices, food riots and other pressures would be met with a great outpouring of relief, a phenomenon that would become a prominent characteristic of Victorian benevolence. Altogether the forms of charitable giving were shifting. Between the endowed trust and the simple gift new types of institution and association were becoming prominent which would subsist mainly on subscriptions and collections to be spent as received. On this basis humane activities, such as hospitals and schools, missionary work and slavery abolition, as well as self-protective objects like the prosecution of felons and the abolition of vice, were attracting the donations and the energies of the respectable. As the leisured grew in numbers, charity would provide an immense outlet for sympathy, self-importance and the placation of discontents.[31] The nineteenth century forms of paternal supervision were beginning to take shape in earnest.

(b) The Elizabethan Poor Law

Tudor governments had been drawn into the direct control and maintenance of the destitute not only by the break-up of the monasteries and the other institutions of the old church but by their increasing regulation of the economy as a whole—prices, wages, apprenticeship and labour. A vagrant population had roved the country since the time of the Black Death and the first movement for enclosure. Brutal measures of suppression including whipping, imprisonment and even death, had been given Parliament's authority, notably in periods of wider unrest.[32] There had also been experimentation with special houses of correction—the Bridewells.[33]

It was with this repressive policy in place that a movement to regularise the provision for the less threatening destitute had evolved into the parish poor law. This was given its final Elizabethan form in Acts of 1597 and 1601.[34] These required each English parish to raise a rate for poor relief and, through those parishioners appointed as overseers, to put children out as apprentices; to provide relief for the "lame, impotent, old, blind and such other being poor and not able to work"; and, above all to secure a set of materials upon which the able-bodied poor should be put to work.

This last requirement was something different from forcing vagrants to work as a punishment and it posed the recurrent dilemma of all who have tried to utilise work as a means of solving destitution: labour is always easiest to provide when times are good

---

[30] Owen (1964), pp. 86–87; Tompson (1979), pp. 83–84.

[31] For the patterns of eighteenth-century philanthropy, see Owen (1960) Chaps. 1–3.

[32] See A. L. Beier, *Masterless Men* (1985).

[33] See, *e.g.*, F. Aydelotte, *Elizabethan Rogues and Vagabonds* (1913), E. M. Leonard, *The Early History of English Poor Relief* (1900); J. Pound, *Poverty and Vagrancy in Tudor England* (1971).

[34] 39 Eliz. I, c. 3 (with accompanying statutes), 43 Eliz. I, c. 2.

and the able-bodied can best fend for themselves.[35] What was important for the future about the Elizabethan legislation was not its solutions for ill-defined and shifting problems so much as its structure of legal obligation.

It settled a continuing interrelation of church and civil government by making the administrative unit the parish, thus spreading responsibilities among some 15,000 small authorities. The parish meant the assembly of incumbent, churchwardens and parishioners—the open vestry—unless, by immemorial custom, bishop's faculty or statute, there had been established some form of closed or select vestry.[36] These latter were to become relatively common in parts of the metropolis and other towns where destitution pressed. A select vestry replaced the popular assembly with a self-perpetuating enclave of the propertied, closely resembling the borough corporation. Both forms of governance were open to selfish manipulation. Often a select vestry was instituted to rid a parish of older corruptions and inefficiencies and might for a time succeed; but equally it could become enmeshed in similar evils. It would not, however, be until the democratic stirrings of the early nineteenth century that the oligarchic nature of the select vestries would come under sustained attack—particularly in London—and reforms providing for elective vestries would form the first precedents for local government reform—initially by Sturges Bourne's Acts of 1818–19,[37] then, more radically, by Hobhouse's Act of 1831.[38]

Given that the parish was mostly a small unit in a layered society, the office of overseer tended to pass to the minor ratepayers—the tradesmen and small tenants—who in the nature of things were likely to be grudging with disbursements.[39] The main check upon such meanness was provided not so much by the applicants themselves as by the justices, the ultimate arbiters of local affairs. Not only quarter sessions but also an individual justice had power to order overseers (not necessarily of his own parish) to grant assistance. The

---

[35] Marshall (below, n. 39) Chap. 4.

[36] See generally on the constitution of the parish, Webb *The Parish and the County* (1906), pp. 37–40, 173–214.

[37] Both these Acts were reactions to the soaring rate of poor law provision described below. The first (58 Geo. III, c. 69) confined parish meetings to ratepayers and by a novel system of plural voting it greatly strengthened the position of large ratepayers. The second (59 Geo. III, c. 12) provided that a parish committee could be elected annually to supervise the overseers of the poor. It also made large poor-rate increases subject to a referendum among owners (not occupiers). It was adopted by some 2,000 parishes and in some places achieved substantial cuts in relief; but the result could be cumbersome and the committees were often abandoned after a time: Webb above, n. 36, pp. 152–163; B. Keith-Lucas, *The English Local Government Franchise* (1952), pp. 23–28.

[38] 1 & 2 Will. IV, c. 60. This substituted an elected vestry for all purposes, upon a franchise given to all ratepayers (including women) without plural votes. The election was by secret ballot (a vital precedent) but a high property qualification was required of those who sought election. Adopted mainly in Metropolitan parishes, it produced a "shopkeeper democracy" that frightened many: Webb, above, n. 36, pp. 274–275.

[39] Unless, as was not uncommon, the overseer was able to supply the workhouse or turn the job to some other account. The inadequacies of overseer administration is a main theme of D. Marshall, *The English Poor in the Eighteenth Century* (1926).

appeal to quarter sessions permitted the airing of issues at county or borough level; the application to an individual justice allowed for some playing on the sentiment of those who might not themselves be obliged to pay.

The parish thus became the defining unit for those who must meet the poor rate and those who might seek relief. Both the duty to pay and the entitlement to claim were the subject for regular legal contest. The rate which the overseers set had to cover the demands upon it, and it was open to challenge first at Quarter Sessions and occasionally thereafter before King's Bench. The liability to be rated was imposed upon tenants rather than landlords and upon those with premises even if they were not residents. This was a simplification which emerged only out of rounder ideas about the ability to pay, taking account of land, stock-in-trade and other property, money income and the expense of dependants. Indeed even in the 1830s the question whether stock-in-trade fell into the assessment was moot.[40] Those who sought the assistance of the overseers were rarely in a position to dispute an unfavourable decision formally, though sometimes they would have the help of more substantial "friends"; and, particularly after 1782, the law permitted them to appeal to any justice, who might order their relief.[41]

Between parishes there was constant skirmishing over liability. From the earliest association of the parish with poor relief, some notion of "settlement" of paupers had of necessity been used to identify those for whom a parish bore responsibility. The basis had shifted with time. At first, custom had largely dictated the outcome, but statute had begun to add to the patina of rules, relating settlement partly to birth and partly to periods of residence. In the later law, an Act of 1662 was regarded as the starting point.[42] Under it, and its surrounding case-law, a wife was treated as settled in her husband's parish, and a legitimate child in its father's parish; but given the mobility of much of the population, determining settlement could require a tortuous climb up the family tree. By contrast an illegitimate child, filius nullius, took settlement where it was born.[43] However, the Act also gave settlement on the basis of 40 days' residence,[44] thus committing the overseers to remove newcomers at once

---

[40] For the history, E. Cannan, *The History of Local Rates in England* (2nd ed., 1927) Chap. 4. The Poor Law Commissioners of 1834 found themselves obliged by a Queen's Bench decision (*R.* v. *Lumsdaine* (1839) 10 Ad. & E. 157) to advise that stock should be rated; whereupon the legislature reversed the rule: 3 & 4 Vict., c. 89.

[41] Gilbert's Act (below, n. 59) explicitly gave justices as well as overseers the power to grant relief in the unions that it created. But the practice was older and occasionally gave rise to arguments for mandamus before King's Bench; see, *e.g.*, *R.* v. *North Shields* (1780) 1 Dougl. 331.

[42] 13 & 14 Car. II, c. 12. For the evolution of the law, see Marshall (above, n. 39) Chaps. 5, 6; Webb (1927) Chap. 6; P. Styles (1963) 9 U. Birmingham Hist. J. 33; J. S. Taylor (1976) 73 P. & P. 42; M. E. Rose in D. Fraser (ed.) *The New Poor Law in the Nineteenth Century* (1976), p. 25.

[43] See, *e.g.*, M. Nolan, *Laws of Relief and Settlement of the Poor*, (4th ed., 1825); G. A. Lewin, *Summary of the Law of Settlement* (1827).

[44] Or paying an annual rent of £10—a form of tenancy beyond the prospects of an ordinary labourer: on the law, see Cranston (1985), pp. 23–25.

or put up with their later claims for relief. It was late seventeenth-century enactments which replaced this with severer rules: that, for instance, completion of an apprenticeship or a yearly hiring was needed to give a new settlement.[45]

Even so this change did not affect the regular practice, particularly in places worried by the itinerant poor, of examining new arrivals in order to decide whether they should be removed—since the overseers were entitled to haul them off to their parish of settlement even before they made any claim.[46] It was part of local policing and became one way of dividing the "sturdy beggars and incorrigible rogues" from the respectable poor who must tramp for work.[47] In bad years there could be many thousands of removals around localities and some even to great distances.[48] Through the first half of the eighteenth century, it was regular practice not only to "badge" those in receipt of relief (as a mark of shame) but to issue them with a certificate acknowledging liability to other parishes.[49]

Adam Smith, Bentham and others, who would attack the law of settlement as a real impediment upon the mobility of labour, may not have appreciated sufficiently that, in a country which did its policing through overseers' and justices' examinations, this system may have been a positive incentive to go off looking for work. A parish with a surplus of labour could escape its immediate liability to provide support at the possible cost of having to do so later; a community with the good fortune to be able to supply the work would get it without having to bear that ultimate cost—in effect a rural subsidy to growing industry.[50] To this process the judges contributed significantly: they refused to hold that a work-force at (say) a new mine or factory acquired any settlement there, even if their contracts ran for a year or longer, if they were hired only for given days and given hours.[51]

Settlement probably had a less evenly balanced impact on relations between agricultural parishes. A "close" parish—dominated by a great landlord and his tenants, and building its efficiency around a successful enclosure—would often do what it could to reduce its casual labour, clearing squatters and cottagers away to less resistant, "open" parishes where eventually they or their descendants would

---

[45] See, in particular, 3 & 4 Will., c. 11 (1691)—other bases were paying parish rates (after 1795, of an annual value of £10 or more) or serving in an annual parish office. For the changes from 1834, see below, p. 428.

[46] Until 1814, however, the overseers were supposed to accompany them personally.

[47] Vagrants could also be tackled under the penal measures of the vagrancy laws: the eighteenth century version (17 Geo. II, c. 5) added conscription into the army or navy to a list of sanctions which stretched from whipping and incarceration in houses of correction to mutilation, transportation and death for the habitual "offender." The nineteenth century version (5 Geo. IV, c. 83 (1824)) modified these somewhat but extended the range of liability.

[48] The surviving records not unexpectedly suggest that that removal was used most aggressively against those likely to become long-term burdens—large families, the old, single mothers and their children.

[49] Certification was given regular backing by 8 & 9 Will. III, c. 30 (1697).

[50] See esp. Taylor (n. 42 above).

[51] Even if these amounted to 13 hours a day (less meal-times), six days a week: see, e.g., R. v. Kingswinford (1791) 4 T.R. 219; Nolan (above, n. 43), I pp. 375–385. For a study of practices in Yorkshire, J. W. Ely (1986) 30 Am.J.Leg.Hist. 1.

become settled.[52] The close parish would supply work but would not have to shoulder relief in slack periods, or during sickness or old age. In such circumstances it cost a watchful squire-justice nothing to order neighbouring overseers to grant relief.[53] When, in the name of humanity and Smithian freedom of movement, overseers were prevented from removing the poor in advance of actual claims upon them,[54] this only increased the ease with which the unwanted could be encouraged to live in surrounding parishes.[55]

In the early seventeenth century, the Privy Council had striven to see that parish relief was actively organised throughout the country and not merely in those towns where demands had led in any case to action in advance of general legislation. But after the Restoration, any central supervision had been reduced to shadowy form, through visits of the judges on assize, judicial decisions on settlement, rating and other aspects of the law, and the communications between justices of the peace and the Secretaries of State. The centre of gravity of domestic government had shifted decisively, leaving the benches at quarter sessions the major devisers of policy, the individual justices and the parish overseers the day-to-day administrators. What therefore a parish did for its poor, how far its system was used for the private benefit of the overseers and their friends, how far pauperism imposed its presence on the local community and called for constant assistance, varied in countless shades.

The obligation to maintain a House of Correction for disciplining vagrants could be met in various ways, for instance by merging it with a county or borough gaol. An Elizabethan statute had given authority for parishes to build poor-houses for the aged and disabled poor.[56] In some places by local Act, or under a general Act of 1722, parishes had set the able-bodied to work by constructing a workhouse.[57] Some did this by themselves, others in combination. Between 1753 and 1771, East Suffolk built eleven huge Houses of Industry with the aim of providing paid work for those without it. But they could not be made profitable and soon enough proved unmanageable. These differing institutions tended to coalesce into a general workhouse, farmed out, in eighteenth-century fashion, to a keeper to make what he could from the enterprise. Their detailed history remains largely unknown, but in some places they became hell-holes into which the unfortunate in every guise could be tipped; filthy, infested, fever-ridden, dissolute, their populations were kept down by frequent deaths. Occasionally the results burst as scandal.

---

[52] Short of threats or fraud, it was not unlawful to secure a settlement for a pauper elsewhere—by getting a woman to marry, or arranging an apprenticeship: *R. v. Seward* (1834) Ad. & E. 706.

[53] Brundage (1978), pp. 3–4, contrasts "close" Compton Winyates (poor relief in 1785, £9) with "open" neighbour Tysoe (poor relief in the same year, £469), the population in the latter per acre being five times that in the former.

[54] 35 Geo. III, c. 101, a statute which buried the dying practice of certification.

[55] The person being examined might, it seems, contest a removal order at quarter sessions, and how often this occurred deserves research. Parishes in dispute with one another would often resort to the common law courts: Cranston (1985), pp. 23–24.

[56] 39 Eliz., c. 5.

[57] Knatchbull's Act, 9 Geo. I, c. 7; Webb (1927), pp. 277–280.

In the 1760s Jonas Hanway revealed the terrible death rate of children in London parish workhouses; after Parliamentary investigation an Act was passed to limit their stay in such places to three weeks.[58]

In 1782, the reformer, Thomas Gilbert, promoted an Act which allowed parishes to combine for building and maintaining a poor-house for the sick and aged while supporting the able-bodied by out-relief.[59] In the first wave of popularity, about sixty Gilbert Unions were established to build poorhouses. But more significant was the Act's explicit blessing for the growing practice (with or without a union) of money doles as a substitute for, or a supplement to, wages. Conditions of grave economic uncertainty were approaching which would place the various provisions against destitution under unexampled strain.

II. The Crises of Pauperism

(a) Charity

As the eighteenth century drew to its close the typical patterns of early industrialisation were beginning to emerge: prosperity and wages in the developing areas (mainly in the north) were advancing, while stagnation and decline affected much of the south. Agriculture, particularly in the wheat-growing areas, which had long provided sporadic employment for much of the labouring population, was moving to a condition of endemic under-employment, the process exacerbated by enclosure and then, in the 1790s, by the sharp inflations of bad harvests and war conditions. In a few places proto-industrial out-work was beginning to be displaced by factory production on new machines which brought in its train a different form of redundancy.

Under this abiding sense of strain, radicals began to question once again how far charitable endowments were being deflected from their proper purposes. Criticism of this kind faced formidable opposition, for institutions of high position—the colleges of Oxford and Cambridge, the London hospitals and livery companies—were leading administrators of such funds; and above all, the Court of Chancery stood as the law's appointed supervisor of the whole multifarious activity.[60] It is one measure of the spreading unease that Brougham and his associates, starting from a determination to foster

---

[58] 7 Geo. III, c. 39; and see 2 Geo. III, c. 22; Webb (1927), pp. 298–300; Inglis (1971), pp. 23–31 (including an account of Hanway's later campaign to protect pauper apprentices in the dreadful trade of chimney-sweeping). For the relation to the gaols, see below, p. 560.

[59] 22 Geo. III, c. 83; Webb (1927), pp. 272–276.

[60] In 1812, Romilly managed to secure two acts (52 Geo. III, c. 101, 102), one for the registration with Chancery of charitable donations; and the other allowing the institution of simplified proceedings for enforcement of charitable trusts: but both failed to have an appreciable effect: Tompson (1979), pp. 90–93.

the cause of popular education, were able in 1818 to procure a new investigation by Commission. In this they were helped by the long tradition of such investigations,[61] even Lord Eldon was obliged to temper his hostility when it was settled that the Commission would report misapplications of funds to the Attorney-General for his reference to Chancery.[62]

Nonetheless half of the twenty Commissioners were to be salaried and were to undertake the long labour of touring the parishes to take evidence, compile returns and make references.[63] The other honorary commissioners were there essentially to monitor the twice-yearly reports and so to temper the stridency of criticism. The whole survey, which would take more than twenty years to complete, established the "briefless Whig barrister" as the new instrument of social investigation.[64] He was in harness for the great commissions of policy innovation—on factories, boroughs and the poor law—which were to follow with the Reform Act. At the end of their long years of "legal drudgery," the Commission had reviewed more than 29,000 endowments,[65] with an annual income of about £1.2 millions per annum. Because of exclusion of many of the richer, more powerful charities from the inquiry[66] this amounted to perhaps a fifth of that available to charity as a whole. Up to a half of that sum was directed once more to proper ends, thanks to the Commission's intervention, in the majority of cases the trustees proving ready enough to collaborate in changes. Only 400 cases were referred to the Attorney-General; these would include some notorious tussles with borough corporations and bishops that would end in Chancery condemnation.[67]

As the work drew to a close, there were moves to establish a permanent body which would continue the same kind of interstitial supervision and assistance. This was one recommendation of a

---

[61] Owen (1964), pp. 183–188 and Tompson (1979) Chap. 4, for details of the establishment of the Commission. The Commission of 1818 was limited to educational trusts and confined in various ways by comparison with Brougham's proposals. The following year the government, despite Eldon, was moved to widen its scope to all categories of charity and to restore most of Brougham's plan: 58 Geo. III, c. 91 and 59 Geo. III, c. 81. This may well have been in order to avert the appointment of Commissions into other more delicate matters, such as government spies. The Commission was renewed in 1831 and, with enhanced powers, in 1835.

[62] See the powers given in 59 Geo. III, c. 91. Towards the end, in 1832, the Commissioners were given power to appoint the incumbent and church-wardens to be recipients for the time being of annuities and rentcharges for charity, when the trustees had died or disappeared: 2 & 3 Will. IV, c. 57.

[63] The 1818 Act required them to act in groups of three, but in 1819 this was reduced to two, as Brougham had proposed.

[64] The taunt was scarcely applicable to the salaried Charity Commissioners, who were mostly barristers with several years of practice; their problem was to find time in between cases to do Commission work: Tompson (1979), pp. 118–120.

[65] Eventually an Analytical Digest of them all was published in 1842. For procedure before the Commissioners, see Tompson (1979), Chap. 6.

[66] For which, see 59 Geo. III, c. 81, ss.7, 8.

[67] Bishop Tomline of Lincoln's insistence on preferring his son as warden of the Mere Hospital (where the latter made £13,000 from renewed leases) was a grotesque example: see *Att. Gen.* v. *Pretyman* (1845) 8 Beav. 316. There was evidence enough of charities sorely depleted by the expense of Chancery proceedings: Owen (1964), p. 198.

rather curious Select Committee in 1835,[68] and Brougham (by now the Chairman of the Charities Commission) promoted the same plan. But as so often, his advocacy only roused opposition. Every Lord Chancellor from Lyndhurst (in 1844) brought forward a proposal on the subject, until eventually, in 1853, Cranworth procured the creation of a permanent Charity Commission of three salaried members, together with a fourth member who was to be in the government and so answerable in Parliament.[69]

Though the early Commissioners tried manfully to make something of their responsibilities, they could only achieve some minor channelling of voluntary benevolence. They had two inspectors to investigate maladministration and charities were under a duty to file their annual accounts with the Commission, but the Commissioners were given no power of audit. Two Official Trusteeships were instigated into which charities could put their lands and funds, if they wanted assistance with administration and a permanent body in place of changing trustees, but the Commissioners could not require this to be done.[70] By an amendment in 1860, they were also given power to sanction cy-pres schemes for application of funds to new purposes (subject to an appeal to Chancery).[71] In this they were tied to the scrupulous respect for the settlor's "dead hand," which Lord Eldon had insisted upon, and which remained the guiding spirit of the Chancery judges, at least until 1881.[72]

While benevolence continued in spate, it was a commonplace that donors should be free to select their own objects without interference. For all their talk of self-reliance, the Victorian propertied classes regarded it as a prime duty, a form often of religious expression, not only to give to charity but to participate, to organise, to bestow. Here lay innumerable outlets for the pent energies of ladies and gentlemen bountiful—sick and maltreated animals, battered and abandoned children, a national lifeboat service, Sunday observance, temperance, preservation of the countryside and amenities in the cities, the distressed in every guise, but particularly gentlefolk fallen on hard times. Through all the fund-raising, committee-work and visiting could be expressed a genuine feeling for suffering, the desire to maintain social order, a distaste for drawing-room tedium, a determination to mix and climb socially.[73]

This was a powerful motive force, but it did not go uncountered.

---

[68] Its chairman was Daniel Whittle Harvey, who for several years had campaigned against the feebleness of the Commissioners, some of them suspecting him of unscrupulous self-interest in doing so: Tompson (1979), pp. 168–170. Its Report (P.P. 1835 (449) VII) did lead to an increase in the size of the Commission in order to bring its work to an end.

[69] 16 & 17 Vict., c. 137. Lord Cottenham, interestingly, proposed to make use of the new County Court judges: Tompson (1979), p. 211. The need for a political spokesman clearly reflected the bitter experiences of the Poor Law Commission (below, p. 432) and the General Board of Health (above, pp. 160–162). It did not, however, become a full-time office; and after 1887, when the Commissioners had lost all their original impetus, a backbencher sufficed.

[70] 16 & 17 Vict., c. 37.

[71] 23 & 24 Vict., c. 136. Cranworth had sought such a power in 1853, but it was thought too threatening.

[72] See below, p. 433.

[73] On the character of Victorian philanthropy, see esp. Owen (1964), Chaps. 4, 5.

The criticism of radicals, instigated by Brougham with an eye to educational reform,[74] soon spread to other fields, notably dole charities. Trusts providing handouts of money, food, clothes, blankets or coals for the parish poor had been accumulating in an uneven sprinkling over the country and in many places trustees were one port of call in a round that would also include the poor law authorities. Nothing was more non-plussing than to find that aid graciously bestowed on the needy had in fact fallen to sharp-eyed scroungers. This was indulgence of idle profligacy and it received short shrift, for instance, in the 1834 Report on the Poor Law.[75]

At that period, the criticism had a certain impact on charity work and saw the appearance of visiting societies which would give only after investigating family circumstances.[76] But their impact was small and the object received no legal backing. Chancery, indeed, began at this period to disapprove the older practice (still accepted by Eldon)[77] of using charitable endowment to reduce the poor rate.[78] Complaints about the ill-consequences of doles continued to rise with the level of gifts.

(b) Parish Support: Towards a new Poor Law

As the difficulties of the destitute grew increasingly apparent in the last decade of the eighteenth century, a war of books and pamphlets on the subject raged.[79] In 1797, Whitbread sought to persuade Parliament to re-institute wage regulation to relieve the wants of the "labouring poor." Upon this Pitt might turn withering scorn, but his own proposal—for the encouragement of small-farming under state support, inspired by Arthur Young and his Board of Agriculture— found an equally lukewarm reception.[80] Instead, in the troubled areas of agricultural under-employment, the justices and overseers turned to some form of supplementation of earnings out of the poor rate, for this allowed them much more flexibility than wage-setting. Of the various policies, the best-known was the Speenhamland scale adopted by the Berkshire justices in 1795 and taken up in numerous places beyond.[81] The scale tied the amount that a labourer should receive (from wages, poor relief, or both) to the cost of the "gallon" loaf and the number of dependants—wife and children—that he supported. Other schemes paid a family allowance of some kind (in

---

[74] See below, p. 436.
[75] Report (below, n. 95), at pp. 204–205: "In some cases [dole charities] have a quality of evil peculiar to themselves," (*i.e.* of attracting a pauper host).
[76] See below, pp. 432–433.
[77] *Att.-Gen.* v. *Exeter Corp.* (1827) 2 Russ. 45.
[78] *Att.-Gen.* v. *Exeter Corp.* (1828) 3 Russ. 395; *Att.-Gen.* v. *Wilkinson* (1839) 1 Beav. 390; *Att.-Gen.* v. *Bovill* (1840) 1 Ph. 762.
[79] On the ideological contests over pauperism, see esp. J. R. Poynter, *Society and Pauperism* (1967); Inglis, (1971) Chaps. 2–4; R. G. Cowherd, *Political Economists and the English Poor Laws* (1978).
[80] Poynter (above, n. 79), pp. 55–61, 75–76.
[81] The justices met at the Pelican Inn, Speenhamland, outside Newbury. Their scheme was effectively sanctioned by 36 Geo. III, c. 23, which also reaffirmed the power of a single justice to order any form of relief. The scale became general in some counties, mainly in the south and east.

many parishes only for the fourth child or more) or introduced a scheme for roundsmen,[82] or occasionally for labour on a parish project such as road-building.[83]

Thomas Malthus' black depiction of the effects of these practices[84] soon captured the attention of ratepayers. Through his eyes they accepted as inevitable the propensity of population to increase out of proportion to the available food supply and were ready to suppose with him that only the "natural" controls of hunger and sickness could check the process; certainly all forms of wage supplementation—and especially family allowances—only stimulated an ability to breed, thus darkening the cloud of fate. Malthus, supported at this point by the more abstract rationalising of Ricardo and other political economists, advocated abolishing the existing forms of relief for those able to work. In 1818 the level of relief would reach a peak of some £8 millions per annum. Yet since other surviving elements in the Tudor economic scheme were being deliberately dismantled,[85] the case for treating the poor law likewise became very much more than the theorising of a radical clique. At local level there seems to have been considerable shift from Speenhamland supplements to subsidies only for large families[86]; and the reorganisation of some parishes under Sturges Bourne's Acts gave a particular impetus to this retrenchment.[87]

Nonetheless there was a rampart of established opinion which could not easily be persuaded to so dramatic a course as complete abandonment. Poor relief, however deplorable its results, had become a crucial element in the paternalist balance between the equal dangers of absolute hunger and undue feeding. The organisation of both public and private assistance was likely to be well controlled in the "close" parishes where large proprietors and tenants dominated the hierarchy, but more problematic in the uneasy conditions of "open" hamlets and the slum quarters of towns. Social order had so far been maintained without any systematic organisation of police (partly thanks to the examinations and removals under the law of settlement) but premonitions of breakdown were frequent, as in the food riots of the war period, and the loom-breaking and marches of the cottage knitters in 1812 and 1817, protesting against the harsh effects of new production techniques. Those who governed hesitated to revert to an Irish condition in which there was no public responsibility for even the most desperate deprivation and charity offered the sole life-line.

In the upheavals which finally propelled electoral reform, the poor

[82] This obliged farmers to take on and pay a proportion of the surplus labour force. A variant—the labour rate—gave them the option of additional workers or an additional rate.

[83] For all these variants, see esp. Webb (1927), pp. 168–196; Henriques (1979), pp. 27–28.

[84] *An Essay on the Principles of Population* (1798); see above, pp. 66–67. After 1810 a considerable anti-Malthusian literature would begin to grow, but it did not have so ready an impact: see Inglis (1971), pp. 225–240; J.P. Huzel (1969) 22 Ec.H.R. (2d) 430.

[85] See above, pp. 292–293.

[86] See esp. Blaug (1963) 23 J.Econ.Hist. 151, (1964) *ibid.* 229; the scale of payments was also reduced substantially in the 1820s.

[87] See above, p. 418. Sturges Bourne himself was a leader of reform, rather of abolition.

law hung in heavy pall, its future shrouded by the fierce arguments between abolitionists and mere adapters. The influential were accordingly in a condition to be captivated by a proposal that was presented as a tertium quid. Its principal progenitor was Edwin Chadwick, who found his inspiration partly in the ideas of Jeremy Bentham on governmental administration and social discipline enforced through the Panopticon plan, and partly in a renewal of experiments in deterrent institutions. He drew in alliance the economist Nassau Senior, converting him (it seems) from strict Malthusianism, and George Nicholls, who had used a disciplinary workhouse in Southwell, Nottinghamshire, to cut the poor rate by a half and had already done a good deal to publicise his results.[88]

Their thinking began from Malthusian premises: wage-supplementation was held to drag wages down by lowering the incentive to increase earnings through greater productivity—cause rather than effect. It was not to be countenanced that an endemic labour surplus might independently have produced a wage-level so much on the border-line of subsistence that the labour force lacked the physical capacity for more work; or that, as a corollary, wage supplementation might be the efficient way of giving the poor the means to fight for themselves. Instead it was taken to exacerbate the slothful, fecund failings of a class unable to feel the virtues of self-help, saving and abstinence. To break this cycle of moral decline, the new plan had at its root the workhouse test: the able-bodied who applied for relief would in all circumstances be turned away to look for work, and if they returned without finding it they would be provided for only upon entering a workhouse whose conditions would be designed to deter—"less eligible" by the diet provided, the drudging work required, the separation of families imposed. Nonetheless, according to Chadwick's view of the psychology, the prior search for work would induce a positive desire to enter the workhouse on such terms. At the same time other institutions would provide "collateral aids" for the young and the aged, the sick, the mentally ill and the retarded.

The programme was no longer a simple laissez-faire, but rather an administrative strategy calculated to heighten the essential values of self-sufficiency and hard work.[89] In the consequent lifting of wage levels would be the greatest happiness of the greatest number. Significantly, from our perspective, it was to be a uniform national policy, put into effect by the edicts of a central bureaucracy.[90] The localities—regrouped as unions of parishes—would continue to pay for

---

[88] In the same district, the Rev. J. T. Becher and the Rev. Robert Lowe vied with similar plans, for prison as well as poor law reform: see below, pp. 578–579; and Brundage (1978), pp. 39–40.

[89] In this it bears comparison with the contemporary planning for factory regulation and for incarceration of criminals and lunatics: see below, pp. 434–435, 569–571, 578–585; Finer (1952), Chaps. 1–3; MacDonagh (1977), Chaps. 3, 6; M. A. Crowther, *The Workhouse System, 1834–1929* (1981), F. M. L. Thompson (1981) 34 Ec.H.R. 205.

[90] Despite his later claims, there are signs that Chadwick was not so strong a "centraliser" as Senior and leant in favour of allowing leading magistrates a strong executive role on boards of guardians: Brundage (1978), pp. 32–42.

their own poor but they would act under direction from the centre.[91] Here was a novelty just about conceivable in the atmosphere of 1832 but nonetheless a paper proposal of quite extraordinary daring. Chadwick and Senior had some feeling for the shift in power being sought. Indeed, they proposed that the central authority be constituted a court of law with the right to impugn for contempt those who challenged its authority.[92]

The Royal Commission to inquire into the poor laws, which Grey's government felt obliged to appoint in February 1832, became the medium through which the plan was put to the public, Senior being appointed a member and Chadwick one of the salaried assistants who were to tour the parishes on Benthamic fact-finding missions.[93] The pressure on the government to produce results allowed Chadwick to write up a preliminary version of his ideas in an interim Survey of 1833,[94] and then, when the assistants' reports were ready, to be largely responsible—with Senior—for the Commission's Report in the following year.[95] Both documents were widely acclaimed for their promise of reduced expenditure.[96]

A broad framework of law to implement the plan could be pushed through with little opposition. By the Poor Law Amendment Act 1834,[97] unions of parishes were to be run by elected guardians. The franchise was given to landowners as well as occupiers, under a plural voting system which reflected their proportional responsibility to pay.[98] The guardians had themselves to meet a substantial property qualification.[99] Accordingly the larger landowners had considerable opportunities for influence. At the same time, each parish remained bound to contribute for its own poor; and so the old law of settlement and removal continued in operation with modifications only at particular points.[1]

At the centre, a three-man Poor Law Commission was established with considerable powers. In the hope of distancing it from the

---

[91] As a consequence, settlement and removal continued, though with modifications, notably the abolition of settlement by apprenticeship, and hiring for a year (1834); and irremovability after five years residence (1846); See A. Digby. *Pauper Palaces* (1978) Chap. 4; Henriques (1979), pp. 57–58.

[92] See below, n. 9.

[93] For its membership and operation, see Brundage (1978) Chap. 2.

[94] Extracts . . . as to the Administration . . . of the Poor Laws (1883); Chadwick was then promoted to be a Commissioner.

[95] P.P. 1834 [44] XXVII–XXX.

[96] *The Times*, however, was critical, its proprietor, John Walter, having clashed with Chadwick; and so were other Tory voices: Brundage (1978), pp. 42–44.

[97] 4 & 5 Will. IV, c. 76. For its enactment, Webb (1929), pp. 90–100; Brundage (1978), Chap. 3. For its provisions on bastard children, see above, pp. 373–374.

[98] s.40: the plural voting for owners was taken from Sturges Bourne's Acts of 1818 and 1819 (see above, p. 418); occupiers had one vote for every £200 annual value, up to a maximum of three votes.

[99] The Commissioners set the qualification for guardians in each union, the minimum required being a £40 annual value for poor rate: s.38.

[1] ss.64–68. Senior and Chadwick followed orthodox economic thought in seeking abolition of settlement as restrictive of labour mobility. If anything the law became more cumbersome to use under the 1834 Act and an amendment in 1846. Within a union, the introduction of a common fund in 1865 (by the Union Chargeability Act) eliminated the problem. The vestige of the concept would survive on until 1948: see J. S. Taylor (1976) 73 P. & P. 42, 53–54.

ordinary toils of patronage, Senior insisted that the Commissioners should not be Members of Parliament[2]—though this would leave them fatefully exposed to political storms. The administration of poor relief throughout England and Wales was placed under their "direction and control" and they were to make rules, orders and regulations over the entire field, which were subject only to disallowance by the Privy Council and laying before each House of Parliament.[3] They and their assistants could require information to be given on oath and documents to be produced.[4] The accounts of local administrators were to be the subject of quarterly audit, as a result of which improper expenditure could be disallowed and recovered from the individuals concerned.[5]

The legislation did not emerge in a form that was as strong as Chadwick and Senior had sought. Chadwick had wanted above all an explicit embargo on outdoor relief to the able-bodied. But this the House of Lords had amended, leaving it to the Commissioners to settle the extent to which this should not be allowed.[6] Local administrators were also given power to delay the introduction of new orders (upon notification to the Commission) and to grant out-relief upon emergencies (again with notification).[7] Likewise Chadwick had wanted power to order unions to raise rates sufficient to build or adapt the necessary workhouse accommodation. But in the end they could compel the raising of only £50 per annum, or one-tenth of the poor rate, if this was less; greater expenditure, up to the level of the whole poor rate, had to be by agreement with the board of guardians.[8] Again his proposal that the Commissioners be a court of record was lost. Instead, discipline (including the recovery of disallowed payments) required summary proceedings before justices, with an appeal to quarter sessions and the right to test the legality of the Commission's orders before King's Bench by means of certiorari.[9]

Beside these structural weaknesses, stood political dangers of equal magnitude. When the Cabinet appointed the three Commissioners, Nicholls became one; but the other two posts went to the parties—Shaw-Lefevre, feeble and cautious, for the Whigs; Frankland Lewis, ponderous and self-important, for the Tories. Chadwick, who had come to expect inclusion, was fobbed off with a form of per-

---

[2] s.8; the Home Secretary in general spoke on their behalf, but not as minister responsible for their behaviour.

[3] s.15.

[4] s.12. The Assistant Commissioners (16 of them by 1837) provided the essential link with boards of guardians, once the latter were established.

[5] s.44. It was not until 1868 that the central authority acquired the unequivocal power to appoint the auditor, thus ensuring that the task could not be put in the friendly hands of the guardians' nominee. In 1878 it was possible to institute a single staff of district auditors over the financial aspects of all local government: Webb (1929), pp. 210–215.

[6] s.52; the Act's preamble referred to the "evil" of out-relief and also to the "difficulty" of attempting "any immediate and universal remedy."

[7] *Ibid*. The justices, however, lost their former powers to intervene save in cases of absolute necessity: s.54 (and note s.27 on the out-relief of the aged incapable of work).

[8] ss.23–25.

[9] ss.98, 103, 105.

manent secretaryship which was itself to prove a major rub.[10] The Commission stood witness to the widespread failure to appreciate the rigorous, highly specific nature of Chadwick's plan. Lewis, in particular, represented the rural squire's view that the problem lay with undue wage supplementation in the countryside. Accordingly the Commissioners concentrated their first efforts at unionisation in the south, Chadwick trying in vain to insist that the north be penetrated while trade conditions remained relatively good—an all-too-percipient premonition of events to come.

Even in 1834 Shaw-Lefevre wanted to issue a circular allowing guardians to institute a labour round when other work failed. In 1837, he and Lewis[11] were on the point of securing a General Order under which assistance to large families would be rendered by allowing some of their children to be taken into the workhouse. By immense effort, Chadwick put a stop to both, but it was plain that neither Commissioner had any real commitment to his principles.[12] Relations between Commission and Secretary declined so drastically that Chadwick's main energies would soon be directed to his favourite subject—the effect of disease and debility upon poverty—with dramatic results for the whole future of public health.[13]

In the shires the new legislation was largely accepted not so much for its technique as for its political adjustment at the local level. Power moved from the individual parishes to unions more easily dominated by large landowners.[14] In particular they could impose a curb upon "sentimental" grants of relief which some local overseers and justices had been prone to allow. In country areas, the new boards were early at work cutting into the lists of those dependent upon out-relief. In this they might need little urging from the Assistant Commissioner of their district.[15] On the issue of providing and staffing a union workhouse, the Commissioners could scarcely insist and were confined to respectful persuasion. It was apparent from the outset that a regular network of separate institutions for the able-bodied, the young, the old, the sick and the lunatic was pie in the Senior-Chadwick sky. Typically, in the geographical heart of a union would emerge a single mixed workhouse, dominated for all its

---

[10] Finer (1952), pp. 106–111, 116–123. Despite the internal feuding, Chadwick was a staunch champion against outside critics and was in particular able to call on the loyalty of the Assistant Commissioners: thus they routed a Select Committee of Inquiry set up in 1836 by John Walter of *The Times* and the dubious Daniel Whittle Harvey: *ibid.*, pp. 129–133.

[11] Chadwick's ally, Nicholls, was at that time despatched to Ireland to help set up the first statutory poor law there.

[12] Finer (1952), pp. 120–121, 136–137.

[13] See above, p. 159ff.

[14] The influence of leading aristocrats, during the enactment of the bill and in the early stages of its implementation, was considerable: Brundage (1978) Chap. 5; *cf.* P. Dunkley (1973) 88 E.H.R. 836; A. Digby, *Pauper Palaces* (1978), pp. 207–214. But the policy of 1834 nonetheless amounted to a very real shift of direction: W. Apfel and P. Dunkley (1985) 10 Soc.Hist. 37; *cf.* A. Digby (1975) 28 Ec.H.R. 69.

[15] In some places, however, a relatively kindly attitude continued at least until the economic pressures of the 1840s: see N. McCord (1969) 14 Int.R.Soc.Hist. 90; P. Dunkley (1974) 17 Hist.J. 329. The Webbs ((1929), pp. 115–116) blame this on the lack of perception of the Royal Commission of 1832–1834. They detail the steps by which the exceptions were gradually suppressed: p. 226.

inmates by some version of the deterrent regimen needed for the "test of the House." It would be managed by a salaried master who was expected to follow a dietary plan prescribed by the Commissioners on a budget that the guardians kept as frugal as they could. A likely consequence was that all the inmates were subjected to the primitive, dreary existence originally intended for the able-bodied alone.

The establishment of unions did not proceed so smoothly elsewhere. In various towns, Gilbert and local Act unions and statutory vestries were able to go their own way, because the Act gave no power to supersede them compulsorily.[16] In the North the policy of the "three Bashaws" of Somerset House became a focal point in the deep discontents expressed by the Chartist movement.[17] Their attempts to set up unions, begun when trade was descending into one of its worst troughs, met with fanatical resistance. The factory owner, Fielden, the minister, J. R. Stevens, the rousing journalist, Feargus O'Connor, found common cause in the campaign. The country had an early experience of civil disobedience directed at a policy deliberately embodied in law and supervised by central bureaucracy.[18] With sudden and massive unemployment striking town after town, the workhouse test was entirely impracticable; but it was not until the Commissioners were brought to an admission of this that the last centres of opposition could be unionised.[19] To some extent a compromise was fashioned around the concept of a labour test—outdoor relief on condition of some drudging work in a union yard.

For all these reasons, Chadwick and Senior's specific regimen was not imposed across the country by central authority. Local autonomy survived to a very considerable extent, expressing its degree of sympathy towards or against a tightening up of relief by its own decisions and its own appreciation of local unemployment patterns and other factors. A large measure of discretion was effectively retained to provide outdoor relief. The Commissioners might have power to impose rules upon unions, but for their first decade they could exercise it only case by case, mainly after persuasion and agreement with the guardians. The results were eventually reduced to a sort of system by placing unions within one or other of a series of General Orders. The first of these grouped the unions applying the Outdoor Labour Test, the next listed those under an Outdoor Relief Prohibition. In the end, there had also to be an order merely regulat-

[16] There were of course legal issues about ultimate powers to enforce compliance with workhouse and labour tests. On their side the authorities were given certain powers to discipline the refractory within the workhouse, and ultimately they might prosecute them under the Vagrancy laws: see Cranston (1985), p. 43.

[17] See generally, N. C. Edsall, *The Anti-Poor Law Movement 1834–1844* (1971); E. C. Midwinter, *Social Administration in Lancashire 1830–1860: Poor Law, Public Health, Police* (1969).

[18] The disintegration of the situation into rioting and distress for rates was preceded by various arguments about the proper constitution of boards of guardians and authority over them: Edsall (above, n. 17) Chap. 7.

[19] The Commission came up for renewal in 1839 (an indication of the hope of some that its interventions need only be temporary); it was not until 1842—in face of the great hostility—that it was given more than an annual extension.

ing outdoor relief and it proved impossible even to lay down that a third of this should be provided in kind. By 1854, 84 per cent. of recipients were on outdoor relief.[20]

Despite this, the Commissioners were a focus for resentment against new severities and distresses, whatever administrative turn they took. The conditions in many general workhouses were grim, the "cruelty" marked by such requirements as silence at meals and the splitting up of families. Some of these rigours were relaxed by the Commissioners as scandals began to be exposed.[21] But in 1845, the report that paupers in the Andover workhouse were eating the bones which they had been set to crush blew into a major row.[22] Two years later the Whig government decided that the Commissioners and their rebarbative Secretary should be replaced by a Poor Law Board comprising a minister and two secretaries, one of whom would also be an MP.[23] It had become necessary that a bureaucracy at such a political nerve-centre should be headed by a member of the government responsible for it in Parliament; its policies would in consequence be determined within the established framework of national politics. It was a lesson of first significance in the trial and error of British constitution-building.[24]

The new Board accepted its essentially supplementative role. Even after 1871, when it was merged with public health branches into the Local Government Board, it would remain a rather pedestrian monitor of developments, an information-gathering central intelligence from which a board of guardians could learn much if it had the will. The LGB remained the authority for sanctioning building projects and loans, as well as deviations from the standard systems of relief administration prescribed in the Orders. But it was no longer the herald of any total solution which needed only invariate adoption for success. Economic growth under capitalism was not going to abolish destitution, and central and local authorities alike settled to the business of coping as cheaply as they could.[25]

Even so, by the 1870s the costs of poor relief had begun to grow,[26] and there was a new attempt to re-inforce the fundamental ideal of 1834—that the way out of pauperdom lay in individual moral resolve. A Chadwickian call went out for common implementation by all dispensers of relief, charity administrators as much as guardians. But the method was now to be the obverse of Chadwick's: instead of

---

[20] Outdoor Labour Test Order 1843; Outdoor Relief Prohibitory Order 1844; Outdoor Relief Regulation Order 1852. The governance of workhouses was eventually covered by the General Consolidated Workhouse Order 1847. For a detailed description of the law embodied in these Orders, see Webb (1910), pp. 22–87.

[21] In the wake of the northern protests, came a radical movement against "cruelty," which drew distinguished literary support from Dickens and others: cf. D. Roberts (1963) 6 Hist.J. 97; Henriques (1968) 11 Hist.J. 365.

[22] See S.C. Report P.P. 1846 (663) V; I. Anstruther, *The Scandal of the Andover Workhouse* (1973).

[23] 10 & 11 Vict., c. 109.

[24] For immediate repercussions in the equally sensitive field of public health, see above, p. 161.

[25] See generally, Webb (1929).

[26] In 1834–44, the level of expenditure in England and Wales had gone down to £4½–5 millions p.a.; in 1844–64 it was £5–6 millions; in 1864–74, £6–8 millions; thereafter its rise was inexorable.

using nasty medicine to drive all to find other means of support if they could, it required a much more careful diagnosis of the moral potential of each applicant, drawing upon a wide net of information. The concept of "visiting" paupers in order to assess their needs already had a history in the world of charity administration as a means of lowering the evils of indiscriminate doles. The Scots minister, Thomas Chalmers, had demonstrated its possibilities in his Glasgow parish in 1819–23. From 1843, a Metropolitan Visiting and Relief Association, led by Blomfield, Bishop of London, had tried the same plan on a substantial scale.[27] But it was the Charity Organisation Society, founded in 1869, that would give real impetus to the system.[28] Through its "visitors" it sought to divide paupers into the deserving, who would be referred to private charity for the assistance needed to establish themselves in a decent independence; and the undeserving, who would be subjected to the rigours of less eligibility by the guardians.

The case-work techniques which grew out of COS visiting would eventually become the basis of modern social work practice.[29] But its initial thrust, perhaps inevitably, was in the detection of scroungers, the putting down of those who toured the charities with well-practised sob-stories. It was a middle-class commonplace that the poor were by nature lazy and mendacious, and the COS attracted ready support. The courts would approve their policy: the Society's unfavourable report upon an applicant for relief was not actionable as a libel since, being given in all honesty, it attracted qualified privilege.[30]

No attempt was made to impose the visiting system by law. It had considerable appeal within the Local Government Board, which urged it on Boards of Guardians. Many charity trustees and organisers were attracted by the idea. For a time at least, they were able in some cases to get the Charity Commissioners (backed by an important decision of the Court of Appeal) to approve cy-pres schemes altering dole charities, for instance, into trusts for pauper education or pensions for the aged.[31] But this shift in legal attitude lasted only thirty years before the Court of Appeal reverted to the old strictness—a direction to give doles was to be followed even though, "according to modern views, they are productive or more harm than good."[32] This ebb and flow of attitude corresponded with the fortunes of the COS's campaign as a whole. Its plan was never sufficiently adopted in London for it to have real effect. All too soon

[27] Owen (1960), pp. 141–143, 225–228.

[28] Owen (1960) Chap. 8.

[29] See C. L. Mowat, *The Charity Organisation Society 1869–1913* (1961); K. Woodroffe, *From Charity to Social Work* (1962).

[30] *Waller* v. *Loch* (1880) 7 Q.B.D. 619. Another manifestation of the new rigour was the tendency of Unions to introduce rules excluding outdoor relief to the elderly who had relatives able to support them: see D. Thompson [1984] L. & H. Rev. 265.

[31] The case was *Re Campden Charities* (1881) 18 Ch.D. 310, which built upon the House of Lords earlier judgment in *Clephane* v. *Lord Provost of Edinburgh* (1869) L.R. 1 Sc. 417—detailed means could be altered provided the end was preserved.

[32] *Re Weir Hospital* [1910] 2 Ch. 124 at 131 (Cozens Hardy M.R.).

experience bred doubt: the causes of poverty seemed too complex for a simple divide to be cut between the deserving and the undeserving.

One root error of 1832–34 had been the failure of all concerned—Commissioners, government, parliament—to assess the degree to which poor relief went on support of the non-able-bodied—especially the sick and the aged.[33] Chadwick, of course, was deeply interested in the relation of disease to poverty and had certainly proposed "collateral aids." The pressure upon poor law authorities to provide some form of rudimentary medical relief was older than 1834, just as voluntary effort had by then become increasingly concerned with providing hospitals and "public" dispensaries of medicines. Chadwick, however, appreciated, more than any other publicist, the unique contribution of sickness in reducing the poor to inescapable pauperism. However much providing a little medicine to those living at home might smack of greater eligibility rather than less, however much it might make inroads into the workhouse test, it had to be admitted. From the outset guardians used their power to appoint medical officers. Indeed they were soon providing a wholly novel service: in 1840 vaccination against smallpox was made available free to anyone (without pauperising them)[34]; in 1853 it became compulsory for infants.[35] Very gradually the medical service would extend the possibility of treatment in and out of hospital to those who would otherwise be left to folk specifics and quack doctoring.[36]

In the 1870s and 1880s the sick were coming to be dealt with separately, just as the young were beginning more regularly to be moved away to "scattered homes" and fostering families, and the aged were being given separate wards.[37] Belatedly the local Boards, despite a governing concern to keep down their rates, were coming to perceive that these categories were the major recipients of in-house relief, rather than the able-bodied.

At the end of the 1880s the first results of careful investigation of the conditions of the poor—Booth's Surveys of London households—suggested the dreadful statistic that a third of the population might be living in actual want; on even a truly cautious estimate, they had

---

[33] The whole method of the Commissioners of 1832 had been to build their case out of egregious examples rather than overall statistics: Blaug (above, n. 86).

[34] For the establishment of the vaccination service, see R. J. Lambert, *Sir John Simon* (1963), pp. 249–258, 322–328, 356–365, 391–394, 563–567.

[35] Victorian Parliaments did not hesitate to override personal scruples in the name of the public good; but it led to a counter-campaign of hysterical intensity and ultimate success: see R. M. McLeod [1967] Public Law 107, 180.

[36] In 1853, a Poor Law Board Order allowed medical relief to those who could not afford a doctor's fee, even where the head of the family was earning. In London, the hospital services were placed under the Metropolitan Asylums Board and paid for from a common fund from all the unions: Metropolitan Poor Law Act 1867. For the various steps by which the service expanded, see B. Abel-Smith, *The Hospitals 1800–1948* (1964); M. W. Flinn in D. Fraser (ed.), *The New Poor Law in the Nineteenth Century* (1976), p. 45.

[37] The incarceration of the mentally sick in asylums, which raised major issues of personal liberty in respect of both public and private institutions, cannot be explored here. See esp. K. Jones, *Lunacy, Law and Conscience 1744–1845* (1955) and *Mental Health and Social Policy 1845–1959* (1960).

barely enough to get by for most of the time and no possibility of saving for crises such as spells without a job.[38]

PART 2: SCHOOLS: LEARNING AND MASS LITERACY TO 1890

Until the nineteenth century, neither central nor local government would play any real part on the other major front of social provision, the running of schools and other sources of education. But the demand for learning, as a passport to material and social improvement, had already grown, with the middling ranks, over several centuries. A period of formal education between infancy and adolescence was becoming part of childhood for a growing number of boys and even of girls. In eighteenth century London and other commercial centres, proprietary schools were burgeoning in response to the demand. Yet over a longer period charitable endeavour had built up the bulk of what schooling there was.

The abolition of the monasteries had been badly disruptive of the medieval inheritance; but thereafter benefactors had been active in endowing grammar schools, with the classical languages at the fulcrum of their teaching.[39] In some places there were foundations for elementary schools. The early eighteenth century had seen a determined effort, especially through the Society for the Promotion of Christian Knowledge, to extend the number of such schools as a means of inculcating religious feeling, a sense of duty and a modicum of knowledge in some part at least of the lower orders.[40] Education was clearly a key to economic development; but to teach beyond the capacities of the economy to absorb was to invite dissidence. Equally education was a machine for promoting disciplined and loyal order; but in the wrong hands a dangerous threat to existing governance.

The gradual spread of literacy was, to the radically inclined, the great prospect for social progress, to the conservative an object of fear.[41] A stage had arrived at which the education issue was crucial to the future of the polity, yet deeply divisive. The courts, Parliament, central and local government would all become closely involved in its development. By the late Victorian period, all classes would be compelled into a modicum of schooling. However, more advanced education, very largely the preserve of the propertied, would still be in the grip of a voluntarist ideology, allowing within that notion not

---

[38] Booth estimated that eight per cent. of his sample were "very poor." His results were broadly confirmed in Seebohm Rowntree's subsequent study of York. Both were later criticised by the statistician, A. L. Bowley, as serious under-estimations of the levels of poverty: for a summary of the debates, E. H. Hunt, *British Labour History 1815–1914* (1981), pp. 120–125; and see J. H. Treble, *Urban Property in Britain* (1979), pp. 139–148; E.P. Hennock (1976) 1 Soc.Hist. 67.

[39] See, *e.g.*, K. Charlton, *Education in Renaissance England* (1965).

[40] M. G. Jones, *The Charity School Movement* (1938) Chaps. 1, 2 (Pt. II studies the spread of the movement in the differing conditions of Scotland, Ireland and Wales).

[41] For the latter in the Court of Chancery: " . . . though at the reformation greater invitations were made to bring the poor to schools, that is not so proper now, for at present the poor had better be trained up to agriculture": Lord Hardwicke, *Att.-Gen. v. Middleton* (1751) 2 Ves.Sen. 330. See further, H. Silver, *The Concept of Popular Education* (1965), Chap. 1.

only provision through market forces but the considerable support of charitable resources. In support of these developments, a legal structure had to be set up which with time became increasingly complex.

I. GRAMMAR SCHOOLS

Apart from the ancient universities of Oxford and Cambridge, England's main institutions of serious learning were the grammar schools. In 1818 over 550 grammar foundations were recorded, some 130 having been established in the preceding century, the rest earlier.[42] Their governance and operation had frequently fallen prey to eighteenth-century notions of property and place. The Church of England retained a general hold over these schools by the requirement that any teacher appointed to a foundation should have an archbishop's licence.[43] This meant that most of the places were filled with graduates of the universities, whose colleges often held the power of appointment. Once appointed, the master of a school was normally conveyed a life interest in the school-house and left to his own devices during his tenure, in many cases working without assistance and in some doing nothing to attract pupils at all.[44] A more active master, however, rather than turning the school into a sinecure, might use it as a base for profit. As well as fulfilling whatever the foundation required of him, he might add places for paying boarders or introduce (for payment) subjects outside the "grammar" curriculum of Latin and Greek.[45]

It was not until the beginning of the nineteenth century that local communities began in earnest to challenge the condition of their grammar schools. Three main issues would emerge in the procession of Chancery suits that followed. All show the court at work in highly instrumental vein, shaping the schools to the patterns of which the judges most approved. First, could the master add to the classical languages, or indeed replace them, by "modern" subjects in his curriculum? Lord Eldon ruled against the governors of Leeds grammar school (led by the mayor) who sought the addition of modern languages, writing and arithmetic to the master's Latin, Greek and divinity. Following Dr. Johnson's definition of "grammar school," the Lord Chancellor held that the trust had been established only for the latter, and there could be no cy-pres order just because the endowment might be put to better use—a decision of fundamental

---

[42] Nicholas Carlisle, *Endowed Grammar Schools of England and Wales* (1818).

[43] But it applied only to grammar schools, according to *Cox's case* (1700) 1 P. Wms. 29; *R. v. Douse* (1701) 1 Ld. Raym. 672. In *R. v. Archbishop of York* (1795) 6 T.R. 490, Lord Kenyon warmly upheld the Archbishop's power to test the sufficiency of an applicant for a licence.

[44] The Brougham Commissioners found the problem of removing inactive masters one of the most intractable facing them: Thompson (1979), pp. 76, 188.

[45] Accordingly, as much as in proprietary schools, relationships between master and parents became a matter of contract. See, *e.g.*, the minor *cause célèbre, Fitzgerald* v. *Northcote* (1865) 4 F. & F. 656: son of Irish Judge held improperly expelled; the allegation against him was that he ran a secret society to stir up trouble between fee-paying pupils and "church boys" of lower caste.

significance to the whole law of charity.[46] In any case, he had no taste for converting the Leeds school into a "commercial academy," where "the clerks and riders of the merchants are to be taught French and German, to enable them to carry on trade"; indeed the classical scholars might be turned out altogether.[47] By way of reaction to such unprogressive ideas, radicals, including James Mill, Bentham and Romilly, led an indignant campaign for utilitarian curricula. But their Bill seeking to reverse the outcome of the Leeds case was defeated.[48] As it was, the teaching at Leeds was somewhat altered on the accession of the next master, and it is clear that many grammar schools at some stage followed a similar course.[49] Eventually, in Eardley Wilmot's Act of 1840, Chancery was given somewhat larger powers to alter grammar school endowments by introducing new subjects, though the court remained reluctant to intervene with any vigour.[50]

Secondly, there was the question of admitting boarders to those schools which had been established to educate poor boys of the parish or town. The restriction to a classical curriculum was here used for an unequivocal piece of class preference. A few of the best-known schools were developing from local institutions towards being "public" schools in the Victorian and present-day sense. In 1807, Lord Eldon ruled that the foundation of Rugby need not be preserved entirely as a free school for local boys; Sir William Grant M.R. then held likewise of Harrow,[51] where only six locals were attending because, in his view, parents did not want classical education for their sons.[52] The Whig aristocracy and gentry could accordingly continue to send their sons there; trust funds were held to have been properly spent on building a new boarding house because the original deed allowed the admission of "foreigners."[53] Under later Chancellors, somewhat lesser schools were required to pay rather greater respect to the local interest, but attitudes varied: Lord Cottenham wanted to oblige the trustees of Manchester Grammar School to cut back their intake of boarders; but when the case came to Lord Lyndhurst he would not accept the new regulations that Cottenham had

---

[46] *Att.-Gen.* v. *Whiteley* (1805) 11 Ves.Jun. 241 (true to type, the case took eight years to dispose of). See generally R. S. Tompson, *Classics or Charity* (1971), pp. 116–126.

[47] The numbers in attendance had already sunk to 44; Eldon also refused to make the master's and usher's salaries dependent upon the number of pupils. In *Att.-Gen.* v. *Mansfield* (1826) 2 Russ. 501, he disapproved the action of the Highgate School trustees in allowing it to become purely an elementary school.

[48] See Simon (1960) Chap. 2.

[49] According to *A Letter . . . on the Best Method of Restoring Decayed Grammar Schools* (1818), about half of 500 grammar schools were teaching every variety of subject, or only "English" subjects, or a choice of English and classical. Some modification is apparent in *Att.-Gen.* v. *Dixie* (1825) 3 Russ. 534n; *Att.-Gen.* v. *Haberdashers' Co.* (1827) 3 Russ. 530.

[50] 3 & 4 Vict., c. 77; classical studies could be abandoned altogether only if there was insufficient finance. The application had to be within 6 months of appointing a new master, which caught out some trustees. For the Court's attitude, see Evidence to the Taunton Commission (below, n. 86), Qs. 13451–52, 12840–44.

[51] For both cases, *Att.-Gen.* v. *Clarendon* (Earl) (1810) 17 Ves.Jun. 491.

[52] The parishioners said this was the result of upper-class bullying.

[53] For the later exclusion of locals, see Simon (1960), pp. 312–318; and below n. 83.

caused to be drafted,[54] stating that it was in the interests of the community as a whole that boys from all classes should receive a classical education together.[55] Shadwell V.C. banished boarders from Tiverton; but Turner V.C. allowed them to remain at Kidderminster.[56] By 1860, Bethell, the Attorney-General, put, and Lord Romilly M.R. accepted, the case against re-admitting boarders to Bristol Grammar School. It did not belong to the class of superior boarding schools (such as Eton, Harrow and Rugby) which had emerged as leading establishments for the education of gentlemen and as such were "governed by another set of principles." Accordingly it should remain a separate school for "intelligent humbler boys" who (*pace* Lord Lyndhurst) were better treated thus.[57]

The third issue, of the right of dissenting parents to withdraw their children from religious instruction at a grammar school (which would necessarily be in Anglican doctrine), did not emerge in the courts until the 1840s, when non-conformists were locked with Church and state in other educational battles.[58] In 1842, Knight-Bruce V.C. was prepared to insert a "conscience clause" allowing withdrawal in a new scheme for Bury St. Edmunds School; but Lord Lyndhurst refused, in the case of Warwick, to bind the master with any such fetter.[59] Subsequently it seems that conscience clauses became usual in any case where the foundation document did not positively require the teaching of a particular dogma.[60] But Nonconformist, Catholic, Jewish and other parents had still to brave the displeasure of determined headmasters, so that the right might mean little in practice. And the hold of the church over appointing headmasters continued, the Lords Justices refusing to admit dissenters as trustees of Ilminster Free School in 1858.[61]

II. ELEMENTARY TEACHING

The small portion of the populace who went on to the further teaching provided by the grammar and like schools received their first teaching from parents or tutors, or from school masters and mistresses in a small, or sometimes more substantial, way. But beyond them was another fraction who would acquire a little learning between the ages of six or seven and ten or even twelve. In the earlier eighteenth century the movement to endow charity schools led to the provision of 1,500 or more schools catering particularly for this segment, but by the end of the century it was losing way. In its place came organisations and models for Sunday schools, schools of indus-

[54] He purported to follow Eldon's view in *Att.-Gen.* v. *Coopers' Co.* (1812) 19 Ves.Jun. 187.

[55] *Att.-Gen.* v. *Stamford (Earl)* (1839–1842) 1 Ph. 737.

[56] *Att.-Gen.* v. *Devon (Earl)* (1846) 15 Sim. 193; *Att.-Gen.* v. *Worcester (Bishop)* (1851) 9 Hare 328.

[57] *Re Bristol Free Grammar School* (1860) 28 Beav. 161.

[58] See below, pp. 440–441.

[59] *Att.-Gen.* v. *Cullum* (1842) Y. & C.C.C. 411; *re Warwick Grammar School* (1845) 1 Ph. 564

[60] See further below, p. 445.

[61] *Re Ilminster Free School* (1858) 2 De. G. & J. 535.

try, schools for apprentices in factories, and above all schools on the monitorial system, using older pupils as the medium for inculcating learning by rote.[62]

This last movement, which spread rapidly at the outset of the new century, would first channel the heated rivalry of Anglicans and Non-conformists on which so much else would come to depend. The established Church supported the National Society for the Education of the Poor and drew its inspiration from Dr. Andrew Bell; the non-conformists came to dominate the British and Foreign Schools Society, which was guided by Dr. Joseph Lancaster, an influential figure for many radicals, including Bentham and Brougham. Each Society strove to swell its own numbers and to resist any sign of favoritism to the other.[63]

It was in the shade of this determined competition that the first prospects of legal compulsion in education were aired. The older Peel's Act of 1802 to protect apprentices in factories[64] had required their masters to provide them with instruction during "some part" of each working day in their first four years; but without effective machinery for enforcement, it remained the expression of pious hope.[65] A more ambitious plan was contained in Samuel Whitbread's Bill of 1807 requiring each parish by rate to provide a school for at least two years of education. This provoked a violent reaction, led by Eldon and the Archbishop of Canterbury: the poor would become "factious and refractory" by reading "seditious pamphlets, vicious books and publications against Christianity." In 1820 Brougham sought to follow up his Committee of inquiry into education of the Metropolitan poor[66] with a somewhat similar plan which specified that the schoolmaster be chosen by the parish vestry, even though religious instruction would be limited to the scriptures without the addition of Church doctrine. But his Bill had to be abandoned in the face of the passionate hostility of Non-conformists against so irrevocable a tie to the Anglican persuasion.[67]

Brougham himself thereafter turned back to his old hope of voluntary effort, but the radical demand for state support was by no means wholly lost. The Factories Act of 1833 contained new requirements for the schooling of factory children in general, which again came to very little, since the new inspectors were preoccupied with hours of work and other basic questions.[68] More importantly, the Whig government decided in that year to cope with the religious hostilities that so plagued educational advance by establishing a fund of

---

[62] See esp. M. G. Jones (above, n. 40) Chaps. 2, 5; Curtis (1967) Chap. 6; Barnard (1961) Chap. 6.

[63] Barnard (1961) Chap. 6; Simon (1960) Chap. 2; Sturt (1967) Chap. 2.

[64] See above, p. 301.

[65] There were, of course, some factory owners who felt it their paternal duty to set up schooling.

[66] This Committee, thanks to Brougham's penchant for dramatising particular scandals, did a good deal to point up the deficiencies and neglects in administering school trusts and other charities; for the Reports, see P P 1816 (427, 469, 495, 497) IV; 1818 (356) IV.

[67] Simon (1960), pp. 151–152. In areas of Irish immigration Catholic schools were also growing, and with them another sectarian voice.

[68] See G. Ward (1935) 3 Ec.H.R. 110.

£20,000 for school building, to be given to organisations which had raised half the costs themselves, and would maintain the school afterwards. The sum, increased to £30,000 in the following year, was divided between the two major societies, the National and the British and Foreign.[69]

The need for some permanent supervision of this grant, however, led to a distinctive experiment in bureaucracy building. In 1839 Lord John Russell announced the establishment of an Education Committee of the Privy Council.[70] It would not need the kind of rule-making authority that had been a mainstay of the Poor Law Commissioners; unlike them it could exert the easy authority of the purse and needed only to minute its principles for distributing the grant.[71] It at once imposed inspection as a prerequisite of aid. The Church tried to insist that it should inspect its own schools but only managed (by an administrative Concordat of 1840) to secure the right to instruct the Committee's inspectors in the assessment of religious teaching. The Committee's secretary, Dr. Kay (later Sir James Kay-Shuttleworth), proved a forceful but discreet counsellor who steered it past various religious shoals.[72] Until his retirement from exhaustion in 1849, the inspectorate became a strongly progressive force, working to replace monitors with teenage pupil-teachers, who were effectively apprentices in a rising profession.[73]

The largest controversy—over factory schooling—ultimately served to bolster the system evolved in the 1830s. Worried by the indiscipline of Chartism and hustled by Tractarian demands for Church domination of elementary education, Peel's Home Secretary, Graham, returned to this long-avoided subject. His bill in 1843 required factory children to be given three hours teaching a day, where necessary in grant-supported schools. These would mostly fall under Anglican auspices, with no more than a conscience clause for dissenters. Their outrage was immense. All that Graham could secure in the Factories Act of the following year was that a child spend three whole days a week, or six half-days, at school. The factory master might deduct 2d. a week from wages as a contribution to the cost, but the nature of the school was left undefined.[74] The voluntary societies were to continue to their programmes with grant-aid where they satisfied the Committee's inspectors. It was this combination of religious enthusiasm and state support that made possible the first significant measure of legal compulsion in education. While children were beyond the question to remain part of the labour force in indus-

---

[69] See J. L. Alexander (1977) 20 Hist.J. 395; Sturt (1967), pp. 62–73.

[70] Barnard (1961), pp. 69–70.

[71] Sturt (1967), pp. 73–92. For the attitudes of the inspectors, see R. Johnson (1970) 49 P. & P. 96.

[72] One of Kay's most far-seeing experiments was in the establishment of a teacher-training school. The Committee's own attempt at this foundered upon the religious antipathies; but Kay saw to the establishment of a private school which was soon handed over to the National Society and led to the establishment of 22 such schools by 1845: Sturt (1967) Chap. 5.

[73] See N. Ball, *Her Majesty's Inspectorate 1839–1849* (1963).

[74] 7 & 8 Vict., c. 15, ss.39, 40. See J. T. Ward and J. H. Treble (1969) 20 J. Eccles. Hist 79; I. Pinchbeck and M. Hewitt, *Children in English Society* (1969), II 414–430; and for the education of pauper children in workhouses, Chap. 17.

try, it was their master's responsibility to see them redeemed from total illiteracy.[75] They were no longer to be left simply in the thrall of drudging routine until put out of work by a down-turn in trade; the social consequences were too threatening, the economic too short-sighted.

By the mid-1850s the Privy Council Committee was distributing over £500,000, four-fifths of which, thanks to inspection, was going to the Church of England's National Society. In 1852, the Committee was able to use its authority to impose a conscience clause, giving parents the right to withdraw children from religious instruction, as a condition of grant.[76] In 1856, the Committee also took over from the Board of Trade two small departments administering separate grants for further education, one for science and the other for industrial design. Although the two branches—the Education Department for schools in Whitehall and the Science and Art Department in South Kensington—continued to operate separately, the whole activity came to need the political responsibility of a regular ministry. The Lord President of the Council continued, as in the past, to answer for the Committee in the Lords, but he was given a Vice-President in the Commons who was also a member of the government.[77] A rapid process of bureaucratic evolution was completed just as the debate upon educational needs at all levels entered a truly momentous phase.

III. The Royal Commissions

The traditional institutions for the education of gentlemen—the ancient universities and great public schools which supplied most of their entrants—were not readily moved by calls for greater relevance, sterner purpose or wider access. Yet by mid-century, Oxford and Cambridge could begin to be measured against other institutions— the university colleges in London and Durham and the colleges for medical teaching in other towns; and the public schools were facing substantial competition from new private schools for the ever-growing middle classes.[78] The two universities were obliged, despite high-handed protest, to undergo criticism by Royal Commission and to submit to legislation which, in particular, lifted the religious tests and other forms of preference for members of the Established Church.[79]

In 1861 a Commission chaired by the Earl of Clarendon reported on the nine leading public schools,[80] which together educated some 3,000 upper-class boys and received £65,000 in annual income.[81] The

---

[75] See Simon (1960), pp. 170–177; Macdonagh (1977), pp. 63–66. The part-time system would remain until 1918: E. and R. Frow, *The Half-Time System in Education* (1970).

[76] Minute of 1852.

[77] An arrangement achieved by Order-in-Council in 1856, after failure of a Bill.

[78] See, *e.g.*, Barnard (1961) Chap. 14.

[79] On the abolition of religious tests, see A. V. Dicey, *Law and Opinion in England in the 19th Century* (2nd ed., 1914), Appendix.

[80] P.P. 1864 [C. 3288] XX, XXI.

[81] They were: Eton and Winchester (old ecclesiastical foundations linked to university colleges); Shrewsbury, Harrow and Rugby (originally grammar schools); Westminster and Charterhouse (London foundations); and St Paul's and Merchant Taylors (City livery foundations).

Commission had no criticism of the essential ethos of these schools and their devotion to the formation of the governing class.[82] In particular, it supported moves to eliminate local boys from those which had developed out of grammar schools for the poor.[83] But it allowed some criticism of means—particularly in comparison with what was being achieved in the newer proprietary schools: there should be a broadening of curricula from the dominant, stereotyped study of classical languages and, in some cases, a greater devotion of funds to teaching.[84] Most of the Schools needed a transformation of their governing bodies to make them more representative of the upper echelons of society and without pecuniary interest in the foundation. In 1868, the Public Schools Act provided the legal machinery to achieve this, requiring a scheme to be submitted for Privy Council approval.[85] But, as with the two universities, this was temporary intervention, leaving the schools completely self-governing and subject to no element of inspection.

At the next level down, came the other endowed schools. The Commission chaired by the Earl of Taunton, using the well-tried machinery of investigative assistants, collected an overview of some 3,000 schools, 705 of them "grammar" schools, a further 70 to 80 providing more than elementary education.[86] Its opinion of the direction in which these schools should be moving was, like the Clarendon Report, marked by a strong feeling of class division. Its model was the Prussian *Realschulen*—separate schools for each social class—rather than the American precedent of free schools for all. There must be classical-cum-modern schools, preparing for university the sons of those of independent means, professional and business men, the clergy and gentry; schools of a second category teaching (to the age of sixteen) Latin and a good grounding in modern subjects to the sons of the larger tenant farmers, shopkeepers and rising men of business, for entry into the army, the lesser professions, civil engineering and the like; and schools of a third category—for the families of small tenant farmers and tradesmen and superior artisans—teaching (to the age of fourteen) "very good" reading, writing and arithmetic. For the ordinary labouring class, elementary education was all that the current economy and their expectations within it could allow.[87]

The Commissioners considered that many of the existing schools met these various needs in extremely poor fashion, scraping along with wholly inadequate staff and premises. Their recommendations covered not only a major refurbishing of existing endowments,

---

[82] "Character" was properly implanted by the boys' self-government—including (with qualifications) the practice of fagging.

[83] This completed, for Harrow, a process already set in train with the approval of Chancery—see above, n. 51.

[84] The finding that the schools were sending out too many "men of idle habits and empty and uncultivated minds" rather undermined the earlier statements of approval.

[85] St. Pauls and Merchant Taylors did not need to be dealt with by this machinery.

[86] P.P. 1867–1868 [3966] XXVIII (in 19 parts). See generally, Owen (1960) Chap. 9.

[87] The thinking was primarily about boys, though, after impressive evidence from Miss Buss (North London Collegiate School), Miss Beale (Cheltenham Ladies College) and other pioneer figures, it expressed a general wish to see endowments, where possible, used for the education of girls as well: Owen (1961) Chap. 6.

which would include the adaptation of trusts by vigorous cy-pres intervention, but also the marshalling of public resources, drawing both central Commissioners and local Poor Law Guardians into the process of assessing local needs and organising the building of new schools, if necessary by means of a local rate. Endowments and rates would together provide and maintain buildings, while parents would meet teaching costs out of fees.[88] Education to these levels was to remain an advantage that must be purchased.

The major novelty would be the rejuvenation of charitable endowments under bureaucratic rather than judicial supervision: this would prove to be the point at which a Brougham-like imposition of overall policy would most substantially be realised in the whole history of charity reform. Gladstone's government promoted the Endowed Schools Act 1869; a three-man Commission was given power to alter existing educational endowments (not only for grammar schools) by schemes that would be "more conducive to the advancement of education of boys and girls or either of them."[89] In addition it was made possible to divert charities from other purposes (loans and doles, marriage portions, apprenticeships, imprisoned debtors etc.) which had failed or outgrown their object, even in some cases ignoring the "next-nearest" requirement of the cy-près rule, but in this case only with the trustees' consent.[90] Chancery was sidestepped: schemes were to be approved by the Education Department (with appeal to the Privy Council itself) and laid before Parliament as a final endorsement.[91]

The first Commissioners moved somewhat aggressively and met the kind of opposition from large well-funded institutions which had long bedevilled this sort of instrumentalist interference.[92] When Disraeli took over in 1874, his government refused to renew the Commission, transferring its role to the Charity Commissioners. Under their more accommodating regime, slow progress continued, something under half the 1,200 or so schools within the Act having received new schemes by 1884 and about 100 other trusts (with annual incomes of £16,000) having been diverted to education. It was a record of useful, but limited, achievement.[93] The mid-Victorian settlement, leaving more advanced education strictly within the voluntary sphere, could not prove final. The pressures, to which the

---

[88] For teacher training, the Commission refused to countenance state-run *écoles normales* of the French type, preferring the system of government grants to efficient private establishments on the lines already operating for elementary schoolteachers: Owen (1961), pp. 611–617.

[89] s.9. There were various exceptions: see s.14 and the Elementary Education Act 1870, s.75.

[90] The endowment had to have been created before 1800. Chancery judges had sometimes been prepared to act in the same way in non-contentious cases: Evidence to the Taunton Commission, (above, n. 80) Q.13,197, *cf.* 13, 310.

[91] Two Commissioners, Lord Lyttelton and Arthur Hobhouse Q.C., were well-known advocates of rigorous re-direction.

[92] The House of Lords threw out their scheme for the Emanuel Hospital, Westminster: Owen (1960), pp. 257–259.

[93] Owen (1960), pp. 259–268. A Select Committee, whipped up by Chamberlain and Collings' Birmingham Education League, nonetheless refused to make major criticisms of the Commission's activities in the educational field: P.P. 1886 (191) IX; see Simon (1960), pp. 329–344.

Taunton Commission had responded, would continue to grow until government would be obliged unequivocally to intervene, but not for another thirty years.[94]

In the aftermath of 1867, it was in the realm of strictly basic education that the state would interfere. One view of the reformed franchise was Robert Lowe's despairing plea to "educate our masters"; but the shift in perceptions was a great deal more complex than that. In the preceding years there had been one extensive survey of elementary schooling, conducted by the assistants to the third of the Royal Commissions, that under the Duke of Newcastle into popular education.[95] As this found, the requirement imposed on factory proprietors in 1844 to furnish opportunities for part-time teaching had done something to reduce the entire absence of schools for the masses in industrial districts. In twenty years the proportion of the population being taught something had improved from perhaps 1:16 to 1:8.[96] Quite as significant was the fact that, of those said to be in school, the great proportion were very young, irregular attenders, and in part this was because the teaching was so inadequate. Nearly a million pupils were in schools supported by Education Department grants but rather more were enrolled at private establishments, many of them the most meagre of "dame schools."[97] Their standards came nowhere near the requirements of the Department's inspectors.[98]

The Commission had been appointed at a time when a lobby for further state grants faced a voluntarist movement which took as a principle of high liberalism that education should be entirely beyond the intervention of the state, a combination of private contract and benevolent aid.[99] In the report a voluntarist minority among its members reported in favour of this position while the majority moved to an uneasy compromise, which rejected radical plans for compulsory state education (on the Prussian model); but it proposed an increase in the central grant on the existing basis of average attendance, and the introduction of rate assistance to private schools on the basis of examinations conducted by the Department's inspectors.[1]

No government could easily accept that education should fall to the mercies of local politicians, with their penchant for sectarian strife. In the immediate event, the central grant remained the sole source of aid, but upon a different version of liberal principle from the voluntarists': this was largely the brain-child of Robert Lowe, who had become Vice-President of the Education Department in 1859, and his friend, Lingen, who had succeeded Kay-Shuttleworth as the Secretary. The qualifying conditions for a grant would become more

[94] See below, p. 474ff.

[95] See below, n. 1.

[96] Statistics were much bandied in the 1850s, but it proved very difficult to get an accurate picture.

[97] But some of the worst were set up by masters, rather than mistresses.

[98] In the 1850s the prime measure of efficiency was the requirement that a child attend for at least 176 days a year.

[99] A leading voluntarist figure was the Congregationalist, Edward Baines, editor of the *Leeds Mercury*. He was to lead the Minority on the Commission.

[1] P.P. 1861 [2794] XXI—in 6 Parts; Sturt (1967) Chap. 12.

closely analogous to market forces: the Newcastle notion of supplementation after examination was now erected into a rigorous organising principle. The "payment-by-results" of Lowe's Revised Code of 1862,[2] gave a third of the grant per child for sufficient attendance, but two-thirds for satisfying the inspector's standards. These gave strictest attention to the necessary skills in reading, writing and arithmetic,[3] rewarding the successful school and impoverishing the weak.[4] It horrified at the outset those like Kay-Shuttleworth and Matthew Arnold, who conceived education to be altogether a larger, more fulfilling ideal, and its yoke lay heavy upon teacher and pupil alike for nearly forty years.[5] But it was a crucial instrument in reconciling the liberal conscience to the uncomfortable fact that while some measure of literacy and learning was becoming essential for life in industrial society, the demand lay beyond the resources of voluntary endeavour and private purchase. Thus education became the root example of what, in neo-liberal thought, the state should guarantee to all.[6]

IV. Compulsion

In any case, the stark fact of franchise reform in 1867 made participation at local level seem inevitable. The Elementary Education Act 1870, promoted by Gladstone's Education Vice-President, W. E. Forster, required new local authorities—the School Boards—to provide schools for education to the age of thirteen where the denominations and charities had not done so. It only foreshadowed compulsory attendance and it did not make provision free (save for the very poor); but it was the crucial precursor of both these steps.[7] The passage of the Bill was dominated by the question of religious teaching in the new schools but the new sense of urgency prevented it from foundering. In the end it was left, by the "Cowper-Temple clause," that there should be no teaching of any "catechism or religious formulary distinctive of any particular denomination."[8] Thus did the radicals of the Birmingham Education League and their nonconformist allies secure the exclusion of the Anglican priests from the Board School classroom.[9]

The churches were given a period of grace within which to set up

---

[2] The concept had the approval of the Newcastle majority.

[3] In 1860, the Privy Council Committee's Minutes had been collected by Lowe into a Code. After 1870, new Minutes became ordinary delegated legislation requiring to be laid before both Houses.

[4] The amounts were originally 4s. and 8s. for a day child, 2s. 6d. and 5s. for an evening child.

[5] For each child there were six Standards of attainment to be achieved; see generally, Sturt (1967) Chap. 13.

[6] See above, p. 112ff.

[7] See Simon (1960), pp. 360–367; Sturt (1967) Chap. 14; G. Sutherland, *Policy Making in Education 1870–1895* (1973) Pt. I.

[8] s.14(2).

[9] The denominational schools in receipt of the Privy Council grant continued under the obligation of a "conscience clause." As further support against domineering Anglicanism, they were required to restrict religious instruction to the first and last periods of the school day: s.7. So great was hostility on the subject that the government could do no less.

further denominational schools under the existing system,[10] but once it was over the radical new machinery began to turn. The Education Department surveyed each district, leaving out of account non-elementary schools, those which charged more than 9d per week and denominational schools which would not accept a conscience clause.[11] If, on its estimate of children requiring schooling, it found a short-fall of places, it would establish a local School Board for the area, with the duty of making up the deficiency. The necessary finance would comprise pupils' fees of up to 9d a week, a central grant from the Education Department under the "payment by results" conditions of the revised Code, and—for any additional expenditure—a local rate.[12]

Once more local government had increased by spawning novel units, this time for a purpose that would soon impose a considerable burden on ratepayers. The development would leave public education to central and local authorities in a way that would in time bring them into serious conflict, largely because their respective areas of authority were ill-defined in law.[13] In 1880 only a sixth of all children were in Board Schools, whereas by 1900 it was over half. Altogether the proportion of the school-age population in adequate schools improved from 7.7 per cent. (1:13) in 1870 to 16 per cent. in 1885 (1:6).[14]

Compulsory attendance grew through the power given to local authorities in 1870 to impose it for their areas: the London School Board led the way and many towns followed. Lord Sandon's Act of 1876 imposed on parents the duty of seeing that their children received efficient elementary instruction, with criminal penalties for failure. As an enforcement machine, it established School Attendance Committees for districts that lacked School Boards.[15] In 1880, A. J. Mundella—like Forster, a radical Vice-President of the Board—secured an Act requiring children to attend school between the ages of five and ten, though local authorities could extend this and also create exemptions. Basic education had become a responsibility of the state and with it a set of correlative duties which the state could impose on parents. With the arrival of the truancy officer came a complex of legal powers—to prosecute those who would not comply,

---

[10] The churches responded vigorously to this stimulus: over ten years the National Society made more than a million school places available:

[11] This followed from the definition of "elementary school" in the 1870 Act, s.3. While this amounted to "a euphemism for 'Education of the Children of the Poor' " (Eaglesham (1956), p. 7), the better-off were not prevented from sending their children to Board Schools, a proposal for doing so having been dropped from the Bill.

[12] If the Board of Education found a School Board to be in default it could take control by appointing nominees, and it had power to block applications for loans. A School Board, once established, became the primary provider, with voluntary schools being the first to lose grant if a surplus of places arose; numerous bitter contests accordingly continued into the next decades.

[13] See below, p. 474.

[14] Average attendances improved from 68 to 76 per cent. in the same period: Cross Commission (below, p. 474, n. 69) App. A (2).

[15] For the results, see esp. G. Sutherland (above, n. 7) Chap. 5; D. Rubinstein, *School Attendance in London 1870–1904* (1969); J. S. Hurt, *Elementary Schooling and the Working Classes 1860–1918* (1979), esp. Chap. 3.

to take children into care and so forth.[16] The continual press of new children into the schools made it difficult to keep up the requirement of fees and a central grant in lieu was introduced in 1891, rendering the Board Schools effectively free.[17] The strict Standards of the Revised Code proved less and less appropriate to the range of children in the schools and they were modified and then in 1890 very largely dropped as a basis of financing.[18] One of the root arguments about the nature of the protective state—whether its benefits should be universal or means-tested—had been resolved for elementary education in favour of the former. It was to be a significant precedent.

PART 3: POOR RELIEF AND ITS ALTERNATIVES

I. EDWARDIAN INITIATIVES

(a) Analysing Poverty

The moral view that self-reliant endeavour alone could solve the long-term problems of the poor had reached its greatest strength in the buoyant mid-century years. There had been temporary upsets—the terrible disruption of cotton supplies to Lancashire during the American civil war, for instance.[19] To deflect such disasters the propertied gave with unexampled willingness. But in the ordinary run, those out of work had to search until they found more and charity was supposed only to carry them forward in their hunt. Those who did not succeed were by definition shiftless; those who did not save risked the consequences of sickness and old age. People could not be left entirely to starve, but short of that they should be given little quarter; hence the whole policy of the Charity Organisation Society.[20] The same perception was expressed by orthodox economists in their own terms: there could be no ultimate imbalance between supply and demand for labour; unemployment demonstrated the unwillingness of labour to accept lower wages in times of falling demand; the market must be left to teach its lesson.[21]

Only in the 1890's did "poverty" and "unemployment" begin widely to be perceived as distinct problems of the economy which might not be explicable in terms of individual lack of responsiveness and which might accordingly justify state intervention by way of cor-

---

[16] For the numerous legal difficulties, see Sutherland (above, n. 7), pp. 146–150, 157–159.

[17] The elaborate structure in the Conservatives' Act allowed individual schools to charge fees and many voluntary schools continued to do so. The cost to the Treasury was £2 million per annum, making education the largest home spending department. See generally, Sutherland (above, n 7) Chap 6

[18] For extensions of the Standards, see below, pp. 472–473.

[19] Owen (1960), pp. 511–514.

[20] See above, pp. 433–434.

[21] Harris, (1972), pp. 9–11.

rective.[22] The persistent depression in particular industries and parts of the country, the widespread disruptions during downswings in the general cycle of trade, the sullen and occasionally threatening gatherings of the unemployed in London and other cities, the investigations into the conditions of the unskilled working-class, the emergence of a distinctive political representation of labour—all these contributed to the change. Only gradually did anything like an adequate analysis of the whole conspectus emerge. It was not until the appearance of William Beveridge's *Unemployment. A Problem of Industry* (1909) that there was any adequate distinction between the skilled worker temporarily laid off and the casual unskilled, endemically under-employed, who gradually got less and less work as depression deepened. It was a period in which understandings of the difficulties shifted in tandem with proposals and actual attempts to solve them. First the Conservative governments of Salisbury and Balfour, and then the Liberals, triumphant in 1905, realised that they were facing a central preoccupation of their political futures.

A major focus for the debate came to be the Royal Commission on the Poor Law, established by the Balfour Government in its last months and concluded only four years later in 1909.[23] It was composed almost entirely of those with a strong personal or professional interest in the subject, with a large representation of both the COS and the LGB.[24] Giving evidence at an early stage, J. S. Davy, Chief Inspector of the LGB, made an uncompromising plea for a return to the "principles of 1834."[25] On the Commission, Beatrice Webb conducted a campaign against any such move, going at the business with such determination that an immense body of information about every aspect of the poor law, and not merely relief to the able-bodied, was amassed and eventually published.[26] Her determination would mean in the end that she and three other Commissioners wrote a Minority Report which in some respects went beyond the Majority Report of the other fifteen. But what was chiefly remarkable was that the majority were carried so far towards perceiving "poverty" as much more than a need to discourage "pauperism." The minority's call for a "break-up" of the poor law and the guarantee of a national minimum for all was too dramatic for the majority's taste; but they accepted that the state must provide distinct solutions to a variety of problems, using separate administrations for the purpose. Like the minority, the majority wanted services for the poor to pass mainly to the county-level authorities (under the blander title, "public assistance") and to be backed by national provision for labour exchanges and perhaps national contribution to unemployment insurance.[27] The majority still hoped for collaboration with charitable bodies in a

---

[22] *Ibid.*, pp. 11–26; Thane (1982), pp. 14–18, 57–63 and generally, J. A. Garraty, *Unemployment in History* (1978); Fraser (1983) Chap. 6.

[23] P.P. 1909 [Cd. 4499] XXXVII; [Cd. 4630, 4922] XXXVIII (Scotland and Ireland).

[24] The chairman was Lord George Hamilton; the Minority Report was written by Beatrice (and Sidney) Webb; its other signatories were George Lansbury, Francis Chandler (a trade unionist) and the Rev. Russell Wakefield.

[25] See P.P. 1909 [Cd. 4625] XXXIX, esp. Qs. 2230, 3285–87.

[26] P.P. 1909 XXXIX–XLV; 1910 XLVI–LV.

[27] The Majority, if anything, favoured contributory schemes, the Minority, non-contributory.

programme of social casework,[28] a tradition which the minority wished to replace with forceful action by local government officials. But even they did not propose any wide range of entitlements not conditioned upon means tests. This was why it seemed so important to determine who would administer relief.

The minority's largest vision was of means and methods for providing a guaranteed minimum income to those suffering unemployment. Their proposals for compulsory labour exchanges, and for participation in retraining schemes as a condition of relief, together with the organization of large-scale public works for periods of trade depression,[29] amounted to a reflationary programme by major state intervention. Only a long train of bitter experiences still to come could convert it into Keynes-inspired orthodoxy.

(b) Tackling Unemployment

Faced with enduring, widespread unemployment from 1903 onwards, the Conservative government was eventually moved to legislative intervention. In the field of employment they had been prepared to impose on the employer the obligation to compensate in small measure for accidents at work which resulted in incapacity.[30] If this invasion of free contracting must be regarded, in the light of the coming arrangements for social security, as a transitional stage, the same is true of their Unemployed Workmen Act 1905. Here was the first legislative acknowledgment that central government must intervene in tempering the effects of an economic phenomenon that was beyond the power of the individual to avert. At the same time, its main technique was to support the effectiveness of charitable giving by means of a special rate.[31] Relief committees were to be set up in all metropolitan boroughs and urban districts of more than 50,000 inhabitants, in order to organise the relief of distress by work provision, labour exchanges, labour colonies in the country and emigration assistance.[32] The Committees were accordingly to contain representatives of charities and boards of guardians and were to act very much on COS principles: they would investigate the degree of need among applicants and give whatever assistance was warranted. This was machinery which would side-step the drudge-labour test, upon which poor relief to the "able-bodied" was still in principle dependent. Walter Long, the President of the LGB, had hoped that in London this Act would also prove a means towards equalising the

---

[28] The local authority would have a voluntary aid committee to which an applicant would first be passed for judgment; if he failed he would be sent to the public assistance committee for relief that was in some measure less eligible: Report (above, n. 23), p. 425 (cf. the Minority at p. 1006: an arrangement intended "to withdraw the whole relief of distress from popular control.")

[29] They did not hesitate to recommend forced labour camps for the recalcitrant.

[30] See below, p. 528ff.

[31] ss.1(6), 2(3).

[32] The LGB was empowered to extend the arrangements to other areas where they were needed: s.2(1).

cost to rate-payers across the metropolis, thus alleviating the spiral-ling difficulties of the poorest boroughs, like Poplar and Bermond-sey. The richer, however, could not be induced to co-operate.[33]

Long also hoped that the new Committees might become perma-nent fixtures. However, the Cabinet insisted upon a three-year limit in the Act, choosing to establish the Royal Commission on the Poor Laws as a preliminary to final decisions upon the whole future of social provision. With little by way of resource and no real commit-ment either from the outgoing Conservatives or the incoming Liber-als, the Committees had a faltering existence not serving even to dispel the disturbing marches and demonstrations of the unem-ployed themselves. It was scarcely possible to provide suitable work for the skilled at times when they could not find it for themselves; and for the unskilled, the size of the problem was simply too great. The committees were mostly abandoned when their first life deter-mined.

The experience of the 1905 Act was not, however, wholly a waste. Through the collation of information, both politicians and planners could learn a great deal about the perplexing character of unemploy-ment. In the metropolis and elsewhere the labour exchanges con-tinued in existence and were seen by Beveridge and others (and eventually both Royal Commission Reports) as vital instruments for the future. Churchill brought Beveridge into the Labour Department of the Board of Trade to prepare for their introduction as a national network and a corollary of his proposed unemployment insurance. By 1909, it was possible to institute them by central funding without division between the major parties.[34] The only real concern came from trade unionists who feared, behind the exchanges, the pros-pects of compulsory labour and the undermining of strike action.[35] In consequence, they became a voluntary service, without any require-ment that jobs should be filled only through their auspices and with an explicit acknowledgment that no disqualification or prejudice should follow from refusing a job under strike conditions or at a rate below that prevailing in a district.[36] This went part of the way to meet Labour objections. By 1914 there were 423 main exchanges, fill-ing over 3,000 positions a day. But only 1 in 4 applicants found work through them, and many employers continued to fill jobs from those who presented themselves at the works.[37]

In no part of Europe, America or Australasia had state schemes of

---

[33] Harris (1972), pp. 157–158, and see generally, Chap. 4; Gilbert (1966), pp. 237–246; K. D. Brown, (1971) 43 J.Med.Hist. 615, and *Labour and Unemployment 1900–1914* (1971) Chap. 2.

[34] The Labour Exchanges Act 1909 was skeletal in form, leaving details to be worked out in regulations and orders of the Labour Department. 61 exchanges from the 1905 Act were taken into the new scheme. See generally, J. Harris (1972), pp. 199–208, 278–295, and *William Beveridge* (1977) Chap. 7; J. A. M. Caldwell (1959) 37 Pub.Admin 367.

[35] The Webbs, particularly in the Minority Report of the Royal Commission, were leading advocates of a compulsory role for the exchanges.

[36] s.2(2).

[37] Thane (1982), p. 93. For the contemporaneous attempt to improve wages in the sweated trades through Trade Boards, see above, pp. 337–338.

protection been extended to the plight of those out of work.[38] It was Beveridge in 1907 who first raised the real possibility of unemployment insurance as a complement to labour exchanges. Once the plan for the latter had taken shape, he and Llewellyn Smith,[39] with Churchill's backing, could turn to the insurance prospect. Existing provision against unemployment through trade unions covered only some 1.5 million workers.[40] The unions argued that state subsidy of unemployment should be administered by them, and that it should be funded by the Treasury out of general revenues. But the government was kept to a contributory scheme by its own predilections and by the grave uncertainties underlying the whole venture, since there were no adequate statistics of unemployment on which to make projections.[41] To secure union co-operation it proved sufficient to add a Treasury grant (initially 1⅔d. per man per week) to contributions (initially 2½d. each) from employer and employee.[42]

However, the major decision to reduce a risk—a significant piece of experimentalism—was to confine the scheme to selected industries: building and construction, shipbuilding, engineering and vehicle construction, iron-founding and sawmilling connected with all these trades.[43] All employed a substantial proportion of skilled workers and so had a considerable measure of unionisation; and they tended to be subject to short-term fluctuations in demand for labour which was dealt with by termination of jobs rather than short-time working. The scheme was meant only for alleviating such conditions, its model being the typical conditions on which unions provded for unemployment: the beneft of 7s. per week was to be available only after seven days out of work and to last for a maximum of 15 weeks in any one year.[44] To qualify a worker must have contributed for 26 weeks. Under all these conditions, the scheme was calculated to cost the Treasury just over £1 million per annum.[45]

The scheme had been largely worked out in 1909 but its enactment was arrested by the House of Lords' rejection of Lloyd George's Budget. Since unemployment insurance was a counterpart not only to labour exchanges but to the workers' health insurance which the Chancellor himself was planning, it had to await the clearing of the constitutional storm. It did not in itself produce political counteroffensives on the scale that engulfed health insurance.[46] Inevitably,

[38] The one attempt to provide such a scheme (in the Swiss canton of St Gall (1895–1897)) was remembered as a failure: Gilbert (1966), pp. 265–266.
[39] Permanent Secretary, Board of Trade, 1907–1919.
[40] *i.e.*, some five per cent. of the workforce.
[41] For the enactment of this part of the National Insurance Act 1911, see Gilbert (1966), pp. 274–288; Harris (1972), pp. 295–334.
[42] In addition, unions which provided their members with better unemployment benefit could reclaim three-quarters from the insurance fund (up to its own rate of benefit) and a Treasury subsidy of one-sixth: s.106.
[43] It covered about 2¼ million workers, almost entirely male.
[44] As had been the case for friendly society pensions since 1904, the first 5s. of benefit was to be discounted in assessing a claim to poor relief.
[45] Much less than the old age pension of 1908 had been expected to cost. By 1914 the scheme was £3 million in credit and by 1920, £20 million; but this was soon to be wiped out: (see below, p. 459ff.). A refund scheme for substantial contributions (s.95) proved unworkable.
[46] See below, pp. 454–455.

however, there was the question whether the work-shy should be disqualified from benefit and if so how they should be identified. Within the Board of Trade, Llewellyn Smith thought it essential. But Churchill maintained that the conditions for obtaining benefit were in themselves strict enough to confine the problem and that in any case once a man had qualified by making contributions he must be given his entitlement.[47] The delay in legislating meant that Llewellyn Smith was left to get his way from Churchill's successor, Sidney Buxton.[48] The claimant had to be capable of work but unable to obtain suitable employment.[49] He would be disqualified if he voluntarily left his job, or if he was out of work because a trade dispute at his place of work had caused a stoppage.[50] While none of this undermined the "neutrality" of the labour exchanges, they became the institution through which claims were made and they were at least in some position to test whether a person was refusing work.

(c) Old Age Pensions

The Liberals' first steps in social reform were a major break in principle since they provided means-tested assistance out of general taxation or rating, without any element of personal contribution in advance. To side-step the insurance concept could only be justified by some extreme need of the community as a whole. In the provision of school meals and medical testing, which were introduced in 1906 and 1907,[51] the future health of the nation was in issue. In the case of old age pensions, it was necessary to accept that anyone who had lived to an advanced age without having even a subsistence was entitled to support without an ignominious application to the guardians. The COS was among the voices insisting that such a step could never be justified.

Certainly a non-contributory solution was not the only course open. Many variants, contributory and non-contributory, had been bandied in discussion over the previous thirty years, against a background of foreign example and co-operative provision at home, mainly through the friendly societies and trade unions. In Germany (1888), Bismarck had attached compulsory contributions towards a pension to his scheme of sickness and other social insurance. In Denmark (1891), and then in New Zealand (1898) and the Australian states (from 1900), non-contributory pensions were made available to those who satisfied a lack-of-income test.[52] In England, Wales and Scotland, it appeared that nearly half the adult male population belonged to a friendly society or benefit union, a movement which had been growing for more than a century. In the 1890s, official

---

[47] In a characteristic memorandum, his final shot was "I do not like mixing up moralities and mathematics": see Gilbert (1966), pp. 272. It was an issue of central significance for the future of social provision.

[48] Gilbert (1966), pp. 270–279.

[49] s.86(3)—cf. the later requirement that he be "genuinely seeking work" (see below, p. 460).

[50] s.87. For the system of tribunals, see below, pp. 455–457.

[51] See below, p. 476.

[52] For these comparative developments, see Thane (1982), pp. 102–103.

inquiries were on balance still against state intervention and in favour of broadening co-operative saving, even though evidence was beginning to emerge that the stability of the societies was not assured: the rate of survival into middle age, particularly among skilled workers, was going up too fast. Joseph Chamberlain, however, was a powerful advocate of a contributory scheme on German lines, while Charles Booth argued for an expensive, non-contributory scheme. Their campaigning was dropped only with the outbreak of the Boer War.[53]

Asquith, who as Chancellor took up the question in 1908, approached the matter from the Liberal orthodoxy of the 1890s—that in the longer term, economic progress could be expected to allow each worker to provide for his own old age through co-operative societies or insurance. He accordingly was against a contributory scheme imposed by the state. He accepted, however, as a temporary expedient that the very poor elderly should be given assistance, and for them it was too late to consider a contributory solution. Thanks to the moves to increase income tax, which began with his Budget of 1907, the Treasury could find £7 millions a year and accordingly he planned to make the pension available to those over seventy.[54] It was an astute manoeuvre: it allowed some of the unalterably poorest a pittance which they could simply draw at a Post Office (and it was claimed at once and with gratitude by nearly half a million people, predominantly women); at the same time it transferred some part of poor law relief to the Exchequer and so relieved the restless municipalities and their ratepayers.[55]

The Old Age Pensions Act 1908 was actually put through by Lloyd George (for which he saw himself remembered). The amount finally settled was 5s. a week for those over 70 whose annual income did not exceed £21, with a reduced amount on a sliding scale for those with incomes between £21 and £31 10s.[56] In addition to this simple, if severe, test of personal (not family) means, a wraith of moralising remained. Various categories were disqualified: those in receipt of poor relief or in a lunatic asylum; those who had been in prison in the previous ten years; those who had received non-medical poor assistance (though this was applied only for two years after January 1, 1908 and then not renewed); and those who had habitually failed to work according to their ability, opportunity and need—a COS inspiration which could not in practice be administered within the straightforward framework for pension claims.[57]

---

[53] Gilbert (1966), pp. 161–202; P. Thane (ed.) *The Origins of Social Policy* (1978) Chap. 5; R .V. Sires (1954) 14 J.Ec.H. 279; D. Collins (1965) 8 Hist.J 246; J. H. Treble (1970) 15 Int.R.Soc.Hist 266.

[54] There was, however, considerable evidence that many could not continue to work after 65.

[55] See above, pp. 449–450.

[56] Originally the proposal was for 5s. a week to those with under £26 a year. The sliding scale aimed to save money and appears to have done so, only a small proportion of claimants proving to fall within its ambit. For the passing of the Act, see Gilbert (1966), pp. 202–226; Thane (1982), pp. 81–84.

[57] s.3(1).

(d) Health Insurance

The central plank of Bismarck's insurance scheme was cover for employees against sickness, and after returning from a visit to Germany in 1908 Lloyd George made this idea his own.[58] It would emerge in 1911, alongside unemployment insurance, tied to compulsory contribution through employment, and directed therefore to the impact of sickness upon earnings.[59] Its range, however, was not confined to the selected industries within the unemployment scheme. It extended to all employment save for a few exceptions: civil servants, railwaymen and spouses being the chief categories.[60] In addition, in the interests of protecting private medical practice, non-manual workers earning more than £160 per annum were not qualified.[61] Each insured man was to contribute 4d. a week, each woman 3d. and his or her employer 3d.; to this the state added 2d.[62] There were two main forms of benefit: *medical benefit*—treatment (mainly by a general practitioner) which was available as soon as contribution started; and *sickness benefit*—a weekly payment for up to 6 months of 10s. for a man or 7s. 6d. for a woman during incapacity for work through sickness (starting from the fourth day of absence). For this at least 26 contributions were necessary. After the 6 months and with at least 104 contributions, there was *permanent disablement benefit* of 5s. per week, for both men and women.[63] Thus to this limited degree, the scheme guaranteed some medical treatment and income to bread-winners. It did nothing directly for their families during their absence from work or on their death.

Health insurance was immediately disturbing to three interests: the medical profession[64]; the friendly societies and trade unions as the traditional form of mutual protection for skilled workers against sickness[65]; and the "industrial assurance" companies, which had been building business in cheap insurance for the cost of a funeral, their method being door-to-door salesmanship and weekly collections of premiums.[66] Lloyd George was obliged, in pyrotechnic negotiations, to accommodate each of these within his insurance scheme, partly by restricting its scope and partly by giving them

---

[58] The civil servant chiefly responsible for health insurance was W. J. Braithwaite: for the record he kept, see H. J. Bunbury (ed.) *Lloyd George's Ambulance Wagon* (1957).

[59] For Lloyd George's attempt to annex unemployment to health insurance, see Harris (1972), pp. 320–327.

[60] National Insurance Act 1911, Sch. I, Pt. II. That masters—and even more, that mistresses—should have to contribute to the insurance of their domestic servants induced a sense of class outrage and this was fanned by *The Daily Mail*. The press had its own anxieties—in particular not to lose the advertising of patent medicines.

[61] App. II(g).

[62] See ss.3–7.

[63] There were special provisions for tuberculosis treatment and a maternity benefit of 30s. to the wives of insured men.

[64] For the conditions of general practice before the 1911 Act, see R. M. Titmuss in M. Ginsberg (ed.), *Law and Opinion in the 20th Century* (1959), pp. 305–312; and for the State's earlier reluctance to intervene, R. M. McLeod (1967) 11 Med.Hist 15.

[65] In addition to the traditional friendly societies, some employers had established their own clubs—and these had been regulated quite stringently by the Shops Clubs Act 1902. There were also small, informal clubs of which general practitioners were often catalysts.

[66] See generally, Sir A. Wilson and H. Levy, *Industrial Assurance* (1937) Chaps. 3–9.

roles in its administration. The companies led him to surrender his hopes for death benefits and widows' and orphans' pensions. The medical practitioners insisted that they should help to administer medical benefit, which they did by membership of local Insurance Committees. They also succeeded in breaking the old reliance of the friendly societies on a single "contract doctor"; and much was heard of the consumer's freedom to choose his own doctor by way of justification for this spreading of work among general practitioners.[67] The friendly societies and the assurance companies secured the right, as "approved societies," to administer the financial benefits (sickness, permanent disablement, etc.) for those who insured through them. Each person on their books entitled them to an annual sum out of the fund being built up by the central Insurance Commissioners.[68] They accordingly had an interest to pay no unnecessary benefits and to insure only the better risks. They could use surpluses to offer benefits additional to the state cover. Those workers who did not find their way to a society or company, could insure through the Post Office. This complex administrative net preserved elements of competition and free choice as well as adhering to the strict insurance principle of building a reserve fund to cover all future claims.[69]

Thus, apart from the minor proportion contributed by the Exchequer, once more the government's risk of having to underwrite the scheme was remote. The contributory nature of both insurance schemes ensured that their impact was regressive, taking a much higher proportion of the income of the lowest paid workers than of those further up the scale, while in their different ways only providing an incomplete answer to need.

(e) Settling Disputes

The three main benefit schemes of the new deal—old age pensions and the two distinct forms of national insurance—were notable in adding to the array of special tribunals for government departments. Each benefit was conceived in terms of a right granted on the fulfilment of conditions and avoided, to a substantial degree, any assessment of general worthiness that was a crucial part of poor relief. Even so there was scope for differences over who satisfied the basic requirements for benefit and who were disqualified by the various grounds specified. Each scheme had its own administrative structure—pensions through the Post Office, the local pensions committees and the LGB; unemployment insurance through the labour

---

[67] The British Medical Association, dominated by specialists, tried to stage a revolt but general practitioners were induced by the rates offered for treatment (compared with their previous earnings) to join the insurance panels in large numbers. The BMA lost a great deal of prestige from the debacle: Gilbert (1966), pp. 400–416; J. L. Brand, *Doctors and the State* (1965).

[68] The government was to make no demands on existing friendly society funds for the liabilities that they were taking over, thus providing a prop for the finances of those which were ailing: see s.72.

[69] Lloyd George had reluctantly accepted this form of "being virtuous," rather than following the German precedent of a fund which balanced yearly income against outgoings. For critical assessments of the scheme in operation, W. A. Brend, *Health and the State* (1917); H. Levy, *National Health Insurance* (1944).

exchanges and the Board of Trade; health insurance through the local Insurance Committees (for medical benefit), the approved societies and the Post Office (for other benefits), with the central Insurance Commissioners above them (and ultimately the LGB).

The disputes mechanisms reflected these differences. In the case of pensions, the initial power of decision lay with the local pensions committee which was to use the pension officer attached to each labour exchange (a central appointee) to investigate and report to it. From the Committees either the pensions officer or the claimant might appeal to the LGB, whose decision was to be final and conclusive.[70] The pensions officer was thus an embodiment of the system, defending it as need be both against undue claims and against wayward local democracy.

For unemployment insurance, the local element was provided not through channels of the counties and county boroughs but through Boards of Referees for each labour exchange. These comprised nominees chosen by employers and workmen in each district (in equal numbers on any board), together with an independent chairman appointed by the Board of Trade. The insurance officer at the labour exchange could either decide a disputed question himself, in which case the claimant might appeal to the Board of Referees and a decision against the officer might be taken by him (but not by the claimant), with the Board's assent, to the Umpire appointed by the Board of Trade. Alternatively, the officer might refer the dispute without decision to the Board of Referees, in which case their decision was final.[71] Again the officer had a role in containing local enthusiasms by pressing for a special appeal to the Umpire.

In the case of health insurance, disputes with Insurance Committees or approved societies were made to lie to the Insurance Commissioners alone; certain matters (notably the definition of insurable employments) were for the Commissioners themselves to decide, and in such cases an aggrieved claimant might appeal to a county court and thence to a judge of the High Court.[72]

More generally, legislative statements that a decision of any of these bodies was "final" were unlikely to preclude the ordinary courts from reviewing the basic equities of the procedure by which it was reached, any more than they had felt the impact of "no certiorari" clauses in the past.[73] But they were allowed no regular part in day-to-day decision-making. The disputes procedures were allowed to take a bureaucratic turn with scarcely a hesitation because of the unsettling experience of giving over the workmen's compensation scheme to adjudication in the county courts and those above.[74] Equally the civil servants involved wanted to control the course of their experiments, not only through their very considerable powers to make regulations but also by bringing in nominees for the business of settling disputed claims.[75] By this combination of means,

[70] Old Age Pensions Act 1908, s.7.
[71] National Insurance Act 1911, ss.88–90.
[72] Ibid., ss.66–68.
[73] See above, p. 32.
[74] See below, p. 533ff.
[75] See Fulbrook (1978), pp. 138–41.

administrative rules were generated in abundance wth a minimum of outside engagement. So far as decisions were concerned, only some of the more important—notably those of the unemployment insurance Umpire—were systematically published.[76] This allocating of authority within the collectivising state established permanent patterns; it merits comparison with the manner in which, in earlier times, the magistrates had acquired administrative-cum-judicial powers in their quarter and petty sessions.[77]

Lawyers would be given a certain place: in particular, the Umpire and chairmen of Courts of Referees were normally legal practitioners.[78] But it was made difficult or impossible for claimants to have their own legal representation, particularly before those tribunals which were involved in implementing unpopular, contentious policies.[79] Many observers would find their mixture of despatch, informality, dignity and fairness decidedly preferable to the atmosphere and proceedings of ordinary courts.[80] It was important that they should command some confidence as they had to handle considerable case-loads.[81]

II. Tribulations of the Inter-War Period

(a) Health Insurance, Pensions and Poor Relief

The circumstances that would overtake the arrangements of 1908–11 have much to tell about the political and social order of a country fractured by a whole-scale war effort and then by long-term unemployment. By way of summary of an increasingly complex history, we will concentrate attention on two aspects: the range of benefits offered, and the division of authority in their administration. Together they underscore how social provision was becoming a central issue of the political divide, and one on which the emergent Labour Party would have to resolve anguished conflicts within its own ranks.

Of the schemes of 1908–11, the least affected by subsequent change

---

[76] For an analysis of some of the more important, see E. Wight Bakke, *Insurance or Dole?* (1935), pp. 31–35, 44–55; H. C. Emmerson and E. C. P. Lascelles, *Guide to Unemployment Insurance Acts* (5th ed., 1939).

[77] According to Horridge J., a Court of Referees discharged only administrative duties; in consequence communications to it were not entitled to absolute privilege against libel proceedings: *Collins v. Whiteway* [1927] 2 K.B. 378; *cf.* below, n. 19.

[78] See Report of the Morris Committee on the Determination of Claims for Unemployment Insurance Benefit P.P. 1929 [Cmd. 3415] XVII; D. Scott Stokes in R. S. W. Pollard, *Administrative Tribunals at Work* (1950), pp. 19–21.

[79] Originally, for instance, courts of referees were left to settle their procedure, but then representation by barrister or solicitor was specifically debarred: Unemployment Insurance Regs. 1921, r. 4(2); similarly, the Unemployment Assistance (Appeal Tribunals) Rules 1934, r. 4(1); Lynes, (below, n. 17), pp. 15–17.

[80] See, *e.g.*, J. Millett, *The Unemployment Assistance Board* (1940), p. 278, quoting W. A. Robson

[81] See further, below pp. 463–464. In the first year of operation of unemployment insurance, for instance, nearly nine per cent. of the 420,802 claims were disallowed by an Insurance Officer or a Court of Referees: J. L. Cohen, *Insurance against Unemployment* (1921), pp. 246.

was national health insurance. There were financial adjustments to take account of inflation and a modest degree of legal tinkering.[82] But the essential limitations of the 1911 scheme were conserved, a Royal Commission advising in 1926 that the country could afford no more.[83] Only contributors were entitled to the benefit for being off sick from work, its duration and scope varying with the "success" of the approved society through which they insured.[84] Dependants acquired no entitlement or other place in the benefits. Medical provision remained limited—there being in general no hospital treatment, consultation with specialists, use of adequate diagnostic aids, or nursing assistance. For almost everything except access to a general practitioner, even the contributor was thrown back on his private resources, or the poor law and charitable medical services, such as they were.[85] It would take another war for a truly national health service to seem a necessity.

In another direction, health insurance did begin to build links. The old age pension had originally provided very small amounts for those over 70 with very low incomes from other sources; the levels had to be adjusted upwards under war-time inflation and the costs to the Treasury grew.[86] Even so, the inadequacy was acknowledged by the concession, in 1919, that a pensioner might also be granted poor relief. Nonetheless there were strong arguments that there should be some general provision for the 65–70 age group, since many had by 65 become physically incapable of work (and so lost their contributor's status in health insurance); likewise there were the extreme difficulties faced by widows and dependant children of bread-winners who died before retirement age. The Conservatives accordingly came back to their earlier preference—that state pensions should be based on contributions while in work. The original pension for those over 70, paid through post offices, would remain, with its means test. Those already within the health insurance scheme would (with their employers) become liable for additional contributions; through their approved society (or the deposit scheme of the post office) they then became entitled to a pension of 10s. a week between 65 and 70, and

---

[82] See National Health Insurance Act 1920, raising insurance benefits and doctors' fees. The government contribution to the scheme was cut in 1926 (Economy (Miscellaneous Provisions) Act) and benefits were cut as part of the 1932 package: Thane (1982), p. 192.

[83] P.P. 1926 [Cmd. 2596] XIV. Both majority and minority on the Commission did, however, recommend dependants' allowances along the lines introduced into unemployment insurance, but without avail. Earlier, the first Minister of Health, Christopher Addison, and his Medical and Administrative Services Council, had sought to foster a consolidated health service; but as a reconstruction plan, it had not survived. See generally, Gilbert (1970) Chap. 6.

[84] Only the minority on the Royal Commission wished to replace the approved societies with local authorities.

[85] The government had given the voluntary hospitals £500,000 in 1921 as some recognition of their increasing difficulties, but had refused any permanent subvention. The public hospitals came to be aided by a 50 per cent. central grant.

[86] The increase of a half, made general in 1917, was to have been removed at the end of the war; instead, after the investigations of the Adkins Committee, the Government raised the basic pension from 5s. to 10s. The first Labour government allowed a certain amount of earnings to be disregarded in calculating the income limit for the pension: Old Age Pensions Act 1924.

their pension after 70 would not be means tested; their widows became entitled to a pension of 10s. a week and their orphaned children 5s. a week to the age of 14.[87] It was expected that the original, non-contributory pension would be phased out and indeed the million recipients in 1926 had fallen to under 600,000 in 1938 while the numbers receiving contributory pensions was continuing to grow.

(b) Unemployment

It was to be unemployment provision that came under constant battering in the inter-war period. It had, moreover, to survive two quite distinct forms of attack. With time the war had absorbed surplus labour.[88] But in the transition back to peace-time conditions large numbers of service personnel were suddenly discharged into a world of high-priced boom—which lasted till mid-1920. The restive disillusion of thousands was to some degree met by an "Out-of-work Donation"—the original "dole"—which was paid from national revenue and at a significantly higher rate than the other benefits,[89] with allowances for dependant children. It was transitional and temporary, but it convinced even the Treasury that the unemployment scheme must be broadened: in 1920 it was made to cover all manual workers and non-manual workers earning less than £250, with certain exceptions.[90]

This was a plan executed as post-war employment seemed to be picking up. As with so much that would follow, its assumptions were almost immediately thrown out by events, in this case the downturn in the economy which heralded long-term unemployment. For 20 years a million would at any time be jobless; and in the worst moments up to three million (out of an employable population of some 30 millions). It was soon enough apparent that, without further Treasury subsidisation the unemployment insurance fund would be in deficit, and that many contributors would outrun the fifteen weeks benefit to which they were entitled, often with no recourse other than charity or the poor law. Still disturbed by signs of revolutionary fervour, the coalition government did two things: it added allowances for dependants to the basic benefit[91]; and, even more significantly, it introduced "uncovenanted" or "extended benefit."[92] The

---

[87] Old Age, Widows and Orphans Contributory Pensions Act 1925.

[88] During the war, Beveridge and Llewellyn Smith had worked at increasing the range of those insured until a quarter of the work force was covered. But they found considerable resistance to programmes for the de-casualisation of labour in the docks and elsewhere, which were a necessary pre-condition of further extension.

[89] Men received 29s., women 24s. with 6s. for a first and 3s. for each subsequent child. The Donation lasted until May 1921, by which time it had cost £62 million.

[90] The main exceptions were: domestic servants, agricultural workers, civil servants and teachers. Benefit had become: 15s. for men and 12s. for women, over 18, which could be claimed for a maximum of 15 weeks a year.

[91] This followed the precedent set by the Out-of-work Donation.

[92] Unemployment Insurance Act 1921, s.3. The Act of 1922 sought to spread this benefit over three five-week periods with equal gaps in between (with resort if necessary to the guardians). It proved unpopular with both claimants and poor law authorities and was later discontinued.

latter was inevitably conceived as a temporary measure and its cost was to be covered partly by an increase in contributions, partly by repayments after a return to work (it being assumed that the economy was about to absorb its labour surplus).

It was this intermediate stage—between the initial contributed protection and poor law relief—that underwent monotonous political buffetting. It was subject, first, to the test that the applicant be genuinely seeking work[93]—and the Rota Sub-Committees of the Local Insurance Committees tended to take a severe line on the question[94]; but in addition to this the Conservatives imposed a limitation that particularly affected single persons living with relatives, married couples one of whom was working, and short-time workers.[95] This was the first point at which family means testing would be carried across from its poor law setting. It was deeply resented and was abolished by the first Labour government in 1924, only to have the Conservatives reinstate it in the following year.[96]

In 1927, in the uneasy mood after the General Strike, a Committee under the Conservative Law Lord, Blanesburgh, recommended that, following a short transitional period, the distinction between the two forms of unemployment benefit should be abandoned. There should be a lower threshold for qualification (30 contributions over two years) and those who crossed it should have benefit without limit of time, subject to a "genuinely seeking work test" which would have to be rigorously applied to those not re-employed within a reasonable period.[97] With this spur, new legislation turned "extended" into "transitional" benefit; but the lull in unemployment (on which the Committee had pinned its hopes) proved very temporary and the division remained in effect.[98]

In 1930, the second Labour government would lift from the claimant the onus of proving that he was "genuinely seeking work"—by then a regular basis for refusing benefit; only those who positively refused a job offer, or would not comply with a direction from the labour exchange, would lose entitlement.[99] But this contributed, in

[93] 1921 Act, s.3(3) (cf. the test for covenanted benefit, above, p. 452).

[94] It was used particularly against married women: Thane (1982), p. 174.

[95] Unemployment Insurance Act 1922, s.1.

[96] Unemployment Insurance Acts, 1924 (No. 2), s.3; 1925, s.1.

[97] Report of the Unemployment Insurance Committee (1927—not a Command paper). As one result, the "genuinely seeking work" test was given extended scope after a "reasonable" period on benefit: Unemployment Insurance Act 1927, s.2(ii). As another, family means testing (see above, n. 95) for a time disappeared.

[98] Even before 1927, the Umpire had delivered a crucial decision placing at the heart of the inquiry into whether a claimant was "genuinely seeking work" the question of his or her own motivation. But what would show the continuing desire to work of a man or woman who had tried for months without success to find a job? A depressing game set in of acquiring rejection slips from employers as evidence to satisfy benefit officers. The process was so pointless that the Morris Committee recommended reversing the onus of proof on the question (see above, n. 78).

[99] In the previous year, the government had tried informal Boards of Assessors without decision making powers, but they were a failure: see W. Hannington, *Ten Lean Years* (1940), p. 16. The Morris Committee (above, n. 78) recommended reversal of the burden of proof. In the year 1928–1929, four million people made 10 million claims, of which 340,045 were refused by Officers or Courts of Referees for "not genuinely seeking work"; and 37,568 for being "able to obtain suitable employment."

the depths of the Great Depression, to the high cost of unemployment relief and, from this directly, came the government's own internal crisis and downfall in the summer of 1931.[1] A Cabinet majority refused to succumb to pressure from the Treasury and the City for substantial cuts in the benefit and MacDonald and Snowden joined a team mainly of Conservatives in a National Government. The immediate results included not only cuts and other restrictions on all benefits but the re-imposition of a means test for the transitional benefit.[2] This "transitional payment," as it became called, remained a central charge, but it was given over to the Public Assistance Committees (the new poor law bodies[3]) to administer at county level until 1934. Then a central Unemployment Assistance Board (UAB) would take it over.[4]

(c) The Authorities

The second factor for discussion is that of governmental organisation. The increasing significance of social provision to central government was marked at the end of the war by the creation, first, of a Ministry of Labour from the Labour Department of the Board of Trade; and secondly, in place of the LGB and the Health Insurance Commissioners, of a Ministry of Health.[5] At the local level, both reports of the Poor Law Commission had envisaged that the administration of services to those in poverty would be transferred to the largest units, the counties and county boroughs. Only at such a level could the distinct elements of poverty administration be efficiently organised. A Reconstruction Sub-Committee at the end of the war, containing both Lord George Hamilton (for the previous Majority), and Beatrice Webb (instigator of the Minority), reiterated this premise and sought to bury the differences between the earlier Reports.[6] But nothing was immediately done on the local government side and in the course of the 20s, the Conservatives became interested in replacing the poor law guardians for other reasons. Some boards adopted non-deterrent, sympathetic programmes of relief which could be used to show up the grim parsimony elsewhere.[7] In 1921, the Poplar Borough Council was led by George Lansbury in a well-calculated act of civil disobedience, which obliged the government to

---

[1] See e.g., R. Skidelsky, *Politicians and the Slump* (1967), pp. xi, 365.

[2] Unemployment Insurance (National Economy) Orders, October 1931, supplemented by the Transitional Payments (Determination of Need) Act 1932: see E. M. Burns, *British Unemployment Programs 1920–1938* (1941), Pt. III.

[3] See below, p. 462.

[4] *Ibid.*

[5] The latter step met some spirited resistance from the approved societies and the LGB, which feared that it heralded a break-up of the poor law on Webbian lines: Gilbert (1970), pp. 98–137.

[6] The McLean Committee Report (P.P. 1918 [Cd. 9151] XI) was an influential statement of the case for a Ministry of Health.

[7] In particular they might allow reasonable out-relief to able-bodied applicants who elsewhere would still be subjected to a labour test.

introduce an equalising scheme between rich and poor unions of the metropolis.[8] In the strikes of 1918 to 1921 and the General Strike, some boards took a more helpful attitude towards strikers' families than others. Increasingly, the Ministry of Health sought to curb the enthusiasm of the more generous, mainly through its power over sanctioning loans[9]; this led in 1926 to special legislation allowing the Ministry to put in commissioners to replace the guardians, a power actually used against three boards.[10]

In 1929 Neville Chamberlain finally pushed through a wholesale reorganisation, giving to Public Assistance Committees of the county authorities the administration of the poor relief (by a new name) to those capable of working. The functions of looking after the young, sick and aged in institutions were to be dispersed among other committees of the local authorities.[11] Resistance was bought off by at last introducing a central contribution to the cost of these social services and the reorganisation brought a measure of rate equalisation to areas outside London. It was an intervention that ended a crucial element in local autonomy and one that heralded the transformation of social support into a central function. PACs in general followed the line that had still been pursued by many Boards of Guardians: those applying for out-relief were to be treated with great suspicion, since the deserving prima facie could turn to unemployment or sickness benefit or a pension and be expected to manage on it. Even the institutional provisions, in difficult economic circumstances, were run on threadbare support, very little going into building or equipping for a more adequate service.[12] If this was a move very largely to anaesthetise the politically heterodox within the forms of democracy, it was paralleled in the related trouble-spot of unemployment insurance by moves to take the issues "out of politics." Again echoing the changes of a century earlier, the Unemployment Insurance Statutory Committee (concerned with the contributory scheme) and the Unemployment Assistance Board (concerned with means-tested benefits for those not covered by contributions) were established as bodies on which MPs could not sit.[13]

The UISC, which was chaired by Beveridge, was indeed expert. Its judicious management of the contributory side helped to restore the

[8] Poplar refused to pay the precept of the London County Council upon it until an equalising measure was introduced. Their action was duly held illegal and they spent a tumultuous six weeks in prison for contempt of court but were let out without ever purging their contempt: B. Keith-Lucas, [1962] Pub.L.52; P.A. Ryan in P. Thane (ed.) *The Origins of British Social Policy* (1978), p. 56; N. Branson, *Poplarism 1919–1925* (1979).

[9] Tightened by the Local Authorities (Financial Provisions) Act 1921 (amended in 1923).

[10] Board of Guardians (Default) Act 1926. The three unions dealt with were West Ham, Chester-le-Street and Bedwellty, all in areas of severe distress. The Audit (Local Authorities) Act 1927 increased the scope of surcharge control by making individuals liable to the amounts spent without legal authority as civil debts and subject in some circumstances to disqualification from local authority office for five years.

[11] Local Government Act 1929. It was preceded by a consolidation of legislation in the Poor Law Act 1927, and by consolidated Public Assistance Orders and Relief Regulation Orders.

[12] See generally, Gilbert (1970), pp. 219–235.

[13] Unemployment Act 1934.

original 1911 insurance fund to order. By the outbreak of war, thanks to the economic turnabout, it was in robust surplus.[14] The UAB, its offices around the country staffed by a hasty cull of civil servants and local authority employees, began as a bureaucratic parallel to the PACs. It did not, however, any more than did the Poor Law Commissioners of 1834, determine the amount of public funds available for distribution through its scheme. It was the Treasury that set the rate of benefit, since the funds were to be entirely a central charge. So preoccupied was the Treasury with the desire for cuts and the administrative organisation to achieve them, that the benefit rates it set proved to be below those being paid by the PACs in over half the country.[15] In deep embarrassment the government had to permit the UAB to pay the PAC rate in any district where it was higher.[16] The Board was rescued by the improving economy from any long-term accusation of undue meanness when measured against local authority action. Late in 1936 the UAB scales could be improved and still remain below both wages and contributory benefit.

One element in the "de-politicisation" of the UAB was the creation of Appeal Tribunals to which disappointed applicants might proceed for a re-hearing of their case.[17] Betterton, the Minister of Labour, argued that they were a necessary absorbent in making the scheme acceptable; and Neville Chamberlain, the Chancellor of the Exchequer, agreed, subject to the filter of leave from the Chairman. The Tribunals were in subtle ways closer to the administrators than were, for instance, the Courts of Referees. Thus they consisted of a chairman appointed by the Minister of Labour, a workpeople's representative from a list nominated by the Board and a Board nominee.[18] The Board itself and outside commentators saw their functions as "quasi-judicial" (in the Donoughmore-Scott conception),[19] directly involved in enunciating the Board's own policy and retaining some measure of discretion in determining individual cases[20]; this was said to justify the political influence over their constitution.[21]

The Board's policy was, however, elucidated in detailed instructions, which were initially (though never subsequently) published.[22] Accordingly, the Tribunals' functions were in reality not easily dis-

---

[14] Under his chairmanship it became not only a manager but the generator of policy ideas for the future. See Gilbert (1970), pp. 179–180; J. Harris, *William Beveridge* (1977), pp. 357–361.

[15] For examples of the deprivations which resulted, see Gilbert (1970), 186–187.

[16] Unemployment Assistance (Temporary Provisions) Act 1935 (the "standstill Act").

[17] See G. Lach in R. S. W. Pollard (ed.) *Administrative Tribunals at Work* (1950), p. 36; T. Lynes in M. Adler and A. Bradley, *Justice Discretion and Poverty* (1978), p. 5; Fulbrook (1976), pp. 164–170.

[18] Unemployment Act 1934, Sch. VII. The Board nominee could even be a district officer of the Board, though this was not usual in practice. See generally Lynes (above, n. 17) pp. 8–15, 23–28.

[19] See above, p. 95ff.

[20] See Lynes (above, n. 17), pp. 7–8.

[21] Note the exclusion of legal representation: above, n. 79.

[22] Memorandum P.P. 1934–35 [Cmd. 4791] XIV. From these instructions would evolve a detailed code which, in 1948, would form the basis for assessing claims for national assistance. It became known as the A Code and was for long assiduously kept secret.

tinguishable from those of courts of referees, and indeed from magistrates and courts more generally. True, not all their ground rules had been embodied in delegated legislation and so could be changed informally; otherwise the degree of individual judgment that went into deciding particular cases did not seem exceptional. The insistence upon "discretion" could spell confusion: when, for instance, the Board instigated a "doctrine" of the constructive household (*i.e.* that those who left a household were to be considered still a part of it unless compelled to go), it was not clear whether individual chairmen and Appeal Tribunals had to apply it.[23] But a certain ambiguity in matters of authority and role seemed to suit an institution which was meant to parry discontents. When relief was refused to the Jarrow hunger-marchers on the ground that marchers were not available for work, it was undoubtedly useful to Ministers to have decisions of Appeal Tribunals in support.[24] The machinery would become part of the transference of the poor law from a local to a national charge and administration. In 1940, the UAB would become the Assistance Board, in order by then to take on the pressing task of supplementing pensions[25]; and in 1948, it became the National Assistance Board, in each case with Appeal Tribunals on the model established in 1934.

III. THE "WELFARE STATE" PROGRAMME

(a) The Beveridge Report

As Britain recovered from depression and faced the inevitability of war, the acute crisis to which unemployment had subjected the social provision schemes eased and it was possible to contemplate reform. At some points, government departments were anxious for change—the Home Office in workmen's compensation, the Ministry of Health in hospital and medical services, divided as they were between health insurance, local authority provision and voluntary effort. But there were many antagonisms—from an over-cautious Treasury, from employers anxious not to shoulder greater contributions to government schemes, from trade unions for whom contributions were a fetter upon wage rises and national insurance an alternative to their own benefit activities.

Without ever becoming the sole cause of change, war nevertheless affected the prospects for state social services.[26] They were to be one element in a wider strategy by which the country was first to be geared up to war-time production through government intervention on an unprecedented scale; and then returned once more to peace-

---

[23] Lynes (above, n. 17), pp. 19–23.

[24] H.C. Deb. CCCXVII 1024, 1895; J. D. Millett, *The Unemployment Assistance Board* (1940).

[25] Old Age and Widows' Pension Act 1940. Despite controls, wartime inflation made this essential.

[26] For the view that war bred a new social consensus, R. M. Titmuss, *Problems of Social Policy* (1950), pp. 506–508, 514–516; but *cf.* J. Harris, in W. Mommsen (ed.) *The Emergence of the Welfare State in Britain and Germany* (1981).

time conditions without (it was hoped) the savage disruptions that followed 1918. A conservative approach, favoured by Churchill at least until the war was won and, as a longer strategy, by the Treasury, was to continue with the inherited structure until the prospects of peace could be realistically assessed. But at least from the end of 1942, as defeat of the enemies seemed a matter of time and the political parties began to define their post-war positions, it became clear that the subject was not one that could be left on one side. In December of that year, Beveridge's celebrated report, *Social Insurance and Allied Services*,[27] was published. The immense interest that it generated showed how close it was to common aspirations and current morale. Nor was it merely a focus of general yearning. It had come about because Ernest Bevin, Minister of Labour in the Coalition cabinet, had made Beveridge chairman of a committee of civil servants to plan the co-ordination of social insurance. The content of the Report accordingly drew on their expertise and that of the many outside whom they consulted, particularly through sub-committees on the different types of need.[28]

The final presentation was a brilliant synthesis and simplification and it was largely to be responsible for the social security arrangements of the coming "welfare state."[29] Beveridge did not hesitate to call for a revolution in social provision, but his plans were as much an enlargement of what has gone before, a building upon foundations that he had helped to lay from 1907 onwards. The Report's most compelling novelty was its insistence that there should be a set of arrangements universal in their scope. Everyone was ultimately at risk of poverty from myriad causes and the various schemes should no longer be planned for particular categories of employee, as had so far been the case for national insurance and contributory pensions. Universality had various implications. It would mean, in particular, that most benefits would not involve any form of means test but would arise simply through qualification. On the question of qualification, however, Beveridge remained close to his original premises: there would be across-the-board provision on two fronts that by then already had a substantial following, a national health service and a child allowance for large families. Beyond these, however, benefit would depend upon contribution, mainly by employees in work and their employers.[30] To Beveridge, the psychology of participatory saving outweighed the regressive effect in terms of income distribution. The contributions and benefits moreover would be the same for all and would seek to provide no more than subsistence; anything better was to be left to private thrift. Of this it was a corollary that there would have to be a separate system for those who had not

---

[27] P.P. 1942–43 [Cmd. 6404] VI.

[28] The Report was published under Beveridge's signature alone because the Cabinet wished to avoid any suggestion of official acceptance.

[29] For the evolution of Beveridge's ideas, including those (particularly directed at improving the position of women) which he had to drop from the final Report, see J. Harris, *William Beveridge* (1977) Chap. 16.

[30] The self-employed would contribute at a rate which entitled them to some of the benefits; working wives would be offered a choice of benefit from their husband's insurance or their own.

qualified through contribution, a vestige—though it was hoped no more—of poor relief (or public assistance, as it had become).

(b) Financial Benefits

The plans for contributory benefits at the heart of Beveridge's Report nonetheless had to face some influential scepticism, understandable in the light of the previous twenty years' experience. The Coalition government did not respond in any definite way for two years and its White Paper, *Social Insurance*,[31] was particularly wary about expensive elements in the proposals, such as the principle that pensions and other benefits should reach a level of real subsistence. But for the Labour Government of July 1945 social security was a prime field for state intervention. Its legislation, taken as a whole, drew heavily on an administrative tradition that had roots back to the world of Senior and Chadwick: operation in the hands of a centralised, expert bureaucracy, and a structure of entitlement which largely avoided administrators having to assess the "worthiness" of individual applicants.

A new Ministry of Social Security was put in charge of the contributory schemes[32]; the "long-stop" of national assistance went to a Board that was effectively the successor of the UAB and continued its measure of "detachment" from politics.[33] The administration of unemployment insurance in the Ministry of Labour and sickness insurance and pensions in the Ministry of Health was taken over in a single department; the participation of the commercial and mutual interests in health insurance—the insurance companies, friendly societies and trade unions as "approved societies" was terminated.[34] Above all, the ancient association of local ratepayers with relief to those in need came to its end.

Thanks to the plan for national health services, national insurance had no longer to provide medical attention and would be confined to financial support. It would provide, at a single rate (initially 26s. a week, plus 16s. for an adult dependant and 7s. 6d. for each child) for the unemployed, those incapable of working through sickness[35] and those of pensionable age or entitlement.[36]

Beside these, was instituted a novel scheme for assisting parents with large families: a weekly family allowance of 5s. was payable to all for each dependant child after the first.[37] The entitlement was universal in the full sense, depending neither upon contribution nor upon tested need. Even the unions, initially suspicious of the plan as a cheap substitute for wage increases, had come to accept that the

---

[31] P.P. 1943–44 [Cmd. 6550] VIII.

[32] National Insurance Act 1946; National Insurance (Industrial Injuries) Act 1946.

[33] National Assistance Act 1948.

[34] So also commercial insurance disappeared with workmen's compensation: see below, pp. 536–537.

[35] But for historical reasons, victims of industrial accidents were allowed a higher rate: see below, *ibid*.

[36] Beveridge had expected a 20-year transition period to bring retirement pensions up to this level, but the government boldly initiated them from the outset.

[37] Family Allowances Act 1945. Beveridge had proposed a rate of 8s.

problem posed by large families was too acute to be left to the gradual course of improved earnings.[38]

As a whole, these benefits were thought sufficient for a frugal subsistence anywhere in the country, despite evident differences in rent, food costs and other variables between districts. Whether even this would prove an unduly optimistic basis for provision remained the great unknown. The whole balance depended upon two truly basic conditions. First, wide-scale unemployment would be averted by judicious interventions of government, which would attract industrial investment to areas with serious long-term problems and would bolster the supply of work during short-term downturns in the economy as a whole—ideas very much of the Webb-Keynes axis. Secondly, working-class wages would continue to move ahead of living costs, as they had begun to do between the wars, to an extent that allowed real differences in level between the earnings, the contributory benefits and national assistance. Only then would it be possible to maintain the incentive to seek employment—that crucial differential that had so long eluded moralists intent on less eligibility. Keynes and a younger generation of economists had argued the possibility of full employment at more than bare subsistence wages.[39] Beveridge had done much to sustain the possibility in the popular imagination. The political expression of that faith was the Labour victory of 1945. Fortunately for the future of social security the predictions would gradually come to be realised as the country regained its peace-time momentum.

As with all great expressions of social aspiration, the Beveridge plan and its implementation was formed by its history and immediate environment. At the time the grim realities of the inter-war years were economic collapse and mass unemployment, while the prospect of persistent inflation was a mere shadow. Yet as with unemployment in the past, inflation would in time render the insurance base of the plan merely decorative, even if the consequences would be less damaging (since general taxation would itself swell with inflation and could more easily be made to bear the added weight). Beveridge's flat-rate, fixed benefits would however give social insurance the old political prominence, being constantly under the attack for falling behind and as constantly the subject of competing promises to make improvements. This in turn would keep means-tested national assistance much more in play than had been expected. Thanks both to the assessment of actual need and to the political remove at which it was made, its payments could rise significantly above the insurance and pension levels and it would acquire a regular function of supplementing those benefits in particular cases. Indeed, what is truly surprising is the capacity of the insurance concept to survive. It is, of course, liked by Chancellors of the Exchequer as an employment poll-tax that can be kept somewhat apart from arguments over rates of income taxation. But that in turn depends upon Beveridge's

---

[38] For the convoluted campaign for family allowances, see P. Hall et al, Change, Choice and Conflict in Social Policy (1975), pp. 179–230; J. MacNicol, The Movement for Family Allowances 1918–1945 (1980).

[39] For the place of Keynes' proposals in the evolution of social provision, see Thane (1982) Chap. 7.

keen perception that contributions which earn benefits—or which
appear to do so—have an enduring appeal in a society which retains
powerful elements of economic self-determination in its make-up.

(c) National Health

The most vibrant resonance in the cry of universality was the
notion of a national health service, or at least services—at general
practitioner, hospital and local authority levels. The concept had
been accepted by Ministry of Health officials and approved by an
influential commission of doctors[40] even before the Beveridge Report
where it was treated as an essential underpinning of all else. That
every member of society, from gestation to the grave, should be guaranteed the medical treatment that he or she needed was a highly
attractive ideal. The many gaps and deficiencies in existing provision
gave strength to the case that the state should put its general
resources to the task. The mid-War enthusiasm declined subsequently—among doctors particularly—as the details began to be
planned, and the Coalition's last views suggested that a rather conservative, piecemeal development of existing organisation might be
the only outcome.[41] The energy of Aneurin Bevan, Minister of Health
in the Attlee Cabinet, saw to it that Britain would indeed emerge as
the one country among those immediately comparable in which
medical attention for individuals would shift from an incomplete,
contributory scheme, run in conjunction with commercial and
mutual organisations outside government, to a truly collective
responsibility. In his vision the scheme would be led and financed
from the centre, but local authority contributions would continue in
the field of public health (including school health services) and in
creating and maintaining health centres for medical practice
throughout the country. The legislative foundation for this was laid
in the National Health Service Act 1946, to come into effect two years
later. The service was to be free, save where specific charges were
prescribed[42]; and no upper income limit was to be imposed, so that it
was not even a law of positive discrimination.

In the course of the preceding century, the doctors had built their
professional reputation upon a unique blend of caring service and
unchallengable expertise. In place of practising a liberal profession,
they were being invited to become the key element in a state service.
As 1911 had made plain, they would not have accepted the qualification of their independence implied by such a change if financial
exigencies had not been a compulsive force. The outcome would,
however, show that a major profession might perfectly well arrive at

---

[40] Established by the BMA, and other leading organisations of doctors, its report went
much further than had the BMA in 1938. Leading specialists had in the interim been
involved in planning the war-time Emergency Medical Service. See generally H.
Eckstein, *The English Health Service* (1958); G. Forsyth, *Doctors and State Medicine*
(1966); A. Lindsey, *Socialised Medicine in England and Wales* (1962); A. J. Willcocks,
The Creation of the National Health Service (1967).

[41] White Paper, *A National Health Service*, P.P. 1943–44 [Cmd. 6502] VIII.

[42] National Health Service Act 1946, s.44; charges were to be levied for spectacles and
apparatus, dental services and drugs.

an accommodation with government which left it quite distinct from a salaried arm of the state and in a strong position to influence a great range of decisions on policy. It was a lesson of significance to others—in particular, the legal professions.

The gravest problems of finance lay in hospital treatment—because of medical advances, the effects of war, and the poor quality of existing institutions as they had developed under charitable endeavour and poor law provision. The consultant specialists secured from Bevan arrangements by which they could do part-time work for the NHS and keep a private practice as well, which might make use (on a paying basis) of beds in NHS hospitals.[43] They were to be supervised by twenty Regional Hospital Boards appointed by the Minister (after consultation with interest groups); each was to be run by its own management committee.[44] The nationalisation of the hospitals was accordingly a matter of relief rather than antagonism and Bevan used the specialists to influence the doubting ranks of general practitioners.

At the eye of their unease was the fear that they would be regimented and used by politicians in a way which would undermine the close trust of the doctor-patient relationship. Only at the last moment did the BMA membership feel sufficiently reassured to collaborate.[45] In particular, GPs were to have lists of patients (to a maximum of 3,500, or 5,000 in partnership) for which they would receive a fee per head per annum—they would not even be partly salaried.[46] They could also have private patients and normally they could refuse to accept particular individuals, just as patients might seek to be transferred to another doctor's list.[47] Thus were the essential freedoms of the doctor-patient relationship, previously couched in contractual terms, preserved by administrative rule. Bevan, however, insisted that practices should henceforth not be saleable, a sum of £66 million being allocated for compensation to those who would lose thereby. However disturbing it might be that the commercialisation of goodwill in a practice could no longer continue, it was scarcely compatible with payment by the state and with the measures to distribute practices more evenly across the population. A Medical Practices Committee would supervise this last question: it would not be able to require existing practices to move elsewhere but it would be able to restrict the opening of new practices in over-supplied neighbourhoods.[48]

Partly because of their experience with national health insurance and poor law services, the medical profession harboured considerable suspicion of local authority control. In consequence, Webbian orthodoxy had to be eschewed in the supervision of GP services: it

---

[43] Bevan thought this arrangement preferable to causing an upsurge of private hospitals.

[44] National Health Service Act 1946, Part II. The influential teaching hospitals were left with their own boards of governors and allowed to keep their endowments: s.8.

[45] See Eckstein (above, n. 40), pp. 140–163.

[46] Dentists however negotiated rates for work performed: with them the danger was unnecessary, rather than skimpy, work.

[47] Subject to an ultimate power given to the Executive Council to allocate the unacceptable: s.33.

[48] s.35, 36, Eckstein (above, n. 40), pp. 200–202.

would not be undertaken by the counties and county boroughs, but by Executive Comittees covering the same areas but composed half of representatives of central and local government and half of the medical, dental and pharmacist professions, with a Chairman appointed by the Minister.[49] Local authorities would continue to employ medical officers and other staff for their own services in the field of public health. Although they were no longer to provide GP or hospital services to the poor, a number of ancillary supports—maternity, child care, health visiting, ambulances—would remain with them and would in some cases be made mandatory for the first time.[50] But the local authority health centres, for all their place in Bevan's Act,[51] as the essential link between GPs, hospitals and local authority services, had to be abandoned. Only a few were set up to answer particular needs; beyond this, professional hostility and financial exiguity would prove insuperable.

(d) The Future of Charity

The fact that the state was taking over so much that was basic in social provision had repercussions for charitable effort in many of its manifestations. There were those, led in this also by Beveridge,[52] who would argue that voluntary work and organisation must positively seek out new roles, complementing the state services by pioneering novel types of provision and finding the cases where additional help would be most efficacious. In this direction some notable efforts would be made. With an NHS operating nationalised hospitals, there was a noticeable growth of charitable work for particular disability groups, such as spastics and the mentally handicapped, medical research and experimental health centres.[53] But the fact that Beveridge's flat-rate financial benefits in the new state system would fall behind levels of inflation meant that there remained continuing scope in the traditional field of helping those in need.

Between the wars, charities had been left largely to their own devices to choose among the many demanding causes of difficult, hard-stretched times. The Charities Commission had continued in existence but only as a marginal agency, sometimes able to help bodies out of difficulties but otherwise ineffectual.[54] Yet it was just those years, when high taxation became a fact of peace-time existence, which provided a new reason for the state to concern itself in the usefulness and effectiveness of voluntary organisations. Over the course of the nineteenth century there had grown a form of negative advantage to charities arising out of various types of relief from fiscal liability—both rates and taxes. One of the earliest instances had occurred in Pitt's first income tax of 1799 and thereafter the process

---

[49] Sched. 5.
[50] Part III.
[51] s.21 imposed a duty on local authorities to provide them.
[52] *Voluntary Action* (1948); for the spate of literature, see Owen (1960), pp. 531–537.
[53] Owen (1960), pp. 544–547 and more generally, Chap. 19.
[54] Accordingly they attracted a good deal of criticism before the Nathan Committee (below, n. 63): see Owen (1960), pp. 584–586.

had followed the pattern of that example.[55] Where relief was given, it generally went to all trusts and other bodies which were in law "charitable"—a classification which had therefore to serve a number of quite distinct purposes. Occasional politicians and others concerned with public efficiency had worried about giving relief so unselectively: Gladstone had sought as Chancellor of the Exchequer to do away with the income tax exemption in 1863; in 1920, the Colwyn Commission on Income Tax had wanted a more limited definition of the objects that would qualify.[56] Parliament, however, was not prepared to take such a stand.[57] The House of Lords, equally, had refused to hold that for tax purposes "charity" meant anything more confined than the rough four-fold classification of objects drawn from the preamble of the Act of 1601.[58]

However, once the fiscal advantages of charitable status acquired major significance, the courts would bring a somewhat more scrupulous appreciation to the question. By the end of the Hitler War, they were insisting that there should be a public benefit element in educational and other charities; the beneficiaries could not be confined to the members of one family or the employees of one firm.[59] The purposes, moreover, had to be exclusively charitable[60] and this could not include as a substantial object the securing of law reforms[61] or the provision of merely recreational facilities.[62] The novel severity of this litigation helped to make inevitable a political review of the ground rules for charitable donation and administration. The Attlee government would appoint a Committee under Lord Nathan which would in essence accept Beveridge's case for the crucial supplementative role of voluntary action; and from this eventually would come legislation designed to put the Charity Commission on a more effective

---

[55] For the modern position, and for the gradual establishment of general rules concerning exemption from rates, see Chesterman (1979) Chap. 10; also Owen (1960), pp. 340–345.

[56] Owen (1960), pp. 330–336 (noting a further recommendation to the same effect from the Royal Commission on Taxation of 1955).

[57] A provision of the Finance Act 1922 (s.20) ended the device of effectively transferring income from one (high-rated) taxpayer to another (low-rated) by the device of a covenanted gift; but an exception was still allowed for such a gift if it extended for seven years or more. This was picked up by charities in the 1920s as a means of attracting donors and became standard fund-raising practice: see Owen (1960), pp. 336–338.

[58] In *Baird's Trustees* v. *Lord Advocate* (1888) 15 S.C. (4th) 688, the Scottish Court of Session had agreed with the Revenue's view that, for tax exemption, there must be an element of poverty relief in the charity's object. But, following English precedents on other aspects of charitable status, in the well-known *I.R.C.* v. *Pemsel* [1891] A.C. 531, a majority of the House of Lords adhered to the broader view. See Chesterman (1979), pp. 58–61.

[59] *Wernher's Trustees* v. *I.R.C.* [1937] 2 All E.R. 488; *Re Compton* [1945] Ch. 123; *Gilmour* v. *Coats* [1949] A.C. 426; *Oppenheim* v. *Tobacco Securities Trust* [1951] A.C. 297. See Chesterman (1979), pp. 153–157, 160–163, 170–171; and for the special exception traditionally allowed to "poor relations" charities, pp. 144–147.

[60] *Chichester Diocesan Fund* v. *Simpson* [1944] A.C. 341 (and see above, p. 115); *Oxford Group* v. *I.R.C.* [1949] 2 All E.R. 537; *Ellis* v. *I.R.C.* (1949) 93 S.J. 678.

[61] *National Anti-Vivisection Society* v. *I.R.C.* [1948] A.C. 31.

[62] *I.R.C.* v. *Baddeley* [1955] A.C. 572; this however was to be reversed by the Recreational Charities Act 1958; see Chesterman (1979), pp. 171–174.

footing as registrar, supervisors and assistant of charities. Among its powers would be a broader ability to re-direct funds cy-pres, which had been presaged almost a century before by the Endowed Schools Act 1869.[63]

PART 4: EDUCATION—THE MODERN STRUCTURE

I. THE ACT OF 1902

Of all the conflicts generated by the Victorian forms of government, that over education came last and took its particular tone from the encircling religious divisions. The determination to use schooling as the principal means of inculcating sectarian dogma had led to an educational structure which allowed the churches to take the lead but to look to the central state for backing—on the elementary side by Education Department grants, and for certain types of further study by Science and Art Department grants. In order to move to compulsion and free provision of elementary education, novel local authorities, the School Boards, had been brought into being under the 1870 Act and had filled the gaps left by the denominations. The latter had not achieved any entitlement to support from the rates. For more advanced schooling, the churches and charities alone had been left to provide (in addition to purely private enterprise), some legal assistance in the matter of revising endowments having been the state's only contribution.

In the late nineteenth century, the most insistent demand on the state was for further education above the elementary level. Employers wanted school leavers with basic training in technical and design skills and they looked enviously at the development of technical education, directed particularly at the lower middle-class, in France, Germany, Switzerland and Austria. This call was taken up by the Royal Commission on Technical Instruction[64]; and eventually Salisbury's government empowered the county and county borough councils, which it had just created, to raise up to a 1d. rate for establishing their own technical schools, making grants to existing institutions, or providing scholarships, for technical education.[65] Soon afterwards, these authorities received their share of "whisky money" tax (on wines and spirits)[66] which they were entitled to devote to technical education (or in reduction of the rate for it).

The Education Department, the Science and Art Department, the School Boards and the new county authorities each had an interest in penetrating this middle ground and watched the others with increas-

---

[63] Report, P.P. 1952–53 [Cmd. 8710] VIII. Implementation had to wait until the Charities Act 1960.
[64] P.P. 1884 [C. 3981] XXIX, XXX.
[65] Technical Instruction Act 1889.
[66] For this, see above, p. 88.

ing suspicion. Crucial to the whole difficulty was the absence of any definition of "elementary education" in the 1870 Act, beyond the statement that it must form the "principal part" of teaching in Board schools. At that stage most effort had been concentrated upon teaching the "3Rs" to the standards required in Lowe's Revised Code; but soon enough teachers were striving to add subjects that would satisfy the abler pupils and prove more stimulating to teach. The Education Department sought to regulate this pressure by claiming the standards in its Code to be the determinant; and in 1875 it admitted English, History, Geography and Elementary Science as "class" subjects; in 1882 a Seventh standard was added and encouragement given to "specific" subjects such as French, physiology and drawing; finally, in 1890, grants for evening schools were liberalized to allow concentration on "class" and "specific" subjects after Standard V, a response to a very considerable demand. School Boards which used the rates to go beyond these perimeters were, on this view of the law, overstepping their powers and might be liable to surcharge on the expenditure.

The Boards had been placed under the audit and surcharge arrangements that applied to poor law and sanitary authorities.[67] These led ultimately to an appeal either to the Local Government Board or, on a question of law, to the Divisional Court of the Queen's Bench Division. The LGB, which heard some 2,000 appeals a year on surcharges of all kinds, became the regular place of recourse in education cases and followed the practice of consulting the Education Department over them. By this important administrative machinery, in the 1880's school boards were disallowed rate-supported nursery schools, special instruction for pupil teachers and separate science schools. Their schools might receive a further education grant from the Science and Art Department, but the auditor might then find it difficult to distinguish the spending on advanced classes from the rate-support of the rest of the school.[68] But still the demand for new opportunities pressed at many points.

Education was in a condition to provide the first, irrefragable confrontation between the new, active collectivism and an older, conservative tradition of non-intervention. Educational opportunity was, after all, a unique desideratum for a range of progressive opinion, which included the ever-vocal nonconformists. There would nevertheless be deep divisions on this front over priorities and over the institutional arrangements for policy and finance. Those whose first concern was efficient management favoured the county councils as local education authorities, those intent on independence backed the School Boards. Fear of too much advancement in education, the wish to keep it largely to the inculcation of simple Christian virtues, combined on the conservative wing with Anglican interests in dismantling the barrier which the Cowper-Temple clause placed against the Church in Board Schools, and even more in securing financial support for its elementary and more advanced schools.

[67] Elementary Education Act 1870, ss.8–10, 63.
[68] See Eaglesham (1956), p. 18ff.

Here the preference was all for the county councils, which retained the Tory complexion of Quarter Sessions.[69]

Hostilities intensified as it became clear that further schooling would have to be extended in some measure. The Bryce Commission on the subject reported in 1895 that the hope of satisfying demand through voluntary provision, which had been the tactic adopted by Gladstone's first government, was beyond redemption. The Commission favoured extending the course of 1870 upwards by introducing a rated element into the financing of secondary schools; and also by publicly-financed scholarships and exhibitions for pupils from the local elementary and higher grade schools to charitable and proprietary schools recognised as efficient. But the authority in charge at local level was to be the county council, rather than the school board, since planning ought to be on a substantial scale.[70]

The competing claims were resolved principally in the Conservatives' Education Act 1902.[71] In the political strategy for achieving the statute, litigation was made to play a tactical role. The politician chiefly in charge was the Education Vice-President, the prickly Sir John Gorst, who tussled with his principal civil servant, George Kekewich, but found an able ally in his private secretary, Robert Morant. The step which showed their intended course was to give the county councils the power to take control over Science and Arts grants for their areas.[72] This the London County Council did, to the chagrin of the London School Board. Gorst then discreetly engineered a challenge to the latter's multifarious activities in support of advanced teaching to school-children and adults. The auditor disallowed and surcharged three items of rate expenditure which had been used in conjunction with Science and Art grants.[73] Appeal was then taken, not to the LGB (as in the 1880's), but to the Divisional Court, and then the Court of Appeal; but with no success. A sense of outrage informed the judgments in *R. v. Cockerton*,[74] Wills J., for instance, branding the Board's activities as "the ne plus ultra of extravagance. . . . "

In the wake of this, the Act of 1902 made the County and County Borough Councils the education authorities for their areas at both the primary and secondary levels; school boards disappeared, though boroughs of 10,000 inhabitants and urban district councils of more

---

[69] These divisions were clearly reflected in the Majority and Minority Reports of the Royal Commission, chaired by Lord Cross, on the Elementary Education Acts: P.P. 1888 [C. 5485] XXXV. For all the disagreements the two groups were unanimous in condemning the constricting effects of payment-by-results and paved the way to a less judgmental basis for the central grant.

[70] P.P. 1895 [C. 7862] XLIII.

[71] The Bryce Commission revived the concept (earlier found in the Taunton Commission of 1867) of an integrated central ministry. This was effected by the Board of Education Act 1899. Inter alia it gave the educational functions of the Charity Commissioners to the newly constituted Board of Education: see P. Gosden (1962) 11 Br.J.Educ.St. 44.

[72] After an unsuccessful attempt in 1896 to create a new local authority for education in competition with the School Boards, this was achieved by adding a clause (Clause VII) to the conditions for grants from the Science and Art Department (South Kensington); see generally Simon (1965) Chap. 6.

[73] For the episode in detail, see Eaglesham (1956).

[74] [1900] 1 Q.B. 322; followed up with *Dyer v. London School Board* [1902] 2 Ch. 768.

than 20,000 could become authorities for primary education.[75] The minimum age for leaving school had been raised from eleven to twelve in 1899[76]; "elementary" teaching could now be provided up to the age of fifteen, but not normally beyond.[77] It would rest with the Local Education Authorities (the LEAs) to settle what provision should be made for "higher" education but they would have the power to raise rates for the purpose.[78] The Board of Education was able to insist that central grants were to be used only for advanced teaching and not for the light-weight, often recreational courses which had proved so popular in London evening schools.[79] The secondary schools were a rung on the ladder towards university for the ablest of the new generation, and LEAs acquired power to grant scholarships to those who would mount it.[80]

The largest concession to Conservative interests, however, came in permitting the voluntary schools of the churches (which remained predominantly Anglican) to be supported by the rates as well as by Board grant. The non-conformists could only secure the pre-condition of a conscience clause allowing withdrawal from religious instruction (the "Kenyon-Slaney clause").[81] The church (or "non-provided") schools now acquired very substantial underpinning from public finance in return for a minority of places on their managing boards going to LEA representatives.[82]

Morant, like his associates, Sidney and Beatrice Webb, believed that progress in education was necessary to produce the expert leaders of the coming society.[83] It was essential that the Board of Education should have an oversight of the whole, but it was to work, largely in an advisory capacity, in collaboration with large, professional authorities at the local level. Morant was prepared to give so much to the Church in order to keep the government on course with the Bill and thus to put an end to the School Boards. The Bill's passage provided evidence enough of the strength of non-conformist antagonism.[84] But perhaps even this was not sufficient warning that it would take a decade to secure acceptance of the new deal (very much as with the New Poor Law of 1834). In a persistent campaign of civil disobedience, occupiers refused to pay their rates; many were prosecuted or had their possessions distrained.[85] Local authorities in

[75] s.1. As a result there were some considerable variations in size.

[76] Elementary Education (School Attendance) Act 1983 Amendment Act 1899.

[77] s.22(2).

[78] s.2(1). The LGB had to consent to a rate higher than 2d. in the £.

[79] Education Regulations 1904.

[80] s.23(1). The process of aiding universities had begun with an annual central grant first made in 1889 (then £15,000; by 1902 £24,000). From this would grow the gradual absorption of major financial responsibility for universities, administered through a University Grants Committee.

[81] s.4(2).

[82] s.6(2) and for other controls, s.7.

[83] See generally, P. Gordon and J. White, *Philosophers as Educational Reformers* (1979) Chaps. 6–8.

[84] See Sturt (1967) Chap. 19; Simon (1965) Chap. 7; J. E. B. Munson, (1977) 20 Hist.J. 607.

[85] The leading figure in the campaign was the nonconformist Minister, Dr. John Clifford: see S. Koss, *Nonconformity in Modern British Politics* (1975), pp. 45–54; J. Murphy, *Church, State and Schools in Britain 1800–1970* (1971) Chaps. 6, 7.

Wales and elsewhere refused to cooperate and the Board took power to make direct payments to voluntary schools rather than include the amounts in the grant to the LEA.[86] Yorkshire County Council adopted the tactic of reducing teachers' pay for the time spent in religious instruction but the (judicial) House of Lords eventually ruled this illegal.[87] The Swansea LEA calculated payments to teachers in voluntary schools at a lower rate than for teachers in their own schools, using the argument that there had previously been such a differential. This gave rise to the well-known decision on proper administrative procedures, *Board of Education* v. *Rice*.[88] The House of Lords in effect upheld the Board's view that such a practice was inadmissible; and there was clear acknowledgment of the Board's arbitral capacity—given to it alone—to settle disputes between an LEA and a voluntary school's managers, subject only to judicial review where basic procedural requirements of natural justice had not been observed. The judgment was powerful confirmation of the position which Morant had sought for the Board.

On the political front, the Liberals had attracted votes in 1905 with a pledge to reverse the religious preference of the 1902 Act. But it was over their Bill tô do so that the House of Lords first determined to assert its independence; and the Liberals in the end chose to bide their moment for battle with the Upper House.[89] Instead the government was pushed towards a first measure of social protection through the education system. They took up (in weakened form) a Labour M.P.'s Bill for subsidised school meals,[90] and they allowed Morant to engineer an Act on medical testing in schools which he (with the Webbs) hoped to use as the starting point for local health services.[91] Both feeding and doctoring had a certain attraction even for those who remained generally opposed to state support systems, for the extent of unfitness in the populace, revealed in the scare stories of the Boer War,[92] boded ill for the maintenance of a vast, scattered empire. The House of Lords accordingly held its fire on these issues and the Liberals were encouraged enough to see larger possibilities in social provision.[93]

---

[86] Education (Local Authorities Default) Act 1904: applied to two Welsh authorities, despite Lloyd George's threat (empty as it proved) that chaos would result throughout Wales.

[87] *Att.-Gen.* v. *West Riding C.C.* [1907] A.C. 29.

[88] [1911] A.C. 179; see above p. 96.

[89] The first Bill, presented by Augustine Birrell, was followed by two government attempts in 1908 (one directed by McKenna, the other by Runciman) at the same objective; they were lost not only among religious factions but also through opposition from teachers, who for the first time were beginning to mobilise. See Simon (1965) Chap. 8.

[90] Education (Provision of Meals) Act 1906—an act which deliberately avoided the taint of pauperism: see Gilbert (1965), p. 108.

[91] Education (Administrative Provisions) Act 1907. In the event, it was not until the NHS of 1948 that the schools medical services provided treatment as well as diagnosis.

[92] Officially investigated by the Royal Commission on Physical Training (Scotland): P.P. 1903 [Cd. 1507] XXX, and an Inter-Departmental Committee on Physical Deterioration (highly critical): P.P. 1904 [Cd. 2175] XXXII.

[93] For Dicey, the school meals legislation was a particular thrust of the collectivist wedge: *Law and Opinion in England in the Nineteenth Century* (2nd ed.) (1914), pp. xlix–li.

The skirmishes against the 1902 Act were distracting, but in the end they remained at the periphery of the developing system of public education. Gorst and Morant had decided, in the wake of the *Cockerton* judgment, that the new distribution of governmental power should not be founded upon a clearer definition of legality. On the contrary, the statutory rubrics were general enough to make it difficult for opponents to challenge in the courts what was or was not done by administrators. This left the Board of Education free to encourage experimentation in methods of elementary teaching and to strengthen the arrangements for the training of pupil-teachers. In post-primary education, its preference was for the modernised "grammar" type, with strong emphasis on the humanities as necessary accomplishments for the future leaders of men. It was a model that filtered down from the elite public schools and it treated the technical and practical as craft skills which could be picked up in employment. British education was thus taking a turn crucially different from that in most European countries, where the urge to catch up in the industrial race fostered the growth of technical and other useful training.

II. THE INTER-WAR PLANS

The pattern of collaboration between central and local authority was such that real initiative lay with the LEA. If it was inclined to action, the Board could do a good deal to shape and direct. If its main aim was to keep down rates and to prevent the expectations and accomplishments of the lower orders from too rapidly rising, the Board had few sticks in its armoury. Some new obligations would be imposed in the period after 1918, mainly because education became a major instrument in reconstruction plans. Even before the War ended a new Education Act in 1918 set forth a bold proclamation: "With a view to establishing a national system of education available to all persons capable of profiting thereby, it shall be the duty of the councils of the counties and county boroughs to contribute thereto by providing for the progressive development and comprehensive organisation of education . . . " and they were required to put forward schemes of action to the Board. The age of compulsory schooling was raised to 14 and fees in public elementary schools completely abolished.[94] The Act explicitly encouraged new ventures in terrain neglected during the Morant era: advanced instruction for those who stayed in the elementary system from the age of 14, the introduction of practical subjects and physical training, and aid for nursery schools.[95] Central financing of local authorities ceased to be related to particular schools, and became instead a block grant of at least half the total expenditure.[96]

The staunch progressivism behind the 1918 Act, however, was to be severely battered by the economic emergencies of the inter-war

---

[94] s.8. As a corollary the restrictions on the employment of children under the leaving age were tightened: ss.13–16.

[95] ss.2, 17, 19. See generally Simon (1965) Chap. 3.

[96] s.44.

years. In the hands of the Treasury, education proved a delicate plant, succumbing readily to retrenchment pruning: the Geddes axe of 1921 cut out a great deal of the new plans for secondary and continuation schooling. Ten years later, the National government reduced building grants to local authorities, cut teachers' pay and introduced a parental means test for free places at grant-aided secondary schools. The condition of some of the voluntary schools in this period deteriorated so badly that by 1936 they were ready to surrender more of their independence in return for government assistance towards new building costs.[97]

In such conditions, the inter-war years were more notable for ideas than achievements. A number of official inquiries began to shape the policies which would dominate the period after 1944, the voice of the education expert becoming ever more penetrating. The first Labour government gave the Board's Education Committee, under the chairmanship of Sir W. H. Hadow, the task of reviewing education for the general run of adolescents. In 1926 it recommended the crucial strategy that would eventually underpin the Butler Education Act of 1944[98]: compulsory education should continue until 15 and all state schooling should divide into primary and secondary levels at "11-plus." In the second stage, pupils would, according to ability and inclination, go either to a grammar school or to a new form of "modern" school which would bring a practical, non-abstract approach to learning. In addition there would be some scope for trade and other strictly technical schools, though their relation to the secondary modern schools was not worked out in detail. The basic "11-plus" division would be made through the new science of educational psychology which proferred intelligence testing at that age as a reliable guide to the future capacities and development of each child.

These were influential ideas from the start and a number of LEA's began, despite the set-backs of 1931, building up their secondary school resources to achieve the primary/secondary division. In 1939, the Consultative Committee, now chaired by Sir Will Spens, again confirmed the desirability of splitting secondary education into streams: it now placed more emphasis on the need for a third, technical channel, but it specifically rejected as too cumbersome and difficult the notion of a "multilateral" school (or "comprehensive" as it later became).[99] This was a step back from the Hadow Report, which had at least warned of the danger that the secondary modern schools might become second-rate in every form of provision and so embalm an inherent division between middle- and working-class schooling. Only subsequently, in the Norwood Report, would there be some consideration of restoring to the basic plan the Webb-Morant notion of a ladder for all of ability whatever their social background: the

---

[97] Education Act 1936, s.8; Simon (1974) Chap. 5.

[98] *Education of the Adolescent*: see Simon (1974) Chap. 3. The Committee later reported on *The Primary School* (1931) and *Infant and Nursery Schools* (1933).

[99] *Secondary Education*. The Education Act 1936 had provided for the introduction of compulsory education to fifteen, but the war intervened just before implementation was due. See D. Rubinstein and B. Simon, *The Evolution of the Comprehensive School 1926–66* (1969) Chaps. 1, 2.

possibility of a "13-plus" change of school from modern to grammar for the most able was recommended.[1] Still the central concept remained that separate schools would best foster the pupil's "special cast of mind," his "special interest and aptitudes."[2] It was a division with considerable appeal to all who would preserve the social and economic advantages of the few to black-coated, or at least white-collared, salary-earning in a world where the many would remain bound to the wage of factory floor or service labour.

III. THE ACT OF 1944

In the second World War, the planning of educational reconstruction was in train by 1941.[3] Thanks particularly to the determination of the President, R. A. Butler, it came early to fruition. Despite Churchill's reluctance to carry such planning forward before victory, Butler secured an Education Act in 1944 which put the modern education system on a centrist-Conservative, rather than a Labour, base. The place of the essentially private, "public" schools—charitable or sometimes proprietary in organisation—was preserved, while making them subject to state inspection for minimum standards.[4] Likewise the direct grant schools, were allowed to continue in receipt of state aid for a proportion of local authority places, while keeping their autonomy over all decision-making and maintaining a largely middle-class intake.[5] The role of the religions in education was also secured, not only by the requirement of a daily act of worship in all state schools, together with teaching of religious knowledge,[6] but by financial arrangements which would allow LEA's to take over the full responsibility for the costs of a school in return for a majority on the governing body. A church might choose to put a school under this "controlled" status, or keep it as an "aided" school, if it met half the capital costs.[7]

The Act carried forward much of the spirit of the Fisher Act of 1918 in its determination to make education at all stages—now classified as primary, secondary and further—available to all who could bene-fit. The minimum leaving age was to be fifteen[8] and most pupils were to pass to secondary schools. The mark of the Norwood Committee— the belief that grammar, technical and modern schools were needed

---

[1] Between the wars, economic and cultural barriers had prevented many working-class children from climbing the Webb-Morant ladder: J. E. Floud (ed.) *Social Class and Educational Opportunity* (1956); D. V. Glass in M. Ginsberg (ed.) *Law and Opinion in England in the 20th Century* (1959), pp. 329–334.

[2] *Curriculum and Examinations in Secondary Schools* (1943). The social assumptions of this Report would subsequently be seriously criticised.

[3] A Green Book had been circulated confidentially, but widely, in 1941, even before Butler arrived at the Board; it was followed by a White Paper, Educational Reconstruction, P.P. 1942–43 [Cmd. 5458] XI. See N. Middleton and S. Weitzman, *A Place for Everyone* (1976) Chaps. 7–10.

[4] Even so, the provision of the 1944 Act (s.77) would not be brought into effect until 1957.

[5] This system had first been instituted in 1926.

[6] 1944 Act, ss.25–30.

[7] s.15.

[8] As already planned (see above, n. 99); there was also provision to raise the leaving age to 16 at a later date: s.35.

to fit the requirements of three types of aptitude within the population—in the end found no direct expression in the Act. Instead, the ability of central government (now significantly a Ministry of Education,[9] rather than a Board) to impose its will upon local authorities was considerably strengthened, through the established mechanism of the plan. Local authorities were to submit a plan to meet their immediate and prospective needs. The Minister then had power to define in detail their duties by issuing Local Education Orders,[10] duties which would ultimately be enforceable by mandamus or by reduction of the central grant. These legal controls were of vital importance even if they did not have to be directly implemented. Educational provision—above all at secondary level—was more than ever to be a subject of direct political antagonisms, and the powers of compulsion and financial discipline became a crucial ingredient in the mixture of cooperation, negotiation and confrontation between the local and central "partners" in modern education policy. Conservative governments and local authorities would in general prefer a division at "11-plus" into grammar and secondary modern schools. Much of the Labour movement, sensing in this distinction a social division rather than one truly intellectual, was already drawn to the concept of "multilateral" or "comprehensive" education. The Butler Act would survive the hostilities engendered by this controversy because of its sophisticated legal structure. In its first phase of operation, for instance, the Attlee government would allow LEA's intent on divided secondary schools to pursue their establishment, while encouraging some (like London), where their allies were in power, to experiment with comprehensive secondary schools. A decade later this programme would begin to provide evidence undermining the capacities of psychological prediction which for a quarter-century had informed so much educational planning. The Act would prove flexible enough to allow later Labour governments to press towards a comprehensive policy in a much more determined way.

Education was a service which in very large measure had passed into the hands of government. While political parties had considerable power to determine what was to happen at a national level, in different localities and even in particular schools, individual parents were left with little by way of specific entitlement, when it came to fulfilling their own legal duty to ensure the education of their children to the minimum leaving age.[11] As with health services, they were entitled to some provision but they could not insist that a child could be placed in any particular school; but then, they could not in general be obliged to accept a place in a given school either.

In contrast with the essentially preservative system for financial support and health care, education—potentially the most dynamic factor in social provision—was not wholeheartedly redirected by the Butler Act or the subsequent Attlee government. The new policy was evidently derived from what had gone before. For all its egalitarian potential, there remained much that pandered to the root assumption

[9] Part I.
[10] ss.11, 12.
[11] See ss.35–40.

among the propertied elites that they shared an intellectual a well as a moral superiority. This fond belief, which so readily translated in the British imagination into judgments about class, was reinforced not only by the continuing place of private education but also by the selective elements in the public system, including those created by the organisation of universities and other further education. Public provision may be the instrument of social transformation, but equally it may represent the cost of resisting truly threatening change. The educational system devised for the New Deal of post-war Britain was in good measure motivated by the latter consideration, which after all played its part in shaping the entire New Deal of social policy.

FURTHER READING

General

Bruce, M. *The Coming of the Welfare State* (3rd ed., 1966).
Chesterman, M. R., *Charities, Trusts and Social Welfare* (1979).
Cranston, R., *Legal Foundations of the Welfare State* (1985).
de Schweinitz, K., *England's Road to Social Security* (1943).
Fraser, D., *The Evolution of the British Welfare State* (2nd ed., 1984).
Hay, J. R., *The Origins of the Liberal Welfare Reforms* (2nd ed., 1983).
Henriques, U. R. Q., *Before the Welfare State* (1979).
Jones, G. H., *History of the Law of Charity 1532–1827* (1969).
Macdonagh, O., *Early Victorian Government* (1977).
Ogus, A. I., "Great Britain" in Köhler P. A., and Zacher H. (eds.), *The Evolution of Social Insurance 1881–1981* (1982).
Owen, D., *English Philanthropy, 1660–1960* (1964).
Tompson, R., *The Charity Commission and the Age of Reform* (1979).
Thane, P., *The Foundations of the Welfare State* (1982).

Poverty

Brundage, A. *The Making of the New Poor Law* (1978).
Finer, S. E., *The Life and Times of Sir Edwin Chadwick* (1952).
Fulbrook, J., *Administrative Justice and the Unemployed* (1978).
Gilbert, B. B., *The Evolution of National Insurance in Great Britain* (1966).
Gilbert, B. B., *British Social Policy, 1914–1939* (1970).
Harris, J., *Unemployment and Politics* (1972).
Inglis, B., *Poverty and the Industrial Revolution* (1971).
Webb, S. & B., *English Poor Law History*, Part I: *The Old Poor Law* (1927); Part II: *The Last Hundred Years* (1929).

Education

Barnard, H. C., *A History of English Education from 1760* (2nd ed., 1961).

Curtis, S. J., *History of Education in Great Britain* (7th ed., 1967).

Eaglesham, E. J. R., *From School Board to Local Authority* (1956).

Eaglesham, E. J. R., *The Foundations of Twentieth Century Education in England* (1967).

Simon, B., *Studies in the History of Education 1780–1870* (1960).

Simon, B., *Education and the Labour Movement 1870–1920* (1965).

Sturt, M., *The Education of the People* (1967).

Chapter Seven

ACCIDENTS

Courts and lawyers have had little enough to do with the social problems of poverty, sickness and old age, if those phenomena are considered in the round. But, in the industrial period, they have been concerned with accidents and the disruptions, emotional and medical as well as purely economic, which they cause. It has by no means been their exclusive preserve, since their main involvement has been in the process of compensating after the event and only to a lesser extent in the enforcement of criminal laws whose aim is prevention. In the course of a century and a half there has built up a legislative armoury of safety measures which it is principally for technical experts in government inspectorates to enforce. Even within the sphere of compensation, the use of insurance—both private and state—has become so widespread that claims adjusters and civil servants are now as much involved as lawyers.

Yet the role played by lawyers in the course of evolution has been so distinctive as to call for a separate treatment of accidents—and in particular of the personal injuries that they cause. The common law view of the proper scope for compensation claims exposed the legal system to perhaps the most sustained allegations of class bias that have befallen it. For politicians and leaders of labour in the generation after 1867 the issue acquired a striking degree of acerbity. The problems were limited enough to seem soluble by positive action. The main outcome of the campaigns against the common law—the workmen's compensation scheme of 1897 and 1906—introduced a measure of "private" social protection which would itself prove transitional. Its own propensity for dysfunction was to contribute to the adoption of state-run insurance schemes against unemployment and sickness of 1911; and ultimately in 1945 the accident scheme would become a part—though still a distinct part—of national insurance.

The economic debilities which flow from accidents do not of necessity demand more favourable treatment than the adversities of sickness, old age or any other cause, and, in pre-industrial England they seem rarely to have been distinguished. With the coming of industrialisation the level of risks "took off" in the wake of economic growth and so made the preventability of accidents a problem of real significance. A world learning the capabilities of utilitarian calculation could think in terms of incentives to take future precautions and these might take the form of compensation to past victims. Even so, it was not until the second half of the nineteenth century that collection began of statistics of the occurrence of accidents, the nature of the injuries and their relation to the particular population at risk.[1]

Transport provided the most dramatic evidence of increasing risk.

---

[1] See Bartrip and Burman (1983) Chap. 2 and pp. 75–76, 87, which presents a useful analysis of what figures there are for injuries at work in mines, railways and factories.

The improvement of eighteenth century roads through turnpike trusts and new techniques of construction brought a growth of road traffic that constantly threatened the very advances.[2] Yet speeds increased: from 4–5 m.p.h. in mid-century to 10–14 m.p.h. by 1830.[3] Keen competition between coaching firms only added to the dangers. "Lay out before such thoughtless creatures [the 'lower orders of people'], a road like a race-course and you produce races innumerable, in which a fall is not like that of a slow beast under its burden, but productive almost of certain death."[4] Even after the coming of the railways, highway accidents took a high toll, for the horse was a notoriously uncertain animal. One estimate puts the rate in the 1870's at 100,000 per annum, costing some £500,000.[5]

In their turn the railways produced disasters which at their worst could be on a large scale, attracting the morbid glamour that is today reserved for air crashes. Beside these ran a succession of more minor collisions, derailments and crossing and shunting accidents which remained common enough throughout the nineteenth century.[6] But it was travel by sea that provided the greatest hazards of all, given the immense risks posed by natural forces. In the 1820's Parliamentary opinion began to be stirred against the condition of ships in a new world.[7] Yet still in the 1870s well-insured "suicide ships" were allegedly sent to their doom and Samuel Plimsoll secured, over the opposition of the shipping interest, the first version of his well-known "line."[8]

Transport accidents provided illustrations enough of the different types into which disasters may be classified. The loss of a ship at sea might well leave no evidence from which cause could be traced.[9] Likewise on land it might be impossible to identify the cause. But at sea, and even more upon rail, there might be a failure in the system which was being operated. Trains were run at excessive speeds, not out of the driver's foolhardiness but because competition between the companies could sometimes be as keen as in the days of coaching. Staff made mistakes because they had too much to do and worked too long at a stretch. Companies refused to pay for the most advanced braking and other safety devices. Yet there were also the cases where the only apparent cause was the casual inadvertence or

---

[2] Not till the techniques pioneered by Macadam was it possible to contemplate the principle that "the roads must be made to accommodate the traffic, not the traffic regulated to preserve the roads": S. and B. Webb, *The Story of the King's Highway* (1913), p. 172.

[3] See W. T. Jackman, *Transportation in Modern England* (1916) I, Chap. 4, esp. pp. 312–318.

[4] T. D. Whitaker, *Loidis and Elmete* (1816), p. 81.

[5] W. A. Dinsdale (1954), p. 179, quoting from papers in the Walford Collection. Deaths from horses and horse-conveyances: in 1875, 1,589; in 1876, 1,732: P.P. 1877 [C. 1786] XXV 235; 1878 [C. 2075] XXIII, Q. 202.

[6] The fatal running down of the former Cabinet minister, Huskisson, at the opening of the Liverpool—Manchester Railway in 1830, formed the first precedent.

[7] For the regulation by a central inspectorate that was the result, see above, p. 54ff. and below, p. 516.

[8] When first introduced by the Merchant Shipping Act 1876, ss. 25–28, it was left to the owner to fix, and so was of little avail.

[9] Hence the courts refused to presume that the loss of a ship was from negligence until the owner showed otherwise: *Scott* v. *London Docks* (1865) 3 H. & C. 596, 599.

foolhardiness of an individual and this in circumstances against which there could be little by way of planning.

Equally, transport accidents showed that there were distinct classes of victims. There were, first of all, those passengers who were being carried under a contract with the business that in some sense caused the accident. Then there were outsiders who were injured by collision on the highway or with someone else's conveyance. Again there were employees engaged in running the transport business. In the case of railways, workers were more exposed to risk of personal injury than passengers or strangers such as crossing-users. As the century progressed a passenger's chance of being killed in a rail accident had steadily declined.[10] Yet in 1875–99, 12,870 railway servants were recorded as being killed at work, and 68,575 injured. In 1899 alone this amounted to 1:1000 killed and 1:115 injured.[11]

There were many other dangerous employments, where outsiders were only occasionally under any risk at all. Worst of all—in the earlier nineteenth century to be ranked beside seafaring—was mining, where injuries to individuals were a commonplace hazard and even major disasters could pass without sustained concern.[12] A Select Committee of 1835, reacting to the quest to exploit deeper, more dangerous seams, did no more than put to mineowners the question:

> "how far any object of pecuniary interest or personal gain, or even the assumed advantages of public competition, can justify the continued exposure of men and boys in situations where science and mechanical skill have failed in providing anything like adequate protection."[13]

The owners did a great deal to ensure that any answer came from themselves rather than from outside interferers.[14] Despite the first timid steps towards inspection they were able for another quarter-century to treat their workforce as an expendable resource in the quest for industry's essential fuel.

The complex machinery of the new factories also exposed workers to serious hazard. Rapidly revolving parts and shafts caught up limbs and clothing (particularly women's dresses) with fearful conse-

---

[10] For the role of the Railway Department of the Board of Trade in imposing improvements in braking, etc.: H. Parris, *Government and the Railways in Nineteenth Century Britain* (1965) Chap. 6.

[11] According to the Royal Commission on Accidents to Railway Servants (P.P. 1900 [Cd. 41, 42] XXVII) shunters were particularly exposed to risk, suffering as many deaths in a year (1897: 0.52 per cent.) as merchant seamen (*cf.* manual rail-servants other than mechanics in general: 0.12 per cent.; underground coal miners: 0.13 per cent.). A consequent statute, the Railway Employment (Prevention of Accidents) Act 1900, does seem to have induced as a noticeable improvement: see P. S. Bagwell, *The Railwaymen* (1963) Chap. 4.

[12] The 216,000 employed in the mines in 1851 had grown to nearly 807,000 by 1901; this was 2½ times the number working on the railways: Bartrip and Burman (1983), p. 45.

[13] Select Committee on Catastrophes in Mines, P.P. 1835 (603) V, p. 5.

[14] See generally, above, p. 55; and below, p. 515.

quences; equally dreadful results could follow from cleaning machines while still in motion.[15] Steam boilers, the immediate source of power, could cause terrible havoc when they exploded.[16] The risk of injury was exacerbated by the long hours of repetitive drudgery, often in humid, hot, dusty conditions. Despite the constant cry from millowners against the foolhardiness and stupidity of the operatives, the frequency of accidents suggested failures of system. Accidents were not separable as a problem from the other dehumanising conditions of industrial work, particularly the long-term threats to health from exposure to gases, dust and effluents. Very little attention could be given by labour unions in the 1830s and 1840s to the specific problems of the injured, though there would be signs of change by the 50s. The 40s would however prove to be the period in which the first attempts at imposing direct safety measures were undertaken, through the legislation on factories and the inspectorate which enforced it.

While from the 1840s onwards, there was an interweaving of common law compensation and statutory regulation, the frame of reference was in various essentials set by the former. Provided that the overlap is not forgotten, the story deserves to start in the realm of litigation designed to shift the burden of an accident (so far as money can) from victim to perpetrator. The first part of this chapter accordingly deals with the evolution to the tort of negligence to the 1860s. Then we deal with concomitant developments by way of spreading risk through insurance and avoiding dangers by safety measures (Part 2). The third part concerns the reaction against the mid-Victorian pattern.

PART 1: COMPENSATION BY CIVIL SUITS

I. An Emergent Tort

At the close of the eighteenth century, the growing dangers on the roads produced an outburst of reported litigation about highway accidents. In these cases, with only minor ripples, it was accepted that liability to pay compensation arose if the plaintiff proved that the defendant's negligence caused him injury or loss. This was by no means inevitable, for the common law knew no general principle by

---

[15] Engels' observation of the deformed and maimed in Manchester—"it is like living in the midst of an army just returned from a campaign"—is probably overcoloured: cf. *The Condition of the Working Classes in England* (1955 ed.), pp. 186–188 with the hostile introduction and notes to that edition, pp. xix–xx. Nonetheless a medical observer, Dr. Charles Thackrah, *The Effects of Arts on Health* (2nd ed., 1832) and a victim, William Dod (*Memoirs of a Factory Cripple* (1841)) suggest, as did the Factory Commission of 1833 and Shaftesbury's Select Committee of 1840–1841, that there was a grave problem; cf. the apologists referred to by Bartrip and Burman (1983), pp. 10–11 and see more generally pp. 9–14; for later statistics, *ibid.* p. 43 ff.

[16] See P. W. J. Bartrip (1980) 25 Int.R. Soc. Hist. 77.

which to settle the basis of such liability.[17] It had defined, by means of the precedents governing its forms of action, a variety of limited situations which gave rise to responsibility for injury to others or damage to their goods. There were a number of commercial relationships which were recognised to create duties not to cause injuries or loss.[18] In particular, those who exercised the "common callings"— carriers, for instance, and innkeepers—were obliged to protect both persons and goods in their care. In the case of goods, so great was the opportunity of defalcation offered to them, that they had come under a strict duty to look after the objects entrusted to them.[19]

Many of the accident cases of the 1790s involved such a relationship, being actions brought by passengers against those who undertook to carry them for reward. It was argued for one defendant that liability did not arise in such a case even for carelessness; but the courts would not accept that passengers travelled on coaches at their own risk.[20] Nor would they agree that a coach-owner was liable merely upon proof that he or his servant caused the injury, irrespective of any neglect: unlike goods, passengers were not entrusted in strictest confidence. The coach-owner and the ship-owner were to be responsible to their passengers only for neglects and defaults.[21]

These were not the only accident cases. There were also disputes arising out of collisions on the highway and at sea between strangers unrelated by any contract of carriage. In 1676, *Mitchil* (or *Michael*) v. *Alestree* had affirmed that the action on the case lay "for negligence" against a man who sent his servant to break in horses amid the crowds of Little Lincoln's Inn Fields and so brought about an injury to the plaintiff.[22] The precedent was, it seems, the source of a steady trickle of similar actions through the eighteenth century, though very little more on the subject was to appear in the reported case-law until the 1790s.[23] In the age of Blackstone and Mansfield, one well-known practice book, *Buller's Nisi Prius*, could propound a generalisation familiar to any student or tort law today:

"Every man ought to take reasonable Care that he does not injure his Neighbour; therefore, where-ever a Man receives any Hurt through the Default of another, though the same were not wilful,

---

[17] P. H. Winfield characterised a process of continuous development from the time of Bracton as "a skein of threads most of which are fairly distinct" (1926) 42 L.Q.R. 184. See also (1934) 34 Col L.R. 41.

[18] Blackstone had confined his discussion of negligence to these cases of "prior relationship" based upon "implied contract": *Commentaries*, III pp. 163–165, *cf.* p. 208.

[19] Other bailees of goods, however were only bound to take care of them in the degree prescribed by Lord Holt in *Coggs* v. *Bernard* (1703) 2 Ld. Raym. 909 (above, p. 237).

[20] *White* v. *Boulton* (1791) Peake 113, the first reported case in the spate of litigation.

[21] *Aston* v. *Heaven* (1797) 2 Esp. 533; *Christie* v. *Griggs* (1809) 2 Camp. 79. Lord Ellenborough's remark in *Israel* v. *Clarke* (1803) 4 Esp. 259 that "he would expect a clear land worthiness in the carriage itself to be established" needs to be understood in the context of the defendant's plea that he need only comply with the statutory prohibitions against overloading his coach. Similarly *Sharp* v. *Grey* (1833) 2 B. & Ad. 169.

[22] (1676) 1 Vent. 295; 3 Keb. 650; 2 Lev. 172; Baker (1979), pp. 344–345. As Prichard (1964) shows, this was not merely an instance of a *scienter* action respecting animals known to be dangerous; it was taken to create a broader form of liability, the essence of which was an injury consequent upon negligence.

[23] See Prichard (1964); Baker (1979), pp. 345–348.

yet if it be occasioned by Negligence or Folly, the Law gives him an Action to recover Damages for the Injury so sustained."[24]

Here, in primal innocence, is very much the proposition to which, after long and painful experience, Lord Atkin would again lead the common law in *Donoghue* v. *Stevenson*. Its broad sweep could justify the courts in shifting the financial consequences of negligently caused injury onto the shoulders of the injurer in circumstances of ill-defined variety. Yet the logical possibilities had only to be sensed for the courts to begin a search for modifications and qualifications that would staunch the fecundity of the notion. In the end their most telling restraint would lie in the concept of duty of care; and it would take all Lord Atkin's daring to suggest once more that there was in principle a duty owed to any "neighbour."[25] But the historical process of retraction from Buller's brave new world is best understood by leaving aside for the moment the uses of "duty of care." We must first note how vicarious liability, already established in principle, added a separate dimension of significance to the emerging tort of negligence; and how the increasing measure of damages gave real cause for concern. It was in face of these combined prospects that the courts turned to a clutch of ideas concerning comparative fault and the need for self-protection as the first means of precluding liability in many situations, but above all for accidents at work.

One initial episode, however, had about it a curious air of inconsequence. It constituted that last major argument about the scope of the common law forms of action before their abolition. The question whether an accident claim should be formulated upon the writ of trespass or that of case had to do with the settled distinction that trespass lay for direct injury, case for indirect[26]: to throw a log into the highway and hit a man was a trespass, to leave it there so that he fell over it was actionable in case.[27] It was a distinction whose application could be arbitrary, as the celebrated "squib" case showed the common lawyers.[28] In accident cases plaintiffs came to be faced with a serious procedural hazard, largely because any vicarious liability had to be asserted in case. Hence, in King's Bench, where there was a nice adherence to the dichotomy: a collision caused by the negligence of the defendant as driver was direct and required trespass;[29] but if his servant had been driving, the vicarious nature of the responsibility obliged an action on the case.[30] It was an insistence upon due form that was perhaps symptomatic of a deeper malaise about the direction in which the common law was turning. Nonethe-

---

[24] 1st ed., 1768, pp. 35–36; 4th ed. 1785, pp. 25–26 (by which time the work was under Buller's editorship).

[25] [1932] A.C. 562 at 578; see below, pp. 511–512.

[26] For the evolution of the distinction, see Milsom, *Historical Foundation of the Common Law* (2nd ed., 1981) Chap. 11; Baker (1979), pp. 240–242.

[27] *Reynolds* v. *Clarke* (1729) 1 Str. 634, per Fortescue J.

[28] *Scott* v. *Shepherd* (1773) 2 W. Bl. 892; Prichard (1964). Common Pleas (Blackstone J. dissenting) held it trespass for a man to throw a lighted squib into a crowd, where it was thrown on until it exploded and injured the plaintiff.

[29] *Day* v. *Edwards* (1794) 5 T.R. 648.

[30] *McManus* v. *Crickett* (1800) 1 East 106; *cf.* the uncertainty in *Savignac* v. *Roome* (1794) 5 T.R. 648; Prichard (1964), pp. 238–239, 242–248.

less it proved to have no direct bearing on fundamental issues; there was no coherent argument, for instance, that trespass lay for any "direct" injury, while case demanded substantiation of fault.[31] Accordingly, the dispute had become vestigial within three decades and would finally disappear with the forms of action under the Judicature Acts.[32]

II. VICARIOUS LIABILITY

The idea that, if a person used an agent to act on his behalf and the agent caused actionable loss, damage or injury in the course of doing so, the principal as well as the agent might be sued, can be found in the medieval common law and in the law merchant.[33] Its place in modern law was fostered particularly by Lord Holt, who showed a lively awareness of its desirability.[34] He held, for instance, that a shipowner was vicariously liable where the ship's master had let cargo be damaged, that a stage-coach owner was liable when his driver lost luggage, and that a farmer was liable for fire damage caused by his servant "in way of husbandry."[35] In the first two instances, a relationship existed in which the law imposed strict duties upon the carrier. It was the third case that had a particular potency, since it affected the general obligations owed even to strangers. Even so, fire was a special danger and strict liability had been imposed for its escape. It was still not clear in the eighteenth century how far a principal would suffer vicarious liability when the agent's wrong involved proof of his personal fault. In what degree was it necessary to show that the principal had ordered commission of the injuring act? Must he be shown to have required it to be performed in a manner that created undue danger? Must he have been careless in choosing the agent? Must there at least have been a relationship between him and the victim—most obviously, a contract from which responsibility could be implied?

In Blackstone's view there was vicarious liability when the agent was acting upon a general command—carrying out the task that he had been set in broad terms; it was not necessary to show that he had been expressly commanded to act in the wrongful way.[36] Blackstone

---

[31] Earlier precedent had established that "inevitable accident" might be a defence to trespass; and the modern view is that, in the nineteenth century, the basis of liability was not treated as differing in trespass and case, see Baker (1979), pp. 341–342. At the height of the controversy, Lord Kenyon saw only one practical consequence: that costs went to the plaintiff in trespass only if he secured a verdict of 40s. damages, a rule not applicable to case. There was, in fact, also some difference in limitation period (trespass, four years; case, six years).

[32] Common Pleas showed an early preference for case: and King's Bench began to give way in *Rogers* v. *Imbleton* (1806) 2 B. & P. (N.S.) 1175. The rule finally settled in *Williams* v. *Holland* (1833) 10 Bing. 112 was that trespass had to be brought only for wilful acts causing immediate injury; in all other circumstances case might be used. The matter had worried the Common Law Commissioners two years earlier: P.P. 1831 (92) X, p. 7.

[33] Holdsworth, III pp. 382–387; VIII p. 472.

[34] See J. H. Wigmore in *Essays in Anglo-American Legal History*, (1909), III p. 520.

[35] *Boson* v. *Sandford* (1691) 2 Salk. 440; 3 Mod. 231 *Middleton* v. *Fowler* (1699) 1 Salk. 82; *Turberwill* v. *Stamp* (1698) Skinner 681, Comb. 459, 1 Ld. Raym. 264.

[36] *Commentaries*, I p. 429.

did, however, refer in justification to the trust that others placed in a principal to see that he employed proper agents, a notion which might be read as limiting the responsibility to fault in selection or to pre-existing contractual relationships.[37] Blackstone, however, also referred to a concept of identification: *qui facit per alium, facit per se.* As Lord Brougham was later to put it, in terms explicitly utilitarian:

> "The reason I am liable is this, that by employing him I set the whole thing in motion: and what he does, being done for my benefit and under my direction, I am responsible for the consequences of doing it."[38]

Some Western legal systems, notably the German, were unable to accept a notion of vicarious liability wide enough to require masters to shoulder responsibilities for the faults of their servants in the absence of any undertaking to do so. If the issue had arisen for settlement in England only at the outset of Victoria's reign, a similarly scrupulous notion of moral responsibility might have pointed in the same direction.[39] As it was, Georgian courts had seen no contradiction in making a blameless principal liable for the personal fault of his agent, as was made plain in the running down decisions of the 1790s. Only on the obfuscating issue of the proper form of action—trespass or case—did the factor of vicarious responsibility add its own complication.[40] Even at the time a moralist such as Archdeacon Paley could regret that the principle stood "rather upon the authority of the law than upon any principle of natural justice."[41] It was a viewpoint that was not entirely to be lost. Eighty years later, Bramwell L.J. would remark sardonically, "the only reason for going against the employer is the great convenience of his always having his pockets full."[42] But having started in the business of selectively compensating the victims of accidents, the common lawyers by and large accepted vicarious responsibility as a practical necessity. The live issues went rather to its scope.

Of these, the most fundamental was to define the range of relationships imposing vicarious responsibility. As we have seen, the notion of employment for a cash wage is a modern one which was emerging with industrial capitalism.[43] Older patterns of agricultural labour by living-in servants and out-working labourers, and of craft trades with their apprentices and journeymen, belonged to a world in which there were many gradations between the close-connected and the casual. Much early industry and construction work depended upon arrangements which today we would call sub-contracting.

---

[37] See also *Boson* v. *Sandford* (above, n. 35) and Tindal C.J., *Laugher* v. *Pointer* (1826) 5 B. & C. 547 at 549–550.

[38] *Duncan* v. *Findlater* (1839) 6 Cl. & F. 894 at 910.

[39] See Baty, *Vicarious Liability* (1916); H. H. Seiler (1967) Jur. Zeitung 525.

[40] See above, pp. 488–489.

[41] *Moral Philosophy* (12th ed., 1827), I 168.

[42] P.P. 1877 (285) X, Q. 1179; see below, XXX; even in 1916, Dr. Baty mounted a sustained attack on the concept in *Vicarious Liability*; and see F. Pollock, *Essays in Jurisprudence and Ethics* (1881), p. 125.

[43] Above, p. 286.

Large-scale factories under the direction of a single employer in our sense were only emerging in the early nineteenth century. The language of "command" which the common lawyers had already used to define the imposing of vicarious liability accordingly cast a wide net of obligation in typical conditions. In *Bush* v. *Steinman*, the defendant had been repairing a house which he did not occupy. He employed a surveyor who employed a carpenter who in turn employed a bricklayer to do some of the work. The servant of the bricklayer left a pile of lime in the highway, which led to the plaintiff's carriage being overturned. The Court of Common Pleas held that the defendant liable as the person "from whom the authority flows, and for whose benefit the work is carried on."[44]

Heath J. gave as an instance: "where a person hires a coach upon a job, and a job-coachman is sent with it, the person who hires the coach is liable for any mischief done by the coachman while in his employ, though he is not his servant."[45] Yet it was this very situation that was to cause a major difference of opinion amongst later judges and an eventual narrowing of doctrine. In 1826, a case of this kind was argued not only before the Court of King's Bench, which was equally divided, but also before the judges of the other common law courts—and they too appear to have been unable to agree in a way that would resolve the deadlock.[46] When the issue arose once more in *Quarman* v. *Burnett*, Parke B. led the Court of Exchequer into requiring the relationship of master and servant before vicarious liability could arise.[47] If it were otherwise, he objected, "the purchaser of an article at a shop, which he had ordered the shopman to bring home for him, might be made responsible for any injury committed by the shopman's carelessness."[48] As elsewhere this court judged the issue by its impact upon the domestic responsibilities of the pater familias. Only the occupier of land, in respect of nuisances occasioned on it, was regarded as being under a wider responsibility for the acts of outside contractors as well as servants. By this exception, cases such as *Bush* v. *Steinman* were confined within a narrow bound.[49]

The formula that the employee must be "acting in the course of his employment" became common form in the early nineteenth century. It was later to be complemented by the notion that there was no vicarious liability when the servant had gone off on his own affairs— "on a frolic of his own," as the judges, with evident disapproval, put it.[50] But what of the servant who deliberately committed a wrong

---

[44] (1799) 1 Bos. & Pul. 404. But Eyre C.J. was greatly troubled by the breadth of the decision; see further *Sly* v. *Edgley* (1806) 6 Esp. 6.

[45] 1 Bos. & Pul. at 409.

[46] *Laugher* v. *Pointer* (1826) 5 B. & C. 547; see also *Brady* v. *Giles* (1835) 1 M. & Rob. 494; *Randleson* v. *Murray* (1838), 8 Ad. & E. 109.

[47] (1840) 6 M. & W. 499.

[48] At p. 510.

[49] F. H. Newark, (1949) 65 L.Q.R. 480 shows how cases of the *Bush* v. *Steinman* kind after about 1840 came to be spoken of as cases of nuisance rather than negligence. This treatment of one kind of personal injury liability as subject to the stricter obligations of nuisance was to produce some curious anomalies and confusions.

[50] The expression appears to originate with Parke B., *Joel* v. *Morrison* (1834) 6 C. & P. 501.

when otherwise about his master's business? Lord Kenyon thought
that there should be no vicarious responsibility in such a case, unless
the servant was acting on the master's express instructions.[51] But this
was modified in 1821,[52] so as to make the master liable when the servant's act was an "injudicious" attempt to execute his general
instructions. And eventually, the employer was made liable, however reckless the employee had been, provided that the latter was acting in the course of his service and doing whatever he thought best
met the interest of his employer. So where bus companies were competing for passengers, and one driver, by running his bus in front of
another, caused an accident, his employer was liable unless it could
be shown that the driver had been motivated by some private spite.
Moreover—and this had the greatest practical importance—the
employer could not exclude his liability by giving his employee
specific instructions not to do what he did.[53]

We shall consider below how, at the outset of Victoria's reign, the
judges began to protect the entire category of employers against one
aspect of vicarious responsibility—that for injuries to one employee
occasioned by a "fellow servant."[54] The concept of such an exception
was, however, no novelty. In the case of the Crown, the base-rule
that the monarch could not in his own courts be considered capable
of wrong imposed a blanket protection against liability, personal or
vicarious.[55] But equally, those who managed an activity without any
immediate chance to share in a profit—such as a turnpike, dock or
town improvement trust or commission—had a special claim to
exemption from any responsibility for the faults or others: theirs was
a public duty. With the early running down cases came those in
which servants left rubble unlighted on the highway in the path of
unsuspecting vehicles. By 1815 the employing authority was beginning to be exempted from vicarious liability in such cases.[56] Some
judges would support this upon a formal application of the *vires* concept: the statute establishing the authority was taken to confer no
power to expend assets in meeting tortious liabilities unless it was
expressly given.[57] Not till the 1860s would it come to be said that, in
exploiting statutory powers, it was still necessary to see that no

---

[51] *McManus* v. *Crickett*, above, n. 30.

[52] *Croft* v. *Allison* (1821) 4 B. & Ald. 590; see also *Sharrod* v. *L.N.W.R.* (1849) 4 Ex. 580.

[53] *Limpus* v. *LGOC* (1862) 1 H. & C. 526. This was ultimately carried to the extreme
that the employer remained liable even where the employee's wrong (a fraud) was
criminal and intended only to benefit himself: *Lloyd* v. *Grace Smith & Co.* [1912] A.C.
716.

[54] See below, p. 496ff.

[55] Nor could indirect pressure be brought by making the actual supervisor vicariously
liable: *Lane* v. *Cotton* (1701) 1 Ld. Raym. 646 (Postmaster-General); *Whitfield* v. *Le
Despencer* (1778) 2 Cowp. 754 (captain of man-of-war). This rule became of general
application.

[56] *Harris* v. *Baker* (1815) 4 M. & S. 26 at 29; *Hall* v. *Smith* (1824) 2 Bing. 156; *Duncan* v.
Findlater (1839) 6 Cl. & F. 894 (imposing the same rule upon Scots law).

[57] Esp. Lord Cottenham, *Duncan* v. *Findlater* (above, n. 56) at 907–908; this was an
extension of cases such as *British Cast Plate* v. *Meredith* (1792) 4 T.R. 794, which held
that it was no tortious invasion of property to do precisely what the incorporating
statute authorised (such as paving a street so as to make entry onto premises difficult).

unnecessary damage was done.[58] Blackburn J. would find justification for this in a new perception of reality: that such statutes were
intended to impose liability "either . . . by incorporating them, or by
enabling them to sue and be sued in the name of the clerk, and
restricting the execution to the property which they hold as Commissioners."[59]

III. Measure of Damages

The effectiveness of compensation suits in inducing caution on the
part of those who ran potentially dangerous enterprises clearly
depended upon the level of damages which they were liable to pay.
Assigning a monetary value to the consequences of personal injury is
inevitably to some degree arbitrary; in consequence the process was
left in the hands of the jury, with few rules as to the instructions
which the judge was to give them on the question. Arguments about
the proper basis of assessment reached the courts *in banc* only very
rarely and it is very difficult to collect information about the awards
which were becoming daily more frequent in the trial courts.

By the 1840s, at least, it seems to have been accepted that while
damages could be given for losses of earnings, both actual and pro-
jected, as well as for medical and other expenditure, these pecuniary
"heads" were not the only factors to be taken into account. Claims for
the pain and suffering occasioned to an injured person were well-
established by the time that the King's Bench ruled that relatives
claiming under the Fatal Accidents Act 1846 had no right to a solatium for *their* grief.[60]

In the first decades of the nineteenth century, injuries which left
the victim severely handicapped rarely resulted in awards even of
£400–£500. £100 for the loss of a limb or an eye seems to have been
common enough, a sum which represented three or four year's
wages to a labourer. The advent of the railways as defendants
encouraged juries to think on a more expansive scale. The three companies which produced detailed statements of compensation paid by
them, to a Select Committee investigating railway accidents in 1857,
showed one verdict of £4,981 and another of £4,000; five were for
£2,000 or more and thirteen for £1,000 or more.[61] Protests by the railways against the size of these verdicts became increasingly strident.
Much play was made of cases where the jury had been touched by
(allegedly) exaggerated, or even fabricated, displays of suffering. For

---

[58] *Mersey Docks Trustees* v. *Gibbs* (1866) L.R. 1 H.L. 93. The shift was achieved through
a curious side-excursion: public purpose trustees were first held no longer to be
exempt from poor rates despite their beneficial activity; see the culminating
decision: *Jones* v. *Mersey Docks Trustees* (1865) 11 H.L.C. 433.

[59] *Gibbs* case (above, n. 58) at 116.

[60] *Blake* v. *Midland Rly.* (1852) 18 Q.B. 93 at 111. But 10 years before Pollock Q.C. had
surrendered any claim to damages for pain and suffering when appearing for an
injured surgeon against the Brighton Railway—the idea was then too new: *ibid* at
104; for claims on death, see below, pp 501–504.

[61] Select Committee on Accidents on Railways P.P. 1857–1858 (362) XIV Appendix. The
three companies were the Great Northern, the Midland, and the Lancashire and
Yorkshire. Thirteen railway companies supplied figures showing payments under
awards and settlements of £368,355 over a period of 10 years.

this, legal and medical practitioners who sought out claimants were held partly to blame. Four judges, who showed a distinct sympathy for the companies before another Select Committee in 1870, admitted that such things did occur but said they were able to detect and control them.[62] In the same spirit, they blamed juries for thinking in large terms against substantial defendants; their own juries did not generally return excessive verdicts, but Baron Martin spoke darkly of "some judges who take the view, that damages ought to be high, and in all probability they lead the jury to think so too."[63]

Despite this to the commoner judicial attitude seems to have been to encourage caution. Baron Parke directed one jury: "scarcely any sums could compensate a labouring man for the loss of a limb, yet you do not in such a case give him enough to maintain him for life."[64] Such remarks were commonplace. One attempt to provide juries with systematic information for calculating pecuniary loss led to a new trial being ordered.[65] To supply them with life expectancy tables and the like, it was feared, would lead them to ignore the various contingencies which might have reduced the earning capacity of the individual plaintiff; instead they would think simply of giving him the price of a government annuity. And so a pattern was settled that was to survive even the eventual decline of jury trial and the consequent growth of detailed rules about the "heads" of personal injury damages. As with other torts, damages were assumed to represent complete compensation for the wrong—in this case for financial loss, suffering and loss of prospective happiness. But in practice much effort was to be devoted towards ensuring that the total amount would err on the side of moderation. While the occasional rich plaintiff (or his estate) was winning a verdict of £10,000 or even £13,000 in the 1870s,[66] the general expectation of a humbler person rendered totally unfit for work was thought to be some three years' wages. Indeed this would be the justification offered for introducing such a limit into the Employers' Liability Act 1880 when that statute saved injured workmen from the harshest restrictions of common law doctrine.[67] It was nonetheless the scale of compensation which contributed significantly to the whole search for limitations.

IV. Contributory Negligence

By providing defendants worth pursuing, vicarious liability fulfilled one precondition for the common law to have practical effect. But any plaintiff still needed the means and the resilience to engage in the litigation: in particular, he had to face the difficulty of establishing

---

[62] Q. 877 (Martin and Bramwell BB.), Qs. 1146–47 (Hannen J.); Q. 2242 (Willes., J.).
[63] Q. 866.
[64] *Armsworth* v. *South East Ry Co.* (1877) 11 Jur. 748.
[65] *Rowley* v. *L.N.W.R.* (1873) L.R. 8 Ex. 221.
[66] In *Phillips* v. *L.S.W.R.* (1879) 4 Q.B.D. 406; affirmed. 5 Q.B.D. 78, the plaintiff, a surgeon, had been earning £6,000–£7,000 a year and had been rendered totally incapacitated. A verdict of only £7,000 was held to be against the weight of the evidence.
[67] See below, p. 524.

that the defendant's negligence was the cause of the accident. This was the first point at which limitations began to constrict the entitlement to sue. It was natural for a defendant to allege that the plaintiff was to blame for the injury that befell him and this turned the law to a strategic but difficult judgment. It had long known the concept of "direct" or "proximate" cause as a precondition of civil liability.[68] But what was to be the position if both plaintiff and defendant had in a significant degree contributed to the result by acts or neglects?

The relative closeness in time of these events to the accident was often decisive. If the plaintiff's act occurred after the defendant's, then the defence of contributory negligence would be likely to succeed. In the initial outcrop of accident cases, contributory negligence was accepted as a complete defence with no suggestion that the question was then a novelty. In *Butterfield* v. *Forrester*, the defendant left a pole needed for building repairs sticking out into the road; the plaintiff rode full tilt into it. Bayley J. directed the jury that if, with reasonable care, the plaintiff could have seen and avoided the pole, they were to find for the defendant. This they did and his direction was upheld.[69] On the other hand, the time sequence might be reversed. In *Davies* v. *Mann*[70] the plaintiff tethered a donkey in the road and the defendant ran into it. He was held liable for injuring it because the jury found that had he exercised ordinary care he might have avoided it. From this case in particular (though it was by no means the first) developed the notion that the defendant would be liable if he had the "last opportunity" of avoiding the accident. Constantly pressed into service, this became a concept of arcane refinement.[71] But most difficult of all were the cases where, if either plaintiff or defendant had been negligent, it was at the same time: as, for instance, in collisions between carriages and riders or between coaches and pedestrians. By the 1840s there was a fair consensus that if the plaintiff's negligence had made a substantial contribution to the accident then he should be wholly non-suited.[72] The proportional reduction of damages, which was the means by which contributory negligence was brought into account in admiralty law for a collision on the high seas, was beyond the imagination of the common law.[73]

Yet, as was regularly acknowledged, juries who were not prepared completely to overlook the plaintiff's negligence might achieve an apportionment *sub rosa*. In *Raisin* v. *Mitchell*, for instance, the plaintiff's contributory negligence in causing a collision at sea had been put in issue by the defendant, and the jury awarded exactly half the

---

[68] Holdsworth, VIII pp. 459–462.

[69] (1809) 11 East 60.

[70] (1842) 10 M. & W. 546.

[71] See esp. *Radley* v. *L.N.W.R.* (1876) 1 A.C. 759; *British Columbia Rly.* v. *Loach* [1916] 1 A.C. 719; *The Eurymedon* [1938] P. 1.

[72] E.g., *Sills* v. *Brown* (1840) 9 C. & P. 601; cf. *Hawkins* v. *Cooper* (1838) 8 C. & P. 473, where Tindal C.J. directed the jury to find for the defendant if the accident "can be attributable in any degree to the incautious conduct of the plaintiff herself." This severer test did not survive.

[73] "One person being in fault will not dispense with another's using care for himself," said Lord Ellenborough at a formative stage: *Butterfield* v. *Forester* (1809) 11 East 60 at 61.

plaintiff's estimated damage.[74] In a case where a widow was awarded only 40s. in respect of her husband's death Cockburn C.J. remarked tartly: "It is obvious that the jury have evaded their responsibility of a decision by a kind of compromise."[75] Yet to upset a verdict for the plaintiff on the ground that he should have been considered contributorily negligent obliged the court *in banc* to find the jury's verdict to be against the weight of the evidence. It was inherently difficult to interfere in this fashion. And so other factors began to emerge as questions of law on which judges might rule for themselves.

V. Common Employment

In *Priestley* v. *Fowler*[76] a butcher's servant sued his master, alleging that the master had allowed a van to be overloaded with goods, apparently by other servants; as a result it gave way and the plaintiff was thrown out, fracturing his thigh. The Court of Exchequer, clearly startled by the novelty of the proceedings, upset the plaintiff's verdict of £100 damages, after looking "at the consequences of a decision the one way or the other." So far as is known, this was the first action by servant against master, at least in the superior courts, in respect of injuries caused by negligence.[77] Workers such as seamen had mounted actions for unpaid wages, and groups of workmen had occasionally gone before the higher courts, for instance to seek enforcement of the Statute of Artificers. Yet at best a servant must have expected sustenance for the rest of his hiring if he became incapacitated by sickness or accident. To think of a remote court awarding monetary compensation for fault, above all against a master, required considerable daring.

Priestley, at least, was emphatically denied his verdict. Lord Abinger C.B., speaking for the court in a reserved judgment, touched upon enough possibilities for refusing the action to provide subsequent courts with many ways of interpreting his judgment. Though the jury had found that the master positively knew the van was overloaded, the fact would have been equally apparent to the servant. It was thus a case where notions of contributory negligence and voluntary assumption of risk might have been the reason for excusing the master. But to settle the matter on this footing might have left each subsequent case to the verdict of its jury, and the Court sensed the real danger:

"If the master be liable to the servant in this action, the principle of that liability will be found to carry us to an alarming extent. He who is responsible by his general duty, or by the terms of his contract, for all the consequences of negligence in a matter in which he is the principal, is responsible for negligence of all his inferior

---

[74] (1839) 9 C. & P. 617. The foreman of the jury admitted that "there was fault on both sides"; Tindal C.J. allowed the verdict to stand, saying: "There may be faults to a certain extent."

[75] *Springett* v. *Ball* (1865) 4 F. & F. 472.

[76] (1837) 3 M. & W. 1; and see Smith (1981), pp. 259–262.

[77] Bartrip and Burman (1983), pp. 24–25 cannot believe it, but have no positive counter-evidence.

agents. If the owner of the carriage is therefore responsible for the sufficiency of this carriage to his servant, he is responsible for negligence of his coach-maker, or his harness-maker, or his coachman."[78]

The willingness to treat vicarious liability, which was thus put in issue, as arising in respect not only of the acts of servants but of all contractors highlights the Court's state of alarm.[79] Yet it was the attitude expressed in this passage that later courts were to find so pertinent. The doctrine of Common Employment, as it became known, was to prescribe that an employer was not vicariously liable to one of his employees for an injury occasioned by the negligence of another.

Lord Abinger did admit that the employer "is, no doubt, bound to provide for the safety of his servant in the course of his employment, to the best of the judgment, information and belief." This personal duty on the employer, which was quite distinct from any vicarious responsibility, was to be preserved, at least as a theoretical obligation.[80] But cases such as *Priestley* v. *Fowler* suggest that the role of this separate duty was severely limited by prevalent attitudes to responsibility for safety. If an employer's cart is sent out overloaded, it is possible to find that there is negligence at three points. The employer may be deemed negligent in not setting up some system for checking against this dangerous condition ever arising. Equally, the employee responsible may be deemed negligent for the particular act of overloading. And the victim may be similarly treated for going off in the overloaded cart. For most of the nineteenth century it remained difficult to persuade judges, government inspectors and established opinion generally,[81] that the servant should have a claim in any circumstance where he could perceive the danger. To require employers to adopt a system of safety bore the taint of paternalistic precaution and was almost always expensive. It was tempting instead to denounce the wanton recklessness or crass stupidity of the servant who brought about or suffered the accident.

The judgment in *Priestley* v. *Fowler*, being concerned to impose a formidable limit on accident liability in the realm of employment, displays the same preoccupation with contract that would restrict the range of liability for faulty goods.[82] Master and servant would have a contract which said nothing expressly about liability for accidents. Two consequences were held to follow: their mere relation could never "imply an obligation on the part of the master to take more care of the servant than he may reasonably be expected to do of himself"; while on the other hand, "the servant is not bound to risk his safety in the service of his master, and may, if he thinks fit, decline

---

[78] (1837) 3 M. & W. 1 at 5–6. The domestic possibilities are pursued through several more examples.

[79] The question was at that time open, but a live issue: see above p. 491.

[80] See below, pp. 508–509.

[81] But not jurymen confronted with an injured plaintiff and a solvent enterprise as defendant!

[82] Below, pp. 507–508.

any service in which he reasonably apprehends injury to himself."[83] This conception of the servant as a "free agent," able to protect himself either by extracting an express guarantee of his safety from the master, or else refusing to undertake risky work, owes an obvious debt to the lingua franca of political economy.[84] Indeed more overtly economic considerations were soon to creep into the rationale of the common employment doctrine: "I am quite sure," remarked Lord Cranworth, "that what was meant in the Court of Exchequer, was, that if men engage for certain wages in a work of great risk, it is to be supposed that the risk forms an element in their contemplation in agreeing to accept the stipulated remuneration."[85] The courts, be it noted, did not imply from the lower price of a third-class railway passenger's ticket that he had taken the risk of accidents upon himself. At the root of common employment lay the judgment that the cost of accidents to employees was not one that developing industry could or should normally have to bear. Examples of such a concession are by no means limited to the mid-nineteenth century,[86] but in its breadth of application the common employment rule was unique.

It was accepted without qualms by almost all the English judges.[87] "There never was a more useful decision," said Pollock L.C.B., "or one of greater practical and social importance in the whole history of the law."[88] In Scotland, however, some of the judiciary proved to be decidedly antagonistic, the Lord Justice Clerk going so far as to hold that "the master's primary obligation in every contract of service in which his workmen are employed in a hazardous and dangerous occupation for his interest and profit, is to provide for, and attend to the safety of the men . . . The obligation to provide for the safety of the lives of his servants by fit machinery, is not greater, or more inherent in the contract, than the obligation to provide for their safety from the acts done by others whom he also employs."[89] But the House of Lords forced Scots law to take on the English mould, pronouncing that "it would be most inexpedient to sanction a different

---

[83] (1837) 3 M. & W. 1 at 6.

[84] The "free agent" had attained his political majority in the debates of 1831–33 on factory regulation: above, p. 302ff.

[85] During argument in *Bartonshill Coal Co.* v. *Reid* (1858) 3 Macqu. 265 at 275. The doctrine that the worker has assumed the risk of injury at a price was spelled out with the utmost clarity in the Supreme Court of Massachusetts by Shaw C.J. in 1842: *Farwell* v. *Boston & Worcester RR.* 45 Mass. (4 Met.) 49. See L. M. Friedman and J. Landinsky, (1967) 67 Col.L.R. 52. This judgment was warmly received by the House of Lords in the *Bartonshill* cases.

[86] By 7 Geo. II, c. 15, shipowners had secured exemption from vicarious liability for wrongs committed by their masters and mariners beyond the value of vessel and freight. In the Warsaw Convention 1927, governments were to agree upon limitations of liability for the young airline industry.

[87] In 1862, Byles J. suggested that it should be confined to the domestic situations that so exercised Lord Abinger's imagination in *Priestley* v. *Fowler,* but he attracted no followers (*Clark* v. *Holmes* (1862) 7 H. & N. 937). Only Martin B., amongst the mid-century generation of judges, said that he could not understand the common employment doctrine (*Smith* v. *Howard* (1870) 22 L.T.N.S. 130).

[88] *Vose* v. *London & Yorkshire Ry. Co.* (1858) Ex. 249, 252; quite exceptionally for Exchequer, this was a case where the plaintiff succeeded upon the employer's failure personally to institute a proper safety system.

[89] *Dixon* v. *Rankin* (1852) 14 D. 420, 424–25; and see *O'Byrne* v. *Burn* (1854) 16 D. 1025.

rule to the north of the Tweed from that which prevails in the south."[90]

In two situations a few judges (notably in Scotland) had found common employment particularly unfair—both of them cases where there was little room for Lord Abinger's justification of the doctrine on the ground that nothing must be done to weaken the vigilance of a servant to prevent the negligence of his fellows.[91] The first was the case where the negligent employee had authority as a manager; he could give orders to the injured man but would not take directions from him. The second was the case where the two employees worked at entirely different tasks for the same employer.

The notion that an employer might be held responsible for the negligence of a "vice-principal" was at one stage adopted by the idiosyncratic Byles J;[92] but in *Wilson* v. *Merry & Cunningham*[93] the Lords rejected a decision by Scots courts to treat a mine manager as representative of the owner. The Scots view that, for common employment to avail the employer, the two workers must be engaged as "collaborateurs" on a common task, was one of the propositions overruled by the Lords in *Bartonshill* v. *Reid*.[94]

VI. Voluntary Assumption of Risk

If a worker must be taken, vis-à-vis his master, to have shouldered the risk of all fellow-servants' negligence, there was no particular extravagance in applying the same presumption to other circumstances. In the early running-down cases, assumption of risk was a notion not clearly distinguished from contributory negligence, and both might well apply to given facts.[95] *Volenti non fit injuria* soon became a maxim in regular use in other cases of work accidents, particularly where the master himself was in some sense responsible for the hazard. In *Seymour* v. *Maddox*[96] a theatre-owner had left an unfenced hole in a passage; the plaintiff, an actor, fell down it but was unable to recover because he knew it was there. In *Dynen* v. *Leach* a labourer in a sugar works had been required to hoist up sugar moulds, not as previously with a net, but with a clip—a device (according to his counsel) adopted "from motives of economy." He was killed when a mould fell on him, but the Court of Exchequer agreed that his dependants had properly been non-suited by the trial

---

[90] *Bartonshill* v. *Reid*, above n. 85, at 285, per Lord Cranworth.

[91] 3 M. & W. at 7.

[92] *Clark* v. *Holmes* (above, n. 87); *Gallagher* v. *Piper* (1864) 33 L.J.C.P. 329 (dissenting); for subsequent case-law, see Bartrip and Burman (1983) 118–119.

[93] (1868) L.R. 1 H.L. (Scot) 326.

[94] Above, n. 85. For later instances, see *Morgan* v. *Vale of Neath Rly.* (1864) 5 B. & S. 570; Bartrip and Burman (1983), pp. 117–118. In the mid-50's, the Court of Exchequer extended the defence to workers for different employers and even to voluntary helpers who joined in a common task (*Wiggett* v. *Fox* (1856) 11 Ex. 832; *Degg* v. *Midland Rly.* (1857) 1 H. & N. 773); but this was soon rejected as too extreme: *e.g., Abrahams* v. *Reynolds* (1860) 5 H. & N. 143; *Fletcher* v. *Peto* (1862) 3 F. & F. 368. For later developments, see below, p. 520ff.

[95] *Cruden* v. *Feltham* (1798) 2 Esp. 695; *Clay* v. *Wood* (1803) 5 Esp. 44; Bohlen, *Studies in the Law of Torts* (1926), p. 446.

[96] (1851) 16 L.T.O.S. 387.

judge. Bramwell B., with his penchant for spelling out the rigours of economic liberalism, said:

"There is nothing legally wrongful in the use by an employer of works or machinery more or less dangerous to his workmen or less safe than others that might be adopted. It may be inhuman to carry on his work so as to expose his workmen to peril of their lives, but it does not create a right of action for an injury which it may occasion when, as in this case, the workmen has known all the facts and is as well acquainted as the master with the nature of the machinery and voluntarily uses it."[97]

It was only where the employee could not have appreciated the danger in the system of work or was protesting about it that he could succeed upon the employer's duty (always acknowledged in principle) to provide a safe system of work. Moreover, the judges were careful to keep the issue where possible out of the reach of juries. Willes J. remarked on one occasion:

"This is one of a great number of cases which have occurred in which the jury have invariably found for the employee—cases where a servant chooses to enter into an employment of which the system is well-known, and one of them after an accident has happened suddenly finds out that the master was exceedingly wrong not to have a greater number of servants . . . , but under such circumstances a servant has no ground to complain of the master in a court of law . . . (C)ases of this kind ought not to be left to the jury on a mere spark of evidence."[98]

Inevitably, subtleties of argument coalesced around *volenti non fit injuria*. Bowen L.J. summarised the result of twenty-five years of case-law when he remarked:

"The maxim, be it observed, is not *'scienti non fit injuria'* but *'volenti.'* It is plain that mere knowledge may not be a conclusive defence. There may be a perception of the existence of the danger without comprehension of the risk: as when the workman is of imperfect intelligence, or, though he knows of the danger, remains imperfectly informed of its extent."[99]

Whether a workman was *volens* or merely *sciens* was a nice question on which a trial judge's direction to the jury might easily be found improper or a verdict might prove unacceptable.[1]

VII. IDENTIFICATION

The contractual constraints upon negligence liability reached their ultimate severity in an extraordinary extension of the contributory

---

[97] (1857) 26 L.J. Ex. 221 at 223.
[98] *Saxton* v. *Hawksworth* (1872) 26 L.T. 85.
[99] *Thomas* v. *Quartermaine* (1887) 18 Q.B.D. 685.
[1] For the correlation of the doctrine to the employer's duties of care, see below, pp. 508–509; and for its retrenchment, pp. 509–510.

negligence principle which employed the fiction of "identification" in a novel guise. If a traveller on a bus belonging to Company A was injured in an accident involving a bus belonging to Company B and the accident was due to the negligence of servants of both companies, the traveller was debarred from suing Company B because he was "identified" with Company A and so affected by the contributory negligence of its servant. The only possible basis for this identification lay in the contract of carriage. According to Maule J., "the passenger is not altogether without fault. He chose his own conveyance and must take the consequences of any default of the driver whom he thought to trust."[2]

To one whose first concern was to prevent the spread of indiscriminate liability for negligence, the idea had a certain plausibility: the injured victim could proceed against the outside company (B in our example) if it alone had caused the accident by negligence. But if A had contributed, the traveller should be left to sue A for breach of its contractual obligation to carry each passenger with due care.

In practice, the rule left the passenger victim in the cross-fire of two enterprises each attempting to put responsibility upon the other. And, of course, its effect was completely debilitating, if the victim was an employee of one of the companies.[3] For common employment and *volenti* reared up to prevent him in most cases from having any cause of action against his own employers. The doctrine of "identification" operated in tandem with them to close off recourse against third parties. Though this form of "identification" enjoyed a vogue for nearly forty years from its debut in 1849, it did not attract universal admiration. The editors of *Smith's Leading Cases*,[4] in the years when it had merely been mooted, though it is "inconceivable" that the judges would accept it (though they did). Not only was it rejected in Scotland, when the more extreme forms of common employment had had to be forced on the courts by the House of Lords, but also in the United States, where common employment had made headway.[5]

VIII. Death

The death of a breadwinner in an accident could bring catastrophe to the other members of his family. Yet if the death was due to another's negligence the dependants found themselves precluded from suing for compensation, either for the grief they suffered or their loss of financial support. Holdsworth attributes this development in part to muddled history.[6] Some deaths that were caused by another's fault were also murder or manslaughter and had therefore been subject to the medieval rule that a felony could not give rise to a civil action.

---

[2] *Thorogood* v. *Bryan* (1849) 8 Q.B. 115, 132. The same predicament might arise in respect of railway passengers, owing to the growing use by one company of another's lines. Indeed, as early as *Bridge* v. *Grand Junction Ry. Co.* (1838) 3 M. & W. 244, it was assumed that the defence of "identification" might succeed.

[3] Its application to an employee-plaintiff was not settled until *Child* v. *Hearn* (1874) 9 Ex. 176 and *Armstrong* v. *London and Yorkshire Ry. Co.* (1875) L.R. 10 Ex. 47.

[4] J. W. Smith, *A Selection of Leading Cases* (4th ed., 1849) I, p. 132 a, b.

[5] For its abandonment, see below, p. 510.

[6] *History of English Law*, III 333–335, 676–677.

When gradually it was recognised that the presence of felony only postponed civil proceedings until after prosecution, the possibility of a suit by those who suffered from the death was not faced on its merits. Amongst the early spate of running-down cases, *Baker* v. *Bolton* was decided by Lord Ellenborough at Nisi Prius.[7] He was reported as laying down the sweeping proposition that "in a civil court the death of a human being cannot be complained of as an injury." He accordingly held that a publican whose wife had been killed in the accident had no right to complain of the loss of her services in his business. Yet for the period of a month during which the wife lingered alive, he did, as a husband, have an established cause of action, the *actio per quod consortium amisit*.[8] When the sufferers were the widow or children of a man killed in an accident, there was not even a known basis on which they might have sued but for the death. There was no principle, as there was in Scots law, that for their distress they might claim a sum by way of *solatium*. As for the personal representatives bringing an action on behalf of the deceased victim himself, such a claim was regarded, so it seems, as barred by the long-familiar maxim, *actio personalis moritur cum persona*.[9] Whatever pains the machine of criminal justice might heap upon the person whose neglect or wilful action caused a death, he (and his employer) went free of the claim for damages that would have lain had the victim remained alive.

Only one possibility presented itself as a remedy for this situation. Ancient superstition had decreed that articles which "moved to" a death were deodands forfeit to the King's Almoner for charity. The practice had evolved that deodands taken by the coroner investigating the cause of death, would be declared and valued by his jury; the amount had to be paid by the owner of the thing and it was divided amongst the dependants of the victims.[10] The coroner might thus extract financial aid for a distressed, resourceless widow without demanding any proof of negligence on the part of the owner of the deodand. For the most part, however, this opportunity was not realised. The amount recoverable was limited by the value of the moving part that caused the injury, and the records studied by Smith suggest that, in the 1820s at least, deodands were being valued at only a few shillings.[11]

In the late 1830s an attempt was made to breathe life into the system, largely it seems through the efforts of Thomas Wakley M.P., corruscating editor of *The Lancet* and in Middlesex a controversial

---

[7] (1808) 1 Camp. 493.

[8] The illogicality of allowing the husband to claim before death, but not afterwards, was to strike Bramwell L.J.: *Osborn* v. *Gillett* (1873) L.R. 8 Ex. 88 at 94–96 (criticising the reporting of *Baker* v. *Bolton*). But his colleagues maintained the established rule and so subsequently did the House of Lords: *Admiralty Commissioners* v. *S.S. Amerika* [1917] A.C. 38.

[9] Hence neither of these possibilities seems even to have been contested in the early nineteenth century.

[10] The dependants had no claim of right, but their interest was recognised. In the cases mentioned in n. 13 below, the widows were made parties to the proceedings.

[11] H. Smith (1967) 11 A.J.L.H. 389. In a dreadful accident at Hyde, Cheshire, in 1829, when 30 people were killed after a club-room floor collapsed, the jury assessed the timber at 5s.

coroner.[12] Suddenly, in various parts of the country, the owners of the new steam-boats and railway engines found them being valued as deodands at several hundred pounds. But coroners' inquisitions were subject to review upon motion in the Queen's Bench, and that Court took exception to the new turn of events. At first the successful objections, in time-honoured fashion, when to the lack of exact description in the inquisition of the event or the deodand.[13] In the Sonning railway disaster, where the jury valued the engine at £2,000, Wakley took the precaution of having his inquisition drafted by the celebrated Sergeant Stephen; but still it "was cast aside and treated almost worse than waste paper."[14] This was because the Court had discovered the principle that deodands could be awarded only in the case of a death by misadventure rather than by felonious act[15]; and at the inquest in question the jury had been moved to return a verdict of "wilful murder." The deodand system was thus rendered inoperative in cases of fault, the very cases where, if injury alone had resulted, the common law would have given an action for damages to the victim.

At the height of the "railway boom," Edwin Chadwick campaigned to publicize the dreadful conditions under which the railway navvy worked.[16] One complaint which the Select Committee on Railway Labourers endorsed was the lack of protection or assistance offered to dependants of those who were killed.[17] Even before that Committee's report, Lord Campbell had taken up the cause, but could not be persuaded to do more than seek a remedy for this small part of the whole injustice. Accordingly two bills became law. One abolished deodands,[18] the other gave dependants certain opportunities to claim compensation by civil action.[19] This Fatal Accidents Act, although in many respects obscure, was nonetheless drawn with a degree of cunning. For it did not give the dependants of the deceased their own right of action, as would have followed from the Scots example of the *solatium*. Instead, the personal representatives of the deceased person were permitted to maintain an action in any case where, if he had not died, he himself might have sued. Nevertheless the damages were to compensate those dependants who fell within a limited range—wife, husband, parent or child of the deceased. If necessary the jury was to apportion the damages amongst them.

Any defence that would have been open to the defendant against the deceased ran equally against a claim by his estate on his depend-

---

[12] *Ibid.* 393–394. See J. Hostettler (1984) 5 J. Leg. Hist. 60.

[13] *e.g. R. v. Brownlow* (1839) 11 Ad. & E. 119 (steamboat boiler and engine: £1500; inquisition quashed for failure to state time of explosion and death); *R. v. West* (1841) 1 Q.B. 826 (railway engine and carriage: £500, failure to describe deodand.)

[14] (1846) P.D. LXXXVII 1372–1373.

[15] See *R. v. Polwart* (1841) 818 (steamboat boiler: £800, verdict of manslaughter). *Cf.* the rule precluding civil action upon a felony, above, n. 6.

[16] Below, p. 515.

[17] P.P. 1846 (530) XIII, p. x–xi; R. A. Lewis (1950) 3 Ec.H.R. 107.

[18] 9 & 10 Vict., c. 62. For the Parliamentary proceedings, see Bartrip and Burman (1983), pp. 98–103.

[19] 9 & 10 Vict., c. 93 (known as Lord Campbell's Act, it was first introduced by Lord Lytellton).

ants' behalf; not only contributory negligence,[20] but also common employment, were to prevent claims from succeeding under the Act.[21] In 1846, *Priestley* v. *Fowler* was still a unique precedent standing against a wholly unfamiliar type of action and it was certainly assumed by some employers that they were being made vicariously liable to dead employees' relatives under the new Act.[22] Yet the first case to reiterate the *Priestley* v. *Fowler* rule refused relief under the Fatal Accidents Act to the widow of a deceased railwayman who, as admistratrix, sought to make her husband's employers vicariously liable for the negligence of a fellow-worker.[23] In the mines, where colliers died in their hundreds each year, the position was the same. The first inspectors of mines were appointed in 1850 and soon recognised the uselessness of Lord Campbell's Act. Their early proposals included a reversion to the system of deodands.[24]

The families of deceased passengers did gain some benefit from the Act—indeed verdicts of £13,000 in 1871 and £16,000 in 1880 are recorded. But even they found that the courts interpreted the Act cautiously. Thus the judges refused to allow that the "injury" suffered by the dependants could include their distress as well as their financial loss. The Scots precedent of the *solatium* was rejected, Coleridge J. pointing out that the Act applied "not only to great railway companies but to little tradesmen who sent out a horse and cart in the care of an apprentice."[25]

IX. DUTIES OF CARE

By mid-nineteenth century, the judges had determined that "negligence" was to be measured by an objective standard. Alderson B. gave a much-repeated definition: "Negligence is the omission to do something which a reasonable man, guided by those considerations which ordinarily regulate the prudent conduct of human affairs,

---

[20] *Tucker* v. *Chaplin* (1848) 2 Car. & K. 730. In Scotland, under the right of action accorded to dependants, there was support for the view that "mere rashness on the part of the workman would not exclude a claim of reparation, if the employer had neglected his duty." But the House of Lords insisted that this generosity be surrendered: *Paterson* v. *Wallace* (1854) 1 Macq. 748, 754; see below, pp. 508–509).

[21] Equally, if the deceased man expressly contracted out of his right to sue, his dependants were bound. The issue only became a live one after the Employer's Liability Act 1880 partly reversed the implications of common employment: see *Griffiths* v. *Earl of Dudley*, below, p. 526.

[22] See the letter from the Coal Owners of North England to the Home Secretary, referred to by Bartrip and Burman (1983), p. 103.

[23] *Hutchinson* v. *York Newcastle and Berwick Rly. Co.* (1850) 19 L.J. Ex. 296.

[24] See O. MacDonagh, in Robson (ed.) *Ideas and Institutions of Victorian Britain* (1967), p. 58 at 78; Bartrip and Burman (1983), p. 110.

[25] *Blake* v. *Midland Rly.* (1852) 18 Q.B. 93 at 111. Lord Campbell, who was a member of that Court, also held that where a dependant had received insurance moneys in the estate of the deceased man, these had to be brought into account in determining whether he had suffered a loss by the death; *Hicks* v. *Newport etc. Rly. Co.* (1857); 4 B. & S. 403n. *Pym* v. *Great Northern Rly.* (1863) 4 B. & S. 396. By contrast, a person injured but not killed did not have to bring insurance moneys into account when himself claiming damages; they came to him through his prevision: *Bradburn* v. *Great Western Rly.* (1874) L.R. 10 Ex. 1.

would do, or doing something which a prudent and reasonable man would not do."[26] This set the "reasonable man" on an early omnibus to Clapham. But it did not settle that liability arose "wherever a Man receives any Hurt through the Default of another." The precocious generalisation to this effect in *Buller's Nisi Prius* had too indiscriminate a potential for imposing costly responsibility.[27] The practice books of the nineteenth century show that the thrust of arguments in court stuck closely to the common law's usual technique of cautious analogy. Precedents for highway accidents, building accidents, shipping accidents had to be relied upon to provide the next nearest case. Plaintiffs would then argue that there must be a duty to take care in some new situation; and to such claims the judges might respond that there was no duty at all, or one that was owed only to a limited class of people, or one that was to guard only against certain hazards.[28]

The concept of duty was unquestionably a matter of law and so gave the judges a power to remove cases from juries that was in a sense more fundamental than any of the defences already considered. The best-remembered examples of this process were in the realms of occupiers' liability, manufacturers' responsibility for defective products and employers' liability for safety. They are worth recalling briefly for the different applications of the duty of care concept which they provided.

(a) Occupiers' Liability

The occupier of land became a potential defendant in many different circumstances: injurious things might fall, spread or escape from his land, and harm property or people on other private land or on the highway. If his boundary was on the highway, there might be dangers, such as trap-doors or protrusions, which might cause an accident.[29] Within his own bounds, untoward events might occur or dangerous conditions arise, which equally might result in injury. It is scarcely surprising that in the earlier nineteenth century, there was considerable confusion about the different aspects of the liability for occupiers. As regards the occupier within his own bounds, it was never contemplated that he should be in any sense strictly liable for injuries occuring to entrants upon his premises. At the other extreme, if he deliberately set traps with the intention of injuring people, it was held in the early nineteenth century that he would become liable even to trespassers who were injured as a result, if they themselves did not know of the hazard.[30] This judicial opinion indeed coincided with the radical and humanitarian campaign

---

[26] *Blyth* v. *Birmingham Waterworks* (1856) 11 Ex. 781 at 784.

[27] See above, pp. 487–488.

[28] See esp. Prichard (1976).

[29] In early instances, the liability was put in negligence (*e.g.*, *Payne* v. *Rogers* (1794) 2 H Bl. 350; *Bush* v. *Steinman* (1799) 1 B. & P. 404); later, such cases might be put in nuisance, particularly to draw upon an extended notion of vicarious responsibility: see above, n. 49.

[30] *Deane* v. *Clayton* (1817) 7 Taunt 489, 58; *Holt* v. *Wilkes* (1820); *Bird* v. *Holbrook* (1828) 4 Bing. 629. See Roscoe Pound (1940) 53 H.L.R. 365.

against setting spring-guns and man-traps to catch poachers, a practice also rendered criminal in 1826.[31]

The difficult ground concerned negligence. By the 1830s it appears
that shopkeepers were being held liable if they carelessly left trap-
doors open and caused injury to unsuspecting customers.[32] But the
prospect of transplanting a commercial risk of this kind into the
domestic circle of family, guests and servants was as worrying in this
context as it had been to Lord Abinger in *Priestley* v. *Fowler*. In 1856,
a private guest visiting the owner of an hotel sued after being injured
by a falling pane of glass. His host was not alleged to have known
about this defect in the premises; the injury it was said, had come
about through his "carelessness, negligence, default and improper
conduct." It was held on demurrer that no action could lie. Pollock
C.B. drew upon *Priestley* v. *Fowler* and broadened its armour by
holding that no member of a household should be liable to claims by
"any other member of the establishment." Just as one servant had no
claim under the fellow servant rule, so a visitor might not sue either
master or servant, since for the time he was part of the household.[33]

This was an extreme view that would soon be modified. The contrast between the protected customer and the unprotected guest
appeared too stark. Moreover, the entrant onto premises might be an
employee sent by his employer on business to visit the occupant: in
the heyday of common employment, some at least of the judges were
reluctant to treat him as they treated business customers. For
instance, in *Wilkinson* v. *Fairrie* a carman, calling on his employer's
business at the defendant's premises, was directed into an unlighted
passage; he fell down an open stairwell. Bramwell B. and Pollock C.B.
brusquely rejected his claim: "if he could see his way, the accident
was the result of his own negligence; if he could not. . . . he ought
not to have proceeded without a light." In any case the defendants
were under no duty to fence the well off; it was to be distinguished
from a "hole" or "trap-door."[34]

Under pressure of a growing number of decisions, a degree of clar-
ification was achieved. In *Indermaur* v. *Dames*, a gasfitter had been
sent by his employer to work in a sugar refinery with a warning to
take care, "because sugar refineries are very peculiar places: they
allow neither candles nor lucifers." He was shown the way in the
dark but later fell through an open shaft. A verdict of £400 for a
broken spine was upheld on appeal since he belonged to the class of
entrants on premises who are there as "invitees" of the occupier
upon his business. Willes J. said:

> "With respect to such a visitor at least, we consider it settled law
> that he, using reasonable care for his own part for his own safety,
> is entitled to expect that the occupier shall on his part use reason-

---

[31] 7 & 8 Geo. IV, c. 18.

[32] *Parnaby* v. *Lancaster Coal Co.* (1839) 11 Ad. & E. 230, 9 L.J. Ex. 338, 541; see also *Chapman* v. *Rothwell* (1858) E.B. & E. 168.

[33] *Southcote* v. *Stanley* (1856) 1 H. & N. 247.

[34] (1862) 4 B. & S. 396. *Cf.* also *Bolch* v. *Smith* (1862) 7 H. & B. 736 (servant failed because
visiting for personal reasons).

able care to prevent damage from unusual danger which he knows or ought to know."[35]

On the other hand, mere "licensees"—volunteers, guests, servants, or persons "whose employment is such that danger may be considered as bargained for"—were expected to look after themselves, save exceptionally, as where the occupier wilfully deceived them or did some positive act which placed them in danger.[36] Willes J.'s judgment came to be read as if it were a statute. Around the ambiguities which existed in his formulation—such as the notion of "unusual danger" and the position of the visiting servant—was to be spun much forensic filigree.[37] But the basic distinction between invitee and licensee was to remain for a long period. Only in 1957 (after the abandonment of common employment) was it to be replaced by a "common duty of care."[38] And by then the whole issue fell to the judge, since juries had all but disappeared in negligence actions.

(b) Products Liability

Thanks to industrial production, the ordinary person not only came across more varieties of article in the course of life and work, but he had to deal with objects that were more complex and dangerous. Where injuries and other damage resulted from the defective condition of an article, the claim could often be formulated in contract. The rapid development of the law concerning warranties and implied terms in sales of goods was directed not only towards giving damages for failure to provide the goods contracted for, but also to impose liability for such consequential losses as injuries caused to people or their property by the defective goods.[39]

The question of liability in tort for negligence arose only when a contract action was not possible, and so the law did not develop rapidly. The most likely case was where the person injured was not party to any contract with the manufacturer or supplier of the dangerous article. Strict notions of privity of contract meant that there was no contract between a manufacturer and the ultimate retail purchaser unless the manufacturer sold direct to the public. The increasing scale of commerce made this the less likely. Equally there was no contract between a retailer and members of the purchaser's family or his servants. This absence of privity was to be seized upon as a reason for denying that any liability for negligently caused injury arose. In *Winterbottom* v. *Wright*[40] a coachman employed to drive the Holyhead mailcoach was lamed for life when the coach broke down thanks to a latent defect. He sued the supplier of the coach, who was not his employer, it being accepted that he would have no action against the latter in consequence of *Priestley* v. *Fowler*.

---

[35] (1866) L.R. 1 C.P. 274.
[36] Willes J. carried his formulation further in *Gautret* v. *Egerton* (1867) L.R. 2 C.P. 37.
[37] See *e.g.* P. H. Winfield, *Law of Tort* (2nd ed. 1943), Chap. 22.
[38] Occupiers' Liability Act 1957.
[39] See above pp. 205–206.
[40] (1842) 10 M. & W. 109.

Against the supplier also he had no cause of action. "By permitting this action, we should be working this injustice that after the defendant had done everything to the satisfaction of the employer, and after all matters between them had been adjusted, and all accounts settled on the footing of their contract, we should subject them to be ripped open by this action of tort being brought against him." If the manufacturers of vehicles could be sued by all who used them "the most absurd and outrageous consequences, to which I can see no limit, would ensue."[41]

While this nice contractualism came normally to limit the scope of a manufacturer's liability for his faulty products, the rule was never quite firm. The Court of Exchequer itself had recognised five years before that deliberate lying could give rise to liability outside a contract: a gunsmith who sold a gun to a father for his son, warranting it falsely to be by a reputable maker, could be sued by the son when injured by it.[42] Thereafter there was always some temptation "to substitute the word 'negligence' for 'fraud' " in such cases. In *George* v. *Skivington*, a later Exchequer court allowed a claim by a woman, whose husband had bought her hair-wash from the defendant; the latter had specifically stated that it was suitable for her hair.[43] "Few cases can have lived so dangerously and lived so long."[44] Eventually it would be given new and more substantial existence in *Donoghue* v. *Stevenson*.

(c) Duties in Employment

In the realm of work accidents, the notion of duty of care was fashioned to reflect the values embodied in the defences of contributory negligence, common employment and *volenti*. From *Priestley* v. *Fowler* onwards, it was always accepted that an employer owed some duty to see to the safety of his servants and, as with duties such as those of occupiers, the experience of case-law led to an elaborate process of definition. Here was a concept around which plaintiffs could press a case that an accident involved a failure of system, rather than a casual inadvertence. If permitted a liberal interpretation, the duty might have made masters responsible for failing to provide adequately trained operatives or supervisors, or for failing to make good defects in plant or materials, or for failing to set up proper safety procedures. In the mid-1850s, the House of Lords did show signs of moving in such a direction. Thus in *Paterson* v. *Wallace*,[45] the House directed a retrial in which it was to be left to the jury to decide

---

[41] Per Lord Abinger C.B., *ibid.* 114. Alderson B. (p. 115) remarked, *a propos* the virtues of privity: "The only real argument in favour of the action is, that this is a case of hardship, but that might have been obviated, if the plaintiff had made himself party to the contract." Perhaps so, but hardly likely!

[42] *Langridge* v. *Levy* (1837) 2 M. & W. 519; affirmed (1838) 4 M. & W. 337.

[43] (1869) L.R. 5 Ex. 1.

[44] Lord Buckmaster, *Donoghue* v. *Stevenson* [1932] A.C. at 570.

[45] (1854) 1 Macq. 748 (Scot.).

whether the colliery owner had broken his duty to secure his workman's safety by leaving a dangerous stone in a mine roof, as well as deciding whether the deceased miner had recklessly courted injury by going under it instead of waiting. In *Brydon* v. *Stewart*,[46] the House upheld an award of damages to the relatives of a deceased miner killed by unsafe planking at the pit-mouth. It is against the potential of such decisions that the contemporaneous determination to give full scope to the concepts of common employment and voluntary assumption of risk must be judged. Just as common employment prevailed even against vicarious responsibility for the negligence of supervisory staff, so it proved very difficult to assert the master's own negligence in selecting the supervisor.[47] Just as *volenti* prevailed when a worker stayed on the job knowing of the risk to him, so it proved possible only rarely to show that the master continued to have a duty to make good the defect.[48] The miners' cases were treated as exceptions for specially hazardous work or as going only to circumstances where the worker could not appreciate the danger.[49] It was in the Court of Exchequer that opposition to compensating for work accidents was most steadily maintained. Occasionally in the other common law courts, a less rigid attitude found expression. But looking at the gravamen of the reported case-law, there can be no doubt that Exchequer set the prevalent tone.[50] Summarising a half-century's development, Bowen L.J. pointed out that the duties to look to safety placed upon an employer ensured that an employee was placed in no better position than "the rest of the world who use the master's premises at his invitation on business."[51]

X. LATER CHANGES IN THE COMMON LAW

We may end this account of the constraints that inhibited the growth of the negligence action at common law, by noting what was to happen subsequently to the key factors. Certain of the evident artificialities would with time be abandoned by the judges themselves. Thus the assumption that a worker, or anyone else, assumed the risk of injury once he knew of the danger began to be pared away. In 1891 the House of Lords boldly decided, in *Smith* v. *Baker*, that a drill operator was not to be taken to have consented to the risks of having crane-loads of stones swung over his head simply by continuing at work. "I believe it to be contrary to fact," said Lord Herschell, "to assert that he either invited or assented to the act or default he com-

---

[46] (1854) 25 L.T. 58, yet another appeal by Scots miners.
[47] *e.g. Ormond* v. *Holland* (1858) E.B. & E. 102; *cf. McAulay* v. *Brownlie* (1860) 22 D. 975.
[48] *cf. e.g., Dynen* v. *Leach* (above, n. 97).
[49] *e.g. Roberts* v. *Smith* (1857) 2 H. & N. 213 (Exchequer Chamber); not applied in *Williams* v. *Clough* (1858) 3 H. & N. 258; *Griffiths* v. *Gidlow* (1858) 3 H. & N. 648; *cf. Vose's* case, above. n. 88.
[50] Note, *e.g., Skipp* v. *Eastern Counties Rly.* (1853) 9 Ex. 223; *Assop* v. *Yates* (1858) 2 H. & N. 768.
[51] *Thomas* v. *Quartermaine* (1887) 18 Q.B.D. 685 at 693.

plains of as a wrong."[52] Here was a judicial response to a quarter-century's pressure by radicals and trade unionists to improve the lot of the injured workmen. The strange concept of identification was also given up at the same period. No longer was a passenger, by taking a ticket on a train or coach, assumed to have control over the driver.[53]

At other points, however, the legislature intervened. In the case of common employment, the Employers' Liability Act 1880 would remove only the more extreme applications of the doctrine (to vice-principals, and in some cases, non-collaborateurs).[54] This left the rule rather more firmly in place for other cases—for it is a standard assumption that, once legislation interposes, future changes must follow the same political process. Eventually in the 1930s the courts would show a new readiness to side-step common employment by giving larger range to the employer's own duties to provide safety at work.[55] But statute in 1948 was needed to kill it off.[56]

It also took statute at that period to modify contributory negligence into a factor which proportionately reduced damages rather than abnegating the entire claim.[57] The first statutory intervention in the field, the Fatal Accidents Act 1846, with minor modification,[58] would also serve to settle the range of claims open to dependants of a deceased victim. Not till 1934 would Lord Ellenborough's assumption, that the deceased's estate retained nothing of his own rights in tort, be overturned and then by a statute which gave little enough heed to the role of Lord Campbell's Act.[59] In the event combination of the two Acts has allowed the dependants their financial loss under the latter and an additional sum under the former, supposedly representing the deceased's lost expectation of happiness but in effect granting a solatium. This the courts have kept to a small, conventional amount, set in 1941 at £200 and later raised to account for inflation.[60]

As for duties of care, when attitudes began to change in the last

---

[52] [1891] A.C. 325 at 263. *Cf.* the unrepentant Lord Bramwell, dissenting:
"It is said that to hold that the plaintiff is not to recover is to hold that a master may carry on his work in a dangerous way and damage his servant. I do so hold, if the servant is foolish enough to agree to it. This sounds very cruel. But do not people go to see dangerous sports? Acrobats daily incur frightful dangers, lion-tamers and the like. Let us hold to law. If we want to be charitable, gratify ourselves out of our own pockets" (p. 346).
Five days later, the House held that common employment could not apply as between employees of a main contractor and a sub-contractor, *Johnson* v. *Lindsay* [1891] A.C. 371.
[53] *The Bernina* (1887) 13 A.C. 1.
[54] Below, p. 524ff.
[55] Notably in *Wilsons and Clyde Coal* v. *English* [1938] A.C. 57; R. B. Stevens, *Law and Politics* (1978), pp. 297–298.
[56] Law Reform (Personal Injuries) Act 1948, s.1; following the Report of the Monckton Committee on Alternative Remedies, P.P. 1945–46 [Cmd. 6860] XIII.
[57] Law Reform (Contributory Negligence) Act 1945, implementing a recommendation of the Law Reform Committee, Eighth Report, P.P. 1938–39 [Cmd. 6032] XII.
[58] 27 and 28 Vict., c. 95 (1864) provided for action by the dependants directly, when there was no personal representative, or none willing to take action.
[59] Law Reform (Miscellaneous Provisions) Act 1934; and see Atiyah (1980), pp. 83–88.
[60] *Benham* v. *Gambling* [1941] A.C. 157; *Yorkshire Electricity* v. *Naylor* [1968] A.C. 529.

quarter of the nineteenth century, a more sophisticated attempt at generalisation made its appearance as part of a unified theory of tort law grounded in liability for fault.[61] In *Heaven* v. *Pender*—a work accident claim against a site-owner who was not the plaintiff's employer—Brett M.R. (afterwards Lord Esher) stated:

> "Whenever one person is by circumstances placed in such a position with regard to another that every one of ordinary sense who did think would at once recognise that, if he did not use ordinary care and skill in his own conduct with regard to those circumstances he would cause danger of injury to the person or property of the other, a duty arises to use ordinary care and skill to avoid such danger."[62]

As a novel advantage to plaintiffs' counsel, it was greeted by other judges with alarm. When Chancery courts were tempted into accepting that merely negligent misstatements should ground a claim for consequent economic loss,[63] the House of Lords and Court of Appeal (the latter containing a temporising Esher) announced that there was no such duty of care.[64] "*Heaven* v. *Pender*," lamented A. L. Smith L.J., "is often cited to support all kinds of untenable propositions". The discriminating approach of the earlier law resumed sway.[65] The House of Lords would confirm, for instance, that the wife of a tenant could not sue the landlord after being injured by the defective state of the premises, for which under the lease he was responsible.[66] The Court of Appeal insisted that farmers and other animal owners were under no duty to prevent them from straying onto the roads, however dangerous they might be to the new motor traffic.[67] It is difficult to accept Holmes' proposition that all this represented a judicial distillation of the wisdom embodied in successive jury verdicts.[68] The judges were pursuing their own notion of what was politic.

Eventually, in *Donoghue* v. *Stevenson*, a bare majority of the House of Lords placed manufacturers under a general duty to take care that faults in their products did not injure ultimate consumers. The "contractualist" limitation of liability that had dominated judicial thought since *Winterbottom* v. *Wright* was abandoned and, in Lord Atkin's famous pronouncement, liability was derived from breach of a general duty to avoid foreseeable harm to one's neighbours—persons, that is, "who are so closely and directly affected by my act that I ought reasonably to have them in contemplation as being so affected when I am directing my mind to the acts or omissions which

---

[61] Such a theory was made explicit particularly in O. W. Holmes' *The Common Law* (1881) Chap. 3.

[62] (1883) 11 Q.B.D. 503 at 509. This was taken up with some enthusiasm in the United States.

[63] *E.g. Peek* v. *Derry* (1887) 37 Ch.D. 541; *Cann* v. *Willson* (1888) 39 Ch.D. 39.

[64] *Derry* v. *Peek* (1889) 14 A.C. 337; *Le Lievre* v. *Gould* [1893] 1 Q.B. 491; but it cannot be said of Esher (as does Fifoot, *Judge and Jurist in the Reign of Victoria* (1959), pp. 38–39) that his "retreat was unequivocal."

[65] Hence Thomas Beven's magisterial *Principles of the Law of Negligence* (1889), analysing many distinct duties of care.

[66] *Cavalier* v. *Pope* [1906] A.C. 428.

[67] *Heath's Garage* v. *Hodges* [1916] 2 K.B. 370.

[68] *The Common Law* (1881), p. 110 ff.

are called in question."[69] Even so, to those trained not to jump, a great leap forward is not easily imitated. The innate caution which the bulk of judges had shown on the question changed little. While Atkin remained in the House of Lords, it is true, there was some very modest growth in the range of liability. But in the years after his retirement there came a succession of leading decisions which in general attitude and specific result showed a marked resemblance to those which had prevailed half a century before. It would not be until the 1960s that the pendulum would swing more definitely in the direction set by Lord Atkin's impetus.[70]

PART 2: PLANNING AGAINST ACCIDENTS

I. INSURANCE AND LIMITATION OF LIABILITY

Once the Common law opted for the principle of fault liability in the arena of accident compensation, its power to intervene was necessarily intermittent, whatever its precise scope. That range might be varied by explicit contractual arrangement, though it was not at the outset clear how far this could be allowed in terms of public policy. However, the possibilities were undoubtedly enhanced as the courts began to make free with notions of implied contract as a device for limiting the scope of the general law. There were two directions in which contractual arrangements might develop, towards insurance of liability and towards exemption from liability, and both deserve some exploration.

Insurance which paid a benefit to the victim of an accident had been developing in the eighteenth century. The early mutual benefit organisations—friendly societies, widows' protection funds and other workers' clubs—frequently included sickness or death after an accident amongst the conditions upon which they paid benefit. In the realm of commercial insurance also, the risk of certain consequences of accidents had long been the subject of cover. The earliest life policies were often for the term of a single voyage and were taken precisely because of the special risks involved; the analogy to the insurance of ship and cargo in a marine venture had been easy to draw.[71] But while the insurance of property on land developed steadily towards longer-term risks (for instance, in the case of fire and burglary insurance), the spread of insurance covering the person was mostly confined to the growth of longer-term life policies. In the earlier nineteenth century therefore some bought their families security against their death (which would include premature death in an accident). But their numbers were confined to those who could afford substantial premiums and who were attracted by the novel type of security offered.[72]

---

[69] [1932] A.C. 562 at 580. The differences of view were presaged in *Oliver* v. *Saddler* [1929] A.C. 584 and *Excelsior* v. *Callan* [1930] A.C. 404.

[70] On the later history, see Atiyah (1987), pp. 68–69.

[71] H. E. Raynes, *A History of British Insurance* (1948), pp. 118–119.

[72] *Ibid.*, Chap. 7.

It was not until the great railway boom that commercial insurance extended its activities beyond death to other injuries. Between 1845 and 1850, three companies were incorporated to provide accident cover to passengers against the risks of their journey. The most successful proved to be the Railway Passengers Assurance Company,[73] whose terms were originally:

> "The sum of 3d for a First Class Passenger to Insure £1,000 in case of Death; Second Class 2d to Insure £500; Third Class 1d to Insurance £200 and in case of Accident only a sum of money to be promptly paid in proportion to the extent of Injury sustained."[74]

Railway ticket offices were used to sell the insurance, but in its early years it was a modest operation.

The offer of insurance to passengers against the consequences of accidents to themselves posed the question whether the companies could insure their liability to pay compensation. This was indeed one aspect of a wider issue: was it right that a person should be able to plan in advance to spread or avoid the risk of liability normally imposed on him by the law? Would such steps not lead to indifference and carelessness in exposing others to danger? In the mid-century years there was a widespread belief that any deflection of liability to pay compensation was both morally wrong and legally ineffective; but by the 1870s that opinion was being dispelled.

When it was in the process of being formed, the Railway Passengers Assurance Company declined a suggestion that the railways should be able to insure against liability under the Fatal Accidents Act "on the ground of its being contrary to public policy—a view strongly held by the Board of Trade."[75] In another field, the Manchester Steam Users' Association, formed in 1855 to aid in the prevention of steam boiler explosions, opposed insurance, "as it would induce a carelessness which the committee think should be punished rather than rewarded." The Association's chief inspector, however, left it to form the Steam Boiler Assurance Co. This was at once successful in providing cover against damage to property caused by explosions and by 1876, the company and its competitors explicitly covered liability for injuries to third parties and for damage to their property. At that time, the London and Provincial Carriage Insurance Co was formed to offer the first compound policies to the owners of road vehicles: this undertook to indemnify against damage to the vehicle and against liability to third parties.[76] Here was the forerunner of the modern motor-vehicle policies, third-party and comprehensive. But for it and the eventual addition of statutory compulsion to carry third-party cover, it is evident that common law negligence liability would not have survived to carry the realm of traffic accidents.

---

[73] Incorporated by statute in 1849.

[74] The justification for the proportionately higher premiums for second and third-class passengers was that they were more at risk. The construction and positioning of first-class coaches made them safest.

[75] F. H. Cox, *The Oldest Accident Office in the World* (1949). Once, however, the Act of incorporation was obtained, the company foresook moral purity and attempted to attract liability business: *ibid.*, p. 41.

[76] Dinsdale, (1954), pp. 40, 179–80.

Liability insurance was also to blossom with the imposition of new responsibilities upon employers towards their workmen in 1880.[77] It was indeed one of the ironies of the "common employment" rule that the mutual insurance funds for the protection of employees, to which some employers were beginning to contribute in the seventies, were able to develop free of any threat of being declared void as contrary to public policy. The employer had virtually no liability to insure against: that was the point of the fund.

There was another way in which enterpreneurs liable to pay compensation for accidents might seek to protect themselves: by contracting in advance with those who might suffer accidents that their liability should be limited, or indeed entirely eliminated. Limitation of liability for the loss of goods had been long known, and in 1854 the railways had been subjected to a special statutory compromise on this question.[78] But, as with liability insurance, there was at the outset a definite opinion that, without Parliamentary sanction, to limit liability against personal injury would be of no avail. Judges might strike out the relevant term from contracts on the ground that it was contrary to public policy; juries might refuse to find that passengers had been given sufficient notice to bring the term into the contract.[79] In 1854, shipowners (typically) obtained the statutory right to limit their personal injury liability, arguing that the Fatal Accidents Act had exposed them to a wholly new order of financial risk, which had gone unconsidered when the Act was passed. The railways tried to follow suit on a string of occasions, but only a few companies secured the right to limit liability for injury in the case of the cheap workmen's trains which they undertook to run.[80]

The case-law however, reveals that in the 1860s the railways were beginning to write limiting terms into certain kinds of ticket, without waiting for Parliamentary assistance. Drovers who accompanied their flocks free of charge, for instance, were held to agreements excluding liability; so, later on, were passengers on cheap excursions.[81] The cases were to come before the courts in the very period when modern judicial attitudes to exemption clauses were largely settled. The judges strove to make these clauses commercially feasible, first, by keeping the issues largely in their control and out of the hands of the juries, and second, by prescribing the "objective" test for incorporating them into contracts.[81] In place of the earlier suspicion of exemption from personal injury liability, had grown a sym-

---

[77] Below, p. 524ff.

[78] Above, p. 269.

[79] In 1870, Hannen J. told the Select Committee on Compensation for Railway Accidents, "it has always been assumed, up to this time, by those who advise railway companies, that they cannot limit their liability and they have always acted upon that up to this time": P.P. 1870 (341) X, Q.1737. To the same body Willes J. marked the shift of opinion by saying that twenty years before he would have thought that a limiting stipulation could not have been made, but that the course of modern decisions was to admit them and leave as a question of fact whether the special contract had actually been made: *ibid.*, Q.2223. Bramwell B. enthusiastically supported the latter view: Q.842.

[80] See Royal Commission on Railways, P.P. 1867 [3844] XXIV, paras. 131, 158.

[81] *e.g., Duff* v. *G.N.R.* (1879) 41 L.T. 197.

pathy, in particular, for "open-ended" risk that was felt to threaten great enterprises such as railways.[82]

II. Safety Legislation

To the extent that it imposed liability to compensate, the common law indirectly stimulated systems of inspection and safe operation which might prevent the occurrence of accidents. There were two ways in which such an incentive might be made more rigorous. One was to increase the range of circumstances in which compensation was payable—even to the extent of imposing strict liability; the other to institute inspection from outside in order to ensure that set standards were maintained.

The first of these approaches did not go entirely unremarked in the earlier nineteenth century, though it would make no political headway. Edwin Chadwick preached strict "pecuniary responsibility" as a means of reducing injuries to workmen. Even as the Factories Commission was preparing recommendations on hours of work which carefully preserved the position of adults to act as free agents,[83] he was writing in a passage on accident prevention that would harness the employers' self-interest by simple utilitarian calculation: they were to pay all injured employees half wages and for medical attendance during absence from work, save for those (over 14) who were guilty of culpable temerity in causing the accident.[84] Once he sensed a rightable wrong, Chadwick (like his master Bentham) was quick to qualify the freedom of the market. The idea got nowhere, but Chadwick returned to it in the "railway boom" of the mid-40s, when he received detailed information about the degraded conditions of the navvies working to cut the Woodhead tunnel on the Manchester, Ashton-under-Lyne and Sheffield Railway, and of the frequent accidents. He lobbied MPs and provincial newspapers and induced a Select Committee to recommend the introduction of both government inspection and employers' no-fault liability in railway construction.[85] Despite this, the latter idea would again lie fallow for a long period. The railway interest in parliament, and the repression of combination among railway workers were among factors which would leave the industry free of anything much in the way of regulation, a monument to the potential of free enterprise.[86]

In other areas, a movement towards the second prospect—external inspection—was beginning, though it was, in matters of safety, halting and fitful. The coaching business in its heyday had been subject to limitations which sought to prevent overloading of passengers as well as to preserve the condition of the roads.[87] The laws had been

---

[82] Above, pp. 493–494.

[83] See above, p. 303.

[84] P.P. 1833 (450) XX, p. 77. It seems that Tooke and Southwood Smith, the other Commissioners, did not appreciate what the proposal was.

[85] P.P. 1846 (530) XII; R.A. Lewis (1950) 3 Ec.H.R. 107; Bartrip and Burman (1983), pp. 68–73.

[86] See generally, H. Parris, *Government and the Railways in Nineteenth Century Britain* (1965) Chap. 4.

[87] P. Bagwell, *The Transport Revolution from 1770* (1974), p. 49, referring to 30 Geo. III, c. 36 and 46 Geo. III, c. 136.

left to be enforced mainly by informers who shared in any fines. From the late 1820s the shipping of emigrants came under central inspection which grew in efficacy by turning to the legislature for enhanced powers.[88] Even the railways came under a degree of surveillance from 1840 onwards, so far as concerned standards of line construction—something which directly affected the safety of passengers; inspectors working under the Board of Trade's Railway Department (later Commission) even acquired the power to prevent the opening of a sub-standard line.[89] Passengers could in any case sue for negligent injury. Here also the prime need was to protect workers, but nothing significant would happen on this front until the next century.

However, textile factory owners, mine operators, and then owners of other factories and workshops were brought under regimes which placed safety alongside other conditions within the aegis of government inspection. The terrible accidents with machinery that occurred in textile mills could be observed by anyone willing to look. The use of children to clean parts while they were still in motion, and the failure to fence off rotating shafts and other bits of the main gearing (in which women's clothing could easily become entangled) were common causes of dreadful mutilations and deaths. Lord Ashley fought a case as next friend of Elizabeth Cotterell, who at seventeen had been crippled for life after being caught and revolved 200 or more times in an unboxed upright shaft. By agreement he secured the admission of the defendant's liability, £100 damages and costs.[90] The factory inspectors of 1833, who were then asked by the government for special reports, also favoured measures against failure to fence, though they differed about what to do.[91] Not surprisingly for a pioneering body seeking to control employers who could be ruthlessly hostile they wanted Parliament to provide a clear statutory code of conduct, leaving as little as possible to be decided upon their own responsibility.

After a good deal of Parliamentary skirmishing, the Factories Act 1844 emerged with a number of provisions regarding safety.[92] In particular, owners of the textile factories covered by the legislation were obliged to fence certain machinery, including "all parts of the Mill gearing," under threat of a fine of £5–20 (or £10–100 if injury or death resulted); they were obliged to inform the inspectors of any accident where the worker did not return to work next day, and the inspectors were given power (subject to an appeal to arbitrators)[93] to designate other machinery "dangerous" by notifying the occupier—but apparently the only consequence of this was to render the employer liable

---

[88] O. MacDonagh, *A Pattern of Government Growth* (1961).

[89] 5 & 6 Vict., c. 55, s.6; Parris (above, n. 86), pp. 50–55.

[90] P.P. 1841 (56) IX, pp. 24–29. In the Factories Bill that he had taken over in 1833, Ashley had included fencing provisions and a power for coroners' juries to indict factory owners for manslaughter whose neglect caused death: M. W. Thomas, *The Early Factory Legislation* (1948), p. 225.

[91] See P.P. 1841 [311] X, p. 206 ff: the severest view was Leonard Horner's: see M. W. Thomas (above, n. 90), pp. 228–231.

[92] 7 & 8 Vict., c. 15, ss.20–23, 59, 60.

[93] For the problems posed by this form of arbitration, see T. K. Djang, *Factory Inspection in Great Britain* (1942), p. 153.

to the increased penalties if subsequently the machinery should cause an accident.[94] In addition, the inspectors acquired two subsidiary powers to give factory workers the help they so clearly needed if they were ever to secure any real compensation for their sufferings in accidents. An inspector might, with the Home Secretary's approval, institute civil proceedings on behalf of a factory worker injured by machinery. Or, in a criminal prosecution for failure to safeguard mill-gearing, the court might award an increased penalty of up to £100 if a worker has been injured, and the inspector might apply any part of this sum for the benefit of the victim.[95]

These new safety measures took their place beside the limits on the working hours of women and children that in 1847 were conceded to the Ten Hours Movement. The small inspectorate was hard enough pressed in enforcing the new rules on hours, and seem to have made little impression on matters of safety. Part of the blame lay in the complacent attitude that some of them adopted,[96] part in the antagonism shown by some benches of magistrates.[97] But once the question of the relay system had been settled,[98] the inspectors were encouraged by Palmerston, as Home Secretary, to take a firmer line in securing the fencing of all mill-gearing. The Act appeared to require this without qualification, and the inspectors drew attention to the need for an all-embracing law by publicising cases in which workers were unexpectedly caught even in high shafts. The manufacturers, who banded together in a vociferous National Association of Factory Occupiers, sought to denounce this as oppressive interference by the state.[99] There was a flurry of litigious activity to determine whether some qualification should be read into the absolute words of the statute,[1] but the question was determined against the manufacturers in a civil action, *Doel* v. *Sheppard*, by the Court of King's Bench.[2] So they sought protection from Parliament, and while they did not undermine the entire legislation, they obtained an amendment which reduced the duty to fence gearing to parts "with which children and young persons and women are liable to come in contact, either in passing or in their ordinary occupation."[3] This left the inspectors

---

[94] So s.60 was understood in 1856, when failure to comply also became the subject of an ordinary penalty: 18 & 20 Vict., c. 38, s.6.

[95] 7 & 8 Vict., c. 15, ss.24, 25, 60. For the employee's right to sue independently for breach of statutory duty, see below, pp. 518–520. The Law Officers took the view that no such claim could be made where the victim was killed: P.P. 1852 [1439] XXII, p. 32.

[96] Thus Sir John Kincaid's Reports explain away the many accidents in his district (Scotland) as nearly always the fault of the victim.

[97] Horner, for instance, reported that the Bolton magistrates refused to convict in a clear case of failure to fence: P.P. 1845 [639] XXV, p. 15, and see many of his succeeding reports.

[98] See above, p. 307.

[99] They were assisted by Harriet Martineau: *The Factory Controversy: a Warning Against Meddling Legislation* (1855).

[1] Horner, incensed by the refusal of the Oldham bench to convict two millowners for a failure to fence which had caused a fatal accident, took proceedings against the three mill-owning justices for failing to fence, even though there had been no accidents. Their convictions were quashed by Quarter Sessions and the case stated to the Queen's Bench. See next note.

[2] (1856) 5 E. & B. 856; see further below, p. 519.

[3] 19 & 20 Vict., c. 38, s.4; see R. Dickson (1981) 2 J. Leg. Hist. 276; (1986) 7 J. Leg. Hist. 188.

deeply dissatisfied, because it allowed manufacturers to escape having to box many shafts which they considered dangerous, unless they first gave notice (with the prospect of protracted arbitration) under the 1844 Act.[4]

Any counter-thrust had to await the political shift of 1867. During the 1860s, when the position of children in employment was once more investigated and the factory legislation was extended to many new forms of employment,[5] scarcely any new provisions were introduced to deal with safety. It was not until the last quarter of the century, largely under trade union pressure, that safety legislation began to increase in scope and severity, and there was a significant expansion in the inspectorates that had the duty of enforcing it.[6]

The provisions in the Factory Act 1844 and subsequent legislation which permitted the inspectors to ensure compensation for the victims of accidents,[7] were of very little formal use, though they sometimes moved an employer to make some payment *ex gratia*.[8] But the safety requirements of legislation concerning working conditions were to have a much more lasting effect as the basis of civil actions claiming compensation for injury. For even in the 1850s it was recognised that where a breach of such a statutory duty resulted in injury to a worker, this in itself gave him a cause of action. None of the statutes said so in terms, and so this development was entirely a matter of judicial determination. The argument was certainly put that, by providing a penalty for breaking the statute, Parliament had intended that no other consequence should ensue; but it was rejected, and in broad terms. Lord Campbell C.J. seized upon a statement in *Comyn's Digest*:[9]

"in every case when a statute enacts or prohibits a thing for the benefit of a person, he shall have a remedy upon the same statute for the thing enacted for his advantage or for the recompense of a wrong done to him contrary to the said law."[10]

In a brief space there emerged the contours of legal argument that were to reappear to this day in industrial accident cases based on

---

[4] The inspectors refused, in protest, to issue such notices: Bartrip and Burman (1983), p. 65.

[5] See the Factory and Workshops Acts of 1864 and 1867.

[6] Esp. by the Factory and Workshops Act 1878, which *inter alia* repealed the Act of 1856; S. & B. Webb, *Industrial Democracy* (1897) Chap. 7. For the special problem of explosives manufacture, see J. H. Pellew (1974), 172 Vict. St.

[7] Above, n. 95.

[8] R. W. L. Howells (1963) 26 M.L.R. 367, found no instance of a compensation claim being pursued by civil action; see also Bartrip and Burman (1983), pp. 55–63.

[9] Comyns' text is drawn from Lord Holt (*Anon.* 6 Mod. 26–27) who was talking of an action of debt arising at law from the Statute of Wills (32 Hen. VIII, c. 1); as E. R. Theyer pointed out, it involved a defence of Holt's prerogatives against the encroachments of Chancery, and deserved to be understood in its context: (1913) 27 H.L.R. 217, 332.

[10] *Couch v. Steel* (1854) 3 E. & B. 402. The statutory provision broken (7 & 8 Vict., c. 112, s.18) required a shipowner to maintain a proper supply of medicines on board. A crew member was held entitled to sue for breach of this duty. It was part of an early, but overdue, attempt to regulate the conditions of merchant seamen.

breach of statutory duty. *Doel* v. *Sheppard*,[11] that temporary victory of inspectors over manufacturers, determined that a breach of the terms of the statute was all that had to be proved. The statute was not to be read as though the plaintiff had also to prove that his employer had been negligent in failing to provide a safe system of work. If the Factory Act said that certain gearing had to be fenced it was not relevant whether a particular piece of gearing created a real danger. On the other hand, the first important attempt to found an industrial claim on breach of statute—the case of *Coe* v. *Platt*[12] four years earlier— showed that it was necessary to prove a case falling exactly within what was required by the statute. The thirteen-year-old plaintiff had been caught in an unfenced shaft which was under repair. The court found that there was no breach of the fencing regulation since at the time the shaft was not under power "for any manufacturing process" as the Factory Act prescribed.[13] Thousands of subsequent claims have hung upon the nice interpretation of statutory regulations in relation to particular circumstances—provisions, it has been remarked, which "vary a great deal, often (and perhaps always) for no discernible policy."[14]

Later courts were to show their mistrust for Lord Campbell's view that those protected by a criminal statute by implication could base a civil action upon it unless the statute said to the contrary. When in the 1870s attempts to do this were made in cases which involved injury to property rather than to the person, reasons were found for refusing such claims.[15] Cairns L.C. took issue with Campbell and insisted that each statute must be separately examined to determine whether Parliament's intention had been impliedly to accord a civil cause of action when prescribing a criminal penalty.[16]

Such a change of tide was bound to wash against the industrial accident claim based on breach of statute. In *Groves* v. *Lord Wimborne*, Grantham J. felt its pull and refused judgment to a plaintiff whose right arm was irretrievably injured in a winch that had lost the fence required for it by the Factory and Workshops Acts 1878. But the Court of Appeal refused to disturb the established approach to such provisions:

"The Act in question . . . is not in the nature of a private legislative bargain between employers and workmen, as the learned judge seemed to think, but is a public Act passed in favour of the

---

[11] Above, n. 2.

[12] (1851) 6 Ex. 752, (1852) 7 Ex. 460, 923. The case was organised by Leonard Horner. He wished to publicise the victory at first instance, but the Home Secretary, Grey, would not agree: Bartrip and Burman (1983), p. 56.

[13] 7 & 8 Vict., c. 15, s.21.

[14] Atiyah (1987), p. 158.

[15] See esp. *Gorris* v. *Scott* (1874) L.R. 9 Ex. 125 (shipowner's duty to provide pens for sheep was to prevent contagious disease, not sweeping overboard); *Atkinson* v. *Newcastle Waterworks* (1877) 2 Ex.D. 441 (water company not liable for consequences of fire even in failing to keep pressure at required level).

[16] *Atkinson's* case (above n. 15, at p. 448): when the Act was a "private legislative bargain" the duty was not to be implied.

workers in factories and workshops to compel their employers to
do certain things for their protection and benefit."[17]

The Court of Appeal's attitude in the atmosphere of 1898 is not
hard to understand: the campaigns that had resulted, first in the
Employers' Liability Act 1880 and then the Workmen's Compensation Act 1897, had induced a somewhat more generous attitude to
industrial accident claims, a change already manifest in the modification of *volenti non fit injuria*.[18] By this time, the great value of basing a
claim upon breach of a specified obligation was transparent. Not
only did the plaintiff avoid the uncertainties that were inevitable in
seeking to convince a jury that an employer's system of work was not
safe (an advantage which remains today). Even more important,
there was no defence of common employment since no one's negligence was in issue.[19]

Queen's Bench created breach of statutory duty at just the moment
when Exchequer was so intent upon leaving the worker responsible
for his own misfortunes. The principle accordingly represented some
countervailing moderation. Its appeal also went to those who would
place responsibility on employers to the extent that their liability was
defined in advance; and since the modifying effects of the Factory
Amendment Act 1856 limited those liabilities severely for a generation, breach of statutory duty set up only minor tensions with common employment, *volenti* and the employer's circumscribed duties of
care at common law. It would only be upon the abolition of common
employment (in 1948) that the essentially strict nature of statutory
duty would seem to pose a real incongruity.[20] An attempt then to
allow reasonable care as a defence in such an action would founder
under trade union objections.[21] Only in the courts would piecemeal
interpretation introduce an element of fault in particular instances.[22]
But the fundamental concept, in modern law an admitted exception,
has survived, with striking resilience.

PART 3: RESETTING THE VICTORIAN FRAME

I. EMPLOYERS' LIABILITY

The challenge to the common law limits upon compensation for work
accidents came from two main quarters. Middle-class criticism—
particularly that of lawyers—surfaced in the proceedings of the

---

[17] [1898] 2 Q.B. 402 at 406. The "penal compensation" provision (see above, n. 95),
which an unfriendly court might well have taken to show the extent to which Parliament was providing personal redress, was brushed aside. The Home Secretary had
a discretion to determine whether the penalty would be paid over to the accident
victim; the section therefore determined nothing about his *rights*.

[18] This defence was held inapplicable to breach of statutory duty (*Baddeley* v. *Earl
Granville* (1887) 19 Q.B.D. 423), even before it was more generally paralysed by *Smith*
v. *Baker* (above, pp. 509–510).

[19] *Groves* v. *Wimborne* (above, n. 17) at 410, *cf.* pp. 417–419.

[20] See Atiyah (1987), pp. 33–34 on levels of strictness.

[21] See below, pp. 537–538.

[22] See R. B. Stevens, *Lawyers and Politics* (1978), pp. 594–598.

National Association for the Promotion of Social Sciences. The views to be found in its proceedings ranged from outright demands for the abolition of common employment to reaffirmations of the law's current wisdom. Yet by the mid-1870s the Association was coming to lend its considerable weight to the cause of reform.[23]

The stronger challenge in political terms came from the emergent organisations of the workers themselves. The Parliamentary Committee of the Trades Union Congress, in particular, had established its position in the course of fighting for the new legislation on union organisation and the freedom to picket. The return of two Scottish miners—Macdonald and Burt—in the 1874 election gave new impetus to the Parliamentary Committee's initial campaignings over accident compensation.[24] Miners had a peculiarly severe experience of disasters, which inspection had been able to do little enough about; and Scottish miners—with Macdonald latterly at their helm—had promoted much of the litigation which had served only to consolidate the walls of common employment.[25] The two MPs and the Parliamentary Committee found ω.'ies among radical liberals, including large employers such as A. J. Mundella, the younger Thomas Brassey and Michael Bass. The representatives of the colliery owners and railway companies now found that they could no longer blow the issue away, as had happened when A. S. Ayrton had raised it in 1862, with a bill to secure pecuniary responsibility by abolishing common employment.[26]

In the Select Committee, which was the response to MacDonald's first Bill to sweep away both common employment and *volenti*,[27] much argument that had become familiar through the court cases was once more rehearsed. The opponents of change relied upon the economic presumptions that were taken to justify writing into the contract of employment the employee's assumption of risk for injuries caused to him by the negligence of fellow servants or from other known dangers[28]; those who took such risks upon themselves were assumed to receive higher wages than they would if the employer had to bear financial responsibility.[29] There were even those who claimed that the higher the risk the greater the wage actually applied across industry. The Attorney-General had already spoken of miners

[23] See Bartrip and Burman (1983), pp. 126–128, 140–145; Smith (1981), pp. 262–267.

[24] See also above, p. 320.

[25] See above, pp. 498–499.

[26] See Bartrip and Burman (1983), pp. 111–115.

[27] MacDonald's first Bill, in 1876, had been preceded by similar attempts in the two previous years, stemming from the representations of the Amalgamated Society of Railway Servants.

[28] Bramwell L.J., the most vocal judicial opponent of change among the judges, admitted the unreality of implying a term into the contract of employment and so sought to base the argument on the employee's failure to extract any positive undertaking from the employer. This might be consistent with his general attack on the "injustice" of vicarious liability, but it failed to explain why the railway passenger got the advantage of that liability without having to bargain expressly for it: P.P. 1877 (285) X, Qs. 1103, 1122.

[29] Despite some well-publicised evidence to the contrary, A. J. Balfour could still say: "If insurance against accidents is included in the present rate of wages, which I believe it to be in fact, workmen, by the operation of this [Employers' Liability] Bill, will be paid twice over for the same risk": (1880) P.D. CCLIII 1406.

"whose favourite daily beverage was champagne," a phenomenon indignantly denied by Burt.[30] There was much talk about the ruin that would follow from placing responsibility for accidents upon employers, and dark threats that the cost of compensation could be met only by cuts in wages.

One relatively new factor amongst the economic considerations, however, was the growth of aid funds that paid compensation to accident victims during periods off work. Not only might this arise from a worker's independent thrift through joining a friendly society or trade union; some of the larger, more sympathetic employers had been prepared to contribute to mutual assistance funds operated either by their own workers or by themselves.[31] Others felt their moral obligations discharged by dispensing charity on the occasion of an accident, even if it was only the coffin and guinea that were the customary solace of the miner's widow. The masters duly pleaded that the proposal for legal liability to compensate some for injury would leave them without resources to show paternal generosity to all; indeed the proposed legislation would induce a litigious atmosphere that would "set class against class."

This was a response to the terms in which the radicals and the Parliamentary Committee put their case. They insisted that the judges had deliberately created and then extended a special discrimination in the law which distinguished one class—the workers—from the general public. The doctrine of common employment (and, more generally, that of *volenti*) was denounced as based upon economic assumptions that bore no resemblance to the realities of wage bargaining. The Select Committee was shown that, but for occasional exceptions such as explosives manufacture, levels of wages did not increase for danger. The solution was therefore to abandon the special defences in their entirety.

Moderate sympathisers were alarmed at so sweeping a prospect and looked for a compromise. Common employment had been said to encourage vigilance by each employee over his fellows.[32] But if this was the true justification of the rule, it was hard to see why it should have been extended to include cases of negligence by supervisory employees and by those in a wholly different job. Even the Select Committee of 1876–1877,[33] which was glad enough to accept

---

[30] P.D. 1876 CCXXIX, 1161, 1179–1180. Burt stated that a miner's weekly wage had at best been £2.10s. but that in present conditions he might be getting only 3s. or 3s. 6d. a day.

[31] Thus the Lancashire colliery owner, Thomas Knowles, held up for admiration the Northumberland and Durham Provident Society for Pitmen to which the employers contributed 20 per cent. of the funds. In addition they paid "smart money" of 6s. a week to a miner off work through accident however caused: *ibid.* 1176.

[32] "Now I do not say that workmen will injure themselves for the sake of compensation, but I do say that whatever tends to lessen their reasons for care and good conduct, as compensation would, tends to make them less careful in themselves and more disposed to conceal want of care in others": Lord Bramwell, *An Open Letter to Sir Henry Jackson M.P.* (1880), p. 6.

[33] P.P. 1877 (285) X, p. iv ff; Evidence Q.1116. The other judicial witness in 1877, Brett L.J., accepted the same premise but regarded vicarious liability as an immoveable fixture. Accordingly, he reached the opposite conclusion to Bramwell: that the "class

Bramwell L.J.'s view that it was vicarious liability that was unjust and the common employment exception just, thought that there should be one modification: the employer who delegated the day-to-day running of the concern to a "competent" manager should be made liable for his delegate's negligence.[34] This would at least put an end to the objection that the large employer could avoid obligations that the small employer had to bear.

A somewhat broader proposal was to place all supervisors outside the range of common employment save those who were actually engaged in manual labour.[35] This became the mainstay of the successful Bill taken up by the Liberal party in order to honour a prominent electoral promise. The Employers' Liability Act 1880 allowed industrial manual workers[36] to sue their employers vicariously for the negligence of non-manual superintendents and for certain other defaults.[37] In addition railway companies became liable to all their employees for injuries caused by the negligence of signalmen, pointsmen, drivers and others in charge or control of engines or trains.[38] In all cases damages were limited to a maximum of three years' earnings for an employee of the plaintiff's type[39]:

The radicals also took up, as a prominent part of the campaign, the idea of pecuniary responsibility that Edwin Chadwick had long before tried to impose on factory owners and railway constructors: safe systems of work would be most effectively achieved if accidents were made expensive to employers. As it became apparent that some modest concessions were likely to succeed, the "expensive accident" theory came to impinge on two subsidiary questions. First, should the employer be permitted to contract expressly with his labour force that he should not bear the new liabilities. A plausible case could be made for allowing him to do so if he already contributed, or proposed to contribute, to a mutual protection fund for accident victims.

---

distinction" against employees should be abandoned: Q.1926. On this question (as opposed to industrial disputes, see above, 319) he stood prophet of the gradual shift in judicial attitudes that was to become apparent only in the 1890s.

[34] There were obvious difficulties in determining which employees were "delegates" of the managerial function. Although the distinction was not attempted at this juncture, it was later to be undertaken by the judges in treating the top management of a company as its "alter ego." At a late stage, this was to supply a judicial exception to the common employment rule: *Rudd* v. *Elder Dempster & Co.* [1933] 1 K.B. 566. Even Bramwell L.J. would have approved: P.P. 1877 (285) X, Qs. 1117, 1176–1177.

[35] This formed the basis of a proposal by its Chairman, Robert Lowe, that was rejected by a majority of the Select Committee in 1877. It was embodied in the Bill promoted by Thomas Brassey in 1879 and subsequently annexed by the Liberal leadership.

[36] The Act excluded not only domestic servants but also seamen; but it covered all railway workers: s.8; see generally, Smith (1981), pp. 267–273.

[37] These included unremedied defects in the condition of "ways, works, machinery, or plant"; compliance with the orders of a negligent servant; and actions in comformity with rules prescribed by the employer or his delegate. A plaintiff who knew of, but did not notify, a defect could not normally succeed; ss.1, 2.

[38] *Ibid.* s.1. Injuries on the railways had been the subject of a separate Royal Commission, which had recommended a special rule of this kind: P.P. 1877 [C. 1637] XLVIII.

[39] *Ibid.* s.3; there were also restrictive time-limits: ss.4, 7. Cases were generally to be tried in the County Courts; s.6.

Secondly, should the employer be permitted to insure against his liability? Both possibilities could substantially weaken the prophylactic effect of liability in damages by allowing the employer to cover himself in advance and so calculate the comparative cost of positive safety measures. "Full unguarded insurance," Chadwick now pronounced, "is the mother of murder, of shipwreck and of fire."[40] But neither insurance nor even "contracting-out," though it was subsequently to become an issue of real political moment, was seriously contested as the 1880 Bill passed through Parliament. Once it was enacted, there was lively business in liability policies for some employers,[41] just as others insisted that the workers sign away their rights and join a mutual protection club. In reality the increase in liability brought about by the Act of 1880 was modest in the extreme. A Tory M.P., Sir Edward Watkin, remarked with some prescience, that it would deal with 5 per cent. of the problem, whereas the other 95 per cent. ought to be dealt with by insurance.[42] Other conservatives took the same position, notably the "Fourth party" of Lord Randolph Churchill and his friends, who used the 1880 Bill to needle both the government and their own front bench. Already schemes existed, in some European countries, for the protection of workers in industries such as mining against accidents or sickness. But during the 1880s a much more striking comparison was to appear as the result of developments in Germany. Bismarck established his network of social security legislation, in which schemes for sickness insurance and for old age and invalidity pensions were linked together with compulsory accident insurance for workers. But while in the sickness and pension schemes the worker was a contributor to the fund, in the case of accident insurance, the fund was provided by the employers and the state in the proportion of 3:1.[43] Thus the accidents at work were singled out as the responsibility of the employer and of society at large, the manual worker was not required to sell his life or health in addition to his labour.[44] But it allowed what Chadwick would never admit—that the payment of an insurance premium should settle the extent of the employers' liability in advance. This was precisely the attraction of the scheme to employers fearful of the 1880 Act, and to all those who were coming to feel that "social" legislation was a necessary bulwark against "socialist" power.

In social planning, as in imperial design, Joseph Chamberlain aspired to be the English Bismarck.[45] As President of the Board of Trade in Gladstone's government, he had been one of the sponsors of the Employers' Liability Act. But by then his advocacy of municipal

[40] *Fraser's Magazine*, May 1881, p. 684; and see his *Preventive Legislation as against Curative Legislation* (1888).

[41] The Employers Liability Assurance Corporation, formed to meet the demand, did particularly well: H. E. Raynes, *A History of British Insurance* (1948), p. 303.

[42] P.D. 1880 CCLII 1134–1135. Subsequently, it became a common guess that one accident in ten fell within the Act; see, *e.g.* G. Drage, *The Labour Problem* (1896), p. 132.

[43] The British learned much about the German scheme from the Royal Commission on Labour 1891–94: P.P. 1893–94 [C.9063–VI] XXXIX Pt. II (Report by G. Drage).

[44] See S. & B. Webb, *Industrial Democracy* (1898), I p. 385.

[45] See W. C. Mallalieu (1950) 10 J.Ec.Hist 45; Hanes (1968), pp. 96–100.

socialism in Birmingham had already shown how far removed was his radicalism from the orthodoxies of his party. He looked upon the 1880 Act merely as a temporary victory in the quest for greater protection of the worker, and during the eighties he campaigned vigorously for new statutory measures to increase safety in employment (particularly for merchant seamen).[46] His break with Gladstone over Home Rule led him into alliance with the Conservatives, especially with that small fringe of Disraelian reformists who strove to entice the working-class voter into the Tory fold. Eventually he would become the chief proponent of the Workmen's Compensation Act 1897, which would oblige employers to give some assistance to injured employees, irrespective of fault. The leading spokesmen of the unions long maintained their original position on the question. In 1877, a London compositor had put to the Trades Union Congress a plan for accident compensation out of a tax upon commodities, but this had been denounced by the miner, Thomas Halliday, on the ground that "what they wanted was not money, but their lives and limbs preserved."[47] Even through the years that saw the emergence of the "new unionism," the unions' efforts continued to be directed towards eliminating the inadequacies of the fault liability system.

The Act of 1880 was soon enough shown to provide few injured workmen with the chance to sue for compensation. Even those whose case fell within its ambit found themselves obliged to bring a personal action against their own employer—something which for many was put beyond possibility by a long habit of dependence, if not by fear of dismissal. Only slowly were the unions organising themselves to provide the moral and financial support that such an undertaking required.[48] Moreover the man audacious enough to claim might be met with a denial of liability, and before long he would find himself facing the hazards of negligence litigation: proving that he was a "workman" as defined by the Act,[49] proving the negligence of a supervisory fellow-servant or that a "defect in the ways, works, machinery, or plant" had gone unremedied by the appropriate supervisor[50]; warding off counter-assertions of contribu-

---

[46] For his later attachment to "experimentalism," see below, p. 530.

[47] Webb (above, n. 44), pp. 382–383. For early Conservative interest in insurance, and Joseph Brown Q.C.'s paper on the subject to the NAPSS in 1878, see Bartrip and Burman (1983), pp. 139–145.

[48] Before 1880, craft unions, such as the Carpenters and Joiners, Building Workers and Amalgamated Engineers, were paying various benefits to injured workers, but only supported litigation in occasional cases. But the prospects opened by the Employers' Liability Act led to substantial union support for injured members in litigation.

[49] Above, n. 36. Omnibus drivers, but not conductors or drivers of horse trams, were held to be within the definition: *Morgan* v. *London General O.C.* (1884) 13 Q.B.D. 832; *Cook* v. *North Metropolitan T.C.* (1887) 18 Q.B.D. 683; *Smith* v. *Associated O.C.* [1907] 1 K.B. 916.

[50] The reported decisions on these central provisions were voluminous. The supervisory fellow-employee had to be distinguished from the man who was ordinarily engaged in manual labour (s.8), and this raised many nice questions of degree. On the failure to detect defects, the appellate courts insisted on their right to review findings at first instance: see the line of cases reviewed in *Walsh* v. *Whiteley* (1888) 21 Q.B.D. 371.

tory negligence,[51] *volenti*,[52] or failure to give the employer notice required by the Act.[53] There were many nice points of interpretation raised by the Act and he could not rely on sympathy if his case came before the high judiciary:

> "Some judges have construed the Act as narrowly as possible with a view to preventing what they conceived to be injustice to masters. Other judges have considered that the Act, having been passed to extend the liabilities of masters, in favour of workmen, ought to be construed liberally in favour of the workmen."[54]

In so saying Lord Esher M.R. claimed allegiance to his own second category, but he does not seem to have been joined by many of his fellows.

The resulting sense of frustration might have been somewhat alleviated by the total abolition of the "common employment" defence, and indeed this was sought. But the great vehemence was kept for the hated practice of "contracting out." During the 1880 debates, unionists and their spokesmen seem to have been preoccupied with combating amendments that would have imposed mutual insurance schemes on workers without their assent.[55] Though it was pointed out on occasion that the Bill left employers free to insist that their work-force contract out of their new rights,[56] there seems to have been no serious attempt to secure an amendment that would have outlawed the practice. When the London and North Western, amongst the railways, and the Lancashire proprietors amongst the mine owners, proceeded to insist on "contracting out" as a term of employment, they were faced with substantial strikes, which, however, they successfully withstood.[57] Moreover the courts accepted the legality of a "contracting out" condition, the leading judgment being couched in staunchly liberal terms by Field J.: if the Act were to negate an express term in the contract "the workman might obtain the benefits of the contract for years in the form of higher wages to cover the risk of injury, and then claim full additional compensation when he was injured."[58]

It was economic brocards of this kind that working men found so remote from reality. As speech after speech records, employees who

---

[51] *e.g.*, disobeying works rules: *Bunker* v. *Midland Rly.* (1882) 47 L.T. 476 (boy under 15 ordered to drive van by foreman, but contrary to rules; action lost).

[52] Applied to actions under the 1880 Act in *Thomas* v. *Quartermaine* (1887) 18 Q.B.D. 685 (C.A., Esher M.R. dissenting); but already this and other decisions showed a new readiness to use the defence much less severely against workers who continued work while appreciating the danger: see above p. 509 and Bartrip and Burman (1983), pp. 182–184.

[53] See above, n. 37.

[54] Esher M.R., *Walsh* v. *Whiteley* (above, n. 50) at p. 375.

[55] Charles Bradlaugh, for instance, reported to the Commons a meeting of 40,000–50,000 Durham miners declaring their hostility to any clause which would put upon them a system of compulsory assurance: P.D. 1880 CCLV 362.

[56] See *e.g.* Lord Shand's letter in *The Times* (August 24, 1880) (advocating compulsory insurance): Wilson and Levy (1939) I, pp. 41–44.

[57] For these events, and the extent of contracting out, see Bartrip and Burman (1983), pp. 158–173.

[58] *Griffiths* v. *Dudley (Earl)* (1882) 9 Q.B.D. 357 at 364.

had accepted "contracting out" as a condition of keeping their jobs felt that they had had no real choice in the matter.[59] The consequence was not that they were left entirely without provision regarding accidents, for employers did not go so far; instead they contributed to a mutual fund which, while it could give broader and better cover than under the Act, was often run on a wholly inadequate basis: the benefits paid out to injured workmen might be very small or the solvency of the fund might be precarious[60]; worst of all, the proportion of the fund contributed by the employer might be very low.[61] The worker saw no evidence that such shabby substitutions for the guarantees of the Act brought him the higher wages posited by economic theorists. Running in tandem with these grievances was a natural dislike amongst unionists for mutual funds which performed a protective role often assumed by unions, and which linked employer and employee together in a collaboration inimical to the bargaining strength of the union. Since benefits were often cumulative, it became increasingly difficult for an employee to leave his employment voluntarily or do anything that might lead to his dismissal.[62] But these matters of self-interest were accepted to be secondary to the main argument against the mutual funds, at least by the governments which moved progressively towards acting on the workers' case.

Much of the argument about "contracting out" was concerned neither with the inadequacies of the meanest mutual funds nor with their effect on labour relations generally. The root issue remained the question of safety. Attempts were made to substantiate the assumptions of the "expensive accident" theory by demonstrating statistically that accident rates had gone up in concerns which insisted on contracting out, but had gone down in comparable organisations which accepted liability under the Act. But the figures proved nothing, save to those determined to find what they sought, partly because the Act itself had an impact too slight to produce noticeable improvements.[63] Even supposing, proclaimed *The Daily Chronicle,* an amendment that "entitled twice as many cripples to a fling at the law, and that the damages were twice as heavy, does the reader imagine that shipowners would risk a day's demurrage or slow down their operations or see that everything was taut and shipshape on that account?"[64]

---

[59] T. H. Green, who found the whole subject an apposite example for his revised liberalism, lent his weight particularly to this argument: *Liberal Legislation and Freedom of Contract* (1881), p. 14.

[60] The four largest miners' societies had an accumulated deficit of £159,400 in 1889: *Westminster Rev.* (1 May 1889), p. 495.

[61] Subsidies varied from 3.9 per cent. (Midlands) to 25.2 per cent. (North Wales): *ibid.*

[62] John Burns put the TUC view, alleging that the "real object of the masters in promoting the mutual insurance schemes is to prejudice the workmen, to damage the friendly societies and to impede the cause of Trade Unionism": P.D. 1893 XXI, 439–440. This was hotly denied.

[63] See G. Drage, *The Labour Problem* (1896), pp. 144–157; but note Bartrip and Burman (1983), pp. 171–173, 181–189, pointing out that while contracting out only ever affected a minority of workers, it prevailed in some of the most dangerous localities, such as Lancashire and South Wales mining.

[64] *The Workers' Tragedy* (1896).

In Parliament there were two main tussles about the future of employers' liability, as first the Conservatives, and then the Liberals sought to attract the working-class vote so substantially increased by the Third Reform Act. During Salisbury's government of 1886–90, it became necessary to give the 1880 Act life beyond its original seven years. Two Bills to abolish "contracting out" were referred to a Select Committee under Sir Thomas Brassey.[65] The Committee's report, in general rather complacent, did propose that in future a "contracting out" term would be valid only if given for some consideration other than just the worker's labour. This "separate consideration," as it came to be defined in the Government's Bill of 1888, comprised an "adequate" contribution by the employer to an insurance fund which protected against all accidents at work and "a benefit equivalent to the compensation under the Act."[66] But so great was the opposition on both flanks to this tortuous substitute for a simple prohibition of "contracting out" that the Bill foundered. The original Act was extended without alteration.[67]

In 1893 Asquith, the Liberal Home Secretary promoted a Bill accepting the unionists' case—both common employment and "contracting out" were to be abolished. The Lords inserted an amendment allowing "contracting out" where the arrangement was "deemed fair" by the Board of Trade and it was adopted by the workers affected in a secret ballot. But the antagonism remained extreme and the new Bill was also lost. Though compensation for work accidents was lively issue in the 1895 election, the Webbs, writing in the following year, considered that a slackness had come over the whole controversy, and also that systematic provision for all injured workers irrespective of fault was a "suggestion as yet scarcely whispered by Trade Unionists."[68] Yet within a year Chamberlain had persuaded them, albeit with reluctance, that beside the "preventive" action for damages based on negligence, should be placed a "curative" entitlement to smaller sums for all victims of accidents.[69]

II. WORKMEN'S COMPENSATION

(a) The 1897 Act

The Workmen's Compensation Act 1897 was built around two principles. First, the employer was liable to pay compensation where personal injury was caused to any of his workmen "by accident arising out of and in the course of employment."[70] Secondly, compensation was to make good in part the losses that flowed from incapacity

---

[65] From 1881, Thomas Burt and Henry Broadhurst introduced annual Bills to secure the abolition of common employment.

[66] The employer was to guarantee the fund and the Board of Trade would assess the adequacy of the scheme if necessary. See Bartrip and Burman (1983), pp. 176–178.

[67] This was done annually as a matter of course until 1948.

[68] Webb (above, n. 44), I pp. 382, 385.

[69] See Hanes (1968) 104; the Bill was introduced by the Home Secretary, Sir Matthew Ridley, who had taken an interest in the subject for twenty years.

[70] s.1(1). See generally, Bartrip (1987) Chap. 1.

to earn: if the injured worker survived the accident he was to receive one half of his average weekly earnings up to a maximum of £1 a week; if he died his dependants were to receive a sum equal to his last three years' earnings from the employer, subject to a minimum of £150 and a maximum of £300.[71]

The scheme did not embody the concept of mutual insurance which had previously been prominent in the thinking of Tory democrats and socially-conscious employers. As in Bismarck's scheme, the worker was not obliged to make any direct contribution towards his own protection. But an element of risk participation was preserved by the principle of a half-pay pension to the incapacitated survivor of an accident.[72] Unlike the German system, however, there was no obligation placed upon the employer to take insurance cover with an industry-wide indemnity organisation supervised by the state.[73] A workman who caused his own accident by "serious and wilful misconduct" could not claim.[74]

The Act did not abolish common law actions for damages for negligence[75]; but their numbers windled.[76] An application for compensation acted as an election not to seek damages.[77] The experience of the 1880 Act, particularly the political tension generated by "contracting out," left its mark in the absence of any requirement that the worker should contribute. "Contracting out" itself was still permitted because employers demanded it in the name of liberty. But the contract had to be "not less favourable to the general body of workmen and their dependants than the provisions of the Act."[78] Though in the debates of 1897 there was still a good deal of anxiety from the unions, the power to "contract out" in this form was little used. Some

---

[71] Cf. the complex averaging that had been used under the 1880 Act: above, n. 39. The compensation was payable only after two weeks off work: see s.1(2), Sched. 1.

[72] Many mutual insurance schemes were wound up, but friendly society and union provisions were little affected: Wilson and Levy (1939), I pp. 79–80.

[73] In introducing the Bill, Ridley disdained the German as "an extremely elaborate system, one which is utterly foreign to this country.": P.D. 1897 XLVIII 1431. The German precedent remained to the fore during the debates, since the second reading revolved around a motion by Geoffrey Drage (in palindromic echo of Chamberlain four years before) that the house could be satisfied with no bill that did not provide for prevention of accidents as well as compensation. In this he drew on his comparative knowledge (see above, nn. 42, 43) to attack the Bismarckian system as destructive of industrial harmony in that it gave rise to great difficulty with malingerers, caused a huge number of appeals and passed the cost of accidents back to the worker: P.D. 1897 XLIX 636 ff. But his warnings were not take up by the Liberal front bench and at the end of the debate he withdrew his motion.

[74] This qualification (s.1(2)(c)), admitted into the Bill upon an amendment, raised in spectral form some aspects of contributory negligence. Attempts to modify it in later Acts were subjected to evasive interpretation by the courts: see below, pp. 534–535.

[75] It also preserved the power of magistrates under the factories and mines legislation, to award penal compensation: s.1(5) (see above, pp. 517–518). But it seems that magistrates refused to apply the provision, saying that the workman could apply for compensation: see the Report of the Digby Committee (below, n. 82) para. 47.

[76] Employers' liability actions in 1898 numbered 879 and in 1908, 405; in 1922, 35 came to trial, a level which did not afterwards change; see Bartrip (1987), pp. 219–223 (also referring to statutory duty actions).

[77] 1897 Act, s.1(2)(b), 1(4); the election was made at the moment of applying for workmen's compensation: Edwards v. Godfrey [1899] 2 Q.B. 333; cf. Beckley v. Scott [1902] 2 K.B. (Ir.) 504.

[78] s.3(1). The Registrar-General of Friendly Societies was to certify this.

employers, however, did deduct the premiums for workmen's compensation insurance from wages.[79]

(b) Reviews of the Scheme

Chamberlain conceived his Act as a legislative experiment, following the economist Stanley Jevons, who argued that "the state use the experimental method: in the usual absence of certain evidence as to how to remedy a particular evil, Parliament must observe it closely, propose a remedy, try it out, and if it works, keep it."[80] The Act was to last for seven years, and it only affected railways, factories, mines and quarries, engineering works and certain building works.[81]

The results therefore soon required assessment. A Departmental Committee under Sir Kenelm Digby reported in 1904 in terms that were cautiously optimistic.[82] The Act had not so far imposed any crushing burden on industry and it worked reasonably where labour was permanent and unionised and employers were insured or sufficiently large to cover their own risks adequately. As a result the system was expanded in 1906 to cover all industrial accidents involving manual workers save in certain exceptional categories[83]; and some diseases commonly associated with types of employment were also brought within it.[84] In addition, the Act of 1906 strove to support the system against its first wave of critics. In this aim it achieved little and after the 1914 War another Committee, chaired by a Liberal M.P., Holman Gregory, suggested more fine-tuning.[85] Some of these recommendations, though by no means all, were eventually made law in 1923.[86] Largely in this form, the scheme survived through to the end of the Second War. But by then it had been subjected to some devastating criticism, notably by Levy and Wilson; and Beveridge, in his Report on the future of Social Insurance, accepted the case for integrating accident compensation within a structure of state-run benefits. The National Insurance (Industrial Injuries) Act 1946 provided for the replacement of workmen's compensation with the

---

[79] Digby Committee Report (below, n. 82) para. 62. Equally, a few employers (*e.g.*, of stevedores) passed the cost of insuring onto customers by separate charge: *ibid.*

[80] Hanes (1968), p. 100. A great deal was heard of the "experiment" as Parliament worked through the provisions delimiting the employments covered.

[81] s.7., extended to agricultural workers in 1900; for which, see Bartrip (1987), pp. 27–33.

[82] Departmental Committee on Workmen's Compensation P.P. 1904 [Cmd. 2208] LXXXVIII; Bartrip (1987), pp. 38–45.

[83] Workmen's Compensation Act 1906, s.13, bringing employed seamen in particular into the scheme; see generally Bartrip (1987), pp. 45–54. Note also the broadening decisions, *Fenton* v. *Thorley & Co.* [1903] A.C. 443; *Brintons* v. *Turvey* [1905] A.C. 230.

[84] s.8, Sched. 3; see Wilson and Levy (1939) I, pp. 104–110.

[85] Departmental Committee on Workmen's Compensation P.P. 1920 [Cmd. 816] XXVI. Bartrip (1987), pp. 88–96. In the war conditions of 1917–19 it had been necessary to increase the amount of some benefits, to include children even if illegally employed, and to introduce a special, industry-funded scheme for silicosis: *ibid.*, pp. 74–82, and for an extension in 1924, pp. 144–145.

[86] The Workmen's Compensation Act 1923 resulted from a Bill sponsored by the Conservative government. It had been provoked by a Bill from the Labour member, J. H. Thomas, which attempted to enact the whole range of Holman Gregory proposals: see generally Wilson and Levy (1939), I Chaps. 12 and 14; Bartrip (1987), pp. 96–110.

industrial injuries scheme of social insurance. Workmen's compensation proved to be a transitional experiment in social policy.

Through its half-century, there was in fact a constant stream of criticism. Between the two sides of industry, an atmosphere of antagonism built up over the settlement of claims; and among the exacerbating factors lay the fact that claims were in the end handled by lawyers following ordinary court procedure. Though under no legal obligation to do so, the majority of employers did insure their liability to pay workmen's compensation, either with a private insurance company in the business for its own profit or in an indemnity association with other employers. Private insurers already had, by 1897, considerable experience of compromising their liability under various forms of policy by direct approach to the victim. Cheap and quick settlements were to be secured from men who had rarely possessed any capital sum before and who in any case feared a dispute involving their employers. With the increase of liability insurance brought about by workmen's compensation, the insurance companies began to build up their corps of claims adjusters. Not only union representatives, but officials of the Home Office, factory inspectors and county court judges complained to the Digby Committee of the plausible approaches to men still sick in hospital and the persistent visiting and even the bullying that they might suffer at home. A. H. Ruegg K.C.[87] said of the claims settlers, particularly from the smaller insurance companies, "they are smart young men and they think they have done a very commendable thing when they have settled for a small amount."[88]

The workers' representatives sought legislation to render inoperative lump sum commutations of the right to weekly payments. But the employers and insurers, as well as expounding the virtues of freedom of contract, could point to some situations in which it was in the injured man's interests to be paid a lump sum—for instance if his incapacity meant that his future was best secured by purchasing a shop or other small business.[89] The Digby Committee agreed that "improvident or oppressive settlements for lump sums are much too frequent" but would only recommend that there should be supervision over settlements by the County Court registrars and judges.[90] The Act of 1906 provided that certain settlements would not be binding unless registered with a county court, and the court might refuse registration or make a different order if the sum was inadequate or the agreement had been obtained by "fraud or undue influence or

---

[87] Ruegg, subsequently a County Court judge, became the foremost legal exponent and critic of the scheme: see his *Laws Regulating the Relation of Employer and Workman in England* (1905); (with Stones) *The Workmen's Compensation Act 1906* (1922) and his evidence to the Digby Committee, and the Gregory Committee (on behalf of the Council of County Court judges).

[88] Report (above n. 82), Q.1372.

[89] The Gregory Committee also stressed the phenomenon of compensation neurosis: settlement by a lump sum once for all did lead to a marked physical improvement in some cases: Report, para. 83.

[90] Report (above n. 82), para. 239—given effect by the 1906 Act, Sched. 2(9), (10); this built upon a less effectual registration provision in the Act of 1897, Sched. 2(8).

other improper means."[91] But failure to register carried no criminal
or other sanction, and insurers and employers tried to ensure that the
worker did not do so. During this period, the unions were increasing
their ability to combat the activities of the claims adjusters. Yet in
1920 union membership stood at 8.3 millions, while the number
covered by workmen's compensation was some 15 millions.[92]

Before the Holman Gregory Committee, even the representative of
the London Chamber of Commerce acknowledged that some insurance offices continued to be "unsympathetic" towards injured
workers. The Committee was not prepared to recommend either a
ban on settlements or penalties for failure to register them; and so the
problem persisted. The union representatives argued instead for a
system of state insurance. "I cannot conceive," said Samuel Chorlton
for the National Union of Railwaymen, "under State insurance and
investigation by a State representative, that the desire for bargaining
and profit could accentuate itself to the extent that it does now."[93]

The Committee itself was disturbed by evidence of the insurance
companies' practice. After some intensive price competition,[94] rates
had begun in 1911 to stabilise and income to increase (through being
calculated as a proportion of wages at a time when wages were rising). As a result, for every £100 of premiums, only £52 went as compensation or into a compensation reserve; the rest went on profits
(£15), managerial expenses (£19), commission to agents and brokers
(£12) and transfers to additional reserves (£2).[95] The Committee
acknowledged that a state scheme had the attraction of "relative
cheapness." Nonetheless, it actually negotiated with the Accident
Offices Association for a working arrangement by which the proportion of premium income devoted to compensation would rise to
70%.[96] In the event the Association gave no actual undertaking until
1923 when they were able to satisfy the Secretary of State with 60%,
rising after three years to 62.5%.[97] Thus by these careful manoeuvrings and the sympathy of the Gregory Committee, they maintained
their position within the system. The most that the Committee was
prepared to see by way of state intervention was a requirement that
the 250,000 "self-insuring" employers (many of them, small traders)
should take out cover.[98] Eventually, in 1934, this solution would be
imposed on a single industry—mining—where the problem was
acute.[99]

[91] Judge Sir Edward Bray to the Gregory Committee (above, n. 85), Q.15037. At one
   point the C.A. even held that there need be no registration unless a weekly payment
   had later been commuted into a lump sum (*Ryan* v. *Hartley* [1922] 2 K.B. 150); this
   was not accepted by the H.L. (*Russell* v. *Rudd* [1923] A.C. 309).
[92] Report (above n. 85), para. 4; and see paras. 83–88.
[93] Gregory Report, Q.2626; the Committee rejected his case.
[94] A tariff association was formed, but to little avail. The Employers' Liability Insurance Companies Act 1907 required new companies to deposit £20,000, as was the
   system for life insurance under Acts of 1870–1872: Bartrip (1987), pp. 64–67.
[95] Gregory Report, paras. 10–12. For the costs and benefits of the scheme generally,
   Bartrip (1987), pp. 67–72, 120–128.
[96] Report, paras. 22, 23.
[97] Wilson and Levy (1939), I p. 166.
[98] Gregory Report, paras. 20, 25.
[99] Workmen's Compensation (Coal Mines) Act 1934; Bartrip (1987), pp. 157–162.

The promoters of workmen's compensation in 1897 claimed that it would be straightforward and uncontroversial to operate. Disputes would be settled by voluntary joint committees of employers and workmen, with ultimate resort to an arbitrator—if necessary a county court judge. The government first tried to foster the informality of this by providing for the arbitrator's award to be without appeal and proceedings before him to be without legal representation (save with leave). "The Government," said Chamberlain, "were as strongly persuaded as any one could be that the constant interference of the lawyer would be an absolute injury. ['Hear, hear!']"[1] In the end, however, they gave in to pressure from the Law Society. The Court of Appeal and the House of Lords were to take appeals on points of law in the interests of uniform interpretation. Professional representatives were to be constrained only by a scale of maximum fees.[2]

In the upshot, the joint arbitration committees rarely materialised and the normal forum became the county courts, which by 1900 heard 1,145 claims. The effect upon appeal business was even greater, quadrupling Court of Appeal work in four years.[3] Chamberlain had derided Asquith's Bill of 1893, for "not being an Employers' Liability Bill so much as a Lawyers' Employment Bill." The foolhardiness of the jibe was soon apparent. The consequences of choosing a "self-administering or court" type of dispute settlement, as opposed to the "board or commission" type commonly adopted in North America, were to be the subject of many criticisms. The experiment would not be repeated in the pension and national insurance schemes of 1908–11.[4] Workmen's compensation, which Dicey denounced as collectivist would induce a sharp hostility to the rule of the common law so paramount among his constitutional virtues. The opinion became widespread that the judges, by training and temperament, were unsuited to handling claims under such schemes and that the use of ordinary court procedures as the model for arbitrations was a mistake.

The stream of cases which reached the Court of Appeal, though never more than a very small part of swelling tide of claims, produced results notable for their narrow construction of the Act and fine interpretative glosses upon it. The 1897 Act, indeed, invited difficulty by its "experimental" restriction to employment in a "railway, factory, mine, quarry or engineering work," etc. Each of these terms proved to have a contentious penumbra: for instance, the Court of Appeal held a ship repairer working in a dry dock was not employed "on in or about a dock"; fortunately, in this instance, a further appeal to the House of Lords procured a reversal.[5] In 1914, a County Court judge would write of such cases:

"Nearly all . . . and there are, I regret to say, many, where the

[1] P.D. 1897 L 272.
[2] *Ibid.*, 670. Despite some pointed needling from radicals the government would admit only to being swayed by the advice of county court judges.
[3] B. Abel-Smith and R. B. Stevens, *Lawyers and the Courts* (1966), p. 116; and see generally Bartrip (1987), pp. 59–63, 129–30, 133–36.
[4] Above, pp. 455–457.
[5] *Raine v. R. Robson & Co.* [1901] A.C. 404.

Court of Appeal has overruled the County Court, and the County Court judgment has ultimately been restored by the House of Lords, the error has been in the Court of Appeal striving to find a reason to hinder the payment of compensation, rather than searching for the principle which brought an admitted injury within the scheme that Parliament has made to compensate the injured. After all, the Act was one for the compensation of workmen, and every case of injury that is found not to be provided for is a blot on the scheme."[6]

The division amongst the judges according to their sympathy either for employers or for workers, which Lord Esher had remarked, seemed to have become a division between one appellate court and the next. The Court of Appeal, led initially by A. L. Smith as Master of the Rolls,[7] displayed a thoroughly legalistic caution. The Lords, which contained Liberals such as Davey and Shand, as well as Halsbury and McNaghten, who were close to Salisbury's government, were undoubtedly more robust in approach.

Later, however, the Lords showed their own divisions.[8] In the process they caused the learning heaped up around the phrase, "accident arising out of and in the course of employment," to acquire a distinct list in the employer's favour. The workman's claim was precluded in many situations where he was not actually working at his job, but was, for instance, in transit to or from it, or was taking a break during the working day. Most remarkable of all was the development of the doctrine of the "added peril." Parliament on two occasions tried to express the idea that serious and wilful misconduct by the worker should not count against him if, as a result, he was killed or seriously and permanently disabled.[9] But the Lords read these provisions as subject to the overriding consideration that the accident would not arise out of the employment at all if the claimant caused his own injury "through the new and added peril to which, by his own conduct he exposed himself, not through any peril which his contract of service, direct or indirect, involved or at all obliged him to enter."[10] The young miner who broke a pit rule by riding in any empty coal truck, the shunter who rode on a truck bumper instead of walking in front as his job required, the railwayman who passed between trucks to get to a mess-room, all lost their claims on this account.[11] Despite Parliament's intervention in 1923,[12] the House of Lords continued to insist that an agricultural worker who

[6] Sir E. Parry, *The Law and the Poor* (1914), p. 91.
[7] Parry (*ibid.*, 89) wrote affectionately, "the social creed of 'A.L.' was something between that of the Church catechism and the *Sporting Times*."
[8] Remarking on the two opposed "tendencies of construction," Lord Dunedin said: "to mention names, I think it will certainly be found that the protagonist of the one is Lord Loreburn and of the other, Lord Atkinson,": *Simpson* v. *L.M.S. Rly.* [1931] A.C. 351 at 357. See generally, R.B. Stevens, *Judges and Politics* (1978), pp. 164–170.
[9] Workmen's Compensation Acts 1906, s.1(2)(c); 1923, s.7.
[10] Thus Lord Atkinson, sternest proponent: *Barnes* v. *Nunnery Colliery* [1912] A.C. 44 at 50.
[11] *Barnes* v. *Nunnery Colliery* above, n. 10; *Herbert* v. *Samuel Fox* [1916] 1 A.C. 405; *Lancs. & Yorks. Rly. Co.* v. *Highley* [1917] A.C. 352.
[12] Above, n. 9.

went to fasten the chains of a reaping machine by walking along a pole, instead of getting off, lost his claim, since he had added gratuitously to the risk "by a foolhardy act of bravado."[13] Only on the eve of war did the Lords begin to efface their own gloss upon the terms of the statute.[14]

The story of the "added peril" provides one instance of the "armchair tests" to which some lawyers, closer to the grass roots of industrial accidents, objected strongly. "In very many cases these tests are quite inapplicable to the actual conditions of the industry concerned but they are seized upon by County Court Judges as a ready means by which to decide difficult cases."[15]

Even those claimants who did not become the subject of a test case on appeal might be daunted by the formality and expense of a County Court arbitration. It was generally recognised that legal representation was vital and only trade union assistance enabled the system for settling disputes to work at all. Part of the formality, however, was the direct result of the suspicion with which each side regarded the other. For instance, a claimant was required to give notice of his accident "as soon as practicable" after its occurrence.[16] This was intended to give employers some protection against claims that they could not check because of lapse of time. But given the stress and disruption of a serious accident, there were many perfectly genuine claimants who put themselves out of time by hesitating, not least because they feared losing their job as a result of complaining.

The most serious problems concerning claims, however, related to medical issues, since these were the crux of so many disputes. Many cases were dealt with upon the assessment of the claimant's own doctor. But in others—where, for instance, permanent disability was likely, or the insurers smelt a malingerer—they required medical examination by their own doctor. This was often antagonistic in atmosphere and could be used as a means of pressing for cheap settlement.[17] If medical issues spilled over into arbitration, they might be resolved in three ways. The County Court judge might choose between the views of the forensic experts; or the question might be passed to one of the medical referees appointed for each court, or a referee might be appointed to advise the county court judge in determining an arbitration. But even the system of medical referees proved problematic. The proposal of the Digby Committee that they should be made state officials made no headway, even when later it was suggested that their functions should be given to the medical officers appointed under the national health insurance scheme.[18] As a result, they fell under the suspicion of bias which was

[13] *Stephen* v. *Cooper* [1929] A.C. 570.
[14] *Harris* v. *Associated Portland Cement Mfrs.* [1939] A.C. 71.
[15] Charles Muir, *Justice in a Depressed Area* (1936), p. 152.
[16] Workmen's Compensation Act 1897, s.2(1). There was also a six-month limitation period for claims. See further Gregory Report (above, n. 85), p. 51 and the 1923 Act, s.10.
[17] According to James Sexton, speaking on behalf of the TUC Parliamentary Committee to the Gregory Committee, insurance companies sometimes required regular medical assessments, and "things get so nauseous to the man that sometimes he may refuse to go," Report (above, n. 85), Q.3860.
[18] Report, (above, n. 82), para. 265; *cf.* Gregory Report (above, n. 85), para. 97.

liable to infect medical assessment at all its stages.[19] The Stewart Committee in 1938 considered that Medical Boards, composed of three members, should become appeal tribunals from the referees.[20]

The workmen's compensation law gave a great many people who suffered a work injury or contracted an industrial disease a measure of protection which had simply not existed for their Victorian counterparts. Its founders had presented it as a mere starting point. A failure to admit that first strides were not the whole race was the great error of the governments which inherited its surveillance. After 1906 there were only meagre increases in the rate of benefit.[21] Adequate medical treatment was never introduced; nor were schemes to rehabilitate claimants, retraining them for suitable employment where possible.[22] State insurance was rejected, and state supervision under a Home Office commissioner, though it had been a vital element in the Gregory Committee's plans for building up the existing structure, formed no part of the remedial legislation of 1923. Once economic recovery had begun in the thirties there was considerable agitation for improvements.[23] If war had not intervened, it may be that the system would have survived with substantial emendation, instead of being swept away.

As it was, the task set for a Royal Commission in 1939 was passed on to Sir William Beveridge, for consideration as part of his plan for the social services of the future. It was the much broader base that he proposed for social security which made possible a radical recasting of protection against industrial injury and disease. Compared with the assurance that characterises so much of Beveridge's Report, his proposals regarding industrial injury have a tentative air.[24] They represent only a transitional step towards the transformation achieved by the National Insurance (Industrial Injuries) Act 1946. Some basic elements in his proposals were to survive: industrial injury benefit as part of the state scheme was to supersede workmen's compensation, replacing the employer's sole responsibility by a joint insurance fund with contributions from employers, employees and the state. Nonetheless the industrial injuries scheme ought to remain a distinct part of social insurance and provide more substantial aid than sickness or unemployment benefit, so Beveridge argued, because of the dangerous nature of certain industries vital to the economy; and because a man at work was "under orders." The first argument, which Bever-

---

[19] Cases occurred in which medical referees to one court regularly appeared as expert witnesses for one side in other courts: *Ibid.*

[20] Departmental Committee on Certain Questions arising under the Workmen's Compensation Acts, P.P. 1937–38 [Cmd. 5657] XV.

[21] In 1906, the position of those under 21 was improved; in 1923 the maximum payable was raised from £250 to £350 and certain other improvements were introduced.

[22] A. F. Young, *Industrial Injuries Insurance* (1964), pp. 84–85, discusses the great importance of retraining in any adequate programme for the victims of accidents.

[23] A succession of private members' bills provoked the limited inquiries of the Stewart Committee (1938, above n. 20) and then the appointment of the Henderson Royal Commission (1939). In decisions such as *Dover Navigation* v. *Craig* [1940] A.C. 190; *Noble* v. *Southern Rly.* [1940] A.C. 583; *Weaver* v. *Tredegar Iron* [1940] A.C. 955, the House of Lords brought a more benevolent approach to issues before it.

[24] *Social Insurance and Allied Services* P.P. 1942–43 [Cmd. 6404] VI, para. 80 ff; and *cf.* the ensuing White Paper, *Social Insurance* P.P. 1943–44 [Cmd. 6511] VIII, Pt. II; see generally, Bartrip (1987), Chaps. 8, 9.

idge himself considered the more significant, was, however, directed only to the dangerous sectors of industry. In any case, Beveridge qualified his proposal for a separate benefit by suggesting that it should operate only in relation to those so seriously injured that they still needed assistance after thirteen weeks. This would be regarded by the government as undermining the whole case for a more generous industrial injuries benefit and was not taken up.

As Miss Young noted, the true force for maintaining the distinction has been political rather than rational.

> "Workmen's compensation has been part of most workers' armoury as long as they can remember. It was offered a better rate of benefit than sickness insurance, and so long as there is a chance to obtain this higher rate, even if for selected cases only, so long will the scheme be supported. It is in truth a protest against the general principle of fixing national insurance benefit at or below the level of subsistence."[25]

So equally with regard to "alternative remedies": should the injured worker be entitled to a claim for common law damages in addition to or as an alternative to his social security benefit? Many places which had adopted the British model for workman's compensation had also, in effect, made the common employment rule permanent: actions by worker against employer were precluded except where the employer was shown to have been guilty of personal negligence.[26] Beveridge, indeed, offered as his third justification for maintaining a special rate of injuries benefit within the social security system that only then "would it appear possible—as on grounds of equity and for the avoidance of controversy it is desirable—to limit the employers' liability at Common Law to the results of actions for which he is responsible morally and in fact, not simply by virtue of some principle of legal liability"[27] (i.e., vicarious responsibility).

But an important current of opinion was already flowing the other way. In 1939 the House of Lords had limited the scope of common employment to exclude the case of "fellow servants who are engaged to act on independent jobs, which do not necessarily or in the ordinary course bring them into relation." Only the force of precedent prevented its abandonment in toto.[28] The whole issue was referred to the Monckton Committee in 1944, which accepted the old arguments against the artificial implication that employees consented to the risks of common employment. The doctrine was therefore to be abolished, and so also was the rule that an injured workman must elect between a common law claim and injury benefit, which had dogged workmen's compensation. Both proposals became law. But nonetheless a majority of the Monckton Committee thought it right to apply

---

[25] Above, n. 22, p. 92; see also V. N. George, *Social Security: Beveridge and After* (1968) Chap. 9; Atiyah (1987), pp. 19–23.

[26] *Cf.* Monckton Committee on Alternative Remedies, P.P. 1945–46 [Cmd. 6860] XIII, para. 75–77.

[27] Report (above, n. 24) para. 81; and see paras. 258–264.

[28] *Radcliffe* v. *Ribble Motor* [1939] A.C. 215 (collision between bus drivers of same company; no common employment); but *cf. Graham* v. *Glasgow Corp.* [1947] A.C. 368; *Glasgow Corp.* v. *Bruce* [1948] A.C. 368.

the Beveridge principle that "no injured person should have the same need met twice." So a majority proposed that any injury benefit should go to reduce an award of common law damages. The courts had long accepted that an injured person who had received money under a private insurance policy against an accident did not have to bring the sum into account in an award of damages: the insurance benefits had been separately paid for by premiums that were the result of thrifty foresight.[29] The Monckton majority refused to regard national insurance benefits resulting from compulsory contributions of employers and employees as well as the state in the same light; the minority argued the contrary. The ultimate compromise put forward by the government, allowed the injured person to keep part of his benefit out of the damages calculation.[30] Though sometimes attacked as irrational, it could be viewed as an arrangement for allowing the employee extra provision towards his needs which reflected his personal contribution to the insurance fund.[31]

III. Postlude

During the nineteenth century, the common law had come increasingly to treat liability for non-contractual harm in terms of liability for fault. The tort of negligence emerged as the mode of compensating for accidental injury to person and property and it grew to encompass some of the consequential losses which might also ensue. In general the territory into which fault liability moved was previously unoccupied by common law rules. Where there were established principles, their strength was not likely to be overcome by large generalisations, however morally attractive. Thus most of the settled instances of strict liability—and notably such torts as conversion which served to protect private property—kept their established character; likewise torts which were dependent upon intentional wrongdoing, such as deceit, were not to be remoulded.

Liability for personal fault had undoubtedly appealed to the strongly individualistic strain in Victorian moralising; but as a basis for a workable system of accident compensation it had required significant compromise. From the outset, vicarious liability made the employing enterprise liable alongside the negligent employee and so provided a defendant who was likely to be worth suing. Where the judges decided to exclude vicarious responsibility—as in the common employment rule—a more limited type of compensation, applicable equally to non-negligent accidents, had to be imposed by legislation, and it was expected that this liability would be backed by insurance cover. More generally, insurance came to be accepted as a necessary planning device for the risks of injury in the field of transport. First, accident insurance gave victims their own protection; and

[29] See above, p. 504.

[30] The Law Reform (Personal Injuries) Act 1948, s.2, provided that in calculating common law damages, any cash benefit received under national insurance, other than half that received or likely to be received for five years from the accident, should be brought into account.

[31] Cf. Atiyah (1987), pp. 405–407; for the effects of the transition in general, see Bartrip (1987) Chap. 11.

then liability insurance was allowed to cover enterprises against their legal responsibilities even for personal injury.[32] The view that such insurance would induce a feckless disregard for precautions gave place to the hope that, through differentials in premiums and perhaps even safety advice and inspection by insurers, this arrangement for compensation could also foster prevention. At the same period the right to "contract out" was accepted not only for the extended liability of the Employers' Liability Act 1880 but also under the terms of contracts in the realm of transport.

This became particularly apparent once the motor vehicle began to replace the horse as the main hazard of the roads. Even before the first restrictions on motor traffic were slackened in 1903,[33] the Law Accident Insurance Society was offering a comprehensive policy, combining liability cover for injury to other people and property with accident cover for injury to the car insured, its driver and passengers. The new field was not covered by the deposit system of financial guarantee[34] and intense competition made motor insurance unprofitable for a decade. The leaders eventually organised themselves under tariff cartels—for private cars (1913–14), commercial vehicles (1915) and finally motor cycles (1921)—which proved enduring enough to bring "stability." During this period shipping insurance would fluctuate somewhat in profitability, but would, in the 1920s, be supplemented by new business in aviation insurance.[35]

In 1930, it was finally required that "third party" liability insurance be carried for all motor vehicles on public highways.[36] Though short-term pre-occupations led insurers to regard this move with some coldness, they would soon realise its opportunities of an assured and growing market. The non-tariff insurers led the way in introducing discriminatory devices such as no-claims bonuses (at first non-cumulative) and regional zoning for premiums; soon these became general practice. By 1946, the position of motor insurance would be sufficiently entrenched for the whole industry to be drawn into collaboration in a Motor Insurers' Bureau.[37] All in the business undertook to finance this institution which acted as third party liability insurer to those who suffered injury or damage by an uninsured driver (including one whose policy could be avoided for fraud or breach of condition by his own insurer).[38] Insurance thus became the life-support system of liability in this field and insurers' staff played an influential role in determining what compensation should be paid, negotiating with individual victims and their solicitors, or, where the victim had accident cover, with his own insurer.[39] The common law rules for liability, requiring proof of negligence, and

[32] See above, pp. 514 515.
[33] The Motor Car Act of that year raised the speed limit from 12 to 20 m.p.h.
[34] This would be required by the Road Traffic Act 1930, ss.37, 42.
[35] See G. Clayton, *British Insurance* (1971), pp. 119–120.
[36] For the political developments, see Dinsdale (1954), pp. 327–329.
[37] The contract was with the Ministry of Transport.
[38] See Clayton (above, n. 35), pp. 157 158, 374; Atiyah (1987), pp. 247 252.
[39] A whole range of understandings were generated between insurers when they were the real interests on each side of a dispute—notably such arrangements as "knock-for-knock" agreements, under which each indemnified its own client in a collision, whatever the truth about fault.

absence of contributory negligence or other defence, underpinned
the structure of such negotiations. Accordingly litigation continued
to evolve from them, as it did with common law claims for accidents
at work and (on its different premises) workmen's compensation. A
major role of this litigation was to set values upon the less readily
quantifiable elements allowed in damages, such as the pain and suffering and "loss of amenity" for (say) the loss of an eye or a limb. It
was in the insurer's interest to have an accepted scale for these factors, for then premiums could be more accurately set. So long as
juries were allowed to assess damages there could be considerable
variation in awards. Indeed, plaintiffs' advisers looked to them as the
only hope of preventing damages from settling down at conservative
levels which would be hard to adjust even to keep in line with
inflation, let alone to improve the victim's deal. On the whole the
judges sympathised with insurance interests. As one economy
measure in 1933, the High Court acquired a discretion to order that a
negligence action be tried by judge alone without a jury.[40] Gradually
juries would become infrequent. Courts were reluctant to order them
and plaintiffs gave up asking.[41] Judges settled to the notion of evolving tariffs from themselves.[42]

In 1945 the present-day position was still emergent. The moderating of contributory negligence and the abolition of common
employment would prove politically acceptable at this juncture,
partly because the growth of insurance made the broadening of liability less fearful. By the same token, transport authorities would be
prevented from entirely excluding liability through the terms on
their tickets.[43] So there were modifications of the nineteenth-century responses to the problems of accidental injury. But what
impresses nonetheless is the continuing grip of those responses.
Other jurisdictions, working from the same starting points, have
chosen to treat fault liability as no longer pivotal—in the field of
employment accidents by making some form of workers' compensation the only basis for responsibility, in the field of traffic accidents
(and perhaps even in all spheres) by introducing a "no-fault" liability scheme. This latter idea has had its airing in Britain.[44] But the
deliberation with which it was discussed, the qualified verdict upon
the alternative that was returned by Royal Commission, the lack of
any subsequent action, all suggest that the compensation system for
accidents has little of the political momentum that it enjoyed in the
late nineteenth century. Without such impetus, it is likely that
the forms evolved by a particular history will continue to underpin
the British approach to the subject.

---

[40] Administration of Justice (Miscellaneous Provisions) Act 1933, s.6; the power,
which had already been tried as a wartime measure from 1918–25, applied to all civil
actions save those involving personal reputation or fraud: see R. M. Jackson (1937) 1
M.L.R. 132.
[41] The process was completed by *Ward* v. *James* [1965] 1 Q.B. 273.
[42] Kemp and Kemp's *Quantum of Damages* (1st ed., 1954–56) collected the requisite
information together for them.
[43] A movement which began with the Road Traffic Act 1930, s.97; see now, Unfair
Contract Terms Act 1977, s.2(1).
[44] See generally, Atiyah (1987), Chap. 25.

FURTHER READING

Atiyah, P. S., *Accidents, Compensation and the Law* (3rd ed., 1980; 4th ed., 1987, by P. Cane).

Bartrip, P. W. J. and Burman, S., *The Wounded Soldiers of Industry* (1983).

Bartrip, P. W. J., *Workmen's Compensation in 20th Century Britain* (1987).

Baker, J. H., *An Introduction to English Legal History* (2nd ed., 1979) Ch. 19.

Dinsdale, W. A., *History of Accident Insurance in Great Britain* (1954).

Hanes, D. G., *The First British Workmen's Compensation Act 1897* (1968).

Manchester, A. H., *Modern Legal History of England and Wales 1750–1950* (1980), pp. 280–301.

Prichard, M. J., "Trespass, Case and the Rule in *Williams v. Holland*" [1964] C.L.J. 234.

Prichard, M. J., "*Scott v. Shepherd* and the Emergence of the Tort of Negligence," (Selden Society Lecture, 1976).

Smith, H., "Judges and the Lagging Law of Compensation for Personal Injuries in the Nineteenth Century" (1981) 2 J. Leg. Hist. 258.

Wilson Sir A., and Levy, H., *Workmen's Compensation* (1939).

Chapter Eight

CRIME

In this final Chapter we focus—for the first time systematically—upon the criminal law and its administration: law at its most evidently proscriptive.[1] Throughout our period the punishments of criminal justice have given force to commands that life, liberty and property be respected, that good order and government be maintained and that social life be rid of a host of offensive, disruptive and immoral practices. Since the country claimed at the root of its politics a rule of law in place of tyrannical discretion, the criminal law and its procedures also marked out a prime frontier of state power. The long testing, so intensely pursued during the stuggles against Stuart authoritarianism, allowed the eighteenth-century Englishman his claim to be free-born. No grown man or woman (at least, if sane) could be punished or restrained by the state without being tried and convicted of a nominate offence. The most serious accusations of crime, moreover, had generally to be upon the presentment of a grand jury and had always to be made out to the satisfaction of a trial jury.[2] Here was the incontrovertible advance—the "unqualified human good," as E. P Thompson was moved to put it[3]—which made criminal law so crucial an element in the constitution.

For Thompson, certainly, it was an advance despite all, since no historian has done more to demonstrate the scope that remained for the powerful to turn the constraints of law to their own advantage. A student of the history of criminal justice must seek to characterise the degree to which, in each period, the law is primarily an instrument of class or other sectional repression; or, on the contrary, the extent to which its benefits of security and order inure to a substantial part of the whole community. But issues of this sort are profound and complex. They depend upon a knowledge of what constituted criminal conduct, who were likely to be prosecuted as offenders and who sought to put the law's machinery in motion. Equally one must understand the very considerable changes that were wrought in the machinery of criminal justice through the period under review. As so often in preceding chapters, these shifts are typically in the direction of professionalisation. This is true of the criminal trial, and accordingly of the substantive law around which it was based. But even more it marks the machinery of prosecution, which was transformed by the introduction of modern police forces; and it alters the mechanics of punishment, with resort to capital sentences giving place to

---

[1] For the courts in which criminal law was administered, see above, p. 33ff.

[2] See further below, pp. 561–562. The ideal was secured primarily by the writ of habeas corpus, by which one who detained another could be required by a royal court to establish the legal justification for doing so. It became tarnished whenever, in times of great tension, Parliament was led to suspend habeas corpus (as in 1794 and 1817) and it was permanently spotted at the edges by the preventive powers of the magistracy: see below, pp. 547–548.

[3] In a celebrated peroration to *Whigs and Hunters* (1975), p. 266; see further below, pp. 566–568.

transportation, then to imprisonment, and ultimately to a whole range of further alternatives. It is a progression of means and ends which vastly increases the power of government to regulate behaviour in the community. We shall look at it in three cross-sections of time: in its mid-eighteenth century condition, when little had happened to re-shape a long inheritance; in the period to 1877, when, the essential design of the new system was sketched; and in the earlier part of the twentieth century, when a growing body of experts developed its operation, but when the disruptions of war and economic collapse put it under new forms of stress.

PART 1: THE ERA OF THE BLOODY CODE

I. The Range of Criminal Law

The idea of criminal law, as a distinct type of social sanction, had begun to emerge in the early middle ages.[4] The assertion of central authority which required that private vengeance be subordinated to official processes was then passing through the stage when communities were made responsible for the misdeeds of their members and was reaching the condition of individual responsibility for wrong-doing. The juridical forms of redress for wrongs which had originally given the victim or his relatives the appeal of felony had divided into distinct processes: civil action gave compensation to the person injured, criminal prosecution imposed death or other punishment in the name of the larger community.[5] The state, indeed, sought to insist that serious crime be prosecuted. The law would not in theory allow a victim to withdraw an accusation of anything more serious than a simple assault[6]; and there was continuing anxiety over private compromises by which, for instance, stolen goods were to be returned on condition that no one was prosecuted—Jonathon Wild, indeed, had made such deals into an early Georgian art-form.[7] But, for all its assertion of primacy in the criminal process, in the eighteenth-century the Crown was still largely dependent on the energies of individual victims of crime to undertake prosecutions. In most of the country, the only representatives of authority were the justices of

---

[4] For the early history, Holdsworth, II, pp. 43–50; IV, pp. 492–532, VIII, pp. 301–346; J. G. Bellamy, *Crime and Public Order in England in the later Middle Ages* (1973). For the early modern period, J. H. Baker and J. S. Cockburn in Cockburn (1977) Chaps. 1, 2; Cockburn, *A History of English Assizes, 1558–1714* (1971); J. A. Sharpe, *Crime in Seventeenth Century England* (1983), Sharpe (1984); M. R. Weisser, *Crime in Early Modern Europe* (1979).

[5] Only the appeal of murder survived on to the eighteenth century, as a means by which occasionally the relatives of the victim might challenge an acquitted murderer to a second trial. When the appeal was acknowledged still to be open to trial by battle in *Ashford* v. *Thornton* (1818) 1 B. & Ald. 457, it was promptly abolished (59 Geo. III, c. 46); see D. R. Ernst (1984) 28 Am.J.Leg.Hist. 164.

[6] The modern practice by which the Attorney-General alone may enter a *nolle prosequi* had no meaning in the eighteenth century: see D. Hay (1983) 21 Osgoode Hall L.J. 165 at 169–171; W.W. Pue (1983) 21 Alberta L.R. 335. For the compromise of assaults, see Beattie (1986), pp. 457–458; and generally, pp. 8–9.

[7] For whom, see G. Howson, *Thief-Taker General* (1970).

the peace and the parish constables (who, like the overseers of the poor, filled a rotating office). They could supply only spasmodically the executive energy which today we associate with the police.[8] Accordingly, a prosecution required two preconditions: evidence which would bring the crime home to the accused; and a prosecutor sufficiently exercised by the wrong to follow the proceedings through, despite the inconveniences and, in some cases, the prospect of reprisals. Yet, even in remote counties, there was regular business for the criminal assizes and quarter sessions. They provided the formal, external reckoning against real threats to community order, particularly from the disruptions caused by roving beggars and trampers after work. Other techniques for settling scores survived for a long period, especially among social equals.[9] The Duke of Wellington and his generation still fought the stylised duels demanded by their militaristic code for insults to honour and manliness.[10]

The scope of criminal law had expanded somewhat erratically over time. Almost all the earliest and most heinous offences were defined by common law.[11] Much of this law was imprecise and was based upon the most rudimentary principles of liability in general.[12] By 1760 there was an ever-increasing volume of statute law specifying particular offences, some in effect reiterating common law, some embracing new territory, much designed primarily to impose death as the penalty for crimes against property—the notorious "Bloody Code." Considerably earlier than in the sphere of civil law, Parliament was becoming the regular source of legal change, both in the substantive criminal law and in its procedures.

If the eighteenth-century criminal law were represented in a Venn diagram, it would be composed of three overlapping Sets. Set I would comprise the major crimes against person and property—in particular, murder and manslaughter, rape, buggery and bestiality, aggravated assaults and affrays, robbery and piracy, burglary and housebreaking, the various forms of larceny (theft) and forgery, arson and malicious damage to property. Most of these were classed as felonies, exposing a convict to death or other punishment and (at least in theory) to forfeiture of estates and goods. There were, however, certain lesser crimes that had come to be grouped as misdemeanours. In this Set they would include, for instance, most assaults, as well as false imprisonment and receiving stolen goods.

Set II would consist of the offences concerned with threats to the state, the established religion and the social order: at the pinnacle the

---

[8] See below, p. 551ff.

[9] Earl Ferrers' conviction in 1760 was for murder of a steward, not a gentleman. It demonstrated the indiscriminate reach of the criminal law, and was much feted in consequence; in reality, it was a highly unusual event. For another much vaunted instance—the trial of Dr. Dodd for forgery in 1777—see Radzinowicz (1948), I Chap. 14.

[10] V. G. Kiernan, *The Duel in History* (1988).

[11] The eighteenth-century King's Bench also made plain their power to hold conduct criminal, as and when they found it contra bonos mores: see esp. *R. v. Delaval* (1763) 3 Burr. 1434 at 1438–39 (Lord Mansfield) (and above, pp. 371, 381); Holdsworth, VIII pp. 407–408.

[12] See below, pp. 565–566.

gravest crime, high treason; below this the misdemeanours of seditious and blasphemous libel, the principal curbs upon freedom of
speech and publication; and at their side, the public order offences,
of which the most usual had become unlawful assembly and riot.[13]
These likewise were misdemeanours, but rioters became guilty of
felony if they failed to disperse within an hour of a magistrate reading the proclamation under the Riot Act 1715.[14] In this Set would also
fall the range of offences aimed at protecting Crown revenues (such
as smuggling), the administration of justice (such as perjury), the
armed forces (such as mutiny and desertion). Overlap with the first
Set would occur where, for instance, rioters were shown to have committed assaults or damage to property. How they were charged might
well depend on the prosecutor's feeling for the case. A Set I charge
could play down the politics of the riot and underscore the ordinary
wrongfulness of what had happened; a Set II charge could make an
example of protesters who had gone beyond tolerable limits in their
confrontation with authority.

Set III would cover a wide miscellany of controls over personal
morality, vagrancy, public health and safety, land and trade regulation. Some of these had earlier been matters for the church courts,[15]
but increasingly they were given over to justices of the peace sitting
separately or in pairs to hear the charge summarily, upon pain of
relatively minor punishments, such as a fine, whipping or a brief
term in a gaol or house of correction.[16] The link connecting these proceedings to major crime was the enduring belief that the worst
offences were only the product of loose, unsupervised living—
drunkenness, prostitution, irreligion, rootless wandering, festering
disrespect for those in higher station. As the extent of property crime
came to seem more fearful, the campaigns to stamp out "vice," in its
protean manifestations, would become more strident. By the end of
the eighteenth century, there were well-supported prosecution
societies which policed the morals of many towns.[17]

---

[13] Unlawful assembly was the gathering of three or more for a common purpose in a
manner that caused a reasonable fear of breach of the peace. Riot was a tumultuous
disturbance by three or more intending to execute their enterprise violently to the
terror of the people and to assist one another against any opposition.

[14] 4 Geo. I. St. 2, c. 5, a modified version of Tudor legislation: Holdsworth, VIII pp.
328–331, X pp. 705–713.

[15] See above p. 28. Some attempts at policing morality, such as the ecclesiastical
offences of adultery and fornication, had made no transfer permanently into the
secular jurisdiction, and in one case—incest—this would be long delayed (see
below, p. 612).

[16] Until 1857, the church courts continued occasionally to deal with such matters as
brawling in churchyards and defamation not serious enough to be the subject of
common law prosecution: see the Ecclesiastical Courts Commission, P.P. 1831–32
(199) XXIV, pp. 53–64.

[17] Such societies were by no means a new phenomenon, expressing as they did an
evangelical yen to impose a religious awakening on the lower orders. But they multiplied and diversified from the late eighteenth century. Typical examples such as
the Proclamation Society of 1787 and its later emanation, the Society for the Suppression of Vice, were inspired by Wilberforce and the Clapham sect. Much of this
activity spilled over into more general plans to regulate poor relief through efficient
marshalling: see Radzinowicz (1956), III pp. 143–180; (1968), IV pp. 43–59.

The many overlaps between this and the other Sets make it crucial to see criminal law in a broad perspective, and not simply confined to conduct which was prosecuted at assizes and quarter sessions.[18] It was, indeed, along the lower perimeter of Set III that concern for a rule of law counted least. Here we find laws that abandoned even the appearance of social equality. The main external discipline upon employed labour—the Master and Servant Laws—had come, as we have seen, to impose much severer sanctions upon those employed than upon those who employed them.[19] In the countryside, the Game Laws, also mainly a matter for petty sessions,[20] stood as a naked symbol of landed exclusivity. The hunting and appropriation of deer, game birds, rabbit and hare, did not originally give rise to charges of theft, since the common law did not admit ownership of animals in the wild.[21] Instead a labyrinth of specific statutes imposed controls.[22] Their apogee was reached in 1671, when it became a summary offence for a person to hunt game if he was not a substantial landholder, heir to person of "higher degree" or owner of a chase or park.[23] Further buttresses were added in the eighteenth century, making it, for instance, an offence to possess hunting equipment, or to deal in game as a trader; and the penalties were increased for hunting at night. In 1784, a hunting licence with a two-guinea Exchequer stamp was required.[24] Blackstone could wax sarcastic about these "questionable" crimes, "which the sportsmen of England seem to think of the highest importance." [25] They were, moreover, administered by justices within their own fiefs in a manner that was sometimes highly partial.[26] But they would remain an inviolable canon of social distinction until at least the eve of Parliamentary reform.[27]

---

[18] On this, see esp. Sharpe (1984), pp. 4–5, taking Elton to task for some remarks in Cockburn (1977), pp. 2–3.

[19] Above, pp. 294–295.

[20] In the earlier seventeenth century, prosecutions for poaching still went mainly to quarter sessions.

[21] But as deer and rabbits came to be "enclosed" they were treated as private property; later the same was done for game-birds.

[22] For a summary, P. B. Munsche, *Gentlemen and Poachers* (1981) App.; for the subject in general, see Munsche's book and M. J. Ingram in Cockburn (1977) Chaps. 5, 9; also C. Kirby (1931) 38 Am. Hist. R. 253; and in *Essays in Modern English History in Honour of W. C. Abbott* (1941), p. 380; A. Howkins in S. B. Burman and B. E. Harrell-Bond, *The Imposition of Law* (1979) Chap. 15.

[23] The maximum punishment became a fine of £5 or 3 months in a House of Correction: 5 Ann., c. 14, s.4; there were higher penalties for "deer-stealing": 3 & 4 Will. & Mar., c. 10.

[24] See Munsche (1981, above, n. 22), pp. 21–27. The Waltham Black Act and other capital statutes also struck at some poaching activities.

[25] *Commentaries*, IV pp. 174 75, 409.

[26] It was probably the disgraceful trial of a farmer, Beller, by the Duke of Buckingham in 1820 which allowed Brougham, in a famous squib, to call "a brace of sporting justices" on a game case, a tribunal "worse constituted than that of the Turkish cadi"; for the context of this remark, Munsche (1981, above, n. 22), pp. 76–80.

[27] In 1831, reformist pressure led to removal of the most evidently discriminatory provisions in the Game Laws. But still £3.13s.6d. was needed for a licence; and still the game rights over the land remained the landlord's, unless expressly granted to the tenant, an arrangement which generated long resentment (often for good economic reason) and eventual legislation in the Ground Game Act 1880 (above, p. 171): Jones (1982), Chap. 3; H. Hopkins, *The Long Affray* (1985).

They were said to keep the aristocracy and gentry on their estates; and to the Georgian ascendancy that was apology enough.[28]

The proper limits of a libertarian criminal law were blurred on a different front: that presented by the preventive powers of the justices of the peace. Since the middle ages it had been part of the magistrates' duty to inhibit those who might otherwise commit crimes or threaten public order. Justices might bind persons over to keep the peace or to be of good behaviour, requiring them to enter recognizances and frequently to find persons who would stand surety for them. Breach of the obligation would make them and their sureties liable to pay a sum set at the time of making the order.[29] Alongside these powers lay the authority given to the justices under the vagrancy laws to deal with the "idle and disorderly," "rogues and vagabonds" and "incorrigible rogues" by fines, committal to a house of correction, and, in the last two categories, whipping and return to place of settlement.[30]

II. THE AMOUNT OF CRIME AND ITS NATURE

Even today attempts to quantify the amount of crime become lost in the shadows of offences that go unreported. In an age before regular police forces, there was little incentive to report crimes committed by unidentified culprits. Even such complaints as were received by parish constables and justices were not the subject of regular records.[31]

Until the nineteenth century we are left in the main with the lists of those who were prosecuted at Assizes and sometimes at Quarter Sessions, very largely for Set I crimes. Around 1800 it was a common guess that not one in ten of the crimes actually committed were prosecuted. The records of prosecution are however, some measure of how perturbed the victims and the respectable community at large were by the different types of crime. They help to identify both short-term variations and long-term trends in the extent to which prosecutors were able and willing to set the law's processes in motion, instead of either seeking some less formal resolution of the grievance or simply letting the matter rest.[32]

A number of studies have now confirmed that the great bulk of eighteenth century prosecutions concerned property offences, mostly without violence.[33] The cases of murder and physical attack not connected with property were always a small proportion which in most

---

[28] An attitude solemnly adumbrated by a lawyer such as Joseph Chitty (1816) 9 *The Pamphleteer* 181.

[29] N. Landau, *The Justices of the Peace, 1679–1760* (1984), pp. 23–24.

[30] The Vagrancy laws were consolidated and strengthened in 1744 (14 Geo. II, c. 5) and 1824 (5 Geo. IV, c. 83); Jones (1982) Chap. 7.

[31] On the records of crimes and prosecutions before the appearance of central statistics in the nineteenth century, see Sharpe (1984), pp. 34–63; Beattie (1986), pp. 4–5, 19–22.

[32] Informal settlement was clearly important and widespread here as elsewhere, see, *e.g.*, M. J. Ingram in Cockburn (1975), pp. 125–127.

[33] See esp. Beattie (1974) 62 P. & P. 47 and (1986) Chaps. 2, 3; D. Hay (1982) 95 P. & P. 117.

instances had declined over the previous two centuries.[34] In the same period even the number of property indictments had fallen considerably. But that was not a trend which in urban areas would continue to the end of the eighteenth century.[35] In the fringes of Surrey which abutted the metropolis, for instance, there was a worrying upsurge which by the 1790s seemed in full spate; and this was symptomatic of a growth in property prosecutions which would embrace more and more of the country in the ensuing 50 years.[36]

As for short term variations, the most notable shifts came in the aftermath of war. The discharge of soldiers would suddenly increase the numbers tramping in search of work or other subsistence; and a miasma of rumour would spread around the real threat which they posed. In response, more victims would prosecute, grand juries would be readier to approve indictments, trials would less often lead to acquittals, more convicts would be left for the gallows. Within a few years, as the surplus labour was absorbed, the remedy was thought to be effective and use of the criminal machine fell back. The cycle can be seen, after the European wars, during 1749–1752 (when Henry Fielding and others became so incensed against the increase of robberies and thefts); after the Indian and American wars, during 1763–1765; and again in the mid-1780s as the conflict with the thirteen colonies drew to its close. In each case the eventual return to "normality" only strengthened the belief that existing procedures could be made to work well enough; plans for radical change could be belittled.[37] At times of bad harvest and hunger, the same phenomenon was observable to some extent, but it tended to be moderated by a factor that was unlikely to operate so strongly in the wake of war. The waves of sympathy for the plight of those who must suffer most dreadfully from shortages would find expression, not only in special doles and other charitable relief, but also in a certain reluctance to proceed against those who stole out of necessity. But even so the moral balance might still send the rate of prosecutions up. Beattie notes an increasing tendency at such times to proceed against older men—those between 20 and 40, who would accordingly have wives and young children to feed and clothe.[38]

Theft out of immediate need is a first form of that elusive phenomenon, "social crime," which has recently been much discussed.[39] There are other, rather different cases that might be included in the category. Prime among them are organised protests with some defined objective which have become criminal by disintegrating into riot or attacks on property or individuals. These, of course, were pro-

---

[34] Homicides reduced by perhaps two-thirds between 1600 and 1800: see Beattie (1986), pp. 107–112. For the special offence of concealing a birth (referred to in the literature as "infanticide") see R. W. Malcolmson in Cockburn (1977) Chap. 8; P. C. Hoffer and N. E. H. Hull, *Murdering Mothers* (1981); Beattie (1986), pp. 113–124. Rape and other attacks on women and children were doubtless common enough but were at all stages prosecuted only occasionally.

[35] Sharpe (1984), pp. 57–63.

[36] Beattie (1986), Chap. 5.

[37] Hay (above n. 33); Beattie (1986), pp. 213–235.

[38] Beattie (1986), pp. 202–212, 235–252; Hay (above, n. 33).

[39] The debate was opened by E. J. Hobsbawm (1972) 25 Bull. S.S. Lab.Hist. 5. For a summary and criticism, Sharpe (1984) Chap. 6.

minent and persistent enough to have played an important part in generating the Set II offences and they would continue to recur down to modern times.[40] A different instance covered attacks on property where the attackers claimed to have been deprived of an interest or share, generally through some manipulative use of legal rights or powers, as for instance in an enclosure.[41] Certainly it was a phenomenon of rural existence that, as landed estates came to be organised on an ever-growing scale, the lesser commoners and farm-workers tended to lose their expectations over grazing for animals, sources of fuel, material for building, and gleaning after threshing, in ways that could stoke deep resentment and retaliation.[42] One justification offered for poaching was that the landed class had expropriated by means of legislation something in which all should have a natural right, since wild animals were not properly the subject of private ownership.[43]

Tensions of this type could arise equally in the realm of productive industry, particularly before the money wage had become the single expectation of reward. If a manager, in the name of profitable efficiency, chose to stamp out some established practice of taking home waste or by-products, his workforce would have no provable right to set against him but nonetheless would feel a very real grievance at the deprivation.[44] Different again were cases where the "social" element is supplied merely by the fact that a large portion of some community engaged in, or connived at, an activity which the law designated criminal: wrecking, smuggling, coining and poaching, have each been posited as eighteenth-century examples.[45]

But these rough categories are a considerable miscellany. True, they are all cases where the governing orthodoxy defined by the criminal law was challenged directly by some more or less large portion of the lower orders. But motivations differed very considerably. In the last category, in particular, a nakedly acquisitive instinct predominated, in the case of wrecking in a form peculiarly bloodthirsty; in the case of smuggling, to an extent which would teach eighteenth century governments that to impose high tariffs upon merchandise would be counter-productive because of the opportunities for illicit

[40] See, e.g., below, p. 597.
[41] See above, p. 137ff. For the Kingswood colliers' rejection of turnpikes, see R. W. Malcolmson in Brewer and Styles (1980) Chap. 3:
[42] Detailed evidence from the early eighteenth century on annexation of forests forms the major substance of E. P. Thompson's *Whigs and Hunters* (1975); on wood gathering, see R. W. Bushaway in Rule (1982), p. 65; on gleaning, Sharpe (1984), p. 123.
[43] Blackstone claimed an equal right to hunt to be part of the law of nature, limitations upon it a matter of social interest: *Commentaries*, II 411–412.
[44] Phillips (1977), pp. 180–195, shows Black Country employers increasingly using the criminal law of theft against their employees; embezzlement by servants and bailees of what was entrusted to them was only made a general crime in 1799 (39 Geo. III, c. 85).
[45] These provided the subjects for various essays in Hay *et al.* (1975): Chap. 3 (C. Winslow—smuggling in Sussex); Chap. 4 (J. G. Rule—wrecking and coastal plunder); Chap. 5 (Hay—on the Paget family's war with local poachers on Cannock Chase). For the coiners and a dismissal of the idea of social crime, see J. Styles in Brewer and Styles (1980) Chap. 5.

profiteering that would ensue.[46] This motivation equally tended to blur the range of the other categories. Sheep-stealing, for instance, might be the crime of a man desperate to provide for a starving family; but equally it might be the work of a butcher.[47] The game laws came to be used with particular determination against gangs which trafficked on the black market, as distinct from locals seeking a bit of meat for their diet or demonstrating their disgust for the manorial lord and all he symbolised.[48] The reaction of the ordinary community likewise could be most varied: there might be widespread feeling that what was done was wholly justified, or there might be sympathetic regret, or aversion and denunciation.

The historical record is in no condition to allow any quantification of what might properly count as social crime, though there are demonstrable instances enough of each of its manifestations. The attempt to identify it is at least useful as one of the indications that the values enshrined in the criminal law derived from the ideology of the propertied and respectable and not necessarily that of the lower orders. Equally, the difficulty of classifying many cases shows how varied was the moral impact of criminal justice, which accordingly retained a broad acceptability that would have been hard to secure if it had been a simple, unrelenting tool of class aggression.

III. POLICING

The twin pivots upon which eighteenth century criminal justice turned—policing through the efforts of the local community, and a narrow, summary range of punishment—now deserve elaboration. It is only with some knowledge of their part in the overall balance that it is possible to understand the central legal step—the trial.

Policing had come primarily to be a function of the smallest units of country and town, the parishes.[49] The office of parish constable rotated amongst those who had a holding in the parish, as did those of churchwarden, surveyor and overseer of the poor. Of them all the constableship was most burdensome and so had perhaps sunk lowest.[50] In earlier times the parish constables had to some extent come under the supervision of the high constable of each hundred; but after the Restoration this role had mostly passed to the local justices of the peace.[51] Indeed, the areas covered by their petty sessions formed

---

[46] Winslow (above, n. 45) shows how the tea duties had to be reduced in 1745; and how nevertheless smuggling continued its growth towards big business.

[47] J. G. Rule (1982) Chap. 5, analyses the manifold causes of this crime.

[48] See P. B. Munsche in Cockburn (1977) Chap. 9.

[49] The most detailed account of the traditional arrangements in the eighteenth century is Radzinowicz (1956), II; see also Critchley (1967) Chap. 1; Emsley (1983), pp. 20–31; and for earlier work still of value, F. W. Maitland, *Justice and Police* (1885); W. L. Melville Lee, *A History of Police in England* (1901) Chaps. 1–9; S. and B. Webb, *The Parish and the County* (1906), pp. 25–29, 39–40; note also J. J. Tobias, *Crime and Policing 1700–1900* (1979) Chaps. 1, 2.

[50] Defoe had called it "an unsupportable hardship."

[51] With time, it became the justices, rather than the courts leet who actually appointed the constable, thus giving it some appearance of an office of the Crown. For the earlier role of the constable as mediator between central government and local community, see Sharpe (1984), pp. 76–77.

the structure that counted for most in the communal policing of the pre-industrial era. To the constable fell the ancient duty imposed upon the parish to preserve the peace.[52] The constable had to apprehend wrongdoers of all kinds and take them before a justice. At the same time, he was to take action against individuals who caused nuisances and to investigate failures of the parish as a whole, for instance over the upkeep of highways and bridges.[53]

The parish constable ought therefore to have been the first recourse of all who were victims of serious crime or had a complaint about community affairs. By our period, however, there were certainly places where the office was carried on with an inept or casual disregard of duty.[54] Where once parishioners of real substance had involved themselves directly in disciplining their rough, quarrelsome inferiors, the task had lost urgency; so they instead took advantage of the ability to buy their way out of being constable which many parishes permitted.[55] Or sometimes they became entitled to an exemption from parish office which a court might grant to the prosecutor of a criminal.[56] Moreover, those who did serve were allowed increasingly to work through a deputy (or even a sub-deputy); there came to be individuals, some of humble station and mediocre capacity, who carried on the job even while the nominal holder changed from year to year.

It is hard to estimate how inadequate the essentially amateur scheme of policing was becoming in the later eighteenth century.[57] The advocates of a complete reorganisation of policing would soon be pouring immense scorn on the parish constables, and their accounts have been rather uncritically accepted in histories of later "progress." Through much of the country, those who ran the system liked it because it was theirs and could, perhaps with a degree of adaptation and improvement, remain a net stretching around their own communities. To such people the instances of abuse and inefficiency only demonstrated the immense difficulties of establishing a paid civilian force that would operate in some ideal, non-partisan spirit.

Under the parish constable system, prosecution was most often a matter for the victims themselves or for other private individuals who could be persuaded to take a sufficient interest in the matter. The result was a splay of inducements. Statutes dealing with felonies against property had come to prescribe "Parliamentary rewards"— better known as "blood money"—the sum amounting to £10 or even

---

[52] Some communities were still capable of being raised on occasion by the constable's "hue-and-cry" to go in pursuit of the perpetrators of some outrage; but the informal help of bystanders was undoubtedly a more frequent occurrence: see Beattie (1986), pp. 36–37.

[53] For the evolution of the office, S. & B. Webb, *The Parish and the County* (1906), pp. 26–28.

[54] For attempts at supervising neglectful constables, see Radzinowicz (1956), II pp. 161–167.

[55] For details see, *e.g.*, Select Committee on Police in the Metropolis P.P. 1817 (484), VII p. 473.

[56] These "Tyburn tickets" were prescribed in 10 & 11 Will. III, c. 23. They were abolished in 1826 by 7 Geo. IV, c. 64, s.32; Radzinowicz (1956), II pp. 155–161.

[57] See Beattie (1986), pp. 70–71.

£40, depending on the crime.[58] In addition, the Home Office regularly offered sums for the detection and prosecution of particular criminals in whom they had an interest, and parishes and boroughs would do the same. The Home Office would intervene only if persuaded that there was some special cause for public alarm. In the last, troubled years of the eighteenth century, it would be spending nearly £8,000 a year on rewards. By 1814 the figure would rise to some £11,000.[59] The victim who could not persuade any public body to act might well offer a reward himself, particularly if he had reason to believe that the crime had been committed by a gang, one of whom might be induced to split by the reward and the hope of a pardon.[60] In the latter eighteenth century, the burgeoning of mutual protecting associations provided another source for reward offers, as did banks and insurance houses.[61]

Clearly this reliance on personal inducements was open to abuse, not least among the parish constables and their deputies and watchmen. A Royal Proclamation of 1750 denounced the incidence of perjury among prosecutors who were after rewards and lamented the consequent reluctance of juries to convict. Six years later, McDaniel and his confederates procured the wrongful conviction and execution of two young men in order to claim the blood money.[62] The scandal was long remembered but the system was much too useful to be abandoned. The Select Committee on Police of 1817 roundly criticised the inherent dangers and wanted the total abolition of the government rewards. But the Law Officers would go no further than to replace the specified sums with a reward to be set at the judge's discretion.[63] This, it would seem, was by no means enough to dispose of the problem.

Offers of reward and pardon were mostly used in an effort to uncover major offenders. For minor offences of the Set III type, common informers were encouraged by the offer of a share in any fine imposed. Again the temptations were great: Coke had long before described common informers as "vituperative vermin," and they continued to excite detestation and occasional violence. Even if well-intentioned, they appeared to be enriching themselves by officious snooping; at their worst, they were totally unscrupulous—ready to distort the facts, perjure themselves or extract hush money.[64] Yet here

[58] The Royal Mint and the Customs authorities also paid statutory rewards. Some statutes coupled the reward with a free pardon, so as to induce accomplices to turn King's evidence. See Radzinowicz (1956), II pp. 40–45, 57–82; Beattie (1986), pp. 50–59.

[59] See Radzinowicz (1956), II pp. 83–111.

[60] The Home Secretary might be induced to advertise a pardon in the hope of stimulating a private offer of reward: Radzinowicz (1956), II pp. 45–52. On private rewards, generally, *ibid.*, pp. 112–137; and in relation to threatening anonymous letters, E. P. Thompson in D. Hay *et al*, (1975) Chap. 6.

[61] At least 450 such associations flourished in the century before the introduction of modern police forces: A. Shubbert in Bailey (1982) Chap. 2; D. Hay (1983) 21 Osgoode H.L.J. 167.

[62] In the alarms about crime after 1748, the Crown had been prepared to offer large rewards in particular cases, which stimulated the business of "thief-taking." For the scandals, see Radzinowicz (1956), II pp. 326–332; Langbein (1983–(i)), pp. 110–114. For the associated questions of accomplice evidence, see below, p. 563.

[63] Radzinowicz (1956), III pp. 74–82.

[64] Radzinowicz (1956), II pp. 14–18, 138–155; Beattie (1886), pp. 134–135.

again, until the gradual spread of administrative inspectorates in the mid-nineteenth century, the arrangements would continue and new legislation would add to the informer's opportunities.

The patterns of cooperation within small rural communities, which left policing in the hands of the respectable and prosecuting to the initiative of victims, tended to break down as conurbations emerged, with their pockets of the very poor, constant shifts of population, and periodic outbreaks of violent protest. In the smaller towns, the old system might be adapted with a modicum of reorganisation. Leaders of the community would together secure a local Act, which typically appointed Commissioners to establish a paid watch, as well as arrange the lighting and paving of at least the main parts of the town and the removal of rubbish and excrement: all of which was to be paid for by a rate. The watch would then ease the burden on the constables of the parishes.[65]

But in the largest cities these expedients were beginning to show serious signs of strain. Even in the seventeenth century, the City of London had organised a very large night watch, and in 1737 Common Council had added a day watch.[66] These bodies at least had the advantage of operating over a relatively wide area. At the same period the surrounding Metropolis was expanding so as to absorb great numbers of parishes and in many of them conditions sank to a disturbing level. As the eighteenth century advanced most of the 150 or so parishes would acquire a watch force under a local improvement Act. But self-interest and jealousy militated against much cooperation between them and the difficulties would continue to grow rapidly.

The magistracy, moreover, had come into the hands of "trading" justices—so called because they charged fees for their services—who were widely suspected of being more or less venal.[67] However Sir Thomas de Veil, who lived and held office in Bow Street, marked himself out in the eyes of the government as a justice to be trusted with its interests; and when in 1748, the novelist Henry Fielding succeeded to his position, the collaboration advanced. Fielding organised "the most reliable among the parish constables" into a body which succeeded in breaking a notorious gang of robbers in 1750, a year when post-war panic against rising crime was running high.[68] This developed, particularly after Henry Fielding was succeeded in 1754 by his blind half-brother, Sir John, into a regular band for which the government contributed a grant. On occasion they could be supplemented by special constables.[69] They were more active than the general run of watches and provided some protection in and around the very seat of government at Westminster. After John Fielding's death in 1780, these "Bow Street Runners" would become notorious

---

[65] The first provincial town so to act was Liverpool in 1748; the question could become intensely political, as with Bristol: see S. and B. Webb, *The Manor and the Borough* (1908), II pp. 483, 456–458.

[66] See D. Rumblelow *I Spy Blue* (1971); Critchley (1966), p. 30.

[67] Critchley (1967), pp. 19–20; *cf*. Langbein (1983–(i)), pp. 57–60.

[68] The next year, Fielding produced his well-known *Enquiry into the Causes of the Late Increase of Robbers*.

[69] For which, see below, p. 556.

as colourful, unscrupulous characters, largely concerned with private commissions for fat rewards. But by then the Bow Street office was an established institution of metropolitan life. Soon enough there would be moves to emulate it which, even against the many suspicions, would prove irresistible.[70]

There was another side to the control of social disorder which aroused fierce controversy in the debate over policing. As earlier chapters have evidenced, crowds gathering to denounce or protest were a frequent occurrence in eighteenth-century life. They came together from many causes: in opposition to rising food prices; in resistance to tithes, enclosures, turnpikes and press-gangs; to make demands over wages and other working conditions; in condemnation of vicious husbands, adulterous couples and other misfits. These were all, in their different ways, social crusades, to be distinguished from the drink-sodden rowdiness that was prone to occur at fairs and other festivities.[71] Actual gatherings might be instigated by the appearance of publications or the sending of written threats, which the authorities might seek to treat as criminal. Equally there might be clandestine attacks on individuals or property.

Group protest had long roots: living in small inward-looking communities the humbler orders had little other hope for remedies to their deepest grievances. Their social superiors, at whom complaints were so often directed, would understand that a process of communal negotiation was under way, because tensions subsisted which could not simply be dispelled by suppression. The paternalist attitude of the eighteenth-century upper class was expressed often enough with patrician hauteur. But it did involve some acknowledgment of social responsibilities towards the lesser orders under protection, and that meant a degree of respect for their moral expectations. When, therefore disruption threatened it required caution as well as force, and a willingness to give way on matters that did not seem of first moment.[72]

In the case of truly major threat, the government might be persuaded to send in troops, a detachment of men who would face the harsh disciplines of army life, if, out of sympathy for the protesters, they disobeyed their officers.[73] But in a country often enough at war, and very suspicious of the need for an army in peace-time, this was an occasional resort. Mostly local communities had to rely on their own resources, and in marshalling them much reliance was placed

[70] Below, pp. 587–588.

[71] J. Bohstedt, *Riots and Community Politics in England and Wales 1790–1810* (1983), shows these disturbances to have been most common and effective in rural towns, where vertical controls were less complete than in the countryside, but horizontal cohesions were greater than in the new industrial areas.

[72] Group protest, an essential element in eighteenth century social relationships, now has a considerable literature: see esp. G. Rudé, *The Crowd in History 1730–1848* (1964); E. J. Hobsbawm, *Primitive Rebels* (1959); E. P. Thompson (1968), pp. 66–83; and (1971) 50 P. & P. 76; [1978] Soc. Hist. 133; Stevenson (1979) Chaps. 2–6; R. B. Rose (1961) 6 Int.Rev.Soc.Hist. 277; W. J. Shelton, *English Hunger and Industrial Disorders* (1973); R. W. Malcolmson, *Life and Labour in England 1700–1780* (1981) Chap. 5.

[73] Insubordination that was labelled "mutiny," however, was by no means unknown in either the army or the navy of the period: see Stevenson (1979), pp. 145–150; for military discipline, J. R. Dinwiddy (1982) 97 Eng.Hist.R. 308.

upon the essential loyalty of the middling ranks. If they could be shaped into units of defence, their solidarity was likely to be more persuasive than sheer numbers or superior weaponry. Under a power given by the Law of Settlement 1662, the justices could swear special constables to defend a parish against "actual tumult, riot or felony" and their occasional service was generally rewarded—in London by the government, elsewhere out of the county rate, commonly at 5s. a day.[74] This was a frequent practice in towns, though in some places property owners chose to organise privately, sometimes as part of mutual defence tactics against looting and theft.[75] During the wars with Revolutionary France these associations proliferated, sometimes taking a decidedly militaristic turn, with organised training in arms.[76] The London Foot Association, indeed, became large enough for the constitutional legality of maintaining in effect a private army to be raised with the Recorder of London.[77]

In the countryside, the state itself had a traditional quasi-military force, the militia. This was selected and raised by the Crown's chief representative in the shires, the Lord Lieutenant.[78] In the earlier eighteenth century these local brigades had declined; but hostilities with France led to a revival under a statute of 1757, which instituted compulsory service by ballot, with the opportunity to buy out for £10: the result was to build up a part-time force comprising a labouring infantry commanded by propertied officers.[79] Later, during the post-Revolution wars with France, Pitt would add to this a voluntary force, partly on foot but partly also on horse.[80] The latter, an amateur cavalry of tenant farmers and others who could equip themselves, was the yeomanry. Being by social rank much more dependable than the old militia or the volunteer foot force, they survived longer: it was the yeomanry which would make the fateful charge on the crowd hearing Orator Hunt at St. Peter's Fields, Manchester, in 1819, derisively nicknamed Peterloo.[81]

As with crime in general, public disorder in London posed a unique threat. Any prolonged disturbance there raised the spectre of true insurrection. In the early years of George III's reign, the Commons' repeated refusals to admit John Wilkes as M.P. for Westminster, despite his successes at the polls, provoked tumultuous meetings and strikes, against which troops had to be used.[82] In 1780 every resource—troops, special constables, watchmen, bellmen—

---

[74] 13 & 14 C. II, c. 12, s. 15.

[75] Radzinowicz (1956), II pp. 209–211.

[76] 57 Geo. III, c. 17, empowered justices in general sessions to require men over 17 to assist in preserving the peace in an emergency; see J. L. and B. Hammond, *The Town Labourer* (1917), pp. 81–82.

[77] His answer was equivocal: Radzinowicz (1968), IV pp. 107–110.

[78] This was also part of the Restoration settlement: 13 Car. II, c. 6; 13 & 14 Car. II, c. 3; see J. R. Western, *The English Militia in the Eighteenth Century* (1965).

[79] 31 Geo. II, c. 26; Critchley (1970), pp. 67–68.

[80] For the deployment of these different forces in face of the Luddite disturbances, see F. O. Darvall, *Popular Disturbances and Public Order in Regency England* (1934) Chaps. 12, 13.

[81] On which see esp. D. Reid, *Peterloo* (1958); *cf.* R. Walmsley, *Peterloo: the Case Reopened* (1969); Thompson (1968), pp. 734–768.

[82] See esp. G. Rudé, *Wilkes and Liberty*, (1962); J. Brewer in Brewer and Styles (1980) Chap. 4.

were needed to quell the week-long anarchy of the Gordon riots.[83] Yet so set was the opposition to permanent police that even this terrifying outburst brought no immediate change. In 1785, the younger Pitt proposed a police force for the whole Metropolis, but this was voted out.[84] In the following year, Parliament was prepared to set up what became the Royal Irish Constabulary. But there the strains of subjecting the local populace to the will of English landlords and their agents were of a wholly different order.[85] Beside the Irish problem, even the Gordon riots appeared a passing phenomenon. They were not the expression of any lasting animus against the country's rulers as a whole, or any section of them. Even through the coming decades of war with France, and the extraordinary economic and political consequences which would pertain at home, the established techniques for controlling disorder would continue to be applied. During the "Luddite" attacks on the new production machinery in 1811–13, the panoply of troops, militia, spies and informers, and ultimately prosecution, had to be brought into play. But still they were enough for the government's purposes.[86]

IV. THE PUNISHMENT OF CRIMINALS

If the notion of a professional police excited alarm and revulsion, the idea that the state should itself take charge of convicted offenders for substantial periods by way of punishment was not a serious prospect for much of the eighteenth century. Notions of punishment were crude and summary. The common law prescribed death as the penalty for treason and felony, occasionally with horrendous additions.[87] For misdemeanours, brief exposure to censure and shame in public—mostly by whipping or placing in the pillory— were the old forms.[88] Fines were also possible,[89] but Stuart judges had imposed such massive amounts on some political offenders as to lead to the declaration against "cruel or unusual publishments" in the Bill of Rights.

Under this schema, the death penalty lay not only for murder and violent offences, such as rape, but for all serious property crimes. In Jacobean England something like a quarter of those accused of capital

---

[83] J. P. De Castro, *The Gordon Riots* (1926).

[84] Radzinowicz (1926), III pp. 108–121.

[85] Radzinowicz (1956), III pp. 121–123. For the uprising of 1798, R. Wells, *Insurrection: the British Experience, 1795–1803* (1983).

[86] For the official perspective, F. O. Darvall, *Popular Disturbances and Public Order in Regency England* (1934); for other perceptions, J. L. and B. Hammond, *The Skilled Labourer, 1760–1832* (1919) Chaps. 4, 6, 8, 9, Thompson (1968), pp. 569–659; M. I. Thomis, *The Luddites* (1970); P. Holt, *Threats of Revolution of Britain, 1789–1848* (1977).

[87] For treason a man were liable to be hanged, cut down while alive, disembowelled, castrated, beheaded and quartered; women to be burnt at the stake: see Beattie (1986), p. 451.

[88] Whipping was often while being dragged behind a cart; but as the century progressed, it was coming to be carried out in private; the pillory was used particularly for offences likely to arouse great resentment, such as child molesting: Beattie (1986), pp. 461–468.

[89] See Beattie (1986), pp. 456–461: a small fine was the common upshot of an assault case, perhaps as part of a private settlement.

offences were actually executed.[90] From that harsh severity there had been some gradual remission,[91] a complex process in which two important developments had already taken place by eighteenth century.

The first concerned that most protean of privileges, benefit of clergy.[92] Originally a concession by Henry II in remorse for Becket's murder, it allowed the church to punish those in its own orders even of great secular crimes. By the sixteenth century, common law and statute had laid it down that the most serious offences were not "clergyable"; but by this time the benefit had been opened to others besides clerks in holy orders. All men who could read might claim it once and so secure their freedom, subject to branding on the thumb in order to prevent a second claim.[93] In the latter seventeenth century, the reading test was being used to limit the numbers who would suffer capital punishment, for illiterate defendants were being allowed to pass it in considerable numbers. In 1692 the privilege was extended to women. Then in 1706 the reading test was abolished.[94] Thus for all but the most serious crimes, there came to be a general exemption from the death penalty for all first offenders. Against this development came a second, Parliament's stream of additions to the notorious "Bloody Code"—the ever-lengthening list of offences that were "non-clergyable." Sometimes in reaction to particular outrages, sometimes during the post-war fears of increasing crime, the legislature would add to the ultimate category of crimes particular property offences which in the main had previously been clergyable felonies.[95] We know from assize lists that capital charges continued mostly to be from the old list,[96] but the additions stood as some warning from the landed governors that their toleration was being unduly strained.

These changes were affected in turn by the increasing use of transportation as an alternative to execution.[97] Banishment had been a medieval practice, in form a voluntary abjuration, in reality a means of avoiding execution. With the establishment of colonies in the Americas, the states of Europe began to dispatch criminals there in punishment. The English had started such experiments by the early seventeenth century and the numbers transported had gradually increased. In 1718, the arrangement was rendered more systematic: it became a condition of benefit of clergy that the offender submit to

[90] Sharpe (1884), p. 47.

[91] Sharpe estimates the proportion in the early eighteenth century at around 10 per cent.

[92] Blackstone applauded the process of adaptation, extracting "by a noble alchemy rich medicines out of poisonous ingredients": see *Commentaries*, IV Chap. 28.

[93] Peers could claim the privilege without demonstrating their literacy. The culminating statute was 18 Eliz., c. 7.

[94] See 3 & 4 Will. & Mar., c. 9, 4 & 5 Will. & Mar., c. 24, 5 Ann., c. 6; and note the earlier 21 Jac. I, c. 6 concerning women; Beattie (1986), pp. 451–452.

[95] The most notorious instance was the Waltham Black Act of 1723 (9 Geo. I, c. 22). The 50 or so capital offences of 1688 were quadrupled. The exact number of new offences created cannot be given, since it depends upon how far elaborate and specific provisions should be broken down; see esp. Radzinowicz (1948), I App. 1, for a listing.

[96] See, esp. Beattie (1986) Chap. 4, analysing the Surrey records.

[97] For the evolution of this form of punishment, see Shaw (1966) Chap. 1; Beattie (1986) Chap. 9; A. E. Smith, *Colonists in Bondage* (1947).

transportation for seven years; and equally, many of those reprieved from capital punishment were pardoned only upon accepting transportation for 14 years.[98] The North American colonies had a growing demand for labour; it became good business for contractors to ship the transportees away for assignment into the service of a settler.[99]

What had evolved, accordingly, was a scheme of enforced exile under conditions often close to private enslavement, The British government was involved in nothing more than a small payment to relieve the country of "real" troublemakers.[1] From an official perspective, it was compendious form of "secondary" punishment, an alternative which could leave death as an awful example to be visited upon the worst few. The arrangement was prey only to the twin doubts that would later afflict transportation to Australia: the fear that the flourishing conditions of the colony would convert dreaded removal into desired release; and the danger that the colonists would react against the dumping of human dross in their increasingly respectable midst.

By 1770, both these problems were assuming real dimensions. In the event, the outbreak of revolutionary war in American colonies put a sudden end to the exercise. As a necessary expedient, those marked for transportation were holed up in old ships—the "hulks"—and put to work in gangs dredging and maintaining the Thames.[2] For a considerable time the hulks would continue under a contracting system, but nevertheless the government was obliged to be regularly concerned over what was done with the prisoners there. In any case, it was not a sufficient expedient. There was a sudden interest in building national penitentiaries, and legislation was passed in 1779 to enable construction. Nothing however, would actually happen for another thirty years.[3] Eventually—with the loss of the American states confirmed—the immense experiment of sending transportees out to the scarcely-known east coast of Australia was decided upon by Pitt's government; and this put the whole maintenance of the convict establishment, at least initially, into government hands.

The pressures created by the war with the Americans were being felt not only by the King's ministers but by those who administered assizes and sessions up and down the country. In the early modern period, the gaols maintained in the name of the Crown by the county sheriffs, the borough corporations and the holders of gaol franchises, had two classes of inmate: prisoners awaiting trial on criminal charges, and debtors who could not or would not pay their creditors.[4] Imprisonment had been used as a punishment for serious crime in

---

[98] 4 Geo. IV, c. 11.

[99] The same contractors dealt in indentured servants, but convicts were often preferred by settlers as their term of assignment was longer.

[1] In the fifty years after 1718, some 30,000 were transported to North America, mainly to Maryland and Virginia. In the earlier eighteenth century, perhaps a fifth died on the journey: Shaw (1966), p. 35. The numbers declined in periods of war, when convicts could instead be sent into the army, navy or dockyards.

[2] For their long drawn history, W. Branch Johnson, *The English Prison Hulks* (1957).

[3] See below, p. 579.

[4] For the diffuse early history of the gaols, see Webb (1922), pp. 1–12; McConville (1981) Chap. 1.

the Middle Ages[5] but the practice had since largely disappeared. It was however still used as a disciplinary measure against threatening elements in the vagrant population. Jacobean legislation had required the erection of county and borough "bridewells"—houses of correction where justices could send "rogues and vagabonds" for short spells of hard labour.[6] In many counties and boroughs, these institutions had not remained distinct from the gaols. Moreover, some summary offences (for instance, under the game laws) provided for incarceration in a house of correction; and so short-term imprisonment had gradually acquired some place as a criminal punishment. But before 1775, imprisonment seems rarely to have been used *per se* as a punishment for felony or misdemeanour.[7] Thus for petty larceny (theft of goods under a shilling), the court could choose between transportation and a whipping, the latter being much the more frequent.

The gaols and houses of correction were often in poor condition, ramshackle places from which escape was by no means precluded. They were often filthy, infested and insanitary. Ultimate responsibility for the more important of them lay mostly with county benches or town corporations. But the day-to-day running was given over to a gaoler who made of his office what he could from charges to the prisoners. Those inmates who were destitute accordingly received only the barest sustinence. They might have to sleep in rags on bare boards in rooms with unglazed windows. When the gaols came under unusual strain—as in post-war upsurges of prosecution—they might be wracked by deadly gaol fever, a disease which might be transmitted to constables, turnkeys and even judges and jurors.[8] To expect these places to take in substantial numbers of convicts for months or years was a tall order. Yet it was a prospect which had to be faced after 1775. The judges at assizes, and—more reluctantly—the justices at sessions, began to pass sentences of imprisonment for months or years. The convicts were put back into a local gaol for the whole period, not merely in order to be moved to the hulks or a transport ship.[9]

This novel role for prisons was an imminent prospect as the single-minded John Howard set out from Bedford on his famous tour which would record their serious drawbacks even for their old limited pur-

---

[5] For this period, R. Pugh, *Imprisonment in Medieval England* (1968); Harding *et al* (1985), Pt. I.

[6] For their emergence, see above, p. 417.

[7] There had, however, been an Act of 1706 (5 Ann. c. 6) which allowed, as a sentence for clergyable felony, a term of six months to two years hard labour in a house of correction. It was used to some extent until overtaken by the transportation arrangements of 1718: Beattie (1986), pp. 492–500.

[8] As in the long remembered "Black Session" of the Old Bailey in 1750, when infected prisoners from Newgate spread the disease to two judges, jurymen and various other officers. From this time onwards a concern to do something about sanitation in gaols began to grow and in 1774 Popham's Act (14 Geo. III, c. 59) authorised justices to order annual whitewashing, better ventilation and supply of running water. Howard would find that the Act was used and that the fever had been much reduced in consequence: Beattie (1986), pp. 297–309.

[9] For this shift of opinion, and variations in practice, Beattie (1986), pp. 530–582, 601–618.

poses.[10] With the War of Independence, in other words, the eighteenth-century penal system reached a climacteric.

V. THE PROCESS OF TRIAL

Between the complaint of crime to a magistrate and the decision whether to acquit or to punish lay the processes of accusation and trial. An understanding of this central ritual is a prerequisite to any true characterisation of the criminal process as a whole[11] and our knowledge of it has recently grown through a burst of detailed research.[12]

Let us first say something of the various stages. If the justice's examination of the complainant and his or her witnesses gave a sufficient basis for going further, the accused would normally be sent to the county gaol[13] to be held for the next assize or quarter session (the choice depending primarily upon the seriousness of the charge, with non-clergyable felonies going almost always to assizes).[14] As the date of the hearing approached, the prisoners would be moved to the town of the sitting, to be held in readiness.[15]

Both events—assizes for meeting the visiting judges, quarter sessions for settling the course of local affairs—were high points in the justices' annual round of governing.[16] The sittings would open with a charge—by the senior judge at assizes, the chairman or recorder at quarter sessions—which would dwell on the state of law and order, a homily often enough on the evils of loose and shiftless living and on the duties of those assembled to see to the maintenance of order and public safety.[17] For the criminal business of both courts, the formal indictments had to be carefully drawn, generally by the clerk of assize or clerk of the peace (for sessions).[18] Errors could well lead the judge to direct a discharge: for instance, for naming the wrong person as owner of stolen goods, or misdescribing what was

---

[10] See below, p. 569ff.

[11] For an account of the legal requirements from the early modern period, J. H. Baker in Cockburn (1977) Chap. 1; and see J. H. Langbein, *Prosecuting Crime in the Renaissance* (1974).

[12] This work draws particularly upon the records of assizes and quarter sessions (though the latter exist only patchily) and upon popular accounts of cases, such as the chapbooks which developed into the Old Bailey Sessions Papers in London: see, in particular, Beattie (1986); Hay (1982); P. King (1984) 27 Hist.J. 25; Langbein (1978) and (1983–(i)); and for somewhat earlier periods, J. S. Cockburn, *A History of English Assizes 1558–1714* (1972) Chap. 6; J. A. Sharpe, *Crime in Seventeenth Century England* (1983).

[13] Bail could be sought but was not likely to be granted to those who could not put up trustable sureties or recognizances.

[14] A person held for the assizes could be in gaol for up to six months. In London and Middlesex, however, the Old Bailey needed eight sessions a year for its lists. Quarter sessions differed in the amount of criminal work they would undertake: for the position in Surrey, see Beattie (1986), pp. 285–288, 309–311.

[15] For the hazards, see Beattie (1986), pp. 311–313.

[16] E. Halévy, *History of the English Peoples in the Nineteenth Century* (2nd ed., 1949), I pp. 110–115.

[17] See Beattie (1986), pp. 331–333, and for other grand preliminaries to the assizes, pp. 316–318.

[18] Baker (above n. 11), pp. 32–33.

taken or the place of a robbery.[19] The indictments would then be sent
to the grand jury—at assizes, a large body of county notables, mostly
justices[20]—to hear the prosecution witnesses and decide whether
there was a "true bill" on which the accused should stand trial.[21] This
was not idle ceremony: something like a fifth of all charges were
"ignored" by the grand jury in "ordinary" years, when there was no
particular need either for severity or for clemency.

Those sent forward for trial would then have to face their trial jury,
made up typically of men from the ranks of small property: craftsmen, shopkeepers, tenant farmers.[22] On the arraignment of each
defendant the charge in the indictment would be read out and his or
her plea taken—almost invariably of Not Guilty.[23] The prosecutor
would then give his own evidence and would be followed by his witnesses. Before 1730, it was extremely unusual for either prosecutor or
defendant to have a barrister to provide professional representation
and this older mode remained common practice throughout the
eighteenth century and beyond.[24] Trials were mostly simple and
rapid; a court getting through 10 or 15 cases in a day's sitting of eight,
ten or even more hours.[25] It was for the judge (or, at sessions, the
chairman or recorder) to elicit the evidence from witnesses and to
probe it to the extent that he might feel was warranted.[26] The accused
might be drawn into this process by being asked what he accepted
and what he wanted to challenge.

The separation of cross-examination from examination-in-chief

---

[19] Formalistic construction of indictments was sometimes carried to extravagant
   lengths; but then the system had no regular means of challenging a jury's conviction
   on appeal and this device probably acted as surrogate: see Stephen (1883), I pp.
   273–297; J. H. Baker in L. Knafla, *Crime and Criminal Justice in Europe and Canada*
   (1981), pp. 17, 22–23: "In many cases the ethic of the sporting contest was enough to
   carry the day; if the Crown did not follow the rules it could be declared out."

[20] The minimum number was 12, but could rise to 50. At Sessions the social status of
   grand jurors was more middling: Beattie (1986), pp. 318–331.

[21] One of the earliest manifestations of due process was the requirement that a person
   accused on indictment be presented for trial by these representatives of the community. In the same tradition was presentment of a person accused of homicide by
   the inquest of the coroner's jury. Such communal processes could be sidestepped by
   information to the King's Bench, but only in the case of misdemeanours: see above,
   pp. 236–245.

[22] The property qualification for trial juries had come to include £10 freeholders (4
   Will. III c. 24, s.15) and £20 long leaseholders (3 Geo. II, c. 25); but there would be
   many local variations until Peel achieved a standardisation in 1825 (56 Geo. IV, c.
   50); Beattie, pp. 378–380.

[23] The occasional defendant who refused to "put himself on his country" by pleading
   would be left to the jury to decide whether he stood mute "of malice" or "by visitation of God." In the latter case he would probably be detained as a lunatic, but in
   the former he was liable to *peine forte et dure*—torturing by weights until he submitted or died. The practice was still recorded in the eighteenth century even
   though the old reason for refusing to plead—avoiding forfeiture of goods—had disappeared. Scrupulous feeling led in 1772 to the substitution of a plea of guilty: 12
   Geo. III, c. 20. In 1827, this became a plea of not guilty: 7 & 8 Geo. IV, c. 28, s.2; Beattie, pp. 333–340.

[24] Langbein (1978) (1983(i)), pp. 123–34; Beattie (1986), pp. 352–362. The latter estimates that at the Old Bailey in the late eighteenth century perhaps one defendant in
   six had counsel: p. 360.

[25] Langbein (1978), pp. 277–278; (1983(i)), pp. 115–123; Beattie (1986), pp. 376–378 and
   on jury deliberations, pp. 395–399.

[26] Langbein (1978), pp. 282–284.

would become the norm only with the arrival of counsel in the criminal courts. But even before that stage was reached, the judges were beginning to apply limiting rules of evidence—in particular, to the accusations of an accomplice who had turned King's evidence; and to confessions already made by those accused.[27] Both kinds of evidence often formed the nub of the case for the Crown—perhaps more so in a pre-police state than is the case today. In cases of burglary and robbery by gangs, it might only be possible to discover and prosecute the leaders by turning one of the members against them. The inducement that was regularly offered at the Bow Street Office was immunity from prosecution in return for Crown evidence[28]; and since this meant escape from hanging or transportation it could be a powerful incentive. It worked well when small fry provided true evidence against big fish; but there were obvious dangers of distortion or total fabrication. The magistrate might indeed have to choose between competing accomplices each seeking to split on the other— with results sometimes revealing and sometimes perplexing.[29]

Clearly the judges felt the dangers of this system and their concern may have intensified as the consequences of having a regular police office in the Metropolis became apparent. There is some evidence that in the 1750s they would direct the jury to acquit if the Crown case depended on the uncorroborated evidence of a turn-coat accomplice. This in turn would place grave impediments in the way of getting up some of the most serious cases. In 1788 the twelve judges, at the instance of Buller J., temporised. It was enough that the judge should instruct the jury of the danger of convicting on the accomplice's uncorroborated evidence.[30]

At much the same time, it was ruled that evidence of a pre-trial confession could not be given if, instead of being "free and voluntary," it was "forced from the mind by the flattery of hope, or by the torture of fear."[31] The reason for keeping it from the jurors was said to be the difficulty they might have in appreciating its possible unreliability. A half-century later, with defence counsel to press the issue on many occasions, the judges would show themselves very willing to exclude confessions obtained upon threat or promise[32]; but the first emergence of the rule,—a striking act of self-denial—occurred as professional detection was being set up at Bow Street. The whole evolution is one expression of that deep suspicion of "police" which pervaded so much of the thinking of the respectable.

---

[27] For the emergence (from about 1740) and operation of these rules, see Langbein (1978), pp. 300–306; (1983(i)), pp. 81–105; note also B. Shapiro, *Probability and Certainty in Seventeenth Century England* (1983) Chap. 5.

[28] The medieval practice of approvement, under which the accomplice pleaded guilty and was then pardoned, had fallen into disuse as exposing him to too grave a risk.

[29] In *R. v. Rudd* (1775) 1 Leach 115, it was held proper that a duplicit Crown accomplice should later herself be prosecuted; but that an honest turncoat would be protected, having "an equitable title to a recommendation for the King's mercy." For the obscurities introduced by this reference to a pardon, see Langbein (1983(i)), pp. 92–96; cf Radzinowicz (1956), II pp. 40–42.

[30] *R. v. Attwood* (1788) 1 Leach 464; Langbein (1983(i)), pp. 96–103.

[31] *R. v. Warickshall* (1783) 1 Leach 263; Langbein (1983(i)), pp. 102–105.

[32] See below, pp. 620–621.

Once the evidence was completed and the accused had made any statement he chose,[33] it was for the judge to direct the jury, making his view of the case as plain as he felt inclined.[34] It was, however, the jury which had the ultimate power to decide whether or not to convict, for the Restoration judges had seen fit to surrender their power to imprison a jury which refused to convict.[35] It was a signal concession which libertarian writers had soon erected into an ultimate bulwark of the constitution.

Juries were a major form of rotational government, but the process of selection made it likely that there would be members who already had experience of the duties. In the main they understood the upshot of their verdicts, whether or not the judge chose to spell it out.[36] In a case of theft, if they convicted of "aggravated" larceny, the offence was capital, though a pardon might afterwards be granted, often on condition of transportation; if they found grand larceny, (theft to the value of a shilling or more), the punishment was transportation to the American colonies; if they found only petty larceny, it was for the judge to decide upon transportation or a whipping. Accordingly a jury might ameliorate a sentence by deliberately undervaluing what had been stolen. This "pious perjury" was an accepted part of their function in dealing with the general run of property crime.[37] For other more serious charges the scope for manoeuvre was not so broad, but still there remained the power to acquit, which was used with considerable frequency.[38]

At the end of the criminal session the convicts were brought up for sentencing. [39] Those convicted of non-clergyable felonies would be condemned to death, but the judge would then proceed to reprieve a substantial proportion of them. This was in form a recommendation to the King-in-Cabinet, but it was decisive for most of the pardons the King subsequently granted.[40] There were in addition also a trickle of cases where petitions from "friends" succeeded in securing

---

[33] This statement was, of course, unsworn, since the accused was not a competent witness under oath and would remain excluded until 1898: see below, pp. 618–619.

[34] The judge might direct an acquittal, *inter alia*, by adopting a limited interpretation of the statute said to have been offended. This "equitable" or "merciful" tendency was particularly manifest over the less serious non-clergyable offences: see J. Hall, *Theft, Law and Society* (1952), pp. 87–95; Radzinowicz (1948), I pp. 83–91, App. 1.

[35] The power to imprison recalcitrant juries had been foresworn in the trial of the Quakers, Penn and Mead: see above, pp. 19–20.

[36] For the social composition and method of selection at Assizes and Quarter Sessions, see esp. Beattie's evidence for Surrey: (1986), pp. 378–395. It was common practice to have a jury hear a succession of quick trials before returning verdicts on each accused: pp. 395–399.

[37] See Blackstone, *Commentaries*, IV, 239; Beattie (1986), pp. 419–430; and for a French observer's acute account of the practice: M. Cottu, *On the Administration of the Criminal Code in England* (1820).

[38] Beattie (1986), pp. 406–419.

[39] Before sentence, the allocution afforded the defendant his opportunity to claim benefit of clergy, or to raise a motion in arrest of judgment, *e.g.*, by way of objection to the indictment: see Baker in Cockburn (1977), pp. 41–42. A woman whose pregnancy was confirmed by a jury of matrons would be reprieved from execution at least until the birth of the child (and mostly, it would seem, for good).

[40] On the process, see esp. Radzinowicz (1948), I Chap. 4; Langbein (1983(i)), pp. 5–10, 18–21.

royal clemency,[41] but only after the judge had been given an opportunity to comment. If the judge was dissatisfied with the convictions, he might propose a free pardon. Much more likely it would be a pardon conditional upon transportation.[42] Typically this might be either because the offence was against property only, without any element of personal violence, or because there was something to be said for the defendant—an innocent led astray, a person with a credible character witness, a youngster, a pauper overwhelmed by temptation. By contrast, the shiftless vagrant, the gang-leader, the pimp or brothel-keeper, the incorrigible offender—these were the people to be made an example of on the scaffold, if their offence warranted it or if a wave of fear called for a tough demonstration of authority's power.[43]

VI. Defining the Law

Criminal process contained no effective machinery for referring general issues of law from assizes or quarter sessions to an appellate bench. This helps to account for the amorphous condition of much of the substantive law, particularly at the level of general principle. In addition, so long as counsel were rare participants, there was no incentive for reports to appear of points decided at trial.[44] Some judges kept private notes of their decisions and during the eighteenth century these were assembled into a repository which passed down the line of Chief Justices.[45] Not till the last decades of the century did reports from criminal assizes begin; and soon after came the first text collations of the subject, which drew on the reports in the private sources, as well as the classic writers and the great bulk of statutory material, much of it concerned to specify exactly which types of felony were non-clergyable.

Nonetheless the criminal law did gradually acquire some firmer underpinning but by no means necessarily so as to extend the range of its operation. The most striking illustration of this caution concerned attempts to expand the range of the property offences beyond the standard notions of theft and malicious damage. Where one person entrusted his money or property to another, or where he was induced to transfer it to the other by some deception, and in either case the upshot was a defalcation, it was difficult to find a basis for criminal, as distinct from civil, liability. The longest standing exception made it larceny for a servant or carrier to "break bulk" and misappropriate parts of what was given into his possession.[46] But this notion was not

---

[41] Hence the controversy generated by Hay: for which see below, p. 566ff. Gentlemen also intervened occasionally to oppose a pardon: Beattie (1986), pp. 444–445.

[42] The usual period was fourteen years: Radzinowicz (1948), I p. 113 has examples.

[43] For the factors which were likely to sway decisions, see Radzinowicz (1948), I, pp. 114–118; Langbein (1983(ii)); P. King (1984) 27 Hist.J. 42; Beattie (1986), pp. 430–449; cf. Hay in Hay et al. (1975), pp. 43–49.

[44] The fact that the defendant's plea was reserved until the trial left no scope for the development of an exchange of written pleadings: see generally, S. F. C. Milsom, *Historical Foundations of the Common Law* (2nd ed., 1981) Chap. 14.

[45] See the preface to the first of the new texts, Sir E. H. East, *Pleas of the Crown* (1803), pp. v–xv.

[46] See, e.g., J. Hall, *Theft, Law and Society* (2nd ed., 1952) Chaps. 1, 2.

easily expanded. In the early modern period, it is true, cheating had also become a common law misdemeanour.[47] But in 1761, Lord Mansfield insisted that there must be some element of public danger for there to be any offence: the trader who regularly used false scales was liable, but the seller who supplied less than full quantity on a single occasion was not.[48]

Twenty years later, this caution did begin to crumble: the hirer of a horse who from the outset meant to sell it off became liable for "larceny by a trick"; but this was at once limited so as to cover only a case of hiring and not one where the initial owner was duped into conferring ownership on the trickster.[49] Then the latter situation was argued to be within a general provision of the statute regulating pawnbrokers which the Fieldings had inspired in 1757.[50] King's Bench were prepared to accept that this misdemeanour of obtaining goods by false pretences did not require proof of public danger in the same way as cheating at common law.[51] But again there was considerable concern lest any deliberate breach of contract should ground the new offence and the crime was held not to arise in the case of extravagant puffs for goods or of statements about future intention.[52] Like the scrupulousless over form, this was something more complex than just a cynical insistence on the virtues of "legality." That may have been one convenient consequence, just as adherence to established precedent was a natural principle of common law technique. But there were other reasons enough: in a system without legal representation many allegations about transactional frauds and misappropriations set the prosecutor's version of events against whatever story the defendant managed to produce. One reason why the "breaking bulk" exception had emerged early was probably that the act of pillage left its independent evidence as a manifestation of criminality. Quite apart from this, in a world that thrived on self-sufficiency, victims were encouraged to look out for themselves. Why indeed, should the state do more than provide a civil remedy against a trickster—a process which in any event included a power of mesne arrest?[53]

VII. CHARACTERISING THE SYSTEM

What ultimately is to be made of the pre-industrial scheme of criminal justice? In Douglas Hay's mordant view, it dressed actions of the state that were grossly arbitrary in the trappings of impartial legality, thereby playing upon two emotional nerve-centres—terrible fear (of

---

[47] See *R. v. Ward* (1727) 2 Ld. Raym. 1462, generalising a statute of 1542 (33 Hen. VIII, c. 1).

[48] *R. v. Wheatley* (1761) 2 Burr. 1125.

[49] *R. v. Pear* (1780) 1 Leach 211; *R. v. Harvey* (1787) 1 Leach 467; *R. v. Parkes* (1793) 2 Leach 614.

[50] See 30 Geo. II, c. 30, s.1.

[51] *R. v. Young* (1788) 1 Leach 505.

[52] See, *e.g.*, *R. v. Goodhall* (1821) R. & R. 461; *R. v. Roebuck* (1855) Dears. & B. 24; *cf. R. v. Pywell* (1816) 1 Stark. 402; *R. v. Codrington* (1825) 1 C. & P. 661.

[53] For an over-emphatic exploration of this theme, G. Fletcher (1976) 89 Harv.L.R. 469; *cf.* Weinreb (1980) 90 Yale L.J. 294, with reply, *ibid.* 319.

the death penalty) and servile gratitude (for merciful forgiveness). In this it is seen to typify the wider social relations between patrician elite and common people.[54] Most historians who have since written on the subject have acknowledged that Hay has provided a significant perspective.[55] It is useful in particular in correcting versions of the longer history, such as Radzinowicz's, which see eighteenth century practice simply as outmoded and negligent, and accordingly ripe for a modernisation that was both more just and more humane.[56] Yet, save for those who insist that criminal justice is mere superstructure given over to the preservation of property within capitalism, the picture must be moderated. It has also to take account of several salient features which explain why, in most of the country, the "amateur" system of criminal justice could continue on for so long with only interstitial change.

First, the age in which Parliaments cavalierly increased the range of capital offences, was equally a period in which the rate of prosecution for most crimes had fallen noticeably. The homicide rate was certainly much lower than in medieval times. Even the prosecution rate for theft and associated property offences, until recently thought to have risen with the advance of capitalism, seems rather to have declined in many places. In early modern England, aside from London and the next largest towns, great stretches of the country had reached an equilibrium which left formal enforcement of the criminal law an occasional, even marginal, activity, with increases only in periods of particular dearth or disruption.

How this had come to be admits of many explanations. Important among them must be counted the myriad vertical ties in the social structure, landlord over tenant, farmer over labourer, master over servant, poor-law overseer over recipient, parson over parish, squire over village. In particular, the increasing use of the poor law regime to police vagrancy and to contain the worst effects of destitution is likely both to have prevented property crime and to have reduced the need to deal with offenders by prosecution.

Second, a system which depended mainly on the efforts of individual victims, sustained to some extent by the justices and lesser amateurs, inevitably reflected the values of the community rather then just those of the landed governors. It is clear from lists of prosecutors at assizes and quarter sessions that those who made use of the system were a wide cross-section of the whole: relatively few came from aristocracy and gentry, the great bulk from the farming tenantry and small-traders, together with a not inconsiderable number of labourers.[57] This is only to be expected. Great wealth lay primarily in sources of income—in rents, investments, the profits of office. It was the lesser owners—of livestock and grain, tools and manufacturers, money in purses and under beds—who were commonly exposed to

---

[54] In Hay et al. (1975) Chap. 1.

[55] Note, however, J. H. Langbein (1982), who accuses Hay of performing the "legitimation trick," whereby whatever happened, aggressive or circumspect, is explained as evidencing the determination of the governing class to impress its authority.

[56] See Sharpe (1983), pp. 57–63; Beattie (1986), pp. 107–112; cf. B. Lenman and G. Parker in Gatrell et al, (1980) Chap. 2; Jones (1982), pp. 3–8.

[57] P. King (1984) 27 Hist.J. 25; Langbein (1983(ii)); Beattie (1986), pp. 192–198.

direct predacity. People in the middling and lesser ranks needed recourse to the protective discipline of the criminal law and some of them felt obliged to devote very considerable efforts towards its workings. Third, if the system operated to bring only occasional criminals to justice and even fewer to actual execution, the choice of those to suffer was by no means at the whim of the influential. Certainly, criminals who could call upon the words of a well-placed "friend" would not hesitate to do so. But it is clear that the question of pardon from a death sentence depended much more upon the assessment of the judge; and he was likely to look broadly for the sort of factors which still today go to mitigate sentence: ill-fortune, mental stress, passing lapse from general righteousness and so on.[58] He might have little go go on, and not be prepared to spend long on the question, but the outcome was not wholly haphazard.

Finally, for all the parading and sermonising that accompanied trials and executions, the operation of the criminal law remained essentially reactive. It was not a deliberate reign of terror which can so easily evolve where an alien government is striving to impose its authority on a resistant populace, as MacFarlane has sought to show.[59] On the contrary the community was already peaceable enough to be able to contain most of its tensions by its own efforts. Its governing class and their lesser supporters had the confidence, underpinned as it was by such a variety of economic buttresses, to deal with social unrest and general crime as one commitment of this station in life.[60] It was at points where economic advance was already transforming social existence—notably in the towns and along the trade routes—that the traditional system was least adequate, for it was there that the absence of vigilance through employment, religion, expectations of "friendship" and the like, was most plainly felt. There, accordingly, began the demand that the state take over the imposition of civil order from the community. After 1800, the new trend was coming to appear irresistible. Its course is certainly the dominant feature of the next part of this Chapter.

PART 2: CRIMINAL JUSTICE TRANSFORMED

I. THE BECCARIAN STRATEGY

In a prodigious essay of 1764 the young Count Beccaria put the case for change before the states of Europe in terms largely utilitarian.[61]

---

[58] See above, pp. 564–565.

[59] *The Justice and the Mare's Ale* (1981), pp. 173–200.

[60] See Munsche, above, p. 547, n. 22; contrast, *e.g.*, the outbreaks of poaching and destruction which followed suppression of the agricultural riots of 1830: A. Peacock in J. P. D. Dunbabin, *Rural Discontent in Nineteenth Century Britain* (1974); Jones (1982) Chap. 3.

[61] *Dei Delitti e delle Pene*; appearing in English as *Of Crimes and Punishments* in 1767 or 1768; for his influence in Continental Europe, see Radzinowicz (1948) I Chap. 9; and generally, C. Phillipson, *Three Criminal Law Reformers* (1923) Pt. I. Beccaria's debt to Montesquieu was considerable.

Crime was not being prevented, so he argued, by the occasional exaction of exaggerated penalties, such as public killing or mutilation. Punishments needed to be of moderate proportion, and to be imposed by law rather than judicial discretion. Beccaria's revulsion against gross exemplarity was, however, not just a psychological perception of how the calculus of pains and pleasures operated upon others; behind it lay the retributive ideal by which punishments ought to be proportionate to crimes and criminals ought to suffer for their wrongs, but should not be sacrificed purely as a means of deterring others.

In England Beccaria's ideas attracted a number of influential writers, including Blackstone[62] William Eden, Samuel Romilly and Jeremy Bentham.[63] Though this early interest would be deflected by the years of war with France, it would lead eventually to a major change on both the policing and the punishment side of the balance: full-time, paid police would be installed, first in London, then in the municipal boroughs and finally in the counties. In place of capital punishment for all the most serious offences, would come renewed use of transportation, and increasingly also a willingness to imprison at home, which would in time breed penal servitude as a replacement for transportation. These were complex shifts which, as respects policing, aroused all the English gentleman's liberal sensibilities. The arguments tended therefore to concentrate upon the techniques of punishment and these will accordingly be our starting point. Among them, repeal of the "Bloody Code" would come to occupy a position of great prominence. But even the issue of the death penalty was dependent upon the organisation of viable "secondary punishments." It is these which form the true connecting link with the previous period.

II. PUNISHMENTS

(a) The Drive for Imprisonment

The formula of locking up in order to set to work had been used since the Elizabethan era in dealing with rogues, vagabonds and lesser vagrants, and in the eighteenth century there had been experiments with Houses of Industry for the discipline of all the able-

---

[62] In the *Commentaries*, Book IV, Blackstone adopted a far less complacent view of the condition of English criminal law than pervades his account of civil obligation.

[63] Eden produced his *Principles of Penal Law* in 1771 at the age of 26; Romilly his *Observations* in 1786 at 28 (these latter were in response to Madan's *Thoughts on Executive Justice*—for which see below, p. 574). During these years, there were distinct signs of restiveness in Parliament and elsewhere over the unthinking extension of the death penalty to new crimes. e.g., the Commons Committee on Capital Offences, (1771) J.H.C. XXXIII 365. See Radzinowicz (1948) 1 Chaps. 10, 11, 13–15; and on Romilly and Bentham, C. Phillipson (above, n. 61) Pts. II, III. Bentham's first major publication on the issues came as part of his *Introduction to the Principles of Morals and Legislation* (1789).

bodied seeking poor relief.[64] The coalescing of the houses of correction and the local gaols, which occured in many places, demonstrated an elision of thought which opened the possibility of subjecting the general run of criminals to reformatory discipline. Such a prison could become an outcrop in the "carcerial archipelagoes," which have been charted in high relief for much of Europe by Michel Foucault,[65] and which are undoubtedly characteristic of the social policies of governments facing rapid industrialisation.[66]

In England it is in the 1770's and 1780's that a new belief in the punitive prison began to catch attention, as we have already had occasion to note. As with the contemporaneous faith in workhouses for the relief of poverty, it would attract only a coterie of adherents. But their inspiration would smoulder on for a couple of generations, before bursting into unquenchable flame. John Howard, whose *The State of the Prisons* (1777) fired the new movement, was by nature an ascetic disciplinarian, responsive to the evangelical stirrings around him.[67] His proposals for reforming the neglected, overparted lock-ups around the country were directed to turning them into institutions for the conditioning of men and women who must be changed. There must be a place for regular, supervised work, with provision for separate arrangements for sleeping in the interests of health, sexual decency and "non-contamination," and enough food and clothing to make the strict regime endurable. But the punitive nature of the regime was never to be forgotten, for that was its whole purpose. Even as the book was in the writing, the Duke of Richmond began rebuilding the Sussex county gaol at Horsham with provision for separate confinement by day as well as night.[68] And when later the House of Correction was also remodelled their reputation became so fearsome that the intake was said to have been halved.[69]

In 1779, Howard, with Eden and Blackstone, did much to promote the Act for setting up two national penitentiaries, one for men and one for women. These were to provide some permanent establishment in which convicts reprieved from the gallows could serve out sentences.[70] Separate confinement was to be provided, with labour of the "hardest, most servile kind," so that the work could not be spoiled. Nonetheless it was to be useful—sawing stone, polishing marble, beating hemp, rasping wood, chopping rags and the like.[71] The warders would be salaried and carefully supervised, so as to eli-

---

[64] Above, pp. 421–422. For an attempt to relate this form of punishment to emergent modes of capitalist production, G. Rusche and O. Kirchheimer, *Punishment and Social Structure* (1939).

[65] Notably in *Discipline and Punish* (English translation, 1977); the long development of the incarceration idea in England suggests an over-dramatic quality in Foucault's presentation of the shift in perception: see P. Spierenburg, *The Spectacle of Suffering* (1984), pp. viii–ix and Chap. 12.

[66] For this theme in Anglo-American context, G. Himmelfarb, *Victorian Minds* (1970), p. 32.

[67] See esp. M. Ignatieff (1978), pp. 47–57; and, in variation of Foucault, in D. Sugarman (ed.) *Legality, Ideology and the State* (1983) Chap. 8; R. Morgan (1977) 62 Hist. 388.

[68] Howard had criticised its condition before a Select Committee in 1774.

[69] See Webb (1922), p. 54; McConville (1981), pp. 89–98.

[70] 19 Geo. III, c. 74, a pallid reflection of its planners' original intentions.

[71] s.24; the Act also provided for a three-stage system, rewards for meritorious work and even remission by an assize judge: see ss.24, 38–39, 45, 47, 49.

minate the old corrupt relationships between keepers and their charges.

So novel a plan ran into Treasury opposition and other difficulties, and once it was decided to start transportation afresh, it came to nothing.[72] In 1794, its place was eventually taken by the government's agreement with Bentham that he should construct and run a penitentiary in accordance with his Panopticon model.[73] This too became the subject of long delays and prevarications until eventually the Holford Select Committee in 1811 reported in favour of a different project and a disillusioned Bentham was left with a solatium of £23,000 for his efforts.[74]

At least this continuing interest of the central government in reformed prisons gave some stimulus to the justices to alter the structure and administration of local gaols. This would occur in a few places, such as Reading and Dorchester. At Southwell the Revd. Thomas Becher was responsible for a well-publicised adaptation of the Nottinghamshire House of Correction, which made disciplined useful labour the central activity and allowed earnings to prisoners during their term and on release, all in the hope of installing a sense of worthwhile occupation.[75] In Gloucester, Sir George Onesiphorus Paul saw to the building of a penitentiary and five houses of correction which aimed at a fearsome evangelical target: by subjecting an inmate to a largely solitary existence removed from all moral contamination, he or she would be brought to a Christian conversion and so to inmost repentance. In this, prison work was meant to play only a secondary part—as a relief from the dreadful tedium of separation, just as in life it must be understood as the one hedge against destitution and despair.[76] In practice this regime proved very difficult to operate. After twenty years of unremitting effort, Paul was obliged to recognise that without his personal drive the Gloucester prison was likely to relapse into its former condition. While the first generation of prison reformers had engaged in fervent debate and a degree of experimentation, they nonetheless appeared to be hammering against a wall of unconcern and venality. As their impact continued so small, their enthusiasm inevitably waned. Theirs was a pre-echo of a great blast still to come.

(b) Transportation Reformed: Australian and other Colonies

As we have noted already, any real interest in penitentiaries at the national level was deflected by the revival of transportation. The suspension caused by the American war, and resort to the hulks, served to reduce earlier doubts about a system which relieved society of its

---

[72] See McConville (1981), pp. 107–111; Harding *et al* (1985), pp. 117–119.
[73] His completed ideas appeared in the tract *Panopticon. Or, the Inspection House* (1791) (*Works* (1843), IV p. 43). See R. Evans, *The Fabrication of Virtue* (1982).
[74] The tortured story is traced by L. J. Hume (1973) 61 Hist.St. 703, (1974) 62 Hist.St. 36. For the Holford Committee and the building of Millbank prison, see below, pp. 578–579.
[75] Webb (1922), pp. 60–62; McConville (1981), pp. 116–117.
[76] Webb (1922), pp. 56–60; E . A. L. Moir in H. P. R. Finberg, *Gloucestershire Studies* (1957); Ignatieff (1978), pp. 103–109; McConville (1981), pp. 98–104.

most troublesome elements.[77] In consequence the government dith-
ered on the penitentiary project and canvassed various places in the
West Indies and on the African coast as penal settlements. Eventually, Australia's East coast was selected.[78] Trading prospects and
colonial rivalries probably played some part in this choice, but the
immediate dictate of policy was the stock-pile of convicts.[79]

The whole venture had of necessity to be undertaken by the
government. The complements of soldiers and prisoners who set
forth in the first fleet of 1787 survived the initial stages of settlement
in New South Wales only with immense difficulty; but the experiment gradually pulled through. Convicts from all over the British
Isles began to be despatched regularly and their labour was used to
build up the colony—under government direction, and then in conjunction with the energies of free settlers.[80] Maintaining discipline
and preventing escape were major hazards for the administrators
throughout this phase of transportation. The punishments that were
the only resort at the outset—lashings and harsh labour in chain
gangs—would later have added to them the threat of transfer to
special penal settlements for the refractory.[81] As the economy
expanded, inducements to good behaviour could be added: grants of
land to those whose sentences were expiring, remission of sentences
by the grant of tickets-of-leave, and during sentence, assignment to
private masters as domestic servants or labourers. Under the gover-
norship of Macquarie (1809–1821) these routes towards emancipation
developed considerably, particularly as he succeeded in raising the
permitted rate of free immigration.[82]

By 1820, after some 30 years of growth, 20,000 transportees had
been sent to New South Wales, and over the next 20 years, more than
80,000 would follow.[83] In the life of the colony, the penal establishment was becoming part of a more complex history, but for the criminal law system at home it allowed a resumption of eighteenth
century method, though at a public cost substantially greater than
transportation to the American colonies had ever been. Questions of
expense would keep a curb on the numbers actually despatched. One
reason why the hulks continued their dreary existence not only as the
staging post for those actually transported but also as a prison for

---

[77] A Commons Committee in 1779 voiced the demand: J.H.C. XXXVI 310.

[78] 24 Geo. III, c. 56 gave the general authority, and another Commons Committee continued to press: J.H.C. 1785 XL 954, 1161: see Shaw (1966) Chap. 2; Hughes (1987)
56–77. For the relationship of transportation to the general history of the new colonies,
C. M. H. Clark, History of Australia (1962–1973), I–III. For the grave difficulties of establishing a judicial system, A. C. Castles, Australian Legal History (1981) Chap. 1.

[79] There is little hard evidence that larger considerations played any direct role: Clark
(above n. 78) I pp. 69–70; Shaw (1966), pp. 49–57; but cf. Blainey, The Tyranny of Distance (1966), pp. 24–26.

[80] Shaw (1966) Chap. 3; Hughes (1987) Chap. 4.

[81] Of these, the most notorious were Port Arthur in Van Diemen's Land, Moreton Bay
(later the site of Brisbane) and Norfolk Island: Shaw (1966), pp. 203–216; Hughes
(1987) Chap. 13.

[82] Shaw (1966) Chap. 4; Hughes (1987) Chap. 9. During this period, the British took
little enough interest in the venture, though there was a review by Select Committee
in 1812: P.P. 1812 (341) II.

[83] For the numbers overall, and break-down by sex and country of origin, Shaw (1966)
App.

those kept behind was that they were irresistibly cheap.[84] But finance was not the real root of an increasingly vociferous debate over transportation. Macquarie's administration became ensnared in battles with leading colonists and these raised in the home country a growing unease that the punishment might be positively sought by the hopeless and destitute as the one chance to survive.[85]

In 1819, a Commissioner, J. T. Bigge, was despatched to New South Wales to investigate with a view to tightening up the penal administration. His first report was severely critical of Macquarie and to some degree the governors who succeeded him toughened their practice.[86] Yet much of what he had instituted remained essential to the system. Free emigration continued to grow and the demand for cheap labour was still met by allowing colonists with some capital to take assigned convicts "off the store." How they then fared differed from master to master, and this inequality of treatment featured prominently in the utilitarian critique of the system. The ticket-of-leave for good behaviour was also retained, the normal practice by 1830 being that a transportee for seven years got his ticket after four, the transportee for fourteen years after six, and the transportee for life after eight.[87] Opinion in the colony became more sharply divided between those whose interest lay in continuing the supply of convict and ex-convict labour and those who wanted to see the country emancipated from the shackles of penal administration so as to develop into an independent, self-respecting community.[88]

The conflicting desires were not much appreciated in England. A number of witnesses from Australia tried to explain them to the Molesworth Select Committee of 1837, but the Committee, which included Lord John Russell (the Home Secretary), argued against the existing system in the terms taught by Bentham.[89] Apart from a host of incidental abuses, it was inevitable that some masters would prove too hard, others too soft. If they treated their assignees with consideration they might hope for some diligence and respect; if they did not, they could become slave-masters embroiled in a running battle to subdue insubordination, drunkenness and crime. Whatever the consequences for the colonial economy, the Committee recommended that in future convicts would be put to gang labour in public works such as road-building. Moreover, the Committee did not doubt the superiority of imprisonment at home and proposed that transportation to New South Wales should cease.[90] This recom-

---

[84] Accordingly the hulks survived occasional outbursts of concern over their dreadful conditions, as by the Select Committee on Secondary Punishments: P.P. 1831–1832 (547) VII, pp. 12–16; and that on Gaols and Houses of Correction (H.L.): 3rd Report 1835 (440) XII, pp. iv–v. However, transportation did remain cheaper than building model prisons.

[85] Shaw (1966), pp. 101–106.

[86] P.P. 1822 (448) XX; Shaw (1966) Chap. 9.

[87] Shaw (1966), pp. 229–231.

[88] See generally Shaw (1966) Chaps. 10, 11; Hughes (1987) Chap. 12.

[89] The young Sir William Molesworth was an ardent Benthamite and seems to have been chosen by Russell after he had made up his own mind that there must be great change. Also on the Committee was Lord Howick (Earl Grey), who as Colonial Secretary would preside over the dismantling of the system.

[90] P.P. 1837 (518) XIX; Shaw (1966), pp. 266–274; Hughes (1987), pp. 493–498.

mendation Melbourne's government put into effect in 1840, a last contribution of the post-Reform whigs to change in the criminal system.

It was by no means the end of the whole system. A number of further experiments would be tried—notably the "probation" system thought up by Peel's Colonial Secretary, Stanley, with its stages of seclusion, gang labour and pass to work for wages outside. Here was a parallel to the regimen for long-term prisoners at home, to which we shall return later.[91] The new burden had to be borne by Van Diemen's Land (Tasmania), a decision which within six years had so overwhelmed the resources of the island that transportation there had to be suspended.[92] In the succeeding years, while Earl Grey at the Colonial Office was searching with little success for other colonies to which convicts could ultimately be exiled, his cousin, Sir George Grey, at the Home Office, was driving forward the national prison building campaign. Early in the next decade, orthodox opinion gave up its faith in the dread of banishment across the globe.

By 1853 legislation was in place for long-term "penal servitude" at home.[93] Some transportation would continue for a time to Western Australia and to hulks in Gibraltar and Bermuda. But the whole system would be wound up in 1868.[94] Three-fifths of all convicts sent to Australia went after 1830. That bald statistic suggests the crucial role of transportation in altering attitudes to the death penalty. For, as we shall now see, it was around that date that the main decisions to give up the awful threat of the supreme penalty were taken.

(c) The reduction of capital punishment

Under eighteenth century conditions, those who debated capital punishment for serious crime remained much preoccupied with questions of deterrence.[95] Should the ultimate penalty be more regularly extracted, as Henry Fielding argued during the upsurge of crime after 1748?[96] Or should occasional examples suffice? In the crime surge of the 1780s, the Rev. Martin Madan,[97] demanded the elimination of all reprieves, while Archdeacon William Paley became the popular exponent of exemplarism.[98]

But the basic premises shifted as the practicalities of the moment and the arguments of the Beccarians led to the revival of transportation and the beginnings of long-term imprisonment. Once the Australian experiment was properly under way, the proportion of

---

[91] See below, p. 583.

[92] Shaw (1966) Chap. 13.

[93] 16 & 17 Vict., c. 99; and see below, pp. 583–585.

[94] Shaw (1966) Chap. 15.

[95] For a full analysis, see Radzinowicz (1948), I Chaps. 8, 12; also J. Heath, *Eighteenth Century Penal Theory* (1963).

[96] His celebrated *Inquiry into the Causes of the late Increase of Robbers* (1750) also argued strongly for better organisation of policing, a call which was taken up by an ensuing Commons Committee. That Committee however was not happy with the proliferation of capital statutes and did not press for more frequent executions.

[97] *Thoughts on Executive Justice* (1785); Radzinowicz (1948), I pp. 239–248.

[98] *Principles of Moral and Political Philosophy* (1785) VI, Chap. 9; Radzinowicz (1948), I pp. 248–259.

those actually executed after capital conviction began to fall away. Paley, with his case for occasional exaction, came to be much vaunted by those who administered the current policy.[99] However, the prospect of formally abandoning the death penalty, at least for property crimes, would be resisted through the first two decades of the new century. Sir Samuel Romilly, the leader of the abolitionists, attributed this above all to the tensions engendered by the French Revolution and the wars, which in his view infused many with a "stupid dread of innovation" and a "savage spirit."[1] Romilly kept the issue before Parliament with a succession of bills seeking to remove the death penalty from offences for which it was least justified. But his two successes, in 1808 and 1811, acted mainly as warnings to his opponents not to relax their guard.[2] No matter how assiduously he constructed a utilitarian case to show the ineffectiveness of the death penalty as a deterrent—pointing up the reluctance to prosecute, the loopholes in trial procedure, the extent of commutation—there were those who insisted that any relaxation of the existing regime would undermine the whole edifice of authority.[3] They were led in the Lords by several of the bishops, and by the Lord Chancellor and the Chief Justice of the King's Bench (Eldon and Ellenborough); the latter claimed to speak for the whole bench of judges and asserted that on a law reform issue they must first be consulted.[4]

In the years after 1815, the mood shifted and the debate began to acquire resonances of larger political tensions. Those who were amassing the newest forms of wealth did not view the haphazard brutalities of the existing system as an adequate means of putting down crime and increasingly they were worried by the purloining of their manufactures and the forgery of bills, warrants and other commercial paper. The petitions of factory owners, bankers and insurer's, which poured in upon Parliament, demanded that the death penalty be given up and adequate policing be instituted instead.[5] After Romilly's untimely death in 1818, leadership of the reformers was taken up by Mackintosh and Fowell Buxton. In 1819 Mackintosh secured a Commons Select Committee inquiring into the Criminal Laws and became its chairman.[6] Like Romilly, the Committee eschewed large moral arguments. It built up the case against the present law with a use of statistics that was quite novel. Attorneys, magistrates, prison chaplains and gaol keepers were called to give evidence of current inadequacies. The judges were not consulted, the excuse being that their position precluded them from offering criticism.[7] The Report was the first mature demonstration of

[99] His authority was such that even in 1835 the Criminal Law Commissioners were obliged to mount a sturdy assault upon it: see below, n. 17.

[1] P. Medd, *Romilly* (1968), p. 215.

[2] 48 Geo. III, c. 129 (pick-pocketing—but Romilly had to accept transportation for life as the substitute); 51 Geo. III, c. 39–41 (stealing from bleaching grounds—supported by petitions from owners of grounds).

[3] See esp. P.D. 1811 XI, App. 1–43; Radzinowicz (1948), I pp. 322–331 and Chap. 16.

[4] J N J Palmer (1976) 3 B.J. Law & Soc. 1.

[5] P.D. 1811 XIX App. 87–122; Radzinowicz (1948), I pp. 506–511.

[6] For its Report, P.P. 1819 (585) VIII; Radzinowicz (1948), I pp. 526–551.

[7] Only the retired Chief Baron, Macdonald, was consulted—as a known supporter of reform.

a proselytising strategy that Benthamites were to make peculiarly their own in the decades of Reform.

In the Committee's view, capital punishment should be removed from numerous (though by no means all) property offences, including the notorious Waltham Black Act, and such varied offences as abducting a woman, failing to surrender as a bankrupt and being found disguised in the Mint. Their list included the three forms of aggravated theft which for so long had been the centre of Romilly's efforts—shoplifting to the value of 5s., stealing from a dwelling house and stealing from a vessel to the value of 40s. But for all this, Mackintosh and Buxton were without real strength in Parliament. All that came of a series of Bills was that the limit on the shoplifting offence was raised to 15s. and a few innocuous crimes were removed from the capital panopoly. But Mackintosh's Forgery Bill was persistently whittled down by opposition from the law officers and others and even so was voted out by surprise.[8]

As with the question of police, it was Peel's arrival at the Home Office in 1822 which shifted the political balance. He appreciated that some reduction in the capital statutes was a necessary part of the package of modifications on which he was determined and something on which he might make quick progress. He opened conciliatory discussions with the judges and found a positive ally in Ellenborough's successor, Lord Tenterden.[9] Already in 1823, he could secure the substitution of transportation or imprisonment for shoplifting and stealing above 40s. from ships; and similarly in various statutes concerned with malicious damage and sending threatening letters.[10] Assaulting a customs officer and other revenue and quarantine offences ceased to be a capital in 1825. Two years later larceny from a dwelling house became capital only at the value of £5, while capital burglary and housebreaking were confined to entry into a dwelling house or its connected buildings, not merely its "curtilage."[11] At the same time, benefit of clergy was abolished, and its distinction between first and subsequent offenders, ceased not to be so important.[12]

These then were significant moderations. Furthermore they took place beside a series of statutes designed to consolidate, clarify and modernise enactments on serious crime, which over time had become an incoherent morass.[13] But Peel was intent on the type of conservative adaptation which to him needed to become the very talisman of Tory policy. In his bill on forgery in 1830 he was prepared to lift capital punishments only from its less threatening forms; he

[8] 1 Geo. IV, c. 115, 117; Radzinowicz (1948), I pp. 551–566.

[9] Radzinowicz (1948), I Chap. 18.

[10] 4 Geo. IV, c. 53, 54. The latter repealed the Waltham Black Act, save for two provisions which would be carried into the malicious injuries consolidation, 7 & 8 Geo. IV, c. 31.

[11] 6 Geo. IV, c. 78, 7 & 8 Geo. IV, c. 29 (larceny consolidation: ss.6, 7).

[12] Crimes that were previously non-clergyable remained capital; those that were clergyable became punishable with seven years' transportation or up to two years' imprisonment: 7 & 8 Geo. IV, c. 28, ss.6, 7; and note the abolition of the distinction between grand and petty larceny: 7 & 8 Geo. IV, c. 29, s.2.

[13] As well as the three mentioned in nn. 10 and 11 above, there was 9 Geo. IV, c. 31—offences against the person.

would retain it for the forgery of securities representing money, wills of personalty and the seals of the realm and for false entries relating to public stock. Mackintosh and his associates, supported by massive petitions from bankers and others who said the current law was virtually unenforceable, steered amendments through the Commons. But they were defeated in the Lords, where Peel had the support of Tenterden and the Lord Chancellor, Lyndhurst.[14]

Here then was an issue on which the radical wing of the reforming Whigs could mount a persistent campaign. It would lead first to the lifting of the penalty from most of the non-violent property crimes to which it still applied: coinage offences, sheep and cattle stealing, larceny from a dwelling-house, all forgeries save wills and powers of attorney to transfer stock (which had to be kept as a concession to the Lords).[15] But this remained action in the territory of punishments which unquestionably exceeded the limits of retribution. Beyond it lay robberies, piracies, rapes and other forms of actual or threatened physical violence; and beyond again the crime of murder. In 1833 a number of attempts to have violent property crimes made non-capital failed, but when Lord John Russell became Home Secretary in 1835 he put the matter to the Commissioners whom Brougham had set upon a Benthamic investigation of the criminal law.[16] They delivered a sustained attack on Paleyean ideas of exemplary punishment and proposed lifting the death penalty from most crimes of violence (robbery, burglary, arson and piracy in particular) where there were no aggravating circumstances.[17] Russell pushed through a whole series of enactments in implementation and in 1840 went so far as to have the death penalty removed from rape.[18]

Beccaria had long before taken the view that death was not an effective or justifiable punishment for murder and Bentham, for one, had been willing to follow him. By 1840 the radical campaigns had succeeded so far that abolition of the penalty even for the deliberate killing of another began to be widely advocated, attracting the persuasive pens of Dickens, Thackeray and even Carlyle. Many of the arguments would be repeated over the next century, though at this stage comparatively little was heard of the danger of hanging an innocent convict. But it was a matter on which literary and intellectual opinion ran counter to the root feeling of the respectable population and their political leaders. When, twenty years later, the question again arose upon the bills to consolidate the statutory criminal law, the death penalty was lifted from attempted murder and buggery; it was kept for murder, treason, piracy with wounding and arson of naval ships, stores and dockyards.[19] An ensuing Commission only served to confirm that this, in legal, medical, governmental and similar circles, was a necessary minimum. The

---

[14] 11 Geo. IV & 1 Will. IV, c. 66; Radzinowicz (1948), I pp. 590–595.

[15] 2 Will. IV, c. 34; 2 & 3 Will. IV, c. 62, 123; and also 3 & 4 Will. IV, c. 44 (housebreaking with larceny).

[16] For the Commission, see below, p. 599; for Russell's impact, Radzinowicz (1968), IV pp. 303–326.

[17] Second Report, P.P. 1836 [343] XXXVI.

[18] 7 Will. IV & 1 Vict., c. 84–89, 91; 4 & 5 Vict., c. 56; Radzinowicz (1968), IV pp. 316–326.

[19] Ibid., pp. 326–343.

Commission confined its recommendations for change principally to two: first, there should be a non-capital offence of infanticide (causing death of a child at birth or within seven days thereafter); secondly, executions should cease to be public spectacles and instead be confined behind prison walls.[20] Of these nothing was to be done in the short term about the former. Juries would continue to try and sometimes to convict mothers who killed their children at birth for murder. The judges mostly disliked having to pass the death sentence in these cases, even knowing that the chances of a reprieve were high (the power of reprieve, however, had passed in 1861 to the Home Secretary). It was to be their pressure which eventually saw to the creation of a separate non-capital crime of infanticide—but this would not be until 1922.[21] However, public execution—that macabre spectacle of the law's might—was replaced in 1868 by a hidden terror, the dreadful passing being signalled to the world by a notice and certificate on the prison door.[22] It was a change in which a certain fastidiousness mingled with concerns over crowd control. For executions all too easily generated the lurid excitement of the bullring. But equally the change had become possible though the great programme of prison building accomplished in the middle decades of the century. It is to that all-powerful thrust of policy that we must now turn.

(d) The Prison Triumphant

The great Victorian prisons—impenetrable Gothic fortresses louring over the county towns and cities—were mostly erected with an immense burst of energy in the decades after 1840. They represented a remarkable moral and financial commitment from both central and local government, the former charged with convicts sentenced to transportation (and later to penal servitude), the latter with those sentenced to simple imprisonment. We shall mention first the inter-relationships between these authorities. But then we shall come to the underlying clash of theories about the aims and organisation of imprisonment, which, far from leading to frustrated inaction, seemed at this juncture only to spur the whole enterprise forward.

In the age of Howard and his immediate followers, as noted earlier, the experiments with new prison treatments were a matter for local initiative, central government having been diverted from its penitentiary plan by the revival of transportation.[23] The enthusiasms of the Duke of Richmond, Becher, Paul and their adherents did not pass wholly away. In 1808, for instance, a Society for the Improvement of Prison Discipline was founded and received a second burst of life in 1816; and in that same year, the charismatic Elizabeth Fry began her transformation of the women's wards in Newgate Gaol into hives of

---

[20] P.P. 1866 [3590] XXI.
[21] See S. Davies in J. W. C. Turner and L. Radzinowicz, *The Modern Approach to Criminal Law* (1945), pp. 301–343.
[22] Radzinowicz (1968), IV pp. 343–353.
[23] See above, p. 569ff.

orderly industry.[24] But from this period increasingly it would be the Home Office which led and the justices who followed. In 1811, the Holford Select Committee recommended that the long-postponed national penitentiary be built on lines deriving from Becher and Paul, rather than from Bentham.[25] The construction of Millbank prison in accordance with this recommendation began in 1812. With it ended the Panoptical notion that visitors would ensure due administration by regular observation of the keepers. Prisons were to become closed against all save those charged with inspection or permitted to visit for some other reason. The general deterrence which prisons were unquestionably intended to promote was to be achieved by indirect repute rather than public display. There were many other aspects to the central programme for testing ideas of penal philosophy and practical management. To begin with they were concentrated upon Millbank, which opened in 1816 for the reception of those sentenced to transportation, and would serve as the only alternative to the hulks until the late 1830s.[26] At that point, as the future of transportation began seriously to be questioned, two further national prisons were begun, Parkhurst (Isle of Wight) for the reception of young offenders, and Pentonville (north London) for adult men.[27]

Alongside this, the Home Office sought to impose new standards and higher purpose on those responsible for the local gaols. By the 1860s, the campaign would ensure that these gaols were either converted from their eighteenth-century condition, or were closed down. But the movement was a gradual one, for there were few benches of justices ready to find the necessary funds for rebuilding their institutions. The process of raising standards began with an Act of 1815 which required that the gaoler be paid a salary.[28] This was followed by the Gaols Act 1823 (an early achievement of Peel's), which sought to place careful classification of prisoners at the centre of a reformed, severe discipline.[29] Then in 1835, four Home Office Inspectors of Prisons were appointed.[30] They were given little power to command—they were after all dealing with committees of J.P.s— but they had a wide brief to make investigations and to publish reports. Among the first appointees, two sturdy publicists from the Prison Disciplinary Society, William Crawford and the Rev. Whitworth Russell, were to have an uncompromising effect on the course of the debate about imprisonment as a punishment, not only at the

---

[24] For the founding and early years of the Society, including the close support of Mrs. Fry's Quaker connections, see Webb (1922), p. 72. For her work, *e.g.*, J. Kent, *Elizabeth Fry* (1962).

[25] First Report, P.P. 1810–1811 (199) III, see above, p. 571.

[26] A. Griffiths, *Memorials of Millbank* (1875); McConville (1981) Chap. 6.

[27] These were to accommodate prisoners undergoing the pre-transportation stage of Stanley's revised policy: see above, p. 574.

[28] 55 Geo. III, c. 50; McConville (1981), pp. 247–248.

[29] 4 Geo. IV, c. 64, following upon a Select Committee Report, P.P. 1822 (300) IV; Webb (1922), pp. 73–75; McConville (1981), pp. 248–250. It applied only to county prisons and those of the City of London, Westminster and 17 provincial towns, not to the three debtors' prisons of London or the 150 in the lesser boroughs and franchises.

[30] A Lords Committee, chaired by the veteran Duke of Richmond, favoured their creation: see generally the five Reports: P.P. 1835 (438–441) XI, XII; 5 & 6 Will. IV, c. 38.

local level but also in the central system itself.[31] Soon enough they were beginning to extend their power, for instance by acquiring the right to inspect the many gaols left outside Peel's Act and to prescribe prison rules and dietaries.[32]

Nevertheless, it would not be until 1865—after ten years of the penal servitude system and considerable public alarm about the release of major criminals back into the community—that the local authorities were required by statute to rebuild so as to provide separate accommodation and a regime of hard, demeaning labour.[33] Twelve years later it would prove possible to "nationalize" the local prisons entirely, placing them under Prison Commissioners who were responsible to the Home Secretary.[34] It was a unique transfer for its time and brought a ripple of protest from those who feared all extension of the central fiefdom. But it was one way of relieving the burden on the rural ratepayer, and to that Disraeli's government were firmly pledged.

Behind this changing pattern of administration lay intense debate about methods and objectives. It was conducted from three main redoubts, each of them positions which had been manned in earlier generations. The first adopted that limited social determinism which had long sustained the houses of correction: the inmates were to be subjected to the discipline of purposeful work; this would endeavour to fit them for release back into the labour force. It was a programme readily justified in utilitarian terms. Bentham argued for useful work executed in small groups, selected so as to reduce the risks of "contamination"; from the sale of products, the diligent convict would earn a share.[35] At Southwell, Becher actually organised a scheme with incentive payments of this kind.

For all her determination to organise the salvation of others, Elizabeth Fry shared much the same ideas about prison activity. The upsurge of prison visiting which she inspired spread her practices to many parts of the country. In the wake of this enthusiasm came Peel's Gaols Act, with its call for "constant employment and labour" in association, the prisoners being divided according to a simple, five-fold classification.[36] The 1820s must rank as the one decade in the nineteenth century when essentially optimistic notions of prisons as reformatories gained some real ground. Soon enough this enthusiasm would meet suspicion and criticism. Alexander Maconochie, for instance, was given charge of the penal settlement for refrac-

---

[31] They were closely involved in planning Parkhurst and Pentonville: see generally, McConville (1981), pp. 170–176.

[32] See 2 & 3 Vict., c. 54; McConville (1981), pp. 254–256.

[33] Prisons Act 1865; see below, p. 564.

[34] Prisons Act 1877; McConville (1981), pp. 468–482; and below, p. 585.

[35] However, it was only in the final version of the Panopticon plan that Bentham moved away from ideas of solitary labour, uncontaminated by association.

[36] This required division of men and women; and then into convicted felons, convicted midemeanants, those awaiting trial for felony, those for misdemeanour, and vagrants: 4 Geo. IV, c. 64, s.4. The appointment of a chaplain and a surgeon was for the first time required. The chaplain was to pass on complaints to the justices—a source of tension with the governor, which McConville shows to have been of major significance in prison administration throughout the period: (1981), pp. 130, 160–163.

tory transportees at Norfolk Island off the New South Wales Coast.[37] He was permitted to introduce a "marks" system of rewards and punishments by which a prisoner's progress towards privileges and release was conditioned by his behaviour. It was however soon wound up, not because it was felt to be capable of degenerating into unchecked manipulation, but because it was adjudged too benificent. In 1849 the Birmingham justices appointed Maconochie the governor of their prison,[38] but they too became alarmed at his benign methods and forced him to retire after two years.[39]

The second theoretical position drew deeply upon the judgemental and authoritarian strains of evangelical feeling. From this perspective the great object was to rescue the sinful soul of the prisoner by securing his conversion to the path of Christian enlightenment. The change of heart could come only from within; but it was most likely to be secured by solitary contemplation, and this at least the prison could insist upon. Paul had managed for a time to impose such a system at Gloucester.[40] The role of silent self-communion was an essential part of the Quaker faith and its introduction into the regime of the prisons in Philadelphia acquired international renown in the 1820s. William Crawford of the Prison Discipline Society returned from an investigation of American prisons[41] convinced of the superiority of the Separate System (no longer called solitary confinement, because the prisoner was to have regular, wholesome contact with prison officers, chief among them the chaplain). When he and Whitworth Russell were appointed the first central inspectors (under the 1835 Act) for the Home District, they argued the need for rebuilding to accommodate a Separate regime, and they poured much scorn upon the Silent System—a rival regimen, already employed in the Coldbath Fields House of Correction and elsewhere—which put the prisoners together for exercise, work and meals but forbade all communication between them.[42] Certainly, the great problem of silent association was the constant policing and punishing of surreptitious

[37] Maconochie, who had made contact with utilitarians as professor of geography at University College, London (1830) went as Governor Franklin's Secretary to Van Diemen's Land in 1837; whereupon he conceived his ideas for the proper treatment of transportees and sent them back in a memorandum that was published officially: P.P. 1837–1838 (309) XLII and P.P. 1838 (687) XL; see Shaw (1966), pp. 268–272, J.V. Barry, *Alexander Maconochie of Norfolk Island* (1958).

[38] He gave an account of his system in *Crime and Punishment* (1846) which became well-known among reformers, one of whom, Matthew Davenport Hill, as Recorder of Birmingham, was influential in securing his appointment.

[39] He came into increasing conflict with his second-in-command, William Austin, who was allowed to succeed him. But the switch to a pathologically severe regime brought scandal in its wake, Austin eventually being sentenced to three months' imprisonment for inflicting unauthorised punishments. See the Report of an investigating Commission: P.P., 1954 [1809] XXXI. At the same time there was similar condemnation of the management of Leicester Gaol: P.P. 1854 [1808] XXXIV.

[40] See above, p. 571.

[41] Distinguished investigators from France, Belgium and Germany also visited and published long commentaries. For Crawford's Report, undertaken for the government, U. R. Q. Henriques (1972) 54 P. & P. 61; M. H. Tomlinson, below, n. 52.

[42] Crawford had seen it in operation in the Auburn prison, New York state. The denunciation came in their Third Report as Prison Inspectors (P.P. 1837–1838 (141) XXX). But a fellow inspector, Captain Williams, favoured the silent system and the governor of Coldbath Fields, G. L. Chesterton, continued vigorously to defend it.

whispering and sign-language. With such temptations prisoners were unlikely to feel the powers of solitary reflection. Crawford and Russell were able to influence the Millbank Committee into appointing the chaplain also as governor, which led to a veritable inquisition of soul-saving. Even more important, they were involved in the plans for ensuring that the government's Pentonville Prison was erected with separate accommodation, in which inmates underwent long months of segregation.[43] Both experiments, however, showed the tendency of such a "separate" system to drive those subjected to it not along the path of righteousness but into insanity or suicide.[44]

The third position, which would emerge unquestionably the victor in the Battle of the Systems, insisted that deterrence was the overweening objective of criminal justice and regarded both the prison labour factory and the evangelical forcing-house as undermining that one dreadful end. In a celebrated attack on the reformism of the Fry school, the Rev. Sydney Smith wrote: "There should be no tea and sugar, no assemblage of female felons round the washing-tub—nothing but beating hemp and pulling oakum and pounding bricks—no work but what was tedious, unusual and unfeminine."[45] This fixation with punitive work was wholly typical. The deterrent prison had to be least eligible, nastier than life outside or within a poor law workhouse. There must be no incentive for a pauper or vagrant to become a proven criminal. The deprivation of freedom was not of itself enough. Diet, clothing and bedding could be made unpleasant,[46] but reducing the diet too far could overwhelm the institution with sickness, as happened at Millbank in 1823.[47] So the argument came back to work. An instrument for unremitting labour, the treadwheel, was perfected by William Cubitt in 1818. It formed an "everlasting staircase" which could be used to power corn-grinding, water-raising, hemp-beating and so on, not that this was the object. It was soon taken up by various benches of justices, who put their charges on it for long stretches each day.[48] A later alternative, utterly without useful function, was the crank, which the prisoner could be required to turn so many times per hour or day.[49] Besides these instruments of terror there were always the dreary occupations like oakum-picking (shredding rope for ship-caulking) which had been listed in the Penitentiaries Act 1779. When it came to

[43] Initially the period was set at eigthteen months, but it had to be reduced over the ensuing years, settling eventually at nine months.
[44] Crawford and Russell both died in 1847, and their critics, led by The Times, then had a field-day: McConville (1981), pp. 206–210.
[45] Edin. Rev., Feb. 1822.
[46] See McConville (1981), pp. 356–362.
[47] Reduction of the diet in 1822 led to an outbreak of scurvy so serious that the prison had to be abandoned for months: McConville (1981), pp. 144–146. The episode inhibited similar experiments, despite later jibes about "prison palaces": for which, see M. H. Tomlinson [1978] Bull.Inst.Hist.R. 60.
[48] For the debate about its effects, see esp. P.P. 1823 (113) XV; 1824 (45, 247) XIX; 1825 (34) XXIII; and James Mill's attacking article in the Encyclopedia Britannica (1823); Webb (1922), pp. 96–100.
[49] Introduced into Pentonville in 1846; Mayhew and Binny calculated that performing 10,000 revolutions—a typical daily requirement, would take 8 hours and 20 minutes: Criminal Prisons of London (1862), p. 308.

practical organisation, there proved to be considerable overlap between this third position and the second.

The advocates of uncompromising deterrence often favoured separate confinement because the lack of contact with other prisoners added an insufferable measure of tedium to the rigours of hard labour. It was an approach well-comprehended by the bulk of retired officers from the army and navy who were now filling the governorships of prisons and the central administration.[50] Chief among them in the middle decades of the century was unquestionably Sir Joshua Jebb, R.E., whose career began as Crawford and Russell were at the brief zenith, and who became Surveyor General (1844) and then Chairman of the Board of Directors of Convict Prisons (1850).[51] He was able to build up his own, rather more pragmatic, position as the excesses of religiously inspired separation became apparent. For him, short-term sentences could consist only of unpalatable medicine and he pressed for the conversion of the local prisons, where most of these prisoners were sent, to separate-cell accommodation in which dreary labour could be required. For the longer-term convict he did much to shape the regime which would become penal servitude, and he did so at a time when the influential and respectable were becoming increasingly alarmed at the consequences of abandoning transportation.[52] Working under a like-minded Home Secretary, Sir George Grey, he pressed forward a plan for a stage of gang labour, to follow upon several months of separate confinement and to act perhaps as some stimulus to personal reform.[53] Portland prison in Dorset was built to house labour for naval construction: Dartmoor, Portsmouth and Chatham were soon added. At last, the hulks could be replaced with conditions more apparently civilised.[54] If gang-work had as its most immediate model in the forced labour to which transportees were subjected, so also did the final stage of penal servitude—release on licence for a period under police supervision.[55]

---

[50] For prison administration in this period, see McConville (1981), esp. Chaps. 8–10, 13; J. E. Thomas, *The English Prison Officer since 1850* (1972) Chaps. 1–4.

[51] The Directorate was created in that year as the central system grew in importance and came under increasing criticism: McConville (1981), pp. 215–217.

[52] A Lords Committee, chaired by Brougham, for instance, convinced itself that prisoners soon became inured against the effects of their punishment, whereas even returned transportees went in living dread of a repetition: P.P. 1847 (534) VII, p. 4; and the judges believed that there was nothing to equal the horror caused by passing a sentence of transportation: Select Committee on Transportation, P.P. 1856 (244) XVII, pp. 293–301, 318–326, 440–446 (Creswell and Erle JJ., Lord Campbell C.J.). See generally M. H. Tomlinson in Bailey (1981) Chap. 6; D. Smith (1982) Cr. Hist. J. 21.

[53] Gang labour had been an anathema to Crawford and Russell. Jebb would also get rid of some of the ultimate refinements of "separation," such as divided cells in chapel and face-masks for exercise.

[54] Scandal broke over their administration in 1847 and a highly critical report by the Prison Inspector, W. J. Williams, condemned their squalor and "contamination." The Home Office became determined to phase them out and the last British hulk was given up in 1857; they continued for a while to be used in Bermuda and Gibraltar during the final stages of transportation: W. Branch Johnson, *The English Prison Hulks* (1957) Chaps. 18–20.

[55] This in turn would form a precedent for the idea of probation: see below pp. 626–627. The new regime was accepted by a Select Committee which Grey chaired in 1850: P.P. 1850 (632) XVII; it was prescribed formally by 16 & 17 Vict., c. 99.

The desire to punish, which becomes so dominant a characteristic of Victorian Britain after 1850, is a complex phenomenon, the product certainly of abandoning transportation, but also of that aggressive, often high-minded determination to govern, which was one element in the country's economic triumph and imperial urge. Any balanced view of it has to understand not only the pro-active attitude that social order needed mustering around a clear sense of duty and effort, but also the reactive fear that the wens of the great cities were producing a disaffected dross which could no longer be cowed by threat of the noose or kept down by transportation. There remained an insistent opinion that imprisonment at home could never be an adequate substitute for transportation, which tore the criminal entirely from his home and friends and probably placed him beyond the hope of return.

The sense of impending crisis is marked by the succession of Parliamentary committees and Royal Commissions which inquired anxiously into the new deal. In the mid-1850s the administrators were still able to convince a Lords' Select Committee that penal servitude was workable—the minimum sentence was even reduced to three years.[56] But five years later, sparked by an outbreak of "garrotting" robberies in London, feeling ran so strongly the other way as truly to amount to "moral panic."[57] A Royal Commission sought to insist that transportation should more regularly be the last stage of penal servitude and that the preceding home stage should be increased in duration to five years, or seven years on a re-conviction.[58] Flogging, which for adult males, had largely been phased out in the consolidating Acts of 1861, was restored for robberies and similar violent crimes.[59]

At the same juncture, a Lords Select Committee, chaired by the Earl of Carnarvon, enthusiastically adopted Jebb's recipe of "hard labour, hard fare and a hard bed"; prison regimes at the local level must be based on separate cells and work that was "penal, irksome and fatiguing."[60] The result was the Prisons Act 1865, with its requirement that the justices transform local prisons in accordance with the model, so as to provide either a separate or a silent routine with separate accommodation for sleeping.[61] The Inspectors were now armed with powers that should have ensured due execution of the Act.[62] The stage certainly was set for the step of "nationalisation"

---

[56] P.P. 1856 (244) XVII; resulting in 20 & 21 Vict., c. 3.

[57] See J. Davis in Gatrell *et al.* (1980) Chap. 7; P. W. J. Bartrip in Bailey (1981) Chap. 7.

[58] P.P. 1863 (3190) XXI. The minimum periods of penal servitude were increased: and licence conditions were tightened in ways that gave supervising police considerable way-leave to harass; and for legislation against recidivists in 1869 and 1871, see below, p. 611.

[59] Feeling that corporal punishment was too savage a brutality for the state to inflict had grown gradually, it being stopped for women in 1820. After its re-introduction for robbery there were a series of campaigns to extend it, particularly to sexual offences, but they did not succeed: see Radzinowicz and Hood (1986), V Chap. 21.

[60] P.P. 1863 (499) IX.

[61] The Act was remarkable for setting out detailed prison rules in the primary legislation, thus making them unalterable except by a further Act; it was not a precedent to be followed.

[62] There proved still to be many obstructions: Webb (1922) Chap. 11; McConville (1981) Chap. 11.

12 years later.[63] In the interim, central direction passed to the formidable figure of Sir Edmund du Cane, who succeeded Jebb as Director-General of Convict Prisons. In 1877, he would become Chairman of the Prisons Commission which was established to run the amalgamated prison and penal servitude regimes. Under him, a uniform policy could be directly achieved. For long-term convicts, the "progressive stages" of penal servitude would remain; but otherwise there was to be no real distinction by sex, age, physical condition or mental capacity. The justices were reduced to the role of visitors. More than ever before, the prisons imposed their dreary, arduous routines, unregarded by the world outside.[64]

(e) Juvenile Offenders

As adult prisoners came to be regarded as past praying for, the reformers moved their attention towards children and adolescents. An age which looked to education to mould each rising generation to economic usefulness and social duty believed that it could inculcate right principles in those still growing up, however lacking they might be in parental restraint and guidance. The eighteenth century policy of deterrence by example had remained indiscriminately crude: once a child was seven, and so at common law capable of committing a crime, it might be subjected to any of the punishments applied to adults. A few children of nine or ten were, indeed, still executed, while many were imprisoned or transported.[65] Of all those convicted of serious crime, a considerable proportion were under 21. Nonetheless, the gradual appreciation of childhood as a distinct condition encouraged a new philanthropy towards those who suffered most: waifs, strays, foundlings and orphans, as well as those picked up for crime. As early as 1756, the Marine Society had started a school for the children of convicts. In 1788, the Philanthropic Society set up cottage homes for delinquent and destitute boys, first in Hackney, then in Bermondsey. At Stretton in Warwickshire, farm-colonies were started in 1818. Sometimes the Crown was prepared to pardon convicted juveniles on condition they went into homes of this type.[66]

The concern over young criminals in the towns and cities parallels the growing concern with adult crime. The Bow Street magistrate, Sir John Fielding, had noted the emergence of gangs of young thieves, set to work by Fagin-like masters; and as the problem became increasingly evident so did the attempts to rescue the more redeemable among them. But it was not until the great age of prison building that any really substantial arrangements for dealing separately with juveniles was set in train. For some time there had been criticism of the way in which young felons were sentenced and treated without distinction, being put into Millbank or the hulks before, in many cases, being transported. One hulk-vessel was eventually set

---

[63] As to which, see L. Blom-Cooper, in J. C. Freeman (ed.) *Prisons Past and Future* (1978) 65.

[64] For the "Du Cane era," see Webb (1922) Chap. 12.

[65] See Radzinowicz (1948), I pp. 11–14, B. E. F. Knell (1965) 5 Br.J. Criminology 198.

[66] See Radzinowicz and Hood (1986), V Chap. 6; J. Carlebach, *Caring for Children in Trouble* (1970) Chap. 1.

apart for boys. But only in 1837 did the government begin the construction of Parkhurst prison on the Isle of Wight, as part of the programme of subjecting them to two or three years imprisonment and then sending them to Australia to work for private masters.

Once, however, the end of transportation began to approach and penal servitude became its replacement, the whole question of reforming young offenders at home took a new prominence. But as with adults, there were very different views of how this reformation could be achieved. At the one pole, there were optimists who sought to encourage, particularly by removing youngsters from city slums and giving them healthy work outdoors. Revd. Sydney Turner, chaplain of the Philanthropic Society, became a leading spokesman of this approach, having organised the Society's farm school at Redhill on the lines of De Metz's *colonie agricole* at Mettray. At the other pole, pessimists believed that only severe discipline and constant exhortation could provide the necessary corrective. Barwick Lloyd Baker imposed a deterrent regime of hard work on his Gloucester Reformatory; and Mary Carpenter, the best-known publicist in the whole movement, made her own establishment at Kingswood a stern and gloomy place.[67]

A flurry of discussion led to general legislation. In 1854, courts were empowered to sentence offenders under sixteen, first to fourteen or more days in prison, then to a period of 2–5 years in a reformatory school. These schools were to be privately run but would receive a government grant per capita in return for Home Office inspection. Three years later, industrial schools were established to receive those sentenced by courts as vagrants.[68] A considerable number of both types of school were set up and institutional discipline became the standard means of dealing with the refractory of both sexes, as much a feature of the penological scene as the separate-cell prisons for adult offenders.[69] Not until the 1880s was much concern shown over conditions within the schools; and even then a Royal Commission returned a largely complacent verdict: "Over and above their effect in reducing the amount of both juvenile and adult crime, these schools are successfully training a vast number of children for honest and useful lives."[70] The schools were by no means the sole recourse in dealing with juvenile offenders. The most heinous still sometimes went to prison.[71] Much more frequent was

---

[67] Mary Carpenter's *Reformatory Schools for the Children of the Perishing and Dangerous Classes and for Juvenile Offenders* (1851) was particularly influential—the title reveals much: see G. Pearson, *Hooligan* (1983) Chap. 7.

[68] 17 & 18 Vict., c. 74; 20 & 21 Vict., c. 48 (the latter following a Scots precedent of 1854); see generally Carlebach (above, n. 66), pp. 59–81; M. May (1973) 17 Vict. St. 7; J. A. Stack, *Social Policy and Juvenile Delinquency in England and Wales 1815–1875* (1974); G. Parker (1976) 26 U. Toronto L.J. 140; Radzinowicz and Hood (1986), V Chap. 7.

[69] There were over fifty English reformatories by 1858; the number of industrial schools climbed to over 140.

[70] P.P. 1884 [C.3876] XLV. The Commission did recommend abandoning the preliminary fourteen days in prison; but School managers objected strongly and the requirement was phased out only in two stages (in 1893 and 1899).

[71] Young offenders over 15 continued to have no special arrangements made for them, until the development of the Borstal institutions: see below, p. 626.

corporal punishment. "A good hiding" was after all the means of control mostly used by parents and school-teachers. There were few who stopped to question whether it should be inflicted by courts on juveniles, even though a certain decorum was leading to its gradual elimination in the case of adults.[72] Statute continued to permit both the superior courts and magistrates to award whippings for indictable offences committed by those under sixteen, if necessary in conjunction with some other punishment. The beating was administered by prison officers or, with growing frequency by the police.[73] Some of them regarded it as a minor blood-sport and occasionally parents and friends reacted in protest. But, for the most part, public opinion seemed unquestioningly to support the use of the state's new arm to knock the country's youth into shape.[74]

III. POLICE REFORM

(a) The London Metropolis

A reformed police—the other factor in the Beccarian equation—trailled somewhat in the wake of changes to the scheme of punishment, and moved only in the face of deep prejudice. The growing problems of controlling the London metropolis had led to the government's support of the Bow Street office.[75] For several decades it had been possible to treat this as an exceptional necessity. But in the end organisations of this kind began to spread. From the late eighteenth century a foot patrol was attached to Bow Street to guard the metropolis and the roads to it at night; later this was supplemented by day and horse patrols. These were responses to a growing fear of gangs of thieves and highwaymen. They had some effect: travellers into the city began to express their relief at the safer conditions.[76]

The Bow Street model, moreover, was replicated in 1792, when seven more police offices were established in strategic parts of the capital, each with three magistrates and six police officers, all of them salaried.[77] Amongst the first batch of magistrates was Patrick Colquhoun, who would unremittingly promote the case for a single professional body of adequately disciplined, uncorrupt police, run by special commissioners accountable neither to the justices nor to the parish.[78] His *Treatise on the Police of the Metropolis* (1795) was widely read, and he was soon afterwards invited by a group of Thames

---

[72] See above, n. 59.

[73] J. R. Gillis (1975) 67 P. & P. 96.

[74] Radzinowicz and Hood (1985), V 711–719. The Howard Association, the Y.M.C.A. and the NSPCC all supported whippings as part of sentences.

[75] See above, pp. 554–555.

[76] See Critchley (1967) 43–45. Yet even such gruesome scandals as the Ratcliffe Highway murders in Wapping (1811) led to no decisive action: Radzinowicz (1956), III Chaps. 11–13; see generally, D. Philips in Gatrell et al. (1980) Chap. 6; C. Reith, *The Police Idea* (1938) Pt. I.

[77] 32 Geo. III, c. 53. Radzinowicz (1956), III pp. 123–140; Emsley (1983), pp. 48–52.

[78] For Colquhoun, see Radzinowicz (1956), III Chaps. 9, 14 (for his collaboration with Bentham, and the differing ideas of Blackstone, Smith and Paley), Chap. 15.

dock-owners to assist in setting up a professional river police to curb
the massive pillaging of cargoes from ships, barges and wharves. The
first experiments were successful, and in 1800 the Thames River
Police became publicly maintained through an additional police
office at Wapping with its own magistrates and officers.[79]

Yet Colquhoun's arguments aroused fierce controversy. Not only
the landed gentlemen and their tenants, but also the middle classes
of the towns, felt a deep pride in their ability to maintain control of
those beneath them without paid organisation on a large scale. If, in
order to meet the deteriorating conditions of London, there had to be
some departure from the voluntarist tradition, it was on an ad hoc
basis which still paid lip service to the magistracy and the parish
constable.[80] The result might be a chaos of small authorities, incapable of properly coordinated action, either against day-to-day property crime or against excitable crowds. But still there was inbred
resistance to change which ran deeper than a concern about cost.
"Police" conjured a vision of French officials, hounding the vagrant
poor certainly, but also regulating the economic and social existence
of the respectable at many junctures, and prying into their political
loyalties.[81] By 1750, the Paris police of the *ancien régime* had been
built into a force of some 3,000 men, which could be used for the surveillance of all levels of society. The Revolution brought its own terrible histories of accusation and retribution and on Napoleon's
accession to power, the police would be built by Fouché into an
instrument which many saw as even more fearsome. These visions of
excess played upon an acute English sensibility.

The governments of the younger Pitt and his successors resorted to
agents provocateurs in order to get up cases of treason and sedition
among suspected Jacobins, but they found themselves derided in the
press and in the acquittals which defence counsel (notably the commanding Thomas Erskine) were able to wrest from juries.[82] As Peel
found in 1822, the francophobic horror of "police" was unremitting. A
Select Committee pronounced that "improvements in police or facilities in the detection of crime" were irreconcilable with "that perfect
freedom of action and exemption from interference, which are the
great privilege and blessing of society in this country."[83] This epitomised equally the feelings of the country justice with his division of
parish constables and the borough alderman with his nightwatch and
his concern to keep away those who might pry into his affairs. The
press were largely of the same opinion, as were those further down
the social scale who could gain any public voice. Indeed, given

[79] 39 & 40 Geo. III, c. 87; Radzinowicz (1956), II Chaps. 12, 13.

[80] In any case, the London parishes continued their own police and watching arrangements.

[81] For comparison with the French situation, Emsley (1983) Chaps. 2, 3; note also, Radzinowicz (1956), III App. 8.

[82] The latter despite considerable evidence that juries were handpicked by the Crown
(on which see J. Bentham, *Elements of the Art of Packing Special Juries* (1821)). Erskine
often played upon the comparison with France: see generally, L. P. Stryker, *For the
Defence* (1949); F. K. Prochaska (1973) 13 J.Brit.St. 63.

[83] P.P. 1822 (440) IV, 107. This outcome was reached despite Peel being in the chair and
for all the criticism of the existing arrangements made by an earlier Committee,
steered for Romilly by Grey Bennet: P.P. 1818 (423) VIII.

the none too propitious experience of London, the arguments of Colquhoun, Bentham and their circle in favour of a civilian police,
commanded neither by landed squires nor military elite, were
remarkable. To imagine that there could ever be a "professionalised"
service which, with active, democratic monitoring, could be made to
promote the interests of the greatest number, was a very considerable act of faith. Yet, as with prisons, and with so many other plans
for institutionalisation, it was the very core of the proposal.

Robert Peel's thinking in the matter was principally the result of
his experience of the Royal Irish Constabulary.[84] Formed in 1786 on
para-military lines to maintain order against continual, unnerving
attacks on English rule, the RIC had survived sufficiently to have
some significance for the intermittently disturbed conditions of the
English towns and countryside. As Peel built his position at the
Home Office with his range of measures on criminal law, trial and
punishment, he began to formulate his plans for a single metropolitan police, though he accepted that the City of London was too
powerful and independent a place to be included as well. In 1828 he
was able to carry a Select Committee with him[85] and in the following
year, when political nerves were frayed by the question of Catholic
emancipation, he steered through his bill without any substantial
opposition.[86] He had the support of his Prime Minister, Wellington,
who had been convinced since Peterloo that amateurs on horseback
were no way to control crowds. But the tactical skill was Peel's and he
displayed it not least in his emphasis of the new force as a means of
protecting property against predation, rather than as an instrument
for curbing the volatility of crowds.[87]

There were aspects of the new scheme which linked it to the recent
developments in the Metropolis. The Commissioners in charge of the
force were nominated J.P.s and appointed Metropolitan magistrates,
even though they were without judicial functions. They were at the
same time responsible to the Home Secretary. But the scale of operation was unquestionably different. Here was a single force, ultimately in the hands of central government, which could be
maintained at the ratepayers' expense up to a rate of 8d. in the
pound, and above that out of public funds.[88] One of the two Commissioners first appointed, Colonel Charles Rowan, had a military
background; the other was a young barrister, Richard Mayne. While
they did what they could to distance their force from army models—
the first "Peelers" were arrayed in top hats and red waistcoats[89] and

---

[84] For his experience as Chief Secretary for Ireland (1812–1818), N. Gash, *Mr. Secretary Peel* (1961) Chaps. 4–6; and see Chap. 14 for his Metropolitan police campaign; also, C. Reith, *The Police Idea* (1938) Pt. II.

[85] P.P. 1828 (533) VI. It was to this committee that the young Edwin Chadwick first presented a memorandum on "preventive police" which became a much-read article in
the London Review (1829, Vol. I, p. 252); for his later influence see below, p. 592.

[86] 10 Geo. IV, c. 44; Radzinowicz (1968), IV Chap. 5; Emsley (1983), pp. 59–67.

[87] In the same year, Peel also promoted a reform of police in Cheshire, following the
earlier London model of stipendiaries (called high constables) each with a paid force
in support (see 10 Geo. IV, c. 97). But the experiment did not become a direct precedent.

[88] 10 Geo. IV, c. 44, s.23.

[89] Hence "Robin Redbreasts."

carried nothing but a rattle and truncheon—it was inevitable that
much about them would be military in character. There was little else
by way of precedent. The men were regularly drilled, they acted
under specific orders from their superiors, they were left little discretion in seeking to resolve arguments and tensions.[90]

The two commissioners did prevent their force from being drawn
either, as to officers, from those with commissions in the services or,
as to men, from the old bodies of watchmen and constables. Against
the former they set the pay at 3s. a day and established a policy of
appointing sergeants from the ranks; against the latter they prescribed that recruits be under 35, of good physique, at least five feet
seven inches, literate and of good character. Even on these criteria
they could at once find some 3,000 men. It was retaining them which
would prove much more problematic.[91]

The first appearance of the new police created a furore, which
would turn into long-lasting hostility and sporadic rioting. It was a
reaction that would be repeated in many parts of the country as
police reform fanned outwards. In accepting Peel's case, Parliament
may have broadly represented a shifting attitude in the governing
class. But below them, many traders and others of the middling ranks
felt their liberties to be under siege and their comfortable relations
with the old constables and watchmen to be at an end. And the
ordinary workers of the capital, now that they could see the organisation that might be turned against so much of their behaviour, were
readily mobilised into action. Placards urging resistance were to be
seen all over London. Officers were manhandled even when trying to
direct the traffic at Hyde Park Corner.

In the febrile months of the Reform Bill the police were having
regularly to restrain large, excitable crowds. But it was in 1833 that
they reached the nadir of their fortunes, when they faced at once
three allegations of abusing their power, each typical of its kind.
First, Sergeant Popay was found to have infiltrated the National Political Union in disguise. Second, the police were obliged to fight a
pitched battle with demonstrators at a rally of the National Union of
the Working Classes in Coldbath fields, which Melbourne, the Home
Secretary, had chosen to ban.[92] Third, the principal Bow Street
magistrate, Sir Frederick Roe, took up the cause of a prostitute who
claimed she had been raped by Sergeant Wovenden in a police cell.
The outcome of these scandals demonstrated how essential the force
had already become to the government and how far respectable
opinion had been won over. One inquiry found Popay to have been
acting without his superiors' knowledge (but the affair helped to

---

[90] The contrast of style in New York policing at the same period is the theme of W. R.
Miller, *Cops and Bobbies* (1977); see also C. Reith, *A New Study of Police History* (1958)
Chaps. 9–13.

[91] Of the 2,800 original recruits, only 562 were still serving in 1834. It was a problem
that would be repeated in most new forces; for the social origins of the first constables, Emsley (1983), pp. 64–65.

[92] A constable was killed, but juries returned hostile verdicts at the inquest and a murder trial: *re Culley* (1833) 5 B. & Ad. 230; *R. v. Fursey* (1833) 3 St. Tr. (N.S.) 543; G.
Thurston, *The Clerkenwell Riot* (1967).

delay the creation of detective branches for a long period).[93] Another inquiry exonerated the police for their conduct of the Coldbath Fields operation.[94] And Roe's allegations eventually foundered, though not before he had made a great deal of trouble; with time it became fairly apparent that he had been seeking a cause by which to reassert the power of the magistracy over the police.[95] Yet another Parliamentary Committee returned a highly favourable report on the Metropolitan force as a whole, and recommended that it absorb the Bow Street horse patrol, the Runners and the other police office constables. Eventually even this would be achieved.[96]

(b) The Municipalities and the Counties

An even clearer sign of the new drive in established opinion came with that local counterpart of franchise reform, the democratisation of the boroughs. In 1830 and 1833, those who sought credence for the old police system secured Acts which would give ratepayers the power to vote for a paid watch without the need to procure a special improvement Act.[97] But the Royal Commission on the future of the boroughs wanted more[98] and under the Municipal Corporations Act 1835, the new councils were obliged to establish Watch Committees which were to appoint a "sufficient number of fit men" as constables.[99] The committees had power to make regulations for this force and to dismiss those who broke them. But the Act did not even provide for a chief constable to have executive authority, let alone state what the relationship between the force and the Watch Committee was to be. It conferred on the men the powers of a constable at common law and instructed them to obey the lawful orders of a justice of the peace; and so further blurrings of authority arose, which would not begin to be resolved until the 1960s.[1]

Nor did the 1835 provisions lead directly to any marked change in borough policing. There was no way of insisting that the corporations honour their obligations. Some—particularly those which had set up a force of some size and efficiency already—used their new power quite extensively and sought advice from the Metropolitan Commissioners in the process. Others, if they did anything, continued with the old, frequently corrupt, bodies of watchmen.[2]

The tide of police reform had still further to run; for there were many well-populated areas where property crime and violent dis-

[93] P.P. 1833 (627) XIII; see C. Reith, *British Police and the Democratic Ideal* (1943), pp. 152–158; Radzinowicz (1968), IV pp. 185–189.

[94] P.P. 1833 (718) XIII; Radzinowicz (1968), IV pp. 180–185.

[95] Reith (*op. cit.*, n. 93), pp. 167–182; Radzinowicz (1968), IV pp. 173–180.

[96] P.P. 1834 (600) XVI; 2 & 3 Vict., c. 47, absorbing the police offices and the Thames police into the Metropolitan. In 1839, the City police were also reformed into a single force with its own Commissioner and 500 men.

[97] 11 Geo. IV, c. 27; 3 & 4 Will. IV, c. 90.

[98] First Report, P.P. 1835 (116) XXIII, 43.

[99] 5 & 6 Will. IV, c. 76, s.76.

[1] Partly from this, would emerge the view that a constable was not an employee of the police authority (see *Fisher* v. *Oldham Corp.* [1930] 2 K.B. 364). See generally, Critchley (1967), pp. 67, 131, 270–272; G. Marshall, *Police and Government* (1965) Chap. 3.

[2] See J. M. Hart (1955) 70 Eng.Hist.R. 411.

turbance were frequent, which were not within the bounds of the boroughs.[3] Even as Lord John Russell took over the Home Secretary-ship in 1836 there were signs enough of a roused political conscious-ness in the working masses. As the various strains of the Chartist movement proceeded to develop, the proponents of physical force, with their organisation of night-drilling on Yorkshire moors and other parts of the north posed an insurrectionary threat on a scale which in England had not occurred even in the 1790s, the Luddite disturbances or the Swing riots.[4] At the outset of his term, Russell established a Royal Commission on the police in rural areas, com-posed of Rowan of the Metropolitan Police, Chadwick and the timid Shaw-Lefevre. Chadwick was by now an old hand at inquiries designed to mobilise influential opinion and the Report, which took until 1839 to complete, bears his stamp.[5] A disturbing picture of ever-growing crime against property—farm animals, agricultural produce, and above all, commercial goods in transit—was built up from the evidence of witnesses, questionnaires administered to rural magistrates and even, through them, to criminals in gaol.[6] The canals, the roads and now the railways were plagued by marauding vagrants, who had a network of nogging houses in which to dispose of their plunder.[7] For this increasingly insecure and dangerous con-dition, the Commissioners considered the improved policing of the Metropolis and the boroughs to be responsible since it had the effect of driving robbers and thieves to quieter pastures: in fact, there is precious little evidence that enough had been achieved in the boroughs in the short period since 1835, to make much difference.[8]

But this assumption of the Commissioners indicated their overall objective. Peel's plan for the Metropolis could be looked at from two poles: either the creation of a force responsible to the Home Secretary was to be regarded as a special arrangement for the seat of central government, which ought to have no counterparts elsewhere because civil power ought not to be further concentrated; or it could be taken as the model from which a national police would be built. The arrangements for the boroughs had done nothing to heighten the latter vision. But that posed no hurdle for Chadwick and his col-leagues. Their Report boldly proposed a professional force for the whole country, regulated on the lines of the Metropolitan police and placed under the authority of the Metropolitan Commissioners (and above them, the Home Secretary). The intent was plain: the county magistracy would remain involved in police management but would lose their ultimate authority. There were, of course, recommen-

---

[3] Some of the inefficiencies of the small rural units of police were pointed up by a Royal Commission on County Rates, P.P. 1836 [58] XXVII, at pp. 12–13; Radzinowicz (1968), IV 215–227.

[4] See further below, p. 595ff.

[5] For his views on police, see above, n. 85; and S. E. Finer, *The Life and Times of Sir Edwin Chadwick* (1952) Chap. 5.

[6] First Report, P.P. 1839 [169] XIX.

[7] Much was also made of the activities of wreckers who lured ships to their doom in order to pillage the cargo; but this was no novelty: see above, p. 550.

[8] See Hart, above, n. 2; *cf.* Tobias (1967), pp. 232–236.

dations to soften the blow. The force would be extended in stages over the whole country, in order to allow the "Met" to help train sufficient men and to give the justices the chance to say when they wanted the new system introduced into their area; and the justices would exercise the power of dismissal over the force in their county (the county rate would after all be expected to meet three-quarters of its cost). As the Report reiterated, the only way towards efficient policing was to give up the outmoded, heirarchical inheritance which was dependent on the voluntary efforts of justices and parish constables.[9] In place of "impotence" there was to be "strict responsibility."

The Commissioners made their case, much as Peel had done a decade before, on the need to control day-to-day property crime. But for the authorities, central and local, the rising tide of Chartist and other protest made that issue quite as pressing. Birmingham, Manchester and Bolton, despite their expanding populations, had not been old boroughs which were converted in 1835. Each had been given a municipal corporation by subsequent charter and the transfer of political power (in each case from Tories to Whigs) had led to challenges to the legality of the charters and hence to the legitimacy of the new police Watch Committees.[10] After listening to Peel, Russell proposed to sidestep this challenge by setting up town forces under a Commissioner responsible to him. At the same time, while appreciating the political hazards of going as far as the Royal Commission wanted, he proposed legislation permitting the county magistrates to set up professional forces with his approval. This too had Peel's support, though the young Disraeli chose it as the opportunity to lead a resistance within the Tory ranks on the libertarian grounds which had so long appealed to rural feeling.[11]

In this state of alarm, all the Bills went through[12]: 25 of the 56 counties set up professional forces within three years; some of them were substantial, others merely token. The Commissioners for Manchester, Birmingham and Bolton were appointed and were able to hand over their forces to the Watch Committees by 1842. In various parts of the country, as the new style of policing became a reality, the London experience spread. There was grave difficulty in finding working-class men who had the resilience to maintain the blameless standards required by their regulations while policing the communities from which they were drawn. They had to withstand regular butting and sneering and to be ready for serious assault. Turnover would continue high for decades. Ordinary people were often suspicious and sometimes outraged at what the police were called upon to do and

---

[9] Much play was made of the inability to get the community to come out on a hue-and-cry: Report (above, n. 6), pp. 90–92, 95–96.

[10] In July 1839, a scarcely controllable Chartist demonstration in the Bull Ring, Birmingham, showed that it was not enough to stiffen the old arrangements with a detachment of Metropolitan Police; the army had to rescue them: Critchley (1967), pp. 80–88; Radzinowicz (1968), IV pp. 252–259.

[11] Radzinowicz (1968), IV pp. 259–270; Emsley (1983), pp. 68–75.

[12] The general Act was 2 & 3 Vict., c. 93, amended the following year by 3 & 4 Vict., c. 83.

this popular antagonism would modify only gradually. There were serious anti-police riots in many places through the 1840s.[13]

Those counties which did not take advantage of Russell's Act of 1839 were not necessarily locked in a torpid conservatism. Since the Reform Act, there had been various signs that the landed governors would reassert their powers over local affairs. The administration of the poor laws was one instance, their willingness to take out their commissions as active J.P.s another.[14] In policing matters, this might lead to revitalising of the petty sessional organisation, in which a justice, or pair of justices, took active command of the local parish constables. Once Peel's government took over, it responded to this with an Act allowing vestries to pay parish constables out of the poor rate and the division to appoint a superintending constable.[15] Thirteen counties made use of its form in the belief that a voluntary response from within the social heirarchy, drawing on the tradition of the eighteenth-century militias, afforded the answer to civil insurrection.[16]

Within little more than a decade this would prove to be a last stand. More than anything the completion of the network of professional forces was demanded as a rationalisation of hodge-podge proliferation.[17] As boroughs and adjoining counties came to devote more resources to policing, territorial jealousies began to plague their operations. And the frustrations were even greater when a local force lay supine in the clutches of local interests, such as brewers and slum landlords. Palmerston arrived at the Home Office in 1852 determined to put down such arrangements as prevailed in Romsey, the borough by his seat of Broadlands.

A Select Committee at once sat to hear complaints about these matters from the police, county magistrates and landowners. It recommended that all counties should be obliged to establish professional forces under the control of Quarter Sessions, but that was in a sense only a preliminary. Small borough forces were to be merged, and large borough forces amalgamated, in these new organisations.[18] The borough watch committees, which had been virtually ignored in the process of consultation, were outraged: they proclaimed themselves the last bastions of liberty against a government determined to spy and oppress. Even so imperious a figure as Palmerston was forced to withdraw first one and then a second Bill.[19] Not until 1856,

---

[13] See generally, R. D. Storch (1976) 9 J.Soc.Hist. 481; Bayley (1977) Chaps. 2 (Storch), 3 (P. T. Stead), 6 (W. R. Miller); E. C. Midwinter, *Law and Order in Early Victorian Lancashire* (1968); R. Reiner, *The Politics of the Police* (1984) Chaps. 1, 2.

[14] See above, pp. 20–21, 430.

[15] 5 & 6 Vict., c. 109; Radzinowicz (1968), IV pp. 271–77; Steedman (1984) Chap. 1; C. Emsley (1982) 7 Midland Hist. 73.

[16] Central government became increasingly reluctant to afford local areas the support of detachments from the army or the Metropolitan force when they were not themselves prepared to pay for police: see Radzinowicz (1968), IV pp. 277–283.

[17] The Royal Commission had pointed up this problem as it applied to the policing of canals and waterways. One solution was to allow proprietors to establish an essentially private brigade of constables under the supervision of two justices: 3 & 4 Vict., c. 50.

[18] P.P. 1852–1853 (603, 715) XXXVI.

[19] For Palmerston's role, Critchley (1967), pp. 101–115.

when he himself had become the Prime Minister of a country ending a war—a country, moreover, which was having to face the consequences of substituting penal servitude for transportation—could anything be achieved. The Home Secretary, the effective Sir George Grey, pushed through a County Police Act, despite still sturdy resistance.[20] his tactic, not previously tried on such a scale, was this. The Home Secretary would have no direct authority over the county forces which county Quarter Sessions would now be required to maintain. But there would be a central grant-in-aid towards the cost in return for annual inspection of the efficiency of the force. The grant could be justified as a reflection of the national interest in having adequate police in each area: neither crime in general nor popular disturbances were any longer exclusively local, and the police also had a role against the threat of invasion.[21] The Act could not go far towards suppressing the inefficiencies of the borough forces, but a borough would only qualify for the grant-in-aid if its population was over 5,000. The pressure of the inspection would contribute towards some 58 borough forces being consolidated with those of an adjacent county by 1870.[22] But against this there was steady creation of new boroughs, and with them separate forces, until legislation in 1877 put an end to police powers being given to boroughs of less than 20,000.[23] In 1888, as part of the county government reforms, forces in boroughs of less than 10,000 were required to merge with a county force.[24]

(c) Protest Movements and Police

Although it was sometimes understated, the desire to have a regular force for the control of crowds and the monitoring of dissidents was undoubtedly a powerful motive behind the movement for the new police. Until at least 1850, forms of protest continued which were deliberately violent. There were attacks on crops, machinery, buildings, or even whole towns—as in the Chartist attempt on Newport; or which easily disintegrated into violence.[25] In the countryside, these outbreaks were tailing away: the "Swing" disturbances in the south-east during the winter of 1830–1831 and a decade later the "Rebecca" riots against Welsh turnpikes and other symbols of propertied power would prove to be be the last prolonged instances.[26] In the towns, however, the trend seemed to be the other way, as strikes, elections, political demands and periods of poor trade each contri-

[20] See D. F. Smith, *Sir George Grey at the Mid-Victorian Home Office* (1972).
[21] 19 & 20 Vict., c. 69; J. Hart (1956) 34 Pub.Admin. 405.
[22] For the early inspections, H. Parris [1961] Pub.Law 230; and for conditions and reactions, Steedman (1984), pp. 25–59; Critchley (1967), pp. 118–123.
[23] Municipal Corporations (New Charters) Act 1877.
[24] Local Government Act 1888, s.9.
[25] For detailed histories of protest in the period 1815–1850, see Stevenson (1979) Chaps. 9–12; Mather (1959); Critchley (1970) Chap. 4; F. C. Mather, D. Philips and R. Quinault in J. Stevenson and R. Quinault (ed.), *Popular Protest and Public Order* (1974) Chaps. 3–5.
[26] As to these events see, E. Hobsbawm and G. Rudé, *Captain Swing* (1969); D. J. V. Jones, *Before Rebecca* (1973); D. Williams, *The Rebecca Riots* (1955); G. A. Williams, *The Merthyr Rising* (1978).

buted to spasmodic unrest. The attacks of the "Luddite" hand-workers would, a generation later, burgeon into the better-organised and more persistent campaigns against the new Poor Law, the Corn Laws and above all, the political settlement of 1832, as evidenced by the demands of the Charter.

The new police, so it was hoped, could fill an essential gap in the authorities' armour against popular disturbance and guerilla sabotage: they would provide a general preparedness and, even more, an accumulated knowledge of successful tactics, which magistrates so often lacked.[27] They could gather intelligence of proposed meetings and demonstrations, parley with leaders and perhaps bring them into negotiation with their antagonists, station themselves and move in with batons in ways calculated to keep order as long as possible and to isolate outbreaks of violence. In the event, the police would undergo a slow, somewhat tortured, education in what was effective, and what counter-productive. They could not at once be a substitute for putting in the army or swearing in special constables for a display of middle-class solidarity. But the Home Office was always most reluctant to turn to the military, and had often to remind agitated mayors and justices of their prime responsibility for civil order and accordingly for maintaining a sufficient police force as a trunk to which other support could be grafted.[28] While those in charge of the police sometimes paraded them in troop-like formation,[29] on the whole they appreciated the value of unprovocative response based on good preliminary information and mutual contact. As late as 1893, the tragic shooting at the Featherstone miners' strike would stand as a reminder of how a situation could disintegrate if troops, for some reason, had to replace police.[30]

What even a coolly commanded police could achieve in this sphere, however, depended on the attitudes and expectations of those whom they sought to control. In the second half of the nineteenth century, a major part of the English working class came to understand the advantages of sober, patient demonstration in the hope of legislative change through Parliamentary machinery. It was a perception with a striking effect on upper- and middle-class opinion, adding notably to the campaigns to extend the franchise and to legitimate trade unions.[31] It formed a dramatic contrast with the violence of anti-English and sectarian feeling in Ireland.[32] The experience of English police in crowd control and associated matters was accordingly gained in increasingly propitious circumstances, which

---

[27] In particular, on the second Lords rejection of the Reform Bill in October 1831, Bristol saw three days of rioting on a scale similar to the Gordon riots. The mayor, magistrates and even the military commanders proved irresolute, and some afterwards had to face trial: Critchley (1970), pp. 123–125.

[28] See above, p. 554ff.

[29] For examples, see Steedman (1984), pp. 32–38.

[30] The police were withdrawn on this occasion in order to attend Doncaster races.

[31] See above, pp. 16, 316–317.

[32] Together with elections, ramifications of Irish tensions continued to be the main source of continuing troubles of the later Victorian period, notably in Fenian terrors and the rabble-rousing of the rabid anti-Catholic, William Murphy—both at the end of the 1860s: see Richter (1981) Chaps. 2, 3 and 5.

allowed the occasions on which there were serious errors of judgment afterwards to be excused, if not wholly forgotton.

As in the previous century, the greatest demonstrations tended to occur in London and to arise out of causes addressed directly to government or Parliament. In the post-war tensions of 1817, when many could still remember the anarchy of the Gordon Riots, Sidmouth's Seditious Meetings Act had rendered meetings of more than fifty people illegal if they took place within a mile of the Palace of Westminster when Parliament was sitting.[33] In 1855, a demonstration was called in Hyde Park against a Sabbatarian Bill which proposed to prohibit all Sunday trading. Mayne, the Metropolitan Police Commissioner, issued a notice banning it. A large crowd nonetheless gathered, which the police eventually attacked with truncheons. A mêlée ensued, for which the superintendent in charge was blamed by a Royal Commission. But no basic concessions were made after this post mortem.[34] In 1866 a banning order issued by the Commissioners with the Home Secretary's approval, against a massive meeting of the Reform League. An angry crowd tore down railings and the Guards had to reinforce the police in restoring order.[35] After some years, Gladstone's first government admitted a limited right of meeting in the Royal Parks, under the authorisation of the Commissioners of Works.[36]

Similar arrangements did not operate for Trafalgar Square, which in the mid-1880s became a collecting point for the unemployed. The "Bloody Monday" meeting in 1886 disintegrated into violence and attacks of shops and clubs in the vicinity, largely because the police organisation was so inept.[37] In the following year, a new and authoritarian Commissioner of the Metropolitan Police (Warren) persuaded the Home Secretary (Matthews) that another such meeting should be banned in advance. Despite the ensuing fracas on "Bloody Sunday," the Conservative government insisted on maintaining a total ban of meetings there, which its opponents continued to denounce as provocatively high-handed.[38] Asquith, as Liberal Home Secretary, later resolved the issue by a system of police permissions—a compromise in the same mould as that for Hyde Park.

Yet while special arrangements had to be hammered out for the meeting sites of the Metropolis, no general powers of control over

---

[33] 57 Geo. III, c. 6.

[34] See B. Harrison (1965) 8 Hist.J. 219, who shows that the government and Mayne feared an insurrection fomented by Chartists and French refugees: P.P. 1856 [2016] XXIII.

[35] Next year, the Home Secretary, Spencer Walpole, refused to act against another such demonstration by the Reform League and was obliged to resign. How far the violent first demonstration contributed to the impetus for the Second Reform Act has been much disputed: cf. R. Harrison, Before the Socialists (1965) Chap. 3 (stressing its effect); G. Himmelfarb (1966) 6 J.Brit.St. 97 (a nuanced view); M. Cowling, 1867: Disraeli, Gladstone and Revolution (1967) (dismissing its role).

[36] Royal Parks and Gardens Act 1872.

[37] The government reacted by prosecuting four speakers from the Social Democratic Federation—including H. M. Hyndman and John Burns—for sedition, with no success: Richter (1984) Chap. 8.

[38] After this confrontation, Burns and Cunningham Graham (defended by Asquith) were prosecuted on various charges but convicted only of unlawful assembly: Richter (1984) Chap. 9; for the legal background, Williams (1967) Chap. 3.

demonstrations would be given to the police throughout the country until the Public Order Act of 1936.[39] On the contrary, the right of peaceful demonstration and meeting could be placed in the pantheon of true English liberties. In 1882 Field J. could proudly rule that the Salvation Army was not to be banned in advance from holding a temperance march in Weston-super-Mare, because a thuggish faction, calling itself the "Skeleton Army," would set upon them.[40] It was an achievement made possible by the change in social and political relationships. The comfortable classes might be apprehensive about the accumulation of slums in the great Victorian cities, but they no longer slept in fear of their safety as many had done a generation earlier. The sobriety and maturity of what had been "the mob" earned it a measure of recognition.[41]

IV. Criminal Law and Procedure: the Fate of a Utilitarian Ideal

(a) Codification

The criminal law which had evolved for the non-professional process of pre-industrial times was beginning to change at the end of the eighteenth century, in response to the arrival of the lawyers.[42] A substantive law compounded largely of rough general rules (which left much scope to individual judges and juries) and a maze of statutory detail (which sought to delimit the range of the death penalty) was coming to seem seriously inadequate to the reform-minded, and in particular to the circle of utilitarians around Bentham, Romilly and Colquhoun. Peel put some order into the statutory profusion with the consolidating Acts which accompanied reduction of the supreme punishment.[43] But this was far from meeting the exacting standards demanded by Bentham and his school.

Bentham's own *Principles of Penal Law* sought to elucidate the factors which would justify treating conduct as criminal and determine the extent to which it should be punished—in particular, the degree of pain, terror, disgrace, damage and special suffering that it would inflict on the victim or his property (evil of the first degree) and the degree of alarm that it would cause in others (evil of the second

---

[39] See below, p. 616.

[40] *Beatty* v. *Gillbanks* (1882) 9 Q.B.D. 308. It was not long before the making of deliberately provocative speeches, such as those of the anti-Catholic preacher, Pastor Wise, were held to fall into a different category: *Wise* v. *Dunning* [1902] 1 K.B. 167. For the attacks on the Salvation Army, see Bailey (1981) Chap. 9; Richter (1981) Chap. 6. At an earlier stage, even Eldon was of opinion that an unlawful assembly such as Peterloo had to have become an unquestionable riot before it could be dispersed: see H. Twiss, *Life of Lord Chancellor Eldon* (1844), I 583.

[41] See Critchley (1970) Chap. 5.

[42] See above, p. 565.

[43] See above, p. 576. In his endeavours, he was much aided by the legal writer, Anthony Hammond: see the latter's evidence to a Select Committee on the subject, P.P. 1824 (205) IV, pp. 43–54.

degree).[44] He did not proceed with an actual draft of the contents of a Criminal Code. But partly because the system was itself beginning to be transformed, the criminal law proved to be the arena in which codifiers became notably active. In the 1830's, the Council in India prepared a draft Code (which with amendments would be enacted in 1866).[45] In Louisiana, Edward Livingston wrote and saw through a Penal Code.[46] And in 1833, Brougham,[47] as Lord Chancellor secured the appointment of a Benthamic set of Criminal Law Commissioners to consider, not just consolidation of the statute law, but even codification by incorporation of common law principle and statute into a single statement of rules.[48]

The Commissioners proceeded critically but cautiously, well aware that at root their project was at odds with the judges' power to develop and adapt a common law that was often little refined. As their Digest emerged in four Reports (1839–1843)[49] their procedure became apparent: where the existing law was clear they would incorporate it in their rules, though they might well criticise it in their introductions or notes (which often referred to foreign penal codes, notably those of France and Germany). As to punishment, they found the existing morass of statute so confused, that they proposed a Bentham-like classification of forty-five heads and sought systematically to select an appropriate level for each crime in their code.

After nine years of much interrupted work, their Draft Act of Crimes and Punishments stood complete, a monumental restatement that would influence all future treatments of the subject. It proved impossible, however, to pass the code directly into law. Brougham, as its godfather, promoted a bill for its enactment. Lyndhurst, Tory Lord Chancellor, and Denman, Whig Chief Justice of Queen's Bench, expressed the widespread unease of the legal community. The subject aroused general interest in the upper chamber, for criminal justice in the shires was a part of aristocratic life.[50] Lyndhurst had the draft sent to a newly constituted Commission for revision and the preparation of a code of criminal procedure; and this exercise was completed in five further Reports (1845–49).[51] Again it was Brougham

---

[44] *Works* (Bowring ed., 1843) I.

[45] The first version was chiefly drafted by T. B. Macaulay, during his term as Law Commissioner: see E. Stokes, *The English Utilitarians in India* (1959), pp. 223–224.

[46] Written in 1822 and adopted as the Penal Code of Louisiana, it was quoted substantially by the Criminal Law Commissioners in their First Report, below, n. 48, pp. 35, 43–49.

[47] The condition of the criminal law had been criticised at length by Brougham in his law reform speech of 1828. The members comprised Starkie, Amos, Wightman, Bellenden Ker and Austin (replaced in 1836 by Jardine): see Sir R. Cross in P. R. Glazebrook (ed.) *Reshaping the Criminal Law* (1978), pp. 5–6.

[48] Their first report was a demonstration of the need for codification of common law as well as statute. Their example was the outmoded and contorted law of larceny: P.P. 1834 (537) XXVI.

[49] P.P. 1839 [168] XIX; 1840 [242] XX; 1841 [316] X; 1843 [448] XIX. There was a further Report containing a procedure code: 1845 [646] XIV. Among the delays were Russell's requirements that they inquire into the felon's right to counsel and the need for capital punishment (P.P. 1836 (343) XXXVI), juvenile offenders (1837 [79] XXXI), and (separately) promulgation of statutes (1835 (406) XXXV).

[50] On this factor, see A. H. Manchester (1973) 2 Anglo-Am. L.R. 395.

[51] P.P. [1845] 631 XIV; 1846 [709] XXIV; 1847 [830] XV; 1847–48 [940] XXVII; 1849 [1100] XXI.

who attempted to obtain legislation and again he failed. When, during his brief Chancellorship in 1852, St. Leonards proposed bills drawn from the reports on offences against the person and property, the judges thought it necessary to act in a body. Their determinedly critical comments showed what a formidable opposition they constituted: they held codification to be an instrument which would cast basic principles in too inflexible a mould to allow for necessary development and the eradication of error.[52] According to Coleridge J., the public already knew enough about the criminal law and had no need of a code to guide it.[53] Moreover, in the view of The Attorney-General, Cockburn, codification would only be successful if it could be so complete as to eliminate all need for judge-made rules.[54]

It was plain that, for the mid-Victorian generation at least, only consolidation had any hope of success. Cranworth, Palmerston's Lord Chancellor, dared to envisage a Code Victoria, restating the entire statute law, and a Statute Law Revision Board set about this task, led by the indefatigable Bellenden Ker.[55] The grand design came to nothing, but revisions of Peel's consolidations, aided by the researches of the intervening Commissions, were eventually put through by Westbury as Chancellor.[56] These on occasion expressed common law rules which were beyond controversy, and they eliminated some statutory overlaps and inconsistencies. But still they were taken up with eighteenth-century legacies. Much clutter was kept by attempts to define the aggravating circumstances which would justify an increased maximum penalty. The Larceny and Malicious Damage Acts in particular read like inventories of the great objects of mid-Victorian wealth.

In the 1870s the codification campaign would again enjoy a brief prominence, when FitzJames Stephen returned from his term as Law Member of the Governer-General's Council in India. His draft of a Homicide Bill (1874) and *Digest of Criminal Law* (1877)[57] attracted attention enough for Cairns and Holker, Disraeli's Lord Chancellor and Attorney-General, to invite him to prepare a draft Code. When, with prodigious energy he completed it, it was revised by a Royal Commission of which he was a member.[58] Yet once again the judges marshalled their opposition just as the final straight was being entered. Cockburn, long-proclaimed perfectionist and now Chief

---

[52] P.P. 1854 (303) LIII.

[53] "The truth is you might as well make every man his own lawyer, to any useful purpose, by such means as these; nor do I believe that they would be happier or better if you did": *ibid.*, at p. 401.

[54] See, *e.g.*, pp. 1854–1855 [1963] XV, p. 14.

[55] See Sir C. Carr, *A Victorian Law Reformer's Correspondence* (1955).

[56] 24 & 25 Vict., c. 94–100; for Brougham's annoyance, see Carr (above n. 55), pp. 23, 25–26. The main draftsman was C. S. Greaves Q.C., whose *Criminal Law Consolidation Acts* (1862) rather disparaged the efforts of the Commissioners of 1833–1850.

[57] The Homicide Bill derived from criticisms by the Royal Commission on Capital Punishment of the definition of murder (P.P. 1866 [3950] XXI); objections to the Bill led Stephen to advocate the need of codifying the whole criminal law. The *Digest* was a product of Stephen's appointment as Professor of Common Law to the Inns of Court (as were his Digests of *Evidence* (1876) and *Criminal Procedure* (1883)).

[58] P.P. 1878–79 [C. 2345] XX; the other members were Lord Blackburn, Lush L.J. and Barry J.

Justice, wrote to the Attorney-General making detailed criticisms of the drafting, the content and the incompleteness of the proposals on general principles and punishment; and he promised further objections to the rest of the draft.[59] The uncompromising tone of the attack—taking every type of debating point—showed that the real leaders of the profession were virtually unmoveable on the subject. Stephen's draft, now standing as the culmination of a half-century's Benthamic effort, might be of use to distant parts of Empire[60]; but it went unheeded in the settled conditions of the motherland.

(b) Substantive Law Problems and Codification

Through codification the utilitarian reformers claimed the ability to lay down acceptable solutions to problems even in advance of their actual occurrence. This in particular struck many as a monstrous self-assurance; indeed it became a commonplace that codification could succeed only where case-law was sufficiently developed to have provided the necessary answers. By that token mid-nineteenth century criminal law still had some way to grow. And to appreciate this it is worth looking at some of the major perplexities which it raised then—many of them of long standing and some still unresolved even today. The best examples concern the mental element in the definition of crime and it is on these that we will concentrate.

(i) *Homicide*

The unlawful taking of life fell into two principal categories, murder and manslaughter. A killing became murder if it was carried out with malice aforethought. Yet definition of this mental requisite had long proved extremely difficult, since it had to resolve a tension that would run high as long as murderers continued to be hanged. On the one hand, in cases (typically) of domestic violence, there was a desire to confine the greater crime to cases of real premeditation—true malice aforethought. Yet in cases (typically) of robbery, burglary, arson or rape, where killing might be the accidental outcome of other serious crime, the desire was to deter the initial dangerous conduct by making an example of the case where death unexpectedly ensued; and this was a particularly strong motivation where highwaymen or housebreakers had killed in resisting arrest. In his *Institutes*, Coke had presented the law as containing both these contradictory tendencies.[61] In Foster's account, written at the outset of our period, the

---

[59] P.P. 1878–1879 (232) LIX. Stephen had to rest content with his judgeship, though he wrote a spirited riposte: (1880) 7 Nineteenth Century 1936. See generally, L. Radzinowicz, *Sir James Fitzjames Stephen* (1957).

[60] It was adopted, more or less completely, in Canada, and in Queensland, Tasmania and Western Australia. In England, even a Bill to enact the procedural part fell under the weight of amendments (in 1883).

[61] III, pp. 47–56 (published 1641); nor had Hale managed any more coherent account of the two crimes: *History of the Pleas of the Crown* (published 1736), I Chap. 23. The subject was confused by 2 Jac. I, c. 8 (1604) making certain manslaughters by stabbing non-clergyable: see Stephen (1883), III pp. 47–79; J. M. Kaye (1967) 83 L.Q.R. 365, 569.

disparities were somewhat reduced: malice in its primary sense no longer required the proof of distinct premeditation, though it could be displaced by proof of provocation; and on the other hand, older ideas of "constructive malice" were confined to cases where the intention was to commit at least felony or to resist arrest by an officer of justice (death having accidentally resulted). In practice, the divide between the two motions was glossed by the judges taking the power direct juries, as "a matter of law," whether or not the accused had "a heart regardless of social duty, and fatally bent on mischief."[62]

While this served the raw, intuitive world of eighteenth-century assizes, it could scarcely satisfy the codifiers of an age which was confining the death penalty very largely to murder. Both the Commissioners of the 1833–1850 and those of 1878–1879 criticised the wide embrace of the rule which found constructive malice aforethought in an intent to do some act other than killing or injury in conditions likely to cause death, however irresponsible it might be.[63] In 1839, the proposal was to confine this type of murder to an endeavour to commit a crime of violence to the person or habitation of another. In 1879, the proposal was to make it murder to intend grievous bodily harm for the purpose of facilitating the commission of a list of dangerous offences. Both discussions acknowledged that the law had introduced fictional extensions in pursuit of particular deterrence, and that once this step had been taken there was no obvious stopping point. The on-going argument about the issue indeed stood as a prime example of the difficulties in seeing the Codes into law.[64]

(ii) *Negations of mens rea*

A similar evolution affected possible "defences" to a criminal charge—matters, that is, which in appropriate circumstances might negate the existence of the requisite mens rea for a given crime.[65] A few of these had inevitably acquired some prominence in the classic texts. Self-defence, for instance, was a well-recognised concept. When it came to be incorporated in the Draft Code of 1879, distinctions could be drawn from established precedents between what was being defended—one's own person, some other person, one's dwelling house, other land or possessions—and between cases where the defendant had, and had not, provoked the situation in which he had then to defend himself.[66] It was also acknowledged that mistakes and accidents might excuse, though there was little definition of what would suffice, apart from the rule that mistakes of law would not. But beyond this most was in shadow. Compulsion might in extreme situations excuse, but there was no basis for saying that necessity could do so. Both sets of Commissioners avoided introducing any pro-

---

[62] Sir M. Foster, *Discourse on Homicide* (1762), II pp. 256–265.

[63] Fourth Report, P.P. 1839 [168] XIX, pp. xxviii–xxix, xl.

[64] P.P. 1878–1879 [C. 2345] XX, pp. 23–24, 100. The rather more limited test in the Bill promoting Stephen's Homicide Code is there discussed.

[65] For the difficulties relating to the burden of proof in homicide cases, see below, p. 623.

[66] See, esp., the "Stephen" Code: P.P. 1878–1879 [C. 2345] XX, ss. 55–63.

vision about necessity, though in 1884 the case of the "Mignonette" shipwreck, when two crew members cannibalised the cabin-boy in order to stay alive, led the judges into insisting this remained murder, however, much it might be a case for executive clemency.[67] Drunkenness likewise was treated in the courts with the gravest suspicion: if lack of criminal intent could be self-induced, who would not plead it? At most, inebriation might be taken to negative "specific intent," particularly when that went to aggravate the seriousness of a basic offence (as, for example, with the "aggravated" larcenies.)[68]

The most difficult of all the defences, perhaps, was insanity. It was finally settled in 1800 that the jury might return a verdict of not guilty by reason of insanity, particularly to murder charges, and in consequence the accused would be detained at His Majesty's pleasure.[69] In formal terms however, the plea could succeed only where the accused was "totally deprived of his understanding and memory and [did] not know what he [was] doing, no more than an infant, than a brute or wild beast"; he must not be "a man who knew what he was doing good or evil, and understood what he did."[70] The "right-from-wrong" distinction at the nub of this direction to the jury set the issue as one of cognition rather than of emotional drive; and it would have a long appeal to lawyers and laymen alike. But judges might on occasion express some wider sympathy for a defendant who had succumbed to an abnormal wave of feeling. In 1784, Eyre B. admitted a notion of irresistible impulse as insanity, describing it as "rage which is the effect of distemper . . . brought upon them by act of God."[71] And at the trial of Hadfield for shooting George III under the delusion that only his execution for treason could save the world, Lord Kenyon C.J. invited the jury to find him insane, a clemency permitted despite the fact that Hadfield's whole motivation stemmed from knowledge that his act would be unlawful.[72]

The issue took an extraordinary turn in the 1840s, however, when Daniel M'Naghten shot Peel's secretary, believing him to be the Prime Minister and so the agent of persecution in his deranged

---

[67] R. v. *Dudley and Stevens* (1884) 14 Q.B.D. 273: the death sentence was commuted to six months in prison. For the absorbing history of sea practices, and also the determination of the authorities to resolve the case in the way that occurred, see A. W. B. Simpson, *Cannibalism and the Common Law*. (1984).

[68] The Stephen Commissioners acknowledged this in their Report, but omitted any mention in the Code; since "it might suggest misunderstanding of a dangerous kind." Above, n. 66, p. 18.

[69] R. v. *Hadfield* (see below, n. 72). The issue had been discussed by Coke (*Institutes*, III Chap. 1) and with considerable perception by Hale (*History of the Pleas of the Crown* (1736), I Chap. 4). For the occurrence of insanity pleas in the Old Bailey Sessions Papers, see Walker (1967) Chap. 3.

[70] So put by Tracy J. at the trial of *Arnold* (1724) 16 St.Tr. 695.

[71] This was recorded only in an Old Bailey Sessions Paper, so formed no part of inherited precedent: see Walker (1967), p. 64.

[72] R. v. *Hadfield* (1800) 27 St.Tr. (N.S.) 1281; Walker (1967) Chap. 4; *cf.* the similar attitude of Denman C. J. trying Oxford forty years later for shooting at Queen Victoria: (1840) 9 C. & P. 525 at 545; and also the short shrift which Mansfield C.J. showed to Bellingham, the man who shot Spencer Perceval in 1811—on which see Walker, App. D; J. Biggs, *The Guilty Mind* (1955), pp. 68–69.

imaginings. After evidence from "mad-doctors"[73] that he had been "deprived of all self-control" by these delusions, Tindal C.J.C.P. initially directed an acquittal on the ground of insanity.[74] Again, it was by no means clear that the assassin did not appreciate the wrongfulness of what he did and the verdict provoked a public outcry. In response to a Lords debate, Lyndhurst, the Lord Chancellor, called upon the judges, to their considerable embarrassment, to restate the law in response to five questions. Their answers largely preserved old doctrine, stemming from Coke and Hale, by the well-known formulation that a man is presumed sane until it is proved that he was "labouring under such a defect of reason, from disease of the mind, as not to know the nature and quality of the act he was doing, or if he did know it, that he did not know he was doing what was wrong."[75]

Generated by this unorthodox procedure, the M'Naghten Rules provided a text of almost legislative authority. Yet it held elements of ambiguity, notably on the question whether the issue was the accused's inability to understand the morality of his action or to comprehend its illegality. The distinction was well-enough appreciated at the time; and indeed the Criminal Law Commissioners in their Reports, changed their minds about which approach would be preferable.[76] More fundamentally, despite the beginnings of medical knowledge of homicidal mania, pyromania and kleptomania, the Commissioners, like the judges, would not allow any direct acknowledgment of the idea of irresistible impulse. Later, FitzJames Stephen would prove almost alone in favour of considering whether the accused had the will-power to restrain himself. He was unable to persuade his fellow commissioners of 1879 to include an additional provision to cover the case. As so often before, to do so was said to run "the risk of a jury being misled by considerations of so metaphysical a character."[77] Subsequent decisions of the courts would only confirm the Rules in their more restricted interpretation.[78] The judges, it is plain, felt the need for a circumscribed law when working with juries who most often had to deal with insanity pleas on

---

[73] A common description of the time, which nevertheless easily acquired pejorative overtones from the lips of a non-believer such as Lord Campbell: see P.D. 1843 LXVII 741.

[74] Cockburn, for the defence, quoted from Dr. Isaac Ray's *Treatise on the Medical Jurisprudence of Insanity* (1838) which had attracted considerable debate by its condemnation of the restrictive, "right-from-wrong" test and argued for a much broader causative test.

[75] The other answers concerned (i) insane delusions—the judges held the relevant question to be whether the accused knew that he was acting contrary to law; and (ii) the practice of calling experts who had only seen the accused in court—which was held not to be normal practice and soon died out (after *R. v. Frances* (1849) 4 Cox C.C. 57). On the answer concerning insane delusions, "nobody was tactless enough to point out that if the judges' answers represented the law, then M'Naghten should have been convicted": Walker (1967), p. 102.

[76] At first they preferred to allow the defence if the accused believed his act to be legally or morally justified; but subsequently a majority thought the latter issue too uncertain to be determined by a jury: P.P. 1843 [448] XIX, p. 31; 1846 [709] XXIV, pp. 9–11, 50–51.

[77] Walker (1967), pp. 106–107; cf. P.P. 1878–1879 [C.2345] XX, p. 186.

[78] See below, pp. 622–623.

capital charges: the Rules must be severe enough to warn against undue sentiment in "inappropriate" cases; there were ways enough outside rules for encouraging the exercise of mercy where it was warranted. One danger of a Code was that it might set out some ideal measure that ignored the workday business of imposing justice in the existing courts. Once again it was a type of interference which could seem a deep threat to those in charge of the adjudicative system.

(iii) *Irrelevance of mens rea: strict liability*

The illiberalities of nineteenth-century criminal law by no means ended with the presumption that an accused intended the necessary consequences of his acts. The lack of any over-arching principle requiring the prosecution to establish a prescribed element of intention, recklessness or at least want of due caution, varying with each crime, left open the possibility of criminal offences which could be committed despite mistake or accident.

One foretaste of what might happen emerged with the idea of vicarious criminal liability, which by the end of the eighteenth century had been recognised in those highly political crimes, seditious and blasphemous libel. A printer was not allowed to escape liability for these misdemeanours by showing that a servant had organised the publication of the offensive material without his knowledge.[79] Through the decades when governments regularly resorted to these charges to suppress attacks on themselves and their church, the judges insisted that printers should not be permitted to slough off the blame by such a plea. Only in 1843 did the one-time journalist, Lord Campbell, secure reversal of an oppressive principle.[80]

Yet as the new bureaucracies began to spread after 1832, their ability to insist on their policies derived mainly from criminal sanctions in the form of summary offences. The civil servants, commissioners and inspectors had much to do with the precise form of their particular legislation and they often found, not only in government circles but also in Parliament, a ready sympathy for their uphill tasks as prosecutors. There were always defendants seeking to plead ignorance or mistake if they could thereby escape a penalty; and if they were shopkeepers on charges of selling adulterated food, or factory owners allegedly running dangerous machinery or polluting air or water, they stood a definite chance of success before a borough bench of people more or less of their own class. Legislation began to cope with this dilemma in purely pragmatic terms. A regulatory statute might prescribe that its more serious offences could be committed only with knowledge or intent; but the lesser offences could then

---

[79] Originally stated as an evidential presumption by Lord Mansfield (*R. v. Almon* (1770) 5 Burr. 2686), it became an independent rule in *R. v. Walter* (1799) 2 Esp. 21 (Kenyon C.J.).

[80] 6 & 7 Vict., c. 96, s.7. By this stage, the idea of vicarious criminal liability had spread to nuisance indictments (*R. v. Medley* (1834) 6 C. & P. 292); and this in turn provided a justification for indicting corporations (*R v. Great North of England Rly.* (1846) 9 Q.B. 315.

by omission be said to impose strict liability. On a very rough calculus, proof of a mental element—knowledge, recklessness, or in some cases negligence—would depend on the seriousness of the crime and the lobbying power of the interest being regulated.[81] In some instances particular compromises would be adopted: an innocent defendant might escape liability by naming a servant or other person who was actually responsible[82]; or the defendant might be given the burden of proving that he acted with all due diligence.[83] But there was not much consistency about what happened. The judges were not the originators of the legislation, but their views were decisive in settling what prosecuting authorities and statutory draftsmen could seek for. For the most part they reached their judgments under the rules for statutory interpretation, striving to read the edicts of Parliament according to "ordinary grammatical meaning," and seizing on logical clues to resolve an ambiguity. So in the catalytic decision of *R. v. Woodrow*,[84] a tobacco dealer was held properly convicted (at the behest of the Commissioners of Excise) of possessing adulterated tobacco, despite his belief that it was pure, because the Commissioners were given a discretion not to prosecute a defendant who acted "without any intention to defraud." By the 1870s, when the Liberal government promoted a severer Licensing Act and various pieces of public health legislation, offences requiring wilful conduct or action with knowledge were placed alongside offences which contained no such apparent condition. The latter were interpreted as offences of strict liability.[85] At least for summary offences of a regulatory character, it became the usual implication that unless a mental state was specified (or was an inherent part of a particular verb such as "permit") the offence would be strict.[86]

Nor was any necessary distinction perceived between summary and indictable offences. In 1872, Brett J. held that a man who remarried, believing that his first wife was dead, would still be guilty of bigamy.[87] In 1875, virtually the whole bench, sitting on a Crown Case Reserved, held the offence of abducting a girl under sixteen from her father to be committed by a man who reasonably believed the girl to

---

[81] I. Paulus, *In Search of Pure Food* (1974) traces the complex lobbying which occurred where groups of producers had an interest to keep out competitors who made substitute products of different quality or composition (*e.g.*, margarine in place of butter); see also E. W. Stieb, *Drug Adulteration* (1966).

[82] Factory owners secured this type of re-directing protection as early as the Factories Act 1833: 3 & 4 Will. IV, c. 103, ss.30, 31; *cf.* 7 & 8 Vict., c. 15, s.41; see generally, W. Carson in G. Geis and E. Stotland (ed.) *White Collar Crime* (1980), p. 142. The mine operators, who were even better organised, had a defence to charges under the early mines legislation, where an act was done without their personal consent, concurrence or knowledge: see *R. v. Handley* (1864) 9 L.T. (N.S.) 827.

[83] An early instance occurred in the Sale of Food and Drugs Act 1875, s.5; and note also, s.25.

[84] (1846) 15 M. & W. 403.

[85] On adulteration of food, see esp. *Fitzpatrick v. Kelly* (1873) L.R. 3 Q.B. 337. On licensing, *Mullins v. Collins* (1873) L.R. 9 Q.B. 292; *Cundy v. LeCocq* (1884) 13 Q.B.D. 207.

[86] For the growth of the modern law, see C. Howard, *Strict Responsibility* (1963); L.H. Leigh, *Strict and Vicarious Liability* (1982).

[87] *R. v. Gibbons* (1872) 12 Cox C.C. 45; Brett J. would, however, dissent vigorously in *Prince* (below, n. 88).

have been over sixteen.[88] Some of the judges admitted their sympathy for this outcome by saying that the defendant still knew that he was morally wrong in what he did. But the decision was said to turn mainly on points of highly technical comparison. The upshot was that mistakes about age were deemed equally irrelevant to charges of having sexual intercourse ("carnal knowledge") with girls under ten, or under twelve.

With this bridge crossed, the possibilities of disregarding pleas of ignorance seemed considerable.[89] But there were judges who worried about the application of the idea to further circumstances. The test case proved to be the bigamist who believed his wife dead. By 1889, Crown Cases Reserved was moved, by a majority, not only to accept his defence where his belief was reasonable but also to assert a presumption in English criminal law that a person could be convicted of an offence only if of a guilty mind.[90] This general principle was arrived at only after extensions of the contrary approach had been carried a considerable distance; and certainly after the treatment of mere "regulatory" or "private" offences had so often been held to impose strict liability that there could be no substantial alteration of course in that territory.[91]

(c) Criminal Process

In comparison with the substantive law, criminal procedure showed some greater signs of adaptation, if not of very marked change. In the later eighteenth century, as we have seen, barristers and attorneys were beginning to undertake business in the criminal courts and their involvement would continue to grow thereafter. It would be long before even the prosecution, let alone the defence, had professional representation as of course at assizes and quarter sessions. In mid-century, it was not unknown for a defendant to be without assistance even on a charge of murder, for there were those who could not even raise the fee for a dock brief.[92] On the prosecution side, the principal change came with the expansion of professional police. Gradually they took over from individual victims of crime, prosecution associations and common informers, as well as their own predecessors in the parishes. When the new police insti-

---

[88] R. v. Prince (1875) 2 C.C.R. 154; R. Cross (1975) 91 L.Q.R. 540. It had already been held that if the man believed that the girl had no father he would have a defence: R. v. Hibbert (1869) 1 C.C.R. 184.

[89] Thus the offence of harbouring lunatics could be committed by persons who reasonably thought they were dealing with the sane: R. v. Bishop (1880) 5 Q.B.D. 259.

[90] R. v. Tolson (1889) 23 Q.B.D. 168, reviewing the conflicting case-law.

[91] Tolson did provoke passing hesitation even over a licensing offence (Sherras v. de Rutzen [1895] 1 Q.B. 918); but soon an increasing severity was apparent: a person could be guilty of selling adulterated milk, even if a third party had actually added to it after he had despatched it: Parker v. Alder [1899] 1 Q.B. 20.

[92] It was only in 1836 (6 & 7) Will. IV, c. 114) that a person accused of felony acquired the clear right to counsel who could address the jury on his behalf. The change was recommended by the Criminal Law Commissioners (above, n. 49) over the fervent objections of some judges.

gated prosecutions, they acted as any citizen might, without acquiring special powers or the ability to stop prosecution by others.

In this continuity lay some small comfort for those who most feared their potential for abuse. The creation of salaried forces did not obliterate the grasp and graft of the Bow Street runners and the parish watchmen. Individual officers could expect their "successes" in prosecution to advance their careers, and forces as a whole had likewise to justify themselves to their paymasters. These pressures contributed to the many frustrations in the way of building a reasonable measure of trust in the police.

At the same time there was signal reluctance to create a prosecution service of professional lawyers who would take charge of the prosecution process and act as some check upon the police. From Bentham and Colquhoun onwards, the idea had not been without its advocates.[93] One of its attractions was that the business of eliciting confessions from suspects and of allowing an accomplice to turn King's Evidence might be kept in check. After 1850, there would be a stream of bills to secure public prosecutors. But they made no progress until eventually in 1879 the office of Director of Public Prosecutions was set up on a small scale, restricted to specially serious and difficult cases.[94]

In the way of any whole-scale system stood the old attachment to private prosecution and the interests of the legal professions in a preserve of private practice.[95] Equally there was the tradition that it was the justices who supervised the police. In tandem with the other shifts, the justices' duty to take depositions upon complaint of crime was modified into the notion of a preliminary hearing. King's Bench accepted that an accused person had a right to be present at these proceedings, and to question the prosecutor and his witnesses.[96] Thus a crucial stage was reached in converting what had been a strategy for organising prosecution into a process which in some measure protected the accused from having to face unsustainable accusation. The result was an inquiry, at a relatively early stage, which would in effect be repeated before the grand jury, and there were those who thought that the latter step had lost its purpose. But the grand jury was an integral bond between London and the provinces in matters of law and order. It would survive until long after the Victorian rearrangements had themselves become traditional.[97]

To the majority of those who contributed to the running of criminal justice, the three tiers of due process—justices' inquiry, grand jury deliberation and trial—seemed more than adequate. When their views were canvassed in the 1840s, there were few who worried about controlling the excesses of the police, far more who thought of

---

[93] See J. L. Edwards, *The Law Officers of the Crown* (1964) Chap. 16.

[94] On the long campaign, see P. Kurland and D. Waters (1959) 9 Duke L.J. 493.

[95] In particular, attorneys commonly acted as clerks to the justices.

[96] *R. v. Arnold* (1838) 8 C. & P. 621; buttressed by 6 & 7 Will. IV, c. 114, s.4 and 11 & 12 Vict., c. 42, s.17.

[97] The grand jury was finally abolished, amid lamentations from the counties, as a cost-cutting measure in 1933: Administration of Justice (Miscellaneous Provisions) Act, s.1.

crime as a blight spreading across the country which the new authorities needed every encouragement to eradicate.[98]

An equal reluctance surrounded the prospect of a regular appeal court to review convictions after verdict and sentence. From the 1830s bills promoting this cause were presented with weary regularity, but without success. The old tradition by which an assize judge might reserve an issue of law for discussion with his fellows at Sergeant's Inn, with the possible outcome that a person wrongly convicted might be offered a "pardon" by the Crown, was modified, it is true, by one of Sir John Jervis's Acts of 1848: a Court of Crown Cases Reserved was set up, composed of the common law judges.[99] While it could order an acquittal, it still received cases only with the assent of the trial judge and it dealt only with questions of law. In consequence it would hear only a handful of cases each year.

No forum existed in which a person who claimed that he was wrongly convicted on the evidence presented against him could reopen the jury's verdict. Equally there was no judicial body before which the severity of sentences could be questioned, even though Sir Joshua Jebb, for one, thought the "extraordinary diversity" in the matter "the most marked failure of the law."[1] Both matters were sometimes dealt with by the Home Office through the pardoning power. But it was always hard to convince the Home Secretary and his officials. Incontrovertible injustices came to light from time to time, and fuelled the campaigns for judicial review as of right. But for long the pressure would not be forcible enough to do away with secretive discretion, which in practice checked all but the undeniable cases that were pushed with unquenchable persistence.[2]

V. The Causes of Crime

Much of what happened to criminal justice in Victorian England was a pragmatic response of those in authority aiming at the suppression of criminal activity, without any undue concern for the deeper tensions and deprivations of which it might be an expression. However it might be explained in causative terms, physical violence, the misappropriation of property and damage to it, rowdyism and rioting had, so far as possible, to be stopped without waiting for answers to questions about cause. Yet these were questions that could scarcely be avoided. To debate the extent and type of policing required, the effectiveness of the various forms of punishment, or the most efficient length of sentences, demanded the collation of social facts— about crimes known and crimes prosecuted, the incidence of crime in different places, the age, sex and social background of criminals,

---

[98] See in particular the evidence collected by the Criminal Law Commissioners, P.P. 1845 [646] XIV; Cornish in Glazebrook (above, n. 45), p. 305; W. W. Pue (1983) 21 Alberta L.R. 335.

[99] 11 & 12 Vict., c. 78, and see the Select Committee Report on the Bill, P.P. 1847–48 (523) XVI. The Court's views were weighty, since all the judges might sit.

[1] In evidence to the Carvarvon Committee: P.P. 1863 (499) IX, Q. 1198.

[2] Radzinowicz and Hood (1986) V 758–764; and for subsequent developments, below, pp. 619ff., 631.

and above all the extent of recidivism—that first measure of the success or failure of a punitive régime.

It was part of the scientific strain in utilitarian thought to use social statistics and other apparently "hard" information in the process of felicific calculation. Colquhoun used figures to demonstrate the extent of predation when seeking professional policing for London and its river, as did Romilly in showing the inefficiencies of capital punishment. At the latter's insistence, annual returns of basic information about prosecutions and punishments began in 1810, and the keeping of statistics thereafter passed through a series of stages.[3] At the end of each, serious inadequacies were identified and a new start begun, thanks both to superior practice in France, Belgium and elsewhere, and to growing interest at home.[4] In 1834, the Home Office took over the collection of criminal statistics and introduced a division of offences prosecuted into six major classes. However, little information was provided about the background of prisoners and any interpretation offered was crude. In 1857, statistics from police and prisons were included with those on prosecutions and a certain amount of material was thus provided on the population being put through the mill of criminal justice. The information provided by the police, however—notably on the number of crimes known in their area and on the background of prisoners—has to be treated with considerable reserve; for there are signs that some forces used the opportunity to gild their record of investigating and clearing up crime.[5] In 1893, the work was taken over at the Home Office by John McDonnell who brought to it a new degree of intelligence and commitment.[6]

Objective inquiry tended to lead explanations of behaviour away from individual moral fault, either towards the external determinants of social circumstance or to matters of genetic inheritance, physical or psychological. In the eighteenth century, when the gallows provided the occasional dreadful example to the community at large, there was scope enough, in a rough and ready way, to take account of social misfortune, physical defects and mental abnormality in deciding which convicts should be reprieved and on what conditions.[7] Real poverty was commonly thought to account for much property crime, and, to some degree at least, to excuse it if not wholly to justify it. But the introduction of the model prison expressed a determination to add individual deterrence to more general discipline, and once that point was reached external explanations of the causes of crime would inevitably seem threatening. It is at this juncture that much of the literature on criminality became preoccupied with demonstrating that crime was not endemic to the lower classes as a whole, but was the indulgence of individuals who refused to accept the basic

---

[3] Radzinowicz and Hood (1986), V pp. 49–54, Chap. 4. For Colquhoun's sometimes ludicrous attempts at precision, see Tobias (1967), p. 15.

[4] The influence of the French pioneers, Guerry and Quetelet was strong. In 1834, the London Statistical Society was founded and gave much attention to questions of crime: T. P. Morris, *The Criminal Area* (1957) Chap. 3.

[5] See esp. Tobias (1967) App.; but for the value of what can be extracted from the nineteenth century records, V. A. C. Gatrell and T. B. Hadden in E. A. Wrigley (ed.) *Nineteenth Century Society* (1972) Chap. 8.

[6] See O.R. McGregor, *Social History and Law Reform* (1981), pp. 27–32.

[7] See above, pp. 564–565.

restraints of the social order around them. Thus the long-remarked association between drunkenness and crime was now employed to show that poverty could not explain a crime committed under the influence of alcohol, for drinking required initial expenditure; equally the desire for alcohol might lead to the theft of its price. The investigations of the Constabulary Commission 1836–1839 were used by Chadwick to demonstrate that individuals became regular criminals because of the profit that they saw in it when compared with the toiling struggle of the honest poor. Even the old view that crime increased in hard times was thought by a number of influential observers to have been reversed: good times now brought more drinking and so more daring.[8]

Yet there co-existed uneasily with these moralistic analyses, the view that crime was largely confined to the lowest segment of the population, those "dangerous or perishing classes" which were quite distinct from the industrious workers. They tended to congregate in the worst slums—the rookeries—of the towns and lived by crime, sometimes in whole families,[9] Their environment made it hard to behave otherwise. Much of the effort to rescue juveniles was based on the premise that they must be wholly removed from such surroundings and given adequate food, clothing and bedding to endure a regular routine of physical work, schooling and the inculcation of moral probity. However, those who had already reached adolescence, in the view of many who took up the cause of punishment, could no longer be reached by a change of environment and moral fervour. A proportion might still be frightened by harshly deterrent imprisonment, but some were incorrigible, and that fact, while in one sense an admission of failure, also opened the prospect of detaining an habitual offender for long periods to protect the public, for much the reason that many lunatics, criminal or otherwise, were locked away.[10] The first strategy actually adopted was to expand and tighten the requirement that offenders with substantial records report monthly to the police for seven years after discharge. But heavy-handed surveillance of this kind proved largely unworkable.[11] The experience would teach that aid societies, and not the police, were the only realistic way of securing cooperation from those discharged.

In the late nineteenth century, the theory gained some currency that habitual criminality was biologically determined—an atavistic throwback to an earlier, nastier type in the chain of human evolu-

---

[8] Tobias (1967) Chaps. 8–10; Radzinowicz and Hood (1986), V pp. 54–73.

[9] Henry Mayhew's detailed portraits of lower-class London life in mid-century contributed significantly to these overall perceptions: *Life and Labour of the People of London* (1861–1862) I–IV and (with J. Binny) *The Criminal Prisons of London and Scenes of Prison Life* (1862). They were drawn from his articles in *The Morning Chronicle*. See generally Radzinowicz and Hood (1986), V pp. 73–84.

[10] Early exponents of these and other measures were Matthew Davenport Hill and Walter Crofton: Radzinowicz and Hood (1986), V pp. 243–253.

[11] Habitual Criminals Act 1869, substantially re-written by the Prevention of Crimes Act, 1871 and 1879. The new system applied not only to those discharged from penal servitude on ticket-of-leave but also to any second offender, if so ordered by the court. There were also provisions strengthening the Vagrancy Act against landlords and publicans who harboured thieves. See Radzinowicz and Hood (1986), V pp. 253–261.

tion.[12] The Italian criminologists Lombroso, Ferri and Garafalo, relentlessly measured criminals in order to show their ape-like physical characteristics. In the rest of Europe their studies were mostly greeted with scepticism or rejected outright. In England, Dr. Charles Goring of the Prison Service undertook a controversial study of 3,000 convicts which eventually rejected the anthropometric thesis of the Italians. But family and social background was also investigated, leading Goring to his own set of deterministic conclusions. He claimed to have shown that the professional criminal in large measure inherited his propensity from his parents, and that beside this all environmental factors, including even the likely lack of moral example in his family circumstances, were of little significance. The study was a landmark in the advance of eugenic thinking and carried with it the overtone, equally to be found in Lombroso, that society would be justified in adopting measures to control and condition its inferior stock, in which individual rights would be subordinate to the administration of "treatment."

In his turn, Goring had to face criticism from many influential people, who felt some of the sinister implications of what he was saying, and refused to accept that criminal behaviour could be so categorically related to inherited factors. But even before his Report appeared, growing concern over the recidivist would lead in 1908 to the introduction of additional periods of detention for those found to be "habitual criminals."[13]

One factor which helped to mark the habitual criminal out for special treatment was the belief that the Victorian campaign against crime was producing a definite diminution overall. It was a view firmly espoused by Sir Edmund du Cane and many others.[14] The statistics on which they relied were capable of demonstrating the conclusion that crime was after all on the increase, or at the very least that the question could not be resolved either way.[15] For one thing the prison population had been reduced by the tendency to give shorter sentences.[16] Yet only a minority of those who ran the system doubted du Cane's view. The propertied and respectable mostly comforted themselves that social progress on many fronts—the rise in real wages, the proper organisation of poor relief, the clearance of slums, the spread of education and opportunity—had contributed to the reduction of the animal unruliness of the early industrial cities and towns. And so had the perfected instrument of criminal justice with its police forces and its fortress prisons. Accordingly the ques-

[12] One of the outworks of social Darwinianism: see above, p. 111.

[13] See N. Morris, *The Habitual Criminal* (1951) Chap. 2; Radzinowicz and Hood (1986), V Chap. 1. For the Habitual Criminals Act 1908, see below, p. 631. In the same year, incest was finally made a crime.

[14] See his *Punishment and Prevention of Crime* (1885); V. A. C. Gatrell in Gatrell *et al.* (1980) Chap. 9; Radzinowicz and Hood (1986), V pp. 113–124.

[15] In 1892, *The Nineteenth Century* published an article by the Wandsworth chaplain, W. D. Morrison, taking the first position, and by Edward Troup of the Home Office, taking the second; Du Cane defended his corner. Morrison's criticisms of the prison regime under Du Cane (see esp. *Crime and its Causes* (1891)) were influential in engendering the doubts which led to the Gladstone Committee: see below, p. 623ff.

[16] The tendency was anything but uniform, since sentencing was open to no form of judicial review until 1907: see below, p. 612; Radzinowicz and Hood (1986), V pp. 741–758.

tion which could afford to be asked was whether the uniform severity of punishment could not be made somewhat more discriminating, so as to select out the better prospects for a somewhat more
humane and hopeful programme of rehabilitation. But that was a
prospect which would begin to gain momentum only at the very end
of Victoria's long reign.

PART 3: INTO THE TWENTIETH CENTURY

The professional machine which had replaced amateur hand-labour
in the business of criminal justice operated, during Victoria's reign,
with a unifying rhythm. Most of those in charge—senior police officers, judges, magistrates and lawyers, prison governors and their
aides, civil servants—shared a common outlook: crime must be
stamped out; the battle was against serious odds; unswerving
resolve was therefore needed in the task. Crime largely meant lower-
class invasions of property, with a certain measure of homicide and
lesser forms of personal violence. In the first half of the twentieth
century, the machine was enlarged and to some extent adapted to
new functions. But more importantly it began to acquire a pitch from
tensions between those manning its parts, and it is with this new
characteristic that we shall be primarily concerned, in carrying the
story up to the period after the Second War.

I. THE POLICE

(a) Structures of Organisation

In 1857, immediately after the counties were obliged to establish
professional police, there were over 19,000 paid officers in England
and Wales—a third of them in London, slightly fewer in the
boroughs and slightly more in the counties. By 1901 the overall figure
would have more than doubled (to 44,260), and by 1939 there had
been further increases (to 60,500) which in the provinces, if not in
London, would run ahead of the increase in population.[17]
Through this steady expansion, the relations between central and
local authority, and between the political superiors and the executive
heads of a force, which were initially the outcome of particular compromises, were built by custom into pillars of the constitution. In
1888, when elected county councils replaced the bench of justices in
most matters of county government, a special Committee was created
as police authority, which was drawn half from the new county council and half from the Quarter Sessions bench.[18] The relationship
which the justices had traditionally maintained with "their" police
had to receive due recognition.
By that time, the system of central grant in return for inspection

---

[17] See J. M. Hart, *The British Police* (1951), p. 34.
[18] Local Government Act 1888, ss.9, 30.

had become standard. The initial disdain for central funds, which some borough watch committees and county benches had shown, had worn away and by 1890 all of the 183 forces still in existence were passed as efficient by the Home Office Inspectors of Constabulary.[19] National interest found expression through this indirect means, and through occasional steps of rationalisation, such as the centralisation of criminal records with the Criminal Investigation Division of the Metropolitan Police. But there was no real resumption of the campaign, so vigorously mounted by the Commissioners of 1836–1839, for a nationally-directed force.[20] After the first world war, the Desborough Committee did favour compulsory absorption of non-county borough police serving less that 50,000 inhabitants into surrounding forces.[21] It was a modest enough proposal in the name of efficiency, but nothing immediate would come of it. In the second world war, the Home Secretary required a number of amalgamations for strategic reasons,[22] and this was followed in 1947 by the abolition of 45 separate forces in boroughs that were not county boroughs for local authority purposes.[23] Certain additional powers were given to require amalgamation after local inquiry, but it would take another two decades for much to change.[24] On no other issue, has local suspicion of central pretensions remained so easy to arouse, and with such reason.[25]

(b) Social Background of Officers

During this period much more significant change occurred in the social derivation of the police. The Victorian forces had been secured largely from the unskilled working class; and to a considerable extent the intermediate positions of command—the sergeants and inspectors—were filled from those in the ranks.[26] But it was a policy at all times difficult to maintain, as the rapid turnover of constables made plain. In the early years of the twentieth century, the police authorities were prepared to allow wages to fall against the cost of living, and even before the outbreak of war there were signs, despite threat of summary dismissal, that constables were interesting themselves in trade unions—indeed, in 1913 a Metropolitan Police Union was

---

[19] The forces had in any case been subject to inspection whether or not they sought the grant.

[20] Not till the Willink Commission in 1962 would it even receive much active debate.

[21] P.P. 1920 [Cmd. 874] XXII.

[22] For the police in this war period, Critchley (1967) Chap. 7.

[23] Under the Police Act 1946; the debates during its passage echoed old fears of nationalisation.

[24] There were three voluntary amalgamations at the time. For the forms of amalgamation before and after the 1946 Act, see Critchley (1967), pp. 239–245.

[25] See Critchley (1967), pp. 140–157; Steedman (1984) Pt. II.

[26] Since Lord Normanby's Rules of 1840, the Home Office had set ranges within which officers of different ranks were to be paid. There were adjustments upwards in 1866, 1873 and 1886; see Critchley (1967), pp. 165–175, for these and other issues over the conditions of service, such as pensions and weekly rest-days.

formed under cover.[27] War-time inflation pushed many police families into real poverty, and this at a time when most forces were working at full stretch. In the summer of 1918, the Union made peremptory demands and then came out on strike. Lloyd George was obliged to concede a first pay rise and, in the following year, to appoint the Desborough Committee to made a hasty further investigation.[28] The government accepted its recommendations on pay: that uniform conditions of service should be introduced, and, for instance, a constable's starting salary should increase from around 30s. to 70s. At the same time, it proposed counter-measures against unionisation. A second strike against these soon faltered and the men involved were thrown out without quarter.[29]

The Police Act 1919 imposed a structure for future industrial negotiations, comprising a Police Federation to represent the interests of all ranks up to that of inspector and a Police Council to act as a central advisory body. It was however a condition of service, spelled out in the Act, that no police officer should join a trade union. The new deal accordingly owed something to Whitleyist hopes for industrial collaboration and something more to the government's determination not to allow unionism to spread to a point where it might penetrate the armed forces. It was a compromise purchased at a price which gave a constable half again over an unskilled wage, and in the coming deflation that differential was more than maintained.[30]

Recruiting and keeping police ceased to be the same problem. They could now be attracted from a somewhat higher social level with better educational attainments. This was said to be justified by a growing sophistication in police work. Certainly, the business of detecting and preventing crime, of controlling motor traffic as it rapidly expanded, of dealing with motoring offenders whose social position differed markedly from the general run of criminals, of understanding and applying a growing miscellany of legisation, lent its support to this claim.[31] But a change in the quality of the police was welcome to those in authority for other reasons. There had been signs enough before the war that social tensions were mounting to a level scarcely known since the 1840s. The police and the army had come under grave strain in keeping order during the massive strikes of 1910–1912[32]; and there were other contributory factors, such as manifestations of Irish nationalism and the Suffragettes' stratagem

---

[27] The initial protagonist was an inspector, John Syme, for whom it was one step in a lifetime of personal protest: see G. W. Rowlands and A. Judge, *The Night the Police Went on Strike* (1968) Chap. 2 and App. 3; and for earlier "mutinies" within the Metropolitan police (in 1872 and 1890), Apps. 1 and 2; also Steedman (1984) Chap. 7.

[28] See their First Report, P.P. 1919 [Cmd. 253] XXVII.

[29] On these events, see Rowlands and Judge (above, n. 27); Critchley (1967), pp. 184–194.

[30] Rowlands and Judge (above, n. 27) App. 4; Critchley (1967), pp. 194–198.

[31] Much was made of all this by the Desborough Committee in its Second Report, P.P. 1920 [Cmd. 574] XXII. Even after the improvements, there were those, such as Arthur Dixon of the Home Office, and Lord Trenchard, who took charge of the Metropolitan Police in 1930, who were deeply dissatisfied with the quality of senior officers and set about founding an elitist Police College: Critchley (1967), pp. 203–209.

[32] Notably in the Tonypandy riots in November 1910 and the Liverpool unrest of August 1911: Critchley (1967), pp. 179–181.

of confrontation. Continuing industrial agitation during the war left the government and its supporters wary of the syndicalist potential within the trade unions and worried about the impact of the Russian revolution on working-class loyalties.

All this formed the background which brought such an immediate response to the first police strike. The benefits to the authorities were transparent: they were able to depend on the police during the great strikes of the 1920s. After the General Strike in 1926, subscribers expressed their gratitude for the helpful neutrality of the police to the tune of £250,000, which went into the Police Fund.[33] The police were able, in that immense confrontation, to observe the high traditions of Rowan and Mayne, since the leaders of the unions insisted that the rituals of sober, peaceable demonstration be observed.

On less public occasions, there were signs of other tactics. The politically suspicious—which for much of the period primarily meant members of the British Communist Party and other organisations of markedly socialist aspiration, such as the National Unemployed Workmen's Movement—found themselves harassed at speeches and demonstrations[34]; and, until a court imposed some curb, they were liable to have the police searching their premises for incriminating material under the pretext of making an arrest.[35] By contrast, the first manifestations of rightist militancy, attracted much less concern. On one notorious occasion in London's East End, the police removed a Communist speaker and put a Fascist in his place. Eventually, however, the bully-boy antics of Mosley's British Union of Fascists became truly apparent, particularly after the notorious rally at Olympia in 1934.[36] In 1936, the government finally moved against such manifestations as political parades in militaristic uniform, with the Public Order Act.[37] From this time, police treatment of demonstrations became less noticeably partisan.

The anxieties which the police aroused were by no means confined to political confrontations. The business of detection had gradually

---

[33] Critchley (1967), pp. 198–200.

[34] The courts proved ready to support authority: the police were held entitled to move a speaker (from the NUWM) away from a place (outside an Unemployment Training Centre in London) even if it was only on thin evidence that they had reason to believe that a breach of the peace might ensue: *Duncan* v. *Jones* [1936] 1 K.B. 218. Equally they were entitled to attend a meeting on private premises (of the International Labour Defence League in Wales) where they feared sedition: *Thomas* v. *Sawkins* [1935] 2 K.B. 249. See generally Williams (1967) Chaps. 5, 6.

[35] *Elias* v. *Pasmore* [1934] 2 K.B. 164: even then, Horridge J. held illegally seized evidence to be admissible; some of it (taken from NUWM headquarters) was used to prosecute Elias successfully for inciting disaffection. It was a measure of the government's anxiety, that it insisted on pushing through an Incitement to Disaffection Act in 1934, a milder but wide-ranging version of Pitt's Seditious Mutiny Act 1797: Williams (1967), pp. 187–192.

[36] On the BUF generally see R. Skidelsky, *Oswald Mosley* (1975); M. F. Mandle, *Anti-Semitism and the British Union of Fascists* (1968). After the Suffragettes' first confrontation with Lloyd George at the Albert Hall in 1908, a Departmental Committee had stated that the police had no right to enter private premises unless invited (P.P. 1909 [Cd. 4673] XXXVI, p. 6]). This was used by the government as the reason why Blackshirt stewards were left to police Olympia without external restraint. *Thomas* v. *Sawkins* (above, n. 34) was decided only afterwards: Williams (1967), pp. 142–144.

[37] The Act contained some important strengthening of police powers over those granted by the Public Order Act 1908; see Williams (1967), Chaps. 6, 7, 9.

become more elaborate and many forces had set up special detective departments, following the model of the Criminal Investigation Department, Scotland Yard.[38] To a degree, the work was improved by advancing technology: notably through the arts of finger-printing and forensic pathology.[39] But much of the work continued to consist of keeping contact with criminal circles, interviewing witnesses, organising identifications, interrogating suspects and collecting evidence from the scene of the crime. Since all this work was rarely supervised by any outside body (only occasionally was the Director of Public Prosecutions involved), the police had opportunity enough for oppressive tactics. A Royal Commission, which had to be conceded in 1929 as the result of demonstrated instances of corruption and other suspicious incidents,[40] heard a considerable round of complaint: in particular, that the police often detained suspects for unlimited periods of time, and that during interogations they handed out some rough treatment. The questioning of suspects had long been a difficult issue, over which the judges had sought to exercise some control through the rule that only a confession shown to have been voluntary was admissible in evidence. Beyond that, they had on occasion sought to instruct the police in the limits of acceptable practice, and in 1912 they were moved to issue guidance in the form of Judges' Rules.[41]

The Royal Commission in the main sought to allay fears of untoward police behaviour, dismissing most allegations as nothing more than the occasional over-enthusiasm of young constables. Nevertheless it felt obliged to accuse the CID at Scotland Yard of "a tendency . . . to regard itself as a thing above and apart, to which the restraints and limitations placed upon the Ordinary Police do not, and should not apply."[42] The distrust of the police as the strong arm of a snooping state, which was endemic among the lower working class,[43] thus filtered occasionally upwards. Particularly after their partisanship in political demonstration became well publicised, the threat to individual freedom once more became a serious talking point. The National Council of Civil liberties was formed in 1933 with numerous prominent names among its members.[44] The experi-

---

[38] In the Met, there had been a small, unpublicised detective department from 1842 onwards. A corruption scandal in the 1870s led to the setting up of the CID in 1877 under Howard Vincent, which soon had 800 men and spawned a political sub-wing, the Special (Irish) Branch: Critchley (1967), pp. 160–162.

[39] Finger-printing, which became established after 1893, made the identification of recidivists much more certain and so stimulated the discussion of how to treat them: see below, p. 631.

[40] In particular, the bribes proved to have been received by Sergeant Goddard, and the curious case of the arrest of Sir Leo Chiozza Money with a Miss Savidge in Hyde Park.

[41] See below, pp. 620–621.

[42] Royal Commission on Police Powers and Procedure, P.P. 1929 [Cmd. 3297] IX.

[43] A feeling well-captured in the writings of Stephen Reynolds: see esp. (with B. and T. Woolley) *Seems So! A Working-Class View of Politics* (1911); see also S. Humphries, *Hooligan or Rebels* (1981) Chap. 6.

[44] Its secretary, Ronald Kidd, published *British Liberty in Danger* (1940); other significant contributions to the movement were W. H. Thompson, *Civil Liberties* (1938); A Barrister, *Justice in England* (1938), Chap. 9; and also the accounts of Wal Hannington of the NUWM, esp. *Unemployed Struggles 1919–1936* (1936), *Ten Lean Years* (1940).

ence of economic collapse and political confrontation roused all the old fears of the respectable against a civil force which was not constantly monitored and publicly criticised.

II. Criminal Law and Procedure

(a) Altered Procedures

As the work of preparing and prosecuting fell increasingly to the police, a larger proportion of cases came to be dealt with entirely before magistrates in petty session. Under the traditional system, all indictable offences went either to assizes or quarter sessions and, unless the accused pleaded guilty, a jury tried the issue. But a first breach had come in Peel's Larceny Act of 1827; and after that there were a series of expansions, notably (for adults) in 1855 when all larcenies of objects worth less than 5s became triable summarily at the accused's option; in 1879, the maximum value was raised to £2, in 1915 to £20, and in 1925 it was removed entirely.[45] Many defendants chose to go before the magistrates, mostly to plead guilty in the hope that they would get no more than the maximum penalty open to the summary court. Equally it suited the police to avoid the delays, expense and uncertainties of a jury trial. As common offences such as larceny were opened to summary trial, there was an immediate increase in the number of charges actually proceeded with.[46] If the matter could be despatched before the local bench, the police often carried the whole process through, even to the extent of presenting the case in court. There did not need to be active complicity with the bench, for the police to be able to expect a measure of trust from justices and stipendiaries who often enough were case-hardened to the round of defendants before them; criminal business, after all, had become the central function of their office. Many justices also sat on Watch or Police Committees and took a rather proprietary view of "their" force.

There were other changes in the details of procedure which worked towards greater efficiency. Notable was the Criminal Evidence Act 1898, which at last made the accused competent to give sworn testimony, though he could not be compelled into the witness box.[47] The shift could be seen as a response to other changes: in particular, many defendants had come to have counsel to defend them, with the result that they were often not heard from the dock, while being kept from the witness stand.[48] Equally, it could be presented as

---

[45] For a full account, R. M. Jackson (1937) 1 M.L.R. 132. Other crimes were also added to the list; and for juveniles the range of crimes triable summarily was at all times greater, leading eventually in 1908 to the establishment of juvenile courts in which those under sixteen were to be tried. There were also some "hybrid" offences where the prosecutor could choose whether the trial should be summary or on indictment; and some summary offences could be sent by magistrates for trial on indictment. But the division of work was largely dictated by what happened in larceny cases.

[46] See Jackson (above, n. 45).

[47] s.1.

[48] Cf. above, pp. 562–563.

an obvious rationalisation, as Bentham had argued decades earlier, necessary to give the truly innocent the opportunity to defend themselves.[49] Nonetheless, the promoters of the measure seem to have been primarily concerned to put all defendants on the spot: without directly invading their "right to silence," failure to take the stand risked the jury or bench of magistrates drawing adverse inferences.[50]

(b) A Court of Criminal Appeal

Above and beyond these factors stands one structural change of decided consequence. Against the better judgment of many judges, lawyers and Home Office officials, a Court of Criminal Appeal was at last established in 1907. This came to pass only because of the government's embarrassment over the misconvictions of Adolf Beck and the highly dubious conviction of the Birmingham solicitor, George Edalji.[51] In consequence, a convicted offender would be able to appeal not only as of right on questions of law, but also in order to challenge the jury's verdict on questions of fact, or mixed law and fact, or to seek a reduction of sentence.[52] From this there was to be further appeal to the House of Lords, but only if the Attorney-General certified that a point of law of exceptional public importance was at stake. The conviction might be quashed or maintained, but no power to order a re-trial was introduced.[53]

The standard counter-argument, which had put paid to so many earlier bills on the subject, claimed that an appeal would undermine the finality of the jury's verdict to an unnecessary degree, since the trial judge could already decide to refer a question of law to the Court of Crown Cases Reserved; and the Home Secretary could grant a "pardon" in the Crown's name either so as to free an accused entirely—and this would be done if he could establish his innocence—or to reduce a sentence that was manifestly too severe. Plainly a regular system of appeals was feared as a time-consuming and

---

[49] Bentham's assaults on the preclusion of evidence by treating potential witnesses as incompetent (in the *Treatise* and the *Rationale of Judicial Evidence*) led to the practice being reversed for civil litigation between 1843 and 1851. On the criminal side, Bentham had no patience even with a privilege against self-incrimination: see G. W. Keeton and O. R. Marshall in Keeton and G. Schwarzenberger (eds.) *Jeremy Bentham and the Law* (1948) Chap. 5; W. L. Twining, *Theories of Evidence: Bentham and Wigmore* (1985), Chap. 2.

[50] See Lord Halsbury L.C., P.D. 1898 LIV 1173.

[51] The mistaken identification of Beck as a fraudster, Smith, led to two convictions and prison sentences for defrauding women; Edalji was convicted of attacking a horse, but the attacks continued after he was detained; there were indications that the police had set out to get him. A Committee of inquiry into the Beck case, recommended a right of appeal only on issues of law, a question about the exclusion of evidence having been crucial to that case: P.P. 1905 [Cd. 2315] LXII. Accordingly it was the Edalji case (also the subject of an inquiry—P.P. 1907 [Cd. 3503] LXVII) which obliged the government also to provide for appeals relating only to the facts.

[52] An appeal on sentence, however, risked the possibility of it being increased. The Court came to warn those for whom this was likely when they applied for leave to appeal.

[53] Criminal Appeal Act 1907.

expensive device which might be manipulated by adept villains so as to escape their just deserts.[54]

Many of the judges who sat in the new court had been amongst those most sceptical of the need to create it.[55] However, in the years 1909–1912, the Court heard an annual average of 450 applications to appeal and 170 actual appeals. Of the latter it quashed the conviction in 20 per cent. of the cases and varied sentence in another 22 per cent.[56] The need for the court would not continue to be questioned. As on earlier occasions when an ability to appeal burgeoned, the most apparent progress proved to be in matters of procedure.[57] On a variety of fronts the new court strove to limit the opportunities for oppressive tactics by the prosecution: the simultaneous trial of more than one defendant, of more than one indictment, and of multiple and disparate counts in a single indictment, were in various circumstances held improper; the introduction of rebutting evidence after the defence had closed its case was curtailed; the production of an offender's record after conviction and before sentence was made to comply with procedures which previously had obtained only on the Northern Circuit. The court insisted at numerous points that it was not for the judge to invade the jury's province by converting an issue into a matter of law, or by giving some other mandatory instruction. Nor were judges to hound witnesses or to insist that a defence proceed despite an inadequate prosecution case. It is apparent that the old absence of control had allowed a great deal that was aggressive or slipshod to occur. The new tightening from the centre did much to improve the treatment of those under trial and the new Court's record must be accounted very real progress towards procedural fairness.[58]

Equally the court became regularly engaged in considering and refining the law of evidence as it applied to the protection of defendants. The trend was inevitable since it was a peculiar consequence of modern jury trial that the rules were to be strictly followed: failure constituted in most cases an error of law, giving an appeal as of right.

It was at the outset of the Court's career, that the King's Bench judges conferred official status on the Judges' Rules laying down the proper course for police questioning of suspects.[59] It then fell to the Court of Criminal Appeal to oversee the Rules in practice, through the doctrine that confessions were inadmissible in evidence unless

---

[54] In relation to sentencing, see Radzinowicz and Hood (1986), V Chap. 22.

[55] Of which, on average 111 were granted; the remaining appeals were those brought as of right.

[56] For an assessment of the Court, made at the end of our period, S. Davies (1949) J.S.P.T.L.(N.S.) 425.

[57] But the older predilection for seeking errors or inconsistencies in the record had disappeared.

[58] See Davies (above, n. 56), pp. 428–431.

[59] They required a caution ("anything you say may be used in evidence") to be given when an officer decided to charge a suspect with an offence, when a person in custody was questioned and when a prisoner wished to volunteer a statement. They derived in particular from Hawkins J.'s Preface to (Sir) Howard Vincent's *Police Code* (1882). They were issued at the Home Secretary's request in 1912. The Court later said that they did not have the force of law, but that failure to observe their "spirit" might lead a judge to exclude the confession at trial: *R.* v. *Voisin* [1918] 1 K.B. 531.

shown to have been obtained voluntarily. The Court did not require a confession necessarily to be excluded because of a breach of the Rules. The result was a discretion which, the police would say, made their task on occasions unduly difficult, and, defendants would complain, did little to stop them being pressured and mistreated in police stations.[60]

The Court strove to make sense of the plethora of case-law on the need to show corroboration of the evidence of accomplices, victims of sexual crimes and children not on oath. It achieved a certain clarity by insisting once more that the judge must advise the jury of the danger of convicting on an accomplice's word without independent corroboration implicating the accused.[61] The same approach was applied to sexual victims and the Court also occasionally upset a conviction where the correct warning had been given, because the conviction appeared "unreasonable."[62]

Beyond this, there was a whole range of perplexing issues concerning the accused's previous criminal record and his conduct on other occasions. For all the surprise that it could occasion to foreign observers, it had become the practice to exclude evidence of both matters for fear that otherwise the jury would too readily infer guilt.[63] But equally there was an exception, at least where the defence was accident or misapprehension or other mishap, which allowed in the accused's record to show that he had in the past followed a particular pattern or "system." An unfortunate tendency, however, set in to stretch the exception and so downgrade the rule, and nowhere more than in charges of alleged homosexual activity. In these cases evidence of what had happened or had been discovered on other occasions was held admissible even to defeat a defence of alibi or mistaken identity.[64]

In connection with the opportunity, first afforded in 1898, for the accused to go into the witness box there were further problems about the accused's prior conduct. He could not normally be cross-examined on his past record, but there were exceptions: if the evidence showed "system," if he had set up his own good character or had attacked the character of prosecution witnesses.[65] Here the Court on the whole steered a fair course, allowing the accused a certain scope to pursue his defence without courting the introduction of his previous record. But there were lapses: when the Appeal Court held that a doctor accused of manslaughter in the course of an abor-

---

[60] For subsequent revisions and criticisms, see Report of the Royal Commission on Criminal Procedure, P.P. 1980–1981 [Cmnd. 8092] XLI, App. 13.

[61] R. v. Baskerville [1916] 2 K.B. 658.

[62] R. v. Dent (1943) 29 Cr.App.R. 120.

[63] But the rule about "similar facts" remained uncertain for most of the nineteenth century: see J. Stone (1933) 46 Harv.L.R. 954.

[64] R. v. Thompson (1918) 13 Cr.App.R. 61. In upholding the C.C.A.'s decision, Lord Sumner in the H.L. characterised a whole attitude by saying: "Persons who commit the offences now under consideration, seek the habitual gratification of a particular perverted lust, which not only takes them out of the class of ordinary men gone wrong but stamps them with the hallmark of a special and extra-ordinary class, as much as if they carried on their bodies some physical peculiarity." (p. 81).

[65] Criminal Evidence Act, 1898, s.1(f).

tion could be asked about his *acquittal* for a similar offence, the House of Lords fortunately over-ruled it.[66]

It is over matters of substantive law that the Court's record is least adequate. The judges had insisted that the essential elements of criminal law were best left to be developed at their hands and not through any embracing code. Indeed, once the new Court was finally conceded, nothing much would be heard of the codification for which Victorian reformers strove so long and hard. On Lord Loreburn's initiative, there was some work on statutory consolidation.[67] But no permanent review machinery, even of a part-time nature, would be established before the Court reached its half-century.

Yet the tone of many of the court's decisions on matters of basic principle betray a bluff, sometimes hasty dogmatism: for the run of common lawyers, the real danger remained the reduction of the criminal law to a formal order which could inhibit the reactions of judge and jury to any particular case. When for example, the court was called upon to provide a general test of what acts sufficed to constitute an attempt to commit a crime, they managed only a bald distinction between what was "immediately connected" and what was "remote."[68] The sparest of judgments sufficed to affirm the existence of the drag-net crime, public mischief; the judges could conceive no lack of wisdom in leaving themselves with such an expansive power.[69] As had its predecessors, the Court also wrestled with such awkward questions as the proper scope of crimes of fraudulent appropriation,[70] but secured no effective grip on the hydra.

For the most part the death penalty was now confined to murder. A defendant on a murder charge might show that he had been so provoked by his victims as to be entitled to a verdict of manslaughter. The notion had long been kept on short rein. The Court nonetheless worked to pull it tighter: by confining the circumstances which could ever amount to provocation; by requiring that the act of antagonism would have provoked a reasonable man—a man indeed of teutonic stoicism; and by insisting that the killing should have been a reaction so immediate as to allow no chance for second thoughts.[71]

With the growth in psychiatric knowledge, pleas of insanity came to be supported by more sophisticated evidence from experts than before, but this seemed to cut little enough ice with the bench. Certainly the Appeal Court insisted upon strict adherence to the terms of the M'Naghten Rules. In applying the "knowledge of right-from-wrong" test, it was held to be knowledge of legal, not of moral, wrongfulness which was alone relevant.[72] Nor was there scope for now admitting the notion of irresistible impulse. The Court dis-

---

[66] *Maxwell* v. *D.P.P.* [1935] A.C. 309.
[67] He created an Advisory Committee on Criminal Law Consolidation, whose work led to the Forgery Act 1913 and the Larceny Act 1916.
[68] *R.* v. *Bloxham* (1943) 29 Cr.App.R. 37.
[69] *R.* v. *Manley* (1933) 24 Cr.App.R. 25.
[70] *R.* v. *Hudson* (1943) 29 Cr.App.R. 65.
[71] Culminating in *Mancini* v. *D.P.P.* [1942] A.C. 1; *Holmes* v. *D.P.P.* [1946] A.C. 588; *R.* v. *McCarthy* [1954] 2 Q.B. 103 and *Bedder* v. *D.P.P.* [1954] 1 W.L.R. 1119.
[72] *R.* v. *Codere* (1916) 12 Cr.App.R. 21; and see *R.* v. *Windle* [1952] 2 Q.B. 826.

approved of a direction by the idiosyncratic McCardie J., which virtually admitted that conception in the case of Ronald True,[73] although his bizarre killing of a prostitute suggested sufficient mental abnormality for the Home Secretary to grant a reprieve from execution. In the ensuing public outcry, the government was obliged to set up a Committee of inquiry under Atkin L.J. and this (to the surprise of many) recommended introducing irresistible impulse as a new M'Naghten category.[74] The Court of Criminal Appeal, led by Lord Hewart C.J., however, remained opposed to a "fantasic theory" whose introduction would be "merely subversive."[75] Accordingly nothing happened.

The ultimate respect of the common law for the liberty of the individual was often claimed to lie in the principle that a man was presumed innocent until proven guilty. Early in its life, the Court of Criminal Appeal affirmed that, once there was evidence from which a defence might be inferred to a charge of receiving stolen goods, the burden of proof lay with the prosecution.[76]

But when it came to claims that a defendant charged with murder lacked the necessary malice aforethought (through accident, self-defence, drunkenness or provocation), the rule was the other way, or so it appeared from the classic authorities. In 1934, a farm labourer, Woolmington shot his wife. Although there was strong evidence of premeditation, he claimed that he had been attempting suicide and had somehow killed her instead by accident. At his first trial, Finlay J. directed that the onus was on the Crown and the jury disagreed; at the second, Swift J. put the burden on the defence and Woolmington was convicted. The Court of Criminal Appeal refused to hold such a direction wrong, relying on various precedents.[77] Fortunately the House of Lords took the occasion to state unequivocally that the prosecution bore the burden on issues of malice aforethought in murder, as it did in respect of other crimes, unless Parliament provided otherwise.[78] By such decisions the basic principles of a liberal criminal jurisprudence were slowly coming to confine the scope of pragmatic discretion. But so long as the judges in the Court of Criminal Appeal considered the first function of the courts to lie in stamping out crime, the movement could be nothing other than gradual.

III. Punishment: New Ventures

(a) The Change of Course

By the 1890s, frissons of doubt were beginning to shake the established social creed of Victorian England: poverty, for instance, might

---

[73] (1922) 16 Cr.App.R. 164.

[74] P.P. 1923 [Cmd. 2005] XII. For this and Lord Darling's ill-fated attempt to pursue it with a Bill: Walker (1968), pp. 108–109.

[75] R. v. Kopsch (1925) 19 Cr.App.R. 50.

[76] R. v. Schama and Abramovitch (1914) 11 Cr.App.R. 45.

[77] In particular, Foster's Crown Law (1762), p. 255 was repeated in subsequent texts and digests.

[78] (1936) 25 Cr.App.R. 72; [1935] A.C. 462; J. C. Smith (1987) 38 N.I.L.Q. 223.

after all not be curable by helping those who would go back to useful employment and by subjecting the irredeemable to the discipline of a less eligible workhouse; a sufficient education might not be installed in the mass of children through "payment-by-results." And so with the punishment of convicted criminals. The militaristic deterrence of the prisons, the regimented rigour the reformatories and industrial schools began to lose their aura of infallibility even before Du Cane's retirement from the Prison Commission. In 1894 a Departmental Committee on prisons, chaired by Gladstone's son, Herbert, was set up in response to jarring criticism.[79] Its Report, which would come to be venerated by subsequent penal reformers, certainly faced the basic issues of ideology and policy squarely.[80] It began with the question, "Is the present Prison System sufficiently deterrent?" and concluded that, at least for first offenders, it was.

The Committee accepted the evidence of a number of experts that a more encouraging set of stages within prisons had a real chance of reclaiming "some of (the community's) worst and most dangerous products" who had descended into a life of habitual crime. As to how these people would be aided on their return to the outside world, the report had relatively little to say, since "the improvement of general social conditions is the work of the community."[81]

The document was stamped with that cautious reformism which was beginning to accommodate the state's manifold interventions to a world in which the working class was no longer without a political voice. It did lead to some modification in the severity of the prison regime. Du Cane was retired off and a cultured civil servant, Ruggles-Brise, took over the Prison Commission, acting much in the spirit of the Gladstone Report. Furnished with new powers by the Prisons Act 1898, the regimes for both penal servitude and imprisonment were modified.[82] The former had its initial nine months of separate confinement somewhat reduced—and this would be carried further in 1910, thanks to a public campaign mounted by Galsworthy, the novelist.[83]

The latter, when it took the form of "first-class hard labour" (the usual case), had involved the thankless drudgery dictated by the 1865 Act—this had been condemned by the Gladstone Report and was abandoned. Work, which tended to centre around the needs of the

---

[79] Particularly that of W. D. Morrison: see above, n. 15; and generally, Radzinowicz and Hood (1986), V pp. 573–583; Harding et al. (1985), pp. 214–217.

[80] P.P. 1895 [C. 7702] LVI. The Committee took a bold view of its terms of reference. The Report spawned a number of further official inquiries: into education in prison, dietaries and aid on discharge: see P.P. 1896 [C. 8154] XLIV; 1799 [C. 9166 and 9514] XLII; 1897 [C. 8299] XL.

[81] But it was critical of earlier neglect and offered cautious encouragement to Discharged Prisoners' Aid Societies which provided charitable help.

[82] The Act had a stormy passage from Liberals who considered that the Gladstone Report stood for more radical change: see Radzinowicz and Hood (1986), V pp. 579–583.

[83] In 1899 the period was reduced to six months, only to be split into periods of three, six and nine months for first offenders, intermediates and recidivists in 1905. Galsworthy's concern, published by his play, Justice, led Churchill, as Home Secretary, to reduce the period to one month for all save recidivists, who got three: see Radzinowicz and Hood (1986), V pp. 588–599. "Separation" was abolished in 1922 after Ruggles Brise's retirement.

prison itself, was mostly done in associative silence, though this was less severely controlled than it had been. Living conditions were made a little less degrading, there was a small improvement in the diet, and punishments for insubordination and other breaches of rules became less severe, with flogging becoming rare instead of commonplace.[84] Nonetheless routines remained drearily standard and would, by the time of Ruggles-Brise's retirement in 1921, have been severely criticised by a succession of eloquent inmates, including suffragettes and then wartime conscientious objectors.[85] Equally, while Ruggles-Brise actively fostered the setting up of special places for the custody of late adolescent convicts (which he labelled Borstal institutions) he was not greatly concerned to avoid a prison-like atmosphere in them, and they in turn would come under increasing attack, notably from the Borstal Association.

In truth Ruggles-Brise, once a pupil of T. H. Green, remained suspicious of techniques for rehabilitating criminals which would compromise the notion that they had been sent for a prescribed measure of punishment. Whether that punishment was penal servitude or imprisonment, it must proceed in accordance with general criteria.[86] It was for the individual prisoner to make what he chose of the opportunities those criteria provided. It was dangerous to give the authorities the sort of discretion which would allow them to restrict privileges and retard release until they were satisfied with the prisoner's "progress."[87]

(b) Alternatives to Institutions

Sir Godfrey Lushington, Permanent Under-Secretary at the Home Office, however, gave evidence to the Gladstone Committee in more radical vein: "the true mode of reforming a man or restoring him to society is exactly in the opposite direction" from life in prison, where inevitably "the status of a prisoner throughout his whole career was unfavourable to reformation."[88] Soon afterwards, Lushington was himself to chair a Committee on Reformatory and Industrial Schools which was heavily critical of the majority of these establishments, for their harsh and discouraging regimen. A minority of the Committee, moreover, denounced the "asylum theory" adopted by some magistrates and school authorities, which led to children being sent to the schools whenever they would be "better off," and not only when the step was necessary in order to protect them or the public. One result of this criticism was a marked reduction in the numbers being sent, particularly to industrial schools.[89]

---

[84] For details see Radzinowicz and Hood (1986), V pp. 583–588; Harding et al. (1985), pp. 211–232.

[85] Culminating in S. Hobhouse and F. Brockway (eds.), *English Prisons Today* (1922).

[86] Accordingly he would be proud to claim that in all prisons, at any time, "the same things in general are being done, and . . . in general they are being done in the same way": *ibid.*, p. 97.

[87] See Radzinowicz and Hood (1986), V pp. 596–599. Ruggles-Brise was equally suspicious of the Lombrosian theory of inherited criminality; see above, p. 612.

[88] Referred to in the Report, P.P. 1895 [C.7702] LVI, § 25.

[89] P.P. 1896 [C. 8204] XLV.

The schools had come to be looked upon with some complaisancy; their successes led the Gladstone Committee to favour similar institutions for the 16–21 age group which became the Borstals.[90] To attack the very idea of institutional isolation, to seek to confine it to the cases of last resort, was accordingly a fundamental challenge. Its adoption by experts both in the prison service and at the Home Office showed how far their professional idealism had carried them from the disciplinary tenets of those who led the previous generation. Their criticism, however, could make little headway without some practical alternative to offer and this they found primarily in the concept of probation. The idea of releasing a convict back into the community under a measure of supervision had not been entirely unknown in the nineteenth century.[91] The justices had long had power to discharge persons on recognisances to be of good behaviour; dedicated reformers, such as M. D. Hill, had encouraged experiments in supervised freedom as an alternative to a custodial sentence; the final stage of penal servitude became a release on licence; and in 1871, and then again in 1886, legislation made it possible to place offenders under the supervision of the police.[92] It was not, however, until the movement to establish university and charity settlements in the working-class districts of London and other great cities, that the concept began to gain real support. "Missionaries" were attached to police courts, originally in pursuit of temperance, but soon enough in a wider role.[93] Where offenders were convicted for the first time, or for some other reason might be expected to keep out of crime in future they might be placed under the supervision of one of these workers'.

In 1907, all criminal courts were given power to appoint regular probation officers. Offenders might be placed under their supervision for a set period, the consequence of failure to comply with the order being that offenders could be recalled and sentenced into custody.[94] In 1922, such appointments were made mandatory. For some time afterwards, most probation officers would come from charitable bodies dealing with delinquency. Their introduction was part of that larger shift by which voluntary visiting was translated into trained, salaried social work. So far as penal practice is concerned, it constituted the most basic re-direction of the Ruggles-Brise era. It gave new impetus to the conception that a proportion of those convicted (and in particular young offenders) could be helped toward lives of social conformity and economic independence by skilled counselling and a degree of watchful supervision. And this in turn depended on a perception of crime as largely a social phenomenon—a pattern of

---

[90] Report (above, n. 80).

[91] See Radzinowicz and Hood (1986), V pp. 633–642.

[92] Prevention of Crimes Act 1871, Probation of First Offenders Act 1887, promoted by Sir Howard Vincent, the creator of Scotland Yard.

[93] The Church of England Temperance Society played a catalytic part.

[94] Probation of Offenders Act 1907; Radzinowicz and Hood (1986), V, pp. 642–647. A contemporaneous movement succeeded in reducing the number of cases in which fine defaulters would be sent to prison: see the Criminal Justice Administration Act 1914; *ibid.*, pp. 648–651. It was also a period when the treatment of the mentally ill, the feeble-minded and the habitually drunk received independent consideration: *ibid.*, Chaps. 9, 10.

behaviour most often stimulated by an unfavourable environment—particularly in family life—but capable of being changed by training in work skills and practice in self-control. The thesis seemed confirmed by the disruptive conditions of the First World War,[95] which saw a considerable increase in convictions of young offenders; yet by the early twenties the rates would sink back roughly to pre-war levels.

(c) The Paterson Era

The two decades between wars stand out for their dominant optimism in matters of penal treatment. On Ruggles-Brise's retirement there emerged a number of dedicated, high-principled leaders—as chairmen of the Prisons Commission, Maurice Waller, Harold Scott and Alexander Maxwell[96]; as Chief Inspector of Reformatories and Industrial Schools, Dr Arthur Norris; as assistant in charge of the Home Office's Children's Branch, Sydney Harris; and prime among them all, the Prison Commissioner, Alec Paterson.[97]

The punitive, deterrent object of imprisoning, which Ruggles-Brise had sought to maintain, and to secure in the new Borstal institutions, lost way in face of rehabilitative concerns. In Paterson's watchword, "Men are sent to prison as a punishment and not for punishment." Determined efforts were made to provide more varied opportunities for work, with a particular emphasis on training for release. Prison earnings were increased as a real incentive to good behaviour; the lumpy patchwork of after-care arrangements was sewn into an effective cover, maintained by the state and voluntary associations in real coordination. With this drive the old differences between the two types of custodial sentence were reduced; indeed penal servitude became uncommon and could be phased out after the next war.

Nonetheless, financial stringencies obstructed much that was most imaginative in this replanning. A Departmental Committee under Sir Isidore Salmon catalogued the modest level of achievement and helped create a run of opinion in favour of more substantial progress.[98] In the 1938–39 session the government promoted a wide ranging Criminal Justice Bill, but the outbreak of war would leave it on the shelf until 1948.[99]

Paterson's special achievement was in re-directing the thrust of Borstal so as to make it primarily a training for older adolescents.[1] The regimented discipline and prison-like work schedules were replaced by more substantial periods of education and training, following the pattern of jobs outside. The most promising "lads" were selected for open Borstals and the first groups actually built the prem-

---

[95] Particularly, in this interpretation, because so many mothers went to work in factories.

[96] The last went on to be Permanent Under-Secretary at the Home Office.

[97] Bailey has called him "the 'Beveridge' of the penal system": (1987), p 4

[98] Report on the Employment of Prisoners, P.P. 1933–1934 [Cmd. 4462] XV.

[99] See below, p. 630.

[1] See generally, Bailey (1987) Part IV.

ises while living in camps.[2] Under strong leadership, they appeared
to be turning out young men who did not afterwards quickly appear
again before the courts.[3] The whole initiative radiated success for
progressivist ideals. It seemed to demonstrate that the spirit of comradely striving, which those in charge had learned at public school,
and applied in the settlements and clubs of the slums and the
trenches of France and Flanders, could equally be inculcated at the
most difficult social levels.

(d) Juveniles

As for children and young offenders, they had come to be separately treated in the juvenile courts set up as distinct units of summary jurisdiction by the "Children's Charter" of 1908.[4] Some of the
justices and stipendiaries who sat in these courts took a strong interest in rehabilitative treatments.[5] The reformatories and industrial
schools which were the main custodial institutions for these age
groups came under renewed criticism for their unimaginative regi-
mentation from a Departmental Committee in 1913, and thereafter
the pressure did not relent.[6] Psychological and psychiatric study suggested that there should be much more careful assessment of the
physical and mental condition of juveniles before and during punishment.[7] A more sympathetic approach made it easier to equate
behaviour which in the lowest classes became crime with the disobedience and daring not uncommon in children of the respectable.
There were of course, divisions of opinion among those who argued
for changes of approach. In particular, there were those who opposed
custodial treatment so long as any alternative (including now probation) had a chance of working; and those who were convinced that a
period in a home at the age of twelve or thirteen was much more
likely to have an effect than if it were put off for two years or so; and
that indeed in some cases it should be possible to send boys and girls
to a home for a shorter period in order to bring them up sharp.[8]

A Departmental Committee on Young Offenders of 1925–1927 was
chiefly preoccupied with deciding the merits of rival progressive
theories and its important recommendations formed the basis of
legislation in 1932.[9] The most profound question before the Committee arose from the recognition that over a considerable course of

---

[2] The small number of girls receiving this sentence could be accommodated in a
single Borstal (at Aylesbury) but they proved difficult to manage: Bailey (1987),
pp. 208–210.

[3] Another important experiment was the establishment of hostels to which young
offenders could be sent as a condition of probation.

[4] See above, n. 45.

[5] Notable among them were Clarke Hall of London's East End and Geraldine Cadbury
of Birmingham: see Bailey (1987), pp. 21, 25.

[6] P.P. 1913 [Cd. 6838] XXXIX; Bailey (1987), pp. 47–57.

[7] The dominant influence was that of the psychologist, Cyril Burt. His *The Young
Delinquent* appeared in 1927: Bailey (1987), pp. 12–17, 31–33, 85–90.

[8] See Bailey (1987) Chap. 2, pp. 92–95.

[9] P.P. 1927 [Cmd. 2831] XII; Bailey (1987), pp. 17–21, Chaps. 2–4. The 1932 Act was
consolidated with earlier legislation in the Children and Young Persons Act 1933.

time the retributive content of punishment for juveniles had been drained away. The sentence they received had, in most cases, little to do with the comparative gravity of their offence and much more with their prospects for rehabilitation. If they were sent to a reformatory, their release would become a matter for those then in charge of them, and not the court. It was clear, moreover, that the police, education authorities and social workers were quite frequently reluctant to involve the courts in dealing with delinquent children because the process would brand them with the stigma of conviction. According, for instance, to the Howard League for Penal Reform, the logical step would be to make the handling of juveniles a guardianship procedure on the model of chancery, rather than a criminal process.[10] The Committee, and some officials of the Home Office, however, balked at so transparent an acceptance of social welfare ideals, and the latter disliked a re-arrangement of strategies which might transfer too much authority to the probation officers of the courts.[11]

The juvenile courts were therefore retained, though their benches were now specially trained and the words "conviction" and "sentence" were no longer used.[12] The distinction between reformatories and industrial schools was abolished, both becoming "approved schools," by virtue of their Home Office inspection. The period of detention was also limited to three years or until school leaving age.[13] This had the object of encouraging schools to let their inmates out on licence to start work rather earlier (something which, as private institutions with declining rolls, they were often loath to do). It was hoped thereby to make magistrates less reluctant to send juveniles to the schools, and to encourage local authorities to make more use of the juvenile courts instead of putting children in trouble directly into homes under their own supervision. At the same time enlarged powers of guardianship were given to local authorities for dealing with cases which did not warrant the intervention of the juvenile court.[14] All in all, the new Act confirmed the crucial roles of the new welfare experts in the business of helping a considerable range of those under sixteen to employable and law-abiding maturity.

(e) Counter-movements

Despite this unmistakeable change of tide, old currents were by no means submerged. By the early thirties, there were statistics showing that rates of prosecutions were once more rising, particularly of juveniles.[15] Pessimists, among whom peers, judges, magistrates and senior police officers were prominent, saw in these figures evidence of the "futile sloppiness" of "sentimental justice." They demanded that the arm of the law be strengthened in a number of particulars. Juvenile courts should once more become places of awesome judg-

[10] Cf. above, p. 402ff.
[11] See Bailey (1987), pp. 22–30, 73–84.
[12] Children and Young Persons Act 1933, s.59(1).
[13] Ibid., ss.57, 58, 60–74, 79–83, Bailey (1987) 95–103, 151–152.
[14] Children and Young Persons Act 1933, ss.61, 62, 77, 78, 80, 84–85.
[15] One explanation of the increase, of course, was that the 1933 Act had succeeded in encouraging more use of the courts.

ment rather than "nice consulting rooms."[16] Corporal punishment, particularly for younger offenders, needed to be restored to regular use. When in its 1938 Bill the government included a welfarist clause to replace beatings entirely as a punishment which a court could order, it became apparent that they would be defeated in the Commons. If they wanted to pursue the argument, they would have to work out some alternative form of "short, sharp shock," perhaps on the lines of the "defaulters' drill" once proposed by Churchill.[17] In consequence, the Criminal Justice Act 1948 would purchase the abolition of corporal punishment sentences with the introduction of detention centres; to these adolescents between 14 and 21 would be sent for three or six months spells of disciplining redolent of the parade ground.[18]

Capital punishment for murder and treason continued a prime article of the pessimists' faith. However in the 1920s, the Howard League revived the case of abolition,[19] and the Quaker, Roy Calvert, published a sustained argument against the death penalty which attracted considerable attention and sympathy.[20] He expressed deep abhorrence at the idea of the state destroying life and could find no countervailing evidence that the penalty was a necessary deterrent, pointing particularly to countries which had abolished execution without experiencing an upsurge in the rate of killings. To the central moral argument could be added the objections that the punishment could not be reversed in cases of wrongful conviction, that executions were degrading for those who must carry them out and disturbing for the whole prison community involved, and that the press took a morbid and mercenary pleasure in purveying the details. During the second Labour government, a Select Committee was in consequence moved to recommend a five-year suspension of hangings.[21] But the succeeding National government took little interest and failed to put an abolition clause in the Criminal Justice Bill of 1938.[22] In 1948, the Labour government did include it; but although passing in the Commons, it fell in the Lords.[23] As our period draws to a close, the issue was joined but far from resolved. The Gowers Royal Commission was set under way and from its Report in 1953 would flow the compromises of the Homicide Act 1957 and the eventual majority for complete abolition in 1967. In 1950, it could not have been predicted with any certainty that such a point would ever be reached.

---

[16] Bailey (1987), pp. 188–121.

[17] During his vigorous Home Secretaryship in 1910: Radzinowicz and Hood (1986), V pp. 770–775. The idea continued to attract officials: see generally, Bailey (1987), pp. 129–146.

[18] s.48; Bailey (1987), pp. 295–297, 299–302.

[19] A. G. Rose, The Struggle for Penal Reform (1961).

[20] Capital Punishment in the Twentieth Century; for this and the later history of the abolitionist cause, see E. O. Tuttle, The Crusade against Capital Punishment in Great Britain (1961); and for the last stages J. B. Christoph, Capital Punishment and British Politics (1962).

[21] P.P. 1930–1931 (15) VI.

[22] A Commons resolution calling for its inclusion was passed, but nothing followed.

[23] While the Law Officers had supported it, the Lord Chancellor, Jowitt, was firmly against; and the Lord Chief Justice, Goddard, gave chapter and verse for his view that in many cases, "the murderer must be destroyed": Christoph (above, n. 20), p. 59.

As the rounds of debate evidenced, advocates of the death penalty for murder were moved by a web of arguments. They believed in its peculiar deterrent value; but often they also wanted to wreak vengeance, a feeling mostly expressed in the retributive mode, life for a life. The conception of just proportion in sentencing generally had achieved a place among ideas of punishment only as the Bloody Code was replaced by measures capable of variation in time or amount. The first Criminal Law Commissioners had given it classic expression, as a necessary part of their Benthamic view of punishment as a deterrent: those who committed more serious crimes should know that they risked severer punishment. Their forty-five categories of sentence were attached to the crimes in their code as measures of the regular sentence, from which a court might make reductions for extenuating circumstances.[24] Equally the maxima set in the statutory definitions of the 1820s and 1861 were for some time treated in this light. But gradually sentences became shorter and the maximum was given only for exceptionally aggravated cases (although what constituted the norm still varied very considerably throughout the nineteenth century.)[25] When the Court of Criminal Appeal was finally created, with a power to review sentences, its very existence emphasised the strength of the retributive ideal. The Court indeed moved cautiously towards the idea of a "tariff" for typical forms of a crime.[26] The trend held the approval of those most anxious to retain the deterrent impact of the legal machine, as well as those, like Ruggles-Brise, who mistrusted the enthusiasms of the scientific rehabilitators.

It was the persistent offender who particularly roused the antagonisms between these viewpoints.[27] The appropriate method of dealing with both the hopeless petty offender and the determined major criminal was much in issue at the time of the Gladstone Committee. That Committee asknowledged that a class of criminal did exist who did not respond to the threats of the existing system; but they were vague about who fitted within it and about what special punishments ought in consequence to be introduced.

They did however hint at the possibility of some indeterminate additional sentence and in the succeeding discussion various models were proposed.[28] In 1908, Herbert Gladstone, now Home Secretary, saw through the Prevention of Crime Act, the second part of which essentially accepted the positivist case that persistent offenders, like those mentally disturbed, should be placed in custody (though their treatment should be somewhat more benign than prison regime in

---

[24] Seventh Report, P.P. 1843 [448] XIX; see Sir R. Cross in P. Glazebrook (ed.) *Reshaping the Criminal Law* (1978), pp. 16–20; Radzinowicz and Hood (1986), V Chap. 22.

[25] On this gradual evolution, D. A. Thomas *Constraints on Judgment* (1978); *The Penal Equation* (1978); the first text on the subject was E. W. Cox, *The Principles of Punishment . . .* (1877). See also Radzinowicz and Hood (1896) Chap. 23.

[26] See also above, p. 609.

[27] It used the expression, *e.g.* in *R. v. Woodrow* (1909) 2 Cr.App.R. 67; Thomas *Penal Equation* (above, n. 25) traces the usage back at least to Lush J., P.P. 1875 [C. 1138] LXI, p. 8, and see J. F. Stephen (1885) 17 *Nineteenth Century* 755.

[28] Radzinowicz and Hood (1986), V pp. 265–287.

general) until, in the view of an Advisory Board, they had been rehabilitated. As a sop to retributive feeling, and at the same time as a hedge against overloading, those subjected to sentence as an habitual offender would first have to be given (and undergo) penal servitude of at least three years for the crime committed; and the court would set a ceiling on the further detention up to a maximum of ten years (with a minimum of five). To begin with the Home Office set up facilities for the new sentence at Camp Hill and began to encourage courts to use the new punishment, but the scheme soon ran against the feeling that it discriminated unfairly against those picked out for it. Churchill, as Home Secretary, became an outspoken opponent and ran the scheme very largely into the ground. Gladstone had predicted that 6,000 might be held as habituals at any time; but by 1911 only 53 received the additional sentence, and after the war the average was even lower.[29] By 1948, the sentence was virtually defunct and the Criminal Justice Act attempted a different formula. A scheme of corrective training sought to make available Borstal-like conditions for those in the next age-group in the scale—those over 21. For those over 30, with at least three previous convictions on indictment since 17 (for two of which there had been a custodial sentence), a sentence of preventive detention between five and fourteen years could be passed without any initial period of ordinary imprisonment.[30] But this too would not be much used. The idea that punishments should respect the principle of equal treatment was by then too firmly engrained.

The 1948 Act was a legislative representation of the extent to which the Victorian penal system had been modified. While it contained new initiatives designed to give bite to its bark—notably the plans for detention centres and preventive detention—its main object was to foster progressive penal reform which Paterson had led between the wars. A careful balance of threats and incentives, administered in humane spirit by idealistic professionals, was the true path towards realisation of Beccaria's utilitarian model, sketched two centuries before. In the four decades which have since passed, every element in the 1948 package has either undergone profound change or has been abandoned. The growth of crime which has accompanied increasing prosperity has given a cutting edge to the jeremiads of the pessimists and has led many in the progressive camp from optimism to scepticism. But when the scheme was enacted it was to take its place beside the other programmes of a protective, watchful state, securing for all a basic income, adequate housing, all necessary medical care, education to the limit of potential and care against the other major disasters and difficulties of life. Crime might not be irradicable, any more than poverty, but the community that was rebuilding out of the ashes of war, led by its first majority Labour government, was thought to have the key to reducing and containing it in the future.

---

[29] Departmental Committee on Persistent Offenders P.P. 1931–1932 [Cmd. 4090] XII, esp. App. 3.

[30] These followed largely from the recommendations of the 1932 Committee.

FURTHER READING

Bailey, V., (ed.) *Policing and Punishment in Nineteenth-Century Britain* (1981).

Bailey, V., *Delinquency and Citizenship* (1987).

Baker, J. H., *An Introduction to English Legal History* (2nd ed., 1979) Chap. 24.

Bayley, P. H., *Police and Society* (1977).

Beattie, J. M., *Crime and the Courts in England 1660–1800* (1986).

Brewer, J. and Styles, J. (eds.) *An Ungovernable People* (1980).

Cockburn, J. S., (ed.) *Crime in England 1550–1800* (1977).

Critchley, T. A., *A History of Police in England and Wales* (1967).

Critchley, T. A., *The Conquest of Violence* (1970).

Donajgrodski, A. P., (ed.) *Social Control in Nineteenth Century Britain* (1977).

Emsley, C., *Policing and its Context 1750–1870* (1983).

Gatrell, V. A. C., Lenman, B. and Parker, G., (eds.) *Crime and the Law* (1980).

Harding, C., Hines, B., Ireland, R., Rawlings, R., *Imprisonment in England and Wales* (1985).

Ignatieff, M., *A Just Measure of Pain* (1978).

Hay, D., "War, Dearth and Theft in the Eighteenth Century . . . " (1982) 95 P. & P. 117.

Hay, D., Linebaugh, P. and Thompson, E.P., (eds.), *Albion's Fatal Tree* (1975).

Holdsworth, Sir W., *A History of English Law*, esp. XI, pp. 556 594; XIII, pp. 317–322, 386–403; XIV, pp. 227–230; XV, pp. 143–167.

Jones, D., *Crime, Protest, Community and Police* (1983).

Knafla, L. A., *Crime and Criminal Justice in England and Canada* (1981).

Langbein, J. H., "The Criminal Trial before the Lawyers" (1975) 45 U. Chicago L.R. 263.

Langbein, J. H., "Shaping the Eighteenth Century Criminal Trial . . . " (1983—(i)) 50 U. Chicago L.R. 1.

Langbein, J. H., "Albion's Fatal Flaws" (1983—(ii)) 98 P. & P. 96.

Manchester, A. H., *Modern Legal History* (1980) Chaps. 7–11.

Mather, F. C., *Public Order in the Age of the Chartists* (1959).

McConville, S., *A History of English Prison Administration* (1981) Vol. I.

Miller, W. R., *Cops and Bobbies* (1973).

Milsom, S. F. C., *Historical Foundations of the Common Law* (2nd ed., 1981) Chap. 14.

Phillips, D., *Crime and Authority in Victorian England* (1977).

Pike, L. O., *A History of Crime in England* (2 vols, 1873, 1876).

Radzinowicz, L., *History of English Criminal Law and its Administration from 1750*: I. *The Movement for Reform* (1948); II. *The Enforcement of the Law* (1956); III. *The Reform of the Police* (1956); IV. *Grappling for Control* (1968); V. (with Hood, R.) *The Emergence of Penal Policy* (1986).

Richter, D. C., *Riotous Victorians* (1981).

Rule, J. R. (ed.), *Outside the Law . . .* (1982).

Sharpe, J. A., *Crime in Early Modern England 1550–1750* (1984).

Shaw, A. G. L., *Convicts and the Colonies* (1966).

Steedman, C., *Policing the Victorian Community . . .* (1984).

Stephen, J. F., *History of the Criminal Law* (3 vols., 1883).

Stevenson, J., *Popular Disturbances in England 1700–1870* (1970).

Thompson, E. P., *The Making of the English Working Class* (2nd ed., 1968).

Tobias, J. J., *Crime and Industrial Society in the Nineteenth Century* (1967).

Walker, N., *Crime and Insanity in England* I (1968), Vol. I.

Webb, S. & B., *English Prisons under Local Government* (1922).

Williams, D., *Keeping the Peace* (1967).

BIOGRAPHICAL LIST

The following list gives brief details of those lawyers and others who play some part in the history described in this book. It does not include reference to familiar political figures, such as Prime Ministers and members of their Cabinets.

Readers who wish for fuller biographical information about the persons referred to should consult in particular:

J. B. Atlay, *The Victorian Chancellors* (1906)
J. Campbell, *Lives of the Lord Chancellors* (1846–1847); *Lives of the Chief Justices of England* (3rd ed., 1874)
Dictionary of National Biography (1885–1971)
E. Foss, *Judges of England* (1848–1851); *A Biographical Dictionary of the Judges of England* (1870)
R. V. Heuston, *Lives of the Lord Chancellors 1885–1940* (1964)
W. S. Holdsworth, *A History of English Law* (1903–1952)
E. Manson, *The Builders of our Law during the reign of Queen Victoria* (1895)
Reporter (W. D. Foulkes), *A Generation of Judges* (1886)
A. W. B. Simpson (ed.), *Biographical Dictionary of the Common Law* (1984)

Each entry begins by referring to father's occupation, university attended and professional qualifications. The following abbreviations have been used:

s.	Son	JCP	Justice of the Common Pleas
Adv.	Advocate		
Att.	Attorney	JKB	Justice of the King's Bench
AG	Attorney-General	KC	King's College
BEx	Baron of the Exchequer	LApp.	Lord of the Appeal in Ordinary
Barr.	Barrister		
CJ	Chief Justice	LC	Lord Chancellor
CCJ	County Court Judge	LCB	Lord Chief Baron
CJKB	Chief Justice of the King's Bench	LCJ	Lord Chief Justice
		MR	Master of the Rolls
CJCP	Chief Justice of the Common Pleas	PDA	Probate, Divorce, Admiralty
CBEx	Chief Baron of the Exchequer	SG	Solicitor-General
		VC	Vice-Chancellor
GGC	Governor-General's Council (India)	TC	Trinity College
		UC	University College
JC	Judicial Committee of the Privy Council		

Abbott, Charles (Lord Tenterden) (1767–1832) s. of substantial barber in Canterbury; Oxford. Barr., Treasury devil. JCP 1816, JKB, 1816. Moderate, but still Tory, successor to Ellenborough as CJKB 1818–32. Reformed limitation of actions (1832).

Alderson, Sir Edward (1786–1857) s. of barr.; Cambridge. Law reporter, barr., Common Law Commissioner 1829–30, JCP 1830, BEx 1834–57, in the high age of Parke B.

Abinger, see *Scarlett*

Amos, Andrew (1791–1860) s. of Russian merchant; Cambridge. Barr., Professor, UC London, 1829–37, Cambridge 1841–60; legal member, GGC (India) 1837–43, Criminal Law Commr. 1833–45; CCJ 1847–52.

Anson, Sir William Bt. (1834–1914) s. of 2nd Bt., Oxford. Jurist. Major works on contract and the constitution; Warden, All Souls, Oxford (1881–99); Unionist MP 1899, Parl. Sec., Board of Education 1902–05.

Arden, R. Pepper (Lord Alvanley) (1745–1804) s. of gentleman; Cambridge. Barr., MP 1787–1801. MR 1788, CJCP 1801.

Ashhurst, Sir William (1725–1807) s. of VC Duchy of Lancaster. Commercial barr., JKB 1770. His denunciation of the 1792 Massacres in France provoked Bentham's *Truth vs. Ashhurst* (pub. 1823).

Astbury, Sir John (1860–1939) s. of chartered accountant; Oxford. Barr., Liberal MP 1906–1910, JChD 1913: claimed to have rescued the nation from the General Strike.

Atkin, James (Lord) (1867–1944) s. of emigré from Cork to Queensland. Commercial barr., JKBD 1913, LJ 1919, LApp 1928. Formidable judge, esp. in CA with Bankes and Scrutton. Author of the "neighbour" test of liability for negligence; revered for his anti-executive stand in the *Liversidge* case (1942); sometimes trenchantly conservative.

Atkinson, John (Lord) (1844–1932) s. of Ulster protestant physician, Galway. Barr., Conservative MP 1895–1905, LApp 1905–28, direct from office of Irish AG. Prejudiced and perfunctory lawyer, arousing Canadian hostility in JC; personally disliked.

Austin, John (1790–1859) s. of successful miller. Jurist, cautious follower of Bentham, being neither convinced democrat nor religious sceptic. *The Province of Jurisprudence Determined* (1832) distinguished positive law (the command of a legally illimitable sovereign) from positive morality and religion in a manner broadly sympathetic to common lawyers. After his death, his wife published two volumes of his *Lectures* (1861).

Bannatyne, Robert (Lord Finlay) (1842–1929) s. of doctor; M.D. Edin. Barr., MP (Lib. Unionist) 1885–92, 1895–1905, SG 1895, AG 1900; LC 1916–19.

Barnes, Gorell (Lord Gorell) (1848–1913) s. of shipping agent; Cambridge. Barr., JPDA and leading spirit in the post-Hannen years, matrimonial law reformer, chairman, R.C. on Divorce (1909–12).

Bentham, Jeremy (1748–1832), s. of prosperous att.; Oxford. Read for bar. Philosopher renowned for the systematic application of utilitarian principle to law reform, and to governmental, social and economic problems. In an immense oeuvre, his founding ideas appeared in *A Fragment on Government* (1776) and *An Introduction to the Principles of Morals and Legislation* (1789); his unfinished masterwork was *The Constitutional Code* (see, in part, *Works* (ed. Bowring, 1843, IX)).

Best, William (Lord Wynford) (1767–1845) s. of gentleman, Oxford.

Barr., MP 1802–19 SG, AG to Prince of Wales, JKB 1819, CJCP (1824–29), ennobled 1829. Whig turned Tory, vehement opponent of Reform Bill and of liberal sentiment.

Bethell, Richard (Lord Westbury) (1800–73) s. of doctor; Oxford. Astute and successful equity barr., Whig MP 1851–61, SG 1852, AG 1856, LC 1861–65 (resigned after Commons censure concerning corrupt officials). Corruscating wit. Espoused a number of law reform projects, including professional education of lawyers.

Beveridge, William (Lord) (1879–1963) s. of judge (in India); Oxford. Studied for bar but turned to social reform. At Toynbee Hall, and through connections with progressives and Fabians, provided analysis crucial to the Liberal social reforms 1908–1911 (esp. *Unemployment: A Problem of Industry* (1909). Director, LSE, 1919–1937, Master, UC Oxford 1937–1944. Chairman, Unemployment Insurance Statutory Committee, 1934. His report, *Social Insurance and Allied Services* (1942), became the template for post-war welfarism. MP (Liberal) 1944, peerage, 1945.

Birkenhead, see Smith, F.E.

Bickersteth, Henry (Lord Langdale) (1783–1857) s. of doctor, studied medicine (Edinburgh), senior Wrangler (Cambridge). Chancery barr., MR 1836. When young, a Benthamite protagonist of democracy and reform of the courts. Helped draft Wills Act 1837 and founded Public Record Office. Advocated division of the Lord Chancellorship, active in the JC.

Blackburn, Colin (Lord) (1813–96) s. of Scots gentleman; Cambridge. Commercial barr., appointed JQB by Campbell over other expectants (1859); became dominant figure of Court and in 1876 one of the first Law Lords. Sometimes hesitant, his judgments still command high authority.

Blackstone, Sir William (1723–80) s. (posthumous) of silk merchant, Oxford. Fellow of All Souls, first Vinerian Professor of English Law (1758–66). His lectures formed the basis of the celebrated *Commentaries*, the first modern presentation of English law in Digestible (and therefore influential) form. Barr., MP 1761–70, Queen's SG 1763, JCP 1770–80.

Bovill, Sir William (1816–73). s. of gentleman. Commercial and patent barr., Tory M.P. 1857, SG 1866, CJCP 1866–73. Originator of bills which emerged as the Petition of Right Act 1860 and Partnership Law Amendment Act 1865.

Bramwell, George (Lord) (1808–92) s. of banker. Special pleader and common law barr., Mercantile Law Commr. (1850–55), BEx 1856, LJ 1876, ennobled 1882. Proponent of strict economic liberalism, prominent in Wemyss' Liberty and Property Defence League.

Brett, Sir William Balliol (Viscount Esher) (1815–99). s. of clergyman, KC, London and Cambridge. Commercial barr., MP 1866–68, SG 1869, JCP 1868, LJ 1876, MR 1883–97. Outstanding neither as lawyer nor judge, though some controversial judgments were remembered.

Brougham, Henry (Lord) (1778–1868) s. of gentleman; Edinburgh. Barr., M.P. 1815, Queen Caroline's AG and hence counsel in the divorce proceedings. Prominent Whig Politician and advocate of political and law reform, LC 1830–34. Too abrasive to hold high office thereafter, but a ceaseless advocate of technical law reform. Formed Society for the Amendment of the Law, 1844; prominent in National Association for Promotion of Social Science from 1856.

Bryce, James (Viscount) (1838–1922) s. of schoolteacher; Glasgow, Oxford, Heidelberg. Regius Prof. of Civil Law, Oxford, 1870–93, important historical and comparative work (*The American Commonwealth* (1868), *Studies in History and Jurisprudence* (1902)). MP (Liberal) 1882, Chancellor of Duchy of Lancaster, 1892–94. Chief Secretary for Ireland, 1906–07, Ambassador to US 1907–13.

Buller, Sir Francis (1746–1800). Author-cum-editor of *Trials at Nisi Prius*, standard common-law practice book. Special pleader then barr., JKB 1778, reflecting Mansfield's "friendship"; JCP 1794 because of ill-health. A considerable lawyer, though in court arrogant and impatient.

Byles, Sir John (1901–84) s. of timber merchant. Commercial barr., MP 1831, JCP 1858–73. Author of *Bills of Exchange* (1829); a paternalist among mid-Victorian judges.

Cairns, Hugh McC. (Earl) (1819–82). Of Scots-Irish descent; TC Dublin. Chancery and commercial barr., MP (Tory) 1852, SG 1858 AG, LJCh. 1866, LC 1868, 1874–80, and so saw into effect the new Judicature. Played larger part in generation of land law reforms of 1881–2 (though no longer in office) than of the Chancery Reform Act 1858 which goes by his name. Deeply conservative, evangelical protestant.

Campbell, John (Lord) (1779–1861) s. of Scots minister; St. Andrews. Barr., in early years a reporter (later came his forthright *Lives of the Lords Chancellors* and *of the Chief Justices*). Chairman, Real Property Commission 1830, MP (Whig) 1830, SG 1832, AG 1834, LC Ireland 1846, CJQB 1850–59, LC 1859–61. Introduced a number of useful law reform statutes.

Carson, Edward (Lord) (1854–1935) s. of civil engineer; TC Dublin. Barr. (Irish), considerable advocate. MP (Unionist, Conservative) 1892–1921, SG (Ireland) 1892, SG 1900–05, AG 1915, First Lord of Admiralty 1917. LApp 1921–29. Leader of the Ulster cause, prepared to organise even for rebellion. Dogged persistence secured partition of his country.

Chadwick, Sir Edwin (1800–1890) s. of journalist. Barr., turned social administrator and reformer. Secretary to the aged Bentham, 1829–1832. Assistant, then commissioner, RC on Poor Laws (1832–34); then combative Secretary to the permanent Poor Law Commission (1834–1846). Also member of RC on Factories (1833) and RC on Police (1839–1839). Growing influence on sanitary policy, esp. after his Sanitary Report (1842) and those of the Health of Towns Commission (1844, 1845). In 1848 a member of General Board of Health until its eclipse in 1854, partly caused by his aggressive determination to impose his own solutions. Thereafter an outsider in seeking to influence social policy on many fronts.

Chalmers, Sir MacKenzie (1847–1927) s. of clergyman; KC London and Oxford. Barr., counsel to Board of Trade, CCJ 1884–96, Birmingham. Principal author of commercial codes and statutes: Bills of Exchange Act 1882, Bankruptcy Act 1883, Sale of Goods Act 1893, Marine Insurance Act 1906.

Chelmsford, see *Thesiger*.

Colquhoun, Patrick (1745–1820) s. of Records Registrar, Dunbarton-shire. Provost of Glasgow, 1782, London stipendiary magistrate 1792; indefatigable reformer of police and the criminal law system, as well as other social issues. His *Population and Wealth of the British Empire* (1814) is an amalgam of social fact and surmise.

Copley, John Singleton (Lord Lyndhurst) (1772–1863) s. of American painter of same name; Cambridge. Common law barr., MP (at Lord Liverpool's behest) 1818, SG 1818, AG 1824, MR 1826, LC 1826–30, 1834. Began Chancery reform in wake of Eldon. Attractive, sardonic, amateur of the social scene; able, but not a devotee of the law.

Cottenham, see *Pepys*.

Crompton, Sir Charles (1797–1865) s. of gentleman-doctor; TC Dublin. Barr., Assessor, Liverpool Court of Passage, 1836, JQB 1852. Strict liberal in matters of labour pressure.

Denman, Thomas (Lord) (1779–1854) s. of physician; Cambridge. Barr., MP (Whig) 1818, SG to Q. Caroline 1820, AG 1830, CJKB 1832–1850. Supporter of criminal and procedural law reform.

Dicey, Albert Venn (1835–1922) s. of newspaper proprietor and related by marriage to the Stephens; Oxford. Barr., esp. in revenue law. Vinerian professor, Oxford, 1884–1911. Among the greatest of his generation of legal scholars: *Law of the Constitution* (1885), *Conflict of Laws* (1896). Whig-individualist values made him a great opponent of collectivism: *Law and Public Opinion in England in the 19th Century* (1905, 1914). Vehement adversary of Irish home rule.

Du Cane, Sir Edmund (1830–1903) s. of major; Royal Engineer. Organised labour of transported prisoners, Western Australia, 1851–1856. A director of Convict Prisons, 1863–1877 (chairman of Board from 1869); chairman of Prison Commission (1877–1895), moulding the prison service into a unitary system for deterrent punishment.

Duke, Edward (Lord Merrivale) (1855–1939) s. of clerk at granite works. Journalist, barr., MP (Conservative) 1900–05, 1910–18, Chief Sec., Ireland 1916–18. Pres. PDA 1919–33; strove to rein in divorce.

Eldon, see *Scott*.

Ellenborough, see *Law*.

Erle, Sir William (1793–1880) s. of vicar; Oxford. Barr., MP (Whig) 1837–41, JCP 1844, JQB 1846, CJCP 1859–66. A believer in moderate reform of the common law. Chairman, RC on Trades Unions, 1866–69, signatory of the Majority Report.

Erskine, Thomas (Lord) (1750–1823) s. of Scottish earl; St. Andrews. LC 1806–07. Highly successful advocate, particularly as defence counsel in political trials from 1780 onwards.

Esher, see *Brett*.

Fielding, Henry (1707–1754), the novelist, and his blind half-brother, Sir John (1721–80), who in turn made the office Bow Street Magazine into the first Metropolitan police organization.

Fortescue-Brickdale, Sir Charles (1857–1944) s. of conveyancing counsel. Barr., Assistant, Registrar, Chief Registrar, Land Registry, 1888–1923. Author of numerous books and reports, mainly on his great subject, titles registration.

Fry, Sir Edward (1827–1918) s. of liberal man of letters; UC London.

FRS, FBA. Chancery barr., JChD 1878, LJ 1883–92. Chaired RC on Irish Land Acts (1897). Author of *Specific Performance of Contracts* (1858), works on mosses etc. Father of Roger (artist) and Margery (penal reformer).

Gibbs, Sir Vicary (1757–1820) s. of chief surgeon; Cambridge. Barr., MP (Tory) 1804–1812, SG 1805, AG 1807, JCP 1812, CBEx 1813, CJCP 1814. Eldonian in politics, dour as a judge.

Gifford, Hardinge (Earl of Halsbury) (1823–1921). s. of newspaper editor; Oxford. Barr., high Tory MP 1877, LC 1886–92, 1895–1905. Responsible for several poor or uninspiring appointments to the bench; also for Land Transfer Act 1897 and Criminal Evidence Act 1898; prominent opponent of Parliament Bill 1911.

Goddard, Rayner (Lord) (1877–1971) s. of solicitor; Oxford. Barr., stood for Parl. (Ind. Cons.) 1929, JKB 1932, LJ 1938, LCJ 1946–58. Commercial barr., who, as Chief Justice, became strongman of the criminal law.

Green, Thomas H. (1836–1882) s. of clergyman; Oxford. Idealist philosopher, Balliol College, Oxford, influencing many pupils towards a modified liberalism (*Liberal Legislation and Freedom of Contract* (1881); *Lectures on the Principles of Political Obligation* (1885)).

Gorell, see *Barnes*.

Hailsham, see *Hogg*.

Halsbury, see *Gifford*.

Haldane, Richard B. (Viscount) (1856–1928) s. of Writer to the Signet; Edinburgh and Göttingen. Chancery barr., MP (Liberal) 1885. Minister of War 1905–12, transforming the British army. LC 1912–15 and 1923–24 (for Labour). A Hegelian and Liberal Imperialist. Greatly interested in adult education.

Hannen, James (Lord) (1821–1894) s. of wine merchant; Heidelberg. Lib. candidate, 1865; JQB 1868 JP&D 1872; Pres. PDA 1875, LApp 1891.

Hatherley, see *Page Wood*.

Herschell, Farrer (Lord) (1837–1907) of Jewish extraction, s. of dissenting minister; UC London. Barr., MP 1874 (Lib.-Rad.), SG 1880, LC 1886, 1892–95. Influential in labour law cases, *Smith* v. *Baker* (1891), *Allen* v. *Flood* (1898).

Hewart, Gordon (Lord) (1870–1943) s. of draper. Barr., MP 1913 (Lib.), SG 1916, AG 1919, LCJ 1922–40. Denounced the pretensions of bureaucracy in *The New Despotism* (1929), his particular bogey continuing to be Sir Claud Schuster.

Hobhouse, Leonard T. (1864–1929) s. of archdeacon, Oxford. Martin White professor of sociology, LSE (1907–29), journalist (*Manchester Guardian*). Critical of the Oxford idealism in which he was bred, he developed his own liberal socialism. Among numerous philosophical, political and sociological works, he wrote *The Labour Movement* (1893); *Social Evolution and Political Theory* (1911); *Liberalism* (1911); *The Metaphysical Theory of the State* (1918); *The Rational Good* (1921); *The Elements of Social Justice* (1922), *Social Development* (1924).

Hobson, John A. (1858–1940) s. of newspaper editor; Oxford. Economist and social scientist whom Keynes acknowledged as a forerunner; journalist (*Progressive Review, Nation*), internationalist, esp. in the critical *Imperialism* (1902). Advanced liberal, moving towards a discriminating socialism.

Hogg, Douglas (Viscount Hailsham) (1872–1950) s. of Quintin, West Indian sugar producer and founder of Regent Street Polytechnic. Common law barr., MP (Conservative), AG 1922, LC 1928–29; Minr. of War, 1931–35. More politician than jurist.

Howard, John (1726–1790). s. of successful furnisher who left him able to devote himself to good works. From a non-conformist background, developed a severe evangelical conscience. As High Sheriff of Bedfordshire began to tour and report on the dreadful conditions of gaols (*The State of the Prisons . . .* (1777)) first at home and then abroad; hence the father of penal reform.

Hyndman, Henry M. (1842–1921), English Marxist, leader of Social Democratic Federation; *England for All* (1881) offered a welfarist, directory interpretation of Marx.

Isaacs, Rufus (Marquess of Reading) (1860–1935) s. of Jewish fruit merchant. MP (Liberal) 1904, SG, AG 1910. Involved in Marconi scandal, LCJ 1913–21, Ambassador to USA 1918, Viceroy of India 1921–26, Foreign Secretary 1931.

James, Henry (Lord James of Hereford) (1828–1911) s. of surgeon. Engineer turned barr., MP 1869–96 (Whig Lib. Unionist), SG 1873, AG 1874, 1880–85. Chanc., Duchy of Lancaster 1895–1902. Thereafter labour arbitrator and LApp. Bachelor.

Jervis, Sir John (1802–1856) s. of judge; Cambridge. Barr., M.P. (Whig) 1832–50; AG 1846–50; CJCP 1850–56. Responsible for Jervis' Acts 1848 simplifying criminal procedure; chaired Common Law Procedure Commission 1850.

Jessel, Sir George (1824–1883) s. of Jewish diamond merchant; UC London. Chancery barr., MP (Lib.) 1868, SG 1871–73, MR 1873–83. Sharp-witted, knowledgeable exponent of equity in the Judicature Act period.

Jeune, F.H. (Lord St. Helier) (1843–1905), s. of bishop; Oxford. Barr., common and ecclesiastical law. Stood for Parl. 1880 (Cons.), J, then Pres, PDA, 1891–1905.

Jones, Sir William (1746–1794), s. of mathematician; Oxford. Barr., J. Calcutta 1783. Remarkable scholar of law, Sanskrit and oriental languages. Author, esp. of *Essay on the Law of Bailments* (1781), *Institutes of Hindu Law* (1794).

Kelly, Sir Fitzroy (1796–1880) s. of naval captain. Common law barr., MP (non-Peelite Tory) 1837–41, 1843–47, 1852–66; SG 1845–46; 1852, AG 1858–59; LCB 1866–80. Polished advocate, sometimes unscrupulous; crotchety old judge.

Kenyon, Lloyd (Lord) (1732–1802) s. of Flintshire gentleman. Articled to att., then barr., MP 1780, AG 1782–84, MR 1784–88, CJKB 1788–1802; successor to Lord Mansfield, but no innovator.

Ker, C.H. Bellenden (1785–1871), s. of naval captain, botanist and wit; Oxford. Conveyancer, law reformer and popular educationist. Criminal Law Commissioner 1833–50, Chairman, Statute Law Consolidation Commission 1853.

Keynes, J. Maynard (Lord) (1883–1946) s. of philosophy don; Cambridge. Economist renowned above all for his vigorous criticisms of the Treaty of Versailles (*The Economic Consequences of the Peace*

(1919) and his *General Theory of Employment, Interest and Money* (1936) which, by rejecting any natural tendency in an economy towards full employment, argued that such a condition was attainable by study aimed at balancing saving and investment. Treasury adviser during World War II, influential in settling the Bretton Woods Agreement (1944) on currency fluctuations and in shaping domestic policy for the coming peace.

Law, Edward (Lord Ellenborough) (1750–1818) s. of bishop; Cambridge. Barr., defended Warren Hastings, MP 1801, AG 1801, CJKB 1802–18. In Fox's cabinet, 1806. Eldonian Tory, prominent in opposing reforms to capital laws and creditors' remedies.

Laski, Harold J. (1893–1950), s. of Manchester merchant; UC London and Oxford. Taught at Harvard 1916–20 (leading to fruitful correspondence with Justice O.W. Holmes (pub. 1953)); LSE 1920–50. Early pluralism (*Studies in the Problem of Sovereignty* (1917), *Authority in the Modern State* (1919), *Grammar of Politics* (1925)) gave place to concern for working-class dominated democracy (*Parliamentary Government in England* (1938)). Intellectual force in Labour party.

Lindley, Nathaniel (Lord) (1828–1921), s. of botanist and horticulturist. Chancery barr., and author of leading works on partnership and companies (1860), translated Thibaut's *System des Pandektenrechts* (1855). JCP 1875, LJ 1881, MR 1897, LApp 1900, persuaded to resign 1905.

Llewellyn Smith, Sir Hubert (1864–1945) s. of grocer; Oxford. Worked at Toynbee Hall, then entered civil service as commissioner of labour 1893; permanent secretary, Board of Trade, 1907 and so responsible for trade boards, labour exchanges and unemployment insurance. Chief economic adviser to government 1919–1927 and renowned personality in international trade negotiations.

Loreburn, see *Reid*.

Loughborough, see *Wedderburn*.

Lushington, Stephen (1782–1873) s. of chairman of East India Coy.; Oxford. Civilian adv., MP 1806–08, 1820–41 (Radical), JAdm. 1838–67, Dean of Arches 1858–67. Important contributions to admiralty and ecclesiastical law and its reform.

Lushington, Godfrey (1832–1907) s. of Stephen; Oxford, All Souls fellow. Civil servant, permanent secretary, Home Office, 1885–95.

Lyndhurst, see *Copley*.

Macaulay, Thomas Babington (Lord) (1800–59), s. of Clapham sect evangelical, Zacariah; Cambridge. The great portrayer of Whiggish history, he was also barr., commissioner in bankruptcy, MP 1830, Law Member, Supreme Council of India, 1833–37, during which service, chiefly responsible for the draft Indian Penal Code, archetype of further Indian codification.

McCullough, John Ramsay (1789–1864) s. of Laird of Auchengool. Editor of *Scotsman*, regular contributor to *Edinburgh Review* on economic issues, professor of political economy, UC London 1828. Leading economic writer in generation after Ricardo.

Mackintosh, Sir James (1765–1832) s. of army captain, Edinburgh (medicine). Barr. and lecturer, MP 1813. Succeeded Romilly as a leader of the campaign against capital punishment.

MacMillan, Hugh (Lord) (1873–1952) s. of religious writer; Edinburgh. Scots adv., Lord Advocate 1924 (Labour government). LApp 1930. Articulate judge, with moderate reforming instincts.

Macnaghten, Edward (Lord) (1830–1913) s. of N. Irish gentleman; Cambridge. Chancery barr., MP 1880 (Conservative), refused Home Secretaryship 1886, LApp 1887–1913, building a considerable reputation; chaired Council of Legal Education 1895–1913.

Maconochie, Alexander (1787–1860) s. of naval captain and Professor of Geography, University College, London, 1833–1836. Penal administrator in the Australian colonies and in Birmingham. Early proponent of the "marks system".

Maine, Sir Henry (1822–1888) s. of doctor; Cambridge. Jurist and Legal Member of GGC (1862–69). Professor of law both in Cambridge and Oxford. Inns of Court Reader, Common Law and Jurisprudence in 1850's, from which came *Ancient Law*, an evolutionary theory of law on the analogy of geology, rather than biology (though often taken to be Darwinian). Historical and anthropological interests combined with a non-positivist utilitarianism. *Popular Government* (1885) argued against democracy as inherently unprogressive.

Maitland, Frederick William (1850–1906) s. of Secretary to Civil Service Commission, Cambridge. Barr., reader, then Downing professor, Cambridge. Brought to legal history a remarkable technical mastery, lucidity and breadth of judgment. Founded Selden Society.

Malthus, Revd. Thomas (1766–1834) s. of Gentleman; Cambridge (9th wrangler). Taught political ecomony at Haileybury. Attacked Rousseau and Godwin in *Essay on the Principle of Population* (1797), claiming as inevitable the tendency of population growth to outstrip food supply and the inefficacy of social intervention as a remedy. Popularised the image of natural selection, afterwards of influence on Darwin.

Mansfield, (Lord), see Murray.

Mansfield, Sir James (1733–1821) s. of att. MP 1779–84, leading barr., CJ Chester, 1799, CJCP 1804–14. Competent, but inclined to shortness of temper in court.

Maule, Sir William (1788–1858) s. of doctor. Barr., BEx 1839, JCP 1839–55. A good mind, rather arrogant; sometimes outspoken on the bench, as in dealing with the bigamist, Hall, in 1845.

Merrivale, see *Duke*.

Mill, James (1773–1836) Journalist and civil servant (India Office, 1819–36). Friend of Bentham and Ricardo, promulgator of their ideas. His contributions to *Encyclopedia Britannica* became basic texts for the Philosophic Radicals.

Mill, John Stuart (1806–1873). Intellectual prococity force fed by his father, James; nonetheless, the ultimate force behind mid-Victorian liberalism, carrying it from the utilitarian radicalism of the 1830's to a new vision of collective responsibility. His writings were highly influential: on philosophy and logic; economics (*Principals of Political Economy* (1848); political theory (*On Liberty* (1859), *Parliamentary Reform* (1859), *Representative Government* (1861), *Subjection of Women* (1863 – much influenced by association and marriage with Harriet Taylor). MP 1865–68.

Montagu, Basil (1770–1851) s. of Earl of Sandwich; Cambridge (5th wrangler). Barr., bankruptcy commissioner and accountant-general in bankruptcy (1835–1846). Associated with many radical campaigns for law reform, above all criticising bankruptcy administration. Essayist and editor of Bacon.

Morant, Sir Robert (1863–1920) s. of decorative artist; Oxford. First experience of educational administration as tutor to King of Siam's nephews, 1886–1894. Civil servant in Education Department with great influence on content and administration of Education Act 1902. Chairman of National Health Insurance Commission, 1911; first permanent Secretary of Ministry of Health 1919: hence pioneering administrator with strong sense of purpose.

Moulton, John Fletcher (Lord) (1844–1921) s. of Wesleyan minister; Cambridge. FRS 1885 (electrical research), leading patent counsel. MP 1885–1906, LJ 1906–12, LApp 1912–21. Liberal of the non-interventionist school.

Owen, Robert (1771–1858) s. of saddler-ironmonger. Flair in managing cotton-spinning factories, and partnership in Dale's New Lanark mills, led to advocacy, by practice and writing, of cooperative production as an answer to capitalist competition: *A New View of Society* (1813) etc. Pursued and encouraged numerous cooperative and trade union ventures, including the Grand National Cooperative TU. Save in distribution, permanent success eluded him and his influence declined.

Page Wood, William (Lord Hatherley) (1801–1881) s. of City alderman. Chancery barr., FRS 1834; MP (advanced Liberal) 1847–53, SG 1851–52, VC 1853, LJ 1868, LC 1868–72. Honest, painstaking, fervent supporter of the Established church.

Paley, William (1743–1805) s. of minor canon and headmaster. Archdeacon of Carlisle. A conservative utilitarianism pervades his much-read *Principles of Moral and Political Philosophy* (1785).

Palmer, Roundell (Lord Selborne) (1812–1895) s. of clergyman, Oxford. Barr., Chancery, MP 1847 (Peelite, then Liberal), SG 1861, AG 1863–66, LC 1872–74, 1880–85. Chief progenitor of the Judicature Acts and campaigner for reform of legal education. Deeply religious, supporter of establishment; later of Home Rule.

Parke, James (Lord Wensleydale) (1782–1868) s. of Liverpool merchant; Cambridge. Barr., JKB 1828, BEx 1834–56. Formidable exponent of the niceties of pleading under Hilary Rules 1834, and dominant figure of common law courts. Life peerage (1856) converted into hereditary title after loud constitutional objections.

Parkes, Joseph (1796–1865), s. of Glasgow worsted maker. Att. and Whig-Benthamite politician. Influential in Birmingham during Reform crisis; sec. and shaper of Municipal Corporations Commission (1833–34), taxing master in Chancery, 1847.

Passfield, see *Webb*.

Paterson, Sir Alexander (1884–1947) s. of solicitor; Oxford. From social work in Bermondsey, he became increasingly concerned with the need for humane, positive treatment of all sent to prison and similar institutions. In 1922, as a Prison Commissioner, he began to work with prison staff and in Borstals towards this end. He inspired the whole administration for a generation and acquired an international reputation.

Patteson, Sir John (1790–1861), s. of vicar; Cambridge. Successful barr., Common Law Commr. 1829. JKB 1830–52, thereafter active in JC. Able; by governments, trustworthy.

Penzance, see *Wilde*.

Pepys, Charles (Earl of Cottenham) (1781–1851) s. of Chancery master; Cambridge. Barr., MP (Whig) 1831, SG 1834, LC 1836–41, 1846–50.

Phillimore, Joseph (1775–1855) s. of civilian; Oxford DCL. Leading advocate. Regius Professor of Civil Law, Oxford 1809–1855. MP 1817 with some radical sympathies.

Phillimore, Robert (1810–85) Oxford DCL. Like his father, Joseph, primarily a civilian. Last J.Adm. 1867; then JPDA, 1876–83. Important contributions to maritime law.

Plumer, Thomas (1753–1824) s. of wine-merchant; Oxford. Common law barr., Tory MP 1807, AG 1812. First VC 1813, MR 1818–24.

Pollock, Ernest (Viscount Hanworth) (1861–1936) grandson of Sir J.F.; Cambridge. Barr., MP (Conservative) 1910–23, SG 1919–22, AG 1922, MR 1923–35. Presided successfully over a CA of considerable men.

Pollock, Sir Frederick (1845–1937) grandson of Sir J.F.; Cambridge. Corpus Professor of Jurisprudence, Oxford (1883–1903). Formidable scholar of history and ideas of common law. Founding editor, Law Quarterly Review (1885–1919), editor of the Law Reports (1895–1935). Renowned correspondent with O.W. Holmes J. (pub. 1942).

Pollock, Sir John Frederick, Bt. (1783–1870), s. of George III's saddler; Cambridge. FRS 1816, FGS 1818. Successful barr., common law, LCB 1844–66. Believer in individual striving; had 24 children.

Pothier, Robert Joseph (1699–1772), judge in Orleans for 50 years. His systematic Digest of the Roman *Corpus Juris* led to his celebrated *Traité des Obligations* and a number of works on particular contracts and other aspects of French private law. Influential not only on the *Code civil* of Napoleon but on the common law.

Pratt, Charles (Earl Camden) (1713–1794) s. of judge; Cambridge. Barr., MP (Whig), AG 1757, CJCP 1761, LC 1766–70, Pres. Council, 1782, 1784. Burkeian liberal renowned for his stand against general warrants, upheld in *Entick* v. *Carrington* (1765).

Reading, see *Isaacs*.

Reid, Robert (Earl Loreburn) (1846–1923), s. of CJ of Ionian Is.; Oxford. Common law barr., MP (Liberal) 1880, AG 1894, LC 1905–12. Untemporising radical, who saw Parliament Act 1911 through.

Ricardo, David (1772–1823) s. of Jewish stockbroker, he himself amassed a fortune in the same business. The most considerable economic theorist of his day, he developed Adam Smith's ideas into a coherent set of ideas about value, wages, rent, etc., esp. in *Principles of Political Economy and Taxation* (1817).

Rollit, Sir Albert (1842 1922) s. of Hull solicitor; Cambridge. City solicitor and director. President of Chambers of Commerce and of Municipal Corporations Assocn. Progressive Conservative.

Romilly, John (Lord) (1802–1874), s. of Sir Samuel; Cambridge. Barr.,

M.P. (Whig) 1832–36, 1847–52, SG 1848, AG 1850. MR 1852–73. Chaired Chancery Commission, 1850.

Romilly, Sir Samuel (1757–1818), s. of jeweller. Equity barr., MP 1806–18, SG 1806. Through Shelburne's circle, met Wilberforce and Bentham. Advocate of many legal and social reforms, associated above all with the Beccarian campaign to reduce the "Bloody Code".

Ruggles-Brise, Sir Evelyn (1857–1935) s. of MP; Oxford. Articulate and effective civil servant, 1880. Private Secretary, Home Office 1881–91; Prison Commissioner, 1891 and chairman of Commission, 1895–1921. Responsible for modifying the High Victorian scheme of carcerial punishment, by measures such as the first version of Borstal.

Sankey, John (Viscount) (1866–1948) s. of draper-cum-undertaker. Barr., JKB 1914, LJ 1928, LC 1929–35. Chaired government commissions, including that on coal industry (1919), acquiring sympathy for Labour politics which led to Woolsack.

Scarlett, James (Lord Abinger) (1769–1844) s. of Jamaica estate-owner. Barr., MP 1819 (Whig, later Tory), AG 1827–28, 1829–30, CBEx 1834–44.

Schuster, Claud (Lord) (1869–1956) s. of merchant; Oxford. Barr. for a short period, then civil servant, first in the Education Department under Morant. In 1915 succeeded Muir Mackenzie as permanent secretary in the Lord Chancellor's Office, an astute organiser of the judicial system and the other aspects of government over which the Chancellor held sway. Held in mistrust among the judiciary mainly by Hewart LCJ.

Scott, John (Earl of Eldon) (1751–1838) s. of Newcastle coal-merchant, br. of Stowell; Oxford. Married after elopement, 1771. MP 1782, SG 1788, AG 1793 – the "best-hated man in England" for his treason and sedition prosecutions; CJCP 1799; LC 1801–06, 1807–27. Ultimate Tory supporter of Kings. Long, dilatory reign as the fount of equity made his judgments venerable; though process became snail-like.

Scott, William (Lord Stowell) (1745–1836) br. of Lord Eldon; Oxford DCL. Civilian adv., J London Consistory Court 1788, J Admiralty 1798–1827, MP from 1784. During the wars with France, able to develop maritime and prize law considerably, in learned, lucid judgments. Like his brother, politically Conservative.

Scrutton, Sir Thomas (1856–1934) s. of shipowner; London and Cambridge: four times Yorke prizewinner. Commercial barr., (writing the text on Charterparties). JKB 1910, unpopular enough to court organized protest; LJ 1916–34, where, although his tone moderated, he was still a masterful figure.

Selborne, see Palmer.

Senior, Nassau (1790–1864) s. of merchant from West Indies; Oxford. Barr., practised as conveyancer because of throat condition; Chancery master 1836–1853. Professor of political economy, Oxford, 1825–1830 and 1847–1862. Member, RC on Poor Law 1832. Hostile to trade unions, inventor of the profit-from-last-hour notion of factory work.

Shaw, Thomas (Lord Shaw of Dunfermline; later Lord Craigmyle)

(1850–1937), s. of baker; Edinburgh. Scots barr., MP (Liberal) 1892–1909; SG for Scotland 1894–95, Adv.-G. 1906–09, LApp 1909–27.

Simon, John (Viscount) (1873–1954), s. of Congregational minister; Oxford. Barr., MP 1906–18, 1922 (Liberal; from 1930, National Liberal); SG 1910, AG 1913, Home Sec. 1915–16. Chairman, Indian Statutory Commission 1927–30. Appeaser Foreign Sec. 1931–35, Home Sec. 1935–37, Chanc. Exchequer 1937–40, LC 1940–45. Distinguished analytical lawyer and judge; as a politician, a cold fish.

Simon, Sir John (1816–1904) s. of stockbroker of French descent. Surgeon and pathologist, St. Thomas' Hospital. First medical officer of health, City of London 1848, medical officer to the reconstituted Board of Health 1855, then to the Privy Council 1858. By adept administration became highly influential over the range of public health issues: cholera outbreaks, vaccination, sanitation. After the creation of Local Government Board in 1871, he was the subject of new constraints and retired in 1876 after friction.

Smith, Adam (1723–1790) s. of Writer to the Signet; Glasgow and Oxford. Professor of logic, later of moral philosophy, Glasgow, 1751–63. From his *Theory of Moral Sentiments* (1759) he was led to analyse the nature of legal duties, and some of this jurisprudential writing has survived; thence to his masterwork *The Wealth of Nations . . .* (1776).

Smith, F.E. (Earl of Birkenhead) (1872–1930) s. of estate agent, mayor of Birkenhead; Oxford. Barr., MP 1906, SG 1915, AG 1915, LC 1919–22. Deployed in all he did (which included supporting Carson's moves towards Ulster revolt) a dashing, insolent style, surpassing even Bethell.

St. Helier, see *Jeune*.

St. Leonards, see *Sugden*.

Stephen, Sir James Fitzjames (1829–1894), s. of "King" Stephen, Under-Secretary to the Colonies, brother of Sir Leslie and so uncle to half Bloomsbury; Cambridge. Barr., journalist and essayist, Professor of Common Law, Inns of Court 1873; utilitarian of Hobbesian mien, he became deeply mistrustful of democracy and its roots in Millian liberalism (*Liberty, Fraternity and Equality,* (1873)) and an advocate of British imperialism. As Law member of GGC (in succession to Maine) 1869–72, drafted Indian Evidence Act and became promoter of criminal law codification at home. JQB, 1879–91.

Stowell, see *Scott*.

Sugden, Edward (Lord St. Leonards) 1781–1875) s. of Canterbury barber. Conveyancer and dominant Chancery barr., Author of the standard tomes on *Vendors and Purchasers* and *Powers*. MP (Tory) 1828, SG 1829, LC of Ireland, 1834, 1841–46, LC 1852, implementing Chancery procedure reform. His will was allowed to be proved by his daughter's oral evidence.

Tawney, Richard Henry (1880–1962) s. of college principal in India; Oxford. Economic historian of gritty integrity, known above all for *Religion and the Rise of Capitalism* (1926). Taught at Glasgow, LSE and widely for the Workers' Education Association. Unsuccessful Labour candidate, abiding influence on Labour Party, esp. *Labour and the Nation* (1929).

Thring, Henry (Lord) (1818–1907), s. of rector-squire; Cambridge. Barr., drawn by drafting bills for Board of Trade to become the first general Parliamentary draftsman officially appointed. Did much to raise standards.

Thesiger, Frederick (Lord Chelmsford) (1794–1848), s. of customs collector, St. Vincent. Common law barr., MP (Peelite) 1840–58, SG 1844, AG 1845–46, LC 1858–59, 1866–68.

Thurlow, Edward (Lord) (1732–1806), s. of Norfolk parson; Cambridge (sent down). Barr., gradually gaining considerable success. MP 1768, SG, AG 1770, LC 1778–92. A stern presence, but often a perfunctory judge. Lived with his mistress near Streatham.

Tidd, William (1760–1847), s. of merchant. Barr., celebrated special pleader (*Practice of the Court of King's Bench*, 1790).

Tindal, Sir Nicholas (1776–1846) s. of att.; Cambridge. Sp. pleader, barr. MP (Tory) 1824–29, SG 1826. CJCP 1829–46. Judge of good sense and considerable learning.

Truro, see *Wilde*.

Webb, Sidney (1859–1947) and Beatrice (née Potter) (1858–1943) (Lord and Lady Passfield) he s. of public accountant, she d. of industrial magnate, married 1892; together a formidable partnership in social reform, education and historical writing. He joined the Fabian Society in 1885 and soon exerted formative influence, she came to social injury through rent collecting and work on Charles Booth's survey of London. Jointly wrote *History of Trade Unionism* (1894), *Industrial Democracy* (1897) and extensive studies of local government history, etc. She served notably on Poor Law Commission 1905–1909 and they were much engaged in influencing social policy after 1906. He drafted for the Labour Party, *Labour and the Social Order* (1918) and they continued deep interest in forms of socialist government (esp. *Constitution for the Socialist Commonwealth of Great Britain* (1920); *Soviet Communism: a New Civilisation?* (1935). Launched the foundation of LSE, 1895.

Wedderburn, Alexander (Lord Loughborough, Earl of Rosslyn) (1733–1805) s. of Scots adv.; Edinburgh. Chancery and Parliamentary barr., MP (under Bute's patronage) 1766, SG 1771, AG 1778, CJCP 1780, LC 1793–1801. Able lawyer, politically ambitious and rather unscrupulous.

Wensleydale, see *Parke*.

Westbury, see *Bethell*.

Wightman, Sir William (1784–1863) s. of gentleman; Oxford. Sp. pleader, barr., junior counsel to Treasury. Common Law Commissioner, 1830, Criminal Law Commissioner, 1833, JQB 1841–63. Learned, sound judge.

Wilde, James (Lord Penzance) (1816–1899), s. of solicitor, nephew of Truro; Cambridge. Barr., BEx 1860, JP&D 1863. Ennobled 1869 and then supported a number of family law and church reform measures. Retired 1874, but from 1875 sat as ecclesiastical judge.

Wilde, Thomas (Lord Truro) (1782–1855), s. of att. Sp. pleader, then barr., MP (Whig) 1832, SG 1839, AG 1841, CJCP 1846, LC 1850–52. Sound, though long-winded judge. Assisted in reform of Chancery and common law procedure.

Willes, Sir James Shaw (1814–1872), s. of Irish doctor; TC Dublin.

Barr., JCP 1855–72. Highly regarded for his learning, a number of his judgments acquiring classic status.

Wilmot, Sir Eardley (1709–1792), s. of gentleman; Cambridge. Barr., JKB 1755, CJCP 1766–71. Refused thrice to be LC; judge of distinct ability.

Wright, Robert (Lord) (1869–1964), s. of marine superintendent; Cambridge. Commercial barr., JKB 1925, LApp 1932–47, MR 1935–37. A considerable intellectual force in the HL.

TABLE OF CASES

TABLE OF STATUTES

Note: Until mid-nineteenth century, statutes were not officially accorded a short title. In this Table, statutes from before this period have been given common identifications or other appropriate titles. In the text they are identified chiefly by regnal year reference.

INDEX